8/98

3000 800030 08050
St. Louis Community College

WITHDRAWN

D0075285

 St. Louis Community College

Forest Park
Florissant Valley
Meramec

Instructional Resources
St. Louis, Missouri

Government in Kano
1350–1950

St. Louis Community College
at Meramec
Library

AFRICAN STATES AND SOCIETIES
IN HISTORY

Series Editors
Philip Curtin, Paul E. Lovejoy, and Shula Marks

Government in Kano, 1350–1950,
M. G. Smith

Family Identity and the State in the
Bamako Kafu, *c. 1800–c. 1900,*
B. Marie Perinbam

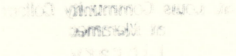

Government in Kano
1350–1950

M. G. Smith

WestviewPress

A Division of HarperCollins*Publishers*

All rights reserved. Printed in the United States of America. No part of this publication may be reproduced or transmitted in any form or by any means, electronic or mechanical, including photocopy, recording, or any information storage and retrieval system, without permission in writing from the publisher.

Copyright © 1997 by Westview Press, A Division of HarperCollins Publishers, Inc.

Published in 1997 in the United States of America by Westview Press, 5500 Central Avenue, Boulder, Colorado 80301-2877, and in the United Kingdom by Westview Press, 12 Hid's Copse Road, Cumnor Hill, Oxford OX2 9JJ

A CIP catalog record for this book is available from the Library of Congress.
ISBN 0-8133-3270-2

The paper used in this publication meets the requirements of the American National Standard for Permanence of Paper for Printed Library Materials Z39.48-1984.

10   9   8   7   6   5   4   3   2   1

Contents

Tables

Foreword

Government in Kano is the third in a set of five studies on the processes of political change in northern Nigeria. The first two, *Government in Zazzau* (Oxford University Press, 1960) and *The Affairs of Daura* (University of California Press, 1978), are both currently out of print. The remaining two studies, on Katsina and on Sokoto, though written as long ago as 1968, are still unpublished (the typescripts are available for consultation at University College London). A short, sixth book was planned, to close the series and draw out the conclusions. In 1992, at the enthusiastic urging of the historian Professor Paul Lovejoy, M.G. Smith finalised the text of *Government in Kano* for publication by Westview Press. On Christmas day that year, however, he was taken ill, and died on January 5th 1993, aged 71. That this text did not return to the archive is due to the editorial persistence of Mary Smith and the generosity of Professor Don Brown.

It is a matter of great regret (and some surprise) that *Government in Kano*, perhaps the most important of these five histories, has taken so long to appear in print. The existence of the histories has been no secret; for years historians of Hausaland have been waiting eagerly to read them. There is a certain irony here: professionally researched *before* African History became a leading discipline in the new universities in Africa, the text is at last offered to readers only *after* the popularity of the pre-colonial period among researchers has sharply declined. The forty years, between 1958 and 1998, have witnessed the giddy rise of History in Africa; in Nigeria alone, it is now taught in some forty university departments. In those years the city of Kano, with over five centuries of source material, has been the focus of doctoral and master's dissertations in a range of disciplines. Yet M.G. Smith's account of the transformations in the government of Kano constitutes, forty years on, still a very important contribution to the analysis of Kano society: there has never been anything quite like it in Kano studies, offering as it does both empirical rigour and a theoretical overview. And it is unlikely to be superseded.

The significance of this study lies partly in the fact that it contains important material from oral sources that no other scholar has ever had access to—the eighty-year-old elders with whom M.G. Smith worked have long been dead; and partly too because Kano is the key emirate in northern Nigeria—it was the economic engine of the region for both the nineteenth and the twentieth centuries. Demographically the most densely populated with its rich farmlands, industrially the most productive with its range of skilled craftsmen, the best financed and the most widely connected with its networks of merchants, bankers and transporters, the Kano hinterland was *the* entrepot, to which inevitably the railway came in

1912 and where the international airport was sited. Metropolitan Kano today has over two million inhabitants. Its traditions of government, particularly as they have adapted to changing conditions and ideologies over the last two centuries, are an important resource within the broader political culture of Nigeria.

But there is a third reason for this study's significance: it offers the reader a dissident view of jihad and colonial history—reflecting not some alien theoretical perspective but rather the rarely expressed hurt of the exploited and the oppressed. The voices that come through are often those of the loser, of the deceived. M.G. Smith was not as impressed as have been other scholars, particularly historians, by the elite practitioners of either Islam or "benevolent colonialism."

M.G. Smith is not, however, writing as a historian but as a social anthropologist interested in political organisation and the dynamics of organisational change. He covers the same periods as a historian would, but with an eye for material on which to draw out inductively the generalisations that would illuminate the underlying principles of Hausa political practice. The insights from this Hausa "lab" could then be applied to, and tested in, other contexts. The "scientificness" of social science was important to M.G. Smith: it demanded a seriousness and a rigour—of evidence, of analysis—that drove him to cross-examine his informants, as if they were in a court-room, with a persistence that sometimes annoyed. Indeed, he was apt to seek in his material a tidiness and a truthfulness that belong more properly to a lab book than to people's memories. It is not for nothing, perhaps, that as a young student M.G. Smith was fascinated by (and rather good at) Chemistry; here, in *Government in Kano*, it is formulae for the political chemistry of Hausaland that constitute his ultimate quest, with an experimental algebra in which to express them.

By taking these five polities as his sample he could, he hoped, eventually eliminate the idiosyncratic and isolate what seemed to be the consistent patterns of change—and identify the specific variables that brought about one type of change and not another. It was a bold project: but rarely do you find five basically similar polities with their own histories intact and in sufficient detail to be analysable. Furthermore, all five polities went through the same two basic changes—the desperate struggles of the jihad c. 1804–1808; conquest by the colonising British a century later, c. 1903. The idea for the project had come to him as early as 1952, when two northern Nigerian scholars, M. Hassan (who taught Hausa in London to M.G. Smith and others in the School of Oriental and African Studies) and M. Shuaibu together published their remarkable study of Abuja, now the name of Nigeria's new federal capital, but then the small town known today as Suleja. The study showed that it was possible to reconstruct in detail the political system of pre-jihad Zaria. Might one now go further and decode the patterns underlying all the structural change that had taken place in a single administrative system over two centuries—first under the "Habe" *sarakuna*, then under the Fulani *umara'*, and finally under the British colonial residents and the emirs they appointed? The answer was not only "yes," but it also yielded exciting results, as the resulting classic study, the prize-winning and twice-reprinted *Government in Zazzau*, proved. Having written that monograph, M.G. Smith (who was then at the Institute for Social and Economic Research, University of the West Indies) proposed comparing the processes he had just uncovered in Zaria (or "Zazzau") with apparently similar processes in Kano, in Katsina and the anti-Katsina state of Maradi, in Daura (where Zango was the counter-state) and, finally, in Sokoto where the model of administrative practice drew not only on Abbasid handbooks of Islamic government but also on local traditions from Kebbi and Gobir. Bornu was added in, for good measure.

In 1958–59 he took leave from ISER in Jamaica, joined the Nigerian Institute for Social and Economic Research, and carried out the necessary fieldwork. In Kano he and Mamman Yola were given lodgings with the Turakin Soro, in the slaves' section at the back of the Emir's palace. He concentrated particularly on talking, in Hausa, to those elders, both Hausawa and Fulani, who had reached adulthood before the British took over Kano, and therefore knew the old system first-hand.

It was not of course his first fieldwork in northern Nigeria. From April 1949 to December 1950 he had carried out the economic study which was published in 1955 as *The Economy of Hausa Communities of Zaria*. This was both his doctoral dissertation, for Professor Daryll Forde at University College London, and a commissioned report to the Colonial Social Science Research Council. The thesis and the report differ in one important point: chapter six of the thesis is missing from the report. In that chapter, mildly titled "Economic aspects of political activity," M.G. Smith detailed the way farmers were systematically defrauded and the various corrupt practices of the Native Authority, and its staff. He was not simply repeating standard rumours or merely scandal-mongering; to put his case beyond doubt, he conducted a series of experiments, sending farmer-assistants with pre-weighed consignments of cotton to the buying stations; he could then calculate the extent of the systematic underpayment of farmers by officials. The farmers had to be ready to swear on a complete copy of the Qur'an to the truth of their evidence. M.G. Smith was angry, and blunt—a bluntness that Daryll Forde as his supervisor turned into language that became in its cool acceptability perhaps an even sharper critique of the colonial collusion between local elites and British officialdom. That chapter was kept back until 1964 and published as "Historical and cultural conditions of political corruption among the Hausa" in *Comparative Studies in Society and History* (6:2, 164–194).

His criticism of the system was, however, well known; he was, he thought, already *persona non grata* in Nigerian government circles. Hence his academic attachment to NISER, on a project to write comparative histories, was intended to seem anodyne. At a time when the Sardauna of Sokoto, as Premier of the new northern-regional government, was reviving the symbolism and certain forms of the nineteenth-century Sokoto Caliphate, the history of local administrative systems was in no sense an antiquarian's hobby: it was of real contemporary significance. M.G. Smith's accounts, researched in 1958/9 and written up between 1965 and 1968/9, do not always buy into the "golden dream" that was the common currency of the day; he was not part of the new academic scene in the Nigeria of the 1960s nor experiencing first-hand the growth of that new nation. Instead, his analysis draws its subtleties and its flavours from a different soil; for a good text is like good wine—the complexity derives from the particular combination of limestone and climate that together affect both root and fruit.

It was as a Jamaican that M.G. Smith was born (in 1921) and educated, under colonial rule. This meant not only a British-style training at Jamaica College but also being part of the 1930s nationalist awakening; as a sixth-former he spent his school holidays in the household of Norman Manley Q.C., whose son Michael was a younger school fellow and later Jamaica's Prime Minister—M.G. Smith's own mother had died at his birth, and he was rather distant from his quarrelsome father, who was then growing bananas on a small scale in a remote valley of the Blue Mountains. Winning in 1939 the one annual Jamaica Scholarship for study at a university abroad, M.G. Smith first chose Bombay but was sent instead to McGill to read English (he was already writing a lot of poetry); after a year, however, he joined a Canadian armoured regiment, refused to go for training as an officer, and was shipped to England. In 1944 he took part in the Normandy landings and was in the thick of the action through France, Holland and Germany until the end of the war.

It was, then, as a 24-year-old demobilised soldier that he came to University College London to study Law. This was "the real world"—not the world of poetry and the "Paradise Lost" that he used to quote to pass time in a slit-trench. Disappointed to find that Law was not in fact about justice, he turned to Social Anthropology, doing the combined degree in Philosophy, Psychology and Anthropology in two years—with such good results that the external examiner, Professor Max Gluckman, recommended him for postgraduate work in anthropology. Hence, his Colonial Social Science Research Council studentship, and his economic survey of Zaria Province under Daryll Forde's supervision. The survey involved not just Hausa communities but also the non-Muslim societies of Kadara and Kagoro in southern Zaria; these areas had been the butt of jihadi attacks and subsequent (mal-)administration—they were as much an under-class as were the slave settlements that M.G. Smith included in his sample of households around Giwa in northern Zaria.

It was at this time, in Giwa and in Zaria, that M.G. Smith's wife, Mary, completed her famous autobiography of *Baba of Karo*. Baba dictated the episodes of her life's story to Mary Smith in Hausa. As an experienced secretary (and wartime radio-operator, as well as a qualified social worker), Mary Smith was able to take Baba's own words down verbatim in long-hand, with Baba herself taking care to speak in a Hausa that was not so colloquial or idiomatic that Mary would make mistakes (the Hausa original is now in print and readily available). It was truly a collaborative work, one of the first African autobiographies of an ordinary working woman; but it is all the more important as a document that takes the reader back into the rural world of southern Kano before the colonial conquest.

In short, in writing *Government in Kano* M.G. Smith was drawing upon several years of previous research experience in Hausaland. He had already become familiar with the lives of ex-slaves, "pagans," poor farmers, petty traders and women as well as with the manners of titled office-holders with power and wealth. As an antidote to authority and its myths he brought, too, a scepticism honed both as a soldier in war and as a radical schoolboy within a colonised society. Ethnicity was a matter of personal experience too; his mother was not "white," he grew up in the plural society of the West Indies where skin-colour had potential consequences socially, and now, 1952–8, he was back in Jamaica at the University, publishing on Caribbean culture and the nature of pluralism. In West Africa therefore he was readier than many to recognise the real power of ethnic labelling and the (ab)uses to which people put "tribal" and lineage identities. When reading *Government in Kano* we can hear a distinct voice—the lawyer-realist, the might-have-been scientist, the romantic radical in the M.G. Smith who once wrote and learnt poetry. All this may help the reader to take the measure of M.G. Smith's driving passion for exactitude, accuracy and reliability in matters intellectual; he had a formidable memory and expected no less of others. Truth mattered. Untruths, polite fictions, fudges had to be contested—and contested now. There was an urgency to what he wrote because, he felt, it had real implications, whether for policy or for the hearing accorded to the victims of government.

The publishing history of this book and the other two unpublished typescripts in the set (the 800-page *The Two Katsinas*, the 1000-page *The State of Sokoto*) can be briefly told for the record. When M.G. Smith moved to University of California at Los Angeles in 1961 and received two years (1965; 1968) of National Science Foundation grants to write up all the histories, the University of California Press agreed to publish them as a set. The typescripts were drafted by 1969; M.G. Smith then left Los Angeles that year for London. *Government in Kano* and *The Affairs of Daura* were revised for the University of California Press in 1972. A final version of *Government in Kano* was sent to the Press in 1976. Nothing happened. In the event, only *The Affairs of Daura* was published by them—and that was in 1978. That same year M.G. Smith moved to Yale (between 1969 and 1978 he had been at University College London and in Jamaica); the Department of Anthropology at Yale then expressed interest in publishing the remaining unpublished histories in their Series in Anthropology and had the thousand typescript pages of *Government in Kano* typed onto their computer system. Nothing more however came of it (except for a disk) by the time M.G. Smith retired from Yale in 1986. Yale University Press did, however, reprint Mary Smith's *Baba of Karo* in 1981. Finally, Professor Paul Lovejoy was interested in including *Government in Kano* in his African History series with Westview Press, and prevailed on M.G. Smith to dig out the unopened parcel containing the text and to prepare the typescript once again for publication. He did so, and Mary Smith edited Yale's existing disk. There was then a further delay waiting for funds to get everything into the camera-ready form required by Westview, but this difficulty was overcome with assistance from Don Brown, an old student and colleague of M.G. Smith's at the University of California.

In the meantime, with M.G. Smith now dead, there was no one else but Mary Smith to proofread, index, prepare the tables, and clear up all the niggling queries that arise in preparing a text for the press. Even for someone as closely involved in the creation of these histories as Mary Smith, it is difficult to reconstruct what would have been M.G. Smith's preferred reading of a passage or a problem. If there are, then, errors and shortcomings in the text, the reader will surely forgive them in the circumstances. A particular problem has been the eight missing maps and the five genealogies; they were not with the rest of the text in the parcel returned from Berkeley and are nowhere to be found amongst his other papers. Given how meticulous M.G. Smith was over maps and genealogies, their absence is a serious gap. The maps included here are cobbled out of those found in the publications of other scholars—and do not necessarily match his conceptions exactly (as he did not "walk" the Kano countryside, he did not know some sites and the problems of their exact location).

A final question. M.G. Smith in 1992 did not substantially update the text of *Government in Kano* (he had done so in 1972/6). Though he kept abreast of the main issues in Hausa studies, his research interests had moved on to such subjects as the comparative analysis of political conflict within nations worldwide, or to the problems of education and society in the Caribbean. A reader new to Kano studies may then well ask, given that thirty years of scholarship have passed since the first typescript of *Government in Kano* was finished: how out-dated is this analysis? What has been written that would seriously call into question, let alone add depth to, this study? Different scholars would offer different answers to these questions, but few would deny, I think, that the pace of northern Nigerian scholarship and research has never been as fast or as radical as in some other branches of academia. More importantly, intellectual interests have shifted, away from "straight" political history towards more socially oriented topics with greater contemporary relevance and a wider range of source materials. A brief survey of the literature on Kano will indicate some of the directions scholars have taken in recent years.

The major area where scholarship on Kano has grown dramatically has been in economic history, where pioneering studies—for example, of merchants (Uba Adamu, Ahmed Beita Yusuf, Ibrahim Tahir, Paul Lovejoy; Mahdi Adamu on the Kano diaspora, Sabo Albasu on the Lebanese); of the manufacture or trade in cloth (Philip Shea), calico (Marion Johnson), leather (Ifeanyi Anagbogu), ironworking (Philip Jaggar), groundnuts (Jan Hogendorn); on changes in slavery (Paul Lovejoy, Jan Hogendorn), urban labour (Paul Lubeck), secluded women (Enid Schildkrout, Barbara Callaway), industry (Alan Frishman), peri-urban farming (Polly Hill), urban food-supply (Michael Watts), taxation (Tijani Garba), to name but a few—have transformed our knowledge. Add to these the studies of geographers (e.g., Michael Mortimore and his many colleagues at Bayero University on Kano's close-settled zone; and J. M. Baba on Kura) and the various scholars, based mainly at Ahmadu Bello University, who analysed the political economy of colonial Kano and its region (Abdullahi Mahadi, Sule Bello, Robert Shenton, for example; and Ahmed Bako on Sabon Gari)—and the new reader will realise not just the wealth of detailed work on widely different aspects of Kano's economy, but also the widely divergent intellectual approaches to the field of economic history.

Another important area of research has been the intellectual history of Kano, by historians (for example, M. A. al-Hajj and Priscilla Starrett on early scholars; John Chamberlain and Ismail Abdulla on the legal and medical tradition; Salah Hassan, Neil Skinner, Abdullahi Mohammed and John McIntyre on the materials of traditional scholarship and schooling; Ousmane Kane, Auwalu Anwar and Roman Loimeier on Muslim radicals and sufis). Religious culture has similarly been studied by political scientists such as John Paden, by the Islamists under the leadership of Professor Sani Zahradin at Bayero University and by their colleagues the specialists on Hausa custom, language and literature (such as the late

Professor Ibrahim Yaro Yahaya and Kabiru Galadanci, Bello Said on jihadi poetry or Baba "Impossible" on the tradition of Kano magic). There have been studies of Kano's music (Monty Besmer), of Kano's architecture, its city walls and rural strongholds (Tukur Sa'ad, Len Moody, N. I. Dantiye); of the culture of the palace (Beverly Mack, Ruqayya Ahmed Rufai and Heidi Nast for example) and inter-ethnic relations (Z. O. Ogunnika). Above all, the historians such as John Lavers (with his creation of the Kano Museum), Halil Said on the Kano jihad, Adamu Fika on the civil war, C. N. Ubah on Kano government, Allan Christelow on the emir's court records, as well as the proceedings of the two international conferences on Kano history run (and published) by Professor Bawuro Barkindo and his colleagues, have made distinctive contributions which over the years attracted M.G. Smith's attention.

Much less has been done on the early history of Kano, but this was marginal to M.G. Smith's concerns. Given how the longevity of a specifically Hausa political culture has now been called into question, there is an urgent need for an archaeology of Kano to give substance to a re-analysis that is clearly overdue (Murray Last, Patrick Darling). At the other end of the period covered by M.G. Smith's analysis, there is surprisingly little published on the internal workings of Kano's Native Authority. But what the new reader has to remember is that published work represents only the tip of an iceberg whose underside is made up of innumerable small (and not so small) dissertations done in Nigerian university departments not just for the Ph.D. but also for both the M.A. and even B. A. honours degrees, some of which are listed in the special issue on Kano (vol. 4, 1993) of *Sudanic Africa*. Finally, there are small studies still being published and sold in Kano outside the university milieu—booklets with historical material in Arabic, Hausa or English (for example by Ibrahim Ado-Kurawa).

M.G. Smith, had he been writing *Government in Kano* today, would have enormously enlarged his understanding of Kano in all its complexity by reading this mass of new material. Given his meticulous system of indexing all the notes he ever took, he would certainly have extended the text well beyond its current six hundred pages of typescript. I am not so sure, however, that he would have drastically altered the core substance of his work; he would have added many footnotes, included more caveats, corrected detailed errors of date or place or name. But the central project—the comparative analysis of the dynamics of political change—is scarcely amenable to updating. The intellectual vision that M.G. Smith had in the 1950s and 1960s of the contribution that a truly searching analysis of Hausa political dynamics could make to history not only in Africa but beyond remains both a challenge *and* a contribution. The study of African society and culture was not a matter, for him, of only parochial significance. *Government in Kano*, though enormously detailed and close-worked, offers to the reader both the materials and the leads for exploring much further.

Murray Last
University College London
January 1997

References

Abdulla, I.H. 1981. "The influence of Islamic medicine on Hausa traditional practitioners in northern Nigeria." PhD thesis, University of Wisconsin.

Adamu, M. 1978. *The Hausa Factor in West African History.* Zaria: Ahmadu Bello University Press. [Based on PhD thesis of the same title, University of Birmingham, 1974.]

Adamu, Muhammad Uba 1968. "Some notes on the influence of north African traders in Kano," *Kano Studies* 4, 43–49.

Ado-Kurawa, I.D. 1989. *The Jihad in Kano.* Kano: Tofa Press. [Cf. his 1988 *History and Genealogy of the Gyanawa* and his 1990 *Sullabawan Dabo*, both with Tofa Press]

Albasu, S. 1989. "The Lebanese in Kano: an immigrant community in a Hausa Muslim society in the colonial and post-colonial periods." PhD thesis, Bayero University.

Anagbobu, I. 1986. "The history of the indigenous leather industry in Sokoto and Kano, northern Nigeria." PhD thesis, University of Birmingham.

Anwar, A. 1989. "Struggle for influence and identity: the ulama in Kano 1937–1987." MA thesis, University of Maiduguri.

Baba, J.M. 1975. "Induced agricultural change in a densely populated district: a study of the existing agricultural system in Kura district and the projected impact of the Kano River irrigation project." PhD thesis, Ahmadu Bello University.

Bako, A. 1990. "A socio-economic history of Sabon Gari, Kano, 1913–1989." PhD thesis, Bayero University.

Barkindo, B.M. (ed.) 1983. *Studies in the History of Kano.* Ibadan: Heinemann Educational Books.

___ . 1989. *Kano and some of her Neighbours.* Zaria: Ahmadu Bello University Press.

Bello, S. 1982. "State and economy in Kano, 1894–1960." PhD thesis, Ahmadu Bello University.

Besmer, F. 1983. *Horses, Musicians and Gods: the Hausa cult of possession-trance.* South Hadley: Bergin & Garvey.

Callaway, B. 1987. *Muslim Hausa Women in Nigeria: tradition and change.* Syracuse: Syracuse University Press.

Chamberlain, J.W. 1975. "The development of Islamic education in Kano city, Nigeria, with special emphasis on legal education in the 19th and 20th centuries." PhD thesis, Columbia University.

Christelow, A. 1994. *Thus Ruled Emir Abbas: selected cases from the records of the Emir of Kano's Judicial Council.* East Lansing: Michigan State University Press.

Dan Asabe, A.U. 1987. "Comparative biographies of selected leaders of the Kano commercial establishment." MA thesis, Bayero University.

Dantiye, N.I. 1985. "A study of the origins, status and defensive role of four Kano strongholds (ribats) in the emirate period (1808–1903)." PhD thesis, Indiana University.

Darling, P. 1986. "Fieldwork surveys in and around Kano State, Nigeria," *Nyame Akuma,* 27: 39–41.

Fika, A.M. 1978. *The Kano Civil War and British Over-rule, 1882–1940.* Ibadan: Oxford University Press. [Based on his 1973 London PhD thesis, "The political and economic re-orientation of Kano Emirate, Northern Nigeria, ca. 1882–1940."]

Frishman, A. 1977. "The spatial growth and residential location of Kano." PhD thesis, Northwestern University.

Garba, T. 1986. "Taxation in some Hausa emirates, c. 1860–1939." PhD thesis, University of Birmingham.

al-Hajj, M.A. 1968. "A seventeenth century chronicle on the origins and missionary activities of the Wangarawa," *Kano Studies,* 1.4: 7–16.

Hassan, S. el M. 1988. "Lore of the traditional malam: material culture of literacy and ethnography of writing among the Hausa of northern Nigeria." PhD thesis, University of Pennsylvania.

Hassan, A., Naibi, A.S. 1962. *A Chronicle of Abuja*. Lagos: African Universities Press. [First edition, 1952.]

Hill, P. 1978. *Population, Prosperity and Poverty: rural Kano 1900 and 1970*. Cambridge: Cambridge University Press.

Hogendorn, J. 1978. *Nigerian Groundnut Exports: origins and development*. Zaria: Ahmadu Bello University Press.

Jaggar, P. 1993. *The Blacksmiths of Kano City, Nigeria: tradition, innovation and entrepreneurship in the twentieth century.* Koln: Koppe Verlag.

Johnson, M. 1976. "Calico caravans: the Tripoli-Kano trade after 1880," *Journal of African History,* 45:4, 95–118.

Kane, O. 1993. "Les mouvements islamiques et le champs politique au nord du Nigeria: le cas du reformisme musulman a Kano." Doctorat en science politique, Institut d'etudes politiques de Paris.

Last, M. 1985. "The early kingdoms of the Nigerian savanna," *History of West Africa* (eds. J.F.A.Ajayi, M.Crowder) 3rd edn.: volume 1, 176–224. London: Longman.

Lavers, J.E. [1992] *Guide to Gidan Makama Museum* (revised edn.; first edn. 1985).

Loimeier, R. 1993. *Islamische Erneuerung und politischer Wandel in Nordnigeria. Die Auseinandersetzungen zwischen den Sufi-Bruderschaften und ihren Gegern seit Ende der 50er Jahre.* Munster: Lit Verlag.

Lovejoy, P. 1980. *Caravans of Kola: the Hausa kola trade, 1700–1900*. Zaria: Ahmadu Bello University Press. [Based on his 1973 University of Wisconsin PhD thesis, "The Hausa kola trade: 1700–1900."]

Lovejoy, P. and J.Hogendorn, 1993. *Slow Death for Slavery: the course of abolition in northern Nigeria, 1897–1936*. Cambridge: Cambridge University Press.

Lubeck, P. 1987. *Islam and Urban Labour in Northern Nigeria: the making of a Muslim working class*. Cambridge: Cambridge University Press.

Mack, Beverly, 1992. "Royal wives in Kano," in *Hausa Women in the Twentieth Century* (eds. C.Coles, B.Mack), 109–129. Madison: University of Wisconsin Press.

Mahadi, A. 1982. "The state and the economy: the sarauta system and its role in shaping the society and economy of Kano with particular reference to the 18th and 19th centuries." PhD thesis, Ahmadu Bello University.

McIntyre, J.A. 1982. "Context and register in Qur'anic education: words and their meaning in the register of Kano malams," in *Sprache, Geschichte und Kultur in Afrika*, 356–389. [Hamburg.]

Mohammed, A. 1978. "A Hausa trader-scholar and his library collection: the case study of Umar Falke of Kano." PhD thesis, Northwestern University.

Moody, H.L.B., 1969. *The Walls and Gates of Kano City.* Lagos: Department of Antiquities.

Mortimore, M. and J. Wilson, 1965. *Land and People in the Kano Close-Settled Zone*. Zaria: Ahmadu Bello University Dept. of Geography.

Nast, H. 1992. "Space, history and power: stories of spatial and social change in the palace of Kano, northern Nigeria ca. 1500–1900." PhD thesis, McGill University

Ogunnika, Z.O. 1982. "Mechanisms of tension management in a plural society: a study of interethnic relations in Kano city, Nigeria." PhD thesis, New School of Social Research, New York.

Paden, J.N. 1973. *Religion and Political Culture in Kano*. Berkeley: University of California Press. [Based on his 1968 Harvard PhD thesis, "The influence of religious elites on the community, culture and political integration of Kano, Nigeria."]

Rufai, Ruqayyatu Ahmed, 1987. "Gidan Rumfa: the socio-political history of the palace of the Emir of Kano with particular reference to the twentieth century." MA thesis, Bayero University.

Sa'ad, H.T. 1981. "Between myth and reality: the aesthetics of traditional architecture in Hausaland." PhD thesis, University of Michigan.

Sa'ad, Bello, 1978. "Gundunmawar masu jihadi kan adabin Hausa." 2 vols. MA thesis, Bayero University.

Sa'id, H.I. 1978. "Revolution and reaction: the Fulani jihad in Kano and its aftermath, 1807–1919." PhD thesis, University of Michigan.

Schildkrout, E. 1983. "Dependency and autonomy: the economic activities of secluded Hausa women in Kano," in *Male and Female in West Africa* (ed. C.Oppong), 107–126. London: Allen & Unwin.

Shea, P.J. 1975. "The development of an export-oriented dyed-cloth industry in Kano emirate in the 19th century." PhD thesis, University of Wisconsin.

Shenton, R. 1986. *The Development of Capitalism in Northern Nigeria.* London: James Currey.

Skinner, Neil, 1980. *Alhaji Mahmudu Koki: Kano malam.* Zaria: Ahmadu Bello University Press.

Smith, Mary F., 1954. *Baba of Karo: a woman of the Muslim Hausa.* London: Faber. Re-issued by Yale University Press, 1981. [Hausa text: *Labarin Baba, Mutuniyar Karo ta Kasar Kano,* Bayero University Library, Kano; 1991.]

Smith, Michael G., 1951. "Social and economic change among selected native communities in northern Nigeria." PhD thesis, University of London.

____ . 1955. *The Economy of Hausa Communities of Zaria: report to the Colonial Social Science Research Council.* London: HMSO. Re-issued by Johnson Reprint Corporation, 1971.

____ . 1960. *Government in Zazzau.* London: Oxford University Press for the International African Institute.

____ . 1964. "Historical and cultural conditions of political corruption among the Hausa" in *Comparative Studies in Society and History,* 6:2, 164–194.

____ . [1969] *The Two Katsinas.* (unpublished typescript)

____ . [1969] *The State of Sokoto.* (unpublished typescript)

____ . 1978. *The Affairs of Daura.* Berkeley: University of California Press.

Starrett, P. 1993. "Oral history in Muslim Africa: al-Maghili legends in Kano." PhD thesis, University of Michigan.

Tahir, I. 1977. "Scholars, sufis, saints and capitalists in Kano, 1904–1974: the pattern of bourgeois revolution in an Islamic society." PhD thesis, Cambridge University.

Ubah, C.N. 1965. "Kano emirate in the 19th century." MA thesis, University of Ghana.

____ . 1985. *Government and Administration of Kano Emirate 1900–1930.* Nsukka: University of Nigeria Press. [Based upon his 1973 Ibadan University PhD thesis, "Administration of Kano Emirate under the British, 1900–1930."]

Watts, M. 1987. "Brittle trade: a political economy of food-supply in Kano," in *Feeding African Cities* (ed. J.I.Guyer), 55–111. Manchester: Manchester University Press for the International African Institute.

Yahaya, I.Y. 1988. *Hausa a Rubuce: tarihin rubuce-rubuce cikin Hausa.* Zaria: NNPC.

Yusuf, A.B. 1975. "Capital formation and management among the Muslim traders of Kano," *Africa,* 45.2: 167–182.

Acknowledgments

The author's acknowledgments of assistance received at Kano from the Emir, Alhaji Sir Muhammad Sanusi and others during his field work there in 1958–59 will be found in Chapters 1 and 2. In addition, I reproduce the following from his Preface to *The Affairs of Daura*, published in 1978:

> For the opportunity to undertake the field enquiries on which the following monographs [on Daura, the two Katsinas, Kano and Sokoto] are based I am indebted to the Nigerian Institute of Social and Economic Research for a fellowship and to the University College of the West Indies for granting leave [in 1958–59]. The preparation of the following monographs was made possible by two generous awards, G8-605 in 1965 and GS-2175 in 1968–69, from the National Science Foundation, Washington, D.C. Together these awards enabled me to devote twenty undistracted months to the analysis of my data and the preparation of the documentary accounts of the five states I had studied. The University of California, Los Angeles kindly approved two requests for leave for this program. ... Without this generous support from the National Science Foundation and the University of California I cannot imagine how it would have been possible to prepare these monographs for publication.

The final appearance of *Government in Kano* is due to the efforts of Professor Paul Lovejoy of York University, Ontario. I wish to thank him for arranging the publication through Westview Press, and the typesetting of the manuscript by Peter Obst, who has patiently worked his way through my "raw" word-processing, not forgetting the twelve tables, to produce the present handsome camera-ready copy. For generous help in financing this I thank M.G. Smith's erstwhile student, colleague and friend since UCLA in the 1960s, Professor Don Brown of UCSB and his wife, Carrie. At Yale in the early 1980s, Liz Kyburg with infinite patience entered my typescript into the IBM system, and in London in 1987 our son David Smith converted that into Apple Macintosh form and taught me how to deal with it. Since M.G. Smith's sudden death in 1993 our sons, Daniel, David and Peter, have each in his own way helped me to complete the project. Finally, I thank Professors Murray Last and Phil Burnham at M.G.'s old department at University College London for unfailing advice and help. I am responsible for the index, a pale shadow of what the author's would have been.

Mary F. Smith
January 1997

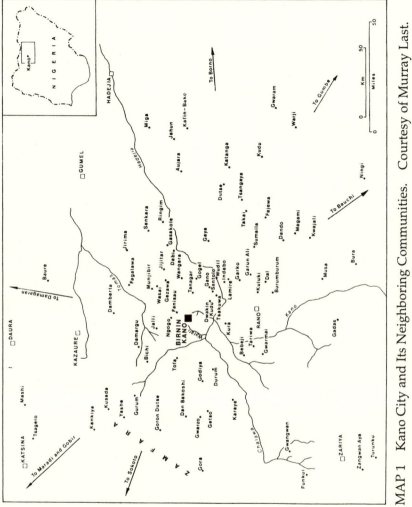

MAP 1 Kano City and Its Neighboring Communities.   Courtesy of Murray Last.

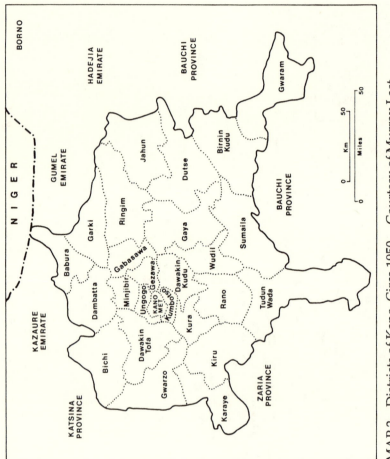

MAP 2   Districts of Kano, Circa 1950.   Courtesy of Murray Last.

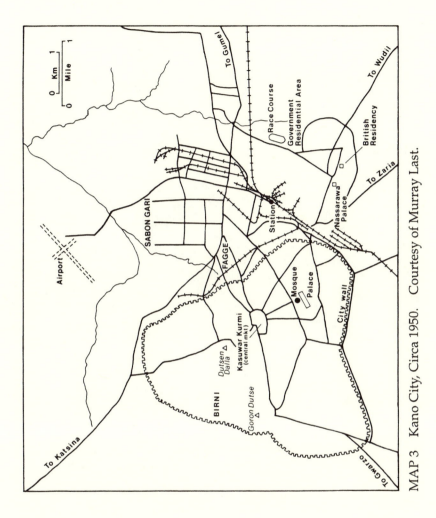

MAP 3 Kano City, Circa 1950. Courtesy of Murray Last.

1

Introduction

The Problem

The Hausa city of Kano, situated at 12 degrees north and 8 degrees 30 minutes east, has long been world famous for its arts and industries, its commerce, wealth, and position in the network of trans-Saharan and trans-Sudanic trade. This city long served as a terminus for one of the two central caravan routes which crossed the Sahara from Tripoli via Ghadames, Ghat, Tintellus, Agades and Katsina, while the other, 300 miles to the east, ran parallel from Murzuk through Kauwar and Bilma to Bornu. Standing in the southern Sahil, in an area of dense population, Kano was also one of the major centres of the trans-Sudanic traffic by which Kukawa and Wadai in the east were linked commercially to Gwanja and Timbuktu on the Niger bend, to Kumasi, Bida in Nupe, the old Yoruba capital at Katanga, and to Zamfara, Kebbi, Katsina, Zaria, Zinder and Agades; so that all were brought into a common, continuous intercourse.

In this book I try to describe the growth and organisation of the Kano state as far as my materials permit and my analytical objectives require. This is not a history of Kano, although it may serve as an interim substitute, and may perhaps stimulate others to prepare such an account. It is rather a historical study of the Kano polity undertaken by a social anthropologist with two major purposes in view. This account forms one of a series designed to advance our understanding of political organisation and the processes of political change. This general enquiry is comparative in its framework and methods. It encompasses parallel but separate studies of several Muslim emirates of the central Sudan, namely, Katsina, Daura, Maradi, Zazzau (Zaria), the Fulani sultanate of Sokoto, and Kano. Most of these states adjoin one another and all share certain major historical experiences and cultural traditions. Together, these six units include the majority of the people and territory of western and central Hausaland. In effect then, in pursuing the comparative analysis of political changes in these several states, I must first provide adequate and comparable accounts of their political ethnography and history over a uniform time span long enough to ensure that most of the developmental tendencies which are intrinsic to these variable political structures may be brought to our notice. Indeed, in a sense, we may consider these several states and their histories as variations on a common theme; but to isolate the constants in this theme and to seek out their fixed relations, an inductive procedure is neces- sary. Not until I have independently analyzed each historical continuum as a sep- arate coherent formation can I abstract their common structures and tendencies or attempt to generalize about the processes of political change on the basis of these comparative studies.

I can neither claim that these several accounts are authentic and comprehen- sive histories of the states to which they relate, nor that their ensemble constitutes an adequate basis for universal generalisations about the structure of the pro- cesses of political change. Our inquiries are restricted as to their typological range, and being subject to numerous historiographic contingencies, some of which are discussed below, are correspondingly limited in their scope. At best I am merely hoping to elucidate some constants in the processes by which these polities of the central Sudan have persisted or changed over the past 200 years. Even if I am so fortunate as to derive some regularities from the mass of historical and ethnographic detail these studies present, such generalizations could at best apply only to units of a similar base, structure, and geosocial context, that is, unless it can be shown that these regularities are logically necessary and invari- able expressions of fixed relations between the determinate elements that consti- tute political organization. This theoretical possibility, however exciting, does not immediately concern us. My present problem is rather to indicate the utility and adequacy of the data presented below for the description of the Kano polity and its development and for the analysis of political change. Some critical assessment of our materials and approach should logically precede the narrative and descrip- tion; and it is with these questions that the present chapter is concerned.

Hausa Historical Periods

The broad outlines of recent Hausa history are well known. Between 1804 and 1810 the Muslim Fulani reformer, Shehu Usman dan Fodio launched a *jihad* or holy war for the revival and expansion of Islam against the Sarkin Gobir Yunfa in whose territory the Shehu and his kinsmen lived. The approaching conflict between Shehu Usman and Yunfa attracted general attention among the Fulani who were scattered widely throughout other chiefdoms of Hausaland. When Yunfa and the Shehu came to blows in 1804 at Matankare and shortly after at Tabkin Kwotto many Fulani from distant areas rallied to the Shehu's cause; and when the reigning Hausa chiefs responded favorably to Yunfa's appeal for sup- port, the initial conflict between the ruler of Gobir and the Shehu's *jema'a* or com- munity was rapidly extended throughout and beyond Hausaland. By 1810 all of the *Hausa bakwai* —the seven Hausa states—had been conquered by the Shehu's forces and representatives. West of Bornu only Kebbi withstood the Fulani assault. Thus between 1804 and 1810 Hausaland experienced a major political upheaval. By the latter year the traditional Hausa states had been incorporated as provinces of a new Muslim caliphate under the Shehu Usman dan Fodio as *Amir- ul-Mu'minin*, or Sarkin Musulmi, the Caliph or Commander of the Faithful. With one exception, namely Bauchi, all the conquered territories were placed under Muslim Fulani rulers whose status and relation to the Shehu and his successors were those of emir to sultan or caliph. Some of the defeated Hausa chiefs withdrew from their capitals to establish successor states in other areas; and for most of the last century, the successor states of Katsina at Maradi and of Gobir at Tsibiri, as well as recalcitrant Kebbi, pursued an unrelenting war against the Fulani sultan, his emirs and chiefs.

This conflict only ceased with the partition and occupation of the central Sudan by France and Britain at the turn of the present century. Under the Convention of Paris and its subsequent modifications, the French obtained control over the two independent Hausa states of Gobir and Maradi together with Adar and Kwonni northwest of Sokoto, the sultan's capital; while the rest of the Fulani empire or caliphate came under British rule. By 1899 the French had imposed their authority in Agades and Zinder; but it was not until 1903 that the British, moving northwards from the coast under Sir Frederick Lugard, overran Kano, Katsina and Sokoto, the three most populous Fulani states. Thenceforth till 1914 Hausaland formed part of the British Protectorate of Northern Nigeria. Between 1914 and 1922 Northern Nigeria was integrated with other southern areas under British control to constitute the modern territory of Nigeria. Following World War I, that part of the German Cameroons which lay due east of Nigeria was attached to it as mandated territory under British administration.

In effect then, all the traditional Hausa states have experienced common conquests first by the Fulani and then by the British. They have also been exposed equally to two different systems of rule, direct administration by their Fulani conquerors and indirect administration under the British. This community of historical experiences distinguishes the Hausa-Fulani emirates of northern Nigeria from other polities within that or adjoining regions. It accordingly establishes a useful framework for controlled comparison and analysis, enabling us to see how variegated were the political organizations and sequences of development of these states before, during, or after the period of unqualified Fulani rule. Moreover by comparing developments at Maradi during the present century under French rule with those of adjacent and cognate Katsina under the British, we may in some measure explore differences in the methods and effects of these alternative systems of colonial administration.

Between 1951 and 1960 Hausaland underwent yet another major political transformation as its people and their British rulers together set about constructing and introducing all the poltical and administrative machinery requisite for internal autonomy of the Northern Region on the basis of free elections by universal suffrage as part of an independent Nigerian Federation. In March 1959 during my field study of Kano, Northern Nigeria achieved full internal autonomy under a cabinet whose members were all born in the region. Within two years the Nigerian Federation had obtained dominion status as a fully autonomous unit of the British Commonwealth; and shortly afterwards the federal constitution was revised to replace the British Queen as head of state by a native president, Dr. Namdi Azikiwe. These in broad outlines are the changing contexts within which our study of Kano is centered; and although my inquiry is not directed to the general problem of modernization in traditional regimes, it is possible that political developments in Kano since 1925 may shed some light on that theme.

The Twentieth Century

Looking back at Kano's past we may usefully distinguish three periods by reference both to the quality, kind and abundance of data available about them, and to their differences of political regime. It is perhaps no accident that these documentary differences coincide with abrupt and extensive changes of political direction and, to a lesser extent, of administration also. For the twentieth century, as might be expected, we have a fair and steadily increasing supply of useful materials available from administrative files, reports and official sources of various kinds. The reliability of these data varies greatly by time and topic. It is presently uncertain how far population returns, whether by periodic census or those compiled annually as a basis for tax assessment and collection, merit confidence. We should also be ill advised to accept administrative enumerations of the numbers of Fulani pastoralists or their cattle as accurate. The amounts officially collected as *jangali* (cattle tax) or *haraji* (the Muslim land tax which in this century has been levied as a capitation tax) are set out clearly in the Native Administration (emirate) accounts as verified by British administrative officers. That this officially reported tax represents only a variable portion of the gross actually collected from the *talakawa* (commoners) by local chiefs is not in doubt. But precisely what proportions of the total population have been officially subject to tax, and what proportions of the amounts levied as tax have been officially reported at any period, no one can confidently say.

Until the closing days of British rule, village and district chiefs augmented their personal incomes by receipts from unregistered individuals and communities; often fairly substantial numbers of persons were simply not reported by the local village chief. Administrative files illustrate the continuance of this practice throughout the colonial period in the periodic discoveries of divisional officers. If the district and emirate returns of population enumerated in the 1952 census are compared with returns from these units for purposes of tax assessment and collection, the generality and scale of this practice can be seen. In short, quantitative data available in the administrative files on local conditions during this century vary greatly in their validity and historical value.

Much information of immediate relevance to our knowledge of the processes of political development and change is also missing from the files, either because it was not recorded in the first place, or through vicissitudes of time and chance. As late as 1932 some Kano files dating from 1907 and 1908 onwards were available at the secretariat of the regional government in Kaduna; however in 1959 I was unable to trace any unpublished administrative documents on Kano written before 1915.[1] Thereafter divisional files and semi-annual reports of provincial residents provide substantial data; but these documents record only such information as the British officers thought relevant or worthy of note. Much that the student of the indigenous society wishes to learn cannot be found in such sources. Perhaps some of the information I sought was familiar to particular administrators; much may not have been. Perhaps also some of the missing data I need may be scattered in personal correspondence, unpublished diaries, or similar places. No attempt has been made in the course of this study to pursue such fragments and personal relics. It is doubtful whether the memoirs and souvenirs of British administrators would yield sufficient new and relevant data to warrant such a survey; and it is virtually certain that such information collected from expatriates could not equal in its range, intimacy or significance the corresponding body of historically relevant data from this period that perished with the contemporary chiefs and rulers. Fortunately, even in 1959 much could be learned about these decades from elders alive in Kano. Moreover, despite inevitable shortcomings and data gaps, our information on affairs at Kano during this century is so superior to the material available on earlier centuries in its range, abundance, systematic detail and verifiability, being often simultaneously and independently recorded by two or more officials, that we may treat our account of twentieth century Kano as set on reasonably firm foundations.

The Nineteenth Century

For the political organization and development of Kano under Fulani rule during the nineteenth century we are also greatly indebted to the detailed historical inquiries of numerous unidentifiable divisional officers who sought in the course of their rural tours to learn the traditional distribution of political allegiances and authority among the local communities of modern administrative districts. Most of this valuable, concrete and readily verifiable historical data is to be found in the district notebooks compiled for each administrative division of the emirate. Of the twenty-six territorial districts extant at Kano in 1959, I obtained district notebooks for twenty-one. For other units which had once served as separate districts but no longer did so, I could only obtain by these means such historical data on the nineteenth century organization as had been transferred to the notebooks of those districts in which they were currently incorporated.

Some allusions to Kano are present in the various historical writings available from Sokoto, the imperial state, during the last century. In his account of the Fulani *jihad* thecaliph Mamman Bello, son and successor of Shehu Usman, mentions its conquest briefly.[2] Al-Hajj Sa'id, in his invaluable first-hand account of Sokoto under caliphs Bello, Atiku and Aliyu, that is, from 1817 to 1849, also makes scattered references to Kano and adjacent emirates.[3] The present *waziri* (vizier) of Sokoto, Alhaji Junaidu, in his excellent history of the Fulani, also provides valuable occasional material.[4] In addition the *waziri* and his senior student, Malam Halidu, graciously translated into Hausa from the original Arabic most if not all of the imperial correspondence between the sultans and viziers of Sokoto on the one hand and successive emirs of Kano on the other that still remains in his personal care at the *waziri's* compound in Sokoto. Of about 200 letters from Kano that Malam Halidu translated into Hausa for me, I copied 50 from his dictation for their historical value.[5] However as most of this correspondence dated from the last three decades of the nineteenth century, I have no knowledge of the correspondence between earlier Fulani emirs of Kano and their suzerains at Sokoto. That some relics of this earlier imperial correspondence may still exist at Sokoto or elsewhere is quite probable in view of materials published by Mr. Bivar.[6] Moreover, I failed to seek the permission of Alhaji Sir Muhammad Sanusi who ruled Kano in 1959 to peruse such historical documents as remained in his care. Finally, in the writings of the Shehu Usman and his brother, Abdullahi dan Fodio, there are occasional references to Kano, together with much else of great interest to historians of Hausa society and the Fulani *jihad*.

A selection of 131 letters from the Fulani imperial correspondence was published in translation in 1927 by H.F. Backwell with an introduction and notes.[7] However, Backwell's selection concentrates mainly on the correspondence that passed between Fulani capitals during the last five years of the autonomous caliphate, while my transcriptions of correspondence between Kano and Sokoto relate to the preceding thirty years.

At Kano itself through the kindness and courtesy of Alhaji Muhammadu Nasiru, I transcribed Hausa translations of two local histories, the older of which was completed by the Alkalin Kano (the senior *qadi* of the emirate) Malam Zangi on the sixth *Zulkida* 1281 A.H., that is, in 1864–1865[8] while the latter was written by a local Arab, Malam Adamu na Ma'aji, around 1940.[9] Both texts were located at the Shahuci Judicial School in Kano city of which Alhajji Muhammadu Nasiru was, in 1959, the principal. Following the technique of Muslim *isnad*, the Alkali Muhammad Zangi begins his account of the affairs of the Shehu's community at Kano by citing in detail his chain of authorities and eye-witnesses to the events that he reports, namely, the *jihad*, and concludes by describing certain campaigns of the emir Abdullahi under whom M. Zangi served as chief judge. In quite different style, Malam Adamu, who seems to have been born in Kano and to have set out on pilgrimage during the early years of World War II, begins by listing all the holders of some fourteen senior offices of state, each official being identified by his paternity, as is usual among Arabs. Malam Adamu then proceeds to review briefly the history of Kano, beginning with the pre-jihadic Hausa chiefdom, its dynasties, political and ritual forms, and its fall. This is followed by data on the six leading Fulani clans in Kano on the eve of the *jihad*, their leaders and locations, and the work concludes with a chronicle of the reigns of all Fulani Emirs up to 1938.

It would seem that Malam Adamu belonged to the local colony of Arabs from Ghadames who lived near Dalla rock in the city and who have long served as its commercial elite. It is perhaps to these naturalized Arabs that Kano owes its famous Arabic chronicle; but it seems clear from internal evidence that although quite familiar with this document, Malam Adamu had access also to other sources of information on the history and organization of Kano before the *jihad*. Whereas the Alkali Zangi's narrative compiled from the statements of participants is especially valuable in providing details of the *jihad* in Kano and the campaigns of the emir Ibrahim Dabo (1819–1846), Malam Adamu gives greatest attention to such institutional patterns as office holding and succession, dynastic change and ritual observance. Thus these two Arabic histories complement one another nicely and furnish much valuable information.

In September 1972, when the early draft of this monograph had been twice revised, the Sudanese historian, Dr. Muhammad Al-Hajj, kindly dictated an English translation of a second history of Kano, *Al-ilan bi ta'rikh Kano*, which was completed in 1352 A.H. (1933–34 A.D.) by another local Arab, Malam Adam Muhammad ibn Adam el-Funduki, who lived near the Kadiriyya mosque in the city.[10] While covering the same time-span as the work of Malam Adamu na Ma'aji, the two accounts are clearly independent in authorship and preparation. *Al-ilan bi ta'rikh Kano* differs from the book of Malam Adamu na Ma'ajji in details as well as construction and scope, and five chapters of geographical interest precede its chapters on the origins and foundations of Kano state.

For the reigns of the Fulani emirs, Muhammad Bello (1882–1893) and his son, Tukur (1893–1895), whose accession precipitated the bloodiest civil war experienced by any Fulani emirate in the last century, I was able to obtain a translation of the *Faid al qadir ausaf al-malik al-khatr*,[11] a work of anonymous authorship prepared for H. R. Palmer in about 1908 by some well-informed supporter of the emirs Muhammad Bello and Tukur, whose testimony accordingly helps to balance hostile accounts from other sources.

Recently, at the request of the former emir, Alhaji Sir Muhammadu Sanusi, the late Dokajin Kano, Alhaji Abubakar, son of the vizier Alhaji Muhammadu Gidado compiled a fuller history of the state for publication.[12] I visited Kano before the Dokaji's book came off the press; but he graciously provided me with a typescript of his earlier draft and generously advised about the selection of knowledgeable elders on the Fulani and pre-Fulani periods of Kano. Though busy with affairs of state as one of the emir's councillors and district chiefs, he nonetheless found time to discuss various areas and problems of Kano history and thus gave me the benefit of his experience and knowledge. Clearly, this work owes a great deal to the Dokaji Alhaji Abubakar and to Malam Nasiru, though its shortcomings and errors are mine.

Unlike Malam Adamu na Ma'aji, the Dokaji based his account of Kano under the Hausa and early Fulani squarely on the famous chronicle translated into English by the late Sir H. Richmond Palmer;[13] but like Malam Adamu na Ma'aji and Malam Adam Muhammad, the Dokaji Abubakar supplemented this chronicle in various places with data from other sources. In the foreword to his book, Alhaji Abubakar lists several local elders on whose oral traditions about the pre-Fulani state he had drawn. Several of the Dokaji's informants also came to my assistance, for example, Malam Buhari, Malam Maigida Hausawa, M. Maikano na Isan Taba and others named below. Thus, having access to the texts of Alkali Zangi, M. Adamu na Ma'aji, and the then unpublished work of the Dokaji Alhaji Abubakar, as well as most of the historically relevant administrative files, in my interviews with these Kano elders and repositories of oral tradition, I naturally tried to extract further unrecorded information by discursive and systematic inquiries alike.

Finally, however fragmentary and incidental in many respects the observations of such explorers as Horneman, Clapperton, Barth, Baikie, Staudinger, Wallace, Robinson and Monteil, they also furnish information of great value on social and economic conditions in Kano at different points in the last century, as do the periodic reports of administrators and others for this. Though they rarely provide appropriate materials on such intimate features of the social order, the reports of these explorers enable me to check, supplement and extend the account of Kano's government derived from systematic compilations of oral and other data that bear directly on the conditions and processes of political organization and change. Accordingly, I draw readily on all remarks by those first-hand observers that may enrich and deepen my understanding of Kano and its development under Fulani rule.

Kano Before the Jihad

Though they all treat Kano under its successive Hausa, Fulani and British rulers, the Kano Chronicle and recent histories by the Dokaji Abubakar, Malam Adamu na Ma'aji and Malam Adam Muhammad together supply the most consecutive accounts of pre-jihadic Kano available to us. Here also, while corresponding in many particulars, each of these accounts contains some information not to be found in the others, while omitting some data recorded elsewhere. Undoubtedly these differences illustrate the attempts of these authors to scrutinize independently all the oral and other materials on this period they could find. Malam Adam Muhammad, for example, often refers to divergences in the reign-lengths of the five king-lists he had consulted in preparing his account of Kano before the *jihad*.

Another valuable historical document which incidentally provides a new perspective on the famous chornicle is a folk poem, "The Song of Bagauda," which is commonly sung by beggars and destitutes in Kano city and which is now also available in written form. This long poem is evidently a collective creation, as Mervyn Hiskett, who recorded, translated and studied it, has shown.[14] It seems clear from Hiskett's collation of alternative versions that the poem is revised and extended during succeeding reigns; and by collating this text with previously unrecorded information on Hausa Kano from Malam Adamu and the Dokaji Alhaji Abubakar, it is clear that the poem preserves part of a complex tradition that has passed through song and story from generation to generation in a stereotyped form. Perhaps it was this or some parallel tradition which formed the basis for the original compilation of the local chronicle, of which the current though not the final form was translated by Palmer in 1906 or 1907 while he was still British Resident in Katsina and unfamiliar with details of the Kano regime. The Arabic script of the chronicle from which Palmer worked broke off in the reign of the emir Muhammad Bello (1883–1892), who had ordered the text that Palmer used to be prepared. Palmer notes that the authorship of this chronicle

> is unknown, and it is very difficult to make a guess. There is an almost complete absence of bias or partisanship ... The style of the Arabic is not at all like that usually found in the compositions of Hausa malams in the present day; there are not nearly enough "classical tags," so to speak, in it. A young Arab in the employ of the writer who, though he can read and write colloquial Tripoli and Ghadames Arabic, finds it difficult, and in fact impossible, to construe the Arabic books which are most commonly found in Hausaland, read and translated the manuscript without difficulty. That the author of the work was thoroughly *au fait* with the Kano dialect of Hausa is evident from several phrases used in the book ...The original may perhaps have been written by some stranger from the north who settled in Kano, and collected the stories of former kings handed down by oral tradition.[15]

With the publication of the "Song of Bagauda" and the new information independently cited by Dokaji Alhaji Abubakar, by M. Adamu na Ma'aji and by Malam Adam Muhammad in their writings, the persistence and character of a substantial part of this complex of traditions has been revealed. Perhaps the Arabs or other *literati* resident in Kano first recorded and then preserved these ancient traditions, and subsequently added to them on the death of each chief a summary account of the salient features and personalities of his reign. In like fashion the Wakar Bagauda lengthens gradually by a couplet or stanza at the death of each chief.[16]

In 1933 Dr. R. M. East, then head of the Translation Bureau at Zaria from which the Gaskiya Corporation and newspaper both derived, published a Hausa translation of the Arabic chronicle of Kano for the growing body of Hausa literate in the Roman script.[17] In his general evaluation of the text Dr. East follows Palmer closely; however, in preparing his Hausa version for publication, East followed the method as well as the spirit of local tradition, and by careful study of the relevant literature, he brought the chronicle forward forty years from Mamman Bello's reign to that of Abdullahi Bayero who ruled Kano in 1933. Intentionally or otherwise, East's version illustrates the pattern by which the chronicle has evidently grown, as he argues strongly in his preface.[18] This is also the way in which the celebrated chronicles of Songhai and Timbuktu came into being before Mahmoud Kati[19] and Es Sadi[20] gave them their present shape. The date of completion of those two chronicles, especially the earlier, coupled with internal evidence from the Kano chronicle, some of which is allusively cited below, strongly suggests that the initial attempt to sift and record the oral traditions of early Kano and its rulers probably took place not long after 1500 AD. It is moreover likely that the impetus for this literary effort was external in its source; but whether this initial edition and transcription of Kano historical traditions reflects the stimulus of Mali in the 14th century or influences from Songhai or Bornu, both imperial states with vigorous literary cultures, which at one time actively contested domination of Kano and Hausaland, we cannot say. The fluent Arabic in which the text is written suggests an Arab author, while the author's evident familiarity with the Hausa language and culture and with the political institutions of Kano indicates long local residence.

Besides carrying forward the narrative of the Chronicle, East made important contributions by correcting the many mis-spelt proper names of places, titles and people which, given the nature of the Arabic script and his unfamiliarity with the toponymy, titles and names of Kano personalities when he undertook the translation, Palmer could hardly avoid. Because of these frequent mis-spellings of place and personal names, titles and the like, his pioneer work has remained at best an opaque guide to the interior details of Kano's early history. Often Palmer's translated version frustrates rather than facilitates identification of the units to which it refers. It is here especially that East's Hausa version of the Arabic text proves most rewarding. By 1933 the modern Roman orthography of Hausa had been officially adopted; and this, coupled with East's linguistic interests and skills, and his deep knowledge of northern Nigeria, enabled him to correct those misdirections of identity which inevitably resulted from the many minor slips in spelling proper names that makes Palmer's script so difficult to use for detailed reconstruction of the ancient polity. A systematic collation of place and personal names, titles and unfamiliar terms in these two translations enables one to identify most of the local institutions and units mentioned in the Chronicle. It is thus possible, having established the principal forms and details of the Hausa polity on the eve of the *jihad*, by employing the information available in this ancient text, to outline earlier phases of the political organization and to identify some of the processes by which it developed and the principal factors that helped to promote this.

We have numerous external checks on the validity of the Kano Chronicle. Many specific statements about the relations of Kano to such nearby polities as Azben, Bornu, Katsina, Gobir or Jukun, have been verified from the traditions of those units.[21] For developments at Kano during the reigns of Muhammad Rumfa and his successor Abdullahi that together span the years 1463 to 1509, I have been able to check, verify and supplement many statements in the text. The writings of Muhammad El-Maghili, Leo Africanus and the letter that Abdurrahman Es Syuti addressed to the ruler of Tekrur and to Ibrahim, the chief of Katsina[22] are valuable contributions in themselves and also furnish external corroborations of events reported in the local Chronicle. As far back as the reign of Dawuda, the son of Kanajeji (AH 824–841; AD 1421–1438) we can verify salient local events from the court chronicles of Bornu.[23] During Dawuda's reign the Chronicle reports the arrival of a great prince with a host of supporters from southern Bornu. This is almost certainly the deposed Mai (sultan) Othman Kalnama, who withdrew to Kano between 1425 and 1432.

Such external data demonstrate the accuracy and specificity of the information recorded in the Kano chronicle; but of course the Chronicle does not record everything. It was neither written for strangers nor with a view to publication. Its compilation and preservation may well have been known to the rulers and probably had their support; but as the accounts of individual reigns demonstrate, such court patronage did not insinuate any obvious bias or misrepresentations into the document. This was probably due to the fact that the accounts of individual reigns were only compiled for inclusion after the deaths of chiefs whose immediate successors had little interest in glorifying them. In effect the prevailing context of dynastic rivalry and court intrigue allowed the chroniclers to record the most striking events of each reign with equal freedom and neutrality. Intimate details of the considerations underlying decisions and policies of various sorts are rarely given. Instead the Chronicle reports the public actions of chiefs and officials, those events that were indubitably common knowledge, and others which, being unusual, seemed most worthy of note.

Accordingly the Chronicle omits much routine information of the utmost interest to us. It neither describes nor "explains" the traditional patterns of territorial and administrative organization. As it was a purely local document that recorded the reigns of successive chiefs in Kano, successive compilers of this Chronicle could validly assume that their audience would be fully acquainted with the political and administrative systems, the geography and social composition of the state whose history they preserved. Thus instead of describing familiar and traditional arrangements, the chroniclers recorded such significant innovations, deviations, changes and events as the appointment of eunuchs to state offices, wall building, the establishment of new markets, currency innovations, changes in military organizations or techniques, the introduction of new texts on Muslim theology and law, changes in commercial and foreign relations and in the internal distribution of power, famines, wars, eclipses, some creations of new office, some local revolts, the arrivals of notable sheikhs or unfamiliar ethnic groups and similar unique incidents. To appreciate the considerations that governed selection of the items recorded, and to assess their significance to the community and chiefdom, it is therefore necessary to reconstruct in sufficient detail the general patterns of the society and its government. On this basis we may then derive the greatest benefit from the many discrete and apparently bizarre items recorded in the Chronicle. Against such a background, that which at first seemed bizarre often becomes meaningful as an index or moment of innovation and change in the structure, content or context of the traditional regime. But to reconstruct this regime with sufficient detail and depth to illuminate the concrete references in the Chronicle we must draw on other bodies of data including, besides available documentary materials, a structurally systematic collation of oral traditions and an equally intensive study of political developments at Kano from the *jihad* to the present day. With this knowledge we can reconstruct in outline the Hausa state of Kano on the eve of the *jihad* with reasonable detail and verifiability. Such reconstructions are developed by algebraic methods of exclusion and restoration, that which is known to have been modified subsequent to the Fulani conquest being restored to its original state as far as our information permits, while all that is known to have been introduced after 1803 is eliminated from our account of the previous regime, and all that is known to have been discontinued, abolished or replaced following the *jihad* is also restored. The hypothetical and fragmentary nature of the reconstructions that result from such procedures, however meticulous and exhaustive, is not in question. All historical statements, descriptions, narrative and analyses are unavoidably and unfortunately hypothetical and incomplete. Were they otherwise, if they were total representations of the events or forms to which they refer, their historical reproduction and analysis would be simply postponed to some future date, since history is inevitably a selective, implicitly synthetic summary of knowledge of past conditions and events.

Some Problems and Criteria of Adequacy in Historical Reconstructions

For scholars whose historical inquiries fall squarely within a range for which there is an abundance of contemporary documentation, historical reconstructions such as those presented below may seem too weakly grounded to possess historical validity. It is necesary then to discuss this central question briefly but carefully.

Any historical statement or series of statements integrates three dimensions of reality: certitude, significance and adequacy; and it is only by combining these separate scales that we can evaluate historical statements with reasonable confidence.

As regards certitude, historical statements must be evaluated at two levels. Directly or indirectly, such statements presume or refer to concrete events and conditions that prevailed at specific times and places in the recent or remoter past. These events or conditions constitute the irreducible raw material for historical presentation and analysis. We may designate them briefly as facts or as pseudo-facts. In the most mundane senses of the term it is essential that the events or conditions to which any historical statement refers should be verifiable fact rather than pseudo-fact. By a fact here, as elsewhere, one merely means any observation whose particulars can be verified objectively, that is, by independent observers or by external evidence.[24] However, assertions of concrete character which are not directly verifiable vary in their status, probability and base. Some of these assertions may be valid inferences from other verified data. Others may lack such supports; and in all cases the unverifiable assertion can only have a probability value that varies with the relative uniqueness of the events or conditions to which it relates in its particular historical context.

Unverifiable assertions vary in their probability values also as a correlate of the events or conditions to which they refer. Institutionalized practices, being routine, standardized and often obligatory, normally possess high degrees of generality and persistence in traditional regimes whose fabric and continuity are both identified with the validity, maintenance and operation of a traditional order. Thus to delineate the form and history of such an order, we need two major categories of fact. First, we need a sufficient body of relevant information to delineate the institutional forms, categories, procedures and relations that constitute the traditional order. In the nature of the case, these institutional categories, procedures, forms and relations will be collective rather than unique. For example, the forms and modes of taxation, the law and its administration, patterns of community organization and the relations of the chief to officials of various sorts, to the dynasty and to the commoners—these and similar categories of institutional fact, being constitutive, are general throughout the regime, and being standardized are subject to limited variations of content and form. To establish the historicity of such institutional patterns, it is merely necessary to observe the current practice, to record and segregate all known historical changes since the period to which the reconstruction refers, and independently to collect and examine the statements of traditional relations and practice during this earlier phase, collecting these from as many qualified sources, documents or informants as are required to furnish a reasonably full account of such practice by their concordance with one another and with the model extracted by the method of residues. Once these antecedent institutional patterns and categories have been adequately determined, it is then relatively easy to identify the statuses of differing units, offices and collectivities of varying kinds. This step enables us to specify the modal patterns of relationship by which those units were formerly integrated into a common polity; and by this process we are able to move from a general description of the institutional order to specific identifications of its component units and their interrelations. This briefly is the method that I shall employ in the following reconstructions of Kano during the eighteenth and nineteenth centuries.

It is evident that definitions of past institutional patterns based on a systematic combination of contemporary observations, on the specific identification and exclusion of intervening changes, and on the collation of documentary and oral accounts of earlier periods, warrant high degrees of confidence, especially insofar as these patterns are adequately reported and describe a coherent and viable social system. The historical description of such an institutional system consists largely in a series of statements about its institutional categories, procedures, relations and forms. The statements that constitute such an historical account of an institutional order thus differ in form, focus and kind from those that specify the detailed composition of this order, that is, the distribution of component units among its prevailing categories. They also differ in kind from equally specific statements about the conditions or processes by which this order emerged or changed. It is these specific distributional statements and reported incidents of change that are most easily isolated as discrete representations of fact for verification from alternative sources, documents, field inquiries and subsequent institutional or material evidence.

In the nature of the case, specific statements of organizational or processual events fall into three broad categories: those that are verified with or without supplement or modification; those that are falsified with or without qualifications; and those to which uncertainty attaches either in consequence of conflicting assertions about them, or because appropriate external and/or internal checks are not immediately available.

If we seek the same sorts of data and level of details for all eras of Kano history, it can be expected that the relative incidence of verified fact will decline as we move backwards in time from the present. However, this tendency for verifiable data to diminish over time is not uniformly constant. The incidence, quality, and scope of verifiable data fluctuate unevenly as a function of historical perspectives, events and developments within and around the unit concerned. The Fulani conquest and the British occupation both terminated historical periods at Kano; and in consequence both events shed an intense light on the society at these dates. Information of comparable quality and scope is also available for the years 1450 to 1550 and for the reigns of most Kutumbawa rulers, that is from 1620 onwards. Even so, as we move backwards in time, our knowledge of Kano's organization and history steadily decreases, while uncertainty and ignorance take its place. Even as regards the details of Kano's organization on the eve of the *jihad*, there are many gaps in our data. Much that we should like to know is obscure or lost, while other conditions are the subject of conflicting assertions. However, such deficiencies and ambiguities of data are a common condition of historical inquiries; and they need not dismay us. It is merely necessary to practice caution and parsimony in sifting our data; and to separate clearly the verified from the uncertain materials. Provided that we can establish the major institutional forms and their relations, we neither need an exhaustive inventory of the composition of the system, nor do we need to employ unverified or uncertain data. Provided that our verified materials enable us to understand and describe adequately the constitution and operation of the regime, and to identify instances and processes of change, we can pursue our political history without undue distress over the gaps or uncertainties in our information. Provided only that the body of verified fact available does furnish an adequate understanding of the nature and conditions of the regime and its change, we can rest our account and analysis on this hard core of established observations while reporting uncertain events and reserving uncertain data for further study. However, if we cannot verify the institutional framework which constitutes the substance and subject of historical change, then even the most extensive list of verified concrete data about its components and their activities can by themselves neither define the order nor indicate in detail its processes of change. In effect then, given a valid and adequate account of the institutional structure, we can usefully study the historical processes of political change provided that our verified data, although incomplete, are sufficiently abundant and detailed. Conversely in the absence of an adequately grounded account of the institutional organization, this sort of analysis can scarcely be pursued unless an adequate outline of the order is implicit in the valid materials at hand.

Undoubtedly the following account contains many errors of asserted fact and interpretation, perhaps even of chronology also. Though I have made strenuous attempts to avoid or reduce such mistakes, it seems fairly certain that I must have made many; and though naturally I cannot now identify these errors, it is to be hoped that others will correct them. Assuming then that besides its uneven coverage of the composition and development of the Kano polity under the Hausa and, to a lesser extent, under the Fulani, the present text includes various erroneous statements and interpretations apart from those reported but segregated as unverified, it is necessary to ask whether its account or analysis may still be useful or valid. Subject always to correction by subsequent research, and being presently unaware of the errors assumed but acutely conscious of various gaps in my information, it seems clear that, however provisional, our study does enjoy adequate validity on various counts. While numerous shortcomings should elicit corrective research and data, and may thus contribute to the promotion of a more detailed and authentic history of Kano, at the analytic level, errors of asserted fact and interpretation in the present text can hardly determine our theoretical approach or conclusions, since this study is merely one of several that are presumably subject to equal degrees of error of many differing kinds. The comparative framework of the general inquiry thus provides some measure of protection against the derivation of erroneous generalities from analysis of erroneous "fact." However, as we shall see, a serious effort has been made to guard against erroneous reporting and interpretation.

Verified or probable facts are merely the indispensable data of history. They are by no means identical with it. Chronicles such as that of Kano differ from history—as I use the term—in their determination to record events or "facts," including opinions and value judgments, to the virtual exclusion of any analysis of their interconnections. History as practised by Western writers since Thucydides, and as conceived by Ibn Khaldun, has been progressively concerned with the interconnections of events, conditions and other social facts. According to their interests historians of different persuasion pursue relations of differing sort between varying bodies of fact. Some merely seek to establish objective sequences in developments integrated as a series by the presence of one or more common participants, by their occurrence in a common community, or by reference to some other variable. Other writers are preoccupied with seeking causal relations or perhaps correlations within and between sequences of historical events. Some sociological historians seek to reduce a given historical ensemble to a meaningful integration of ideas or orientations, whose internal consistency and compatibility with the social environment, may then be analyzed. It is at this level that historical statements vary most widely in their significance. A typical historical statement asserts one or more relations of varying evidential status between two or more apparently discrete facts, conditions or events. The "typical historian" rarely indicates the theoretical models or axioms that guide his predication of such relations or his assessment of their relative significance. By contrast, as we have seen, Hausa chroniclers tend to regard innovation and change, the unexpected and the bizarre, as significant in themselves and worthy of record, while treating the traditional structure of political relations as too mundane and familiar to note.

Historians document, relate, describe and analyze processes of social change, economic, legal, religious, political or other. Such change occurs always in the interstices or relations between and among antecedent and correlative events. It is inherent in social milieux that many significant interconnections between the same sets of simultaneous and successive facts or events can be produced by scholars with different orientations, assumptions and methods of procedure. Philosophies of history probably differ no less in their range and variety than do the theories of society advanced by sociologists and anthropologists. These differences are nonetheless evidence of the uncertain significance of the relations adduced by different historians with regard to various types of development. Levels of significance vary; and any given social fact, however unique, can be shown to stand in some "significant relations" to a wide range of other social facts, whether these are antecedent, subsequent or simultaneous. However, since historical interpretation typically selects one or some of these various connections as significant to the exclusion of others which may be equally relevant for analysis, and since historians characteristically eschew general theories or models of the sequence or system under analysis, it is often difficult to determine the degree or level of significance possessed by a specific datum or set of relations in regard to a determinate system or sequence of events. Thus historical selectivity, conditioned in part by sheer abundance of documentary materials from those western communities with which historians have traditionally been preoccupied, in part by differences of methodology and interest, in part by the traditional hostility of some historical schools to the framework of social science, and doubtless by various other factors, seems often to defeat its own ends; assertions of significant connection demonstrated by such a theoretical and whimsical selection of data are often purely subjective at best.

It is appropriate then to ask in what respects and by what means the present inquiry may avoid similar subjective assertions of significance or selectivity in the assemblage and presentation of fact.

The comparative research of which the present study forms one part was preceded by an intensive study of the society and history of Zaria emirate,[25] which lies directly south of Kano. This study of Zaria served to identify the institutional forms and relations that together constitute Hausa society; it served also to identify the forms, procedures and relations that together constituted the native system of government; and it is accordingly by reference to their place and roles in these social and political systems that units, procedures or forms of different type are seen to differ in their significance. In effect, the standard and measure of relative significance which has guided the present field work and analysis alike rests on an analysis of the part played by institutions and units of different level and type in the maintenance or change of these traditional polities. This significance varies with the relative centrality or marginality of such elements or events in the Hausa political structure.

The field study of Zaria served also to identify the minimally requisite framework of units, forms, processes, conditions and relations concerning which verified data are essential in order to describe a Hausa polity or allow us to analyze its development and change. It also indicated the most rewarding techniques of field inquiry and methods of data analysis.[26] My field inquiries in Kano have accordingly followed the procedures employed in Zaria, Daura, Katsina and other chiefdoms; they have pursued the same general topics together with any recognizably significant local patterns or developments; and these data have been analyzed by the same techniques.

For this analysis, on quitting the field, an exhaustive index of all recorded materials, oral or other, was first compiled. Some years later, the accuracy and completeness of that index was checked by compiling another, following which all references were summarized and tabulated under every entry in the index. By this means all my information on each particular item—place, person, event, institution or other—has been systematically brought together, thereby juxtaposing data from different sources, oral and documentary, as well as data from the same informants on different occasions, in a form that simultaneously facilitates the identification of inconsistencies and the collation of all my information on each verifiable item. The same tabular inventory and re-organization of data under these index headings serves also to objectify and indicate the relative significance of items and events of the same or different sorts, since the more significant the item, the greater the number of cross-references under various index headings that relate to it. Such measures of relative significance are clearly crude and imperfect. However, significance is a qualitative attribute of structural relations which it is not always easy to measure quantitatively by relative frequency of index entries or by other means. Relative significance can only be demonstrated by the processes of historical change or by an intensive sociological analysis of the connections between various elements that constitute a common structure or system and isolates their several contributions toward continuity or change. To validate such analyses and estimates of significance, it is necessary then to study historical sequences of continuity and change with special care; and unless that is done, sociological specifications of necessary or contingent relations of varying types among the components of a common structure are subject to the same reservations that apply to the general run of asserted historically significant relations.

The third dimension of historical analysis is its adequacy for the understanding or representation of the conditions or sequences under review. Often that which is said to be most significant is merely one of a multiplicity of the relevant or related aspects or relations of given units or events. But adequacy at the representational or analytic levels neither entails nor consists in the complete viridical reconstitution of the total complex situation or ensemble to which the events or elements under study belong. Rather it seems that the criteria of an adequate historical or sociological representation and analysis consist in the minimum sum of verified data required to identify the forms, processes, conditions and interconnections of the institutional units or relations under study, and of the sequence and processes of change to which the account and analysis relates. In effect, then, like its significance and certitude, the adequacy of an historical or sociological account is contingent on the scope and character of the structure to which it refers.

This study of Kano is explicitly conceived as part of an inquiry into the structure of the processes of political change. It accordingly concentrates almost exclusively on the political and administrative institutions and relations of the Hausa society. Together these political and administrative subsystems constitute the gov-

ernment by which the polity and territory of Kano are identified. But this governmental order represents merely one of several institutional systems that together
constitute and define the Hausa society. Assuming that I can list all elements and
relations that enter into the government of Kano, it is relevant to ask whether an
account or analysis of this system of political relations abstracted from its social
milieu is likely to prove adequate or meaningful.

To this query, the appropriate reply is presented in the following chapters. As
a Muslim state, the society and government of Kano were variably subject to the
prescriptions and proscriptions of Muslim law. Society and government alike
were supported by an economy based on rural agriculture, pastoralism, urban
commerce and craft production. The government drew its revenues and remunerated its representatives by arrangements and procedures which varied in their
legitimacy, legality and public acceptance, but which are also easily recognizable
accommodations of the rulers to their social and economic milieu. In like fashion
the structure of social categories and stratification characteristic of Kano at different periods finds full expression in the organization of the government as a
system of offices differentially allocated among persons of differing category and
status. Besides the dynasty and hereditary nobles identified by offices reserved
for their particular lineages, the Muslim intelligentsia of malams (clerics), community chiefs, craftsmen, slaves, ennuchs and such ethnic groups as the Tuareg,
resident Arabs, Nupe, Kanuri from Bornu, pastoral Fulani of different "clans" and
provenience, settled Fulani, princes, or others of royal descent, were all distinguished by specific political arrangements and provisions as related below. In this
way each major social category or unit was represented in the official hierarchy
directly or indirectly. Likewise, all the major interests and institutional processes
of Hausa society, law, cult, economy, kinship, marriage, stratification and descent,
pastoralism, landholding, slavery, and the long distance caravan trade are relevant to a study of the political system, as they furnish necessary conditions of its
operation and subjects of its regulation.

Clearly at Kano the political order attempted to integrate and regulate the
interests and relations of all other institutional systems. Thus, to describe or
analyze the society as an integrated order of interdependent activities and relations, we must examine its political structure and processes of government. Alternatively, we may usefully segregate these political institutions for descriptive
analysis and historical study, provided only that due attention is paid to the relevant and variable social conditions, for example, crop failures and famine, epidemics, population movements, population growth and loss, economic
fluctuations, ideological movements and religious changes, and to many social re-
orientations or alterations in the internal status structure. Thus, given the multiplicity of social conditions and factors that entered into the constitution and operation of the traditional polity, it is neither necessary, valid nor useful to assume
that changes in or of the political system were governed by constant factors, such
as economy or cult. The best answer to such deterministic interpretations of
Hausa political history is given by the data directly.

In Kano as elsewhere the relation between government and society has always
been complex and flexible. The variety of social interests and elements that enter
into the form and substance of the regime as essential constituents, themselves

served to protect the political order against domination by any single institutional interest for very long, however imperious its claims. As shown below, this was equally the case after the *jihad* and after the British conquest. In effect, this means that changes in the form, content and orientation of the local government developed in consequence of internal or external events of an explicitly political character, for example, the conquests by the British or Fulani, decolonization or the like. This means, briefly, that it should be possible to identify the forces and conditions of change within the political regimes of Kano without undertaking an exhaustive analysis of the societal order and its various non-political subsystems, such as economy, kinship and cult, to seek the ultimate sources of these developments. Thus, providing only that our account of the essential institutional elements of the local government and of the conditions and courses of its historic changes is sound and analytically adequate, we may examine its form, content and change without continuous attention to other types of institutional data.

In its general plan the present study follows freely the pattern of my earlier book on the political history of Zaria. I shall begin by trying to describe the polity of Kano on the eve of the *jihad,* using all the recorded and verified oral information at my disposal. Next I shall try to sketch the development of the Hausa polity by confronting my reconstruction of its eighteenth-century form with a detailed study of the Kano Chronicle. Besides thus checking my reconstruction, this confrontation should also advance further our understanding of the Hausa polity and of the Chronicle that records its development. Next I shall describe the Fulani *jihad* and the development of their state up to the time of the British conquest. The chronicle is then carried forward to 1954 in an account that includes summary descriptions of the political regime in 1932 and 1950. I shall then proceed to analyze these data.

Notes

1. Mary Bull cites an official minute which suggests that the first British Resident of Kano, Dr. F. Cargill, allowed or ordered "the destruction of all the old provincial letters, ... an extraordinary thing for a sane man to do," before his retirement in 1908. See Mary Bull, "Indirect Rule in Northern Nigeria, 1906–1911," in Kenneth Robinson and Frederick Madden (Eds.), *Essays in Imperial Government presented to Margery Perham* (Oxford: Basil Blackwell, 1963), p. 77. In addition I was told by British officials at Kano in 1959 that the Provincial Office and records had been destroyed by fire in 1915, but have no independent confirmation of this report.

2. E.J. Arnett, *The Rise of the Sokoto Fulani, being a paraphrase and in some parts a translation of the Infaku'l Maisuri of Sultan Mohammed Bello* (Kano 1922), pp 77–80, 86–87, 99–100.

3. C.E.J. Whitting, *History of Sokoto* (Translation of Al-Hajj Sa'id's *Ta'rikh Sokoto* (Kano, IFE-OLU Printing Works, 1947).

4. Wazirin Sakkwato, Alhaji Junaidu, *Tarihin Fulani* (Zaria, Northern Region Literature Agency, 1957).

5. Most of these letters date from the reign of the fifth Fulani emir of Kano, Muhammad (Mamman) Bello, 1882–1893, and are cited in the account of his reign.

6. A.D.H. Bivar, "Arabic Documents of Northern Nigeria," *Bulletin of the School of Oriental and African Studies*, vol. 22, pp 324–349, 1959.

7. H.F. Backwell, *The Occupation of Hausaland, 1900–1904* (Lagos: The Government Printer, 1927).

8. Alkalin Kano, Muhammad Zangi, *Taqyid Al-akbar* (Kano: 1281 A.H./1864–5 A.D. Unpublished Ms. at the Library of the Shahuci Arabic School)

9. Adamu Na Ma'aji, *Ta'rikh Kano* (Kano: n.d., ?1938–9. Unpublished Ms. in the Library of the Shahuci Arabic School).

10. Adam Muhammad ibn Adam el-Funduki, *Al-ilan bi Ta'rikh Kano* (Kano: 1352 A.H./ 1933–34 A.D. Unpublished Ms. in the possession of Malam Muhammad Al-Hajj, Department of History, Abdullahi Bayero College, Kano).

11. Anon., *Faid al-qadir ausaf al-malik al-khatr.* (Jos, The Museum: n.d. ?1908. Unpublished Ms. in the collection of H.R.Palmer's papers, 372 X 51, 52). For a note on this text, suggesting a possible author, v. Murray Last, *The Sokoto Caliphate* (London: Longmans, 1967), p. xliv.

12. Alhaji Abubakar Dokaji, *Kano ta Dabo Cigari* (Zaria: Gaskiya Corporation, 1959).

13. H.R. Palmer, "The Kano Chronicle," *Journal of the Royal Anthropological Institute*, Vol. XXXVIII, 1908, pp 58–98. Hereafter quoted as KC.

14. M. Hiskett, "The 'Song of Bagauda': A Hausa King list and homily in verse." *Bulletin of the School of Oriental and African Studies* (BSOAS), Vol 27, part 3, 1964, pp 540–567; Vol. 28, parts 1 and 2, 1965, pp 112–135, 363–385.

15. H.R. Palmer, KC, pp 58–59.

16. For a neat demonstration of the growth of the 'Song of Bagauda' by additions at the end of each reign, see M.Hiskett, 1965 *op.cit*, pp 364–365. For his evaluation of the Chronicle, see M. Hiskett, "The Kano Chronicle," *Journal of the Royal African Society*, 1957; and M Hiskett, "Materials relating to the Cowry currency of the Western Sudan - II," *BSOAS*, Vol 29, part 2, 1966.

17. Anon. (R.M.East), *Labarun Hausawa da Makwabtansu* (Zaria: Translation Bureau, 1933), Vol. 2, pp 15–74. Hereafter quoted as LH.

18. Ibid., pp 5–6.

19. Mahmoud Kati, *Tarikh El-Fettach* (Paris: Adrien-Maisonneuve, 1964: translated with notes by O.Houdas and M.Delafosse).

20. Abdurrahman Ibn, Es-Sa'di, *Tarikh Es-Soudan* (Paris: Adrien-Maisonneuve, 1964. Translated by O.Houdas).

21. v. H.R. Palmer, KC, pp 59–60; LH, Vol. 2 pp 5–7; M. Hiskett, "The Kano Chronicle," ; and *idem.*, "Materials relating to the Cowry currency of the Western Sudan" *BSOAS*, Vol. 29, 1966, pp 354–358. See also Abdullahi Smith, "The Early States of the Central Sudan" in J.F. Ade Ajayi & Michael Crowder (Eds.), *History of West Africa* (London: Longman, 1971) pp 193–199.

22. *The Obligations of the Princes, An Essay on Moslem Kingship*, translated by T.H.Baldwin (Beirut: Imprimerie Catholique, 1932); H.R. Palmer, "An Early Fulani Conception of Islam," *JRAS*, Vol. 14, No. 1, pp 55–59; part 2, pp 185–188; Leo Africanus, *The Historie and Description of Africa* (London: Cambridge University Press for the Hakluyt Society, 1896) translated by John Pory, 1603, Vol. 3, Book 7, pp 829–831.

23. H.R.Palmer, KC, p. 60; *idem.*, *The Bornu Sahara and Sudan* (London: John Murray, 1936), pp 93, 219.

24. Bertrand Russell, *The Limits of Human Knowledge.* (London:)

25. M.G.Smith, *The Economy of Hausa Communities of Zaria*, Colonial Research Studies No. 16 (London: Her Majesty's Stationery Office, 1955); *idem.*, *Government in Zazzau, 1800–1950* (London: Oxford University Press, 1960).

26. M.G. Smith, "Field Histories among the Hausa," *Journal of African History*, Vol. 2 part 1, 1961, pp 87–101; *idem.*, "History and Social Anthropology," *Journal of the Royal Anthropological Institute (JRAI)*, Vol. 92, part 1, pp 73–85.

2

Kano under Alwali (1781–1807)

The Society

Sources

To construct the following account of Kano under the last Hausa ruler, Mohamman Alwali II, I have drawn on all the information at my disposal. This includes the Kano Chronicle which says little about Alwali's early years, the later histories of Kano by Malam Adamu na Ma'aji, Malam Adam Muhammad, the Alkali Mohammad Zangi, and the Dokaji Alhaji Abubakar; the fragmentary notes of Horneman, C.L. Temple, W.F. Gowers, and others who have discussed pre-jihadic Kano; the observations of Clapperton in 1824 so far as they permit regressive extrapolations; administrative files and District Notebooks which provide valuable if unsystematic data on Kano organization before the *jihad*; and especially the oral data collected from several elderly men in Kano City who were widely respected as local "authorities" on the pre-Fulani government and society. Besides Malams Buhari, Maikano Abdullahi, Dan Isa and Maigida, the pre-Fulani institutions of Kano were also discussed at length in several interviews with each of the following: the Wamban Sankira Zubairu, Malam Mamman Zango, Malam Mohamman Sani, and the Magajin Dakwara. About one-half of these interviews were individual and private. On other occasions the groups interviewed varied freely in composition. Of these local informants, several traced descent to senior officials who served in the Hausa government under Mohamman Alwali II. For example, Malam Maikano is three generations removed in the direct line of descent from Alwali's senior slave official, the Shamaki Mohamman. Muhamman Zango and Malam Maigida can also trace descent to free senior officials of Alwali's regime. Another, the Wamban Sankira Zubairu, as one of the emir's senior Hausa praise singers, had memorized a great deal of valuable historical material in the stereotyped praise songs which it was his duty to address to officials on appropriate occasions. In addition, out of personal interest, the Wamban Sankira had gathered other traditions about the last Kutumbawa rulers in his early youth. All my informants on Hausa Kano before the *jihad* were of Hausa ("Habe") descent. In 1959 all were over 60 years of age, and Malams Maikano, Mohamman Sani, Magajin Dakwara and Maigida were then past 80. In addition, while in Maradi, Niger, earlier that year, I visited the Hausa Sarkin Kano

Abubakar, Alwali's descendant and the 8th successor to the empty title at Maradun, where this branch of Alwali's lineage have been settled for several generations; and for most of one forenoon we discussed the pre-Fulani organization of
Kano in as much detail as the dispossessed chief, who had never visited his ancestors' domain, could recall.

To derive the following account of Kano under Alwali, I tried to integrate all
these uneven and disparate data by tabulating my information under an extensive series of index categories. This procedure identifies corroborative, conflicting,
complementary and supplementary information obtained from the same or different sources on the same or different occasions. It thus facilitates the classification and assessment of all available items of data for reliability. In the following
description I shall indicate my reservations with regard to the accuracy or completeness of my information wherever necessary; thus unqualified statements are
assumed to be historically correct.

Kano, Katsina and the Caravan Trade

Kano under Alwali was one of the greatest and most ancient states in the
Central Sudan. Possibly then the most populous and prosperous Sudanese city, it
formed a natural terminus for the central Sudanic caravan trade that flowed
through Ghat and Ghadames to and from Tripoli. It also stood on the main
highway between Gonja and Gasrgamu, the Bornu capital on the Yobe River some
80 miles west of Lake Chad; and by reason of its large dense population, which
probably numbered over 400,000 souls at that date, the state provided an attractive market for visiting merchants. By 1800 the city may have contained about
30,000 residents within its walls. During the long dry season between November
and May when the trade routes and markets were busiest, its population may
have swelled by another ten thousand, most of whom were probably part-time
traders and craftsmen from the densely settled districts round about who moved
into town at this season to pursue their occupations in the vicinity of its market.

By 1780 Kano had lost commercial leadership in the trans-Saharan traffic to its
rival Katsina, which lay just under a hundred miles to the northwest. From 1565
until c. 1650 these neighbouring states had waged a long destructive war, probably in part to determine who should engross the lucrative Saharan trade. However, it is possible that this strife was promoted or encouraged by the rulers of
Bornu, who had earlier sought to dominate the Hausa states to their west. Finally
peace was made with Katsina on Kano's initiative during the reign of Shekarau
Dan Alhaji (1649–1651) through the good offices of three leading Kano clerics, the
Shehu Atuman, the Limamin Yandoya and a certain Malam Bawa. To ensure that
the peace would be kept, the Shehu Atuman pronounced a formal curse and
invoked Allah's wrath on all who broke it; and thereafter Katsina and Kano have
been at peace.

Cessation of these hostilities in 1650 ushered in a period of great prosperity for
Kano. For the next 80 years, it was the unchallenged commercial capital of the
Central Sudan, an emporium that engrossed the desert and trans-Sahilian trade
linked by frequent caravans to Nupe, Ashanti, Asben and Gwanja and eastwards
to Gasrgamu, Bilma and Wadai. It was probably at this time that Kano's indigo-
dyed cloth became a standard article for fashionable wear from Timbuktu and

further west in the Sudan to Murzuk, Fez and Tripoli on the Mediterranean. Katsina, the center of finest Hausa leatherwork, lay too far north in the Sahil to compete with Kano in this clothing trade. The cotton and indigo on which Kano's prosperity and commercial dominance was largely based at this period require an average annual rainfall of about 35 inches, such as southern Kano receives, unlike the area of Katsina's densest population, one degree of latitude further north.

To visiting merchants, Kano's cloth industry was a major attraction. During the 17th century standard strips of cloth, the *turkudi* (pl. *turkuda*), of uniform size, weave, and dye served as an accepted currency throughout the central Sahara and Sudan. These *turkuda* were produced in southern and central Kano, in northern Zaria and adjacent Rano, the regions best suited to cultivation of cotton and indigo. Farmers, weavers, and dyers in those areas thus had a ready and almost illimitable market for their cloth currency; and of course, although the values of *turkuda* varied regionally and seasonally, its currency value always corresponded in some degree to its local demand as clothing and thus to its local price. Under such conditions, the Kano cloth industry expanded to supply extensive markets opened to it by the increasing caravan traffic; and in consequence of the profitability of this clothing trade to merchants as well as to the local producers, the caravan traffic to and through Kano seems to have grown equally with local increases in the output of quality clothing, and of cloth for currency or wear. Caravans also visited Katsina, bringing salt, copper, paper and northern goods, and purchasing the beautiful Katsina leather goods, water skins, some fine clothing, and the like; yet even then Kano was probably the major market. There the large densely nucleated population around the capital provided an excellent market; and local traders as well as resident Arabs were eager to serve as middleman by purchasing surplus goods for export further south, east or west to Nupe, Katanga (Oyo), Zazzau, Kumasi, and perhaps also to Jukun. Thus Kano merchants learned commercial skills and techiques by competition with Ghadames traders resident in the city.

Besides clothing, leather, metal work, foodstuffs and other standard Hausa products in which visiting merchants were interested, slaves, a major staple of the Saharan traffic, were also exported to Bornu in the east and southwards to Oyo and Nupe for further shipment to the New World. Once again, Kano was better placed to supply the foreign markets with slaves than was its major rival, Katsina. Slaves were generally recruited from nearby communities whose members were neither Muslim nor spoke the Hausa language as their native tongue. Raiding, the major means by which slaves were secured for export, had always been state-organized and regulated. It was thus exclusively an official enterprise; and by comparison with Katsina, Kano City lay much closer to substantial slave reservoirs.

Due south one hundred miles was the city of Zaria, capital of another ancient and powerful Hausa state. Today Zaria City still stands only 60 miles north of the limits of continuous Hausa occupation. By orientation as well as their geo-social context the Hausa of Zaria relied on slaves as their staple export. Unquestionably many slaves from Zaria were marketed at Kano and probably by local traders who visited Zaria to purchase these profitable commodities. Probably few caravans then passed beyond Kano to the Zaria slave markets, as Kano could supply their demands. The rulers and merchants of Kano also were concerned to keep their city as the terminus of the trans-Saharan trade by supplying its needs as fully as possible.

By 1700 Kano was clearly the leading economic center in this region. The overwhelming bulk of the lucrative caravan trade, both trans-Saharan and trans-Sudanic, passed through its market. Not long afterwards, Mohamman Sharefa (1703–1731) sought to increase his revenues by introducing monthly market taxes.[1] Sharefa's son and successor, Muhammadu Kumbari (1731–1743) increased this market taxation, perhaps in response to inflationary conditions linked with the introduction of cowrie currency during Sharefa's reign.[2] In consequence, "there was so much disturbance that the Arabs left the town and went back to Katsina, and most of the poorer people in the town fled to the country."[3] From then until some decades after the *jihad*, Katsina replaced Kano as the commercial capital of Hausaland; and by 1770 in consequence Katsina enjoyed an unprecedented wave of prosperity and expansion.

The new cowrie currency did not immediately displace the old cloth currency. As late as 1824, Clapperton notes that cowrie currency had penetrated no further eastwards than Katagum, then under Fulani rule. In Bornu and to the north, "native cloth, or some other commodity of standard price, had been the common medium of exchange."[4] On Barth's observations, it seems that cowries had little part in the Bornu exchange system before the mid or late 1840s, that is, more than a century after they circulated in the Kano market.[5] Thus, despite the relocation of Arab and Tuareg trading agents in Katsina following Kumbari's reign, *turkuda* and other Kano cloth was still in great demand for currency and for wear. Perhaps some Katsina merchants undertook to supply the visiting caravans with this Kano product. It is also probable that slaves were then brought north from Kano and Zaria to Katsina for re-export to and across the Sahara. By these and other means Katsina retained the economic leadership of Hausa which it owed to Kumbari's policy until the Fulani conquest and subsequent struggles destroyed it.[6]

Nothing in the Kano Chronicle suggests that Kumbari's successors retrieved the fortunes he lost. Rather we are told that shortly after his accession, Muhamman Alwali, the last Hausa chief of Kano, anticipating famine, collected huge stores of sorghum and millet; "nevertheless, famine overtook him."[7] Alwali's policy may reflect some economic reorientation at Kano, at least in ruling circles. Perhaps Alwali sought to compensate for the loss of Kano's lucrative commerce by renewed emphasis on agriculture. In any event, while there was no famine at Kano before 1804–1807 during Alwali's reign, the state had lost its chief commercial assets, and probably the expansion of its cloth industry had also slowed to a halt. There may even have been a significant economic depression at the urban center. The wave of prosperity that swept Kano along from 1650 until 1731 had now passed to Katsina.

Bornu and the Hausa Bakwai

At longitude East 8 degrees 30 minutes, Kano City stands due south of Daura and north of Rano and Zaria, all capitals of ancient Hausa states. Eighty miles eastwards stood Biram (Garun Gabas) in modern Hadeija. Northwest lay Katsina, and beyond that Gobir. These states identified themselves as a group that shared common kinship and descent. According to the famous Hausa origin myth, all were founded by the descendants of one Bayajidda or Abuyazid who married the Queen of Daura after slaying a mythical snake which denied her people access to their only well.[8] Bayajidda is said to have fled westwards from Kanem-Bornu where the Magumi dynasty of Sefawa descent had long ruled. On his westward flight Bayajidda left his wife, the Magira or senior princess of Bornu, at Garun Gabas where she bore his son Biram who later ruled this region as its first chief.

In Daura, besides a son, Bawo, by his wife the queen, Bayajidda is said also to have begotten another, Karba Gari, by a Gwari concubine given to him by his spouse. From Karba Gari, according to the myth, were descended the *Banza Bakwai* or seven non-Hausa states. The latter, Kebbi, Zamfara, Nupe, Gwari, Yauri, Yoruba (Oyo), and the Jukun, or Kororofa as Hausa call them, are thus said to share common descent. Of these, Zamfara and Kebbi lay due west of Katsina, while Yauri stands on the Niger about 100 miles south of Birnin Kebbi. Nupe and Yoruba (Oyo) lay several hundred miles further south. The Gwari occupy a territory that stretches northeast from Nupe to the southern limits of Katsina and into central Zazzau. Of the *Banza Bakwai*, only the Jukun (Kororofa) are east of Zaria. Notably neither of these contraposed lists of states includes Bornu, from which Bayajidda is said to have come and to which all the *Hausa Bakwai* at one time rendered tribute, recognizing its sultan as their suzerain for many years. Of the *Banza Bakwai*, only Yauri and perhaps Nupe were similarly subordinate to Bornu. In addition the seven Hausa states were distinguished as a common cultural group from the societies on their southern and western borders by two basic features. All *Hausa Bakwai*, Daura, Kano, Katsina, Rano, Zaria, Gobir and Auyo, share Hausa as their common native tongue. Despite some differences of dialect their speech is mutually intelligible, and their customs and forms of society are very similar. By contrast the *Banza Bakwai* include several peoples such as the Jukun, Yoruba, Gwari, and Nupe whose native speech differs radically from Hausa. Of the remaining states, Kebbi, Yauri and Zamfara, only the last is preponderantly Hausa in population. However, Zamfara always remained beyond the reach of Bornu imperialism, and perhaps for that reason has not been assimilated to the *Hausa Bakwai* by mythological descent from Bayajidda and Bawo, but is classified among the non-Hausa states instead.

Between Kano and Bornu lay a region known as Bornu Nguderi that contained several minor chiefdoms during the eighteenth century, Tashena, Shirra, Auyo, Gasia, Kazura, Gatarwa, and Garun Gabas or Biram among them.[9] Like Kano and the other major Hausa states at this period, all these minor chiefdoms rendered tribute to Bornu. At Murzuk in 1799 the explorer Horneman learned from a Hausa marabout who may have hailed from Katsina that that state then paid an annual tribute of 100 slaves to Bornu.[10] Despite the military vigour of Gobir at that date, Horneman's informant regarded Katsina and Kano as the two "most powerful" Hausa states.[11] In 1851 another explorer, Henry Barth learned that on their accession, the chiefs of Katsina each had to forward a *gaisuwa* or tribute of 100 slaves to the court of their suzerain at Gasrgamu.[12] Neither explorer estimates the tribute from Kano to Bornu. However, it was probably similar in periodicity, form and value to that furnished by Katsina.

It is said that in the eighteenth century Bornu received Yauri's tribute through Zaria, together with its own; while tribute from the northern states, Kano and Rano, Gobir, Katsina, and Daura, was collected at Daura for transfer east.[13] This may be true since, of all the states thus far studied, only at Daura and at Zaria have I found special officers charged with the care and transfer of these tributes.[14] My data also confirm Barth's observations that under Bornu domination, provided a chief met his tributary obligations regularly, "it does not appear that his sovereign rights were in any way interfered with."[15] Thus, despite its vassal status, the political autonomy of Kano may not have been severely affected by Bornu overrule. Perhaps Kano's obligation to render annual tribute as the price of peace merely reflected prevailing estimates of the balance of military power. However, during Alwali's reign at Kano, the aggressive chief of Gobir, Bawa Jan Gwarzo (1776–1796) repudiated Bornu's claims for allegiance and tribute, and led his army eastwards to assert his independence in the field. Not long before, Kano had had to wage a brief but bitter defensive war against Soba, then chief of Gobir; and it is probable that, despite the demonstration of Bornu's weakness, Alwali was well advised to retain his link with Gasrgamu, the Bornu capital, as an insurance against the armies of Gobir which were then resolutely attacking Katsina.

The Boundaries of Kano, 1780–1800

Alwali's chiefdom included most of the present territory of Kano emirate. However, there have since been several important changes. In the late eighteenth century, when the Kazaure chiefdom did not exist, its present territory was distributed among the adjoining emirates of Katsina, Kano and Daura. The settlement of Kazaura was then a stockaded village (*keffi*) on the northwesterly frontier of Kano; and all Kazaure territory to its south came under Alwali's rule. At that date, the northeastern frontiers of Kano may also have included most of the territory of Gumel that lies west of Kukalbaldi and Shabiru. Most of this area was sparsely populated except for Fulani pastoralists and their herds. The Manga chief from whom the rulers of modern Gumel trace descent then lived further north in Bornu or Niger. The present boundary between Gumel and Kano was established later by severe fighting after the Fulani conquest of Kano.

In outline, the present boundary between Hadeija and Kano emirates corresponds fairly well with the limits of eighteenth century Kano; but in Alwali's day Hadeija was merely a village within the chiefdom of Auyo, and the present territory of Hadeija emirate was divided among several petty states, all mutually independent and subject to Bornu. Between 1768 and 1776, Auyo, perhaps the oldest of these states, suffered a severe attack from Kano, for reasons I do not know.[16] On this occasion, if I interpret the Kano Chronicle correctly, the ruler of Bornu may have ordered the chief of Kano, Babba Zaki, to desist.

At the start of Alwali's reign, the Kano boundary ran southwest from its southernmost junction with Hadeija and past Birnin Bako, Magami and Kongura, before pushing south towards Riruwe. The district of Birnin Kudu formed an independent chiefdom at Alwali's accession, but during his reign the chief of Birnin Kudu is said to have made voluntary submission (*cafka*) to Alwali, and his country was incorporated within the Kano domain as an internally autonomous substate.[17] Birnin Kudu was thus the last of several ancient chiefdoms to be absorbed by Kano under Hausa rule. From its list of local chiefs, that chiefdom may have been founded before Kano during the tenth century AD. It then probably occupied most of the present district of Birnin Kudu and included some territory in the modern province of Bauchi. The walls of Birnin Kudu were over three miles in length and had twelve fortified gates. Its chiefs and people were Hausa of the same stock as Kano to their northwest.

Between 1768 and 1786, the Sarkin (chief of) Kano Babba Zaki, having overrun Auyo "built a house at Takai and almost lived there, but the court refused to live there."[18] Takai lies about 25 miles west northwest of Birnin Kudu, and about the same distance east northeast from Burumburum, then the capital of another independent chiefdom. From Takai, Babba Zaki "made war on Burumburum, (and) took the town by assault, capturing many of the inhabitants and cutting the throats of some, whilst the others fled."[19] Thereafter, Babba Zaki incorporated Burumburum into Kano state. Perhaps it was fear of similar treatment that later led the chief and people of Birnin Kudu to place themselves under Alwali's protection and control without a struggle. The proximity of Takai, which was garrisoned by throne slaves under the command of the Jekadan Garko, a senior military slave official, was probably critical in promoting this decision.

Until Birnin Kudu was incorporated in Kano by Alwali, the territories of Kila and Gwaram which lay beyond it to the southeast were also probably independent. Administrative sources suggest that Gwaram was founded by Fulani from Bauchi after the *jihad* in Kano, and Kila by Hausa before it.[20] Whether this entire southeastern corner of modern Kano was formerly subject to the chiefs of Birnin Kudu, and was thus transferred by them to Kano in Alwali's reign, remains unknown, though probable.

Another obscurity surrounds the status of Rano. According to the Hausa myth of origin, Bagauda, the first chief of Kano, and Zamnakogi who founded Rano were either twins or full brothers. Under the version current at Kano, as Bawo's youngest son, Zamnakogi was denoted by the special term, *auta* and to this day the chiefs of Rano are sung as *Autan Bawo*. The Dokaji Abubakar relates the Kano tradition that their mother placed Zamnakogi under Bagauda's protection. Politically, these kinship idioms probably indicate that the formerly independent chiefdom of Rano, which by descent and antiquity was Kano's equal, had long since been incorporated into the senior state as an internally autonomous local chiefdom bound to Kano by ties of vassalage and kinship. This interpretation fits all explicit statements on relations between Rano and Kano at this period that I could gather.[21] According to the Kano Chronicle, Rano was the target of assault from Kano under Yaji who ruled from 1349–1385.[22] Thereafter, the Chronicle makes no mention of further conflicts between these units; but, apart from numerous assertions that Rano formed an internally autonomous chiefdom within the eighteenth century Kano state, circumstantial evidence indicates this.

Ten miles southeast of Rano lay Burumburum, a town which at this date was said to be equal to Rano in population and wealth. We have seen how Burumburum was forcibly incorporated in the Kano state by Babba Zaki between 1768 and 1776. That conquest brought Kano all its present territory which lies south of Burumburum to the borders of Zaria and Bauchi and northwestwards from Burumburum to Tudunwada. The major unit in that area was the small chiefdom centered at Riruwe in the extreme south. According to my information Riruwe was subordinate to Burumburum before Babba Zaki's conquest; and although subsequently separated for administration and supervision by the Kano chiefs, Riruwe still ranks below Burumburum in the Kano order of precedence.

From Tudunwada westwards, the boundaries of Kano have been virtually unchanged from Alwali's day to ours. All major local units in this area, Bebeji, Kofa, Kiru, Karaye, Gwarzo, Getso and Shanono, were ancient components of the Kano state; and, following the peace of 1650 between Katsina and Kano, the boundary between these states was never disputed until the Fulani emir of Katsina, Mamman Bello (1844–1869) began to build walls around Dan Zabuwa in southeastern Katsina. His neighbour, the emir of Kano Abdullahi, promptly claimed the site and its adjoining territory. To avert strife the dispute was referred to the Sultan of Sokoto, and settled by his decision as related below.[23]

The Population: Ethnic Categories

Before proceeding to describe the political institutions and organization of Alwali's day, it is necessary to give a general account of the Kano population and society. As might be expected in view of its commercial and ecological situation, the population was heterogeneous both in its ethnic composition and with respect to status. Besides Islamised Hausa, the country contained many substantial enclaves of pagan Hausa, or Maguzawa as they are called. In the south on the borders of Bauchi, there are other pagan groups, Warjawa, Ajawa, and 'Mbutawa from whom Kano recruited slaves as tribute (*gandu*) or by raids. These southern pagans spoke unfamiliar languages of the Niger-Congo or semi-Bantu type, and were accordingly subject to harsher treatment from the Muslim Hausa than that meted out to Maguzawa. In Islamic terms these pagan Hausa were classified by their Muslim cousins as protected and friendly heathen (*kahiran amana*); Warjawa, 'Mbutawa and Ajawa who differed in language and culture were regarded as hostile heathen whose subjugation was desirable on religious and secular grounds.

The Hausa chiefdom ruled by Alwali also contained large numbers of Fulani, many of whom had settled permanently in the city or rural towns while others lived as pastoral nomads, moving across the country with their herds from wet season homesteads in search of grass and water, as their descendants do to this day. Kano Hausa accordingly distinguish two major categories of local Fulani, the Bororoje or pastoral nomads, who are also called the "Bush" or "Cow" Fulani, and the Settled or Town Fulani, the Fulanin Gida. Fulani, of course, make many other and different distinctions among themselves, only a few of which concern us here.[24]

All Fulani share with Muslim Hausa an emphasis on agnatic descent and relationships in the allocation of jural status, inheritance, succession and liabilities. Moreover, as with Muslim Hausa, agnation entails no exogamy among pastoral or settled Fulani, whereas among the Maguzawa and southern pagans agnatic descent groups are exogamous. This feature of their social organization accordingly serves to segregate the pagans from surrounding Muslims, both Fulani and Hausa. Lacking exogamous localised lineages ordered by prescriptive relations of descent, patrilineal kin groups among the Muslims, being subject to various situational pressures and contingencies, are labile in their boundaries, composition and social implications. Today most Hausa commoners, despite their agnatic transmissions of property and status, find it difficult to name their grandfather's father;[25] but free nobles and slaves who have interests in particular titles are much better informed on these questions; and patrilineal descent groups of considerable depth and span are characteristic of privileged Hausa. They are even more stringently defined and sustained among the urban Fulani, most of whom practised clerical occupations as malams, jurists and Islamic scholars, and accordingly upheld Arabic values, notions and techniques of genealogical recording.

Pastoral Fulani, subject to very different social and ecological conditions, frequently move their wet season residence as their pastoral programs or social situations seem to require.[26] In consequence of such progressive dispersals of Fulani descent-groups throughout the Sudan from Lake Chad to the Atlantic, Hausa have for long classified Fulani by reference either to the areas in which they reside or to those from which they have come. This mode of classification is of course welcome to pastoralists for its anonymity and the opportunity it offers to shed one's previous local identity. Under the Hausa system of classification, to establish a new identity it was merely necessary for the pastoralists to relocate their wet season residences at intervals.

The cores of these pastoral communities are recruited by kinship, patrilineage and marriage; and irrespective of their relocation, among the Fulani themselves, patrilineal relations are immutable and determine individual identity. Thus while Fulani may periodically assume new identities among the Hausa by serial relocations, among themselves their relations are constant and ascriptively defined.

I know no comprehensive study of the organization of Fulani society. Being so mobile and widely scattered across the central and western Sudan, such studies are difficult to design and execute. Perhaps our best guide on this subject, as on so many others, are the observations of Henry Barth. He distinguishes four tribal groups or stocks among the true Fula, Fulbe, Pullo, or Fulani, as they are known in different places, namely the Jel, the Ba'a, So and Beri.[27] Each of these stocks contains a plurality of tribes, clans and unilineal descent groups. Many of these lesser units are endogamous and occupationally specialized, thus giving the Fulani community the appearance of a caste-stratified social order. As a correlate of these emphases on tribal endogamy and occupational inheritance, Fulani society is an ascriptively defined status order in which prestige and leadership vest prominently in some units to the exclusion of others. This ancient status structure accordingly furnishes a firm but flexible framework for *ad hoc* assemblages of migrating pastoralists, and also orders their relations with the clerical Fulani intelligentsia of the towns. Once an individual's lineage identity is known, his position in the status hierarchy is fixed, and his relations with other members of the Fulani community are consequently determinate and predictable. Their status structure serves further to segregate the Fulani as an ethnic group from other people, wherever they may reside. This follows because the status order, which regulates intra-Fulani relations, being fixed and defined by the myth of their common descent from Ukuba, an Arab progenitor,[28] restricts the incorporation of non-Fulani peoples by extension or fictions. For example, enslavement only permits indirect incorporation of descent lines within the community at the lowest level of slaves and serfs. By the same token, once senior representatives of high ranking Fulani clans and tribes initiate collective action on behalf of the community as a whole, other Fulani tribes and clans of lower caste readily mobilize under their leadership. Their high mobilization potential is thus a function of the social structure of this dispersed, endogamously oriented and internally stratified people, whether nomadic or settled; and during the eighteenth century this capacity for rapid mobilization over wide areas was important in facilitating a number of successful *jihads* led by Toronkawa clerics who, although assimilated in the highest Fulani stratum with the Suleibawa or Sussulbe, are more correctly classified with the Zoromawa, and certain other groups as *rimbe*, or assimilated people, than as true Fulani.[29]

Hausa distinguish also a third category of semi-sedentary Fulani who typically occupy discrete settlements close by a rural town. While these semi-sedentarized Fulani normally have small herds of cattle, they depend primarily on agriculture, craft production and trade. Such groups are generally distinguished as Agwai, the term Rahazawa being apparently reserved for those Agwai who combine seasonal transhumance with subsistence agriculture.

Besides designations by provenience, many Fulani communities settled in Kano are also known by Hausa names which either allude to some specific event in the history of the group or misstate its correct Fulani lineage designation, thereby assimilating its Hausa identification to the category of groups distinguished by reference to place. Some examples will illustrate how these Hausa schemes of denotation conceal Fulani identities and relationships. One of Alwali's senior Fulani headmen was the famous Malam Maiyaki (warrior), also known as Dan Tunku, a name which may refer to some title Maiyaki once held. This Dan Tunku claimed leadership of the Yerimawa Fulani who were settled in northwestern Kano, adjacent to Daura and Katsina, and who formed a distinct community identified by common descent, history and internal leadership. Their name has two complementary etymologies. Some say that their forbears moved to this region from the district of Yeri in western Bornu, the fief of the crown prince or Yerima; but it is also said that the Yerimawa migration from Bornu to Kano followed a clash in which these ancestral Fulani slew the Yerima (Crown Prince) of Bornu. Thus the term Yerimawa, by which this group is currently known in Katsina, Kano, Kazaure and Daura, simultaneously refers to the unit's provenience and to its formation as a distinct group in response to a particular historical event.

An equally famous example of historical differentiation perpetuated by change of name occurs in the descent group now known as the Jobawa. During the reigns of Alwali and his predecessors these Jobawa were settled at Utai near Suma'ila in southeastern Kano. On learning the reputation of the Shehu Usman dan Fodio, it is related that one of these Fulani of Utai, Malam Umaru, took his children to the Shehu's home at Degel in northwestern Gobir and asked the Shehu to accept his daughter Habiba as a pupil. When the Shehu agreed, Habiba immediately asked if he would also consent to teach her younger brother Ahmadu, who later acquired the *lakabi* or nickname of Malam Bakatsine. The Shehu is said to have replied in Fulfulde, "ja ba do," meaning "your wish is granted." According to this tradition, the agnatic issue of Malam Umaru and his two sons, Ahmadu (Malam Bakatsine) and Sa'idu, were subsequently identified as a distinct descent group, and named Jobawa to honor this event. However, it seems certain that

Malam Umaru and his agnates were by birth Fulani of Waijobe stock[30] and that the structurally significant condition which differentiated Malam Umaru's *zuri'a* (agnatic issue) from other Waijobe was the Shehu's recognition of Malam Bakatsine as one of his senior representatives at Kano during and after the *jihad*.

To illustrate conversion of Fulani descent names in Hausa speech into designations for local descent groups, we may cite two lineages settled near Dutse in Alwali's reign. In Fulani speech these two groups are identified as segments of the Jelube or Jelbe and of the Yan Lagi'en respectively. Hausa designate them as Jelubawa (the people of Jelbe) and Yeligawa, the latter being the Hausa equivalent of Yan Lagi'en. Other Jelbe settled in Kano city at this time were distinguished for undetermined reasons as Gyenawa (S. baGyeni). In like fashion the Fulanin Jayen are regarded by Hausa as a segment of the Bebedawa Fulani who take their name from Bebeji in southwestern Kano where their headman resides. Again, the Fulani of Jahun in northeastern Kano came to this area from Mali during the seventeenth century; but such identification of their provenience reveals nothing about their descent, tribal affiliations, and status within the Fulani community. Another important group, the Yolawa who were settled in northwestern Kano in Alwali's day, are Fulani of Ba'a stock. Whether the group owes its common name to its former or current location remains obscure. It is sometimes said that the capital of Adamawa emirate which was established by Modibbo Adamu during the Shehu's *jihad* was named Yola to honor this Ba'a lineage of Kano. However within the city, during and after Alwali's reign, the leading members of this Ba'a group lived in the ward known as Tudun Yola (the Yola rise or slope). It is thus quite possible that this Ba'a group at Kano received its name from the city ward in which its leaders dwelt. In like fashion, one branch of Jelubawa are known as Kurawa because their members lived in that ward of the town.

Merely to list some of the more important Fulani groups who had long dwelt at Kano under Hausa rule may indicate their variety and importance. Apart from the Yolawa, Jobawa, Yerimawa, Jelubawa, Yeligawa, Gyenawa, Bebejawa, Fulanin Jayen, Agwai and the Mallawa at Jahun, there were large, internally diverse Suleibawa communities in southwestern Kano and adjoining Zaria; Danejawa concentrated at Zuwo and Kiru close by one branch of Suleibawa; Dambazawa, under the leadership of Malam Dabo of Dambazau in northern Kano, Mundubawa or clerics (Modibbawa), concentrated in Kano city and its immediate environs; Dokajawa, Daurawa, Jelurawa, Dugujawa, Cilabawa and several Fulani groups from Bornu, one of whom, the Zarawa, achieved prominence later.

Hausa-Fulani Relations

The political and administrative arrangements by which this large diverse Fulani population was incorporated into the Hausa state are briefly discussed below. Here we should note that besides differentiation through dispersion, descent and status in Fulani society, Fulani groups were also differentiated by occupation and ecology. Bororoje, Rahazawa, Agwai and Fulanin Gida occupied mutually distinctive social and economic contexts in view of their differing measures of nomadism or sedentarization. As we would expect, members of many Fulani tribes or clans were ecologically differentiated by distribution within these categories.

Relations between Fulani and Hausa varied as an aspect of the sedentary or nomadic habits of the various Fulani groups. Pastoralists in transit had very limited and specific relations with the sedentary Hausa across whose lands they moved. The pastoralists were most closely linked to those Hausa communities in which they had their wet season homes and gardens. Rahazawa, having long established local communities in specific areas, were more or less continually engaged in a wide variety of social interactions with the Hausa grain farmers and craftsmen, officials and traders around them. Nonetheless, following Fulani traditions, however sedentary, these localized groups, although freely taking women from other groups as wives or concubines, disapproved the transfer of Fulani girls in return. Even in the Hausa capitals, the Fulanin Gida likewise maintained their distinctness by avoiding intermarriage and kinship assimilation with the Hausa ruling group. Hausa-Fulani relations accordingly lacked those basic solidarities with which ties of kinship, affinity and marriage furnish communities at these levels of social and economic development. Instead, even in the Hausa capitals, Fulani strenuously preserved the social distance they found essential to maintain their ethnic closure and traditional status within the distinctive order of Fulani society.

Whereas the Bororo, Rahazawa and Agwai categories of Fulani were clearly subject to Hausa institutions and variably dependent on Hausa goodwill, the Fulanin Gida occupied a somewhat different position, particularly that large segment of this group which specialised in clerical Muslim occupations and served as teachers, priests, scribes, copyists, jurists, marabouts, and in cognate roles that presupposed literacy in the Maghrebine Ajemic script, and a working knowledge of Arabic and Islamic teachings on theology and law. At Kano such Fulani clerics probably constituted the bulk of the local Muslim *'ulama* or learned men (*malamai*, s. *malam*), indispensable for the organization and guidance of a Muslim community. As we have seen, they were also segregated by ethnicity and language from other local *'ulama* as leading elements of a very numerous and widely dispersed Fulani community. Besides their routine clerical functions, many of these Fulani malams devoted themselves to intensive study of the available Islamic texts, and in their schools, writings and addresses they discussed and disputed such critical but apparently innocuous questions as Jibril's assertion that innovation constituted disbelief and apostasy.[31] Many of these Fulani clerics were already enrolled in the Kadiriyya order (*tariqa*), knew of the Fulani *jihad* in Futa Toro, and were sensitive to the Islamic revival launched by Shaikh Jibril of Agades throughout the central Sudan. Preoccupied in their religious fraternities and schools with such doctrinal questions, the Fulani *'ulama* kept aloof from their immediate environment, whose Islamic status seemed to them ambiguous and questionable. However, many Fulani held important official positions in Hausa government, typically as headmen of semi-nomadic pastoral communities. Others served as judicial assessors, scribes and imams (*limam*, pl. *limamai*). A few clerics probably served as scribes; and those Fulani whose secular orientations allowed them to accept the ritual syncretisms that characterised the accommodations of paganism and Islam in eighteenth-century Kano could freely assimilate to Hausa society by pursuing political, military and administrative careers. The Hausa chiefs of Kano were always ready to welcome and reward such supporters.

Tuareg and Arabs

Scattered throughout the northern districts of the chiefdom were numerous discrete settlements in which the Tuareg of Agades and Damargu had, with the consent of local chiefs and the king's permission, settled their *Buzaye* (s., *Buzu*) slaves and serfs. Annually the Tuareg visited Kano, bringing salt in caravans that sometimes exceeded 3,000 camels. Having deposited their salt with local agents for re-export or sale, they would purchase the supplies they needed and visit these serf estates to collect their shares of the grain harvests. One-tenth of the total crop was transferred to the local chief for the ruler, as required by the Muslim law of *zakat* (*zakka*). In addition Tuareg slave-owners were expected to make appropriate gifts to chiefs of the areas in which their estates lay and to its ruler before setting out for home.

At Kano city, besides local communities of Kanuri (Beriberi), Nupe, and Hausa from other states, the most notable trading group were those Arabs from Ghadames and Ghat, who had remained in Kano despite Kumbari's "oppression." Those who remained in Kano after that served as local agents for their merchant kinsmen at the Katsina capital.[32] Like other communities of resident aliens, these Arabs occupied a special ward in the city supervised by an officially recognized headman whom they selected from among themselves. Equally at home in Hausa and Arabic and in close, continuous contact with their kinsmen at Tintellus, Ghat and Tripoli, these Kano Arabs acted as bankers, warehousemen and trading agents for much of the trans-Saharan traffic, administrative and commercial alike. As the journals of European explorers show, Arabs at Kano or Katsina would often provide local travellers or merchants with the goods or currency they sought in return for written undertakings to pay specified sums to other Arabs living near or on the Mediterranean.[33] Conversely, a trader or traveller could make a deposit at either terminus in return for a promissory note instructing its receiver's partner or agent en route or at the journey's end to pay a specified sum or to transfer the equivalent in goods if desired after a stated interval of time. The network of credit and commercial relations those Arabs maintained solely on the basis of mutual good faith and co-operation spread from Chad to Timbuktu and from the Mediterranean to the Sudan.

Like Fulani, the local Arabs willingly accepted native women as wives or concubines while reserving their daughters for their kinsmen and fellow Arabs; but while Fulani exclusiveness helped to reinforce their specializations as pastoralists or as a closed intelligentsia in which Islamic learning and ideals were preserved and transmitted within lineages linked by kinship and marriage, among the Arabs ethnic closure enabled them to preserve their delicate and extensive commercial arrangements as a corporate ethnic monopoly. However they may have disapproved the local practice of Islam, as a protected group of alien merchants, these Arabs apparently withheld their comment and confined their public interests to the market and the caravan trade. Some adopted the local practice of slave farming in internally autonomous settlements under resident slave headmen. Occasionally, they served the chief or his treasurer, the Ma'aji, as scribes, creditors, commission agents or simply as translators and computers. As we have seen, they were also probably responsible for compiling and maintaining the local chronicle,whether with the ruler's support we do not know. Otherwise, they kept away

from the court, and administered their community affairs after their own customs, as their descendants still do.[34]

Incorporated Communities and Chiefdoms

In Alwali's day, the majority of Kano's people were Muslim Hausa, whose
religion and law were pragmatic mixtures of Islamic and heathen practice. Nonetheless, these Muslim Hausa distinguished themselves from their Maguzawa
ancestors and cousins by their formal attachment to Islam, and from all other
ethnic groups in Kano by their historic identification with the state and its territory. This native population of Muslim Hausa were the *Kanawa*, the "people of
Kano" in the fullest sense. The decisive elements that served to unite and distinguish them as a single collectivity from other Hausa populations nearby and from
other groups within Kano were the polity and the state, the former consisting in
those systems of implicitly or explicitly political relations that spread serially in
intersecting and concentric circles at differing levels of organization to the limits
of Kano society, while the state was identified with and regulated and symbolised
by a highly centralized official hierarchy, whose members were differentiated by
their status, scope, relations, resources, place, history and procedures of action.

As we have seen, even in Alwali's reign, the Kano polity was still expanding
by the incorporation of formerly independent communities and chiefdoms as
subordinate components. For several centuries the Kano chiefdom, that is, the
state and polity conceived as a single integrated structure with these two aspects,
had grown by similar processes to its present dimensions. Besides Rano, Burumburum and Birnin Kudu, in Alwali's day Kano had long since forcibly absorbed
the large adjacent chiefdoms of Gaya, Dutse, and Karaye, together with many
smaller ones such as Santolo, Gano, Dal, Sarina, Debbi and others, either unrecorded or previously themselves incorporated by Gaya, Rano, Dutse, Karaye and
Birnin Kudu, before they in turn fell prey to Kano. In addition, some small chiefdoms had been founded within the territory of Kano by Fulani immigrants at
Jahun, Bebeji, Shanono, Dambarta, Aujara and Minjibir; and others by movements from the city, such as that which established Godiya in the reign of Shekarau, immediately after peace was made with Katsina c. 1650.[35] Residents of these
local chiefdoms and other rural communities participated indirectly in the political life of the state by responding to its ruler's policies and measures under the
guidance of local officials and chiefs whose appointments and authority were, at
least in theory and tradition, to some degree contingent on distributions of power
and support within the local community. Thus, in effect, each group of local communities identified by common subordination to a specific local chief constituted
a discrete political unit whose population was frequently organised in contraposed factions (*kunjiya*; pl., *kunjiyoyi*) which competed for dominance or independence. Apart from the numerous ties of kinship, marriage and affinity by which
the members of such politically demarcated units were internally differentiated,
bound together, and variably linked to others elsewhere, besides their general
espousal of Islam, and their individual participation in the markets of adjacent
communities, the framework that held these hundreds of discrete units together
consisted in a complex hierarchic administrative structure that bound wards and
hamlets to villages and often several villages to a common local chief, himself

subject to the authority and supervision of officials at Kano. Often, but by no means always, adjoining communities or collections of settlements sprung from a common centre were distributed among several chiefs or officials of similar or different status, each separately responsible to the ruler for the administration of particular units. Alternatively, relatively large blocs of territory were locally organized under resident chiefs typically recruited by descent from leading members of the local dynasty as at Rano, Dutse, Birnin Kudu or Gaya. In miniature such incorporated chiefdoms replicated the administrative pattern of Kano polity. In scale they constituted social units whose internal integration through interconnected hierarchies of command and obedience and labile structures of alliances, oppositions, clientage, factional and dynastic strife distinguished their aggregates as intermediate in size between the discrete communities previously mentioned and the polity as a whole. To illustrate the point, before proceeding to particularize the institutional structure of this inclusive unit, let me briefly summarize the essential elements of Hausa social organization.

Principles and Forms of Social Organization

Like Fulani, Arab, Kanuri and other Muslim residents in Kano, Muslim Hausa emphasize patrilineal descent with respect to residence, occupational inheritance, status, succession and the transmission of property or liabilities. In the higher strata of Hausa society, this patrilineal emphasis, coupled with family interests in status, property and office, usually generates agnatic descent groupings of significant size and depth; but these groupings are neither exogamous nor internally uniform. Their members differ sharply in status and prospects largely as an effect of differences in the political rank of their fathers. Moreover those kinsmen whose father or fathers held the same office or offices of similar rank are unavoidably competitors for such positions. This follows from the structure of Hausa kinship and status allocation.

From the late fifteenth century onwards, Hausa society has been characterized by a marked stratification. It is easy to trace the specific development of this status order and the conditions which served to promote it at Kano in the local Chronicle. This has already been done in outline and need not be repeated.[36] Long before Alwali's day, Hausa society had assumed its traditional form, much of which still persists today.

A major distinction within this society lay between the slave and the free; but slaves were themselves distinguished initially by the condition that attached them to their particular owner, namely, captivity, purchase or birth within the estate of the owners' family. Slaves of the latter sort were distinguished as *dimajai* or *cucanawa* whose alienation was prohibited by morality and law unless their conduct enjoined it. In contrast, purchased or captive slaves could be disposed of at their owner's pleasure, being normally pagans and alien by birth, language and culture. *Dimajai* and *matankara*, slaves of the third or succeeding generations, differed by virtue of their socialization from infancy to Hausa society, culture and language. Though not jural persons under Muslim law or Hausa custom, they knew no other culture or form of social organization. Though members of the society, with positive interests and many private rights, particularly against their owners, the law denied them the status and initiative it granted to free men.

Women also, under this local mixture of custom (*al'ada*) and Muslim law (*shari'a*) remained jural minors, subject to numerous incapacities in relations with their agnatic guardians and husbands alike. However, by Muslim law women may demand divorce, recover debts from their husbands or others, and hold property in their own name. By contrast, Hausa custom denied women the right to inherit valuable capital goods (*dukiya*) such as land, farms or compounds, except when widows acted as trustees for their sons. Women could, however, inherit slaves, cattle and other *res mobiles*;[37] but pastoral Fulani oppose female inheritance of cattle, their major capital good. Finally, except for certain offices reserved to the chief's kinswomen as mentioned below, all females were entirely excluded from the political system. They nonetheless participated passively in this sector of social life whether by transfer as brides to cement political alliance, to reinforce selective kinship links, or as concubines (*kuyangi, kwarakwarai, sadaku*) who ranked among the greatest rewards the system had to offer. Under Muslim conventions, concubines, if they have borne him offspring, become free on their master's death. Moreover descent being traced agnatically, a man's offspring by his concubine have the same status at law as those by his wife. Normally, however, offspring of concubines receive smaller shares of their father's estate than the children of free wives.[38]

Slave status varied substantively as a reflex of status differences among the slave-owners. The extremes in this variation are presented by the senior slaves of a chief and those of a lowly commoner. While the ruler's senior slaves often had reason to fear him, they had no reason to fear anyone else. Indeed, as throne slaves they were often far freer than the free; and this condition of political immunity attached also to their juniors, since commoners feared lest they should challenge the chief's authority by challenging that of his slaves. Throne slaves were thus widely regarded as representatives of the chief, and as manisfestations of his will and personality. Public attitudes towards the slaves of senior officials, royal and other, were similar in content and expression. However, only those slaves who held administrative or political roles as agents or official subordinates (*lawanai*) of their lord received such deference from the free community. Others whose lot was labor on the official's farm, herds or compound, whether born in slavery or not, had no special claims to public deference independent of their master's favor.

Eunuchs formed a very small but highly esteemed and distinct social category. It is said that Kano obtained its eunuchs from Zaria, Nupe, Bornu and other centers of supply; but probably some were manufactured locally. Eunuchs were usually familiar with Hausa society and culture by virtue of their socialization within it or in similar Muslim societies, before or after castration. Even more than the captive slave, the eunuch was a kinless person, finally and totally divorced from his family and kinsmen by virtue of his condition, and equally incapable of marriage and offspring. Moreover a eunuch's status was immutable and his condition could not normally be hidden. He accordingly approached closely the most stringent criteria of a loyal disinterested servant fully identified with his master's interests. Lacking heirs, kin, and all essential qualifications for offices other than those specifically reserved for males of his condition, the eunuch was free of familial interests, ambitions and antagonisms. At best he could merely hope to increase his influence with his master by demonstrating his ability and loyalty among the limited and select company of his fellows. He was usually also too valuable to destroy. Chiefs who wished to rid themselves of suspect eunuchs might thus either send or permit them to set out on pilgrimage, that is, informally set them free; or they could donate them to rulers of other states; or, at Kano, they might send them as tribute to Bornu; or, more rarely, sell them in the open market or present them as gifts to senior subordinates. Characteristically, eunuchs served in the harems of the chiefs and senior nobles. At Kano in an earlier age, absolutist rulers had aggrandized power and centralized authority by appointing trusted eunuchs to senior public office,[39] but by Alwali's day the ruler's eunuchs had lost such public authority, and took no part in affairs outside the palace.

The major categories of the Hausa status structure are the *masu-sarauta* or officialdom, the *malamai* or Muslim intelligentsia (*'ulama*), the *attajirai* or wealthy merchants and *talakawa* or commoners, themselves internally classified by reference to occupation, age, wealth and place of residence.[40] Of the *masu-sarauta*, some held their office on grounds of descent (*asali*), or traced descent from hereditary officials. Such people are generally distinguished as *sarakuna na asali*, or simply *sarakuna*, that is, rulers by origin or descent, while other *masu-sarauta* having no hereditary claim to the offices they held are generally described as *shigege* or *kat-siro*, that is, as socially and occupationally mobile self-seekers. Of two men holding offices of similar level, the hereditary official always outranks the *shigege* in status and prestige. Likewise, of two men who practice the same occupation, the one who claims it by inheritance (*gado*) always takes precedence over the colleague who adopted his occupation independently. Thus occupational and social mobility is disvalued and discouraged as the repudiation of one's paternal inheritance, an innovation which if unduly frequent could threaten the continuity of the status order on which the stability of the political structure depends. Nonetheless, there are no legal or other proscriptions against individual changes of occupation. Men may apprentice their sons to affines, neighbours or friends whose occupations differ from their own. Orphans are commonly subject to this contingency. More often in adult life, men seek their fortunes in the marketplace, and, if successful, gradually abandon their paternal craft.

Malanci, or Islamic scholarship, is an inherited occupation among Hausa, as among the Fulanin Gida. But whereas at this date it was the most prestigious occupation among Settled Fulani, among Hausa it had competing attractions in the market and government. Relatively few Hausa lineages therefore maintained rigorous clerical traditions characteristic of Moorish or Fulani clerical clans over a span of three or more successive generations. With certain strategic exceptions such as the clerical community at 'Yandoto in southwestern Katsina, who were probably of Mandinka (Wangarawa) stock, Hausa malams were generally recruited from other occupational groups through early attachments to the cleric's life during childhood in the Koranic school of some benevolent or inspiring teacher. Such Koranic schools abound throughout Hausaland, and cluster especially in and around its capital cities; but various rural towns also achieved renown for the number and quality of their resident malams and Koranic schools. Often clerics moved to places where their calling was respected and where they could share the company of colleagues advanced in studies of theology, Arabic and law. Such communities existed at Fatika in Zaria, 'Yandoto in the Guangara (i.e., Wangara, Katsina Laka) of Leo Africanus, and at Degel in Gobir during the Shehu's lifetime. There were several such centres of learning in rural Kano during Alwali's reign. For the most part, however, clerics and their pupils concentrated in such communities were drawn from the settled Fulani intelligentsia. Islamic scholarship remained peripheral to Hausa culture; and for such guidance in Muslim law and doctrine as they required, the Hausa often had to look to Fulani or foreign clerics.

An important and characteristic Hausa institution is clientage (*barantaka, baranci*). This is a relation between two individuals, groups, or social units of different status, for example, suzerain and vassal, principal and agent, lord and courtier, teacher and pupil, the object of which is the reciprocal and mutual promotion of one another's welfare and interest by mutual loyalty and good faith (*amana*) within a competitive context. Clientage thus links members of the various layers of Hausa society from the chief to the lowliest commoner. Chains of clientage are joined together through the alliances and convergent allegiances of their patrons; and thus several sets of such relations may be organized in a loosely pyramidal structure, adjacent levels of which are pinned together by immediate loyalties of patron and client, while the aggregate as a whole derives its validity from political competition with some parallel structure or from collective enjoyment of some political advantage.

It is inherent in the Hausa institution of clientage that the client may only have one political patron to whom he relates immediately, whereas the patron, to pursue power and influence requires many influential clients. It follows from the structure of Hausa kinship and local organization that young men can neither establish relations of clientage independently of their father nor often, after his death, though less prescriptively, of their father's brothers. This reflects the fact that the political and administrative relations of all who live in joint families (*ganduna*, s. *gandu*) are subsumed by those of the *gandu*-head. Administrative relations include direct and indirect obligations of obedience to the orders of the local chief or his representatives. The strictly political relations are those of clientage and patronage through which factional associations (*kunjiyoyi*) are developed to support or oppose the chief and his officials, to compete for office or to press particular policies, appointments and programs. At any level of the social structure, clientage presupposes loyalty and good faith; but hierarchic groupings built by serial chains and combinations of these relations are naturally weakest at their points of linkage where the leaders of important aggregates indirectly affiliate themselves as clients of some superior patron through some intermediate link. It is thus at such points that the general framework of Hausa political association is often most unstable.

Religious Syncretism

The Fulani conquest of Hausaland in 1804–10 is legitimized by the Shehu Usmanu's call to local Muslims to join his *jihad* (holy war) for the defence, purification and expansion of Islam in this area. In proclaiming this *jihad*, the Shehu initially restricted his interest to the chiefdom of Gobir, whose rulers he classified as heathen because they combined Islam and pagan rituals, and directed or permitted attacks against his Muslim *jema'a* (community) at Gimbana, Matankare and elsewhere.[41] Only later was the *jihad* extended beyond the boundaries of Gobir to Kano and other nearby chiefdoms. The Shehu's son, Mamman Bello relates how the Hausa rulers of Katsina, Kano and Daura, then all under Bornu protection, brought their forces against the attacking Fulani and consequently identified themselves to the Shehu's community as heathens.[42] Since ultimate justification of the Fulani conquest of Kano rests on the charge of heathenism against its Hausa rulers and specifically against Alwali and his immediate predecessors, it is inevitable that subsequent discussions of the Hausa regime by local Fulani and other Muslims should stress its heathen elements.

The Kano chronicle merely reports that on Alwali's accession he immediately collected stores of grain against anticipated famine:

> His chiefs said to him, "sarkin Kano, why do you refuse to give cattle to Dirki?" The Sarki said, "I cannot give you forty cattle for Dirki." They said, "What prevents you? If any Sarkin Kano does not allow cattle for Dirki, we fear that he will come to some ill." Alwali was very angry and sent young men to beat "Dirki" with axes until that which was inside the skins came out. They found a beautiful Koran inside Dirki. Alwali said, "Is this Dirki?" They said, "Who does not know Dirki? Behold here is Dirki. Dirki is nothing but the Koran."

In Alwali's time the Fulani conquered the seven Hausa states under the plea of reviving the Mohammedan religion.[43] Thus at best this contributor to the chronicle neither accepted the Fulani justification of their conquest nor does he provide any evidence of Alwali's heathenism. Rather, the Muslims could applaud Alwali's desecration of the central fetish of the Kano chiefship which Malam Adamu na Ma'aji, writing 150 years later, plausibly attributes to Usumanu Zamnagawa (1343–1349), though the Chronicle cites Muhammadu Zaki (1582–1618).[44] However Malam Adamu also mentions certain heathen practices current at Kano under Babba Zaki (1768–1776) and during Alwali's reign. He describes a royal fetish which was said to drink blood and which was sometimes used by the chief as a substitute for the Koran when requiring witnesses or litigants to take the oath in court. He says also that on the Idi festivals the Hausa chief closeted himself with the Magajiya, his senior kinswoman, presumably for certain heathen rites. On the Id-el-Fitr and Id-el-Kabir, according to Malam Adamu, the Hausa chief was also obliged to dress in a special loin cloth (*banten dabazau*) and cap, wearing silver armlets and a silken cord (*tsakiya*) around his neck. Further, according to Malam Adamu's account, on those days and at other times, the chief would leave his palace to watch a pagan dance of naked men and women, the *Rawar Toji*, which was held at the site of the present city mosque between the palace and the residence of a senior throne slave, the Shamaki.[45]

The only comparable incident reported in the Kano chronicle occurs in the reign of Muhamma Kukunna (1652–1660) after the Jukun had captured Kano. Kukunna summoned

> all the Maguzawa to the city to salute him. They remained 21 days, and played a game in which they beat each other's heads with iron. The Sarki gave them many gifts, and asked them who was their chief. On their saying it was Zanku, the Sarki

said to him "Next year come again and let all your men come with their *hauyias* on their shoulders. If you do so, Zanku," said Kukunna, "God willing, no Sarkin Kano will be driven out again."[46]

It is thus possible that the Rawar (dance of) Toji had its origin in this event; and clearly its purpose, character and timing classified it as heathen, a repudiation or syncretistic corruption of Islam.

Undoubtedly there were many ambiguous or explicitly heathen elements in Hausa ritual practices at Kano and elsewhere during the latter eighteenth century, and perhaps even more so at an earlier date. All the evidence we presently have indicates that beneath the Muslim overlay, various pagan or non-Islamic concepts and orientations persisted; but this was equally true among Muslim Fulani, Arabs and Hausa. Undoubtedly also, the Hausa government and legal administration deviated from Islam in various ways; but so do many polities, including the succeeding Fulani regime, which strenuously protest their Muslim purity. In his eloquent critique of Hausa government and incisive summary of Muslim administrative ideas, the Shehu lists several abuses current in Gobir and other Hausa states during his day.[47] On the evidence available such illegalities had relatively little place in the civil administration at Kano, perhaps because the scale and wealth of this unit assured officials of ample revenues from more acceptable procedures. Nonetheless in this respect also, the Fulani performance at Kano during the last century compares indifferently with such information as we have on its government during Alwali's reign.

The Hausa Government

Scope

The Hausa ("Habe") government of Kano was a complicated structure which regulated the public affairs of the country and the population by means of diverse and elaborate procedures. Affairs defined as public and thus directly subject to governmental regulation included all foreign relations of a corporate kind, that is, relations between collectivities in Kano and collectivities elsewhere, for example, immigration, war, peace, alliance, or vassalage, maintenance or development of the city and its administration, town building and defensive fortifications of all sorts, and collective relations between the Muslim Hausa of Kano and all other ethnic groups within its territory, such as the Maguzawa, Warjawa, Arabs, Fulani, Nupe, etc. The Hausa government also reserved to itself regulation of all local rights in land, including rights of grazing, mining, or building, the use of trade routes and occupancy of farm land. Only rarely and with due cause did the government interfere with established rights of land occupancy or use held by individuals, families, or communities; but at all levels of territorial organization its representatives exercised reversionary and residual claims to currently occupied land as an element in their roles as trustees and guardians of the territory on behalf of the king and the wider political community, including future generations. By virtue of such comprehensive claims to land, the government, through its official hierarchy, exercised control on all immigration and all movements and relocations of people within the territory. Thus on shifting their homesteads to new farm sites, family heads had to inform the local chief, and to obtain his approval of their occupancies. It follows that the subjects of one village chief were not permitted to farm land in areas under the jurisdiction of another. This practice, known as *noma jidde*, was quickly suppressed whenever discovered, since it was inconsistent with the fundamental requirement that jurisdiction over clearly demarcated territorial units should be exclusively vested in local chiefs who were each individually responsible to the ruler for the administration of their respective communities and territories. In effect, this meant that men lived and farmed within the same community, subject to administration by a single local chief. Adjacent communities were thus politically and territorially discrete units with separate structures; and their territorial limits and closure were determined by an explicitly political regulation from above. As defined and organized at Kano, territorial units and claims were thus established by political action and were accordingly liable to change by these means in their form and content.

Regulation of the Caravan Trade

The government undertook to secure the major caravan routes within its territory. For this purpose it restricted farming along particular tracts, fortified strategic towns along these routes, garrisoned the perimeter and other vulnerable spots against bands of Tuareg raiders or local brigands, sunk wells to service the travellers, and encouraged the growth of settlements and markets along the route. Special provisions were made for reception of caravans at the capital and at market-towns along the route, to facilitate trade and encourage their regular return. The caravans were thus met by a special official, the *Sarkin Zango*, who was responsible for their supplies and accommodation. Camels would be unloaded at the Kofar Ruwa, the watering gate, on the northern wall where they were corralled at night against prowling hyena, and pastured by day. The Sarkin Zango distributed his guests in many well designed compounds built by city traders for this purpose. The Ghadames Arabs probably owned most of the hostels which stood around the Dalla rock away from the unhealthy Jakara pond and the borrow-pits that adjoined the market. Normally the visitors conducted their trade through the agency of the man who served as their host; and in this way, the compound owner reaped profits on his investment. The visiting merchant would itemize his stock and deposit it in the care of his host for sale at fixed minimum prices which were set after inquiries about the current state of the market. The visitors were then free to call on their friends in the city, or to leave for their slave farms in rural areas. They would normally select appropriate articles from their stock for presentation to the chief and senior officials in charge of the city. Their host would expect a smaller gift before the caravan departed, as a gesture of satisfaction and goodwill. The host could retain all receipts in excess of the minimum prices set by his guests for their articles; or he might understate the excess and seek a commission on this. Normally the host also served his guests by changing their currency and purchasing at low current rates such local commodities as grain, cloth, slaves, leather or metal goods as they required. The visitors accordingly enjoyed excellent protection against bad faith or cheating by the local agents, especially since all transactions were regulated by the principle of *caveat vendor* under which the seller remains responsible for the good condition of the article sold. All sales were thus conditional on the purchaser's satisfaction with the quality of the article bought. Credit was available from wealthy local merchants, Arab and other, who also acted as currency changers; the great bulk of market transactions proceeded by cash transfers. Wealthy merchants also provided warehouse facilities to visiting traders. Any disputes about the price or condition of articles transferred could be referred to leading members of the commercial community for informal arbitration, failing which they were first referred to the Sarkin Zango, and if necessary to the local court for adjudication by the *qadi* and his assessors. Local factors and commission agents risked exclusion from this traffic by official order if they were guilty of sharp practice or cheating. Their trade prospects also depended on their individual reputations among the Arabs, visitors and other foreign merchants. This external traffic was not subject to any official dues or exactions. No toll (*kudin fito*) was levied on caravans or itinerant traders (*fatake, madugu*) throughout Kano country, though such levies were then general in other Hausa states. It seems probable that the rulers of Kano deliberately refrained from instituting them to protect the caravans against illegal exactions represented as tolls and so, by reducing their expenses en route and at Kano, to attract and engross the caravan trade.

Law and Order

The state also regulated through its courts and senior executives all local actions that breached or threatened peace and order—assaults, thefts, woundings, kidnappings, violence of any kind; and all manifestation of disaffection (*renon sarauta*, contempt of office or official authority), rejection of official orders (*kin umurnai*) or plotting and threats of insurrection or of foreign attack, engaged its attention immediately. Individuals suspected of such offences would be taken into custody by the ruler's police or by the retainers of the local chief, and brought before the Muslim court where the *alkali* (Muslim judge) would investigate and adjudicate the case. If the *shari'a* (Muslim law) prescribed mutilation or execution for the offence, the judge would report his findings to the chief for reference to the Sarkin Kano, to whom the authority to order executions or mutilations was reserved. This aspect of his authority distinguished the paramount as a *Sarkin Yanka* (chief having powers of execution) from other *sarakuna*, whose status neither entailed nor conferred this ultimate right, whether these were officials or hereditary chiefs, within or beyond his domain. In effect then, all punishments for homicide and comparably serious offences were subject to the ruler's discretion, following adjudication of the particular charge by the local *qadi*. As mentioned below, the chief's mother, and perhaps his "elder sister," who was entitled Magajiya, also had a certain constitutional authority to overrule and suspend certain of his decisions. It is unlikely, however, that this power was frequently used in routine cases of private injury and offence. Explicitly political offences such as disloyalty, conspiracy, *kin umurci* (rejection of orders), *renon sarauta*, or usurpation and trespass of authority were dealt with by executives of appropriate levels under the Muslim doctrine of *siyasa*.

Such civil issues as debt, inheritance, property damage, divorce, trusteeship, manumission and commercial transactions of all sorts were referred to local courts or chiefs for adjudication, the plaintiff being responsible for initiating the suit. Under Muslim law, bastardy, the remarriage of women without proper observance of *idda* after divorce, or the stipulated mourning period (*takaba*) are criminal offences; and so are certain forms of libel or slander.[48] However, initiatives for action in all of these cases except the first rested with the individual whose rights had been transgressed.

Islam prescribed an extremely close and comprehensive integration of law, polity and ritual observance.[49] As a Muslim state, the Hausa government of Kano maintained the usual complement of malams and Muslim courts. Its chiefs also commissioned malams to administer the inheritance of estates, to canvass military and political success by prayers and rituals, to serve as assessors in executive courts, to advise on particular issues of policy or law, and to act as agents in various affairs. For such services clerics were richly rewarded with cash, slaves, grain, clothing and other local valuables. Further, the government routinely celebrated the main Muslim festivals of Al Muharram and the two Idis; its clerical and legal officials supervised the observance of Ramadan; and, besides levying the various revenues and tithes authorized by Islam as mentioned below, the Hausa government treated non-Muslims as heathen from whom *jizya*, the punitive capitation tax, was due, and on whom slaves could be levied as tribute or by raids on grounds of their heathen status.

To discharge this wide range of regulative tasks, as resources and administrative instruments the government employed slaves recruited by raids or descent, purchase or inheritance; stockpiles of arms and an exclusive concentration of military resources and organization; revenues levied locally in tithe or tax as described below, or derived from such state property as large slave farms, and the workshops Alwali maintained within the palace, including its dyepits that produced *turkuda* for export. Government resources also included police, prisons, state compounds, territorial claims, and rights to levy corvée labor and to impress individuals or their property for service on occasional official undertakings. Only the chief could authorize construction of such major earthworks as town walls or defensive trenches; but in these and similar major undertakings he relied on the corvée labor of his free subjects. Likewise only the chief could authorize military expeditions, though all able-bodied men were expected to take full part in the defence of their communities and districts against external attack.

The Chiefship and Islam

Besides this ensemble of material resources and means, the central government identified itself as the final and overriding authority in the territory of Kano, to which all other local collectivities and units were subject and on which all depended for the legitimation of their rights and resources. Thus the regulative order and the supreme regulative organ reciprocally validated one another. The nature and scope of the processes of public regulation identified their source and basis as the kingship and its official representatives. A profound, pervasive integration of state, people, and territory identified the chiefship as the central public institution in three intimately connected senses. First, the chiefship constituted the state and polity; and, as we shall see, this logical priority of chiefship is equally evident in the history of Kano's emergence and in the structure of its governmental regime. The chiefship was also the only institution that embraced and represented the entire public as an indivisible unit inseparable from itself. It was thus the sole institution simultaneously endowed with final validity at all levels of the corporate organization and, conversely, the only common center to which all individuals in Kano could appeal for relief, support, justice or protection. It was therefore the central and supreme agency of public regulation and integration.

The chiefship was endowed with this supreme authority on several mutually reinforcing grounds. Historically it preceded and created the chiefdom and the political order. Of all local elements this institution was most closely identified with the indigenous ethnic group, the Hausa of Kano and with their homeland. Custom and tradition merely reinforced the many powerful and ramifying ties that bound people, territory and chiefship into a single polity and state, the pragmatic advantages of which, reinforced by the unthinkable alternative of its dissolution, habituated most natives to accept the current order and its form as the decisive, presumably perpetual conditions of their social life. Only as a centralized collective unit could the residents of Kano in this historical context hope to maintain their integrity as a single distinct political entity, their internal autonomy, or their favorable social and economic milieu. But only some of the many pragmatic considerations that sustained the current order were clearly instrumental; and even these, examined closely, are sometimes only partially or conditionally so.

There was also a salient concentration of resources and force at the command of the chief; and though never before the Fulani *jihad* employed to crush a widespread popular revolt, these military resources were frequently used against rebellious chiefs, ambitious officials and conspiring dynasts. Indeed, as the territorial administrative structure systematically insulated adjacent communities from one another, it minimized the opportunities for popular movements and disaffections to spread their roots. Even so, the prompt suppression by central authorities of such revolts and rebellions as periodically broke out, demonstrated the dangers and disadvantages of dissidence and collective protest. The equally prompt apprehension of recalcitrant individuals and their summary punishment by the chief's *siyasa* jurisdiction on charges of *renon sarauta* or *kin umurci* instructed everyone to practice compliance. Thus the order and regime were reinforced by special administrative arrangements, superior organization, and by a control of overwhelming force and resources. Further, as we have seen, Muslim Hausa were encouraged by the ethnic heterogeneity of the population in Kano to identify their interests and rights closely with the structure, policies and procedures of the state. Only thus could they assuredly remain masters in their own land. The presence of Tuareg, Arab, Kanuri, Fulani and pagan collectivities in Kano, all distinguished by various privileges or disabilities and all in differing ways dependent, probably crystallised to some degree the conscious ethnic identification of Muslim Hausa with the state as their own representative and regulative organization.

Beyond these secular considerations hung the mantle of Islam which prescribes the centralized organization of Muslim communities under an appointed imam or leader in order that they may pursue and maintain *ibada* or the good life.[50] Islam abjures acephalous political organizations such as those of the Bedouin or the Warjawa and other local pagans. In practice also it often differentiates the religious and political leadership of the Muslim community, although ideally these imamates are one. It prescribes the exclusion of heathen from the political community of Muslims, enjoins their domination by Muslims, and ordains continual holy war (*jihad*) between Muslims and heathen, wherever the situation favours victory by Muslims. Islam prescribes or permits many political institutions and forms of procedure that prevailed at Kano in Alwali's day, for example the administration of the *shari'a* by formally appointed *alkalai* (*qadis*), the levying of tithe (*zakka*) on grain or cattle, state appropriation of one-fifth (*humushi*) of the booty of war, state inheritance from kinless people and state rights to specified shares of estates under certain other conditions. Allowing for circumstances, Islam likewise empowers a Muslim chief to suspend certain rules of *shari'a* in favor of local custom (*'ada, 'urf*), or as reasons of state (*siyasa*) seem to require. The decisive criterion which legitimates such deviations is fixed by Islam as the welfare and power of the Muslim community.

For several centuries this zone of the central Sudan and southern Sahara had been dominated by Muslim states and empires of varying scale and duration. Throughout this period Kano had steadily grown in area, population and wealth, although subject to demands from Bornu, to devastating invasions by the pagan Jukun (Kororofa) based on the Benue, and frequent strife with adjacent Hausa chiefdoms such as Katsina, Zaria or Gobir. Excluding the Jukun, no pagan power within reach of Kano presented a threat; and although liable to attacks, conquests and subordination by other Muslim states, as a Muslim polity Kano enjoyed many securities in its relation with these units. Its people were not unconditionally liable to wholesale slaughter or enslavement; nor, if conquered, could they be utterly dispossessed under the Muslim law that regulates the treatment of conquered Muslims.[51] The government could also expect sympathetic reception of its requests from many adjacent and distant Muslim polities. Arabic provided the prestigious medium and patterns of diplomatic communication. Further, as a Muslim state Kano qualified for its strategic place in the trans-Saharan and trans-Sudanic caravan traffic which was then almost exclusively in the hands of Muslim Berbers and Arabs. Thus in effect, its Islamic identity provided the Hausa state with many important advantages in its relations with other centrally organised polities from Lake Chad to Timbuktu and in its commerce with the wider Muslim world. Thus the chiefs of Kano may well have thought that their long-standing identification as Muslim rulers of a Muslim state, guaranteed their protection against Muslim *jihads*, though not against assault by other Muslim states for secular political reasons.

Like other theocratic systems, Muslim doctrine concerning the legitimacy of rebellion by Muslims against an unjust ruler of their own faith is complex and variable. In discussing this topic the Shehu Usuman dan Fodio adopts the view that prohibits the rebellion of Muslims against their unjust leaders, provided these latter do not commit apostasy.[52] This qualification is especially significant for the Shehu, since it furnished the base that legitimated his call to *jihad* against the chiefs of Hausaland. From the Shehu's argument, it appears that although oppressive, secular maladministration neither justifies Muslim revolt nor the

summons to *jihad*. However, syncretisms of pagan and Muslim ritual, together
with deviations from other orthodox Muslim forms, are regarded as evidence of
heathenism or apostasy and should therefore be uprooted by means of *jihad*. The
Shehu's doctrine accordingly cut through those secular securities with which
their Muslim allegiance had long protected the chiefs and people of Kano by
forthrightly denying their status as Muslims and denouncing their Islam as a
hollow fraud, dangerous because it positively obstructed the observance of Islam
and, because of its stability and convenience to chiefs and people alike, conta-
gious and liable to thrive and spread. Thus the Shehu's critique effectively
reversed those traditional principles that had served to legitimate the Hausa
regime by denying their consistency with Islam and by categorically representing
their bases and manifestations as modes of syncretism or paganism.[53]

Office

Having outlined its scope and conditions or means of regulation as well as its
structural and ideological bases and justifications, we can now discuss the regulative structure of the Hausa state and its modes of operation and perpetuation.

The basic unit of Hausa government at Kano as elsewhere is *sarauta* (pl.,
sarautu). The term denotes a unique titled office having determinate rights,
powers, resources, responsibilities and relations with other units of similar character whose common organization constitutes the government of the state and
exercises an integrated jurisdiction throughout its territory. The fundamental
sarauta, that from which all others in Hausa political doctrine derive their authority and status, is chiefship, and never the chief. In theory the chiefship possesses
very wide authority and discretion. However, this is neither arbitrary nor unde-
fined. Like other offices, Hausa chiefship enjoys authority within restricted
spheres, however wide, by virtue of the many rules and institutions which
together constitute and regulate it. It is by reference to these constitutional precedents, procedures and rules that the actions of a chief or his representatives may
be classified as legitimate or illegitimate, that is, as consistent or inconsistent with
the authority constitutionally vested in the office over issues of those kinds.

Official action in accordance with routine procedures or directions by superior
authority possessed corresponding authority. Official actions that contravened or
exceeded customary and accepted procedures or directions from above, together
with any usurpations of superior authority, were implicitly illegal though often
unpunished. To enforce official conventions and restrictions following such illegal
activities, superior authority had to overrule and check displays of power by infe-
rior officials. Normally, such *ultra vires* activities were conducted at the expense of
inadequately affiliated commoners, and were rarely pursued or punished. By contrast, aggrandizements by officials at the expense of their superiors or peers were
rather infrequent, being promptly exposed and sternly punished. Illegalities at
the expense of commoners were probably no less common in Alwali's day than
under the Fulani or more recently the British; but given the hierarchic organization of offices and authority, it was difficult for humble individuals to secure
redress or relief against their immediate superiors. To attempt this was often
rather risky. Such illegal or extra-legal activities of officials which, though known,
escaped correction, manifestly expressed the power latent in the relation of their

office to the collectivity they administered. Such displays of power *(iko)* always involved trespasses beyond convention and the constitutionally prescribed bounds of official authority. They were sometimes undertaken to protect the interests of clients, sometimes to further those of patrons, and sometimes with the agent's assurance of adequate political protection from patrons or superiors. However, unpunished exercises of power by officials tended to become routinized in form and scope, so that the prescriptions that governed official authority only covered a portion of the jurisdiction actually exercised. We lack the necessary data to determine the exact situation in this regard during Alwali's regime.

The Capital and the Court

The city was the heart of the kingdom, but the city itself had two hearts, one of which, the market, is discussed below, while the other, the palace or Gidan Rumfa (Rumfa's compound), was the king's residence and center of government. There the ruler granted audience to foreign emissaries and distinguished guests including *shareefs*, *sa'ids* and clerics of great repute. There also he presided over the chiefdom's highest tribunal at the council chamber in the forecourt known as Fagaci. In theory, anyone, however humble, was free to bring complaints to this court even without first seeking redress from the *qadi*. Several palace officials were especially responsible for presenting these complainants to the chief at Fagaci; and indeed that was apparently the chief official duty of the Kilishi. To ensure that complainants were not obstructed permanently by these ushers, custom also permitted anyone thus frustrated to voice his complaint loudly outside the palace forecourt on Thursday evenings when the Muslim sabbath begins, or in the early Friday afternoons when the chief set out for the city mosque. Such importunate complainants would then address the chief indirectly in stereotyped phrases as follows: "Since God has given you (the chief) your rightful portion (inheritance), in God's name give me my due for the sake of God and for His Prophet upon whom be the blessing of God and peace." Declaimed loudly, a few repetitions of this invocation usually brought free passersby and some throne slaves from the palace forecourt to the spot where the complainant sat ritually wailing; and before the group dispersed he would normally be conducted to some usher he had not previously contacted, whose duty it was to provide him with accommodation and food and present him to the chief when the court met next at Fagaci. Thus determined complainants could indirectly invoke public pressure against obstructive palace attendants whose exploitive tactics tended to support injustice. However it does not seem that there was otherwise any institutional machinery by which the chief was routinely informed of such malpractice by his attendants.

On Friday mornings, the sabbath, the entire court assembled; and on these occasions, the titled clerics and other senior members of the clerical order also came to greet the chief and to invoke blessings upon him. In such court assemblies the chief sat among his slaves close by one wall of the large, elaborately decorated audience chamber on a raised dais, while the malams sat directly opposite to him near the entrance in order of rank, and his free officials, royal and other, were distributed on his right and left, seniority being expressed by closeness to the king. On these occasions, after greetings, the chief distributed kola nuts and addressed whoever he wished, after which the gathering would disperse. These court assemblies were highly formal affairs regulated by protocol under the guidance of the senior throne slaves, the Shamaki, Dan Rimi, Sarkin Dogarai, and others. Following dismissal of the court, senior *hakimai* usually remained behind for a council meeting with the chief. The council met in a special chamber further in the palace interior, near the king's private quarters. By tradition, from Rumfa's day (1463–1499) the Kano state council consisted of nine senior officials, the Galadima, the Madaki, the Sarkin Bai, the Wambai, the Makama, the Dan Iya, the Sarkin Dawaki Tsakar Gida, and a ninth who was generally either the Barde Babba, the Turaki Manya, or, less frequently, Sarkin Dawaki the cavalry commander. Over the generations and during relatively long reigns the council sometimes underwent minor changes in its official composition; but on available evidence these were less than we might expect.

Councils and the Constitution

Between sabbaths the chief visited his main audience chamber daily after a preliminary meeting with his senior slaves and chief eunuch, the Sallama, in chambers adjoining his quarters reserved for that purpose. Having taken his seat on the dais that served as a throne, the chief signalled his slaves to announce the audience and admit the courtiers and officials waiting outside. As usual the chief sat among his slaves removed from his free officials. Apart from those who visited the palace daily as councillors, few princes attended these sessions unless they were specially requested to do so or figured among the chief's confidants and advisers. For the most part, the daily audience consisted of non-royal *hakimai* and courtiers (*fadawa*), some of whom sought commissions, others favors, gifts or office; but on these occasions the chief might discuss matters of interest or instruct individuals to undertake particular tasks. Observing the traditional formalities that regulated their posture and speech, courtiers and *hakimai* might also take the chance to bring to the chief's notice matters of personal or general interest. However, as court etiquette reflected relations of authority, it imposed severe restrictions on free expression of opinion or information. The senior throne slaves who accompanied the chief on these occasions and ranked among the most powerful men in the state never spoke to the chief unless directly addressed by him. If their opinion or information was sought, each spoke in turn strictly according to rank, first the Shamaki, then the Dan Rimi, then the Sallama. Thus *lawanai* (subordinate staff) did not attend court, being represented by their immediate superior.

The state council of Nine, the *Tara ta Kano*, discussed and decided issues of foreign relations including those with Bornu, alliances, defence, movements or relocation of population, the siting and construction of new towns and walling of old ones, the administration of local Fulani, pagans, and other ethnic groups, agricultural prospects, harvest yields and levies of tithe and tax, the condition of the export and import trade, relations with such major local chiefdoms as Rano, Karaye, Gaya, Dutse, Birnin Kudu and Jahun, any instances of official disloyalty or maladministration that had come to the chief's notice, together with such official appointments, dismissals, decrees, territorial reallocations, promotions, transfers or role redefinitions as seemed relevant to the chief, his councillors, or the senior slaves. The chief might also issue general summons or directives which would be publicised later through the subordinate staffs attached to each major office.

According to Kano constitutional doctrine, a chief was not expected to over-rule the joint advice of the four senior non-royal councillors, the Madaki, the Makama, the Sarkin Bai and the Wambai. However, by Alwali's day, the Wambai was usually one of the chief's agnatic kinsmen, normally his elder "brother," and another prince often served as Madaki. The Alkali Zangi allusively suggests that in 1805 the Madakin Kano was one of Alwali's sons.[54]

On the death of a chief, the four senior non-royal members of the state council, the Makama, the Madaki—when not a prince—the Sarkin Bai and Dan Iya, together with the Sarkin Dawaki Tsakar Gida, who though a kinsman of the king, was ineligible by descent for the succession, constituted themselves as an electoral council to choose and appoint the successor. During this interregnum the *limam* of Kano, its senior Muslim priest, acted as formal head of state; and according to some informants, the *limam* and leading city malams had a final say in selecting the new chief. There are also indications that of the throne slaves at least the Sha-maki and the Dan Rimi were probably consulted, though this was informal.

Women were rigorously excluded from active participation in Hausa politics; but perhaps as a symbolic compensation, most Hausa states reserved at least one lofty office, which might be invested with extremely wide prerogatives, for some senior kinswoman of the chief. In Hausa Kano the precise designation of this office remains uncertain. In some contexts it is identified as the Babar Daki, and in others as the Maidaki, since both terms have similar meanings, as "owner" ("mother") of the house (hut). In yet other contexts the title Magajiya is cited. It is thus possible that at different times these superior powers passed from one posi-tion to the next perhaps as an effect of personality differences. The Babar Daki was generally the ruler's mother who actually bore him; the Maidaki was usually one of his aunts, and probably a paternal aunt, though this is not clear. The Maga-jiya title was generally reserved for an elder 'sister' of the ruler who had nursed him as an infant. Another title, Dauduwa, which carried little authority, was gen-erally given to the ruler's younger sister.

It is said that during Hausa days the Babar Daki, and occasionally also the Magajiya, could overrule decisions of the chief and reprieve or exonerate anyone, irrespective of their offence. It is also said that this constitutional power was most generally invoked by the non-royal councillors to prevent a chief from pursuing courses he had decided to follow against their joint advice in the council. It is said too that should the chief choose to ignore their joint opinions, the non-royal coun-cillors under the Madaki's leadership could constitutionally proceed to depose him. However, the last reported instance of such action is the deposition of Mohammed Kukuna by the Madaki Kuma in 1652, following which the Galadima recalled Kukuna and defeated the Madaki and his nominee, Soyaki, in battle at Hotoro.[55] Thus either these constitutional doctrines are recent misconceptions of the Hausa organization; or they preserve principles such as the council's right to depose the chief which, though rarely given dramatic political form, effectively restrained his arbitrary rule and enhanced or preserved the significance of the council as the highest forum of state, its final deliberative organ, and custodian of the kingship. The traditional powers of veto and reprieve that were formally vested in the Babar Daki and exercised during and after her lifetime by the Maga-jiya on the advice of senior non-royal councillors may thus have been a device to secure the state against autocratic rule.

On the most important decisions of State, including issues of peace and war, the senior territorial chiefs of Rano, Gaya, Dutse and Karaye were generally consulted. On such occasions, these chiefs would be summoned by couriers to Kano for a full discussion of the situation and the alternatives under review. It is said that the chief could not independently dismiss any of his councillors except for certain grave offences, namely, failure to answer his summons, whether to court or to war, military cowardice, or treason in either of its three major forms, namely, contempt of the chief or his office, rejection of orders (*kin umurnai*), or conspiratorial plotting against the chief. However, serious or frequent failures of duty were probably acceptable as grounds for dismissal. The senior territorial chiefs of Karaye, Rano, Dutse and Gaya, thus enjoyed corresponding securities in their tenures of office. Lesser *hakimai* and rural chiefs were dismissible by the ruler independently, but since most of these offices were hereditary, such dismissed officials were usually succeeded by kinsmen, in some cases on the king's choice, in others on the choice of the group's senior members, in yet others after consultation with a local council of elders. Under these conditions, territorial officials generally enjoyed high security of tenure in their positions which, even when not hereditary, were not entirely at the ruler's free disposal. Indeed the chief risked alienating his councillors and senior *hakimai* by ill-advised or frequent dismissals of these staff. The rule that a chief could not dismiss any councillor without the council's general assent was probably necessary to preserve the council's integrity against encroachments by the chief; but it also enabled the council to dissuade the chief against over-hasty dismissals of important territorial officials.

Oral traditions relate that in Alwali's day, the Maidaki Hauwa took such an active interest in state councils and affairs (as her wide prerogative allowed), that she enhanced her power greatly. It is related that on one occasion she summoned a corvée of citizens of the capital to divert the Jakara pond southwest of the main market, since it overflowed seasonally and had recently destroyed some nearby compounds. The Jakara is really a marsh that was progressively extended by removal of soft earth on its margins for the construction of compound walls and buildings. All Hausa cities have many borrow pits made in this way; but of such inner-city depressions the Jakara is the largest, best known, and most troublesome, being also a marsh and unhealthy. However, Kano traditions identify the growth and prosperity of the city and state with the Jakara pond, where the early pagan inhabitants worshipped their god. Alwali's aunt, the Maidaki Hauwa, is also credited with the unusual feat of diverting the Jakara overflow by means of a canal that ran eastward through the city wall, in a tradition that reports several significant innovations. It is also said that the Maidaki Hauwa attended Alwali's court and councils freely and took an active part in discussions of policy and State affairs. Though previously married, during this period Hauwa remained unwed, administering her distant fiefs through male clients, including princes, under her senior slave, the Shamaki Zodo, who levied tax therein on her behalf and had charge of her revenues. The Kano Chronicle also mentions an earlier Madaki (Maidaki) Hauwa who achieved a similar position under Muhammadu Kisoke (1509–1565) and also ascribes to Madaki Mariana, the mother of Muhammadu Sharif (1709–1739), a similar ascendancy.[56] It is thus equally possible that during Alwali's time the Maidaki achieved the influence described above by these unwritten traditions; or that traditions have transferred to her some of her predecessor's legendary attributes. In either event, it is clear that the extensive immunities and positive privileges that together defined the Maidaki's status enabled her, if so inclined, to wield considerable influence in the government and the city by exercising the initiatives of her unusual position.

Revenues and Taxation

In general outline the nature and scope of the Hausa revenue system is reasonably clear, although many details remain uncertain. As enjoined by Islam, the State claimed a death duty of ten percent (*ushira*) on the assessed value of all vendible property left by private individuals after payment of their debts. The state also inherited any residues after eligible heirs had received their specified shares from the estates of private individuals. Further, the chief had rights to one-third of the personal estate of deceased officials and to one-half the estates of those dismissed from office. In either case state properties and rights with which the office was endowed passed without reduction to the next incumbent.[57]

Following Maliki law, the State also claimed one-fifth (*humushi*) of the war booty (*ganima*) seized during state campaigns. Slave raiding was perhaps the most rewarding type of campaign; and this was a state monopoly. Booty collected in wars with such other Hausa states as Katsina or Gobir was subject also to the rule of *humushi*. However, these engagements carried high risks of defeat and loss to the Kano forces.

Under Muslim law the State also received *ushira* (one-tenth) of all values transferred in civil transactions through its court, for example, refunds of bride wealth, recovery of debt and property, or compensation for damages. In addition, the state properly received all monies and properties levied as fines; and under a chief's *siyasa* jurisdiction this principle was sometimes extended to "legalize" confiscation of an offender's estate and the translation of his immediate kin into bondage. At Kano these latter punishments seem to have been very rare.

Muslim law was locally interpreted to prescribe annual transfers to the state of one-tenth of the harvest of certain crops, notably the cereals which are Hausa food staples. Other tithes, also known as *zakka*, were due from stock keepers and miners. Accordingly the state claimed and received one-tenth of iron, tin, natron or other locally produced minerals, resident head-men in the mining areas being responsible for the collection and transfer of those revenues. In like fashion territorial chiefs and head-men were charged with local collection and storage of the valuable grain tithe at the harvests in August and late November. It is also possible that a tithe was collected as in other states on the harvest of locust bean (*dorowa*), another essential foodstuff. Maliki law further allots the state a tithe of dates harvested within its boundaries. Of all Hausa chiefdoms, Kano had most successfully naturalized the date tree, following its traditional introduction during the

reign of Muhammad Rumfa by Abdurrahman, who is identified by local traditions as Sheikh Muhammad El Maghili.[58] At Kano all groves of date trees belong
to the chief as head of state, and at Dutse about sixty miles east of Kano, the ruler
had a valuable date plantation before Alwali's reign.

Being bulky, the grain tithe was stored in specially large granaries under care
of the local chiefs and head-men who collected it. When the chief was informed
by the latters' *hakimai* of the amounts, types and locations of the grain involved,
this was recorded by his scribes. He might then distribute set portions of this to
courtiers, malams, sharifs, visitors, or to his kin; or he could order its conveyance
as needed to the palace for allocation to the numerous throne slaves settled within
and immediately around the palace walls. Alwali, it is said in the Kano chronicle,
collected stores of sorghum and millet as reserves against war and famine.[59] Presumably some of these stores were kept within the palace and in the adjoining
compounds of the Shamaki and the Ma'aji, the latter being the public treasurer;
but customarily, the ruler left the bulk of in state granaries distributed throughout
the country at compounds of the local chiefs who undertook its initial collection.
These grain stores were mainly held as reserves against famine due to drought,
locusts and other pests, or to devastation by enemies; but they were also drawn
on by the chief to assist invalids and paupers or to provide subsistence for immigrants during the first year or two in which they could not normally secure adequate grain supplies by their own cultivation. Finally these grain stores were
scattered over the country at strategic points to serve as food dumps on which the
army could draw when campaigning in the neighbourhood.

Like other sources of revenue, *zakka* was shared by the chief with his *hakimai*
and local head-men. In this manner, the state remunerated its officials. As a rule a
local chief and his immediate superior, the *hakimi* resident at the capital, received
equal shares from local revenues. At most the ruler may have received forty
percent of the local intake while the *hakimi* and local chief shared the rest.

Since most *hakimai* held several local units in fief, and the ruler received a
similar share from all *hakimai*, although in principle approximately equal shares
prevailed at all levels of revenue collection, given the systematic inequalities of
territorial authority on which the administrative organization was based, the
incomes legitimately received by officials at different levels of the organization
differed sharply in accordance with their status, responsibilities and resources.
Even among officials of the same rank, legitimate revenues varied widely in
accordance with the number, size and prosperity of the units under their control.
This was equally true of *hakimai* as a category, of local village chiefs, and ward-
heads. Thus, at the highest level of their officialdoms the Hausa chiefs of Kano
and Katsina enjoyed far greater wealth and prosperity than their peers and kin in
Daura and Zazzau. As regards the chief's receipts at Kano from the four senior
sub-states south of the city, Rano, Karaye, Dutse and Gaya, proportions remain
uncertain. By one account, those chiefs retained the bulk of their local *zakka* themselves, transferring about one-tenth of it to Kano. On another account, they
reserved for the chief of Kano approximately one-third of the *zakka* they received.
A similar ambiguity attaches to the king's customary share in the cash and livestock revenues collected by these four senior rural chiefs and by the rulers of
Birnin Kudu.

Cattle Tithe and Taxation: bin kanu

Under Maliki law *zakka* levied on cattle, including sheep, represents approximately one-thirtieth of the total herd each year, provided the herd exceeds a certain size.[60] Allowances are made for loss of cattle by disease, accident or other misfortunes, following which the amount due by law is computed and compared with the increase of the herd in the preceding year. Thus Maliki law prescribes that *zakka* on cattle should be computed and transferred in kind; but it does not clearly proscribe its conversion into cash values for collection.[61]

This tithe on livestock fell almost exclusively on the Fulani pastoralists (*Bororo*), the Agwai and Rahazawa. *Fulanin gida* were liable only so far as they held stock herded for them by their serfs or clients. The Kano Chronicle relates that Kutumbi (1623–1648)

> was the first sarki at Kano who collected the *Jizia* from the Fulani which is called *Jangali*. He collected a hundred cows from the Jafunawa, the chief clan of Fulani, 70 from the Baawa, 60 from Dindi Maji, 50 from the Danneji, and others too numerous to mention. When he had collected the cattle, he said to his slave Ibo, "I make you Serkin Shannu" (chief of the cattle).[62]

Thus as this quotation shows, *jangali* was instituted as *zakkan shanu*, the stipulated Moslem tithe on cattle collected in kind from resident Fulani; however the Chronicle describes it as *jizya*, the punitive tax levied on heathen, thus suggesting either that Kutumbi was oppressive or that the pastoralists were heathen.

During the dry season, transhumant Fulani herdsmen frequently cross over state boundaries in their ceaseless search for good grazing, water, tsetse-free areas and better markets for their milk, butter, cattle manure, and old or ailing livestock. As the rains approach such transhumants generally head homeward to their wet-season pastures, where the poorer ones may cultivate. In like fashion, Fulani settled at Kano during the rains ranged far afield in the dry season and often crossed into other states. As Stenning has shown, these patterns of transhumance are fairly stable; and the pastoralists' routine changes little from one year to the next, provided their social contexts remain favourable. However, over time there is a tendency for these patterns of seasonal migrancy to change their direction and routes by gradual processes of cumulative drift.[63] In general the dry season routines of transhumants change more readily and frequently than their wet-season locations. Thus, bands of pastoral Fulani coming from other territories in the dry season presented the Kano rulers with a different administrative problem from the resident Fulani. These incoming bands would often return annually to adjacent districts before discontinuing their visits. Their homes and future movements were thus uncertain and difficult to determine. Their migrancy enabled these pastoralists to evade the liabilities they incurred on their routes through damage to the persons or property of sedentary folk. As migrants, moreover, they were often ill-informed about local regulations on grazing and other matters. Transhumants settled in Kano were better informed about its local arrangements and more easily reached through administrative channels. Such resident pastoralists were called on to furnish *zakka* in cattle; and each distinct collectivity was organized under some senior male who served as headman (*Ruga, Ardo*).

The senior headman of each major group of Fulani was accredited by the king as their representative and chief; and usually the heads of such segments were appointed to special offices created for this purpose. Almost without exception these officially appointed Fulani headmen were designated *Sarakunan Fulani* (s. *Sarkin Fulani*, chief of [pastoral] Fulani), each being further distinguished by locality. Thus in Alwali's day there were Sarakunan Fulani at Sankara, Dambarta, Bebeji, Jahun and elsewhere. All the Fulani chiefs just named held *tambari*, the kettledrums characteristic of hereditary territorial chiefs among the Hausa. The *Sarakunan Fulani* of Bebeji and Jahun, and perhaps those of Dambarta and Sankara, also exercised the territorial authority and function vested in resident local chiefs of equivalent rank.

Sarakunan Fulani were recruited within Fulani groups on criteria of descent, seniority, personal performance, and support within their communities. Normally, each of these *Sarakunan Fulani* exercised a representative authority for all members of his ethnic division, wherever dispersed within the chiefdom, unless they were explicitly subordinated to other officials. For example, the baYerime Sarkin Fulanin Dambarta claimed authority over all Yerimawa Fulani in the chiefdom, whether located at Dambarta or not. Thus, in Alwali's day, the role and authority of the *Sarakunan Fulani* were not simply territorial; nor were their differing jurisdictions always distinct. For example, Yerimawa Fulani resident in Jahun were simultaneously subject to the territorial authority of the Sarkin Fulanin Jahun and to that of their ethnic chief, the Sarkin Fulanin Dambarta; and though the implications and interests of these differing relations were normally segregated by the social situation, on certain occasions they would conflict. Presumably in such cases, the local Fulani chief turned over to the head of the ethnic unit such issues as were usually reserved on ethnic grounds for administration by Fulani headmen, while claiming the same treatment from other local chiefs in similar situations; but this is mere inference, and even then, numerous juridical ambiguities remain. The chiefs of ethnic divisions among the Fulani pastoralists in Kano traditionally administered such inheritance and civil suits as arose in their ethnic community, together with other suits of serious character such as bastardy, assault or theft. Chiefs of these ethnic divisions also presided over the appointment of subordinate *Ardos* and *Rugas* who served as their immediate representatives within each mobile segment of their collectivities. Further, as head of an ethnic unit, a Fulani chief supervised the enumeration of livestock and collection of *zakka* among his people. He acted as the Hausa ruler's official channel of communication and representative to the group. Issues involving members of his group and subjects of other lesser chiefs would be reserved for joint settlement by these lords when the Sarkin Fulani or his appointed representative was present. Probably within the territory of Kano the attributes and claims of ethnic chiefship were modified to accommodate the minimal requirements of an administrative organization based on a firm devolution of executive authority over distinct areas or collectivities to resident chiefs and headmen. At the very least, the territorial authority structure presupposed the subordination of local communities to a relatively uniform pattern of legal administration in all matters of common interest, irrespective of their differing provenience. It is thus possible that the local headmen exercised jurisdiction over serious torts or crimes even when the Fulani in their areas were involved, and irrespective of ethnic affiliations. They also probably settled all issues that arose between the Fulani and local people in their executive courts. Even so, the absentee head of a Fulani segment retained the rights to administer inheritance and other civil issues arising among members of his segment, to decide appointments to sub-segment headships, and to handle its communications with the throne and *zakka* collection.

The administrative arrangements just outlined go by the local name of *bin kanu*, which means roughly "following heads."[64] *Bin kanu* was a flexible institution designed to ensure to Hausa officials a constant administrative control over mobile resident Fulani, wherever they were. Its major interests were the regulation of relations in each ethnic division, corporately through the appointment of headmen, and individually by the administration of civil suits; the regulation of relations between members of an ethnic division and individuals or groups in the wider community; and the enforcement of state claims for *zakka*, labour dues, and obedience to its representatives and order as the essential condition of continued residence within its territory. This institution prevailed in Katsina and other Hausa states during the eighteenth century. It probably developed in the sixteenth and seventeenth centuries as the Fulani influx to this region increased, and may have then been modelled on the Bornu institution of the *chima jeribe*. How far afield the ethnic headmen of this period pursued their mobile 'subjects' to assert their jurisdiction remains obscure; but within Kano resident Fulani were free to move as and where they pleased, subject only to the ruler's regulations and the conditions of *bin kanu* administration just described. It seems also that before 1750 *bin kanu* jurisdictions were at least periodically, and perhaps regularly exercised across some state frontiers, presumably by bilateral agreements. For example, a Fulani chief of Kano might follow his people into Katsina territory and vice versa. However, on this question the data remain uncertain.

During Sharefa's reign at Kano (1703–1731) cowries were introduced as currency from the southwest;[65] and according to the Shehu Usuman, by the end of the century Hausa rulers were levying cash taxes on pastoralists. The Shehu cites these taxes by their local name as *jangali*;[66] and, as shown by the Chronicle's reference to its introduction already cited, *jangali* originally denoted *zakkan shanu* or statutory cattle tithe paid in kind. However, by the Shehu's day *jangali* had come to denote cash taxes levied on Fulani. Against this type of levy the Shehu protested vehemently and often, condemning the practice as illegal, but whether because Muslim law forbids transfer of *zakka* in cash equivalents, or because these *jangali* levies represented a form of double taxation is not entirely clear from the contexts of his remarks. Undoubtedly, much of the support that Shehu's *jihad* received from the predominantly pagan pastoral Fulani of Hausaland and elsewhere illustrates their response to his criticisms of *jangali* and other administrative arrangements that oppressed them, and the Shehu's evident desire to remove these burdens.

At Kano in Alwali's time, *zakkan shanu* was levied in kind from locally resident Fulani pastoralists. However, *jangali* was also collected, not so much from these Kano Fulani, as from the *masu-ketare*, that is, from those who entered Kano during the dry season. Such migratory groups would normally have already paid *zakka* to officials of their home states. Thus the *jangali* levied against immigrant Fulani at Kano in cash appeared oppressive to them on two grounds: firstly, it was an innovation and an added burden, especially severe because they rarely had the currency required, since they had marginal relations with the urban market economy in which cowrie currency circulated; secondly, the Kano levy ignored their previous payments of tithe (*zakka*) in their home countries. Pastoralists thus conceived these *jangali* levies as demands for double tithe by oppressive Hausa chiefs across whose lands they were merely moving their flocks, and not settling as residents. However, it does not seem that Hausa chiefs consciously regarded *jangali* as a second tithe levied on Fulani from other states. Rather, in their view the new tax was a legitimate charge on immigrants for dry-season grazing rights in their territory. Nonetheless, like tithe, *jangali* was estimated by a head count of the herd on which it was charged; and it is probably the identical basis of these two levies that encouraged pastoralists to assimilate them and to represent the new tax to their Muslim kinsmen and patrons in the towns as illegal and oppressive. Moreover, as we have seen, the new cash tax went by the same local name as the older cattle tithe.

Inflation and Tax Policy in the Eighteenth Century

Two conditions that probably contributed to the introduction of the *jangali* cash tax were the increasing use of cowries, and the disputes that periodically arose across state boundaries concerning the scope and span of territorial and *bin kanu* jurisdictions over Fulani. As indicated above, the introduction and increasing in-flow of cowries as currency during the century disturbed traditional price levels and perhaps upset the fundamental price structure of the major urban markets, with inflationary results. This developed partly because cowrie imports increased the volume of currency in local circulation without corresponding increases in demand or supply of goods. The more ancient cloth currency, of which the *turkudi* was a standard unit, continued to function alongside the new cowrie currency; and as the volume of cowries increased, the relative value of the *turkudi* in cowrie equivalents should tend to increase in proportion to the cowries in circulation, provided only that the numbers of *turkuda* involved remained constant. Evidently this did not occur. To extrapolate from the observations of Clapperton and Barth in the early and mid-nineteenth century, with minor fluctuations such as correlating currencies everywhere display, in any area the values of *turkuda* and cowries maintained fairly stable relations. In consequence, given the stable supply of *turkuda* at different periods, as against any expansion in the volume of circulating cowries, the inflationary price movements initially linked with the introduction of cowrie currency probably continued at increasing rates over the decades.

During Barth's visit (1851–54), major Hausa markets embraced two sectors distinguished by striking disparities of price levels. Locally produced subsistence goods fetched very little, while such export articles as fine clothing had relatively high values, and imported luxury goods fetched a very great deal.[67] We can thus distinguish two market sectors by the two major categories of market commodities: the one, local and rural in origin, which served Hausa subsistence needs, attached very low values to its goods and services; while the other consisted of export or import articles of urban manufacture and demand which carried much higher values. In the altered economic contexts associated with the spread of cowrie currency, the chief's court and officialdom were constrained to seek new sources of revenue and increased revenues from the resources available, in order to maintain their traditional standards of living and the many customary disbursements expected of them. As these changing and depreciating currency values provoked and coincided with its loss of the major part of the trans-Saharan caravan trade, Kano experienced a sustained inflation from Kumbari's reign until the *jihad*; and the essential features of this development were the steady increase in the volume of cowry currency and a steady decline in the volume of imported luxury goods, matched by rising prices.

As regards the jurisdictional disputes that may have promoted the introduction of *jangali* cash charges on immigrant herds, we lack direct data;[68] however, there are suggestive clues. During the nineteenth century, disputes arose between the Fulani emirs of Zazzau and Kano concerning precisely this issue. Being unhealthy for cattle, Zaria contained relatively few resident pastoralists. Local provisions for their administration varied in consequence. Lacking Kano's striking economic advantages, but having similar status demands and obligations, the chiefs of Zaria thus had to exploit the resources at hand more rigorously than their peers in Kano. If we interpret the juridical dispute over the migrant Fulani that arose between Zaria and Kano during the last century in structural terms, this clash probably had several precedents. Its essentials are quite straightforward. The Fulani emir of Kano asserted the jurisdiction of his Fulani chiefs over their transhumant communities in Zazzau, as in Kano or elsewhere. The Fulani Sarkin Zazzau rejected this, and like his Hausa predecessors, levied *jangali* on immigrant Fulani from Kano. To forestall war the caliph resolved the dispute in Zazzau's favour, treating that emirate as a special case, since, although extensive, it was relatively poor, and lacked an adequate number of resident Fulani. In fact, climate and latitude were probably decisive. Zaria falls squarely in the southern, relatively humid belt of the central Sudan. Kano lies equally in the Sudan and the Sahil, the better zone for grazing. In consequence, most pastoralists cluster in Kano and similar latitudes, while avoiding Zaria, Niger and other low-lying southerly regions where tsetse prevails.

These nineteenth century data suggest that the cash taxation of incoming Fulani at Kano during the late eighteenth century may have begun following disputes over extra-territorial *bin kanu* jurisdiction with other states in contexts of inflation, currency change and economic decline. Possibly the *jangali* then levied at Kano was intended to force dry-season immigrants either to avoid Kano territory or to settle within it, since either course would relieve them of further cash taxation by Kano. On available data it seems that at this date Katsina and Kano recognised one another's *bin kanu* rights over their pastoral residents. Thus at Kano, the cash tax levied on incoming Fulani as *jangali* was probably selective. Pastoralists from Katsina and other states with which Kano had agreements for reciprocal recognition of *bin kanu* administrative rights were not so taxed.

As his title implies, the Sarkin Shanu was originally a slave official[69] but by Alwali's time he supervised the herds of cattle and sheep collected for the chief as *zakkan shanu*. Unfortunately, we cannot say certainly how this supervision was organized. Oral traditions indicate two alternatives. In the first case the Sarkin

Shanu is represented as dealing with each Sarkin Fulani individually through his own personal staff of *jekadu* (intermediaries, agents) and *lawanai* (titled subordinates employed as the senior *jekadu* and agents). Alternatively, it is said that the several Fulani chiefs in eighteenth century Kano were grouped under two senior Fulani officials, the Dokaji and the Ja'idanawa, both of whom lived in the city near the Sarkin Shanu, the Ja'idanawa being in charge of the western Fulani chiefs, while the Dokaji supervised those in the east. It should be noted, however, that this Hausa dichotomization of east (*gabas*) and west (*yamma*) rarely corresponds with our usage of those terms. At best this tradition indicates that supervision of rural Fulani chiefs was perhaps divided between two senior officials of Fulani stock and of equal rank, each directly responsible to the Sarkin Shanu.

It remains uncertain whether the offices of Ja'idanawa and Dokaji existed before or during Alwali's reign. Administrative records identify a certain Malam Husamatu as the first Sarkin Fulanin Ja'idanawa appointed after the Fulani *jihad*.[70] This appointment may be consistent with an earlier establishment of the office under the single designation of Ja'idanawa, or with its tenure by others, including Hausa. Likewise the Hausa title of Dokaji, following the *jihad*, became known as the Sarkin Fulanin Dokaji. By 1959 when Alhaji Abubakar, the historian of Kano, held it, the office was generally designated as Dokaji, though correctly it remained a Fulani chiefship.

Concerning the etymology of the name Dokaji, I could learn nothing; but Ja'idanawa is clearly a Hausa term for the Ja'en Fulani who form a distinct ethnic division among Fulani descent units. To my knowledge, Ja'idanawa is the only title said to date from Hausa days which explicitly employs a Fulani descent term as its referent. The names, status, role-descriptions and histories of these two offices, Dokaji and Ja'idanawa thus present various unresolved puzzles. Until further research elicits decisive data, it is wise to suspend judgment.

The Territorial Organization, Karo and Other Levies

Besides grain received from their fiefs as *zakka*, all *hakimai* and territorial chiefs, including village chiefs, had the use of state compounds and farms reserved to their particular offices. Usually such a senior office as that of the *hakimi* or an important rural chiefship, was also endowed with an adequate number of slaves to execute the official's routine cultivation and domestic or public service. The great majority of office-holding throne slaves in the king's household and in the government also had compounds reserved for them within or immediately around the palace; but only such senior slave officials as the Shamaki, Dan Rimi, Sallama, Magajin Dakwara, or Jakadan Garko, were usually allocated farm sites attached to their titles. These plots were generally set within or beside the chief's official farms which lay in different parts of the country. During the last century, Fulani emirs of Kano had estates and country houses at Birnin Bako, Takai, Nassarawa, Garki, Gurjiya, Arkau, Gogyen, and Panisau. Most of these royal estates were simply taken over by Fulani emirs from their Hausa predecessors. It was on these estates that specific plots were reserved for senior slaves holding public office. Such plots were worked by locally resident slaves under slave overseers, the total labour force being subdivided into work teams separately responsible to the officials whose plots they cultivated.

There was no land tax in Kano under Hausa rule, but cash taxes were then collected at a rate of 500 cowries per family head for married men of moderate means. In Alwali's day, the wealthy were also taxed at 1,000 cowries each. Slaves, officials, royals and clerics were traditionally exempt from tax; nor did a man have to pay tax on behalf of his slaves. Pastoral Fulani, being subject to *zakkan shanu* and onerous labour dues, were exempt from other taxes. As protected pagans, Maguzawa paid a much heavier *jizya*, levied at the rate of 3,000 cowries per family head. This *jizya* was specially punitive to Maguzawa because they had very peripheral relations with the urban cash economy. It accordingly reinforced their institutional preferences for large households and joint families.[71] Whether Muslim tax collectors then demanded *jizya* from each married man we cannot say; but this seems unlikely. Warjawa, 'Mbutawa and Ajawa were expected to render tribute in slaves and/or local products; but the volumes involved remain unknown.

Although it is highly probable that these cash taxes were collected routinely and without protest when they were due, and although oral traditions assert this, further study of these transactions is desirable. The Kano Chronicle says that Muhamman Sharefa (1703–1731) "introduced certain practices in Kano all of which were robbery,"[72] one of these being *karo*, the tax on family land. Sharefa's son and successor, Kumbari "collected *jizya* in Kano (that is, in the city) and made even the malams pay."[73] At this stage, "the Arabs left the town and went back to Katsina, and most of the poorer people in the town fled to the country."[74] The Chronicle expresses the public reaction to this new impost, the *karo*, most succinctly by describing it as *jizya* or illegitimate, since under Muslim law, Muslims are not liable to *jizya* though they are usually required to pay *haraji*, (*kharaj*) the traditional Islamic land tax.[75] At Kano the Muslim Hausa evidently regarded Sharefa's *karo* as *zalunci* (oppression).

To this day the cash tax levied on Kano Muslims by Hausa chiefs is known only as *karo*; and it is this designation which obscures its status, periodicity, and normalcy. The term *karo* currently has two meanings; it denotes a cash levy of any kind; but it is also used at Kano to describe levies made by chiefs and *hakimai* on their appointments to office. Following custom, candidates for office recommended themselves to those who controlled the appointment or could influence the decision, by gifts that simultaneously served as declarations of loyalty, as demonstrations of the candidate's substance and support, and as material inducements.[76] Apart from these informal expenses, on appointment the new official was required by tradition to transfer a certain sum that varied for offices of differing resources and rank. This payment, known as the *kudin sarauta* (money for office), served three main functions. It compensated the chief for the outlays he had to make on each official appointment. For *hakimai* and senior rural chiefs these chiefly expenses of installation included garments appropriate to clothe the individual completely, namely trousers, robe (*riga*), turban and burnous (*alkyabba*), besides a fully clad horse that symbolised the official's political and military obligations. On these occasions the ruler did not present appointees with swords, each official being expected to purchase his own. However if a new official had limited private means, as was often the case in appointments to hereditary office, the chief might select four slave women (*kuyangi*) to wait upon him, and send them to the official's compound a day or two after the formal installation which was always held at the palace. *Hakimai* and senior rural chiefs were installed in the ruler's presence at the palace forecourt, while village chiefs were appointed publicly at the southern gate, the Kilishi presiding. *Hakimai* and senior territorial chiefs, being vested with considerable discretionary power (*iko*) and responsibilities, were required to make an act of allegiance on their appointment. This consisted of shaking the ruler's hand, the new official bowing meanwhile. Those were the only occasions on which the ruler shook hands with any of his subjects. Village chiefs, being either subordinate to *hakimai* or to senior rural chiefs did not make this act of allegiance (*mubaya'a*) directly to the ruler. The fundamental principle on which the administrative hierarchy rested can be stated simply: only the chief could dismiss anyone whom he or his predecessors had appointed.

The *kudin sarauta* was paid to the chief on most appointments. Even those paid by village heads served also to express their submission to the reigning chief and their support of the political order. Finally *kudin sarauta* served as a valuable source of occasional revenue. In less prosperous states such as Daura the institution was systematically exploited for revenues.[77] This was not the case in traditional Kano, perhaps because the ruler's income relieved him of any need to do so. Indeed, by some accounts at Kano, the chief was expected to present all *hakimai* on their appointments with four *kuyangi* to serve as concubines and handmaidens. If this was always the case, the ruler's expenses on some appointments probably exceeded his receipts of *kudin sarauta*.

Slaves, clerics and princes did not pay *kudin sarauta* on appointment at Kano, nor did the rulers' titled kinsmen. Thus, in effect, *kudin sarauta* was due mainly from non-dynastic offices endowed with territorial authority and usufruct of state resources.

On their appointments, territorial officials could levy "*gaisuwa*" from all householders subject to their authority. This levy simultaneously served to declare the new official's authority, the people's acceptance and recognition of it, and remunerated him for his appointment expenses, including both the unofficial *gaisuwa* and the official *kudin sarauta*. The levy on appointment was known to officials as the *kudin wankan sarauta*, that is, money for washing the office; and when levied by *hakimai*, it was also sometimes called *kudin wankan takobi*, meaning money for washing (purchasing) the sword. To its collectors and subscribers it was more laconically known as *karo*. Under Kano conventions, the collection was undertaken within seven days of an official's installation, during the period when he was expected to remain within his new quarters, receiving visitors and gifts and distributing largesse. The *kudin wanka* thus enabled the new official to clear off some of the pressing debts incurred in his pursuit of office, to reward some supporters, and to supply some of his immediate needs.

Data available do not indicate whether the *karo* introduced by Sharefa and collected in Kano city by Kumbari refers to this occasional levy or to the recurrent annual demand for cash tax from household heads. In this case as with *jangali* and Ja'idanawa, uncertainty hinges on the multiple connotations of specific terms and on some discernible shifts of meaning and usage. For such reasons, several questions about pre-jihadic Kano may remain permanently unresolved.

Among Sharefa's seven oppressive innovations, the Chronicle mentions market taxation, and *murgu* (ransom?), here used for payments due on the first marriage of maidens which among Hausa generally occurred between their 13th and 15th year.[78] This *murgun buduruwa* was still collected in Alwali's day; and some informants cited its rate then at about 20,000 cowries which, even 80 years later when cowries abounded in Kano, would be highly excessive, equalling 8–10 Maria Theresa silver dollars. (These were first minted in 1783 for export to the Sahara and Sudan as currency.) At most the *murgun buduruwa* may then have stood at 2,000; but even this figure seems rather high, given the relative scarcity of cowries in Alwali's day.[79] Evidently, this innovation did not diffuse to Gobir, the Shehu's home, as it escapes mention in his list of those administrative abuses and oppressions against which the *jihad* was in part directed, these being condemned by the Shehu as modes of apostasy and incompatible with Islam. Like the annual tax, this *murgu* on maidens was collected locally by village chiefs for transmission to the Sarki.

The term *murgu* is of interest. *Murgu* is a rent or cash payment by slaves for free time in which to pursue their own enterprises. This was a standard source of income to slaveowners in Kano City and other important towns during the eighteenth and nineteenth centuries. Thus, in describing Sharefa's demand for payment on the first marriage of maidens as *murgu*, the Chronicle implicitly condemns the marriage tax by assimilating it to the payments levied on slaves for free time. Implicitly then, by this term the Chronicle suggests that the chief regarded all Kano maidens as his concubines or property, and consequently, claimed a portion of their marriage fee, approximately equal to that which a slave owner would receive on the marriage of his female slaves.

Our information as regards the *kudin wankan sarauta* is ambiguous in one important particular. Some informants assert that this was payable to the chief on the seventh day after the official's appointment, while others suggest that at least the majority of the sum collected remained with the new official.

Market Dues and Taxes

We have seen that Mohamman Sharefa introduced monthly taxation at the main city market, the *kasuwan kurmi*, which Mohammed Rumfa had established to service the growing caravan trade.[80] Under Sharefa's successor, Kumbari (1731–1743) these market taxes became a burden, probably because their form and modes of collection permitted or encouraged various extortions. Arab merchants withdrew to Katsina; and when tax was later demanded of the city folk, many moved away from the town.[81] The Chronicle says nothing further about this market taxation under Kumbari's successors; but some inferences may be tentatively drawn from occasional comments. It is possible that Alwali's father Yaji (1753–1768) reduced, regulated, or even suspended it. The Chronicle describes him as a "just and good Sarki, and a man of mild disposition ... In his time there was no trouble ... There was no difficulty either with his Sarkis (officials) or his chief slaves, or his household, or anyone. Many men came and settled in Kano land in his reign."[82]

Yaji's immediate successor and senior son, Babba Zaki quickly established an autocratic regime by playing off his official courtiers and slaves against one another, and by imposing new burdens and far more rigorous control on them than they had known. "He curbed the power of the Sarkis (the rural chiefs and *hakimai*) and head slaves and plundered them every day. He forced them to give presents under compulsion, and to go to war unwillingly."[83] Babba Zaki's power seems to have been achieved at the expense of his officialdom rather than the general public. His autocracy consisted in subordination of his administrative staff by novel political means. Despite his constant campaigning and domineering regime, the Chronicle indicates that many Arabs had already returned from Katsina to Kano where their influence on the chief was pronounced. Babba Zaki "imitated the Arabs of Kano in almost everything."[84] Evidently, following Yaji's reign the Arabs and the chief had achieved a rapprochement and some had returned. It seems likely that this concord involved some concessions of immunity against market taxes to the Arabs by the chief. Five years after Babba Zaki's death Alwali succeeded; and for his reign our only specific data on market taxation at Kano comes from local oral traditions.

In his critical contrast between the Hausa ("Habe") governments of his day and the ideal government ordained by Muslim traditions, the Shehu Usuman dan Fodio cites as abuses of Hausa government that "the superintendent of the market takes from all the parties to a sale, and the meat which he takes on each market there from the butchers, they call this *tawasa*, and ...the cotton and other things which they take in the course of the markets, ... they call this *agama*." Further, "one of the ways of their government is to impose tax on merchants, and on other travellers."[85] Referring specifically to Kano in 1826 the explorer Clapperton remarks that "a small duty is also levied on every article sold in the market; or, in lieu thereof, a certain rent is paid for the stall or shed; a duty is also fixed on every tobe that is dyed blue and sold. On grain there is no duty."[86] Twenty-five years later Barth mentions a standard charge of 500 cowries on "every slave sold in the market."[87] And rather less clearly he indicates that loads of natron carried by pack oxen or asses paid a toll (*kurdin fito*) of 500 cowries for rights of transit through the territory.[88] On this point, Barth's phrasing is unfortunately ambiguous and suggests that the "passage money" he mentioned may be the minimum average profit or commission charged by city merchants for handling the re-export of this natron. If the "passage money" was an official toll, then some official would have been specifically responsible for collecting it. However, neither in Fulani nor in Hausa Kano did I find any official authorized to collect *kurdin fito*.

Concerning the market taxation that prevailed in Alwali's day, our oral data are in some respects conflicting. By one report, butchers paid a slaughter fee of approximately 1,000 cowries per beast to their chief, the Sarkin Pawa, who exercised administrative control over the city markets. Commission agents dealing in cloth were taxed according to their goods and turnover at rates that varied from 200 to 1,000 cowries over unspecified periods, this sum being also collected by the Sarki Pawa. Further, a fee, equivalent to 5 percent of the price, was charged on all slave sales, the vendor being liable. This was collected for the Sarkin Pawa by his agent in charge of the slave sheds, who was often called the Sarkin Turawa. Presumably, vendors of other standard articles who were not liable either to these fixed charges or to the customary exactions mentioned below, were obliged to pay small monthly fees for the use of market stalls. This tradition states that the Sarkin Pawa was obliged to transfer a fixed sum to the local chief after each market day, thus implying that these modes and rates of taxation were not restricted to the city markets but were general throughout Kano. The putative amounts claimed by local chiefs from the Sarkin Pawa for each market day varied with the size and wealth of the town and market. Figures of 5 to 10,000 cowries sometimes cited assert modal variations as matters of fact, rather than precise or probable rates.

Each Sarkin Pawa was personally responsible for supplying his local chief with appropriate portions of meat on market days. At the city, there were several daily markets, and perhaps a night market also. In other larger towns the market met daily. Further, in Kano City and probably in the more important rural administrative centers, the Korama, who was always a woman, appointed by the Sarkin Pawa over all grain sellers and other vendors who used standard measures of capacity in their trade, was obliged to provide the local prison warder with the grain he needed for his wards. In effect, the market bore the major costs incurred by government for subsisting prisoners.

In certain nearby states, markets were subject to customary levies by chiefs or their slaves and agents on the Muslim Idi festivals. Such levies were commonly known as *agama* and are cited thus by the Shehu. Their incidence varied widely.[89] Whether this custom or oppression prevailed in rural Kano at this period I do not know; but on the data available it certainly had no currency within the city in Alwali's day.

The alternative account of market administration at Kano in Alwali's day asserts that, excepting slaves, no market sales were subject to official tax. This tradition admits that certain categories of market activity were subject to demands for fees; but it expressly defines these imposts as unofficial and perhaps illegal abuses of their administrative positions by the Sarkin Pawa and his assistants. Being in charge of the market and its conduct, these men could suspend or otherwise punish vendors who opposed their demands. Their authority thus enabled them to aggrandize their incomes and positions by the exercise of power. On this tradition such payments as the Sarkin Pawa made at the palace did not go to the chief but to his senior slaves to retain their support. On this account, stall charges were perhaps the sole official form of market taxation in cash at Kano on the eve of the *jihad*. In addition the San Kurmi in charge of the city prison drew his grain supplies from the Korama; and the Sarkin Pawa supplied the chief with meat. When he wished to sell some of his livestock, the chief employed the Sarkin Pawa as his agent.

Craft Taxes and Organization

Three craft activities of special interest to the chief were metalwork, tanning and leatherwork. All three were organized and controlled by the administration through formally appointed craft heads. Metal workers were distinguished as blacksmiths and those who worked "white metal," namely, silver or tin. Goldsmithing is not a characteristic Hausa craft. The senior metalworker was the Sarkin Makera, chief of the blacksmiths. The Sarkin Makera Fari, chief of the silversmiths, supplied the court with necklaces, bracelets, armlets, anklets and fine work of various types; but the head of the blacksmiths was responsible for producing such war weapons and tools as the chief required; he was also expected to keep himself informed about the local production of pig-iron (*tamma*), thus providing the ruler with an indirect check on his receipts from local smelters. As necessary the chief would instruct his senior slaves, normally the Shamaki, to supply the Sarkin Makera with sufficient raw metal to furnish a set quantity of standard articles such as arrows or spearheads, crowbars, axes, stirrups and other horse gear, throwing knives and the like. The Sarkin Makera was then responsible for completing the order by the date agreed; and to this end, he simply distributed the pig among blacksmiths in and outside the city with appropriate instructions. The smiths were then required to set aside all other work till they had finished that of the chief. Standards were maintained by Sarkin Makera's inspection of the articles produced. In return for these services, blacksmiths at Kano were exempt from official *karo*. So were silversmiths whose corvée production on similar lines provided valuables for the court and for export to other Hausa states and beyond. Likewise tanners and leatherworkers, being subject to labor impressments by the chief, were exempt from *karo*. Such exemptions and obligations applied throughout the country to all who practised these crafts.

Tanners and leatherworkers were primarily required to produce the heavy leather shields and suits of armor known as *lifida* (s. *lifidi*), which together with chain mail (*sulke*) and quilted cotton distinguished the heavy cavalry used for assault and defence. *Lifida* were commonly made from cowhides. The chief's prerogatives included rights to the tusks and hide of locally slain elephants, and to all lion and leopard skins. The chief's leather was tanned under the direction of the *Sarkin dukawa na ajema* (the head of the tanners) who distributed it among his craftsmen within and outside the city as he saw fit. Thus leatherworkers had to prepare articles requested by the chief through their headman, the Sarkin Dukawa.

These four craft officials, heads of the butchers, blacksmiths, tanners and leatherworkers, were recruited from particular descent groups of craftsmen at the city; and each headman usually recruited his assistants from his agnates and friends. Having a final voice in the allocation of work imposed by the chief on his craft, craft headmen could use their administrative authority for personal ends by relieving those who furnished adequate gifts (*gaisuwa*). The craft chief might also send his agents annually on tour through the countryside or visit leading rural centres himself; and his incomes from rural specialists in his craft would guide his distribution of state work during the coming year. Like some of the market collections reported above, some receipts of these craft-heads were extra-legal and unofficial. They accordingly illustrate the use of public authority for private ends; but given the concentration of authority in Hausa government, the difficulties of supervision and complaint, and the general acceptance of a social order based on differential privilege and liability, these abuses were probably unavoidable.

Despite occasional statements to the contrary, it does not seem that dyers or dye pits were subject to tax under Alwali or his predecessors at Kano; and no official was authorised to collect such taxes. As we have seen, the chief had a *marina* (set of dye pits) at the palace to produce dyed cloth for currency and export. Builders were also exempt from *karo*, but had to work as required on public buildings, such as the palace, official compounds and the city mosques, especially on their roofing, the town gates, wall construction and repair. Under the Fulani in the nineteenth century, one of the senior non-royal *hakimai*, the Makama, had charge of all royal building in the chiefdom under the emir's direction. This was also the Makama's responsibility under Hausa rule. Wall repairs at the capital and other towns were undertaken as necessary by local corvée. At the capital, responsibilities for wall repairs were initially distributed among the *hakimai*, each having to complete a certain section of the wall with labor summoned for that purpose from his followers and fiefs; but city folk could also help.

Palace construction and repair was distributed between the three senior slaves, Shamaki, Dan Rimi and Sallama, the last being a eunuch, each having charge of set areas. Slave compounds were built by palace slaves, while the royal apartments and court chambers, which were elaborate in design and decoration, were constructed and maintained by expert builders under the Sarkin Gini (head of the builders). In Hausa days it seems that the Sarkin Gini was a free hereditary official attached to the throne, who supervised the repair and maintenance of state compounds and mosques within the city.

Excluding metal workers, tanners, leatherworkers, builders and malams, *karo* was levied on all craftsmen and traders along with the general population. However, until Kumbari's reign, cash taxes were not collected within Kano City; and whether Alwali maintained Kumbari's practice in this respect we cannot say. Certainly, *zakka* was collected in Alwali's day on grain grown within the city walls; and the three gate keepers at each of the fourteen city gates were then each remunerated by rights to *zakka* from specified farms within and outside the walls. These benefices were designated as *hurumi*, a Muslim institution, by which a ruler could allocate revenues from specific resources for such varying purposes as the remuneration of functionnaires, the support of religion, charity, or as rewards to favorites, *sayids*, princes, and so on. In addition several crops not liable to *zakka* were cultivated for subsistence and marketing, for example, cassava and sweet potato were grown as reserves against locusts, and cotton, groundnuts and indigo for local trade. During the nineteenth century these marketable crops were subject to taxes known as *kudin shuke* or crop taxes. Under Hausa rule it seems that no tax was levied on these crops at Kano, although such taxation prevailed elsewhere.[90] However, on this matter also traditions differ; and though Hausa administrative organisation includes no official specifically authorized to collect such crop taxes, this question merits further study, as such taxes could have been collected through the territorial organization, as was done by Fulani during the nineteenth century.

Besides its revenues in cash and kind and from the services of specialist craftsmen, the government had extensive claims against commoners for free labor on public works or business. Corvée was employed to build and repair town walls, mosques and state compounds at the capital and in rural towns, to clear and hoe the farms of *hakimai* and *dagatai* (rural village chiefs; s. *dagaci*) as well as those belonging to the king, and to transport loads or run errands as required. Officials claimed the right to impress local beasts for these purposes.[91] They were also authorized to conscript all able-bodied men for the defence of their community and adjacent units against attack. While commoners were not obliged to volunteer for expeditions against other countries, military service was obligatory for territorial officials, *hakimai* and *dagatai* being dismissible for failure to turn out with adequate contingents when instructed. The Shehu's criticism of Hausa

("Habe") government for levying fines in commutation of military service[92] may thus refer primarily to cash payments levied by despotic chiefs on members of their officialdom, as, for example, was done by Babba Zaki at Kano.[93] However, it is clear from his context and phrasing that the Shehu's criticism of this practice, known as *gargadi*, refers primarily to its use against settled Fulani and other "Muslims" on whose behalf he protests.[94] It is indeed likely that during the eighteenth century labor burdens and levies on the pastoral Fulani steadily increased; but whether such Fulani liabilities increased faster than those of the local Hausa, remains uncertain. Pastoralists, being exempt from tax, craft liturgies and corvée cultivation, were frequently impressed, together with their beasts, for the transport of public supplies; and they were also recruited for wall building. Unless commuted by appropriate gifts, their chiefs were also liable to dismissal for failure to turn out on campaigns or furnish adequate contingents as required. Being segmentally assimilated to Hausa society, various Fulani communities apparently regarded these state demands as forms of ethnic oppression; but without adequate data on their relative distribution among Fulani and Hausa, we cannot now determine the validity of this view.

The Legal Administration, Police and Prisons

The Shehu also criticizes "Habe" (Hausa) governments for various practices that violate Muslim law: the bribery and corruption of judges, the commutation of physical penalties such as mutilation into fines, decisions according to customary law rather than the *shari'a*, and illegal appropriations of property left by deceased travellers.[95] In substance, these charges are undeniable; but they are equally true of succeeding Fulani regimes. In general Hausa deviations from or suspensions of *shari'a* procedures, rules and punishments represent accommodations of this sacred law to their social milieu and cultural conditions. Offenders for whom the *shari'a* prescribed such punishments as amputation or stoning were normally reprieved if they or their kin could furnish fines that varied with the character and context of each offence. Clearly, such fines enriched the judicial and political officials who shared them; but given their collective character, they were also effective punishments.[96] Even if reserved only for first offenders, they were certainly more humane than the punishments prescribed by the *shari'a*; but equally, they allowed an offender's agnates to be compelled to furnish the fine levied on their kinsman. These enforced compositions were also described locally as *karo* (levy, fine); and it is possible that this was one of Sharefa's "oppressive" innovations.

In Hausa days, besides the senior *Alkali* or judge in Kano city, there were appointed *alkalai* at Gaya, Dutse, Rano, Karaye, Kura and perhaps at other centers also. It is said, too, that most senior rural chiefs who held the hereditary offices of which *tambari* were critical insignia, appointed local *alkalai* to administer the current mixture of Muslim law (*shari'a*) and Hausa custom (*al'ada*) within their domains, for example, Burumburum, Birnin Kudu, Suma'ila, Dambarta, Bebeji, Jahun, Gwaram, Babura and similar units. I cannot verify these specific attributions; but it is clear that, however numerous the distribution of formally appointed and adequately trained *alkalai* in rural Kano during Hausa days, most rural people still remained subject to territorial chiefs for the administration of justice. These chiefs normally employed senior local clerics as court assessors and jurisconsults on technicalities of Muslim law. Their local imam was often responsible for administration of the Koranic oath. The territorial chief generally reserved the right of decision, following interpretations of the evidence and law by his malams. As the ruler's representative, he also administered all suits involving claims to local land, compounds and economic trees. Likewise, following the ruler's practice, he decided the appropriate action in cases of local maladministration by his subordinates. If a matter was serious he might either report it to his *hakimi* or refrain from public, though not necessarily private, action.

Those rural chiefs who appointed *alkalai* kept local prisons and police staff at their headquarters. Though not empowered to order or execute any physical punishments beyond those whippings the *shari'a* prescribed, these territorial chiefs could levy and collect fines. Such restrictions accordingly encouraged them to substitute fines for punishments they could not ordain. To apprehend offenders and to enforce their decisions, the rural chiefs maintained police known as *dogarai*. The prison warder had custody of suspects awaiting trial, and of convicts whose fines remained unpaid.

At the capital the ruler had three prisons, in the larger of which commoners were placed under the San Kurmi's charge. This prison was within the *gidan* (compound of) San Kurmi away from the palace, the prisoners being kept in deep pits within a central courtyard. At Kano, the San Kurmi provided his wards with a minimal diet. Imprisonment for debt was unknown. The second prison was reserved for persons of high rank such as officials or princes, and stood within the palace. It was controlled by the Sarkin Yara who, though junior to the San Kurmi in rank, was not his subordinate. Alternatively the ruler could dispatch noble prisoners to the Shamaki whose compound then stood on the site of the modern mosque. Stocks and chains were sometimes used to immobilize noble prisoners, but as a mark of their status, such persons were isolated within guarded enclosures, and not placed in pits. The king's executioner had the title of Hauni. Routine executions were publicized by impaling the victim's head on a pole beside the market or on the city walls. However, executions of noblemen or princes for reasons of state varied in their context, publicity and form.

Fief Administration

It is said that in Hausa, as in later, days, ward heads in rural areas of Kano could appeal for protection and redress against their immediate superior, the *dagaci* or village chief, to the *hakimi* who held the unit in fief. In theory this was the situation; and undoubtedly on many occasions such appeals were made and some may have proved effective. However, whether wisely or not, the administrative organization tended to discourage such appeals. A *hakimi* normally administered the various units under his care through titled agents (*jekadu*; s. *jekada*), each directly responsible for the levies and good order of one or more discrete communities. To have access to the *hakimi* who formally appointed him, a ward-head normally had to win the support of his *jekada*; but this depended on the *jekada's* interest in supporting, replacing or subordinating the local chief.

Likewise, in theory a village (local) chief could appeal to the ruler against oppressive administration by his *hakimi* or to the *hakimi* against oppressive

administration by his *jekada*. In practice *jekadu* were probably assured of the
hakimi's favor by ties of kinship, clientage and long service. The *hakimi* could normally rely on the senior court ushers, Kilishi, Ciroman Shamaki, and Makaman
Dan Rimi to obstruct complainants with various excuses until he had either composed the matter or insinuated his view with the chief through the appropriate
throne slaves and eunuchs. We cannot now determine how this leap-frogging
authority structure actually worked in different cases. Though directly subject to
the *jekada*'s administration, the village chief was formally only the *hakimi*'s subordinate; and, although the *hakimi* could engineer the *dagaci*'s dismissal, he could
not effect this independently. Only the ruler could dismiss anyone he appointed.
The *jekada* was appointed and freely dismissible by the *hakimi*. He was accordingly vulnerable to complaints from the *dagatai* he supervised. The *hakimi* normally appointed ward heads on the guidance of his *jekadu* and village chiefs; and
he could dismiss them freely. By alliance with the *jekada*, a ward head could preserve his position against encroachments by the village chief and might even
secure his dismissal. Unless he had such alternative routes of access to the king as
those discussed below, a *dagaci* could only address the ruler by personal appeal to
his judicial court. However, the king could summon the village chief or address
enquiries to him without restraint. Clearly this set of counterbalancing structures
which linked each pair across an intermediary administrative level, was designed
to facilitate and stabilize central direction and control. Babba Zaki evidently capitalized its value in this respect. At the centre power was formally dispersed
between the chief and his council, and informally between the chief and those
senior slave officials on whom he depended for communications with and
beyond the *hakimai*. It is thus probable that inferiors at any level of organization
were encouraged to seek redress or protection against their immediate superiors
through political relations of alliance and clientage with officials further up the
hierarchy rather than through judicial or administrative appeal. The hereditary
character of most important central offices served to protect the regime against
subversion by insulating the administration with protective political shields of
kinship and clientage while restraining its inherent tendency to aggrandizement
and autocracy. Most *hakim*ships vested in specific descent groups; and as indicated above, these units were deeply cleft by rivalries for lineage office and
cognate values. Often then, the clienteles of successive incumbents and rivals differed sharply in their social alignments and relations of patronage. The probability of successive alternations in local distributions of power that was implicit in
this political system thus furnished some constraints on those holding authority
at any moment.

The Military Organization

Despite the strength latent in its population and prosperity, Kano has always
had a mediocre military record. Evidently the chiefdom lacked both the military
spirit and sense of "national" unity that characterized Katsina and Gobir. Kano
had grown great by dominating and incorporating several old chiefdoms, its
equals in age and once in status; but this incorporation was formal rather than
complete. Local particularism reinforced communal antagonism to the central
government. Further as indicated above, the polity included many Fulani com-

munities under chiefs of their own. Though dispersed, divided and clearly subordinate, these collectivities were only loosely attached to the Hausa state, and certainly not part of its corporate body. Moreover, even among the Muslim Hausa its political stratifications weakened Kano. Commoners (*talakawa*) were normally not required to take part in offensive campaigns, and when attacked in force, they were often best advised to flee. Rarely could the chief mobilize his army in time to relieve them. Campaigns were thus in form always offensive; and even when undertaken for defensive purposes, the general object was to defeat the enemy in battle. Offensive action often consisted of raiding and devastation.

Commoners could participate in these campaigns only as foot soldiers or bowmen, unless provided with a horse and armor by their patrons; but all who sought and received mounts simultaneously undertook to present themselves whenever summoned by their patrons for campaigns or such other services as escorting their *jekadu* to rural areas, or attendance at Sallah in the patron's retinue.

By virtue of their positions, *hakimai* were well placed to acquire horses; but they were expected to distribute them among their kin, slaves and ablest clients. The chief likewise presented horses to his *hakimai*, to his titled and untitled courtiers, and to his palace slaves.

The core of the chiefdom's fighting force consisted of the king's slave soldiers. Many of these, equipped as *lifida*, were held in reserve around the chief and the commander for defence or final assault in phalanx formation. Lightly armed cavalry (*barade*) were used for scouting, raiding and swift attacks. The vanguard contained a cluster of *lifida*, spearmen, and bowmen, infantry sheltering between the horses.

The chief himself rarely took the field except for ceremonial attacks against Wasai. Though Babba Zaki was unusual in this respect, even he placed the eunuch Muradi in charge of his cavalry.[97] As field commanders (*tirikai*), the chief usually relied on the Madaki, Makama, Barde Babba, or Sarkin Dawaki; however, he could also commission other captains of known prowess though lesser rank as he pleased. The field commander (*tirika*) had tactical discretion but defined objectives. He supervised the distribution of booty following the campaign and received a share of the state's portion for his services. Senior throne slaves only went on campaigns with the chief. Clerics and certain specialized officials remained at the capital, for example, the Alkali, the Limam, the Ma'aji (treasurer), and the Sarkin Shanu who formally administered the government during the ruler's absence from the city.

Campaigns were planned by the chief in council, following which state forces would be mobilized by detailing *hakimai* to summon levies from their fiefs at a given date and place. Usually the force was marshalled in or near Kano City. It set out with a numerous train of concubines, camp followers and a reserve of riderless horses for use as replacements. The four senior rural chiefs, Rano, Gaya, Dutse and Karaye, held high military rank and could be given independent commands. These chiefs could also independently levy their forces to intercept raiders or to join the Kano armies in attack. However they lacked authority to raid or campaign independently, even against the pagan tribes in Bauchi.[98] While this prohibition was clearly designed to prevent internal violence and war within Kano itself, it reinforced the dominance of the central authority by reserving to it all rights of military agression. To further enhance this dominance, Babba Zaki created a unit of slave musketeers as royal guards,[99] following the practice of Gobir and Bornu. At that time even the senior rural chiefs lacked such weapons.

Rulers and Ruled, Officials and Subjects

The state consisted of an organization of offices, each distinguished by specific duties, resources, powers and rights. Its authentic representatives were the officials, their commissioned agents (*jekadu*) and their *fadawa* (courtiers). Though numerous, these office-holders and their agents were only a small part of the population from which the officialdom was recruited. At any moment most of those who were eligible for office at any level of the organization lacked it. Such eligible persons who lacked office consisted mainly of senior agnatic kinsmen of current officials and other members of those lineages for which specific titles were traditionally reserved; but senior clients, slaves, clerics and eunuchs and warriors of proven valour were also included.

This reservoir of potential office holders should not be regarded as a determinate stratum. Rather it contained several discrete groupings, scattered across the various ethnic and territorial divisions of the society; and within each local unit, these elements were drawn from such distinct status-categories as slaves, free men, clerics, hereditary nobles and others, most offices being prescriptively identified with particular collectivities and status-categories, local and/or ethnic. Thus eligibility for a particular office or discrete set of offices generally excluded an individual from all others. For example, those eligible for hereditary offices at Dutse were thereby ineligible for office at Rano, Gaya, Karaye and other local units. Occasionally some of these rural officials and nobles were selected by the king for appointment to central offices of state or for promotion and transfer to other communities whose chiefships were not prescriptively closed by descent; but such occasions were relatively rare; and most officials, local and other, were unlikely to be transferred or promoted from positions identified with their local ethnic or occupational segment and reserved for members of their own status category within it. Promotion was thus restricted in range and scope by this combination of segmental and status criteria which normally defined the social locus and context of office, and its relations with the central authority. Citizenship was correspondingly qualified by this segmental ethnic and local structure.

In theory citizenship derived from allegiance to the chief rather than simple residence in the chiefdom. It was the primacy and exclusiveness of this political allegiance (*capka*) that underlay extra-territorial assertions of *kanu* jurisdiction over Kano Fulani adrift in other countries. However, as we have seen, *jangali* taxation of migratory pastoralists revealed the ambiguous relations of these two principles, territoriality and political allegiance. In like fashion Ghadames Arabs at Kano city were not citizens of Kano, though either native or effectively naturalized by long residence; neither were Kano immigrants in Zazzau or Katsina, citizens of those states until they formally made allegiance to their rulers directly, or to some senior official who stood proxy for the chief. Such declarations of allegiance (*capka*) from individual immigrants or small family groups were neither required nor general; but they were obligatory for the leaders of large and ethnically alien immigrant groups, such as a Fulani Ruga, Ardo or lineage head.

While it was sufficient for individual immigrants to report to the local village chief and ask his permission to settle, leaders of immigrant collectivities, being obliged to preserve their corporate boundaries and their internal autonomy, had first to establish good political relations with the ruler by declaring allegiance, presenting gifts, and undertaking to uphold his order. In return, the ruler usually directed such immigrants to some suitable unoccupied sites; and, provided their rank or number merited, he might appoint a headman among them, thus creating a new segmental title. Alternatively he might place the immigrants under one of his *hakimai* or reserve their administration temporarily for himself. In the latter case a senior throne slave normally served as the official channel of communication (*kofa*, door) between the chief and the immigrant community.

Irrespective of theory, in practice citizenship, at Kano as elsewhere, and under the Hausa as under the Fulani, was pervasively particularistic at base. Most men became citizens of Kano because they were citizens first of local or ethnic communities located there. Resident aliens, though subject to Kano, were not Kano citizens until they made declarations of personal allegiance. Members of such dispersed ethnic communities as the pastoral Fulani, were only conditionally subject to Kano. Should they formally transfer allegiance on relocation elsewhere, for example, in Katsina or Bornu, they simultaneously ceased to be subject to jurisdiction by Kano, but remained under their headmen. Thus pastoral Fulani, although residents and conditional subjects, were not citizens of Kano state in any prescriptive sense. Instead they were primarily citizens of their particular ethnic groups. Likewise, local Arabs, Nupe and administratively discrete Kanuri groups remained incompletely assimilated to the degree that their membership was circumscribed by the boundaries of their corporate groups. This was also the situation of Maguzawa and other pagan groups.

Among the Muslim Hausa of Kano, citizenship was also qualified in content and form by community membership. Men were citizens of Kano state because the communities with which they were identified were corporate components of that polity. Only at the centre, and even there, only for the limited population of rulers and their slave staffs, was citizenship directly and exclusively identified with the state. The Muslim Hausa derived his identity within the polity from his membership in a community or ethnic segment that it incorporated.

Normally, rural folk participated indirectly in the political life of their village communities under the heads of the wards and hamlets in which they lived and were organized. Their participation in the political life of the state was thereby mediated through the institution of community chiefship. In several rural areas this structure of allegiance and citizenship was further qualified by intermediate levels of social and administrative organization. For example, such large substates as Gaya or Birnin Kudu, Rano, Karaye, Dutse and Burumburum were historic polities organized as hierarchies with several levels under resident hereditary chiefs. In these districts, individual citizenship was mediated serially through affiliations in wards, villages, fiefs, and subdistricts, all of which were integrated as a separate system by allegiance to the hereditary local chief. In consequence of their constitutions, the citizenship of people living in such areas was more intensively bound to the local unit than that of any others in the chiefdom. Structurally and historically, Kano was an aggregate of local and ethnic segments of differing complexity, extent and kind, coordinated as a heterogenous but distinctive polity by their differential subordination to a common central authority that demanded uniform obedience to its orders, but distributed these differentially in accordance with local differences of history, ethnicity, organization and scale. In effect, the polity was an aggregate of disparate parts unified by subjection to a common central executive; but neither were all its component parts equally and continuously coordinated, nor was the whole a genuine unity. Indeed to some extent, despite many shared values and institutions, this was equally true even within local segments, including both the once independent substates and communities of simple structure.

For example, if residents of Gaya distinguished themselves from those of Rano or Dutse, they also contraposed their collective interests and citizenship with those of Kano state and the community centered at and around the capital which had served as its historic core, and which continued to dominate the country, while reaping the major economic benefits from the regime. However, even within that central community, whose history the Chronicle revealingly relates as the history of Kano chiefdom and state, citizenship was conditioned by differences of descent, community and status. As the primitive chiefdom grew by the subordination and partial absorption of similar units on its borders, its chiefs and officials progressively lost their initial exclusive identity with the central community and expanded their interests and claims throughout the territory. Thus, in the course of expansion, as the Kano chiefship and state organization became progressively segregated from its immediate communal context, the stratification at the centre deepened, its chieftaincy was magnified, elevated and isolated in an increasingly elaborate complex of ceremonial organization and activities; and inevitably the officials were progressively differentiated from other strata. Thus, paradoxically, solidarities based on communal interests and citizenship were often weakest within the dominant central community; and to a lesser extent, a similar situation also obtained in such substates as Gaya, Rano, or Karaye, where the elevated status and authority of the local chiefs and courts generated corresponding social disjunctions. However, in consequence of their variable positions within the inclusive hierarchic structure, such internal divisions differed in kind and intensity among communities of different constitution, history and complexity.

Only the capital concentrated the entire span of differential status, power, wealth and authority characteristic of Kano; but there the structure was at once predominant and ubiquitous. The population of the capital was rigidly divided into categories distinguished by status, political position and prospect. Clientage ramified extensively to link individuals and families of different levels into pyramidal structures, whose internal solidarities varied as a function of their constitution and their immediate administrative and political context. Some social mobility was institutionalized within and through frameworks of clientage; and all officials sought to maintain and increase their clienteles by appointing one or more senior clients to offices on their staff. The ruler likewise made variable use of such *shigege* appointments. Though strongly stratified, the official order was neither fixed nor closed; and though firmly based on differential status over most of its range, its differential statuses were sometimes specific and sometimes diffuse in their authority elements and political connotations. Together these conditions furnished the social framework of Hausa government.

The Governors

Tambari Titles

In Kano, as in other Hausa states, officials were differentiated by various criteria as free or slave, hereditary or *shigege*, royal or other, central and resident in the capital, or local and resident in rural communities, territorial or nonterritorial, military or civil, secular or religious, senior (*shugaba*) or subordinate (*lawani*), and by other specifically functional or structural criteria. This combination of dichotomies does not exhaust all the critical factors that differentiate particular offices. For example, some territorial officials (*hakimai*) held large continuous tracts of territory (*yanki; jiha*), while most did not. Further, as we have seen, such chiefs as Gaya, Rano, Karaye, or Dutse held distinct though equivalent positions. These senior chiefs were usually distinguished from the *hakimai* resident in Kano as rural chiefs (*dagatai*); but they all exercised a wider territorial authority than the *hakimai*; and though generally ranked with other *dagatai*, these chiefs and others like them had many *dagatai* of their own as direct subordinates. Indeed, it seems likely that, unlike *hakimai*, these senior rural chiefs may have themselves appointed local *dagatai* over their subject communities.

In status, jurisdiction, and provenience, important local chiefs could be regarded as vassals, though their autonomy was rather reduced by comparison with the vassalage at Zazzau, for example. In Kano, "vassals" were subject to central taxation, whereas in Zazzau and elsewhere, vassals paid tribute. In Kano also these rural chiefs lacked authority to mobilize their forces or wage war without permission of the chief at Kano. Moreover, the four chiefs listed above were only the most senior of many hereditary chiefs of rural communities whose titles carried *tambari* (kettle-drums), the common symbol of former political independence. It is said that in Hausa days, as under the Fulani, there were about 50 rural chiefs in Kano territory, who held *tambari* as insignia of hereditary and formerly independent office. Most of these territorial chiefs were recruited by descent from lineages that had traditionally held these offices; but in some cases *shigege* appointments to such positions had been institutionalized long before Alwali's reign. Moreover, in their political significance, these drum-chiefs, as we may call them, differed widely. Several administered large compact areas that contained many communities and substantial populations. Others presided over single villages or towns, for example, at Gano, Sarina or Dal; and it is quite likely that several community chiefs in such large substates as Dutse or Gaya also held *tambari* and hereditary office by traditional right.

This distribution of *tambari* chiefships at Kano has persisted from Alwali's day to the present despite two major changes of regime. *Tambari* titles are not lightly abolished but rather tend to be preserved for their value in expressing and reinforcing the political order. Thus the historic and current distribution of these drum titles, each differentiated by locality, lineage and history, furnishes a vivid institutional record of the processes by which these lesser chiefdoms grew in

TABLE 2.1   Some Eighteenth Century Office Staffs *(lawanai)*

GALADIMA	Madakin Galadima	(Agnate)
	Dan Ruwata	"
	Dan Darman	(Cognate?)
	Dan Goriba	(Free client)
	Dan Gaje	" "
	Shentali	" "
	Dan Tama	(Rural chief)
	Sangetso	" "
SARKIN SHANU	Ja'idanawa	——> Sarkin Fulanin Bebeji
	S.F. Sankara	
	S.F. Dambarta	
	S.F. Kunci	
	S.F. Jahun	
	Gyerengi	
	Azaure	
	Dokaje	——> Gezawa
		Other Fulani Ardos
SARKIN JARMAI	Jeru Kusheyi	
	Madakin Jarmai	
	Galadiman Jarmai	
CIROMA	Shentalin Ciroma	
	Madakin Ciroma	
	Makaman Ciroma	
MADAKI	Ciroman Madaki	
	Galadiman Madaki	
	Shentalin Madaki	
	Barden Madaki	
	Barwa	
	Dawaki	
BABBAR DAKI	Shamakin Babbar Daki	
	Sarkin Gida	
SANKURMI	Sarkin Yara	

earlier centuries at Kano, sometimes absorbing one another before they were themselves in turn subjugated and incorporated by the Kano chiefs. In consequence of such variable antecedents, *tambari* titles in Kano do not constitute a separate distinctive order; but are generally assimilated to other local chiefships that lack such insignia and traditions, in the order of *dagatai*. Their position, while variable, is structurally ambiguous. The most important *tambari* titles carried rights to a voice in the councils of state, while the less important were administratively little different from ordinary *dagatai*. Between these extremes there were great variations in status, importance and authority, which sometimes expressed the differing histories of these units.

Dynastic Offices

Titles reserved for the ruler's kinsmen differed likewise in their political and administrative significance, seniority, and traditional distribution. Some offices were by tradition reserved for the ruler's cognatic kin, who were ineligible for the succession; for example, the offices of Sarkin Dawakin Tsakar Gida, Dan Kade, and Barde Kereriya. Such senior hereditary office holders as the nonroyal councillors and the four senior *tambari* chiefs were also usually linked to the ruler by ties of kinship and marriage, it being customary for the royal lineage to intermarry extensively with these descent groups. Nonetheless, since these titles passed by agnatic descent, though their holders were often also cognates of the ruler, they were sharply distinguished at Kano from those reserved for the king's cognatic kin.

As indicated above, some titles were reserved for the king's womenfolk, specifically for his mother and probably for his paternal aunt, for his elder and younger sisters, and for his favourite concubine, the *uwar soro* (mother of the bedchamber). Likewise, the more numerous and administratively important offices reserved for princes were traditionally distinguished by their distribution among differing categories of the king's agnatic kin. Thus, such offices as Ciroma, Tafida and Dan Lawan were usually reserved for the ruler's sons, while the titles of Wombai and Galadima were reserved for his elder brothers who were unlikely to succeed him under Hausa conventions. Such titles as Dan Maje or Dan Buram were traditionally allocated among the chief's younger brothers, while the position of Turaki Manya was reserved for the chief's agnatic parallel cousins, and normally for the grandsons of previous chiefs, and the office of Dan Ruwata was generally held by the Galadima's senior son. Other princely titles such as Sarkin Shanu or Dan Makwayau could be alloted to the chief's sons or brothers equally. Each of these various categories of titled royal kin differed in their relations with the ruler, their relative rank, political prominence and promotional prospects. While some titles were allocated to leading candidates for the succession, others went to princes who, though formally eligible to succeed, were unlikely to do so on personal, political or constitutional grounds. Yet other princes however, such as the Galadima or Wombai even if ineligible for the throne, ranked first among princes in authority, power and wealth.

The throne itself was an object of constant strife. Alwali and his immediate predecessors belonged to that dynasty or segment known as the Kutumbawa after their ancestor Muhamman Alwali I (1623–1648), who was nicknamed "El Kutumbi." These Kutumbawa had evidently displaced an earlier "dynasty" or segment of their own dynasty, who were identified as Rumfawa after their out-standing member, Muhamman Rumfa (1463–1499). Muhamman Alwali II is said to have faced a revolt of Rumfawa and their supporters shortly after his accession in 1781. This incident is well remembered, though not recorded in the Kano Chronicle. Other traditions also relate rebellions of Rumfawa during Sharefa's reign (1703–1731). According to the Dokaji Alhaji Abubakar, the Kutumbawa ruled Kano for 186 years till Alwali's death, following 163 years of Rumfawa rule.[100] Malam Adamu na Ma'aji assigns the Kutumbawa 195 years and distin-guishes them from their predecessors as Tubawa, that is, Muslim converts.[101] Both the Dokaji and M. Adamu associate the Rumfawa with Gaya, but Dokaji Abubakar also identifies them as a segment of the Daura dynasty which had immigrated to Kano via Gaya and displaced an older line of Daurawa, the Gaud-awa, who had founded and ruled Kano since Bagauda's day around 1000 A.D.[102] According to the kinship ascriptions reported in the Kano Chronicle, both Rumfa and Kutumbi descend from their immediate respective predecessors, Yakubu (1452–1463) and Muhammadu na Zaki (1618–1623); however for neither does the text of the Chronicle specify paternity, although, following Temple and Palmer, East lists these rulers as sons of earlier chiefs.[103] It is thus possible, as tradition affirms, that the Kutumbawa are merely that segment of Rumfawa which success-fully excluded others from the throne over a series of reigns. Whether or not this is the case, under Kutumbi rulers, many Rumfawa remained within the Kano population, a constant threat to their power; and it seems clear that senior Rum-fawa, though untitled, were widely regarded as princes formally entitled to rule provided they could seize the throne. Thus, even the category of princes and royals had obscure and variable boundaries, since presumably the Rumfawa dynasts rejected Kutumbawa status claims.[104]

It is said that before the *jihad* the rulers of Rano, Dutse, Gaya, Getso, Godiya, Suma'ila and Burumburum, were linked to the Kutumbawa chiefs by ties of kinship and frequent intermarriage that influenced appointments of local chiefs. In addition, Kutumbawa princes consolidated their rule by marriage alliances with noble lineages that held senior offices in the capital and the outer districts. The Rumfawa faction accordingly found little support among the senior officials.

Hakimai—*the Fiefholders*

As already indicated, in popular opinion, the relative importance of *hakim-*ships of similar rank held by members of the same status category varied with the number, size and wealth of their respective fiefs. Though many central offices lacked fiefs, fief administration was the characteristic mode of official action; and territorial jurisdiction was the prototype for senior offices directly subordinate to the throne. Routine objects of this territorial administration included the mainte-nance and enforcement of law, order and peace within the local units concerned; the transmission and enforcement of royal commands; the organization of a steady inflow of detailed information on affairs in the fief and its immediate envi-rons; the administration of land rights, inheritance suits and similar civil issues in the area; the supervision and control of local officials by various means, including the exercise of influence on local appointments and dismissals; routine levies of tax, *zakka*, corvée, or military contingents as directed by the king; provision of safe conduct for caravans in transit, the public transport of state goods; and the maintenance of local state property in good repair. In addition to customary shares of revenue and *zakka* from their fiefs, and customary rights to free labour on their local farms, *hakimai* normally sought to extract further incomes to meet their continually increasing personal and administrative expenditures by exploiting the various opportunities the administrative structure provided.

Hakimai administered their distant fiefs through titled staffs of *jekadu* recruited from their kin, clients or slaves. On his appointment to the official staff of a *hakimi* as a *jekada*, the subordinate (*lawani*; pl., *lawanai*) usually received one of the titles derivatively attached to that of his superior. Thus, the Madaki's *lawanai* bore such titles as Barden Madaki, Shentalin Madaki, Ciroman Madaki, Galadiman Madaki, Shamakin Madaki. The designations of these subtitles corresponded with prototypes attached to the chief, but distinguished their holders by specific reference to the Madaki. Thus, while the title of Ciroma was reserved for the ruler's senior son, the Ciroman Madaki was normally the Madaki's eldest son; and while the office of Barde was usually reserved for the chief's client, Barden Madaki was usually the Madaki's client, though the office might also be given to a collateral. Likewise Shamakin Madaki was usually the Madaki's senior slave. Under Kano conventions, slaves were not usually given territorial authority; nor were they formally put in charge over collectivities of free men. Accordingly slave members of the Madaki's staff had limited public roles; and their offices were generally regarded as having purely household relevance.

A *hakimi* with several fiefs would allocate them among his *lawanai* and modify established precedent and custom to fit his situation. Some fiefs attached to an office were traditionally reserved for its holder's Ciroma, others for his Galadima, and the like. The *hakimi* was required, on appointment, to remain at the capital and attend the ruler's court regularly. Unless otherwise instructed, he only visited his fiefs once or twice a year. The *jekada* maintained contact with his fief directly or through his own messengers and agents. The *jekada* thus relayed instructions and requests from the centre and information, supplies and tax from the fief, dealing with the unit through its official head and the latter's titled subordinates. The chains of communication and command were identical; and it was formally at once a serious affront, a breach of procedure and a trespass of authority for the *jekada* to communicate with ward heads directly rather than through their superior, the village chief. However, the consequences of such conduct varied with the situation and its content. Likewise a *hakimi* avoided routine dealings with his village heads except through *jekadu* he had officially appointed.

One brief example, the Madaki's administration, illustrates the general form and scope of these territorial jurisdictions. In Alwali's day the Madaki had several fiefs in a large compact area in northwestern Kano. These were divided among his titled *lawanai*, each of whom was responsible for collecting the tax, *zakka*, and other local supplies from the units under his care, for referring serious local disputes to the Madaki for settlement, for levying labour and troops, and for keeping the Madaki informed about all local incidents and conditions of administrative relevance. The Madaki selected and appointed his *lawanai* personally, with turban, robe and horse, at his official compound in the city; and thereafter he alone could dismiss them.

Village heads were selected by the Madaki and *jekadu* for recommendation to and formal appointment by the Chief, who alone could dismiss a village head. Ward-heads were selected by the *jekada* and village head concerned for commendation to and appointment by the Madaki; and he alone could dismiss them. Each *jekada* kept a customary share of the revenues from his fief, whether *zakka*, *jangali*, or cash, and turned the rest over to the Madaki who transferred the Chief's share to the Ma'aji or Shamaki as required, and retained a portion for himself. When an expedition was planned, the Madaki ordered his *jekadu* to have their village chiefs announce in the local markets that *talakawa* warriors should renew or prepare their weapons and war medicines by a set day, and all horsed clients should see to their mounts and gear. The village chief would lead his contingent to the *jekada* at Kano, and the Madaki would report to the palace when his contingents had all come in. Neither the Madaki nor his subordinates had any independent legislative power, but such legislation (*doka*, law; pl. *dokoki*) as the chief decreed would be announced locally at the village market by the town-crier in the presence of the village chief and *jekada*.

In theory, the Madaki could promote subordinates to senior offices on his staff. In practice the differing status qualifications of these offices restricted his freedom. Thus instead of promotion, the Madaki might reallocate administrative control of fiefs as he deemed appropriate. I did not learn whether any Hausa Madaki or his peers had claims against the estates of *lawanai* who died in their service, or against those they dismissed. However, it seems unlikely in the context that a Madaki would assert such claims unless the subordinate's disloyalty or cowardice seemed to merit punishment, in which case he could either impose a heavy fine on his agent or dismiss him.

The Madaki's official estate consisted of public property, including the horses, state compounds, farms, economic trees, slaves and other wealth endowed to the office. This aggregate remained for his successor. On his death, the Madaki's personal property was usually divided into three portions of theoretically equal value. One of these went to the late Madaki's immediate family, the second to his successor, and the third to the Chief, who might, if he wished, distribute it as he pleased among his courtiers or among his late Madaki's clients and kin. By Muslim law, the Madaki's fertile concubines were freed by his death. Under Hausa practice, all the personal property he had given away in his lifetime was excluded from the inheritance. However, horses transferred to clients or slaves would be returned to his estate. After those belonging to the office were removed, the remainder were distributed as already described, with their riding gear and weapons. The chief normally appropriated these and other military equipment from the estate of *hakimai* as his share. That reserved for the fief holder's issue and widows was usually divided unequally according to the relative rank of the women's lineage, the largest portion going to those children whose mother was of royal rank.

In such adjacent Hausa states as Zaria, Katsina and Daura, the office of Madaki, or Kaura, its traditional equivalent in Katsina and Daura, whether hereditary or not, normally ranked second only to the chief. This was not so in Kano. At

Zaria, the Madaki, and in Katsina and Daura, the Kauras, were the officials in charge of war. They normally commmanded the field force, unless too old or ill; and even when the king campaigned, they directed the cavalry operations. At Kano, the chief had several *tirikai* or field commanders; and the Madaki himself had a subordinate, entitled Dawaki, to direct the field operations of his horsemen. Thus, at Kano the Madaki was not primarily a military office. Perhaps by deliberate policy of successive chiefs, there was no senior military office in Kano. At an earlier date, the Chronicle suggests that the Mai-dawaki (owner, i.e., commander of horses, i.e., cavalry chief, of which Madaki is the abbreviated form) did serve as the state's war leader; but by 1780 that was long past. Learning from experience, chiefs enhanced their position by dispersing military leadership among several offices such as Makama, Barde, Sarkin Dawaki, Madaki, Sarkin Jarmai and others, while concentrating supervision of the civil administration in the hands of the Galadima, who was usually an elder kinsman of the chief either unlikely to survive him or ineligible to succeed. Indeed at Kano, even in Fulani days, the Galadima was regarded as the Sarki's vizier (*waziri*); and whenever his executive powers passed to another, usually some favourite of the chief, the Chronicle remarks this unusual development. Only after some major upheaval would the Galadima's powers and functions be reduced by the formal appointment of a vizier; until then the Galadima constitutionally exercised many powers of decision that were otherwise reserved for the chief, together with wide territorial authority. As vizier, the Galadima's functions were consistent with his close kinship with the chief, and his decisions were only subject to modification by the chief. Responsibilities for routine and *ad hoc* administrative decisions and action were delegated to him by the chief directly or in council. One effect of this transfer of executive powers to the Galadima as vizier was to deny throne slaves the chance to dominate the state by dominating or manipulating its chief.

The Throne Slaves: Babba Zaki's Reorganization

At Kano senior slaves served as administrative heads of police departments, supervising and directing the work of other slaves. The power of the cadre of senior throne slaves, was dispersed by their division under three *shigege* heads of equivalent rank and diverse function. Beyond the ruler's household, two senior slaves, Shamaki and Dan Rimi, and the eunuch Sallama, served as the main channels of communication (*kofofi, wasidodi*) between the chief and his free officials. In his unpublished history of Kano Mallam Adamu expressly attributes this administrative innovation to Babba Zaki (1768–1776);[105] and oral data on the distribution of these communication channels among the throne slaves during Alwali's reign tend to support M. Adamu's assertion that this communication structure developed during the closing phases of the Hausa regime.

Apart from throne farms and a few scattered communities reserved for allocation among his *fadawa*, slaves and untitled kin as *jekadu*, the chief held no land directly in fief, being lord of all. The territory was thus entirely parcelled out among his *hakimai* for administration; and such substates as Rano or Karaye, also came under particular *hakimai* who served as *kofas* and originally handled all their communications with the king.

For various reasons Babba Zaki evidently regarded this arrangement as unsatisfactory, perhaps because it concentrated excessive power in the hands of the senior *hakimai*, thereby reducing the ruler's freedom and control; but also because these arrangements permitted such powerful rural chiefs as Dutse and Gaya to plan and initiate revolts with security. As we shall see, there were several such outbreaks under Babba Zaki's predecessors during the eighteenth century. Evidently by establishing a new set of communication channels Babba Zaki simultaneously sought to reduce and undermine the power of his *hakimai* and to bring the senior rural chiefs and others holding *tambari* under closer central supervision. Apparently he made no attempt either to abolish or to modify in any major way the prevailing distribution of administrative responsibilities for these units among his *hakimai*, probably because such action might have promoted his deposition. Instead Babba Zaki sought to abolish the *hakimai*'s strategic positions as exclusive intermediaries between the *tambari* chiefs and the court by two measures he introduced simultaneously. First he placed his senior slaves in charge of his official communications with *hakimai*, and distributed the latter among these *wasidodi* (intermediaries). Simultaneously he made these slave "doors" responsible also for his communications with the *tambari* chiefs. For the most part it seems, from the oral data collected, that communications with the *tambari* chiefs were then segregated from those with their *hakimai*, and passed through differing slave *kofa*s, thereby enabling the king to play off the *tambari* chiefs, the *hakimai* and his slave *kofa*s against one another, *kofa* against *kofa*, *hakimi* against *tambari* chief, *kofa* against the official whose communication he handled, or the *hakimi* and his *kofa* against the *tambari* chief and his. In any of these situations the king's political independence and initiative were greatly enhanced.

The Kano Chronicle corroborates this interpretation. Having stressed Babba Zaki's ability and power, the Chronicle reports that he "curbed the power of the Sarkis (hakimai and drum chiefs) and head slaves and plundered them every day. He forced them to give presents under compulsion, and to go to war unwillingly."[106] Contemporary praise-singers, perhaps the most reliable if cryptic reporters, acclaim Babba Zaki as "the three-pronged fork for roasting elephants" (*Jan Rino Gasa Giwa*).[107] Such terms as "elephant" or "lion" denote powerful territorial chiefs. Babba Zaki's name, "great lion," itself indicates his unusual dominance and power. The three-pronged fork clearly refers to the new communication structure, with its dislocated alignments and new facilities for "roasting elephants." Moreover, having listed Babba Zaki's five senior war captains, his chief eunuchs, chief malams, leading Arab advisors— "he imitated the Arabs in almost everything"[108]—and several senior slaves, the Chronicler summarizes the situation curtly. "In all there were 42 ('great men'). Each of them thought he was greater than the rest in the Sarki's eyes. Thus the Sarki planned. Babba Zaki ruled Kano eight years."[109] To no other chief does the Chronicle attribute such mastery.

Indirectly, the Chronicle confirms Malam Adamu's direct statement that Babba Zaki introduced the system of slave *kofa*s (*wasidodi*); and its context explains the basis and purpose of this peculiar formation, the major characteristic of which is its systematic segregation of *hakimai* from the *tambari* chiefs they had previously administered under different slave *kofa*s. In Table 2.2 that summarizes these alignments as revealed by oral data, the dispersal of communication networks and administrative allignments is immediately clear. However I do not claim that the chart is either complete or accurate in all its details. Many gaps and problematic or controversial affiliations may be detected by comparing this catalogue with others given below; yet even with these qualifications the underlying structure is equally remarkable and clear. Babba Zaki's innovation was a masterly device for centralising control at the throne while simultaneously reducing the political potential of *hakimai* and *masu-tambari*. By this measure, even those *masu-tambari* who shared a common *kofa* with their *hakimai* were brought into direct contact with the Sarki, exclusive of the *hakimi* who administered their affairs. Moreover, Babba Zaki's innovation also placed those senior territorial Fulani chiefs who held *tambari* under palace control by establishing direct links with them through throne slaves, thus enabling them for the first time to communicate with the chief as seemed necessary or desirable, and to transmit their complaints, requests and reports through their *kofa*s to him. By these means Babba Zaki simultaneously sought to bring the throne into more immediate and continuous contact with senior rural chiefs, and to bring the latter more directly under his administrative control. The various revolts under his predecessors probably stimulated Babba Zaki to redesign and centralize the communication system in this way. Until the *jihad* none of his successors experienced similar difficulties; and even though Alwali had first to suppress the Rumfawa and later to fight the Fulani, our information indicates that several Fulani chiefs brought into relation with the throne through the new *kofa* system remained aloof from the *jihad*, at least until its triumph was clear. Only one of Alwali's territorial Fulani chiefs, Dan Tunku, the Sarkin Fulani of Dambarta, figures among the leaders of the Kano *jihad*; and although in the end Dan Tunku betrayed Alwali, it remains uncertain whether he openly opposed him before the final battle at Dan Yayya.

At the top of Table 2.2 I have inserted those offices for which the chief reserved communications to himself, namely, the San Kurmi, who had charge of prisons, the Sarkin Dogarai in charge of police, the Sarkin Shanu who was responsible for supervision of the Fulani *sarakuna*, for administration of the royal herd, and for the government of Kano in the ruler's absence, and the Ma'aji or public treasurer who had charge of the chief's stores of cash, grain, and other valuables. It is revealing that Babba Zaki reserved communications with these specialized and critical offices to himself, and refused to place them under the eunuchs or slaves. Through the Sarkin Dogarai, the chief dealt with Hauni, the public executioner; and through the Sarkin Shanu, he could also communicate with the rural Fulani chiefs independent of their slave *kofa*s.

In summarising my data on the territorial organisation of Kano during Alwali's day, I have set out the distribution of local units among central offices at that time for comparison with the corresponding organization under the Fulani before and after the civil war of 1893–4. Here again, despite the care and patience of my informants, and an exhaustive tabulation of all the relevant data recorded in the administrative files and district notebooks available to me, there are undoubtedly many errors and omissions. Moreover, these omissions and errors affect our representation of the Hausa territorial distribution under Alwali more severely than that current at Kano under the Fulani until the latter half of the last century for two reasons. Firstly, several informants on Fulani Kano, being themselves over 80 years of age in 1959, had witnessed the territorial organization

82

TABLE 2.2 Babba Zaki's Communication Structure, c. 1770

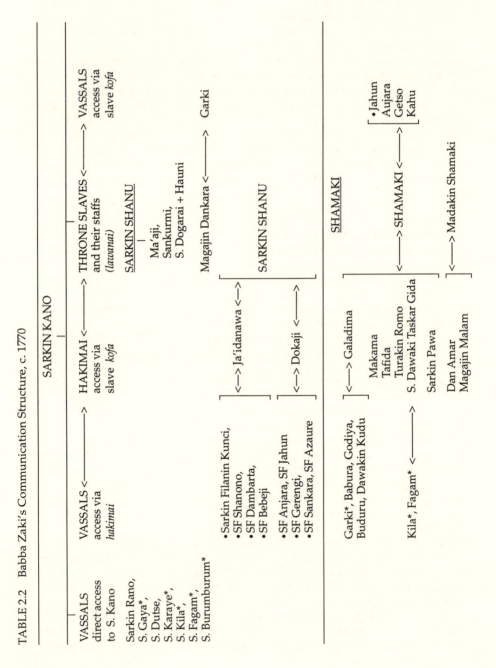

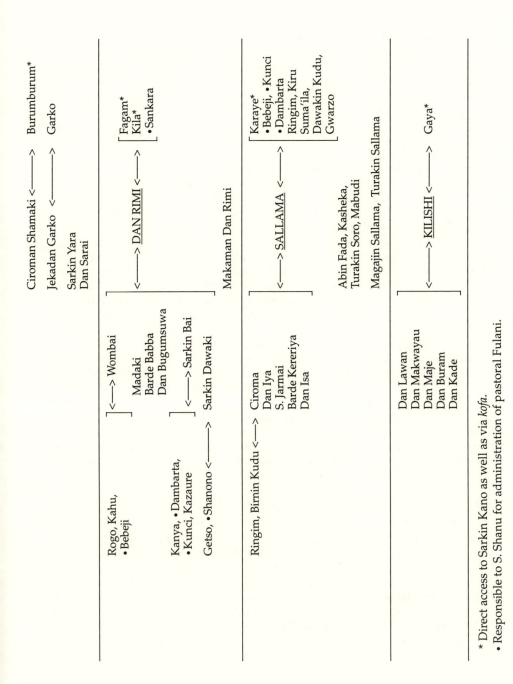

* Direct access to Sarkin Kano as well as via *kofa*.
• Responsible to S. Shanu for administration of pastoral Fulani.

before and after 1893–4. Two of these men, both aged 86 in 1959, supplied much of my data on these distributions during the last decades of Fulani rule. Their initial statements sometimes concurred and sometimes disagreed, but their disagreements were then brought forward at joint discussions in the presence of other knowledgeable elders, with the results presented below. Being by then reasonably informed about the history and details of Fulani organization, I could check the criteria and differing sources cited as evidence in these discussions. However, on this score also we are fortunate. These elders were men of fine character and good faith, who sought to recall and report what they could of the Kano of their youth as fully and accurately as possible. In addition, there are ample administrative materials available on this period to supplement, check and verify their oral information. Much of these administrative data had been recorded 40 or 50 years earlier when the territorial organization of Kano during the late nineteenth century was still highly relevant to the distribution of territorial offices under the regime introduced by the British, and in circumstances when detailed examination of contradictory reports by the field investigations of administrative officers was equally necessary and rewarding.

For the Hausa period, on the other hand, we merely have such data on territorial organization as accidents of personal, family or collective history have helped to preserve, overlaid or obscured by later modifications and redistributions under and after Fulani rule. To recover the exact pre-jihadic Hausa territorial organisation accurately is doubly difficult, especially because the Fulani simultaneously revived, employed and modified the preceding structure. All my specific distributive data for Hausa Kano are subject to qualifications of this sort. All require independent verification, correction and extension by more intensive study, especially by enquiries within the rural areas, than the resources or time at my disposal allowed. Nonetheless, having given special care to their collection and collation in recognition of these uncertainties, I believe that most of these data are substantially correct.

Table 2.3 indicates some of the gaps and ambiguities in our information. The relative importance of different territorial offices may be provisionally assessed by the admittedly inadequate criterion of the numbers and names of fiefs attached to them. Implicitly also the Table identifies those offices that lacked fiefs under Hausa rule. These are easily listed.

The Officialdom Under Alwali: Some Status Shifts

We can now review the specific composition of the officialdom in Kano under its last Hausa ruler, Alwali. Table 2.4 represents the main categories and details of this organization as far as I can reconstruct it. Information summarized there is largely derived from field discussions with city elders who enjoyed particular repute as authorities on Kutumbawa Kano; but the Table also includes data from District Notebooks and other administrative records, from the Kano Chronicle and the histories of the Alhaji Abukakar Dokaji, Malam Adamu na Ma'aji, Malam Adam Muhammad and the Alkali Mohammad Zangi. Much information required to tabulate completely the official organization at this period is undoubtedly lost; and much that remains is variably ambiguous in relevant particulars or uncertain

TABLE 2.3   Territorial Organization Under Alwali, c. 1800

Office	Vassal-states (bolded) and fiefs
Sarkin Kano	**Rano**, **Dutse**, **Gaya**, **Kila**, Panisau, Takai, Kahu, Garko
Galadima	Garki, Godiya, **Babura**, Buduru, **Dawakin Kudu**
Turaki Manya	**Bebeji**, Kura, Kofa, Gora, Madobi, Rafin Mallam
Wombai	Taura, Majiya, Ringim, **Sankara**, **Karaye**
Makama	Wudil, **Suma'ila**, Utai, Barkum, Sarina, Kademi, Indabo
Madaki	Yan Karma, Rimin Gado, Gude, Tora, Garza, Kwanyawa, Gadanya, Gurum, Dan Zabuwa, Bagwai
Dan Lawan	**Jahun**, Aujara
Sarkin Bai	Kanya, Chambo, Kyambo, Garun Gudunya, Kazaure, Kuki, Dambarta, Yakehuya, Kunci
Ciroma	Fogolawa, Harbau, Ungogo, Rantau, **Birnin Kudu**, **Burumburum**, Gargai, Ranka, Malikawa
Dan Iya	**Kiru**, Gwarzo, Farin Ruwa, Kasuwan Kuka, Bici, Tsakuwa
Sarkin Dawaki	
Tsakar Gida	**Gwaram**, **Fagam**, Shanono
S. Fulani Dambarta	Dambarta, Shiddar
Sarkin Dawaki	Yelwa, Massanawa, Dugabau, Kabo, Guru
Turakin Romo	Minjibir, Hotoro, Garo, Yataikyau, Galori, Dandake, Ruwantsa, Maraki
Dan Maje	Getso
Barwa	Bado
Soyaki	Ringim
Alkali	Dingare, Gero
Sarkin Shanu	Kano city
Magajiya	Duja (in Gaya)
Iya	Gulu
S. Fulani Sankara	Sankara, Sabon Gari, Dan Ali
Tafida	Gabasawa, Zakirai, Dabi
Ma'aji	Watari, Cishema, Rimin Gata, Rimin Azbenawa
Ja'idanawa	Azare, Gyerengi
Dokaji	Gezawa
S. Kurmi	Tudun Mazadu, Jayen, Anguwan Kwari

Vassals and *Tambari* Chiefs

Gaya	Jahun	Sankara	Shanono	Suma'ila	Tudun Wada
Rano	Kiru	Birnin Kudu	Dawakin Kudu	Garko	Riruwe
Karaye	Babura	Ringim	Dambarta	Fagam	Buji
Dutse	Kila	Bebeji	Getso	Garki	Aujara
Gwaram	Burumburum				

in its foundations. Such uncertainties and ambiguities are indicated by appropriate marks on the chart.

Much of the obscurity in the available information may faithfully reflect historical conditions of political structure. For example, the Kano Chronicle cites several cases in which Alwali's predecessors had appointed slaves or eunuchs to offices traditionally reserved for free nobles or princes. Conversely, in some cases, offices initially alloted to eunuchs had been transferred to other status categories by Alwali's day. Thus, of public offices to which Mohammed Rumfa (1463–1499) appointed eunuchs, in Alwali's day the Ma'aji or treasurer was a free *shigege* official, the Sarkin Bai, a senior hereditary *hakimi*, the Dan Turbuna, one of the throne musicians, and the Sarkin Ruwa, a slave in charge of state ferries at different points of the Challawa and Kano Rivers near the city.[110] We read also of eunuchs holding such offices as Sarkin Dawaki, Turaki Manya, and, possibly, Dan Maje in Babba Zaki's reign,[111] though the Turaki Manya was a princely office under Muhammadu Sheshere (1573–1582).[112] We read also that slaves were appointed to the senior princely title of Wambai, and that the Wambai Giwa was given Karaye by Mohammed Zaki (1618–1623) after Giwa had independently extended the southeastern city walls from the Kansakali gate to its present junction with the older wall midway between the Kofa Gadankaya and Kofa na'Isa.[113]

Such irregular and changing distributions of office among persons not traditionally eligible by status to hold them are inevitable and frequent features of patrimonial chiefship among the Hausa. Until Babba Zaki solved the problem of centralizing control over *hakimai* and major rural chiefs by superimposing a new communication network on the older chain of command, to strengthen themselves against their entrenched and powerful officialdoms, his predecessors had often tried to attach strategic offices to the throne by *shigege* appointments such as the Sarkin Dawaki, or even to such senior princeships as the Wambai.[114] They might also confer an informal viziership on some able and trusted favourite, though that was a risky step. As effects of these deviations from the prescriptive order on which allocation of office was routinely based, the distribution of certain offices among status categories varied over time and thus remains unavoidably obscure. In other cases, despite some deviant appointments, the status designation of an office was never in doubt. However, in several cases, an office might be given to slaves or freemen indiscriminately as the ruler willed. In others, an office firmly reserved for members of a single status category such as throne slaves, might be filled by *shigege* appointments although traditionally ascribed to a distinct lineage as a hereditary (*gado*) status. The resulting obscurities accordingly reflect the traditional politically expedient manipulations of distribution by rulers concerned to preserve or enhance their positions and to penalize disloyalty or incompetence among officials of various ranks. In such cases, if the culpable official had held a hereditary title, this could either be transferred to a rival segment of the holding lineage; or if the occasion warranted, it might be given to some member of the same status category who had no hereditary claim to the office.

Ostensibly the initial transfer of *gado* office to a *shigege* appointee served to warn the titular lineage that it risked losing its traditional rights to the post; but the consequences often varied. Sometimes a *shigege* incumbent established hereditary claims to the office for his sons or kinsmen. This might occur if his early demise created the urgent need for an equivalent replacement, such as a son or a younger brother, or as an effect of long and distinguished tenure of the office. Sometimes also descendants of the *shigege* holder managed to pre-empt the position exclusively for themselves, as for instance the Kutumbawa dynasty was thought to have done. Alternatively, through serial but not necessarily successive appointments to the office, the *shigege* lineage might gradually develop hereditary (*gado*) claims upon it, in which case during that period, the status and lineage locus of the office would remain obscure. Finally if some dissident or unsatisfactory official originally held a free *shigege* title, the ruler might replace him by a eunuch or slave. Subsequent appointments would then be made to the office from these or other status categories at the king's discretion.

Shigege titles were thus more directly exposed to risks of reallocation among members of different status categories than hereditary titles, which were normally reallocated in the first place to other descent groups of the same status category. However, here also, alternative procedures could obscure the traditional status of an office. While princeships retained their royal identity even though alloted to slaves, free or slave offices appropriated to princes exhibited status uncertainty, unless thereafter exclusively filled by royals for successive appointments. While certain princeships were frequently allotted to free noblemen, for example, the titles of Dan Iya, Barde Kereriya, Dan Kade, Dan Maje, and Dan Makwayau, other princely titles were exclusively reserved for specific categories of royal kin as related above. Although even these latter might be allocated by the king to agnates of other categories, it was unusual for him to appoint non-royals to these royal ranks. Thus such offices as Ciroma (crown prince) Galadima, Wambai, Dan Lawan, or Tafida were unlikely to pass beyond the king's immediate kin, some of whom might also be appointed to titles normally reserved for collateral agnates, as the conditions of dynastic rivalry allowed. Alternatively, positions reserved for the ruler's collaterals were sometimes allocated to trusted free clients, affines, or cognates to exclude possible rivals eligible for the succession from territorial office. Similar considerations influenced the distribution of titles traditionally identified with the ruler's cognatic kin.

In short, the prescriptive identifications of office by traditional reservation for members of distinct status categories and for particular lineages within them, furnish an ideal model of the Hausa officialdom which reveals the normative design that underlay and justified their distribution. By reference to this scheme we may segregate the various political principles that regulated the actual allocations of office on different lines. However, the rigidity and specificity of the traditional model made such variation necessary if the structure was to endure and adapt as the exigencies of internal or external conditions required. Some of these adaptive developments were subsequently institutionalized as traditional prescriptions. Others being strictly situational and temporary, for example, displacements of the Galadima as vizier by favourites, although recurrent, were inconsistent with other fundamental elements and never institutionalized. Yet other developments were clearly institutionalized either as ambiguities or as legitimate alternatives through which the structure maintained the flexibility requisite for its efficient operation and survival. Thus beyond the normative model with its clear distributions of office among status categories, sometimes overlying this, and in part arising from and sustained by it, are numerous alternatives and variant practices and relations, some institutionalized, others not, but all equally generated by their structure and context, and reflecting or servicing these in different ways.

Transfers of Resources and Functions

Just as offices were frequently transferred from traditional lineage groups and status categories as situations required, so fiefs and functions were also periodically reallocated piece-meal between offices for similar reasons. By such means chiefs sometimes sought to strengthen themselves and their leading supporters within the officialdom. They could also be employed to weaken an official whose authority and power they wished to reduce. However, when such powerful officials held senior hereditary seats on the council of state, the chief had to move warily. His office was not that of a despot, and he was subject to numerous traditional prescriptions that restricted his independent direction of the state. Indeed, to rule, the chief depended on his entire officialdom, and particularly on those senior territorial officials who constituted his council. Thus, although he could transfer fiefs or functions between offices, that was usually done piece-meal; and such action rarely escaped notice by the public or officialdom, since it always represented a possible extension of royal power which, if unchecked, could undermine the total structure and, through successful usurpation, promote despotism. For the regime as constituted identified the king as the individual most capable of such usurpation; and to avoid this charge, in their piece-meal reallocations of functions and fiefs, rulers normally refrained from appropriating further powers or domains directly to the throne. Thus by such transfers of fief or function, they simply enhanced some offices at the expense of others.

Unless there were good reasons for so doing, rulers were otherwise well-advised to leave the traditional distribution of official functions fairly intact. If for various reasons it was thought desirable to reduce an office to strengthen the throne, the chief, having dismissed the official, might simply place the units' fiefs under the temporary but indefinite administration of his courtiers or slaves. His successor could then decide whether to retain administrative control of those units or return them with the office to the lineage or status group concerned, or he might reallocate the fiefs and office, separately or together, within or across the boundaries of status groups. In either event it was essential that the chief should not aggrandize his immediate territorial jurisdiction at the expense of his officialdom.

Two important patterns of functional transfer and reorganization have been cited above, namely, the periodic displacement of Galadima as vizier by chiefly favorites, and the fundamental centralizing innovation of Babba Zaki. While developments of the first sort remained contingent and anomalous, and were thus recurrently revoked, Babba Zaki's communication system persisted as a permanent feature of the regime and supplied the basis of its remarkable political centralization. No other pre-jihadic state in Hausaland displays a degree of centralization comparable with Kano; and when reconstituted in the following century, this structure also distinguished Kano as the most intensively centralized emirate in the Fulani empire.

It was simpler for the chief, and less offensive to his officials, to create new functions and distribute these as he pleased than to transfer routine ones from offices that had traditionally discharged them. Likewise it was simpler for the chief to expand his territory by diplomacy or conquest as opportunity allowed; and by distributing those units to alter the relative status and power of officials and descent groups, than to effect such redistributions of power by reallocating the fiefs already incorporated under particular offices. On the available data, no wholesale redistribution of state functions or fiefs was ever attempted for simply structural reasons in Kano under the Hausa. On the other hand, such outstanding chiefs as Rumfa, Kutumbi, Sharefa and Babba Zaki all added new functions, offices and territories to the state, and distributed these to promote the royal power. Such innovations were readily institutionalized, largely because they simultaneously expanded the size, revenues and scope of the officialdom, but also because they disturbed no one and enhanced the strength of the state. In effect, those structural considerations that enjoined the conservation of traditional forms themselves generated and encouraged institutionalization of new structures and functions through continuous processes of internal complication and territorial expansion. Both tendencies and developments were closely associated. Both had their roots in the same structure.

These considerations together indicate that reservations are advisable with regard to many statements of the concrete allocations of fiefs or function between offices, and of offices among status groups and between the hereditary or *shigege* categories, in any detailed reconstructions of Hausa government at Kano under Alwali. The same considerations also account for numerous apparent obscurities or inconsistencies in the available oral and documentary materials on the Hausa polity of this period. Given such variations and modifications of pattern mainte-nance through internal redistribution and elaboration, and through external growth, it is clearly unlikely that sources that refer with different levels of preci-sion to different aspects or phases of the system will furnish perfectly corrobora-tive data. Thus the numerous specific ambiguities or uncertainties indicated in the tabular data and accompanying text may reflect structural features or variant tra-ditions, or both together. It is not always simple to determine at this stage on the available data the source of present uncertainty in any particular case; even to gauge its extent we have concretely to relate the alternatives before us to their common systemic contexts. It is thus certain that our errors and ambiguities have diverse sources both in the traditional structure and in the structure of the tradi-tions themselves; but they are distributed irregularly at different points in both these representatives of "reality."

Another set of distortions in Table 2.4 has much simpler foundations. Follow-ing Hausa practice, though I have classified these offices by status categories and, where relevant, by the presence or absence of hereditary restrictions on their allo-cation, the result corresponds closely with the basic division between territorial and other officials of state. All princely offices and others reserved for the king's kinsmen, together with most hereditary titles held by freemen, had territorial fiefs and accordingly ranked as *hakimai*. However several *shigege* offices alloted to freemen lacked such fiefs, and besides *hakimai* resident at the capital, several *tambari* chiefs and *Sarakunan Fulani*, though not normally ranked as *hakimai*, being themselves supervised by their *hakimi's jekadu*, enjoyed the essential powers and status of *hakimai*. Further, even excluding princes, *hakimai* resident at the capital varied widely in status and power. Such differences usually correlated with parallel differences in the number and value of fiefs attached to these offices, and with their hereditary or *shigege* distribution. However, it is by no means clear that relative status or power always or only had these bases. It is equally possible that such differing distributions of office and fiefs might reflect initial differentiations of status and power and derive therefrom. Probably both alternatives held for different sets of offices and both developed in different historical contexts. Similar effects or institutional patterns often have very different historical roots and processes of growth.

Ambiguities of Structure or Information?

In Table 2.4, by classifying offices in the status categories for which they were reserved, I have inevitably assimilated territorial and functionally specific offices concentrated at the capital. These assimilations fall within the order of *barori* ranks in the table. Most of the functionally specific offices reserved for free men were *shigege* positions filled on the basis of capacity or chiefly favour, rather than by seniority within a noble descent group. Several of these functionally specific positions had strictly military roles, for example, the Sarkin Jarmai, Sarkin Karma, Sarkin Baka, and their *lawanai*. Except possibly the Sarkin Jarmai, who commanded the *lifida*, none of these titled captains administered fiefs. However the senior military post filled by free *shigege* clients, the Sarkin Dawaki, was an important territorial office.

Most of the craft heads appointed in Hausa Kano were recruited by descent. This is established for the two metal working chiefs and for the heads of dyers and leatherworkers; but it is not beyond doubt for the Sarkin Gini or Sarkin Pawa who had charge of the market. The Korama appointed by Sarkin Pawa over the grain vendors was a *shigege* appointment. None of these several craft heads administered fiefs. Following Hausa practice I have therefore separated them from other free officials as a distinct order of occupational officials (*masu-sana'o'i*).

Certain functionally specialized officials such as the San Kurmi and the Ma'aji Babba may well rank as *hakimai*, being entrusted with the administration of specific fiefs. Though described as the state jailer, San Kurmi administered Jayen, Unguwan Kwari, and perhaps also Tudun Mazadu and Samagu. Besides the state treasury, the Ma'aji Babba was also responsible for routine administration of the capital, including the selection, appointment, remuneration and discipline of its fourteen gate keepers, and the selection and supervision of the many ward heads through whom the city population was immediately organised. As necessary the Ma'aji dealt with these ward heads directly or through messengers, but directed cases arising from the wards to the city judges, or, if land and political issues were involved, to the court of the chief. His jural powers and responsibilities were thus very slight. Likewise until Kumbari's day, the Ma'aji did not collect *karo* within the city. Under Sharefa (1703–1731) when the city markets were first taxed, the Ma'aji was charged with supervising this tax collection through the Sarkin Pawa and his market staff. The Ma'aji also received as personal income all *zakka* due to the state from farms within the city walls and their immediate environs, apart from those areas reserved for the various gatekeepers; and this tithe provided much of his legitimate income. The Ma'aji lived in a state compound which served also as the treasury; and his office was endowed with a farm and certain field slaves. It seems doubtful whether this combination of attributes assuredly placed the Ma'aji among the *hakimai*.

As mentioned above, such *hakimai* as the Madaki, the Makama, or the Sarkin Bai administered extensive continuous tracts of country that contained contiguous fiefs. Other *hakimai*, such as the Barwa, Dan Goriba, Magajin Malam, and Dan Jigawa, had a few small units which were widely scattered. The Barwa, for example, was the king's senior messenger to other independent chiefs in Zazzau or Katsina who were authorized by tradition to levy capital punishment, tribute, tax, or war, and were accordingly distinguished as *sarakunan yanka* (chiefs of execution). The Dan Jigawa, Sarkin Yaki, Ubandawaki and Barden Goriba were titled courtiers who served as agents (*jekadu*) of the chief and sometimes received particular fiefs. However, such allocations were optional and often revoked by succeeding chiefs. Formally, when holding fiefs, these men ranked with the Madaki or the Makama as *hakimai* since *hakim*ship consists in territorial administration through fief-holding, and with its civil jurisdiction went distinctive military and political obligations to constitute the role. However, differences of status and power between such senior *hakimai* as the Madaki and the Sarkin Bai who held positions on the electoral and state councils by hereditary right, and such minor functionaries who occasionally served as *hakimai* as the Barwa, Magajin Malam or Turakin Romo, all of whom held *shigege* appointments and hence depended on the chief's continued favor, are of such an order that indiscriminate assimilation of these titles as *hakimai* would seriously misrepresent the political structure and their several positions within it.

Similar variability of status and power also appears among and between *masu-tambari* and other *dagatai*. *Tambari* chiefs differed widely among themselves in status, power and domain. So did *dagatai*; and some *dagatai* undoubtedly administered larger units than several *masu-tambari*. Nonetheless, though assimilated to the general category of *dagatai*, *tambari* chiefs took precedence, and the most senior among them also ranked above *hakimai* on grounds of *asali* (origin, descent, i.e., dynastic status).

Of the various Fulani chiefs settled in rural Kano, several held *tambari* on differing historical grounds; but one or two did not. Though these Fulani chiefs were distinguished by their specific titles, they were evidently not regarded by the Kano Hausa as constituting a separate rank order. However in segregating them from strictly territorial Hausa *hakimai* I have indicated those who held *tambari* by appropriate marks. These Fulani chiefs also differed among themselves in the degree to which their authority had been institutionalized on strictly territorial grounds. That development had probably gone furthest at Bebeji and Dambarta, where the territorial and ethnic orientations of the Fulani chiefships were equally prominent, and sometimes pulled in opposite directions. By contrast, the Shanono chiefship seems at this date to have been predominantly ethnic in its orientation and exercise. Such variations are masked by our uniform classification of these titles; but it is for this reason, among others, necessary to segregate the Fulani chiefs supervised from the city by the Sarkin Shanu. Thus, with reservations mentioned above, Dokaji and Ja'idanawa are classified in the *barori* category among *hakimai* and *fadawa*.

Precedence and Seniority

Two further comments are necessary before presenting summary role descriptions of unfamiliar titles in this list. Both centre on relations of precedence and leadership among these offices. The Hausa term *shugabanci* carries both connotations. In several senses the Galadima could be described as *shugaba* (senior or leader) of the royal ranks and the Madaki or Makama as *shugaba* of the *barori*; but such usage denotes relations of precedence rather than the leadership expressed in direct administrative responsibility and control. The typical instances of direct leadership are structures of *lawanai* attached to senior offices. Such *lawanai* may themselves differ in relative rank, characteristically by their relations of kinship or clientage with their common chief; and in consequence, these *lawanai* titles may form an order of precedence. However, unless specifically authorized by their common superior to do so, no subordinate exercised direction over others. All ranked equally as their superior's subordinates and proceeded independently with their tasks, unless directed otherwise. A similar pattern of administrative segregation prevailed among the primary offices of state. For instance, the Madaki conducted his administration without reference to Makama, or any official except the chief, unless specifically directed otherwise by the latter.

Such relationships are not the only type of administrative supervision institutionalized within the officialdom. For example, the Sallama supervised all throne eunuchs; but as each normally had his own clearly defined role, their offices were all distinct; and these eunuchs were not Sallama's *lawanai*. By contrast his subordinate staff bore the titles of Makaman Sallama and Turakin Sallama respectively. Similarly, the Shamaki supervised those free and slave officials directly attached to the throne such as the Sarkin Yara, the Jekadan Garko, the Dan Sarai and others; but these men, though responsible to Shamaki, were not his subordinates. The latter held *lawanai* ranks derived from the Shamaki title, such as the Ciroman Shamaki, etc. Thus administrative relations of *shugabanci* had at least two modalities, one identified by a discretionary power over the subordinate that vested directly in the superior, the other by the absence of such discretionary power. Likewise relations of precedence had at least two modes—the Ma'ajin Watali ranked below the Madaki and Sarkin Bai in all respects, individually and as an office. In other cases, offices might form a promotional series through which individuals could pass. For example, in Hausa days the routine *cursus honorum* to the office of Galadima usually proceeded from the village chiefship of Badari to the *tambari* title of San Getso, in charge of Getso, and thence to the office of Dan Tama in charge of Godiya which lay between Getso and Kano. Alternatively such senior titled princes as the Dan Lawan, Tafida or Dan Buram who had been passed over for the succession might be promoted to the Galadima office. Notably none of the Galadima's senior subordinates, including the Dan Ruwata, his son or kinsman, the Dan Goriba, Dan Gaje, or the Dan Darman, were eligible to succeed him. However the Dan Ruwata was often promoted to some other royal office, such as Turaki Manya, after the Galadima's death.

As befitted his unique position under the king, the Galadima alone had discretionary power (*iko*) over these four offices, Dan Ruwata, Dan Goriba, Dan Gaje and Dan Darman, though each was formally an independent unit of the state organization. A fifth, the Shentali, arouses controversy among Kano savants who dispute whether this office was then attached to the Galadima or to the Kano *sarauta* (chiefship) directly. It seems probable that like the other four state ranks assimilated as *lawanai* to the Galadima's office, the title of Shentali was initially attached to the Kano chiefship, but in due course came under the Galadima's direction. Perhaps such relational ambiguities merely evidence processes of institutional change linked with the development of the Galadima as the unofficial vizier at Kano, its senior state councillor and civil official.

Some Official Roles

To conclude this descriptive account of the state and government over which Alwali presided at Kano, I briefly cite the salient features of those offices which remain undiscussed. To review the structure of this officialdom it is convenient to follow the order of presentation in the preceding Table of organization (Table 2.4). Most of the critical data on the roles and relations of the titles reserved for the ruler's kinswomen have already been presented. It seems likely that the Hausa terms of Maidaki and Babbar Daki are synonyms; alternatively the Maidaki may have designated the king's paternal aunt, or occasionally his father's mother, and rarely became prominent during the ruler's mother's lifetime. Failing both Babbar Daki and the Maidaki, the Magajiya might exercise their powers of intercession and overrule. Thus these three offices constituted a series that preserved the oligarchic distribution of power and authority between the chief and his councillors against erosion or dissolution by aggrandizement of the chief. Whether the Dauduwa was ever eligible for promotion to these positions remains unknown. It is said that on their accession chiefs were expected to replace their predecessor's Babbar Daki by their own mothers. Presumably, this principle applies also to the Maidaki.

Of princely titles, little need be said. Dan Ruwata, as the Galadima's kinsman or son, was normally an agnate of the king, the Galadima being usually the ruler's brother. The Ciroma title was reserved for the ruler's eldest son, his predecessor's Ciroma being usually transferred to some other royal office with reduction in status and power. Except for the Sarkin Shanu, a title initially created for slaves, and subsequently appropriated to princes and cognatic kinsmen of the king, all princely ranks functioned as *hakimai*. Two of them, the Galadima and the Wambai, had permanent positions on the council of state; a third, the Dan Iya title, was sometimes held by royals eligible for the throne, at other times by the ruler's cognatic kin, and alternatively by noblemen of non-royal descent. When the Dan Iya was ineligible to succeed, he served on both the electoral and the state councils. The Sarkin Dawakin Tsakar Gida was generally a uterine cross cousin of the king. He was traditionally expected to remain near the ruler, whenever the latter left the palace. Presumably kings appointed to this office their favourite cross cousins and joking relations. Several of these cognatic (*wajen mace*) ranks had ambiguous distributions, being alternatively allocated to the ruler's agnates or to noble free-

TABLE 2.4 Status Structure of Alwali's Officialdom, c. 1800

Status Category		Hereditary	Non-Hereditary	Uncertain
ROYAL	Female	Babbar Daki, Magajiya, Maidaki, Daudawa, Iya	Uwar Soro	
	Male	Galadima, Wombai, Turaki Manya, Ciroma, Dan Isa, Dan Lawan, Dan Buram, Tafida, Dan Ruwata	Sarkin Dawaki Tsakar Gida, Dan Iya, Dan Kade, Sarkin Shanu, Dan Darman, Dan Makwayau, Barde Kereriya, Dan Maje	
NON-ROYAL				
Hakimai and Courtiers (fadawa)		Madaki, Makama, Sarkin Bai, Barde Babba, Dan Atuman	Turakin Romo, Dokaje, Soyaki, Sarkin Dawaki, Ma'aji, Sankurmi, Barwa, Sarkin Karma, Dan Jigawa, Madawakin Gawo, Ubandawaki	Dan Goriba, Dan Gaje, Ja'idanawa, Sarkin Jarmai, Dan Bugumsuwa, Sarkin Yara, Dan Amar, ? Shentali, Gadomasu, Jeru Kusheyi, Sarkin Fada, Sarkin Karma
RURAL CHIEFS (a) Hausa tambari chiefs * Direct access to Sarkin Kano		S. Rano*, S. Gaya, S. Dutse* S. Karaye*, S. Birnin Kudu, Sangetso, S. Godiya, S. Burumburum*, S. Gwaram*, S. Buduru, S . Babura*, S. Aujara, S. Riruwe, S. Fagam, S. Kahu, S. Garki (= Dirani), S. Garko, S. Kiru, S. Gwarzo, S. Ringim, (Soyaki) S. Garza*, S. Kila*, Dawakin Kudu, S. Suma'ila*		

b) Fulani chiefs	Sarkin Fulanin Sankara, S.F. Dambarta, S.F. Bebeji, S.F. Kunci, S.F. Shanono, S.F. Jahun		
CLERICS	Limam, Na'ibi, Alkali, S. Sherifa S. Ladanai: (? S. Malamai)	Magatakarda, Mala, Magajin Malam	
FREE CRAFT HEADS	S. Makeran Baki, S. Makeran Fari, S. Dukawa	Korama, S. Baka	S. Gini, S. Pawa, S. Dillalai, S. Kasuwa
Musicians	S. Kakaki, S. Busa, S. Tambari, S. Jauje, S. Kida na Kuso	Dan Kwando, Dan Turbuna	
EUNUCHS		Sallama, Abin Fada, Mabudi, Kasheka, Turakin Soro	
PALACE SLAVES	Jekadan Garko, Dan Rimi, Hauni, Magajin Dankama, S. Dogarai, Madakin Zarbabi.	Shamaki, S. Bargo, S. Ruwa, Lifidi, Garkuwan Karfe, Ubandawaki, S. Hatsi, Kilishi, S. Rakuma, Maje Sirdi	
FREE OR SLAVE status obscure			Dan Sarai, S. Zagi, S. Masu, S. Takuba, Butali, Hangaza, S. Garka, Jekafada, S. Sirdi

men. For example, the Dan Darman, usually a cognatic kinsman of the Galadima, and thus sometimes of the chief, could be appointed to other cognatic ranks following the Galadima's death. Alternatively, the Galadima's "cognate" might also be a prince in the direct line of descent, given the Hausa practice of cousin marriage within as well as beyond agnatic groups.

Much has already been said concerning the complexity of offices classified as *barori* (free non royal) ranks in the preceding list. Occasionally it seems in Hausa times the Madaki office was given to princes. Thus the Alkali Zangi mentions that Alwali's Madaki was his son; but this may be an error. Of unfamiliar hereditary free titles on this *barori* list, the Ma'ajin Watali, Barde Babba, Dan Bugumtsua and Dada all ranked as lesser *hakimai*. However only for Ma'jin Watali are fiefs now known. The Makama, Sarkin Bai and Madaki had seats on both electoral and state councils. Of those *barori* whose hereditary or *shigege* modes of recruitment remain uncertain, only the Dan Tama has not been mentioned. This office exercised *hakimi* functions. So did the Dan Goriba and Dan Gaje, both subject to the Galadima. In the eighteenth century the Sarkin Yara seems by contrast to have lacked fiefs. He served as warder of the palace prison reserved for men of high status. Though formally subordinate to the San Kurmi, he was also subject to Shamaki's guidance and supervision, the latter being in charge of this palace department. The Sarkin Jarmai was a free official sometimes recruited from a particular lineage to command the chief's *lifida* and was rewarded with valuable fiefs. The Jeru Kusheyi (lit. "lines of graves") was the senior *lawani* of the Sarkin Jarmai, and served as his *jekada* and military captain. The Soyaki is said to have been placed in charge of Ringim following a serious revolt there in Kumbari's reign.[115] The roles of Dan Goriba, Ma'aji Babba, San Kurmi, Barwa, Sarkin Karma, Sarkin Baka, Dokaji and Sarkin Dawaki have already been indicated. The latter, who was sometimes placed in command of the state forces, retained the position by prowess and chiefly patronage. Through the latter, he often had a seat in the king's councils. The Ubandawaki was a less prominent master of horse. The Dan Jigawa like the Barwa served the chief as courtier and messenger (*jekada*), and was occasionally remunerated with minor fiefs.

The office of Turakin Romo, classified here as a free *shigege* title, had evidently passed to throne eunuchs before Alwali's day. Several informants identified this with the title of Turakin Kuka which is mentioned frequently in the Kano Chronicle. It seems rather that these were distinct positions initially allocated to palace eunuchs. The Turakin Kuka title may once have been designated Turakin Soro. Under Alwali, freed men, presumably former throne slaves, were appointed to the title of Turakin Romo which then carried fiefs northwest of Kano and Panisau in an area of immediate strategic interest to the ruler. Concerning the Madawakin Gawo little is known, except from the Kano Chronicle. There, creation of this office is attributed to Jaji (1349–1385) who replaced his Madaki Gasatoro by the Mandinka warrior Goje. "Gasatoro who was turned out of the post of Madawaki, built a house at Gawo, and for that reason was known as Madawakin Gawo, to distinguish the two."[116] By Alwali's day, the Madawakin Gawo had become the Kano equivalent of Sarkin Daji (chief of the bush) with a vague authority over local hunters and certain military functions, perhaps serving as a scout. It was through the Madawakin Gawo that elephant tusks, lion and leopard skins were presented to the chief annually by successful hunters. Periodically also the chief required hunters to capture lions for "palace customs" that were probably pagan rites.

Of the clerical order, only the Alkali is said to have held official fiefs in the Hausa state. This title was thus provided with sufficient independent revenues to make it unnecessary for the judge to accept bribes from litigants. Evidently appeal could be made from the Alkali's court to that of the chief. Of the other hereditary clerical offices, the Na'ibi was the Limam's deputy, close kinsman and probable successor. The Limam then conducted both the Friday mosque and the Idi prayers. The Sarkin Ladan was head of the Kano muezzins. Although not subordinate directly to the Limam he worked along with him. The title of Sarkin Sherifai is said to date from the reign of Mohamma Zaki (1618–1623). According to oral traditions, its holders are recruited from the descendants of Sidi Fari, the white or first *sa'id*, Malam Isa, who is generally said to be El Maghili's senior son whom he left at Kano in Muhammad Rumfa's reign (1463–1499) with the necessary instructions and materials to establish Islam. Since the Sherifai descended from Sidi Fari are concentrated at Zainawa, it was placed under the Sarkin Sherifai as their lineage head.[117] However, the Sarkin Sherifai had no strictly territorial jurisdiction, his authority at Zainawa being based solely on kinship and ritual status. Like titled clerics other than the Alkali, he depended on the chief's largesse, receiving gifts of grain, clothing, money, slaves and other valuables at the major Muslim feasts, and irregularly at other times during the year. Of other clerical titles attributed to Alwali's Kano, the office of Sarkin Malamai (chief of the malams) is the least well established. Magatakarda, the sole *shigege* cleric, served as the chief's scribe responsible for correspondence with Bornu and with nearby chiefs, for compiling lists of *zakka*, and for assisting the Ma'aji (treasurer) as necessary.

As indicated above, clerical skills were in great demand at court whenever military and political success seemed uncertain. Clerics were then required to divine the future, to manipulate Providence and to guide the ruler propitiously. In return they received substantial payments in cash and kind, evidently whether their rituals succeeded or failed. Officials and private citizens also appealed for similar aid in times of need, presumably at lower rates. Most important offices had such ritual agents attached to them, often as their *limam*, though generally without formal appointment.

The Abin Fada relayed messages and information to the chief in his private quarters. The Turakin Soro was in charge of the chief's personal apartments, to which his concubines were summoned. Most chiefs had such large harems they refrained from entering them. The Kasheka was the Sallama's senior assistant and likely successor. He may also have served as a *kofa* at this time. Presumably one of these two senior eunuchs accompanied the chief when away from the palace, the other having charge of the harem and state insignia. From his title, it seems likely that Kasheka ("Kill you") controlled the harem guards. The Mabudi (Opener, key) supervised entrances to the chief's private quarters, while the palace entrances were under the Sarkin Dogarai who was responsible to the chief. It is said that there were several other eunuchs with strictly domestic functions. Sallama, Shamaki and Dan Rimi were the chief's senior palace staff and advisors. They were expected to keep him abreast of events and opinions within the palace and the town.

Of Hausa slave offices that are still remembered, some were hereditary, others were not. Of the hereditary offices, Dan Rimi was senior; of *shigege* ones, the Shamaki. Our data indicate that of these two, the Shamaki had the more important role. However, influence over palace staff was divided between the three senior slaves, each of whom had many clients within the palace, among the free official-dom, and among city folk with political aspirations. Their free clients frequently visited the palace to pay court to these senior slaves, and if they then attracted the favourable notice of the chief, these freemen might be gradually admitted among his circle of *fadawa* (courtiers), and could then aspire to intermittent and subse-quently to continuous appointment as *jekadu*, often on the staff of some *hakimi* who frequented the court. Each of these senior slaves had one *lawani* always with the chief. For the Sallama this was the Yora, for Dan Rimi his Makama, and for Shamaki his Ciroma. These slave *lawanai* reported all significant events to their superiors who would visit the chief together early in the morning and at noon, being otherwise summoned as they were wanted.

As we have seen, the senior throne slaves served as communication centres for the chief. Each accordingly directed a staff of mounted messengers. The Shamaki also supervised the Maje Sirdi who had charge of the chief's stables, the Lifidi who had charge of the palace stores of cotton and leather armour, the Sarkin Rakuma who looked after the chief's herd of camels, the Sarkin Masu who cap-tained the slave spearmen, the Sarkin Takoba who captained the swordsmen, and other minor figures. The Garkuwan Karfe was slave commander of those *lifida* who guarded the chief in battle. This title, meaning "shield of iron," indicates its role. The Ubandawaki commanded a troop of slave horsemen. Sarkin Garko was another slave warrior who also served as one of the chief's *jekadu* to the estates and rural areas that formed part of his domain. Sarkin Hatsi administered the palace stores of grain under the Dan Rimi. Sarkin Dogarai commanded the police and palace guards, and was directly responsible to the chief. When the latter went on campaign, the Sarkin Dogarai proceeded a day's march ahead of him to prepare his quarters. Besides a marginal communications role, the Magajin Dakwara had some responsibilities for the chief's estates. Further, like the Sha-maki, the Sallama, and the Dan Rimi, the Magajin Dakwara administered a segment of the palace slaves, having responsibility for the repairs and order of a ward in the palace. The Jekadan Garko was placed at Takai by Babba Zaki with a sufficient slave force to consolidate his recent conquests in that region and overawe nearby pagans. The Madakin Zarbabi was a slave jester and *zagi*, that is, a footman who accompanied the chief as he rode to the mosque or elsewhere, clearing his way with a litany of standard jokes. Kilishi, who may have been a hereditary slave official, served as the senior court usher along with the Makaman Dan Rimi and the Ciroman Shamaki. Another official who was required to remain at the court and palace in close contact with Kilishi was the Mala. This title which is of Bornu origin was given to the senior *lawani* of the San Kurmi in charge of the public prison. Mala, with his staff of warders, escorted prisoners between the palace and public prison. The Hauni's role has been described above. That of the Dan Sarai at this date remains obscure. He appears to have served mainly as a *jekada* and court attendant, but may also have been a spy.

Hausa chiefship required an elaborate musical and poetic setting to celebrate its magificence and glorify the chief. This aspect of the institution and court is indeed most impressive, and difficult to recapture in the cold language of an ethnographic report. Most court musicians were free persons of low status whose offices were hereditary. As senior trumpeter, the Sarkin Kakaki bugled the royal presence on slender horns of beaten metal six feet long. The Sarkin Busa was a virtuoso on the *algaita*, a reed instrument as penetrating as the bagpipe, which he played on horseback as well as on foot. The Sarkin Tambari, recruited from Tambarawa where his lineage lived, repaired, guarded and played the royal kettledrums, which were beaten on the Sabbath eve (Thursday night), nightly in Ramadan, and whenever the chief mounted for the Idi festivals or for war. These drums ranked among the central insignia of the chiefship, of which the most important, until Alwali destroyed it, was the fetish Dirki whose possession finally established the chief's accession. The Sankira was the ruler's chief praise-singer, and like other court officials, he recruited titled *lawanai* from his kinsmen and clients. Together these eulogists memorized the traditional praise songs (*kirari, taki*) of the chief and leading officials of state. The Dan Kwando and the Dan Turbuna, like the Madakin Zababi, were court jesters, dancers, and entertainers. The Sarkin Kidan Kursu and the Sarkin Kidan Lauje headed drum troupes that played instruments of differing type. There were probably other titled court musicians and attendants not listed here.

Concerning the *sarakunan Fulani* and the *tambari* chiefs, the basic information has already been presented. There is also no need to itemize the titles and roles of village chiefs or ward heads. Such rural chiefships as Dan Tama, Dan Akasan, Dan Ataman, Madawakin Gawo, Dirani and Sarkin Maji'a had distinguished antecedents, while most had not.

Two titles of special interest remain, Jarmai and Sarkin Fada. Jarmai was an honorific conferred on individuals for distinguished military exploits.[118] *Jaramawa* (its plural) might be free or slave, royal or other. They were respected and rewarded by the chief with gifts and horses, concubines and the like, and might be given small commands on dangerous missions. The honorific title, Jarmai, carried no military or administrative authority. It merely distinguished its holder as a warrior of proven valor.

The last title which should be mentioned is not a true Kano title at all. This is the *lakabi* or folk designation, Sarkin Fada, "chief of the palace." This term was usually applied to those untitled favourites or upstarts whose influence with the chief seemed to subvert traditional constitutional procedures and authority for policy formation and execution, before or after the temporary transfer of vizieral functions from the Galadima. Such unofficial power attracted public notice and elicited two folk descriptions. The favourite was commonly described as Sarkin Fada without mentioning his name, while the chief was described as his vizier, to indicate his favourite's influence.

These popular terms, which reflected court gossip and intrigue, and focussed attention on usurpations underway, identified a basic feature of the political order with typical Hausa terseness and clarity. By the unwritten constitution that underlay this oligarchic regime, with its complex but flexible dispersal of administrative and political initiatives, all executive authority or influence on policy formation or implementation exercised by untitled persons was unconstitutional and subversive. That is to say, in theory, public authority was exhaustively distributed among the offices of state, their duly appointed staffs and subordinates in the central and rural administrations. Unofficial influence and executive capacities over public affairs were thus inconsistent with this exhaustive distribution of administrative responsibilities among the offices of state. Accordingly such informal authority was neither public nor legitimate, but an insidious expression of private influence.

Notes

1. Palmer, KC, p. 89; East, LH, Vol. 2, p. 53.

2. KC, p. 90; LH, Vol. 2, pp 54–55.

3. KC, p. 90; LH, p. 55. See also Muhammad Uba Adamu, "Some Notes on the Influence of North African traders in Kano," *Kano Studies*, Vol. 1, No. 4, 1968, pp 43–49.

4. Major Denham, FRS, Captain Clapperton, and the late Doctor Oudney, *Narrative of Travels and Discoveries in Northern and Central Africa in the years 1822, 1823 and 1824.* (London: John Murray, Second Edition, 1826), Vol. II, p. 220.

5. Henry Barth, *Travels and Discoveries in North and Central Africa.* (London: Ward, Lock & Co., 1890) Vol. 1, pp 308–309. For further discussion of this question, see Hiskett, "Materials relating to the cowry currency of the Western Sudan - I," *BSOAS*, Vol. XXIX, 1966, pp 339–366.

6. H. Barth, *op. cit.*, Vol. 1, pp 278–281; Muhammad Uba Adamu, *op. cit.*: M.G. Smith, *The Two Katsinas* (Unpublished Ms.)

7. Palmer, KC, p. 93; East, LH, Vol 2, p. 59.

8. For further discussion of this myth, see M.G. Smith, "The Beginnings of Hausa Society," in J. Vansina, R. Mauny and L.V. Thomas (Eds.), *The Historian in Tropical Africa* (London: Oxford University Press for International African Institute, 1964) pp. 339–357; and M.G. Smith, *The Affairs of Daura* (Berkeley & Los Angeles: University of California Press, 1978).

9. See Y. Urvoy, *Histoire de l'Empire du Bornou*, Memoires de l'Institut Francais d'Afrique Noire, No. 7) Paris: Librairie Larose, 1949), Figure 6 and p. 90; W.F.Gowers, *Gazetteer of Kano Province* (London: Waterlow & Sons, 1921), p. 21; J.M.Freemantle, "A History of the Region Comprising the Katagum Division of Kano Province," *JRAS*, Vol X, 1910–11, pp 298–307.

10. E.W.Bovill (Ed.), *Missions to the Niger* (London: Cambridge University Press for the Hakluyt Society, 1964), Vol. 1, pp 115–116, 121.

11. Ibid., p. 117

12. H. Barth, *op. cit.*, (1902 Edn.) Vol. 1, p. 278.

13. P.G. Harris, *Gazetteer of Sokoto Province* (Unpublished Ms. at Sokoto Government Office, n.d., ?1939), pp 20–21.

14. M.G. Smith, 1960, *Government in Zazzau, 1800–1950*, pp 6, 61, 131, 142 and 338 for references to the Magajin Mallam whose duty this was. For his northern counterpart, the Magajin Dankakulema at Daura, see M.G. Smith, 1978, *The Affairs of Daura*, chapter 2.

15. H.Barth, *Travels & Discoveries* (1902 edn.) Vol. 1, p. 278.

16. H.R. Palmer, KC, p. 92; R.M.East, LH, Vol. 2, p. 57.

17. *Birnin Kudu District Note Book (DNB)*, revised 1955. Unpublished Ms. at the Provincial Office, Kano.

18. KC, p. 92; LH, Vol. 2, p. 57.

19. KC, p. 92; LH, Vol. 2, p. 57.

20. *Gwaram District Notebook.* Unpublished Ms. at the Provincial Officed, Kano

21. See Dokaji Alhaji Abubakar, *Kano ta Dabo Cigari*, p. 19.

22. KC, p. 70; LH, Vol. 2, pp 28–29.

23. v. below, chapter 4, and M.G. Smith, *The Two Katsinas.*

24. For Fulani classifications of Fulani, see C.L. Temple (Ed.), *Notes on the Tribes, Provinces, Emirates and States of the Northern Provinces of Nigeria* (Lagos: The C.M.S. Bookshop, 1922), pp 396–404; also Henry Barth, *Travels & Discoveries* (1890 edn.), Vol. 2, pp 167–170, especially the second footnote on p. 169; also Wazirin Sakkwato Alhaji Junaidu, *Tarihin Fulani*, pp 7–8; and E.J. Arnett, *The Rise of the Sokoto Fulani* (translation of Caliph Mamman Bello's *Infaq'ul Maisur*, pp 137–139.

25. M.G. Smith, "Hausa Inheritance and Succession" in J. Duncan Derrett (Ed.), *Studies in the Laws of Succession in Nigeria* (London: Oxford University Press, 1965); *idem., The Economy of Hausa Communities*, pp 41–48; *idem.,* "The Hausa System of Social Status," *Africa*, Vol. 29, 1959.

26. v. D.J. Stenning, *Savannah Nomads* (London: Oxford University Press (OUP.) for International African Institute (IAI.), 1959); C.J. Hopen, *The Pastoral Fulani Family in Gwandu* (London: OUP. for IAI.); F.W. de St. Croix, *The Fulani of Northern Nigeria* (Lagos: The Government Printer, 1945).

27. H.Barth, *op. cit.* (1902 edn.), Vol. 2, footnote on p. 169.

28. Wazirin Sakkwato, Alhaji Junaidu, *op. cit.*, pp 7–8; E.J.Arnett, *The Rise of the Sokoto Fulani*, pp 137–139.

29. H. Barth, *op. cit.* (1890 Edn.), Vol. 2, pp 167–170; J. Spencer Trimingham, *A History of Islam in West Africa* (London: Oxford University Press, 1962), pp. 47, 160–162, and footnote 2, p. 195.

30. For a record of this tradition, see *Suma'ila District Note Book*, unpublished Ms. in the Provincial Office, Kano, 1959. However, Barth lists the Waijobe as a section of the Jel or highest ranked stratum of Fulani clans. See Barth, *op. cit.*, (1890 Edn.), Vol. 2, p. 169.

31. M. Hiskett, "Material on the State of Learning among the Fulani before the Jihad" (*BSOAS*, Vol. 19, pp 550–578; A.D.H. Bivar and M. Hiskett, "The Arabic Literature of Nigeria to 1800 - A Provisional Account" *BSOAS*, Vol. 25, pp 104–148; H.R. Palmer, "An Early Fulani Conception of Islam," *JRAS*, Vol. 13, 1914, pp 407–414, Vol. 14, 1915, pp 53–59, 185–192; E.J. Arnett, *The Rise of the Sokoto Fulani*, pp 17–20, 132–137; 'Abdullah Ibn Muhammad, *Tazyin Al-Waraqat*, translated by M. Hiskett (Ibadan University Press, 1963), pp 5–8, 85–105.

32. v. Muhammad Uba Adamu, (*op. cit.*, 1968) writes as though all Arabs deserted Kano for Katsina during Muhammadu Kumbari's oppressive reign, 1731–1743, and only returned to Kano during the reign of Ibrahim Dabo (1819–1846) by Dabo's invitation. Other evidence indicates that while most withdrew to Katsina during Kumbari's reign, there were Arabs at Kano in the reign of Babba Zaki (1768–1776), who is said to have imitated them in almost everything; v. KC, p. 92; and LH, Vol. 2, p. 58; and footnote 84, *infra.*

33. Denham, Clapperton and Oudney, *Travels and Discoveries, 1822–24*, Vol. 2.

34. See C.W.Rowling, *Report on Land Tenure in Kano Province* (Kaduna: The Government Printer, 1949), pp 24–26.

35. KC, p. 86; LH, Vol. 2, p. 48.

36. See M.G. Smith, "The Beginnings of Hausa Society," 1964 *op. cit.*; and *idem.,* "Historical and Cultural Conditions of Political Corruption among the Hausa," *Comparative Studies in Society & History*, Vol. 6 No. 2, 1964, pp 165–170.

37. v. M.G. Smith, "Hausa Inheritance and Succession," *op. cit.* 1965.

38. Ibid.

39. KC, p. 38; LH, Vol. 2, p. 38.

40. M.G. Smith, "The Hausa System of Social Status," *op. cit.*, 1959; *idem.,* "Kebbi and Hausa Stratification," *British Journal of Sociology*, Vol. 12, 1961, pp 52–63.

41. E.J. Arnett, *The Rise of the Sokoto Fulani*, pp 17–20, 43–53, 99–120, 122–126; 'Abdallah Ibn Muhammad, *Tazyin Al-Waraqat*, p. 107–8; H.R.Palmer, "An Early Fulani Conception of Islam," *JRAS*, Vols 13 (1914) and 14 (1915); M.G. Smith, "The Jihad of Shehu dan Fodio:

Some problems" in I.M. Lewis, *Islam in Tropical Africa* (London: O.U.P. for I.A.I., 1966), pp 408–420.

42. E.J. Arnett, *The Rise of the Sokoto Fulani*, pp 54, 77–79, 104–5, 117–120.

43. KC, p. 93; LH, Vol. 2, p. 59.

44. M. Adamu na Ma'aji, *Ta'rikh Kano*. (Unpublished Ms. at Shahuci Arabic Library, Kano). For the Chronicle's version of the creation of Dirki, v. KC, p. 82, and LH, Vol. 2, pp 43–44.

45. Adamu na Ma'aji, *Ta'rikh Kano*.

46. KC, p. 87; LH, Vol. 2, p. 50.

47. M. Hiskett, "Kitab all-farq: a work on the Habe Kingdoms attributed to Uthman dan Fodio," *BSOAS*, Vol. 23, part 3, 1960, pp 558–579; M.G. Smith, 1964, "Historical and Cultural Conditions of Political Corruption among the Hausa."

48. F.H. Ruxton, Maliki Law (London: Luzac & Co., 1916).

49. J.N. Anderson, "Law as a Social Force in Islamic Culture and Theory," BSOAS, Vol. 20, No. 1, 1957, pp. 13–40.

50. G.G. von Grunebaum, *Islam: Essays on the Nature of a Cultural Tradition*. Memoir of the American Anthropological Association No. (Chicago: Chicago University Press, 1955)

51. For further discussion, see M.G. Smith, "Hausa Inheritance and Succession," pp. 264–266.

52. Shehu Usman dan Fodio, *Bayan Wujub al-Hijra 'ala'l-'ibad*. Unpublished Ms. 1221 A.H./1805 A.D.

53. See Shehu Usman dan Fodio, *Bayan Wujub Al-Hijra 'alal-'ibad*; and his Tanbih al-ikhwan, translated into English by H.R. Palmer, "An Early Fulani Conception of Islam," *JRAS* Vols. 12 & 13, 1913 & 1914. See also E.J. Arnett, *The Rise of the Sokoto Fulani*, pp. 54, 77–79, 104–105, 117–120 for expressions of Sultan Mamman Bello's views on this issue.

54. Alkalin Kano Muhammad Zangi, *Taqyid al-akhbar*. Unpublished Ms. completed 1865, at Shahuci Arabic Library.

55. KC, p. 86; LH, Vol. 2, p. 49.

56. KC, pp. 79, 90; LH, Vol. 2, pp. 40, 54.

57. M.G. Smith, "Hausa Inheritance and Succession."

58. Sheikh Mohammed Al-Maghili of Tlemsen, *The Obligations of Princes: An Essay on Muslim Kingship*, translated by T.H. Baldwin (Beirut: Imprimerie Catholique, 1932). See also KC pp. 59, 77; and LH, Vol. 2, pp. 37–38; Alkali Muhammad Zangi, *Taqyid al-Akhbar*.

59. KC, p. 93; LH, Vol. 2, p. 59.

60. F. Edgar, *Litafi na Tatsuniyoyi na Hausa* (Belfast: Mayne & Co., 1913), Vol. 1, pp. 376–388.

61. Ibid., and see F.H. Buxton, *Maliki Law.*

62. KC, p. 90; LH, Vol. 2, p. 54. This was one of the practices denounced by the Shehu Usman. See M. Hiskett, "Kitab al-farq" *BSOAS*, Vol. 23, part 2, 1960, pp. 567–574.

63. D.J. Stenning, "Transhumance and Migratory Drift" *Journal of the Royal Anthropological Institute*, Vol. 90, 1960

64. For a fuller account of this institution, see M.G. Smith, *The Two Katsinas* (unpublished). Its origin was probably the Kanuri (Bornu) institution of *Chima Jeribe*. See J.R. Patterson, *Special Report on Borsari District, Bornu*, 1918 (unpublished Ms. at the Provincial Office, Maiduguri, Bornu), p. 16, para. 46.

65. KC, p. 90; LH, Vol. 2, p. 54; and see M. Hiskett, "Materials Relating to the Cowry Currency of the Western Sudan - II," *BSOAS*, Vol. 29, part 2, 1966, pp. 353–356.

66. M. Hiskett, "Kitab al-farq," *BSOAS*, Vol. 23, part 3, 1960, p. 567.

67. H. Barth, *Travels and Discoveries* (1902 Edn.), Vol. 1, pp. 269–271, 300–308 & *passim*; Vol. 2, pp. 146–147 and footnote, p. 147; and see also Clapperton's observations at Kano in Denham, Clapperton and Oudney, *Travels and Discoveries, 1822–1824*, Vol. 2, pp. 251–258; 266–267; and at Sokoto in Hugh Clapperton, *Journal of a Second Expedition into the Interior of*

Africa from the Bight of Benin to Soccatoo (London: John Murray, 1826) pp. 222–223; also M. Hiskett, "Materials Relating to the Cowry Currency of the Western Sudan," *BSOAS*, Vol. 29, part 2, 1966, pp. 359–364.

68. For further information on *bin kanu*, see M.G. Smith, *The Two Katsinas* (unpublished Ms.).

69. KC, p. 85; LH, Vol. 2, p. 47.

70. Dutse District Notebook, unpublished Ms. in the Provincial Office, Kano.

71. v. Joseph Greenberg, *The Influence of Islam on a Sudanese Religion*. Monograph of the American Ethnological Society, No. 10 (New York: J.J. Augustin, 1946), p. 17.

72. KC, p. 89; LH, Vol. 2, p. 53.

73. KC, p. 90; LH, Vol. 2, p. 55.

74. KC, p. 90; LH, Vol. 2, p. 55.

75. Concerning *kharaj* and *jizya*, see Reuben Levy, *The Social Structure of Islam* (London: Cambridge University Press, 195)

76. On inducements (*gaisuwa*), see M.G. Smith, *The Economy of Hausa Communities of Zaria* (London: H.M.S.O., 1955) pp. 88–93

77. v. M.G. Smith, *The Affairs of Daura* (Berkeley & Los Angeles: University of California Press, 1978).

78. KC, p. 89; LH, Vol. 2, p. 53.

79. In 1824, Clapperton reports that 2000 cowries exchanged for a dollar (thaler) at Kano. In Alwali's day, the rate may thus have been nearer 1500 cowries. See Denham, Clapperton and Oudney, *Travels and Discoveries*, Vol. 2, p. 253.

80. KC, pp. 77, 89; LH, Vol. 2, pp. 53, 58.

81. KC, p. 90; LH, Vol. 2, p. 55.

82. KC, p. 92; LH, Vol. 2, p. 57.

83. KC, p. 92; LH, Vol. 2, pp. 57–58. This report is corroborated by the histories of Malam Adamu na Ma'aji and Malam Adam Muhammad, and by the sketch of Babba Zaki's regime in the beggar's song. See M. Hiskett, "The 'song of Bagauda': A Hausa King List and Homily in Verse - II," *BSOAS* Vol. 28, part I, 1965, p. 118. For an account of Babba Zaki's political arrangements, see Ch. 3.

84. KC, p. 92; LH, vol. 2, p. 58. See footnote 32 *supra*.

85. M. Hiskett, "Kitab al-farq," *BSOAS*, Vol. 23, part 3, 1960, p. 568.

86. Hugh Clapperton, *Journal of a Second Expedition*, p. 215.

87. H. Barth, *Travels and Discoveries* (1890 edn.), Vol. , p. 309.

88. Ibid., p. 304.

89. For the Shehu's reference, see M. Hiskett, "Kitab al-farq," *BSOAS*, Vol. 23, part 3, 1960, pp. 568 and 575. For historical accounts of this practice in the eighteenth century Hausa states, v. M.G. Smith, *The Affairs of Daura*, and *The Two Katsinas*.

90. For examples, see M.G. Smith, *The Affairs of Daura* and *The Two Katsinas*.

91. v. M. Hiskett, "Kitab al-farq," *BSOAS*, Vol. 23, part 3, 1960, pp. 568, 573–4.

92. Ibid, p. 568.

93. KC, p. 92; LH, vol. 2, p. 57.

94. v. M. Hiskett, *"Kitab al-farq,"* pp. 568, 573, 576.

95. Ibid., pp. 567–569.

96. This was another practice condemned by the Shehu Usman; v. Ibid., pp. 568, 574.

97. LH, Vol. 2, p. 58; KC p. 93.

98. For the conditions of vassalage in other states, see M.G. Smith, *Government in Zazzau, 1800–1950*, pp. 35–6, 73–79 etc.; *idem, The Affairs of Daura* and *The Two Katsinas*.

99. KC, p. 92; LH, Vol. 2, p. 58.

100. Dokaji Alhaji Abubakar, Kano ta Dabo Cigari, pp. 44–45.

101. Malam Adamu na Ma'aji, *Ta'rikh Kano*. Unpublished Ms. In his history, Malam Adam Muhammad lists three successive Hausa dynasties at Kano—namely the Gaudawa

(issue of Bagauda) who supplied 18 chiefs and ruled for a total of 435 Muslim years; the Rumfawa, who displaced them, and had 9 chiefs who ruled for 125 years; and their successors, the Kutumbawa, also called the Alwaliya and the Tubawa, whose 15 chiefs held the throne for 202 years, thus yielding a total of 42 pre-jihadic chiefs who ruled for 762 Muslim years. The Dokaji Abubakar lists 19 chiefs and 477 years for the first dynasty, 9 chiefs and 163 years for the second, Rumfawa dynasty, and 14 Kutumbawa chiefs, who ruled for 186 years, yielding a total of 42 chiefs and 826 years, as against 43 chiefs over a span of 833 years, listed in the Kano Chronicle.

Incidentally both M. Adamu na Ma'aji and M. Adam Muhammad divide the Kutumbawa dynasty into 3 sections, namely, the Warjawa who hailed from Burumburum but were expelled and replaced by the Maguzawa from Chola in Suma'ila District, who were also heathen. Finally, the Kutumbawa proper, who were Muslim syncretists, replaced the Maguzawa. Whether the two latter segments coexisted and competed, or ruled in the order given above, remains unclear on the data available. In either case, Kano then contained a Rumfawa segment that still sought to recover the throne.

102. Dokaji Alhaji Abubakar, *Kano ta Dabo Cigari*, p. 29; M. Adamu na Ma'aji *Ta'rikh Kano*. Interestingly Malam Adam Muhammad says nothing directly about the provenience of the Rumfawa, though identifying Muhammad Rumfa as the paternal half-brother of his immediate predecessors, Abdullahi and Yakubu. Perhaps Rumfa's mother, Fatima, was a princess from Gaya and thus kin to the Gaya chief who, in M. Adam Muhammad's account, rebelled with the Madaki and Galadima against Umaru (1410–1421) and was finally defeated. The Chronicle does not record this rebellion, but relates that Umaru abdicated on religious grounds. v. LH, Vol. 2, pp. 33–34; KC, p. 74.

103. See R.M. East, *Labarun Hausawa*, Vol. 2, pp. 36, 45; H.R. Palmer, "The Kano Chronicle," pp. 36, 45; and also C.L. Temple (ed.), *Notes on the tribes, Provinces, Emirates and States of Northern Nigeria* (Lagos: C.M.S. Bookshop, 1922) p. 466 for a Genealogical Tree of Kano. As noted in Footnote 102, though Malam Muhammad says nothing about the paternity of Muhammad Alwali I, el-Kutumbi, the founder of that dynasty, he does state specifically that Muhammad Rumfa (1463–1499) and Yakubu (1452–1463) were both paternal half-brothers of Abdullahi (1438–1452), and identifies their respective mothers as Fatima, Tasafe, and Takarda. It is thus possible that all three were sons of Dauda (1421–1438), whose father was Kanajeji (1390–1410).

104. M. Adamu Na Ma'aji, *Ta'rikh Kano*, says that on his accession in 1781, Muhammad Alwali II had to suppress a rebellion by Rumfawa aimed at his throne.

105. Of Babba Zaki, Malam Adam Muhammad relates in his *Ta'rikh Kano*: "Next Babba Zaki, son of Yaji (1753–1768) and Zainabu, a very powerful man. It was he who organized the affairs of state. None of his predecessors had organized the state the way he did. He first introduced the system of gatekeepers (Ar. *haijab*: H. *wasidodi*) so that even his women could only reach him through an intermediary. Nobody could see him except through his slaves. It was Babba Zaki who first organized spying (secret communications concerning people). He used to go through the city with his slaves, some armed with muskets that made a loud noise. He did so throughout his reign and his successors followed his example. Three of the documents (king-lists consulted by the author) say he reigned for nine years and 2 say he reigned for twenty years, but God knows best."

106. KC, p. 92; LH, Vol. 2, p. 58.

107. LH, Vol. 2, p. 58. Compare with H.R. Palmer's version in "The Hausa Chronicle," p. 92; and with that of G.P. Bargery, *A Hausa-English Dictionary and English-Hausa Vocabulary* (London: Oxford University Press, 1934), p. 858. See also M. Hiskett, "The 'song of Bagauda': A Hausa King List and Homily in Verse - II," *BSOAS*, Vol. 28, part 1, 1965, p. 118. Palmer's translation of this passage obscures the meaning by misplacements of vowels. Palmer's phrase "Jan Rano, well-named disturber of elephants" presents an elegant puzzle.

108. KC, p. 92; LH, Vol. 2, p. 58.

109. KC, p. 93; LH, Vol. 2, p. 38.

110. KC, p. 78; LH, Vol. 2, p. 38.

111. KC, p. 93; LH, Vol. 2, p. 58.

112. KC, p. 81; LH, Vol. 2, p. 42.

113. KC, p. 83; LH, Vol. 2, p. 25.

114. Alkali Muhammad Zangi, *Taqyid al-Akhbar*, says that Muhammad Alwali II (1781–1807) appointed his son as Madaki.

115. (1730–1743). For a reference to this revolt, see Dokaji Alhaji Abubakar *Kano ta Dabo Cigari*, pp. 38–39. The Chronicle refers to an attack by Kumbari on Dutse; v. KC p. 90.

116. KC, p. 72; LH, Vol. 2, p. 31

117. Dokaji Alhaji Abubakar, *Kano ta Dabo Cigari*, p. 31.

118. For references to this title, v. KC, pp. 84–85; LH, Vol. 2, pp. 46–7; and Dokaji Alhaji Abubakar, *Kano ta Dabo Cigari*, p. 85.

3

The Development of Kano State

Introduction

Before proceeding to relate the history of Kano state from Alwali's day to ours, we should check the preceding reconstruction of its final Hausa phase for completeness and validity by tracing as best we may the development of its specific units and institutions over as many centuries as the data allow. Among Hausa states only rarely can we recover specific material on their early political organization and history from indigenous sources. Such data are relatively abundant for the imperial courts of Bornu and Gao.[1] For pre-jihadic Zazzau an illuminating account of traditional political organization was published in 1952 by Malams Hassan and Shua'ibu at the request of their brother, Suleimanu, then Emir of Abuja.[2] Those authors also relate the history of Abuja after its foundation by the defeated Hausa chief of Zazzau and his officials, following the Fulani *jihad*. Their recent history of Abuja contrasts sharply with the arid king list which is still our only published fragment on the pre-jihadic "history" of Zaria under the Hausa;[3] but for pre-jihadic histories of Katsina, Daura and Gobir, our data are almost equally fragmentary;[4] nor does the recently published "Chronicle" of Zamfara furnish the kind of detail essential to any systematic analysis of the early development and organization of that state.[5] Even so, we may still learn much about the institutional organization of these states before the Fulani period by collating such information with accounts of the polities that developed after the Fulani *jihad*. Thus by comparing details of state organization among the independent Hausa of Katsina who relocated at Maradi with similar materials from the Fulani conquest state of Katsina, and by doing likewise for the Hausa successor state of Zazzau at Abuja and the Fulani conquest state of Zaria—or for the various independent states that emerged in Daura, Gobir, or Zamfara following the *jihad*—we may, at least provisionally, abstract the main elements of the antecedent regimes from which these different polities derived.[6] For Kano this procedure is not practical. Its expelled Hausa dynasty never managed to establish a successor state, and the Hausa "Sarkin Kano" Abubakar whom I visited at Maradun in Maradi in January 1959 was unable to distinguish the traditions of Kano from those of old Katsina that still flourished in Maradi. No independent Hausa polity derived from

107

Alwali's Kano which could be compared with Fulani Kano to allow us to distinguish those pre-jihadic elements that were common to both or selectively retained by either.

Accordingly in the preceding reconstruction of Alwali's state, I have had to rely primarily on oral data gathered at Kano in 1959 and collated with documentary materials, whether scattered like the observations of explorers, or systematic in character, and such information on Kano under its Hausa rulers, recorded in local histories, as I could find. Accordingly, to check the reconstruction based on such material, to indicate its limitations, and perhaps to enrich its detail and scope, we need an independent body of precise information with which concrete comparisons can systematically be made. Elsewhere independent Hausa successor states supply controls that allow direct comparison with the Fulani conquest regimes in their homelands, thus enabling us to identify the major units and forms of organization in the pre-jihadic polity from which they both derived. Lacking such contemporary sources of comparative materials for independent verification of the pre-jihadic Kano state as reconstructed from current local traditions, we may still assess the validity of our account by examining its congruence with the relatively rich documentary information on Kano history that is available.

Fortunately we have an unusual body of valuable historical data on the Hausa polity in the celebrated Kano Chronicle. To this we may add further information from the histories of the Dokaji Alhaji Abubakar, Malam Adamu Muhammad and Malam Adamu Na Ma'aji, from the Beggar's Song (the "Song of Bagauda"), the Bornu Girgams, the Chronicles of such nearby states as Songhay, Kebbi, Katsina, Agades, Gobir and Zaria, the "king lists" of such local chiefdoms as Gaya and Rano that became subject to Kano before Alwali's time, and the writings of such Muslim scholars and travellers as El Maghili, Es Suyuti and Leo Africanus. Together these documentary materials may provide a reasonably firm control on the preceding account of Alwali's state extracted from current traditions and recently recorded data.

Clearly these sources of information overlap substantially with current oral traditions and contemporary or retrospective records. For example, the "Song of Bagauda" which is a central element in the current oral tradition, has clearly grown over the centuries by accretions that mark successive reigns; it has probably incorporated some elements from documentary sources, and has been consulted by some local scholars who have recently written histories of Kano. Nonetheless there is a marked divergence in the data, context and character of the ancient and contemporary materials. Most of the information on which my reconstruction of the Hausa polity rests is not available in any previous records, although preserved as categories or elements in oral traditions. Most of the information in the Kano Chronicle and other historical texts were recent or contemporary observations when recorded. Thus in order that I could employ these textual data to check the account derived from current oral traditions, they were deliberately excluded from the preceding summary based on field enquiries. Hence we may validly use these old historical documents and other texts of equal age to check the form and details of the preceding account of Alwali's Kano.

A systematic re-examination of historical texts for information on the growth and organization of Kano state is long overdue, but that cannot be fruitfully undertaken without prior reconstruction of the Hausa polity, since this alone can furnish adequate guidance to significant and appropriate data. For example, unremarked, we have listed many titles that bear the prefix "Dan," such as Dan Buram, Dan Lawan, Dan Tama, and Dan Akasan. Others have the suffix "-ma," for example, Galadima or Ciroma, both of which are clearly Kanuri terms institutionalized as official titles at Kano under Bornu influence. To trace the growth of the Kano state or the history of specific offices, we should therefore index our documentary references to all titles. We shall then find that such titles as Dan Tama and Dan Akasan, though minor central offices in Alwali's time, initially denoted chiefships reserved for the sons (*'ya'ya*; s., *"da"* = son, *dan* = son of) Tama and Akasan, while other titles of similar form, such as Dan Shanono, are either toponymous or ethnic rather than eponymous, the term Shanono denoting both a place and an ethnic aggregate (*Shanono*: milk drinker, i.e. Fulani). We may thus identify the differing historic antecedents of such titles as Dan Tama and Dan Shanono. One derives from an individual whose successors simultaneously identified their lineage boundaries, hereditary claims and common ancestor by retaining his name as their title. In the other case, a certain Fulani group localised in an area which was then named with them after their diet.

Unless we are sufficiently familiar with the ethnic and social composition of Kano and with its formal and informal social categories and organization, most of the data in its famous Chronicle remain a closed book, a meaningless and therefore bizarre jigsaw of concrete particulars of *ad hoc* and indeterminate character which we must either politely ignore or regard as decisive evidence of its compilers' perceptual incapacity and preference for the concrete and bizarre. Nothing could be further from the truth. As we shall see, the Chronicle records many significant developments, and reports in detail the growth and transformation of Kano; but its meaning eludes outsiders unless they already have a fair knowledge of the units whose development it reports. Lacking such knowledge of the Hausa polity, the Chronicle and other historical texts that refer to Kano have been valued by foreign scholars primarily for their evidence of its contacts with other states, notably Bornu, Jukun, Mali, Songhai and the neighbouring Hausa chiefdoms. This orientation, which is shared by such writers as Temple, Gowers, Hogben, Urvoy and Palmer,[7] is the opposite of Barth's,[8] who correctly perceived that neither the history nor the internal organization of Kano could be understood in isolation. Accordingly, without an adequate background for interpretation of those strictly local events and details the Chronicle reports, foreign scholars have unavoidably had to concentrate on Kano's increasingly complex relations with nearby states, and have made little effort to relate these external contacts to the internal structure and growth of the state. However, to the people of Kano such external developments were primarily significant for their local implications; and since Kano supplied the reference point and the audience of the Chronicle, unless we are initially familiar with its constitution, we can hardly appreciate the events it reports, the reasons that underlay its selection of items, and the information that it omits. To treat the Chronicle as significant mainly or solely because of the external relations it reports, grossly underestimates its content and value; but to appreciate its internal significance, the outsider needs a key to its many concrete and apparently disconnected data, which only a reasonably detailed and accurate model of the native polity at some point before the *jihad* can provide. For lack of such a key the central body of data in the Chronicle has so far been virtually ignored. Thus, in using these and other ancient texts to check my reconstruction of Kano during the late 18th century, I shall also be employing our reconstruction to illuminate much unused data in these texts.

The state owed its form, composition and growth to its particular combinations of internal and external elements. These differed in provenience, kind, and importance at different phases of its development and organization; but we can neither understand the significance of its external relations and influences without tracing their institutional impact on Kano society, nor can we understand the form and development of the state in isolation from its changing context.

At the earliest, the first attempts to record the traditional history of Kano in writing may have been made during the latter half of the fourteenth century after Mandinka Muslim missionaries first reached Kano from Mali in the west. However it is more likely that these local traditions were not reduced to writing before the middle or end of the fifteenth century when Kanuri influence at Kano was very strong. The Hausa word for writing, *rubutu*, is a loan word of Kanuri origin.[9] Following the flight of Mai Othman Kalnama from Bornu to Kano c. 1425 in the reign of Abdullahi Burja (1438–1452), the Hausa state became subject to Bornu. It is thus appropriate to regard this as the earliest likely date at which attempts to reduce local historical traditions to written form were probably made. If so, then for the immediately preceding century the original chronicler could recover and check traditions from elders by methods similar to our own; but for earlier periods the basic materials recorded in the Chronicle were probably traditions preserved within the current social organization and culture, in folk tales, songs and monuments, and in stories attached to particular places, people, or events. At most then the time-span in which reliable data on the history of Kano could have been recorded in the middle or late fifteenth century would probably reach no further backward than 1350 when the chiefship was already centuries old. The earliest Chroniclers must accordingly have assembled traditions that differed in their specificity and reliability with the time levels to which they referred, and fused these into a single continuous record organized serially by the reigns of successive kings. Thus, while their accounts of Kano in the fourteenth and fifteenth centuries are increasingly reliable and specific, for the earlier period these first chroniclers probably recast some traditional materials, reinterpreted or misinterpreted others, lost a great deal and inserted, perhaps unwittingly, perhaps deliberately, some elements of their own. We should therefore distinguish the legendary account with which the Chronicle begins from the more concrete and historical narrative that forms its bulk.

However, while recognizing the importance of this distinction between mythical and "empirical" history, for convenience I shall periodize the following narrative into three sections to correspond with the pre-jihadic dynasties distinguished by Dokaji Abubakar, M. Adam Muhammad and other local historians. To simplify the exposition, I shall place supplementary materials, including some observations that bear on the Chronicle, in footnotes.

The Gaudawa (Daurawa)

The Legend of Origin

By tradition and perhaps correctly, chiefship was introduced to Kano from Daura where Bayajidda (Abu Yazid) and his son Bawo had ruled. At that date, Kano and its immediate environs were occupied by Hausa-speaking pagans whom Malam Adamu identifies as Warjawa,[10] and local traditions as Abagiyawa, that is, people of Gaya stock. These pagans were apparently organized in sizeable clans, each settled in a particular locality under a senior elder who served as clan-head. The Chronicle identifies several of these legendary lineage heads and collectivities, their locations and distinctive occupations. However, to ascribe such specific occupational differentiation to these localized exogamous patrilineages is probably an unconscious reinterpretation of their differing ritual responsibilities by which the Chroniclers and their informants assimilated the pre-existing social organization to the occupationally stratified and differentiated urban society of their day. It is empirically unlikely that the original pagan collectivities centered around Kano at this period were thus prescriptively differentiated in occupational terms.[11] However, according to tradition these pagans were united as a community by a common cult which was presided over by members of a particular patrilineage settled within the present city walls around the Dalla Rock and Jakara pond, which was then a sacred *kurmi*, or thickly wooded grove. The Chronicler's Muslim bias is only too evident in the various anachronisms and solecisms that enliven his account of this cult. For example, he says that its two annual festivals were held on the Muslim Idi, that it centered on the tree called Shamuz,[12] and that only black beasts, dogs, goats or fowls, were used for sacrifice. However, these anachronisms do not entirely invalidate the account of the native cult and community with which the Chronicle begins. For some indirect confirmation of its outlines, we need only observe current practices among the Maguzawa and other Hausa-speaking pagans of Kano and its neighbours.[13]

At this early date, according to the Chronicle, the territory immediately around the site of Kano was sub-divided into named tracts occupied by different groups. Barbushe, the priest of Tsumburbura, the nature spirit who inhabited the Shamuz tree at Jakara, then lived on Dalla rock in seclusion, and wielded a ritual authority over this congregation. Beyond the boundaries of Barbushe's community lay several others, presumably of similar character and organization.

Before Bagauda came from Daura, by way of Gaya according to the folksong,[14] other people from Daura had settled at Gano and Debi in southeastern Kano as immigrant communities. These early Daura immigrants were not of royal stock; "but Buram, Isa, Baba, Kududdufi, Akasa, and others of the Kano chiefs, men of princely clan, came with Bagauda."[15] In one of its rare footnotes the Chronicle adds "for this reason all their descendants were called after these, their forefathers. The names have remained as titles of princes to this day. Such titles are Dan Buram, Dan Isa, Dan Baba, Dan Akasan, Dan Kududdufi, and others like Dan Darman, and Dan Goriba."[16] Thus several of the princely titles current in Kano in Alwali's day are traditionally derived from those Daura "princes" who accompanied Bagauda to Kano. By Alwali's time several of these "princeships" had lost their princely rank; or, even when reserved for princes, they had lost their early meaning by transformation into local community titles. Thus in Alwali's day, as the village head of Gora, Dan Akasan was subordinate to the Ciroma, while Dan Kududdufi administered a ward of Kano city and perhaps also a village immediately beside its walls. Others, such as Dan Isa and Dan Buram, had retained their historic positions in the rank of princely offices; but by Alwali's reign, Dan Goriba was allocated to free noblemen while Dan Darman was normally reserved for a Galadima's cognate.

The "Song of Bagauda" preserves a different version of these early days. It presents Bagauda as a mighty hunter from Gaya who first cleared the bush where Kano city stands.

> He remained there, and his relations came after him,
> Hunters all of them …
> There were no women; indeed it was men who cooked.
> The encampment became extensive …
> Then they sent for the women.[17]

The hunters gradually settled the area and began to cultivate.

> Then came a killing famine
> And there was no corn to be had; only by coming to them,
> Could it be had, and they doled it out in small quantities.
> They became well off in slaves and horses too.

Immigrants settled among them seeking corn. The community expanded as the famine increased. The Jakara marsh may indeed have furnished the Kano community with good harvests during a time of irregular or inadequate rainfall.

> The people were living widely dispersed over the open country, not subject to any authority.
> There was no chief, no protecting town wall.
> Tunbi together with Washam saw an easy prey.
> And they joined forces conquering the people of Kano.
> The elders said: Let a chieftaincy be established.
> They appointed Bagauda, the protector.[18]

Thus on this tradition famine first drove many strangers into Bagauda's community, the prosperity of which attracted attack, following which the local chiefship was established, presumably to organize effective defense.

According to yet another tradition preserved by the Dokaji Abubakar, the Kano pagans, having fallen into feuds with one another after Barbushe's death, sent to Daura, whose dominion they had anciently recognized, asking for someone to keep the peace among them.[19] We do not have to choose between these alternatives. They may be mutually consistent, and perhaps neither Bagauda nor Barbushe represent historic individuals.

The Kano Chronicle says that Bagauda and his son Warisi (1063–1095) both died at Sheme about 40 miles north-northwest of Kano City close to Kunci. According to the Chronicle, Warisi's successor Gijimasu moved further south into the district of Gazarzawa which then stretched from Damargu to Kano City. There he settled among the pagans and persuaded them to set up a stockade. When the question of intermarriage with the immigrants arose, the indigenous people decided against it. Thus the stockaded town came to include two endogamous collectivities, one of which, the indigenous people, reserved its ancient ritual to itself. Such chiefship as Gijimasu may have exercised was thus conditional, tenuous, and probably restricted to the immigrants. The autochthonous people preserved their collective cohesion by excluding the immigrants from cult and marriage.[20] It is said that Gijimasu left Kano "walled with eight gates"; but the earliest wall of which traces remain may have been about seven miles in circumference;[21] and it is most unlikely that this structure was initiated or completed by Gijimasu, if indeed he really existed.

The Chronicle is clearly anachronistic in naming the Galadima, the Barwa, the Maidawaki, Makama, Barde, Jarmai, and Dawaki as the chief's senior assistants even before Gijimasu's day, together with the Maidalla (owner, i.e., chief, of Dalla) and Magayaki, the latter title being also common to Katsina and Daura.[22] It is true that legend and ethnology indicate the probable derivation of the Daura chiefship from Kanem-Bornu directly or otherwise; and even at this early date there may have been Galadimas in Kanem, and perhaps at Daura also.[23] However, we may question the early establishment of such titles as Barwa, Makama, Magayaki, Barde, Dawaki, and Madawaki, and Jarmai at Kano. Perhaps the early chroniclers, finding these titles already ancient in their day, attributed indefinite antiquity to them, and accordingly assumed their prevalence among those Daura immigrants who first settled at Kano. Such retrospective projections merely indicate that these titles were already current and reasonably ancient in the fifteenth century. Significantly, none of these offices, including the Galadima's, are said to have been ascribed to princes, at this date. Rather the text implies that their holders were drawn from different lineages of the immigrant group, presumably the largest and most powerful. Thus, however erroneous, the chronicle indicates the age and place of these titles in the government of fifteenth century Kano.

The new chiefship remained uncertain in its base, form, and scope for many years. Following Gijimasu, the Chronicle reports the simultaneous accession of the twins, Nawata and Gawata, as chiefs, while the "Song of Bagauda" distinguishes sharply between these rulers.[24] It is probable that several divergent traditions have been scrambled in one or both accounts at this point. Though noteworthy, such errors have little significance to our enquiry.

Immigrants vs. Natives

Gijimasu had already begun to expand his influence or domain by political and military pressures. Following East's Hausa version of the Chronicle, it seems that he imposed his rule on other communities of Daura immigrants at Danbakwanyaki, Dabi, Dabu, and Gano, 15 to 25 miles south and east of Kano. Beyond Dabi Gijimasu also laid claim to Ringim, whose chief does not seem to have hailed from Daura. Thus, according to the Chronicle, several independent communities under local "chiefs" existed at this date within a radius of one to three days' march from Kano. However, Gijimasu's attack on Santolo ten miles southeast of Kano, near contemporary Tsakuwa, was in vain. Santolo then contained a large native community which practiced a different ritual from the Daura immigrants. In thus attacking Santolo Gijimasu revealed his desire to dominate the indigenous folk whose exclusive local cults and rejection of intermarriage segregated the two communities as corporate units; inevitably, the ritual monopolies of one emphasized the secular status and interests of the other. This contraposed them both and generated drives to political dominion within the ritually excluded group, whose aggregation under a common senior chief greatly enhanced its political and military capacities.

Yusa (1136–1194), Gijimasu's son, directed his expansion westward, attacking the chief of Karaye, and subjugating the country from Gwarmai 25 miles south of Kano, past Badari, west of Karaye, to Farin Ruwa in the northwest on the Katsina border. Some of Yusa's warriors are mentioned in the Chronicle by name but without title. In Gijimasu's reign the first chief of Rano, a close agnatic collateral of the Kano chief, had established his capital at Zamnagaba, south of Kano. There, following Gijimasu's example, this prince walled a considerable site; and from that base he also proceeded to subjugate nearby communities. Thus Gijimasu and his immediate successors did not have the field entirely to themselves. The community from which historic Rano derived was also seeking further population and territory; and perhaps this or some other competition stimulated the Daurawa at Kano to greater exertions. We know from their king lists that even at this date Gaya and Birnin Kudu, and perhaps Dutse and Burumburum also, were chiefdoms whose survival may likewise have involved their territorial expansion. How many of these local units may have derived from Daura is not known; but the traditions of Gano, Dabu and Dabi suggest that, even if of Daura origin, such chiefdoms were not established by members of its royal house.

The conflict long latent between the immigrants under their chief and the Kano natives who were loosely united as a separate group by their cult and priesthood flared into the open under Naguji (1194–1247) who succeeded Yusa. Having subjugated the territory from Kura ten miles south of Kano to Tsangaya 40 miles southeast beyond the boundaries of the Dutse and Gaya chiefdoms, like Gijimasu, Naguji sought to reduce Santolo, the only native stronghold in this area that still withstood him.

> He camped at Basaima two years for the purpose of attacking Santolo, but he was worsted in the war and returned to Kano. He found the pagans there on the verge of revolt; so he cajoled them with talk and executed their leader ... When he was dead the rest of the people said, "we are willing to follow you, O Sarki, because we must." The Sarki said ... "If you are willing to follow me, show me the secrets of this god of yours." They replied, "We will not show you the secrets of our god." Therefore the Sarki punished them. Naguji was the first Sarki who collected a land tax of one-eighth of the crop from all husbandmen," a truly legendary feat.[25]

Naguji's successor Guguwa (1247–1290) also sought to destroy the ritual centres of native opposition at Kano and failed. Characteristically, the Muslim chronicler says that Guguwa was smitten blind on the night of the Idi festival by an apparition, a manifestation of the god, "a man with a red snake in his hand," but whether or not Guguwa was blinded thus, he was replaced, the first of many deposed chiefs.[26]

Guguwa's councillors, the Galadima Bangare and Barde Kirmau, had advised him to attack the cult centre. Shekarau (1290–1307), Guguwa's successor, was likewise pressed by his courtiers to subdue the natives by force; but the indigenous people diverted this threat by diplomatic appeals to the chief. "If the domains of a ruler are wide, he should be patient; if they are not so, he will not obtain possession of the whole country by impatience." The Sarki said to them, "Your talk is true," and left them their customs and power. They said, "Were it not for fear of what may result, we should have told the Sarki the secrets of our god." The chief of them, Samagi, said, "If we show him the secrets of our god, we shall lose all our power, and we and our generation will be forgotten." And so the dispute continued until the Sarki died."[27] The political character of this struggle between the immigrants and indigenous people is evident. Under their leader Samagi, which may have been a title rather than a name,[28] the natives clung to their cult to preserve their corporate solidarity and internal autonomy against threats of domination by the immigrants. Samagi emphasized the secrecy of the ritual and the secular consequences of revelation. Thus the ancient cult was driven underground to become a mystery religion which the immigrant chiefs regarded as a threat to their rule.

Tsamiya (1307–1343) who succeeded Shekarau, attacked the cult centre after refusing to accept a tribute of 200 slaves to permit its maintenance. At this point the chronicler is almost certainly recording relatively recent traditions rich with detail, perhaps those his informants had learned from their fathers and grandfathers. Already, Tsamiya's captains bore such titles as Dan Kududdufi and Dan Buram which derived from the names of Daura nobles who accompanied Bagauda to Sheme. The institution by which the names of eminent men persisted as titles reserved for their descendants may thus be almost as old as the Kano chiefship; and if so, then Hausa conceptions of office may have evolved from older institutions of positional succession. Other prominent warriors who helped Tsamiya to seize the pagan cult centre included the Madawaki, the Barde, the Jarmai, Makama, the Sarkin Damargu whose village lay to the northwest between Kano and Sheme, Jekafada, the chief's messenger, a title that also appears at Daura and Katsina, and the Dan Unas, whose title later lapsed.

By this time the pagan deity and cult had changed its identity from Tsumburbura to Cibiri while remaining centered on the tree that was known as Shamuz in Barbushe's day. Its capture was Tsamiya's objective; and he successfully destroyed the sanctuary and all within it. Following his triumph, three of the pagans explained the nature of the ritual to the chief. In return he gave them new titles as Sarkin Cibiri, Sarkin Gazarzawa, and Sarkin Kurmi and placed them over their people. This is the first occasion in which the Chronicle explicitly records the creation of a new title by the chief; and the context indicates its purpose clearly. Having broken the ritual unity of the city pagans, Tsamiya consolidated his control by dividing them under three headmen of equal status who all owed their positions of authority to him.[29]

Tsamiya met a violent death at the hands of Usumanu Zamnagawa, whose ancestry is not entirely clear. Usumanu's nickname, Zamnagawa, derives from his subsequent seclusion at the palace with the corpse (*gawa*) of the dead chief; but the name Usumanu suggests he was a Muslim, being the first Muslim name in the list of Kano chiefs. Thus his obscure ancestry and violent accession may indicate a conquest of Kano by Muslims, perhaps by Malinke. Zamnagawa reigned between 1343–1349 when Mohammed Korau, another Muslim, became chief of Katsina, due northwest. This Korau was also probably of Mandinka descent and subject to Mali, since his chief assistant and immediate successor, Ibrahim Sura, bears a Muslim name and a Mandinka title.[30] It is thus possible that Zamnagawa's reign represents a brief subjugation of Kano by Mandinka forces of the Mali empire.

Following Tsamiya's victory, the indigenous people of Kano developed three different responses to the immigrant chiefship; some, like the contemporary Maguzawa, withdrew from the city environs to rocky areas at Fankui. Another larger group, called Rumawa, asked the chief to appoint someone to administer their affairs. On receiving this request Zamnagawa consulted his courtiers and appointed his son as the Rumawa chief. The third native response, defiance, was represented by Santolo. Thus, despite our uncertainty about Zamnagawa's origin and mode of achieving power, it seems that by his day, the natives of Kano had been more or less divided and subdued. Their remaining strongholds were few and scattered. The majority had been brought under immigrant rulers by force of arms or by political pressure. The Kano chiefdom already extended east and south to the boundaries of Gaya, Dutse, and Rano, the capital of which was still Zamnagaba, and westwards from Gwarmai to Farin Ruwa and Sheme.

The Historical Threshold: Yaji and Kanajeji

Zamnagawa's successor was Ali, better known as Yaji, who is generally regarded as Tsamiya's son, although the text of the Chronicle does not state this. Zamnagawa himself is said to be Shekarau's son, although nothing in the text indicates this. Critical omissions are probably inevitable in any chronicle, however thorough, simply because our curiosity attaches to that which is obscure and makes it critical.

Yaji drove his kinsmen and rivals from Zamnagaba to Rano[31] and pushed the Ajawa, Warjawa and Arawa pagans further southwards. "In Yaji's time, the Wangarawa (Mandinka) came from Meli (Mali) bringing the Mohammedan religion … forty in all,"[32] several of whom are named in the text. The chief converted and appointed some of these Mandinka to ritual offices of state as imam, *ladan* (muezzin) , and *alkali* (judge). Yaji then commanded his subjects to practise Islam by observing the obligatory prayers, and when the Sarkin Gazarzawa objected, he and his people were struck blind by Allah. Yaji celebrated this event by reappointing the Sarkin Gazarzawa as Sarkin Makafi or chief of the blind; and by common belief the title is still held by descendants of its first holder.[33] Evidently then the ancient conflict between immigrants and indigenous people still persisted despite Tsamiya's policy. It flared up once more on Yaji's conversion and decision to impose Islam. This miraculous blinding of the Kano pagans encouraged Yaji to consider reducing Santolo, a desire the presence of his Mandinka allies reinforced. With the Mandinka and 111 picked men of his own, Yaji entered Santolo and destroyed its cult centre. The leading Mandinka warriors removed the Santolo cult objects, a battleaxe, "leg irons," a bell and two horns. The Sarki commanded all the inhabitants to be killed except women and little children.[34] This marked the end of effective resistance by the natives of Kano to the Daura immigrants. Disabled by their social organization from combining against the immigrants, the indigenous people had been reduced piecemeal, until only Santolo remained defiant following Tsamiya's triumph in Kano. However, only when the chief accepted Islam and had Mandinka support was this last tribal stronghold finally destroyed. Its fall occurred under the aegis of Islam and was probably due to the superior military techniques of the Muslim Mandinka.

The Chronicle gives so many circumstantial details concerning this attack on Santolo that its author probably drew on very fresh traditions or perhaps on survivors' accounts. Evidently neither side used horses in the battle. The warriors whose efforts turned the tide were Goji, Kosa, the chief's slave, and Gurgu. In appreciation Yaji asked Goji to "'Choose whatever you want.' Goji said, 'I only want to become Madawakin Kano.' The Sarki said, 'I give you the office.'" Gasatoro, who was turned out of the post of Madawaki, built a house at Gawo, and for that reason was known as Madawakin Gawo to distinguish the two.[35] According to the Chronicle, Yaji also appointed Kosa Dawaki and Gurgu Dan Maje.[36] These events reveal the chief's eagerness to strengthen and extend his power by attaching the strangers to his service and rewarding them with high office. This is also the first time that the Chronicle mentions the dismissal of an official by the chief; and in the context its basis and purpose are equally clear. By appointing the Wangarawa to high office, and attaching them to himself directly, the chief decreased his dependence upon his own immigrant community. Thus, having reduced the rest of the natives with the aid of his Daura people, Yaji could aggrandize his power by employing his foreign allies to reduce his traditional obligations to his people. These appointments also indicate the relative antiquity of two offices, Madawakin Gawo, which may date from this time, and Dan Maje, which was probably older and may have the same origin as Dan Buram and Dan Akasan. It is possible that in appointing these warriors as Madawaki (Madaki), Dawaki and Dan Maje, Yaji was merely acting to retain his throne; but it seems more likely that he thereby increased his autonomy.

Following his victory at Santolo, Yaji attacked the Warjawa (Warji) and conquered all tribesmen from Bere to Panda, following which he raided the Kworarafa or Jukun for the first time, driving them up the rocks at Attagara. Being unable to farm while Yaji camped below, the Jukun are said to have made their peace by giving Yaji a hundred slaves; however the Chronicle suggests that they may have killed him.[37] The Jukun (Kworarafa) have long lived along the Benue northeast of Tiv.

Yaji's achievement in raiding thus far and occupying Jukun territory for seven months indicates a considerable access of strength at Kano following the end of organized local resistance. If Yaji's reign established the chiefship as the dominant unit in the Kano state, this development owed a great deal to his Mandinka allies and supporters. We lack further data concerning their numbers and status at Kano, and cannot say whether the Chronicle correctly records essential facts of Kano's first known interaction with a foreign power. Fortunately for Kano, even before the Mandinka arrived, the prolonged struggle between the immigrants and native tribesmen had ended, and the chiefship and chiefdom had consolidated; but the duration of this conflict is certainly exaggerated by the abnormally long reigns with which tradition credits the earliest rulers. The record clearly telescopes a process, whose elements and details were imperfectly recalled and written down after literacy had been introduced with Islam.

Although it seems that the Chronicle specifies the descent of successive chiefs so clearly that Temple could tabulate these relations genealogically, while Palmer and East have used them to subdivide their printed versions, precise connections between the early chiefs and several of their successors remain uncertain.[38] While the Chronicle cites by name the mother of each chief, the text often omits the father. However, this tendency to identify chiefs by their mothers has no matrilineal implications. From Barbushe's and Bagauda's day, as far as we know, both the immigrants and the natives of Kano have always practiced agnatic descent. Moreover, if the Arabic texts translated by Palmer and East contained specific statements about the paternity of these chiefs, the Chronicle would be unique in this respect among Hausa king lists, which merely cite the names of successive rulers together with the lengths of their reigns where these are known, while leaving many agnatic links unspecified.[39]

In these circumstances we cannot confidently say much more about the principles that regulated succession to the chiefship than that the office, being hereditary in an agnatic group, would pass collaterally and lineally at different times. Nonetheless, following Temple's example, I constructed a genealogy for these chiefs, based on the relations of descent specified by Palmer, East, the Dokaji Alhaji Abubakar, M. Adam Muhammad and M. Adamu na Ma'aji. Which was clearly subject to all the qualifications that attach to the data on which it rested. However, if the pedigree correctly indicated the kin relations of these chiefs, then the interval between Gijimasu's accession and that of Yaji was probably less than 150 years, instead of 250 as the Chronicle claims. Further, if the pedigree was correct, the first explicit instance of collateral succession was Yusa, the fifth chief, who followed Nawata and Gawata. However, in identifying these chiefs as twins and co-regnants, the Chronicle probably distorts the historical displacement of strict lineal succession from father to son by the collateral alternative, and represents this in a figurative form. Yusa was succeeded by his son, Naguji; but following Naguji, the succession passed to Guguwa, Yusa's brother; and after Guguwa, Shekarau, who is said to be Yusa's son, became chief. Thus if Usumanu Zamnagawa was the son of Shekarau, the following four appointments were equally divided on lineal and collateral lines.

However uncertain in their particulars, such data indicate two important conditions of succession. Only direct descendants of former chiefs were formally eligible to succeed. Thus the brothers and sons of a late chief or his father were equally eligible and probably competed for the throne. Princes who failed in this contest accordingly disqualified their issue from the chiefship by their failure to realise the full potential of their birth-status. If Usumanu Zamnagawa was indeed Shekarau's son and slew Tsamiya personally as the Chronicle suggests, collateral rivalries for the throne had even at this early date revealed their tendencies to violence. However, as indicated above, Usumanu's name and actions suggest a Muslim conqueror.

By piecing together fragments from various sources, it seems that collateral succession first began when Yusa, who was also called Dariki and Makankari, succeeded from the office of Galadima.

Makankari was first Galadima;
Then he reigned for a long time.[40]

If so, collateral rivalry for the Kano throne may be as old as the appropriation of the Galadima's office for the rulers' agnates, who were normally his collaterals.

Yaji was succeeded by Bugaya whom the Chronicle describes as a posthumous son of Tsamiya, though circumstantial evidence suggests that he was probably Zamnagawa's son. Bugaya's most notable act was to order the Maguzawa, clustered in the rocky area at Fankui, to disperse, thus preventing the growth of yet another centre of tribal resistance to the chiefship. To assure his control, Bugaya then placed the Maguzawa under his Galadima. Thereafter chiefs had no cause to fear further tribal resistance. In Bugaya's time "the country was ... peaceful, and regular tribute was paid to the Sarki. No one knew anything of his character even to the day of his death. He reigned five years," 1385–1390.[41] In placing the Maguzawa under his Galadima, Bugaya followed Zamnagawa's method of incorporating the Rumawa by appointing his son as their chief. Zamnagawa in turn had merely adapted the innovation of Tsamiya who designated three headmen as tribal community chiefs. Thus the state had grown by successive creations of ethnic and local chiefships which were supervised by a progressively segregated central officialdom of which the Galadima, Madawaki, Dan Buram, Dawaki, and Dan Maje were the senior members, administrators and councillors, together with the new Mandinka Alkali and Limam.

At his request, Bugaya was buried at Madatai by the local Limam with Muslim rites. The Chronicle mentions that his body was washed by Turbuna, Jigawa and Kusubi, who are said to have come to Kano in Yaji's day with the Mandinka who accompanied Abdurrahman Zaite. The Limamin Madatai and Lawan who officiated at Bugaya's funeral are listed as members of Zaite's group.[42] If Turbuna, Jigawa and Kusubi were not Mandinka immigrants, they were probably body servants or slaves of the chief. By Alwali's day the title of Dan Turbuna was reserved for one of three lineages of court musicians and entertainers (*maroka*) of low status though attached to the throne; whether the Dan Kusubi title flourished then remains obscure. However in Alwali's reign the title of Dan Jigawa was given to free *shigege* courtiers who served the chief as *jekadu*. In reporting Bugaya's burial, the Chronicle accordingly records an event from which two or three Kano offices derive. Thus the significance of recording this superficially bizarre item consists firstly in emphasizing the Muslim status of the chiefship, and secondly in establishing the charter, functions, and foundation of these three offices.[43]

Bugaya's successor was Kanajeji the son of Yaji, an aggressive chief who reigned from 1390 to 1410. By then the chiefdom was sufficiently pacified and powerful for its rulers to attempt further expansion; but in place of territory, the chief now mainly sought tribute and slaves, whether for export to Mali and other foreign markets or to retain in Kano as labour and throne staff we cannot say. Following his father's footsteps, Kanajeji levied a tribute of 200 slaves on the Jukun and claimed this as a traditional due. Thereafter he sent horses to the Jukun, receiving slaves in return. This exchange was political in base, diplomatic in form, and perhaps commercial in aim. He next attacked the 'Mbutawa, who had settled in a rocky area of southern Kano and adjacent Bauchi for defensive purposes. Kanajeji lost many men without much profit. The cavalry, on which Hausa armies for the first time relied in attacking, could not operate effectively in the 'Mbutu country. "Kanajeji was the first Hausa Sarki to introduce *lifidi* and iron helmets and coats of mail for battle. They were introduced because in the war at Umbatu ('Mbutu) the losses had been so heavy."[44] Kanajeji probably introduced this military gear on the advice of Mandinka (Wangarawa) at his court. Previously unknown in Kano, such equipment was long familiar to Bornu and Mali. Kanajeji may thus have imported coats of chain mail (*sulke*) for his warriors from the north or west. *Lifida* were locally made suits of quilted cotton with leather covers. Their use marks the stage of Hausa military development at which the heavy cavalry became specialized as a unit for defense and assault while light cavalry were employed in raiding, scouting, flanking movements, attacks and pursuit.

After further military failures despite his new equipment, Kanajeji occupied the 'Mbutu farm lands for two years until the tribesmen capitulated from hunger. Yaji had used the same technique earlier against the Jukun; but while Yaji then received 100 slaves, Kanajeji levied four thousand from the 'Mbutu, two thousand children and as many adults. While many hundreds of these 'Mbutu slaves did not remain in Kano, we cannot say how they were disposed of. Encouraged by this victory, Kanajeji then attacked Zazzau, and besieged its capital, Turunku, some seventeen miles south of Zaria, but was defeated.

Returning to Kano, Kanajeji sought counsel before resuming the war with Zazzau. The Sarkin Cibiri, ritual head of the native tribesmen at Kano, advised him to "re-establish the god that your father and grandfather destroyed."[45] The local tribesmen attributed Kanajeji's defeat to Tsamiya's desecration of Cibiri and to his acceptance of the foreign religion of the Mandinka. They were willing to fight with Kanajeji against Zazzau under the protection of their own god but not under the banner of Islam. Thus despite his improved military equipment and technique, Kanajeji's defeats at 'Mbutu and Turunku revealed the ruler's isolation from the subjugated natives. Kanajeji decided to abandon Islam and therewith his dependence on the immigrant Mandinka. In re-establishing the Cibiri cult he sought the local support he needed to overrun Zazzau and also tried to base his power on the subordinated native tribesmen. He therefore apostasized. At the Sarkin Cibiri's directions, new cult implements were made and Kanajeji himself executed Barbushe's ritual. In the following year he invaded Zazzau, and camped at Gadas, then a semi-autonomous state in the north. Perhaps Kanajeji there sought allies against the chief of Zazzau who duly came out to meet him. In the following battle the Sarkin Zazzau was slain and his army scattered. Kanajeji then moved southwest to Shika, twelve miles northwest of the site of Zaria city, which had not yet been built, and devastated the country for eight months, seizing whatever he wished. Such large scale brigandage, which was neither territorial conquest nor a formal levy of tribute from subordinates reduced to vassalage, reveals the motives and nature of Kanajeji's aggression.

Among Kanajeji's leading warriors the Chronicler lists the Barde, Maidawaki, Makama, Dan Buram, Jekafada, Jarmai and Janbori Sarkin Zaura, who ruled one of the ancient districts of Kano, the Lifidi Buzuzu, and Dan Akasan. Thus by this date the titles of Dan Burum and Dan Akasan which derived from Bagauda's princely companions had been established, and moreover, having introduced *lifida*, Kanajeji had appointed the first Lifidi Buzuzu, to command these troops. Thus development in military or other fields generated new functionally special-ized formations; and new titles were instituted to integrate and administer these units as permanent elements of state structure.[46]

Kanajeji's militarism and apostasy, his crippling slave levy at 'Mbutu, his exchanges with the tributary Jukun, and his attacks on Zazzau, expressed tenden-cies inherent in the stucture and orientation of the Kano chiefship at this time. Evidently Kanajeji wanted booty and wealth, particularly in the form of slaves and tribute. It apparently mattered little to him whether such exactions were made against nearby pagans in the name of Islam or against other Hausa chief-doms under the aegis of Cibiri. Having subdued the environs of Kano, territorial domination was no longer the prime concern of the chief. Slaves, to be traded, sold, given away, put into production or converted into political capital as the chief's slave staff and soldiery, seem to have been his primary objective.

Islam and Bornu

Kanajeji was succeeded by Umaru (1410–1421), "a malam earnest in prayer,"[47] whose friend, Abubakar, another devout Muslim, protested when he accepted the chiefship, arguing that Umaru was deserting religion for the world and its lusts. According to the Chronicle, when Umaru resisted this appeal, Abubakar with-drew from Kano to Bornu, but returned after eleven years to repeat his warning. On this occasion "Umaru called together all the Kanawa (the people; i.e., notables of Kano) and said to them: 'This high estate is a trap for the erring; I wash my hands of it,' and he resigned and went away with his friend. He spent the rest of his life in remorse for his actions as Sarki."[48] Umaru had reigned peacefully and without personal extortion; but he had placed "the affairs of Kano ... into the hands of the Galadima (Babba)," who was popularly sung as "head of the city, great dust heap of all affairs."[49] This *kirari* (praise-song) neatly describes the Gal-adima's role as the vizier responsible for regulating the daily business of the city-state.

A principal theme that recurs in the Chronicle, and which is more explicit and insistent in the "Song of Bagauda" is the conflict between the demands of religion and those of the world, which Muslim chiefs can rarely escape. In the "Song of Bagauda" and most eloquently in the poem that Abdullahi dan Fodio wrote at Kano in 1809, religion and government are contraposed as good and evil, so that the devout prince is virtually obliged to withdraw from the world.[50] The Kano Chronicle provides particularly useful data on this tension, since as a work of many hands, it is a relatively impersonal record. Undoubtedly the Muslim *malamai* who compiled it were familiar with this element in Muslim theology and political theory. However even if they did not tend to stress the antinomy, the theme recurs in different forms throughout the text. Umaru's abdication in 1421 following Kanajeji's revival of the pagan cult his ancestors had suppressed, introduces the conflict without comment by presenting a radically contrasted pair of solutions to the chief's dilemma. Other evidence suggests that on this as on other matters, the Chronicle faithfully reports the publicly accepted truth. The Song of Bagauda has for its theme,

> The promise of the world is untrustworthy.
> Let there be less of your haughty arrogance; this world is but transitory.
> That which she gives does not abide.
> Look behind you; then look before.
> If you have good sense and much prudent reflection,
> Look at the kings who have flourished in the past,
> Their story is near to being obliterated.[51]

But of Umaru it says,

> Now Umaru was one learned in Islam; he it was who escaped (Hell-fire);
> He lit a fire which defied extinction.
> He drove out the pagan Hausa and they fled to the bush.
> He reigned a full twelve years.[52]

Umaru is one of the few chiefs in more than fifty whom the Song credits with religious devotion or escaping "hell fire." It seems likely that the poem and the Chronicle allude here to the same events.

Umaru is said to have studied Islam under Dan Gurdamus Ibrahimu. Gurdamus himself is listed as one of the Mandinka who came to Kano during Yaji's reign.[53] Ibrahimu was his son and hence called Dan (son of) Gurdamus. Whether this designation is official and titular or merely genealogical, we cannot say. No such title is known to have persisted at Kano in Alwali's day; but it may have flourished and lapsed during the period between Alwali and Yaji. This apparently minor point is significant because many Kano titles preserve the descent of individuals in a style familiar to Islam and Arabic culture, the Hausa *dan* (son of) being equivalent to the Arab *ibn*, but, as we have seen, this Hausa idiom was indigenous and in general use long before Islam arrived, being a feature of the patrilineal organisation. Proceeding hypothetically, the son of Umaru's teacher, Ibrahimu, might thus either be called Dan Ibrahimu or, since his father's father, Gurdamus, was especially distinguished, he might be spoken of as Dan Gurdamus, followed by his given name. Accidents of chiefly and public preference probably decided which of these alternatives prevailed; but if Ibrahimu's son's son still retained the designation Dan Gurdamus, this term would probably be reserved for one of many genealogically equivalent individuals, the senior descendant of Gurdamus.

Thus ancestral names, perpetuated to distinguish descent groups and within them their senior members and descent lines, might easily be transformed into titles, provided only that the descent group, its founder, or both, were politically prominent and that the chief for variable reasons of state had decided either to recognize and formalize current practice or to direct this by creating an office named after the ancestor for whose descendants (*zuri'a*) it was reserved. Once instituted by a chief, such offices remained hereditary and depended for their per-

sistence down the centuries on the status and political performances of their holders, and on the solidarity, wealth and number of the groups in which they were
vested. Vicissitudes of various kinds eliminated some of these hereditary titles
while perpetuating others. Those with the best chance of indefinite continuity
were offices hereditarily reserved for close agnates of the chief. This developed
partly because of the unusually high reproductive rate of the dynasty, which
reflected its strategic position in the distributive system; and partly as an effect of
the scale and character of political competition within the dynasty between men
interested in assuring the succession of their sons and their brothers, whom either
the chief or his father had appointed as trusted assistants and probable heirs.
Under such conditions the number of royal offices would tend to increase steadily
over the generations.

At Umaru's accession in 1410, his other-worldly friend, Abubakar, unwilling
to maintain their relation, had moved from Kano to Bornu. In 1421 Abubakar
returned and persuaded Umaru to abdicate. Between 1425 and 1432 a deposed
sultan of Bornu, Othman Kalnama, came westwards to Kano "from south Bornu
with many men and malams. He brought with him horses, drums and trumpets
and flags and guns."[54] Almost certainly Othman's Kanuri clerics initiated the
spread of literacy among the Hausa. Evidently the literate Mandinka who preceded them had reserved such knowledge for themselves to protect their position.
However, if Kalnama's men taught some Hausa to read and write at their chief's
direction, they could hardly have had muskets, which were not yet invented.

It is just remotely possible that the visit of Umaru's friend, Abubakar, to Bornu
between 1410 and 1421, may have influenced Othman Kalnama's decision to
move west. Until this time the interests, power and population of Kanem-Bornu
had centered east of Chad, but its Magumi rulers (Mais) were then under heavy
pressure from rebel Bulala, and not long after they were forced to relocate their
forces west of Chad. For thirty or forty years after Kalnama's migration to Kano
the Mais (s., Mai) moved their courts restlessly across the northern Bornu plains,
from Nguru through Geidam, west of Chad. Finally, between 1484 and 1488 Mai
Ali Dunama built a permanent capital at Gasrgamu on the Komadugu Yobe, into
which the Challawa that flows eastward past Kano empties.[55] Thus between 1420
and 1490, the Kanuri relocated, reoriented their state, and developed new interests in the west.

Farther west at Gao on the Niger, Ali Kolon, a prince of Songhai who had
spent some years at the court of Mali, had revolted to reassert the independence
of his people. This was the beginning of the Songhai empire which Sonni Ali
(1464–1493) established from headquarters at Gao. Following Sonni Ali, his
general el-Hajj Askia Mohammed (1494–1528) usurped the throne and pressed
the Songhai expansion. These imperial developments in Bornu and Songhai later
affected Kano severely, but Othman Kalnama's arrival may have marked the mild
beginning of Kano's subjugation to these imperial states. Once the Kanuri had
quit Kanem for Bornu west of Chad, Kano could hardly escape their attention, not
only because of the rewards its subjugation offered, but also because its control
seemed essential to the Kanuri for their own security.

The Chronicle merely identifies Othman Kalnama as "Dagaci, a great prince
... from southern Bornu."[56] Nowadays at Kano the term *dagaci* denotes the resi-

dent head of a rural community which may vary widely in its size or political status. Elsewhere, for example, in Zaria, the term normally means a "village," or minor rural, chief. As we have seen, both in Alwali's day and after at Kano, such major rural chiefs as Gaya and Dutse were classified with village heads as *dagatai* (s. *dagaci*). Although the word is clearly Hausa, it does not occur in the Chronicle before this. It is thus possible that the title of Dagaci was initially applied exclusively at Kano to Othman Kalnama, who settled the Kanuri immigrants at Bompai outside the walls of Kano until Dawuda (1421–1438), having consulted his Galadima, formally welcomed him and brought him within the city, before placing the government of Kano in his hands when he went on campaign in Zaria. Thus for five months Dagaci (Othman Kalnama) administered Kano in Dawuda's absence and "became very wealthy."[57] According to the Chronicle it was at this time that Zaria, under its legendary "Queen" Amina, conquered Nupe and Jukun, thereby discontinuing the traditional Jukun tribute to Kano. It is said that Amina received forty eunuchs and ten thousand kola nuts from the Sarkin Nupe; "she first had eunuch ministers and kolas in Hausa land."[58] This may have provoked Dawuda's attack on Zaria. Thus, having already established relations with Zaria, Kano was now linked indirectly to Nupe and the Yoruba city-states of the southwest. Othman Kalnama's visit had also brought Kano into relations with Bornu.

Under Dawuda's successor, Abdullahi Burja, another son of Kanajeji, the Mai of Bornu, Mohammed Ibn Matala (c. 1448–1450), imposed Kanuri suzerainty on Kano. Abdullahi Burja (1438–1452) "was the first in Hausa land to give Bornu "*tsare*" (tribute) to secure its favour. In his reign the way was opened from Bornu to Gwanja"[59] in northern Ghana, thenceforth for centuries the major source of kola nuts imported to Hausa. Burja also obtained camels through his Kanuri contacts, the first known in Kano. Shortly after Kano submitted, the Mai of Bornu attacked the Tuareg chiefdom of Azben several hundred miles northwest of Chad and Kano. The long struggle between Bornu, Azben and others over the central caravan routes had begun. "The next year every town in the west paid him (the sultan of Bornu) "*tsare*" (tribute)."[60] It is difficult to determine the specific scope of the phrase "every town in the west." Certainly Kano, Biram (Garun Gabas) and Daura north of Kano were reduced to vassalage by Bornu at this date. Whether Katsina, Zaria, Gobir and Nupe followed suit remains unclear.[61] For our purpose it is sufficient that historical records in Kano and Bornu independently date Bornu's dominion over Kano to this time.

Instead of diminishing Kano's aggressive tendencies, at least initially its vassalage intensified them. Following his submission, Burja marched south to raid for one year and six months. Karmashi, one of Burja's captains, subjugated Miga about 80 miles northeast of Kano on its present boundary with Hadeija. Perhaps Bornu's activity persuaded Burja to expand his chiefdom eastwards before Bornu incorporated these territories itself. Immediately after the conquest of Miga, Burja marched against the important independent chiefdom of Dutse that lay between Miga and Kano. Dutse capitulated and accepted a tributary relation modelled on that which linked Kano to Bornu. This left the powerful independent chiefdom of Gaya due west of Dutse, almost wholly enclosed within the territory of Kano.

Following these successes, Burja's Galadima Dawuda took over the field command and, moving south from Dutse, he raided the Warjawa and other pagan tribes south of Suma'ila with great success. "Every month he sent a thousand slaves to Sarkin Kano. All the people of Kano flocked to him. No one was left in Kano except the Sarki and very old men."[62] For seven years the Galadima campaigned southwards in adjoining areas of the modern province of Bauchi.

> Slaves because very numerous in Kano. The Sarki sent a message for him to come back, so he returned. On his way back he halted every three miles and built a town. At each he left a thousand slaves, 500 males and 500 females. He thus founded 21 towns, before he came to Kano. On his arrival he gave the Sarki three thousand slaves and said to him, "I have founded 21 towns, and in each I have left a thousand slaves, all yours." The Sarki asked him, "What are the names of the towns you have built?" Galadima said, "Their names are *Ibdabu* (throne slave-estates)." The Sarki said, "I make you ruler of all these towns and of their domains."[63]

Fortunately for the nearby tribesmen, Kano soon found a new activity in the caravan trade and ancillary industries that was even more lucrative than slave raiding. Thereafter slave raiding became the specialism of the Hausa in Zaria. For pagan tribesmen, however grievous, this was perhaps the lesser of two evils.

No other record from this region matches the Galadima Dawuda's campaign in scale, length, and in its systematic decimation or devastation and wholesale enslavement of primitive tribesmen incapable of defense or escape. Kanejeji's massive toll at 'Mbutu shrinks in comparison. He had merely shown what was possible with the equipment, organization and force at Kano's disposal. It was left for Galadima Dawuda to realize the full extent of these possibilities; and it is clearly not accidental that this campaign which followed the subjugation of Miga, Dutse and the intervening territory came immediately after Kano's subordination to Bornu. How much of this slave harvest flowed east as tribute from Kano to the Magumi court we cannot guess; but many of Dawuda's captives remained in Kano as throne slaves settled in separate communities (*rumada*) on the road southwest from the city past Sumai'la and Wudil where at least one is still known as *Ibdabu*.

Three aspects of these events merit attention. Firstly, as Dawuda's captives arrived, many able-bodied men left Kano to join the Galadima and share the plunder. Thus the numbers cited above as state property represent only a fraction, perhaps a small one, of the total number of tribesmen enslaved. Had Muslim law regulating the distribution of booty been observed, the share retained by the state would represent one fifth of the total. Even this was enough to establish twenty-one separate villages, and the three thousand presented to Burja at Kano were probably exported in tribute or trade. Thus, even if the chief merely retained one-tenth of the slaves presented to him, he received a substantial increment of resources and force. In short, Dawuda's slave raiding capitalized and transformed the chiefship by investing it with substantial numbers of captured men as a versatile resource. Those twenty-one thousand slaves settled afield furnished annual tributes of grain and other crops that could support a large number of slaves and freemen employed at the capital in increasingly specialized political and military roles. With this new force attached permanently to the throne as slaves with few jural rights, the chief could at last shed his dependence on both the Mandinka and Daurawa elites, and the native Kano tribesmen. Thus the previously traditionalistic patrimonial order could now evolve towards sultanism, provided first that dynastic strife did not erode the basis of chiefly pre-eminence and enable senior officials to reduce the chiefship by advancing the latter's rivals; and, secondly, that Bornu remained content with Kano's tribute and assured its autonomy. Never again to my knowledge did any Hausa ruler undertake or achieve such wholesale enslavement. For the time being at least, the Galadima Dawuda had saturated Kano's demand for slaves. He had also established a slave population sufficiently large to perpetuate itself by reproduction. Impolitically the chief had placed the new throne estates under the Galadima's care, as his predecessor had done with the Maguzawa. Its initial pre-eminence accordingly facilitated the progressive expansion of the Galadima's power and role until his office had no peer below the chief within the state.

While Burja was at Dutse, Dagaci, that is, Othman Kalnama or his successor, "had assumed great power in the country, and collected wealth without end, and had built houses from his house as far as Salamta. It was Dagaci who made the market of Karabka."[64] Perhaps Burja had again left the government of Kano in Dagaci's hands while campaigning in the east at Miga and Dutse as Dawuda had done while campaigning in Zaria. If so, then Dagaci had once again taken advantage of the opportunity to increase or restore his wealth by compensating himself as the chief's deputy for the chief's failure to provide him with adequate income. However, on this occasion, Dagaci made a fundamental innovation. He established the market at Karabka in the city, the first market in Hausa land of which we have report, and one that was urgently needed to handle the increasing long-distance trade in slaves and other commodities. As a Bornu prince, Dagaci may long have puzzled over the primitive state of commerce at Kano. Coming from Kanem and Bornu where markets were ancient and indispensable, when the opportunity presented itself, he accordingly introduced this essential institution at Kano, thereby furnishing an alternative basis for its future development and prosperity. There is no indication that Dagaci sought to retain power either after Burja's return to Kano, or on Dawuda's return from Zaria some years before. However, his presence in Kano evidently stimulated Bornu's desire to subordinate the chiefdom; and it is possible that as a prince and former Mai of Bornu, he governed Kano in the absence of the chief on behalf of Bornu.

Following the Galadima Dawuda's return to the capital "the Sarki sent to Dussi (Dutse) to ask for a wife. He was the first Sarki who married a daughter of Sarkin Dussi, Sarkin Shirra and Sarkin Rano, and also the daughter of the Galadima."[65] In short, the ancient Kanuri practice of strategic political marriages by which alliances of vassalage were converted into ties of kinship and affinity was adopted at Kano in Burja's reign, following Kano's vassalage to Bornu. Dutse had only recently been reduced by Burja to the status of vassal; and perhaps this was already the position of Rano following Yaji's original assault on its former capital, Zamnagaba. The Sarkin Shirra ruled a district east of Miga as a minor independent chief of Hausa stock. By taking his daughter in marriage, Burja ostensibly assured Shirra of his goodwill. Evidently Burja considered it politic to maintain friendly relations with the small buffer states that lay between Kano and Bornu. He also thought it politic to marry the Galadima's daughter, thereby attaching the powerful Galadima to himself and his offspring, particularly the Galadima's grandsons, in the forthcoming succession struggle.

An Unstable Throne

The Chronicle relates that on Burja's death a dumb prince, Dakauta, was appointed in the hope that his enthronement would give him speech. This experiment was abandoned the following day when Dakauta remained dumb. However, neither Baikie's king-list compiled in 1862, nor Malam Adam Muhammad's, nor the "Song of Bagauda" mention Dakauta's accession. Neither do they cite Atuma, Dakauta's son, whom the Chronicle lists as his immediate successor.[66] Of Atuma the Chronicle reports that "he was king for seven days only. He was turned out of the chiefship for fear of trouble with the Galadima Dawuda."[67] The chiefship now depended on the Galadima's support, and its base had become unstable. Without the Galadima's blessing, the chief could neither reign nor rule. Yet, the Chronicle suggests that the Galadima could not prevent the appointments of Dakauta and Atuma. Whether these selections had been made by Bornu or by others at Kano, we cannot say; but unless there was a Bornu supervisor resident in Kano, the brevity of both reigns excludes Bornu's manipulation. Evidently, some electoral procedure had developed before Burja's reign since succession had long ago ceased to be routine, and alternated irregularly between collateral and lineal heirs. However, we lack information on the existence and composition of any electoral councils at this time and can merely draw inferences from particular cases. Perhaps the successive depositions of Dakauta and Atuma within eight days of Burja's death marks the point at which electoral powers were lost by the dynasty to public officials, without the establishment of accepted procedures or an electoral council to regulate the succession. This is mere speculation; we lack the critical data; and Dakauta and Atuma do not figure in all lists of Kano chiefs.

The Rumfawa

Yakubu

Yakubu (1452–1463) is generally identified as Burja's son; but with little evidence. During his reign, "Agalfati came to Kano. He was Sarkin Gaya, the son of Sarkin Machina. He came with his three brothers who became Sarkin Hadeija, Sarkin Dal and Sarkin Gayam. Sarkin Hadeija became Sarkin Gabas, and was given Hadeija. The Sarkin Gaya came to Kano and was given Gaya. The Sarkin Dal came to Kano (Rano) and was given Dal. Sarkin Gayam went to Zaria and was given Gayam."[68] Thus, apparently Gaya either secured Yakubu's accession and claimed these rewards, or submitted to Kano peacefully following its territorial encirclement in Burja's reign. Perhaps Yakubu's accession and these territorial appointments were the price of Gaya's incorporation in Kano. Agalfati, the Sarkin Gaya, then brought three kinsmen ('*yanuwansa*) who were not necessarily brothers, one of whom moved to Zazzau where his descendants retained the title of Sarkin Gayam in Alwali's day as their descendants still do in contemporary Abuja.[69] On Palmer's translation, Yakubu invested one of Agalfati's kinsmen with the *tambari* chiefship of Dal and placed him strategically near Rano, Burumburum and the pagans of southern Kano. According to East, this appointment was made by the chief of Rano. Yakubu also seems to have either forfeited or asserted an indirect claim to the territory beyond Auyo and Shirra by appointing Agalfati's kinsman as Sarkin Gabas (chief of the east, or more probably chief of Garun Gabas, the town once ruled by Biram) over "Hadeija," thus perhaps creating yet another buffer state as Kano's ally between Bornu and Kano. However by Alwali's day the Galadima of Bornu administered the seven petty states of this region, Bornu Ngaundere, for the Mai.[70]

Perhaps the true import of this passage is to record Gaya's role in changing the dynasty and its entry into the Kano state. With Gaya's incorporation following the conquest of Dutse and Miga, the territorial expansion of Kano was temporarily complete. Gaya was the last major unit to be incorporated by Kano before Babba Zaki conquered Burumburum, and Birnin Kudu submitted to Alwali. It seems clear that by this date Rano had long been reduced to vassalage in return for military and political protection, and high prestige at Kano on grounds of its ruler's descent from Bawo of Daura, Bayajidda's son; but it is also possible that Rano supported Gaya in securing Yakubu's accession.

> In Yakubu's time the Fulani came to Hausa land from Mele (Mali) bringing with them books on divinity and etymology. Formerly our doctors had, in addition to the Koran, only the books of the Law and the Traditions. The Fulani passed by and went to Bornu, leaving few men in Hausa land ... At this time too the Asbenawa came to Gobir and salt became common in Hausaland. In the following year merchants from Gwanja began coming to Katsina; Beriberi came in large numbers and a colony of Arabs arrived. Some of the Arabs settled in Kano and some in Katsina. There was no war in Hausaland in Yakubu's time. He sent ten horses to the Sarkin Nupe in order to buy ten eunuchs. The Sarkin Nupe gave him twelve eunuchs.[71]

The Mali empire, then in its final phase, was shortly overthrown by Sonni Ali, the chief of Songhay, whose attitude towards Islam was pragmatic.[72] The Fulani missionaries who came eastward brought Maghrebi Muslim books and doctrines with them, thereby enriching local knowledge of Islam and re-orienting the *'ulama* of Kano away from Egypt and the Muslim heartland towards the west and the north. Malam Adamu na Ma'aji dates the "true" conversion of Kano to Islam in Yakubu's reign.[73]

The route from Gwanja to Bornu had been open long before Yakubu's reign; and as its trans-Sudanic commerce grew, Katsina and Kano, having regulated markets in which Muslim merchants were protected by the chief, provided excellent centres for this trade. While Gwanja merchants came to Katsina, Kanuri merchants moved to Kano, followed by Arabs from Ghadames not long after the Tuareg of Azben began carrying salt by caravan to Gobir. The market at Karabka in Kano city which Dagaci had established now proved its worth. Dagaci or his successor may also have told the chief how to administer the market so as to increase the number of visiting merchants. At this time Kano became the crossroads of two great trading routes and finally lost its former isolation. The growth of its market transformed the town from a local capital into a major commercial city; and in the process, its ethnic heterogeneity increased. First Arabs and Kanuri settled at Kano; then came other traders from different lands,—from Katsina, Nupe, and perhaps from Gwanja also. Even so, the chief of Kano still had to import his eunuchs from Nupe. Evidently, at this date Kano did not produce eunuchs itself. That development came later with the elaboration of the chiefship.

Muhammad Rumfa (1463–1499)

Yakubu was succeeded by Muhamman Rumfa (1463–1499), whom the Chronicle expressly identifies as his son. However, M. Adam Muhammad says that Rumfa, Yakubu and Abullahi Burja were paternal half-brothers. Kano traditions distinguish the dynasty founded by Rumfa from that of Bagauda. The Dokaji Alhaji Abubakar relates that Rumfa came from Daura by way of Gaya; and Malam Adamu, who divides the history of Hausa Kano into three dynastic periods distinguished by their deviance from Islam, also identifies Rumfa as founder of the second dynasty, saying that he came to Kano from Kula in northern Gaya.[74] Palmer gives his mother's name as Fasima Birana, which vaguely suggests a Kanuri origin, while East expressly identifies her as Fadimatu, a woman of Rano, and M. Adam as Fatima.[75] Thus Rumfa's origin remains obscure. It is equally possible that he was installed as chief at Kano under pressure from Bornu; or that, although Yakubu's son, and thus one of Bagauda's *zuri'a* (descendants), he was regarded as founding a new dynasty since he introduced a new political order, which, although clearly based on the preceding regime, transformed it thoroughly. Alternately, as suggested here, Yakubu may have founded the dynasty. Since the Hausa mode of historical periodization assimilates major structural changes in the role and relations of chiefship with the emergence of new dynasties, it is quite possible that, although belonging to Bagauda's stock, Rumfa and his immediate successors are distinguished dynastically, by their regime rather than their genealogy. However, the brief and uncertain reigns of Dakauta and Atuma suggest that turbulent successions were resolved by a dynastic change at Yakubu's accession. Otherwise, as the Dokaji Abubakar observes, Rumfa's origin remains ambiguous.[76]

During Rumfa's reign the character and context of the Kano chiefship underwent a fundamental and irreversible change; and by the same process the state was thoroughly transformed. These developments are generally attributed as innovations to Rumfa. However, in Tsamiya's reign and Yaji's their bases had been laid, and in Burja's and Yakubu's, the remaining preconditions were established. It is even possible that some developments of this kind were inevitable at this time. The demands of Bornu suzerainty, coupled with influences from the Arabs, from Kanuri and from others in the city, accelerated and supported the reorganization attributed to Rumfa. Left in its early isolation, the Kano chiefdom might well have remained organizationally at the level established by Tsamiya. However, Tsamiya's successors were only enabled to advance their authority with the aid of their Mandinka guests. The earliest phase of local Islam that this Mandinka mission initiated was expressed as an unbridled militarism which harnessed the Kano people to the chiefship for continuous slave raiding, legitimated by Muslim doctrines of *jihad,* and motivated by secular appetites for slaves that were available only through participation in the state-organized forays that remained the chief's main monopoly. This sudden influx of slaves at Kano attracted the attention of Kanuri and other foreigners, including Tuareg and Arab traders. When Bornu levied tribute on Kano, slaves were probably the principal item. In consequence Kano's slave-raiding increased sharply in intensity and scale. One result of Dawuda's campaign was to endow the state with an unprecedented mass of permanently attached manpower, only a small part of which was concentrated at the court in the capital.

Inevitably these new resources increased the chief's capacity to dominate his officials and subjects; but initially they elevated the Galadima's power above that of the chief. First Tsamiya had mobilized the Daura immigrants to subdue the local pagans; next Yaji had used his Mandinka allies to increase his power over pagans and Daurawa alike; and finally, Kanajeji had maintained his dominance by an alliance with the natives rather than his Daurawa or Mandinka elites. Following Bornu's imposition of sovereignty and the Galadima Dawuda's campaigns, the chief had cause to fear his officials and nobles, but not his subjects. Only the Galadima at Kano, the suzerain at Bornu, and the major rural chiefs of Gaya and Rano now had the power to threaten his position. Burja's death revealed the instability at the centre produced by this sudden access of new resources and power concentrated at the throne and under the Galadima. Two successive chiefs were deposed in eight days, the second explicitly for fear of the Galadima; and even in Yakubu's reign, it is clear that the Galadima dominated the government. Indeed it is possible that the Galadima Dawuda installed Yakubu and terminated the Gaudawa rule in alliance with the Sarkin Gaya Agalfati and the Sarkin Rano. Thus while concentration of slave manpower at the throne freed the chief from dependence on Mandinka, Daurawa or other free strata among his subjects, the resulting centralization increased his dependence on that senior executive, the Galadima, who now controlled most of these throne slaves. In effect, the large body of throne slaves simultaneously increased the predominance and vulnerability of the chiefship by replacing its former dependence on popular support with new relations of dependence on the Galadima, the chiefs of Rano and Gaya, and the suzerain at Bornu or his local representative.

Rumfa evidently perceived this central imbalance. The circumstances of Dakauta's and Atuma's depositions and Yakubu's and his own succession had exposed its nature and base. Several of his "twelve innovations" were clearly intended to resolve the structural problems generated by recent changes in the content and character of the chiefship and in its relations to other basic elements of the state. These developments excluded atavistic regressions. The semitribal chiefship of Tsamiya's day could not be restored. The special bonds between the chief and the Daura immigrants had been effectively destroyed by Yaji and Kanajeji; but in any event they were inadequate bases of chiefly power in Rumfa's day. The increasing ethnic complexity of the capital and the chief's new subordination to Bornu together obstructed programs of "restoration." Indeed, given their tributary status and new responsibilities for Kano's relations with foreign units, including those communities of strangers who had settled within the city, Rumfa and his successors had to rely primarily upon the authority and capacity provided by their resources. Rumfa accordingly tried to stabilize and augment this central power as an indispensable condition for the preservation and government of the state in its changing context. To achieve these goals without endangering his supremacy as chief, it was essential to reduce the Galadima's power of decision and execution.

"Rumfa was the author of twelve innovations in Kano."[77] Together, these transformed the chiefship and redefined its relations with the people and with the officials of state. Rumfa first built himself a new compound which still stands, the Gidan Makama. He then extended the city by building a new wall from the Kofar (Gate of) Dagaci, opposite Fage, now called Kofar Wambai, past the Women's gate (Kofar Mata), to the Kofar Gyartawasa, which is now known as the Kofar Nassarawa, south to the Kofar Kawaye, which is now the Kofar Dan Gundi, west to the Kofar Na'Isa, and so northeastwards, to the Kofar Kansakali, the gate of slave warriors.[78] Having finished the wall, Rumfa then built a new palace, the Gidan Rumfa, or house of Rumfa, within the area enclosed by the new wall. This new palace, which is still the emir's residence at Kano, was much larger than Rumfa's first compound; and this difference in size had a patent political significance. During the interval between building these two compounds, Rumfa evidently decided to settle several hundred throne slaves within and immediately around the palace. He could not expand his first compound to accommodate this population, due to its central position in the densely settled part of town; but Rumfa had probably decided to place the slaves who staffed such palace departments as the armory, the storehouses, treasury, police, prisons, and communications, within the palace precincts. To this end he selected a large open area between the new and older wall as the site of his palace, and on its completion he gave his former home near the city market to the Makama as his official compound.[79]

At this time, Mai Ali Dunama was also building the new capital of Bornu at Gasrgamu where his palace was walled with brick.[80] Whether Rumfa acted at Mai Ali's direction or under the influence of his example, or himself set the pattern is not known; but thereafter at Kano the palace where the ruler lived was virtually a separate town shut off from the rest of the city by a high wall with guarded gates on three sides, the Kofar Fada at the front, the Kofar Kudu facing south, and the Kofar Bai or slave gate at the rear. Free men were only permitted to enter or leave the palace through the front gate that led on to the various chambers in which the king held court, council or audience. The northern wall of the palace had no entrance. The chief's chambers and harem stood deep in the palace surrounded on all sides by compounds of throne slaves grouped in wards under headmen, each responsible to the chief through some senior slave for the good order and condition of his ward and for the disciplined performance of their duties by its members. Effectively, the palace was a garrison-town whose active male residents were organized and equipped for police and military action and for civil administration. A substantial number served as guards and police, others as prison warders, others as messengers on horse or foot, as escorts, store keepers, craftsmen and the like. In this way, the large slave staff attached to the throne were organized and used as instruments of government by the chief. In consequence, his power was greatly enhanced.

These building programs were probably carried out by slave and free labor, the latter being recruited from country and town; but it is probable that in rebuilding and extending the city wall and palace, Rumfa relied primarily on corvée levied from his free subjects within and outside of the town. He must also have commandeered the services of expert builders and blacksmiths, the latter having to furnish the tools required. It is also likely that having set up his new wall and extended the city, Rumfa renewed and repaired the remainder of the old wall between the Kofar Kansakali and Kofar Wambai, to further strengthen the city's defense. While habituating his subjects to obey, this extensive corvée demonstrated that such renovations required the chief's power and initiative. Presumably on its completion, Rumfa settled at his new palace many throne slaves summoned from the *ibdabu* for this work.

Rumfa then followed Dagaci's example and "established the Kurmi market,"[81] beside the Jakara pond in the old heart of the city. By his orders, commerce with foreign caravans and merchants was concentrated at Kurmi. This then became the major city market and, in later days, "the celebrated emporium of central Negro land."[82] But having himself set up the market, Rumfa was obliged to arrange for its regulation; and it is probably at this date or shortly after that the Sarkin Pawa or Sarkin Kasuwa (market head) was first put in charge. The Chronicle indicates that the title of Sarkin Pawa (chief butcher) was already established before Rumfa's reign, a son of one of Yaji's Mandinka visitors, the Limam Jibjin Yanlabu, having held the office;[83] and other evidence suggests that Rumfa placed the Sarkin Pawa in charge of his new market at the Kurmi on the site of the old cult grove.

Several other innovations were clearly designed to glorify and distinguish the chiefship by surrounding it with ceremony and magnificence. From Bornu, Rumfa introduced the long royal horn (*kakaki*), ostrich feather sandals as ceremonial foot wear for the chief, and ostrich feather fans (*figini*) for slaves to keep him cool. He also first "practised *kame*. He appointed Darman to go around the dwellings of the Indabawa (throne slaves) and to take every first-born virgin for him. He was the first Sarki to have a thousand wives. He began the custom of "*kulle*" (purdah, wife-seclusion)."[84] Rumfa thus expanded his harem by levying virgins from the slave settlements, now called Indabu, with which Galadima Dawuda had endowed the throne; and as the harem grew, purdah became necessary to restrain the women. However, Rumfa restricted his *kame* (appropriation, levy) to slave settlements that belonged to the throne, and apparently made no levies on the persons or property of his free subjects. Being throne slaves, Rumfa could legitimately claim these girls as his concubines; and perhaps by these means he deliberately sought to promote the strength and growth of his own family-line, by realizing to the full the reproductive potential of his chiefship while attaching the throne slaves firmly to it.

Two other innovations were more fundamental. Rumfa instituted the "*Tara ta Kano*," the "Kano Nine," as the state council. This institution was obviously modelled on the council of twelve by which Rumfa's suzerain, the Mai (sultan) of Bornu, governed his empire.[85] Whether the Kano council was established at Bornu's direction or at Rumfa's initiative is not clear. Nor do we know how the council was composed at its inception. It evidently contained the Galadima, the Madawaki (Madaki), the Makama, and other senior traditional officials. But Rumfa also created several new offices, some of which he placed on the council in order to strengthen himself against such powerful officials as the Galadima; he appointed the first Ciroma or crown prince at Kano, Bugaya or Bugai, who built his state compound at Dambazau.[86] Bugaya was probably Yakubu's posthumous son. The Ciroma title, like many of Rumfa's innovations, derived from Bornu, where it had long been reserved for the ruler's first son and chosen heir, the crown prince.

Further, Rumfa "began the custom of giving to eunuchs offices of state,"[87] among them the Dan Kusubi, Dan Jigawa, Dan Turbuna, Sarkin Gabas, Sarkin Tudu, Sarkin Ruwa, Ma'aji, Sarkin Bai, and Sarkin Kofa. Four other eunuchs were placed in charge of the royal bedchamber, the *turaka*, whence the title Turaki derives. Another harem eunuch was the Kashekusa from which the eunuch office of Kasheka in Alwali's day is clearly derived. A third, cited by East as Aljara and by Palmer as Aljira, may have been the prototype of the 19th century official Ajiya, the chief's private storekeeper. The fourth is identified by East as Aswara and by Palmer as Al-Soro.[88]

Of these palace eunuchs, one, the Sarkin Bai, seems to have sat on the state council from the start. Three other eunuch offices, Dan Kusubi, Dan Jigawa and Dan Turbuna, clearly identify body servants of the chief whose titles memorialize the three men who had prepared Bugaya's body for burial at Madatai under the direction of Lawan in 1390.[89] As that place thereafter became the Royal cemetery, the event may have been institutionalized before Rumfa's day in titles reserved for body servants of the chief. If so, Rumfa preferred to transfer these positions to his eunuch staff while creating others, such as Ma'aji, Sarkin Tudu, Sarkin Ruwa, Sarkin Bai (chief of the slaves) and perhaps the title of Sarkin Kofa in charge of the palace gates. Yakubu (1452–63) had created the title of Sarkin Gabas (chief of the East) for Agalfati's kinsman, who was given "Hadeija," or more probably, Garun Gabas. Presumably, by Rumfa's reign, "Hadeija" had either fallen to Bornu or become independent of Kano under its own chiefship, thus leaving vacant the title of Sarkin Gabas which Rumfa transferred to the new order of eunuchs. The Ma'aji served as his treasurer.

The Chronicle preceptively cites these appointments of eunuchs to state offices as significant developments. They were probably the most explicit signs of the profound reorientation of the chiefship and of its relations with the people and officials of Kano that Dawuda's slave-raids in Burja's reign had made possible and Rumfa instituted. By creating and appropriating state offices for throne slaves and eunuchs, Rumfa also showed his successors how to extend their power progressively while reducing that of their free officials. This was evidently Rumfa's intention, following the model of Bornu where the Mai was then reducing the power of his *Kona* (council). While several eunuch offices pertained solely to affairs within the palace, others had public functions and authority. Thus by by creating new institutions to alter the preceding distribution of power and placing three eunuchs and slave officials on the state council, Rumfa revealed and achieved his main purpose, namely, a signal enhancement of the chiefship's supremacy. According to the Chronicle, till then the only new offices created by chiefs were the ethnic or territorial chiefships set up by Tsamiya, Zamnagaba and Yaji.

However, Rumfa neither sought nor achieved a despotic chiefship, perhaps because that was inconsistent with his position as a protégé of Gaya and vassal of

Bornu. It is also likely that Bornu's overlordship made the chiefship of Kano vulnerable to complaints from disaffected senior nobles, and may have been manipulated to displace the Gaudawa line.

Instead, Rumfa instituted a new mixture of oligarchy and patrimonialism which assured the chiefship of independent power in such spheres as external relations, particularly with Bornu, in the administration of throne property, including the slave estates that Burja had rashly placed under the Galadima, in the regulation of trade and markets, and in the creation and control of state offices and appointments. Further, to preserve the chiefship against overpowerful officials, such as the Galadima Dawuda, Rumfa instituted the state council to advise on policy, thereby obliging the Galadima to deal with his senior colleagues as well as the chief, and replacing the previous dyadic structure of policy decision by one that combined oligarchic and patrimonial interests, most of the free councillors being senior hereditary officials. Further, Rumfa evidently recognized the need for a formally constituted electoral council both to secure the royal succession against usurpation, and the chiefship against domination by individual kingmakers. He probably perceived that the Council of Nine provided the model and basis for an electoral council; and it is possible that his constitutional reforms included this. However the Chronicle merely relates that Rumfa "began the *Tara ta Kano*"; and it is only by pursuing the structure and tendencies of the polity in sufficient depth that we can dimly perceive the conditions that promoted or followed such events, or the redistributions of power and authority they were intended and served to institute.[90]

We are told that in Rumfa's day the Galadima Dabello built his state compound at Gauda and that the Madawaki Badusu did likewise at Kura. The Ciroma Bugai (Bugaya) also built himself a state compound. The Makama had received Rumfa's compound when he moved to the new palace. Thus, these four senior offices first received state compounds in Rumfa's reign; and with these compounds went slaves, official farms, and other endowments covered by the Muslim law of *wakf*,[91] to create the Hausa institutions of state property. Accordingly, after the Galadima Dawuda had endowed the throne with slave-estates in Burja's reign, similar endowments were made to senior offices, thus generalizing the new form and character assumed by the chiefship to the senior offices of state. Thereafter, senior free offices vested with territorial jurisdiction and/or positions on the state council had compounds, farms and slaves permanently appropriated to them. Moreover, by its phrasing and by their locations, the Chronicle suggests that Rumfa also endowed these offices with territorial fiefs at this time.

Eleven years of Rumfa's reign were spent in war with Katsina; but the struggle was inconclusive and continued under his successor Abdullahi (1499–1509). During this war Rumfa introduced a new military unit, the reserve of fully equipped horses known as *dawakin zagi*, to replace those lost in battle.[92] This innovation confirms that cavalry was already a decisive arm of the Kano force.

Rumfa's final innovation combined his religious and political interests. He instituted the celebration of the Muslim festivals, *'Id El-Fitr* and *'Id El-Kabir*, the two annual Sallahs, at Shadakoko in Kano City in its present form, following Bornu models. After public prayers under the Limam at an open air prayer ground (*Masallacin Idi*) outside the city wall, the Sallah concludes with a dramatic ceremonial as mounted officials and vassals declare and renew their allegiance to the chief in strict order of rank by galloping charges. These declarations of homage and loyalty, that follow immediately after the Muslim prayers, are the central public rites of Hausa government. Once Rumfa had introduced them at Kano, like many of his other innovations, the practice diffused to other Hausa states.

It was in Rumfa's day that the Shehu Mohammed El Maghili visited Kano with a mission of about ten men and many important Islamic writings. Rumfa, a Muslim, welcomed El Maghili and his companions personally, escorting them from Panisau to Kano city, where he provided them with houses, supplies and servants. At El Maghili's direction, Rumfa built a sabbath mosque, the first in Kano; and he also cut down Shamuz, the tree of *cibiri* which still stood beside the Jakara as in Barbushe's day. On its site Rumfa built a minaret, the first in Kano. El Maghili remained in Kano until he was convinced of its conversion to Islam; but when departing to Katsina, where he also had great success, he left three disciples, by tradition his "sons," to continue the mission, of whom Malam Isa, also called Sidifari (the first or white Sa'id), was senior. El Maghili instructed his deputies to strengthen Islam at Kano by preaching to commoners and advising the court. The Hausa classified these disciples as shareefs; and, as his name implies, Sidifari, the senior *sa'id*, was their head.

El Maghili's visit to Kano in Rumfa's reign is well established.[93] Some time after his visit, El Maghili composed an essay on "The Obligations of Princes," at Rumfa's request for his guidance.[94] The Chronicle and other local traditions also stress that "Abdurrahman" came to Kano from the east, from Egypt, Es Suyuti's home; and that, having completed his mission, he returned thither; but El Maghili evidently entered Kano from the northwest. From Kano, El Maghili went northwest to Katsina.

Undoubtedly the news of Kano's wealth, commerce and development had spread, and attracted Muslim savants and merchants from east and west. Local thirst for deeper knowledge of Islam had been shown in Yakubu's reign when efforts were made to arrest Fulani clerics on their way east. Rumfa welcomed visiting scholars liberally and sought their advice, as did his neighbour and rival, the chief of Katsina, Maje Ibrahim (1494–1520), whom Es Suyuti addresses directly in an epistle.[95] El Maghili also wrote an important letter to Abdullahi Mohammed Ibn Yakubu, who was almost certainly Rumfa, in 897 A.H. or 1491–1492 A.D.[96] But if Es Suyuti and/or El Maghili visited Kano during Rumfa's later years, it is unlikely that Rumfa's innovations were made on their advice. Evidently these innovations developed during the early decades of Rumfa's reign and under the influence of Kanuri models, if not with Kanuri guidance and support.

El Maghili was also consulted by the Askia Alhaji Mohammed, the Muslim general who had seized the throne of Songhai in 1494 and assumed the role of caliph in the Western Sudan. From Kano, El Maghili evidently proceeded via Katsina to the Askia's court at Gao and thence homeward to Tlemcen.[97] He could hardly have failed to inform the Askia of Kano's wealth and political situation. At this date Kano was probably as large as Gao, the Songhai capital; and the rulers of Songhai may already have taken due notice of this.[98] Any nearby unit of outstanding wealth, size and organization might be regarded either as a possible threat or as a valuable prize. The Askia may already have learnt by this date of Bornu's westward expansion and overlordship of several Hausa states. The western boundaries of the Bornu empire already approached the dominions of Songhai in Kebbi, Dendi, Azben and Gobir. The Askia perhaps perceived Bornu's expansion as a threat to Songhai control of the caravan routes and traffic southwest from Azben. However, being otherwise engaged, for several years he took no direct action against Hausaland. El Maghili died at Tuat in 1503 A.D. before the Askia moved his armies east.

Abdullahi (1499–1509)

Rumfa's successor Abdullahi (1499–1509) was his son by Hauwa whose "influence was very strong among the rulers of the day. She built the house at Dausayi, that is known as the house of Madaki (sic) Hauwa."[99] This indicates another important innovation, the creation of the office of "Queen Mother" (Mai-daki) for Hauwa before or after Rumfa's death. As befitted its rank and prerogatives, this office was established with a state compound and property that probably included farms, slaves and fiefs. Its title Mai-daki, transcribed Madaki by Palmer and East, means owner (mother) of the hut; and its initial holder was Abdullahi's mother. This innovation was clearly modelled on the position of the Magira, the official Queen Mother of the Magumi sultans in Bornu. At Kano the new office was evidently instituted with support from the state council and senior officials, who perhaps by these means sought to restrain the independent power and centralizing tendencies of the chiefship. Thus Rumfa established a patrimonial regime restrained by oligarchic interests that could dominate the state if the council invoked the Mai-daki's residual powers.

Abdullahi pursued the struggle with Katsina vigorously. Whether this was simply a war over trade routes and prospects or one their common suzerain had promoted to weaken both states, or whether it had other bases and objects, we cannot tell. The Chronicle says that Abdullahi's Limam Ahmadu overcame Katsina and occupied Tsagero east of Katsina City for four months, following which Abdullahi attacked Zaria, defeated its army and moved past Kadaura to Kalam. Evidently this campaign had wide designs and scope; but returning to Kano, Abdullahi found that the Dagaci, presumably Othman Kalnama's successor, and perhaps in his absence the regent of Kano or Sultan's resident deputy, was preparing to "revolt," and that only the Mai-daki Hauwa had prevented this by her influence. "This was the reason that Sarkin Bornu came to attack Kano, and camped at Gunduwawa. The Sarkin Kano went out to meet him together with his Malams and humbled himself before him. Sarkin Bornu went back to his country. As soon as he was gone Abdullahi beguiled Dagaci into submission and then turned him out of his office and gave his own slave the title. He ruled Kano ten years."[100]

The Dagaci referred to in this passage was Othman Kalnama's descendant and titular successor who clearly retained considerable power and may have acted as regent during Abdullahi's absence on campaign, a role that Kalnama had previously performed. But it seems unlikely that this Dagaci had actually contemplated violent revolt against Abdullahi. Abdullahi's campaigns offered a much simpler route to the chiefship, since at this date Katsina and Zaria were either vassals of Bornu, or at very least important chiefdoms within the Kanuri sphere of interest. Perhaps Dagaci, who was himself of Magumi descent, had reported these developments to the Sultan at Gasrgamo as evidence of Abdullahi's independence and disloyalty to Bornu. Perhaps Dagaci was preparing to contest the Mai's power and right to the Bornu throne. Perhaps indeed Dagaci did so as the Sultan's agent or deputy, resident at Kano. As a Magumi prince, Dagaci was particularly equipped to seek the Kano throne, being also deeply familiar with its affairs; and it seems possible that either this Dagaci or his predecessors may have guided Rumfa's "innovations." The Maidaki Hauwa, through her courtiers, kept herself informed of Dagaci's conduct, thus enabling Abdullahi to deal with the situation on his return. But when the Magumi sultan reacted by bringing his army against Kano to reassert his suzerainty and, if necessary, to depose his vassal the Kano chief, Abdullahi, recognizing the alternative, renewed his submission, flanked by the malams of Kano. It seems likely that he paid a heavy fine to remain in office, and he may also have had to promise not to attack Katsina or Zaria again. In return Abdullahi probably persuaded the Sultan to allow him to deal with Dagaci, but in any event when the Sultan returned to Bornu, Abdullahi dismissed Dagaci and gave his office to a slave, thereby eliminating that threat to the chiefship and the dynasty.

Sometime between 1510 and 1515 and perhaps in 1513 the Arab traveller, Leo Africanus, visited Kano, and, when some years later recording his recollections, he remarked the presence of (Fulani) herdsmen among the cultivators who produced corn, rice and cotton.

> In the midst of this province standeth the towne called by the same name, the walls and houses whereof are built for the most part of a kind of chalke. The inhabitants are rich merchants and most ciuill people. Their king was in times past of great puissance and had mighty troupes of horsemen at his command; but he has since been constrained to pay tribute vnto the kings of Zegzeg (Zazzau) and Casena (Katsina). Afterwards Ischia (Askia), the king of Tanboto (Timbuctu; i.e., Songhai), feigning friendship vnto the two aforesaid kings, treacherously slew them both. And then he waged warre against the king of Cano whom after a long seige he tooke and compelled him to marie one of his daughters, restoring him again to his kingdome, conditionally that he should pay vnto him the third part of all his tribute; and the said king of Tanbutu hath some of his courtiers perpetually residing at Cano for the receipt thereof.[101]

Leo's observations are no less terse than those of the Chronicle; but both accounts illuminate and confirm one another. Apparently, though the Chronicle does not mention it, the chiefs of Zazzau and Katsina had allied themselves against Kano, either before or after Abdullahi's victory at Tsagero. Whether it was this alliance that provoked Abdullahi's attack on Zaria or his attack the alliance we cannot say. Perhaps at Gunduwawa the sultan of Bornu ordered Abdullahi to refrain from further wars against both states. Evidently, Katsina and Zaria, seeking revenge against Kano and perhaps also against Bornu, welcomed the overtures of Askia Mohammed who was now preparing to invade Hausa. However, as Leo relates, Askia deceived these chiefs and killed them both before besieging Kano. Despite the Chronicle's silence on these episodes, it is probable that they formed the context of Abdullahi's death. If so, the Chronicle's reticence about Abdullahi's death tacitly corroborates Leo's report; and this could enable us to date Abdullahi's demise precisely within a year or two and thus retrospectively to establish the accession and terminal dates of earlier reigns backwards to Yaji and Tsamiya.

An earlier independent confirmation of the chronological accuracy of the Chronicle is furnished by Othman Kalnama's migration to Kano from Bornu after his deposition in circa 1425 or 1432. Likewise when the Wangarawa (Mandinka) came to Kano from the west, in Yaji's reign, their presence in Katsina is independently attested. The surviving correspondence of Es Suyuti and El Maghili with Ibrahim Maje at Katsina and with Rumfa in Kano, who were contemporaries according to the records of both states, further validates the chronology of these Chronicles for this period. Thus, we are not confronted with a fanciful string of traditions laden with bizarre and disconnected items. The Kano Chronicle is certainly one of the most illuminating and reliable contemporary accounts of the history of any African people or state available to us. As such it is a truly unique document, of which almost every word, its various errors, and its many omissions are equally significant. From the mid–fifteenth century onwards, and perhaps for 100 years before that, it is also sufficiently detailed and reliable to provide a sound basis for structural analysis of the processes of political development at Kano.

Muhammadu Kisoke (1509–1565)

Songhai's domination of Kano was short-lived. The Askia probably overran Kano in 1512–13, shortly after Katsina and Zaria had been subjugated. All territory west of these states to Gao and beyond was then ruled by Songhai. To the north the Tuareg capital at Agades remained independent and hostile, and Tuareg plundered Songhai trade routes as opportunity allowed. Between 1513 and 1515 the Askia attacked Agades, ordering his local governors in nearby regions to join him with their contingents. One of these was the Kotal Kanta, who then administered the Kebbi area from Leka near Gwandu in the Surame district of Sokoto. There are several variant but mutually consistent accounts of the Kanta's rebellion, the most authoritative being that given in the *Tarikh es Soudan*.[102] On that version, Kanta returned from Agades to prepare his revolt against Songhai, being disappointed with his treatment by the Askia after the fall of Agades. Next year, when the Askia Alhaji Mohammed came eastward on his annual tour of inspection, Kanta ambushed his party with a small band near Beibei not far from Kazaure. The Askia, caught unprepared, escaped to Gao and sent an army against Leka six months later. Kanta anticipated this, and inflicted a heavy defeat on the Songhai forces. Thereafter Leka was independent; and with dispatch, Kanta seized control of Katsina, Kano, Zamfara, Zazzau, and other nearby states which had recently been overrun by Askia. It seems that Kanta appropriated control of these states without any serious battle, perhaps by simply asserting his authority as the successor of Askia, or by some other means. He seems also to have driven his forces northwards against Air or Azben and southwards to Nupe, if not beyond.[103]

Between 1516 and about 1550, when he died, Kanta built a small but impressive empire that stretched from Air southwards past Dendi to Nupe and northeastwards to include most of the main Hausa states formerly subject to Bornu. This empire was administered from the new kingdom of Kebbi that Kanta created in the old Leka district of Songhai. Moving from Leka, he built his first capital at Surame and expanded this successively with seven encircling walls, which still remain. Even so, Surame, with a perimeter of five miles, was too small to contain the striking force that Kanta concentrated under his command at the imperial centre. He then built a second town, Gungu, as a military camp close by Surame. Both towns were partially walled with stone, and had deeply recessed gateways, and several other novel features in their construction. Both towns were built by corvée levied on the subject Hausa states. Kanta's revolt took place shortly after Leo Africanus had passed through this area; and perhaps by the time that Leo wrote his account, Surame was already in being. It is said that Kanta built yet a third town near Gungu for the womenfolk of the soldiers settled at Gungu. This indicates the general character of Kanta's regime.

The Chronicle and Kano traditions make no explicit reference to Kanta's revolt or attempt to subjugate Kano; however as we shall see, the Chronicle provides revealing corroborative evidence. Bornu records are also silent about the successive dominations of Hausaland by Songhai and Kebbi. When Askia overran Hausa, the Magumi were unable to oppose him without risking defeat and conquest. It is thus possible that Kanta's revolt was encouraged or initially supported by Bornu; but having thrown off the Songhai yoke, Kanta appropriated control of the Askia's easternmost territories for himself. By then Bornu was equally aware of the immediacy of the threat and ready to reassert its claims.

> The Fulani ruler Mamman Bello (1817–1837), in his quick sketch of prejihadic Hausa history, says that "Kanta's rule extended over Katsina and Kano and Gobir and Zazzau and the town of Ahir (Air) and half the land of Songhai. He also made war on Bornu. The cause of the war with Bornu is said to have been as follows: Mai Ali, Sarkin Bornu was approached by Sarkin Ahir who asked his aid against Sarkin Kebbi Kanta because Kanta was overwhelming the people of Ahir. Mai Ali started from Bornu with his army and marched via Sosobaki, keeping north of Daura and Katsina and south of Gobir. He entered the land of Kebbi and approached Surame (Silame). The Sarkin Kebbi met him on the morning of the feast of Idi. They fought for a time and Sarkin Kebbi was driven westwards by sunset. The Sarkin Bornu settled down to besiege the city, but the city of Surame was too strong for him, so he retreated, taking the southern route via Gandi and retired to his own country. Then Kanta made war and followed after him until he came to Nguru. The Beriberi met him there and he defeated their army in about seven battles and took much spoil from them. Then he retired and was returning to his home when he reached a place called Dugul in the country of Katsina. Now these people were rebels, and Kanta had a severe fight with them in which he was wounded with an arrow. He continued his journey homewards until he reached Jirwa (Zurmi?), and there he died.[104]

The Mai Ali who attacked Surame was most probably either Ali ibn Idris (Ali Gaji Zeinami II) who reigned between 1545 and 1546 or Ali Dunama Ngumarama (1546–1564).[105]

These bare outlines of the changing imperial contexts and affiliations of Kano during the half-century that followed Rumfa's death must be borne in mind to appreciate correctly the erratic conduct of Abdullahi's successor, Muhammadu Kisoke (1509–1565), who may have acted as the Kanta's representative and agent in charge of all the central Hausa states.

According to the Chronicle,

> Kisoke was an energetic Sarki, warlike and masterful. He ruled over all Hausaland east and west and south and north. He waged war on Birnin Unguru (Nguru) because of Agaidam. He entered the town ... and assembling the inhabitants ... reduced them to terrified submission. He gave orders that no men were to be made prisoners but that only clothes and horses were to be taken. Then he left Nguru and lived for a month in the bush. The Sarkin Bornu sent to him and said, "What do you mean by making war?" Kisoke replied, "I do not know, but the cause of war is the ordinance of Allah." The Sarkin Bornu said nothing more. The men of Kano returned to Kano. In the next year the Sarkin Bornu came to attack Kano, but could not take the town and returned home.[106]

Kisoke then commissioned his praise singer, Dunki, to climb the city wall and from its battlements sound forth his praises and those of his officials and chiefs for forty days, mocking meanwhile the power of Bornu and Shirra, its nearby vassal. This was probably the greatest and most extended bout of praise singing in Hausa history. The Chronicle, registering the public wonder at this unusual event, records it graphically and lists many of the thirty-four officials and chiefs whom Dunki and his helpers praised during their "forty days" on top of the wall.[107]

Superficially this is one of the most bizarre events recorded in the Chronicle; and the meticulous report merely intensifies its apparent craziness. However we have already found the equally perplexing account of the preparation of Bugaya's corpse for his funeral important to document the origin and status of certain palace titles. Likewise, though the Chronicle nowhere reveals it, this stupendous praise song was Kisoke's way of celebrating and publicizing Kano's recovery of its independence, after serving three different masters during the past fifty to seventy years.

From the scattered fragments of information still available to us, we can decipher the march of events in outline. Following Kanta's successful revolt and domination of Hausa, he evidently gave Kisoke, the most remote and powerful Hausa chief, a privileged position in the new Kebbi empire. Kano lay on Kebbi's frontier with Bornu, and was treated with care by Kanta, who sought thus to divert the loyalties of its chief to himself from his enemy, the Mai of Bornu. It is possible that Kano provided few workers, if any, for Kanta's continual corvée construction in Kebbi. Instead, Kano may have been charged with supervision of adjacent Hausa states and transmission of their tributes to Kebbi. Kanta probably wished to encourage the growth of Kano's commerce for its value to his empire. It thus appears that Kano enjoyed rather favourable conditions under Kanta's control. However, between 1527 and 1532 the Bornu sultan, Idris ibn Ali, subdued Agades and made treaties with its leading Tuareg tribes.[108] It is unlikely that Bornu attacked Surame, the Kebbi capital, before this date. Until then, Kebbi had remained under periodic attack from Songhai; and the Bornu court clearly awaited the outcome of that struggle, hoping that its rivals would seriously weaken one another. Now, having subdued Agades, Bornu controlled the central Saharan trade routes to Katsina and Kano. Presumably this was one objective behind the Kanuri attack on Agades, then the largest and most southerly settlement in the region of Air which Kebbi had attacked strenuously. Mamman Bello interprets this conquest of Agades as Bornu's response to appeals by the Sultan of Air;[109] and explicit reference to treaties of peace made between Bornu and the Tuareg of Agades seems to support this. The Magumi sultan appointed his slave Ibrahim to represent him at Agades, to supervise it and to handle its communications with Gasrgamu.[110]

Shortly afterwards, Bornu confronted Kebbi directly, probably to free Air and Agades of Kebbi's demands and harassment. According to Palmer, the Kanuri sultan Mohammed Ibn Idrisi marched against Surame and, almost certainly with Tuareg support, he defeated the Kanta outside the city, but failed to take it. Following the usual methods of siege, the Bornu army probably devastated the surrounding farm lands and territory, but being unable to reduce Surame, the sultan withdrew, avoiding Kano on his homeward route. To re-establish his control, and to recover those eastern dominions this Bornu invasion had temporarily shaken loose, Kanta prepared his counter-attack. It seems possible that for this purpose he somehow attached to himself the sultan of Air, Mohammed ibn Shala (c. 1517–1542),[111] whose authority over Agades had been recently reduced by the Bornu conquest. The Kanuri record of these events obliquely indicates that the "king of Asben," that is, the sultan of Air, perhaps Ibn Shala, may have rebelled against Bornu at this date and recovered Agades.[112] The Kanuri at Gasrgamo were then under pressure from Bagirmi and Kanem to the east. Whether Kanta reassumed domination over Air or not, he marched eastwards, presumably with Kisoke's army from Kano, and took Nguru, thus threatening to cut the major Saharan trade route to Gasrgamu southwards from Agades to Geidam. In short, Kanta used Nguru as a decoy to draw the Bornu forces on to successive defeats, his major objective being the northern caravan route from Bilma to Gasrgamu. It was almost certainly in this campaign that Kisoke took part in the capture and looting of Nguru. It seems from the general context that this event took place when the Bornu forces were drawn off from Nguru by Kanta striking northeastwards to Geidam. These campaigns may have occurred in 1544–5. On his return homeward, Kanta was killed, following which his sons, Kanu and Ahmadu, began fighting for the Kebbi throne.[113] The sultan of Bornu immediately sought to re-establish his authority over Kano. He first demanded reasons for his vassal's disloyalty; and when Kisoke referred him to Allah, the sultan attacked Kano but failed to take it. This failure, coupled with the sharp decline in Kebbi's power following Kanta's death and the dynastic struggle among his sons, freed Kano from Bornu and Kebbi simultaneously. It is not surprising that Kisoke celebrated this sudden good fortune by an extended praise song.

It seems clear that by this time, following Kanta's death and Kebbi's decline, Bornu had reasserted its suzerainty over Daura, and perhaps from that base over Katsina also. However, like Kano, Zaria seems to have remained independent of Kebbi and Bornu alike. West of Katsina, Zamfara and Gobir remained subject to Kebbi until 1700 when, with Katsina support, they finally broke Kebbi power. From Kisoke's day to Kumbari's (1731–1743), Kano seems to have remained fully independent, a sovereign state (*iklimi*), and as such simultaneously free to aggrandize at the expense of others, and exposed to similar treatment. Thus in tracing the history of Kano for these two succeeding centuries, we are primarily concerned with its internal affairs rather than its role in a changing system of imperial politics.

The Chronicle cites many of those whom Dumki praised on the city wall by name and title. Such lists enable us to detect some of the continuities or changes in the offices that constituted the government of Kano. This list includes, besides the Galadima and the Madawaki, the Madawakin Gawo, the Dan Kududufi, the Makama Abdullahi and another Makama Atuman who may either have been Abdullahi's successor or perhaps the Makama of Dan Atuman, known as Makama Atuman. In addition, Dumki praised the Dan Yerima, the Dan Buram, the Dan Maje, the Dan Makwayau, the Dan Goriba, the Dan Darman, all, except the Dan Yerima, offices current in Alwali's day; the Dan Bauni, of whom no trace remains, the Maidaki Hauwa, Kisoke's grandmother, the Dagaci, then a slave, the Alkali, the Limam, the Sarkin Bai, the Sarkin Yara, first mentioned at this date and probably already in charge of palace prisons, the Korama, the Sarkin Kasuwa and the San Turaki, then head of the ruler's chamber eunuchs. This list provides the first mention of several state offices, for example Korama, Sarkin Yara, Dan Goriba, Dan Makwayau, Makama Atuman, Dan Bauni and Sarkin Kasuwa, head of the Kurmi market. The Maidaki Hauwa, Kisoke's grandmother, received special praise, though she could hardly have taken an active part in the recent struggle. It is said that "Kisoke ruled the town with his mother, Iya Lamis and his grandmother, Madaki Hauwa and Guli, the brother of Madaki Hauwa. Guli was much respected by the Sarki, he came to have power over the whole country."[114] This is the first of several untitled courtiers reported in the Chronicle as dominating the chief. However, as Guli was Kisoke's father's mother's brother, his influence may not have aroused public hostility.

The quotation also indicates that by this date the title of Iya or Magajiya had been separated from that of Mai-daki. Abdullahi had introduced the Maidaki title for Hauwa as she was the then ruler's mother. Outliving her son, and having captured the affection and respect of the Kano people, Hauwa retained the title, compound and authority of Maidaki until her death. Thus another title was needed for Kisoke's mother Lamis, and perhaps the office of Iya was introduced for her at this time from Daura, Zaria or Katsina, where it is also found. Moreover, as the passage just cited indicates, so long as the Maidaki Hauwa and the Iya Lamis were active, Kisoke consulted them on decisions of policy. Thus, from its inception at Kano the title of Iya or Magajiya shared some of the powers and prerogatives of the Maidaki office, though to a lesser degree. This relation persisted to Alwali's day, as we have seen.

During Kisoke's reign, Kano received further Muslim missionaries, the Shehu Atunashe, i.e. the Shehu from Tunis, and Shehu Abdusallam, who brought with them such books on law as the Mudauwana, Jami'u, 'Ssangiri and *Samarkandi*. "From Zaria a man called Tubi ("convert") came to the Tunisian sheikh and became his leading disciple in Kano. Further, Shehu Korsiki and Magumi and Kabi came from Bornu. They were brothers. Kisoke took a liking to the Shehu Kursi and asked him to become Alkali. He refused and suggested his brother,

Magumi. Magumi agreed and built a portico at the Kofar Fada,"[115] that is, by the palace entrance. Others who came to Kano in Kisoke's day include Burduru, Kudu and Watasanu. By this date Islam was firmly established as the state religion of Kano, and the government appointed leading Muslim scholars as the city judge and imam. Such offices were thus *shigege* at this time.

Lamis, Kisoke's mother, the first known Magajiya at Kano, built her state compound at Banibuki in the city and established there a market for the sale of eunuchs.[116] Thus it seems likely that the trade in eunuchs became a royal monopoly in Kisoke's reign. Perhaps eunuchs were then being made in Kano; if so, by this date the output may have exceeded the palace needs. The new Magajiya was given a monopoly to sell the surplus. The castration sheds and traffic in eunuchs had become state monopolies controlled by the palace and the king's official kinswomen.

Lamis was also "the mother of Dakpare Dan Iya. Kisoke put him in the 'Kano nine' and for that purpose expelled the Barde."[117] This passage identifies the Dan Iya as an ancient princely office; but whether at this date it was reserved for the ruler's uterine kin or for agnates remains obscure. In replacing the Barde, a senior military captain, by his kinsman the Dan Iya on the council of state, Kisoke sought to increase his chiefly power by redistributing council seats among his supporters. This was a patrimonial technique practiced by Rumfa and before him by Yaji and others. Evidently since Rumfa's reign, the constitution of the Kano state council had not changed. However, the Barde's replacement by Dan Iya on the council reveals strains within the constitution Rumfa had created. Its patrimonial and oligarchic interests, though interlocking and mutually reinforcing in certain areas, were contraposed in others. By controlling appointments to office and by redistributing official functions or powers, the chief could usurp the council's power, if not checked. Short of collective rebellion, a difficult project given their mutual rivalries, councillors could probably best preserve their oligarchic rights by seeking the Queen Mother's support and intervention, by backing one another against the chief and other senior officials and, as opportunity arose, by recouping their collective losses and strengthening their position against the chiefship in the contexts of royal succession. In thus replacing the Barde by Dan Iya, Kisoke seems to have initiated a long struggle between chiefship and oligarchy.

Some Turbulence at the Throne (1565–1582)

On Kisoke's death, Yakufu, presumably his son, succeeded; but after four months and twenty days, Guli, the Maidaki Hauwa's brother and Kisoke's unofficial vizier, deposed him. The Galadima Sarkatunya then waged a civil war against Guli and his supporters, Kisoke's uterine kin. After "forty" days the Galadima defeated Guli and killed him. He then sought to re-establish Yakufu on the throne; but Yakufu refused, apparently preferring to retire to clerical studies.[118]

Yakufu had probably been selected by the official electors, presumably the senior rural chiefs and officials, under the chairmanship of the Galadima Sarkatunya. Guli and his faction opposed Yakufu's accession either on personal grounds, considering him unsuitable on unrecorded issues of policy, or perhaps because his appointment reduced their influence and placed the chief under the council's direction. It is also possible that Yakufu was neither Kisoke's son nor his full brother, and thus unrelated to Lamis. Evidently the council sought to assert its central position as the directive organ of state by extruding those unconstitutional supports and procedures employed by Kisoke, and especially the two "queen mothers" and his influential grandfather, Guli. In the ensuing struggle, acting on behalf of the officialdom and with its support, the Galadima had constitutional right on his side. Perhaps Guli, besides his kinsmen, and levies from the Queen Mother's fiefs and some dissident throne slaves, relied mainly on clients in search of power, wealth and position to contest the issue. There is no evidence of any external intervention. However, it is conceivable that Bornu influence was somehow involved.

On Yakufu's refusal to accept reinstatement, his son, Dauda Abasama, was appointed; but at the end of fifty days he too was dismissed; and in this case the Chronicle neither indicates the reason, the context, nor the persons who dismissed him. Whether this reticence implies external intervention by Kebbi or Bornu we cannot say. Dauda could equally have been overthrown by a shift of power among the councillors themselves. This might easily have happened had he first been appointed against the Galadima's wishes and then alienated some of those who chose him, perhaps so sharply that they determined to remove him. Conceivably, Dauda Abasama, and perhaps his father Yakufu also, may have been inclined to resume the old vassalage relation with Bornu for the internal and external security it promised.

Besides Dauda Abasama, Yakufu had several children, four of whom were given local chiefships in northeastern Kano near its borders with Gumel and Hadeija. These chiefships included Majia, Gilima, Gunka and Kazaure, the latter lying far to the northwest near the site of the present town. All four units still persist; and in Alwali's day it is said that at least two of them, Majia and Gilima, had *tambari* to signify the royal descent and autonomous local jurisdiction of their chiefs. Perhaps this was also true of the others. However, when Dauda Abasama was deposed from office, the four princes were also removed from their chiefships and sent with Dauda to Kwarmashe to farm. Their offices were then given to others.

Abubakar Kado (1565–1573), another son of Muhammad Rumfa by the Maidaki Hauwa, who had recently died, was appointed next by the council in an obvious attempt to pacify the faction of Hauwa's clients and kin, of whom Guli had been the recent leader. This was probably the decisive political consideration that overthrew Dauda Abasama.

Abubakar Kado, who was probably over sixty years old at his accession, was an ineffective ruler, and after seven and a half years in office he, too, was deposed. Quite apart from his age and personal incapacities, political cleavages between the councillors and the Galadima on the one hand, and the lineage and clients of the Maidaki Hauwa's faction on the other, reduced cohesion and weakened the central authority. Abubakar was also preoccupied with religion. "He was the first Sarki who made the princes learn the Koran ... Every morning after sunrise the princes assembled. The Sarki came out after early morning prayer. He had seven sons, each of which read a seventh of the Koran."[119] Abubakar Kado built the hall called Fagaci at the palace "for the reading of the Koran." He himself studied also with the Dan Goronduma Kursiyu who had settled at Kano during Kisoke's reign and who had probably received the title Dan Goronduma from him.[120] Abubakar Kado seems to have been reading the Jami'u Sangiri when deposed. "Abubakar Kado did nothing but religious offices. He disdained the duties of Sarki. He and all his chiefs spent their time in prayer. In his time eunuchs and malams (clerics) became very numerous."[121] Evidently the recent conflicts that had unseated Yakufu and Dauda Abasama involved or generated tensions about relations between the state and its official cult, Islam.

While the chief practised his religious offices, the leaderless country suffered. In Kado's time "the men of Katsina worsted the men of Kano until they came to the very gates of Kano. They encamped at Salamta. The men of Kano went out to fight, but they were beaten and scattered and had to take refuge in the town. Devastation went on, and the country was denuded of people. The only place where anybody was found was in walled towns or rocks such as Karaye, Gwangwan, Maska, Tariwa or any other rocky place."[122] Weakened by plague and civil war and made impotent by its own internal divisions and conflicts, the government could not mobilize an effective defence. Perhaps the recent rapid depositions of successive chiefs had made all aware how impolitic it was to place the major forces of the state under any single commander. The southwestern territory was thus left defenceless.

During Kado's reign several important immigrants arrived from Bagirmi or the Logoni region southeast of Chad. Among them were the Malams Sharif Tama, Getso and Wuri, two of whom, Tama and Getso, founded local chiefships. "Tama was the greatest of them. When they first came, they lived in Katsina … Afterwards they moved to Kano and settled at Godiya. The town was called Godiya after a certain woman, a harlot. She and the Sarki reigned jointly over the town. The Sarki said to Tama, 'Settle at Godiya.' So Tama settled at Godiya and married Godiya."[123] Later Tama's successor, the Dan Tama, established a chiefship at Godiya just as Getso's successor, the San Getso, ruled Getso nearby; in Alwali's day as well as in the last century, the two offices administered these two towns. Perhaps it was to record their origins and date of arrival that the Chronicle reports this apparently disconnected incident.

Of those princes who read the Koran daily to Abubakar Kado at the Goron Fagaci, the eldest, Abdullahi, had the title Dan Kade, first mentioned in the Chronicle here and current in Kano today as in 1800. Another was the Ciroma or crown prince. Another was Dan Ashiya, Ashiya being the chief's sister, but whether this last denotation was titular or merely genealogical the context leaves unclear. Perhaps Ashiya had died and Abubakar Kado had created the title for her son in her honour. In this way some of the offices reserved for royal cognates might have been instituted; but by Alwali's day, if it ever existed, the title of Dan Ashiya had disappeared, as Abubakar Kado's successors appointed their cognatic kin to other positions carrying greater prestige and resources.

Political conflicts at Kano continued under Muhammad Shashere, Yakufu's son, who succeeded on Abubakar Kado's deposition in 1573. We can tentatively decipher the principal competing units in this conflict and some of their orientations: the allied lineages of the Queen Mothers Lamis and Hauwa, with their

numerous clients, slaves and subjects; an officialdom divided by differing orientations; the clerical Islamic faction which sought to guide policy by dominating the
chief; and within the dynasty, Yakufu's issue, who had been removed to Kwarmashe but who were now restored to power under Shashere's rule and leadership. Finally, there were the seven sons of Abubakar Kado, and other princes
descended from Abdullahi and Kisoke. There were probably also sharp differences between these groups over the conduct of foreign affairs, particularly the
war with Katsina and relations with Bornu, which in all probability underlay the
war. Finally, there were palace pressures by the chief to centralize control through
the subordination or dissolution of the oligarchy and increase of patrimonial
power.

Shashere "was the first to give a eunuch the title of Wambai (the eunuch was
called Damu.) He gave to another eunuch called Dabba the title of Sarkin Dawaki.
He gave to another eunuch called Mabaiyi the title of Dagaci."[124] The first two of
these three offices, and perhaps the third also, carried seats on the state and electoral councils, large fiefs and military commands. Evidently Shashere's solution
of the political divisions in Kano was to appropriate strategic positions to the
throne, augmenting his own power accordingly. However, this policy served to
unite several mutually hostile factions in opposition against him. Perhaps for this
reason Shashere decided to redress the situation that Kado's shiftlessness had permitted. "He determined on an expedition against Katsina." To mobilise support
from the Muslim pressure group, he appointed Musa Gero as Alkali to the army
on campaign, presumably to preside over all legal issues that arose during the
expedition, and particularly to administer the distribution of booty according to
the law. "The armies met at Kankiya and fought there. The Katsinawa won
because they were superior in numbers. The Kanawa ran away—deserting their
Sarki—with the exception of the San Turaki Manya Narai, San Turaki Kuka Zuga,
and Dan Dumpki (Dunki); hence the songs, 'Narai the wall: ready to answer any
challenge'; 'Zuga does not run away.'"[125] The Dan Dunki who stood by Shashere
in defeat held the title created by Kisoke or his successors to commemmorate
Dunki's great feat of praise-singing on the city wall in Kisoke's reign after the
sultan of Bornu abandoned his siege of Kano. The holder was thus probably the
chief's senior praise singer. The San Turaki Kuka title, then held by Zuga, seems
to have been a eunuch office attached to the Turaka (the chief's bedchamber);
while the San Turaki Manya (Turaki the Greater) Narai was the head of these
eunuchs.

In local idiom, this terse account of Kano's defeat obliquely indicates that its
officials and military captains had plotted to betray their chief by deserting him in
battle, perhaps hoping that the Katsina forces would kill him. Shashere clearly
perceived this. "The Sarki was very grieved. His men said to him, 'Put aside your
grief, next year we will defeat the Katsinawa if Allah wills.' But meantime his
brothers (kinsmen) were treacherously planning to kill him. San Turaki Narai
heard of their plans and told the Sarki."[126] Having apparently diverted the chief's
fears and suspicions, his dynastic rivals plotted his assassination in a perfectly
rational way. There was certainly nothing traditionalistic about their scheme or
conduct. At least in Kano it had no known precedent.[127] The chief also acted in a
highly rational fashion to frustrate their plans.

Having learned that the plotters intended to assassinate Shashere in the mosque on the sabbath evening, the Turaki Manya (San Turaki) Narai requested Shashere to remain in his quarters at that hour. Dressed in the royal robes and with some regalia, Narai waited in the mosque with "nine of his own slaves, and eighteen of the Sarki's household," a reasonable bodyguard. However, the plotters evidently anticipated a force of this size and turned up in strength. "The nine slaves (of Narai) were killed. Twelve of the others were killed and six captured." The Chronicle then names all six of Shashere's household who let themselves be captured rather than fight to the death. One of these was the Sarkin Wawaye (Chief of Fools), a court jester.[128] "San Turaki Narai was buried in the mosque in which he was killed;" but apparently the mosque was then abandoned and not rebuilt until the reign of Ibrahim Dabo (1819–1846), when an antechamber (*zaure*) was built nearby in Narai's honour and named after him. From this date also to commemorate Narai's valour the Turaki Manya (San Turaki) "had the honour of acting for the Sarki, if he were absent" at least throughout this reign and that of Sheshere's successor, Muhammadu Zaki.[129]

To conceal their own identity the plotters held the six slaves of Narai's bodyguard who survived the struggle in the mosque. Shashere could thus take no action against his would-be assassins, partly because he could not establish their identity or guilt at law, but also perhaps because he dared make no move against them. The chief was thus forced totally on the defensive. He became a virtual prisoner within his palace, and was deposed in 1582, but at whose instigation or how long after Narai's death, we do not know.

Shashere's situation indicates how rivalry among dynastic segments further weakened the chiefship. Despite his constitutional pre-eminence and superior resources of slaves and eunuchs, the chief remained insecure. By themselves, slave and eunuch officials could neither administer the state nor defend its head until the oligarchic lineages and dynastic segments had been subdued or dispersed; but this was to prove rather difficult, given the multiple and shifting alliances between princes, councillors and other officials, including the palace eunuchs and slaves; and given also the distribution of territorial jurisdiction among these officials, several of whom held hereditary ranks. During their period of vassalage, the Kano chiefs had been protected against local threats of assassination or violent removal by the superior authority of their suzerain. Rumfa's reforms presupposed such relations; and in part they were designed to furnish sufficient central control to enable the chief of Kano to deal with Bornu from a position of internal strength. But when Kano regained its independence c. 1550, its chiefship lost also this external support; and beset by labile factions too strong and numerous to be destroyed, the chief could neither rule effectively, nor could he ultimately defend himself against his local enemies.

It seems appropriate at this stage to ask in what respect it is either useful or accurate to characterize this chiefship and its political context in such vague and global terms as "traditional" or "rational," as I have done previously. Clearly the political structure of Kano underwent continuous and cumulative change throughout those centuries for which our data are adequate. Clearly the character, context, scope and form of the chiefship changed notably throughout this period. So did the composition, structure, resources and recruitment of the officialdom and its relations with the chief. As we have seen, these changes developed prima-rily under the impact of forces generated by pressures and conflicts of different kinds, internal to the system of political authority. On various occasions develop-ments were guided or stimulated by important external influences; and several foreign patterns, procedures and techniques were selected and institutionalized at Kano by successive chiefs from Yaji to Rumfa. Even so, most of the new corporate units and relations in the local state had emerged through processes of structural change by which individuals or groups who exercised a temporary dominance sought to enhance and consolidate their position in contexts of continuing politi-cal insecurity and struggle. Such conflicts in the central community of Kano are evident as far back in time as the data allow us to go.

Despite periodic injections of new elements, relations, ideas, resources and problems from outside, political developments at Kano have nonetheless been guided primarily by local exigencies, alignments and objectives, normally of a specifically political nature and base. While this pattern presupposes some conti-nuity of structures and orientations, including the persistence or replication of political competition and conflict, our data indicate high degrees of specificity and instrumental rationality in the pursuit of determinate political goals by the parties to such competition. As the context of this continuing competition, the "traditional" structure of the chiefdom underwent continuous modification through processes by which old institutions were either progressively trans-formed or erased, while new elements of very different provenience, form and orientation were institutionalized as traditional and prescriptive.

How meaningful is it to designate a polity in such continuous self-sustaining and self-modifying ferment as "traditionalistic" or "rationalistic"? Likewise, is it meaningful to characterize its central authority structure as patrimonial, feudal or other? Clearly such categories grossly over-simplify the structures to which they refer and they commonly mislead our understanding by misrepresenting and sys-tematically obscuring much that is intrinsically significant to the system, and to the orientations and relations of its principal actors. Repeatedly in the medieval history of Kano we encounter policies and actions of a Machiavellian sort exe-cuted with considerable finesse and guided by equally intense considerations of rationality and "traditionalism." Is it meaningful also to designate this system as governed by consummatory or instrumental values, and as either pyramidal or hierarchic in form? Are such dichotomous conceptions appropriate to Kano, or perhaps to any complex state? Experience shows that empirical structures are substantially rather ambiguous and subtle; but if we are to represent them cor-rectly and penetrate their significance, we shall have to abandon this hoary aca-demic commitment to the Zoroastrian dichotomization of social processes, structures and facts. It is perhaps no less essential in sociology than in history to credit those actors whose courses we observe with at least the same intelligence and capacity to maintain or pursue a plurality of interests, goals, values, beliefs and moral orientations as we ourselves possess, at least until the total range of evidence demonstrates otherwise.[130] We need not cling compulsively to our home-made blinkers; but if we choose to do so, we shall merely reject the enor-mous variability of human experience, pursuits and problems for myopic reflec-tions of our own conceits.

The Last Two Rumfawa Chiefs, 1582–1623

On the deposition of Muhammadu Shashere in 1582, Muhammadu Zaki, son of Kisoke, was appointed. His mother, Hausatu, was the daughter of that immigrant Tama who had married the prostitute Godiya in whose honour her town was named. Presumably, Hausatu was Tama's daughter by another lady, perhaps a princess. On Zaki's appointment, "Tama came to live at Kano together with his men, the Katukawa,"[131] that is, men from the south (of Bornu).

At his accession Zaki received the six captive members of Shashere's household who had witnessed the death of San Turaki Narai at the mosque. He "intended to kill these six, but they prayed and begged him saying 'Spare us and we will be your slaves, we are your grandchildren.' So the Sarki spared them, but each of them chose a task as the price of their lives."[132] As the new chief, Muhamman Zaki could neither formally condone the attempt to assassinate his predecessor, nor the failure of the chief's staff and household to die fighting for him, as Narai had done. Yet it seems that Zaki may have owed his appointment to those princes who had plotted Shashere's death. In thus reprieving their six captives by imposing these onerous burdens, Muhamman Zaki simultaneously indicated his intention to take no action against those who had plotted against Shashere, and sought to educate the household and throne slaves concerning the binding nature of their obligations to defend the chief. Muhamman Zaki was probably concerned to prevent any repetition of a similar incident against himself or his successors, perceiving that if such attempts became frequent, Kano could be destroyed internally.

His efforts to forestall and suppress any similar future attempts to assassinate the chief also took military, political and ritual forms, and combined both rational and traditional calculations and procedures. He "made Aderki (Adarka) build Sarkin Jarmai a house inside the Sarki's compound." The Sarkin Jarmai was the hand-picked captain of the chief's *lifida* or heavily armed slave cavalry, the mainstay of the chief's personal defence. By bringing him within the palace on standing duty, Muhamman Zaki took the final step to prepare the slave cavalry, concentrated at the palace, for instant action. He likewise built near the compound of his senior chamber eunuch, the Turaki Kuka, a barracks for his free *lifida*, the 'Yan Sentali,[133] thereby reducing his personal dependence on slave guards and troops. Until this date, excluding the chief's personal family and harem, none but slaves had compounds in the Gidan Rumfa. Muhamman Zaki now brought in free clients selected for their loyalty and valour and organized directly under the Sarkin Jarmai, himself a free man, who lodged close by the chief's personal quarters. Within the palace these free soldiers were thus surrounded by slaves on all sides; but the slaves were themselves surrounded by free men within the town. The chief no longer vested his personal safety solely in slave guards. Neither did he rely wholly on free men. Instead he could now play off each category against the other.

To reverse the recent increasing secularization of the chiefship, Muhamman Zaki introduced the fetish Dirki together with another element, Cokana, the details of which are not known. Dirki was a copy of the Koran covered with goatskin. Afterwards cowhide was used for the purpose, as many as ten skins being used, and even forty in later times. In Alwali's time (1781–1807) the practice had gone to such a ridiculous length that the chief stopped it altogether.

The people said, "If you stop this practice, God will bring evil fortune upon you." Alwali replied, "Dirki is nothing but the Koran; I swear I will open it and expose its contents." So he ordered young men to take axes and open "Dirki." They did so. Alwali found the Koran inside and took it to his house. The people said, "You will be expelled from this land even as you have expelled the Koran from Dirki." Alwali was afterwards driven out of Kano.[134]

Dirki thus became the central fetish of the chiefship, its ritual foundation and assurance of continuity. Each year the fetish would be covered with new skins. It remained under the chief's immediate care. It conferred a mystique of inviolability on chiefly authority; but clearly it did not guarantee the chief's secular success or even his tenure of office, though Muhamman Zaki probably intended to enhance the chief's security and power by these means.

Precisely when during his long reign (1582–1618) Zaki established Dirki and Cokana is not known; but internal evidence suggests that these cult objects or practices were probably instituted after the first major Jukun assault on Kano during the early half of Zaki's reign. Two centuries earlier, Yaji had raided the Jukun and levied a tribute of 100 slaves before withdrawing. Kanajeji, who followed him at Kano, demanded double this number of slaves as tribute. Thereafter, as noted above, he traded horses for slaves with the Jukun. Later, in Dawuda's reign (1421–1438), Zaria wrested control of the Jukun from Kano. Thereafter the Jukun remained independent of Kano; and by Zaki's reign they were evidently independent of Zazzau also. Indeed, some years before, they had inflicted heavy defeats on the forces of Bornu.[135] For the next 100 years Jukun (Kororofa) remained one of the most formidable military powers in this region; however, their divine kingship and heavily ritualized social institutions made it difficult for them to consolidate their conquests by incorporating defeated peoples through appropriate administrative arrangements of a secular kind.[136] The Jukun power thus expressed itself in sporadic violent assaults and campaigns against Zazzau, Bornu, Kano and perhaps Katsina, their primary objectives being devastation and loot.

In course of time Kano was subjected to three major invasions by this once subordinate "pagan" people. Of these, the first occurred in Zaki's reign, apparently before 1600, the second between 1652 and 1660, and the third between 1670 and 1703. On all three occasions the Jukun directed their main assault against Kano city. On each occasion the people of Kano either fled or failed to put up an effective defense. On the first attack, "the people of Kano left the city and went to Daura, with the result that the Kwororofa (Jukun) ate up the whole country and Kano became very weak. The men of Katsina kept on harrying Kano."[137] When the Jukun had withdrawn homeward to their farms, Muhamman Zaki and his court returned from Daura to Kano. Perhaps the Kano people fled north to avoid being caught between the Katsinawa on the west and the Jukun.

Returning, Zaki determined to square accounts with the Katsinawa, who at this time seem to have dominated most of western Kano. However, the effects of the devastations inflicted by the armies of Katsina and Jukun were intensified and extended by bad weather. "There was a great famine which lasted eleven years."[138] Zaki took counsel with all his officials and malams "to stay this calamity." A Maghrebi Sheikh Abubakar offered ritual guarantees of victory against Katsina, promising thereby to free the western districts of Kano for resettlement and cultivation. Zaki rewarded the Shehu Abubakar handsomely and followed his instructions. He brought the Kano army to the walls of Katsina city on the morning of the Idi Salla at the end of Ramadan. Caught unprepared, the Katsinawa suffered a sharp defeat. Zaki captured 400 horses and 60 coats of quilted cotton armour; but he himself died at Karaye on his homeward march, perhaps from a wound.

Zaki's long reign was a troubled time for Kano. Throughout his reign the Katsinawa overran the western districts from Karaye to Sheme. Perhaps it was partly as an effect of this social and economic disorganization and territorial loss that Kano then experienced such prolonged famine. It thus lacked the strength to withstand the unexpected assault from Jukun; and Zaki and his council wisely decided to conserve their forces for the more critical struggle with Katsina over autonomy and territory rather than to risk disaster and heavy losses against the Jukun. Thus at this period the survival of the Kano people and their polity were both at stake. Zaki seems to have risen to the demands of his situation; but perhaps its successive defeats and general distress during the famine may have weakened the factional rivalries which had reduced Kano to this parlous state. Of Muhamman Zaki's eight leading warriors, six bear familiar titles—Madawaki, Makama, Jarmai, Atuman (Dan Atuman or Makama Atuman), Barde and Dawaki. Two others, Butali and Biyan Kasheka, apparently held no titles, unless the latter was the Kasheka or one of his staff.

On his accession Muhamman Nazaki (1618–1623), probably Zaki's son, "sent messengers to make peace with Katsina. Sarkin Katsina refused his terms and invaded Kano ... The battle took place at Karaye in which the Kanawa defeated the Katsinawa."[139] Karaye, a large walled town thirty miles southwest of Kano, figures prominently in this protracted war with Katsina and furnished one of its principal objects. Since Yusa's day (1136–1194), Karaye had been incorporated into the chiefdom of Kano. For centuries it flourished peacefully but because its situation was strategic, its control became a central issue in the Kano-Katsina war. Whoever held Karaye could control nearly one-half of the enemy's territory and also the direct route from Katsina to Kano. All Katsina territory south of the Karaduwa river was exposed to Karaye; and all western Kano, from Dan Zabuwa in the north to Rano due south of the city. For this reason we find the Katsinawa forces concentrating on Karaye rather than Kano; but the tables turned when Nazaki finally established a powerful force at Karaye itself, thus perhaps initiating the practice of *zaman ribadi* or garrisoning frontier towns.

Following his victory at Karaye, Nazaki campaigned against Kalam. During Nazaki's absence, the Wambai Giwa, who may have been a eunuch or slave, and who had been prevented by illness from accompanying the force, set about extending the city area by building a new section of wall in the southeast from the Kofar Kansakali past the Kofar Gadankaya to join Rumfa's wall near the Kofar Na'isa. Perhaps that section of the old wall was thought insecure; or it may have been breached by invading Jukun in the previous reign. Persisting traces indicate at least four successive extensions of the wall in this area but none to its north.

From the Chronicle's account of the Wambai's wall-building efforts, it seems possible that Nazaki had left him in charge of the government and state during his absence on campaign. At Nazaki's request or on his own initiative, the Wambai wished to complete construction of the wall before the chief returned. Only as temporary head of the government could he enjoy the authority to initiate the work or to summon the large corvée it required; but perhaps this corvée was also intended to encourage commoners to volunteer in future. Further, as acting head of state, the Wambai could employ such state stores and resources as the work required. As reported in the Chronicle, it seems that the Wambai used his own personal wealth to finance the construction; but the outlays involved, together with the precise phrasing of the account, suggest that he also drew on state stores for supplies to complete the task.

> He spent an enormous amount of money on this improvement. Every morning he brought a thousand calabashes of food and fifty oxen for the workmen until the work was finished. Every man in Kano went to work. No man surpassed the Wambai in benevolence to Muslims and the poor. The day when the work was to be finished, the Wambai Giwa distributed among the workmen a thousand tobes (robes). He slaughtered three hundred cows at the Kofar Kansakali and gave the malams many presents. When the Sarkin Kano returned from war, the Wambai gave him a hundred riding horses. Each horse had a mail coat.[140]

Only this gift of horses and *sulke* to the chief may the Wambai have provided entirely at his own expense; but he probably acquired the *sulke* from Arab traders at Kano by purchase and/or other means. Some horses may also have been captured from Katsina during Muhamman Zaki's victory at Karaye. The purpose of this large gift by the Wambai to Nazaki on his return is revealed by its composition. Wambai turned over to the chief a considerable store, perhaps the bulk of his own military resources, to demonstrate his loyalty and lack of chiefly ambitions. This was necessary, given his unprecedented performance as *Wakil* or *Mukaddas* (deputy) by which the Wambai had mobilized the entire city folk to construct the wall, and won a large political following by his lavish provisions.

Nazaki

> was very pleased. He said, "What shall I do for this man to make his heart glad?" Men said, "Give him a town." So the Sarki gave him Karaye. The Wambai left Kano and went to Karaye. Every day he fought the Katsinawa and took much spoil from them in war. He became master of a hundred mailed horsemen and a thousand horses. He was sung as the Elephant (Giwa) who reduced his neighbours to servitude. He became so mighty that it was feared that he would revolt. Hence he was turned out of his office in the time of Kutumbi.[141]

The acute political insight that informs the selection and presentation of almost every incident in this Chronicle is eloquently half-hidden in the critical "Hence" that illuminates this sequence.

This Wambai is only known to us by his *lakabi* (praise-name), Giwa (Elephant). His transfer from Kano to Karaye at the ruler's order served to isolate him from his followers in the city, and thus to eliminate his power as a threat to the chief's;

but it also reasserted Kano's control of the western districts by settling a large garrison at Karaye under an energetic leader vested with the requisite discretionary powers of command. In consequence the tide of war turned in Kano's favour so long as the Wambai stayed at Karaye. Many successful raids on southern Katsina were launched from Karaye and much booty was secured to strengthen Kano and the force at Wambai's command. When the latter seemed sufficiently large to threaten the chiefship, Kutumbi, Nazaki's son and successor, found ways of displacing the Wambai Giwa to secure and increase his own power. The more centralized patrimonial chiefship that Kutumbi instituted could not tolerate a rival concentration of power within the state, whether of a slave or of a kinsman eligible for the throne, as this Wambai may well have been. Yet, even in Nazaki's reign, the traditional oligarchy had given way to two power structures, headed respectively by the Wambai and the chief. No evidence indicates that Wambai was disloyal to his chief. All his recorded activities overtly aimed to strengthen the state and the chief. Their covert motive or unintended effect was simultaneously to enhance the Wambai's personal position. It is thus instructive to compare the Wambai's career with that of the Galadima Dawuda, whose military achievements in Burja's reign brought him the pre-eminence which led to Atuma's rapid deposition. In dismissing the Wambai Giwa, Kutumbi sought to forestall similar developments.

The Kutumbawa

Muhammad Alwali I (El Kutumbi)

It is of interest to observe the various attempts by officials or courtiers to build independent bases of power at Kano. Under successive regimes of differing constitution and context, Dagaci, Dawuda, Guli and the Wambai Giwa, by different methods had each obtained sufficient resources and power to challenge the chief's supremacy. To forestall this, Rumfa had tried to institute a combination of chiefship and oligarchy which dispersed power among the oligarchs and assured the autonomy and support of the major rural chiefs, while concentrating state resources and executive authority at the throne. Evidently Kisoke appropriated power from the oligarchic council with the aid of Guli, the Queen Mother Hauwa, and his uterine kinsmen. Following Kisoke, the council had never quite regained its lost authority. Instead, factions of differing base, composition and aim struggled with one another and with the chiefship for dominance, and sometimes removed chiefs, peacefully or by force. This strife so weakened Kano that it proved incapable of adequate self-defence during the reign of Muhamman Zaki. This situation permitted the chief to reassert a limited power of central direction and leadership; but no sooner had this been done than the chiefship faced a rival concentration of power in the hands of its ablest senior official.

Such recurrent developments and tendencies proceeded without any evident polarization of attitude to the regime. They arose, rather, as direct but unanticipated consequences of the initial concentration of dominant power at the centre. Thus such developments generated administrative and political imbalances throughout the structure, whether this structure institutionalized its oligarchy in specific or diffuse forms, as for instance through hereditary or *shigege* office. His situation obliged the patrimonial chief to exercise his control through one or two senior executives whose status and resources removed them from the officialdom they administered, while preserving their dependence on the chief. This arrangement was intrinsically unstable. It generated rivalry among these unconstitutional "viziers" and made the chief correspondingly dependent upon them. With the emergence in this context of one extremely powerful subordinate, the chief's control of the council and state increased in efficiency and scope, but also in vulnerability, which corresponded closely in its locus and intensity with chiefly use of these means to secure predominance. For unless the power of his agent or favourite exceeded by far the resources that could be employed against him by others, it could not securely enhance the chief's directive capacities; yet to the extent that this unofficial vizier enjoyed unchallenged dominance, he correspondingly became a threat to the position of the chief. In these conditions, the constitution was only maintained in form. By concentrating dominant power in his vizier or himself, the chief had subverted the constitution and facilitated usurpation. He could not therefore validly invoke constitutional norms against his vizier, since in so doing he invoked them effectively against himself. Either the dominant ruler should follow Rumfa's example and promote an oligarchic dispersal of power to assure his supremacy; or if he did not remove the rivals he himself had unintentionally created, he imperilled the throne and the succession.

Patrimonialism, whether oligarchic or centralist in its base, tended to reproduce this recurrent pattern at Kano; and to avoid usurpation or ineffectiveness, chiefs had to prove their capacity to aggrandize and defend their autonomy by appropriate and vigilant action. Sultanism was only one of several outcomes latent in structures of this sort, the relative likelihood of other alternatives being directly linked with the composition and context of the antecedent situation. Another common feature of these mixed regimes that has hitherto attracted little theoretical attention is their propensity to persist over long periods by a series of reversible internal transformations, each of which generates new distributions of power and activates opposing tendencies. At Kano, successive resolutions of such recurrent but formally varied problems enriched, modified and stabilized the structure, thereby preserving with it the forces that generated its continuous internal change.

Muhamman Nazaki's son, Muhammadu Alwali 1, also called El Kutumbi, is generally regarded as the founder of the dynasty that bears his name and retained power until 1807 at the expense of other branches of the Rumfawa, often by violent struggles. Like Rumfa and Bagauda, Kutumbi initiated a new era in the political history of Kano; and perhaps it is on these grounds rather than descent that Kutumbi rather than his father is regarded as the founder of the new dynasty. While the preceding Rumfawa regime had been characterized by unstable dispersals of power between the chief, the dynasty, affiliated lineages that held hereditary offices, the chief's uterine kinsmen, the state council, the city clerics, palace slaves and other officials, the two distinctive characteristics of the Kutumbawa regimes that persisted until Alwali's day, even after Babba Zaki's "reforms," were the predominance of the patrimonial chief and of his official or unofficial "vizier." Under the Kutumbawa, patrimonial interests and tendencies threatened to dominate the government. Under the Rumfawa, dispersed oligarchic power had prevailed, and the throne was subject to sudden upheavals. In neither case did one alternative exclude or suppress the other. Rather each presumed the other, since the oligarchs needed the chief for political reasons no less clearly than the chief needed the oligarchs for administrative ends. Nonetheless, in character and form the two systems differ significantly. The Kutumbawa chiefs enjoyed a predominance in the state which their Rumfawa predecessors had lacked since Kisoke's day. They tended also to rule through selected individuals, not all of whom held office, nor necessarily those offices that normally carried wide executive powers or high status. Occasional chiefs preferred to dominate the state directly and acted as their own viziers. In propitious circumstances the state council might periodically reassert its control, only to lose this once more as the next chief concentrated resources and power in the hands of some private or official favourite. Finally, when this system of personal rule had so entrenched itself that officials accepted the supremacy of the patrimonial chief, the regime increased its pressure on the subordinate public.

Having removed the Wambai Giwa from office, Kutumbi either appropriated or dispersed his resources and power. He preferred to rule through men of his own choice, first the Kalina Atuman, who was either the holder of that title or a member of the holding lineage; and then, after Atuman's death, through the Dawaki Koshi. Of Kalina Atuman it is related that "no one would believe the extent of his power except one who saw it. He ruled over Kano town and country until his power equalled that of the Sarki, while the Sarki was like his vizier. This Kalina Atuman was in power for twelve years, then he died. After his death one of his men, Dawaki Koshi, came to the front. He, too, became so powerful that he seemed likely to revolt."[142] Dawaki Koshi was the "son" of the Turakin Kuka Allandaya, who then held the senior eunuch office, but was not himself a eunuch. The title Dawaki is common in Kano for village chiefs and minor officials with prominent military roles. As a client of Atuman's and the Turakin Kuka's "son," Koshi was well placed to serve as Kutumbi's chief adviser and agent after Atuman's death.However, the Chronicle relates that Koshi "seemed likely to revolt" against Kutumbi. Perhaps because the chief was then concerned to reduce his power, Koshi "went to a place called Bakinkare for several days,"[143] thereby deserting the capital and implicitly signalling his rebellion against the chief. It being forbidden for senior officials and courtiers to quit the city without the chief's consent, their public withdrawal from the city could be regarded as a formal declaration of intent to revolt. From Bakinkare, Koshi went east to Yankusa for three days and thence via Rimin Koshi to Gunduwawa close to the city. There Koshi received declarations of allegiance from a substantial number of city folk who came out to join him. "All the chief men of the town flocked to his standard. He had been there nine days when the Sarki induced him to come back with fine words, then he returned to Kano."[144] The Chronicle says nothing about subsequent developments. In similar cases, as we shall see, after such reconciliations the official who had threatened rebellion normally died quickly, sometimes in prison, sometimes at his home through magic (*sammu*), or perhaps by poison. Evidently Kutumbi neither dismissed the Dawaki nor had any subsequent difficulty or relations with him. Like other careerists, the Dawaki Koshi lacked an independent institutional base for personal power; and with his disappearance, his following dispersed.

It is possible that Koshi's withdrawal and evident "preparations for revolt" may have been incited by Kutumbi's removal of the city ward at the Kabaga gate from the Dawaki's "father," Turakin Kuka Allandaya. The Chronicle links these two incidents in a curious way, and stresses Allandaya's anger when the ward was transferred. Evidently this was considered sufficiently important to stimulate a new praise-song (*kirari*) composed about the Turakin Kuka. "No man of that time in Kano had accumulated such vast wealth and so many eunuchs and ornaments."[145] Whether Koshi withdrew to protest against Kutumbi's treatment of his father, the Turakin Kuka, we cannot say. Evidently Kutumbi was concerned to reduce Allandaya's authority and resources.

Kutumbi had difficulty with another trusted agent, the Sarkin Dawaki Magari who was given command of a force to raid the Bauchi tribesmen for slaves. Returning, Magari "built a town at Ganjuwa and settled there. He sent to Kano two thousand slaves. Kutumbi was very angry about this. The next year he mounted his horse and went off to war there (to attack Ganjuwa). The people paid him *jizia* (tribute). Then he returned to Kano, leaving there five hundred slaves. The place was called Ibdabu (*Indabo*) since the people were all slaves of the Sarki."[146]

Ganjuwa lay about fifteen miles southeast of Fagam, in what later became Bauchi Province. Evidently the Sarkin Dawaki Magari had decided to establish there a small independent chiefship beyond the limits of Kano territory with the force at his disposal. Kutumbi rightly regarded this as a serious breach of allegiance and obligation. As commander in charge of a raiding force, Magari should have returned to Kano with his army and captives. His conduct was in every way delinquent and Kutumbi punished him by leading the attack himself to levy tribute, and by removing a large number of Magari's slaves. The incident is probably included in the Chronicle as a unique instance of this kind of treason and the appropriate response.

Yet another powerful subject during Kutumbi's reign was his son Bako, of whom the Chronicle relates that "no prince could compare with him. In everything, in doing good or doing ill, in courage, anger and generosity he was like a Sarki even while he was only a prince. He had six hundred horses and ninety mailed horsemen. He went to Kurmin Dan Ranko (in Katsina) to war and took much spoil. When he returned to Kano he was given the title of Jarmai for this exploit." Following this, on East's version, prayers were made for the Jarmai Bako's death by those who feared trouble from him when Kutumbi was gone. Evidently these prayers were effective, and Bako died shortly after, presumably by natural means.[147]

Clearly Kutumbi, however powerful, had various difficulties with his leading ministers and generals. Their successive rise and fall neatly expresses the changing character of his regime. Kutumbi evidently preferred to rule through chosen ministers whom he first invested with unusual powers, and later had to reduce in order to preserve his supremacy. The successive rise and fall of royal ministers thus raises certain questions about the stability of Kutumbi's regime. Its two essential elements were a stable supreme centre, the chiefship, and a series of ministers whose personal power lacked independent institutional bases and was accordingly labile, restless and readily dispersed. On various occasions the chief's position may have seemed insecure; yet Kutumbi steadily advanced his dominance by military and political means.

Having punished the Sarkin Dawaki for his desertion at Ganjuwa, Kutumbi attacked Katsina, and isolated its capital for nine months but failed to take it. Next year he marched southeast past Fagam and Ganjuwa against Gombe on the Gongola, sacking it and taking valuable booty. At Kano, he first levied *jangali* in its legal form as cattle tithe on the Fulani clans settled in the country, the Ba'awa, Daneji, Jafunawa, "and others too numerous to mention." To supervise the herds thus gathered, he appointed his slave Ibo (Abu) as the first Sarkin Shanu. Another slave, Mandawari was appointed either as Sarkin Yara or as Sarkin Samari in charge of the young male slaves (*samari*) at the palace.[148] Another, Gunki (Gumki), was made Sarkin Dogarai in charge of the slave police. A fourth, Buwaiyi, was appointed Shamaki, probably the first to hold this title recorded at Kano. Kutumbi also dismissed the Sarkin Sirdi, and appointed another slave to supervise the state stores of horse gear (*sirdi* = saddle).

He sought also to glorify the chiefship by public display. "Whenever Kutumbi went to war or to Sallah, he was followed by a hundred spare horses. Forty drums were in front of him and twenty-five trumpets and fifty kettledrums. ... he had gold and silver ornaments."[149] He built royal compounds and estates at Gunduwawa and Tukurawa near the city for use as military marshalling grounds, mobilizing his levies at Tukurawa before setting out on campaign and demobilizing them at Gunduwawa on his return.[150] Among his leading free warriors were the Madawaki Kimbarni, the Makama, the Dan Maje, the Jarmai, Garaje, the Barde, the Dan Goriba, Dan Atuman, Dan Makwayau, the Dawaki Sunkuce, Kadarko and Dan Kamface, whose titles apparently lapsed before Alwali's succession. Kutumbi created the title of Barde Kererriya which, in the late eighteenth century, was given either to the ruler's cognates, to throne princes, or to favourite noblemen. We do not know on whom Kutumbi conferred the office, or its resources and duties in his reign. In creating this title Kutumbi may have sought to demonstrate his concern for the free officialdom as well as the palace slaves, whose organization he had developed greatly by the various appointments listed above. However, in his closing years, it seems that Kutumbi based his dominance upon an efficient organization of palace slaves as a police and military corps under his own personal direction. This combination of means assured his supremacy.

In 1648 Kutumbi marched once more against Katsina, and camped close by its western wall, perhaps beside the Yandaka Gate. The Katsinawa came out at night and attacked before daybreak, surprising Kutumbi's men and driving them in flight. It is uncertain whether Kutumbi died at Katsina or managed first to reach Kano. This defeat ended the commanding military position that Kano had enjoyed since the Wambai Giwa first went to Karaye; and it thus allowed an early end to this long and devastating war. Kutumbi was the last chief of Kano to die in battle before Alwali fell at Burumburum.

Instability at the Throne

Kutumbi's son Alhaji, who succeeded, was deposed in less than nine months, by whom, how, or for what reason we are not told. Alhaji was sent to reside in a small village and his son Shekarau became chief. Shekarau reigned for about twenty months (1649–1651); and it was during this period that the Shehu Atuman, the Limamin Yandoya, and Malam Bawa managed to negotiate a peace between Katsina and Kano. The Shehu Atuman then sacralized the peace by calling down the curse of Allah on whoever broke it. In Shekarau's reign also, the Dan Tama and the Sarkin (San) Getso quit the city to reside in Godiya and Getso respectively. We are not told how Shekarau's reign ended. He may have died in office or been dismissed. His predecessor and his successor, Kukuna, who is said to be another son of Alhaji, were both dismissed. So was Soyaki, Kukuna's successor, and Kukuna himself eight years after his restoration.

Between 1648 and 1653, excluding Kutumbi, Kano had four rulers, one of whom, Kukuna, was restored after dismissal. It was nearly two hundred years since Kano had had three rulers in one year, Dakauta, Atuma and Yakubu, on Abdullahi Burja's death in 1452. Again in 1565 on Kisoke's death Kano had three chiefs in a year, Yakufu, Dawuda and Abubakar Kado. In both periods these clusters of brief reigns were preceded by evident imbalances and instabilities in the distribution of political power. For example, in Burja's closing years, the Galadima Dawuda was probably more powerful than the chief; and it was at his will that Atuma was replaced by Yakubu. Likewise, in Kisoke's later years, his uterine kinsman Guli directed the government though holding no office; and it was Guli's pressure that led to Yakufu's dismissal and the brief civil war that followed. It is clear from our account of Kutumbi's reign that the shifting distribution of power he had created and manipulated with such skill presupposed his presence, and that, being otherwise unstable, the regime was thrown into confusion at his death. Unusually powerful chiefs like Kutumbi or officials and courtiers, such as the Galadima Dawuda or Guli, in different ways dislocated the basic elements of this political structure, and upset the balances required for its continued operation. No reason is given for Alhaji's replacement by Shekarau; but following Shekarau's end, Kukuna, who succeeded, was dismissed after a year by the Madawaki Kuma who replaced him by Soyaki, his (the Madawaki's) sister's son by Shekarau, Kukuna's brother. In Kutumbi's later years the Madawaki Kimbarmi had obtained considerable influence through his military leadership. Madawaki Kuma seems to have succeeded to Kimbarmi's position of strength; and in the absence of such powerful figures as Kutumbi, he was able to dismiss the ruler and appoint his sister's son. Kukuna fled to Zazzau.

Other senior officials, notably the councillor Galadima Wari, the Dan Iya Babba, Makama Mukhtari and the Sarkin Dawaki Gogori, were caught unprepared by the Madawaki's coup. Either he had not consulted them and obtained their support or, if he had done so, within three months of Soyaki's succession these councillors had changed their position. Conspiring in secret, they sent messages instructing Kukuna to return from Zazzau to Gaya, where the local chief had undertaken to assist them. On Kukuna's arrival at Gaya, the Galadima, the Dan Iya, the Makama and the Sarkin Dawaki then withdrew from the city towards Gaya, leaving the Madawaki Kuma, Soyaki and their supporters at the capital. After taking counsel with his followers, the Madawaki gave battle at Hotoro, but was defeated, and Kukuna entered the town, driving Soyaki from the palace. This was the second succession war in Kano's history, the first being that between the Galadima Sarkatunya and Guli after Yakufu's deposition by Guli in 1565. On both occasions, fortunately, the struggle, though sharp, was brief. As we shall see, this was not always the case.

Kukuna treated Soyaki courteously, sending him to Dakurawa to farm in peace. After sixty days in the palace he arrested the Madawaki Kuma who had previously deposed him, and, summoning the town maidens, "put the Madawaki on a donkey and handed it over to the maidens to drive around town. They did as he commanded. The Madawaki died of chagrin."[151] Given the context and culture, such public humiliation could destoy an individual's ego, his sanity, or his will to live. This incident provides a nice demonstration of the degree to which individual personality and psychic health may be dependent on social personality and public esteem. Following this, Kukuna dismissed Soyaki's mother, the Madawaki's sister Fatsumatu from the Maidaki's compound and office, and reinstated his mother, Goro.

In 1653, within two years of this turmoil, the Jukun under their chief "Adashu" launched their second attack on Kano. Incapable of resisting, Kukuna fled northeast to Yan-magada and after seven days moved to Abewa in Auyo, where he remained for "forty" days until the Jukun withdrew. Returning, he found that they had broken through the Kofar Kawaye into the city, and immediately repaired it, an event the praise-singers celebrated sardonically. Once again the Jukun had struck, and Kano, riven by internal strife, could mobilize no effective resistance. Undoubtedly the Jukun were greatly dreaded at Kano; but it also seems that the chiefs did not trust the strength of their town defenses, perhaps fearing betrayal by enemies at court. Like Muhamman Zaki, Kukuna preferred flight to open defiance. At least in this way he retained his independence and chiefdom, recovering them immediately the Jukun withdrew when he returned to Kano.

Like Zaki before him in a similar context, anxious to ward off further Jukun invasions and chiefly flights, Kukuna appealed to the Muslim clerics to secure "a charm which will prevent any Sarki from being again driven out of Kano." The Limam Yandoya, perhaps the senior city priest, undertook to do this in return for "much silver and gold." The Limam gave him what he gave him, "instructing Kukuna to bury one charm in the antechamber of the Turakin Manya (San Turaki), another in that of the Turakin Kuka, and a third in the chief's bedchamber (*turaka*), each with a fire permanently burning above it. The Limam "assured the Sarki that if his instructions were carried out, no Sarki would ever again be deposed. Kukuna did so and ruled eight years and seven months ... then he was deposed."[152] This incident illustrates the syncretisms of pagan and Islamic practice which had grown up at Kano through the secularization and corruption of Islam in the service of state and chiefs. The venality of the clerical class, official or other, and the gullibility of the chief, are thus recorded without comment. The unreliability of such ritual devices, despite the Limam's promise, is evident from Kukuna's deposition. Otherwise, the Chronicle says nothing about the situation in which Kukuna was deposed. Neither does it indicate who deposed him. However, it seems likely that he was removed by those state councillors who had jointly reinstated him, perhaps with support from the clerical party, with or without the Limam Yandoya, because he had proved so clearly inadequate to rule.

On his return to Kano from Auyo in 1653, Kukuna summoned "all the Maguzawa to the city to salute him. They remained twenty-one days and played a game in which they beat each other's heads with iron. The Sarki gave them many gifts and ... said ... 'Next year come again and ... if you do so, ... God willing, no Sarkin Kano will be driven out again.'"[153] This is probably the historic origin of the Rawan Toji mentioned by Malam Adamu as one of the chief pagan ceremonies of the Kano chiefship in Alwali's day. It was only after he had initiated this annual Maguzawa ceremony that Kukuna turned to the Limam Yandoya for Islamic charms against any future deposition or expulsion of Kano chiefs. Thus Kukuna sought security in pagan and Muslim rites alike. His Islam was no stronger than his political capacity. This conduct was equally craven for a chief and a Muslim and marks the nadir of Kano's political experience. It is easy to understand how Kukuna's councillors and officials, having lost their respect and patience, finally removed him from office; but, while identifying Kukuna as the author of these syncretisms, if the Chronicle points a moral in this case, it is clearly that ritual investments are no substitute for secular administrative and political skills in such governments as Kano's.

Bawa (1660–1670), who succeeded Kukuna, is said to have been Kukuna's son.[154] He was more fortunate but no more effective than his predecessor; but he proved a better Muslim, who devoted his energies and time to the Koran and other Islamic books, built compounds within the palace for his close religious associates, and evidently left the state administration in the hands of his officials and councillors, none of whom are named in the text. The only public actions attributed to Bawa during his ten years as chief are the rebuilding of the Goron Fagaci originally constructed by Abubakar Kado, the building of Fagacin Kishi for study and discussion with his clerical friends, and the appointment of a visiting student with a "wonderfully captivating voice" to the title of Dan Lawan or perhaps Sarkin Lawan to serve as muezzin (*ladan*).[155] Evidently during Bawa's reign, the council ruled, and though Bawa received the credit for a period of good and just government, his senior officials really held the power.

Kano now enjoyed a spell of peace during which the caravan traffic, the city population and the local cloth industry grew together. The long Katsina war had turned at least in part on this Saharan traffic. From Damagaram due north there were two southern routes, one via Gezawa to Katsina, the other through Tumfashi direct to Kano. There may well have been some mutual undercutting and interference with one another's merchants by Katsina and Kano competing to secure the greater part of this Saharan trade. But there may also have been other critical factors. Throughout the sixteenth and seventeenth centuries Katsina seems to have retained its formal vassalage to Bornu, and to have rendered allegiance and tribute. For Katsina this relation offered assurances of powerful military support whenever necessary against Kebbi, which then still held Zamfara and Gobir subordinate. The chiefs of Katsina accordingly relied on their Bornu vassalage to keep Kebbi at bay. However, since Kisoke's day, Kano, lying east of Katsina and west of Bornu, had repudiated its allegiance to Bornu. It is thus possible that Katsina's initial attacks on Kano were launched under pressure from Bornu, following the unsuccessful Kanuri attempt to capture Kano. However, after the peace of 1650 with Katsina, and the council's appropriation of dominance, Kano lost its aggressive potential. As a collegial body, the council had neither the interest, capacity nor resources to pursue an aggressive foreign policy that risked or entailed war. Perhaps with sufficient time, the state council might have developed such tendencies. Meanwhile they were primarily concerned to consolidate their recently recovered powers and to reduce those of the throne. Their focus being almost exclusively on internal affairs, they sought to avoid external crises. In consequence, with such administration Kano enjoyed a much needed breathing spell during which the western districts were resettled by immigrants who followed the examples of Dan Tama and San Getso. Population, agriculture, trade and craft production gradually recovered, and there was probably also an influx of pastoralists to Kano, where they could graze their herds in peace.

Stabilization and the Trend Toward Sultanism

Dadi, who followed Bawa, is said to be his son. He ruled between 1670 and 1703. "He wished to enlarge the city of Kano, but Shehu Mohamma prevented him."[156] The Shehu Mohamma, who is otherwise unidentified, may have been one of Bawa's Muslim teachers, or perhaps a leading local cleric of his day. Dadi's desire to expand the city by yet another extension of its walls suggests simultaneous growth in the city population and inhabited area and in the state revenues and resources requisite for such protracted large-scale public corvée. It further indicates Dadi's interest in reasserting the chiefship's directive capacity. He may even have contemplated increasing his popular support by following the Wambai Giwa's distributions of largesse during and after the work. However, as the chief now lacked autocratic power, he was overruled, and it is possible that the Shehu Mohamma advised against the extension with support from the council.

Shortly after this, perhaps in 1671 or 1672, the Jukun chief led his army against Kano. Dadi "wished to go and fight him outside, but the chiefs of Kano demurred and he remained in his house."[157] This incident again illustrates the central position of the council in regulating policy at this period. "The Kworarofai (Jukun) entered Kano by the Kofan Gadon Kaia, slaughtered the men of Kano and reached Bakin Ruwa,"[158] the western end of Jakara pond. Having entered the uninhabited southeastern part of the city, they now drove eastwards to cut the inhabited area in half at the Jakara pond and city market. "The Galadima Kofakani said to the Sarkin Kano, who was in the Fagacin Kishi with his Jarumai (warriors), "Establish 'Cibiri' at Toji and 'Bundu' at Rimin Bundu,'" a large silk cotton tree reserved for the *bundu* fetish, the nature and details of which we cannot determine. Evidently, despite centuries of Islamization and the use of Islamic charms of various sorts such as *dirki* and the charm Kukuna obtained from the Limam Yandoya, the chiefs still kept basic elements of Cibiri and Bundu, the old pagan fetishes, at or near the palace. "Galadima said to the Sarki, 'Rise up! The Kworarofai have destroyed the best part of your town and have killed many men! They have penetrated to the Kurmi (the market area at Jakara) and will attack the palace.' The Sarki mounted his horse and went out."[159]

There was a sharp struggle around the *Cibiri* and *Bundu* fetishes, which the chief planted as the Galadima directed. The Chronicle mentions Dadi's assault on the Jukun with three to four hundred warriors. "The Sarkin Kano came to the *Cibiri* and took it. On his right hand he had a hundred warriors, in front of him ninety-nine chiefs, all of them malams, and on his left hand a hundred warriors. They were all slaughtered by the Kwararofai; only a few were left alive. Sarkin Kano fled to Daura. The Kworarofai followed him to Jeili (Jalli, about thirteen miles northeast of Kano) and then returned."[160] The list of Kano officials killed in this battle includes several whose titles are not otherwise mentioned in the Chronicle—the Dan Janbori, Dan Bara, Sarkin Busa, Sarkin Dara, Dan Tanadi, Bundu (perhaps the slave who took care of the *Bundu*), Sarkin Zabarau (a village chief), Magajin Bugaji, Sarkin Maru, Dan Garadu, Dan Ragamar Giwa, Magaji Butaci, Dan Kuwamma, Magajin Shegi, Dan Gawaji, Magajin Gantaroro, Dan Dagazau, Magajin Tuntu, Sarkin Makuri, Dan Gauwaji, Magajin Garuji, Dan Tankarau, Dan Kargaje, Magaji Karfasa, Dan Kutuntu, Dan Toro, Dan Zaki, Dan Bambauri, and others unnamed to a total of ninety-seven.[161]

Most offices entitled Sarki or Magaji in this list probably identify village chiefs and/or ward heads. Titles prefixed by Dan (son of), may equally well denote courtiers (*fadawa*), and minor fiefholders, court attendants such as musicians, messengers, entertainers and the like, titled slaves or village chiefs. Notably, none of the senior chiefs such as the Dan Iya, Galadima, Madawaki or Makama died in this battle. They apparently withdrew with Dadi to Daura and safety.

This was the third time the Jukun had broken into Kano city, but the first occasion on which the chief had dared to resist them. From the Chronicle's account of the battle and list of lost personnel, it seems that Dadi opposed the Jukun with his palace staff, courtiers and officials only. The city folk probably took little active part in this engagement. Probably unarmed or fleeing, they were evidently caught by surprise. Dadi seems to have marshalled his palace guards, slave police and warriors to throw against the Jukun at the marsh. After a brief initial success, when the chief fled the small force was overwhelmed and slaughtered.

This was the last assault on Kano by the Jukun. They had also attacked and ravaged Zaria and southern Katsina; and during the sixteenth and seventeenth centuries, they frequently clashed in battle with Bornu; but c. 1680 their military power was finally broken when the sultan of Bornu, Mai Ali Umarmi (Ali Ta'ir), besieged at Gasrgamo, his capital, by the Jukun, defeated them heavily in a battle celebrated by the Katsina poet Dan Marina, which identifies the Jukun as the major current threat to the predominence of Muslim societies in this zone of the central Sudan.[162]

Dadi returned to Kano after the Jukun withdrew. Their defeat at Gasrgamo seven or eight years later relieved Kano of further danger from that quarter; but these successive Jukun occupations and the flight of the Kano chiefs shook the foundation of the Hausa polity. We have seen that almost from its earliest days this chiefship was secular in its basis, character and modes of expression. Islamization did not alter this. Although the chief now figured as political head of the "Muslim community," religious leadership of that community remained with the clerics; and to sacralize and strengthen the chiefship, rulers sought charms and fetishes of various kinds, pagan or Muslim, as properties of office. The futility of these various rituals had been shown by the successive Jukun invasions; and these pagan triumphs over Muslim Kano also revealed the military weakness of its chief. In this context, "the Sarkin Gaya revolted. His name was Farin Dutse, the father of Mariyama." For three years he neither rendered the Sarkin Kano tribute nor tax, "but then the Sarkin Kano enticed him to an interview, he killed him, some say with a razor, some at *'baura'*" (a pagan physical contest between men armed with sharp iron armlets.)[163] Mariyama, Sarkin Gaya's daughter, was Dadi's wife and the mother of Mahomman Sharefa, Dadi's heir. Dadi had therefore disposed of his father-in-law.

The Sarkin Gaya ruled a chiefdom which, formerly independent, was older than Kano, and may well have dominated this territory had his predecessors shown the aggressiveness that Bagauda's successors had cultivated, beset by the defiant pagans immediately around them. In any event, Gaya had probably supported the Rumfawa who still maintained close ties with the chiefdom. Further, the Sarkin Gaya had not so long ago played a leading part in defeating the Madawaki Kuma and restoring Kukuna at Kano. Finally, Gaya was a unit of sufficient size (c. 600 square miles), population, internal autonomy and strength to challenge Kano and reassert its independence. Evidently Dadi did not care to attack it for fear that defeat might spark revolts in other substates of comparable size, such as Rano, Dutse, and perhaps Karaye. Instead he relied on diplomacy, reinforced by his affinal relation with the rebel chief. Having thus tricked Farin Dutse and put him out of the way, Dadi instructed his commander of horse, the Sarkin Dawaki Duba (Debba), to proceed to Aujara and settle there as its chief. "The Sarki said to him, 'I am making you Sarkin Aujara because I am afraid of Miga, Dutse and Gaya revolting.'"[164]

In effect the three Jukun invasions had loosened the chiefdom's fabric. Accordingly, following Gaya's revolt, Dadi took various steps to prevent the polity falling apart by secessionist movements of its major rural components. Aujara stood about 20 miles southeast of Miga and north of Dutse, some ten miles west of Jahun, then a stockaded town, and about 12 miles south of Majia, all relatively strong local chiefdoms which had escaped the Jukun devastations. Of these, Dutse, almost as large and populous as Gaya, was the most formidable and likeliest to attempt secession. As a *tirika*, the Sarkin Dawaki Duba had sufficient discretionary power to order military action as the situation seemed to require, without having to await instructions from Kano. From Aujara, he could threaten both Dutse and Gaya with attacks in the rear if they chose to rebel against Kano. His garrison (*ribadi*) was also well placed to guard the northern route to Kano from Auyo, Machena, Nguru and Gasrgamu. Thus, this assignment neatly integrated political and strategic considerations.

However urgent the Rumfawa appeal, the Sarkin Gaya had clearly been encouraged to revolt by recent evidence of Kano's military weakness. On many occasions his predecessors may have been equally displeased with the government of Kano and with their situation; but they had not dared to challenge the central authority for fear of military sanctions. Kutumbi's treatment of Ganjuwa was not forgotten; but in the reaction that followed Kutumbi's reign, the state was threatened with dissolution by extreme dispersals of power at the centre, following the resumption of oligarchic control. This situation may account for the large number of otherwise unfamiliar titles held by the men who fell fighting with Dadi against the Jukun within the city. Probably many of these titles were recent creations, and lapsed permanently once central concentration of power had been firmly re-established. The leading oligarchs could not reserve entirely to themselves the power, resources and authority they had appropriated from the chief; and they may have distributed many of these assets among units whose resources and jurisdiction were so small that central direction and mobilization became difficult. As the text indicates, these minor officials were classified as expendable by chief and councillors alike. These were the men who perished fighting the Jukun within the city; and it is possible that no successors were appointed to several of these offices on Dadi's return. Even so, Dadi still lacked sufficient strength to assure the defeat of Gaya; and its three years of independence before Farin Dutse was beguiled to his death could hardly have escaped the notice of Gaya's peers at Dutse and at Rano. The means by which Dadi suppressed the Gaya revolt also proclaimed his weakness and may have led others to contemplate similar action. The moral was not overlooked by Gaya's peers.

Like Kukuna after the previous Jukun assault of 1653, Dadi appealed to pagan fetishes for security against the Jukun in the heat of battle. This was done at the direction of his Galadima Kofakani. Perhaps the appearance of *Cibiri* on the battlefield inspired Dadi's men and some city Hausa to fight with greater determination. "The Sarkin Kworarofa told his people to take away the *cibiri*. The Kworarafai tried to charge, but they failed to seize it."[165] However, when Dadi personally removed the *Cibiri*, for reasons unknown, the Hausa resistance was broken. Recurrently we encounter these atavistic appeals to paganism by Kano chiefs in times of stress, especially in times of military danger. Islam had evidently failed to displace many heathen orientations which, being profound, persisted beneath the Muslim veneer and procedures to which the rulers and people were alike committed. But if Islam could not guarrantee security, neither could *Cibiri* nor other pagan cults.

Listed among the captains who "fought under Dadi" are three men who held the title of Dan Iya, four others who held the title of Sarkin Jarmai, the Sarkin Dawaki Sodi, the Barde, the Galadima Kofakani and the Limamin Barde. Evidently throughout Dadi's long reign the titles of Dan Iya and Sarkin Jarmai were reserved for military leaders. So was that of the Sarkin Dawaki, Duba, who was sent to rule Aujara, being selected for military reasons.[166]

Muhammadu Sharefa, Dadi's son by Mariyama, the daughter of Sarkin Gaya Farin Dutse, succeeded in 1703 and ruled until 1731. In his time, the "men of Gaya became very influential in Kano."[167] Perhaps by this appointment the Kutumbawa tried to compensate Gaya for Farin Dutse's death and to win over its chiefs from their Rumfawa rivals. For sentimental and political reasons, Sharefa sought to repair the damage Dadi had done to Kano's relations with Gaya; and by relying on men from Gaya as his advisers and agents, he sought to free himself of dependence on the Kano oligarchy. His mother, the Maidaki Mariyama, a Gaya princess, almost certainly encouraged and may have initiated this pattern. "She was a great personage, there was no woman like her in the seven Hausa states."[168] With such provincial agents, Sharefa gradually established his predominance in Kano.

For reasons that are not explicit, Sharefa sent the Wambai with a force against Kiru, a considerable town twenty-five miles southwest of Kano near Karaye. Presumably Kiru had revolted. The Wambai took Kiru and sacked it. "News came to Sharefa that the Wambai had sacked Kiru, that there was nothing in the town but ashes. Sharefa said nothing, but when the Wambai Duba returned to Kano, (he) asked him what he meant by such work. Wambai said, 'I like Kano,' speaking in riddles."[169] Evidently Kiru had followed Gaya's example, and received harsher treatment. Perhaps the Wambai Duba was the Sarkin Dawaki whom Dadi had sent to Kujara after Farin Dutse's revolt. Malam Adamu says that Sharefa faced more rebellions during his reign than any other ruler during the eighteenth century. Between Tsamiya's day and Dadi's, there had been two civil wars for the throne but no strictly local rebellions. Perhaps the Wambai sacked Kiru ruthlessly to discourage other rebels. Sharefa evidently made no attempt to punish him. The sack of Kiru demonstrated the changed relation between the chiefship and the people. During the Jukun invasions, the people had apparently deserted the chief. Under Sharefa, rebellions were harshly suppressed, and the chief's demands on the people increased sharply.

Around 1700, in alliance with the Tuareg of Azben under their sultan Nakaba, the Gobirawa under Mohammed Dan Ciroma, and the Sarkin Zamfara, Yakuba Dan Baba, finally broke the power of Kebbi and forced it onto the defensive, thus freeing Zamfara, Gobir and adjacent areas from their long Kebbi domination.[170] Yakuba followed this victory by pursuing military expansion at the expense of his neighbours. Shortly after Sharefa came to the throne, Yakuba brought the Zamfara army against Kano. "A battle was fought at Yergana (Yargaya) ... the men of Kano fled and deserted the Sarki";[171] but whether by treacherous design or following defeat remains unclear. Sharefa was left with the Barde Karreriya, two slaves, and the eunuchs Kasheka and Turakin Manya. With some difficulty they found their way back to Kano and Sharefa re-entered his palace, but for some time, "no one was allowed to see him, so great was his wrath."[172] Evidently the chief suspected treachery. He rewarded those who had stuck by him at Yergana with titles and honour. The Kasheka Bugau was later promoted to the senior eunuch office of Turakin Kuka; it is said that he first sent to Yauri for the reed instrument known as the *algaita*. On receiving it, he presented it to Sharefa's mother, the Maidaki Mariyama.

Following his defeat at Yergana, Sharefa "sent out Sarkin Gaya Janhazo and told him to put a wall around Gaya. Walls were built too at Takai, Tsakuwa, Gano, Dawaki, and many other towns."[173] Evidently, after eliminating the rebel Farin Dutse, Dadi and Sharefa had kept succeeding Gaya chiefs at Kano, away from their political and military base. Sharefa was Janhazo's uterine kinsman, and perhaps his cross-cousin. Thus in authorizing him to rebuild or strengthen the Gaya town wall, he publicly declared his confidence in Gaya's support. This program of fortification was also evidently intended to strengthen Kano's defenses in expectation of further raids from Zamfara, but these did not mature. After Yakuba's death, the Zamfara state lost its aggressiveness.

Sharefa is specially remembered for certain innovations that occurred during his reign. One of these, the introduction of cowries to Kano, has already been discussed. There is no other evidence that Sharefa was directly responsible for this development. However, he apparently "introduced seven practices in Kano, all of which were robbery"; ... he invented many other methods of extortion."[174] Local traditions assert that before Sharefa, the Kutumbawa chiefs had ruled "justly," that is, without resorting to oppressive levies; but this may simply reflect the prevailing oligarchic control. Sharefa was the first of Kutumbi's successors to recover a clear political dominance; and with him the chieftaincy began to exert increasing pressure on the people, perhaps as a response to the changing currency situation, but also as an effect of its changing conditions and context.

The seven extortionate or unjust innovations attributed to Sharefa include *karo*, which may either denote an annual tax or the occasional forced levies such as *hakimai* and *dagatai* collected for *kudin wankan takobi* on their appointments; *matar fada*, which may either indicate the use of free women as female agents and messengers (*jekadu*) or some mode of palace prostitution; *karuwa*, which may be palace prostitution as a means of attaching young men as "bully-boys" to the chief; taxes on the first marriage of all maidens (*murgun buduruwa*), discussed above; monthly taxes levied on the Kurmi market; *'yan dawaki* (horse boys), whose role remains undetermined, and *rantsuwa*, probably the use of pagan fetishes (*gwunki*) for administration of oaths (*rantsuwa*) in the chief's court, another regression from Islam to paganism which Malam Adamu reports as current under Sharefa's successors.[175] Sharefa made his village heads directly responsible for collection of the marriage fees and other levies he introduced. Further, *dagatai* and their immediate superiors, the *hakimai* who lived at the capital, were empowered to collect similar levies on their appointment. Thus Sharefa compensated his territorial officials for the power he had appropriated from them by increasing their revenues along with his own, at the expense of the common people. Further, if *karo* was collected in cowries, which were then still scarce, especially in rural areas, this would increase the people's hardship and oblige them to render their dues in goods by the principle of substitution (*rangwame*), to the advantage of the tax collector. Notably, Sharefa's innovations fell into three major classes: those that increased state revenues by new forms of taxation; those that increased the means and power of the chief by exploiting palace women and 'yan dawaki; and, finally, the use of an explicitly pagan form of oaths. These innovations persisted under Sharefa's successors.

In Sharefa's day, the leading warriors and chiefs at Kano included the Fulani chiefs of Bebeji and Sankara, the Sarkin Fulani Dan Iya whose residence is unknown, the Sarkin Damargu, the Barde, Madawaki Dan Maje, Sarkin Bugai and the Dawakin Gawo, perhaps the successor to the old Madawakin Gawo whose abbreviated title of Dawaki now clearly identifies him as a village chief.[176]

Kumbari (1731–1743) was Sharefa's son. According to Palmer's translation, "his councillors liked him but the common people hated him." However East's Hausa version says that he liked his courtiers but disliked the commoners.[177] Evidently Kumbari identified himself with the officials against the people's interests; and perhaps he thus sought to retain and strengthen the loyalty of his officials. Kumbari seems to have faced a revolt led by segments of the Rumfawa who had recently gained new strength and hope from the increasing alienation of government and people that accompanied Sharefa's *zalunci* (oppression). Kumbari had also to face a revolt at Dutse, which he attacked vigorously but did not enter, being restrained by his councillors who probably wished to avoid a general slaughter. In this attack, the Sarkin Aujara Bagau, Duba's successor, lost his life; but Kumbari defeated the Dutse rebels by using the Aujara garrison, as his grandfather had planned. Clearly Dadi had anticipated accurately the implications of Sarkin Gaya's revolt.

Yet another serious revolt that Kumbari had to face was led by the Fulani Ada Gwauro, the chief of Ringim, which lay north of Dutse and Gaya. Though not mentioned in the Chronicle, this event is well attested in Kano traditions.[178] The Sarkin Ringim advanced against Kano, seizing several towns on his route. Kumbari seems to have been caught unprepared. One of his leading warriors, the Jarmai Tagwai, volunteered to go out against Ada. Tagwai seems to have taken a small picked force with him and engaged Ada in a duel which remains the theme of a famous folk song at Kano. Put to flight, Ada Gwauro fled northwards to Damagaram, where he settled. Years later, on the Shehu Usuman's general call to *jihad*, it is said that Ada or his descendants went to the Shehu, seeking appointment as his leader at Kano. The Shehu had already delegated his command in Kano; but the descendants of Ada Gwauro re-established themselves at Ringim, where they still hold the chiefship.

These revolts illustrate the progressive polarization and alienation of the court and the people in the reigns of Sharefa and Kumbari. Perhaps the court's excessive reliance on levies and other forms of taxation accelerated this deterioration of internal solidarity. Since Kutumbi's day the Kano chiefship had become progressively remote from the people, even from those within the capital. It was now either the organ and agent of an oligarchy, the senior officialdom, or its dominant unit and director. Even such major rural chiefs as Gaya and Dutse became sufficiently disaffected with this regime to revolt. Undoubtedly, the new modes of taxation provoked dissatisfaction among rural chiefs and subjects throughout the state. Notably, the Chronicle never mentions taxation until Sharefa's day, when the alien cowrie currency was also introduced. Previously the chiefs of Kano had little need for revenues in cash, since they could themselves manufacture all the cash they needed by producing the *turkuda* that then served as the principal currency from Bilma and Bornu to Ghadames and westwards past Kebbi. The dyepits at the palace in Alwali's day were established nearly two centuries earlier when the *turkuda* first obtained currency as a form of cash, after the Ghadames Arabs had settled in Kano. However, with the introduction of new cowrie currency whose values and inflow he could not control, the chief's traditional reliance on production of cloth currency proved inadequate to supply revenues for the palace and the state. As we have seen, the introduction of cowries generated inflationary trends in the central market. To meet this, Sharefa introduced cash taxation in the form of *ad hoc* levies, marriage fees, and market dues. However, being unprecedented, all were regarded by the people as "robbery" and "extortion" by the chief, whose public image now changed from that of protector and leader to that of oppressor and tyrant.

Kumbari had other difficulties. The power of Gobir was now expanding rapidly. Its vigorous chief, Soba, attacked Kano, a state whose wealth and military record invited predatory assault. "If the Gobirawa defeated the Kanawa one day, the Kanawa defeated them the next. This state of affairs continued for a long time."[179] This war was fought on Kano soil with resulting devastation in the north and western districts.

Around 1734 the Mai Ali of Bornu also attacked Kano, camping for three nights at Fage outside the city walls. Two resident sheikhs are said to have prevented a battle, presumably by negotiating Kano's surrender. From this date Kano re-entered Bornu's vassalage, and again became liable for annual and occasional tribute, thereby increasing the chief's need for revenues.[180] It is said that on this attack the Bornu sultan threatened to burn Kano unless it surrendered. The event has been dated to 1734 by the tradition of an eclipse that occurred at this time.[181] Apparently Gobir's attacks on Kano ceased shortly after its subjection to Bornu. It is thus possible that Bornu may have employed Gobir, at this date its vassal, to reduce Kano before launching its own attack. Bornu was at this stage avidly expanding westwards; but its military peak was long past. Nonetheless, Kano remained tributary to Bornu until the Fulani conquest.

His new obligations may have led Kumbari to increase his taxations on the city market, the major source of cash in the state. In consequence "the market was nearly killed. The next year he collected *jizia* (the capitation tax levied on heathens) in Kano and made even the malams pay. There was so much disturbance that the Arabs left the town and went back to Katsina, and most of the poorer people in the town fled to the country."[182] The innovation here probably consists in Kumbari's extension of the levies (*karo*) introduced by Sharefa from the country to the capital; hitherto, apart from the statutory grain tithe, only Sharefa's market taxes were collected in the city. Kumbari, needing cowries, was driven to exploit the market, their main source within the chiefdom. This apparently led to a substantial exodus. His senior eunuch, the Turaki Kuka, warned Kumbari that if he continued, because of this "*jizia*, there will be no one left in the town but yourself and your servants." "The Sarki listened";[183] but it does not seem that he discontinued the levy.

Kumbari made yet another effort to increase his resources by attacking Kudu Baudam, probably Birnin Kudu, which had escaped Kano's aggression until this date. He marched to Zanga (Zango) and advanced thence against Baudam (who was probably the current chief). A strenuous battle was fought before the defenders retreated behind their walls. Kumbari camped at Zango, some four miles west. "Terms of peace were arranged and Kumbari returned to Kano."[184] It does not seem that Birnin Kudu lost its independence at this date. However, though it remained unconquered, it is likely that the local chief undertook to pay tribute, either annually or periodically, to Kano, to preserve his autonomy.

The Chronicle lists several of Kumbari's leading captains who fought with him against Gobir, Birnin Kudu, Dutse and Ringim. These include, besides Ada Gwauro and his opponent the Jarmai Tagwai, the Dan Tama, the Sarkin Majiya, Sarkin Gano Lifidi, Sarkin Damargu, Sarkin Bebeji, Sarkin Sakiya, Sarkin Birku, Dan Suma'ila, Makaman Dal (a village head), the Madawaki, Barde, Sarkin Jarmai, Dan Iya, Galadima, Makama, Sarkin Dawaki, Janbarde and Madawakin Barde, two *lawanai* of the Barde, together with many minor figures some of whom, such as the Dan Ali, Da-dana and Dan Bugai, were probably village chiefs, while others may have been free or slave palace functionaries or men without formal rank.

Alhaji Kabe (1743–1753), Kumbari's successor, is usually identified as his son. If this is correct, then from 1670, when Bawa died, until 1753 the succession had passed directly from father to son on four occasions. Kabe is remembered as "a Sarki of many wars and terrible ... he did not remain five months in his house without going to war or sending out his Sarkis (officials) to fight. ... No one gave presents to the malams so much as Kabe did ... there was no man of his age who was so ruthless in killing men as Kabe. There was no peace in Kano, only trouble after trouble, what with the war with Gobir and other wars."[185]

On Kabe's accession, the new chief of Gobir, Barbari, sent to make peace, but Kabe refused his overture, probably wishing to inflict damage on Gobir for its role in the reduction of Kano to vassalage once more. But Kabe had picked a tough opponent. In a major battle at Dami (Dumi) the Kano army was routed, and once again the chief was left alone with his police and slave bodyguards, most of whom were killed before he escaped. This defeat did not diminish Kabe's militarism. "The Gobirawa went on slaughtering the Kanawa, and the Kanawa slaughtered the Gobirawa in frequent wars until Kabe's death. No record can be kept of the fighting between them in Kabe's time or the number of wars in which Kabe engaged."[186] Leading warriors of his reign listed in the Chronicle held familiar titles such as Sarkin Dawaki, Jarmai, Sarkin Jarmai, Lifidi, Barde, Makama, Galadima, Sarkin Damargu, Sarkin Ringim among others. There is no report of revolt in Kabe's time. Perhaps the people's energies and attention were otherwise engaged. It seems likely that he inspired considerable fear in Kano as a domineering ruler.

On Kabe's death the electoral council finally reversed the recent pattern of direct succession that had permitted progressive concentrations of power in the chiefship, and appointed instead his collateral Mohamma Yaji, Dadi's son by the Maidaki Mariyama and Sharefa's full brother. Yaji ruled peacefully from 1753 to 1768. The Sarkin Gobir Barbari was busy part of this time attacking his immediate neighbour, the chief of Zamfara Mairoki. If Yaji made a formal peace with Gobir, this is not reported. His nickname, Malam Lafiya, (Mr. Well-being) indicates the popular response to his regime. "In his time there was no trouble ... there was no difficulty with his Sarkis or his chief slave or his household or anyone. Many men came and settled in Kano land in his reign."[187] Some of these immigrants were Fulani fleeing eastwards with their herds from Zamfara and western Katsina to avoid the armies of Gobir and Zamfara, then locked in a deadly struggle. Yaji was already an old man when he was appointed chief; but his peaceful reign is not solely attributable to his age or personal disposition. He had, in fact, no power base of his own from which to govern, and was thus wholly dependent on the councillors who had elected him and who evidently determined policy during his reign. By transferring the chiefship from Sharefa's line to this powerless collateral, the council had recovered much of the power it had lost to Sharefa and his successors.

Not mentioned in the Chronicle or other texts are certain features of Yaji's career which are relevant to later events, including the Fulani *jihad* and subsequent consolidation of power at Kano. With Yaji's succession, Sharefa's descendants lost the throne permanently, and if any survived, they are not easily identified. Current traditions of Yaji's career accordingly present the view of his successors and supporters. It is said that Sharefa had long regarded his younger brother, Yaji, as a rival, and had ordered him to remove from Kano to Kunci at the extreme north western corner of the chiefdom. On this ground tradition relates Sharefa also withheld from Yaji his share of Dadi's inheritance and the resources he needed to maintain his status as the chief's full brother and possible successor. Sharefa evidently sought to impoverish and isolate Yaji in order to ensure the succession of his own sons. Thus for several years Yaji had lacked not only office and slaves, but the essential means for princely subsistence. By status he was forbidden to engage in work other than *malanci* (Islamic scholarship), for which he was evidently untrained. It is said that he lived in poverty at Kunci throughout the reigns of Sharefa and his descendants. During this time, according to the tradition, Yaji was almost entirely dependent on a client from Katagum who was either Dan Mama or Dan Mama's father. This man made snuff from local tobacco for sale in the market. He also farmed and supported Yaji with his income. On his appointment as chief, according to one tradition, Yaji adopted Dan Mama as his son, and instructed his own sons never to divulge Dan Mama's origin.

After his formal accession Yaji's first and best remembered remark was "Today Yaji, tomorrow Yaji, the day after tomorrow Yaji, the day after that Yaji, beyond that who knows?" ("*Yau Yaji, gobe Yaji, jibi Yaji, gata Yaji, bayan wannan, oho.*")[188] This was not mere exuberance but a statement of policy. Yaji apparently promoted Dan Mama and may have appointed him Ciroma, that is, Crown Prince, before his death. It is said that he concentrated unusual resources of fiefs, slaves, horses and power in Dan Mama's hands, to assure the succession of his own begotten sons, three of whom did in fact succeed Yaji serially, namely Babba Zaki, Dawuda and Muhammadu Alwali II. This was what Yaji's cryptic statement intended; he certainly did not anticipate any Fulani conquest, but strove to secure the succession of his three sons to the exclusion of Sharefa's issue. Beyond that he had few interests or goals; but throughout his reign of nearly sixteen years, Yaji quietly built public confidence in his family, cultivated the support of relevant electors, and concentrated the necessary resources in Dan Mama's hands to the exclusion of Sharefa's descendants. Thus when he died in 1768 Yaji was succeeded by his eldest son Babba Zaki, whose exploits and rule have been mentioned earlier.

Sultanism and Reaction

Babba Zaki inherited a position of power, which he greatly increased by war and by the system of *wasidodi* (slave channels of communication) discussed above. According to the "Song of Bagauda":

> It was his sovereignty that has set the standard for Kano.
> It was in his time that horses were amassed.
> He had a strong force of cavalry, his protective quilt, and of bodyguards.
> It was he who introduced remoteness into kingship,
> Setting bodyguards to rebuke the people.
> One could not see him—the Great One—except through an intermediary.
> It was his confidant who would arrange an audience.[189]

Babba Zaki did indeed "set the standard" for Kano. He solved the problem of centralizing power with an oligarchic structure of hereditary territorial office by creating several differing lines of communication. As we shall see, not long after their conquest, the Fulani found it necessary to revive this institution.

The descent, career and personality of the Ciroma Dan Mama remain obscure. It seems unlikely on grounds of age that Dan Mama himself supported Yaji during the latter's long sojourn in the political wilderness at Kunci. More probably Dan Mama was the son of that Katagum Hausa who financed Yaji over this period. The Dokaji Abubakar cites a tradition that Dan Mama was Alwali's son, who was appointed Ciroma on his naming day, that is, when he was only a week old;[190] but this is clearly a mis-identification. Dan Mama held the Ciroma title during Alwali's reign and remained in Kano under the first Fulani emir; but according to oral tradition, Alwali dismissed Dan Mama from the Ciroma title to give this to his week-old son; and it is said that thereafter Dan Mama, who still acted as Ciroma while serving as regent for Alwali's son, was deeply estranged from the chief. This tradition suggests that Alwali may have sought to ensure his son's succession by employing Dan Mama as Yaji had originally done. There is a further tradition related by the Dokaji that in his youth Alwali's son, the Ciroma, damaged the crops on the farm of Shehu Abdullahi Suka at Gwale while riding, presumably with his companions. The Shehu asked Allah never to let the Ciroma become chief.[191] Presumably the Shehu's invocation was directed at the Ciroma who damaged his crops. However, not till 1926 did any Ciroma become chief; and then for some months there was widespread apprehension in Kano.

This last tradition persists for two reasons. Firstly, it attaches to the problematic identity and conduct of Dan Mama as Alwali's Ciroma. Secondly, it provides a convenient mystical basis for the Fulani pattern of collateral rather than lineal succession. Descendants of Shehu Abdullahi Suka are easy to find; but the incident remains somewhat apocryphal. We cannot determine the exact identity of the Ciroma Dan Mama or his relation to Yaji and Alwali; but it seems reasonably certain that he played a major part in securing the serial succession of Yaji's later sons and that he also served as the informal vizier of this dynastic segment, having unusual resources and power placed in his hands. Further, as the dynastic genealogy indicates, there was a major switch in succession on Yaji's appointment. The swift successions of his sons effectively displaced Sharefa's issue and split the Kutumbawa into at least three major factions: the heirs of Yaji, of Sharefa, and the rest. Perhaps several figures have been assimilated by tradition into the complex image of Dan Mama. The Chronicle reports that Babba Zaki's successor, Dauda Abbasama, ruled through his Galadima Makam, the constitutional vizier. He "took the Galadima Makama's (Makam's) advice in everything. The Galadima Makam was like a Sarki, while Dauda was like his *wazir*."[192] There is sufficient similarity in the two names to suggest the possibility that the tradition may have assimilated individual careers also.

The most important features of the regime at this penultimate phase include its dynastic division, the recent extreme centralization of power at the throne, generalized disaffection among the people under the new taxation and levies, and reliance of the chief on one dominant subordinate, whether the Galadima Makam or the Ciroma Dan Mama, to protect his family interests by deploying a reserve concentration of power. It is quite possible in this context that while the chief relied on the Galadima as his formal vizier in dealings with state officials, he may have placed the resources required for the dynastic struggle in other hands. It is also possible that Alwali himself may have created the power base for Dan Mama, instead of Yaji, as the tradition asserts. These alternatives cannot be finally evaluated on the available evidence, but certainly the Ciroma Dan Mama occupied an important and strategic position in Alwali's government, and perhaps also in Dawuda's.

Notes

1. Mahmoud Kati, *Tarikh el-Fettach*, translated by O. Houdas and M. Delafosse (Paris, Adrien-Maisonneuve, 1964); Abdurrahman Es-Sadi, *Tarikh Es-Soudan*, translated by O. Houdas (Paris: Adrien-Maisonneuve, 1964); Sir Richmond Palmer, *The Bornu, Sahara and Sudan* (London: John Murray, 1936); *idem, Gazetteer of Bornu Province* (Lagos: The Government Printer, 1929); A. Schultze, The Sultanate of Bornu, translated by P.A. Benton, 1913 (London: Frank Cass & Co., 1968); Y. Urvoy, *Histoire de L'Empire du Bornou* (Memoires de L'Institut Francais d'Afrique Noire, No. 7, Paris: Librairie Larose, 1947); J. Rouch, "Contribution a l'Histoire des Songhay," *Memoires de L'Institut d'Afrique Noire*, No. 29 (Dakar, IFAN, 1953), pp. 139–261.

2. Malam Hassan, Sarkin Ruwa, Abuja, and Malam Shu'aibu, Mukaddamin Makaranta, Bida, *A Chronicle of Abuja*, translated by F. Heath (Ibadan: Ibadan University Press, 1952).

3. E.J. Arnett, "A Hausa Chronicle," JRAS, 1909, Vol. 10, pp. 161–167; W.R. Baikie, "Notes on a Journey from Nupe to Kano in Hausa," Journal of the Royal Geographical Society (JRGS), 1867, Vol. 37, pp. 102–103.

4. See H.R. Palmer, *Sudanese Memoirs* (Lagos: The Government Printer, 1928), Vol. III, pp. 74–91, 132–146; E.J. Arnett, *Gazetteer of Sokoto Province* (London: Waterlow & Sons, 1920), pp. 10–12; P.G. Harris, *Gazetteer of Sokoto Province* (Unpublished Ms. in Sokoto Government Office, n.d., ?1938).

5. Kurt Kreiger, *Geschichte von Zamfara* (Berlin: Verlag von Dietrich Reimer, 1959). For a review of this interesting text, see M.G. Smith, "Kurt Krieger, Geschichte von Zamfara," *Journal of African History*, 196.

6. M.G. Smith, *Government in Zazzau, 1800–1950; idem, The Affairs of Daura* (Berkeley & Los Angeles: University of California Press, 1978); *idem, The Two Katsinas* (Unpublished ms.); *idem*, "Field Studies of African History," *Journal of African History*, Vol. 2 (1961), pp. 87–101.

7. C.L. Temple (Ed.), *Notes on the Tribes, Provinces, Emirates and States of the Northern Provinces of Nigeria* (Lagos: C.M.S. Bookshop, 1922), pp. 466–470; KC, pp. 58–62; S.J. Hogben, *The Muhammadan Emirates of Nigeria* (London: Oxford University Press, 1930), pp. 68–73; W.F. Gowers *Gazetteer of Kano Province* (London: Waterlow & Sons, 1921), pp. 8–10; Y. Urvoy, *Histoire des Populations du Soudan Central* (Paris: Librairie Larose, 1936), pp. 240–243.

8. Henry Barth, *Travels and Discoveries* (1902 Edn., Vol. 1, pp. 295–299).

9. Joseph Greenberg, "Linguistic Evidence for the Influence of the Kanuri on the Hausa." *Journal of African History*, Vol. 1, 1960, pp. 295–299.

10. M. Adamu na Ma'aji, *Ta'rikh Kano*. Unpublished Ms. at Shahuci Arabic Library, Kano.

11. See KC, p. 65; also Dokaji Alhaji Abubakar, *Kano ta Dabo Cigari*, pp. 13–17; and M. Hiskett, "The 'Song of Bagauda'"—Part II, BSOAS, Vol. 28, 1965, p. 113.

12. LH, Vol. 2, pp. 17–18; KC, p. 63; Dokaji Alhaji Abubakar, *Kano ta Dabo Cigari*, p. 13. Though the Arabic texts translated by Palmer and East were very similar, being copies of a

common original or of texts derived from a common source, they are not identical in all respects; and the two translations frequently differ both in the sense and import of phrases and sentences, and especially in their spelling of proper names for individuals, places and titles. Where such differences seem relevant they are indicated in the text or in footnotes; but for brevity and convenience, as a rule, I shall give East's spelling in parentheses after Palmer's where this seems substantively relevant, remarking any departures from this rule in the text or footnotes.

13. Joseph Greenberg, *The Influence of Islam on a Sudanese Religion* (Monographs of the American Ethnological Society, Vol. X, New York: J.J. Augustin, 1946); M. Landeroin, *Documents Scientifiques de la Mission Tilho (1906–1909)* (Paris: Ministère des Colonies, 1910, Vol. 2, pp. 528–234).

14. M. Hiskett, "The 'Song of Bagauda,'" Part II, *BSOAS*, Vol. 28, 1965, p. 114.

15. KC, p. 66; LH, Vol. 2, p. 23.

16. KC, p. 66 and footnote; LH, Vol. 2, p. 23 and footnote; Dokaji Alhaji Abubakar, *Kano ta Dabo Cigari*, p. 20; M. Hiskett, "The 'Song of Bagauda,'" Part II, p. 114.

17. M. Hiskett, "The 'Song of Bagauda,'" Part II, p. 114.

18. Ibid., p. 115.

19. Dokaji Alhaji Abubakar, *Kano ta Dabo Cigari*, pp. 15–17.

20. KC, pp. 65–66; LH, Vol. 2, p. 23.

21. See LH, Vol. 2, p. 16 for a map, indicating the courses of the successive city walls.

22. LH, Vol. 2, p. 22; KC, p. 65.

23. H.R. Palmer, *Sudanese Memoirs*, Vol. III, pp. 132–138, 144–153; M.G. Smith, *The Affairs of Daura* (1978).

24. KC, p. 66; LH, Vol. 2, p. 24; M. Hiskett, "The 'Song of Bagauda,'" Part II, p. 116. According to M. Adam Muhammad (*Tarikh Kano*, Unpublished Ms., completed 1933), "Nawata and Dagawata were twins, the sons of Munsako. They ruled jointly. Nawata was the older. Dagawata was a nickname like Nagawata. Both referred state affairs to their mother who lived for nearly 100 years for guidance. Near the end of their reign, Dagawata became the more powerful but he died a year later." Considering the discrepancies between the five king-lists that his history was based on, M. Adam remarks that "As some King-lists only mention Dagawata, this may help to explain their discrepancies."

25. KC, p. 67; LH, Vol. 2, p. 24–25.

26. KC, p. 68; LH, Vol. 2, p. 25; M. Hiskett, "The 'Song of Bagauda,'" Part II, p. 116; Dokaji Alhaji Abubakar, *Kano ta Dabo Cigari*, p. 21.

27. KC, p. 68; LH, Vol. 2, p. 26.

28. It seems likely that Samagi may have been the title of the pagan leader rather than his name, since the Chronicle reports that Naguyi, the 6th Gaudawa chief, slew "their leader Samagi" on returning from a campaign against Kura and Tsangaya. See LH, Vol. 2, p. 24; KC, p. 67.

29. KC, pp. 68–70; LH, Vol. 2, pp. 26–27.

30. H.R. Palmer, *Sudanese Memoirs*, Vol. III, pp. 79–80 dates the reign of Muhammad Korau at Katsina from c. 1320–1353, and that of Ibrahim Sura 1353–1355. With no supporting data, but several inconsistencies in his account, A.H.M. Kirk-Greene proposes 1492–3 for Muhammad Korau's accession, on grounds of "recent research" v. *idem*, in S.J. Hogben and A.H.M. Kirk-Greene, *The Emirates of Northern Nigeria* (London: Oxford University Press, 1966), pp. 160–161. Kirk-Greene's chronological error has been adopted with enthusiasm by Abdullahi Smith, presumably for its convenience; v. *idem.*, "The Early States of the Central Sudan," in J.F. Ade Ajayi and Michael Crowder (Eds.), *History of West Africa* (London: Longman, 1971), Vol. 1, p. 196 and footnote 138.

Zamnagawa is listed in the 'Song of Bagauda' (v. M. Hiskett, *op. cit.*, p. 116) by another nickname as Gakin-Gakuma. For the identification, v. Dokaji Alhaji Abubakar, *Kano ta Dabo Cigari*, p. 44.

Concerning Zamnagawa, M. Adam Muhammad in his *Ta'rikh Kano* writes: "He was the son of Randa (i.e., Tsamiya, who was also called Randamasu) and Kumaimaya. He is nicknamed Gakin-Gakuma. He killed many men as chief. During his reign Islam came to Kano, brought by *'ulamma*, who taught him to say his prayers. And that was the reason for his death. At first very powerful, he became arrogant and then died. He ruled 9 years."

The 'Song of Bagauda' also says of Gakin-Gakuma, "When he prayed this became the cause of his death" (M. Hiskett, *op. cit.*, part II, p. 116).

The probability that Zamnagawa's violent seizure of power, obscure ancestry and Islamic name, may indicate an external Muslim conquest of Kano is reinforced by the account of his appointments of chiefs for the Rumawa and Maguzawa pagans, and the withdrawal of the Maguzawa from Kano and its environs to Pankui (Palmer writes Fongui)—the district between Santolo and Barku. Such terms as Rumawa and Maguzawa are ethnic designations of clearly Islamic provenience.

31. KC, p. 90 adds that Yaji "went to Rano and reigned at Bunu two years." LH, Vol. 2, pp. 28–9 reads "He (Yaji) drove the Chief of Rano from Zamanagaba. Then he went to Bono and remained there for two years. Then he moved to Kura together with the Ajawa, Warjawa and Arawa (tribes) and settled there." Presumably this "refers to Yaji, not the Sarkin Rano."

32. KC, p. 70; LH, Vol. 2, p. 29. The text lists Abdurrahman Zaite as the leader of this Mandinka Mission; but with the recent publication of an anonymous text, dated 1061 A.H. (1650/51 A.D.), this incident has been questioned. See Muhammad Al-Hajj, "A seventeenth Century Chronicle of the Origins and Missionary Activities of the Wangarawa," *Kano Studies*, Vol. 1, No. 4, 1968, pp. 7–42. Muhammad Al-Hajj notes that "According to the manuscript under discussion they (Zaite and his companions) left their original home in the year 835 A.H. (1431/32 A.D.) and arrived in Kano during the reign of Muhamma Rumfa" (Ibid., p. 8), after a journey of at least 31 years. Since Yaji is said to have died in 1385 and Rumfa succeeded in 1463, the implication is that Zaite did not leave Mali until nearly 50 years after Yaji's death. Thus either the Chronicle errs in identifying him as leader of these Mandinka missionaries, or more seriously there may have been no Muslim mission such as it records. Besides this statement that Abdurrahman Zaite led the first Muslim Mission to Kano in Yaji's reign (1349–85), the Chronicle contains another passage that could also refer to Zaite. In the reign of Muhammad Rumfa (1463–1499), "the Sherifs came to Kano. They were Abdu Rahaman and his people" (Palmer, "The Kano Chronicle," p. 77); but here the following sentences, although garbled, show clearly that the passage refers to Muhammed ibn Abdulkarim El-Maghili of Tlemcen, rather than Abdurrahman Zaite; and the local "History of the Wangarawa" published by Mr. Al-Hajj asserts that El-Maghili and Abdurrahman Zaite arrived at Kano in Rumfa's reign within 3 days of one another, having set out independently and followed different routes.

The critical questions are simply—was there a mission from Mali to Kano during Yaji's reign, whoever led it, and did Yaji formally accept Islam and employ these Mandinka immigrants to assist him in subduing Santolo and other remaining centres of native resistance, as reported in the Chronicle? The Chronicle's reliability for the century between Yaji and Rumfa hinges on the answer to this question; and the circumstantial evidence in support of the Chronicle is strong. For some of these data see A. Mischlich, "Contributions to the History of the Hausa States," *Journal of the African Society*, vol. 4, 1905, pp. 455–463; and H.R. Palmer, *Sudanese Memoirs*, Vol. III, pp. 79–83; *idem*, "The Kano Chronicle," pp. 58–60; and the Chronicle's accounts of the reigns of Yaji's successors, Bugaya, Kanajeji, Umaru, Dauda, Abdullahi Burja and Yakubu. Concerning Kanajeji, the apostate (1390–1410), and his son Umaru (1410–1421), "The 'Song of Bagauda'" remarks:

Kanajeji, when he had reigned for twenty years, he died.
These were the chiefs of the pagan Hausa.

Now Umaru was one learned in Islam; he it was who escaped (Hell-fire);
He lit a fire which defied extinction.
He drove onto the pagan Hausa and they fled to the bush.
He reigned a full twelve years

(M. Hiskett, *op. cit.*, *BSOAS*, in Vol. 28, 1965, p. 116).

For a fine general sketch of this geo-historical context, see Joseph Greenberg, *The Influence of Islam on a Sudanese Religion*, pp. 1–11.

33. KC, p. 71; LH, Vol. 2, p. 29; Dokaji Alhaji Abubakar, *Kano ta Dabo Cigari*, p. 26, photograph and note.

34. KC, p. 71; LH, Vol. 2, p. 31.

35. KC, p. 72; LH, Vol. 2, p. 31.

36. KC, p. 72, footnote. This item is not included in East's translation, v. *L.H.*, Vol. 2, pp. 30–31.

37. KC, p. 72; LH, Vol. 2, p. 31.

38. In the introduction to his translation of the Chronicle, Palmer says: "The *Chronicle* has been translated as it stands, with the marginal notes of the text, in footnotes. The names of the Sarkis (given in the margin by the author) are merely for convenience of reference. I have added approximate dates worked out by simply reckoning back from the length of reigns given, assuming the date of the Fulani entry into Kano as September of A.D. 1807 (A.H. 1222) which a careful comparison of various accounts has led me to believe is about the right date" (*K.C.*, p. 59).

Unfortunately this phrasing does not indicate whether the paternity of these Chiefs, as listed by Palmer in his translation, was included in the marginal notes to which he refers. The presumption is that they were, since R.M. East follows the same pattern and gives the same details, though working from another copy of the Chronicle translated. On this topic East remarks that "The book (text, copy) that we have followed (translated) was obtained from Zubairu, the son of Sarkin (emir of) Kano Dabo. Sarkin Kano Abdullahi Bayero (1926–1953) had it released (?loaned, changed, copied?—*ya sa aka sake shi*), and then it was translated into Hausa at the Translation Bureau. In translating it, we have followed the Arabic exactly and without changing anything, despite the various commentaries we have in all the versions of this book that we have collected. However, for the reader's convenience, we have separated the story of each chief's reign. So when we come to a new chief, we first give his name and the Muslim years of his reign" (*L.H.*, Vol. 2, p. 5). Here also East's phrasing suggests that the paternity of each was part of his given name, following the usual Arab practice. If so then the genealogy abstracted by C.L. Temple (*Notes on the Tribes etc. of Northern Nigeria*, opposite p. 466) summarises the agnatic relations of the chiefs, as recorded in the Arabic texts translated by Palmer and East. Nonetheless, various problems remain, as illustrated for example by some differing pedigrees reported by Mallam Adam Muhammad in his *Ta'rikh Kano*, though at least one Arabic text of the Chronicle must almost certainly have figured among the five king-lists M. Adam sought to collate. The text of the Chronicle provides another ground for reservation about the paternal designations given by Palmer and East, since it frequently specifies the paternity of chiefs when introducing their reigns. This suggests that the names of these chiefs did not always include those of their fathers. Unfortunately recent copies of the Arabic text of the Chronicle may have incorporated the pedigrees published by Palmer and East; so this question may only be resolved by examining the texts that they translated, which are probably available in Nigerian libraries.

39. For examples, see W.R. Baikie, "Notes on a Journey from Nupe to Kano in Hausa," *JRGS*, Vol. 37, 1867, pp. 102–105; H.R. Palmer, *Sudanese Memoirs*, Vol. III, pp. 79–82, 142–144; E.J. Arnett, "A Hausa Chronicle," *JRAS*, Vol. 10, 1911, pp. 161–167; Malams Hassan and Shu'aibu, *A Chronicle of Abuja* (Ibadan: Ibadan University Press, 1952), pp. 36–37; E.J. Arnett, *Gazetteer of Sokoto* (London: Waterlow & Sons, 1920), pp. 11–15, etc.

40. M. Hiskett, *The 'Song of Bagauda,'* Part II, p. 116; compare KC, p. 67; LH, Vol. 2, p. 24; W.R. Baikie, "Notes on a Journey," 1867, *JRGS*, Vol. 37, p. 102; and the remarks of Mallam Adam Muhammad, *Ta'rikh Kano* (unpublished Ms., 1933), cited above in footnote 24.

Baikie says Makarkari reigned for 2 years and 7 months after Guguwa (Gaogau), but omits Nawata and Gawata. Palmer and East translated texts that credit the twins with a joint reign of two years. The 'Song of Bagauda' says "Nawata reigned for 70 years ... Gawata reigned for 30 years." For Mallam Adam's observations, v. fn. 24 *supra*.

Perhaps these confused traditions reflect some change in the line or patterns of chiefly succession; and one possibility is the assertion of collateral claims against the exclusive lineal succession that had apparently prevailed since Bagauda's death. Could this account for the names, the proclaimed twinship and joint reign of 'Nawata and Gawata'?

41. KC, p. 73; LH, Vol. 2, p. 32.

42. Compare KC, pp. 70 and 73; LH, Vol. 2, pp. 29 and 32; and also Dokaji Alhaji Abubakar, *Kano ta Dabo Cigari*, p. 23.

43. LH, Vol. 2, p. 33, writes Lawan for the name H.R. Palmer cites as Lowal, *idem*, K.C., pp. 70, 73.

44. KC, p. 73; LH, Vol. 2, p. 32.

45. KC, p. 73; LH, Vol. 2, p. 32.

46. KC, pp. 73–74; LH, Vol. 2, pp. 32–33.

47. KC, p. 74; LH, Vol. 2, p. 33; M. Hiskett, "The 'Song of Bagauda,'" p. 116; and Malam Adam Muhammad, *Ta'rikh Kano*, who says: "Next came the learned (*El-Alim*) Malam Umoru, the son of Kanajeji. He was driven out of Kano by heathen, including the Sarkin Gaya, the Sarkin Miga, the Madaki and the Galadima. Then he prayed and was restored, victorious. Then he drove his heathen opponents from the city, including the Warjawa. His mother was Ayatara. He reigned for twelve years, and it was under him that Islam really began in Kano."

48. KC, p. 74; LH, vol. 2, p. 34.

49. KC, p. 74; LH, Vol. 2, p. 34.

50. M. Hiskett, "The 'Song of Bagauda,'" Parts II & III, *BSOAS*, Vol. 28, 1965, pp. 112–135, and 378–385; see also 'Abdallah Ibn Muhammad, *Tazyin al-Waraqat*, translated by M. Hiskett (Ibadan: Ibadan University Press, 1963), pp. 120–124.

For a general discussion of this tension after the *jihad*, see Murray Last, "Aspects of Administration and Dissent in Hausaland, 1800–1968," *Africa*, Vol. XL, No. 4, 1970, pp. 345–357.

51. M. Hiskett, "The 'Song of Bagauda,'" Part II, p. 113.

52. Ibid., p. 116.

53. KC, pp. 74, 70; LH, Vol. 2, pp. 33, 29.

54. KC, pp. 74, 60; LH, Vol. 2, p. 34; see also H.R. Palmer, *The Bornu, Sahara and Sudan* (London: John Murray, 1936), p. 219; and M.G. Smith, "The Beginnings of Hausa Society," in J. Vansina *et al.* (eds.), *The Historian in Tropical Africa* (London: Oxford University Press, 1964), p. 347 ff. For a concordance of the various Bornu king-lists which yields 1421, 1425 and 1431 A.D. as alternative dates for Othman Kalnama's reign, see Ronald Cohen, "The Bornu King-lists," in Jeffrey Butler (ed.), *African History*, Boston University Papers on Africa, Vol. II (Boston: Boston University Press, 1966), pp. 41–83, especially p. 63.

55. H.R. Palmer, *Sudanese Memoirs*, Vol. III, pp. 48, 36 and 40, Note 28; also *idem*, *The Bornu Sahara and Sudan*, pp. 222–224; R. Cohen's data indicates that Ali Gaji Dunama probably reigned between 1472 and 1507 A.D., v. *idem*, "The Bornu King-lists," in J. Butler (ed.), *African History* Boston: Boston University Press, 1966), p. 64.

56. KC, p. 74; LH, Vol. 2, p. 34.

57. KC, p. 75; LH, Vol. 2, p. 34.

58. KC, p. 75; LH, Vol. 2, pp. 34–35. On Amina, see Malams Hassan and Shu'aibu, *A Chronicle of Abuja*, pp. 4–5, which suggests that Amina may have flourished c. 1520–80 A.D.

Baikie ("Notes on a Journey," *JRGS*, 1867, p. 102) and E.J. Arnett ("A Hausa Chronicle, *JAS.*, 1911, Vol. 10, p. 165), both list Bakwa Turunku as the 22nd chief of Zazzau and say she ruled for 30 years. Malams Hassan and Shu'aibu agree on her position in the list of Zazzau chiefs but say she only ruled from 1536–1539 A.D. (Ibid., p. 36). Unfortunately, in the absence of external corroboration, such is the state of the Zaria and Abuja King-lists, the probability of copyists' errors in recording reign-lengths, and the legendary character of 'Queen' Amina and her activities, that we have no ground for preferring the dates assigned by Malams Hassan and Shu'aibu to those implied in the Kano Chronicle, especially as these authors rely on the Chronicle and Sultan Bello for an account of Amina's activities (v. Ibid., p. 5). For further comments on the puzzle and probable implication of the legend of Queen Amina, see M.G. Smith, "The Beginnings of Hausa Society," p. 349 and footnote.

59. KC, p. 75; LH, Vol. 2, p. 35; H.R. Palmer, *The Bornu, Sahara and Sudan*, p. 220; R. Cohen, "The Bornu King Lists," p. 63.

60. KC, p. 75; LH, Vol. 2, p. 35.

61. For further discussion, see M.G. Smith, "The Beginnings of Hausa Society," p. 348 and footnote 35. Also H.R. Palmer, *Sudanese Memoirs*, Vol. III, pp. 80–83; and Malams Hassan and Shu'aibu, *A Chronicle of Abuja*, p. 5.

62. KC, p. 75; LH, Vol. 2, p. 35.

63. KC, p. 76; LH, Vol. 2, pp. 35–36.

64. KC, p. 75; LH, Vol. 2, p. 36.

65. KC, p. 76; LH, Vol. 2, p. 36.

66. KC, p. 76; LH, Vol. 2, p. 36. However see Baikie, "Notes on a Journey" *JRGS*, Vol. 37, 1867, p. 102, and M. Hiskett "The 'Song of Bagauda,'" Part II, p. 116. M. Adam Muhammad likewise omits Dakauta and Atuma in his *Ta'rikh Kano*, and lists Yakubu as the immediate successor of Abdullahi Burja. Almost certainly these disagreements, and the brief bizarre reigns of Dakauta and Atuma, indicate some conflicts over the succession, whether with or without Bornu's participation. The struggles thinly veiled by these discrepant data may have marked the displacement of the Gaudawa (Daurawa) dynasty by the Rumfawa, with the appointment of Yakubu, who is listed by Palmer and East as a son of Abdullahi Burja, but by Mallam Mahammad as Abdullahi's paternal half-brother.

67. KC, p. 76; LH, Vol. 2, p. 36.

68. KC, p. 76; LH, Vol. 2, pp. 36–7.

69. See Malams Hassan and Shu'aibu, "*A Chronicle of Abuja*," pp. 7, 80; and M.G. Smith, *Government in Zazzau, 1800–1950*, pp. 47, 52–3, 130, 338.

70. W.F. Gowers, *Gazetteer of Kano Province* (London: Waterlow and Sons, 1921), p. 21; J.M. Freemantle, "A History of the Region Comprising the Katagum division of Kano Province," *JRAS*, Vol. X, 1910, pp. 299–307; Y. Urvoy, *Histoire de L'Empire du Bornou*, p. 90.

71. KC, pp. 76–77; LH, Vol. 2, p. 37.

72. Mahmoud Kati, *Tarikh El-Fettach*, pp. 81–84, 94–99; see also J.O. Hunwick, "Religion and State in the Songhay Empire, 1464–1591," in I.M. Lewis (ed.), *Islam in Tropical Africa* (London: Oxford University Press for International African Institute, 1966), pp. 296–315.

73. M. Hiskett, "Material Relating to the State of Learning Among the Fulani before the *Jihad*," *BSOAS*, Vol. 19, 1957, pp. 530–598; A.D.H. Bivar and M. Hiskett, "The Arabic Literature of Nigeria to 1804. A Provisional Report," *BSOAS*, Vol. 25, 1962, pp. 104–148; 'Abdallah Ibn Muhammad, *Tazyin al-Waraqat*, translated by M. Hiskett, pp. 6–8; John E. Lavers "Islam in the Bornu Caliphate," *ODU, A Journal of West African Studies*, N.S., No. 5, April, 1971, pp. 27–53.

74. KC, p. 77; LH, Vol. 2, p. 37; Dokaji Alhaji Abubakar, *Kano ta Dabo Cigari*, p. 29. If the Rumfawa did come from Gaya or owed their thrones to Gaya support, then the events chronicled in Yakubu's reign indicate that he was the first of the new dynasty, even though they took their name from his successor and son, Mohammad Rumfa.

75. KC, p. 77; LH, Vol. 2, p. 37; M. Adam Muhammad in his *Ta'rikh Kano* gives her name as Fatima.

76. Dokaji Alhaji Abubakar, *Kano ta Dabo Cigari*, p. 29.

77. KC, p. 77; LH, Vol. 2, p. 38.

78. KC, p. 77; LH, Vol. 2, p. 38.

79. Dokaji Alhaji Abubakar, *Kano ta Dabo Cigari* p. 29.

80. H.R. Palmer, *Sudanese Memoirs*, Vol. III, pp. 44, 80 and footnote; *idem*, *The Bornu Sahara and Sudan*, pp. 222–223.

81. KC, p. 77; LH, Vol. 2, p. 38.

82. Henry Barth, *Travels and Discoveries* (1902 Edn.), Vol. 1, p. 284. Concerning the Wangarawa immigration, v. Muhammad Al-Hajj, "A Seventeenth Century Chronicle on the Origins and Missionary Activities of the Wangarawa," *Kano Studies*, Vol. 1, No. 4, 1968, pp. 7–16.

83. KC, p. 70; LH, Vol. 2, p. 29.

84. KC, p. 78; LH, Vol. 2, p. 38.

85. KC, p. 78; LH, Vol. 2, p. 38. For the Bornu original, see C.L. Temple (Ed.), *Notes on the Tribes etc. of Northern Nigeria*, p. 435; and Y. Urvoy, *Histoire de l'Empire du Bornou*, pp. 37–42.

86. East's spelling "Dambazau' is preferred to Palmer's, "Dambazaro' on linguistic and substantive grounds, but the geography is puzzling. See KC, p. 78 and LH, Vol. 2, p. 38.

87. KC, p. 78; LH, Vol. 2, p. 38.

88. KC, p. 78; LH, Vol. 2, p. 38.

89. KC, 73; LH, Vol. 2, p. 32. Thereafter Hausa chiefs of Kano were usually buried at Madatai.

90. See C.L. Temple (Ed.), *Notes on the Tribes etc. of Northern Nigeria*, p. 467, and M.G. Smith, "The Beginnings of Hausa Society," p. 351. Unfortunately the data are obscure on these points.

91. See M.G. Smith, "Hausa Succession and Inheritance," pp. 264–266, 273 ff.

92. KC, p. 77, LH, Vol. 2, p. 38; Dokaji Alhaji Abubakar, *Kano ta Dabo Cigari*, pp. 29–30, and photograph on p. 30.

93. Ahmed Baba, *The Gilt Brocade*, cited by T.H. Baldwin, in the "Introduction" to his translation of El-Maghili's *Obligations of Princes* (Beirut: Imprimerie Catholique, 1932), pp. 3–4.

94. Sheikh Mohammed El-Maghili of Tlemcen, *The Obligations of Princes* translated by T.H. Baldwin (Beirut: Imprimerie Catholique, 1932).

95. A letter from the Egyptian scholar Abdurrahman As-Suyuti (c. 1445–1505 A.D.) addressed to the Sarkin Katsina, Ibrahim Maje, and the chief of Agades, was also quoted *in extenso* by the Shehu Usuman in his *Tambihu'l Ikhwan*, of which H.R. Palmer's "An Early Fulani Conception of Islam," *JRAS*, Vols. 13 & 14, 1914 and 1915, pp. 407–414, 53–59, and 185–192, is a translation. For As-Suyuti's "Message to the Kings of the Sudan, Hausa and Tocrur (Tekrur)," v. Ibid., pp. 55–59.

96. v. H.R. Palmer, "An Early Fulani Conception of Islam," *JRAS*, Vol. 14, 1915, pp. 185–188, for the text of another treatise addressed to Rumfa by El Maghili in 879 A.H. 1491 A.D., and cited *in toto* by the Shehu Usuman dan Fodio in his *Tanbihu'l Ikwan*.

97. O. Houdas dates El-Maghili's visit to the Askia Muhammad at Gao in c. 1502; El-Maghili first visited the Askia at Cairo in 1498 while the Emperor was returning from his pilgrimage to Mecca. v. Mahmoud Kati *Tarikh El-Fettach*, p. 15, note 2, 132; Mahmoud Kati also refers to the Askia's consultation and correspondence with El-Maghili (Ibid., pp. 22–23); and in his *Bayan Wujub al-hijra ala'l-ibad*, the Shehu Usuman quotes liberally from El-Maghili's replies to legal questions raised by the Askia. See also T.H. Baldwin's Introduction to his translation of El Maghili's "Obligations of Princes," pp. 3–4; and S.J. Hogben, *The Muhammadan Emirates of Nigeria* (London: Oxford University Press, 1930) p. 48.

98. See Mahmoud Kati, *Tarikh El-Fettach* p. 262 for references to an impassioned debate between two Timbuktu scholars in 1589 concerning the relative size, wealth and importance of Kano and Gao, two years before the end of the Songhai Empire

99. KC, p. 78; LH, Vol. 2, p. 38.

100. KC, p. 78; LH, Vol. 2, p. 39.

101. Leo Africanus, *The History and Description of Africa*, translated by John Pory (1896 Edn.), Vol. III, p. 830.

102. Abderrahman Es-Sa'di, *Tarikh Es-Soudan*, translated by O. Houdas (Paris: Adrien-Maisonneuve, 1964), pp. 129–130. See also E.J. Arnett, *Gazetteer of Sokoto Province*, pp. 12–13; C.L. Temple (ed.), *Notes on the Tribes etc. of Northern Nigeria*, pp. 557–559.

103. J. Hogben, *The Muhammadan Emirates of Nigeria*, pp. 100–101; P.G. Harris, *Gazetteer of Sokoto Province* (Unpublished Ms. c. 1938, in Sokoto Government Office).

104. E.J. Arnett, *The Rise of the Sokoto Fulani*; being a paraphrase and in some parts a translation of the *Infaku'l Maisuri* of Sultan Mohammed Bello (Kano, 1922), pp. 13–14; see also E.J. Arnett, *Gazetteer of Sokoto Province*, pp. 12–13, and for identities of the rulers of Air, H.R. Palmer, *Sudanese Memoirs*, Vol. III, p. 48.

105. H.R. Palmer, *Sudanese Memoirs*, Vol. III, p. 45; *idem, The Bornu Sahara and Sudan*, pp. 228–230; R. Cohen, "The Bornu King Lists," p. 64.

106. KC, p. 79; LH, Vol. 2, p. 39.

107. KC, p. 79; LH, Vol. 2, pp. 39–40.

108. H.R. Palmer, *Sudanese Memoirs*, Vol. III, pp. 160, 45; R. Cohen, "The Bornu King Lists," p. 64; and Y. Urvoy, "Chroniques d'Agades," *Journal de la Societe des Africanistes*, Tome IV, 1934, pp. 145–177, especially p. 152. Concordance suggests 1527 A.D. as the likely date for Bornu's domination over or alliance with Agades rather than 1532 as given in Palmer's text; v. *Sudanese Memoirs*, Vol. III, p. 160.

109. E.J. Arnett, *The Rise of the Sokoto Fulani*, p. 13; cf. H.R. Palmer, *Sudanese Memoirs*, Vol. III, p. 48. The identification is ambiguous.

110. H.R. Palmer, *Sudanese Memoirs*, Vol. III, p. 160; *idem*, 1936, *Bornu, Sahara and Sudan*, p. 229.

111. Ibid., p. 48.

112. Ibid., p. 160. For the equation of Asben & Air, v. H. Barth, *Travels and Discoveries*, (1902 Edn.), Vol. 1, p. 151

113. E.J. Arnett, *Gazetteer of Sokoto Province*, p. 13; S.J. Hogben, *The Muhammadan Emirates of Nigeria*, p. 102.

114. KC, p. 79; LH, Vol. 2, p. 40.

115. KC, p. 79; LH, Vol. 2, p. 40.

116. KC, p. 78 merely says "a Market"; whereas LH, Vol. 2, p. 39 says explicitly "a market for eunuchs" (*kasuwar babanni*).

117. KC, pp. 78–79; LH, Vol. 2, p. 39.

118. KC, p. 80; LH, Vol. 2, pp. 40–41. Of this period, Mallam Adam Muhammad in his *Ta'rikh Kano* writes as follows: "Muhammad Kisoke, the son of Abdullahi, the son of Muhammad Rumfa. His mother was Lamis. He was as powerful as Rumfa and very alert in affairs of state. He was feared by his enemies, cunning but helpful. The state prospered in his reign. He ruled for 58 years and near the end of his reign there was a great epidemic (*waba*) and famine which killed many people, including Kisoke. There had never been an epidemic like this at Kano before, and it continued for four years.

Next came Yakubu and Muhammad Sheshe, brothers, both sons of Abdullahi, Yakubu ruled 6 months and died in the epidemic, while Sheshe died 4 months later. Sheshe's mother was A'isha, while Yakubu's was Amina.

Then Abubakar Kado, the son of Abdullahi, the son of Muhammadu Rumfa succeeded. His mother was Hauwa. He ruled for 7 years. During his reign the plague ended …

M. Hiskett, "The 'Song of Bagauda,'" Part II, p. 117, also mentions a plague at this point.

Four months Sheshe was on his throne;
There was a plague, and the people were dropping dead.
It cut down Sheshe. Yakubu, his younger brother succeeded.
Then after six months came death the buffeter.
Seven years only Bubakar (Kado) reigned.

Hiskett suggests that the plague at Kano may have been an intense local outbreak "of the pandemic pattern of plague during the sixteenth and seventeenth centuries" in the near East and Europe. v. M. Hiskett, "The 'Song of Bagauda,'" Part III, *BSOAS*, Vol. 28, 1965, pp. 369–370. Evidently "The 'Song of Bagauda'" was one of the texts that M. Adam Muhammad consulted in preparing his work.

119. KC, p. 81; LH, Vol. 2, pp. 40–41.

120. KC, pp. 81, 79; LH, Vol. 2, pp. 42, 40.

121. KC, p. 80; LH, Vol. 2, p. 41.

122. KC, p. 80; LH, Vol. 2, p. 41.

123. KC, p. 80; LH, Vol. 2, pp. 41–42.

124. KC, p. 81; LH, Vol. 2, p. 42.

125. KC, p. 81; LH, Vol. 2, p. 423; Dokaji Alhaji Abubakar, *Kano ta Dabo Cigari*, pp. 32–33, tactfully omits this incident.

126. KC, p. 81; LH, Vol. 2, p. 43.

127. On rationality and traditionalism, v. Max Weber, *The Theory of Social and Economic Organization*. Translated by A.M. Henderson and Talcott Parsons (London: Wm. Hodge & Co., 1949), pp. 104–121, 152–154, 297–317.

128. KC, p. 81; LH, Vol. 2, p. 43. While Palmer leaves open the status of those "eighteen of the Sarki's household" that Narai took with him to the mosque, East explicitly describes them as princes ('*yan Sarki*); this seems unlikely, but East's version is probably sounder.

129. KC, p. 82; LH, Vol. 2, p. 43. Both authors note that the mosque in which Narai was murdered was abandoned and only rebuilt in the reign of the Fulani Emir, Ibrahim Dabo. Both also note that after the reign of Muhammadu Zaki, no Turaki acted as the ruler's deputy until the Fulani Emir Muhammadu Bello (1882–1893) delegated his son, the Turaki Manya Zakari Ya'u, to do so. Evidently, both footnotes translate identical marginalia to the two texts, the originals of which were thus clearly copied from an older text in Muhammadu Bello's reign, when he ordered the Chronicle to be brought up to date. The shorter versions of the Chronicle should thus be the older, though not necessarily the more authentic. Palmer for example notes that while his text, obtained in Katsina, c. 1907, continues through to the reign of Muhammad Bello, the 48th ruler, the text that Lady Lugard referred to in her book, *A Tropical Dependency*, stops at the 42nd, namely Muhammad Alwali II, the last Hausa ruler. Given the information we have that Mamman Bello had the Chronicle extended up to his reign, this is perhaps as conclusive evidence as we may hope for that the original text which Mamman Bello's scribes copied or extended antedated the Fulani *jihad*; and certainly antedated the accession of Muhammad Alwali II.

130. Cf. Max Weber, *The Theory of Social & Economic Organization*, pp. 297–334, and Talcott Parsons' "Introduction" in that volume, pp. 50–70; see also M. Bloch, *The Historian's Craft* (London: 1954 and R.G. Collingwood, *The Idea of History* (New York: Oxford University Press, 1956).

131. KC, p. 82; LH, Vol. 2, p. 43.

132. KC, pp. 81–2; LH, Vol. 2, p. 43.

133. KC, p. 82; LH, Vol. 2, p. 43.

134. KC, p. 82; LH, Vol. 2, p. 44. Here also both translations footnote identical marginalia to their Arabic texts, which confirm that the original which was copied and extended in Mamman Bello's reign antedates the reign of Alwali.

135. H.R. Palmer, *Sudanese Memoirs*, Vol. III, p. 160; *idem, The Bornu Sahara and Sudan.*

136. For an ethnological account of the Jukun, see C.K. Meek, *A Sudanese Kingdom* (London: Routledge & Kegan Paul, 1931).

137. KC, p. 82; LH, Vol. 2, p. 44.

138. KC, p. 82; LH, Vol. 2, p. 44.

139. KC, p. 83; LH, Vol. 2, p. 45.

140. KC, p. 83; LH, Vol. 2, p. 45.

141. KC, p. 83; LH, Vol. 2, p. 45.

142. KC, p. 84; LH, Vol. 2, p. 46.

143. KC, p. 84; LH, Vol. 2, p. 46.

144. KC, p. 84; LH, Vol. 2, p. 46.

145. KC, p. 84; LH, Vol. 2, p. 46.

146. KC, p. 84; LH, Vol. 2, pp. 46–47.

147. KC, p. 84; LH, Vol. 2, p. 46. While Palmer's translation suggests that Bako invoked his own death, East's indicates clearly that this was prayed for by others.

148. KC, p. 85 says Mandawari was appointed as Sarkin Samari. LH, Vol. 2, p. 47, gives the title as Sarkin Yara. Never having heard of a Sarkin Samari in charge of young male slaves at the palace, I prefer East's version.

149. KC, p. 85; LH, Vol. 2, p. 47.

150. KC, p. 85; R.M. East. *L.H.*, Vol. 2, p. 47.

151. KC, p. 87; LH, Vol. 2, p. 50.

152. KC, p. 87; R.M. East, *L.H.* Vol. 2, pp. 50–51.

153. K.C., p. 87; L.H., Vol. 2, p. 50. For an account of the *Rawan Toji*, see Malam Adamu na Ma'aji, *Tarikh Kano* (Unpublished Ms. in Shahuci Arabic Library, Kano). The dance described in the Chronicle seems similar to the dance performed at the Idi festivals outside the Emir's palace (at least until 1950) in Zaria by the 'Yan-Hoto, who were regarded by local Muslims as pagan magicians, invulnerable to metal by virtue of their medicines.

154. KC, p. 87; LH, Vol. 2, p. 50.

155. KC, pp. 87–88; LH, Vol. 2, p. 51.

156. KC, p. 88; LH, Vol. 2, p. 52.

157. KC, p. 88; LH, Vol. 2, p. 52. For a somewhat different version of this attack, emphasizing the prescience and heroism of Kano's 'national' Saint, the Wali Mai Kargo, v. Dokaji Alhaji Abubakar, *Kano ta Dabo Cigari*, pp. 37–8.

158. KC, p. 88; LH, Vol. 2, p. 52.

159. KC, p. 88; LH, Vol. 2, p. 52. East's text gives 'Bindu' instead of Palmer's 'Bundu.'

160. KC, p. 88; LH, Vol. 2, p. 52.

161. KC, p. 89; LH, Vol. 2, p. 52.

162. H.R. Palmer, *Sudanese Memoirs*, Vol. III, pp. 83–84. For the likely date of Ali Umarmi's reign in Bornu, see R. Cohen, "The Bornu King Lists," p. 64.

163. KC, p. 89; LH, Vol. 2, pp. 52–53.

164. KC, p. 89; LH, Vol. 2, p. 53.

165. KC, p. 88; LH, Vol. 2, p. 52.

166. KC, p. 89; LH, Vol. 2, p. 53.

167. KC, p. 89; LH, Vol. 2, p. 53.

168. KC, p. 90; LH, Vol. 2, p. 54.

169. KC, p. 89; LH, Vol. 2, p. 53.

170. E.J. Arnett, *Gazetteer of Sokoto Province*, p. 10; *idem, The Rise of the Sokoto Fulani*, p. 13.

171. KC, p. 89; LH, Vol. 1, p. 53 names the site 'Yargaya.'

172. KC, p. 89; LH, Vol. 2, pp. 53–4.

173. KC, p. 89; LH, Vol. 2, p. 54.

174. KC, p. 89; LH, Vol. 2, p. 53; likewise Dokaji Alhaji Abubakar, *Kano ta Dabo Cigari*, p. 38; and the unpublished *Ta'rikh Kano* of M. Adamu Na Ma'aji and M. Adam Muhammad. M. Hiskett's argument that cowries were introduced to Kano *because* of Sharefa's slave-raiding activities hangs on his claim that "the oldest extant copy" of the Arabic text of the Chronicle, "and the one from which Palmer took his working copy, "really reads 'In Sharifa's time cowries came to Hausa land *because* he was zealous in raiding'" (v. M. Hiskett, "Materials relating to the Cowry Currency of the Western Sudan," Part II, *BSOAS*, Vol. 29, 1966, p. 355. His italics.). Unfortunately for this argument, as we have seen (v. footnotes 129 and 134 *supra*), Palmer's text, obtained in Katsina, was not a copy of "the oldest extant" version of the Chronicle, since this would be shorter by several reigns. As far as we know, Lady Lugard was shown an older verison than Palmer's since that text had only 42 reigns, as against 48 in those studied by Palmer and Hiskett. Moreover, Palmer's translation of this passage agrees exactly with that of East, whose text was, as noted above (v. footnote 38), obtained for him by the Emir Abdullahi Bayero from Zubairu, the son of the Emir Ibrahim Dabo. Thus it seems more probable that the text examined by Hiskett contains a copyist's error, than that the two distinct copies translated by Palmer and East should contain identical errors on this point. In any event, since Sharefa minted the prevailing *turkuda* currency in his palace, and since this currency was accepted in the Sahara and Sudan, one fails to see why he should have destroyed his lucrative monopoly by importing a currency whose volumes and values he could not control. Hiskett's error illustrates the dangers of placing too much weight on a single word and rejecting older texts or translations as imperfect if they do not support one's thesis. Unfortunately, though Hiskett rarely errs in that respect, this tactic is far too common among Arabists at work in Northern Nigeria, and unless checked will merely generate an increasingly specious and lop-sided view of the past.

175. It is possible that this obscure note marks the introduction of the *Dodo Mai-Shan Jini* (the blood-drinking Spirit) which Malam Adamu na Ma'aji cites in his *Ta'rikh Kano* as a terrifying heathen object employed by Alwali and his predecessors for the swearing of judicial oaths and other purposes.

176. KC, p. 90; LH, Vol. 2, p. 56. I have followed East's spelling of proper names here as in most instances where they differ materially from those in Palmer's translation.

177. KC, p. 90; LH, Vol. 2, p. 54.

178. For example, see Dokaji Alhaji Abubakar, *Kano ta Dabo Cigari*, pp. 38–9. I obtained several independent oral accounts of this incident.

179. KC, p. 90; LH, Vol. 2, pp. 54–55.

180. KC, p. 89; LH, Vol. 2, p. 55. Malams Hassan and Shu'aibu, *A Chronicle of Abuja*, p. 5, remark that "in 1734 ... the Beriberi of Bornu made war on all the Hausa states. It was from this time that the people of Zaria began to pay tribute to Bornu."

181. W.F. Gowers, *Gazetteer of Kano Province*, pp. 9–10. "Apparently while encamped in front of the walls of Kano ... (The Sultan of Bornu) ... issued an ultimatum that he would burn the city unless his tribute was promptly paid. Certain Mohammedan mallamai approached him, and their arguments and entreaties induced him to abandon his intention. One of the members of this deputation, by name Shehu Attahiru, was a direct ancestor of the present Emir (Usuman, 1919–1926), his daughter, Halimatu, being the mother of Dabo. The payment of tribute to Bornu continued until the *Jihad*." See also, H.R. Palmer, *The Bornu Sahara and Sudan*, p. 253; and as regards the identity of the Bornu Sultan, R. Cohen, "The King Lists of Bornu," p. 65. Gowers' account neatly supplies those aspects of this incident that the Chronicle omits. In brief Kumbari submitted without a fight, presumably overawed by the size of the Bornu army.

182. KC, p. 90; LH, Vol. 2, p. 55.

183. KC, p. 90; LH, Vol. 2, p. 55.

184. KC, p. 91; LH, Vol. 2, p. 55.

185. KC, pp. 91–2; LH, Vol. 2, p. 56.

186. KC, pp. 91–2; LH, Vol. 2, p. 56.

187. KC, p. 92; LH, Vol. 2, p. 57.

188. This remark, obtained independently from several Kutumbawa and Fulani informants, is now part of Kano's folklore.

189. M. Hiskett, "The 'Song of Bagauda,'" Part II, p. 118.

190. Dokaji Alhaji Abubakar, *Kano ta Dabo Cigari*, p. 41. It is of interest that although they both report Dan Mama's role in the *jihad*, neither Malam Adamu na Ma'aji nor Malam Adam Muhammad in their *Ta'rikh Kano* offer any information on his identity.

191. Dokaji Alhaji Abubakar, *Kano ta Dabo Cigari*, p. 41.

192. KC, p. 93; LH, Vol. 2, pp. 58–9. While Palmer writes 'Galadima Makama,' which makes no sense, East writes 'Galadima Makam.' Was Dan Mama then Dawada's Galadima, before his appointment as Ciroma by Alwali?

4

Conquest and Consolidation

The *Jihad* in Kano

The Genesis of the Jihad

The eighteenth century witnessed a resurgence of Islamic learning and ardor throughout the Sudan. Starting at Tukolor in 1724, there was a succession of *jihads* which only closed in the middle of the 19th century at Masina, to be followed shortly afterwards by a major outburst of Mahdism in the Anglo-Egyptian Sudan.[1] This, in turn, was followed by the rise of the Sanusi,[2] and by a succession of minor discontinuous movements which sustained the inner cohesion and resilience of West African Muslims under European rule in the present century.[3] Taking many different forms and directions, this Muslim revival continues in West Africa to the present day. Its greatest and most enduring achievement was the creation of a large Fulani caliphate and empire in the *jihad* of 1804–10, which the Shehu Usuman dan Fodio declared.

The Shehu, a native of Gobir descended from several generations of Toronke (Toronkawa) clerics who, though not strictly Fulani, are assimilated to them,[4] had studied Islam with his senior kinsmen and with the Shehu al-Hajj Jibril bin Umar, who died during the closing years of Bawa's reign at Gobir, c. 1778–1794. A.D.[5] It is related of Hajj Jibril, also called Jibirin, that he was Hausa, apparently a native of Gobir.[6] He twice made the pilgrimage to Mecca and is said to have remained in Egypt for eighteen years before returning to Gobir and Agades.[7] He may have been stimulated to condemn syncretisms and heathen elements in Hausa state cults by the doctrines and example of the Wahabbite puritanism in Arabia at this time.[8] Jibril's teaching denounced the Hausa chiefdoms for their lax Islam, pagan retentions, and arbitrary governments. These denunciations involved considerable risk. After Jibril returned to Gobir and preached reform in public and private, the rulers "did not listen to him but rather considered how they might do away with him."[9] Alkalawa, the capital of Gobir, then contained

> many honoured malams, but they only taught in secret, in their houses or in the schools. But Hajj Jibirin knew how to speak the truth openly, and he laboured earnestly and fearlessly; but although they could not kill him, neither did he succeed in

bringing them back into the ways of the Prophet. They only became more obstinate in their heathen practices. At this time Usuman, son of Fodio, was born, and was taught to read by Hajj Jibirin. When Hajj Jibirin died, Usuman began to preach until the time of Bawa Jan Gwarzo's death.[10]

Jibril concentrated his teaching on the fundamental issues of Hausa Islam in his day, proclaiming that the practice of non-Islamic customs and rituals constituted disobedience, and that such disobedience constituted unbelief or apostasy.[11] Jibril directed all committed Muslims to reject the corrupt religious and political order of their day. It is easy to see why the local chiefs "considered how they might do away with him." Jibril was really proclaiming two doctrines. He effectively denounced Hausa governments as non-Muslim and accordingly summoned Muslims to resist and reform. This was the first penetrating call to a *jihad* in Hausaland. It obliged every Muslim to determine where he stood, for or against the lax contemporary practice of Islam.

The Shehu Usuman, Jibril's greatest pupil, later rejected his teacher's main thesis—that disobedience constitutes unbelief; but in various works he used similar arguments to justify the *jihad*.[12] The Shehu's second major justification was that of self-defence, namely, that the Hausa chiefs had attacked his community of Muslims during and after their withdrawal. The Muslims were thus obliged by the Sunna and the need for self-preservation to retaliate forcibly until victory was theirs. Despite this disagreement with his old teacher, the Shehu emphasised that "the beginning of the destruction of these blameworthy customs in our Sudanese towns was by his (Jibril's) hands, and the completion of that was by our hands."[13] He repeatedly declared his indebtedness to Jibril, to the latter's puritanical Islam, and to Jibril's insistence on Muslim observance without heathen admixture; and in one place describes himself as merely one of "the waves" produced by Jibril.[14] As Hiskett says, "the teaching of Sheikh Jibril b. 'Umar set off a controversy in the Sudanese towns, centered on the relation of 'disobedience' (here synonymous with non-Islamic local customs) to unbelief—and in the circumstances of the western Sudan of the day, ... this became a burning question. Thus, the Shehu's movement is to be seen as arising, in part, out of a conflict of doctrine in a climate of theological controversy."[15]

This controversy naturally centred among the Muhammadan *'ulama* of Hausaland, each of whom had to decide this question individually in terms of the dichotomy that Jibril proclaimed between Muslims and unbelievers or apostates. An issue of this sort could spread swiftly throughout the Muslim intelligentsia of Hausaland, most of whom were settled Fulani and belonged to clans that ranked high in the Fulani community. Thus, concentrated mainly among the Fulani clerics in Hausaland, the controversy intensified their inner cohesion and separateness from the Hausa round about. When the Shehu Usuman, following Jibril's death, emerged as the leading Muslim teacher and advocate of reform, Fulani clerics throughout Hausaland increasingly looked to him for guidance and leadership on the theological and practical questions Jibril had raised. Individual salvation was felt to depend upon finding the correct answer and course of action.

Briefly, since the history of the Shehu's *jihad* in Gobir does not concern us here, following the death of Bawa Jan Gwarzo, relations between the Shehu and his *jema'a* or congregation on the one hand, and the chiefs and officials of Gobir on the other, deteriorated rapidly. The Sarkin Gobir Nafata (1800–1802) forbade anyone to convert to Islam whose parents had not practised the Faith. He also prohibited the use by Muslims of turbans, or veils for women. Foreseeing strife, and under increasing pressure for action by his immediate followers and by Fulani Muslims in other areas, the Shehu began to proclaim, "Verily, to make ready weapons is Sunna."[16] Perhaps the ensuing struggle could no longer be avoided. In December 1803, the Gobir forces attacked and captured Gimbana, a settlement to which some of the Shehu's Hausa followers under their leader Abdusallami had already withdrawn (*yi hijra*) from Gobir. The Shehu intervened to release his captive followers, and on the 21st of February, 1804, fled from Degel to Gudu (Sokwai) near Kwonni, across the Gobir border, where his followers accepted him as *Emir el-Mu'minin*, or head (caliph) of the Muslim community, the Hausa equivalent being *Sarkin Musulmi*, Chief of the Muslims. The *jihad* dates from this event.[17]

To halt the flow of people from Gobir to Gudu, the Sarkin Gobir Yunfa, Nafata's successor, sent emissaries requesting the Shehu to return. Conditions were set, but the negotiations broke down and fighting began at Matankare. On June 21, 1804 the Shehu's people won a major victory over Yunfa's army at the battle of Tabkin (Lake) Kwoto.[18] Shortly afterwards, the Shehu moved from Gudu to Magabci, and in July 1804 he wrote letters to

> the chiefs of Soudan (Hausa). ... He explained to them that his cause was that of truth against falsehood, that he was reviving religion and putting an end to evil practices. He called upon them to purify their religion before God and to abandon all that was not in accordance with or opposed to the law. He called upon them to aid him in war against his enemies, not to be deceived by the words of his enemies nor to help his enemies against him; for if they did so, God would give them over to destruction.[19]

However, it is said that the Sarkin Gobir Yunfa had already written "to his brother chiefs, Sarkin Katsina, Sarkin Kano, Sarkin Zazzau, Sarkin Daura and Sarkin Asben. They all answered his letter and undertook what he asked of them, that they should help him and increase his strength to fight against all who allied themselves with Shehu."[20] Thus, shortly after the battle of Tabkin Kwoto, the conflict between Yunfa and Shehu spread throughout Hausaland.

Reactions at Kano

We have seen how on his accession Alwali hoarded grain for fear of famine, and refused to provide the forty cattle his chiefs demanded for the fetish Dirki. When his officials insisted, Alwali confronted them directly, destroyed Dirki by opening it and found "a beautiful Koran inside."[21] "The people said, 'you will be expelled from this land even as you have expelled the Koran from Dirki.'"[22] We are told that famine overtook Alwali despite his precautions, probably before the *jihad*. Oral traditions also mention a revolt of the Rumfawa at the start of Alwali's reign, perhaps after his desecration of Dirki. He suppressed that, but evidently as the years went by he became increasingly anxious about the succession. The

Dokaji Abubakar relates two folk stories of fabulous character[23] which may illustrate his anxiety, but Alwali was certainly more anxious about his dynastic rivals, Sharefa's issue, than about the local Fulani.

Sultan Bello relates that when the Shehu's circular letter was brought to the Sarkin Zazzau in July 1804, he accepted the Shehu's message and leadership. However, his people "refused to follow and he fought with them. He remained steadfast in the faith until the end of his life. After his death his people deserted the Mohammedans and became rebels."[24] The chief referred to is Ishi'aku, also called Jatau, who died two years before the Fulani conquered Zaria under Malam Musa. Jatau, the fifty-seventh chief of Zazzau, "was a very pious Mohammedan, and many manuscripts written by his hand are said to be in existence. His son Makam (Makau), however, was a great backslider."[25] Makau was driven south from Zaria by the Fulani at the end of 1808.[26]

Bello also says that "when they brought Shehu's letter to Sarkin Kano, he was on the point of accepting Shehu's message. Then he refused it and followed the way of his brother chiefs."[27] According to local tradition, Alwali wanted to write, accepting the Shehu's message; but his Ciroma Dan Mama first dissuaded him and then, or shortly afterwards, personally wrote the Shehu, offering to support his affairs at Kano.[28] Alwali knew nothing of Dan Mama's treachery. Indeed, he appears to have accepted Dan Mama's advice against his own inclination and judgment in this matter. Dan Mama remained at court in the city throughout and after the *jihad*. According to one report, Dan Mama was then in charge of Rano, Karaye, Bebeji, Tofa, Aujara, Jahun, Dambarta and Sankara. Together these units constituted a substantial portion of the chiefdom.

At that date several important Fulani clans of high rank were settled in different parts of western and southern Kano. In the southeast at Utai near Wudil were the Jobawa under Malam Bakatsine and his brother Malam Sa'idu. In the southwest at Kiru were the Suleibawa under Malam Jamau. From Kiru to Ricifa and Kwassallo in northeastern Zazzau, Suleibawa were the dominant Fulani group. Five miles northeast of Kiru, the Danejawa centred around Zuwa under Yusufu, who is better known as Malam Dan Zabuwa. Bebeji, due east of Kiru, was then under a Fulani territorial chief, the Sarkin Fulani Bebeji. Further north were the Ba'awa, whose senior segment, led by the Limam Yati's two sons, Malam Abdurrahman Goshi and Malam Jibir, were known to Hausa as Yolawa and had their city compounds at Tudun Yola. Due north of Kano, at Matsidau and Shiddar, were the Dambazawa under their leader Muhammadu Dabo, also called Dabo Dambazau. Five miles further north were some Yerimawa Fulani under the Sarkin Fulanin Dambarta, Malam Mayaki (Dan Tunku), who was one of Alwali's officials. Within the capital there were several clerical Fulani lineages of whom the Modibawa (Mundubawa) under Suleimanu, the Gyenawa under Malam Dikoyi, and the Zarawa should be mentioned.[29]

In the Fulani stratification, the Yolawa segment of Ba'awa probably ranked as the senior of these groups. The Suleibawa under Malam Jamau were probably the strongest and most numerous, but like the Toronkawa, though generally classified by outsiders as Fulani, they were distinguished by other Fulani as *rimbe* or assimilated people, and ranked below the Toronkawa, Ba'awa and Jobawa. Another group of the Shehu's followers were Hausa led by one Malam Usuman, also called Yusufu, who had moved in the late eighteenth century from Tam-burawa to Kura where he became Alkali and may also have served as the town chief. On one report this Alkali Usuman founded Kura; but it seems certain the town is far older. Those Hausa Muslims who supported the Shehu's cause, grouped themselves under the Alkali Usuman's leadership, and formed a section (*kunjiya*) within the Shehu's local followers (*jema'a*) alongside the *jihad*ic Fulani clans. Leaders of these and other Fulani groups had been following the course of events in Gobir closely. They awaited further news and instructions from the Shehu. Malam Bakatsine, who had accompanied the Shehu Usuman from Degel on his *hijra* (flight), had fought at the battle of Tabkin Kwoto and taken part in the first unsuccessful attack by the Shehu's followers on Alkalawa, the Gobir capital, in November 1804. Bakatsine seems to have set out for Kano shortly before the Gobir army defeated the Shehu's forces at Tsuntsua in the following month. He played an important part during the next few months in encouraging the local Fulani to prepare for the *jihad* in Kano.

In 1281 A.H. (1864–1865 A.D.) the Alkali Muhammadu Zangi compiled a detailed account of the Fulani *jihad* in Kano from information supplied by three elderly Fulani, the Malams Ishi'aku and Muhammadu Faladi and the Limam of Panisau, who had all apparently taken part in the campaigns at Kano. Excluding Sultan Bello's account of the *jihad* at Gobir, Zangi's history of the struggle in Kano is perhaps the most detailed and convincing available for a Hausa state. Its con-tents may have been known to W.F. Gowers, at least in part.[30] Otherwise, the pub-lished literature shows little trace of this document. The following account of the Fulani conquest of Kano relies heavily on the Alkali Zangi's valuable text, supple-mented or corroborated by Sultan Bello's brief references, by data in District Notebooks, and by other published information and oral traditions.

The Shehu's letter to his *jema'a* in Kano was taken by the Muezzin Goje and a certain Adama, probably Modibbo Adamu, the founder of Adamawa, to the Daneji leader, Malam Dan Zabuwa (Yusufu), who was then probably at Zuwa. This seems to have given a new urgency to their preparations. Messengers moved backwards and forwards between the committed Muslim groups, and on an agreed date their leaders assembled at Dan Zabuwa's compound in Zuwa to take counsel and set their plans. There the decision was taken to "*yi hijra*," that is, to withdraw all their people, property and dependents from the Hausa communities in preparation for the *jihad* or holy war. It was decided to reassemble around Kwazzazabo, five miles northeast of Kiru, and near Zuwa, the Daneji centre. In this movement, the Yolawa concentrated around Durum and Tofa. The date agreed for the Fulani *hijra* in Kano to begin was the 16th of *Jumada Alaula*. In Arnett's interpretation of Sultan Bello's account, this was probably about the middle of 1805, but other data suggest 1806.[31]

Having assembled as planned, the *jihadis* remained for four months at Kwaz-zazabo, completing their preparations. It was probably at this time that the council of leaders, Malam Bakatsine, Malam Jibir, Malam Jamau, Malam Yusufu, Dan Zabuwa, Alkali Usuman, Malam Dabo Dambazau, and Malam Dikoyi of Gyenawa, decided to send Malam Dan Zabuwa to the Shehu for a flag to bless and authorise their *jihad* in Kano. It does not seem that Suleimanu, the leading Mundubawa cleric, had any part in these councils, or perhaps in the entire *jihad*.

All our evidence indicates that Suleimanu remained in Kano city throughout the fighting, and served the Fulani community there as Limam. Even before the *jihad*, Muslim Fulani had refused to worship under Hausa limams.[32] Suleimanu thus remained in the city as Limam until the struggle was over; but many Mundubawa were almost certainly present at Kwazzazabo.

As Gowers notes, though the Shehu Usuman sent a flag and sanction for the *jihad* to the Kano Fulani, "no single leader was appointed."[33] This was not the Shehu's normal practice; and it has been interpreted as a sign that he feared "dissension and jealousy" among the Fulani of Kano.[34] However, from every other chiefdom and province, interested Fulani leaders had themselves gone direct to the Shehu to seek commissions as his representatives. To my knowledge only the Kano Fulani sent someone to the Shehu to seek a flag authorising their *jihad*, but not to seek a leader. The Shehu accordingly sent the flag, leaving the *jema'a* at Kano under collegial leadership. On his return to Kano, Malam Dan Zabuwa deposited the flag with Malam Jamau, the Suleibawa leader whose home was Kiru. Malam Jamau accordingly became the standard-bearer, and was thence known as *Mai-tuta*, the "one with the flag," its custodian. Perhaps Dan Zabuwa deposited the flag with Malam Jamau to clear himself publicly of any suspicion of asserting personal leadership. However, Malam Jamau probably had the best claim to guard the flag, being the first *Muhajarini* (the first to withdraw), and head of the largest Fulani group.[35]

There was clearly some strain and manoeuvring for position among the Fulani leaders during the *jihad* at Kano; but, as we shall see, they cooperated closely throughout most of the ensuing campaign, grouping their forces together and taking counsel at critical moments. It is true that Malam Bakatsine set out alone against Gaya; but this may as easily have arisen from collective strategy as from personal pique at not being placed in charge. The Alkali Zangi's text can be interpreted to indicate the latter; yet, if this was so, Bakatsine's pique was evidently not treated seriously by the others. Indeed, Bakatsine seems to have returned from Kwazzazabo to Utai before the fighting broke out, probably to mislead the Hausa and prepare for his campaign in Eastern Kano; but perhaps also he had lost patience during the long inactivity that preceded the fighting. In these months the Fulani leaders may have been waiting for reinforcements from Katsina or elsewhere; or they may have hoped that Alwali would soon leave Kano for a spell in the country; or perhaps they merely lacked confidence and cohesion.

The Initial Encounter

Meanwhile, their large following at Kwazzazabo had to be fed. The unusual number of Fulani at Kwazzazabo terrified the nearby villagers who were scattered in small hamlets. According to Zangi, most of these "pagans" (*arna*) fled, defenceless against the Fulani mass and perhaps expecting trouble. The Fulani then emptied their granaries. This went on for a while, until a certain farmer of "Maguzawa" stock refused either to flee or to open his granaries, following which Dandaya, one of the Fulani foragers, slew him with an arrow. His was the first reported death in the Kano *jihad*. The farmer's son, Gainaku, escaped to Bebeji. The Fulani appropriated his father's grain. The Sarkin Bebeji sent at once to inform Alwali of the incident. Alwali had recently moved from Kano to Takai, the town Sharefa had walled and Babba Zaki had used as a rural residence and military base. Alwali appraised the situation acurately; but to test Fulani intentions, he instructed Gainaku to return to Kwazzazabo, and, with the help of his neighbours, to burn the Fulani compounds and seize whom or what he would from among them. Gainaku collected a local force and attacked the Fulani. He was repulsed severely, but only after several Fulani had died, including Ibrahim of the Yolawa.

An official report of this engagement soon reached Alwali. Before proceeding further, Alwali determined to discuss the situation with Malam Bakatsine, who was then at Utai. On one report, Alwali summoned Bakatsine to meet him at Utai. According to another, Alwali sent word to Bakatsine that he wished to visit the latter for prayers, that is, for the formal ritual invocations which chiefs often sought in times of crisis. According to Gowers, "Alwali accused him of treachery, but Malam Bakatsine swore to his innocence on the Koran. On his return from the interview he (Bakatsine) took Gogel (seventeen miles east southeast of Kano) and then proceeded on a campaign in the southeastern parts of Kano in which he was uniformly successful."[36] The Alkali Zangi gives a more ambiguous account, which suggests that Bakatsine told Alwali to proceed to Joda about eight miles northeast of Gogel; but it seems clear from both traditions that Alwali did confront Bakatsine with questions and charges; and perhaps, being without immediate military support, Bakatsine escaped by deceiving Alwali with false words or oaths.

Following this, Alwali consulted his courtiers[37] and despatched the Barde Bakori with a force he thought sufficient to disperse the Fulani. Like Gainaku, Bakori was repulsed, and the Fulani continued at Kwazzazabo. The Barde returned to Alwali, who had apparently moved back to Kano city. Alwali's councillors were divided. Some advocated total mobilisation and immediate assault; others wished to negotiate a settlement without further bloodshed. Alwali supported the second view. He had earlier wanted to accept the Shehu Usuman's letter demanding support. Five clerics, including an Arab, were sent to Kwazzazabo with a letter from Alwali that authorised them to discuss and settle the dispute. The deputation contained Malams Baringimi, Bakada, Nakardayawa, Japbo and an Arab, Aziyan. The Fulani leaders gave them an audience at Gyerta, but instructed them publicly to leave. Encircled by Fulani warriors, Alwali's messengers seem to have been terrified into submission. It is reported that they all "repented" and agreed to support the Fulani, including Nakardayawa, who is said to have died of fright on his return to Kano. The Fulani leaders thus rejected Alwali's appeal for peace point-blank. Alwali then consulted his two senior clerics, the Limam, Malam Abdulkadiri and the Alkali Datuwa, who was probably a baGyeni Fulani. Both men condemned the "*jihad*" at Kwazzazabo as *jahilci* (ignorance, error, falsehood) and thus indirectly condemned the Shehu Usuman, his cause and his followers alike. They advised Alwali to call out his levy and also to summon friendly Tuareg to help disperse the horde at Kwazzazabo. Having little alternative, Alwali summoned the levy and placed his Sarkin Dawaki Ali in command, directing him to capture the Fulani leaders and women, but to slay the rank and file.

Long before the Sarkin Dawaki reached Kwazzazabo, the Fulani had prepared strong defensive positions and cut the trenches from which their archers and spearmen later fought off the Hausa cavalry charges. By then Fulani leaders had apparently withdrawn toward Kogo, a nearby settlement; and when the Sarkin Dawaki's cavalry broke through the Fulani lines into their settlement, he ordered his Barde to set fire to the Fulani huts. Had this order been promptly obeyed the Kano Fulani might not have been able to continue the fight. However, the Barde demurred; "Not yet, have you seen their flag? If you haven't found it, you had better go and get it." Barde then seized the Shehu's flag, whereupon Jamau's Suleibawa counter-attacked with fury, and threw the Hausa horse into confusion. Their retreat was a costly one in confined spaces between the broken homesteads and the trenches, with the Fulani bowmen pursuing. So many Hausa were thrown from their horses in the rout, it is said that Fulani women took part in the slaughter. The Sarkin Dawaki Ali escaped by a trench to report the disaster to Alwali. The Fulani acquired much valuable booty in this engagement—horses, *lifida*, muskets, spears, suits of chain-mail, swords, and other weapons of war. They also gained a confidence they had previously lacked.

As Sarkin Fulanin Dambarta, Malam Maiyaki, better known as Dan Tunku, the founder and first chief of Kazaure emirate, owed allegiance to Alwali. However, having witnessed this Fulani victory, apparently as a member of the Sarkin Dawaki's force, he elected to "convert to Islam" (*shiga Musulunci*),[38] broke faith with Alwali and undertook to assist his embattled cousins as best he could. However, Alwali did not learn of Dan Tunku's change of sides until too late. Zangi dates the "conversion" of Kano, that is, the Fulani conquest, from this first important victory at Kwazzazabo.

The Fulani now felt free to move from their strong defensive positions across western Kano in search of food and military advantage. They first seized Gammo near Godiya, whose people "converted," that is, surrendered. They then took Kabo close by, and Massanawa, following which they attacked Godiya. There the Dan Tama sallied out and repelled them sharply, slaying many of their leading men. Nonetheless, the Fulani managed to enter the town and burnt it utterly, with all its adjacent hamlets. They next moved en bloc to Birnin Malam, which no longer exists. To avoid the fate of Godiya, the people of this village also "converted," and their example was followed by those of Kofa nearby. There, a Fulani called Turmi who later became the chief of Bebeji joined the *jihadis* with his people.

The battle with the Sarkin Dawaki at Kwazzazabo occurred on the last day of Rajab following the opening clashes. The Sarkin Dawaki Ali fled eastward to Mura before returning to Kano. Turmi, the new recruit, moved from Kofa against Bebeji, and then against Karaye during the month of Ramadan. There Dan Zabuwa took command; but failing to capture Karaye, the *jihadis* fell upon a pastoral Fulani group which had refused to join them. This engagement occurred near Karaye at a place called Sapti on a Saturday. The pastoralists were put to flight, their cattle seized, and their leader (*Ardo*) "converted," shortly before his death. The Fulani *jihadis* then set aside their war to observe the fast.

From Kwazzazabo to Dan Yaya

After the fast and the Idi prayers, the Muslim forces occupied Keffi in Dabga, their first break from the field. Thence they moved against Kumasa and again to

Karaye. Here the Fulani were attacked by the chief and his force outside the walls, but by late afternoon they had regained control and entered the town. Almost immediately they saw the Dan Tama of Godiya and the Barde Bakori coming toward them with an army. Evidently the Hausa leaders didn't expect to encounter the Fulani. The latter took up strong positions in the river bed at Karaye and, attacking suddenly, slew many, put the Hausa force to flight, and captured most of their horses. Karaye was the first major town the Fulani had taken. Thereafter Alwali was clearly on the defensive.

The Fulani had occupied Karaye for three days, when Malam Musa Ba Malle arrived from the northwest on his way to Zaria. A Fulani of Malle, Malam Musa was later given the Shehu's flag and commission for the conquest of Zaria or Zazzau. According to Zangi's account, on this occasion the Shehu had sent him to Zaria in response to a request from the Sarkin Zazzau Ishi'aku, who had accepted the call to Islam, for some suitable Muslim scholars to assist him. The Fulani assembled at Karaye delegated Dan Zabuwa, the Daneji leader, to accompany Musa to Zaria and help him. Together Malams Musa and Dan Zabuwa entered Zaria as the Shehu's representatives and were welcomed with official appointments by the chief, who persevered in Islam until his death shortly after. His successor then apostasised, following which Musa returned to the Shehu to receive a flag for the conquest of Zaria while Dan Zabuwa rejoined the Kano *jihad*. Zangi identifies the Muslim chief of Zazzau who adopted Islam as Makau; if so then Musa's visit occurred after November 1806; but Zangi is clearly in error. It was Ishi'aku (Jatau), Makau's father, who accepted Islam. When Makau succeeded, he ejected Dan Zabuwa and Musa, but he also ejected Alwali from Zaria, before being evicted himself.[39]

Karaye provided the *jihadi* forces with a strong defensive position which could serve equally well as a refuge or as a base for attack. Having regrouped, the Fulani set out eastwards, moving by Magami and Hawadi to Gora, midway between Kano and Kiru. There the leaders had a dispute, following which Malam Abdurrahman Goshi led his Yolawa north, while Malam Jamau moved southwards to link up with Bakatsine and the Jobawa who had been campaigning for some months in the southeastern districts from their headquarters at Utai. In part, this dispersion of Fulani forces certainly expressed strain and rivalries among their leaders, but it may also have been guided by strategic considerations. In the discussion at Gora, Abdurrahman argued firstly, that if the armies of the *jihad* remained all in one place, they invited a major attack by the combined forces of Katsina, Daura and Kano; and secondly, that such concentration would leave the rest of the country in Alwali's hands, thereby enabling him to bring all his resources against the *jihad*. Abdurrahman argued further that by dispersing to their various home districts, the Fulani would oblige Alwali to disperse his forces likewise, and could then put their superior mobility and field knowledge to best advantage. Whether or not these counsels won the support of the meeting, Abdurrahman and Jamau then withdrew their forces in different directions.

After some months of desultory campaigning, the Fulani leaders determined once more to reunite their armies and assembled at Farin Tabki near Tofa in the Yolawa homelands. Almost immediately they were attacked by a Hausa force hastily collected from Damargu and Tatarawa. The Fulani repelled this attack, and captured many horses. They then reduced Bici and Tofa to submission, before moving on Marke and thence on Tatarawa. There a new enemy came against them, the Tuareg of Adar under their chief, the Tambari Agumbil.[40] Zangi says that Alwali had paid Agumbil (Agunbulu) four million cowries to bring his people against the Fulani. Reinforced by the local Hausa, Agumbil attacked the Fulani at Tatarawa. The Tuareg attack drove the Suleibawa and Fulani to flight; but the Suleibawa rallied and levelled a steady fire of arrows at the Hausa flank. It seems that Agumbil pressed the attack to relieve the pressure on his Hausa troops; but he was killed at that moment, following which the Hausa resistance broke, and the Fulani attack produced a rout. The Fulani followed the fleeing Hausa up to the river Tomas, and for some days they combed the area for prisoners and booty, and destroyed the village of Tomas, before moving southwards to Jalli and Madaci nearby.

Alwali now tried another tactic. Reinforcing his experienced troops with further levies, he directed them to contain the Fulani at Madaci, and while avoiding open battle, to harrass them by continuous minor attacks that would block their movement elsewhere and wear them down by attrition. This tactic seems to have been effective. Meanwhile the Hausa prepared for another battle, and sent out their raiders to decoy the Fulani. The ruse succeeded, and the Fulani lost many men in that engagement, following which they withdrew to their camp between Madaci and Jalli to regroup; but on the next day, instead of retiring, they threw their entire force against these two towns; Malam Dan Zabuwa, who had returned from Zaria, fell in the fight. By late afternoon the Fulani had taken Madaci and Jalli. Situated about 17 miles north of Kano city, these towns were strategically important.

The Battle at Dan Yaya

On learning of these losses, Alwali himself came out from Kano with a large force, including seven hundred heavy calvalry (*lifida*), and moved directly across the Fulani front before turning westwards to Dawaki, a walled town between Tofa and Jalli, the Fulani stronghold. Alwali first attacked and burned Dawaki, and then occupied the area with his army. The Fulani quickly concentrated against him at Dawaki and kept up a constant harassing attack with arrows and light horsemen, circling the town to draw out the Hausa cavalry in pursuit for piecemeal destruction. It was here that the Sarkin Fulanin Dambarta Dan Tunku, Malam Maiyaki, first openly threw his forces on the Fulani side, thus repudiating his allegiance to Alwali. Here also the Fulani received further reinforcements when "Mai-duniya" ("Owner of the world") sent his men to join them.[41] It seems likely that Mai-duniya may have been the Ciroma Dan Mama. The ex-Ciroma had made his personal allegiance to Shehu by letter after dissuading Alwali from doing so; he had also offered his aid secretly to the Shehu at the appropriate time. It is said that Shehu informed the Fulani leaders about this and instructed them to reserve "one hundred towns" for Dan Mama following Alwali's defeat. Dan Mama himself did not fight on either side, but at Dan Yaya he seems to have placed much of his force at the Fulanis' disposal and, as indicated above, this would normally form a substantial section of the Kano army. While Alwali remained in the city, Dan Mama had stayed with him and may have had little direct contact with the Fulani leaders; but at Dawaki as the campaign approached its crisis he did so.

Alwali was well aware that his situation was serious. He had already offered the Fulani terms twice without success. The challenge and contest were explicitly unconditional. Following Agumbil's defeat and death, Alwali sent letters to his suzerain in Bornu and to adjoining chiefs appealing for aid against the Fulani in Kano, in their own interests as well as his. According to Mamman Bello, the sultan of Bornu, Mai Ahmed (1791–1808),

> sent his waziri … to their aid. … The Waziri directed his forces as he had been commanded. He sent a raiding force to the people of Daura and made preparations in order to come to the aid of Sarkin Daura and Sarkin Kano and Sarkin Katsina even as the Sarkin Bornu had commanded him. When their neighbours, our folk (the Fulani of Bornu) who were there, heard news of his coming they assembled together in one force. The Waziri of the Sarkin Bornu sent his army against them and God turned his army in flight. Then Waziri came forth himself and raided our people and drew up his force in battle against them. God turned him to flight.[42]

Thus Alwali received no reinforcements from Bornu as the Shehu's followers there organised the local Fulani to block their route west. Sultan Bello cites this incident as the beginning and decisive justification of the Fulani *jihad* in Bornu.

Alwali's appeals to the chiefs of Katsina and Daura were more successful. Thus far, those rulers seem to have escaped attack in their territories; but being aware of the trend of events, they were alert to the implications of the Shehu's *jihad*. Mamman Bello, the Shehu's son and ablest lieutenant, seems to have directed these developments. He

> directed Umoru Dallaji (the first Fulani Emir of Katsina) to go as my messenger to Katsina and Kano in order to inform them (the Fulani) there of our affairs. … Umaru became my delegate among the people of Katsina. He found the Katsina people at Yan Tumaki. Then he passed on with the letter to Kano. His arrival at Katsina coincided with the departure of Sarkin Katsina to Kano, together with Sarkin Daura. The chiefs of these countries had never combined before our *jihad*. Even in war they did not unite. But as soon as our *jihad* broke out they became united as one hand. Thus it happened that Sarkin Katsina and Sarkin Daura set out together with a vast army of which God alone knows the numbers. They marched until they approached the villages of our people at Kano. There some of their Fulani kindred joined our folk, followers of the faith. The name of their leader was Dan Tunku; his following was a small one. The army of Katsina and Daura was defeated and returned home empty-handed. The arrival of our messenger Umaru Dallaji coincided with this defeat, and he thereupon attacked at once and captured many of the Katsina towns.[43]

Evidently before proceeding to Kano, Umaru Dallaji had instructed the Katsina Fulani congregated at Yan Tumaki to prepare for immediate action. He probably brought eastwards with him a number of enthusiasts eager to join their kin and fellows in the major battle that was clearly developing at Dawaki to decide the future of Kano; but most of the Katsina Fulani remained in reserve at Yan Tumaki, ready to move east to Kano or north to Katsina as the situation required. Perhaps the Fulani of Kano received few reinforcements from Katsina before this engagement was over. However, Dan Tunku clearly threw his forces against Alwali at this time.

As Sarkin Fulanin Dambarta and head of the local Yerimawa, Dan Tunku was a Kano official who owed allegiance to Alwali and had not been party to the consultations and preparations that preceded the Kano *jihad*. Indeed, of all senior Fulani chiefs who held office under Alwali, he alone seems to have changed sides openly. However, Dan Tunku had no wish to remain subordinate to the council of untitled clan leaders who directed the Shehu's affairs in Kano. Already himself of senior rank, when he saw how the struggle proceeded and was likely to end, like the Ciroma Dan Mama and perhaps on the latter's advice, Dan Tunku made his submission either to the Shehu or to his son, Mamman Bello, and either personally or through a trusted emissary, such as his son Dambo. Thus, while transferring allegiance to the Shehu, he remained independent and outside of the group in Kano to whom the Shehu had sent a flag. Though Dan Tunku had earlier declared his sympathies with the *jihadis* at Kwazzazabo, he had not since moved to help them. However, at Dawaki he joined actively in the fray on their side.

From Dawaki, Alwali moved to Danyaya, twenty-five miles north of Kano.[44] His general, Dan Tama, also moved a force to Beguwa nearby. The Fulani then occupied Sabon Ruwa. At Danyaya, Alwali welcomed the chiefs and the armies of Daura and Katsina, while the Fulani also received further reinforcements from their kinsmen in Ringim, Jahun and other northeastern areas. These contingents concentrated at the nearby village of Gwarmai.

It is sometimes said that the following battle lasted three days.[45] Alkali Muhammed Zangi mentions ninety-three fights over a period of four months at Danyaya and the nearby villages.[46] However, Alwali did not commit the bulk of his force until the last three days. Evidently for three months there was constant skirmishing and raiding between the armies, each playing for time and advantage. Maybe Alwali pursued then the tactics that had won his only success near Madaci, namely, attrition followed by assault. He may also have been awaiting further reinforcements from Katsina, Daura, Bornu or elsewhere.

After three months at Danyaya, Alwali took the field himself on a Monday and attacked the Fulani settled at Sabon Ruwa in strength. Some homes were destroyed by fire, but Fulani moved quickly to Sabon Ruwa from surrounding areas and checked the Hausa assault. On the following day Alwali's men, who may have occupied Sabon Ruwa the day before, were pushed back towards evening after a severe struggle that took a heavy toll on both sides. Only those who had died within the Fulani camp were buried. The battlefield was littered with dead. The Hausa renewed their attack in the late afternoon, and that night Alwali received more reinforcements from Daura. In the morning the Hausa renewed their attack, but without its initial vigour. The Fulani were then running short of food and stores. Their leaders held a meeting to decide the next step.

Bakatsine and his Jobawa were still campaigning separately in the southeast. Having taken Gogel and some small towns nearby, Bakatsine had moved against Gaya but failed to take it. He had then camped outside and harried the nearby villages. One of the leaders present suggested that all should withdraw to Bakatsine at Gaya; and this was quickly accepted. The leaders then considered when and how to move—by dispersing separately or moving together, by night or by day. At this stage Abdurrahman Goshi, the Yola leader, pointed out the difficulties involved in either course. In addition, he argued that to withdraw was to concede defeat, which would weaken Fulani morale and strengthen the Hausa. Malam Jibir, Goshi's brother and another leader, whose opinion was asked next, said bluntly that the Fulani should throw everything into one major attack against the Hausa armies before them and leave the issue to Allah. This way, by the morrow victor and defeated would both be known. Withdrawal merely postponed the day of final decision; but that could not be escaped; and in Jibir's view, this encounter at Danyaya was the best situation for forcing a decision. Jibir's opinion won immediate support, and the Fulani prepared for one last decisive attack.

At dusk around the time of the evening prayer (about 7 p.m.), the Fulani moved from their defenses into the open fields. The Hausa army at once came out against them. In the failing light and early darkness the two forces clashed; and as darkness fell the battle seems to have broken down into thousands of individual combats across the open plain. The struggle went on until 5 a.m. the following day, when the Fulani set fire to the Hausa camp with its tents, huts and bivouacs, its womenfolk, horses and stores of food and weapons. The sight of the camp burning in the rear threw the Hausa into confusion. They began to withdraw towards the flames, and soon the battle became a rout. Alwali quit the camp as the fire spread, and fled to Kano with his sons, the Madaki and Ciroma, accompanied by the Sarkin Shanu, the Sarkin Yara and other officials. The Fulani devoted themselves to looting, prayer, slaughter and rejoicing, according to inclination and opportunity. The chiefs of Katsina and Daura withdrew homeward separately with such forces as they had. Small detachments of the broken armies fled or fought for their lives as best they could.

Gowers briefly mentions the tradition that "the treachery of the Ciroma of Kano decided the event of the battle";[47] but the Ciroma who behaved in this way was Dan Mama, and not Alwali's son who had succeeded to that title.

The Fall of Kano and End of Alwali

The Hausa army having disintegrated and its leader fled, the victorious Fulani proceeded to reduce the major settlements throughout the surrounding area, beginning with Beguwa which Dan Tama vacated, Damargu and Bogwai. Bici and Tofa had surrendered to them shortly before Agumbil's defeat at Tatarawa. From Bogwai they first reduced Gogori and then Farin Ruwa on the Katsina border, following which they moved to Kurkujan across the border to reinforce Umaru Dallaji in his *jihad* against their recent enemy, the Hausa chief of Katsina. At Kurkujan they met Umaru Dallaji and Malam Ishi'aku, whom the Shehu had appointed to conquer Daura. For the next four months the Kano Fulani campaigned in Katsina under Umaru Dallaji's command. For much of this time they fought in west central Katsina in the area around Sabon Gari, Dallaji's headquarters directly south of the city. We are not told whether the Kano Fulani took part in Dallaji's first capture of Katsina city; but this seems likely. They probably withdrew to Kano shortly after Dallaji occupied Katsina, following which he was expelled by a Hausa counter-attack. In response to Dallaji's appeals for aid, Mamman Bello then sent Namoda and the Alibawa Fulani of Zamfara to reinforce him, and the Fulani of Kano, who had withdrawn, returned in time to join the Fulani attack on the Sarkin Katsina at Dankama.[48]

Returning by way of Tabayeni, the Kano Fulani crossed the state boundary near Farin Ruwa and retraced their steps from Gogori to Bogwai, Bici, Damargu, and Tomas on the river of that name. There Zangi relates that Malam Jibir departed with his following to attack Fageni and attacked and burned the town.[49]

Meanwhile at the city Alwali reviewed the situation, counting his losses and remaining assets. He seems also to have consulted several city clerics for advice. Some months after his return from Danyaya when, except for Jibir, the Fulani were still at Tomas, Alwali sent a letter appealing for peace by a delegation of Kano malams—Kabara, Gabdo, Jabo, a Fulani, 'Nguruza, and the Dan Goronduma Isma'ilu, an official cleric. The Fulani leaders assembled at Tomas to hear the chief's message. Alwali undertook to obey the Fulani *jihadis* and to do whatever they wished, and expressed his willingness to come to them on foot if required. The letter was apparently a declaration of unconditional surrender; but Alwali seemed throughout to assume that he would retain the throne as a tributary chief, and rule Kano under the guidance and supervision of the Shehu's supporters. This was clearly not what the *jihadis* wished, nor perhaps was it practicable. Yet so far, with the possible exceptions of Daura and Katsina, no Hausa chiefdom had fallen to the Fulani *jihad*. Perhaps Alwali's was among the first to fall. Thus, lacking relevant precedents, he may have hoped that the letter would preserve his throne by some new mode of vassalage, or at least that it would clarify the new situation created by events at Danyaya.

The Fulani leaders considered Alwali's appeal jointly and made their reply, which was brief and forthright. They claimed they had initially commanded Alwali to abandon paganism and practice Islam as the Shehu directed, that he had refused to do so, and that he had attacked them until Allah inflicted on him the crippling defeat of Danyaya. They wished no further communication with him, but announced that they would attack Kano on the twelfth of *Rabi Al-awal*, which may have been the next month or the one after. Alwali's delegation was instructed to return at once; and on learning their message, Alwali prepared for flight. "Forty" days before the Fulani attack was due, Alwali went to Rano; and when the Fulani occupied Kano city on the twelfth of Rabi Al-awal, recognizing his insecurity at Rano, he then fled further south to Zaria, which was then under Makau.[50] This was probably in the first half of 1807. Alwali spent a year at Zaria before being driven homewards to his end by the scorn and shame of his new situation.[51]

Meanwhile, of the five or six leading Fulani, only Bakatsine remained outside Kano city, bogged down at Gaya on his private *jihad*. Evidently Bakatsine lacked the resources necessary to reduce Gaya; and his Jobe councillors suggested that he withdrew to Wudil, then a large town near Utai, his home. The *jihadis'* council in Kano also sent to Bakatsine advising him to leave Gaya and settle at Wudil. In obeying, Bakatsine called all the Shehu's followers in southeastern Kano to join him at Wudil, thereby increasing the town and ensuring his local dominance. With him to Wudil went the leading members of the Jelbe (Jelubawa), the 'yan Lagi'en, Gyenawa and Zarawa Fulani of Gaya and Dutse. Together these clans remained at Wudil with Bakatsine for nine months before Alwali re-entered the chiefdom and settled at Burumburum about 30 miles due south.

After Bakatsine's withdrawal to Wudil lifted the siege of Gaya, that chiefdom remained outside Fulani control, loyal to Alwali, whose grandmother, the Maidaki Mariyama, was a princess of the Gaya line. Gaya was thus one of the last remaining strings to Alwali's bow. Its successful defiance of the Fulani under Bakatsine encouraged Alwali to make one last effort to recover his throne. Before moving from Zaria to Burumburum, he instructed the Sarkin Gaya Gujabu to call out his levy and attack the Fulani at Wudil. Gujabu did so but was defeated. Bakatsine had assembled a large body of Fulani at Wudil. Gujabu then withdrew to Gaya, losing many horses to Bakatsine's men. They at once attacked Gaya, and on this assault forced an entrance. Gujabu seems to have been slain. Meanwhile Alwali had quit his unpleasant situation at Zaria for Burumburum where his kinsman, the Wambai Tagwai, welcomed him.

At Burumburum Alwali learnt of recent events at Gaya; but by then the Fulani were closing in. Though most of Bakatsine's force had swept on eastwards from Gaya to subdue Aujara and to Taura, which withstood them, to Kiyawa in Dutse, Katanga, Gwandi and Taka, some had remained at Gaya, and many had returned to Wudil. The *jihadis* in Kano instructed Bakatsine to attack Alwali at Burumburum from Takai; and a larger force of Yolawa under Malam Goshi and of Suleibawa under Malam Jamau Maituta, the flag-bearer, moved south from Kano to join them. Together these Fulani forces invested Burumburum, besieged and assaulted it. After a strenuous resistance for several weeks, the defence was broken. In the general slaughter that followed, Alwali was killed and his son Umaru escaped, fleeing north along the border beyond Daura towards Damagaram, where he found the defeated emirs of Katsina and Daura, Dan Kasawa and the Sarkin Daura Abdu. Several years later when Dan Kasawa established his chiefdom at Maradi, Umaru accompanied him westwards from Gafai; but by then the Daurawa under Sarkin Gwari Abdu had moved apart to Kalgo near the modern town of Gumel.[52] In the final assault on Burumburum, Malam Abdurrahman Goshi lost his life. Thereafter his brother Malam Jibir was undisputed head of the Yolawa.

Some months before Alwali's death, the chiefdom had been effectively conquered. Nonetheless large areas remained to be subdued, for example Rano, Dutse and Birnin Kudu and the districts of Gezawa, Gabazawa, Girke, Babura and Dambarta. The Kumbotso area immediately south of Kano, and Kura were also untouched; but the central resistance had been broken. The remaining Hausa forces could not challenge Fulani dominance; and following Alwali's flight, there was no one to mobilize or coordinate them. As their campaign unfolded, the Fulani had also subjugated a number of districts and towns which, being scattered across the country, provided a network of bases and strong points that ensured the swift reduction of intervening areas. In the southeast the Jobawa now dominated their home areas from Gogel past Utai and Gaya southwards. Ringim, Taura, Aujara and Kiyawa were also in Fulani hands, thus sealing off the eastern frontier. Jahun had for centuries been held by Fulani who, although not initial suporters of the *jihad*, had joined the *jihadis* at Dan Yaya. From Kano northeast past Gezawa, Gabbasawa, Sankara and beyond, there had been little fighting; this triangle awaited reduction and occupation. But north and west of the city, the home areas had been effectively conquered. From Damargu to Kunci, Bici and

Farin Ruwa, the *jihadis* held sway. Everything east of the city had fallen before them. Malam Dabo Dambazau dominated Matsidau, Shiddar and the southern half of Dambarta district. Northwards the Yerimawa leader Dan Tunku had seized control. In the southwest where the struggle began, Karaye, Kiru, Gora and Gamo lay within a block of territory completely under Fulani control. Rano as yet had escaped attack; but its fall was a foregone conclusion, and, with the capture of Burumburum, only Birnin Kudu and the districts beyond could still resist.

It is perhaps not accidental that in the course of the *jihad* the leading *jihadi* lineages each managed to establish military dominance over their own home areas, the Jobawa around Wudil and Utai, the Dambazawa at Matsidau, the Yolawa in northwestern Kano from Damargu, Farin Ruwa and Kunci southwards to Tofa, the Suleibawa of Malam Jamau at Kiru and southwards, the Danejawa from Zuwo to Massanawa, the Jelubawa and Yeligawa at Gaya, and the Yerimawa under Dan Tunku in the north from Dambarta to Kazaure. Evidently the Fulani leaders and clans who waged the Kano *jihad* were keenly concerned to pre-empt control over their respective home areas; they were perhaps equally determined not to lose these to other Fulani groups. Such considerations probably prolonged the struggle by reducing the attackers' cohesion. It is doubtful how clearly these leaders were primarily concerned each to seize his clan territory before proceeding further afield, or were motivated by long-term political considerations; but their immediate interests were probably the more concrete. Only by securing exclusive dominance over their respective home areas would these clans and their leaders establish firm bases for their continuing power, resources, and freedom from direct interference and overrule by others.

In effect then, during the *jihad*, Kano had been provisionally partitioned between the leading Fulani clans by this process of local appropriation. Each of the leading *jihadi* clans justified its appropriation and local dominance in identical terms, at once historical and secular, religious and military, for since all had had equal shares in the *jihad*, each could justify the occupation of its home district as essential for successful pursuit of the common campaign. The territories appropriated thus served as lineage bases in which the various clan-contingents could leave their families and cattle while engaged on campaigns. Accordingly, when the Hausa chiefship was finally overthrown and the Fulani began to rule, their governing college consisted of those clan chiefs to whom the Shehu had sent his flag for Kano by Dan Zabuwa, and who had fought the *jihad* together as its generals. These men had common interests and shared a joint dominion, the fruit of their joint efforts and risk; but each was also first identified as head of a distinct Fulani segment, the Dambazawa, Danejawa, Yolawa, Jobawa, or Suleibawa, which each held exclusive jurisdiction over its home territory, and each sought to preserve full autonomy and equality of rights and status with his colleagues. Even during the *jihad* this situation had generated strains and rivalries between the leaders, since their parity obliged each of them first to enhance his position within the group in order to secure his pre-eminence within the clan.

Of the Hausa officials, several are known to have remained at Kano following Alwali's flight, including the Hausa Limam Abdulkadiri, the Alkali Datuwa (a baGyeni Fulani), the Barde Kerreriya, the Ciroma Dan Mama, and probably others. When the Fulani occupied Kano, the Limam Abdulkadiri withdrew to settle at Bangare. If the Alkali Datuwa remained in the city, he then ceased to administer the law, this function being appropriated by the victors collegially under their Hausa colleague, the Alkali Usuman, who served as chairman and judge and delivered sentence on behalf of the court which now met every morning in a city mosque, the Masallacin Hausawa. The Barde Kerrerriya continued to act as head of a city ward; but like other Hausa *hakimai*, he lost his rural fiefs at this period. The new Alkali Usuman Bahaushe (The Hausa) retained Kura and adjacent settlements by virtue of his role as a leading *jihadi*. The ex-Ciroma Dan Mama alone of Alwali's territorial chiefs retained his claim to substantial territorial fiefs. This rested on the role he had played in helping the Muslim forces to victory at Danyaya, on his personal allegiance to the Shehu, and on the latter's unconfirmed order that Dan Mama should be compensated with "a hundred towns." Alwali's senior slaves, the Shamaki Mohamma Jifa and the Dan Rimi, had both accompanied him south from Kano; and either Alwali had dismissed or removed most of the palace slaves when he left Kano, or they had fled of their own volition during the interval of forty days between his exit and the Fulani entry. On their arrival the latter found the palace almost uninhabited, but made no attempt to occupy it. Since the Fulani leaders all shared equal rank and authority in the collegial form of government they had developed during the *jihad*, there was no chief, and so the palace remained empty.

Following Alwali's death at Burumburum, the Shamaki Mohamma Jifa returned to Kano, where he died. His descendants remain there today, being classified as Kutumbawa. Several minor Kutumbawa princes also remained in the city. Perhaps some of these had followed Dan Mama in helping the Fulani against Alwali with information or secret aid; but most of the Hausa officials had fallen in battle or fled with Alwali southwards, and few returned. Several were slain with their chief at Burumburum. Some who survived that battle fled northwards with Umaru, who succeeded Alwali as the forty-fourth Hausa chief of Kano, and the first without a chiefdom. By contrast, many rural Fulani chiefs who had exercised territorial or *bin kanu* jurisdiction under Alwali remained at their posts. Few of these rural Fulani chiefs had been directly attacked during the *jihad*. However, the Sarkin Fulanin Bebeji, having openly assisted Alwali, lost his office and seems to have fled the country. Dan Tunku, the Sarkin Fulanin Dambarta, remained in the north away from the city and, though differentiating himself in this way from the leaders of the *jihad*, did not reveal his intentions immediately. The Ghadames Arabs of Kano continued to occupy their quarter near the market unmolested, being held in high respect by the Fulani as the Prophet's people.

Local history and traditions set 1807 as the year in which the Fulani conquered Kano. Relying on Sultan Bello's history of the *jihad*, which concentrates heavily on events in Gobir, Kebbi and Zamfara and says very little about eastern Hausa, Arnett and Last place the conquest some months before December 1805; but this is certainly an error. If we take the Fulani occupation of Kano city as its decisive event, the conquest could hardly have occurred before April or May 1807; and Alwali probably died at Burumburum in the rainy season of the following year, having left Zaria shortly before its conquest by Malam Musa baMalle. These dates, though tentative, agree closely with the chronology usually employed in summaries of Kano history.[53]

The Interregnum

A Collegial Government

Having conquered Kano, broken the Hausa resistance and occupied the city, the Fulani now faced the task of ruling it. To do so, they had first to develop acceptable procedures and arrangements to regulate their own relations and affairs in order that they might rule the chiefdom collegially. The new rulers had no single leader. Malam Dan Zabuwa, to whom the Shehu had entrusted the flag and near whose home at Zuwa the *jihad* had begun, was dead. His son and successor, Abdullahi, was junior to the surviving leaders by a generation. Abdurrahman Goshi, the original head of the Yolawa, had also been killed; but this left his brother Jibir, who from the start had been one of the council, as undisputed head of the Yolawa. With Jibir, Malam Jamau, Malam Bakatsine, and Malam Muhammadu Dabo of Dambazau, formed the inner leadership.

As the sole Hausa *muhajarini* among these leaders, the Alkali Usuman, though formally equal to his peers and presiding over the daily meetings of their court, lacked their resources, following, ethnic status and power. Usuman could not overrule his colleagues, though he might mediate their differences acceptably. Almost certainly, he could neither understand nor speak the Fulani language his colleagues commonly used in their discussions. The Alkali Usuman was also regarded as a traitor by those local Hausa who resented the Fulani attack and conquest, and who discredited its ideological justifications as a subterfuge that failed to mask the crude secular motives and interests of the *jihadis*. The Alkali Usuman was thus dependent on his Fulani colleagues for their support in his collegial role and public position. This dependence increased his utility to the inner group of ruling Fulani.

Outside their ranks, but closely linked with them through the course of recent events, the ruling college could rely for support on the Mundubawa Fulani settled in Kano city, and on the Gyenawa, Kurawa and Zarawa (Fulanin Bornu), all clerical Fulani lineages long established at Kano, whose identification with Islam committed them implicitly to the Shehu's *jihad*. Of these groups, only the Gyenawa under their leader Malam Dikoyi had taken an active part in planning the *jihad*. Thereafter we hear little further concerning them during this campaign before Bakatsine's withdrawal to Wudil, except for Alwali's consultations with his Alkali Datuwa, who was probably also of the Gyenawa clan, and who then condemned the jihad as *jahilci* (falsehood, error).[54] Throughout the campaign the leading baMundube, the Fulani Limam Sule, had remained in the city. In consequence, those Mundubawa who campaigned for the *jihad*, had attached themselves to other Fulani groups. Thus, both the Mundubawa and the Gyenawa had forfeited their chance of a place in the collective leadership of the Fulani *jihad*. Only those who could mobilize and direct large active forces recruited primarily by clanship were eligible to participate in the councils that directed the strategy of the *jihad*. In brief, the price of leadership was military power.

As the Shehu's senior Hausa adherent and perhaps the only Hausa official who had followed him openly in June 1804, the Alkali Usuman may then have had a following which compared in size with those of his peers; and perhaps the Fulani leaders had hoped that other Hausa would rally behind the Alkali Usuman against Alwali in the course of the struggle. If so, this expectation was mistaken. Those Hausa who later supported the *jihad* voluntarily, and not through conquest or threat of attack, did not submit themselves to the Alkali Usuman or his Fulani peers. These late supporters were marshalled and organized by the Ciroma Dan Mama, who had made his allegiance to the Shehu Usuman direct, apparently before the fighting began in Kano. In like fashion, Dan Tunku flung his Yerimawa Fulani against Alwali at Danyaya without submitting himself to the council of Kano *jihadis*. Like Dan Mama, Dan Tunku had made *capka* directly either to the Shehu or to his son Mamman Bello.[55]

Even within the ruling college, despite its stress on formal equality, there were important differences of power, status and interest among the members. Abdullahi, the son of Malam Yusufu (Dan Zabuwa) and the Alkali Usuman, for different reasons, exercised less influence on collective policy decisions than did the senior leaders. Attached to this group, though not within it, were the Gyenawa, Zarawa, Kurawa and other clerical Fulani lineages, the Ciroma Dan Mama and his Hausa followers, and the Yerimawa of Dambarta under Dan Tunku. Most Fulani clans long settled in Kano had attached themselves to the dominant *jihadi* unit in their local area—for example, the Yeligawa and Jelubawa of Dutse aligned themselves under the leadership of Malam baKatsine and his Jobawa. The Fulani of Karaye were likewise attached to Malam Jamau Maituta, the Suleibawa leader. Those Yerimawa settled at Minjibir who had previously been under the Yerimawa headman Dan Tunku dissociated themselves by making allegiance to the Kano *jihadis*, most probably to Malam Dabo Dambazau in person. Such Fulani realignments and transfers of allegiance had proceeded sporadically throughout the *jihad*, as Zangi's account indicates. In consequence, the balance of forces, power and status among the collegial leaders tended to shift over time in consequence of their differing success in attaching other Fulani groups to themselves. Dan Zabuwa's absence at Zaria for several months, followed by his death at Sabon Ruwa, were critical setbacks to the political prospects of the Daneji clan.

The alignments indicated above, some pre-jihadic and others developed during the *jihad* or after, exerted important influences on the course of developments at Kano during the formative first years of Fulani rule. Substantially these alignments persisted throughout the century, though overlaid and complicated differentially by new relations, structures and events that often had their sources in the distributions of allegiance, status and power that prevailed in 1807. In some cases, later alignments and categories developed slowly and won public recognition gradually, instead of following directly from public acts. In others, the public recognition of categorical criteria, boundaries and contrasts was almost immediate; and though their formal differentiations proceeded over several years, differences of substance were clear from the beginning.

The best example of such immediately institutionalized differentiation concerns the conquered population. As we have seen, their situation obliged the Fulani *jihadis* to distinguish three categories of local Hausa: those who had fought with them under the Alkali Usuman throughout the *jihad*; those who had joined them later under Dan Mama as covert or overt allies; and the rest who had either remained aloof or resisted. These latter, the overwhelming majority, the Fulani described as "Habe," employing the pejorative Fulfulde term for conquered tribal or Black peoples (Ar. Al-Sudan), much as the Fulani conquerors of Massina did later to the Bambara, Dogon and other subjugated Blacks in that area, though not to the resident Tuareg or Arabs.[56]

In Kano the new rulers assimilated several religious and political categories under the term Habe; and as Habe, Hausa were assimilated *kahirai* or *arna* (heathens or pagans). They were the subject people, the conquered, whose collective defeat in the recent struggle entailed their subjugation as a corporate category, simultaneously denied participation in the Kano government and autonomy to regulate their own affairs. Rural "Habe" communities were thus systematically placed under resident Fulani chiefs whose local administrations had the legitimacy of Islamic conquest and the power of the conquerors behind them. Even before the *jihad* was over, many of these local chiefships had been appropriated by senior Fulani for distribution among their leading followers, who then assumed responsibility for maintenance of Fulani control in these conquered areas. Thus, Malam Jamau who conquered Karaye, the first important town to fall into Fulani hands, immediately placed his client Suleimanu Nadoyi there in full command; similar steps were taken by other leaders at Bici, Damargu, Tofa, Farin Ruwa, and other conquered communities. The Fulani appointed to rule these units must initially have formed a small minority of these local populations. Only when the fighting was over could they expect significant Fulani increments to secure their position; and they then found it necessary to recruit such immigrants by providing attractive political and economic opportunities. All local offices were thenceforward reserved for loyal Fulani, while the Hausa or Habe as a defeated category were parcelled out in wards and villages under their direct administration. In this way the Fulani excluded Hausa from almost all administrative positions in rural communities as well as the central government.

The Fulani victors distinguished those Hausa who had attached themselves to the Alkali Usuman and supported the *jihad* from the Habe as Hausawa. As allies of the conquerors, the Hausawa were not among the conquered. They were thus neither by defeat nor by religious alignment subject to the direct administration imposed on Habe, nor were they liable to the harsh treatment meted out to the conquered population. As native Hausa and a minority among the new rulers, they enjoyed various privileges but little power. Their position had been protected by the Shehu Dan Fodio who, in response to appeals from the new rulers at Kano for guidance concerning their Hausa allies, is said to have told them to "leave the Hausawa under their Malam." It was on this occasion also that the Shehu is said to have instructed the Fulani leaders to give Dan Mama "a hundred towns." The Fulani leaders interpreted the Shehu's remark as an order requiring them to leave their Hausa supporters under the Alkali Usuman, who was both a Hausa and a Malam. The term "Hausawa" was therefore initially used to designate Usuman's followers (*kunjiya*). Most of these Hausawa had ranked as commoners (*talakawa*) in Alwali's day; and perhaps only their leader Usuman, who is said to have administered Kura, held high official rank. However the group was sharply distinguished from other Hausa both by its status as *muhajarini*, and by its explicit self-identification as Muslims and supporters of the Shehu. Interpreting the Shehu's remark literally, the Fulani leaders instructed Usuman to settle his followers within the city as a compact group, whose internal and external affairs he could then administer easily. In consequence, Kano city came to contain a new ward, the Anguwan Hausawa, named after this group.[57] In addition to his other capacities, the Alkali Usuman now acted as ward head over his community. Many of their descendants having remained in the Anguwan Hausawa of Kano city until today, the term Hausawa is still used by Fulani of Kano to denote these communities and others of like derivation.

Those Hausa who helped them under Dan Mama's leadership were distinguished by Fulani as Kutumbawa. This designation clearly derives from their leader's identification with the Kutumbawa. As illustrated by the Dokaji's account, Fulani tradition identifies Dan Mama as Alwali's son;[58] and, irrespective of his actual identity and parentage, his tenure of the Ciroma title asserted his status as a Kutumbawa prince. Dan Mama's official and unofficial following were accordingly designated Kutumbawa, to distinguish them from the Alkali Usuman's people, who as clerics and commoners, played little part in Alwali's officialdom. The Kutumbawa group under Dan Mama probably contained few people of Kutumbi descent; however, to the conquerors they were the local representatives of the old regime, their leader ranked as a senior Kutumbawa prince, and the entire collectivity were treated as his kin, clients, slaves and political subordinates. The Fulani accordingly directed Dan Mama to settle his people in the city as a compact group, so that he could handle their internal and external affairs. In consequence, Kano thereafter contained a Kutumbawa ward in which descendants of Dan Mama's people may still be found.[59] Thus, while the Hausa attached to Alkali Usuman were identified as commoners, Muslims, *muhajarini* and early adherents of the Shehu's religious teaching, the Hausa under Dan Mama were distinguished first as *lansaru*, and secondly by their royal and official status in the overthrown "Habe" regime. Spatially the two collectivities were separated from one another and from the victorious Fulani, who settled mainly in the southern part of the town where Rumfa had built his palace.

At the same time that they placed Dan Mama and the Alkali Usuman in direct administrative charge of their separate followings, localized as city wards, the Fulani leaders were, wittingly or otherwise, implicitly asserting separate jurisdictions over their own clans and clan territories, in virtue of their positions in these clans and the clan occupancies of particular areas. Thus after each leader had appropriated an exclusive internal jurisdiction for his clansmen and followers, the problem arose of delimiting these jurisdictions by determining the scope and limits of public affairs reserved for the regulation of the ruling college. To complicate the situation further, two important Fulani chiefs elected not to remain in Kano city. These were Dan Tunku, who had settled at Shiddar near Matsidau and now ruled this northwest corner with increasing independence, and Malam Bakatsine, who likewise remained at Dutse, and held as his domain most of the lands south of Wudil to the borders of Ningi and Warjawa, and east of Dutse to Shirra. Gaya, which was finally captured by Dabo Dambazau, was placed under separate administration, with its traditional dependencies. Meanwhile, Bakatsine ruled Dutse with Isa, his brother's son. To represent him on the ruling college at Kano he sent his son, Mandikko.

Excluding the Alkali Usuman, the ex-Ciroma Dan Mama and Dan Tunku, Alwali's Sarkin Fulani of Dambarta, none of the new rulers had previously held any official titles. The Fulani who led the *jihad* at Kano had based their power on their positions as clan heads and senior clerics, and not on Hausa offices. Being chiefless and equal at this period, there was no one, excluding the Shehu, his closest kin and senior assistants, Mamman Bello and Abdullahi, the Shehu's brother and vizier, who had the authority to distribute titles among them. Certainly at Kano no one, other than the members of the ruling college themselves, could now make such appointments; and it is difficult to see how the college as constituted could formally do so. Moreover, the Shehu had strongly condemned the use of titles and Hausa court ceremonial as vanities conducive to oppression. He had also explicitly prohibited the use or maintenance of such Hausa practices by his lieutenants and representatives.

> Therefore do not follow their way in their government, and do not imitate them, not even in the titles of their king, such as Kukinnu and Ghaladima and Ubandawaki and Dhaghi and Bargha and Serkin Yari. Address your chief emir as "Commander of the Believers," and the emir of each province as "Emir of such and such a province," and the emir of each place as "Emir of such and such a place," and the emir of each village as "Emir of such and such a village," and him who has charge of God's statutory punishments as "Emir of the statutory punishments."[60]

The Shehu's *jihad* was not directed exclusively at the elimination of heathen elements from the ritual practice of the Hausa chiefdoms. It was also directly addressed to the reform of local government by the elimination of all forms of organization or procedure that seemed inconsistent with or opposed to the tenets of Islam and to the pattern of political organization that prevailed under the first four rightly-guided Caliphs.[61]

In Kano the leaders of the *jihad*, on entering the city, rejected Hausa titles and official positions as equally inconsistent with their collegial relations and with the radical Muslim reforms their conquest was designed to institute. Each leader, nonetheless, on moving to the city occupied one or other of the large state compounds traditionally reserved to senior state offices, these having been vacant since Alwali's flight to Rano. Malam Jamau the flagbearer (Mai-Tuta) moved into the compound recently occupied by Alwali's Sarkin Dawaki Ali, who had been defeated at Kwazzazabo. Mandikko, Bakatsine's son, settled himself in the Madaki's compound. Malam Dabo Dambazau took over the house of the Sarkin Bai. Umaru, the son of the baYole, Malam Jibir, moved into the compound of the Ciroma. Malam Dahiru baSuleibe, a kinsman of Malam Jamau, occupied that of the Galadima; and perhaps at this time Dan Zabuwa's elder son, Abdullahi, settled in the Dan Iya's compound. Many other state compounds in the city were taken over by other incoming Fulani or used as temporary accommodation for the conquering group. These state compounds had become vacant when their occupants, the Hausa officials, fled south with Alwali or afterwards dispersed. They provided the readiest and finest accommodation for the new rulers, who clearly neither intended to claim particular titles by occupying compounds reserved for them, nor foresaw that by such occupancy they publicly identified themselves with the titles to which the compounds were severally attached. Thus, though vacant, the titles persisted with their state properties and powers, awaiting future occupants; and when the Fulani leaders moved into these empty compounds, they became captives of the historical situation.

However unwittingly, the Fulani leaders had by this act identified themselves individually with the titles of the compounds in which they lived. For example, the flagbearer Malam Jamau, being already distinguished as Maituta, was thenceforth known as Sarkin Dawaki Maituta, since he had chosen to live in the Sarkin Dawaki's house, thus partially transforming this old military title by investing it with religious significance by his custody of the Shehu's flag, at this date the sole insignia of Fulani government at Kano. Thenceforth the title of Sarkin Dawaki Maituta assumed a higher status in the Kano government than its original, the Sarkin Dawaki, had possessed among the Hausa. Perhaps Malam Jamau's decision to occupy this compound was not entirely random. Jamau had held or shared the command in several important Fulani victories—at Kwazzazabo, at Karaye, and in the final assault on Burumburum. He may thus have intended to assert his military pre-eminence by occupying this particular compound.

In like fashion, Mandikko was identified by his city compound as the Madaki, while his father, Malam Bakatsine, remained at Dutse. Umaru, the son of Jibir, having settled in the Gidan Ciroma, had intentionally or otherwise identified himself as the new Ciroma. Malam Dabo Dambazau, having occupied the compound of the Sarkin Bai, became the new Sarkin Bai. Malam Jibir, who seems to have remained in a private (*talauci*) compound, escaped such designations; and in all probability Bakatsine was simply regarded by the defeated Hausa as the new Sarkin Dutse, or Emir of Dutse, following the Shehu's principles of denotation.

Inevitably, being imperfectly aware of their situation and especially of the implications of their own actions, the new rulers risked becoming captives of the structure they had overthrown, as these early official identifications indicate. Nonetheless, though many units of the old regime persisted more or less intact, others had lapsed, and the traditional Hausa system of relations between politically relevant social categories was initially erased. Many offices provisionally reactivated by reoccupation of their compounds clearly underwent major changes of status at this time. Transformation of the formerly *shigege* title of Sarkin Dawaki into the new office of Sarkin Dawaki Maituta, vested with the Shehu's flag, illustrates this process and its underlying condition. No one, Fulani or Hausa, could then have foreseen the future history of this new office. Neither could they have predicted correctly the careers of the "Madaki" Mandikko and the "Ciroma" Umaru whose fathers, Bakatsine and Jibir respectively, themselves had no place in this unplanned resuscitation of the central office stucture. Likewise, though a senior hereditary slave office under Alwali, the title of Sarkin Bai, now, and perhaps unintentionally, appropriated by Malam Dabo Dambazau, one of the initiators of the *jihad*, had obviously undergone a major change of status. But easily the most fundamental change of all was the vacancy and apparent dissolution of the chiefship. With Alwali's flight and subsequent death, Kano was chiefless for the first time in eight centuries; yet its entire traditional structure of offices, territorial jurisdictions and the state itself were wholly and inextricably identified with a central chiefship. Lacking this necessary centre, the newly reactivated offices spun free in political space without fixed orbits, unsteadily and unpredictably. Thus, following the conquest, itself a major collective experience, in consolidating their rule and constructing their government according to their own ideas and needs, having rooted out the primary institution of state, the Fulani leaders further dislocated and displaced many pivotal connections among the corporate components of the preceding structure.

Much of this was undoubtedly accidental; but these accidents were also in part governed by orientations and relations among the conquerors themselves. These orientations and relations were prevailingly political and structured by numerous antecedents. While none dared to occupy the palace, the Fulani leaders first selected the compounds they regarded as appropriate to their status as clan heads and conquerors. Such compounds, grouped around the empty palace, were probably the most impressive state properties available. The Fulani also segregated their colleague, the Alkali Usuman, and their ally, Dan Mama, in differing parts of the town, thereby pre-empting for themselves the compounds identified with central offices of state. However accidental and informal, it seems clear that this initial distribution of official compounds corresponded very closely to the relative prominence and rank of their occupants within the conquering group. Though Bakatsine and Jibir, two of the most eminent Fulani leaders, occupied none of these compounds and were consequently identified by no title, their sons did so, however unwittingly, on their behalf; and as Madaki and Ciroma, these men were evidently possible candidates and rivals for the vacant chiefship.

Malikite Islam, as practiced in the western Sudan, seems to presuppose or enjoin chiefship for the regulation of the community (*jema'a*) and its affairs. It is on these bases that the Shehu's election at Gudu as *Emir el-Mu'munin* (caliph) was later legitimized by his brother Abdullahi and his son Mamman Bello.[62] However, in their references to this event, Abdullahi and Bello justify the creation of this "caliphate" on instrumental grounds rather than as a religious obligation. The Fulani *'ulama* of Hausaland were quite familiar by hearsay with the republican organization of Kharijite Muslim communities in the Mzab;[63] and though the Kharijites were probably regarded as "innovators" by the Shehu,[64] he made no immediate move to select a chief (emir) for Kano until the local Fulani themselves requested this approximately two years after their conquest. In no other chiefdom conquered or created by the Shehu's delegates did the chiefship remain so long undetermined in its locus and scope. Thus, following its conquest, Kano provides a unique instance of a "republican" experiment by the Shehu's followers. That this experiment ended swiftly in the restoration of the chiefship is perhaps no more significant than its occurrence and duration.

It is not certain how long this collegial regime persisted. Written histories of Kano traditionally set the appointment of its first Fulani chief almost immediately after Alwali's death at Burumburum. However, the Fulani administered Kano for at least twelve months before this, while Alwali remained in Zazzau; and oral traditions assert that the Fulani conquerors ruled collegially for another two years before they sent to ask the Shehu to appoint a chief. It is quite likely that a military administration prevailed throughout most of this period, certainly while Alwali was alive. During those months, the ruling college probably concentrated on the subjugation of the remaining districts in Kano, a military task they had long since learned to handle. Only after Alwali's death did the more fundamental problems of political administration unavoidably assert themselves.

Several structural issues that then arose have been indicated obliquely above. First and foremost was the constitution and cohesion of the ruling college itself. Neither its composition nor its powers had been clearly agreed; and perhaps even its basic procedures remained uncertain in form and effect. Malam Bakatsine chose to remain at Dutse, delegating his collegial functions to his son Mandikko, though properly these were not transferable by his sole discretion. The Alkali Usuman and the Daneji leader Abdullahi, Dan Zabuwa's son, were clearly not the political equals of Jibir, Jamau, or Dabo Dambazau. Problems of parity or pre-eminence were also a fertile source of strain among the latter three. Meanwhile, the country had to be administered. "Habe" village chiefs required Fulani replacements; but the appointments of Fulani by any of these leaders to such positions inevitably strengthened some and weakened other members of the ruling college. For example, when the Yolawa appropriated local chiefships in their northwestern territory, as at Tofa and Gwarzo, for Yolawa personnel or clients, they correspondingly consolidated their dominance of that region. Conversely, if such local chiefships had been allocated to members or clients of other leading clans, Yolawa dominance within their home area would be undercut, thereby weakening their bargaining position in the councils of state. By distributing community chiefships among his clients or kinsmen, each councillor could thus consolidate his hold on his following and on particular districts in Kano. In consequence, councillors found it difficult to agree on appointments to local chiefships in districts which had not fallen to any one of them during the *jihad*. The administrative unavoidability of such allocations generated strains that promoted rivalries; but rivalry reduced the solidarity of the ruling college by stressing conflicts of individual and collective interests among its members.

The territorial appropriations made by differing clans were also highly unequal. Excluding Gaya chiefdom, Bakatsine's Jobawa seem to have established exclusive control over all southeastern Kano up to the frontier of Birnin Kudu, which had thus far escaped attack. Taura and Ringim may also at this time have been attached to Bakatsine. The Yolawa held territories southwest of Damargu as far as Durum, Gammo and Gwarzo. To the south, Malam Jamau's Suleibawa were the dominant lineage, though the Danejawa controlled the small area they occupied between Zuwo and Massanawa. Due south of Kano, Kura remained under the Hausa Alkali Usuman; but he had already administered that town before the *jihad* and he acquired no further territory during the campaign.

Such inequalities in their territorial resources and interests inevitably generated strains among members of the ruling college, confronting them directly with the situation of their political disparity and divergent interests though, as members of its supreme collective unit, they were all equal guardians of the state. As the state at this phase was hardly distinguishable from its ruling college, such issues probably arose most urgently in the context of appointments to local village chiefships, rather than in general terms. Even so, allocations of community chiefships themselves underlined the cleavages of individual and collective interests within the college. To reduce such tensions, the new rulers finally partitioned the territory among themselves; but since this consisted mainly in ratifying one another's appropriations during the jihadic campaigns, it left the unconquered areas undistributed, and merely expressed the intransigence of the situation. Disputes concerning appointments of local chiefs recurrently produced disputes over territorial boundaries, jurisdictions and spheres of interest; and though in principle those councillors who were not immediately involved in the particular case could serve as mediators and arbitrators, being themselves repeatedly and variably involved in alliances and oppositions over other cases, such mediation and arbitration was itself politically conditioned and suspect.

Disputes about clan boundaries generated disputes over the relative scope and primacy of collegial and clan jurisdictions within the districts already appropriated. Such issues as local levies of tax, grain tithe, labour, local appointments to village chiefships, and the central or local administration of the *shari'a* recurred and were difficult to resolve. No clan, separately or with its immediate affiliates, could dispense with the help of the others. Repeatedly the new oligarchs asserted the necessity for cooperation to retain their individual privileges and position. Thus clan autarchy, however strongly desired, was tempered by their recognition of political and military interdependence. Given the structure and composition of this collegial group, the insoluble problems turned on the relative limits and scope of clan autonomy and central collegial jurisdiction, and on the allocations of control over those districts that had thus far escaped conquest. Such issues expressed conflicting interests within the ruling college and impaired its cohesion.

The Selection of Suleimanu

Learning from experience, the new rulers finally appealed to Shehu to appoint a chief over them, but the exact date of this appointment remains obscure.[65] It is therefore necessary to discuss this question.

Alhaji Dokaji Abubakar relates that when the Kano Fulani sent a delegation asking Shehu to appoint an emir over them, he asked who was their *limam*. They replied, "Suleimanu, but he is a *yaro*," a Hausa term which either denotes a boy or a man of no consequence. Since Suleimanu was then over thirty years old, it is in the second sense that the Fulani delegation attempted to discredit his candidacy, but the Shehu, following sound Muslim principle, pronounced in favour of Suleimanu, "Limaminku, emirinku (your imam is your Emir)." The Dokaji dates this event in "1807 to 1808" after Alwali's death.[66]

Malam Adamu relates that after Alwali's death at Burumburum, the five senior Fulani leaders, Bakatsine, Dabo Dambazau, Jibir, Jamau and Abdullahi the son of Dan Zabuwa, sent to ask the Shehu Usuman to choose a chief from among them. To this the Shehu astutely replied, "Whoever settled in the city without fighting, let him be chief." Only Suleimanu, as a *limam* already resident in Kano, fulfilled this condition. Therefore, says this story, Suleimanu became chief.[67]

W.F. Gowers, who studied the *jihad* and early Fulani administration of Kano with some care, presents another view. He sets the appointment of Suleimanu after Alwali's death at Burumburum, but before the Fulani entered Kano city, thereby reversing the order of events presented by the Alkali Zangi, Sultan Bello and others. Gowers suggests that having killed Alwali, and before they entered

Kano city, the leading Fulani appealed to Shehu to appoint a chief in order that they might capture the capital.

> The five leaders of the principal clans went to Sokoto (?), but none of them were selected. The Shehu appointed (probably owing to the disunion and rivalry among them) one Suleimanu of the Modibawa clan, the servant of Dan Zabuwa (head of the Daneji clan). Suleimanu returned and was recognized as the leader. He eventually entered Kano without fighting. ... He was actually appointed by the Shehu in 1809.[68]

According to C.L. Temple, Alwali was killed after a campaign lasting "some three years," that is, in 1807. "The confederates (the Fulani leaders) extended their conquests in the neighborhood, but did not attack Kano itself. After the lapse of some two years, the five leaders went to Sokoto that a Sarki might be nominated. A slave, by name Suleimanu, by birth a Kanawa (Kano) Fulani, was selected and became the first Emir and 44th Chief of Kano."[69] Temple's summary is based on data collected by several British Provincial staff, including Gowers.

Suleimanu was neither a slave nor the servant of Dan Zabuwa, although he may have been the latter's student or client; but neither did he rank among the leading Fulani of Kano, nor was he one of the leaders of the Kano *jihad*. By descent and investiture, originally the Fulani *limam* in Kano city, he probably became the Limam of Kano only after Alwali's Limam Abdulkadiri had moved to Bangere following Alwali's departure. On entering the capital, the leaders of the *jihad* found Suleimanu serving as the Fulani *limam*, and made no attempt to replace him, since the office was essential, prestigious and politically unimportant. Later, when the Fulani chiefs went or sent to seek an emir, hopefully from among themselves, the limam was chosen at Birnin Gada. Whether that was done by the Shehu, as Dokaji affirms, by his son, Mamman Bello, or by the Fulani leaders, as Alkali Zangi relates, is not material; but in either case, as Gowers suggests, this choice was probably intended to avoid endangering the survival of the state by placing either of these five clan chiefs over his rivals. Notably, neither was Suleimanu present at Birnin Gada, nor was the Alkali Usuman, the only Hausa in the council of the Kano *jihadis* who was considered for this appointment.

According to the Kano Chronicle, the new chief acceded in 1807, after Alwali fell at Burumburum.[70] According to Sultan Bello, the Shehu, having summoned "his followers in the east" to meet him at Magami south of Cafe, sent Bello in his stead at the appointed time. Bello met the "people of Kano," that is, the Fulani leaders, at Birnin Gada in southern Zamfara.

> In truth they had captured very many towns. I appointed to be chief over them Suleimanu, son of Jamu, a learned and just man. I gave them all the news and said to them my father saluted them. Moreover I commanded them to pay homage and to listen to all I had to say to them and to follow it. That they should obey the law in private and in public, by night and by day. They listened and promised to do so. Further I informed them that Shehu had told me to congratulate them that God had given the countries to them to dwell in, that God had given them power in the land, but let them take care after this lest they quarrel with each other and be separated, lest they pervert the law of Islam even as the Soudanese people had done. The men

of Kano were pleased with these words and accepted Shehu's warning with enthusiasm. They contributed goods in proportion to what God had given them.[71]

From the location of this passage in Bello's history of the *jihad*, Arnett and others have concluded that Suleimanu was appointed in December 1805; but Arnett, who first proposed this date, also noted that on this interpretation, Bello apparently dated Alwali's flight and death at Burumburum, which preceded Suleimanu's appointment in his account, to the summer of 1805, which is clearly improbable. On Zangi's history of the *jihad* at Kano, it seems that the Fulani entered Kano City on May 20th or 21st, 1807, Alwali having fled to Rano on April 10th or 11th.

Bello's summary of the *jihad* in Kano confirms the much fuller account by Alkali Zangi, which I have followed, in two critical respects. Both accounts indicate clearly that neither the Shehu nor Bello appointed anyone to lead their followers and command the *jihad* in Kano. The Kano Fulani fought their *jihad* under the collegial direction of their senior clan-heads. Secondly, neither Bello nor Zangi mentions Suleimanu in their accounts of the Kano *jihad* until the conquest was over and the capital taken. Had Suleimanu been appointed earlier, it would surely have been impossible for both writers to describe the campaign without one reference to him. Instead, Zangi refers to a flag which the Kano clan-leaders received from Shehu as their collective possession, the symbol of their corporate authority to wage *jihad* in the Shehu's name. This flag was kept initially by Malam Dan Zabuwa, and later by Malam Jamau, who was accordingly given the unusual title of Sarkin Dawaki Mai-Tuta (the flag-bearer) on settling in the Sarkin Dawaki's compound at Kano; but Zangi's report also shows that no one, least of all Suleimanu, who had remained throughout the *jihad* in the city and seems to have taken no active part, ever claimed this flag as his exclusively by the Shehu's gift. It is thus clear that Suleimanu was not appointed before the Fulani entered Kano city following Alwali's flight. It is evidently to this victory that the Shehu's message which Bello delivered at Birnin Gada refers. "Shehu had told me to congratulate them that God had given the countries to them to dwell in, that God had given them power in the land," congratulations which clearly presupposed victory. Continuing, Bello then repeated the Shehu's warning to "let them take care after this lest they quarrel with each other, and be separated, lest they pervert the law of Islam, as the Soudanese had done,"[72] an admonition which echoes the observations of the Shehu's brother Abdullahi, who visited Kano in October 1807, too closely to be unrelated.[73]

Abdullahi relates that he stopped at Kano on his way east to Mecca.

> I found that God had driven the unbelievers from them but their affair(s) had become confused among them because of their preoccupation with the world. I saw among them that from which I had fled in my own country. ... Then I composed for them my book *Diya 'ul-Hukkam*, and I read to them all the commentary on the Qur'an and they repented and put their affair(s) in order.[74]

Alkali Zangi placed Abdullahi's visit during Suleimanu's reign, but since Abdullahi spent several months at Kano, writing his book, building the city mosque, and expounding the law and Koran, it is possible—and likely, on the passage just quoted—that his arrival antedated Suleimanu's appointment. Zangi's account of these events runs as follows: "When the Habe government was over-thrown, Muhammadu Bello appointed him (Suleimanu) with a letter from the Shehu Usuman. He, Mamman Bello, met them (the Fulani leaders of Kano) at Birnin Gada and asked them to choose (an emir). Then they selected Suleimanu and returned home safely."[75] It is clear from Zangi's phrase that the meeting at Birnin Gada occurred after Alwali had fled and the Fulani had occupied the city. Later,

> when Alwali set out northward from Zazzau, Sule ordered Malam Bakatsine to intercept him at Burumburum. So they fought there until Alwali was killed within the town, and all was well. Then Shehu Abdullahi arrived in the year of the eclipse. He conducted the prayers for the eclipse and the Friday service in the month of the Fast. He built the Sabbath mosque (for the city) and expounded the commentary on the Koran, and he wrote the *Diya 'ul-Hukkam* when they asked him for guidance in following the true way.[76]

Thus Zangi sets Suleimanu's appointment in the interval between Alwali's flight and his death at Burumburum, a period of more than twelve months. He also says that Suleimanu was emir when Abdullahi resided at Kano; and implies that Abdullahi arrived after Suleimanu's appointment. However, on other data I suggest that Suleimanu's selection by the Shehu may have been made on Abdullahi's recommendation, after he had reported the confusion he found in Kano among the leaderless Fulani. Probably Abdullahi also nominated Suleimanu as a suitable candidate on grounds of his office as *limam*, his learning, piety and lack of political ambition and power. On this interpretation, the Shehu summoned the Fulani leaders to Birnin Gada, where Suleimanu was appointed in his absence, after receiving Abdullahi's report on the situation in Kano; and since Abdullahi sojourned there until mid-1808 when he returned to Sokoto to lead an army against Argungu, it is even possible that Suleimanu was appointed in 1808 rather than late in 1807. As noted above, Gowers thinks it happened in 1809. However indirect and tentative, this dating seems more consistent with the available information than that which Arnett derived from Bello's brief account.

Suleimanu, 1807/8?–1819

The Emir and the Founding Fathers

Suleimanu was designated emir without an installation ceremony. The Shehu had prohibited resumptions of traditional Hausa practice, and as yet the Fulani had not developed alternatives. There was thus no public installation to provide exterior evidence of Suleimanu's supremacy. He remained poor, without followers, rural desmesnes, slaves, courtiers and the like. He thus lacked both the resources and the means to demonstrate his chiefship, other than the limited number of appointments he could make without contraverting the Shehu's proscriptions. On his accession, he appointed the baGyeni Sule, his namesake, another Fulani of Kano city, as Limam, and perhaps soon after, when those settlements had fallen, he also endowed that office with fiefs at Jijitar, Karmami and Zango, west of Gezawa. In addition the new Limam received Kinosawa hamlet at Bompai, adjoining the city, as his farm (*rinji*). Whether the leading Fulani recognized these allocations as valid remains uncertain. To assist him, the new baGyeni Limam Sule selected his own son Muhammadu as his *na'ibi* (deputy). It is doubtful if either was appointed formally in public.

Suleimanu sought to publicize and demonstrate his position by joining the daily court sessions of the Fulani leaders at the Hausa mosque in Kano city. As emir, responsible to the Shehu for the enforcement of the *shari'a* in Kano, he assumed the role of senior judge in the court, thereby displacing the Alkali Usuman, who now lost his role as Alkali, although retaining the title. By this step Suleimanu sought to associate himself with the lordly Fulani leaders of the *jihad*. Apparently before his appointment as emir, these men had conducted their political meetings at the old Hausa city mosque before, in between, or after their judicial sittings. With the appointment of an emir, the college had lost its formal function as the governing council; but its members probably still continued to discuss political affairs among themselves while ignoring and denying the authority of the new emir. Suleimanu commanded little respect among them. His poverty, his lack of land, cattle, a numerous following of kin and clients, slaves, and strangers appealing for support, coupled with his non-participation in the battles of the *jihad*, his personal failure or refusal to quit Kano and withdraw (*hijra*), and the modest status of his lineage, discredited him thoroughly among the ruling Fulani, who had already habituated themselves and others to their new aristocratic status.

Temple neatly indicates the prevailing relations among these leaders and their clan communities when he describes them as "confederates." Each was now lord of a large domain and its inhabitants. Though potential rivals, these lords also recognized their community of interests. Cooperation was necessary for their collective dominion. Suleimanu's appointment dismayed and upset them. Here was a parvenu by any standards, who had neither fought in the *jihad* nor withdrawn from Kano city, whose resources were not worth mentioning, and who had contributed nothing either to the *jihad* or to the establishment of the new Fulani Muslim state, neither followers nor territory nor cattle nor personal eminence in any field. The aristocratic leadership of the *jihad* closed its ranks; and despite Suleimanu's appointment, they continued their collegial arrangements and discussions of public business at their daily meetings in the Hausa mosque where the court was held as before. However by asserting his right to preside in this court, the new emir had also claimed the right to participate in these policy discussions. Undoubtedly for a while his voice was negligible; but he was the Shehu's chosen representative, and he could appeal to Mamman Bello for support. Bello himself emphasizes that he had ordered the Fulani of Kano to "listen to all I had to say to them and to follow it ... (and to) take care after this lest they quarrel with each other and be separated."[77] Suleimanu could thus invoke Bello's words to support his authority. Where necessary he could also appeal to Bello, who had in fact, anticipating this situation, provided Suleimanu with a confidential messenger, one Malam Jalhi, a Fulani cleric, who moved between Kano and Sokoto, the new capital of the empire, as required for several years. In 1959 Jalhi's descendants held judicial offices in Kano and Katsina, and perhaps elsewhere also.[78]

The Chronicle relates that when Suleimanu "became Sarkin Kano, the Fulani prevented him from entering the palace." He then moved into the compound of the Sarkin Dawaki Tsakar Gida, that being either vacant, or occupied by someone who could be displaced. The palace itself had remained empty since Alwali fled and increasingly needed repair.

> One of the remaining Kanawa said to Suleimanu, "If you do not enter the *gidan Rumfa* you will not really be the Sarki of the city and country" (i.e., You will not exercise real authority over the people in the city or the country). When Suleimanu heard this, he called the chief Fulani, but they refused to answer his summons, and said "We will not come to you, you must come to us, though you be the Sarki. If you will come to Malam Jibrim's (Jibir's) house we will assemble there." Suleimanu went to Jibrim's house and called them there. When they had assembled, he asked them and said, "Why do you prevent me entering the *gidan Rumfa?*' Malam Jibrim said, "If we enter the Habe's houses and we beget children, they will be like these Habe and do like them." Suleimanu said nothing and set off to Shehu Usuman dan Fodio asking to be allowed to enter the *gidan Rumfa*. Shehu dan Fodio gave him a sword and a knife and gave him leave to enter the *gidan Rumfa*, telling him to kill all who opposed him.[79]

This account of the incident is well known. However, it contains serious error. Suleimanu did not go to Shehu Usuman dan Fodio on this or any occasion. Alkali Zangi relates that he once met Shehu in a vision.[80] However that may be, Suleimanu did not visit him on this occasion. Palmer is probably correct in his assessment that "had he (Sule) gone himself, he would never have regained his position."[81]

This incident reveals Suleimanu's weakness neatly and dramatically. The leading Fulani refused to heed his summons or attend upon him, obliging him to visit them instead at the house of Malam Jibirin, the baYole leader, who alone among them had not himself occupied a state compound. Notably, this dispute was thrashed out among the Fulani leaders in private, away from the city mosque; and Jibirin, the senior leader present, replied to Sule on behalf of all. "If we enter the Habe's houses and we beget children, they will be like these Habe and do like them."

It is likely that Jibirin and his colleagues shared this sentiment. Similar ideas were prominent in the teaching of the Shehu Usuman.[82] However, this collective veto may also have had other motives and purposes; as is often the case in such matters, these different interests were mutually consistent. Briefly, in forbidding their Emir to enter the palace, the Fulani leaders of the *jihad* reasserted their collegial predominance and rejected Suleimanu's claim to precedence or supremacy among them. This was made clear in their initial refusal to visit his house for any discussions. By occupying the compound of the Sarkin Dawaki Tsakar Gida, intentionally or not, Suleimanu had identified himself as one of the ruling Fulani, but not their ruler. Other members of this group had occupied compounds of greater splendour, as befitted the Hausa titles to which they were endowed. Thus only by occupying the *gidan Rumfa* could Suleimanu publicly declare his supremacy; and Jibirin's argument that by so doing, Suleimanu committed his descendants to behave like the Habe, was pure political polemic, for the leading Fulani had themselves already occupied Hausa state compounds. On Jibirin's argument they had thereby committed their issue to assimilate "Habe" political culture; but in Kano this culture presupposed a strong central chiefship. Thus, in protesting the chief's occupancy of the compound traditionally reserved for the chief, Jibirin was mainly concerned to prevent this first public assertion of patrimonial chiefship and dissolution of collegial oligarchy.

It is curious to find this ancient theme of the Hausa polity at Kano recur so swiftly and under such different circumstances among the Fulani after their *jihad*. Perhaps the struggle between a patrimonial chiefship and a collegiate oligarchy may be intrinsic to polities of this sort, whether constituted by tradition or erected on the basis of conquest. This incident was formally closed when Suleimanu received authority from Sokoto to occupy the palace, perhaps after referral to the Shehu himself, but certainly on instruction from Mamman Bello. Having appointed Suleimanu as their emir at Kano, the Shehu and Bello had to support and enforce his legitimate demands; and Suleimanu's occupation of the palace was both politically necessary and legally correct. The Fulani leaders were clearly at fault in seeking to prevent their emir from entering his palace. However, it is unlikely that Suleimanu was authorized to "kill all who opposed him" on entering the *gidan Rumfa*, as the Chronicle states. Once he had settled there, the general public recognized him as the only person who claimed to rule as their chief (emir); but to do so effectively, he still had to rule through and over the leading Fulani, each of whom individually controlled greater resources and wealth than Suleimanu possessed. It is clear from subsequent events that Suleimanu failed to translate his formal supremacy into substantive dominance.

Suleimanu's poverty gradually decreased; but being initially extreme, it is well recalled. The palace he now inhabited was a vast empty structure. The new emir had few, if any, slaves. Most of his court ushers and staff were recruited from free Fulani clients who had attached themselves to him, but these were generally men of little account in Fulani society. As emir, Suleimanu could claim those rural estates traditionally reserved to the Kano throne, for example, the chief's properties at Panisau and at Takai; but lacking slaves, he could not exploit these immediately to enrich himself. It is said that he subsisted by writing Muslim charms and by intensively farming certain marsh plots near the city.[83] On one occasion Suleimanu publicly admitted that he lacked a ram for the sacrifice that follows the greater Beiram (Babban Salla), after which each of the leading Fulani sent him a beast, thereby initiating a tradition which was repeated annually until 1954, when the Sarkin Kano Sanusi abolished it.[84]

It is said that in Suleimanu's reign, tax was levied at a rate of 500 cowries per householder (*maigida*) as a tax on farms. Apparently residents at the capital were exempt from this tax; but it is not clear whether the clan-heads as major territorial chiefs collected the tax on Suleimanu's behalf or on their own. It seems likely that initially Suleimanu received little if any of the tax collected by the council of *muhajarini*; but in his later years that was rectified, and the chief's right to a portion of the local tax collected annually in his name was accepted by the oligarchs. Whether the collection and allocation of grain tithe (*zakka*) changed likewise over this period, I cannot say. Such local dues were collected in each *jiha* or clan-appropriated territory by resident local chiefs for their superior, the clan head in the city. For example, in the northwest, local chiefs and community heads collected *zakka* for presentation to Malam Jibirin or his representatives; in the southwest for Malam Jamau and his staff; and so on. Little attention was given to the collection of tithe on Fulani cattle; and it is likely that during the first two years, and perhaps throughout Suleimanu's reign, no tithe was taken from local pastoralists who had supported the *jihad* or assisted the consolidation of Fulani rule. However, Suleimanu did appoint a Sarkin Shanu, a Fulani called Jiji, which suggests that cattle tithes were probably collected during his closing years. Likewise, Suleimanu appointed the first Sarkin Fulani Ja'idanawa and also a Sarkin Fulani at Minjibir who was drawn from the local Yerimawa. Such appointments suggest that Suleimanu may have received cattle tithe at least from those pastoralists who were not directly included among the followings of any of the senior Fulani chiefs. However under Sule, the city people seem to have been free from any tax beside the grain tithe. The old system of market taxation had probably ceased to operate on Alwali's flight and was not restored during Sule's reign.

In October 1807, Abdullahi dan Fodio, morally disturbed at the conduct of his battle companions in the *jihad* against Gobir and Kebbi, "sought to shun the homelands, and my brothers, and turn towards the best of God's creation,"[85] that is, to go on pilgrimage to Mecca. Abdullahi was especially disturbed by the secular interests of the Shehu's warriors, and most profoundly, by his own ambitions. "I considered flight incumbent upon me and I left the army and ... faced towards the East."[86] His departure was soon noticed and a messenger was sent by pony express to Kano, which lay immediately on his route. The Fulani of Kano were instructed to send Abdullahi back to the Shehu; but force was out of the question. Abdullahi relates that "(the people of Kano) prevented me from continuing, and sought from me that I should teach them how they should act in order to establish religion ... their affairs had become confused among them because of their preoccupation with the world. I saw among them that from which I fled in my own country."[87] While in Kano, Abdullahi composed a powerful ode condemning those warriors whose professions of Islam during the *jihad* were merely a cloak for secular purposes,

> Whose purpose is the ruling of the countries and their people
> In order to obtain delights and acquire rank,
> According to the custom of the unbelievers, and the titles of their sovereigns,
> And the appointing of ignorant persons to the highest offices,
> And the collecting of concubines and fine clothes,
> And horses that gallop in the towns, not on the battlefields,
> And the devouring of the gifts of sanctity in booty and bribery.[88]

Abdullahi dan Fodio was widely regarded as the most learned Fulani scholar of his day after the Shehu; and presumably to delay his flight, the "people of Kano" asked him to prepare for them a treatise on the law that they could use to guide their government. He then composed his famous book, the *Diya'ul Hukkam*, and expounded it to the leaders at Kano. During these months, Abdullahi also supervised the building of a new city mosque for the sabbath prayers, and concluded his visit by accompanying the Fulani forces to attack Fagam beyond Birnin Kudu, which had not yet been taken. The Alkali Zangi places this visit during Suleimanu's reign;[89] but perhaps it was earlier. Zangi relates that during the month of the fast when Abdullahi was at Kano there was an eclipse (*kusufi*), presumably an eclipse of the sun, for which Abdullahi led the public prayers that Friday. In his account of the visit, Abdullahi does not refer to Sule or to anyone at Kano by name.

The Problem of Sule's Authority

We lack sufficient detail concerning Suleimanu's administration to establish its character and development definitively. However, available fragments and traditions indicate that despite progressive consolidation, the chief's authority in various spheres remained uncertain and insecure. In part, the Shehu's political prescriptions promoted this. As we have seen, the Shehu forbade his emirs to restore or employ Hausa official structures and administrative procedures because of their past associations and deviant implications. Instead, he prescribed a political organization based on a hierarchy of territorial units ranging from village communities through districts and emirates under the caliphate. In this model of the state, units at every level of organization would be placed under rulers having the status and title of emirs, each solely and directly responsible to his immediate superior in the administrative hierarchy.[90] However, that model would either eliminate the intermediate level of *hakimai*, thus overloading the emir and his vizier with responsibilities and work; or it would place control over the village administration in the hands of "emirs" at the intermediate level of organization, thus reducing the authority and scope of the central chiefship correspondingly.

The Shehu seems to have had in mind a territorial organization based on compact units with resident chiefs or emirs, much as exists in Kano today; but long before Suleimanu's accession, to centralize communications and control, most of the *hakimai* in Kano had been withdrawn to the city. In the traditional scheme of territorial administration, such officials mediated relations between the rural communities and the chief; but under the Shehu's model, the emir would become dependent on such officials for military and political support, revenues, and routine discharge of governmental functions. The Shehu may have intended by his prescriptions to restrain the growth of central autocracy and oppression; but at Kano in Sule's reign those principles reinforced and legitimized pre-emptions of territorial authority in the preceding partition by those clan heads who had organized and led the local *jihad*. Thus, following the Shehu's administrative model, Suleimanu was obliged to treat with these entrenched territorial chiefs, the more so as he lacked the power necessary to override them separately, much less together. He was also bound by the Shehu's precepts not to re-establish the old Hausa system of offices, *wasidodi* and centralized jurisdiction. At Kano the Shehu's political theories could thus be interpreted to sanction collegial rule, but this implied a dispersal of power that weakened the senior central office.

In 1817 the Shehu Usumanu died after a year's illness. Almost certainly, even before his death, many Hausa titles had been resuscitated at Sokoto, Zaria and elsewhere, as well as at Kano. Indeed, as early as 1807, Abdullahi remarked this tendency in the poem just cited. It is true that at Kano Suleimanu had not formally revived the Hausa official structure. However, as we have seen, several important titles had been informally reactivated through continued occupation of the state compounds attaching to them by the leading *muhajarini*. Suleimanu had also revived certain territorial offices which were necessary to the rural administration in Kano. Thus, a Turaki Romo was appointed to administer Minjibir and certain adjacent communities, a San Getso to administer Getso, a Sarkin Godiya in charge of Godiya, and the like. Further, Suleimanu appointed Salihi of the Yeligawa to administer Dutse, and conferred the title of Sarkin Rano (emir of Rano) on its Fulani conqueror, Ishiyaku. Such territorial appointments were probably essential for orderly administration of the chiefdom; but they were more easily made in areas not already appropriated by the major clan chiefs; and once made, in whatever terms, they were rapidly assimilated to the preceding official organization. For example, the new village chief or "emir" of Godiya, the Sarkin Godiya, was inevitably identified with his predecessor, the Hausa Dan Tama. The new Sarkin ("emir" of) Rano was, like Suleimanu himself, merely the latest in a long line of local chiefs. Even new townships, such as the Jalirawa Fulani founded in Rano territory on Suleimanu's direction, were inevitably assimilated to the traditional scheme of organization.

During and immediately after the *jihad*, Fulani in adjoining states frequently assisted one another in the subjugation of their recently acquired domains. For example, after the decisive battle at Danyaya, the Fulani of Kano had moved *en bloc* to Katsina to reinforce Umaru Dallaji and his people. Such cooperation, though occasional and *ad hoc*, was essential under prevailing conditions of war and consolidation. Thus, some time after Suleimanu's succession, he was called on to reinforce Malam Musa, the Shehu's new emir of Zazzau. A force was collected and sent southwards under the command of Dahiru, the baSuleibe who had installed himself in the state compound formerly reserved for the Galadima. With Dahiru went his close agnate and junior, Ibrahim Dabo, another baSuleibe who, like Dahiru, had come to Kano from the Suleibawa centres at Ricifa and Kwassallo in northeastern Zaria. Being already familiar with the geography and society of Zaria these men were well-fitted to lead the Kano army in that area. However, in an engagement at Ifira in northwestern Zaria, Dahiru was killed; and on his death the Fulani forces faced the risk of defeat. Dabo, though relatively junior, at once assumed command and rallied his men to snatch an impressive victory. The contingent returned to Kano with Suleimanu's share of the spoils. In these circumstances, Suleimanu decided to reward Dabo's initiative by installing him in Dahiru's compound and place. In doing so, he formally appointed Ibrahim Dabo to the office of Galadima, thereby reconstituting this office. While this violated the Shehu's proscriptions, these directives had perhaps by then been set aside in many other areas, including Sokoto itself.

Suleimanu made no attempt to formalize the titular identifications of such leading Fulani as Malam Jamau or Mandikko, or Umaru the son of Malam Jibir by investing them with those titles by which they were already commonly known in consequence of their residence. The compound of the Hausa Makama being still unoccupied on his accession, Suleimanu instructed his younger brother Sani to live there; but he does not seem to have appointed Sani formally to this office.

Otherwise, he carefully avoided challenging the titular identities or interests of the Fulani founding fathers. Instead he sought as best he could to establish his rule by incorporating theirs, without displacing them.

Unfortunately with Dabo Dambazau, the unofficial Sarkin Bai, Suleimanu had a serious clash. The Chronicle relates that Dabo Dambazau "raised a revolt. He dared to look for a wife in Sokoto and was given one. Sarkin Kano said, 'What do you mean by looking for a wife in Sokoto?' So Dabo was caught and bound. His relations the Dambazawa, however, came by night and cut his bonds, and set him free. He ran to Sokoto with Suleimanu following him. At Sokoto ... a reconciliation was made and they returned to Kano."[91] The bride sought by Dambazau was a Toronke girl, drawn from the Shehu's kinsmen at Sokoto, and probably one of Sultan Bello's sisters or daughters. Such a marriage alliance implicitly asserted Dabo Dambazau's interest in the succession. On these grounds, Suleimanu challenged Dabo's proposal. This section of the Chronicle, written after 1882 at the emir Mamman Bello's request, errs in stating that Suleimanu and Dabo presented themselves at Sokoto. Having other grudges against Dabo Dambazau, Suleimanu had him arrested and put in jail, his warders being the Sarkin Yara and the San Kurmi, both free Fulani clients who lived at the palace. According to oral traditions, Dambazau's colleagues immediately demanded his release, but Sule refused. Having repeatedly failed to secure Dambazau's release, these Fulani reported the matter to Sokoto and asked Mamman Bello to order Dabo's release. In essence, this incident expresses neatly the conflict over status and authority which persisted throughout Sule's reign.

It is well known that Dabo Dambazau resented Sule's appointment on several grounds; and Sule certainly suspected Dabo of seeking his deposition by Sultan Bello. When he threw Dambazau into the palace prison, Sule placed Dambarta, Matsidau and Kunya under his own son, Musa, who later became Ciroma, thus seeking to strengthen himself by taking over the territory of his "sarkin Bai." On Dambazau's release, Sule did not restore these communities to him, but gave him Gadanya near Shanono in the Yolawa region instead. Dambazau's colleagues from the days of the *jihad* protested at Sule's treatment of Dabo, perhaps on their own behalf as well as on his. The parvenu Emir had overreached himself by imprisoning one of the principal architects of Fulani rule in Kano. To the *muhajarini* leaders of 1804, such developments must have seemed intolerable. Dambazau was one of those to whom the Shehu had sent the Kano flag. His imprisonment indirectly threatened their own positions. Dambazau's colleagues rallied to his cause; and, following his release at Mamman Bello's command, Suleimanu's authority was discredited and his position insecure. Dambazau had now the further motive of recovering his lost domains.

The uncertainty and inconclusiveness of Suleimanu's chiefly authority is also shown by his relations with Dan Tunku, then settled at Shidar. Under the partition that followed the conquest, Dan Tunku held the area north, northwest and northeast of Shidar. As Alwali's Sarkin Fulani Dambarta he also claimed Dambarta, then a stockaded town; but that had been appropriated by Dabo Dambazau, the new "sarkin Bai." Like Malam Bakatsine, Dan Tunku remained in his territory away from Kano; and as the years went by, he exercised increasing autonomy. When Sule gradually established his right to shares of *zakka* and local tax from other clan chiefs holding domains under the collegial partition, Dan Tunku refused to conform. In response to Suleimanu's pressure, he proclaimed his formal independence of Kano, asserting that he had received a flag from the Shehu through Bello that authorized him to conquer and administer a chiefdom of his own. Dan Tunku argued that it was with these aims that he had assisted in the conquests of Kano, Daura and Katsina, whose boundaries previously met two or three miles northwest of Kazaure, then a stockaded village (*keffi*). Dan Tunku's reply to Sule's demands was thus to claim independence and to excise a substantial area from the old Hausa chiefdom of Kano. This was probably facilitated by Sule's removal of Dabo Dambazau from Dambarta.

As he had never made any formal allegiance to Sule or any Fulani at Kano, but to the Shehu and Bello direct, Dan Tunku claimed independence and parity of status with Kano. Though Bello says at Birnin Gada that he had "commanded them to pay homage,"[92] this was probably to himself as the Shehu's proxy; for on his accession, Sule had not dared to demand an act of allegiance (*mubaya'a*) from the Fulani or anyone at Kano, since to attempt this would have been most impolitic and might have provoked an open revolt. Since *mubaya'a* was a public declaration of personal submission to the emir by all who performed it, Dan Tunku thus reminded Sule that he had made no *mubaya'a* to Kano, that being inconsistent with his initial *mubaya'a* to the Shehu. Sule failed to impose his demands on Dan Tunku by negotiation and dared not risk an open conflict, certainly for lack of the military resources and skill, but also perhaps for fear that Dan Tunku would have the support of those Fulani leaders who had acquired extensive territories at the conquest and by subsequent partition. Thus by invoking his separate grant of a flag and his personal allegiance to Sokoto, Dan Tunku advanced the autarchic territorial claims and interests of the Fulani *muhajirini* in their most extreme form. Sule realized that these men, on whose tolerance his regime depended, regarded his chiefship with considerable ambivalence. Their loyalties were already strained; and under these circumstances he continued to assert his claim against Dan Tunku by correspondence rather than arms.[93]

Of those Kano flagbearers who still survived, Sule seems to have received most assistance from Malam Jamau, the Sarkin Dawaki Maituta. Jamau's role as custodian of the Shehu's flag obliged him to support the Shehu's nominee as chief; and in the circumstances he seems to have done the best he could. Ibrahim Dabo, formerly the Limam in the Galadima's ward at the city, originally served as liaison between Sule and Malam Jamau; and on Jamau's death, Dabo became Suleimanu's senior and most important assistant. Like Sule, Dabo was not one of the original Kano flagbearers; but so close was Dabo's association with Sule that for a while Jamau's son, Mani, seemed in danger of losing his father's office. Instead Sule, perhaps on Dabo's suggestion, transferred the baYole Umaru from the Ciroma's compound to Malam Jamau's, and appointed his own son Shehu as Ciroma instead. Sule also appointed the Wombai Abubakar (Habu, of unknown lineage), and relied on him, the Galadima Dabo, Dan Zabuwa's son, Muhammadu Sani, the Alkali Usuman, his successor Yusufu, and various malams for assistance and advice in the government.

Much of Sule's reign was given over to unsuccessful attacks on the Mangawa chiefdom at Tumbi, a vassal of Bornu, with which the Fulani remained at war.

Except for attacks on Shirra by Bakatsine and M. Zara in 1808 and an expedition by Dabo in 1814, until about 1812 Kano seems to have carried on fighting against the Sarkin Gumel Kalgo (1804–11), though inconclusively. Thereafter, under Dan Auwa (1814–1828) the Mangawa raided northeastern Kano with increasing success, until a special force was placed at Garki to garrison the town and close the frontier.[94] Suleimanu seems to have relied on Dabo and others to lead his levies in these raids and counter-raids; and although Zangi says he made 13 campaigns, he himself apparently almost always remained at Kano. There is no evidence to show that he ever visited his suzerain in the new imperial state of Sokoto. Nor, despite the traditions, did he ever meet the Shehu; but the sword and knife which the Shehu sent on his appointment have since formed the key insignia of the Fulani chiefship at Kano.

The Dokaji Abubakar relates a well-known tale that, anticipating his death, Suleimanu wrote to Mamman Bello, who had succeeded his father the Shehu in 1817 as caliph (Sarkin Musulmi) and head of the empire, concerning the succession at Kano.[95] In Malam Adamu's version, Sule implored Sultan Bello not to appoint any of his immediate kin to succeed him, and pleaded his own unhappy experience as chief. Instead he recommended the appointment of the Galadima Dabo as his successor. Jamau had already died, and Malams Bakatsine and Jibirin were then both old. Mandikko, Bakatsine's son, Sule suspected of oppressive inclinations, and Dabo Dambazau of haughtiness and pride. It is improbable that Suleimanu's letter to Bello has survived; and these traditions may thus be merely a rationalization of historical fact, though that is not entirely likely. Sule valued Dabo's energies and abilities highly. He may also have felt that Dabo was likely to succeed where he had failed in ruling the aristocratic Fulani, and that his own kinsmen were likely to follow suit. Having formerly served as Limam in the Galadima's ward at the city, Dabo, then Galadima, was eligible for the succession on religious as well as administrative and military grounds. It is likely that Suleimanu himself had little family interest in the succession. He is said to have died at Kano in 1819, two years after the Shehu.[96]

On the tradition reported by Malam Adamu, Sultan Bello wrote requiring Jibirin, the head of the Yolawa, to assemble all the people, that is, the *jema'a*, the ruling Fulani, in the city, and to inform them of Suleimanu's letter with its specific remarks and requests. Presumably Bello's friend, Gidado, who soon became vizier, was present at the assembly. Following this, Jibirin read the people another, shorter letter from Sultan Bello, which appointed the Galadima Ibrahim Dabo as the new emir. In yet another letter, Sultan Bello directed Malam Jibirin to make *mubaya'a* to Dabo immediately on his formal enthronement on the carpeted dais reserved for the emir. Malam Jibirin executed the caliph's directions faithfully and, having shaken Dabo's hand with the stereotyped invocation, "May God help you, may God grant you success," stood aside while the assembly, in order of rank, presented themselves and did likewise. However, Dabo Dambazau, who should have followed Malam Jibirin in the act of *mubaya'a*, refused to do so. After a pause, the next in rank was summoned and so, excluding Dambazau, the new emir received the allegiance of all assembled Fulani. This event occurred at the new mosque founded by Abdullahi dan Fodio.

For the next seven days, Ibrahim Dabo remained in seclusion at the Galadima's compound where he received *mubaya'a* from others who presented themselves, before moving into the palace. Dan Tunku did not appear. Dabo took due note of this; and on assuming the chiefship, he wrote and summoned Dan Tunku to make *mubaya'a*. Dan Tunku rejected this demand directly; but unlike Sule, Dabo determined to fight. Though the ensuing conflict seemed to centre on claims of status and territory, authority was the central issue. Dabo risked losing the esteem, supremacy and leadership his new responsibilities required, by letting such acts of defiance pass unpunished. Complaisance merely invited denigration by others, thus threatening the central authority with dissolution or usurpation.

Ibrahim Dabo, 1819–1846

The Accession

Dabo had to prove that he was the proper person to succeed Suleimanu. By the standards of the day and the *jihad*, he had a fine Muslim record. He was learned, devout, and a keen champion of Islam. However, he had played a very minor role in the *jihad* at Kano. There is a tale that the Shehu commissioned Dabo to conquer Shirra; but this is probably false. Beginning as a muezzin at Gulu in Nupe, he had moved north to Kwasallo in north-eastern Zaria, where he directed a small Koranic school in the years immediately preceding the *jihad*. On the outbreak of fighting around Kiru in Kano, Dabo moved northwards to Kanwa in Karaye and there attached himself to the Suleibawa leader Malam Jamau, the Kano flagbearer. Though not himself a close kinsman of Jamau, as a fellow baSuleibe, Dabo served as one of Jamau's closest aids and advisers, though he did not take an active part in the opening campaigns of the *jihad* in Kano.

After the capital had been occupied, Malam Jamau asked Dabo to serve as Limam at the mosque in the ward adjoining his compound; and thereafter, Dabo became Jamau's confidential liaison with Suleimanu. In this capacity, Dabo also represented Dahiru, his lineage kinsman, another baSuleibe from Zaria. Though living in the Galadima's compound, as a baSuleibe, Dahiru recognized Malam Jamau as the Suleibawa head and spokesman in Kano affairs. When Dahiru died at Ifira in Zazzau, Dabo was given his compound by Sule and continued to support Malam Jamau and the chief until Jamau's death. Thereafter though not qualified by descent, being easily the outstanding baSuleibe and the chief's most important supporter, Dabo assumed much of Malam Jamau's role in state affairs. Perhaps in order to consolidate this position, Sule did not immediately install Jamau's son as Sarkin Dawaki Mai Tuta, but gave that office instead to Umoru, a son of the baYole Malam Jibir, who then occupied the Ciroma's compound. In Umoru's place as Ciroma, Sule appointed his own son Shehu, thus affirming the old Hausa criteria for allocation of that office. The flag having been thus temporarily removed from the custody of Malam Jamau's issue, Dabo lacked a rival for leadership of the Suleibawa; and since under Malam Jamau's leadership these Suleibawa were the only major segment of conquering Fulani that steadily supported Suleimanu's rule, on Sule's death, Dabo was a prominent candidate for the succession.

It is related at Sokoto and in Kano that, on learning of Sule's death, the Sultan Bello consulted his trusted friend and chief assistant, Muhammadu Gidado, who, although not yet formally installed as vizier (*waziri*) of the empire with direct responsibility for supervision of Kano, already discharged those functions. Gidado and Bello discussed the succession at Kano. While Bello favoured Dabo's appointment, Gidado advocated the selection of Sani, Sule's brother, then living in the Makama's compound. It is said that Bello and Gidado referred the decision to Allah with the historic result. However this may be, Dabo was chosen and appointed, as related above. It seems clear that Sani expected to succeed Sule; and he may have canvassed his candidacy with Gidado personally. He evidently felt confident in Gidado's support, and resented Dabo's succession.

Another important rival was Malam Dabo Dambazau, one of the earliest leaders of the *jihad*. Dabo Dambazau had steadfastly opposed Suleimanu's chiefship, seeking that office himself. He seems also to have canvassed his claims as Sule's successor. Whether this was done before Sule's death or soon, but still too late, afterwards, remains obscure. The story goes that at Sule's death, Dabo Dambazau sent gifts and messages to Mamman Bello seeking the appointment. However, even before these messages arrived, Bello had sent letters to Malam Jibir at Kano ordering Dabo's appointment. Jibir conducted Dabo's public installation before Dabo Dambazau had received Bello's reply to his own approach; and it was perhaps from mixed emotions of hope, anger, chagrin and disbelief that Dabo Dambazau remained motionless when called upon to make his allegiance to Ibrahim Dabo. It is said that to compose the matter and to strengthen the new emir, Sultan Bello then informed Dambazau that he would be the next emir of Kano and that he then directed Dabo to appoint Dambazau formally as Sarkin Bai (Chief of the Slaves) to denote that he was the Sarkin Baya (the chief of (here)after, that is, the successor.)[97] This is an obscure point even in Hausa; and the tale seems to assimilate two distinct events; for even in Sule's reign, Dabo Dambazau was known as Sarkin Bai, having settled in that compound. However, he had not been formally appointed; and his political status and power were based on his chiefship of the Dambazawa and his role in the *jihad*, rather than on formal office. Indeed, on his imprisonment by Sule, Dabo Dambazau would have lost any official position he had formerly held. But as he held none, that could not occur. Sule likewise had no claims on Dambazau's estate, since this was personal rather than official property. On his release from prison at Sokoto's order, Dabo Dambazau seems to have re-occupied the compound of the Sarkin Bai, undoubtedly to Suleimanu's annoyance.

Evidently Sultan Bello promised Dabo Dambazau the succession after Dabo, seeking thus to commit Dambazau to support the throne, since its aggrandisement would facilitate his own rule later. By this means, Bello also postponed the problem of the next succession until the occasion arose; but when it did, Sultan Bello had already died and his successor, the Sultan Atiku, was not committed to honour Bello's promise. It is also possible that Mohammadu Dabo of Dambazau died in 1845 shortly before Ibrahim Dabo. However, even if he did survive Dabo by a month or two, Dambazau was by then too old to receive the appointment and Dabo's dynasty was too strongly entrenched to be displaced.

Dambazau's ambitions and rivalry were well known to those Fulani who assembled to witness Dabo's induction as chief; and his refusal to render allegiance (*mubaya'a*) was remarked accordingly. One of the senior malams present at this event remarked that Dambazau would never become chief; another malam, learning of Ibrahim Dabo's accession, prophesied that henceforward the chiefship would remain with his issue.[98] It is unlikely that such observations did not reach the ears of Dambazau through his numerous agents, courtiers and kin.

The new chief, Ibrahim Dabo, took no immediate action against his powerful rival and namesake, knowing well that the latter had sought the office and was bitterly disappointed. In due course, Sultan Bello instructed Dabo to appoint Dambazau formally as Sarkin Bai; but before this was done a general revolt had broken out.

The Fulani aristocracy had rejected Dabo's accession, despite their overt declarations of allegiance. Though Malam Jibir, who was then quite old, had loyally obeyed Sultan Bello's directions, he may also have had private reservations; but in any case, at this date his son Umaru was now the effective head of the Yolawa, Jibir having retired from routine executive affairs due to age. The Suleibawa of Kano also resented Dabo's displacement of Malam Jamau's lineage and issue, and rejected him as their leader on grounds of descent. As regards the Jobawa, Malam baKatsine still remained at Dutse, leaving Mandikko, his son, to represent their clan in affairs at the capital. Mandikko, then living in the Madaki's compound, resented Dabo's accession, as a rival and on other grounds. Like Dambazau, Mandikko had chiefly ambitions. Like other leaders of the *jihad* or their heirs, he resented the successive chiefly appointments of men who had taken no leading role in the *jihad* at Kano. Dan Tunku expressed this attitude curtly when, in reply to Dabo's summons to make *mabaya'a*, he refused, saying that Dabo had neither withdrawn (*hijra*), nor helped in the conquest of Kano. Mandikko's subsequent conduct reveals his hostility to Dabo, mixed with the contempt he affected as an aristocrat by birth for his successful *shigege* rival. Mandikko's conduct expressed attitudes that were widespread and intense among the new Fulani aristocracy.

Dabo sensed his situation accurately. Though his appointment by Sultan Bello's command entitled him to rule, to do so was another matter. He thus had to create and employ the power he needed to assert his authority. To dramatize his accession and indicate his intentions, on completing his week's seclusion at the Galadima's compound, Dabo ordered his people to cut a new entrance for him through the palace wall, and ordained that hereafter all his successors should do likewise on first entering the palace. Perhaps by this act Dabo wished to stress that he was a *shigege*, the first of a new dynasty. Dabo's innovation attracted public notice immediately, and the resulting speculation focused attention upon him. Evidently, the new chief did not intend to follow his predecessor's footsteps.

The Revival of Hausa Political Forms

On entering the palace, Dabo isolated himself for "forty days," fasting and praying.[99] Much of this period was undoubtedly employed in considering his new situation, and the relative advantages of alternative courses of action. Dabo may also have withdrawn for the period in order to allow himself the necessary time to learn the reactions of rural areas to his accession. Throughout his isolation he was well-informed about current developments and consulted various people. He may also have initiated preliminary steps towards mobilisation at this time.

As Suleimanu's successor, though no Fulani tradition on this score had yet developed at Kano, Dabo was entitled by Muslim practice and local custom to all items in Sule's estate that were of value for such public purposes as administration or war. Some of these items would be given to the caliph at Sokoto; but the bulk of Suleimanu's estate, and especially all items of military significance such as horses, war gear, weapons, male slaves and stores of money or grain, by Muslim precedent, would remain with the throne for the state as *kayan jihadi* (equipment for the holy war). However, Sule had left little wealth—a few slaves, some horses, stores of grain, clothes and cash—perhaps no more than each of his senior subjects, the *muhajarini*, possessed. It is said that his brother, Sani, claimed all Sule's possessions on behalf of his family; and that even the suits of quilted cotton armour (*lifida*) were thus transferred. Since Sule had found both the palace and treasury empty on his accession, and since his successor was not a kinsman, given the character and history of Sule's chiefship, it was difficult to deny the personal status of his estate, and consequently that his kin had some right to inherit.

During his seclusion Dabo took stock of his situation. It is said that immediately afterwards he wrote to Sultan Bello, seeking permission to revive certain Hausa titles and political institutions. In support, he explained to the Sultan that unless this was done, neither Islam nor its laws (*shari'a*) could be firmly established at Kano. Having himself already done this, Mamman Bello granted his request.[100] Dabo began by putting on the large ostrich-feather slippers that Rumfa had introduced centuries earlier in imitation of his Bornu suzerain. He restored the double-headed spear that Rumfa had instituted as the symbol of Kano chiefship. He instructed his courtiers and slaves to shield his rising up and sitting down from public view by placing themselves before his dais and draping their voluminous gowns on out-stretched arms, following a practice Babba Zaki had introduced. Dabo also revived Babba Zaki's organization of court ushers and *kofas* (*wasidodi*), in principle though not in its exact particulars. Since most of the Hausa offices were still unfilled, Babba Zaki's communication structure could not be reconstituted in its original form. Further, given the peculiarities of the Fulani power structure, with its four or five major clan components, Babba Zaki's system would have been inappropriate in detail; but its principles were readily adapted. Dabo then also added certain practices of his own, perhaps the most important being the double-eared turban that distinguishes the emir from other Muslims. This was rationalized as a permanent reminder that Allah, the ruler of chiefs, has two ears to hear all their doings, the wrong as well as the right; but the mundane explanation is at least as important. By these and other means, Dabo emphasized his unique position as emir and his difference from other Fulani nobles. Implicitly, he thus indicated that his authority exceeded theirs in its basis, kind and scope.

An immigrant from Zaria, Dabo was guided in these revivals of Kano chiefship by Dan Mama, who still lived in the city. Being dependent on the caliph's representative for the tenure of his "hundred towns," which were mostly scattered hamlets without stockades, Dan Mama gave Dabo his full support and found that this was welcome. It is said that Dan Mama convinced Dabo that unless the antecedent official structure was substantially revived and used as the basis for administrative organization, he would remain as powerless as Suleimanu. Undoubtedly Dabo learned the details of the traditional Hausa organization from Dan Mama and other informed Kutumbawa residents at the capital. But once he was convinced of the centralizing values of these institutions and recognized their significance for the resolution of the current situation with its divisive and disintegrative entrenchment of segmental powers, Dabo sought formal authority from the caliph to adopt such Hausa institutions as seemed appropriate to coordinate and strengthen the government of Kano. No trace of this request appears to have survived in written form; yet even if it had, to judge by those communications that have survived, the specific content of the letter would probably seem cryptic and general. However, Mamman Bello had himself, some years earlier, accepted the inevitability of reviving Hausa titled offices as governmental units. Under his guidance, the new imperial state of Sokoto had emerged as a distinctive structure of titles drawn from the traditional regimes of Kebbi, Zamfara and Gobir, whose territories it had absorbed.[101] In Katsina and Zazzau, experience had also convinced the Fulani rulers that some selective revival of preceding patterns of political organization was necessary and useful. We cannot say whether Dabo's request initiated the general trend towards the revival of Hausa governmental forms throughout the Fulani dominions and the suspension of the Shehu Usuman's proscriptions on this point. However, late though it was, we know of no other; and in the particular circumstances then prevailing at Kano it is difficult to see how the new emir could have established his predominance without employing these or similar institutional means.

On receiving Bello's approval, Dabo made certain initial appointments. His accession had left vacant the office of Galadima. To this he transferred Sani, his predecessor's brother who had hitherto occupied the Makama's compound. Mandikko, who formerly lived in the Madaki's compound, was then appointed Makama and instructed to occupy the compound Sani had just vacated. Umaru, the son of Malam Jibir, whom Sule had formally appointed as Sarkin Dawaki Maituta on Malam Jamau's death, was now invested with the robes and office of Madaki by Dabo, and directed to take over the compound formerly occupied by Mandikko. Dabo then appointed Mani, the son of Malam Jamau, to the office and compound of the Sarkin Dawaki Mai Tuta, thus establishing the hereditary status of the title held initially by Malam Jamau. Whether Dabo invested his rival Dambazau with the title of Sarkin Bai at this time remains uncertain. He did formally appoint Dabo Dambazau as Sarkin Bai; but this may have happened later; but if indeed Sultan Bello first instructed Dabo to appoint Dambazau to some senior office, most probably that of the Sarkin Bai, Dabo may in fact have seized the opportunity presented by this order to seek permission for a general revival of the pre-jihadic political institutions of Kano with such modifications or exclusions as Islam required.

Dabo and the Ruling Fulani

The appointments just listed were all public, formal, and carried out at the palace according to traditional Hausa procedures. Each appointment was an implicit challenge by the new emir to the appointee to reject his authority and the profferred office, if he dared to risk the consequences. However, in issuing these challenges, Dabo proceeded so as to minimize the probability of direct rejection by the individuals concerned. Thus, he first appointed Sani by promoting him from Makama to Galadima, traditionally at Kano the senior office under the chief, and one reserved for royals only. By this act Dabo honoured Sani and publicly identified him as the senior member of the Mundubawa dynasty and his own personal choice as "wazir," the role that Dabo had filled for Sule and one traditional for the Galadima.

Following this, Dabo confronted Mandikko with the alternative of accepting office at his hands or disqualifying himself by rejection from further participation in the government. Mandikko, hitherto identified by residents as "Madaki," recognized that his appointment as Makama, though endowing him with official status and authority, was a carefully calculated slight, as the Makama ranked below the Madaki in the traditional Kano system. Further to thrust the point home, Dabo simultaneously required Mandikko to vacate the compound reserved for the Madaki, thereby asserting his right as emir to all properties traditionally regarded as belonging to the Hausa state. This claim clearly extended both to occupancy of land and to the administration of rural communities, thus embracing the entire territory. Mandikko found himself in an awkward position. He was already occupying state property without the emir's permission to do so; and although the appointed representative of his father Bakatsine, the head of the Jobawa clan, he was neither himself the Jobawa leader nor one of the Fulani founding fathers. If he resisted Dabo's request, Mandikko simultaneously ran the risk of alienating his own clansmen who might—correctly—interpret such action as a threat to their own rights; and he might also forfeit future prospects of official authority, including perhaps the throne. Mandikko accordingly accepted the defeat and mild humiliation; but it can hardly have increased his affection for Dabo.

Dabo's two remaining appointments were both evident promotions, and thus welcome to the individuals and lineage groups concerned. By transferring the baYole Umaru to the Madaki office, Dabo indicated his recognition of the Yolawa as the senior non-royal lineage among the Kano Fulani. By reinstating Malam Jamau's son in the office of Sarkin Dawaki Mai-Tuta, Dabo sought to reassure the senior branch of the Kano Suleibawa that he intended to uphold their rights. Moreover as both these appointments indirectly reversed Suleimanu's policy, by these means also Dabo disassociated himself from his predecessor. However, as Ciroma or Crown Prince, Dabo retained Shehu, the son of Suleimanu, thereby assuring the Mundubawa that he intended to preserve their dynastic interests in the throne.

By these appointments Dabo also tried to transform the unofficial power of the clan-heads into an official authority that depended ultimately on his personal endowments or assent; but he wisely made no attempt to redistribute fiefs or territories administered by the individuals whose titular positions he had just changed. Mandikko, as Bakatsine's representative and apparent successor, continued to administer the area around Wudil, while Malam Umaru, the new Madaki, administered exactly the same Yolawa territory that he had formerly held first as Ciroma and then as Sarkin Dawaki Mai-Tuta. Likewise, Malam Jamau's southwestern domains, which stretched from Kiru throughout the old substate of

Karaye, remained under Mani, his son. However, Dabo had now implicitly asserted his jurisdiction as emir throughout these areas by investing their holders with official authority and administrative responsibilities. Bearing in mind Dan Tunku's assumption of independence, by these formal appointments Dabo tried to transform the pre-existing appropriations of territorial jurisdiction based on conquest and partition into the corollaries of chiefly appointment to office. Thus each offer of appointment contained a challenge to the individual addressed to revolt if he dare.

The new aristocracy founded on conquest understood this implication of Dabo's appointments perfectly well, and took action accordingly. These men had resented Sule as a parvenu who had neither withdrawn (*yi hijra*) as the Shehu enjoined, nor had taken an active part in the campaigns of the *jihad*. As Sule's successor, Dabo was even less acceptable, being a stranger to Kano, the second emir appointed by Sokoto who had neither withdrawn nor fought in the *jihad*, and because he had revived these Hausa political institutions, which the *muhajarini* had prevented Suleimanu from doing. To intensify their opposition to these developments, Dabo had chosen to resuscitate Hausa titles forbidden by the Shehu and, in so doing, to assert his superior claims to clan territories long since occupied by force of arms. The old aristocracy accordingly regarded Dabo's actions as a direct threat to their rights and status. Unlike Sule, Dabo clearly sought to place himself over them, though, by various criteria, he had little claim to equal rank with them. By comparison with theirs, Dabo's resources, territorial, military and economic, were then quite slender while his commitments were heavy. He was confronted by Dan Tunku with the alternatives of substantial territorial loss or war; and had also to cope with raids launched by Dan Auwa of Gumel. The new chief was clearly in no position to throw his weight around; and thus, though as individuals they accepted office at his hands when formally obliged to do so, the founding aristocracy of Fulani Kano did not accept Dabo's claim to a superior and structurally antecedent jurisdiction over their territories and subjects. To do so would involve forfeiting all their hard-won gains to one who had neither shared in the struggle nor apparently possessed the power to enforce his claims.

According to the Chronicle,

> Dabo made Sani Galadima. He, however, immediately tried to raise a revolt and incite all the towns to disaffection. The country sarkis assembled and became *tawaye* (rebels) from Ungogo to Dambarta, from Jarima to Sankara and from Dusse (Dutse) to Birnin Kudu and Karayi. Dabo said, "I will conquer them if Allah wills." He entered his house and remained there forty days praying to Allah for victory. ... He ... made a camp on Dala hill. Because of this he got the name of "the man who camped on Dala."[102]

The Dokaji Abubakar, following local traditions, identifies Sule's brother, the Galadima Sani, as the man who incited revolt, noting that although appointed Galadima, Sani desired to be chief.[103] Perhaps Sani may have hoped for Dabo's deposition in the face of widespread public protest.

Sani clearly played an important part in inciting the revolt; but it is doubtful if he had sufficient influence to organize it; and perhaps this allegation merely reflects dynastic politics. The revolt occurred throughout the territories hitherto controlled by Dabo Dambazau, the baJobe Mandikko, and the Suleibawa under Malam Jamau; but it was concentrated in the northwest and northeastern districts. Only the Yolawa west of Kano city did not openly rebel. Clearly, given the preceding distribution of territorial control, this general revolt was not solely the work of the Galadima Sani.

Local tradition attributes the revolt to those Fulani leaders who had settled at the city, the founding fathers of Fulani Kano, or their successors and representatives. These men were probably encouraged by the Galadima Sani, but the ultimate decision to revolt rested with them, since they controlled the territorial chiefs. However, neither they nor the Galadima Sani resorted to arms. As usual, they all remained in the city. But having levied the annual tax on their villages, they withheld it, and gave Dabo none. It seems that they also instructed the village chiefs subordinate to them to ignore Dabo's requests for military and other supplies. In short, they struck at Dabo's weakest points—his need for supplies and support, and his dependence on the compliance of his senior territorial officials in order to administer the rural areas. Dabo soon learned how matters stood. He saw that the clan heads presented the immediate source of opposition. He was told that they were withholding his dues of tax, tithe and other supplies. He accordingly sent orders throughout the country forbidding the levy or payment of tax to village chiefs for transfer to these clan heads. This order sparked off the revolt, which was confined almost entirely to rural Fulani, the community chiefs and their supporters.

With few exceptions, the defeated Hausa (Habe) took no direct part; but at Getso and Rano they were troublesome, having long awaited a chance to expel their local chiefs. At Karaye also, Sule Nadoyi, Malam Jamau's appointee, was ejected by the local Habe. Dabo sent Jamau's son Mani, the new Sarkin Dawaki Maituta, to reduce Karaye and restore Nadoyi. Apart from towns that lacked a leader, the "Habe" took little part in the revolt. Thus this was strictly a revolt of the Fulani against the new Fulani chief, and it expressed the general rejection by the leading Kano Fulani of Dabo's claims to pre-eminence. The revolt displayed the political power of the old oligarchy, and aimed to show the new chief's incapacity to rule the country without their willing assistance. When Rano joined the rebels, virtually the entire south and east of Kano territory repudiated Dabo's authority. In the north, besides the followers of Dambazau, Dan Tunku had asserted his independence. In this situation, Dabo relied heavily on the support of Dan Mama, and those Hausawa attached to the Alkali Usuman.

Dan Tunku and Kazaure

Dabo sought first to deal with Dan Tunku, and initially tried to split the Yerimawa by supporting Dan Tunku's rival, Gebi, as their headman. To reinforce Gebi's position as the new Yerimawa leader, Dabo directed the Turakin Romo Abubakar, whom Sule had appointed, to mobilize the Yerimawa of Minjibir, Malaki, Kutoru and other nearby communities behind Gebi's claims. Abubakar, however, remained loyal to Dan Tunku and was accordingly replaced by Gamo, who supported Dabo.[104] Nonetheless, Gebi's aspirations had been discredited and Dan Tunku's leadership of the Yerimawa reinforced.

Dabo then adopted a different approach. On appointing Dambazau to the office of Sarkin Bai, he placed him in charge of all the territory ranging between Ungogo, three or four miles north of the city, and Kunci near the northwestern boundaries of Kano. He restored Dambarta and Kunya to Dambazau, expressly setting Dambazau and Dan Tunku against one another. To formalize the new situation further, Dabo appointed his daughter, Fatsamatu Zara, to the title of Magajiya, the first Fulani Magajiya in Kano; he then gave Fatsamatu to Dabo Dambazau as a bride, together with Kunci as her dowry, thus publicly demonstrating his reconciliation with Dambazau.

I cannot determine the exact chronology of the central events in this confused period of revolt. After central administrative control had broken down in the southeast and in much of northern Kano, the Fulani leaders assembled together privately at the house of the Alkali Usuman in the city to discuss the situation and to decide their course of action. It is not known whether the Galadima Sani attended this meeting. The Alkali Usuman, as a "founding father" but a Hausa and thus with little influence or territory, was an appropriate host for this secret meeting. The discussion seems to have been forthright. Finally, Dabo Dambazau declared that by their recent and current policies, the jihadic leaders threatened to destroy Fulani rule in Kano. Recalling Mamman Bello's warning at Birnin Gada, he stressed the need for unity among the Fulani in order to maintain control over the far larger "Habe" population. He identified such political unity with strong central leadership under the Caliph's emir, and declared in favour of giving Dabo his due share of the tax and tithe that was presently withheld. Dambazau said that he intended to do this immediately, and advised his colleagues to do the same.[105]

Whether this meeting preceded Dambazau's appointment as Sarkin Bai and his marriage to Fatsumatu, or whether, following on Mamman Bello's offer of his future appointment as chief, it expressed Dambazau's reorientation and encouraged Dabo to reward him by increasing his previous territory and giving him Fatsumatu as a bride, I cannot say. It seems certain that these events all took place within a year or two in 1819 and 1820, but I cannot determine the precise order in which they occurred. Further, I lack information on the response that Dambazau's appeal elicited. His colleagues probably interpreted his new stress on unity in realistic or cynical terms as an indication of his political interests and aspirations. It is even possible that when Dambazau transferred to Dabo his withheld share of tax and tithe, Dabo decided to increase Dambazau's territories in the hopes that others would be encouraged to follow his example. We do not know precisely what happened.

In response to Dabo's early demands for allegiance, Dan Tunku had claimed much of the territory recently placed under Dambazau by Dabo. Further, Dan Tunku also claimed Dabi and Sankara, neither of which he had previously administered, and both about thirty miles from his base at Shiddar. Dabo replied that he had no intention of surrendering any territory that Suleimanu had ruled. He sent messengers to rural Fulani chiefs appealing for horses to defend Kano against Dan Tunku's claims, and directed the Madaki Umaru to march northeastwards from Dan Zabuwa and drive Dan Tunku back. Another force moved northwards from Jali against Shiddar; and Dabo sent his Sarkin Dawakin Tsakar Gida Ali against Mazangada. To reinforce Madaki Umaru in the northwest, he summoned Malam Bakatsine from Dutse.

Dan Tunku was an elusive target and skillfully evaded these various attacks. In response, he made several successful thrusts himself. Shortly after the new Sarkin Bai had moved to Ungogo to take over its administration, Dan Tunku invested the area, besieged the town, raided Fage three miles from the city, and gave Kano a severe fright.[106] Dabo mobilized quickly and pushed Dan Tunku northwards, only to lose part of his force in an ambush. Dan Tunku's military success and diplomacy led several dissident Fulani chiefs to take up arms against Dabo openly. The son of the Sarkin Fulani of Sankara quit that town with his followers, established himself at Sabon Gari and raided the environs intensively, subjugating it. From Kunci in the northwest to Sankara and Sabon Gari in the northeast, Dan Tunku's forces raided freely. Dabo sought to push Dan Tunku north by fortifying strategic townships in this area. Ungogo, Panisau and Dawaki were walled to shield Kano, and Panisau was converted into a military camp and marshalling ground. Kunya and Dambarta were fortified as soon as Kano recovered them. Dambazau thereafter occupied Dambarta as the capital of his large fief and his military base against Dan Tunku.

This war occupied Dabo for five or six years; and being waged on Kano territory, it cost the chiefdom much in life and property. Clapperton, who visited Kano in January 1824, met Dabo at Panisau preparing a major assault on Dan Tunku's new headquarters at Kazaure. Before moving west, Clapperton learned that having broken into the town, Dabo was surprised by Dan Tunku's counter-attack and driven back with heavy losses.[107] North of the city, en route to and from Sokoto via Katsina, he frequently remarks the "many villages in ruins which have been destroyed by the rebel Duntungua and the inhabitants sold as slaves."[108] On his return to Kano in June, he found Dabo again preparing another attack on Dan Tunku.[109]

Despite heavy losses, Dabo's determination and superior resources enabled him to force Dan Tunku northwards to the strong defensive position of Kazaure by 1825; but when Kazaure came under heavy attack, Mamman Bello intervened to impose peace between his two vassals, accrediting Dan Tunku's independence of Kano, and delimiting the boundaries of their states at the Jekuradi River north of Dambarta. Nearly one-half of the newly constituted emirate of Kazaure had formed part of Kano territory during the eighteenth century. Dan Tunku appropriated the remainder from Daura and Katsina. Nonetheless, Dabo was probably grateful to Mamman Bello for intervening to end this long struggle. He now had the far more important task of assisting his neighbour, the emir of Bauchi, Yakubu, to defend the eastern frontiers of the empire against a strong attack by the Bornu army under its new leader, the Sheik Alhaji Aminu El-Kanemi. Perhaps Dabo had stubbornly pursued his struggle with Dan Tunku against Mamman Bello's earlier offer of arbitration; or perhaps on learning of El-Kanemi's attack, Mamman Bello decided to impose peace on Dan Tunku and Dabo, thereby enabling the latter to defend Kano. In the following campaign, after initial successes, El-Kanemi suffered a major reverse.

As El-Kanemi marched west towards Kano, Shirra and Misau welcomed him by throwing out their Fulani rulers. El Kanemi proceeded to Garko south of

Wudil where he was held up for 30 days by the siege. Dabo learned of El Kanemi's movements at Dutse and at once returned to Kano "where he was informed all were preparing to follow Laminu (El Kanemi)." Meanwhile, at Mamman Bello's request, Dabo's neighbour, Yakubu, the emir of Bauchi, had assembled his army and marched north to intercept El Kanemi at Fake between Garko and Dutse. Yakubu's victory in that engagement certainly saved Kano for the Fulani, and perhaps some other eastern emirates as well.[110]

Thereafter, recognizing the risks and futility of further conflict with Bello's empire, El-Kanemi reached an understanding with Bello which remained in force, despite periodic breaches, until Rabeh overran Bornu in 1893.

Dabo was also active in assisting Mamman Bello against the independent Hausa of Gobir and Katsina who had established themselves at Tsibiri and Maradi north of Katsina. He campaigned under Bello against these successor-states on several occasions. He also led forces from Kano to assist the Fulani of Zaria as required. Later, in 1843, though then quite old, Dabo brought his army against Matazu in Katsina to assist his neighbour Sidiku, the emir of Katsina, in suppressing a serious revolt of local Hausa under the leadership of Dan Mari, then chief of Maradi. Such expeditions across the frontiers of Kano illustrate the military interdependence and cooperation of the several emirates in defending or extending the Fulani dominion; they indicate important aspects of Kano's imperial context and rule. Just as he was expected to assist Sidiku against the "Habe" revolt in Katsina, Dabo could rely on forces from Bauchi and other emirates to help him repel a Kanuri invasion, or put down any serious threat from the "Habe" of Kano. However, in suppressing the general revolt of local Fulani against him, Dabo received no assistance from other states. Likewise, in expelling Dan Tunku from Kano, he had to rely on his own resources.

The Reconquest of Kano

Dabo is deservedly famous in Kano as the man who restored the pre-eminence of the chiefship by reconquering the country. His praise-name or *lakabi*, "Cigari," means "Taker of towns"—all or nearly all of which lay within Kano emirate. Dabo's reconquest was greatly simplified by disunity among the rebels and by the general dissociation of the "Habe" from the revolt. With the exceptions already mentioned, the rebels were entirely Fulani who ruled local communities by right of conquest, or appointment by Sule or those clan chiefs who led the *jihad*. Following Dabo's accession, these rural chiefs had been encouraged to reject the new emir's authority by the Galadima Sani, Mandikko, and other dissident Fulani leaders at the capital who had hitherto exercised immediate control over them. However, the leaders in Kano did not apparently order the use of arms against Dabo. They sought rather to withhold their revenues until he acknowledged their power and prior administrative right. In reply, Dabo forbade all further collections of revenue that were not transferred to him directly. These directives were relayed initially to the rural chiefs through their territorial superiors in the city, and then by messengers direct from Dabo. Some rural chiefs received Dabo's orders with open defiance. Others quietly ignored them, and continued to levy local tax and tithe without transferring any to Dabo as instructed.

Apparently the "rebel" chiefs made little effort to coordinate their resistance, probably assuming that Dabo would accept the situation as a "fait accompli" as Sule had done. Thus, in moving against them, for initial support Dabo relied mainly on the Hausawa and Kutumbawa at the capital, the Yolawa under Madaki Umaru, and the levies supplied by Dabo Dambazau from his clansmen and extensive fiefs. Once Mani had reconquered the Habe of Karaye for the Suleibawa, Dabo also received some Suleibawa support. Further, in the course of many expeditions against Dan Tunku, Dabo directed his armies against the rebel towns en route. Each was invested separately and few were able to withstand Dabo's assault. The Alkali Zangi catalogues Dabo's local campaigns in roughly chronological order. The list is long and impressive, and only those towns that withstood earlier assaults recur, as, for example, Jijitar. Dabo attacked and reduced Jirima in modern Garki, Gasakole near Dambarta, Sintirma, Jijitar (which he attacked four times before he took it), Dan Yaya, Garun Giginya in Babura, Dagurawa, Kunya twice, Gezawa, Rano, Gwarji twice, Danbarkushi twice, Makori, Dabi twice, Haina, Riruwe, Dogwaram, Shanu, Babuji, Gwarji, Dandayau, Fusatu, Rano, Faragai and Birnin Kudu, among others.[111] It is said that Dabo campaigned steadily for nine years before he succeeded in subduing resistance throughout Kano and established his supremacy. By close cooperation, the Fulani had conquered the Hausa; by their irresolution and failure to combine, they had allowed Dabo to conquer them. The Chronicle notes that "When the Kano towns saw that Dabo would not leave any town unconquered, they all submitted to him."[112]

These long severe campaigns were probably unavoidable if Dabo or anyone was to re-establish an effective central jurisdiction at Kano. The circumstances that prevailed during and immediately after the *jihad* had institutionalized a collegial aristocratic government characterised by dispersals of power and ill-defined jurisdictions among the heads of the more important Fulani clans. Sule had failed to modify or supersede this "confederate" organization. In consequence, although emir, he remained ineffective and poor. Dabo had learned the secrets of Sule's failure; and having first tried formally to subordinate these clan jurisdictions to the chiefship by investing their holders with senior offices of state, he determined to overawe and subdue all rural resistance that remained in Kano, thereby showing the local Fulani that although they now formed the governing "class," they governed under conditions imposed by the needs of state and at the emir's discretion.

These years of revolt and war strengthened Dabo in many ways. Being continuously engaged in a ceaseless struggle to subjugate his chiefdom, to repel the raids of Dan Auwa and Dan Tunku, to withstand El-Kanemi's invasion, and to assist the caliph and other emirs in their campaigns, Dabo needed a large and effective military establishment; and the rewards and opportunities he controlled attracted many men with political ambitions, who saw in military service with the chief the shortest route to territorial office. Dabo himself needed able and energetic captains to mobilize and lead out their troops for raids and defence. To organise these military resources, he revived many of the traditional Hausa war titles, such as Sarkin Dawaki, Sarkin Jarmai, Jarmai, Lifidi, Garkuwan Karfe, Madawakin Gawo, Barde, Sarkin Yaki (Chief of War), Sarkin Karma (Head of Infantry), Sarkin Baka (Chief of Archers) and Ubandawaki.[113] Some of these titles he allocated to slaves, others to free Fulani clients. Those Fulani aristocrats whom he could trust, Dabo employed as field commanders (*tirikai*), for example, Malam

Bakatsine, the Madaki Umaru, the Sarkin Bai Dambazau, and the Sarkin Dawaki Maituta Sani, the son of Malam Jamau; but neither the Galadima Sani nor the Makama Mandikko.

Dabo's campaigns in Kano provided ample opportunities for the redistribution of power and wealth. His attacks devastated certain areas, destroyed or damaged several towns, eliminated many chiefs and officials, and entailed considerable enslavement and loss of life. As emir, Dabo received a fifth of all booty to make good his losses and strengthen his military force. Much of this share consisted of slaves, horses, weapons and other war gear. Dabo's captains had similar though lesser opportunities to enrich and strengthen themselves by their campaigns. As always, prospects of booty attacted many to take part in raids, thereby increasing Dabo's following. Suleimanu had failed to exploit successfully this means of increasing his resources and power. Dabo steadily accumulated large numbers of slaves, clients, weapons, followers and wealth through these years of intense campaigning; and with these slaves he re-stocked the palace and some royal estates in rural areas. Whereas Sule had employed a free Fulani client, Muhamman, as head of his palace staff with the title of Dan Rimi, Dabo restored the offices of Shamaki and Dan Rimi to Alwali's slaves, Nasamu and Barka, respectively; and after Nasamu's death in action at Maradi, he appointed another slave, Ibrahim, as Shamaki. It is likely also that Dabo revived the office of Sallama after conferring the titles of Turakin Romo on Gazare and Turakin Manya on Gamdi. He gave the title of Sarkin Shanu to a BaSuleibe kinsman, Jiji, and that of Barde to a Fulani client, Bagel.

On the death of the Sarkin Gaya Attahiru, whom he had appointed, Sule had promoted his Sarkin Dawaki Muhammadu to administer Gaya, appointing Muhammadu's younger brother, Muhammadu dan Alhaji, as Sarkin Dawaki. At Dutse, after Bakatsine's withdrawal to the capital, Dabo appointed Musa, the head of the Jelubawa centred there. When the Habe at Rano revolted against their Fulani chief, Dabo attacked the town and, in restoring the ruler, also restored the direct relation between the chiefs of Kano and Rano that had virtually disappeared with Alwali's defeat. Dabo also subdued Birnin Kudu, which had escaped Fulani attack during or after the *jihad*. Dan Guri, the last Hausa chief of Birnin Kudu, fled with most of his people to Ningi country on the approach of Dabo's army in 1819. In his place Dabo appointed a Fulani client, Suleimanu, whose descendants still rule the chiefdom. Dan Guri and his followers then returned, settling in the western town in distinct wards. Two years later the Hausa ("Habe") revolted and expelled Suleimanu, restoring Dan Guri. Dabo sent a force southwards against them and called on his new Sarkin Dutse, Musa, for assistance. Dan Guri was put to flight once more, and retired to Ningi. Several years later he was allowed to settle at Badungu on the boundary of Kano with his immediate followers, paying allegiance directly to Dabo. Thus by good fortune and skill, Dabo attached the major rural chiefships of Gaya, Dutse, Rano, and Birnin Kudu directly to the chiefship. At Karaye the local chief, Sule Nadoyi, owed his restoration in 1820 to Dabo and Mani together; but, on Nadoyi's death in 1830, Dabo gave the office to his client, Muhammadu Kaciya, formerly the village chief at Gurum; and on Kaciya's death in 1836 he appointed his kinsman, Muhammadu Sambo, a baSuleibe of Kwasallo, to rule. Kiru was similarly transferred to Dabo's father's brother, Dangi, and placed under the Wambai Haruna, Dabo's brother.[114] Thus, while restoring the Suleibawa chiefship to Malam Jamau's issue, Dabo appropriated substantial Suleibawa domains for his kinsmen from Zaria.

Re-integration

Between 1826 and 1828 Dabo established his predominance at Kano; and thereafter he relied mainly on political and administrative measures rather than military action to consolidate and enhance his position. The initial situation had committed Dabo to the establishment of a strong and effective central chiefship capable of ruling Kano, with or without the active support of the Fulani aristocracy; but he clearly could not govern the conquest state without the consent and help of the conquerors. Moreover, recognizing their rights, status and historical role, Dabo had no wish to rule without or against them. Rather, he sought to win their support for his chiefship by appealing to them for unity against Dan Tunku, El-Kanemi, Dan Auwa of Gumel and other external threats, by assisting the rural Fulani against "Habe" resistance wherever this occurred, and by conferring the highest non-royal offices of state on representatives of these founding lineages. Thus on the death of Dan Iya Abdullahi, Dan Zabuwa's son, Dabo appointed Abdullahi's brother Sani to that office, thereby identifying the Dan Iya title with Dan Zabuwa's issue among the Daneji clan; and on the death of the Ciroma Shehu early in his reign, Dabo appointed Shehu's brother, also called Dabo, to succeed, thereby publicly affirming the dynastic claims and status of Suleimanu's issue.

Dabo sought further to strengthen his regime by marriage alliances with the official leaders of these founding lineages. As mentioned above, he gave his daughter, the Magajiya Fatsumatu Zara, to Dabo Dambazau, the Sarkin Bai, with Kunci as her dowry. He gave Kumboto, another daughter, to the baYole Madaki Umaru, together with the town of Kumbotsu, five miles south of Kano, which was renamed in her honour. He likewise gave a daughter in marriage to the recognized leader of each of the senior Fulani lineages, to the Sarkin Dawaki Maituta, the Dan Iya, the Gyenawa leader, the Limam, and others. Dabo likewise offered one of his daughters to the baJobe Makama Mandikko. Mandikko however refused to accept Dabo's daughter as a bride, thus showing his hostility and contempt for Dabo and, in the context, implicitly challenged him to take disciplinary action. This Dabo promptly did, dismissing Mandikko and appointing Malam Isa, the son of Malam Sa'idu, Bakatsine's younger brother, as Makama in his place. Isa had long been associated with Bakatsine in the administration of Dutse chiefdom during Suleimanu's reign; and after Mandikko, he was by birth and experience the senior baJobe, Bakatsine having died at Wudil in the early 1820's. Thus in dismissing Mandikko and appointing Isa, Dabo simultaneously showed his intention to preserve lineage rights to the offices distributed among these aristocratic families, and his capacity to replace these officials by other members of their families as their conduct warranted.

Mandikko had cultivated the offensive practice of proffering handshakes to Dabo whenever they met, thereby asserting his claim to status parity, a claim which struck at the foundations of the chiefly supremacy Dabo sought to enforce. In rejecting Dabo's offer of his daughter as a bride, Mandikko simultaneously asserted his lineage precedence in terms of the Fulani ethnic stratification, and the aristocratic structure laid down by the Kano *jihad*.[115] By rejecting this affinal link, he also declared his disaffection with Dabo's regime. In the context, such action indicated disloyal orientations and invited dismissal. Yet no titleholder of a founding lineage having been previously dismissed, despite their well-known covert roles in the rebellion of 1819–23, Mandikko probably assumed that Dabo lacked the will or capacity to take such action. He may also have hoped by his curt rejection to provoke Dabo to some hasty act, such as Sule's imprisonment of Dabo Dambazau, thereby giving cause for complaint to Sokoto. Dabo chose instead the colder but more effective route of administrative discipline, and on Isa's appointment as Makama, he gave him the girl Mandikko had rejected as his bride. This event clearly demonstrates that these marriage alliances were public political relations holding between occupants of particular offices, and neither primarily personal nor family relations, though those elements could not be excluded. Dabo may have been guided to establish these marriage alliances with his senior territorial chiefs by Kutumbawa or other Hausa advisers, who recognized the role of such links in binding senior officials closer to the chief; but Fulani culture and the example of the Shehu's family at Sokoto could as well have furnished the guiding ideas. Notably, in replacing Mandikko, Dabo made no attempt to reduce the scope of the Jobawa office or territorial holdings in Kano. He merely rid himself of a troublesome subordinate who had long refused to accept his status. Mandikko's dismissal took place in 1830, when Dabo had already reigned for ten years.

Concerning the Galadima Sani, to whom the Kano Chronicle and the Dokaji Alhaji Abubakar attribute the initial incitement to revolt,[116] reports differ. Current oral traditions say that Dabo dismissed Sani for refusal to obey and support him; but none of the available written records confirms this. I cannot say how or when the office of Galadima passed from Sani. However, following Sani, Dabo appointed Ango, who was formerly his San Kurmi in charge of the public prisons, a Hausa client and the only non-Fulani to hold this office at Kano after the *jihad*. Of the two Galadimas in Kano since 1808 who have not been members of either royal lineage, Ango was the first. Clearly, by appointing this Hausa client to such high office, Dabo was adapting an old Kutumbawa technique to centralize state power in his own hands. Then the sole Hausa to hold high rank at Kano, Ango had to rely entirely on Dabo's support; and as the chief's creature, he was accordingly a valued assistant who could inform Dabo on Hausa techniques and forms of political organization at Kano and advise on their manipulation and modification. Dabo found such Hausa counsellors especially helpful in his dealing with the senior Fulani.

Besides reviving many old Hausa titles, Dabo created several of his own. One of these, the Magajin Malam Na Cedi, was instituted to reward the confidential messenger (*jekada*) who handled Dabo's communications with Malam Jibir and his son the Madaki Umaru. The man concerned was a baYole of junior lineage. On his appointment as the first Magajin Malam na Cedi, Dabo placed him in charge of Cedi, Dawanau, Danbu and Dan Guguwa as a *hakimi*, and so made him formally independent of the Madaki. By thus instituting this office for his baYole *jekada*, Dabo was indirectly honouring and dividing the Yolawa. Once instituted, the office was retained by the issue of its first holder until the civil war of 1893.

Throughout Suleimanu's reign, the Hausa *muhajarini* Usuman had retained the title of Alkali, even though he seems to have lost the substance of the office to Suleimanu himself. The Shehu Usuman and his senior associates had placed heavy stress on the faithful administration of the *shari'a* in listing the duties of Muslim rulers. Moreover, on his accession Suleimanu had found that this was one of the few functions he could appropriate. He presided regularly over the collective court which met at the city mosque; and though Alkali Usuman attended, and may have continued to sum up the evidence and to summarize relevant legal doctrines, judgement now rested with the emir. On his accession, Dabo seems to have tried to move this court to the palace. It is said that the senior Fulani, who had tacitly indicated support for Suleimanu by sitting with him daily in the court, refused to do so with Dabo, thereby publicising their political differences with the new chief. Dabo accordingly appointed a new Alkali, Malam Ashafa of the Gyenawa, thus replacing the Alkali Usuman who had long been identified with the former court. In appointing Ashafa, Dabo also discontinued the pre-existing court by withdrawing its judicial authority. By this response to the refusal of the old tribunal to assemble at the palace, Dabo sharply distinguished his judges from courtiers and executives.

When the Alkali Usuman died, Dabo summoned his heir, and in a carefully calculated phrase that echoed the Shehu's apocryphal remark, asked for "the successor of the Hausa Malam" ("Ina magajin Malamin Hausawa?"), Usuman's eldest son, Malam Dan Adu'a, was duly presented and formally appointed to the title, Magajin Malam na Hausawa—that is, as the "successor of the Hausa Malam." A new title was thus created which memorialized Usuman's role in the Kano *jihad* and fulfilled to the letter the apocryphal remark of the Shehu that the Fulani should leave the "Hausawa" under their malam. However, this edict did not apparently include Kura, which Dabo transferred to Fulani clients around 1836.

When Suleimanu's son, the Ciroma Dabo, died, Dabo appointed his own son, Kwairanga as Ciroma. By then Suleimanu's brother, Sani, had ceased to be Galadima. We cannot specify the exact chronology of the following appointments; however, their rationale and general outlines are reasonably clear. In the second half of his reign Dabo created two new titles and appropriated another traditional Hausa one for the Mundubawa kinsmen of his predecessor, Suleimanu. A new title of Mai Anguwan Mundubawa (the Mundubawa ward-head) was created for Suleimanu's lineal descendants; while the title of Dan Amar was revived and allocated to the Galadima Sani's issue. A second title of Magajin Maude was also created for Sule's issue, probably for those descended through the Ciroma Dabo.

Subsequently, according to tradition, the office of Sarkin Dawaki Tsakar Gida was often allotted to men of Mundubawa descent borne by women of the royal lineage, that is to say, typically to those cross-cousins and joking relations of the reigning chief who were of Mundubawa descent. Mundubawa whose mothers were of royal stock were accordingly eligible for appointment to this office; but so were Danejawa and other Fulani born of the ruler's sisters. Thus the old title of Sarkin Dawaki Tsakar Gida was neither exclusively pre-empted to Mundubawa, nor to any distinct descent line within that lineage, unlike the three preceding titles, each of which was thereafter reserved to the immediate agnates and issue of their first holders, thereby splitting Suleimanu's lineage into as many sections, each identified by its exclusive interest in a particular title. Whether Dabo intended by these appointments to divide and reduce the Mundubawa dynasty with which his own offspring had to compete, we cannot say; but that was their effect.

Dabo ruled Kano for twenty-seven years, during the last ten of which no Mundubawa held offices of the first rank. Clearly, in creating new offices for the Mundubawa, Dabo publicly honoured them and indicated his interest in their welfare. Covertly, he may have provided them with three offices instead of one to reduce their internal solidarity and thus promote the interests of his own line. However, by the time of Dabo's death in 1846, the appointment of further Mundubawa to the chiefship was out of the question. Where Sule had failed to institute an effective central chiefship, Dabo had brilliantly succeeded; and his achievement in Kano greatly strengthened the Fulani empire which, by 1846, was beginning to need all the political and administrative resources on which it could draw. Kano was in many respects at this period the central bastion of the empire. To transfer it from Dabo's line to some other, whether Sule's or a third, carried such high risks of imperial dislocation, that practical considerations excluded the possibility. Few, if any, in Kano on Dabo's death looked beyond his sons for the successor.

The Growth of Central Authority

Traditions from various sources independently assert Dabo's great dependence on the former Ciroma Dan Mama in the crisis that confronted his succession. Dan Mama still held many fiefs, and lived at the capital. In view of his role in the *jihad*, he had a prominent place in the private councils of the Fulani founding fathers. He also had direct obligations to the Shehu and his successors at Sokoto to obey and support their appointed representatives. At Maradi, the "Habe" Sarkin Kano Abubakar (1958–?) related that on Suleimanu's death, Alwali's son and successor, Umaru, returned to Kano to seek the throne. Umaru's arrival was welcomed by some city "Habe" who hid and sheltered him, and made their allegiance. Perhaps the ruling oligarchy did not know of his presence; but acting on the advice of a local malam, Umaru then left Kano for Burumburum to pray at Alwali's grave in the hopes that this would ritually assure his success in the coming struggle. The "Habe" Sarkin Kano asserts that on Umaru's return to Kano, at the orders of the former Ciroma Muhamman (Dan Mama), Umaru was denied entry into the city by the gatekeepers. This may be a dynastic fable treasured by men who have since lost hope; but its particulars are concrete, appropriate and intriguing. There was an interval of thirty to forty days between Sule's death and Dabo's accession.[117] Sule's ineffectiveness had been such that the immediate absence of his successor made little difference to the operation of the local government. It is said that Alwali's son Umaru, after a few days in Kano, having assured himself of Habe support, spent nearly "forty" days before returning from Burumburum; and that even on his return, no Fulani successor to Sule had been appointed. Most strikingly, at this removal of space and time, the tradition preserved by the Habe Sarkin Kano Abubakar identifies the Ciroma Dan Mama (Muhamman) as the immediate and effective opponent of Habe restoration.

From Kutumbawa at Kano we also hear that Dan Mama placed all his resources at Dabo's disposal and undertook to mobilize all the Hausa support he could for Dabo against Dan Tunku and the rebels. Dan Mama still retained the fiefs the Fulani had allocated to him at the Shehu's order, in addition to some he had held in Alwali's day; and on this tradition, by placing these at Dabo's disposal, he fulfilled his pledge to support the Shehu's chosen ruler of Kano. Some Kutumbawa also say that Dan Mama secured for Dabo much of the support and tax withheld from him by the Fulani oligarchs. Fulani oral traditions affirm that Dabo was guided by Dan Mama in his decision to seek permission to reinstitute selected Hausa political institutions. Just how and how well Dan Mama may have helped Dabo, we cannot determine; but when Dan Mama died, Dabo created the office of Mai-anguwan Kutumbawa for his successor, the Kutumbawa being already, as described, concentrated in a discrete city ward.

The new title was thus simultaneously a ward headship, official symbol of the Kutumbawa traditions, a mechanism for their segregation, an index of the decline and subordination of the local Kutumbawa, and as such a device for the simultaneous institutionalization and reinforcement of Fulani rule among the Hausa. Kutumbawa having succeeded in displacing the Rumfawa, the Fulani had now succeeded in displacing them. Representatives of the old dynasty had thus been reduced to the status of privileged ward heads, having reserved for them a place, but not a voice, in the councils of their successors, the Fulani chiefs.[118] Thus, when Dabo, having several years before instituted the new title of Mai-Anguwan Kutumbawa, on the death of Suleimanu's son, the Ciroma Dabo, created another title, the Mai-Anguwan Mundubawa, among the many inner meanings of this act, one that was well understood was to discredit the Mundubawa by assimilating them with the Kutumbawa in the category of dispossessed dynasties. Undoubtedly this was Dabo's intention, since there was then no Mundubawa ward within the city for which the new Mai-Anguwa was clearly responsible. Further, by means of these titles, Dabo systematically segregated the Kutumbawa and their associates, the Hausawa and theirs, and the Mundubawa, who were simultaneously divided into three distinct segments by their differential attachments to three titles.

When his son, the Ciroma Kwairanga died, Dabo promptly appointed another, Mamudu, who had been named after Dabo's father, to succeed. These successive appointments of Dabo's sons to the Ciroma title re-appropriated this office for the ruler's sons as the senior princely title. The Galadima title, traditionally allocated to one of the ruler's senior agnates, was then occupied by Dabo's client, Ango. As Wambai, in succession Dabo appointed his own brother Haruna and a cognate, Adamu, thereby appropriating that office also for the dynasty. As his reign lengthened and his sons matured, Dabo revived other princely titles for them. His son Usuman was appointed Tafida; another son, Abdullahi, became Dan Buram, and yet another, Abdusallami, was appointed Turaki Manya. Meanwhile the office of Turakin Romo was successively filled from the Yerimawa of Minjibir, and commonly by promotion of the Sarkin Filani Minjibir, an arrangement that was clearly designed to dissuade these Yerimawa from assisting Dan Tunku or his successor, Dambo, by withdrawal to Kazaure, or activities disloyal to Kano. Accordingly the Turakin Romo was loaded with many fiefs, including two, Garun Giginya and Baushi, which Dabo in 1821 attached to Gamau's office.

The jurisdictional ambiguities and political accommodations that had accompanied the conquest and slow resurrection of central authority at Kano are neatly illustrated by a case concerning the *limanci* or limam's office that emerged during the first three or four years of Dabo's reign. On his appointment as chief, Suleimanu, a former Limam, had appointed his namesake, the baGyeni Sule, to succeed him. This baGyeni Limam Sule died early in Dabo's reign, probably between 1820 and 1823. Dabo then appointed as Limam Muhamman Zara, head of the Zarawa branch of Fulanin Bornu, a clerical lineage long established at Kano. On appointing Suleimanu Limam, Sule had attached Jijitar, Karmami and Zango, near Gezawa, to the office as fiefs from which the Limam could draw the revenues he needed; and as related above, on his appointment as Limam, the baGyeni Suleimanu had selected his son, Muhammadu, as his senior assistant, the Na'ibi. When the Limam Suleimanu died and Muhamman Zara succeeded, the Na'ibi Muhammadu, who had hitherto administered these fiefs for his father, refused to transfer them to the new Limam, asserting that they were family endowments (Ar. *wakf*) made by the previous emir. On four occasions Dabo attacked Jijitar; but though he was generally successful elsewhere, despite its small size and modest defenses, Jijitar withstood his assaults. We lack, as usual, the information necessary to elucidate these successive attacks; but it does seem that Dabo was irked by the Na'ibi's refusal to transfer Jijitar and other units that his father had held to Muhamman Zara, the new Limam. His repeated failures to seize this town eventually persuaded Dabo to relinquish his jurisdictional claims, perhaps in this case only. Thereafter Jijitar, Karmami and Zango remained as before under the Na'ibi Muhammadu, while Dabo remunerated the Limam by periodic gifts. Much later, in Abdullahi's reign, perhaps to resolve this anomaly, Muhammadu was appointed Limam and required to subsist from his fiefs. On his death, the fiefs and the office were simultaneously transferred to his successor, thereby abolishing the juridically obscure claim of family endowment (Ar. *wakf*) against them.

It is possible that the Na'ibi's conduct was not unique; but his case has been nicely preserved by military accident for our notice. Evidently such claims of *wakf* provided the bases for other assertions of autonomous jurisdictions by founding lineages and their dependents over much of Kano territory at the time of Dabo's accession. Faced with such fundamental claims, Dabo had the alternatives of acceptance and impotence or military conquest. Where successful, his victories automatically abolished such claims and restored the subjugated units to chiefly jurisdiction; but at Jijitar, for reasons unknown, he was repeatedly unsuccessful; and by admitting defeat at that place, he accordingly admitted the probable validity of the Na'ibi's claim at law and its operational validity as tested by arms.

Like Suleimanu, Dabo received occasional reinforcements from Muslim Fulani immigrants who had moved eastwards after the end of the *jihad* or following the Shehu's death. One of these, Muhammad Babi, a baYole of Kano who was distantly related to Malam Jibir, quit Sokoto shortly after Mamman Bello's accession, and was directed by Dabo to set up the new town of Gwarzo near Getso in western Kano with the title of Dan Gwarzo. Administratively, the new Dan Gwarzo was attached to the Dan Iya for communications and supervision. Nearby, at Getso, Suleimanu's appointee Maigada was unable to impose his authority on the local people, who were in part Katsina Hausa and in part Beddes long established at Getso from an early Bornu immigration. Dabo sent money to help his beleaguered San Getso. He also appointed an Alkali to reside at Getso in order that the San Getso's authority might be enforced and the recalcitrants punished without delay. A jail was established at Getso for this purpose, but as usual all sentences entailing amputations or execution were referred to the emir's court at the capital.

Evidently on Hausa guidance, Dabo also revived the three prisons maintained by Alwali—the public jail under the San Kurmi for ordinary cases, and those in the palace and/or the *gidan Shamaki* for offending nobles. However Dabo put the palace jail under the care of his Sarkin Yara, a free Fulani client who served also as his *jekada* to Gaya. It does not seem that Dabo made much use of the Sarkin Yara as a jailer.

Suleimanu in his later years may have imposed taxation at an annual rate of 500 cowries per householder, to be collected by village chiefs in the rural areas for transfer—after the usual customary deductions—to their immediate superiors in the capital who, in turn, would remit appropriate portions to Suleimanu himself. Suleimanu's tax was levied at the rate of the *karo* that prevailed in Alwali's reign, though its periodicity then remains uncertain; but while the Kutumbawa levy was known as *karo*, under the Fulani it became the *kudin gona* (farm, land tax), a significant term, since it excludes all Fulani who do not cultivate, and who were thus liable solely for *zakkan shanu*, the cattle tithe. Thus Suleimanu levied this land tax solely from rural Hausa (Habe).

As he reconquered Kano, Dabo recouped his arrears of revenue by levying this tax at an increased rate of 1,000 cowries per farmer, that is, per Hausa family head. No cash taxes seem to have been required by Dabo from sedentary Fulani. Forced labor was also levied exclusively on Hausa by Dabo, a practice that probably began before Suleimanu's accession and persisted at Kano well into this century. In short, the Fulani victory and Hausa defeat were institutionalized as Fulani exemption from, and Hausa subordination to, state labour, levies and tax demands. To discourage revolt, the mass of Hausa, now classified as "Habe," were forbidden the use of horses and arms by Fulani, who justified their privileges by their role in the *jihad* and their responsibilities for the religion, defence and administration of the state. Since the Fulani addressed these justifications to themselves, they served merely to rationalize their privileged political position in acceptably Islamic terms; but this ideology presumed the classification of "Habe" as heathen (*kahirai, arna*) in contradistinction to the privileged Muslims. Once classified as heathen, the "Habe" became liable to *jizya*, the punitive poll tax prescribed for pagans by the *shari'a*, to forced labour, and to such other demands as the welfare of the Muslim community (*jema'a*), in this case the Fulani rulers, seemed to require. Thus, following doctrines developed early by the Shehu to justify his *jihad*,[119] the conquerors classified the conquered as heathens, and thus citizenship and justice were dichotomized by historic conditions of conquest and domination, the rulers reserving to themselves those privileges they denied to the ruled. In consequence, the regime lacked legitimacy and normative acceptance by the majority subject to it. Moreover, as these unequal institutions bore their fruit, inequality also spread among the rulers, generating other conflicts which further qualified their own perception of the order as legitimate.[120]

With characteristic insight, Abdullahi dan Fodio had identified those interests and tendencies long before. Of his battle companions, the Fulani *jihadis*, he says:

> They were many, but their righteous men were few;
> They showed the dissimulation of wicked people, the people of the squadrons
> And of the sellers of free men in the market.
> Some of them are posing as *qadis* in the clothing of foxes.[121]

The Shehu's doctrines thus bore fruit in the exclusion of conquered Muslims from the *dar-es-Islam*, and in the conversion of the conquerors from religious reformers to a quasi-caste of conservative oligarchs.

Kano in 1824

In January 1824 the explorer Clapperton visited Kano on his way from Kukawa to Sokoto, bearing letters from El Kanemi in Bornu to Mamman Bello at Sokoto. Though the two empires were technically at war and the Shehu El Kanemi at Kukawa was then busily preparing for his ill-starred invasion of Kano, Clapperton's passage was a smooth one, itself a remarkable fact.

Clapperton met Dabo at Panisau which had been converted into a military camp in 1819 on Dabo's accession. He also met Dabo's brother, the Wambai Haruna, "a thin slender man, of a pretty fair complexion, with only one eye, … clad in a rather dirty toga, … said to be the father of fifty sons."[122] Dabo is described as "a Fellata of a dark copper colour and stout make, … (having) the character of being very devout and learned."[123] Clapperton spent the following month in Kano before proceeding westwards, and gives a valuable account of the city and its government at that time. His relations with Dabo were friendly and honourable; and his slender observations strengthen our remoter view of Dabo as a man of considerable integrity, despatch and inner strength, beset by difficulties, but well-equipped to overcome them.

Clapperton estimates that Kano then contained thirty or forty thousand residents, "of whom more than one-half are slaves."[124] Its sanitation was, as now, in need of improvement. He visited the Gidan Rumfa, "a large space … (resembling) a walled village. It even contains a mosque, and several towers three or four storeys high, with windows. … It is necessary to pass through two of these towers in order to gain the suite of inner apartments occupied by the governor."[125] He describes the city as surrounded by

> a clay wall thirty feet high, with a dry ditch along the inside, and another on the outside. There are fifteen gates, including one lately built up … The gates are of wood, covered with sheet iron. They are regularly opened and shut at sunrise and sunset. A platform inside, with two guardhouses below it, serves to defend each entrance. Not more than one-fourth of the ground within the walls is occupied by houses; the vacant space is laid out in fields and gardens.[126]

The market clearly excited Clapperton's interest. He asserts that

> no market in Africa is so well regulated. The sheikh of the *soug* (market) lets the
> stalls at so much a month, and the rent forms a part of the revenues of the governor.
> The Sheikh of the *soug* also fixes the price of all wares, for which he is entitled to a
> small commission at the rate of fifty *whydah* or cowries for every sale amounting to
> four dollars, or eight thousand cowries, according to the standard of exchange
> between silver money and this shell currency.[127]

He then describes the market layout, trade patterns, handicrafts, customs, and the
life of the people, mentioning such particulars as Dabo's regular allowances to the
city blind and the Muslim refusal of burial to slaves (?heathen).[128]

On his way to Sokoto, accompanied by one of Dabo's courtiers, Muhammad
Jali, "a fair complexioned Fellatah," Clapperton travelled with "two loaded
camels and a handsome lead horse of Tuarick breed, sent as the weekly present or
tribute from Kano to the sultan."[129] Passing by Tofa and Gadanya, both severely
ravaged in the struggle with Dan Tunku, he crossed into Katsina at Farin Ruwa.[130]
On his return by the same route some months later, Clapperton passed "the ruins
of several walled towns."[131] He visited Dabo, "who received me with marked
kindness, and enquired particularly after the health of the sultan and of the
Gadado,"[132] that is, the sultan's vizier, 'Uthman Gidado.

Clapperton remained at Kano until the Idi festival; and happening to visit
Dabo then to pay his respects, he was greatly honoured by an invitation "to ride
out with him, according to their annual customs; and we proceeded to an open
space within the city wall, amidst skirmishing and firing of muskets, attended by
his people on horseback, and Arabs and the principal townsfolk dressed in their
gayest raiment—all who could possibly muster a horse for the occasion being
mounted." As usual, "the governor (Dabo) made a speech to the people, declaring
his intention to attack Untungua (Dan Tunku), when he expected every man to
exert his utmost prowess. Their sons, too, should not, as in times past, be left
behind, but should accompany them to the war, and learn to fight the battles of
their country under the eyes of their parents." On Clapperton's final visit to say
farewell, Dabo was again "very kind, and after enquiring if I should ever return,
begged me to remember him to his friend, the Sheikh El-Kanemy, and expressed
his hope that I would give a favourable account of the people I had visited. ... He
then repeated the Fatah, and I bade him farewell."[133]

Clapperton never had the chance to return to Kano; but in Sokoto, during his
last illness, he wrote a brief general account of the countries under Fulani rule and
the pattern of their government, which he describes as "a perfect despotism"
under Sultan Bello.

> The governors of the different provinces are appointed during pleasure, as, in the
> event of any improper conduct, they are displaced; and all their property at their
> death or removal falls to the sultan. The appointment to a vacancy is then sold to
> the highest bidder, who is generally a near relation. ... All the inferior offices in the
> towns of the provinces are sold in like manner by the governors, who also succeed
> to the property of these petty officers at their death or removal.

Of revenues I can say very little. I know only that in the province of Kano they have no regular system of taxation. A great deal of marketable property is claimed by the government, such as two-thirds of the produce of all the date and other fruit trees. ... A small duty is also levied on every article sold in the market; or in lieu thereof, a certain rent is paid for the stall or shed; duty is also fixed on every tobe (robe) that is dyed blue and sold. On grain there is no duty. Kano produces the greatest revenue which the sultan receives, and it is paid monthly in horses, cowries and cloth.[134] At this date "a young male slave from thirteen to twenty years of age will bring from ten thousand to twenty thousand cowries; a female slave, if very handsome, from forty thousand to fifty thousand; the common price is about thirty thousand for a virgin about fourteen or fifteen.[135]

Development of the Central Administration

As Clapperton's observations indicate, even by 1824, though facing a general revolt and engaged in constant war, Dabo had taken many important steps to organize a strong central government. Following his forceful pacification of Kano, he continued to develop and refine this central administration, and reinstituted annual taxation, along with the pre-Fulani structure of local chiefships supervised through titled *jekadu* by *hakimai* resident at the capital. Following traditional practice, Dabo also preserved Rano and Gaya, Karaye, Dutse and Birnin Kudu as major rural units under resident chiefs. At Karaye and Gaya he appointed *shigege* clients, thus discountenancing hereditary claims to these territories. At Dutse, following the baYelige, Salihi, the first Fulani chief, Dabo installed his old colleague in arms, the baJelbe Makaman Dutse Musa, as chief, thus leaving ambiguous the hereditary or *shigege* status of that office. At Rano and Birnin Kudu, however, Dabo appointed agnatic kinsmen of the first Fulani chiefs.

At the centre, territorial offices were distinguished from others with specialized functions, whether military or civil. Specialist religious offices included those of the Limam and the Alkali. Specialist secular offices held by free men at this date included administration of the treasury, the city, the prisons, certain military formations, and the role of court usher then held by Kilishi. Dabo seems to have followed the Shehu's instructions and Mamman Bello's example in separating his public and private treasuries, the former being placed under a Ma'aji, who was also responsible for the administration of the city.

As his first Ma'aji, Dabo appointed a Katsina Fulani, Gado. In his role as city administrator, Gado received daily reports from ward heads within the city, and relayed important matters directly to the chief for instruction. The Ma'aji was also in charge of the town gatekeepers, who were then all free Fulani, remunerated by shares of grain tithe and occasional gifts of money and goods. The Ma'aji may also have supervised the Sarkin Pawa or Sarkin Kasuwa in charge of the city market, receiving its monthly revenues, and he also perhaps acted as Dabo's agent in the purchase of horses and other war gear on behalf of the state. Presumably as public treasurer, the Ma'aji distributed the emir's largesse to the blind and clerics, as directed.

Dabo seems to have retained the greater part of his revenues and wealth in his palace treasury under the care of the Shamaki, his senior slave. One of the Shamaki's primary responsibilities as head of the palace treasury was to furnish a regular flow of tribute to the caliph at Sokoto. Besides the weekly despatch of a horse and camels laden with bales of fine clothing called *kyenkyendi*, each bale containing twenty gowns and trousers, the Shamaki had also to send special gifts as greetings for the caliph at the Biram festival. Further, on the accession of a new caliph, an appropriate gift was expected; and after Mamman Bello had formally designated his close friend Gidado as vizier, the Kano tribute increased by one-half its previous value, the increment being presented to the Waziri. As early as 1821, the caliph had sent on a visiting *sherif* to Dabo at Kano, with a note instruct-ing Dabo to furnish the bearer with hospitality and five hundred thousand cow-ries.[136] As the wealthiest state in the Fulani empire, Kano was also the most frequently called on by the caliph to honour and reward distinguished Muslim visitors, *sherifs, sa'ids*, marabouts and clerics, by similar substantial gifts from its state reserves. To handle these imperial demands and his own recurrent and capital expenditures, Dabo accordingly placed the greater part of his revenue under the Shamaki at the palace, and held him responsible for prompt fulfillment of all approved demands for supplies and disbursements.

The Shamaki's function became a polite imperial joke. It was said that what-ever the Sarkin Musulmi (caliph) demanded for himself or anyone, the stables (*shamaki*) of the Sarkin Kano contained. But in his roles as paymaster and quarter-master, the Shamaki had also to keep Dabo informed about state stocks of war weapons, and cash for purchasing more. In this capacity, Dabo increasingly employed the Shamaki to organize corvée among the local blacksmiths, tanners and leather workers to furnish the equipment needed. By the end of Dabo's reign, the Shamaki, Dan Rimi and Sallama were also employed as the three principal *kofofi* (communication channels) between the chief and free officials. With Kutum-bawa guidance, Dabo had revived Babba Zaki's system of *wasidodi* as a means of administrative control, an effective device for political centralization, and for the enhancement and entrenchment of chiefly dominance. He likewise revived the Hausa institution of state police under the Sarkin Dogarai, appointing a free Fulani to that office. He also established slave formations in the army, under the Garkuwan Karfe, to support and protect the chief, and the office of state execu-tioner (Hauni), which was held by a free man throughout his reign. Besides responsibility for supplying grain and foodstuffs through the Sarkin Hatsi to the palace staff, the Shamaki shared with the Dan Rimi administration of the palace wards, communications with the local headmen of royal estates, and supervision of those rural communities reserved to the throne.

Slaves did not themselves directly administer free communities under Dabo or his immediate successors. Instead the chief instructed individual courtiers to serve as *jekadu* to particular villages under the Shamaki or Dan Rimi. Some but not all of these *jekadu* had honorific titles. Often such commissions were initiated at the suggestion of the senior slaves, following requests by suitable Fulani clients at court. By virtue of their influence with the chief, the Dan Rimi and Shamaki acquired considerable followings among office-seeking freemen at the capital, whose relations of clientage obliged them to keep these senior slaves well informed about events and opinion in their respective city wards. Thus, though Dabo officially depended on the Ma'aji for information on affairs at the capital, he may have relied rather more on that supplied by his senior slaves through their extensive communication networks.

Dabo re-established the office of Sarkin Shanu and endowed it with territorial administrative functions; but he did not attempt to revive its pre-jihadic role and responsibilities for supervising the administration of all Fulani pastoralists resident in Kano. As a Fulani, Dabo was too well informed about the nature and implications of Fulani divisions to perpetuate this basic error, which illustrated Hausa ignorance of Fulani social organization. Dabo initially gave the office of Sarkin Shanu to a baSuleibe kinsman who was not himself a member of the new dynasty. Simultaneously he seems to have segregated his relations with the Ma'aji and with the new Sarkin Shanu. Both these officials had direct access to the emir without overlap of functions. It is also possible that Dabo placed the care of the city and chiefdom under the Sarkin Shanu during his many absences on campaigns in Kano or other territories; and this is likely since his friend, the Hausa Galadima Ango, often accompanied him. However, we lack detailed information. By contrast, for the first campaign after his accession it is related that Dabo placed Dan Mama in charge of the capital, being then perhaps without any alternative.

Several initial appointments that revived Hausa offices were subsequently institutionalized as hereditary by Dabo or his immediate successors. It is obvious that without explicit rulings these initial appointments can neither be classified as hereditary nor *shigege*. Nonetheless, there is indirect evidence to suggest that Dabo did conceive several of his initial appointments as hereditary allocations of office to particular descent lines. Some examples illustrating this have already been cited, for instance, the titles of Mai Anguwan Mundubawa, Mai Anguwan Kutumbawa, Magajin Maude, Dan Amar, Sarkin Dawaki Maituta, Makama, Ciroma, Sarkin Rano, Sarkin Birnin Kudu, Turakin Romo, Magajin Malam na Hausawa, and Magajin Malam na Cedi. Dabo also confirmed traditional lineage rights to particular rural Fulani chiefships, such as those at Sankara, Bebeji, Minjibir, Jahun, etc., while replacing unsuitable titleholders by their close agnatic kin. He also made successive *shigege* appointments to such offices as Barde, Sarkin Jarmai, Sarkin Dawaki Tsakar Gida, Sarkin Yaki, and others of pre-eminently military character, thereby unavoidably reviving the traditional distinction between hereditary and *shigege* office for free and slave alike. It is difficult to see how the traditional offices could be revived and reallocated among the important groups at Kano in Dabo's day without directly or indirectly re-establishing that fundamental distinction.

To attach certain marginal Fulani groups to his regime, Dabo allocated new or old offices among them; for example, the Filanin Ja'en received the title of Ja'idanawa, the Balarawa Fulani were given the office of Dan Darman, the Jelorawa were invested with the title of Ma'ajin Kwatali. My lists of these title-holders do not identify their first Fulani incumbents by name or by dates of appointment; and it is probable that some of these offices may have been created or re-established by Dabo's successors; but in essence, the pattern of such appointments is little affected by the moment of their initiation; and their distribution among the Fulani lineages at Kano strongly suggests that the original allocations of these offices were made in the latter part of Dabo's reign. Inevitably also, given the prevalent system of status categories, such offices were distinguished by their allocation to men of differing status—to royals, namely the Mundubawa and Dabo's lineage, to Hausawa, to the Fulani founding lineages, to other pastoral or settled Fulani groups, to clerics, craftsmen, eunuchs and slaves. Such re-institutionalization of traditional status distinctions within the central officialdom may have been unavoidable, given the composition and structure of the social aggregate from which the incumbents were recruited and to which the government was bound. Moreover, as Suleimanu's situation shows, it is difficult to see how the integration, boundaries and continuity of the state could have been assured without a comprehensive official hierarchy such as Dabo re-established, given the preceding appropriations of indeterminate territorial jurisdictions by the conquering clans whose leaders constituted the central ruling college. Inevitably, given the traditional pattern and Dabo's immediate situational needs, the majority of these state offices were invested with territorial jurisdiction.

As of old, the prototype of office in the new structure was that of the *hakimi*, exercised through titled *lawanai* who themselves directed or served as *jekadu* to the principal fiefs placed under the office, organising their local control, tax collection, military levies, corvée, tithe, legal administration, and the like. Inevitably *hakimai* differed in precedence and rank as their offices differed in scope and significance. Under Dabo, as in Alwali's day, the Galadima, Wambai, Makama, Madaki, Dan Iya, Sarkin Dawaki (Mai-Tuta) and Sarkin Bai ranked as the senior offices of state and held the most valuable and most extensive territories in fief. As before, the five major rural chiefdoms in southern Kano were distinguished from these seven councillors but of almost equal status. Notably, these senior central offices had first been informally appropriated, and then formally reallocated, by Dabo to leaders of the founding Fulani lineages, thereby assimilating the old administrative structure to the new political composition and context; and, at least juridically, Dabo's appointments reduced the autonomy of these clan chiefships by converting their power into an administrative authority prescribed and defined by offices constituted and subsumed within a state under supreme central direction. By allocating high ranking titles of the Hausa state to its senior Fulani leaders, Dabo simultaneously confirmed the pre-eminence of these clans, prescribed the hereditary distribution of these offices, associated them in his reconstruction of the traditional state, and validated its chief official units by assimilating them to the principal Fulani groupings. Clan territories were thus redefined formally as jurisdictions vested in particular offices; and it seems that in redistributing titles between these founding lineages, Dabo may have been governed by the pre-Fulani distributions of their respective fiefs. Thus, in Hausa days the Madaki's fiefs lay mainly northwest of Kano, while those of the Makama lay in the southwest. Dabo accordingly appointed the baYole Umaru as Madaki in place of the baJobe Mandikko, who became Makama. Evidently by these titular redistributions, Dabo sought to effect as close a correspondence as the situation allowed between the territorial allocations of his reconstituted officialdom and those of its Hausa model. By doing so, he could appeal to precedent, and to considerations of consistency, in delimiting the functions and authority of his officials. He thus consciously employed this process of reconstruction to counteract the autarchic and disintegrative pressures of clan jurisdiction by transforming its strategic sectors into state-regulated authority, while leaving the legitimacy of residual clan power open to be mobilized or challenged as developments required.

The Surveillance of Sokoto

Before Dabo died in 1846, the caliph had probably established his control over certain senior offices of state, initially those held by the founding lineages, namely the titles of Makama, Madaki, Sarkin Dawaki Maituta, Sarkin Bai and Dan Iya. Precisely when the caliph proclaimed his final control of these positions, we do not know, nor in which particular context. It is even possible that these imperial rights were not asserted in Dabo's lifetime. We simply lack the data necessary to determine precisely how and when Sokoto first established its control of these positions.

The caliph never attempted to regulate the allocation of these reserved offices by his emir at Kano. He merely required that no one should be dismissed from these five titles without his express approval. Thus the caliph left his emir to select suitable candidates qualified by the appropriate descent to these reserved titles; but, by reserving to himself the final decision with regard to dismissal from these titles, he assured the Fulani founding clans of imperial protection against arbitrary treatment by autocratic emirs who sought to centralize power in the throne by subverting, dispersing or appropriating other centres of independent power. On structural grounds, the caliph's assumption of this supervisory power, and his declared intention to review carefully all complaints by the emir of Kano against officials of these founding families, seem almost indispensable to the constructive resolution of juridical and political conflicts between those aristocrats and the emir that generated the revolt on Dabo's accession.

It is likely that Mandikko, on his dismissal from the office of Makama in 1830, appealed to Mamman Bello or his vizier, Gidado, to review and ajudicate the issue between Dabo and himself. As suggested above, Mandikko may have rejected Dabo's daughter in marriage with such intentions in mind. Mandikko was the first acting head of a founding lineage to be formally dismissed from office at Kano. However, some years before, Suleimanu had arbitrarily imprisoned Dabo Dambazau for seeking a bride at the caliph's court. To stabilize political relations between the founding families and chiefs of Kano, the caliph was thus constrained to assert his supervisory responsibilities, especially perhaps because the founding families of Kano had fought behind the Shehu's flag and in the process appropriated much of the territory, whereas the emirs appointed to rule the country had not.

In later years as we shall see, the caliph and his vizier extended their rights of review and supervision to cover dismissals from other senior offices in Kano, notably those of the Galadima and Wombai, which were usually held by the emir's agnates. Indirectly, such imperial restraints enhanced the stability and power of the Fulani chiefship at Kano by providing the leading local Fulani groups with those political guarantees that were essential preconditions of their willing cooperation with the chief. Lacking effective external assurances of protection and support, these aristocratic lineages could only preserve their power by collectively opposing that of the chief, as indeed they had done in Suleimanu's

reign, and in Dabo's early years; without external support and guarantees of disinterested appraisal, these founding families perceived that their status and rights
remained insecure against pressures from centralizing rulers. They accordingly
sought their security in those instruments by which the chief initially strove to
subdue them.

In obliging the Fulani leaders to accept office at his hands, Dabo had simultaneously assumed the capacity to replace them by others as he saw fit, and thereby
claimed the right to remove clan leadership and power from their hands, while
rendering its scope and exercise conditional always on his assent. Having
accepted office to preserve their status and rights, these Fulani could no longer
reject or forego it; but neither could they deliver themselves or their clan fortunes
and antecedent power into the hands of chiefs bent on autocratic aggrandizement
at their expense. Almost certainly during the revolt that followed Dabo's accession, these leaders impressed their situation and dilemmas on the caliph and
vizier at Sokoto; and perhaps for this reason, Mamman Bello made no effort to
intervene in the struggle at Kano, but left Dabo to deal with Dan Tunku and other
dissidents himself. Later, and most probably after Mandikko's appeal, he may
have asserted his special control over these offices, even though it seems likely
that some such assurance may have been sought much earlier by the founding
families as the condition of their continued co-operation with his governor at
Kano. Since Dabo had restricted their power and autonomy by endowing them
with offices they could hardly reject, only imperial restraints on the chief's arbitrary power of dismissal could preserve the essential autonomy and status of
these clan-heads and assure a continuing and viable accommodation of patrimonial centralism and aristocratic collegiality.

Under later rulers, those senior officials whose positions were protected by the
caliph's right to review complaints against them, formed the council of state, a
direct successor to the "Kano Nine" established by Mohammed Rumfa. Of these
nine, three, the Madaki, the Makama and the Sarkin Bai, collectively held a formal
power of veto to restrain the emir which was not restricted in its scope or range.
This could be invoked on any issue as the councillors felt appropriate; but the
emir could appeal against it to the vizier or caliph at Sokoto if the situation
seemed to warrant. Perhaps this joint veto was rarely used, since the emir could
cultivate the support of one or all of these senior councillors by various means.
Nothing suggests that these three councillors had any such power during Dabo's
reign; nor that there was initially or later any opportunity to employ such
restraints.The Dan Iya and the Sarkin Dawaki Maituta did not share these
restraining capacities, the former because his lineage, through various historical
accidents, had remained relatively weak though retaining its high status; and the
latter because the Suleibawa dynasty had appropriated much of its support from
Jamau's following and former territory. Dabo having entrenched his power and
his dynasty, developed a mutually satisfactory accommodation with the founding
lineages, which enabled them to collaborate with him in the Kano administration,
and probably achieved all the major goals on which he meditated during his forty
days' seclusion and fast on entering the Gidan Rumfa. Perhaps the last eight years
of his reign witnessed few novel developments in the constitution or administration of Kano.

With the death of the caliph Mamman Bello in 1837, an era ended. Though not a *jihadi*, Dabo had identified himself with this founding phase of the Fulani caliphate and empire, one characterised by conquest and creative political organization, by Islamic fervour, uncertainty and conflict. Following Bello's death, his brother Abubakar Atiku (1837–1842) succeeded as caliph. The puritanical Atiku sought to reduce the flow of tribute westwards to Sokoto and to subdue the Hausa of Gobir, Zamfara and Maradi, but without success on either score. In 1842, on the homeward route from an attack on Maradi, he died at Katuru in Sokoto territory. Aliyu Babba (1842–1859), the son of Bello, was chosen to succeed him. The new caliph dispensed with his father's vizier, Muhammad Gidado, and appointed instead his cross-cousin, Abdulkadiri, of Gidado's lineage.[137] Both the caliph and his vizier were thus drawn from the succeeding generation. Dabo died in 1846 when the new vizier of Sokoto Abdulkadiri was visiting Kano city.

Usuman, 1846–1855

Usuman's Regime

Without delay, Abdulkadiri immediately appointed Dabo's son Usuman, the Tafida, as emir of Kano. "Then he returned to Wurno (the caliph's residence) with what the sultan of Kano had left, which was a vast property."[138] Perhaps Aliyu Babba had decided to appoint Usuman before Dabo's death. If so, as his vizier and minister in charge of Kano, Hadeija, Zaria, and certain other emirates, Abdulkadiri apparently knew this. Hence, being at Kano on Dabo's death, Abdulkadiri appointed Usuman without delay and apparently without consulting local opinion. The state council, which had probably begun to take new shape and life in Dabo's later years, did not, on this or any other occasion in the last century, function as an electoral council to decide the succession to the chiefship at Kano. Perhaps the caliph, recognizing the peculiar distributions of power and interest in Kano, had decided to reserve the right to select successive emirs of Kano to himself and his vizier; and among Fulani emirates, Kano may have been unique in lacking an effective electoral council that regulated the local succession. As we shall see, this deficiency, perhaps unavoidable, given the tense and delicate balance of patrimonialism and collegiality, had severe consequences for Kano later on. However, on Dabo's death, despite reservations among those who knew Usuman, his immediate appointment by the vizier was probably welcomed in Kano by those who feared a disputed succession.

Al-Hajj Sa'id, who knew Usuman, says that he "was corpulent, seldom went out and entrusted his business to untrustworthy men."[139] Barth also characterizes Usuman as "lazy and indolent," and compares him unfavourably with his brother and vizier, the Galadima Abdullahi, whose intelligence and energy contrasted with Usuman's langor and effeteness. Usuman reigned from 1846 to 1855, dying in his forty-second year, on Barth's account.[140]

Shortly after his installation at the palace, Usuman recognized his need for an efficient and loyal vizier who would relieve him of the routine tasks and difficult decisions involved in administering the state. Probably on the advice of his mother Shekara, "one of the celebrated ladies of Hausa, a native of Daura,"[141] he then dismissed Dabo's Hausa Galadima, Ango, and appointed Abdullahi, his full brother and immediate junior, as Galadima with the authority and functions of a vizier. Abdullahi had formerly held the title of Dan Buram, which was now given to Dadu, another of Dabo's sons. Shekara had also borne Dabo a third son, Mamman Bello, several years younger than Usuman and Abdullahi, who as yet held no office. One of Shekara's daughters, Fatsumata Zara, had been appointed Magajiya by Dabo and given to Sarkin Bai Dambazau as a bride, together with Kunci. Another, Saretu, had been disposed of in marriage likewise.

Shekara seems to have been Dabo's senior wife, perhaps his favourite. Shortly after his accession, Usuman built a special compound for her, and, observing the normal teknonymy, designated her *Mai Babban Daki*, "the owner (mother) of the great hut"—that is, the mother of the successful dynastic segment, a usage which quickly passed into general currency as an informal title for the widow Shekara. Its general acceptance was greatly enhanced by its evident similarity to the old Hausa title, Maidaki, reserved for the queen mother. Indeed, with Usuman's allocation of certain fiefs to Shekara for her support, as mother of the emir and his vizier, Shekara's position and influence paralleled in all respects that traditionally ascribed to the Hausa Maidaki. In consequence, officials and others sought her favour and support in matters of interest to them. Though the defeated "Habe" had learned to expect very little favour from their Fulani rulers, and probably made few appeals to Shekara for aid, yet almost certainly her role was assimilated by them to that of the traditional queen mother, but with a difference. This queen mother was clearly identified with their Fulani rulers.

Shortly after Dabo died, his namesake the Sarkin Bai Dambazau followed. Usuman then appointed Dambazau's senior son, Muhammadu Kwairanga, to his father's title, thus identifying the office as hereditary (*gado*). Likewise, when the Madaki Umaru died in 1846, Usuman appointed Umaru's younger brother Hadiri, Jibir's son, to succeed; but he then transferred the Kumbotso fief, which Dabo had given to Umaru as his daughter's dowry, to the Galadima's administration. Similarly, on the deaths of the Daneji Dan Iya and the Suleibawa Sarkin Dawaki Maituta, Usuman appointed senior kinsmen from their respective lineages.

On his accession, Usuman appointed his son Aliyu to the office of Tafida which had now become vacant; and on Aliyu's death, during his reign, he appointed Abdurrazaku, another son, to succeed. When Mamudu, the son of Dabo, died, Usuman installed his own son Muhammadu Dikko as Ciroma with sizeable fiefs. Such appointments revealed the familistic orientations of Usuman's dynastic policy, and probably strengthened the determination of his brother Abdullahi, the effective governor, to pursue the succession himself. Usuman also appointed one of Dabo's senior sons, Abdusallame, to the office of San Turaki. As Shamaki to succeed Ibrahim, he appointed the slave Isa. As Magatakarda or scribe he appointed Muhammadu Jali, probably the same individual who had accompanied Clapperton from Kano to Sokoto on Dabo's instruction in 1824. Except that Usuman revealed a narrowly familistic interest in his allocations of princely office, his public appointments followed the lines laid down by Dabo earlier. Perhaps his chief innovation was the appointment of Abdullahi, formerly the Limam of Wudil, as Limam at Kano to succeed Hamma, the son of Muhamman Zara, now dead.

Some say that before appointing Abdullahi as his Galadima, Usuman promoted him from the office of Dan Buram to that of San Turaki, moving him later to the Galadima's position. Others say that Abdullahi was promoted directly from the office of Dan Buram to that of Galadima shortly after Usuman's accession.

Usuman's lassitude excluded significant displays of central initiative at Kano during his reign. His able and energetic brother the Galadima Abdullahi administered the state routinely according to Muslim law and Dabo's accepted precedents. The Chronicle notes that at this time "highway robbers were very numerous because Usuman was so good-tempered and merciful. He could not bring himself to cut a man's hand off nor, because he was so pitiful, could he cut a robber's throat."[142] Barth also comments on the insecurity that prevailed in rural areas due to Usuman's inadequate police and military arrangements.[143] Usuman clearly refused to give his brother the vizier leave to issue the orders necessary to organize an effective defense, either against small marauding bands or against the many destructive raids directed from Gumel at this date.

Farther north, the chief Ibram of Damagaram (Zinder), like Gumel and other Kanuri vassal states, was also active. Ibram was then engaged in a major assault on the capital of the Fulani emirate of Daura, in which his brother and rival Tanimu had taken refuge. As allies he had the independent Hausa chiefs of Gobir, Daura and Maradi. Kano sent reinforcements to the aid of the small Fulani emirate at Daura. In consequence, Ibram raided northern Kano freely and without effective response. At most, Usuman may have organized or reinforced the garrison stationed at Garki, near Kano's border with Gumel. However, this town of 15,000 people had five governors when visited by Barth in 1857, with consequent dispersal of its military capacity.[144] Usuman's performance as chief was not very distinguished. He seems to have withheld from his vizier all major decisions, while himself refusing to initiate effective action.

Revolt, Rebellion and War

In 1847 Kano experienced its first major famine since the *jihad*; and in the following year taxation increased sharply. In these circumstances, three years after his accession Usuman faced the beginnings of a Hausa revolt, the origins of which remain obscure. The revolt was initiated by certain Hausa ("Habe") malams: Maje, Ahmadu, Hamza and Maimazari. In 1848, on the introduction of further taxes and increased demands for forced labour from the "Habe," Malams Hamza and Maimazari left Kano for Tsakuwa, 16 miles southeast of Kano, where they encountered similar spirits in Maje and Ahmadu. At Tsakuwa, Malam Hamza decided to emigrate and instigate a revolt after experiencing further Fulani oppression. With their families and about five hundred supporters, these Hausa malams fled from Tsakuwa by way of Magami, Bashe and Dua to Kuluki, a settlement of Ningi pagans in northwestern Bauchi, where they rapidly built up a strong alliance of Ningi, Warjawa, Ajawa and Mbutawa tribes under their leadership. By 1849 under Maje, the Ningi had attacked and besieged Birnin Kudu, but failed to take it. A small force sent against them from Kano under the Barde Maude was defeated and the Barde was killed, following which Usuman despatched his Hausa client Ango and the Dan Ruwata against Kuluki, the largest Ningi settlement, while Ibrahim the emir of Bauchi sent another force to besiege their stronghold at Jabula. Neither attempt succeeded, the Kano forces withdrawing after two years, the Bauchi army after five.

By 1850 Malam Hamza had consolidated his alliance with the Ningi, the Mbutawa and Warjawa, and thereafter southeastern Kano knew little rest from Ningi raids. From 1850 to 1875 the Ningi concentrated their heaviest attacks on southeastern Kano, inflicting considerable damage. Only later, when they turned their attention to Zaria emirate, did Kano receive some relief. When Kuluki and Tabula were relieved, Maje resumed his attack on Kano, but after some successes, he was cut off by a force from Bauchi at Gasanya on his homeward route and killed in battle. Malam Hamza's son Haruna then assumed leadership of the revolt, Mai-Mazari having died at Tabula, and Hamza himself being then too old. Haruna attacked and took Dal near Sumaila, raided Rano freely, and invested Takai, without moving Usuman to launch a counter-attack. The main struggle took place after Usuman's death; but perhaps had he sent a strong force against Ningi at the first disturbance, Usuman might have spared Kano much later trouble.

From the slender materials available, it seems that Hamza, Mai-Mazari, Maje and Ahmadu began by protesting against the inequities of the Fulani regime with its differential taxation, justice, forced labour and unequal civil, military and religious provisions. According to Malam Adamu, increasing oppression by Fulani princes, *hakimai* and their retainers provoked these Hausa of Tsakuwa to resist. Leaders of the resistance were then summoned by the emir to his court at Kano to explain their conduct, but, fearing the consequences of obedience, they decided to flee, and sought safety among the nearby pagans, whom they promptly organized for defense against the inevitable military attack. All sources identify the leaders of this Hausa protest against Fulani oppression as malams of high repute for magical power. Presumably these Hausa malams also based their resistance and criticism of Fulani rule on Islamic doctrines which forbade the treatment of conquered Muslims as pagans liable to *jizya*, forced labour, arbitrary justice, and similar abuses. Feeling threatened, they fled to the pagans in Bauchi, accompanied by many alienated Hausa from southern Kano and followed by others. As the struggle developed and other dissident Hausa joined the rebels or aided them with reinforcements or critical information about Fulani dispositions and plans, this small population at "Ningi" under the leadership of Hamza, Maje and their successors Haruna and Dan Yaya, achieved disproportionate military success, due largely to the flow of information and support from alienated Hausa in southern Kano.[145]

In 1848–49 Usuman had also to face another threat of revolt from the Fulani Sarkin Dutse, Muhammadu Bello, who had been appointed by Dabo at his father's request when the latter retired from office in 1840 on grounds of age. Again, we know little about the start of this conflict. It is said that by 1848 the Sarkin Dutse Mamman Bello had virtually abandoned his allegiance to Usuman, ignoring the latter's orders and requests, and raiding nearby communities in Jahun and Gaya to extend his domain. The Sarkin Dutse also refused to obey Usuman's repeated summons to come to Kano until he received a message ordering him to accompany Usuman to Sokoto, where the caliph Aliyu Babba would decide the affair. This final message was probably fictitious. On visiting Kano in

1849, the Sarkin Dutse was turned over to the Sarkin Yara and killed in the palace prison. Following Fulani political practice, Usuman immediately appointed the dead man's brother, Suleimanu, to succeed at Dutse. Suleimanu remained loyal until he was killed by the Ningi in 1868.

In Hadeija in 1848, after a succession of short reigns, the Ciroma Buhari succeeded to the chiefship against the wishes of his father, Sambo, the caliph Aliyu Babba, and the vizier of Sokoto Abdulkadiri. Having suffered several rebuffs in his efforts to win the Hadeija chiefship, Buhari had become disenchanted with Sokoto's regulation of Hadeija affairs. Entering into independent relations with the Shehu Umar of Bornu which had once ruled this area, Buhari pursued his own interests and was shortly deposed by the caliph. Buhari's brother, Muhammadu, was next appointed as chief, only to be killed by Buhari in 1851.[146] By then, Buhari had identified himself openly as an enemy of the Fulani caliph and empire. He defeated the Katagum army, secured Bornu reinforcements, and raided nearby Kano and Bauchi. The caliph Aliyu Babba commanded his eastern emirs to assemble their forces in northeastern Kano and attack Buhari. The vizier of Sokoto was sent to Kano to supervise these arrangements. Usuman's brother, the Galadima Abdullahi, led the Kano contingent. The emirs of Zaria, Bauchi, Katagum, Fulani Daura and Katsina turned out their cavalry as directed. Perhaps this was the largest force the Fulani empire had fielded till then. It moved against Hadeija from Ringim and Aujara only to suffer resounding defeat in the *Yakin Duniya* (World War) of 1852. The caliph Aliyu himself took command in the following year, only to suffer another decisive reverse. In 1855 he commissioned Usuman, the Sarkin Kano, to take command of the assembled eastern forces. Usuman directed the army to assemble in northeastern Kano and set out for Ringim, accompanied by his brother the Galadima. At Ringim, Usuman died and Abdullahi assumed the command. His campaign against Buhari was no more successful than those of 1852 and 1853. Buhari knew the territory well and cleverly exploited its marshlands in defense. Besides his Bornu allies, he had substantial forces of his own committed to fight sternly by their unforgiveable "apostasy." Abdullahi returned to Kano without glory to await the vizier of Sokoto, Halilu, who would bring the caliph's letters appointing the new emir.

Kano in 1851

Easily the fullest account of pre-colonial Kano available to us is that furnished by Henry Barth, the explorer, in his visits of 1851 and 1853. Following Clapperton, Barth first visited Bornu and then travelled through Kano to Sokoto to visit the caliph, Aliyu Babba. From Sokoto he went westward to Timbuktu and returned by the same route to Bornu in 1854, before returning homewards across the desert to complete his journey, one of the finest achievements in the history of African exploration. On February 1st, 1851 Barth entered Kano from Katsina, after crossing the desert southwards. On that occasion he spent five and a half weeks in the town before continuing east to Bornu. Three years later, he spent another five and a half weeks at Kano during October and November 1854, on his route eastwards from Sokoto to Bornu.[147] During these visits, Barth conducted a systematic survey of the city, its wards, walls, public buildings, markets, and especially its commerce and trade. One reason for his stay at Kano in 1854 was to complete this task. In preparing his journals for publication, Barth brought these survey data together to provide a complete description of Kano as he first saw it in 1851. This account is no simple diary of random observations by an explorer unfamiliar with the language, culture and history of the people he visited, but a tight professional summary of data gathered in a careful and systematic survey on the secular organization of the city and the state, that demonstrates Barth's unrivalled understanding of the people, their language, society and way of life. Here, thanks to the remarkable diligence and skill of this exceptional observer, who still provides our finest information on the central Sudan for this period, we have precisely those detailed systematic materials that historians and ethnographers usually lack about the ordinary life of people in time long past.

Barth did not have access to the Kano Chronicle; but he was already sufficiently informed about the histories of Katsina, Bornu, Gobir, Zamfara, Kebbi, Sokoto and Songhai to have an excellent general idea of the history of Kano which the Chronicle fully confirms.[148] Here I shall only summarize those data or estimates that indicate the essential outlines of the society and the state, its character and composition. Since both of Barth's visits fell in Usuman's reign, he describes the country at midpoint in its career as an emirate of the Fulani caliphate and empire of Sokoto.

In 1853 Barth estimated that the emirate contained about half a million people, of whom at least one-half were slaves. Conservatively, he reckoned the residents at the capital as about thirty thousand for most of the year. Between January and April, when trade was busiest, he estimated the city's population at about twice that number. Of thirty thousand permanent residents in Kano, Barth estimated that Fulani did not exceed four thousand; and the slaves, though numerous, were certainly less than one-half. He found it impossible to estimate the relative number or proportion of Fulani in the rural population.[149] He remarked on the residential segregation of Fulani, Hausa, Habe, Arabs, Kanuri and Nupe at the capital; and having listed and mapped all its wards carefully, he may have used these areas to estimate the probable number of Fulani in the city.

Like Clapperton, Barth was greatly interested in the commercial and industrial activities of Kano. He saw in the economy of Kano evident parallels with the organization of northwestern Europe in the Middle Ages.

> The great advantage of Kano is, that commerce and manufactures go hand in hand, and that almost every family has its share in them. There is really something grand in this kind of industry, which spreads to the north as far as Murzuk, Ghat, and even Tripoli; to the west, not only to Timbuktu, but in some degree even as far as the shores of the Atlantic; ... to the east, all over Bornu, ... and to the south. ... This industry is not carried on here, as in Europe, in immense establishments, degrading man to the meanest condition of life, but ... gives employment and support to families without compelling them to sarifice their domestic habits.[150]

Having established that 2,500 cowries were currently equivalent to one Spanish dollar, and 10,000 to one pound sterling, Barth sought to estimate the gross annual trade turnovers of the export and import commerce at Kano by the numbers, periodicity, volumes and values of local exports and imports by caravan. He estimated Kano exports of cloth and clothing at a minimum value of 300 million cowries per annum, specifying the amounts and types of clothing exported to different areas. Exports of local sandals and tanned dyed hides and skins he set at 10 and 5 millions per annum respectively. Imports of kola nuts were reckoned at 100 million per annum. Slave exports, estimated at 5,000 per annum to Bornu, Nupe, Ghat and Fezzan ranged between 150 and 200 millions per annum. The transit traffic in natron and potash from Bornu southwards to Nupe and Yoruba, Barth estimated at 20 thousand loads of oxen, asses and other beasts, yielding a minimum income to Kano of 10 million a year. Of three thousand camel loads of salt brought annually to Kano by the Tuareg, he estimated one-third to be locally consumed with a value of between 50 and 80 millions, most of which was spent locally by the Tuareg to purchase grain, cloth and other necessities. He then proceeds to itemize the probable gross traffic in other imports: Manchester cotton cloth—40 million cowries; coarse silk—70 millions; wool—15 millions; beads—20 millions; sugar—12 millions; paper—5 millions; needles—8 millions; sword blades, 50,000 per annum costing 50 millions; muskets, mainly American-made, were available through Nupe in small quantities but not budgeted; razors—2 to 3 millions; French silks—20 millions; Arab clothing—shawls, kaftans, trousers, caps or turbans, sashes, burnouses, etc., mainly imported from Egypt—50 millions; spices, mainly cloves and benzoin—15 millions; rose oil and cheap perfume—40 millions; tin—10 millions; 50 camel loads of copper, 20 of zinc from Tripoli—valued at 15 to 20 millions; cowries were also imported from the west and south for local use, and re-exported eastwards to Bornu. This yields a total for Kano's exports and re-exports of between 525 and 555 millions of cowries, or £52,500 at current rates, and for its imports between 523 and 558 millions of cowries, which is virtually the same.[151] Besides the central market founded by Rumfa, Barth names nine lesser ones in the city, most of which are still current today.

Whereas formerly, the "governor" or emir could muster ten thousand horsemen, in 1853 Barth estimated that Usuman could only raise about seven thousand horse and twenty thousand foot soldiers, a considerable force nonetheless. He reckoned the chief's revenues at about "one hundred millions of *kurdi* besides the presents received from merchants";[152] but whether this represents the total levied or the amounts received by the chief, which were probably about 30 to 40 per cent of the gross, is not indicated. In Barth's estimate, ninety millions or about 90 per cent of the chief's cash income derived from the *"kurdin-kasa"* or "ground rent," that is, *kudin gona* or farm tax, introduced by Dabo after Clapperton's visit. "Every head of a family has to pay two thousand five hundred *kurdi*, or just a Spanish dollar."[153] This was two-and-a-half times the rate levied by Dabo at the end of his reign; and as in Dabo's day, it fell solely on the conquered people, being described alternately by the Fulani as land tax, as ground rent due from the subjects for the right to occupy land, or as the *jizya* levied by the Muslims on non-Muslims, that is, on the "Habe," Hausawa and Kutumbawa being exempted. It is likely that the tax rate increased sharply between 1846 and 1848, provoking Hamza's immediate protest and the withdrawal of the Hausa malams from Kano via Tsakuwa to Ningi.

Although we lack documentation on this point also, it seems likely that this sharp rise in the tax rate at Kano accompanied a similar increase in the scale of tribute demanded by Sokoto from subordinate emirates. This increase in the scale of imperial tribute was instituted by the Caliph Aliyu Babba (1842–1859) whom Barth met later at Sokoto—"a stout middle-sized man, with a round fat face, exhibiting, evidently, rather the features of his mother, a Hausa slave, than those of his father Muhammad Bello, a free and noble Pullo, but full of cheerfulness and good humour."[154] Barth estimated that the caliph's annual revenues from the emirates "certainly exceeds one hundred millions of shells, or about ten thousand pounds sterling, besides an equal value in slaves and native cloth or articles of foreign produce."[155] Thus, excluding the official revenues received by his Vizier, Galadima and other imperial ministers who supervised particular states, the caliph's tributary income was almost twice that of his emir at Kano, though Kano was more populous and prosperous than Sokoto.

Aliyu Babba recognized that his revenues from war and raids had diminished sharply from their initial peak, and thus sought alternative supplies of revenue to maintain his government. These could only be drawn either from Sokoto itself, or from the eastern emirates under its care; but following his father's practice, Aliyu Babba decided not to levy regular taxes on the population at Sokoto, Fulani or other. Revolt and hostility were so frequent and general among the "Habe" of Kebbi, Gobir and Zamfara, within and around the borders of Sokoto that, like his predecessors, Aliyu Babba felt it would be unwise to fan the flames of resentment further by adding new burdens. Thus he had to increase his tributary income from the less turbulent and more effectively subjugated eastern states. Accordingly, between 1845 and 1847 the rates of imperial tribute rose sharply, the eastern emirs being left to collect the amounts required as they thought fit.

In Kano most of this increase in state tribute was transferred to the conquered "Habe" by doubling the land tax. In Katsina and Zaria the emirs sought to collect the additional cash revenues they needed by reviving or instituting comprehensive systems of occupational taxation. This was another, but subtler and more flexible form of doubling the tax load on "Habe," who formed the overwhelming bulk of the local craftsmen and market vendors. Further, to increase the "Habe" tax load in Katsina and Zaria, special crop taxes (*kudin shuke*) were levied on all who cultivated such marketable crops as sweet potatoes, cassava, sugar cane, yams and the like. Since Fulani eschewed farming, while market gardening was a Hausa specialty, these crop-taxes were merely another mode of selective double taxation of the subject "Habe" farmers. At Kano also, Barth reported a variety of *kudin shuke* and "a small tax called *kudin rafi* on the vegetables sold in the market,"[156] listing these crops just mentioned. However, this tax was paid not only on the market sales of such crops, but on the plots in which they were grown, and apparently without much adjustment for differences in plot extent or intercropping. At Kano the *kudin shuke* was first introduced by the Fulani under Usuman, and remained individually variable. It thus resembled an arbitrary impost or instrument of subjugation more closely than a standard tax. Presumably, in each community taxable plots were assessed at rates governed by the need for revenue.

Barth also reports an annual tax called '*kurdin-korofi*' of seven hundred *kurdi* (cowries) on every dyepit or *korofi*, of which there are more than two thousand in the city alone; a "*fito*" or tax of five hundred *kurdi* on every slave sold in the market and an annual tax, "*kurdi-n-dabino*" of six hundred *kurdi* on every palm tree (date tree)."[157] He omits death duties (*ushiran gado*) rated at ten per cent of private property, *zakka* (the grain tithe fixed at ten per cent of the harvest); free labour from blacksmiths, silversmiths, tanners and leather workers for state production, forced labour or corvée, those market taxes listed by Clapperton thirty years earlier; *zakkan shanu*, the cattle tithe, or *jangali*, its cash equivalent, together with the *humushi* or fifth of war booty, *kudin sarauta*, *kudin wankan takobi*, and the yield from official farms cultivated by slaves. In short, the ruler's annual revenue in goods, services and locally produced crops at Kano was probably equal in value to his receipts in cash. If so, then in cash and kind, the "Habe" of Kano may have transferred rather more than one-tenth of their annual incomes to the state as official dues, excluding fines, bribes or extortions by tax-collectors. Indeed perhaps the proportion of gross household incomes given to the state in cash, kind or labour by these "Habe" was nearly twice as high, since Barth estimates that "with from fifty to sixty thousand *kurdi*, ... a whole family may live in that country with ease, including every expense, even that of their clothing."[158] For this calculation, he employed the standards of living observed among the prosperous merchants and malams who befriended him at the capital.

Merely to indicate the abnormality of the urban price structure and the source of much financial instability in these Fulani emirates, we may cite two of Barth's gifts to the Emir Usuman and to his brother the Galadima Abdullahi, both of which equalled in their local value the amounts just mentioned as sufficient to support a family at Kano city in moderate comfort for a year. Barth gave the chief "a sort of bernus, with silk and gold lace ... here worth sixty thousand *kurdi*," besides much else of value. To the Galadima he gave "a piece of French striped silk worth fifty thousand *kurdi*."[159] At that date, while fine war steeds fetched elastic amounts, a horse in poor condition might fetch four dollars (ten thousand cowries), a spacious house in the better part of town rented for one dollar (two thousand five hundred cowries) a month, slaves averaged about thirty thousand cowries each, and camels fifty thousand.[160]

At Kano Barth met the treasurer (Ma'aji) whose name (*lakabi*) Gado, he mistook for his title;[161] the Ciroma Dikko, Usuman's eldest son, "a handsome, modest and intelligent youth of about eighteen years of age";[162] the Galadima, the emir, many clerics and merchants, and an ailing son of the emir of Zaria. He found the palace filled with "hundreds of lazy, arrogant courtiers, free men and slaves, ... lounging and idling here, killing time with trivial and saucy jokes."[163] The Galadima Abdullahi visited the palace every day to administer the government in offices and audience chambers reserved there for his use. As required, he attended Usuman for consultations, instructions, and audience with such distinguished visitors as the vizier of Sokoto. Barth's summary of the prevailing constitution, though incomplete, is clear and accurate.

> The authority of the governor is not absolute, even without considering the appeal which lies to his liege lord in Sokoto or Wurno, if the subjects' complaints can be made to reach so far; a sort of ministerial council is formed, to act in conjunction with the governor which in important cases he cannot well avoid consulting. At the head of this council stands the Ghaladima, whose office originated ... in the empire of Bornu, and who very often exercises, as is the case in Kano, the highest influence, surpassing that of the governor himself; then follows the "sarki-n-Dawakay" (the

master of the horse), an important charge in barbarous countries, where victory depends almost always on the cavalry; then the "barde-n-Kano" (a sort of commander in chief); then the "alkali," the chief justice, the "chiroma-n-Kano" (the eldest son of the governor, or someone assuming this title, who exercises the chief power in the southern part of the province); the "serki-n-bay" (properly, the chief of the slaves) who has the inspection of the northern districts of the province as far as Kazaure; then the "gado," the lord of the treasury, and finally the "serki-n-shano" (the master of the oxen, or rather the quartermaster general), who has all the military stores under his care; for the ox, rather the bull, is the ordinary beast of burden in Negro land. It is characteristic that, when the governor is absent paying his homage to his liege lord, it is not the ghaladima, but the gado and the serki-n-shano who are his lieutenants or substitutes ... The government in general ... is not oppressive, though the behaviour of the ruling class is certainly haughty, and there is, no doubt, a great deal of injustice inflicted in small matters. The etiquette of the court, which is far more strict than in Sokoto, must prevent any poor man from entering the presence of the governor. The Fulbe (Fulani) marry the handsome daughters of the subjugated tribe, but would not condescend to give their own daughters to men of that tribe as wives.[164]

In this passage Barth does not mention the Madaki or the Makama, the Wombai or the Dan Iya, all of whom sat on the official council of state. Neither does he mention the Shamaki and other throne slaves, the Mundubawa, the major rural chiefs of Gaya, Rano, etc., nor the pastoral Fulani chiefs. His list of councillors seems best to represent those whom Usuman usually summoned for advice and counsel on important executive affairs. The Sarkin Shanu, at this time, a baSuleibe client, Muhamman, who was formerly the village head of Yako, and the treasurer, Gado, both lacked traditional claims to seats on the council and held their appointments at the will of the chief. Such appointments committed them to serve as the chief's men or advocates in council, rather than as councillors guided by the interests of state rather than those of the chief.

Nonetheless, Barth's account of the "ministerial council" during Usuman's reign is quite convincing. Evidently the Dan Iya, Wombai and Makama, though formally councillors of state, were called on rarely, perhaps only on the most important issues. As a rule, Usuman preferred to work with a smaller council in which the Ciroma, the Ma'aji and the Sarkin Shanu could be relied on for support, and perhaps also the baGyeni Alkali Malam Datuwa, and the Barde. Usuman probably employed this council to restrict the executive power and political influence of his Galadima. As vizier, the latter administered many routine affairs, military and civil; and, being more alert and informed than his brother, Abdullahi may also have guided many important decisions Usuman reserved for himself as chief. The composition of Usuman's council indicates that its primary function was to serve as a buffer between himself and the vizier, a group to which issues involving some difficulty, disagreements, or interest of the state as a whole could be referred for joint discussion, thereby diverting direct confrontations between his vizier and himself, while preserving Usuman's power of final decision in a forum to which the vizier was routinely though indirectly answerable.

This combination of a strong central vizierate in the hands of his brother, and a council of mixed composition available for consultation and action as required, enabled Usuman to retain final powers of decision while leaving his brother to administer the chiefdom. As a means of permitting the delegation of substantial authority without transferring equivalent power, this political structure was adequate, given the close kinship between vizier and chief, the presence of their mother, the caliph's supervisory role, and the political composition of the Fulani in Kano. The chief defect of this structure was the restraints it imposed on energetic action by the central authority in emergencies or in pursuit of long-term goals. Clearly the decision to double the farm tax to meet Sokoto's demands for more tribute was a serious political mistake which indirectly touched off the Ningi wars by provoking the revolt of Malam Hamza and his colleagues. Oral information from several sources at Sokoto agree in setting the annual tribute required from Kano during and after Usuman's reign as one hundred horses, one hundred slaves, one hundred *kyenkyendi* or bales of twenty fine gowns each, plus one million cowries per month, known as "money for lamp-oil," these being the caliph's receipts.[165] Other gifts, equal to one half the caliph's tribute, were forwarded simultaneously to the vizier.

We need not treat Barth's estimates of the population of the chiefdom and its capital, of the value and composition of its trade, the growth of its cash revenues and size of its army as solemn facts to recognize their significance. These estimates are equally consistent with one another and with all our information about Kano before and after Barth passed through it. It seems likely that there had been a substantial decline in the population of the chiefdom between 1804 and 1853, due mainly to the *jihad* and the subsequent campaigns, including Dabo's wars with Dan Tunku and the Kano rebels, but also to attacks on Kano by nearby enemies, such as Gumel and Hadeija. Perhaps at least a hundred thousand lives were lost in these campaigns. Barth's remark that in the rural areas slaves were no less numerous than free people[166] also suggests that a substantial number of the defeated Hausa ("Habe") had been enslaved by or shortly after the Fulani conquest. Nothing indicates that slavery flourished in Kano under Alwali's rule on anything like this scale.

The most important qualities Barth's observations reveal are Kano's impressive size and wealth. Together, those conditions endowed the polity with remarkable capacities for survival and recovery, despite much waste of its resources and population; yet the same conditions tended to immobilize its political superstructure, since the rulers found that they could only regulate and coordinate this unwieldy diversified mass by means of the official system that had grown up with it historically as the machinery of its central communication and control. In consequence, archaic and structurally discordant features of the old regime persisted in Fulani Kano to structure the orientations of the new and impair its efficiency.

Notes

1. For an excellent general account, see J. Spencer Trimingham, *A History of Islam in West Africa* (London: Oxford University Press, 1962), especially chapters 4 and 5.

2. E.E. Evans-Pritchard, *The Sanusi of Cyrenaica* (London: Oxford University Press, 1949).

3. Thomas Hodgkin, *Nationalism in Africa* (London: 1957); J. Spencer Trimingham, *A History of Islam in West Africa*, Ch. 7: and *idem*, *Islam in West Africa* (Oxford: Clarendon press, 1959); Paul Marty, *L'Islam Noir* (Paris: , 193).

4. Henry Barth, *Travels and Discoveries* (1890 edn.), Vol. 2, p. 168; Wazirin Sakkwato, Alhaji Junaidu, *Tarihin Fulani*, pp. 7–8; 'Abdullah Ibn Muhammad, *Tazyin al-Waraqat*, pp. 97–98.

5. A.D.H. Bivar and M. Hiskett, "The Arabic Literature of Nigeria to 1804: A Provisional Report," *BSOAS*, Vol. 25, 1962, pp. 140–143; S.J. Hogben, *The Muhammadan Emirates of Nigeria*, p. 109.

6. Bivar and Hiskett, "The Arabic Literature of Nigeria to 1804: A Provisional Report," pp. 140–141; J. Lippert, "Contributions to the History of the Hausa States," in J.A. Burdon, *Historical Notes on Certain Emirates and Tribes* (London: Waterlow & Sons, 1909), pp. 93–94.

7. J. Lippert, "Contributions to the History of the Hausa States," p. 93; E.J. Arnett, *The Rise of the Sokoto Fulani*, pp. 19–20.

8. M. Hiskett, "An Islamic tradition of reform in the Western Sudan from the Sixteenth to the Eighteenth century," *BSOAS*, Vol. 25, part 3, 1962, pp. 588–591; *idem*, "Material relating to the state of learning among the Fulani before their *Jihad*," *BSOAS*, Vol. 19, 1957, pp. 560–569.

9. J. Lippert, "Contributions to the History of the Hausa States," p. 93.

10. Ibid., p. 94.

11. M. Hiskett, "An Islamic tradition of reform in the Western Sudan from the Sixteenth to the Eighteenth century," pp. 588–590; A.D.H. Bivar and M. Hiskett, "The Arabic Literature of Nigeria to 1804: A Provisional Account," pp. 140–143.

12. For Jibril's thesis, see A.D.H. Bivar and M. Hiskett, "The Arabic Literature of Northern Nigeria 59 1804: A provisional account," pp. 140–143; and for the Shehu Usman's criticism, see M. Hiskett, "An Islamic tradition of reform in the Western Sudan from the Sixteenth to the Eighteenth century," pp. 588–590. For the Shehu's apologia for the *jihad*, his *Tanbihu'l Ikhwan*, see the translation by H.R. Palmer, "An early Fulani conception of Islam," *JRAS*, Vols. 13–14, 1914–5, pp. 407–414; 53–59, 185–192. For the Shehu's views on the Muslim obligations of segregation and *jihad*, see his *Bayan wujub al-hijra ala'l-ibad* (A.H. 1221; 1806–7 A.D).

13. M. Hiskett, "An Islamic tadition of reform in the Western Sudan from the Sixteenth to the Eighteenth century," p. 591.

14. See M. Hiskett, "Material relating to the state of learning among the Fulani before their Jihad," *BSOAS*, Vol. 19, 1957; p. 566. See also 'Abdullah Ibn Muhammad, *Tazyin Al-Waraqat*, pp. 90–94, for Abdullahi's ode on Al-Hajj Jibril.

15. M. Hiskett, "An Islamic tradition of reform in the Western Sudan from the sixteenth to the eighteenth century," p. 591.

16. 'Abdullah Ibn Muhammad, *Tazyin Al-Waraqat*, p. 105.

17. Ibid., pp. 107–109; E.J. Arnett, *The Rise of the Sokoto Fulani*, p. 51.

18. E.J. Arnett, *The Rise of the Sokoto Fulani*, pp. 50–57; *idem*, "History of Sokoto," in E.J. Arnett, *The Rise of the Sokoto Fulani*, pp. 18–19. 'Abdullah Ibn Muhammad, *Tazyin Al-Waraqat*, pp. 109–111.

19. E.J. Arnett, *The Rise of the Sokoto Fulani*, p. 63.

20. Ibid., p. 54.

21. KC, p. 93; LH, Vol. 2, p. 59.

22. KC, p. 82, footnote 2; LH, Vol. 2, p. 44, footnote 1.

23. Dokaji Abubakar, *Kano ta Dabo Cigari*

24. E.J. Arnett, *The Rise of the Sokoto Fulani*, p. 64

25. E.J.Arnett, "A Hausa Chronicle," *JRAS*, vol. 10, 1911, p. 167; and see Ibid., p. 166 for the reigns of Ish'iaku (Jatau) and Makam in the Zaria king list.

26. For alternative dates for the Fulani capture of Zaria city and Makau's withdrawal, see Malams Hassan and Shu'aibu, *A Chronicle of Abuja*, p. 5 ("Saturday, the tenth day of the month of Zulhaji in the year 1804"): E.J. Arnett, "A Hausa Chronicle," p. 166: "Makkam reigned 2 years 1 month. He was driven from the throne on Saturday in the month of Zulhaji , on the thirteenth day of the month"; M.G. Smith, *Government in Zazzau*, 1800–1950, pp. 3, 34, 1804, follows Malams Hassan and Shu'aibu, *op cit.*; S.J. Hogben and A.H.M. Kirk-Greene, *The Emirates of Northern Nigeria* (London: Oxford University Press, 1966), pp. 236–237 (1804); H.F.C. (Abdullahi) Smith: "The Dynastic Chronology of Fulani Zaria," *Journal of the Historical Society of Nigeria*, Vol. II, No. 2, 1961; D.M. Last, "A Solution to the Problems of Dynastic Chronology in 19th Century Zaria and Kano." *Journal of the Historic Society of Nigeria* (JHSN), Vol. III, No. 3, pp. 461–469, says on p. 467 - Makau "succeeds to the throne c. Nov. 1806/1221 (A.H.); receives Alwali, ex-King of Kano c. June 1807/1223: Alwali leaves c. June 1808/1223; (Makau) evacuates Zaria 31 Dec. 1808/1223."

27. E.J. Arnett, *The Rise of the Sokoto Fulani*, pp 63–64

28. On Dan Mama's conduct in this crisis, Malam Adam Muhammad, *Ta'rikh Kano*, writes that when the Fulani proclaimed their *jihad*, "Alwali asked one of the Malams of Tamburawa, Malam Gawaiya, whether the Fulani affair was the truth so that he should make peace, or whether he should fight them, as they would surely win. But when that Malam left, the Ciroma of Kano Dan Mama said, "Do not make peace, but fight as you'll surely win, since they are weak." Later Dan Mama secretly sent to the Fulani and made his peace with them to save his own life. In other words he betrayed the Chief of Kano ..."

Alkali Muhammad Zangi, *Taqyid Al-Akhbar*, makes no reference to Dan Mama but says that Alwali's Alkali and the Limam of Kano, Adulkadiri, assured him that the Fulani rebels were misguided.

M. Adamu na Ma'aji in his *Ta'rikh Kano* writes that, "After he had opened Dirki, Alwali became afraid as the prophecy went that if any ruler ever opened Dirki to see what was in it, he would be overthrown, and with it the Habe state. Alwali II did so after his appointment and found the Koran in it. He called the malams and showed them, and they said he would certainly be overthrown. He asked a famous Malam, Muhamma na Yandoya, to make prayers to save him. The Malam said there was no possible protection except possibly to "obey (follow) the directions of the Malam of Degel (Shehu Usuman dan Fodio) exactly." Alwali consulted his *hakimai* and they rejected this proposal. He then consulted another famous Malam, M. Gwaja of Tumbarawa who also told him to seek the friendship (trust) of the "Malam of Degel." Alwali then asked the Ciroma dan Mama for his advice. Dan Mama dissuaded him finally, though Alwali wanted to follow the malam's advice. Then the Ciroma dan Mama wrote himself to Shehu Usmanu declaring allegiance; and because of this Shehu (later) ordered the Fulani of Kano to leave him as Ciroma, and the Fulani also gave him 100 towns after their conquest."

Oral traditions iterate this account too fully and consistently for it to be entirely false.

29. M. Adamu na Ma'aji, *Ta'rikh Kano*; Alkali Muhammad Zangi, *Taqyid Al-Akbar*; Dokaji Alhaji Abubakar, *Kano ta Dabo Cigari*, pp. 48–49.

30. W.F. Gowers, *Gazeteer of Kano Province*, pp. 10–12.

31. E.J. Arnett, *The Rise of the Sokoto Fulani*, pp. 77–79; *idem*, "History of Sokoto," in Arnett, *op. cit.*, p. 22. Interestingly, Alkali Muhammad Zangi does not give the year in which the Kano *jihad* started, or that in which the Kano *jihadis* withdrew (*hijra*) but says that "when the Shehu was ready to withdraw, he instructed all around him to return to their homes, saying, 'the time for withdrawal (*hijra*) has come.' He also wrote a letter to all his followers ordering them to withdraw. It was Adamawa (Lamido Adamu) who brought this letter to (the Shehu's) community in Kano. The Muezzin Goje was with him. They handed this letter to Malam Dan Zabuwa; and for some time the leaders communicated with one another by messages."

M. Adamu na Ma'aji in his *Ta'rikh Kano* says: "The Beginning of the Jihad in Kano: Three years after the Shehu Usuman had been appointed as Caliph and received the allegiance (of the faithful), the Fulani in Kano country sent to the Shehu to receive a flag for their jihad. The one they sent was named Dan Zabuwa. Their war leader was M. Muhammadau Jamau. He was the first one to withdraw and settled at Kozaba (Kwazzabo)."

Thus, on M. Adamu na Ma'aji's account, the fighting in Kano did not begin before December 1806. This accords with Gowers who writes: "In 1807, Dan Zabua was sent by the Mahommedan community (of Kano) to Sokoto to obtain a flag and the encouragement of the Shehu to the conquest of Kano for the reformed religion" (*Gazetteer of Kano Province*, p. 11).

Possibly the Shehu's circular to his scattered following was his as yet undated *Wathiqat ahl al-Sudan*, concerning which see A.D.H. Bivar, *The Wathiqat ahl Al-Sudan*: A Manifesto of the Fulani Jihad," *Journal of African History*, Vol. II, part 2, 1961, pp. 235–243.

However, after reporting the jihadis' victory over Alwali's Barde Bakori at Kofa Kogo in the first six months of the *jihad*, Alkali Zangi says "Islam has been estalished since then for 64 years," thus dating that battle to 1217 A.H., if the copyist's date for the completion of the *Taqyid al-Akbar*, Monday, Zulkida 6th 1281 A.H., is accepted. Since the Shehu's *hijra* and *jihad* only began in A.H. 1219, there is evidently some error here, but whether the author's or the copyist's I cannot say.

32. See M. Hiskett, "The 'Song of Bagauda'" - Part II, BSOAS, vol. 28, 1965, p. 129, text and footnote 125.

33. W.F. Gowers, *Gazetteer of Kano Province*, p. 11, reckons that the fighting in Kano "extended over a year" before Alwali fled south. For M. Adamu na Ma'aji's account, which confirms this, see footnote 31 *supra*. For confirmation from the Dokaji Abubakar, see *Kano ta Dabo Cigari*, pp. 48–9; likewise Alkali Muhammadu Zangi, *Taqyid al-Akbar*, and M. Adam Muhammad, *Ta'rikh Kano*.

In Sultan Bello's account (*Infaqu'l Maisur*) we read "I directed Umoru Dallaji to go as my messenger to Katsina ... He found the Katsina people at Yantumaki. Then he passed on with the letter to Kano. His arrival at Katsina coincided with the departure of Sarkina Katsina to Kano with Sarkin Daura." As related below, these Hausa chiefs joined Alwali in the decisive battle of Dan Yaya, of which Bello says, "The army of Katsina and Daura was defeated and returned home empty handed. The arrival of our messenger Umoru Dallaji coincided with this defeat ... After that when I was fighting Yandoto we met Umoru and his men there and our people from Kano. I gave them a flag and set them to attack Ranko and Awai." (E.J. Arnett, *The Rise of the Sokoto Fulani*, pp. 77–78.)

It is obvious that Sultan Bello's account reverses the chronology of events in the Kano *jihad*. Only by some errors in the ordering of the sheets on which his text was written can the chronology of his account be explained. Thus, his account of the Kano campaign provides no basis for chronological inferences, as E.J. Arnett's inferential date of December 1805 for the Fulani entry into Kano and Mammon Bello's appointment of Suleimanu as their first Emir makes plain (v. Arnett, "History of Sokoto," pp. 23–24 in *idem, The Rise of the Sokoto Fulani*.)

34. S.J. Hogben, *The Muhammadan Emirates of Nigeria*, p. 75. For some confirmation, see Alkali Zangi, *Taqyid al-Akbar*, as related below.

35. My account follows closely the *Taqyid al-Akbar* of Alkali Muhammad Zangi. However Gowers, *Gazetteer of Kano Province*, p. 11, reports that the jihad began by an attack of M. Jamau on the Kano forces at Gammo, after which he retired to Kwozaba. That attack is not reported by Muhammadu Zangi.

36. According to Gowers, *Gazetteer of Kano Province*, p. 11.

37. Presumably it was before this confrontation with M. Bakatsine that Alwali consulted the clerics as reported by Malams Adamu na Ma'aji and Adam Muhammad. After returning

to Kano from the discussion with Bakatsine, Alwali consulted the Limam and Alkali at Kano, as Zangi relates.

38. Having described the battle and the Hausa defeat, the Alkali Zangi writes as follows: "Dan Tunku became a (joined the) Muslim(s) when he saw what had happened. Until then he had been with the Habe." (*Taqyid al-Akbar.*)

39. See E.J. Arnett, "A Hausa Chronicle," *JRAS.* vol. 10, 1911, pp. 166–167; D.M. Last, "A Solution to the Problems of Dynastic Chronology in 19th century Zaria and Kano," *JHSN*, vol. 3, no. 3, 1966, pp. 461–469. There are some difficulties and inconsistencies with the chronology Last proposes for Kano on the basis of dates established for Zazzau. There he says the Hausa chief Ishi'aku (Jatau), who accepted the Shehu's call for reform, received his turban from Dan Zabuwa of Kano in January 1806, and died in November, being succeeded by Makau, who fled Zaria on December 31st, 1808. During his brief reign, Makau was visited by Alwali of Kano from June 1807 until June 1808 (v. Last *op. cit.*, p. 467). Last's dating of Alwali's flight from Kano to "the early rainy season, 1807," i.e. May–June, is consistent with Zangi's account of the campaign in the *Taqyid al-Akbar.* But his statement that Mammon Bello appointed Suleiman as Emir of Kano at Birnin Gada in the "dry season 1805–6" merely repeats Arnett's error, noted above (cf. note 33). This statement is also inconsistent with the *Taqyid al-Akbar* on which Last relies for his chronology of the *jihad* in Kano. On this the Alkali Zangi writes, "when the Habe regime was overthrown, Mamman Bello appointed him (Suleimanu) with a letter from Shehu Usumanu. Mamman Bello met them (the Kano leaders) at Birnin Gada and told them to choose (an Emir). They chose Suleimanu."

On this version, then, the appointment was made after Alwali's defeat at the battle of Dan Yaya; and probably after his flight from Kano, i.e., at the earliest in the dry season of 1806–7, since the Kano Fulani campaigned immediately after their victory at Dan Yaya for four months in Katsina. However, Malam Adamu Na Ma'aji writes (*Ta'rikh Kano*): "When Alwali had been killed, the Fulani (leaders) of Kano came together, all five, and sent to the Shehu Usuman asking him to choose an Emir among them. Shehu said "I won't choose an Emir from among you: but you return home; and whoever entered the town without fighting, let him be the Emir."

Dokaji Alhaji Abubakar writes: "When the Fulani drove Alwali out of Kano, he fled south to the Sarkin Zazzau; but the latter refused to help him. Alwali then returned from Zaria but met with the Fulani forces at Burumburum and was killed. When they had conquered Kano, some of the Fulani went and met the Shehu Usmanu at Gwandu and said they wanted him to appoint a leader for them. He asked who was their Limam." (*Kano ta Dabo Cigari*, p. 49.)

Thus on Zangi's account, Suleimanu was not appointed before Alwali fled Kano, which Last dates as June 1807. On the accounts of M. Adamu and the Dokaji he was not appointed before Alwali's death which Last sets after June 1808. Whether the appointment was further delayed by the leading *jihadis* is an open question as indicated below, given the available data: but Palmer is probably not far out in placing the earliest date for Suleimanu's accession as September 1807. (H.R. Palmer, *Kano Chronicle*, pp. 58–9.) More likely it was after rather than before that date.

40. Alkali Muhammadu Zangi, *Taqyid al-Akbar*. D.M. Last, "A Solution to the Problems of Dynastic Chronology in 19th Century Zaria and Kano," *JHSN*, Vol. 3, No. 3, 1966, p. 464, appears to date Agumbil's (Agunbulu's) active participation to the early dry season of 1806, i.e. November 1806–February 1807. Agumbil's Tuareg also supported the Gobir Hausa against the Shehu's community; see E.J. Arnett, *The Rise of the Sokoto Fulani*, p. 51.

41. Alkali Muhammadu Zangi, *Taqyid al-Akbar*. It is unlikely that 'Mai-Duniya' here denotes the Shehu Usman, his son, Mammon Bello, or Bello's messenger, Umaru Dallaji, since his name is coupled with that of Dan Tunku, to indicate that two former supporters of Alwali had switched sides.

42. E.J. Arnett, *The Rise of the Sokoto Fulani*, pp. 99–100.

43. Ibid., p. 77.

44. W.F. Gowers, *Gazetteer of Kano Province*, p. 11; Alkali Muhammadu Zangi, *Taqyid Al-Akbar*.

45. W.F. Gowers, *Gazetteer of Kano Province*, p. 11; S.J. Hogben, *The Muhammadan Emirates of Nigeria*, p. 75; M. Adamu na Ma'aji, *Ta'rikh Kano* also says the battle at Dan Yaya lasted three days.

46. Alkali Muhammadu Zangi, *Taqyid Al-Akbar*.

47. W.F. Gowers, *Gazetteer of Kano Province*, p. 11.

48. Alkali Muhammadu Zangi, *Taqyid al-Akbar*. Sultan Bello's account of events at Kano immediately after the Fulani victory at Dan Yaya are inconsistent and puzzling. In one place (E.J. Arnett, *The Rise of the Sokoto Fulani*, p. 80) he says that after Alwali had fled to Kano from Dan Yaya, "the Mohammedans marched to Mariki and attacked it. The fighting was severe and they remained there one month. Thence they moved on and camped close to Kano. They had not been there more than a few days when God opened the city to them, and the Sarkin Kano fled to Rano. His cause was lost and the Mohammedans settled in Kano. After that when they heard that (the Hausa) Sarkin Katsina had driven out Umaru Dallaji from the city of Katsina they went forth to his aid ... Then the Sarkin Kano returned from Rano with his people, and when they heard the news of his coming, they set out and met him at Burumburum."

In his preceding account, Bello says, "the arrival of our messenger (at Dan Yaya) coincided with this (Alwali's) defeat, and he (Dallaji) thereupon attacked at once and captured many of the Katsina towns.

"After that when I was fighting Yan Doto, we met Umaru and his men there and our people from Kano. I gave them a flag and set them to attack Ranko and Awai. They captured Awai."

49. Alkali Muhammadu Zangi, *Taqyid al-Akbar*.

50. This agrees with the dates suggested by H.R. Palmer ("The Kano Chronicle," p. 58), by the Dokaji Alhaji Abubakar (*Kano ta Dabo Cigari*, p. 49) and by D.M. Last ("A Solution to the Problems of Daynastic Chronology," p. 467), as well as that implied by W.F. Gowers (*Gazetteer of Kano Province*, pp. 11–12). The dates cited in the text are taken from Muhammadu Zangi's *Taqyid al-Akbar*.

51. D.M. Last, "A Solution to the Problems of Dynastic Chronology," p. 467; Alkali Muhammadu Zangi, Taqyid al-Akbar.

52. H.R. Palmer, *Sudanese Memoirs*, Vol. III, p. 139; oral information from 'sarkin Kano' Abubakar at Maradun, in Maradi, 10 January 1959; on Gumel, see W.F. Gowers, *Gazetteer of Kano Province*, p. 25.

53. For Arnett's dating, see the "History of Sokoto" in his *Rise of the Sokoto Fulani*, pp. 22–23; and also *idem*, *Gazetteer of Sokoto Province*, 1920, pp.2 5–6. For the alternative preferred here, see references in footnote 49, *supra*; also LH, vol. 2, p. 59; and KC, pp. 93–94; and Anon. (?R.M. East) *Labarun Hausawa da Makwabtansu* (Zaria: Northern Nigerian Publishing Co., 1971, 2nd printing), vol. 1, p. 15. "In the third year (after the *hijra* (withdrawal) of Shehu Usman), Kano, Daura and Yan-doto were taken." This text is a Hausa translation of the *Raudat al-afkar* by 'Abd. Al Qadir ibn Al Mustafa, probably completed in 1825, concerning which see Murray Last, *The Sokoto Caliphate* (London: Longmans, 1967), pp. xxxiii–xxxiv. Its English translation by H.R. Palmer, "Western Sudan History," *JRAS*, vol. 15, 1915–6, pp. 261–273, seems to be based on an imperfect text, which for example omits events of "the third year after the Shehu's *Hijra*" in its chronicle of these developments year by year, v. Palmer, *op. cit.*

54. See Wudil District Notebook. According to J.M. Freemantle, "A History of the Region comprising the Katagum Division of Kano Province" *JRAS*, vol. 10, 1911, p. 310: "The Shehu had assigned the conquest of Shira to Dabo (afterwards Sarkin Kano), Mallam Bakatsina, Ubangidda, and Mallam Zara. Malam (Ibrahim) Zaki (who obtained a flag from

the Shehu about A.D. 1807) went to Shira and met Mallam Zara who was the flag-bearer and had taken the town. Mallam Zaki claimed that Shira should be given to him and Mallam Zara gave way. The Fulani Kanawa had had a victorious expedition and went on further west (?), but Mallam Zara died at Shellum and the expedition returned."

It is likely that this M. Zara was a leader of one of the Fulani clerical lineages, localized near Dutse east of Kano, but whether of the Gyenawa, Jelubawa, Bornu Fulani (Zarawa) or Yeligawa, I cannot say. Evidently from Alkali Zangi's account, the Fulani of this region campaigned together under the leadership of M. Bakatsine, while the other *jihadis* fought in the Western districts. Unfortunately we have little information about these Eastern campaigns, beyond their success. Evidently they were effective in preventing the forces of Dutse and Gaya from reinforcing Alwali before and after the battle of Dan Yaya.

55. Concerning Dan Tunku, see W.F. Gowers, *Gazetteer of Kano Province*, p. 28; see also Bello's remarks on Dan Tunku in E.J. Arnett, *The Rise of Sokoto Fulani*, p. 97: At Dan Yaya, "Some of their Fulani kindred joined our folk, followers of the faith. The name of their leader was Dan Tunku: his following was a small one" (p. 77); and following the battle: "When the Sarkin Daura returned to his town, the party who had allied themselves with Shehu attacked Sarkin Daura. Dan Tunku and Musa (later) Sarkin Zazzau aided them" (p. 79).

56. See KC; Hampate Ba, *L'Empire Peul du Macina*, Memoires de l'Institut Francais d'Afrique Noire, (Dakar: IFAN, 196–)

57. Henry Barth, *Travels and Discoveries* (1890 edn.) Vol. 1, p. 299.

58. Dokaji Alhaji Abubakar, *Kano ta Dabo Cigari*, p. 41.

59. Dokaji Alhaji Abubakar, *Kano ta Dabo Cigari*, pp. 45–6, photograph; H. Barth, *Travels and Discoveries* (1890 Edn.), vol. 1, p. 298.

60. M. Hiskett, *"Kitab al-farq"* a work on the Habe kingdoms attributed to 'Uthman dan Fodio," *BSOAS*, Vol. 23, part 3, 1960, pp. 571–2.

61. Ibid.; and the Shehu's *Bayan Wujub al-hijra 'ala'l-ibad* (unpublished text, completed in 1221 A.H. (1806–7 A.D.), especially sections 58–63).

62. See 'Abdullah Ibn Muhammad, *Tazyin al-Waraqat*, p. 108; and his *Tanbihu'l Ikhwan*, translated by H.R. Palmer, "An Early Fulani Conception of Islam" *JRAS*, Vol. 14, 1914, p. 191. For Mamman Bello's views, see E.J. Arnett, *The Rise of the Sokoto Fulani*, p. 51. For the Shehu's categorical statements on this point, see A.D.H. Bivar, "The *Wathiqat Ahl al-Sudan*: A manifesto of the Fulani *jihad*," JAH, Vol. II, No. 2, 1961, pp. 235–243.

63. E.A. Alport, "The Mzab," *JRAI*, vol. 84, 1954, pp. 34–44; and *idem*, "The Annelm," *JRAI*, Vol. 195.

64. For the Shehu's views, see M. Hiskett, "An Islamic tradition of reform," *BSOAS*, Vol. 25, part 3, 1962, pp. 595–596.

65. Alexander Mischlich, "Hausa History," in J.A. Burdon, *Historical Notes on Certain Emirates and Tribes* (London: Waterlow & Sons, 1909), p. 96, says: "Kano remained without a ruler after it had been taken, because Dabo of Dambazau and Sulaimana both disputed their right to the throne." Gowers, *Gazetteer of Kano Province*, p. 12, writes that Suleimanu "was actually appointed by the Shehu in 1809." Oral traditions support this statement.

66. Dokaji Alhaji Abubakar, *Kano ta Dabo Cigari*, p. 49. See also S.J. Hogben, *The Muhammadan Emirates of Nigeria*, p. 76.

67. M. Adamu na Ma'aji, *Ta'rikh Kano*; Alkali Muhammadu Zangi, *Taqyid al-Akbar*, gives an account, cited in footnote 39 *supra*, similar to that of Sultan Bello (in footnotes 33 and 48), but with significant differences of detail.

68. W.F. Gowers, *Gazetteer of Kano Province*, p. 12. At this date, Sokoto was not yet built.

69. C.L. Temple (ed.), *Notes on the Tribes … of Northern … Nigeria* (Lagos: C.M.S. Bookshop, 1922), p. 468.

70. KC, p. 94; LH, Vol. 2, pp. 59–60.

71. E.J. Arnett, *The Rise of the Sokoto Fulani*, p. 86.

72. *Idem*, "History of Sokoto," in E.J. Arnett, *op. cit.*, pp. 23–24; D.M. Last, "A Solution to the Problems of Dynastic Chronology," pp. 464–465.

73. 'Abdullah Ibn Muhammad, *Tazyin al-Waraqat*, pp. 120–1, and footnote 5, p. 120, which dates Abdullahi's departure from the Gobir campaign to October 1807.

74. Ibid., p. 121.

75. Alkali Muhammad Zangi, *Taqyid al Akbar*, Chapter II.

76. Ibid., Chapter 2.

77. E.J. Arnett, *The Rise of the Sokoto Fulani*, p. 86.

78. KC, p. 94; LH, Vol. 2, pp. 59–60.

79. KC, p. 94; LH, vol. 2, pp. 59–60.

80. The Dokaji Abubakar lists Suleimanu as one of the three top pupils of the Shehu Usmanu. See *Kano ta Dabo Cigari*, p. 49.

81. KC, p. 94, footnote.

82. M. Hiskett, '*Kitab al-farq*'; Shehu Usman dan Fodio; *Bayan Wujub al-hijra 'ala'l-ibad*.

83. Dokaji Alhaji Abubakar, *Kano ta Dabo Cigari*, p. 50.

84. Ibid., p. 50.

85. 'Abdullah Ibn Muhammad, *Tazyin al-Waraqat*, p. 120.

86. Ibid., p. 120.

87. Ibid., p. 121.

88. Ibid., pp. 121–122.

89. Alkali Muhammadu Zangi, *Taqyid al-Akbar*, Ch. II.

90. M. Hiskett, '*Kitab al-farq*,' pp. 566–570.

91. KC, p. 94; LH, Vol. 2, p. 60.

92. E.J. Arnett, *Rise of the Sokoto Fulani*, p. 86.

93. Alkali Muhammad Zangi, *Taqyid al-Akbar*, Ch. II.

94. For campaigns by Kano forces at this period across its eastern border, v. J.M. Freemantle, "A History of the region comprising the Katagum Division of Kano Province," *JRAS*, vol. 10, 1911, pp. 305, 310, 315.

95. Dokaji Alhaji Abubakar, *Kano ta Dabo Cigari*, pp. 52–3.

96. One of the most obviously biassed entries in the Chronicle concludes its account of Sule's reign: "Suleimanu sent the Galadima Ibrahim (Dabo) to Zaria to make war. Ibrahim conquered Zaria and took many spoils. He returned to Kano. Suleimanu was angry because of the Galadima's success, and had sinister designs against him when he died himself without having an opportunity of carrying them out." KC, p. 94; LH, Vol. 2, p. 60.

These misrepresentations illustrate the dynastic orientations that inspired the author of this passage. Recollecting that the Chronicle was brought up to date from Alwali's reign at the request of the 5th Fulani emir, Muhammadu Bello (1882–1893), a son of Ibrahim Dabo, this attempt to villify Suleimanu and discredit the Mundubawa is easy to understand and ignore. However several incidental inaccuracies in the passage cited, should be noticed. Dabo was *not* Galadima when he was sent to Zaria. Indeed he was not even in charge of the force sent south. Far from envying Dabo's success and harbouring 'sinister designs against him,' Suleimanu promoted Dabo to be Galadima after his return and probably recommended his succession. Likewise Dabo did not "conquer Zaria," though he did help the Fulani emir of Zaria to victory. On Freemantle's statement that while Galadima, Dabo led a Kano force to assist Dankawa of Shirra in 1814, presumably Dabo's expedition to Zaria and subsequent promotion may have preceded 1814, v. J.M. Freemantle, "A History of the Katagum Division," *JRAS*, Vol. 10, 1911, p. 315.

97. Dokaji Alhaji Abubakar, *Kano ta Dabo Cigari*, pp. 52–53. This account of Dabo Dambazau's refusal of allegiance at Dabo's installation, though based on oral traditions, is also found in M. Adamu na Ma'aji's *Ta'rikh Kano*; see also M. Adam Muhammad, *Ta'rikh Kano* for the same story.

98. See Dokaji Alhaji Abubakar, *Kano ta Dabo Cigari*, p. 53; and M. Adamu na Ma'aji, *Ta'rikh Kano*.

99. KC, p. 95; LH, Vol. 2, p. 61.

100. Dokaji Alhaji Abubakar, *Kano ta Dabo Cigari*, pp. 53–54.

101. M.G. Smith, *The State of Sokoto* (unpublished Ms.).

102. KC, p. 95; LH, vol. 2, p. 61.

103. Dokaji Alhaji Abubakar, *Kano ta Dabo Cigari*, pp. 53; but see W.F. Gowers, *Gazetteer of Kano Province*, p. 12.

104. *Minjibir District Notebook* and oral traditions.

105. See Alkali Muhammad Zangi, *Taqyid al-Akbar*, for this account.

106. v. W.F. Gowers, *Gazetteer of Kano Province*, p. 28. My account of this struggle follows closely that given by Alkali Zangi in his *Taqyid al-Akbar*, supplemented by other information from written and oral sources.

107. Major Denham, Captain Clapperton and Dr. Oudney, *Narrative of Travels and Discoveries in Northern and Central Africa in 1822, 1823, and 1824.* (London: John Murray, 2nd Edn., 1826), Vol. 2, p. 251.

108. Ibid., Vol. 2, pp. 275, 349–353.

109. Ibid., Vol. 2, pp. 356–359.

110. For accounts of this campaign, see J.M. Freemantle, "A History of ... the Katagum Division," *JRAS*, vol. 10, 1911, pp. 317–319; Dokaji Alhaji Abubakar, *Kano ta Dabo Cigari*, pp. 54–55; Al-Hajj Sa'id, *Ta'rikh Sokoto*, translated by C.E.J. Whitting (Kano: Ile-Olu Printing Works, n.d.) pp. 9–11; S.J. Hogben and A.H.M. Kirk-Greene, *The Emirates of Northern Nigeria* (London: Oxford University Press, 1966) pp. 457–459.

111. Alkali Muhammadu Zangi, *Taqyid al-Akbar*, Ch. 3.

112. KC, p. 95; LH, Vol. 2, p. 61.

113. For some examples, see KC, p. 95; LH, Vol. 2, p. 62.

114. Oral data and *District Note Books*, Gaya, Dutse, Kano, Birnin Kudu, Karaye, Kiru.

115. Oral traditions and Suma'ila *District Note Book*.

116. KC, p. 95; LH, vol. 2, p. 61; Dokaji Alhaji Abubakar, *Kano ta Dabo Cigari*, p. 53.

117. See D.M. Last, "A Solution to the Problems of Dynastic Chronology ... " p. 468. The oral tradition was given by the Hausa 'sarkin Kano' Abubakar at Maradun in Maradi, Niger, on January 10th, 1959.

118. See Dokaji Alhaji Abubakar, *Kano ta Dabo Cigari*, pp. 45–6.

119. M. Hiskett, "Kitab al-farq," *BSOAS*, Vol. 23, part 3, 1960, pp. 558–579; A.D.H. Bivar, "The Wathiqat ahl al-Sudan: A Manifesto of the Fulani jihad," *JAH*, vol. II, no. 2, 1961, pp. 235–243; H.R. Palmer, "An Early Fulani Conception of Islam," *JRAS*, vol. 13, 1914, pp. 407–414; vol. 14, 1915, pp. 53–59, 185–192.

120. For a general discussion of this classification and its effects, see M.G.Smith, "Historical and Cultural Conditions of Political Corruption among the Hausa," *Comparative Studies in Society and History*, vol. 6, no. 2, January 1964, pp. 170–184, 193–4.

121. 'Abdallah Ibn Muhammad, *Tazyin Al-Waraqat*, p. 122.

122. Denham, Clapperton and Oudney, *Travels and Discoveries ... 1822–24*, (1826 edition) vol 2, p. 244.

123. Ibid., vol. 2, p. 243.

124. Ibid., vol. 2, p. 243.

125. Ibid., vol. 2, p. 253.

126. Ibid., vol. 2, p. 252. Concerning the 'fifteenth' gate, the Kofar Na'Isa, which was made in Suleimanu's reign, see Dokaji Alhaji Abubakar, *Kano ta Dabo Cigari*, p. 52.

127. Denham, Clapperton and Oudney, 1826, vol. 2, p. 253.

128. Ibid., vol. 2, pp. 270–271.

129. Ibid., vol. 2, p. 274.

130. Ibid., vol. 2, p. 275.

131. Ibid., vol. 2, p. 353.

132. Ibid., vol. 3, p. 355.

133. Ibid., vol. 2, pp. 356–357.

134. Hugh Clapperton, *Journal of a Second Expedition into the Interior of Africa* (London: John Murray, 1829), pp. 215–6. As regards Clapperton's report of the Kano tax on date trees, see H. Barth, *Travels and Discoveries* (1890 Edn.) vol. 1, pp. 309–10.

135. Ibid., p. 222.

136. Al-Hajj Sa'id, *Ta'rikh Sokoto* (translated by C.E.J. Whitting) p. 4.

137. Ibid., p. 24; Murray Last, *The Sokoto Caliphate* (London: Longmans, 1969) p. 84.

138. Al-Hajj Sa'id, *Ta'rikh Sokoto* (translated by C.E.J. Whitting), p. 28.

139. Ibid., p. 28.

140. Henry Barth, *Travels and Discoveries* (1890 Edn.) vol. 1, pp. 290–291.

141. Ibid., vol. 1, p. 290. See also Dokaji Alhaji Abubakar, *Kano ta Dabo Cigari*, p. 55: by Shekara, Dabo had five sons, Usuman, Abdusallame, Abdullahi, Muhammadu Bello, Hassan, and two daughters, Fatsumata Zara and Zaretu.

142. KC, p. 96; LH, vol. 2, p. 62.

143. Henry Barth, *Travels and Discoveries* (1890 Edn.) vol. 1, pp. 290–311,315, 317.

144. Ibid., vol. 1, p. 317.

145. This account summarises oral information, the narratives of Malam Adamu na Ma'aji, *Ta'rikh Kano*, the *Taqyid al-Akbar* of Alkali Muhammadu Zangi, and stories collected by Koelle and reproduced in D.H. Olderogge, *Zapadnyi Sudan* (Moscow: 1960) pp. 163–168.

146. For accounts of the succession struggles at Hadeija and Buhari's succession, see W.F. Gowers, *Gazetteer of Kano Province*, pp. 22–23; S.J. Hogben and A.M. Kirk-Greene, *The Emirates of Northern Nigeria*, pp 485–489; Al-Hajj Sa'id, *Ta'rikh Sokoto* (translated by C.E.J. Whitting), pp. 28–9; Henry Barth, *Travels and Discoveries* (1890 Edn.) vol. 1, p. 323; vol. 2, pp. 172–3, 507; and M. Jirgi, Dan Galadiman Hadeija, *Sarkin Arewan Hadeija, Tattagana* (Zaria: NORLA, n.d.) 3 vols.

147. Henry Barth, *Travels and Discoveries* (1890 Edn.) vol. 1, pp. 286–310, vol. 2, pp. 501–507.

148. Ibid., vol. 1, pp. 295–297.

149. Ibid., vol. 1, pp. 299–300, 309.

150. Ibid., vol. 1, pp. 300–301.

151. Ibid., vol. 1, pp. 300–309.

152. Ibid., vol. 1, p. 309.

153. Ibid., vol. 1, p. 309.

154. Ibid., vol. 2, p. 165.

155. Ibid., vol. 2, p. 172.

156. Ibid., vol. 1, p. 309.

157. Ibid., vol. 1, p. 309.

158. Ibid., vol. 1, p. 301.

159. Ibid., vol. 1, p. 291.

160. Ibid., vol. 1, pp. 286, 295, 303, and vol. 2, p. 506.

161. Ibid., vol. 1, p. 289.

162. Ibid., vol. 1, p. 294.

163. Ibid., vol. 1, p. 290.

164. Ibid., vol. 1, p. 310.

165. See M.G. Smith, *The State of Sokoto* (unpublished ms.)

166. H. Barth, *Travels and Discoveries* (1890 Edn.) vol. 1, p. 309.

5

Two Sons of Dabo

Abdullahi, 1855–1882

The Succession

On returning to Kano from the Hadeija campaign, Abdullahi continued to administer the government from the palace as he had done in Usuman's reign. Under the traditional Hausa constitution of Kano, during the interregnum between the death of one chief and the installation of another, the senior Limam had formal charge of the government of the country and its capital. However, though Abdullahi may have recognised the Limam's formal regency, he administered the state routinely while awaiting the vizier, and thus kept control of its affairs and resources firmly in his hands.

To justify his conduct, Abdullahi could plead the threat to Kano posed by the attacks of Tanimu, the new Kanuri chief of Damagaram (Zinder) due north. In 1854–5 Tanimu brought his army against Kandi and Garun Gidinya in northern Kano. Fortunately, that year the water-table was unusually high, and the northern districts marshy. Tanimu's cavalry were thus bogged down and unable to deal with counter-attacking foot soldiers, who exploited the local terrain. Tanimu lost hundreds of horses, men and weapons in that *Yakin Ruwa* (War of Water),[1] but determined to square the account shortly. Abdullahi accordingly awaited another assault from Damagaram at this time.

The Waziri of Sokoto, who administered Kano's affairs for the caliph, was then Abdulkadiri, the son of Gidado; but to supervise Kano directly, Abdulkadiri had selected his son and successor, Ibrahim Halilu, and invested him with the title of Dangaladiman Waziri.[2] On arriving at Kano, the Waziri directed the princes and rulers of Kano to assemble at the city mosque. From conversation with the Waziri and from other sources, the Galadima Abdullahi inferred that he had not been selected by the caliph to succeed Usuman. Two possibilities were rumoured, namely Abdullahi's brother, the Turaki Abdusallami, and another Abdusallami of the Mundubawa dynasty. Abdullahi, who had long effectively governed Kano and was recently ruler in all but name, decided that he would not accept such treatment lightly. He prepared his cavalry, buckled on his arms, and proceeded to the mosque with spear and sword, flanked by his slaves in armour.

Following normal practice, the Waziri bore two letters from the caliph.³ The first consisted simply of a general greeting and invoked Allah's blessing upon the assembly. It served to identify the bearer as the caliph's chief minister, the Waziri of Sokoto. In this letter, the caliph also commiserated with the Muslims of Kano on the recent death of their emir. The second letter named the individual the caliph had selected to succeed as emir of Kano. When Abdullahi entered the mosque and greeted the vizier, the Waziri directed him to have a seat. However, Abdullahi refused, and stood with his hand on his sword. Someone nearby, probably a client or slave, warned the vizier what they were about. Waziri Abdulkadiri assured Abdullahi that he was the chosen emir; but when the scribe (Magatakarda) Mohammadu Jalli moved to read the second letter to the assembly, Abdullahi's slaves reacted quickly. It is said that one of the Waziri's attendants was killed or hurt on the spot. The Waziri was required to read the letter himself, and Abdullahi was duly nominated as the new emir without any sign of opposition from the assembly. He then settled himself on the dais reserved for the emir.

This incident is omitted both from the Kano Chronicle and from the Alkali Zangi's history of Kano. The Dokaji Abubakar alludes to it delicately, and suggests that the scribe Jalli and the Waziri may have intended to misconstrue the caliph's letter.⁴ Jalli was certainly suspected by Abdullahi's supporters of ill intentions; but the caliph's letter, bearing his imperial seal, may well have nominated some other prince than Abdullahi. Malam Adamu Na Ma'aji, who describes this event in detail, says that Abdullahi took the letter from the Waziri immediately the latter had read the passage announcing his nomination. According to oral traditions, Abdullahi tore it up in public, putting the pieces in his pocket, and certainly the letter was never made public. There is little reason to doubt the oral account. This incident took place in full view of a highly alert and interested audience at the city mosque. Its unusual features are too prominent and numerous to be easily mistaken. Abdullahi gave the Wazirin Sokoto the caliph's portion of Usuman's estate, together with valuable gifts for himself, and moved to the palace.

It is possible that the individual named in the caliph's letter was Abdusallami, but whether Abdullahi's brother, the San Turaki, or the Mundubawa prince, we cannot say. The Waziri may have been persuaded to select the baMundube Abdusallami by Mohammed Jalli, who probably saw an opportunity to reap great reward from such an appointment, but Malam Adamu writes that caliph Aliyu Babba had selected the baMundube Abdusallami himself. Nonetheless, the Waziri's replacement of Abdusallami's name or some other by Abdullahi under the latter's open threat of revolt was quite legitimate. As Waziri of Sokoto, Abdulkadiri exercised a wide discretionary power on behalf of the caliph; and in emergencies like this, he had full authority to take such actions as he felt appropriate on his own initiative, with reasonable assurance of the caliph's support. When on tour in the eastern provinces, the vizier "carried ... papers already stamped with the caliphal seal to fill in the appropriate appointments or deposition."⁵ Thus the vizier was indeed the appropriate target for Abdullahi's pressure in the mosque at Kano.

Abdulkadiri probably gave in to Abdullahi because he feared the political repercussions throughout the empire if Kano followed Hadeija's example, its ruler seized the throne and repudiated his allegiance to Sokoto, rather than for his own safety. Abdullahi controlled the greatest body of support and force within Kano at this date. To reject his explicit demand for the succession almost certainly threatened Kano with civil war, and the Sokoto empire with disaster if not collapse. An outlawed Abdullahi could be expected to ally himself with the redoubtable Buhari and Bornu, thereby removing Kano from the empire, at least temporarily, and dislocating the imperial structure, its finances, communications and military organisation. Set against this, the price that Abdullahi demanded for Kano's continued loyalty was relatively small; and he had long shown his fitness for the role he sought. To his credit, the Waziri Abdulkadiri, without pusillanimity or pride, appraised the situation swiftly, realistically and in its wider implications. Having appointed Abdullahi, Abdulkadiri remained a while in Kano to settle him in his office, and returned to Sokoto where the caliph Aliyu Babba welcomed him heartily, having already learned of the affair and Abdulkadiri's wise response. Not long afterwards, to publicise his regard, Aliyu Babba gave the vizier Abdulkadiri his daughter Saudatu as a bride; and many years later Abdulkadiri's son by Saudatu, Muhammadu Adili, succeeded to his father's office.

Though mentioned in none of the published histories, according to Kano traditions Abdullahi later faced the risk of deposition on at least two and possibly three occasions. From Sokoto we learn that he was once summoned by the caliph Aliyu Babba to bring his forces to meet him at Katsina city, which Aliyu often used as a convenient base and marshalling point for attacks on Gobir and Maradi. This was to be Abdullahi's first meeting with the caliph since his unorthodox accession. Aliyu was already in Katsina when Abdullahi came with his contingent and instructed them to quarter in the town. Following obligatory practice, Adullahi then went himself to Aliyu's quarters to pay his respects. He was shown a hall in which to await the caliph's summons, but none came for several hours. Then, in mid afternoon at *azahar*, (the 2:30 p.m. prayer), Aliyu sent an order to Abdullahi to move his troops outside the city to some villages nearby. Abdullahi obeyed and withdrew himself from Katsina.

Three days later Aliyu summoned him to come at once without an escort. Abdullahi obeyed and found Aliyu sitting in an inner hall of the Katsina palace among his senior councillors. It is said that Abdullahi presented himself, sat down, and greeted the caliph humbly. After a pause, Aliyu remarked three times, "Abdullahi, you seized the throne by force," ("*Ka ci da karfe*"), to which Abdullahi astutely replied, "I took it with your blessing (approval)," ("*Na ci da albarkarka*"). Aliyu then asked Abdullahi why he had camped outside the town. Abdullahi replied that he had been ordered to do so. Aliyu then asked why Abdullahi had come to see him. Abdullahi replied that he had been ordered to do so. On this, Aliyu said, "Then why did you remain in the Gidan Rumfa (palace) after Usuman had died?" Abdullahi apologised and attempted to excuse himself. Aliyu then sent to Kano, ordering the non-royal state councillors to Katsina at once. On their arrival, he consulted with them about Abdullahi's accession; and it is said that, having learned of their support for Abdullahi, Aliyu Babba had him formally "crowned" at the Gidan Korau, the palace in Katsina, either before or immediately on their return from the campaign at Maradi. Aliyu then presented Abdullahi with his eldest daughter as a bride and symbol of his forgiveness and goodwill.[6]

While it is known that Abdullahi did, on one occasion, meet Aliyu at Katsina for a joint campaign against Maradi, shortly after his accession, and probably in 1856,[7] this tradition is not known at Kano, and understandably, since Abdullahi was alone at these exchanges with caliph Aliyu, and the latter did not inform the councillors he consulted of the immediate background of his enquiries. Its probability is nonetheless fairly high. As minister for Katsina, the Galadima of Sokoto, from whom this tradition derives, probably remained beside Aliyu throughout that week. We seem here to have the account of Aliyu's first meeting with his most powerful subordinate, relayed by an informed eye-witness to his son. The procedure Aliyu employed on this occasion is very much in character with his procedure on others.[8]

Aliyu had simultaneously to reassure himself of Abdullahi's willing submission, to reprimand him, to strengthen his loyalty to Sokoto, and, with Buhari's revolt at Hadeija in mind, to discourage further usurpations of chiefship at Kano. His peculiar orders to Abdullahi, and deliberate discourtesy in refusing initially to acknowledge his presence and grant him an audience, were calculated tests of Abdullahi's attitude and loyalty. Not long before Aliyu Babba had been constrained to remove Sidiku, then emir of Katsina, for arrogantly rejecting that authority; and at about the same time, Buhari of Hadeija had repudiated his allegiance to Sokoto. Kano lay directly between Katsina and Hadeija. Abdullahi having seized the throne of Kano, the caliph needed to know definitely where he stood. The acid test of Abdullahi's loyalty and confidence in the caliph's good will was the order that he should come to Katsina city to see Aliyu alone and unescorted. In the prevailing context, this could easily be interpreted as a sentence of deposition. We have seen how Usuman tricked the Sarkin Dutse Muhammadu Bello to visit Kano on the pretext of proceeding to Sokoto, thereby leading Dutse to his death. Such practices were common. Had Abdullahi harboured any suspicions or disloyal designs, he would never have dared to place himself thus powerless in the caliph's hands, while surrounded by the flower of the Kano army. Instead he might simply have ordered them homewards and prepared for war. Aliyu Babba thus imposed his authority where the Waziri had failed; but wisely, following his vizier's example, he legitimised Abdullahi's appointment, after the senior councillors of Kano had reaffirmed their support for him. By these means, Aliyu simultaneously sought to erase the dangerous precedent set by Abdullahi's seizure of power and to eliminate the anomalous situation that had produced by publicly appointing Abdullahi as emir despite his initial assumption of the title through force. As usual, Aliyu Babba showed consummate political skill in handling a delicate situation.

The Ningi Campaigns

Abdullahi's early years on the throne were mainly devoted to repelling attacks from Zinder and Gumel in the northeast, and to the Ningi, whose attacks were now increasingly severe. In 1857 Tanimu of Zinder launched his second attack on Kano and sacked Duguyawa, before turning north to sack Kazaure and kill the emir Dambo, Dan Tunku's son, whose submission and vassalage were probably the prime objects of Tanimu's campaign.[9] Thereafter Damagaram left Kano in peace for more than thirty years.

Usuman's lassitude had given the Ningi excellent opportunities to organise their chiefdom and armies for aggression and defense. In 1855, the year of Abdullahi's accession, they penetrated within twenty miles of Kano city in a highly successful raid. However, on their homeward route they were waylaid at Tugugu by the Sarkin Rano Aliyu with all his forces. The Ningi lost most of their booty and many men in that engagement. Two years later they attacked Rano, defeating and slaying the Sarkin Rano Aliyu in an ambush at Rantam. Farther east they attacked Gwaram and ravaged the surrounding area. In 1856 Suma'ila and surrounding towns, Dutse and its dependencies, Rano, Burumburum and theirs, all suffered Ningi attacks in which crops and settlements were destroyed and many were seized as slaves. In 1860, they wiped out the recently founded town at Tudun Wada.[10]

On Barth's reckoning, Abdullahi was probably about 40 years old on his accession.[11] Following the example of his father Dabo, he determined to prove a hardy fighter for Islam; and whereas Usuman only went to war himself when ordered by the caliph, like Dabo, Abdullahi spent most of his early years as emir away from Kano on his Ningi campaigns.

Perhaps Abdullahi's most impressive early act was the summary execution without trial of Usuman's senior slave, the Shamaki Isa. During Usuman's reign, Abdullahi may have experienced some insult or obstruction at Shamaki's hands; or he may have suspected the Shamaki of opposing his accession. We know only that Abdullahi ordered Isa's execution almost immediately he moved to the palace, but we do not know the reasons or circumstances of this act. Such a start could hardly fail to impress throne slaves and palace staff with the personality and power of their new chief. To replace Isa, Abdullahi appointed Maigari, his personal slave, a man from Bebeji; and on Maigari's death many years later, Abdullahi appointed Maiyaki, the former Ciroman Shamaki, a court usher, to succeed.

Together the Alkali Zangi and the Kano Chronicle give many details of Abdullahi's Ningi wars. "The Sarkin Kano was eager to make war upon Umbatu. His first move was to attack Kuluki. Dan Iya Lowal of Kano raided Kuluki, whereupon the Sarki returned home himself."[12] Some years later, Abdullahi

built a house at Takai for the war with Umbatu. He had a house at Keffin Bako where he lived almost two years because of Dan Maji, the neighbour of Umbatu. He fought with Warji after ... Kuluki, and took enormous spoils ... After a short time, the Sarki attacked Warji again, and once more took many spoils. Kano was filled with slaves. Abdullahi went to Sokoto leaving his son Yusufu at Takai. While he was there Dan Maji came to attack Yusufu. A battle was fought at Dubaiya. The Kanawa fled and deserted Yusufu. Many men were slain and captured ... After this Yusufu was made Galadiman Kano, and hence acquired much power. Abdullahi sent him to Dal from Takai to capture Haruna, the son of Dan Maji. Yusufu met Haruna at Jambo, and a battle took place. The Umbutawa ran away deserting Haruna ... About seven hundred were killed. Afterwards Yusufu tried to stir up rebellion and was deprived of his office and had to remain in chagrin and poverty till he was penniless ... At Woso, he (Abdullahi) met Dan Maji in war. It was towards evening when the battle was fought. Dan Maji retreated. If it had not been that the light failed he would have been killed. Abdullahi attacked Betu but failed.[13]

The Alkali Zangi gives a detailed account of Abdullahi's Ningi campaigns for three or four years. Internal evidence suggests that Zangi accompanied Abdullahi much of the time. Thus the date of his completed text, 6th Zulkida, 1281 A.H., places the campaigns he describes before 1864,[14] and most probably between 1859 and 1863, when Buhari had reduced his earlier attacks on Kano, Tanimu of Damagaram had withdrawn his pressure, and the raids by Sarkin Gumel Cheri in the northeast had been repulsed.[15] By then the Ningi were raiding freely in Bauchi, Kano and Hadeija. The emir of Bauchi having failed to bring them to a decisive battle, Abdullahi attempted to do so by fortifying several towns on their route northwestwards to Kano.

For two years he seems to have been mainly concerned with setting up strong points (*ribadu*) at Suma'ila, where he installed his Arab client, Juma, as chief, at Tudun Wada, Falali, Matugwai, Birnin Bako (formerly the Keffin Bako of the Chronicle), and at Takai. Meanwhile, Abdullahi assembled a substantial army to garrison this area under the practice of *zaman ribadi*, by which border towns were garrisoned as military colonies for defense. Abdullahi then asked his neighbour, the emir of Bauchi Ibrahim, to attack the Ningi, Warjawa, Ajawa and their allies from the rear, and drive them northwestwards out of their rocky fastnesses within reach of his troops. He himself sent forces into Ningi country, besieging and burning their towns and crops, to bring them to battle.

The active front stretched about seventy miles from Birnin Bako eastwards to Gwaram and Fagam, where the people supported the Ningi against their chiefs. Fagam was over-run and its elders slaughtered, the Warjawa and Gwaram were overawed.[16] Ningi crops were destroyed, and on occasion Abdullahi simply ringed the Ningi rocks with his army and laid siege till they ran short of supplies. At Tufi the armies of Kano and Dan Maje fought a strenuous engagement for two or three days. Joined by the Bauchi forces at Banga, Abdullahi attacked the Ningi capital, but found it deserted; on learning that Dan Maje had attacked Garun Ali, 45 miles northwest, Abdullahi moved quickly to relieve the town, and garrisoned Falali to the southeast, where he spent the next three years, until summoned to Sokoto. Much booty was taken, but when Abdullahi returned homewards the Ningi were as active as ever; and against less cautious generals they were often very successful.

In July 1862 Dr. W.B. Baikie, seeking to recover the lost journals of Barth's companions, Vogel and Overweg, visited Kano where he was "well received by the Sarin Saru (Sarkin Shanu), brother of the king who was absent at war camp in the southeast."[17] Evidently the Sarkin Shanu acted as head of the government at Kano during Abdullahi's long absence on campaign. Baikie proceeded to Takai only to find that Abdullahi was at Tsangaya, six miles northeast. He received Baikie kindly and took him along to Dutse for "a grand review of his army."[18] Baikie found the entire southeastern district heavily fortified. Dawaki, then containing from sixteen hundred to two thousand inhabitants, was fortified with two ditches and four gates; Girku was walled with two ditches, and had three to four thousand inhabitants; Sarina, walled with two ditches, contained a thousand inhabitants; Takai, walled with a double ditch, had fifteen hundred, and Tsangaya the same. Dutse, with both a wall and a stockade several miles in circumference, had about two thousand five hundred people. Gaya was walled with two ditches and contained four thousand people.[19] Abdullahi had wisely attempted to strengthen the area by concentrating population in walled settlements within striking distance of one another.

When Abdullahi withdrew to Kano the Ningi resumed their attacks. In 1864, they ambushed the chief of Birnin Kudu, south of Dutse, slew him and destroyed his force.[20] They repeatedly attacked Rano, Gwaram and Dutse, while avoiding the cluster of forts Abdullahi had set up between Birnin Bako, Suma'ila and Takai. In 1868 Abdullahi sent his Madaki Isma'ilu, the son of Madaki Umaru, and the Sarkin Dutse Suleimanu, with an army against them. At Fajewa near Falali, the army was destroyed and both leaders were killed. Abdullahi replaced the Madaki by Isma'ilu's brother Hassan, and appointed another baJelbe, Ibrahimu, of the Dutse ruling family. It was probably at this time that he sent his son, the Ciroma Yusufu, to take command of the campaign in this area. Yusufu's initial defeat and later successes have been sketched above; but the Ningi were never brought under control by Kano armies at any time.

Operating in a country where massed forces and cavalry were at a disadvantage, they also enjoyed the support of many Kano people, free and slave, who relayed information to them about Fulani movements and plans, freely or under duress. Hardened by long years of fighting, they had learned much on the way. Their leadership and morale under Dan Maje, Malam Hamza's son, and Haruna were excellent. Biding their time, they struck heavily where least expected. In 1873 they wiped out Tudun Wada once more, and by 1880 they had attached Kila as well as Fegam to their cause. In 1882 the combined forces of Hadeija and Katagum were ambushed and routed while marching against them.[21] Thereafter the Ningi raided Zaria and Bauchi as they pleased, devastating northern Zaria and penetrating to the capital. They also maintained an active interest in southeastern Kano; but thanks to Abdullahi's fortification, they rarely broke through into the central districts of the chiefdom again. Thus, although he failed to break their resistance, Abdullahi preserved Fulani rule over southeastern Kano by forcing the Ningi to avoid its strategic and vulnerable centres of dense population.

Maradi and Zaria

Besides Ningi attacks in the southeast, Abdullahi had also to defend Kano against the Hausa chief of Maradi, Dan Baskore, a formidable raider who had reduced Sokoto's returns from Zamfara and Katsina by raiding them for many years, and who then began to direct his attention south-eastwards to Kano.[22] In the early 1870s Dan Baskore raided Karaye twice, nearly taking the town on his first visit and sacking the village of Karshi on the second. In the interval Dan Baskore attacked Gwarzo and besieged it for two days. Abdullahi, by then too old for combat, sent the Madaki Hassan and the Sarkin Dawaki Dan Ladan against him. In the ensuing battle, Dan Baskore routed the Kano forces and slew both leaders. He then seized Godiya, formerly under the Dan Tama.[23] On later raids he attacked Kiru and Gwarzo again.

The Maradawa raids differed from Ningi attacks in being primarily cavalry affairs. Moving southwards along the borders between Katsina and Kano, the

Maradawa exploited political geography to their military advantage, striking swiftly inwards to targets in either emirate before adequate forces could be fielded against them. Often they ranged deep in one emirate to promote its mobilisation while their main target lay in the other. As a variation, they frequently moved along the boundary south to Zaria, leaving Kano and Katsina untroubled. As Hausa and inveterate enemies of the Fulani, they easily secured information about their enemy's strength and preparation. Fortunately for Abdullahi, before the Ningi menace emerged, Buhari of Hadeija and the people of Gumel had shifted their attention from Kano, though raiding periodically and besieging various towns in the east. Likewise, before the Maradawa directed their raids at western Kano, the Ningi had begun to shift their attention from Kano to Bauchi and Zaria. In short, Kano was not faced with these three aggressive foes simultaneously; yet even had this happened, it is unlikely that Buhari, the Ningi and Dan Baskore could have coordinated their attacks.

Of their attackers, the Kano Fulani had most to fear from the Ningi, on political as well as military grounds. Buhari of Hadeija, despite his ruthlessness and military skill, was identified as a brigand chief, a Fulani apostate (*kahiri*). He might kill and capture Fulani or "Habe" in Kano; but he could not expect their support. The Maradawa, although Hausa, were Katsinawa by origin; and their chief bore the title, Sarkin Katsina. Being Hausa, they could expect little Fulani support; and as Katsinawa, they remained suspect to the Kano "Habe," many of whom regarded the Ningi with sympathy, since their leaders were Hausa malams driven from Kano by Fulani oppression to organise the Ningi for effective defense. For these reasons Ningi victories spread hope among the "Habe" of Kano and alarmed the ruling Fulani. Abdullahi correctly assessed the critical danger of Ningi penetration into the home districts. Hence his thorough fortification along the routes from the frontier; and on returning to Kano in 1863–4 he left a garrison of slave and free troops at Birnin Bako under his slave general, the Jekadan Garko. The "Habe" of Kano meanwhile took keen interest in the Ningi struggle; but given their fragmentation under Fulani village chiefs this generated no revolt.

Despite his heavy military engagements in southeastern Kano, the Chronicle relates that Abdullahi sent "Sarkin Dawaki Dan Ladan and his son Tafida to war in Zaria country. They went to Zaria together. This was in the time of Sarkin Zaria Adullahi Dan Hamada,"[24] who ruled Zaria initially from 1856–1870 and again from 1873–1878.[25] Unfortunately, I do not know whether the Kano force visited Zaria during the emir's first or second reign, nor whether they went to fight or to help the Fulani of Zaria. The latter did have some need of assistance against the Ningi; but it is more likely that the Sarkin Kano Abdullahi sent troops against his namesake in Zaria, who reported the incursion to the caliph, and kept his own forces out of the way until the Kano troops were recalled by orders from Sokoto.

It is possible that this expedition to Zaria arose from the conflict of the two Abdullahis about their respective rights to tax and administer those Fulani pastoralists who crossed over (*ketare*) their common frontiers. The conflict, which is well remembered at Kano, Katsina and Sokoto, was finally referred to the caliph for resolution. As mentioned above, from Hausa days at Kano, pastoral Fulani had been administered under the immediate jurisdiction of their headmen, irrespective of seasonal migration, until they shifted their wet season headquarters to an adjoining emirate and made their formal allegiance to its ruler. As we have seen, this mobile jurisdiction, known as *bin kanu* or *bin Fulani*—that is, "following heads" or "following Fulani"—antedated the *jihad* and provided Hausa territorial chiefs with a flexible means for the continuous administration of their resident pastoralists. However, at Zaria, this arrangement seems to have been unknown, probably because, being relatively wet and infested with tsetse-fly, Zaria is less suited for wet-season homesteads than the dry Sahilian areas further north. Accordingly, Zaria has always had a relatively small population of resident Fulani. Lacking adequate numbers of resident Fulani, the chiefs of Zaria, besides levying tithe or tax on local pastoralists, also taxed those Fulani who moved southwards to Zaria to graze there in the dry season.

Most of these migrant bands came into northeastern Zaria from Karaye, Rano, and remoter parts of Kano. Fulani herdsmen from Katsina , following a similar pattern of southern transhumance, tended at this time to move west of Zaria through Birnin Gwari into the northern areas of Niger province. Thus pastoralists subject to the grazing tax in Zaria were mainly Fulani from Kano. Having already paid tithe in stock at Kano, some resisted the imposts levied on them in Zaria, while those who accepted the demands of the territorial chief whose frontiers they had crossed, paid their dues in cash as *jangali*, thus reviving the practice which Shehu Usuman had condemned, perhaps for the same reasons that initially produced it. Some Fulani who resisted the officials sent to levy *jangali* on them were probably manhandled and imprisoned, or may have had their cattle seized. On returning northwards, some of these Kano Fulani complained through their appointed chiefs to the Sarkin Kano and appealed for his assistance. Abdullahi of Kano proceeded to demand restitution from his namesake in Zaria in order to protect and retain his pastoral subjects.

Directly and without initial reference to Sokoto, the two chiefs contested their claims. Abdullahi at Zaria could claim the right to tax any Fulani entering his territory. Abdullahi at Kano could claim freedom from further taxation for all Fulani who had already paid the statutory tithe on their cattle to his agents in Kano. The exclusive territorial claims of the southern chief denied Kano's jurisdiction over any pastoralists who entered Zaria territory from Kano. Since his juridical claims over these Kano pastoralists were rejected by his namesake in Zaria who continued to levy *jangali* on incoming bands, Abdullahi may have sent an armed force to Zaria to indicate his objections and determination to protect the Kano pastoralists against levies in Zaria. The Sarkin Zazzau then appealed to the Waziri and caliph; and when the matter was finally brought to the caliph's court at Sokoto, the issue was decided in Zaria's favour on the grounds that Zaria state had few Fulani and inadequate revenues.[26]

Its chief was therefore permitted to levy cash taxes on incoming pastoralists who were free to avoid these by going elsewhere. Zaria and other southern emirates with small Fulani populations were thus allowed to assert their territorial jurisdiction over all pastoralists within their boundaries, while the more northerly states, such as Sokoto, Gwandu, Zamfara, Katsina, Kano, Hadeija and Daura, were required to practice reciprocal *bin kanu*, so that pastoralists could roam across them as their herds required, without thereby changing their political alle-

giances or falling subject to additional taxation and new jurisdictions on crossing
state boundaries. Indeed, ecological differences between the tsetse-free sahil with
its open savannahs and fine pasturage and the wetter, southern Sudan which the
pastoralists avoided for homesteading, seemed to require such different administrative arrangements for the supervision and taxation of pastoral Fulani. Before
the *jihad* the same geographical factors may have stimulated that *jangali* taxation
of migrant pastoralists who had already paid tithes against which the Shehu
Usuman protested. Only an extensive polity that embraced most of the pastoralists' terrain could provide a framework in which these problems could be
handled in administrative terms. Though there is no evidence to show that this
jurisdictional dispute was the issue which led Abdullahi to send his troops to
Zazzau, circumstantial data from various states suggest that it may have been,
and the issue is of sufficient interest to justify discussion.

The Governments of Abdullahi and Usuman

Abdullahi's long reign and extensive campaigns facilitated further changes in
the power and status of the chiefship, and thus in the structure of the political
system at Kano. By 1835 Dabo had clearly established his predominance; but his
incessant campaigning was then past. Having established supremacy, Dabo proceeded to consolidate it by associating the senior Fulani leaders with his government, while reviving the old state council in a modified form. By sheer inactivity
Usuman had also advanced the institutionalisation of the chiefship as the
supreme executive and juridical office in the land. Usuman's inaction may have
been the situationally appropriate response for a man of his capacities. Lacking
Dabo's energy, incentives and determination , he was content to reap his father's
political harvest, and let things be, except when required to initiate new action by
Sokoto, as, for example, the increase of revenues, or the Hadeija campaign on
which he perished.

By employing his brother as executive vizier while formulating policy
through the state councils inherited from Dabo, Usuman also habituated the
Fulani founding lineages in Kano to regard the chiefship as a constitutionally
restricted office that provided leadership and support, although neither was
prominent in his performance. Thus unwittingly Usuman presented the chiefship
to the founding Fulani as an office whose capacities for self-enhancement were
limited by external and internal factors, notably by the caliph's supervision, by
the oligarchy of ruling Fulani, by the conciliar organisation, and by the official
machinery of government. Thus Usuman's regime, while permitting the lassitude
that was his wish, by restricting and routinising the chiefly administration of
Kano emirate, reassured Fulani aristocrats that their status and interests would be
respected and preserved. Under his rule, the chiefship apparently lacked both the
capacity and the desire to subordinate them further. Instead, to restrain his vizier,
Usuman needed the support of his councillors.

Abdullahi had been Usuman's vizier. He had thus already assembled the reins
of power in his hands, though in Usuman's lifetime he exerted little independent
pull upon them. Nonetheless he had accumulated considerable military, political
and economic resources and expertise during Usuman's reign, and some of these
had been mobilised for his forcible assumption of the chiefship. Initially, his acces-

sion changed little. The vizier, formerly the senior prince, had now become the chief; and, being already vizier, Abdullahi continued to exercise those routine administrative functions as well as the discretionary powers he now held as chief. He also maintained the traditions of conciliar government initiated by Dabo and developed by Usuman. Initially, his only public demonstration of arbitrary power was the execution of the Shamaki Isa who, despite his important office, as a slave was legally expendable at his master's discretion. Indeed Abdullahi had little desire to encroach on the rights and powers of his officials or the noble Fulani lineages. His main interest on accession was clearly to assure Kano's security against Gumel, Damagaram, Hadeija and the Ningi; and during his long absence from the capital the government continued routinely as before under the supervision of his brother, the Sarkin Shanu Hassan.

As Abdullahi's deputy, the Sarkin Shanu administered the state on his behalf in close association with those councillors resident at the capital. The capital itself remained directly under the Ma'aji, who discussed its affairs with the Sarkin Shanu. That Abdullahi could leave this caretaker administration in charge of the capital and the state for several years while engaged in his southeastern campaigns, demonstrates the stability and authority the chiefship had developed since the revolt against Dabo. Certainly the Sarkin Shanu Hassan kept in close contact with Abdullahi, and routinely relayed all important or unusual issues for his decision or information. He also took care of Abdullahi's requests, and relayed his orders, with or without consulting the council, as seemed necessary. In Abdullahi's absence the Alkali Datuwa, another baGyeni, administered the *shari'a* at Kano without a superior court at the palace. Probably also before moving southwards, Abdullahi had appointed the first Alkalin Kasuwa with jurisdiction over commercial transactions and petty suits arising at the Kano market, while reserving all major issues (*manyan shari'a*) for the senior Alkali's court. It is known that Abdullahi first established this office at Kano, but whether he appointed the first Alkalin Kasuwa before or after 1860 remains obscure. During his absence on campaign, legal sentences involving mutilation or execution were routinely referred by mounted messengers to Abdullahi for his consideration and orders. Thus, for this period, the Sarkin Shanu really served as Abdullahi's vizier; but the parallels between Abdullahi's regime and Usuman's were partly due to their differing situations.

There were, however, at least two important differences between the two regimes. In Usuman's day, the chief discussed matters with the council, of which the vizier was a member. During Abdullahi's campaigns, the Sarkin Shanu, acting as vizier, consulted the city council in the chief's absence. The old collegial organ of policy formation was thus apparently restored. At his field headquarters, Abdullahi likewise took counsel with senior officials and clerics; and evidently the future Alkali Zangi, then with the emir, may thus have recommended himself as Datuwa's successor, while acting as a legal consultant. Ever since Shashere's day (1573–1582), the Hausa chiefs of Kano had taken an *alkali* with them on their campaigns.[27] Their Fulani successors, though not specialising an office for this function, such as the Salenke in Zazzau,[28] having reserved to themselves the right to order executions or mutilations, routinely took along trained jurists on campaigns to advise on matters of law, since all important issues were referred to the emir as chief executive for decision. Thus, although the caretaker government at Kano under the Sarkin Shanu was conciliar in form, Abdullahi retained substantive powers of decision and command at his camp. In effect, his independent authority was enhanced by the caretaker regime with its appearance of collegial rule.

A second difference between the governments of Kano during the reigns of Abdullahi and Usuman lay in their attitude to war. Dabo having re-established Kano's frontiers, Usuman had been content to administer the enclosed area with inadequate defensive arrangements. Despite constant harrassments from Gumel, he seems never to have launched or led a major expedition against it. Even the war with Hadeija was undertaken at the caliph's command. With Abdullahi's accession, Kano engaged in a continuous series of defensive campaigns in the north, east, south and west, all of which helped to mobilise the sentiments of the ruling stratum around the emir, who personally led and directed the country's defense. Though the attacks against Kano were widely scattered, severe and recurrent, they demonstrated how sorely each region (*jiha, yanki*) and Fulani segment depended on the rest for its own survival. Thus, in the southeast, Abdullahi was actively defending territory over which the Jobawa exercised primary jurisdiction. In the west and southwest his armies did likewise for the Suleibawa, Yolawa and Danejawa. In the north Dabo had earlier defended and extended the Dambazawa interests against Dan Tunku. In the east Abdullahi's forces preserved the jurisdictions of those Fulani who administered Jahun, Dutse, Gaya, Ringim and elsewhere. In this military context the founding families and their supporters gradually perceived the necessity for a strong central chiefship capable of mobilising the power of the state in the effective defense of its territory and their interests; and thereafter each of these factions was less inclined to oppose the chiefship on behalf of another, than to preserve its own estate and status with the support of this central authority. Thus, even without employing his power to subvert the preceding balance of rights and responsibilities, Abdullahi's situation and policies enhanced the status of the chiefship by demonstrating its indispensability as the central co-ordinating institution of the state.

Two major famines, the *banga banga*, which occurred between 1855 and 1863, and the *yunwar dagiya* of about 1878, further reinforced the chiefship by emphasising its dormant role as the main agency of public succour.[29] On both occasions the state granaries and reserves were opened for public relief by distributions through the appropriate official channels. On both occasions, Abdullahi also appealed to neighboring emirs for grain to help his people. In the general distress, his office and leadership were thus identified with solicitude and generosity. The emir's office thus acquired new moral status and material significance as the public shepherd; and such sentiments of solidarity as the prevailing inequality allowed concentrated around the chiefship as the symbol of societal unity.

In public esteem, Abdullahi ranks second only to Dabo among the Fulani emirs who ruled Kano during the last century. Of those who have ruled since, only Abdullahi Bayero (1926–1954) achieved a comparable status. However, Abdullahi's reputation does not rest on any single outstanding achievement, such as Dabo's reconquest of Kano, following Sule's failure and the general revolt. Indeed, Abdullahi's campaigns were not notably successful, although none the less decisive. Following Usuman, Abdullahi was appreciated as an energetic ruler and a forceful personality, who sought to discharge the duties of his office as fully and fairly as he could. He is especially respected and remembered for his devotion to the *shari'a* and his long service as a judge.[30] Even in Usuman's reign, as vizier, Abdullahi had presided over the emir's court at the palace, since Usuman was too indolent to do so. On one occasion, the explorer Barth brought a complex case against some Arab merchants who were withholding payments to him for Abdullahi to settle. In its character and principals, the case offered ample opportunities for legal corruption; but Abdullahi, renowned locally as an incorruptible judge, handled the matter expeditiously and fairly.[31]

Abdullahi's judicial role forms the subject of several Hausa folk tales. One tale which may have some foundation in fact relates how Abdullahi, hastily convinced by circumstantial evidence of the guilt of a man accused of theft, ordered the man's hand to be cut off as the *shari'a* required. Later that day the accuser, a woman, returned to report that the shawl she thought was stolen had been returned, having been borrowed by one of her kin. Abdullahi was overwhelmed with grief at his miscarriage of justice, especially because he had not allowed the accused to clear himself by taking the Koranic oath, as the *shari'a* stipulated in such cases. Abdullahi sent for the injured man, expressed his grief, and offered ten of everything—horses, cattle, slaves, concubines and bags of cowries—as tokens of compensation and regret. The injured man declined these gifts, and left the judgment to Allah. Abdullahi went into seclusion for several weeks, grieved at his error. According to some, thereafter he never again judged any criminal charges that involved amputation or execution himself, but left those to the Alkali.[32]

In Usuman's day, as we have seen, robbery was rife and weakly punished in rural Kano. According to the Chronicle, when Abdullahi "became Sarki, he set to work to kill all the robbers and cut off the hands of the thieves. He was called "Abdu, Sarkin Yanka,"[33] —that is, Abdu, the chief of cutting (execution). Nonetheless, it is only Abdullahi among many Fulani emirs to whom Hausa folklore ascribes such contrition for judicial error. With discrimination, the folk traditions single out Abdullahi's concern for justice as a quality that distinguished him from other Fulani chiefs. His Fulani subjects evidently appreciated this feature of Abdullahi's rule which, however stern, sought to be fair and was inspired by Muslim ideals of law and justice.

Abdullahi's increasing predominance at Kano was inevitable given his situation, personality, intelligence, energy, resources and long reign; yet in constitutional terms his record seems virtually spotless. Once enthroned, there is no evidence that he sought to abuse power. He neither threatened the rights of aristocratic Fulani, nor did he increase the burdens upon his "Habe" subjects, except inevitably, given prevailing practice, by his extensive building programme to strengthen Kano's defenses. His ascendancy flowed from his attempt to fulfill the ideal requirements and roles of Muslim chiefship. He was judge, military leader, head of state, provider in times of famine, defender of pastoral Fulani against "extortions" in Zaria, a devout Muslim, the caliph's chief resource in war and peace, and Dabo's outstanding son. His role in the empire was informally that of the caliph's Sarkin Yaki or commander-in-chief. With these assets, and despite his constitutionalism, Abdullahi could hardly have failed to impress the principle of patrimonial chiefship indelibly on Kano. This effect seems to have arisen almost inevitably from the sheer length and success of his reign, which realised to the full the direction of political development that Dabo had initiated.

Official Appointments and Marriages

On his accession from the office of Galadima, Abdullahi appointed his brother Abdulkadiri to succeed him. Abdulkadiri's former position remains unknown; but as Galadima, he outranked all officials under the chief. Following traditional precedent and recent practice, he could expect to exercise the role of vizier with corresponding enhancement of influence, authority, and chances for the succession. However, Abdullahi's absence from Kano frustrated the Galadima's expectations. Following constitutional precedent, Abdullahi left the Sarkin Shanu in charge of the government during his absences. The Galadima Abdulkadiri must certainly have had an important share in the Sarkin Shanu's administration; but the latter's administrative superiority was incongruous with the Galadima's precedence by rank and office. This situation probably frustrated Abdulkadiri and eventually alienated his sympathies.

In 1863–5 when Abdullahi returned to Kano and resumed control of the government, the Sarkin Shanu stepped back to his normal role and the Galadima Abdulkadiri again had prospects of becoming vizier. These hopes were again frustrated; and without undue delay, Abdulkadiri seems to have expressed his resentment indiscreetly. Abdullahi, who may already have had reason to treat the Galadima with reserve, learned from his slaves that his brother Abdulkadiri was spreading a rumour that the chief had placed some new fetish (*gwunki*) within the palace and regularly conducted heathen rituals (*tsafi*) there to increase his physical and political capacities. Whether the Galadima Abdulkadiri actually made this allegation remains unproven. It is possible, but unlikely, that some slaves may have invented the charge. Abdullahi could not forgive an accusation of this sort, especially from the brother he had appointed as Galadima. Given the religious character of the charge, he immediately reported the matter to the Waziri and caliph at Sokoto; and, having thus cleared himself of any taint, he told them he wished to dismiss the Galadima. It is possible that even before this date the caliph had directed his vizier to forbid the emir of Kano to dismiss his Galadima without express approval from Sokoto. The caliph had much earlier instituted similar reservations at Katsina, and in 1880, similar restrictions were imposed by Sokoto on the autonomy of the emirs of Zaria.[34] Whether this extension of the caliph's supervisory power preceded or followed Abdulkadiri's dismissal from the office of Galadima remains obscure; but, given the religious character of the charge, and Abdullahi's innocence, Sokoto had no hesitation in approving Abdulkadiri's dismissal. Abdullahi then replaced Abdulkadiri by his own son, the Ciroma Yusufu.

On his death in 1855, Usuman's eldest son, Muhammadu Dikko, held the title of Ciroma. In 1851, when Barth met him, Dikko was about eighteen years old.[35] On his accession, following Dabo's policy of marriage alliances, Abdullahi gave Dikko one of his daughters as a bride. This represented an assurance of the chief's favour and support of Dikko as Usuman's heir and a leading candidate for the throne. Nonetheless, by 1860 at the latest, Dikko had been peremptorily dismissed from the office of Ciroma and replaced by Yusufu, Abdullahi's eldest son. It is said that Dikko had offended the emir by beating and generally ill-treating Abdullahi's daughter, his wife. Presumably the girl complained to her father. Abdullahi treated Dikko's conduct as a political offence, namely *renon sarki* (contempt or disrespect for the chief), who was also Dikko's father's brother. Dikko was first dismissed and then divorced; and it was probably this incident that stimulated the caliph to impose restraints on the power of his emir at Kano to dismiss the crown prince out of hand, without prior assent from Sokoto.

Inevitably, in dismissing Dikko, Usuman's senior son, Abdullahi had alienated Dikko's brothers and their supporters. On Dikko's dismissal, of Usuman's sons only Abdurrazuku still held office as Tafida, the position his father had given him. Abdurrazuku's fate is unknown; but in due course Abdullahi's son Muhamman succeeded to that title. It matters little whether Abdurrazuku was dismissed or died in office. Two other sons of Usuman were then at Kano without title, namely Malanta and Mustafa. Usuman had shown some restraint in pursuing a familistic policy of appointments. Of his sons he had appointed only three to office, Abdurrazuku having succeeded on the death of his brother Aliyu as Tafida. Thus in Usuman's reign the ruler's sons only held the titles of Ciroma and Tafida. With Dikko's dismissal and the appointment of Tafida Muhamman, Usuman's descendants were entirely excluded from office, thereby characterising Abdullahi's distribution of royal offices as familistic and sectional.

Perhaps by this date Shekara, the mother of Usuman, Abdullahi and Mamman Bello, Abdullahi's successor, had died; but while Usuman had few sons, Abdullahi had many; and over the following years at least 28 of them held senior titles at Kano. Abdullahi himself appointed two sons, Halilu and Sule, successively to the title of Dan Buram. Following Yusufu's promotion from Ciroma to Galadima, Halilu became Ciroma, his brother Sule succeeding as Dan Buram. At this date only three or four offices were available for allocation to the chief's sons, namely the titles of Ciroma, Tafida, Dan Buram, and perhaps the Dan Isa also. Following Hausa precedent, Dabo and Usuman had allocated the senior royal offices—Galadima, Wambai, Turakin Manya and Sarkin Shanu— to their brothers, while the titles of Dan Lawan and Sarkin Dawaki Tsakar Gida were filled by the ruler's cognates, the former being usually allocated to a daughter's son ineligible by descent to succeed. Few offices were constitutionally available at this time for Abdullahi's many maturing sons, although as chief, he had four wives and a large harem. A large royal progeny was valuable for the dynasty and the state, since it ensured sufficient candidates to assure the succession and permit the selection of someone with appropriate qualities. Abdullahi was fortunate in having many sons. However, this fortune created its own problems as Abdullahi's sons replaced Usuman's in princely positions.

As the Chronicle relates, on appointing Yusufu as Galadima, Abdullahi sent him southwards to take command of the Ningi campaign. Yusufu, then about 25 years of age, was unsuited to serve as vizier by reason of filiation and age. Evidently, Abdullahi preferred Galadimas who were his kin and juniors by a generation. As "vizier" at Kano, Abdullahi relied instead on a Fulani client Dogo, who had campaigned with him against the Ningi. Abdullahi conferred on Dogo the title of Sarkin Yaki (war chief) hitherto reserved for the *jekada* to Jahun; and having replaced Galadima Abdulkadiri by his son Yusufu, Abdullahi employed Dogo as his unofficial vizier in charge of audiences and routine communications at the palace, thereby intensifying his personal control over the government. Lacking any independent basis of support, Dogo was rather a functionary than a vizier. Important issues and law cases remained in Abdullahi's hands, while Dogo cleared routine transactions, thereby reducing the trivia that could consume the chief's time. At Kano Dogo is often described informally as the first Fulani "Sarkin Fada"; but in this case, the familiar corollary is lacking. No one claims that Dogo behaved like the chief while the chief behaved like his vizier. Tradition faithfully reflects Dogo's role as a functionary. Abdullahi had thus taken a further step in centralisation by appointing a political nonentity as his chief assistant.

Following Dabo's practice, Abdullahi sought to identify the leading Fulani families with the chiefship by dynastic marriages. He had a large number of daughters to dispose of and few men were eligible to marry them. Some daughters were given to Abdullahi's agnates, as, for instance, the unfortunate Ciroma Muhammadu Dikko. One was given to the caliph's vizier, Halilu. Others went as brides to councillors of state, to the Sarkin Bai, Madaki, Makama, Dan Iya, Sarkin Dawaki Maituta and others. Abdullahi gave his favourite daughter the title of Magajiya, following Dabo's precedent, and married her to the Sarkin Rano Jibir, who took office at Rano in 1857 and fought vigorously and effectively against the Ningi until he was finally defeated and killed in 1892.[36] Jibir's military prowess, coupled with his position as Sarkin Rano, an office traditionally allied to the Kano chief by marriage and kinship, suggested this bond. For her wedding gift Abdullahi placed the town of Bici, which contained large numbers of Tuareg serfs (*bugaje*) under the Magajiya's administration as a fief as Usuman had long since transferred Kumbotso, the town allocated by Dabo to his Magajiya, the wife of Madaki Umaru, to the Galadima.

As customary, Abdullahi gave a daughter, Rahamatu, to the Madaki Isma'ilu, the son of Madaki Umaru, who succeeded on Haliru's death in 1856. Ten years later Isma'ilu was defeated and slain by the Ningi in the military disaster at Fajewa. Abdullahi then appointed Isma'ilu's younger brother Hassan as Madaki, and transferred Rahamatu to Hassan after she had completed the period of mourning (*takaba*). When the Madaki Hassan was slain by Dan Baskore at Godiya some years later, Abdullahi appointed Hassan's younger brother Ibrahim, and married Rahamatu to Ibrahim. Still later, when the fourth Madaki, Muhamman Kwairanga, was appointed on Ibrahim's dismissal, Rahamatu was presented to Kwairanga by her brother Aliyu, who was then chief. Kwairanga escaped by pleading his relative youth, and received a younger substitute.[37] The successive marriages of Rahamatu to these three brothers over twenty years demonstrate clearly the political character of these royal marriages. One might almost say at this period that successive Madakis took over Rahamatu as well as their offices, compounds, horses, fiefs and seats on the council; or, if not Rahamatu, another princess. State councillors were linked to the chief by ties of affinity and often also by cognatic kinship. The dynasty was no longer segregated from or contraposed with the founding lineages. Instead many bonds of marriage, affinity and kinship now identified it as the inner core and most highly ranked group of the Fulani ruling stratum.

Usually the chief pursued this policy of marriage alliance by giving senior officials his daughters as brides, while taking his wives from the leading families at Sokoto, from nearby chiefdoms such as Daura or Katsina, and from his senior vassals, the chiefs of Rano and Dutse. Since Gaya and Karaye, while retaining their status as sub-chiefdoms, were now often ruled by clients who lacked hereditary claim, and thus assimilated to the category of *shigege* officials, the emir did not usually take wives from those units, though he might give his daughters to them in marriage.

Abdullahi departed from this marriage policy on one famous occasion. He fell in love with a woman of the Daneji clan whose descent made marriage imperative. To wed required the transfer of bridewealth from the groom to the lady's kinsmen, and in this case to her elder brother, as her father had died. Abdullahi made the prestations appropriate to his chiefly rank, but clearly felt these were inadequate to express his joy at receiving the bride. He sought to reward the lady's guardian more appropriately, and on consulting the Mai Anguwan Kutumbawa discovered that several important Hausa titles had not yet been re-established. One of these, the title of Dan Makwayau, was revived for Abdullahi's new brother-in-law, the Daneji Gidado; simultaneously, Abdullahi transferred Gora and Dutse to Gidado for supervision. Following this, several other old Hausa titles were reinstated, for example the Dan Maje and Dan Kade, and perhaps also the Barde Kareriya.

Over the past fifty years the number of suitable candidates for *hakimi* offices had steadily increased since the practice of polygyny promoted the rapid growth in numbers of the aristocracy. The population of the state had also begun to increase when Western Kano received a notable influx from Katsina following Sidiku's suppression of Dan Mari's revolt in 1842–4. Some "forty" towns are said to have been founded at that time. To accommodate these increases in the populations of subjects and rulers, given the traditional form of territorial administration, comparable increases in the number of territorial offices were required. However, as relatively few offices had been added during Usuman's reign, Dabo's reconstitution of the Hausa official structure was probably adequate to the needs of the government under his sons.

Following the death of his Alkali Zangi, the only local Fulani who is known to have written a history of Kano during the 19th century, Abdullahi appointed Zangi's younger brother, Rufa'i, as the Alkali at Kano. Following his usual practice, Abdullahi gave Rufa'i one of his daughters in marriage; but not long after, he first imprisoned and then executed Rufa'i without any public trial. The vizier and caliph at Sokoto were both informed, but whether before or after Rufa'i's execution remains unclear. The incident is noted briefly in the Kano Chronicle without elucidation.[38] Though mentioned neither by the Dokaje nor by Malam Adamu, it is well remembered at Sokoto. There I was told that Rufa'i had committed some heinous offence which merited this punishment under the *shari'a*. It was obliquely suggested that he may have violated a girl consigned to him as a ward, thereby committing several offences at once; but of course that allegation may only illustrate the general character of his offence. The caliph took no action against Abdullahi; and though the occasion for this violent act remains obscure, it seems unlikely that by local standards Abdullahi had transgressed the law.

On Rufa'i's death, Abdullahi appointed the Limam of Kano, Sule, as Alkali, thereby disrupting the hereditary succession of Gyenawa in that office. As Limam, however, he appointed the baGyeni Na'ibi, Muhammadu, whose father Sule had been installed by the emir Suleimanu when Sule was promoted from the Limamship to the throne. As mentioned above, since his father's death in Dabo's reign, this Na'ibi Muhammadu had retained the fiefs of Jijitar, Harmani and Zango, which Suleimanu had allocated to the Limam. Thus on his promotion as Limam, those towns were finally recovered by the state as fiefs of the Limam's office. Thereafter the claim that they were family property lapsed.

Some Administrative Changes

Abdullahi seems to have been the first Fulani emir to levy a regular tax on the sedentary Fulani population at Kano. It is said that he collected 500 cowries from each Fulani householder as against 2,000 per annum from each Hausa (Habe) equivalent. If correct, though minor, this change institutes a significant new principle, namely that the Fulani also were liable to regular taxation. There were, of course, numerous exemptions from taxation, and most of these probably applied to men of Fulani descent. Malams, officials, and princes were excused from taxes; and it is not clear whether residents in the capital now became liable to annual tax. As before, blacksmiths, leatherworkers, silversmiths, builders, itinerant traders, the blind, lame and lepers were exempt, together with all slaves, for whom no tax was paid. The *kudin shuke*, the taxes on dyepits, date trees and cattle, the standard legal fees and death duty, the fifth (*humushi*) of booty, and tithes of grain and cattle were collected as before.

By this innovation Abdullahi intended to reduce the tax burden on his "Habe" subjects, probably seeking to win their support in his conflict with the Ningi. In Usuman's reign, "Habe" householders had paid two thousand five hundred cowries per annum. Abdullahi sought to collect an amount equivalent to that by which he had reduced the "Habe" tax rate from each Fulani householder. Manifestly, he was seeking to redistribute the tax load less unequally while maintaining the previous flow of revenue. Like other Fulani, he regarded the unequal distribution of taxation as morally and politically appropriate; but though conservative, this change reflects his recognition of the political dissatisfaction and depressed situation of the "Habe."

It is probably also to Abdullahi's reign that we must date the proliferation of rural courts in Kano. As indicated above, Abdullahi was unusually insistent on the exact enforcement of the *shari'a*, which was also a major objective of the Shehu Usuman and his closest supporters, Abdullahi dan Fodio and Mamman Bello. Certainly, Abdullahi first established a judge in the Kano city market to clear commercial cases quickly. He likewise established the first *alkalai* at Debi and Dingare, and perhaps also at Gano and Jahun. During the latter part of his reign, local limams trained in Muslim law served as judges at Lamire and Wasai. Some of the major rural units such as Rano, Gaya, Karaye and Dutse certainly had *alkalai* from Dabo's reign, and for some of these units we have complete lists of all local *alkalai* since that date. Dabo had also appointed an *alkali* at Getso to support the San Getso Mai Dabo. While on campaign, Abdullahi appointed an *alkali* at Gwaram in the extreme southeast.

Such rural *alkalai* reinforced Fulani domination throughout the country by imposing the stern penalties ordained by Muslim law for political and criminal offences. It is said that besides the towns already named, there were also *alkalai* at Dambarta, Bebeji, Ringim and Godiya during the latter half of the 19th century. Though probably sound, these data remain unconfirmed, and we cannot indicate the probable dates of the initial appointments.

Following his promotion of the San Kurmi Ango to the title of Galadima, Dabo had appointed Ango's son Musa as San Kurmi, in charge of the public prisons. For reasons unknown Abdullahi dismissed Musa, a Hausa, from this office, and appointed Mamudu, his own daughter's son. The office was thereafter reserved for free Fulani.

The palace prison fell under the Sarkin Yara; and from Usuman's reign until the civil war, that office, which also served as the chief's channel of communications with Gaya, was filled by Burde, a Fulani, and his descendants, Aliyu, his son, and Abdu his grandson. Under Abdullahi, the Kilishi remained a free *shigege* office; but the office of Hauni, the executioner, passed to throne slaves, like that of Sarkin Dogarai or chief of police, which was held by palace slaves at an earlier date. Under Usuman, the Sarkin Yara and the Dan Sarai, both free *shigege* officials, took the main annual tribute to Sokoto together. Abdullahi appointed the first slave Dan Sarai, and placed him directly under the Dan Rimi. Thereafter the Dan Sarai seems to have taken the tribute to Sokoto with the Sarkin Yara or the Sarkin Yaki, both of whom were free men and served as the emir's *jekadu* to Dutse, Gaya, Rano and Jahun.

Abdullahi and Sokoto

On the death of Aliyu Babba in 1859, the electors of Sokoto chose Ahmadu Zaruku, the son of Atiku, to succeed as caliph. Thus on two successive occasions the caliphate had been given to grandsons of the Shehu Usmanu, while Ahmadu Rufa'i, the Shehu's surviving son, was passed over. Rufa'i regarded these successive appointments of his classificatory sons as public affronts; and at some time in Zaruku's reign, in chagrin, he quit Sokoto for the East. Like Abdullahi dan Fodio in 1807, he may have intended to go eastwards to Mecca; but at Sokoto it is said that he set out to tour the eastern emirates, beginning with Kano, to seek gifts and support for his succession. However, Abdullahi dan Fodio's earlier flight to the east had created a precedent for future rulers. Thereafter no senior prince of the Shehu's family was permitted to visit the eastern provinces without the caliph's permission.[39] This precaution was probably designed to prevent the spread of dynastic rivalries at Sokoto throughout the empire, with consequent subversions of the loyalties of the eastern emirs; but it was also regarded at Sokoto as necessary to preserve the eastern provinces from unregulated solicitations by the increasing number of Shehu Usmanu's descendants who were dissatisfied with their dependence on the caliph and his officials for recognition and support.

Ahmadu Rufa'i's silent departure was soon reported to the Waziri and caliph at Sokoto. They at once despatched couriers by the pony express to Kano and Bauchi, advising their emirs of Rufa'i's flight, and instructing them to intercept and return him immediately to Sokoto without excessive gifts. On receiving this letter, Abdullahi ordered the Ma'aji, who administered the city, to keep a close watch for

Rufa'i at the gates; and when Rufa'i arrived shortly after, obeying Sokoto's instructions, Abdullahi refused to let him enter Kano, but sent his greetings and substantial gifts to Rufa'i with an armed escort to return him to Sokoto. As Rufa'i did not know that Abdullahi was acting under orders from the caliph and vizier, he held the emir personally responsible for his interception and humiliating return. In these circumstances Rufa'i understandably regarded Abdullahi as personally hostile, particularly since Abdullahi had refused to let him enter Kano after a long and tiring journey. Rufa'i returned to Sokoto, having thus indicated his desire for the caliphate; and when Aliyu Karami died in 1867, he was appointed.

By then Abdullahi had returned to the southern front to attack the Ningi. On Rufa'i's accession, Abdullahi despatched the customary greetings and prestations with a high-ranking delegation, who were instructed to declare his homage (*mubaya'a*) to the new caliph, while excusing his absence on *jihad*. Such an indirect declaration of homage seemed cavalier and ominous to Ahmadu Rufa'i, thus strengthening his belief in Abdullahi's animosity, and encouraging further suspicions. A peremptory order was sent to Abdullahi, requiring his personal appearance at Sokoto. With that order, Abdullahi received information from members of the returned delegation about Rufa'i's hostility and desire to depose him. Abdullahi accordingly set out for Sokoto with lavish gifts and a large force of heavily-armed veterans seasoned in the Ningi campaigns. For two days after his arrival at Sokoto, Rufa'i denied him an audience. The Shehu's daughter, Mariam, a widow of Abdullahi's father Ibrahim Dabo, who had remarried Muhammad Ade, the son of Mamman Bello's Waziri Gidado, was still alive and resident in Sokoto. Abdullahi visited Mariam to solicit her aid, attributing his failure to attend the caliph's accession to the severity of the Ningi threat in southern Kano, and protesting that he had waited in vain to see Rufa'i and render homage over the past two days. Having heard that Rufa'i wished to depose him, he told Mariam he would resist, since he had committed no offence and had served several caliphs loyally. He concluded by saying that he proposed to leave Sokoto and return to Kano on the following day unless Rufa'i consented to see him.

Meanwhile Rufa'i was engaged in long discussion with his *sarakunan karaga*, the imperial councillors of Sokoto, concerning Abdullahi's future. Rufa'i sought to depose him, and cited Abdullahi's armed entourage as evidence of disloyal intentions; but most of his councillors urged the opposite view, stressing Kano's strategic role as an imperial bastion, and Abdullahi's many contributions to its maintenance. Against Rufa'i's personal antipathy, these councillors, and particularly the Galadima of Sokoto, urged imperial considerations, Abdullahi's long service, and devotion to Islam. Mariam's entry and report crystallised the issue. It seems also that Abdullahi may have paraded his troops in Sokoto at this time, receiving a cavalry charge of allegiance (*jafi*) which concluded in volleys of musket-fire. The Council interpreted these signals correctly and Rufa'i, confronted with the risk of destroying the empire by alienating Kano, or accepting Abdullahi's homage, gave in. Abdullahi was summoned to greet Rufa'i and spent the following seven days in Sokoto with Rufa'i, Mariam and the councillors, repairing the recent breach.

Some at Kano say that on this occasion Rufa'i initially deposed Abdullahi and then reinstated him; but this interpretation treats Rufa'i's refusal to grant Abdullahi an audience as evidence of the latter's deposition, and reasons that since his homage had been refused, his right to govern Kano was thereby revoked. It is also possible that Rufa'i may have used words that suggested Abdullahi's dismissal. Evidently Abdullahi himself regarded the situation in this light when he visited Mariam. However, since he was escorted by Rufa'i for the customary distance on his departure and left Sokoto with the caliph's authority to govern Kano, it seems clear that despite the threat, no deposition actually took place.

It is said that Rufa'i imposed a personal tribute or fine of one million cowries a day, known colloquially at Sokoto as the *kudin cefane* (money for stew) on Abdullahi as the price of their reconciliation; and further, that to relieve the finances of Kano of this iniquitous burden, Abdullahi prayed for Rufa'i's death with such diligence and fervour that Allah removed Rufa'i in 1873 before Kano was bankrupt. However, the tale derives from Sokoto, not Kano, and the sum involved is perhaps improbable. On returning to Kano, Abdullahi proceeded to Birnin Bako on the Ningi frontier, where he remained on campaign for the next three years.

In 1871 Ahmadu Rufa'i deposed the Sarkin Zazzau Abdullahi on charges of disloyalty and disobedience. The deposition was questioned on various grounds by Rufa'i's kinsmen and colleagues in Sokoto, where Abdullahi resided after his removal from Zazzau, being replaced there by a dynastic rival.

On Ahmadu Rufa'i's death in March 1873, Abubakar Atiku of Raba, the younger brother of Aliyu Babba, succeeded as caliph.[40] Abubakar had opposed the deposition of Abdullahi of Zaria as unjust, since it had been effected without due process of law. Later that year, when the reigning emir of Zaria died, the caliph Abubakar restored Abdullahi to Zaria as governor without consulting the local electors.[41] News of Abdullahi's return from exile as chief generated alarm in Zaria, particularly among those senior officials who, under established conventions, had received portions of Abdullahi's estate at his deposition in 1870. The Madaki Ali and Galadima Hamman, the two leading officials in Zaria, raised the flag of revolt against Abdullahi's restoration, and collected their supporters at Ifira near Rigacikum, southwest of the capital. Abdullahi of Zaria reported the matter at once to Sokoto and sent his forces against Ifira. At Sokoto the Waziri Halilu was then ailing or already dead, and unable to act in this emergency.[42] The caliph Abubakar accordingly directed Abdullahi of Kano to intervene and negotiate a settlement before the conflict deepened or spread. Abdullahi at once marched with part of his army to Ifira, and camped between the two opposing forces. Of the rebel leaders, only the Madaki Ali was eligible by descent for succession to the throne of Zaria. Abdullahi (of Kano) accordingly persuaded the Madaki Ali to terminate his revolt on the understanding that neither he, the Galadima Hamman, nor their supporters would be punished for their actions, and also that Madaki Ali would succeed Abdullahi as emir of Zaria. When the Madaki accepted these terms, Abdullahi then informed his namesake in Zaria that the disagreement was over, that there had been a misunderstanding, and that he should neither attempt to recover those portions of his former estate which had been distributed to his officials on his deposition in 1870, nor make reprisals. Abdullahi then withdrew with his army to Kano, having successfully forestalled a threatening conflict by provisionally committing the caliph to appoint the rebel Madaki Ali as the next emir of Zaria.[43]

That was one of Abdullahi's last campaigns. He was probably at this time in his early sixties. During the last few years, age had begun to tell. He was also afflicted with haemorrhoids and found it increasingly difficult to ride long distances. Under these circumstances, Abdullahi delegated field command to the Madaki Hassan, the Sarkin Rano Jibir, and Sarkin Dawaki Dan Ladan; but when Dan Baskore of Maradi defeated and killed the Madaki and the Sarkin Dawaki at Gwarzo, Abdullahi decided to resume command himself, and when next

> Sarkin Maradi Dan Baskore came into Katsina, Abdullahi went to meet him. They met at Kusada in Katsina, but did not fight. For this reason the meeting was called *"Yakin Zuru"* (the battle of looks), they looked at each other and went back. There was also a fight between Barahiya, Sarkin Maradi and Sarkin Kano at Bichi. Barahiya ran away and Abdullahi took all the spoils. It is not known how many men were killed and slain.[44]

On Urvoy's reckoning Barahiya Barmou succeeded Dan Baskore at Maradi in 1873 and died in 1877,[45] but some scholars set Barmou's reign between 1879 and 1883,[46] and perhaps Barmou reigned from 1875 to 1879.[47] In any event, Abdullahi's last recorded campaign was his victory over Barmou at Bichi which took place on the differing Maradi chronologies sometime between 1873 and 1879, probably in 1875–6, when Abdullahi was over 65.

Palace Affairs

Yusufu, Abdullahi's son by the caliph Aliyu Babba's daughter, held the office of Galadima for several years in the later part of his father's reign. Some time earlier, Abdullahi had placed Yusufu in command of the southern front during one of his periodic visits to Sokoto. When Dan Maje the Ningi leader attacked, Yusufu gave battle at Dubaya where the Kano forces broke and fled.[48] On his return to Kano, as related above, Abdullahi dismissed his brother, the Galadima Adulkadiri, and gave Yusufu that office, reinforcing Yusufu's command at Takai where Mallam Hamza's son, Haruna, was active. Yusufu inflicted a heavy defeat on Haruna's Ningi at Jambo, thus vindicating Abdullahi's confidence and his claims to the succession. Evidently, following this triumph, Yusufu attracted many supporters and clients who sought influence and fortune in the light of his rising star. In this context, Yusufu sought to convert his enhanced prestige into direct influence on the civil and military administration of Kano. However, although local conventions treated the Galadima as vizier, Abdullahi preferred to be his own executive, and Yusufu was further disqualified for this role as his senior and favourite son. Abdullahi accordingly placed his Fulani client, Malam Dogo, as Sarkin Fada, in charge of palace communications and audiences, while relying on the scribe (*magatakarda*) Malam Ibrahim, for written messages and accounts. By these means Abdullahi kept executive control of Kano in his hands, thus frustrating Yusufu's ambitions and generating dissidence. Moreover when the Tafida Muhamman, another son, was mature enough to handle Mallam Dogo's confidential role, Abdullahi transferred these functions to the Tafida, while leaving Dogo with the title of Sarkin Fada and temporary fiefs. The Tafida Muhamman's political advance intensified Yusufu's resentment at his exclusion from the seats of power.

At this time the Sallama Barka, Abdullahi's senior palace eunuch, as the emir's *kofa*, handled his communications with the Galadima, with the Sarkin Dawaki Tsakar Gida, the Mai Anguwan Kutumbawa, the Dan Maje, and perhaps with the Sarkin Fulani Jahun also. In addition, Sallama monitored the conduct of Kasheka, the eunuch court usher, and supervised communications through other eunuchs such as the Turakin Soro and the Magaji Dankama. The Sallama's senior charge was the Galadima Yusufu, Abdullahi's likely successor. Over the years Yusufu and Sallama Barka developed a close confidential relationship, which kept the Galadima fully informed about palace affairs, including his father's health, dynastic matters, and communications with Sokoto.

As he aged, Abdullahi's preoccupation with the political and military affairs of Kano and the Fulani Empire seems to have increased, thus diverting his attention from developments at the palace. During his absence on campaigns in the south, the palace slaves, effectively subordinated by Shamaki Isa's execution, had discharged their duties with routine efficiency, and in consequence secured the confidence of the emir, his councillors and deputies, including the Sarkin Shanu and the Ma'aji. By custom, on installing a new emir at Kano, the Waziri of Sokoto or his representative would summon the senior throne slaves and eunuchs, Shamaki, Dan Rimi, Sallama, Sarkin Dogarai, San Kurmi and other slave *rukunai* to meet their new master, saying as follows: "This is the man the caliph has selected to govern Kano. Keep him well, and obey him with good faith." ("*Ga wanda Sarkin Musulmi ya ba mulkin Kano. Ku rike shi da amana, ku biye umurcinsa.*") In Kano and especially within the palace, this *amana* (good faith, solidarity, trust) renewed between the emir and his palace slaves at each accession, identified their interests, established their hierarchy, and ordained cohesion, while excluding such slave attempts to subvert the throne as Katsina and Hadeija experienced. Thus by command of the caliph, throne slaves in Kano were politically neutralised, insulated from intra-dynastic competitions, and from sporadic conflicts between the emirs and their powerful subordinates. The palace slaves were thus constituted as an expressly administrative staff charged with routine support of the emir and with implementation of his decisions. We shall see later how gravely the state suffered when dynastic strife finally politicised the slaves and divided their loyalties.

This relation of *amana* between the chief and his slaves was critical in facilitating the political centralisation of Kano by successive Suleibawa emirs to whom it assured control of a large, loyal, and efficiently organised staff at the palace and on royal estates scattered strategically throughout the rural areas. With such resources, the emir enjoyed an unchallenged predominance within the state; and since his slave staff were thus immune to external subversion, he was free to employ them as necessary to overawe the opposition of rival princes, the *jihad*ic aristocracy, or territorial chiefs, or to defend Kano from outside attacks. The palace staff thus provided the emir with unrivalled resources of military manpower, communications, information, wealth and political expertise, which neatly complemented his special relation with the vizier and caliph of Sokoto. Together these attributes made the emir's office indispensable to the unity and routine coordination of Kano, while elevating its significance and magnifying its power as the supreme organ and core of the state. By comparison, in successive reigns the authority, influence and prestige of the founding Fulani families and their offices

had progressively diminished, unless reinforced by the emir's favour and policies.

As *imam* or head of the Muslim community, one of the many non-political
roles that an emir was obliged to assume was the care and guardianship of all free
women who freely came to the palace seeking his aid, whatever their age, status
or previous career. A Muslim woman has merely to present herself at the palace
and claim the emir's protection to be welcomed, fed, clothed and sheltered within
it, for as long as she cares to remain. Throughout their stay, such women are
legally wards of the emir, and he is expected to treat them as if they were his
daughters. Often an emir may not know the women who reside at the palace in
this privileged status. At Kano it was customary to conduct such supplicants to
the Uwar Soro, the emir's favourite wife or concubine, who enquired and supplied their needs. Thereafter they might serve her as free handmaidens until such
time as they were reconciled to their husbands or kin, or had new marriages
arranged for them. Following the *jihad*, most women who thus invoked the emir's
protection by entering the palace were of Fulani stock, and many were daughters
of high-ranking lineages who had rejected the aristocratic husbands selected for
them by their agnatic kin. Such daughters of the Fulani included Yolawa, Danbazawa, Danejawa and others who had temporarily or permanently broken their
family alliances. It is thus possible that the Daneji woman whom Abdullahi
admired and married may have come to his notice initially by this route.

During Abdullahi's long absence from Kano on the Ningi campaigns, his
deputy (*wakil*), the Sarkin Shanu probably administered these women's affairs as
best he could, although unable to enter the women's quarters within the palace.
However in the absence of the Uwar Soro with the emir at Takai, this administration was unavoidably imperfect and perfunctory; and it is probably at this period
that some palace slaves began to court these unattached ladies, the emir's wards,
and eventually married several of them, since Maliki law allows the marriage of
free women and male slaves.[49] Moreover, since the institution of *amana* virtually
vested the emirship in the care of throne slaves, the palace staff enjoyed an unusually privileged status, being themselves, by *amana*, the special wards and charge
of the emir. In the circumstances, there being no legal barrier against intermarriage, it may have seemed to many male throne slaves that the current social bar-
riers to such unions lacked effective sanctions. Whether or when the Sarkin Shanu
and Abdullahi first learnt of these marriages between palace slaves and the emir's
free female wards, we cannot say. However, the emir alone had the authority to
divorce his slaves, and in his absence on campaign, neither the Sarkin Shanu, nor
the women's aristocratic kinsfolk, nor the Alkali of Kano were able to cancel these
anomalous unions, or to prevent their increase. To Fulani aristocrats, who had
steadfastly refused to marry their daughters to free Hausa or Habe, whatever
their official status, knowledge of these marriages to throne slaves must have
been especially humiliating, and their powerlessness to prevent or punish them
even more so; and since they reasoned that such slave insolence was only possible
by virtue of the emir's protection and complaisance, Fulani aristocrats and commoners alike held Abdullahi personally responsible for authorising or permitting
such unions. Some still do so in Kano to this day.

On learning about these marriages between his slaves and Fulani women, Abdullahi was restrained from abrogating these anomalies by various considerations. First, however distasteful to Fulani, such marriages were valid at law and permissible, and Abdullahi's respect for the *shari'a* restrained him from forbidding his slaves to do what the law allowed. Secondly, Abdullahi was also restrained by the relation of *amana* which obliged him to foster and guard the interests of his slaves; under the law, these unprecedented unions were legitimate interests of their slave partners. Abdullahi also recognised his need for staff solidarity and support within the palace. To abrogate slave marriages could disrupt these relations, thereby weakening Kano militarily in its hour of need, and weakening the chiefship politically in various ways. Finally, as he aged and relied increasingly on his throne slaves for civil and military support, Abdullahi may have been positively disinclined to interfere with their unions, preferring instead to hustle his remaining wards out of the palace by early reconciliations, or by early remarriages to free men.

Meanwhile, Fulani disaffection and frustration with these affairs increased. Learning about them from the Sallama and others, Galadima Yusufu felt that his father had lost repute and was held in contempt, and became increasingly impatient for the successsion. During these years, Abdullahi's anal disorder kept him from horseback, and thus from taking the field with his armies, as was his wont. To his impatient son, the ageing emir seemed increasingly incapable of fulfilling his routine responsibilities. Somehow, perhaps through letters from Yusufu, Sokoto was led to believe that Abdullahi could no longer mount or direct his armies. It is related that, while on a visit to Sokoto, these questions were tactfully raised, following which Abdullahi, unaware of their source and implications, demonstrated his physical fitness by leading a charge of salute to the caliph with muskets fired at the gallop. Revealing neither their sources nor their intent, the caliph and Waziri of Sokoto congratulated Abdullahi on his agility and took no further action. Some say that Abdullahi fainted with pain after this display of horsemanship; but in any event, he avoided riding and campaigned no further on returning to Kano. Age was taking its toll.

It seems that Abdullahi's chief eunuch, Sallama, had not been castrated. In Kano and nearby capitals at this time, impotent males and some others incapable of or uninterested in copulation, were sometimes classified as eunuchs along with *castrati* purchased from Damagaram, Zaria, or elsewhere. According to contemporary traditions, Kano lacked castrators and castrating sheds throughout the Fulani period; but this remains uncertain. Understandably, since a critical element in the Fulani conception of man is continuing desire and ability to copulate, physically complete males who were either incapable or uninterested in sexual activity were regarded as congenitally sick and classified as eunuchs (*baba*, pl. *babanni*). Evidently the Sallama Barka was a eunuch of this sort, a natural invalid, and not a castrate. As Abdullahi's senior eunuch and confidential agent, he had free access to the emir's private quarters, including the harem, and as the *kofar Galadima*, his relations with Yusufu were especially close. The Sallama was fully aware of Yusufu's impatience and ambitions, and evidently wished to promote them as best he could.

Abdullahi and Yusufu

At some time during Abdullahi's decline, the Sallama Barka recovered his potency. Since this change of condition endangered his life as well as his office, he concealed it with care and seduced a succession of Abdullahi's concubines, whose fears of death if discovered also bound them to secrecy. One tradition, which is unlikely to be true, alleges that Abdullahi knew or suspected the Sallama's philanderings, but that being already impotent with age, he no longer cared. In due course Sallama Barka confided his secret to the Galadima Yusufu, and argued that Abdullahi knew the situation in his harem, but did not care, being impotent by age. At the Sallama's suggestion or on his own initiative, it is said that the Galadima wrote the Waziri and caliph of Sokoto, urging that Abdullahi should be retired on grounds of senility and physical incapacities which made it impossible for him to fulfill his role.

If these letters from Yusufu urging Abdullahi's deposition survive at Sokoto, I did not see them, though the Waziri Alhaji Junaidu of Sokoto kindly placed such imperial correspondence with Kano as remained in his care at my disposal, and instructed his senior student, Malam Haliru, to translate those letters into Hausa for me to copy. However, of 47 letters in this collection that passed between Kano and Sokoto which had sufficient interest to merit full transcriptions of their Hausa translations, only six date from Abdullahi's reign. Of these, two dealt with differing inheritance claims, two reported gifts of tribute, one was sent by the Wombai Hassan, Dabo's younger brother, to Sokoto with declarations of homage on the succession of a new caliph, and the last was an appeal and complaint that Abdullahi received from Yamusa of Keffi, alleging an injustice he had suffered at the hands of Sarkin Zazzau Sambo (1878–1888), which Abdullahi forwarded to the Waziri Abdullahi (1874–1886) with a comment.[50] These letters all date from the closing years of Abdullahi's reign; as does a letter written by Yusufu to the caliph Umaru (1881–1891) which simply declares his allegiance and good wishes. Another letter from Yusufu congratulating Muhammadu Buhari on his appointment as the Waziri's Dan Galadima seeks Buhari's help in a cryptic phrase that suggests secret correspondence. However, it is unlikely that any letters Yusufu may have written to secure his father's dismissal were available in the Sokoto archives for public inspection by visitors. My information on these events comes from two elderly aristocrats, Malam Abubakar Mai Katuru, a son of caliph Umaru's Galadima at Sokoto, and Malam Babba Bagyeni at Kano, both of whom in 1959 independently confirmed the tale of Yusufu's surreptitious correspondence.

Following the death of caliph Abubakar in March 1877, Mu'azu, another son of Mamman Bello, succeeded; and on receiving the news Abdullahi proceeded to Wurno near Sokoto, where Mu'azu lived, accompanied by his senior kinsmen and officials, "the people (leaders) of Kano," to render homage in person. Following that ceremony, in a private audience with the caliph and Council of Sokoto, Abdullahi expressed the wish to resign on account of age, on condition that his son, the Galadima Yusufu, should succeed. Abdullahi is said to have told Mu'azu that he felt it was now time for him to resign and to give his position (*sarauta*) to his son Yusufu. Mu'azu, having received Yusufu's letters, repeatedly asked Abdullahi if and why he wished to quit. Abdullahi reaffirmed his desire and cited his age. Finally Mu'azu agreed, declaring "In that case, I release (dismiss) you; but I know whom I will appoint, and it won't be Yusufu." Thus, while accepting Abdullahi's request to abdicate, Mu'azu rejected the condition on which Abdullahi resigned, his *wasiyya* or final request. The caliph's decision was quite correct. Abdullahi had already committed Sokoto to offer the throne of Zazzau to Madaki Ali, a man of his own choice. He seemed now to be extending that precedent to Kano by selecting his successor before abdication. *"Ba kai za ka ba shi ba"* (It is not for you to choose your successor") said Mu'azu, directing Abdullahi to return to his lodging at Sokoto. The caliph then questioned the vizier, Abdullahi Bayero, who denied that the emir had consulted him about the matter. But when Mu'azu dismissed his council, they consulted among themselves and agreed to try to persuade him to reinstate Abdullahi as soon as possible, recalling the precedent of Ahmadu Rufa'i's attempted deposition.

That afternoon when the council reassembled, the subject was reopened after an appropriate interval by the Galadima of Sokoto, Shehu, who beseeched the caliph to overlook Abdullahi's error as a weakness of age, and restore him to office. When the caliph demurred, the Galadima remarked that never from the time of Shehu Usuman had any of his predecessors at Sokoto dismissed an emir of Kano, adding that to do so now was an unfortunate innovation, creating a dangerous precedent. Supported by the Ubandoma and other councillors, who collectively undertook to stand surety (*ceto*) for Abdullahi's future conduct, the Galadima then asked the vizier's opinion, but before the vizier could speak, the Galadima concluded by imploring Mu'azu to "forgive him (Abdullahi) unless the Waziri decides otherwise." Thus the Galadima Shehu sought to isolate the caliph in council while persuading him to transfer the final decision on Abdullahi to his vizier, since the latter was formally responsible for the supervision of Kano and had a wide and intimate knowledge of its affairs. At this point Mu'azu gave in and, without awaiting his vizier's decision, announced that he would revoke Abdullahi's abdication and restore him to office; but he then pulled a letter from his pocket, handed it to the scribe who attended the council, and directed him to stand up and read its contents. It is said that the letter was addressed from the Galadima Yusufu to the caliph personally. After greetings and wishes for the caliph's success, Yusufu declared that at Kano he acted as the eyes and ears of the caliph. In this capacity, Yusufu reported that Abdullahi was unfit to hold the emirship under the law (*shari'a*) because of his sexual impotence (*la'ifci*). Concluding, Yusufu declared that he hoped to succeed as emir of Kano by Mu'azu's favour, and had sent gifts (*gaisuwa*) to express his homage and hopes.

When the scribe had finished and the Council had recovered its composure, Mu'azu turned to the vizier Abdullahi Bayero and asked if Yusufu's messenger had brought this letter to him. The vizier denied this. The caliph then asked the vizier whether he knew anything about this or similar letters from Yusufu; and again the vizier declared his ignorance. Clearly, on the preceding day, when Abdullahi made his unexpected request to abdicate in favour of his son, the Galadima Yusufu, the caliph, privy to Yusufu's subversion, suspected a plot; and when his Galadima and Council pressed later for Abdullahi's restoration, urging that the vizier should be allowed to decide, he may have suspected his vizier's complicity in Yusufu's machinations. To forestall further intrigue, the caliph therefore promptly reappointed Abdullahi, publicised Yusufu's subversion, and pressed the vizier to declare his innocence or complicity. When the vizier had established his ignorance of Yusufu's plot, Mu'azu declared that after such conduct he would never appoint Yusufu to rule Kano. The Council was then dismissed, following which Abdullahi was informed that his request to resign could not be accepted, and he should continue to govern Kano.[51]

Abdullahi's surprise and curiosity at this sudden reversal of fortune are easily appreciated; but during the following week, which he spent in Sokoto as Mu'azu's honoured guest, he learned the explanation, perhaps from the caliph himself.

On leaving Kano to render homage to Mu'azu, Abdullahi had taken along the leading notables of Kano to greet the new caliph and other imperial dignitaries, as was the custom. The Galadima Yusufu had thus accompanied his father, both unaware of the other's designs. On setting out homewards from Sokoto, the Kano delegation was escorted the customary distance by the caliph, Waziri and councillors of Sokoto. After the final farewells, the Kano nobles resumed their route, Abdullahi riding towards the front of the column, preceded by slaves. As they neared Raba in the Rima valley, Abdullahi summoned the Sarkin Dogarai, his slave chief of police, and instructed him to remove Yusufu to the very rear of the column and place him under guard. The procession then continued to Kano.

On entering the palace, and without revealing the reason, Abdullahi formally dismissed Yusufu and appointed his scribe Ibrahim as Galadima. He then ordered the Sarkin Dogarai to hand Yusufu to the Shamaki in chains, and for several days Yusufu remained in prison at the Gidan Shamaki. Meanwhile Abdullahi said nothing about Yusufu's conduct but withdrew to his quarters in grief, nursing his wounds. After an interval he instructed the Sarkin Dogarai to empty Yusufu's compound of all its contents; and so, while Yusufu, guarded and chained, was exhibited outside the palace, his wives, children and slaves, horses, armour, clothing, wealth and all his personal stores were brought from the Galadima's compound and placed in the public road. Later when Yusufu's wives and fertile concubines had been separated from his slaves, Abdullahi directed that these women and their children should be put to live in quarters fit for destitutes. Next he ordered that two of Yusufu's infertile concubines should be taken to each of his (Abdullahi's) surviving brothers, warning that anyone who refused these women would be regarded as hostile. By thus distributing Yusufu's concubines, Abdullahi intended to set his brothers against Yusufu permanently. However, when they heard, perhaps from Sallama, that Abdullahi intended next to order Yusufu's execution as a *kahiri* (apostate) on the ground that he foresaw civil strife if Yusufu lived, the emir's brothers, Sarkin Shanu Hasan, the Santuraki Mamman Bello and Husaini, jointly interposed and forbade this at a private meeting with Abdullahi in the palace, demanding their own executions if Yusufu was harmed. Abdullahi was thus forced by his kinsmen's pressure to release Yusufu from chains and jail, and restored to him his wives and children.

Thereafter until his father's death, Yusufu "had to remain in chagrin and poverty till he was penniless," disgraced and confined to the capital where his shame could not be hid. On dismissing Yusufu and appointing Ibrahim Mai Kulutu as Galadima, Abdullahi further expressed his displeasure by reducing the

Galadima's fiefs, and removed Kumbotso, Fari, Tsenti and Kankarawa near Minjibir for distribution to his own untitled sons, some of whom such as Cigari and
Aliyu already administered Sallawa, Garun Malam, Gadan Sarki and other minor
settlements as his *jekadu*. In thus reducing the territorial base of the Galadimaship,
Abdullahi sought to discourage ambitions among future Galadimas. These events
occurred in 1877, according to information collected at Kano.[52]

Appointment Policies

Abdullahi's reign ended in September 1882 when, en route to Sokoto, accompanied by the Kano nobility, he died at Korofi in Katsina. Despite his irregular
succession and periodic difficulties with Sokoto, Abdullahi's long reign had
established the Kano chiefship and defined its relations with the founding aristocracy, with local "Habe," and with such foreign enemies as Hadeija, Gumel, Damagaram, Maradi and Ningi. During his 27 years on the throne, most of Kano had
enjoyed peace and regular government. Population and prosperity had increased,
despite rising taxation; and even the unsettled southern territory on the Ningi
front, thanks to Abdullahi's foresight and vigour, retained a relatively dense population. Abdullahi's tireless if unspectacular attention to the needs and affairs of
state gave Kano the security that enabled it to recover from the losses and devastations of the *jihad*, from Dabo's long campaigns, and from the attacks of Hadeija,
Gumel, Damagaram, Ningi and Maradi. By 1875 Kano was probably the strongest
and most populous state in the Fulani Empire, as well as the wealthiest, most
central and advanced. As its vigour ebbed and imperial capacities declined, the
Fulani leadership in Sokoto became increasingly sensitive to Kano's superiority in
material resources, population, resilience and internal order. There are indications
that ill-judged desires to "put Kano in its place" may have entered into some of
Abdullahi's later difficulties with Sokoto.

Despite his autocratic leanings and manner, Abdullahi had observed the
unwritten constitution of Fulani Kano with scrupulous care. Throughout his reign
he preserved the prescriptive rights of founding lineages to their hereditary titles.
The Danbazawa Sarkin Bai Muhammad Kwairanga exercised his office without
interference. On the death of Abubakar, son of Isa, in 1878, Abdullahi appointed
Haruna, Abubakar's brother, to the Jobawa title of Makama. Successive Yolawa
leaders were appointed to the Madaki title following defeats at Fajewa and
Godiya by the Ningi and Maradi forces respectively. Throughout his reign,
Abdullahi seems also to have appointed only Yolawa to the minor office of
Magajin Mallam na Cedi. Likewise, the Mundubawa retained their titles, Mai
Anguwan Mundubawa, Dan Amar, and Mallamin Maude. The lineage of Malam
Jamau retained the title of Sarkin Dawaki Mai Tuta. The Danejawa retained their
office, Dan Iya, with its attached fiefs, and were also given the newly revived title
of Dan Makwayau, as related above. Descendants of the Hausa Usuman contin-
ued to fill the minor title of Magajin Malam na Hausawa, while the residual
Kutumbi lineage retained the parallel Kutumbawa title.

At Rano and Birnin Kudu, Abdullahi also preserved the rights of the local
ruling lineages. At Karaye and Dutse the chiefship oscillated between two competing Fulani lineages. At Kiru, another important rural chiefship, Suleibawa collaterals of the central dynasty remained dominant, as under the emirs Sule and

Dabo. At Gaya, for reasons unknown, following the death of Sarkin Gaya Faruku in 1870, Abdullahi passed over the ruling Kurawa lineage, and between 1870 and 1883 appointed three *shigege* Fulani students of his own, first Garba, then Aliyu, Garba's younger brother, and finally Mamman, Aliyu having been dismissed for oppression (*zalunci*). As indicated above, the senior clerical offices of Limam and Alkali were given by Abdullahi to men whose learning and character specially qualified them for these posts. Hereditary or quasi-hereditary rights to these critical titles were thus denied. Following the death of the baYole limam of Wudil called Abdullahi, the immigrant Sule held this office until he was made Alkali on the execution of Ahmadu Rufa'i, following which the Na'ibi Ahmadu, son of Sule Bagyeni, was appointed Limam, and on his death, Umaru, son of the Bornu Fulani Muhammadu Zahara who had served as Dabo's Limam.

In his history, Malam Adamu Na Ma'aji lists successive Ma'ajis without further detail about their career or status.[53] According to Malam Adamu, on Abdullahi's accession, the Ma'aji was Malam Na Kazaure, a Kano Habe, who was followed by a slave, Son Allah. After Son Allah, Usumanu, a freeman, was appointed. However, the Kano Chronicle reports that Abdullahi "degraded Ma'aji Suleimanu, Ma'aji Gajere, and Sankurmi Musa."[54] On the data available, it seems that Malam Adamu's list omits Suleimanu and Gajere after Malam na Kazaure and before the slave Ma'aji Son Allah. Son Allah was probably appointed by Abdullahi following the dismissals of Gajere and Suleimanu for misconduct. In like fashion the technically indispensable but subordinate positions of Sarkin Fada, Magatakarda (Scribe), Sarkin Yaki, Jakadan Garko, Sarkin Jarmai, Sarkin Dogarai and Sankurmi were allocated by Abdullahi to men whose service, loyalties and competence recommended them for these roles. Such positions accordingly remained *shigege* appointments, despite the occasional succession of kinsmen, as for example, on the appointment of Malam Dogo's son, Datti, as Sarkin Yaki following Dogo's transfer to this office after the Tafida Muhamman had assumed Dogo's former role as Sarkin Fada and "unofficial" Waziri. Likewise, though Laiyu succeeded his father Haburde, a Fulani, in the title of Sarkin Yara under Abdullahi, that office retained its *shigege* identification. More unusual was Abdullahi's replacement of the Hausa Sankurmi Musa, the son of Dabo's Galadima Ango, by his own daughter's son, Mamudu, and the appointment of his client, Dodo Mai Kwaban Tabo, to the key office of Sarkin Dogarai (chief of police).

Under Abdullahi, setting aside such female titles as Magajiya, Mai Babban Daki and Uwar Soro, the following territorial offices had been appropriated by the dynasty: Galadima, Wombai, Dan Lawan, Sarkin Shanu, Ciroma, Turaki Manya (Santuraki), Dan Buram, Tafida, and perhaps also Barde Babba, following the appointment of Sule, a son of the Wombai Haruna, Dabo's younger brother, to this title in 1849, after the previous Barde, a client called Maude, had been killed by the Ningi at Birnin Kudu. Of these royal offices in Abdullahi's reign, the Wombai, Sarkin Shanu, Santuraki and Danlawan titles were held by the emir's collaterals; the Barde Babba was another collateral, though unable to succeed since only those descended from Dabo were eligible. The Wombai Hassan, Dabo's younger brother, retained his office throughout Abdu's reign, despite increasing blindness. Following the death of the Dan Lawan Dan Mai-soro, the son of Sarkin Kano Usuman's daughter, Abdullahi appointed his own younger brother Yusufu, who died at Sokoto early in the following reign. Of dynastic offices in 1882, the Ciroma and Tafida were filled by the ruler's sons, namely, Musa who succeeded his brother Halilu on the latter's death as Ciroma, and Hamman who replaced Abdurrazuku, Usuman's son, as Tafida. It is presumed that the office of Dan Ruwata, subordinate to Galadima, was also filled by one of the ruler's issue; but the holder's identity in Abdullahi's reign remains unknown.

Early in his reign, Abdullahi had appointed his son Halilu as Dan Buram, following the death of Dabo's son, Dadu. Later, on Halilu's promotion to Ciroma, the emir gave this office to another son, Sule. Likewise in 1862, after the dismissal of his brother Abdulkadiri from the Galadimaship, Abdullahi had installed his son Yusufu, as related above; but following Yusufu's disaffection, Abdullahi replaced him by the scribe Ibrahim, having learned that this office, traditionally allocated to the ruler's elder brothers, was ill-suited to his son. We lack data on the distribution of such titles as Barde Kereriya, Dan Darman, Dan Isa and Dan Maje for Abdullahi's reign and for some that preceded it. However, it is said that the office of Dan Kade was held by *barori* (non-royal clients) throughout this period, whether on hereditary or other grounds we do not know. The office of Sarkin Dawakin Tsakar Gida at this date appears to have been reserved for Mundubawa cross-cousins of the emir. Thus following Yusufu's dismissal and public humiliation, on Abdullahi's death, Mundubawa claims for the succession having long since lapsed, the Santuraki Mamman Bello, the Dan Lawan Yusufu and the Sarkin Shanu Hassan, all sons of Dabo, and the Ciroma Musa, Tafida Muhammad and Dan Buram Sule, Abdullahi's sons, were the only serious candidates for the succession.

Mamman Bello, 1882–1893

The Succession

Having buried Abdullahi at Korofi, the Kano column resumed its route to Sokoto. It is likely that most of the Kano "Electors" had accompanied the column; but on their arrival in Sokoto, there is no evidence that the Council met to select Abdullahi's successor. Rather, on learning of Abdullahi's death by the arrival of his riderless, caparisoned horse, the traditional sign, the caliph and Waziri of Sokoto assumed responsibility for deciding the succession themselves. According to the Dokaji Alhaji Abubakar, caliph Umaru (1881–1891) selected the ex-Galadima Yusufu, while the vizier Abdullahi Bayero chose Dabo's son, the Dan Lawan Yusufu. According to another Kano tradition, the caliph nominated the Dan Lawan, while the vizier selected the ex-Galadima Yusufu. The nominees were namesakes; and neither the caliph nor the vizier dared to overrule the other, the caliph because his vizier was better informed about Kano and directly responsible for its affairs, the vizier because of the caliph's status and final right. Thus if the tale related above concerning Abdullahi's request for permission to abdicate is correct, it seems that the ex-Galadima Yusufu had continued to canvass the succession at Sokoto thereafter to good effect.

In their impasse over Abdullahi's successor, the caliph and his Waziri discussed the question for several days. It is not reported that either the *sarakunan karaga* (imperial council) or the Kano "electoral" council were formally asked to settle the issue. As we have seen, from Suleimanu's day until Abdullahi's, the caliphs of Sokoto had reserved to their viziers and themselves authority to decide the succession at Kano; and usually they had exercised it without formally consulting the Kano council. Later events exhibited the danger of this anomalous procedure, which had been progressively institutionalised by the successions of Suleimanu and Dabo. Abdullahi's seizure of the throne had already revealed some attendant risks of this procedure; but evidently, by reserving to themselves the right to decide the succession, the caliph and vizier of Sokoto sought to retain or strengthen their grip on Kano, which, as its largest, most central and important state, had a particularly strategic place in the imperial structure.

As the caliph and vizier debated the matter, the news and names of favoured candidates leaked to their courtiers. That known, the Kano nobility awaited the final selection. Whether the caliph and vizier, unable to resolve their differences, appealed to Mariam, the Shehu's daughter, who still lived in Sokoto, or whether Mariam, learning of the impasse, decided to intervene, remains unclear; but since the caliph and vizier could not agree, it is said that she suggested that both should defer to her judgment, and then nominated the Turaki Manya Mamman Bello, who was Dabo's son, and Abdullahi's younger brother. Caliph Umaru and Waziri Abdullahi were both relieved, and proposed to instal Mamman Bello at once, but he asked them to defer the installation until Sabbath Eve on the following Thursday. Shortly after this Mamman Bello's brother, the Dan Lawan Yusufu died at Sokoto, thus removing his leading rival. Following the installation, the Kano nobility returned home, and Mamman Bello entered the palace after straightening the affairs of his old office, Santuraki.[55]

During Abdullahi's reign, Mamman Bello had remained in the background, administering his fiefs routinely, but without influence in matters of policy. Abdullahi had rebuilt the Santuraki's compound early in his reign, together with the city mosque. "They had been in ruins for many years."[56] By such means Abdullahi may have wished to show his respect for the Santuraki office which Narai had distinguished when he went to his death at the city mosque in place of Mohamma Shashere (1573–82). Shashere's successor Muhamman Zaki had, in honour of Narai's deed built the *zaure* or audience chamber of Turaki Manya near the mosque, and placed the kingdom in his Turaki's hands while away from the city. However, despite these traditions, Abdullahi seems to have excluded his brother Mamman Bello from policy decisions; and, despite his numerous fiefs— Kafin Agur, Kiru, Dan Hassan, Kabo, Bebeji, Durum, Kerawa, Yako, Culu, Kofa and Karaye—the Santuraki Mamman Bello is said to have remained poor throughout Abdu's reign, perhaps in consequence of his habitual generosity and increasing number of adult sons. For aid in these years Mamman Bello relied heavily on the support and advice of his friend Dan Gyatum, who served as his majordomo (Sarkin Fada).

On moving to the palace, Mamman Bello formally installed Dan Gyatum as his Sarkin Fada. Mamman Bello's early administration and relation to Dan Gyatum are neatly summarised in the Kano Chronicle. "He said to his friend Sarkin Fada Dan Gyatum, 'You are Wazirin Kano; I place in your hands the management of Kano.' The Sarkin Fada was unrivalled as a settler of disputes; Bello was like his Waziri, and Sarkin Fada was like Sarki. When Sarkin Fada died, Muhammed Bello stretched out his legs because he saw that now he must become Sarki in earnest."[57] Apparently, when Mamman Bello held court, Dan Gyatum sat by the edge of the dais before the assembly; and Bello tolerated no rebukes from his courtiers to the Sarkin Fada for the latter's uncouth habits.[58] Unlike Abdullahi, who employed his Sarkin Fada Malam Dogo purely as a functionary, while reserving to himself all decisions on policy, as long as Dan Gyatum lived, Mamman Bello relied on his guidance and vigilance in governing Kano; but that does not imply that Dan Gyatum decided matters of state to the exclusion of his friend the emir. As the Chronicle suggests, Mamman Bello may have employed him chiefly to arbitrate and reconcile disputes, since "the Sarkin Fada was unrivalled as a settler of disputes." By relieving himself in this way of tedious trivia, Bello may thus have reserved his time for more important affairs.

At his accession, Mamman Bello may have been over 50 years of age. His sight was already failing, and continued to weaken, though he never became blind. His accession, followed rapidly by the death of his brother and rival the Dan Lawan Yusufu, left the royal offices of Turaki and the Dan Lawan for him to fill. Mamman Bello gave the office of Turaki to his eldest son Tukur, and appointed Abdullahi's son Ayuba, who probably held the rank of Dan Maje, as Dan Lawan; but when Ayuba died a few years later, Mamman Bello gave the title to his own son, Umaru.

As mentioned above, during Abdullahi's reign, some throne slaves had begun to marry free women who lived at the palace as the emir's wards. Many of these ladies belonged to aristocratic Fulani lineages; but despite public comment and private pressure, Abdullahi had taken no action to dissolve those unions. On entering the palace, Mamman Bello asserted his legal right as owner of the slaves, and dissolved all these asymmetrical marriages by decreeing the divorce of free women from their slave husbands. Bello then enunciated a new law which overrode the Maliki code on these matters and forbade any future recurrence of these irregular unions. "*Bayan wannan, bawa ya aure baiwa, 'yaya ya aure 'yaya.*" (Henceforth, let slave men marry slave women (only), and free men marry free women.) The effectiveness of this law is attested by C.H. Robinson's report that ten years later at Kano "a free man may not marry a slave, nor vice versa."[59] Notably, by this measure Mamman Bello eliminated unions of free and slave without proscribing those between individuals of different "race" or ethnic stock. He then sent all those Fulani women whose marriages to throne slaves he had abruptly terminated back to the homes of their kinsmen, together with the offspring of their slave marriages, since under Muslim law such children belonged to their free mothers and not to their slave genitors. Perhaps recalling Abdullahi's early execution of the Shamaki Isa, the palace slaves made no protest at Mamman Bello's peremptory dissolution of their unions; but they were probably relieved at his restraint, being well aware of the widespread Fulani resentment of these unions, of their incongruity, and of their questionable status and character as abuses of the emir's *amana*.

Not long after this, the Alkalin Kano Sule, whom Abdullahi had promoted to this position from the Limamship, sensing Mamman Bello's antipathy, fled to Zaria, his former home, after consulting the Sarkin Gaya, who probably reminded him of the fate of his predecessor Ahmadu Rufa'i in Abdullahi's reign. Although Alkali Sule had taken no action to prevent or revoke these irregular marriages of the throne slaves to the emir's free wards, it is uncertain whether Mamman Bello regarded him as morally or legally involved in them, since they pertained rather to Abdullahi's palace administration. However, I cannot say what generated the Alkali's anxiety about Mamman Bello. On Sule's flight, Bello appointed Bappa, a baGyeni cleric, as Alkalin Kano, and Bappa discharged the office throughout Bello's reign.

The Development of Dynastic Rivalry

Following the cryptic remark that "in Abdullahi's time Sallama Berka became great," the Kano Chronicle misleadingly reports that "in the time of Mohammed Bello, this man revolted and was degraded. In Abdullahi's time, too, the palace slaves became so great that they were like free men. They all rebelled in Mohammed's time, but Allah helped Mohammed Bello to quell the rebellion."[60] However, careful enquiries failed to disclose any indication or rumour of revolt during the reign of Mamman Bello or any other emir by Sallama Barka or any other slaves.

Bello seems to have heard about Sallama Barka's philanderings during the closing years of Abdullahi's reign. Abdullahi's death gave Bello the opportunity to remove those concubines, fertile and infertile, who may have tolerated or welcomed the Sallama's advances. It also allowed him to exclude the Sallama from the harem. Not long after, while reading an Arabic manuscript in an inner chamber at night, Mamman Bello received an unexpected visit from the Sallama Barka and his friend the ex-Galadima Yusufu. The ageing emir was alone and unattended when confronted by these unwelcome guests. It is related that all Yusufu had to say was that since Mamman Bello lived and occupied the throne, his "father" (*baba*) had not died, a cryptic statement which, while formally correct, since the same term (*baba*) denotes father and father's brother, might be interpreted in two ways: firstly as a declaration of political homage (*capka*); secondly as an implied threat that Bello could expect another such visit if he left Yusufu in his current poverty and disgrace. There being no further communication, Bello replied with equal obscurity, "Na ji," ("I hear," meaning "I understand") and sent the two away.

Next morning when the court had assembled at Fagaci, the emir denounced Sallama Barka as a serious menace, relating what had happened the previous night. Bello said the Sallama had broken his trust ("*amana*") in bringing Yusufu privately to him without warning, while he was unattended and alone, arguing that if Yusufu or anyone brought thus privily intended harm, that could not have been prevented. In short, Sallama Barka, charged with the emir's personal security, had used his position to place Bello in a potentially dangerous situation. Clearly the emir expected that Sallama would do so again at an opportune moment, given another chance. He concluded by ordering the Shamaki's attendant to remove Sallama Barka at once to the jail in Shamaki's compound and keep him there pending further orders. It is said that Mamman Bello then wrote to Sokoto, relating Sallama's disloyalty and seeking permission to dismiss and punish him. Galadima Yusufu, perhaps at Sallama's request, also wrote to the caliph on Barka's behalf, invoking the *amana* relation between the dynasty and throne slaves, and appealing for protection for his friend.

After further correspondence, Mamman Bello learnt of Yusufu's intervention and had him summoned to the morning court at Fagaci. There Bello denounced and cursed him as a *kahiri* (apostate, heathen), accused him of plotting to do him physical harm, and of treasonable interference on Sallama's behalf in his appeal to Sokoto despite Yusufu's knowledge of Sallama's conduct in Abdullahi's harem. Bello then related how he and his brothers had intervened to prevent Abdullahi from ordering Yusufu's execution. Bello concluded his denunciation by forbidding Yusufu ever to return to the palace, and wrote urgently to Sokoto requesting permission to punish Barka. On receiving the caliph's assent, Bello directed Hauni to remove Barka from the Shamaki's prison and execute him in the market place, declaiming the reason therefor to all. This public declaration by Hauni at Sallama's execution, coupled with Mamman Bello's denunciation of Yusufu in the presence of his assembled courtiers, broadcast to Kano those details of palace events and arrangements related above, about which we should otherwise know only what the Chronicle records cryptically, since on these matters the Dokaji Abubakar is tactfully silent, like Malam Adamu before him. However, this account should serve to demonstrate that, though Sallama Barka had grossly overreached himself, neither he nor any other palace slave raised any sign of "revolt" at Kano during the reigns of Abdullahi or Bello.

The emir's long indictment of Yusufu before the assembled courtiers, and his detailed recital of Yusufu's devious conduct and personal failings, had the effect of permanently alienating Mamman Bello from Yusufu and from all those sons of Abdullahi who supported Yusufu as their senior and leader, discreetly or openly, on grounds of kinship and dynastic interest. Mamman Bello may not have intended to generate this sharp cleavage so early in his reign; but recognising that the damage done made an irreparable breach, he took appropriate action to protect his throne and preserve his sons' interests in the coming succession struggle by strategic allocations of royal office. Thus, when the Tafida Muhamman, Abdullahi's son, died not long after, Mamman Bello appointed Malanta, the son of Abdullahi's brother Usuman, to succeed. Later, when Abdullahi's Daneji Danmakwayau Gidado died en route to Sokoto for an attack on Argungu, Bello appointed Mustafa, another of Usuman's sons, who had married his daughter. By this appointment Bello tried to redefine the title of Danmakwayau as one reserved for the ruler's affines, since like Gidado, that was Mustafa's status. However, unlike Gidado, Mustafa was both a Basuleibe prince, eligible for the succession, and a son of Abdullahi's predecessor, Usuman. In appointing Malanta and Mustafa to the offices of Tafida and Danmakwayau, Bello's purpose was perfectly clear. By these means he sought to attach Usuman's sons to his side, hoping thereby to strengthen his issue in the coming struggle with Abdullahi's for the future control of Kano.

If we look back on the development of Suleibawa rule in Kano, the rapidity with which intra-dynastic cleavages followed dynastic pre-eminence is so marked as to suggest some necessary connection. Even in Usuman's reign, familistic policies were evident. Under Abdullahi, despite his general regard for lineage rights to hereditary offices, the distribution of royal appointments was clearly patrimonial, and his brother's sons were excluded, including the heirs of Usuman. Instead, Abdullahi sought to balance the distribution of office between his sons and his brothers, the sons of Dabo, without much further provision for the latter's children; but he could hardly assume that, with the resources at their disposal, his brothers could promote the interests of their sons as well as he could do for his. Nonetheless, with the unfortunate exception of the Galadimaship, he scrupulously reserved the senior royal offices that administered the largest number of fiefs for his collaterals, so that when he died, his brothers and sons held equal numbers of territorial titles. It was thus in Mamman Bello's reign that dynastic rivalry was first unbridled; and perhaps the collusion of Yusufu and Sallama Barka which furnished the occasion for its expression, was incidental rather than intrinsic to this development.

Abdullahi's long reign had not only displaced Mundubawa claims to rule Kano. It had so strongly identified the government of the country with Abdullahi, and by extension with his heirs, that many at Kano, including the ex-Galadima Yusufu, were deeply surprised when Sokoto appointed some other, Abdullahi's brother, to succeed him. By 1882 Abdullahi's surviving male progeny probably outnumbered all other issue of Dabo. To withstand their future domination, Mamman Bello accordingly forged alliances with the heirs of Usuman by appointments designed to make them dependent on his sons.

Since Abdullahi's dismissal of the Ciroma Dikko, Usuman's son, that title had come under the supervision and protection of Sokoto. Thenceforward the ruler of Kano could no longer dismiss his Ciroma without first securing the Waziri's assent. Following Dikko, Abdullahi had appointed his son Musa as Ciroma and, to enrich and enhance the office, in return for Gadanya and adjacent towns, he had transferred to it from the Dambazawa Sarkin Bai Kwairanga the lucrative fief of Dambarta, and perhaps Kunya also. Thereafter, Dambarta remained attached to the Ciroma's office until 1903.

Mamman Bello secured the dismissal of Ciroma Musa by accusing him of withholding half the wealth that he (Mamman Bello) had sent to Sokoto under the Ciroma as prestations and gifts on receiving a bride from the Toronkawa dynasty there. We have no way of determining the truth of this accusation; but the Ciroma would indeed have been rash to appropriate any part of such a consignment, particularly since it was borne by an escort of throne slaves whose loyalty lay to the emir. However, to dismiss the Ciroma, an offence and specific accusation were necessary. Presumably other charges could have been manufactured with equal ease or success to effect this end, despite the vizier's supervision. When my Kano informants were asked why Bello dismissed the Ciroma, they answered simply *"Don ya ba dansa"*—that is, "in order that he (the emir) could give (the office to) his own son." This was precisely what happened.

Following Musa's removal, Mamman Bello installed his own son Abubakar as Ciroma in charge of Dambarta and its other fiefs. Next when Dabo's son Hassan, the Sarkin Shanu, died, Mamman Bello appointed his own son Datti, who retained the office throughout his reign. At some point also the Dan Buram Sule, Abdullahi's son, was replaced by Mamman Bello's son Abubakar under circumstances that remain obscure. Then after the death of his friend, the Sarkin Fada Dan Gyatum, Mamman Bello "expelled the Galadima Ibrahim from his office and banished him to Funkuyi in Zaria, hence his name 'Galadima na Funkuyi.' Bello gave the post of Galadima to his son Tukur, and his son Zakari was made Santuraki."[61] Thus, following the death of the Dan Lawan Ayuba and Bello's appointment of his own son Umaru to that office, none of Abdullahi's numerous heirs held any territorial title, whereas all five adult sons of Mamman Bello had senior offices, as did two sons of the deceased emir Usuman. This completely turned the dynastic tables. Formerly, Abdullahi's sons had enjoyed office to the exclusion of their first cousins. It was now the turn of Bello's sons to hold office and acquire wealth while the sons of Abdullahi looked on in chagrin, fear and envy.

The ancient Wombai Hassan, Dabo's younger brother, who was long since blind, had retained his office undisturbed on grounds of kinship and age from Dabo's reign through Usuman's and Abdullahi's into Mamman Bello's; but when the caliph and vizier of Sokoto realised that Bello had eliminated all Abdullahi's sons from office, they instructed him to retire the Wombai Hassan and give that office with its fiefs intact, to Shehu (Usuman), Abdullahi's son. By this means, the caliph and vizier sought to preserve the interests and claims of Abdullahi's issue in the succession, to provide an official channel for their support, and to warn Mamman Bello that his dynastic policies had not escaped their attention. However, Hassan's retirement and Shehu's appointment had other structural implications. Under the rule that no one could dismiss anyone appointed by his superior, Mamman Bello lost the authority to remove Shehu without Sokoto's permission. Thus with that appointment, Sokoto had restricted the emir's rights to remove his Wombai, Ciroma, Galadima, Dan Iya, Sarkin Bai, Madaki, Makama and Sarkin Dawaki Mai Tuta, all of them hereditary offices. On the other hand it seems that Bello had little difficulty in dismissing the *shigege* Galadima Ibrahim.

As the Wombai appointed by Sokoto, Shehu enjoyed the caliph's protection. He was also the only one of Abdullahi's sons to hold office in the second half of Bello's administration. However, in age, achievements, prospects, and the relative ranks of their respective offices, despite his official status, Shehu remained junior to the ex-Galadima Yusufu, around whom the *zuri'an Abdullahi* (descendants of Abdullahi) clustered, concentrating their resentment and deepening their solidarity by identifying Yusufu's humiliation with their own.

As mentioned above, in his later years Abdullahi had placed some minor rural settlements under his elder untitled sons. Formally these fiefs remained attached to the throne, being administered by princes as *jekadu* whose authority derived from the emir's commissions instructing them to supervise these fiefs on his behalf. Holding no titled offices, those princely *jekadu* could not be dismissed by conventional procedures; but their commissions could easily be withdrawn, whenever the ruler delegated administrative responsibilities for the towns they administered to others of his choice; and this is precisely what appears to have occurred.

In the collection of imperial correspondence between Sokoto and Kano for these decades, there is a letter from Aliyu Babba, Abdullahi's son, to his mother's brother, Muhammadu Mansuru, a son of caliph Aliyu Babba, which obliquely describes Aliyu's displacement and loss of his territorial commission. It will be recalled that when the caliph Aliyu Babba confirmed Abdullahi's accession at Katsina, following the latter's usurpation in Kano, he sealed his approval by giving Abdullahi his daughter as a bride. The first child of that union was duly named Aliyu Babba after his mother's father, the caliph, and brought up as a mallam. Thus, through his mother, the young Aliyu had specially close relations with the Toronkawa dynasty of Sokoto, and especially with those grandsons of caliph Aliyu Babba who were his cross-cousins, joking relations and closest cognatic kin. Caliph Umaru (1881–1891), the emir Mamman Bello's suzerain, was thus Aliyu Babba's senior mother's brother; and perhaps in writing Muhammadu Mansuru, Aliyu Babba hoped that his message would be conveyed to caliph Umaru, Mansuru's brother.

Late in his reign, Abdullahi had placed the town of Garun Malam and its surrounding hamlets under Aliyu Babba, seeking thereby simultaneously to provide adequately for the prince's support, and to retain this strategic town, midway between Bebeji, Kura and Rano, for the crown, while ensuring its effective administration. Holding no office or title, Aliyu Babba administered Garun Malam by his father's commission. In his letter to Muhammadu Mansuru, written during Mamman Bello's reign, after greetings Aliyu Babba continues,

> when we had returned home (to Garun Malam?) we gave our emir (Mamman Bello) the tax he had levied on us by his slave Makama Dandaura, who is well known. He (Mamman Bello) said that he had placed him in charge of these matters and that if any others interfered (?or collaborated) with him he should report this. He (Dandaura) said nobody had interfered (?or collaborated) with him at all, so I told him to depart. Since then nothing has stopped me from writing to you sooner except my fear that he (?Mamman Bello) may say that I have complained to you about him. Farewell and peace.[62]

Presumably other sons of Abdullahi who exercised such irregular commissions, for example, Cigari, who ruled Sallawa, Zakari who ruled Tsenti and Isma'ila at Gadan Sarki, experienced similar displacement as Mamman Bello transferred their fiefs to throne slaves for tax collection and administration.

Tax Policies and the Treasury

Usuman had increased the basic rate of tax from 1,000 cowries per "Habe" farmer in Dabo's day to 2,500, but Abdullahi had reduced this to 2,000 per "Habe" householder, while imposing a levy of 500 cowries on Fulani farmers for the first time. Mamman Bello doubled the Habe rate to 4,000 cowries annually per farming household, and the Fulani rate to 1,000 cowries per farmer. Maguzawa, Warjawa and other pagans throughout Kano were as usual liable to the punitive *jizya* the *shari'a* ordained for heathens at rates that varied with their wealth. In addition, taxes levied on cassava, chilli peppers, cotton, sugar cane, sweet potatoes and other market crops were increased to an average rate of 1,500 cowries per plot, although officially, individual levies varied with the size of the field. This levy on market crops was known as *kudin shuke*, while the basic tax, known interchangeably as *haraji* or *kudin kasa*, was assimilated to the Islamic *kharaj*. *Jangali* was also collected from those transhumant Fulani who remained in Kano during the rains at rates of 2,000 cowries per head on herds in excess of more than 30 beasts, whereas resident Fulani rendered their dues in kind as the law laid down for herds exceeding 30 head. Pastoralists were exempt from *haraji* or *kudin kasa*, which, like *jangali* and cattle tithe, was collected annually during the rainy season. However, following the decimation of Fulani herds between 1887 and 1891 by major epidemics of rinderpest,[63] Mamman Bello suspended collections of cattle tax and tithe, and they were not resumed during his lifetime.

Unlike the *haraji* and *jangali*, *kudin shuke*, the tax on marsh plots of market crops, was collected during the grain harvest by *jekadu* of the village chief and fiefholder, who surveyed, inspected and assessed the taxable plots together. In addition, during Bello's reign 1,100 cowries were levied annually on each date tree in bearing, and on every dyepit. Grain tithe, death duties and *kudin wankan sarauta* were collected routinely. Though princes, the blind, lepers, disabled and malams were exempt from tax, *haraji* was now levied on farmers resident in the capital as well as rural areas. Leather workers, tanners, blacksmiths and silversmiths remained subject to corvée at the emir's direction under craft heads residing in Kano. Smelters turned in one-tenth of the iron they smelted to the village head in whose area the ore had been mined. *Fatake* (long-distance traders), while exempt from tax, were expected to "greet" the chief with appropriate gifts. At the city market, the Chief Butcher (Sarkin Pawa) collected a fee for every beast slaughtered, and Korama, the senior grain seller, who was always a woman, collected grain daily for the San Kurmi and his prisoners. Caravans, sales of slaves and horses, commission agents, weaving, sewing and building, were all untaxed. Such resident hereditary chiefs as those at Rano, Birnin Kudu, Dutse, Karaye and Gaya lacked authority to levy taxes other than *kudin wankan sarauta* on their appointments. As elsewhere, in these incorporated chiefdoms taxes were collected jointly by *jekadu* of the *hakimi* and the hereditary chief touring the local communities together.

As before, the Ma'aji and Shamaki served as treasurers, and besides routine administration of the capital, the Ma'aji administered the public treasury, while the Shamaki had charge of the emir's personal stores and palace expenditure. Much of Shamaki's expenditure passed to or through *fatake* who traded to Lokoja and Nupe and purchased firearms or powder for the royal armoury indirectly from British trading stations along the River Niger. As the emir's military quartermaster, Shamaki was also responsible for securing horses and all types of war gear needed to equip the palace squadrons and to supply forces recruited outside. As required, other moneys for palace expenses were transferred by Ma'aji to the slave Sarkin Hatsi who administered the distribution of grain from the palace stores. While no daily written accounts were kept, payments by the Ma'aji at the ruler's instructions should be simultaneously witnessed by the Ma'aji's agent and by the Shamaki's slave charged with this commission. Such arrangements not only allowed the Ma'aji to procrastinate as the emir directed, but also, with or without the latter's knowledge, in those transactions which he conducted for the emir. In this situation, the Ma'aji could also employ portions of the public fund for his own purposes.

It is said that tax increases at Kano under Mamman Bello were necessitated by increased demands for cash from Kano made by the caliph and vizier of Sokoto. Though undoubtedly important, this is unlikely to be the full explanation. Of the forty letters between Kano and Sokoto dating from Bello's reign that I copied at

Sokoto, only two deal with tributary payments from Kano, and four with local donations at Sokoto's direction, while three others mention taxation in differing contexts. Of the latter, one reports in considerable detail Bello's difficulties with a Sarkin Fulani of Kunci who was formally supervised by the Sarkin Bai. After a year's dispute with this Sarkin Fulani, Mamman Bello wrote to the vizier Buhari relating the source and termination of the dispute. He mentions firstly that the Sarkin Fulani had seized horses, cattle and slave girls from the camps of some transhumant pastoralists who had entered Kano from Katsina and remained there during the rainy season. When these immigrants appealed, Bello sent a message to the Sarkin Fulani ordering him to return these chattels and to avoid repeating his conduct. The Sarkin Fulani procrastinated, and in due course Bello learnt from an agent of the baJobe Makama Haruna, that he had declared his intention to disobey. Bello then sent further instructions to the Sarkin Fulani Kunci to return the property he had seized from immigrant Katsina Fulani. This time the Sarkin Fulani complied; but when tax was collected the following year, Bello writes that he gave Sarkin Fulani his customary fourth (*rubu'i*) from the total of 440 *keso* or 8,800,000 cowries he had collected as *haraji* rather than *jangali*, since the Sarkin Fulani Kunci exercised a territorial jurisdiction as well as *bin kanu*. Nonetheless, Bello reports that Sarkin Fulani refused a summons to support the Sarkin Dawaki and the Kano forces at Dambarta against an attack by the Hausa of Gobir and Maradi. Following this, the Sarkin Fulani Kunci also refused to join the Kano contingent summoned by the caliph to reinforce the Sokoto army in his attack on Kebbi that year. Finally, when Bello had suppressed the rebellion at Dutse discussed below, and arranged to despatch the caliph's share of the rebel chief's slaves to Sokoto in the charge of Sarkin Fulani Kunci, the latter refused to go. By then the Sarkin Fulani's kinsmen had wearied of his conduct and protested to him. Since the Sarkin Fulani rejected their appeals, his kin came to Kano, asked Bello to dismiss him, nominated his full brother, the Galadima of Kunci, to succeed, and joined a squadron despatched under the Sarkin Dawaki to instal him at Kunci. On learning of his dismissal, the recalcitrant Sarkin Fulani quickly bundled up his wealth, assembled his family and slaves, set fire to his compound, and fled across the border to Kazaure.

Of minor importance, this incident, like several others from Bello's surviving correspondence with Sokoto, enriches and deepens our understanding of governmental processes and conditions in Kano during his reign. Whether the Sarkin Fulani Kunci was predisposed to disobey Bello before their initial difference over the cattle, horses and slave-girls he had received in lieu of cash payments of *jangali*, we have no way of knowing from the letters; but thereafter he increasingly set aside the emir's instructions. Nonetheless, he collected the local *haraji* and turned in nearly nine million cowries to Bello, receiving one fourth as his share. Since Buhari, to whom the letter was addressed, became vizier on Abdullahi Bayero's death in 1886, it is probable that Bello's dispute with the Sarkin Fulani arose after the collection of *jangali* had been suspended following the epidemic of 1887.[64] Perhaps the Sarkin Fulani, accustomed to receiving one-fourth of the tax receipts he sent to Kano, viewed the suspension as an unwarranted reduction of his income, and sought to register his protest by these actions.

In another letter addressed to the Waziri Buhari, Bello briefly reports that he had given 2.7 million cowries to an unidentified bearer of the vizier's letter, but asked reprieve in sending 10 million to the caliph and 5 million to the vizier, since neither the *kudin jizya* (*?haraji*) nor the *kudin korofi* (tax on dyepits) had yet been collected. Instead of 15 million, Bello despatched 2 million cowries by the vizier's messenger. This letter sheds light on the state of Kano finances at the time under the heavy, irregular demands for cash from Sokoto. If we assume that Bello normally maintained sufficient reserves of cash in the treasury to meet foreseeable expenditures until the *jizya* (*?kudin kasa*) and tax on dyepits had come in, the 2 million cowries he despatched to Sokoto illustrates his improvidence.

In truth, Fulani rulers had little sense of finance and less interest in summing or balancing their accounts; but nowhere were these failings so severe as at the imperial centre, and there they were particularly evident in the conduct of the caliph and his vizier. Yet even these imperial demands fail to explain the financial stringency which beset Kano after Bello had doubled the rate of taxation and instituted *jangali* levies in cash. Undoubtedly, the Ma'aji Son Allah, a throne slave, exploited his inadequately supervised office; but it is hard to believe that peculations on the scale necessary to ruin the finances of so wealthy a state should for so long escape the ruler's notice. The Kano Chronicle characterises Mamman Bello as a "very generous Sarki"; and so do the traditions recorded by Malam Adamu.[65] He was also a devout Muslim, who is said to have preferred prayers and study to sleep at night. Such orientations could incline Bello to make frequent and handsome donations to city malams, *sherifai* and visiting Muslim *za'ids*, saints, scholars or notables, as well as to his kin, slaves and courtiers It is known also that during his reign, the Shamaki Sa'idu sought to stockpile firearms and powder by purchases at Lokoja from British firms through his agent, the Hausa trader, Damba Dagari. Nonetheless, even these additional expenditures fail to account for Kano's financial state. We must look elsewhere to understand the financial situation.

Some elderly informants who may themselves have paid or collected tax in Bello's reign, report that neither did the central administration at this date specify in advance the amount required from each *hakimi*, nor did the *hakimai* do so in relation to their *jekadu* or village chiefs; neither was there any population count. Instead, once the tax rates were set for taxpayers of different categories, a Village Head might arrange with his *hakimi's jekada* (agent) to understate grossly the amount they had jointly collected. In collusion with his *jekada*, the *hakimi* would also understate his receipts to the emir, but would nonetheless receive one-fourth (*rubu'i*) of the sum he reported as customary remuneration. Under such arrangements, perhaps an emir would only secure about one-third of the total tax levied throughout the country; but unless he had himself served as a *jekada* and *hakimi* in his early career, and so knew the system at all levels at first hand, he had no way of detecting or estimating his losses as emir. It is said that under Mamman Bello taxpayers suffered heavily without much benefit to the emir; and even the official tax rates in Bello's day are still disputed. Officially 4,000 cowries were due from each Habe household and 1,000 from each Fulani; but some informants who were then close to the court cite *increases* of 2,500–3,000 cowries per "Habe" household head, and 1,000 per Fulani household head as the "official" rates under Bello. This would lift the prevailing rates from 2,000 to 4,500 for "Habe" and from 500 to 1,500 for Fulani.

However, even such iniquities and inefficiencies of the tax collection fail to explain the financial difficulties that Bello's improvidence, generosity and subservience to Sokoto prolonged and deepened. If the emir received 6.6 million cowries per annum from the *haraji* at Kunci, after rewarding the tax collector, presumably his receipts from the country as a whole exceeded 500 million a year. From this revenue, on Robinson's reckoning, Kano sent one hundred horses, 15,000 tobes (superior gowns), 10,000 turbans and other commodities to Sokoto as tribute.[66] From Sokoto we learn that throughout and after Usuman's reign, Kano's annual tribute was 100 horses, 100 slaves, 100 bales of 20 gowns each (2,000 gowns), and one million cowries a month for the caliph, with half as much again for the vizier. Over and above this fixed tribute, the emir of Kano was also expected to meet any requests for cash, clothes or any material requirements addressed to him from the caliph and vizier of Sokoto. Even so, these out-payments seem insufficient to exhaust the unused portions of his large annual revenues.

The most convincing explanation of the emir's fiscal difficulties at this period is economic. Evidently during the past 30 to 40 years, the volume of cowries in circulation had swollen with annual imports from the southwest, thereby generating a continuing inflation. Moreover, as cowrie circulation increased, particularly in the city, but also, to a lesser extent, in rural areas, the market economy extended its scope by penetrating and absorbing relations and values which had traditionally eluded commerce. Whereas in 1851 Barth estimated a gross annual revenue of 100 millions for the emir Usuman,[67] on the slender data from Kunci, it would seem that Bello collected over 500 millions as tax; but while in Barth's day £1 was equivalent to 10,000 cowries, by 1893 it fetched 26.6 thousand cowries.[68] In Barth's day the price of a young male slave may have been about 40,000 cowries or £3 (twelve thalers). Robinson, who visited Kano in 1893, shortly after Mamman Bello's death, cites prices that vary from £6 to £10 for young male or female slaves of differing condition. At the then prevailing rate, £6 corresponded to 150,000 cowries as against Barth's £3 or 40,000.[69] In 1851 Barth estimated that a family could live in Kano "with ease, including every expense, even that of their clothing" on 50,000 to 60,000 cowries a year.[70] But in 1894, when he employed a Hausa malam to check the dictionary he was compiling, Robinson had to pay 4,000 cowries a week, which suggests an annual average of 200,000.[71] Other indications of decline in the purchasing power of money at Kano cited by Robinson include average prices of kola-nuts at Kano, which ranged according to quality between 140 and 250 cowries;[72] at this date, also, slaves allowed to work on their own account rendered a monthly rent (*murgu*) of 3,000 cowries, or 100 per afternoon for this privilege. Robinson's report nicely confirms my field account on this arrangement.[73] However, in discussing *murgu* my informants reckoned that a minimum of ten slaves was necessary to maintain their owner and his family in comfort at Kano during the closing decades of Fulani rule with a combined *murgu* of c. 360,000 cowries per year.

Together these data suggest that absolute increases in the state's cash revenues since 1851 hardly kept pace with the progressive decline in the purchasing power of cowries during this period. Moreover, as inflation developed and money bought less, the state and its suzerain both sought more and more revenues to meet their needs, thereby accelerating the import and circulation of cowries, increasing the volume of currency, and depreciating its value further. Moreover, increasingly from Usuman's time onwards, Sokoto had looked to Kano for luxury goods such as fine robes, clothing, carpets, leatherwork and the like, most of which the emir had to purchase locally or elsewhere, at prices that rose rapidly as the cowrie currency depreciated. In Abdullahi's day, slave sales from successful southern campaigns had swollen the emir's income, thus masking the real effect of this rolling inflation. However, while Mamman Bello derived very limited slave incomes, his annual cash expenditures greatly exceeded Abdullahi's, as much because money values had declined as because he was obliged to distribute more in gifts, locally and to Sokoto.

Understandably in these conditions, Mamman Bello sought to increase the central revenues by discouraging peculation and embezzlement among his territorial chiefs through exemplary dismissals of proven offenders. In 1884 the Sarkin Dutse Ibrahimu was dismissed for tax abuses and other matters. Bello's letter to Waziri Abdullahi Bayero at Sokoto reporting the administration of Ibrahimu's estate reads as follows: after the customary greetings,

> I wish to inform you that, having dismissed the *hakimin Dutse* (Ibrahimu), we ordered a list to be made of all that he possessed and a tally of his war equipment, such as horses, swords and muskets; these war gear we left with the office, since they belong to the Dutse chiefship. We took none of their war materials, but we did count up his slaves, and having found 80 male slaves, we divided them into two halves and brought one half to Kano City, following which I divided that half into two equal portions and am sending your portion to you, 20 slaves, 15 for the caliph and five for yourself. Farewell and peace.[74]

This letter neatly illustrates the imperial regulations for administration of the estates of dismissed officials.

In 1888 Mamman Bello also dismissed the Sarkin Gaya Sule for oppression and tax embezzlement. Sule's family, the Kurawa Fulani, had claimed this office on quasi-hereditary grounds, but following Sule's conduct, Mamman Bello appointed a *shigege* Fulani from Gombe, Abubakar, who ruled till 1891 when the Ningi slew him in battle. In 1891 also, Mamman Bello dismissed the Suleibawa Sarkin Kiru Ahmadu for embezzling the *kudin shuke*, appointing Ahmadu's younger brother, Abubakar, to succeed. We have already noticed Mamman Bello's attempt to prevent unjust appropriations by the Sarkin Fulani Kunci. Another letter reports his action to restore three million cowries and two slaves which the Ardon Shanono had appropriated from his kinsman. Two other letters written before 1885, illustrate Sokoto's increasing control of Kano's internal administration. In this case, Bello seems to have suspended the Makaman Jibga for reasons unspecified, and was instructed by caliph Umaru to restore him to office. In the second letter, written to the vizier, after greetings, Bello says, "I am writing to let you know that your messenger, Sarkin Baka, came before us together with Jibga. We understand fully the instructions on his affair in your letter, and accept them. We have therefore returned his town (fief) to him, as well as his compound; but from the beginning we had neither appropriated his estate, nor had we dismissed him. This for your information." Though his identity remains obscure, the Makaman Jigba was probably either a *jekada*, or a village head.

Kano and Sokoto

Our data on the government of Kano under Mamman Bello are richer and more diverse in their sources than those on preceding reigns. Besides information from administrative files, the histories of Malam Adamu and Alhaji Abubakar Dokaje, the Hausa version of the Kano Chronicle, and oral traditions of the normal sort, there are travellers' accounts by J. P-L. Monteil and C.H. Robinson, Mamman Bello's correspondence with caliph Umaru and the Waziris Abdullahi and Buhari, and first-hand reports from some elderly informants within the capital whose privileged status enabled them to observe routine and unusual events freely. Concordance between these differing bodies of data is high; but they serve also to supplement one another, particularly by presenting differing perspectives on complex issues, and so filling out the political ethnography of Fulani Kano in its penultimate phase.

Of 40 letters that I copied at Sokoto which date from Bello's reign, five are purely or primarily ceremonial.[75] Thus Bello wrote to congratulate the vizier when Buhari appointed his son as his Dan Galadima and preferred successor. According to Bello this choice was particularly welcome, since the Dan Galadima's mother was a Kano princess, and probably a granddaughter of Dabo. On returning home from a visit to Sokoto, Bello wrote to inform the caliph of his safe arrival; and when the latter was ill, he wrote to enquire about his health and send his condolence. Once, en route to Kaura Namoda in Zamfara for a meeting with the caliph Umoru and other emirs, Bello was delayed by illness at Panisau for 14 days and at Bici near the Katsina border for 24. He first wrote the caliph from Bici to explain his delay, and despatched the Kano tribute by his son, the Galadima Tukur. It was customary to write letters of condolence to the survivor on the deaths of either the caliph or vizier of Sokoto; and also to write expressing delight and thanks on both these appointments. At both Idi festivals the emir sent separate letters of greeting to the caliph and the vizier. He wrote also to report the safe arrival of imperial couriers en route through Kano to the rulers of Bornu, and to acknowledge receipt of any imperial instructions. He wrote to inform the vizier about arrangements for his annual visit to Sokoto, and of his return home. When the caliph and his council decided to summon provincial armies for imperial campaigns, on receiving his instructions, Mamman Bello would congratulate the caliph on resuming the *jihad*, and wish him success. Though purely formal, his reply indicated Bello's receipt and acceptance of the imperial order. Likewise, when he had installed a new vizier, the caliph wrote to those emirs whom the vizier supervised to inform them of his choice, and thus to accredit his minister.

Such ceremonial correspondence indirectly subserved many practical ends, but it also maintained the links and loyalties between provincial emirs and Sokoto and signified the continuing allegiance of the former to the caliph and his Waziri. Often also this formal correspondence was accompanied by tribute and other donations, and presumably the couriers or tribute bearers were quizzed at Sokoto by the vizier or his agents about conditions or events of particular interest in Kano or other countries along the route, and at Kano likewise about developments in Katsina, Zamfara and Sokoto. Evidently, a provincial emir who failed to maintain these formalities in the conventional manner, unless excused by illness, by absence on campaigns or non-receipt of previous messages, invited suspicions of disaffection or disloyalty to Sokoto.

Several items in Bello's correspondence treat of legal matters, particularly claims of inheritance, debt or appeals to the caliph for redress and protection against such important rural chiefs as the Sarkin Gaya and Sarkin Jahun. One letter describes the subdivision of a dead man's estate and the amounts paid to the malams and administrative agents who officiated. Two letters concerned the debts and intrigues of a Sarkin Dawaki Mai Tuta with whom Mamman Bello was evidently at odds. This Sarkin Dawaki (?Shehu) was said to have hired three venal malams to conduct ritual and prayers on his behalf, providing them with homes at Godiya. Evidently Mamman Bello suspected that these rituals intended him no good; but having dispersed the clerics, he found himself indirectly responsible for their debts, and also for those of the Sarkin Dawaki himself on another occasion. Two other letters addressed to Waziri Buhari referred to a man who, having been sold to slavery in Kano, claimed his freedom by right of birth, and appealed to the caliph's court. Bello duly sent him under escort to Sokoto, but unfortunately the man died at Tofa near Kano. Among various letters that illustrate Bello's role as Sokoto's vassal, one reports his settlement of a client of the vizier who wished to live at Dutse. Bello duly instructed the Sarkin Dutse to provide the man with a suitable compound, farms, grain and other household necessities for a year. Another informs the vizier that Bello had instructed the Sarkin Karaye to escort some unidentified "Christians" (i.e., Europeans) to Kaura Namoda en route to Sokoto. A third informs caliph Umaru (1881–91) of action taken to distribute twelve slaves that he had sent to Kano. Three had been given to the Sarkin Fada Dangyatum, two to another and one to a third man, while six were sold in the Kano market to cover certain purchases specified by Umaru. In another letter Bello undertakes to purchase one million cowries' worth of thalers for despatch to the vizier; and as the caliph's agent, Bello was normally required to hand over specified sums to bearers named by the vizier or the caliph.

Of the 40 letters I copied that passed between Kano and Sokoto during Bello's reign, one announcing Buhari's accession as Waziri, was addressed from caliph Umaru to Mamman Bello, two were from Mamman Bello to the vizier Abdullahi, 14 from Mamman Bello to caliph Umaru, 22 from Mamman Bello to the vizier Buhari, and one from Abdullahi's son, Aliyu Babba to Muhammadu Mansuru, the son of caliph Aliyu. Of these letters only caliph Umaru's letter announcing Buhari's appointment as vizier may be a duplicate, which suggests that copies were not retained in the files at Sokoto, thereby illustrating the informal, non-bureaucratic nature of the imperial communication and organisation. Of 38 letters written by Bello, five deal solely with external affairs, and two others refer to attacks on Kano by Gumel and Ningi. In a cheerful letter, Bello relates how, after the Ningi had surprised and seized Rano in a night attack, the Sarkin Rano assembled his people rapidly and fell upon the invaders at dawn, slaying 1500 and capturing 590 horses, together with many guns and swords. "Let us give thanks to

God for this event. Farewell and peace." This redoubtable Sarkin Rano was Jibir, whose wife was Abdullahi's daughter, the Magajiya. However, Kano was not always victorious.

Foreign and Imperial Affairs

In a letter to the vizier Buhari, Mamman Bello reports the plight of Barbura in northeastern Kano. Dabo had established Barbura as a fortified town (*ribat*) on the Kano panhandle that separates Daura in the west from Gumel, an affiliate of Bornu. He had settled Barbura with Hausa and Fulani immigrants from Damagaram (Zinder) and appointed their leader as chief. Thereafter the community at Barbura prospered peacefully till Bello's day, when their Gumel neighbours, having suffered two devastating attacks by Zinder, suspecting Barbura of treachery, launched a series of punitive raids against it. Bello reports that Barbura had sent to ask him for food, since its crops had been destroyed the year before, and the people were unable to farm due to Gumel's attacks. Bello accepted Barbura's pleas for peace with Gumel as the only condition in which Barbura and nearby districts in the extreme northeast could retain their population; but before communicating with the Sarkin Gumel Abubakar (1872–1896), he wrote to inform the vizier and seek his permission "because our reins and spurs are both in your hands—None the less, neither ourselves nor these people (of Barbura) will have any rest until this peace is made."

In 1884 Suleiman, the son of Tanimu, seized the throne of Zinder after a brief struggle with Ibrahim Gwoto, who had succeeded.[76] Like his father, Suleiman then sought to reduce Kazaure, which lay due south of Zinder between the "Habe" (Hausa) successor-state of Daura, and Kano. However, despite Dambo's defeat and death at Tanimu's hands, Dan Tunku's successors at Kazaure steadfastly maintained their allegiance to Sokoto. In 1885 Suleiman beseiged Kazaure for nine days but failed to take it, following which he raided the surrounding country and returned home. Next year he attacked Kano, and took Madaka with much slaughter and booty, the country folk fleeing southwards to escape his advance. Mamman Bello, disabled by age and failing sight, moved out from Kano to Dabo's marshalling ground at Panisau, and despatched two armies northwards under his son, the Galadima Tukur, and the Sarkin Dawaki to intercept Suleiman.[77] From Panisau Bello wrote the Waziri Buhari about the crisis.

> When the Galadima had set out we received a messenger from Sarkin Dambarta to let us know that Sarkin Damagaram (Zinder) had camped outside the gate of Kazaure and launched two severe attacks against it. Next his cavalry fanned out throughout our country (Kano), about six hundred horsemen, seizing and killing our people from the environs of Kunci, past Maraki almost to Malikawa. We ourselves are at Panisau. Hearing this, we despatched the Sarkin Dawaki and other cavalrymen *(barade)* to Kunci and Dambarta, and they are presently there outside Kazaure waiting; but according to the reports we have had from our scouts, so far there has been no battle.

Three letters discussed the arrival in Kano of some Kel-Owi Tuareg, and Mamman Bello's reaction to them. Evidently, for some years, these Kel-Owi of

Asben had been at odds with Sokoto and had avoided Kano. Since 1860 Tanimu at Damagaram had struggled to capture the entrepot trade from Kano for Zinder, which lay about 120 miles north of the city along the mid-Saharan caravan route. Tanimu had had considerable success in halting or diverting the Tuareg caravans that traditionally by-passed Zinder for Kano market; but I cannot say how far the resulting decline in this lucrative northern trade contributed to the inflation and economic difficulties of Kano in Mamman Bello's reign.

Bello's letter on this matter to the vizier Buhari reads as follows:

> We wish also to inform you that some people from Asben have arrived at Fage out-side our capital, (with) about 90 camels. These men have left their loads (here) and moved on to Gaya; but we have instructed their agents and hosts to withhold these loads until the Asben people return to go home, for they should only enter among us with a letter from you to us about this, or, alternatively, with their own letter assuring us that they have come among us in friendship (*aminci*). Meanwhile, we have forbidden these travellers to return by way of Damagaram. We have told them to go home via Katsina (as) that is their ancient trade route according to our under-standing of it. As greetings for you, we send two robes and a burnous. Farewell and peace.

Not long after, for reasons unknown, Suleiman of Zinder sought to make peace with Kano. It is possible that he was disturbed by news of Rabeh's westerly movements; but he had also fallen out with the Kel-Geres Tuareg of Wancaregwe, and may have modified Tanimu's economic policy. In any event, on receiving the overtures from Zinder, Mamman Bello wrote to inform caliph Umaru and seek his instructions. Following the customary greetings,

> I wish to inform you that Suleimanu (of Zinder) has written to us about friendship (*amana*) and concord (*sulhu*) not once but often, and I have written to let him know that friendship and peace are not established in this way, or so quickly, but require preparation, so that the Leader of the Muslims (*Emir el-Mu'minin*) can write about it to us to set out our conditions and what we must do. However, since he has written to us about this matter first, we ought to reply to him. For this reason I am writing to inform you of these developments so that you can decide the response to their letter. Praise be to God. Farewell and peace.

These letters concerning Gumel, Damagaram and the Tuareg show that in Bello's reign as before, the emirs of Kano lacked authority to negotiate treaties of peace or alliance with foreign powers such as Zinder or Gumel who were formally subor-dinate to Bornu, or with the Tuareg of Asben. The caliph reserved such decisions on foreign affairs to himself and his councillors at Sokoto, since they could affect the empire as a whole.

East of Kano, beyond Jama'are, lay Misau, a minor emirate which the caliph Bello had created for the sons of Gwoni Muktar, the Fulani leader who had first sacked Gazrgamo, the capital of Bornu, in 1807, only to fall in the counterattack led by Shehu Aminu el-Kanemi in the following year. Gwoni Muktar had received a flag from Shehu dan Fodio with authority to conquer Bornu; and in recognition of this, his descendants, the emirs of Misau, were designated as emirs of Bornu by the caliph, although Misau lay west of Bornu. Moreover, to compensate the rulers of Misau for their narrow domain, they were "empowered to levy *jangali* and *haraji* on all the Fulani of Bornu, wherever they happened to be living at the time, a privilege ... (they) exercised till about 1880."[78] Thus the emirs of Misau exercised a general *bin kanu* jurisdiction over all pastoralists who entered Fulani territory

In 1886, during the rinderpest epidemic which forced Mamman Bello to suspend the *jangali* collection in Kano, Muhammadu Manga (1886–1890) succeeded to the throne of Misau on the death of his father, Sale. Manga soon found himself in difficulties with the vizier of Sokoto, Buhari, who supervised Misau's administration. Two undated letters from Mamman Bello at Kano to the vizier illustrate further aspects of Bello's position as the senior provincial emir. In one letter, probably the earlier, after the customary greetings, Bello writes,

> When I received the letter in which you told me that you were not going to send further messages to the emir of Bornu (Misau) until he came before you and made his homage, well, that worried and distressed me, to know for sure that you had ceased communicating with him, so that, assuming your approval, I sent my courier to him in Misau and wrote to ask that he should authorise me to intercede on his behalf with the caliph for his forgiveness. He assented to this suggestion, and authorised me to proceed; and I wish to do so respectfully now. I know that it is said that this was what he (Misau) intended, since there seems to be no other avenue of communication, but I will stand surety (*ceto*) for him to you. I throw myself at the feet of Shehu Usmanu and the other caliphs, interceding that you should forgive him and pass over what he has done in forgiveness and mercy and justice. This is why Allah placed you in leadership over your slaves (subjects). May God help you in this world and the next. Farewell and peace.

In a second letter concerning Misau addressed to the vizier Buhari, Bello writes,

> I wish to tell you that when we had returned home we found that the men of Sarkin Bornu (Misau) Muhammadu Manga had completed the collection of their *jangali*, so we called them and asked them how much they had collected here. They said that they had gathered one hundred *keso* (2 million cowries) as *jangali*. Our man who handled their visit said to us, "The Sarkin Bornu Muhammadu Manga hasn't ceased from sending (messengers) among us (on this matter); and he has already spent 21 *keso* (420,000 cowries) of this money." After I had divided the tax returns and given my agent 160,000 cowries (8 *keso*) I wrote to let him know that I was keeping the remainder of the tax in good faith, but would not hand it over to him until he had gone to the caliph and declared his allegiance (*mubaya'a*) as the vizier had instructed him to do. When he received my letter about this, he wrote me his reactions in a letter of his own. I enclose it for you to read and will leave the matter there. Farewell and peace.

On circumstantial data, it seems probable that these two letters were written in 1887 or 1888, before rinderpest had disorganised *jangali* collection throughout Kano. It seems also that the letters were probably written in the order presented above; and perhaps during the interval between them, the vizier may have instructed Mamman Bello to withhold the *jangali* due to Muhammadu Manga from Kano until the latter had visited Sokoto and made homage. Misau's position on the border between the Fulani and Bornu empires undoubtedly increased the vizier's concern about its emir's intentions, after Manga had ignored repeated letters summoning him to Sokoto. In this situation, the emir of Kano, as a near and senior neighbour first attempted to heal the breach by standing surety for Misau with Sokoto, an act that committed the Kano forces to invade and reduce Misau should its emir prove disloyal. Then, when that offer was rejected, probably after the vizier had consulted caliph Umaru, Mamman Bello was instructed to withhold the *jangali* due to Misau from Kano, thus demonstrating how *bin kanu* rights could easily be converted into economic sanctions against those who held them. It seems likely that it was in this context that Sokoto suspended the *bin kanu* jurisdiction and privileges Misau had formerly enjoyed; but whether Mamman Bello then transferred these *bin kanu* rights over Bornu Fulani in Kano to the Yeli-gawa or Jelubawa chiefs of Dutse, who jointly held their senior territorial title in Kano, or suspended or reserved them for the throne until the caliph restored them to Misau, remains unknown.[79]

Local Rebellions and Revolts

Mamman Bello also wrote at length to inform the vizier of local problems, especially those that required police action. Bello had difficulties with several hereditary chiefs in eastern Kano, notably Gaya, Gwaram, Kila and Jahun; and he wrote frequently and fully to the vizier about the last three.

Gwaram had been founded around 1827 by Malam Lawan, a Fulani of Bauchi whose father, M. Isi'aku had, according to one tradition, initially received a flag to conquer Bauchi from Shehu Usman dan Fodio. Accompanied by his pupil, the future emir Yakubu, a man of Gerawa stock, M. Isi'aku set out from Sokoto to Bauchi but died at Yelwa near Dawakin Tofa in Kano. It is said that the Shehu then chose Yakubu to bear the flag and conquer Bauchi. Disappointed, Isi'aku's son, M. Lawan, attached himself to Suleimanu, the baMundube emir of Kano, and was directed to settle in the sparsely populated southeast near the Ningi, War-jawa, Ajawa and Mbutawa pagans along the ill-defined border between Kano and Bauchi. After some years in that area, Lawan moved to Gwaram and founded the town, which grew quickly as a frontier post. Thereafter the Gwaram chiefship vested in Lawan's issue; but while their Fulani chiefs remained loyal to Kano throughout the Ningi wars, the people of Gwaram inclined to support the Ningi and their rebel Hausa leaders.

In 1884 Lawan's son, the Sarkin Gwaram Musa, died after a long successful reign; and after the death of his successor and younger brother, Isma'ila, in 1887, dynastic rivalries, aggravated by Mamman Bello's errors of judgment and the intrigues of Dan Yaya, the Ningi chief, threw Gwaram into disorder for more than a year, during which three men held the chiefship before the community selected a fourth, Adamu, by popular choice, having forcefully rejected Mamman Bello's nominee, the *shigege* Sarkin Buji, and forcefully evicted Musa's son, Suleimanu, who had tried to seize the chieftainship. Bello reported these developments to the Waziri Buhari as they occurred, to ensure that his handling of this tortuous succession would have the vizier's support.

About ten miles northwest of Gwaram stood Kila, a much older town, which seems to have fallen to Kano shortly after Alwali overawed Birnin Kudu before the *jihad*. Kila was then administratively attached to the throne until the Fulani conquest, when it fell to Dutse, a town forty miles northwest, having been reduced by forces from that area. In terms of political geography, Kila's subordination to the chiefs of Dutse was quite unsatisfactory; Kila lay only 15 miles southeast of Birnin Kudu and 10 miles from Gwaram, either of which could have supervised it more effectively. On the other hand Buji, attached to Gwaram, lay 20 miles to the north and within a day's march of Dutse. Evidently the political alignments of communities in this sparsely peopled frontier zone were determined not by geographical contiguity, but by provenience or military domination. The foundation of Kila antedated Gwaram and, like Birnin Kudu, it had remained independent until Alwali subdued them both.

Throughout the Ningi campaigns, Kila maintained an ambivalent, ambiguous relation with Kano. While Abdullahi's forces stood nearby, the people of Kila, having once experienced Abdullahi's attack, avoided inviting another. However, when the Ningi transferred their attentions to other areas and the Kano garrisons were withdrawn, the chiefs of Rano, Gaya and Dutse being left to contain and repulse the Ningi, the chief and people of Kila entered into collusion with Dan Yaya, the Ningi leader. These relations were nicely facilitated by Kila's geographical distance from Dutse and by its political segregation from nearby Gwaram. In due course, on failing to receive the *haraji* due from Kila, Mamman Bello sent his *jekada* to the Sarkin Gwaram for an escort to collect it. The chief of Gwaram directed one of his men to accompany the emir's *jekada* to Kila and collect the tax. By then the Sarkin Kila Ahmadu had firmly aligned himself with the Ningi and had planned to secede from Kano. It is said that the two tax collectors were both slain at Kila by Ahmadu with the people's support, a clear sign of revolt; so when the news reached Kano from Gwaram, Mamman Bello despatched a force under his son, the Galadima Tukur, to overawe Kila and suppress the rebellion. Resistance being futile, the people of Kila submitted, and declared that the incident had only arisen through an error for which their chief, Ahmadu, was solely responsible. On instructions from Mamman Bello, Tukur then dismissed Ahmadu and appointed as his successor a namesake from the same lineage. However, on the people's request, Tukur left the deposed chief, Ahmadu, at Kila when he withdrew to Kano. Without delay the dispossessed Ahmadu rebelled against his successor, slew him and resumed the chiefship. Ahmadu's revolt was now quite open; yet, despite his repudiation of Dutse and Kano, Ahmadu's intentions and support remained obscure.

Tukur having already withdrawn with the Kano army, while the rebel Ahmadu controlled Kila, the Fulani chief of Jahun, Modibo, decided to act without awaiting the emir's orders, to stamp out Ahmadu's rebellion and restore Kila to Kano. Though Jahun lies over 60 miles north of Kila near Kano's eastern border with Hadeija, Modibo led his troops against Kila without seeking Dutse's help or the emir's permission. However, the rebel Ahmadu had anticipated retaliation from Kano, and had perhaps tried to provoke this by slaughtering his kinsman. In event of such an attack, Dan Yaya had promised to bring the Ningi forces to assist him. Had Modibo of Jahun expected that he would have the Ningi on his hands, he may well have stayed at home. Instead, caught unprepared en route to Kila, he suffered a severe defeat and returned home, broken. Thereafter Kila remained independent of Dutse and Kano until the reign of Aliyu Babba. At Jahun on his return, Modibo soon received a letter from Mamman Bello demanding an explanation of his attack on Kila.

Traditionally the chiefs of Jahun had sought to protect themselves and their community against attacks from Hadeija by marriage alliances with its chiefs. Like his predecessors, Modibo had married a daughter of the Sarkin Hadeija Muhammadu (1885–1906); and the rebel Ahmadu of Kila, to divert attention from himself, exploited that relation to subvert Jahun's loyalty to Kano. It is said that Ahmadu forged a letter to himself from Mamman Bello, in which among other things the emir was represented as saying that Modibo was a *kahiri* (apostate). He then despatched this to Modibo's father-in-law, the Sarkin Hadeija, who immediately informed Modibo of the allegation. Neither Muhammadu of Hadeija nor his son-in-law Modibo, the Sarkin Jahun, questioned the authenticity of the letter, whose contents accordingly remained unknown to its purported author, Mamman Bello.

Modibo is a Fulani term for "learned" (holy) man; and the Sarkin Jahun Modibo may have received this name in recognition of his Muslim learning. In any case, accepting the letter relayed from Hadija as genuine, the Sarkin Jahun was understandably astonished at Mamman Bello's deviousness and treachery. As intended, the letter suggested to him that Mamman Bello was seeking to recover the allegiance of Ahmadu, a rebel and a murderer, by repudiating Modibo's loyal efforts and by blackening his character with dastardly insinuations. Modibo probably feared that Mamman Bello had also written a similar letter about him to the vizier or caliph of Sokoto, although the charge of apostasy was deliberately missing from the peremptory note he had received from Kano demanding the grounds for his recent assault on Kila. Understandably, since apostasy or heathenism (*kahirci*) were the ultimate sins in the Fulani political code, Modibo of Jahun promptly repudiated his allegiance to Mamman Bello under the conviction that the emir had already repudiated him. Thereafter Jahun and its subordinate communities discontinued relations with Kano and seceded, maintaining their independence until Bello's death.

Bello wrote lengthily about this affair to the caliph Umaru as well as the vizier; but since he himself did not understand the cause of Jahun's revolt, these letters record his distress, confusion and efforts to penetrate Modibo's stony rejection, without illumination. Jahun's seccession, following so swiftly on Kila's after Modibo's gallant intervention, certainly disturbed Mamman Bello by revealing how fragile were the bonds which held his emirate together.

After some correspondence, the caliph Umaru instructed the emir to depose Modibo and appoint a loyal chief in his place. Bello then sent his *jekada* the Sarkin Yaki Wada with the caliph's letter to implement the order at Jahun. The town's elders and leading citizens were duly assembled at the chief's compound, the Alkali and Limam among them, and the caliph's letter was read to the assembly. It ruled that if the Sarkin Jahun refused obedience (*biyayya*) the leaders of the town should be instructed to choose a loyal successor. Following this, Modibo asked the Limam and Alkali if they understood the caliph's instructions. On their assent he told them to choose his successor, at which they protested that they lacked the *iko* (authority, power). Modibo then addressed the Sarkin Yaki Wada as follows: "The caliph said that someone should be appointed. Who? The regime (*mulki*) of the caliph is not even a hundred years old; but we, our lineage, we have been here in Jahun for seven hundred years ruling this town. Will he then remove us and appoint another? ..." In reply the Sarkin Yaki heaped abuse and insinuations on Modibo's dead father, the Sarkin Jahun Erkiyo, at which point Modibo seized the Sarkin Yaki and had to be restrained by the assembled malams, who sent the *jekada* out of town.

Bello wisely refrained from attacking Jahun in force, fearing that Hadeija and Kila, and perhaps sundry quiescent communities within Kano, might rally to Jahun's side. But having failed either to secure Modibo's allegiance or to install a loyal successor at Jahun, Bello was still obliged to fulfill the caliph's instructions. As related in letters sent to the caliph and vizier, he then appealed to the people of Jahun to leave Modibo and to settle elsewhere in Kano as a separate community under a loyal chief of their own choice. When this proved fruitless he finally appointed the Chief of Garki, Tukur, a member of Modibo's lineage, as Sarkin Jahun, directing him to move to Garko near Wudil in the Makama's territory, and from this headquarters to collect the *jangali* due from all migrant Jahunawa Fulani in Kano, and to administer their affairs within and beyond the boundaries of Kano under the traditional *bin kanu* jurisdiction of Jahun chiefs. In this case, as in the dispute between Misau and Sokoto, withdrawal of *bin kanu* jurisdiction was used as a political and economic sanction. In retaliation, the Sarkin Jahun Modibo simply collected and kept the taxes of the settlements attached to Jahun and regulated official appointments within these units independently until he freely restored Jahun's allegiance to Kano, after Mamman Bello's death.

It is worth noting briefly that although Galadima Tukur, Bello's chosen heir, senior subordinate, and most effective commander, was then the *hakimi* in charge of Jahun, at no time did the emir send Tukur against Modibo. Bello evidently preferred to handle these delicate and provoking negotiations with Jahun on the one side and Sokoto on the other himself, and avoided employing force against Modibo and the Jahun Fulani, since such action might have alienated other Fulani and widened the breach. Bello's timidity and subservience to Sokoto may have also restrained him from attempting to subdue Jahun by force. However since he was responsible as emir of Kano for effective action regarding Jahun, after considerable delay he appealed to the caliph for decision and guidance. A forceful emir such as Dabo or Abdullahi might simply have summoned his troops and marched on Jahun himself to resolve the matter. Under Bello, three years passed before Jahun's secession was formally clear. Thereafter the region remained independent and isolated from Kano, with covert support from Hadeija, for the rest of Bello's reign. We may therefore set 1888 as the date of Modibo's initial repudiation of his allegiance to Kano, and place the revolt of Kila under Ahmadu to the preceding year.

In 1889–90 Mamman Bello faced yet another threat of withdrawal, this time from the Sarkin Gaya Garba (Abubakar). Garba was an immigrant from Shirra or Misau, a learned malam, whose abilities had impressed Bello. In 1884 Bello appointed Garba as the chief of Balare village, ten miles north of Gaya town.

Then, after deposing Sarkin Gaya Sule in 1888, he promoted Garba to rule Gaya. As a *bako* (immigrant) Garba was thus a *shigege* officeholder with no other claim to the Gaya chiefship than Bello's favour.

As mentioned above, when the Ningi, unable to move freely between Abdullahi's garrison towns in southeastern Kano, directed their attacks elsewhere, the reserves Abdullahi had kept there, ready for swift counterattacks, were gradually depleted and withdrawn to Kano; and the chiefs of Rano, Gaya, Dutse and perhaps Birnin Kudu were given responsibilities for defense of the south-east. Over several years the Sarkin Rano Jibir waged a vigorous and effective defense against Ningi inroads, although several towns in southernmost Kano, notably Tudun Wada, were sacked by Ningi from time to time. In the northeast, Jahun had participated in these campaigns by aiding Hadeija and Dutse against the Ningi. When Garba became Sarkin Gaya, he rapidly asserted his leadership of this central front, and took the offensive against the Ningi with striking success. It is recalled by an eyewitness that on one occasion Garba sent Mamman Bello one thousand Ningi slaves he had seized in a raid. Such successes attracted to Garba's standard warriors and adventurers in search of booty and fortune from all over Kano, so that his successes in the field swelled the forces at his disposal. Informants who knew the Sarkin Gaya Garba and witnessed these events assert that he soon had 1500 well armed horsemen at his command, with proportionate infantry. To keep this large force employed, Garba maintained his offensive against Ningi with increasing success.

At this stage some of Mamman Bello's courtiers and palace staff at Kano began to cast doubt and suspicion about Garba's designs in collecting, arming and retaining such unusual forces. As their intrigues developed, news of these insinuations filtered through to Garba who saw then that his loyalty and intentions were suspect. Under the circumstances, but after some hesitation, Garba decided that it would be wisest for him to leave Kano and withdraw with those who wished to follow him home to Misau, perhaps to secure or establish a chiefdom there. He then assembled his army and marched to Kano City to bid Mamman Bello farewell. On reaching the city, he halted outside the walls and ordered his troops to stack their weapons in bundles, thus disarming themselves, and told them to remain there while he bade Mamman Bello farewell. Garba then entered the city with a few personal attendants, notified the palace of his arrival and seated himself in the Barde's mosque (*Masallacin Barde*) to await the emir's summons for an audience. Meanwhile, having learned of Sarkin Gaya's movements and desire to leave Kano, Mamman Bello discussed the appropriate action with Galadima Tukur and other councillors in a meeting that continued until the *La'asar* prayer (around 5:30 p.m.), the situation being unprecedented and grave.

As the hours passed at the Barde's Mosque, the Sarkin Gaya's distress and anxiety increased, as he recalled the treacherous murder of Sarkin Dutse Bello by Usuman, and his own defenseless situation, separated from the powerful force he had disarmed before entering Kano. A young man, one of my informants, who visited Sarkin Gaya at the Masallacin Barde in the afternoon, found him weeping. Until a message came from his *kofa* summoning him to the palace, the Sarkin Gaya could neither go to see Mamman Bello nor, without compromising himself further, could he withdraw to join his army. At this period, Mamman Bello's son, the

Ciroma Abubakar, was Gaya's *hakimi*, while the Sarkin Yara Abdu, grandson of Haburde, served as *Jekadan Gaya* under the Ciroma. Both men were then at the palace, the Ciroma sitting with Mamman Bello in council on this affair. Eventually after *La'asar*, the Sarkin Yara came to summon Garba, whose nerve by then seems to have broken. In the audience with Mamman Bello, Garba attributed his unusual conduct to magic (*samau*) employed against him by his enemies and rivals for the Gaya chiefship, and renounced his intention of withdrawing from Kano. Mamman Bello and Sarkin Gaya were then reconciled in the presence of the council; and, to demonstrate his appreciation and confidence in Garba, Mamman Bello conferred the title of Sarkin Yaki on him that evening. Garba thus now held two titles simultaneously, the territorial title of Sarkin Gaya and the military one of Sarkin Yaki, which carried with it command of the Kano forces. On returning to Gaya, Garba set out on a campaign of thankfulness (*yakin godiyan Sarki*) for his reprieve, and raided the Ningi, taking about 700 captives. Unfortunately while presiding over the subdivision of the booty to remove his share and the emir's, as the *shari'a* directed, Garba was shot in the eye with an arrow by a Ningi sniper and died immediately, following which Mamman Bello appointed Ibrahim, one of the Kurawa Fulani whose lineage had ruled Gaya since Dabo's day to succeed. Garba died in 1891, the only man to hold two offices simultaneously at Kano before 1894.

Following Bello's troubles with Gwaram, Kila and Jahun, Garba's career as Sarkin Gaya most clearly illustrates the political implications of Mamman Bello's arrangements for the defense of southern and eastern Kano by senior *tambari*-holding chiefs resident in these regions. Such policies could only achieve their aims if the responsible chiefs were able to accumulate sufficient military force to repel or discourage the Ningi. Alternatively, some of these communities and chiefs might enter into subversive relations with Ningi, as Kila had done. More-over, once Kila had seceded from Kano, the political alignment of Gwaram to its southeast became uncertain, since Kila controlled the routes from Kano to Gwaram. The prolonged and successful defense of southern Kano by Sarkin Rano Jibir had suggested this defensive strategy to Mamman Bello; but Jibir's talents and position were both unusual. He had married Abdu's daughter, the Magajiya, and was thus identified with Kano by bonds of dynastic and kinship alliance. Garba, as a *shigege* Sarkin Gaya, had tried to justify his appointment locally and otherwise by vigorous aggressive campaigns against Ningi in their homelands; but the overwhelming force that he later deployed on these objectives identified him to the courtiers and councillors in Kano as a potential political threat, since, as an immigrant, his attachments to Mamman Bello and the Kano state were per-sonal, and lacked any hereditary roots or kinship basis. Thus, while Bello's mili-tary policy required that his rural chiefs of southeastern Kano should concentrate unusual forces under their command, under successful leadership such concen-trations either generated political fears and intrigues at the capital, or attempts to secede or revolt among these major rural chiefs.

Finally, this tale of Sarkin Gaya Garba indicates the difficulties that obstructed the movements of chiefs and their followers across state boundaries at this period.[80] Had he led his men eastwards to Misau at once without securing Bello's approval, by their flight, Garba and his people would invite political ostracism as *kahirai* (apostates, disloyal people) throughout the Fulani empire. Certainly the ruler of Misau would enquire at Kano and perhaps even at Sokoto concerning the circumstances of their flight and how to deal with them. In effect, throughout the empire, with the sole exception of pastoral Fulani, whose *bin kanu* jurisdictions were specially adapted to their seasonal movements, while free individuals enjoyed much freedom of movement, community officials, princes and chiefs were not free to relocate without the prior knowledge and approval of their official superiors and emirs, even within the boundaries of an emirate. For a chief and his followers to cross over emirate boundaries into another Fulani state required the approval of both emirs, and perhaps that of the vizier and caliph as well. Thus Sarkin Gaya Garba, having decided to quit Kano for Misau, found himself constrained by institutional requirements to seek Mamman Bello's permission to do so, thereby precipitating the crisis described above.

The Pursuit of the Succession

Another incident from Bello's reign illustrates imperial arrangements neatly. On instructions from the caliph Umaru, Mamman Bello received a displaced Fulani of Ruma in northwestern Katsina whose father had helped the Sarkin Maradi Danmari in his attempt to overthrow Fulani Katsina. Finding this immigrant energetic and valiant, Bello rewarded him with the chiefship of Were (Waire) village in northwestern Kano, near the Katsina border. Thus stimulated to distinguish himself, Dan Were, the *shigege* client chief, sought Bello's permission to challenge the leading champion of Maradi, the Jarmai Dan Baba, to single combat at Ruma in Katsina. Bello approved and the meeting was arranged. Dan Were won the fight, slew Dan Baba, and achieved renown as a warrior. It is said that after the death of Sarkin Gaya Garba, Bello rewarded Dan Were's valour with the title of Sarkin Yaki; and when the Kano forces supported Sokoto in the following year against Ism'a'ila (Sama'ila), the independent chief of Kebbi at Argungu, Dan Were took a leading role in the Kano contingent. It is said that on this campaign, in one engagement he had three horses killed under him.[81] Presenting himself to the Galadima Tukur who commanded the Kano forces at Argungu, Dan Were asked for yet another mount to re-enter the fray. Tukur refused this, perhaps because Dan Were's recklessness was depleting his reserve of horses. In anger at this rebuff, Dan Were used insulting language to Tukur; and on their return to Kano, the Galadima mentioned this incident when reporting the course of this major Fulani defeat to his father, Mamman Bello. Bello, who was deeply concerned to secure the succession for Tukur, summoned Dan Were, verified the report, dismissed him from the Were (Waire) chiefship, and banished him from Kano. Dan Were then proceeded to Sokoto to seek the caliph's permission to settle at Ruma in Katsina, and received it.

As Bello's reign drew to its close, ominous signs of the darker days ahead for Kano multiplied. In 1891, the caliph Umaru died while attending an assembly of provincial emirs at Kaura Namoda. Umaru was Aliyu Babba's senior son and the third successive caliph selected from Mamman Bello's descendants. Of Abubakar Atiku's issue thus far, only his eldest son, Ahmadu Zaruku (1859–1866), had acceded. On Zaruku's death in 1866 Abdurrahman became a leading candidate among Atiku's sons by sheer seniority, but although, following the conventional alternation of Bello's lineage and Atiku's in the succession, Abdurrahman may have hoped to succeed on the death of Aliyu Karami in 1867, he was passed over on four occasions while in turn Ahmadu Rufa'i, Abubakar na Raba, Mu'azu and Umaru were appointed. Only in 1891, on Umaru's death, did Abdurrahman succeed, and then by the vizier Buhari's independent action, and without the blessing of the Electoral Council. It was not long before all concerned began to regret this.

By 1891, the new caliph Abdu was over 60, and his chronically unstable disposition had been soured by disappointment and suspicion. Soon after his accession, Abdu faced an open revolt at Talata Mafara, formerly part of Hausa Zamfara. When that had been suppressed, Abdu decided to overrun the hostile chiefdom of Kebbi that adjoined Gwandu and Sokoto, thereby eliminating this threat to both imperial capitals. Remembering the defeat his predecessor had suffered in an earlier attack on Argungu, the Kebbi capital, Abdu ordered his provincial emirs to bring half their armies to Sokoto for the attack on Kebbi during the coming dry season. Unable to campaign personally on grounds of age and health, Mamman Bello placed his son, the Galadima Tukur in charge of the Kano force. Although this army was perhaps the largest that any caliph of Sokoto ever commanded, it experienced a resounding defeat outside Argungu at the hands of Sama'ila, the Kebbi chief. Evidently, caliph Abdu did not imagine that Sama'ila would offer open battle against such overwhelming odds. He conceived the campaign as a siege, followed by the assault, destruction and capture of Argungu, and therewith the end of Kebbi's existence. However, Sama'ila elected to raise the siege, and routed the Fulani by a cavalry attack in their rear which took them by surprise. Sama'ila's force first struck the Kano contingent under Galadima Tukur. Tukur strove vigorously to hold his ground and to throw back the Kebbi charge, but after his men gave way, Sama'ila proceeded to roll up the Fulani line outside the walls of Argungu. In this situation the Fulani suffered heavy losses before they fled homeward to Gwandu and Sokoto. But instead of recognising that the defeat was due to his own errors of judgment and tactics, caliph Abdu attributed it privately to the treachery of his imperial councillors (*sarakunan karaga*) and convinced himself that their hostility to him had inclined them to flee, rather than fight in the face of Suma'ila's horsemen. Particularly it seems that Abdu suspected the vizier Muhammadu Buhari, to whom he owed his accession, of hostility and perfidy.[82] For its contrast with the cowardly flight of the main Sokoto force, the caliph warmly appreciated Galadima Tukur's struggle to hold the line, and let this be known.

Mamman Bello's son, the Ciroma Abubakar, had been killed in the battle by Sama'ila's cavalry. Mamman Bello accordingly appointed another son, the Dan Lawan Umaru, as Ciroma; and as Dan Lawan he appointed Galadima Tukur's son, his own grandson Abdu, also called Lele. Lele's appointment as Dan Lawan was immediately interpreted in Kano as decisive evidence that Mamman Bello hoped that Galadima Tukur would succeed him. Opinion divided on the question whether Mamman Bello had already secured the succession for Tukur by bribing the notoriously avaricious and erratic caliph Abdu, whose Hausa nickname, "*Danyen kasko*"—the unbaked pot—aptly described his character. The caliph's admiration for Tukur's efforts at Argungu was well known in Kano; and

Mamman Bello's abrupt dismissal and banishment of the ambitious and ill-tempered Dan Were for insulting Tukur was also interpreted as a sign of Tukur's preeminence. However, the best index of Bello's intentions was his appointment of Tukur's son Abdu to the high-ranking princely title of Dan Lawan, thereby concentrating even more fiefs under Tukur's control than he already administered as Galadima.

I present in Table 5.2 my data on the distribution of fiefs in Mamman Bello's reign in the closing years of Fulani rule, in tabular form to facilitate comparison with parallel distributions in Alwali's day, and in this century under British supervision. It is also convenient to reproduce the official communication structure over which Mamman Bello presided for comparison with earlier and later systems (Table 5.1). The distributions of titles among officially prominent Fulani lineages in nineteenth and twentieth century Kano are presented in tabular form for further study in Chapter 8. Prolonged recitals of such data are not feasible at this point in our narrative. However, to indicate the unusual resources at Tukur's disposal under Mamman Bello's provisions, it is appropriate to list the principal territories that Tukur as Galadima then held in fief, namely Gwaram, Dutse, Rano, Jahun, Fogolawa, Yelwa, 'Yargaza, Minjibir, Tamburawa, Kumbotso, Jigawa, Kacako, Kanya Babba, Dawakin Kudu, Tudun Wada, Riruwe, Burdo, Kiri, Miga, Gadan Sarki, Makori, Harbau, Dan Gyatum, Gammo and perhaps Ringim, Buga, Kiyawa, Taura, Gujingu and Majiya. Whereas Abdullahi, following his dismissal and humiliation of Galadima Yusufu, had removed Kumbotso, Fari, Kankarawa and other fiefs from the Galadima's office to reduce its excessive wealth, on appointing Tukur, Mamman Bello had increased its territorial endowment until the Galadima now administered a much larger territory and population than before. Thus, on his son's appointment as Dan Lawan, Tukur's position as the leading candidate for the succession was even further aggrandized, since that appointment placed the Dan Lawan's resources and fiefs substantially at Tukur's disposal.

Moreover, by then Tukur's brothers also held the well-endowed offices of Ciroma, Santuraki, Sarkin Shanu and Dan Buram. In addition, Malanta and Mustafa, two sons of the emir Usuman, who owed their appointments to Mamman Bello, and were thus aligned behind Tukur, also held office as Tafida and Dan Makwayau. The fiefs administered by Dan Gyatum's younger brother, the Sarkin Fada Malam, were also aligned behind Tukur, as were the more important units administered by the Barde Babba Umaru, whom Bello had appointed on the death of Barde Sule. Quite systematically the emir had transferred authority over nearly one-half the state to his senior son and vizier, the Galadima Tukur, thereby entrenching Tukur's leadership and prospects for the succession. Meanwhile, of Abdullahi's large progeny, only the Wombai Shehu still held an official post, and that under direct instruction and protection from Sokoto, whose fears and forebodings for the Yusufawa faction—that is, the sons of Abdullahi and others who had placed themselves under the leadership of Yusufu—deepened with Abdu's appointment as Dan Lawan and the rumours that caliph Abdu had already assured Bello that Tukur would succeed.

Alhaji Abubakar Dokaji, in his published history, simply asserts that "before the emir of Kano Bello died the caliph, Abdu Danyen Kasko, promised that he

TABLE 5.1   Fulani Communication Structure, c. 1880–1893

EMIR OF KANO			
TAMBARI CHIEFS ** with direct access to Emir	HAKIMAI with direct access to Emir	HAKIMAI <——> with access via slave *kofa*	THRONE SLAVES and their staffs *(lawanai)*
Sarkin Rano	Mai Anguwan Mundubawa*	Madaki	<——> SHAMAKI
Sarkin Gaya	Limam*	Magajin Malam na Cedi	
Sarkin Dutse	Ma'aji	Magajin Malam na Hausawa	
Sarkin Karaye	Sarkin Sherifai	Tafida	Maje Sirdi
	Magatakarda	Dokaji	Lifidi
		Sarkin Bai	Hauni
		Dan Makwayau	Dan Sarai
		Ma'ajin Watali	Sarkin Gini
		Sarkin Shanu	
		Wombai	<——> DAN RIMI
		Sarkin Dawaki mai Tuta	
		Dan Iya	
		Dan Amar	
		Ciroma —— Sarkin Yara	S. Dogarai
		Dan Kade	S. Hatsi
		Ja'idanawa	
		Barde Babba	
		Mai-Anguwan Mundubawa*	
		Limam *	
		Sarkin Filanin Jahun	<——> SALLAMA
		S. Dawaki Tsakar Gida	
		Mai–Anguwan Kutumbawa	
		Dan Maje	Yora
		Galadima	Turakin Soro
			Turaki Manya
			Dan Isa
	S. Jarmai Turakin Romo Gadodamasu		
	Dan Farantama		Magajin Dankama
		Makama	<——> Kasheka
		Alkali	

* Listed as having slave *kofa* and also direct access to Emir.
** Compare VASSALS in Table 2, Babba Zaki's Communications Structure c. 1770.

TABLE 5.2 Territorial Organization under Mamman Bello (c. 1890) and Aliyu (c. 1900)

Title	Vassal-states and fiefs c. 1890	Vassal-states and fiefs c. 1900 (changes: + or –)
Emir (Sarkin Kano)	Jalurawa, Tudun Wada (1860+), Garki, Tsentsi, Jogana, Joda, Butubutu, Dumbulum, Gadan Sarki, Salawa, Garun Malam, Kambarawa	+ Kura, Sakuwa, Rano, Burumburum, Dawakin Kudu, Karaye, Majiya, Dan Hassan
Galadima	Dawakin Kudu, Tsakuwa, Fogolawa, Yelwa, Yargaza, Minjibir, Tamburawa, Kumbotso (*kofar yamma* ward), Jigawa, Kacako, Kanya Babba, Dutse, Tudun Wada (1880+), Riruwe, Burdo, Kiri, Makori, Harbau, Gammo, Ringim (1883–93: Jahun, Taura, Dan Gyatun, Majiya, Miga, Buga, Gujingu)	+ Gazara, Sarina – the following: Ringim, Tsakuwa, Dawakin Kudu, Harbau, Tamburawa
Sarkin Bai	Ungogo, Jalli, Saye, Tinki, Kuka, Kunci, Fogolawa, Kunya, Gwangwan, Takwasa, Gadanya (1870+), Matsidau, Dambarta	– Dambarta
Sarkin Dawaki Tsakar Gida	Kura, Birnin Kudu, Madobi, Kiyawa (near Bagwai), Yadakwari, Yargaya, Tsamiyar Kara, Panisau, Rana, Dimawa Buzaye	+ Daddare – Kura, Madobi
Sarkin Dawaki Mai Tuta	Godiya, Durum, Karaye, Shanono, Gulu, Yelwa, Gogori, Burumburum	+ the following: Yargaya, Butubutu, Gude, Tudun Koya, Danzan, Rogo Sabuwa, Rogo Tsohuwa
Barde Babba	Babura, Wasai, Gwarzo (nr. Kududufawa), Gasgainu	—
Mai Anguwan Kutumbawa	Hausa at Debi, Hauwan Dawaki, Surma, Yakansare, Fagawa, Filatan, Zambur	—
Sarkin Sherifa	Zainawa (nr. Gezawa)	—
Ma'ajin Watali	—	10 small hamlets between Kano and Kunya
Tafida	Rimin Gata, Rimin Azbenawa (= Rimi)	—
Turaki Manya	Dan Hassan, Kabo, Bebeji, Durum, Kerana, Yako, Gani, Wak, Taura, Karfi, Kofa, Gwarmai, Gajali, Jita, Rikadawa, Kiru, Culu, Kifa, Rimi	+ Masanawa, Karaye

(Continued on the next page)

TABLE 5.2 *(continued)*

Title	Vassal-states and fiefs c. 1890	Vassal-states and fiefs c. 1900 (changes: + or –)
Magatakarda	Kanwa, Dawakiji, Juma	—
Ciroma	Gaya, Tsaure, Kofa, Gurum, Gantsa, Lantai, Masanawa, Kantama, Kiyawa, Tsangaya, Dambarta	– Gaya, Dambarta
Dan Iya	Mariri, Tanagar, Gurjiya, Gogel, Gwarzo, Ruwan Bago, Koya, Beli	—
Wombai	Kumbotso (Galadanci ward), Birnin Kudu, Fagam, Debi, Sankara, Buduru, Gezawa, Ciromawa, Kafin Agur, Gazara	– Gezawa, Gazara, Kafin Agur + Ringim, Mallawa, Biyamusu
Barde Kereriya	—	Kiyawa, Tamanyawa
Dan Makwayau	Gora, Bici	– Bici
Dan Goriba	Dansawa, Yan Gunda	—
Jekadan Garko	Garko	—
Sarkin Fulanin Sankara	Sankara, Sabon Gari, Garki and nearby towns, (for defence against Gumel), Gasakole, Kwangi, Beguwa, Karshe, Tsaba	—
Turakin Romo	Minjibir, Baushi, Garun Gudinya	—
Makama	Wudil, Suma'ila, Del, Sarina, Utai, Acika, Gano, Lamire Romo, Matugwai, Fajewa, Falali, Kula, Farin Dutse, Indabo, Senna, Takai, Darki, Lajawa	—
Madaki	Tofa, Dawaki, Dawanau, Bagwai, Gogari, Damlargu, Waire, Dan Zabuwa, Yan Kamaye, Harbau, Kabo, Malikawa, Dan Guguwa, Rimin Gado, Kiyawa, Tattarawa, Dangada, Daddarawa	– Harbau, Kabo + Kunci, Kumbotso
Sarkin Shanu	Kududufawa, Kwanyawa, Danga, Makiya, part of Gabasawa	+ Kafin Agur
Ma'aji	Doko, Dingare	+ Karshi
Dan Maje	Getso, Barbaje, Zarewa, Dan Bakoshi, Lambu, Goron Dutse, Gude	—

Magajin Malam na Cedi	Cedi, Dawanau, Lambu, Dan Guguwa	—
Magajin Malam na Hausawa	Bwam, Shike, Kalangu, Tum, Birji, Zakirai, part of Gabasawa, Zugaci, Tsamiyar Kara, Kumbo, Dadin Duniya, Tarai, Sabon Garu, Gafiyawa, Zawa Ciki	—
Limam	Jijitar, Karmami, Zango	—
Dan Buram	Maddare, settlements near Gabasawa and Fogalawa	—
Ja'idanawa	Gogel, Zara, Zawa Ciki	—
Waziri	—	Gaya, Gezawa, Gammo, Gwaram
Shettima	—	Harbau, Bici, Tanagar, Majiya, Aujara?
Mai Babban Daki	Gude	– Gude
Dan Lawan	Tofa (= 'Yar Tofa)	—
Malamin Maude	Kyarama, Wangara	—
Dan Darman	Balare, Kyaurawa, Zangon Guliya	—
Dan Rimi	—	Gezawa, Mazangado, Shanono
Sarkin Jarmai	Mallam, Bauda	+ Garun Malam, Ciromawa
Ma Anguwan Mundubawa	Wangara, Keffin Zugaci, Gezawa, Gabasawa, Bangare, Kerawa	—
Lifidi	Fagam	—
Alkali	Debigel, part of Dingare	– Dingare
Shamaki	Yan Cibi, Farin Ruwa	+ Gora
Madakin Shamaki	Hugungumai	—
Kilishi	Yola, Bawan Aliyu	—

would give Galadima Tukur the throne (*sarauta*) of Kano after the death of his father."[83]

Although this tradition remains unproven, it is certain that Mamman Bello, by material and ritual means, had made strenuous efforts to secure Tukur's succession. The Dokaji Abubakar also relates another established Kano tradition: "It is said that before he died, Bello gave Galadima Tukur to understand that he (Tukur) would succeed him; and that he even went so far as to give him certain instructions (*wasiyoyi*) concerning the conditions of retaining the throne (*sha'anin rikon sarauta*)."[84] The Kano Chronicle mentions neither tradition; and it is possible that we owe both to the victors in the following conflict, not merely because of their political value to Tukur's opponents, but also because these rumours were widespread and probably true.

Notes

1. M. Landeroin, *Documents Scientifiques de la Mission Tilho, (1906–1909)* (Paris: Imprimerie Nationale, 1911) Vol. 2, p. 444.

2. D.M. Last, *The Sokoto Caliphate* (London: Longmans, 1967), pp 157–62, 187.

3. Ibid., p. 180–1.

4. Dokaji Alhaji Abubakar, *Kano ta Dabo Cigari*, p. 57; The Kano Chronicle makes no mention of this incident. KC, pp. 96–98; LH, vol. 2, pp. 63–66. The relevant page was missing from the text of Muhammadu Zanti's *Taqyid al-Akbar* in the Shahuci Library.

For the account given here I am indebted to the *Ta'rikh Kano* of Adamu na Ma'aji, confirmed by oral traditions.

5. D.M. Last, *The Sokoto Caliphate* (London: Longmans, 1967) p. 180.

6. This story was related at Sokoto by Malam Abubakar Mai-Katuru, a son and assistant of the Galidiman Sokoto Shehu, whose family administered Katsina for the caliph, much as the descendants of Gidado, the Waziris, administered Kano. As Malam Abubakar was born in 1872, and his father was on the Galadima's staff at this time, it is very likely that Malam Abubakar learnt of this incident from his father who was present.

7. M.G. Smith, *The Two Katsinas* (unpublished ms.).

8. For another example, see M.G. Smith, *The Two Katsinas* (unpublished ms.).

9. M. Landeroin, *Documents Scientifiques de la Mission Tilho (1906–1909)*, (Paris: Imprimerie National, 1911), p. 445.

10. *District Note Books*, Gwaram, Tudun Wada, Rano, Suma'ila.

11. Henry Barth, *Travels and discoveries* (1890 Edn.), vol. 1, p. 290.

12. KC, p. 96; LH, vol. 2, pp. 63.

13. KC, p. 97; LH, vol. 2, pp. 63–64.

14. Alkali Muhammadu Zangi, *Taqyid al-Akbar.*

15. W.F. Gowers, *Gazetteer of Kano Province*, p. 26.

16. My account of Abdullahi's Ningi campaigns draws heavily on Muhammadu Zangi's *Taqyid al Akbar*, supplemented by information in *District Note Books*.

17. W.R. Baikie, "Notes of a Journey from Bida in Nupe to Kano in Hausa, performed in 1862," *JRGS*, vol. 37, pp. 92–108.

18. Ibid., pp. 97–98.

19. Ibid., p. 101.

20. *District Note Book*, Birnin Kudu.

21. J.M. Freemantle, "A History of the Katagum Division of Kano Province," *JRAS* vol. 10, 1911, p. 416; *District Notebooks*, Gwaram, Tudun Wada.

22. M.G. Smith, "A Hausa Kingdom: Maradi under Dan Baskore, 1854–75," in Daryll Forde and Phyllis Kaberry (Eds.), *West African Kingdoms in the Nineteenth Century* (London: Oxford University Press for International African Institute, 1967), and *idem, The Two Katsinas* (unpublished ms.).

23. *District Notebooks*, Karaye and Gwarzo.

24. KC, p. 96; LH, vol. 2, p. 63.

25. For the dates of Abdullahi's two reigns in Zaria, I follow D.M. Last, "A Solution to the Problems of Dynastic Chronology in 19th Century Zaria and Kano" *JHSN*, Vol. III, No. 3, December 1966, p. 467.

26. For a summary account of the arrangements for administration of Fulani pastoralists at Zaria, see M.G. Smith, *Government in Zazzau*, pp. 93–4, 132, 142. Very similar oral accounts of this incident were gathered in Kano, Katsina and Sokoto.

27. KC, p. 81; LH, vol. 2, p. 62.

28. See M.G. Smith, *Government in Zazzau*, pp. 95, 97.

29. KC, p. 96; LH, vol. 2, 63; J.M. Freemantle, "A History of the Katagum Division," Vol. II, 1912, pp. 70, 73; W.R. Baikie also mentions a severe cholera epidemic at Kano city in 1862; "Notes on a Journey," *JRGS*, vol. 37, 1867, p. 97.

30. For representative tributes see Dokaji Alhaji Abubakar, *Kano ta Dabo Cigari*, p. 57; and M. Hiskett, "The 'Song of Bagauda,'" *BSOAS*, vol. 28, part , 1965, p. 119, which says

It was a righteous reign, one that held fast to the Shari'a,
Was Abdullahi's; no wrong was done to anyone.

31. Henry Barth, *Travels & Discoveries*, (1890 Edn.) vol. 2, pp. 505–506.

32. F. Edgar, *Litafi na Tatsuniyoyi na Hausa* (Belfast: J. Mayne & Co., 1913), vol. 1, pp. 273–4; vol. 2; pp. 425–7; vol. 3, p. 440.

33. KC, p. 96; LH, vol. 2, p. 63.

34. See M.G. Smith, *The Two Katsinas* (unpublished ms.); and *idem, Government in Zazzau*, p. 179 ff.

35. Henry Barth, *Travels & Discoveries* (1890 Edn.) Vol. 1, pp. 284–5.

36. *District Notebook, Rano.*

37. *District Notebook, Dawakin Tofa.*

38. KC, p. 97; LH, vol. 2, p. 64.

39. Oral information from Sokoto, 1959, confirms data gathered in Kano on these incidents.

40. For the reigns and succession of the caliphs of Sokoto, see Murray Last, *The Sokoto Caliphate*; M.G. Smith, *The State of Sokoto* (unpublished ms.); and E.J. Arnett, *Gazetteer of Sokoto Province* (London: Waterlow and Sons, 1920).

41. According to D.M. Last, Abdullahi was restored as emir of Zaria in August–September 1873 ("A Solution to the Problems of Dynastic Chronology," p. 467). According to J.A. Burdon, Abubakar Atiku na Raba was appointed as caliph on March 16th, 1873 (J.A. Burdon, "Sokoto History: Table of Dates & Genealogy," *JAS*, vol. 4, 1905; pp. 372–373).

42. See Murray Last, *The Sokoto Caliphate*, p. 166.

43. For an oral account of these events collected at Zaria in 1950, see M.G. Smith, *Government in Zazzau*, pp. 174–176. There it was said that Abdullahi sent his Madaki Hassan to Zaria to mediate and resolve the dispute; however the Kano Chronicle says "Abdullahi went to Zaria and sat down at Afira (Ifira) and then at Zangon Aiya. The Madawaki Ali of Zaria was in revolt against Sarkin Zaria. The Sarkin Kano made peace between them and returned home." KC, p. 97; LH, vol. 2, p. 64. Probably Abdullahi took the Madaki Hassan to Zaria with him, and employed Hassan to negotiate with the rebel Madakin Zazzau Ali while he negotiated with his namesake and peer, the emir Abdullahi. On this incident see also S.J. Hogben and A.M. Kirk-Greene, *The Emirates of Northern Nigeria*, pp 225–227.

44. KC, p. 98; LH, vol. 2, p. 65.

45. Y. Urvoy, *Histoire des Populations du Soudan Centrale* (Colonie du Niger) (Paris: Librarie LaRose, 1936) p. 284.

46. M. Landeroin, *Documents Scientifiques de la Mission Tilho (1906–1909)*, vol. 2, p. 464; Edmonde Sere de Rivieres, *Histoire du Niger* (Paris: Berger Levrault, 1965) p. 150; Philippe David, *Maradi: L'ancien Etat et L'ancienne Ville: Site, Population: Histoire*. Documents des Etudes Nigeriennes, No. 18 (Republique du Niger: IFAN-CNRS, 1964) p. 96, dates Barmou's reign as 1873–1878.

47. See M.G. Smith, *The Two Katsinas*; also *idem*, "A Hausa Kingdom: Maradi under Dan Baskore, 1854–1875." In Daryll Forde and Phyllis Kaberry (eds.) *West African Kingdoms in the Nineteenth Century* (London: Oxford University Press, 1967). The genealogical Table of Maradi chiefs on p. 97 of that text, which follows Landeroin's dating in the *Documents Scientifiques de la Mission Tilho*, should be altered to align it more closely with Urvoy's.

48. KC, p. 97; LH, vol. 2, pp. 63–4.

49. F.H. Ruxton, *Maliki Law* (London: Luzac & Co., 1916).

50. These dates follow Murray Last, *The Sokoto Caliphate*, p. 12, and *idem*., "A Solution to the Problems of Dynastic Chronology," p 467.

51. For the preceding account of the incident, I am indebted to Malam Abubakar Maikaturu, son of the Galadiman Sokoto Shehu.

52. Oral information collected at Kano from men whose fathers witnessed these events. Compare with the Kano Chronicle, KC, p. 97; LH, vol. 2, p. 64.

The author of *Faid al-qadir fi ausaf al-malik at-Khatir*, an official scribe of the emir Mamman Bello (1882–1893) and Tukur (1893–5), relates that while at his Nassarawa palace Abdullahi received a visit from the Bunu Abdurrahman of Sokoto, who became caliph in 1891. According to this report Abdullahi told Abdurrahman, the son of caliph Atiku (1837–1842), that he understood that the next caliph would be chosen from Abdurrahman's family. He then warned Abdurrahman, should he be chosen as caliph, never to appoint Yusufu to rule Kano. If correctly reported, this incident probably occurred after the appointment of the caliph Umoru in 1881, when Abdullahi's reign was near its end. In the context, Abdullahi's forceful warning is cited as one of the decisive reasons for Abdurrahman's decision to appoint Tukur rather than Yusufu on Mamman Bello's death in 1893.

53. Adamu na Ma'aji, *Ta'rikh Kano*.

54. KC, p. 97; LH, vol. 2, p. 64. East's version identifies Gajere as Ma'aji.

55. Oral information gathered at Sokoto, 1959. For a similar independent account, see Murray Last, *The Sokoto Caliphate*, p. 170.

56. KC, p. 97; LH, vol. 2, p. 64.

57. KC, p. 98; LH, vol. 2, p. 65. Palmer's translation of the Chronicle stops four lines beyond this point. However East up-dated his Hausa translation to c. 1933, as mentioned above.

58. See Dokaji Alhaji Abubakar, *Kano ta Dabo Cigari*, p. 60.

59. C.H. Robinson, *Hausaland, or Fifteen Hundred Miles through the Central Sudan* (London: Sampson Low, Marston & Co., 1897) p. 132.

60. KC, pp. 97–8; LH, vol. 2, pp. 64–65. The phrase, '*niyyar kangara*' used by East in this context means 'over-reached themselves' rather than 'prepared to revolt' as Palmer has written.

61. KC, p. 98; LH, vol. 2, 65.

62. Unfortunately, I am unable to cite catalogue numbers for those letters from the Waziri Junaidu's collection quoted below, since none had been numbered in 1959 when the Waziri very kindly asked his student to translate them into Hausa for me. I shall therefore identify these letters by the name of their authors and the persons to whom they were addressed.

63. F.W. St. Croix, *The Fulani of Northern Nigeria* (Lagos: The Government Printer, 1945), p. 12ff.

64. Murray Last, *The Sokoto Caliphate*, p. 171. Paul Staudinger, *Im Herzen der Hausalander* (Oldenberg & Leipsig, 1891) reports, p. 525, learning at Zaria of the death of the vizier Bayero shortly after his return from Sokoto in late 1885.

65. KC, p. 98; LH, vol. 2, p. 65; M. Adamu na Ma'aji, *Ta'rikh Kano*. The author of the unpublished manuscript, *Faid al-qadir fi ausaf al-malik al-khatir*, a partisan account of the reigns of Mamman Bello and his son Tukur, on file in the Jos Museum (372 X 51,52), says that from 1886 until the end of the reign of the caliph Umoru (1881–1891), Mamman Bello clandestinely gave the Waziri Muhammadu Buhari (1886–1903), who supervised Kano, 15 million cowries per year, exactly the same as his tribute to the caliph. Previously Abdullahi had given the vizier one-half or one-third of the amounts transferred to the caliph as tribute. Thus by his gifts to the vizier, Bello increased Kano's tributary contributions by 33%–50%, with consequential depletion of the Kano treasury reserves. According to this text, written by the scribe (*magatakarda*) of Mamman Bello and Tukur, when the caliph Umaru discovered these payments, he sent his messenger Ruwashi to Mamman Bello to forbid them. Bello did not obey and continued to give the vizier and the caliph equal tributes until some time after the caliph Abdurrahman succeeded, when he abruptly ceased these lavish donations to the vizier. The author attributes the sufferings of Bello's son and successor, the emir Tukur (1893–5), to the vizier's implacable desire to avenge this abrupt loss of revenues and Bello's favour. See the *Faid al-qadir*, sheets 2–3.

66. C.H. Robinson, *Hausaland*, p. 105. Cash transfers from Kano to Sokoto in Bello's reign from 1886–92 averaged 15 million cowries per annum to the caliph, and an equal amount for the vizier.

67. Henry Barth, *Travels & Discoveries* (1890 Edn.) vol. 1, p. 309.

68. C.H. Robinson, *Hausaland*, p. 92.

69. Ibid., p. 131.

70. H. Barth, *Travels and Discoveries* (1890 Edn.) vol. 1, p. 301.

71. C.H. Robinson, *Hausaland*, p. 105.

72. Ibid., p. 117.

73. Ibid., p. 132. See also M. Hiskett, "Materials Relating to the Cowrie currency in the Western Sudan," Part II, *BSOAS*, vol. 29, 1966, pp. 358–364.

74. For a detailed legal inventory and pricing of the estate of one of the Kano Madakis during the latter half of the nineteenth century, see M. Hiskett "Materials Relating to the cowry currency of the Western Sudan," Part I, *BSOAS*, Vol. 29, Part I, 1966, pp. 122–142. This text gives a vivid idea of the levels of living and wealth sought and enjoyed by senior title holders at Kano during the Fulani period. Clearly such leading figures as the Madaki supplied models for the aspirations and conduct of lesser officials. Presumably Mamman Bello omitted a substantial part of the Sarkin Dutse's estate from his report to the vizier. However, as indicated in footnote 65, *supra*, until the last 24 months of his reign, Mamman Bello regularly gave the vizier cash tributes equal to that due to the caliph. According to the *Faid al-qadir fi ansaf al-malik al Khatir* (sheet 7), Mamman Bello "divided the year into four quarters, and summoned his *hakimai* to the city in every quarter to bring in the revenues they had collected, up to the limits of their ability. They used to bring in these revenues to him at the end of every third month." This illustrates Bello's concern to increase the frequency and volume of treasury receipts.

75. For a general discussion of the imperial correspondence in the care of the Waziri Alhaji Junaidu, see Murray Last, *The Sokoto Caliphate*, pp. 190–198.

76. See M. Landeroin, *Documents Scientifiques de la Mission Tilho*, vol. 2, p. 448; Roberta Anne Dunbar, *Damagaram (Zinder, Niger), 1812–1906: The History of a Central Sudanic Kingdom*, pp. 67–70.

77. See Murray Last, *The Sokoto Caliphate*, pp. 202–203. According to the *Faid al-qadir fi ausaf al-malik, al-Khatir*, a merchant at Zinder, Alhaji Balhi, purchased over 300 of the people Suleiman had captured at Madaka and sent them to Kano free. On learning of this, Mamman Bello sent Alhaji Balhi 300 expensive gowns of equivalent value to indicate his appreciation.

78. S.J. Hogben and A.H.M. Kirke-Greene, *The Emirates of Northern Nigeria* p. 498; J.M. Freemantle, "A History of the Katagum Division," *JAS*, Vol. X, 1910, p. 400.

79. On Misau affairs in the reign of Mamman Manga, see J.M. Freemantle, "A History of the Katagum Division," *JAS*, vol. XI, 1911, p. 189; W.F. Gowers, *Gazetteer of Kano Province*, p. 33; S.J. Hogben and A.H.M. Kirk-Greene, *The Emirates of Northern Nigeria*, pp. 498–9.

80. J.M. Freemantle, "A History of the Katagum Division," *JAS*, vol. X, 1910, p. 417, mentions the suppression of a large movement led by the Limam Yamusa of Dutse to go to Mecca. It has been suggested that the Liman's desire for pilgrimage had Mahdist connections or implications. Nothing similar can be attributed to the attempt by the Sarkin Gaya Garba to return to Misau.

The *Faid al-qadir fi ausaf al-malik al Khatir* gives a different account of these events. Firstly, it says that Bello agreed to a request to allow the Ningi chief Dan Yayya to build a town on the flatter lands north of the iselbergs, on condition that Dan Yayya would cease raids on Kano, Misau, Gombe, Katagum, Shira, Hadeija and other Fulani emirates. Apparently after completing these negotiations, Bello submitted the treaty to the caliph Abdurrahman for approval and ratification, which places this event between 1891 and 1893.

Later, when Rabeh had overrun Bornu and threatened Kano, according to the *Faid al-qadir*, being himself old and nearly blind, Bello actively strengthened the Sarkin Gaya Dabo (Garba) with warriors, horses, and military gear for the defense and policing of the Eastern districts. The text also credits the Sarkin Gaya with the victories that preceded Dan Yayya's overtures of peace; however, shortly after that truce broke down, hostilities were resumed with those Ningi who rejected Dan Yayya's accommodation.

81. On Dan Were, see Dokaji Alhaji Abubakar, *Kano ta Dabo Cigari*, pp. 59–60. For an account of Abdurrahman's attack on Argungu, see S.J. Hogben and A.M.M. Kirk-Greene, *The Emirates of Northern Nigeria*, pp. 251, 407.

82. F. Edgar, *Litafi na Tatsuniyoyi na Hausa* (Belfast: Mayne & Co., 1913) vol. 3, pp. 410–411. The central argument of the *Faid al-qadir ansaf al-malik al Khatir* is briefly that the vizier Buhari consistently deceived and opposed the caliph Abdurrahman and betrayed Tukur, whose ability to resist or overcome the Yusufawa rebels was severely restricted by his obligation to seek the vizier's approval of all his plans and to obey the vizier's orders. This thesis is so heavily and variously documented that it surely requires intensive study in any assessment of the role of Buhari in the catastrophic struggles at Kano, especially in view of the entirely favourable account given by the Wazirin Sokoto Junaidu in his *Tarihin Fulani* (Zaria: N.R.L.A., 1957), pp. 62–68. According to the *Faid al-qadir*, the caliph Abdurahman finally discovered his vizier's treachery when Tukur was at Kamri in Katsina, and Buhari at Keffin Dangi nearby; but, besides being then too late to affect the issue, this merely stimulated the vizier to subvert and negate the caliph's orders openly as well as secretly. Abdurrahman may thus have had good cause for distrusting Buhari; and it is possible that he has had to bear the odium for his vizier's sabotage and obstructions.

83. Dokaji Alhaji Abubakar, *Kano ta Dabo Cigari*, p. 61.

84. Ibid., p. 61. In 1885 while at Sokoto, Staudinger (*Im Herzen der Hausalander*) reports seeing "The 'Galadima' of Kano in the company of the emir of Zaria. He looked for security there because he feared the angry outburst of his lord (the emir of Kano) who wanted to execute him. Such asylum was already mentioned as common by Henry Barth. During my stay at Wurno, a Kano prince with 'the Galadima' visited the caliph (Umoru) to urge him to depose his relative, the Governor (Mamman Bello), because of his various trespasses" (p. 402). Obviously the 'Galadima' to whom Staudinger refers on these occasions is Yusufu, and

not Tukur, Bello's son. According to the *Faid al-qadir al-malik al-Khatir*, before Bello's death, the vizier Buhari had assured Yusufu of the succession, and Yusufu had publicised this widely through Kano. However, the caliph rejected Yusufu and selected Tukur. Thereafter says the *Faid al-qadir*, the vizier betrayed Tukur, sabotaged his plans, and actively abetted Yusufu's revolt.

6

Civil War and Sultanism

Tukur, 1893–94

Accession and Revolt

Mamman Bello died late in 1893, one year after the redoubtable Sarkin Rano Jibir had been defeated and slain by the Ningi; shortly after Rabeh had overrun Bornu, and destroyed Kukawa; and at about the same time that Ahmadu Maje Rinji succeeded Suleiman as Sarkin Damagaram at Zinder. The Kano Chronicle, extended in 1933 under the supervision of R.M. East, relates that Mamman Bello

> died at the palace and was buried there. The vizier of Sokoto being then in the city, Bello's horse and sword were sent to [caliph Abdu at] Sokoto. A message was sent to the Sultan to say that Yusufu should be appointed, otherwise blood would flow in Kano. But the Sultan replied that Tukur should be appointed, even though intestines flowed, let alone blood. The vizier of Sokoto [Muhammadu Buhari] then summoned Dan Rimi Yahaya and [Shamaki] Sa'idu, Mallam Mayaki and Galadima Tukur, and consulted with them, saying, "Who should be appointed to succeed? Tukur or Yusufu?" Shamaki Sa'idu said, "Whoever is appointed from among Dabo's grandchildren, it is the same to us." Dan Rimi Yahaya said it should be Yusufu; and after listening to their speech, the Waziri said "The Sultan has said that Tukur should be appointed."[1]

Oral traditions recorded at Sokoto before 1913 confirm the Chronicle's brief account, but suggest also that following his defeat at Argungu, caliph Abdu's judgment was clouded by suspicions and distrust of his Waziri to such a degree that he may have overriden Yusufu's nomination and designated Tukur from personal pride and pique.[2] Another report, sympathetic to Tukur,[3] holds that for various reasons the vizier wanted to appoint Yusufu but was overruled by the caliph. Thereafter, according to this source, the vizier studiously betrayed and subverted Tukur, assisted Yusufu, and sabotaged the caliph's design. That possibility certainly merits further study; but unlike the deadlock that followed Abdullahi's death, when caliph Umaru and his Waziri Abdullahi Bayero debated the succession without trying to overrule one another, on this occasion neither did any surviving daughter of Shehu Usuman intervene to mediate the matter, nor did the caliph hesitate to overrule his vizier or the elders and people of Kano.

Ironically, and by accident, on this occasion the vizier's presence in Kano when Bello died allowed him to initiate discussions with the leaders of Kano to choose their next chief, an unusual departure from Sokoto's normal procedure for deciding the Kano succession. Accounts differ in their details;[4] but all agree that when the vizier assembled the notables of Kano, he was told that they preferred Yusufu to succeed rather than Tukur. The Dokaji Alhaji Abubakar says that the senior *hakimai*, presumably those officeholders drawn from founding lineages who held seats on the council of state, protested the caliph's choice of Tukur, since Yusufu had the people's support, and that they asked the vizier to write and ask caliph Abdu to revoke his decision.[5] However, a tradition recorded at Sokoto by Edgar confirms the Chronicle's report that Buhari consulted the princes, malams and the throne slaves, who warned him on learning of Tukur's nomination, "Not so! Waziri, do not make the appointment like that. If you give Galadima Tukur the throne of Kano, you will see that Yusufu will rise up and start to wage war until many men have been killed."[6] Even so, despite these warnings of danger, caliph Abdu ordered the vizier to instal Tukur, forbidding him to return to Sokoto otherwise.[7] At that point the Waziri gave in, summoned Tukur to his quarters at night, and appointed him formally but privately, without the customary assembly or fanfare. (*Ba a kirawo kowa ba.*)[8] From the vizier's quarters Tukur proceeded to the palace with a few slaves who constructed a shed (*rumfa*) and attended on him during the conventional seclusion that followed accession. Only when the royal drums (*tambaru*) began to play later that night, announcing Tukur's coronation, did the nobles and people of Kano learn of his accession. Evidently the vizier appointed Tukur clandestinely in this manner for fear of violence in a public assembly at the mosque. During the ten days that Tukur spent in seclusion in the palace forecourt, receiving declarations of allegiance from officials, princes, clerics and other notables, few of Abdullahi's sons visited him to render homage. Of these the Kano Chronicle reports that only the Wombai Shehu and Mamman Mailafiya made formal allegiance; but the Dokaji Abubakar says that Yusufu did likewise.[9]

Tukur ascended the throne grimly in a city silenced by foreboding. By his accession Tukur had vacated the Galadimaship. It is just possible that had he offered this to Yusufu, he might have bridged the breach, at least sufficiently to avert civil war and permit a political resolution of the crisis. However, shortly after he had completed his seclusion, following consultation with the vizier Buhari, who remained at Kano, sending messages to caliph Abdu at Sokoto as the crisis unfolded, Tukur installed the Tafida Malanta, Emir Usuman's son, as his Galadima.[10] While it is possible that Tukur considered Yusufu's restoration as Galadima, it is unlikely that he communicated with Yusufu about this. Perhaps, convinced of Yusufu's hostility and inclination to revolt, he decided against such an appointment. Since Tukur anticipated further opposition from Yusufu and the *zuri'an* (descendants of) Abdullahi, he could hardly have chosen to strengthen them by giving them the most powerful and richly endowed office of state under the throne. Instead, he used the political opportunities presented by that vacancy to promote the Emir Usuman's son Malanta, and thus to strengthen the alliance of

Usuman's and Mamman Bello's sons against those of Abdullahi; but curiously, having transferred Malanta from the Tafida's office, Tukur did not fill the latter, preferring perhaps to keep this post and its resources under palace administration throughout his reign.

According to the Chronicle, when the Wombai Shehu visited the palace to render homage to Tukur, the throne slaves mocked him, saying "Five men defeated a hundred," meaning that the five surviving sons of Mamman Bello had overcome Abdullahi's large progeny. Continuing, the Chronicle says that this taunt so pierced the Wombai's complacency that he then went to visit Yusufu in his compound, although he had never done so since the death of their father, Abdullahi. Following that, the sons of Abdullahi assembled at Yusufu's compound to discuss their situation and decide what to do. Only Mamman Mailafiya, who had paid homage to Tukur, refused to attend the meeting. Having completed their discussions, they all left Kano, assembling at Nassarawa, the summer palace near the city that Abdullahi had built. On the following day they moved further south to Wudil, then to Kademi, and thence to Takai, the town Abdullahi had rebuilt as his headquarters for the Ningi campaigns.[11] At Takai Yusufu established himself in the Emir's compound, his father's old quarters, and despatched letters to *hakimai* and village chiefs throughout Kano calling them to join his side.[12]

The Chronicle reports a long estrangement between the Wombai Shehu and ex-Galadima Yusufu following Abdullahi's death; their rapprochement removed the final obstacle to the Yusufawa revolt. Oral traditions at Kano attribute the initiative for revolt to the Wombai Shehu. According to the Dokaji Abubakar, "Wombai began the discussion saying, 'The only thing we can do now is to quit the city entirely at once; otherwise Tukur will finish us off, since his father has cornered (confined) us.' They all agreed with this opinion, so they went out by the Nassarawa gate, together with all their supporters, heading towards Dawakin Kudu."[13]

If Shehu had avoided Yusufu since Abdullahi's death, perhaps in disgust at Yusufu's shameless ambition and disrespect for Abdullahi, his estrangement may have recommended Shehu to the vizier and Mamman Bello for appointment as Wombai when Sokoto finally intervened to secure this office for one of Abdu's sons. If so, in appointing Shehu, the vizier and Mamman Bello may have hoped to neutralise Abdullahi's sons by dividing them between the Wombai Shehu and the dissident, officially discredited ex-Galadima Yusufu, who was nonetheless their leader. It is possible that Shehu, either on or after his appointment as Wombai, was forbidden to have any further dealings with Yusufu, perhaps by the vizier himself. In either case, throughout Bello's reign the sons of Abdullahi had waited, divided between the contrasting policies represented among them by Yusufu and the Wombai Shehu; but after Bello's death, only Mamman Mailafiya maintained a policy of accommodation, perhaps, like Shehu earlier, because of his disgust at Yusufu's past conduct and his reservations about the future. Mamman's sobriquet "Mai lafiya" reveals the popular evaluation of his conduct, and suggests that temperamentally he sought peace and well being (*lafiya*) at any price. Like other casual, fragmentary data, this *lakabi* illustrates the general sentiment that Abdullahi's sons, and Yusufu in particular, had been treated so harshly and unjustly that they were "entitled" to revolt. When the Wombai Shehu, stung by the the throne slaves' scorn, abandoned his accommodative position and sought reconciliation with Yusufu, the only appropriate proposal he could make was for immediate revolt under the leadership of Yusufu. Following the Wombai's conversion to their corporate cause and his reasoned appeal for revolt under Yusufu's leadership, the sons of Abdullahi acted quickly and fled the city before Tukur could learn their plans or intercept them.

Mobilization by Segmentation

In its chronology and major movements, the general outline of the ensuing Civil War is reasonably clear; but many minor engagements and transfers of allegiance cannot be dated precisely. The Chronicle records that Tukur ruled Kano for eleven months, thus treating his flight from Kano to Katsina as the end of Tukur's reign.[14] Although that event did not terminate the struggle, it initiated a pause of three and a half months, during which the victors established themselves at Kano and prepared for the final campaign against Tukur on the Katsina border. At Sokoto, where Tukur's reign is commonly reckoned as one year and three months, it ends with his death at Tafashiya in 1895.[15] Since Tukur succeeded during the early dry season of 1893, the struggle initiated within two weeks of his enthronement proceeded without interruption except for the rainy season of 1894; and even then sporadic fighting continued in rural Kano.

While at Takai, Yusufu circulated letters to the chiefs of strategic villages throughout rural Kano, summoning them to his side. As replies came in, the "Yusufawa" (rebels, i.e., the active supporters of Yusufu) were able to identify those who refused their aid and others who did not respond as loyalists supporting Tukur. Meanwhile at Takai they corresponded also with leading Fulani of noble families in Kano City, and by these appeals, as well as the prospects of fortune and office, they attracted many warriors to their cause.[16] Broadly, the Yusufawa seem to have drawn most support from east and southeastern Kano, whereas the west and north were generally loyal to Tukur. However, in either half of the country rival chiefs had to deal with centres of resistance; and even within a town or a lineage which had declared for either side, the distribution of loyalties was often complex and unstable.

Nowhere was this bifurcation of collective loyalties more evident than in the southeastern area from Wudil to Takai, Yusufu's headquarters. Since the *jihad* and even earlier, the Fulani of this region had recognised and followed Jobawa leadership; and ever since Malam Bakatsine's son Mandikko, the Makaman Kano had administered the area and the Jobawa as their hereditary chief. Not since Dabo removed Mandikko for contumacy had any Makama been dismissed; nor had any but a baJobe of M. Umoru's lineage held that high-ranking office. Shortly before Tukur's accession, the Makama Haruna died and was replaced by his brother's son, Isma'ila, who died shortly after and was succeeded by Fula'ilu, a son of the Makama Isa who had succeeded Mandikko, and who was himself a son of Bakatsine's younger brother. After thirty days in office Fula'ilu also died, following which Makama Isa's grandson, Iliyasu, succeeded as Makama. These last two appointments to the Jobawa chiefship were made by Tukur in Kano, where many leading Jobawa resided. In turn all three Makamas, Isma'ila, Fula'ilu and Iliyasu, made their homage to Tukur as the caliph's representative and remained loyal to him. All were descendants of Sa'idu, Malam Bakatsine's younger brother; nor had any of Bakatsine's lineal issue held the office of Makama since Mandikko's dismissal by Dabo. Predictably, under such circumstances, while Sa'idu's descendants rallied to Tukur's side under the leadership of Makama Iliyasu, the grandsons of Malam Bakatsine and other Jobawa lines attached themselves to Yusufu under Mujeli, Hamza and Umaru. Moreover, through the good offices of these Jobawa rebels, and perhaps also because of regional loyalties that dated from Abdullahi's and Yusufu's prolonged residence in the area during their Ningi campaigns, with few exceptions Jobawa-dominated communities from Wudil to Suma'ila and Takai rallied solidly around Yusufu and his brothers, so that village chiefs in this area who remained loyal to Tukur were replaced without difficulty. Thus people here turned deaf ears to messages from Makama Iliyasu.[17]

Excluding the Wombai Shehu, all senior officials in Kano remained loyal to the caliph's nominee, Muhammadu Tukur, whatever their personal reservations about the wisdom of his appointment. Without exception, the official heads of all Fulani founding clans, the Yolawa, Jobawa, Dambazawa, Danejawa and the Suleibawan (of) Jamau honored their allegiances to Sokoto and their homage to Tukur, often with their lives;[18] but in almost all cases some close kismen of these loyal titleholders grouped themselves with Abdullahi's issue behind Yusufu's flag, thereby lending the rebels the prestige of their presence and names, while jockeying for their lineage titles when victory was won. Thus while the baYole Madaki Ibrahim fought on Tukur's side, his ambitious maternal half-brother, Muhammadu Kwairanga, fought first for Yusufu, and then for Yusufu's successor. Likewise while the Dambazawa Sarkin Bai Muhammadu Bashiri honored his allegiance to Tukur, another grandson of Dabo Dambazau, Abdusallami, led his kinsmen and supporters to the rebel side. Of Malam Jamau's kin and descendants, a discrete Suleibawa clan, the Sarkin Dawaki Mai Tuta fought for Tukur, while his younger brother Shehu fought on Yusufu's side.[19] Even the heirs of Malam Usuman, the leading local Hausa *muhajarini*, illustrate the determination of individual alignments in this dynastic strife by prevailing distributions of office and intra-familial competitions. Thus Mamman Bello's Magajin Malam na Hausawa Rabi'u, the grandson of Malam Usuman, remained loyal to Tukur and died in battle at the Dan Agundi Gate of Kano City during the first Yusufawa attack on the capital; but his kinsman Sule, eager to obtain the office for which he was eligible by descent, fought for the Yusufawa. Among the lineages that led and fought the Kano *jihad*, only Dan Zabuwa's line, the Danejawa, depleted by emigration and misfortune, remained entirely loyal to Tukur throughout the crisis.

Similar conditions of intra-familial rivalry for hereditary office also decided the alignments of many ambitious men drawn from lineages that had prescriptive rights to such important rural chiefships as Rano, Dutse, Birnin Kudu and Gwaram. At Rano, following Jibir's death fighting the Ningi in 1892, his eldest son Hamadu had succeeded. Predictably, Hamadu's younger brother, Yusufu, sought to displace him, and joined the rebels at Takai. At Dutse, following the death of its chief, Abdulkadir, on the eve of the rebellion, the Madakin Dutse Salihi of the Yeligawa seized power, ostensibly to assure the town for Tukur. His leading Jelubawa rival, Ibrahimu, proceeded at once to Takai, where he declared allegiance to Yusufu. At Birnin Kudu the recently appointed chief, Muhammadu

Nafi, remained loyal to Tukur, while his nephew and rival, Zakari, attached himself to Yusufu.

At Gwaram also, the reigning chief, Musa, stood by Tukur, while his rival, the ex-chief, Suleimanu, seeking to regain office, joined Yusufu. Of the major southeastern chiefships, only Gaya remained solidly behind Tukur. There the Kurawa Fulani had only recovered their hereditary title on the death of Sarkin Yaki Garba in 1891. Under their new chief, Ibrahim, the ruling lineage and people of Gaya fought stoutly for Tukur. In the southwest, at Bebeji and Kiru, the chiefs, their families and people also remained solidly for Tukur. Northeast of Kano about fifteen miles, the communities of Minjibir and Gezawa initially did likewise; but even at Minjibir, while the Turakin Romo Gamdo, its hereditary *hakimi*, supported Tukur, three of his kinsmen, seeking office, joined the Yusufawa, re-entered the town, subverted the people's loyalties to Tukur, and provoked a drastic response. At Gezawa likewise, where the chief Dabugel remained loyal to Tukur, the Dawaki Husaini, Yusufu's ambitious Habe field commander, spread subversive propaganda within the town, and persuaded the people to revolt and install him as chief.[20]

All throne slaves honored their *amana* obligations and obeyed Tukur loyally until he quit the palace and Kano and fled to Katsina. As it is known that several senior slaves personally sympathised with the sons of Abdullahi, their loyal support of Tukur illustrates their corporate discipline. The head slave, Shamaki Sa'idu, had undertaken personally and on behalf of the palace staff, to obey and support the caliph's nominee when the vizier consulted him. On that occasion, the Dan Rimi Yahaya, who administered the royal estates throughout the country, had expressed his preference for Yusufu. Nonetheless, Yahaya remained loyally at his post in Tukur's service throughout the following months.

Two rural chiefs who responded promptly and gladly to the news of Yusufu's revolt were the Madakin Kila Muhammadu and the Sarkin Jahun Modibo, both of whom, as already related, had broken their ties with Mamman Bello and seceded from Kano for different reasons and in different ways. Both chiefs now came in person to declare their allegiance to Yusufu and his faction at Takai during the opening months of the revolt. So did the Sarkin Dal Sambo and the Sarkin Sarina, chiefs of two substantial communities west of Takai, together with the Sarkin Suma'ila Sati, a baJobe.[21]

By timidity and dilatoriness, Mamman Bello had forfeited the allegiance of Kila and Jahun to Kano, and alienated most of the southern and eastern districts on whose support the Yusufawa based their campaigns.[22] Undoubtedly Bello's heavy taxation and military inactivity contributed to this general disaffection, and alienated those territories in southern and eastern Kano that were most directly exposed to threats of attack from Ningi in the south and Gumel in the north. Traditionally administered by hereditary local chiefs, these communities were only partially and indirectly incorporated in Kano. Abdullahi's long residence and tireless efforts in defence of this area had endeared his name and his family to its inhabitants; but in backing Yusufu's revolt, however passively, many whose poverty or low status assured their passive role in this struggle, expressed their frustration and dismay at the twin evils of rising taxation and inflation, both of which enlarged the oppressive tendencies of the Fulani administration.

From Babura in the extreme north, the Jarmai Dila, a notable warrior, set out for Takai to join Yusufu. The Sarkin Fulani of Sankara, the Sarkin Taura Aba, the Sarkin Dabi Tiku and the chief of Aujara, whose territories all lay west of Jahun on the route to Kano, also declared their allegiance. In that region only the Sarkin Ringim at Ture remained loyal to Tukur. Whether on his own initiative, or on the advice of these eastern leaders, Yusufu also sent messages to the Sarkin Gumel Abu and to the Ningi chief Danyaya, announcing his revolt and inviting their help in the attack he planned to launch on Kano. As inveterate enemies of the Fulani state, the chiefs of Ningi and Gumel welcomed this chance to weaken it further; and both subsequently permitted detachments from their forces to join Yusufu's advance on Kano.[23] Yusufu also received a promise of contingents from Misau, but this was not fulfilled.[24] While at Takai, the Yusufawa made several sorties against western communities whose chiefs had refused their allegiance. By such raids and the constant inflow of armed supporters, the rebels built up their strength until it seemed sufficient to throw against Kano.

The First Attack on Kano

Following an approach from Yusufu, the Emir of Hadeija Muhammadu (1885–1906) arranged to meet him to discuss the situation in Kano and his request for aid. To Yusufu the time seemd ripe for a direct assault on Kano, for one decisive battle to settle the issue. Hoping for troops from Hadeija, Yusufu marshalled his forces, ordered them to meet him later east of Kano, and set off to meet Muhammadu. There he found the Wazirin Sokoto Buhari, whom Muhammadu had invited in a last effort to resolve the dispute and avert a civil war. It is not clear whether Yusufu and Buhari expected to meet one another on this occasion. Thus one or both of them may have been surprised when Muhammadu brought them together before the Hadeija nobility and throne-slaves to discuss the succession struggle.[25]

By then caliph Abdurrahman had threatened to dismiss Buhari for protesting Tukur's appointment, and Buhari had been ordered to remain at Kano as long as the rebellion continued.[26] Thus the vizier had no room for diplomatic manoeuvre when Muhammadu demanded that he should replace Tukur as Emir of Kano by Yusufu. Buhari, whose family and possessions were then virtual hostages in the caliph's hands, could only reiterate the latter's orders and disclaim responsibility for the policy he had been obliged to implement. This reply convinced several senior Hadeija officials that there was now no peaceful way for Yusufu to succeed, and that if Hadeija threw its weight on the rebel side and intervened in the war, by widening the conflict, it would either split the empire, or at least repudiate the caliph, since Abdurrahman seemed solely responsible for Tukur's appointment and determined to instal him at any cost. To avoid either alternative, Hadeija officials urged their Emir Muhammadu to abandon Yusufu's cause and remain neutral throughout the coming conflict in Kano. In accepting their counsels, Muhammadu accordingly refused to furnish Yusufu the troops he had promised, although he later claimed that Yusufu had given him the border towns of Miga and Kwanda in return for Hadeija's support.[27]

Buhari's statement thus detached Hadeija from the rebel side; but before the assembly dispersed, Yusufu had moved to Kano, leaving Buhari and Muhammadu together. On reaching Kano Yusufu camped at Fage, just outside the city walls, with a thousand men. On the following day he launched a direct assault. By mid-morning the rebels had broken through the Women's Gate (*Kofar Mata*) , slaying the Dan Iya at the wall; but as the Yusufawa poured through the gate along the narrow paths between compounds, the Sarkin Gaya Ibrahim Dabo cut off these routes, hemmed them in, and threw his troops against them with devastating effect. In these narrow spaces the Yusufawa were trapped, unable to flee, to form defensive ranks or move freely. Many fell among the dyepits near the gate, others within or between the clusters of compounds, while those who could sought safety in flight over the walls or through the gate. In all 340 fell within the city. Those who escaped fled towards Takai through the Dan Agundi Gate, led by Aliyu Babba, the Kofar Mata being now closed behind them. At the Kofar Dan Agundi, the Magajin Malam na Hausawa Rabi'u was killed trying to block their route; but 400 rebels failed to escape and were captured in Kano.[28]

Buhari meanwhile had hurried back to the city, where the victorious Tukur welcomed him and asked what should be done with the captives. Buhari says that he told Tukur to do whatever he wished. Kano traditions credit caliph Abdu with the decision; and the vengeance it authorised was prompt and vicious.[29] According to the Chronicle, after Yusufu's unsuccessful attack on Kano Tukur

> wrote to the Sultan (Abdu) to tell him what had happened between himself and his kinsman. The Sultan replied, saying "Since they have resorted to war, slay them without respect to their ancestry." The messenger returned and gave Sarkin Kano Tukur this message. From then on, whoever was captured was killed; so was anyone suspected of going over (to the enemy) caught and killed. Some of Yusufu's men were seized, divided into fives, and killed at each of the thirteen gates. Not long after, Tukur set out and conquered the men of Minjibir and Dawaki ta Kudu and kept on selling them (as slaves), having ceased execution; because of this a song was made saying "May God reduce our misfortunes, slaves are selling free men at Kano!" ... Then the vizier of Sokoto came to reason with Yusufu; but Yusufu rejected his speech and said, "I will not agree, it is better that everything should be broken up since you have betrayed us." [30]

Minjibir was governed at this time either by the Sarkin Fulani or by his senior kinsman, the Turakin Romo, who held it in fief along with Garun Gudinya and Baushi. Traditionally these two offices were reserved for those Yerimawa Fulani descended from Gamau who had helped Dabo against Dan Tunku. In 1893 the Turakin Romo was Gaudo; but while he supported Tukur, three of his kin, Usuman, Buwaye and Maso, had joined Yusufu at Takai. From Takai, Buwaye led a force of horsemen to Minjibir and won over the town for Yusufu. In retaliation Tukur sent a force against Minjibir under the Kauran Katsina who had brought troops from the Emir of Katsina on Sokoto's orders to assist Tukur.[31] The Kaura's men broke into Minjibir, expelled Buwaye, captured the Ciroma Kadiri of Minjibir and 80 householders, and burnt the town. The captives were taken to Kano, where the Ciroma of Minjibir, Kadiri, was executed and the others were imprisoned.[32]

The war had now taken two serious turns. First, it had spread beyond the route from Takai to Kano across the countryside. The Yusufawa attacked and seized Lamire south of Wudil. They also attacked, but failed to take, Durum southwest of Kano. They sent forces against Bebeji and Karaye. Tukur responded by sending a force against Wudil under his brother, the Ciroma Umaru, and the Sarkin Gaya Ibrahim Dabo. However, finding Wudil heavily manned, the force passed on to attack Lamire where many rebels were seized and removed to Kano.

Throughout the country many local communities, internally segmented by long-standing rivalries for their chiefships, tottered on the brink of internecine strife and ruin, polarised by the increasingly bitter and vicious struggle of the Yusufawa and the Tukurawa. At Getso near Gwarzo, west of Kano, the Katsina "Habe" and Bedde inhabitants seized the chance to expel their Fulani rulers, the Sangetso Danhazo and his Alkali, and drove them both to Musawa in Katsina. The Getso people then burnt the Sangetso's compound and, on their own initiative, elected Dahuwa from among themselves, as their chief. Dahuwa ruled this "Habe" community independently for several months until Tukur's successor removed him. Though to my knowledge unique, this upheaval at Getso indicates how the dynastic war now threatened to engulf the ruling Fulani of Kano and destroy their hold on the state.[33]

Secondly, besides its expanded geographical range, the conflict had also increased its intensity beyond a critical threshold, since on the caliph's orders Tukur now routinely executed or enslaved captive rebels. Hitherto, despite their irreconcilable differences, the two princes and their followers had observed the current conventions of Fulani chivalry. A valiant opponent was respected though not released. The political loyalties and considerations that determined his opposition were probably recognised as mirror images of those that aligned and motivated his captors. In battle, slaughter was necessary for survival and victory. Thereafter it was abhorred. Cold-blooded executions have always appalled the Hausa, who dramatise tyranny by contrasting the situation of the executed and his executioners. Thus when, following caliph Abadu's decree, Tukur made a daily spectacle of his enemies' executions at the gates and markets of Kano, he horrified all, including his supporters, who now feared their own fates, should they fall into Yusufawa hands. Predictably, reports of Tukur's brutalities and terror blackened his name throughout the land, and steeled the Yusufawa to attack and drive him out, thereby ending the slaughter and sale of free people into slavery as soon as possible.

We are fortunate in having an impartial eyewitness report on the situation at this time from Sir William Wallace, who visited the city in 1894 on his way to Sokoto to negotiate a treaty on behalf of the Royal Niger Company with caliph Abdu. Learning that the vizier Buhari was then in Kano, having "been sent at that time to Kano by the Sultan of Sokoto to try and quell the civil war," Wallace came to Kano to meet him, since "it would have been useless, for the purposes of my mission, to proceed to Wurnu, the capital of the Sokoto empire, while the Grand vizier was absent"; but after waiting a month on the vizier at Kano, Wallace regretfully proceeded to Sokoto without him. During that time, as he observes,

> civil war held the entire province in its grasp. Every few days batches of prisoners were butchered in the market place with the customary indignities to the dead, parts of the bodies being utilised as medicines and for poisoning arrows, and the

remains left to the dogs and vultures. Numbers of women were strangled simply because they belonged to the rebel party without the town. All this, combined with the simultaneous destruction of Kuka (Kukawa), the capital of the neighbouring kingdom of Bornu, by Rabba (Rabeh) ... caused an almost entire cessation of the movement of Hausa caravans from the East and North.[34]

His indiscriminate slaughter of captives whose revolt inspired widespread sympathy identified Tukur as a tyrant, particularly by its contrast with the relatively lenient conduct of the rebels until then. The Yusufawa had thus far contented themselves with pillage and foraging, while attacking only those loyalist towns they could not subvert by political means. Having captured or subverted a town, they had merely replaced its chief by one of their own men and garrisoned it with a sufficient force of horsemen and infantry to ensure their control, while avoiding reprisals. However when the news of Tukur's executions spread among them, Yusufawa attacks became more ruthless. On both sides the original struggle for dominance had now become a struggle for survival and vengeance, largely in consequence of the caliph Abdu's vicious order that even Tukur later set aside, unfortunately only after it had done irreparable moral damage.

Yusufu's Last Campaign

Following their setback at Kano, the Yusufawa remained at Takai for nearly three months, replenishing their forces; but they then also attempted to reduce various towns that had withstood them by propaganda and promises, or by displays of force. One area of particular importance for the rebels was Dawaki-ta-Kudu and nearby townships north of the Challawa river about ten miles from Kano on the route to Takai. Had the Yusufawa been assured of support and succour from those towns, following their defeat at Kano, they might have fallen back and regrouped with fewer losses, and thus renewed the contest more quickly and with greater strength. Instead, lacking secure bases near the city, they had lost many men for lack of reinforcements to strengthen the troops that had broken through the wall, and others on their long disorderly retreat to Takai. Anticipating a second longer struggle for Kano, Yusufu and his advisors therefore determined to secure this strategic area within the home districts near the capital as a base for their second assault; and since Gaya supported Tukur, and stood only some twenty miles east of Dawaki ta Kudu and north of Takai, they decided to reduce that also, to forestall any attack from Gaya on Takai, and to eliminate Gaya as a threat on the flank of their second advance against Kano through Dawaki ta Kudu.

Until his accession, as Galadima, Tukur had administered Dawaki ta Kudu, Tamburawa, Tsakuwa and Kumbotso, northwest of Wudil, between Kano city and the Yusufawa stronghold. Kumbotso was then formally divided between the Wombai and Galadima; but while its chief, Gutu, was loyal to Tukur, its people supported Yusufu and the Wombai Shehu. At Dawaki ta Kudu also the chief kept the community on Tukur's side until Yusufu's lieutenant, the Jarmai Dila of Barbura, visited the town and persuaded the townsfolk to support Yusufu by political promises and arguments. Tsakuwa and Tamburawa were subverted in the same way.[35]

While the Jarmai Dila cultivated support for the rebels around Dawaki ta Kudu, Yusufu led a large force against Gaya, where a strenuous fight took place without and within the walls. Resistance ceased when the Sarkin Suma'ila fired the compounds, and the Sarkin Gaya Ibrahim fled to Tukur in Kano. "The slaughter was very heavy and a survivor described the town that day as having been paved with corpses."[36] Leaving the baJobe Umaru, Malam Bakatsine's grandson, in charge of Gaya, Yusufu then turned east towards Dutse, where the baYelige Madaki Salihi had seized the chiefship in Tukur's name on the death of Sarkin Dutse Abdulkadiri. Guided by Salihi's rival, the baJelube Ibrahima, Yusufu's army cut down the resistance at Dutse, driving the usurper Salihi in flight northeast to Hadeija. Shortly after Dutse had fallen, Muhammadu of Hadeija sent his forces to seize the border towns of Miga and Kwanda, ostensibly as the wages for his support, but perhaps in response to appeals from Salihi of Dutse or Sokoto that he should help Tukur. Those seizures later created a border conflict between Hadeija and Kano which remained unresolved until the British came. There is some evidence that Yusufu had agreed to give Kwanda and Miga to Muhammadu in return for field support by the Hadeija army; but for various reasons that was not forthcoming. Perhaps anticipating a prolonged civil war in Kano, Muhammadu thought the moment opportune to seize these desirable units; but it is also possible that the vizier had discussed such boundary changes with Muhammadu in seeking Hadeija's support for Tukur. However, we have no record of that.[37]

Leaving Dutse under his baJelube client, Ibrahima, Yusufu directed his force against Tukur's few remaining strongholds in southeastern Kano, namely, Gantsa, Katanga and Buji, northeast of Birnin Kudu, which also surrendered at this time, its loyalist chief Muhammadu Nafi being replaced by his nephew and rival Zakari. Returning to Takai, Yusufu next sent a force against Rano to expel the chief, Muhammadu, and instal his supporter and namesake. After the fall of Rano, Yusufu then sent his agent Dan A'i to the southwestern border town of Tudun Wada, which had so far remained loyal to Tukur under its *shigege* chief Jaye, a client of Mamman Bello's. Employing the persuasive techniques of Jarmai Dila, Dan A'i subverted Tudun Wada by promising its people tax exemption under a Yusufawa government of Kano. The village chief Jaye was thrown out by a popular riot, and the *shigege* Dan A'i assumed authority in Yusufu's name and cause.[38]

Yusufu fell ill during the Gaya campaign. Having reduced Dutse and Birnin Kudu, he returned to Takai, as mentioned above. While his squadrons campaigned in the west he recovered and awaited their return to march on Kano; but having set out for Kano from Takai, Yusufu's health collapsed and he died at Garko, thereby precipitating a political crisis among his supporters.

Aliyu's Succession and the Fall of Kano

Before dying, Yusufu instructed the Shamaki Harisu, his personal slave, to bring the senior slaves and princes to him. Yusufu then nominated Aliyu Babba as his successor on the grounds that as a grandson of the caliph Aliyu Babba, Aliyu would receive the support of many Toronkawa who were dissatisfied with the caliph Abdu, thereby legitimising the revolt and facilitating the reconciliation of the victorious rebels and the caliph at Sokoto when the war was won. Aliyu's mother, Saudatu, the daughter of caliph Aliyu Babba, was herself among the rebels, though she was probably at Takai when Yusufu died.

After burying Yusufu at Garko, his senior slaves, the Shamaki Harisu, the Dan Rimi Nuhu and others decided to fulfil his final instructions without delay. Accordingly they crowned Aliyu by installing him on the royal dais and present-ing him with the royal insignia, the double-pronged spear, ostrich-feather shoes and other symbols of Kano chiefship dating back to the reign of Muhammadu Rumfa that had been revived by Dabo under Kutumbawa guidance after disuse in Suleimanu's reign. Having enthroned Aliyu, the slaves then sent to summon the princes, Abdullahi's sons. As each appeared in turn and expressed his grief, he was required to present himself before Aliyu and render homage while the slaves stood by with swords drawn to discourage dissent. Several senior princes objected to this procedure on various grounds; firstly, because the slaves had transgressed in enthroning the chief; secondly, because they resented the threat of force by Yusufu's slaves if homage was witheld; and thirdly, some objected that Yusufu's nomination of Aliyu Babba contravened both the usual Islamic proce-dures for settling succession, and those current in Fulani Kano. Nonetheless this display of slave power and loyalty (*amana*) to the throne and to their dead master may have saved the rebels from falling into dispute about the succession, and may thus have prevented their destruction at Tukur's hands.

A Sokoto tradition relates that the rebel baYole leader, Kwairanga, Yusufu's throne slaves, and certain others, having decided on Aliyu Babba, nominated him to the assembly, all of whom assented except the ex-Ciroma Musa, Abdullahi's son, who said "I should be the chief since I am now the most senior (eldest). Oth-erwise I shall return to Takai to wage my own war and kill whoever you choose as chief." Those in control of the assembly replied "Go ahead, you alone; as for us, since Yusufu is dead, we will follow Aliyu." In the end the ex-Ciroma Musa, finding himself without support, abandoned his threat of withdrawal. It is thus possible that had Yusufu failed to select an acceptable successor before his death, and had the throne slaves not acted resolutely to dissolve the succession crisis before it matured, the rebels might have fallen asunder from internal divisions and rivalries at Garko. Lacking any precedent to guide them in their extraordi-nary situation, the rebel leaders, made equal by Yusufu's death, were likely, as Musa's conduct shows, to destroy their enterprise by denying its leadership to one another. In these circumstances, the throne slaves invoked their obligation of *amana* and traditional status as custodians of the chiefship to impose on all assem-bled the fulfilment of Yusufu's last instruction, the *wasiya* which, when delivered by a leader shortly before his death, is regarded as almost sacred and especially binding. Thus they effectively restored the Yusufawa's cohesion and revived their morale by installing Aliyu as their chief.[39]

For some months thereafter the rebels remained at Garko while Aliyu sent urgently to Lokoja and Bida to purchase elephant-guns that shot harpoons with flaming tips, rifles, and other equipment needed for the coming assault.[40] From Garko also Aliyu wrote to caliph Abdu to inform him of his succession.

From the deputy (*wakil*), greetings and friendship, good wishes and increased prestige to our excellent leader, caliph Abdu, son of the late caliph Abubakar

(Atiku). After greetings, the reason for this letter is to inform you that our leader Yusufu died in the month of Muharram, on the day that he withdrew [from Kano?]. His people have not kept anything that he left behind him; but they assembled all of us; and following consultation, both the men from the city and those from the country parts said that after Yusufu there was no other one to lead them except me (Aliyu). So I have accepted, I have taken up their burdens. What is certain is that nothing can resolve our affair except God or his Messenger or Shehu Usmanu or all our leaders, unless it is the hand of the *Amir al-Mu'minin* (caliph). As for me, I stand on the side of Allah, I stand beside his Prophet, I stand beside you. We have not left the ways of our fathers or our grandfathers. Farewell and peace.[41]

If caliph Abdu acknowledged this letter, I have not seen his reply. Having determined to stamp out the rebellion and assure Tukur's succession, Abdu was angered to learn that Aliyu had assumed the leadership of the rebels after Yusufu's death, thereby preserving their power and revolt. On the other hand when she had learnt of her son's succession, Aliyu's mother Saudatu, the daughter of caliph Aliyu Babba, intervened to overrule the ex-Ciroma Musa's divisive threats by appealing to the assembled rebels not to set Yusufu's *wasiya* aside.[42] Thereby, Saudatu aligned herself squarely behind her son's assumption of leadership and responsibility for the revolt. Saudatu moreover was both a cross-cousin and an affine of the vizier Buhari.

Caliph Abdu's response to the news of Aliyu's accession took several forms. He sent letters directing those emirs on Kano's borders to prepare troops for an early campaign against the rebels. He instructed the vizier to exert himself to the utmost to persuade Aliyu to cease the revolt. According to Malam Adamu's account, this led to a breach between the vizier and Saudatu, the mother of Aliyu, who had already taken up his cause. In a cryptic passage Malam Adamu na Ma'aji suggests that, having failed to halt Aliyu's revolt, the caliph or his vizier may later have intrigued secretly with Damagaram to attack Kano, thereby initiating the heavy fighting that later broke out between Zinder and Kano in Aliyu's reign. [43] Nonetheless, despite her failure to persuade the vizier or caliph Abdu that the rebels' cause was just, Saudatu was influential in securing the sympathy of her kinsmen descended from caliphs Mamman Bello and Aliyu Babba for Aliyu and his people.

From Garko Aliyu sent an expedition under the Sarkin Yaki Yusufu of Rano against Bebeji in southeastern Kano on the route to Zaria City, whose Fulani chief was loyal to Tukur. This attack may have been launched merely to weaken Tukur further, but its success also protected the southwestern flank of the rebel advance to Kano by blocking that road against incoming reinforcements from Zaria. At this time also the Dawaki Husaini, a "Habe" lieutenant of Yusufu, overawed Gezawa and drove out its loyalist chief, Dabugel, thereby threatening Kano from the northeast. Meanwhile Aliyu prepared to launch his main attack from the southeast, as Yusufu had done earlier, but from firm bases near Dawaki ta Kudu, closer to Kano.[44]

Tukur perceived the threat and moved to prevent it, sending the pick of his cavalry under the Galadima Malanta and his kinsman the Sarkin Dawaki Tsakar Gida Mamudu to drive the Jarmai Dila from Dawaki and secure the town. The Tukurawa fooled their opponents by moving towards Tamburawa, another rebel stronghold, thus leaving Dawaki on their flank, and appearing to invite an attack. When that was launched, Tukur's cavalry drove the Jarmai Dila and his people headlong into Dawaki, which they sacked, burning the town and seizing many women and children for sale as slaves, while those who could withdrew southwards to Garko, with the Jarmai.

This setback probably determined Aliyu's plans for the coming campaign. Within a month the Yusufawa had moved from Garko to Tsakuwa, four miles southeast of Dawaki ta Kudu. After skirmishing, they sent a body of horsemen under the Sarkin Yaki Yusufu of Rano and Abdu na Gwangwazo, a grandson of the Emir Abdullahi, as a decoy to entice Tukur's troops from Dawaki ta Kudu into an ambush at Salanta, where some 1200 duly met their deaths, including the Sarkin Dawaki Tsakar Gida Mamudu, the Galadima Malanta, his younger brother, Sule Harsa, and many other cavalry leaders and horsemen Tukur could not replace.[45] Immediately after that victory, the Yusufawa marched on Kano, and camped at Anguwar Rimi outside the city.

There Aliyu wrote to Tukur, announcing his arrival. Tukur led out his forces from Kano to Tudun Maliki, where the two armies joined battle, close by the city wall. Tukur's forces were outnumbered and outgeneralled, and the harpoons hurled from Aliyu's elephant guns spread panic among them. After a brief resistance they gave ground and retired to the city. For the next five days Aliyu waited at Fage, presumably for reinforcements due from Gumel, while Tukur remained in a command post opposite at the Women's Gate (*Kofar Mata*). On the sixth day, before the Yusufawa advanced against the city, Tukur fled to Dawaki near Tofa and thence to Bici, Gurum and Kusada in Katsina, leaving Kano through the Waika Gate, which has since been tabooed to his successors.[46] Meanwhile, caliph Abdu ordered his Emir in Katsina, Abubakar, to mobilise the Katsina army and support Tukur. Abubakar unwillingly obeyed, and established his camp at Yashi, just inside his border with Kano. Other imperial directives had been sent to the Emirs of Kazaure, Zamfara and Zaria to do likewise; and the caliph sent the Waziri Buhari from Wurno to the battlefront to direct the campaign. However, neither Kazaure, Zamfara, nor Zazzau sent any troops; and when the Katsina forces were wanted, they were not at hand.

Accompanying Tukur from Kano to Bici and Kusada were those nobles and commoners who, having fought for him throughout, either feared to stay in Kano, or from conviction and loyalty decided to stay by him to the end. Unlike those refugees, the throne slaves remained behind to serve their new master Aliyu as they had served Tukur throughout his days in the palace. Though neither the Shamaki Sa'idu, the Dan Rimi Yahaya, nor any others who had fought for Tukur until his flight had good reason to expect Aliyu's favour, true to their obligations as they interpreted them, the throne slaves awaited his entry to serve as required. Thus in fleeing Kano, Tukur forfeited the slave staff and heavy cavalry ('*yan lifida*) to his opponents.

The Kano Chronicle records that "when Aliyu first entered the palace, his followers began to break into people's compounds, confiscating their property—this is what we call "*basasa*" (raiding and plundering); people were seized and bound, some to be killed, some to be sold, some women to be secluded in harems; some were enslaved directly and remain so to this day (1933). After this Aliyu said,

"Whoever seizes a free man may sell him, except a slave."[47] Though it is probable that these punishments were directed at the compounds of men known to have supported Tukur, it is also likely that in the general breakdown of law and order they were not entirely confined to them. In any event, Aliyu's treatment of his defeated opponents differed little from Tukur's original conduct in its form, scale or violence. We have no way of knowing how many families that had remained aloof and neutral throughout this struggle suffered during the *basasa* that concluded the civil war within Kano, as the victorious Yusufawa wreaked revenge on their enemies and on others believed to have opposed them.

The Death of Tukur

Once in the palace Aliyu worked quickly to reconstitute the territorial administration by allocating its central offices to his leading followers. As the Madaki Ibrahim had supported Tukur, Aliyu replaced him by Muhammadu Kwairanga, his senior baYole supporter. Aliyu's brother, the former Wombai Shehu, was made Galadima, and the Wombai's office was given to Ishi'aku, another son of the Emir Abdullahi. As Ciroma, Aliyu appointed his full brother Mamudu (Muhammadu), another son of the Emir Abdullahi; and since the Daneji Dan Iya Muhammadu had fled with Tukur to Kusada, Aliyu appointed a baSuleibe supporter, Malam Gajere, to hold that office. In place of Tukur's Ma'aji Son Allah, a slave, Aliyu appointed his follower Usumanu, a son of that Ma'aji Gado who had served Suleimanu and Dabo. As Shamaki he replaced Sa'idu, who had served Tukur, by Harisu, who was Yusufu's personal slave and who had taken a leading role in securing Aliyu's accession. As Dan Rimi, Aliyu replaced Yahaya by Nuhu, and as Sallama, the senior eunuch, he appointed a slave called Barde. In addition, to command his slave troops armed with elephant-guns and rifles, Aliyu instituted the new title of Shettima borrowed from Bornu, and conferred it on Shekarau, who had captained his slave riflemen.

To the ex-Ciroma Musa, who had contested his succession, Aliyu gave the title of Magajin Malam na Hausawa. This was a double insult, since it identified Musa with the "Hausawa" and also signified demotion, the office having fewer fiefs and less prestige than the Ciroma title which Musa had held more than ten years earlier. As Turaki he appointed Abdullahi's son Muhammadu in place of Zakari, the son of Mamman Bello, who had withdrawn with Tukur to Katsina; and in place of Tukur's Sarkin Dawaki Tsakar Gida Mamudu, who was slain at Salamta, Aliyu appointed his brother Abbas, another son of Abdullahi, who had successfully commanded the Yusufawa forces against Buji near Birnin Kudu. As Dan Kade, Aliyu appointed his nephew, Abdullahi's grandson, Abdu na Gwangwazo, the first prince to hold this title in Fulani times; and his client Jamau replaced Tukur's Barde Suleimanu, who had been killed with the loyalist Sarkin Dutse Ibrahim outside Fage. As Sarkin Shanu in place of Mamman Bello's son and Tukur's brother, Dati, who had withdrawn to Kusada, Aliyu installed his slave, Dankwari. He also created a new office of Waziri in Kano, and gave it to his brother Ahmadu. Thus on entering the palace, Aliyu promptly filled sixteen offices, two of which, the Waziri and Shettima, were new creations. Of the remaining fourteen, three had been traditionally reserved for palace slaves and seven for free clients of noble family. However, of these sixteen titles, Aliyu gave four to slaves, four to clients, and eight to the sons and grandsons of the Emir Abdullahi, thereby demonstrating beyond doubt the root of their revolt, and his determination to satisfy his kinsmen's desire for office.

Meanwhile, having reassembled his supporters, Tukur had moved from Kusada to Kamri nearby, a more commodious and suitable spot.[48] His brother, the Ciroma Umaru, having died at Kusada, Tukur appointed his own son Lele, also called Abdu, as Ciroma. Until then Lele had held the title of Dan Lawan, but Tukur made no attempt to fill that office at Kamri. At Kamri also he filled the vacant title of Magajin Malam na Hausawa by appointing Zailani, a son of the previous holder, Rabi'u, who had fallen in battle at the Kofar Dan Agundi. Tukur also appointed Modibo as his Alkali, the baGyeni Alkali Batta, who had fled west with him, having died. Finally at Kamri, Tukur also initiated a viziership, probably on learning of Aliyu's innovation, and appointed his son Dibgau to that post. Perhaps Dibgau's role as vizier was merely that of a confidential *magatakarda*, the official scribe or secretary, who was commonly described at Kano as the *Wazirin Waziri*, i.e. the Galadima's chief assistant, being personally responsible for the correspondence and records. In that post the *shigege* Ibrahim had acquired such thorough knowledge of the Galadima's role in the central administration that the Emir Abdullahi did not hesitate to instal him as Galadima, following Yusufu's disgrace. However as Tukur's Magatakarda accompanied him from Kano to Kamri, Tukur probably appointed Dibgau as Waziri with other reasons in mind. [49]

In Kano, where Aliyu is credited with the creation of the vizierate, Dibgau is usually described as the Wazirin Kamri (vizier of Kamri). Unlike Tukur's appointment, Aliyu's vizierate symbolised Kano's assumption of parity with and independence from Sokoto, since in Yusufawa eyes the caliph and vizier of Sokoto were together responsible for the civil war, by their studied refusal to heed local opinion. Since the war, though initially groundless, was necessary to erase the blunders of Sokoto and restore harmony in Kano, the new chief and his supporters were determined that it should not happen again. They therefore united in rejecting further claims for suzerainty over Kano from the caliph or vizier of Sokoto. Indeed at that moment the caliph's Emir, Tukur, still survived at Kamri with his supporters and depended on the caliph for military aid. When Tukur fled from Kano he took with him its allegiance to Sokoto. The new rulers had been obliged to fight long and bitterly to overthrow an emir imposed on them against their will by the obstinacy of an arrogant and politically inept caliph. To punish this rejection of his authority, the latter had ordered that all rebels should be slain without quarter, thereby irreparably destroying the tenuous allegiance of the Yusufawa leaders to his rule. Anticipating that Sokoto would seek to reassert its dominion, after Tukur's flight, Aliyu probably created the office of Waziri to announce to the people of Kano and to other Fulani emirates that Kano was now independent from the caliph and vizier of Sokoto. Those bonds of vassalage and subordination, that had grown so thick in Mamman Bello's reign that they threatened to strangle Kano, in Tukur's were now abruptly cut.

For three months the opposing sides prepared for the final struggle by diplomatic and military means. Caliph Abdu having ordered the Sarkin Katsina to restore Tukur to Kano, "when the Sarkin Kano Aliyu learned this, he sent to the Sarkin Katsina Abubakar to say Kano's affairs were not his business."[50] Presumably similar letters were addressed by Aliyu to the Emirs of Kazaure, Zazzau and Zamfara, who had also received orders from Sokoto to reinforce Tukur at Kusada but failed to do so.[51] Meanwhile Aliyu kept sending to Bida and Lokoja to purchase ammunition, elephant-guns and rifles.

To command the imperial forces supporting Tukur, caliph Abdu had sent his vizier, Muhammadu Buhari, to Katsina. When he felt that preparations were complete and the time opportune, Buhari directed Tukur to move from Kamri to Tafashiya on the border of Kano, thereby signalling his intent to invade Kano and challenging Aliyu to open battle. Aliyu was well informed of Tukur's plans by his spies in Tukur's camp. On Tukur's move to Tafashiya, Aliyu set out from Kano with his army on February 19th 1895, according to the diary of C. H. Robinson, who was then in Kano and witnessed his departure. "It would be hard to imagine a more unwarlike set of men than his warriors are. Dressed in every colour of the rainbow, they are apparently subject to no discipline of any kind."[52] From Kano, Aliyu went to Bici via Dawakin Tofa; from Bici via Dan Zabuwa he moved towards Tafashiya, and pitched his camp at Macinjim on the boundary between Katsina and Kano.

In the preliminary skirmishes, Tukur left the fighting to his Sarkin Gaya Ibrahim, who drove back some of Aliyu's men towards Kano and Zaria. Only when the weight of Aliyu's cavalry had forced the Sarkin Gaya back to Tafashiya and surrounded it, did Tukur himself appear, armed and apparently determined to settle the issue by a single charge. On one report, he set his spear and galloped headlong towards the circle of thickly-corsletted slaves grouped around Aliyu, intending to break through their ring and slay his rival. It was a gallant, unexpected gesture; but unfortunately for Tukur, his horse tripped and fell in mid-gallop. Having disentangled himself, Tukur then settled on his shield with folded hands, in the traditional stance of the noble Fulani warrior who awaits death without fear. At this sight Aliyu shouted an order that Tukur should be captured without harm. In the circumstances only those immediately beside him seem to have heard. One of Aliyu's keenest horsemen, the Dan Kade Abdu na Gwangwazo, grandson of the Emir Abdullahi, who had already broken ranks, galloped to the spot where Tukur sat, and despatched him.[53]

Though desperate, Tukur's decision to seek out Aliyu personally in this fatal charge was not irrational. As Aliyu marched towards Tafashiya, the Waziri Buhari had allowed the Sarkin Katsina Abubakar to withdraw his forces on the pretext that Abubakar had learnt that his enemies, the Hausa of Maradi, were about to attack his capital, an attack that never materialised. Katsina's withdrawal left Tukur heavily outnumbered by the Yusufawa. Under the circumstances, Tukur decided to take the fortune of battle into his own hands, perhaps hoping thus to reduce the general slaughter. This was not to be. Most of the Kano nobles who still stood by Tukur perished at Tafashiya or at Kamri nearby. Those who survived wisely abandoned Kano to settle in Sokoto.

The victorious Yusufawa returned to Kano, where Aliyu shortly received a visit from the vizier Buhari, bringing back some refugees with a letter from the caliph to say that their compounds should be returned. The Waziri also bore with him those traditional insignia of the Kano chiefship which had been removed to Sokoto on Tukur's death. These actions were interpreted as proofs that the caliph finally accepted Aliyu's chiefship and rule over Kano;[54] but in return Aliyu rejected Sokoto's claims to political suzerainty, while not openly challenging the religious leadership of the caliph as the successor of Shehu Usuman dan Fodio. Throughout the remaining years of caliph Abdu's reign, Aliyu steadfastly refused to visit Sokoto or to send tribute; and only after Abdu's death in the face of a grave external threat and at the most inopportune moment did Aliyu set out for Sokoto to make formal reconciliation with Abdu's successor. Thus throughout his reign, unlike his predecessors, Aliyu ruled Kano as an independent Fulani state owing political allegiance to none.[55]

Aliyu Babba, 1894–1903

The Initial Situation

It is said that on his deathbed, having summoned Kwairanga, the future Madaki, and his senior slaves, Yusufu gave Aliyu Babba his turban and robe, as signs of his appointment to lead the Yusufawa, and ordered his slaves to ensure that Aliyu succeeded and received allegiance from all. When Aliyu was finally installed after the forceful intervention of his mother Saudatu, he swore to fulfil all promises and undertakings that Yusufu had made to his followers, after Tukur had been defeated. In the nature of the case, we cannot detail all the commitments that Yusufu had contracted in recruiting and holding together the rebel force; but many of Aliyu's initial appointments were obviously intended to discharge some of these pressing obligations. Moreover, several of Yusufu's promises were inconsistent with the surveillance and close control that Sokoto had traditionally exercised over administrative appointments at Kano. Thus, instead of swearing allegiance to the caliph on his enthronement at Garko, Aliyu had implicitly sworn allegiance to the dead leader of his rebel faction.

Abdullahi's sons and grandsons were the core of that faction; but without the determined support of others seeking hereditary or *shigege* appointments and many adventurers, seekers of fortune, and warriors disaffected by the state of Kano under Mamman Bello and Tukur, the Yusufawa might well have fared badly in the struggle, despite the assistance received from Gumel and the Ningi. Aliyu therefore, on Tukur's flight from Kano, found himself committed to satisfy two important categories of free supporters whose interests were distinct from and potentially at odds with those he had assumed as the ruler of an independent Kano. These two classes of free supporters were princes descended from Abdullahi, and rebel leaders of other lineages, together with some Hausa adventurers. In relation to the princes, Aliyu's position at this stage was rather that of a senior representative, obliged to promote their interests and reward their services, than a ruler. Unless he satisfied the claims of his brothers and nephews for appropriate rewards, Aliyu risked withdrawal of their support for his regime. To alienate them could invite their active revolt, which would certainly be abetted by disaffected persons of non-royal rank, and perhaps by those Tukurawa still resident in Kano. Under such pressures, Aliyu had begun to distribute offices and fiefs as soon as he established himself at the palace after Tukur's withdrawal to Kamri. In these initial appointments, he had few formal obstacles, since almost all *hakimai* and free officials of Kano had fled westwards with Tukur on Aliyu's triumph, thereby vacating their positions; and he could also replace the throne slaves at will. Nonetheless, in allocating these positions, Aliyu's freedom of choice was restricted by commitments inherited from Yusufu. Thus his situation on assuming the chiefship emphasised his dependence on those leading followers and veterans for the continued and active support on which his chiefship relied, in the absence of any alternative political base.

Aliyu's predicament as supreme head of a fully independent Kano, compromised in advance by these conditions and commitments that restrained his autonomy, differs notably from that of his predecessors in several ways. Firstly, unlike preceding emirs of Kano, Aliyu did not enjoy the protection from local revolt that Sokoto's suzerainty had offered until Tukur's accession. Yet if he could not rely on external support against local rivals, neither was there anyone outside Kano whose right to threaten dismissal he now had to fear. Nonetheless, although Aliyu's supremacy in the government of Kano was formally unqualified, it was substantially compromised by the commitments he had made or inherited.

Secondly, unlike previous rulers, having by his accession repudiated the surveillance of Sokoto and with it so many restrictions on the scope and autonomy of the Kano chiefship, Aliyu was formally free to appoint and dismiss all subordinate officials of Kano at his discretion, since his rejection of Sokoto's suzerainty also terminated Sokoto's control of such senior administrative positions as Madaki, Makama, Galadima, Wombai, Sarkin Dawaki Mai Tuta, Dan Iya, Ciroma, Shamaki and the like. Indeed, when Aliyu installed Muhammadu Kwairanga, his senior baYole supporter, as Madaki in place of Madaki Ibrahim (Iro) who had fled west with Tukur, the removal of traditional imperial restraints on the chief's autonomy was made doubly clear, firstly, since the Madaki Iro was then replaced without any attempt to consult Sokoto, and secondly, since no preceding Fulani emir of Kano had ever dismissed a Madaki. In like fashion, Aliyu's initial appointments to the offices of Galadima, Wombai, Ciroma and Dan Iya, together with his creation of the vizierate, proceeded without reference to Sokoto or slavish observance of Kano's political traditions.

By his allocations of these and other offices such as Dan Kade, Sarkin Dawakin Tsakar Gida, Magajin Malam na Hausawa, Barde and Shettima, Aliyu indicated for all who cared to see that he did not regard himself as bound by those traditional norms that had hitherto regulated the distribution of fiefs and office among the various politically prominent lineages and status categories at Kano. As though to force this point on public notice, Aliyu appointed his slave Dan Kwari to the princely office of Sarkin Shanu, which traditionally administered the state during the ruler's frequent absences on "pilgrimage" to Sokoto or on extended campaigns. By this appointment, Aliyu obliquely indicated his intention to control his most powerful but troublesome supporters, namely, his brothers, Abdullahi's sons, who may have expected this title on traditional grounds. Simultaneously, Aliyu also revealed his desire to extend the number and sphere of the slave administrators in the government of Kano, to strengthen his position and control.

Thus on finding his autonomy restricted and his authority correspondingly compromised by political dependence on his free followers, royal and other, very early in his reign Aliyu decided to increase the administrative functions of his most reliable aides, the palace slaves, to whom he owed his initial enthronement, reserving to himself the power to direct or remove them, and thereby centralising the critical control of strategic state structures in his hands. In effect, while Aliyu's circumstances obliged him to regard his brothers and leading supporters as potential threats to his authority as chief, the throne slaves, politically neutralised by their status, their personal loyalties and by their collective *amana* with the throne, provided an excellent instrument through which he could simultaneously extend his authority and recover his independence.

Aliyu's regime differs in so many directions and details from preceding ones that we are constrained either to assume that, despite his familiarity with the norms and conventions of Fulani Kano, he breached or honored them indifferently and without design, or we must seek the meaning and purpose of his actions in his own perception of the constraints, resources and requirements of his situation. If we adopt the second approach, it is necessary to recognise that Aliyu's initial situation on occupying the palace differed no less radically from that of his predecessors than from the position he held during his closing years; and in my view, the striking differences in Aliyu's position at the start and the end of his reign provide the best evidence of his political objectives and achievements.

On entering Kano at the head of a triumphant rebellion, Aliyu's major problems were twofold. He had to legitimate his rule, since violence and force were neither appropriate nor sufficient to stabilise his government, being themselves the antithesis of order. Simultaneously, Aliyu had to convert his power into a superior authority which would be equally valid and binding on his unruly supporters and on his terrified subjects. Traditionally, the Fulani Emirs of Kano had derived their legitimacy and authority by delegation from the caliph of Sokoto, as emirs appointed by and responsible to the caliph for the enforcement of Muslim religion and rule in Kano. By the method of his accession, Aliyu lacked such validation of his claim to rule; in traditional terms, without the caliph's blessing and mandate, his chiefship remained illegitimate. Caliph Abdu's *post facto* ratification of Aliyu's accession could not erase the means by which it was achieved, and carried too many obscure conditions to be acceptable. Like Buhari of Hadeija before him, Aliyu could therefore be described as a rebel or an apostate (*kahiri*) in terms that implied heathenism, despite the caliph's belated gesture of recognition.

However, Aliyu was deeply religious, a learned Muslim, steeped in the conventional Fulani concepts of Islam formulated by the Shehu and Abdullahi dan Fodio. He was accordingly sensitive to the anomaly of his position, with its taints of illegitimacy and apostasy. On the other hand, after such bitter, prolonged and finally vicious conflict, it was equally impossible for him to accept caliph Abdu's gesture of remission and amnesty, or to forgive Buhari and Abdu for the havoc they had wreaked. Least of all could he submit to Abdu, even though the latter condoned his victory by returning the Kano insignia and surviving Tukurawa from Sokoto in the custody of Waziri Buhari. For Aliyu, such tokens of the caliph's recognition and overtures of reconciliation were primarily valuable for their implied endorsement and recognition of his legitimacy as Kano's chief. By the manner and content of his message, Abdu appeared to admit that he had erred in appointing Tukur, and that he no longer regarded Aliyu as an apostate. However, such a convenient resolution of the problem of Aliyu's legitimacy could neither establish his authority in Kano nor his submission to Sokoto.

In repudiating Kano's traditional subordination to Sokoto, Aliyu asserted his own legitimacy as Kano's ruler on grounds beyond the range of the caliph's authority, by asserting Kano's right to self-determination following its sufferings under the mismanagement of Sokoto. Indeed by withdrawing from the city to revolt, Yusufu had simultaneously repudiated the caliph's authority and Tukur's chieftainship; and in subsequently repudiating Kano's subordination to Sokoto, Aliyu was merely honoring this second, "nationalistic" aspect of the Yusufawa revolt. By so doing, he could claim moreover that the Yusufawa had stood and fought for Kano against external tyranny and misrule.

Within the palace, Aliyu's authority was assured. Beyond, despite the submission of a people terrified by the *basasa* his victory had released, Aliyu's authority remained initially contingent on the inclinations and power of his leading free followers. For this reason among others, Aliyu distributed eight of his first sixteen appointments to his brothers, Abdullahi's sons, and four to trusted slaves. Of these eight princely titles, five, namely, the Waziri, Galadima, Wombai, Ciroma and Turaki, were endowed with extensive fiefs and military authority. By such appointments Aliyu sought to associate his senior siblings firmly with his rule, and motivated them to uphold his authority.

From Emir and Oligarchs to Sultanism

Like Dabo, Aliyu assumed the chiefship without assurances of support from the founding lineages of Fulani Kano; but unlike Dabo, who faced a revolt generated by those lineages after his accession, Aliyu had won the throne by revolt against two allied segments of Dabo's dynasty descended from the Emirs Mamman Bello and Usuman. The civil war in fact developed, centred, and concluded within the "*dakin Shekara*," that is, among the descendants of the sons that Shekara had borne to Dabo; but, beginning in strife between descendants of Abdullahi on the one hand and those of Mamman Bello and Usuman on the other, it concluded with the elimination of Bello's and Usuman's progeny from Kano, including Tukur's son, the ex-Ciroman Kamri Lele, who returned to Kano in 1894 on the caliph Abdu's intercession, but soon withdrew to Zinder.

Thus, whereas Dabo had been forced to assert his authority against the opposition of the founding families, the Yusufawa had asserted theirs against rival dynastic segments; and whereas Dabo's triumph had left the founding families in enjoyment of their hereditary titles, extensive domains and privileged political status, Aliyu's triumphs vested the chiefship of Kano in Abdullahi's heirs by eliminating their rivals. Dabo, having conquered, ruled a state in which wide powers and territories had already been endowed to the founding oligarchy. As under its Hausa chiefs, so too in Dabo's day, the government of Kano was an uneasy combination of patrimonial and oligarchic institutions which changed substantially during Dabo's later reign. Under Usuman, and more so under Abdullahi, while the patrimonial power increased greatly, and became predominant in political and military affairs, the oligarchs retained their positions, estates and authority under the express protection of Sokoto. Had Sokoto seen fit to employ these oligarchs as effective electors of the Kano chiefship, it might then have preserved their political power as a counterpoise to those of the dynasty and its chief. Instead, as we have seen, time after time, for reasons of its own, Sokoto completely ignored the "electors" of Kano, and, most recently and painfully, on Bello's death, it had ignored their advice as well. Dabo's authority, though conferred by Sokoto, was initially qualified by the presence of an older, dispossessed and rival dynasty, the Mundubawa, around which the oligarchs could cluster to defend their "rights." With Tukur's defeat and Aliyu's rejection of the caliph's authority, in which he was supported by dissident members of several founding families, relieved of his dynastic rivals, and as heir of the politically predominant partrimonial chiefship, he was now restrained neither by directives from Sokoto, nor by a powerful local oligarchy in his allocations of fiefs and offices.

Indeed the scope and intensity of the Civil War is itself conclusive evidence that, even in the eyes of its members, the original oligarchy had ceased to exist as a solidary political bloc or force capable of resisting or restraining the chief. Since Dabo's day it had owed its continued prominence and high status so heavily to the caliph's protection and favour, that in the general Yusufawa revulsion against Sokoto the oligarchs were doubly compromised, by their relations with Sokoto, and by their services on Tukur's side. Structurally the *basasa* could not have occurred had not the power of the patrimonial chiefship already outstripped all other local institutions to such a degree that within the dynasty, while one segment held the throne, another could simultaneously challenge the chief and his master the caliph, recruit several foreign allies, including Kano's chief enemies the Ningi, and mobilise approximately one-half the country and ruling stratum under its flag. The old unwritten constitution that had persisted from Dabo's day to Bello's and Tukur's was thus no longer consistent with the current structure and distribution of power.

Despite several warnings during Abdullahi's reign, the rulers of Sokoto had failed to perceive that the Suleibawa dynasty in Kano was too deeply entrenched to be regulated at their will. Unlike his vizier Buhari, caliph Abdu had also failed to distinguish between the power of the dynasty and its several segments, and the authority conferred upon its head by his appointment as chief. To Abdu it initially seemed certain that, by virtue of his appointment with Sokoto's support, Tukur would possess sufficient material and political resources to defeat his opponents. Here also the caliph had miscalculated seriously, for without the active support of the largest dynastic segment, the chiefship was neither powerful nor secure. As the contrast between Abdullahi's reign and those of Usuman and Mamman Bello illustrates, following Dabo's rule, chiefly authority at Kano presupposed political power based on sufficiently widespread dynastic support to assure its unquestioned validity. While the original oligarchy had long since lost its coherence and capacity to govern, the Fulani state presupposed effective control of its Hausa population for its continued existence.

Dabo's reign had established a new political constitution at Kano by modifying that inherited from Suleimanu. In essence, under Dabo the pre-eminent chieftainship was restrained by two complementary and co-operating structures, the entrenched local oligarchy and the caliph's supreme authority. Under Dabo's sons the chiefship developed and maintained an excellent *modus vivendi* with the local oligarchy by assimilating the oligarchs to its interests through dynastic marriages, official allocations, reserved places on council, and other arrangements. By such means, the Suleibawa emirs of Kano progressively neutralised the oligarchy as a distinct political force contraposed to theirs. Recognising this, Sokoto progressively reduced the prerogatives of Kano chiefship by assuming the right to decide the final allocations of senior offices, including dynastic positions until, in Abdullahi's reign, as we have seen, the caliphs asserted their decisive control by threatening to depose the emir of Kano without adequate cause.

Notably, no such threats were levelled at Usuman or Mamman Bello despite their incapacities; and none of the various attempts to depose Abdullahi had proved successful. Mamman Bello and Usuman were both rather weak chiefs, temperamentally disinclined to military activity, to vigorous administration or to independent policies. Both deferred willingly to the judgment of Sokoto; and, as Bello's correspondence illustrates, he consulted the vizier and caliph on many minor events and questions that had hitherto formed part of the routine internal administration of Kano Emirate. Abdullahi appears to have handled most of these issues himself without seeking the caliph's guidance or approval for the policies he proposed to pursue. At Kano the repeated attempts of successive caliphs to depose Abdullahi are frankly attributed to their jealousy of Abdullahi's autonomous administration and military strength. caliph Abdurrahman had failed to learn the lessons of Abdullahi's reign, namely, that a powerful and energetic emir who enjoyed sufficient dynastic support at Kano could retain and increase his power despite the attempts of successive caliphs to remove him, primarily because the Fulani of Kano supported his leadership as essential for the preservation of their rule. A weak chief whose familistic policies ensured his political isolation within the dynasty was correspondingly obliged to rely on Sokoto's support and guidance, being himself incapable of mobilising local support for vigorous domestic policies. This was Mamman Bello's situation; and perhaps Bello's subservience misled the rulers of Sokoto to believe that his political weakness, which was partially the result of his familistic policies, was either a desirable or a necessary feature of the Kano chiefship. If so, the lessons of Abdullahi's reign had been rapidly forgotten.

With his victory and repudiation of vassalage to Sokoto, Aliyu had removed the last traditional restraints of an institutional or material kind on the patrimonial chieftaincy of Kano, since the original oligarchic control had long since lapsed, and the oligarchy itself was now divided and weakened. In this situation the only extrinsic restraints on the ruler's power at Kano were those that Aliyu had inherited from Yusufu or contracted himself in leading the revolt. However, by distributing offices to his senior supporters, Aliyu simultaneously institutionalised the rebellion as the decisive condition of his chiefship and terminated it by transforming its champions into state officials and chiefs. Thus while obliged to reward these powerful supporters, on whom he was politically and administratively dependent, Aliyu was constrained by his anomalous situation to seek political security by maximising his resources and autonomy, and to discourage dissidence among his followers and maintain their loyalties while increasing his domination.

In the absence of an effective oligarchy or countervailing external supervision, such policies implied that the patrimonial chieftaincy which had developed from

Dabo's day to Mamman Bello's would progressively be transformed into an autocratic sultanism as fast as the situation allowed.[56] In truth, the civil war that inau-
gurated Aliyu's reign represented the birth pangs of this new political stucture,
with its undiluted thrust towards centralization of military and civil resources
under the chief, to the exclusion of conciliatory imperial restraints. The civil war
had destroyed and discredited the unstable political constitution that had swung
like a pendulum under Dabo's sons between the ineffective and the formidable
variants of a patrimonial state. The Civil War had changed that by eliminating
those dispersals of jurisdiction and constitutional power that had previously
characterised the traditional Fulani regime at Kano as a tripartite structure consisting of a patrimonial chiefship, an entrenched local oligarchy, and an aggressive suzerain. The profound structural transformation and simplification which
the polity of Kano underwent in Aliyu's reign is illustrated with equal clarity by
his distributions of titles and fiefs and by other important events and developments at Kano during these years.

Territorial Replacements

As mentioned earlier, most of the senior hereditary rural chiefs whose title
carried *tambari* had remained loyal to Tukur. Some, such as the Sarkin Gaya,
Sarkin Bebeji and Sarkin Dutse, had fought strenuously on his side. Of Tukur's
captains, the Sarkin Gaya Ibrahim Dabo was conspicuous for his efforts and brav-
ery. So too among the Yusufawa was the Jarmai Dila of Babura, who had won
Dawaki ta Kudu for the rebels almost single-handed. To replace Ibrahim Dabo,
Aliyu therefore awarded the Jarmai Dila the chiefship of Gaya. Later when Dila
died at Bashe fighting the Ningi, Aliyu appointed the Madakin Kila Ahmadu,
whose rebellion against Mamman Bello was reported above, as chief of Gaya; but
when at Gezawa, against the armies of Damagaram, Ahmadu disgraced himself
by cowardice, Aliyu promptly dismissed him and appointed a Kanuri client,
Mamman Kwallo, to succeed. Notably, all three appointments set aside the traditional claims of the Kurawa lineage who had ruled Gaya since Dabo's day, its
members having fought for Tukur. Moreover, whereas in Bello's reign the Ciroma
had supervised Gaya, Aliyu transferred it to his brother the Waziri Ahmadu,
thereby altering Gaya's political situation at two levels.

The Chief of Birnin Kudu, Muhammadu Nafi, had also supported Tukur,
athough constrained to submit to Yusufu's forces when his town was attacked in
the campaign of 1894. Muhammadu Nafi was therefore dismissed and replaced
by his nephew Zakari, who had fought for the Yusufawa. Zakari, "a disreputable
character ... soon embarked on a course of oppression. No property was safe from
his greed, and his henchmen were often guilty of raiding markets and even of
highway robbery. After five years the extortions had become so gross that Aliyu
dismissed him,"[57] and appointed Muhammadu Mazadu, another member of the
ruling lineage, in his place. Mazadu retained the office until 1930.

At Karaye, Hassan, the chief, had remained loyal to Tukur and wisely fled on
his defeat. Aliyu replaced him with a Fulani cleric (*malam*), Ahmadu Dabo, whose
ritual assistance was highly valued during the war; and on Ahmadu Dabo's death
in 1897, Aliyu appointed Dabo's son, Abdulkadiri, as the resident chief of Karaye.

Thus here also the traditional ruling family lost their rights to the chiefship as reprisal for their support of Tukur. However, Aliyu left Karaye under the supervision of the Sarkin Dawaki Mai Tuta who had held the town in fief before the *basasa*.

At Kiru, Mamman Bello had dismissed the hereditary chief, Ahmadu, in 1891, for embezzling the *kudin shuke* tax, appointing in his place Ahmadu's brother Abubakar, who fought for Tukur in the Civil War; but when Yusufu of Rano, the Sarkin Yaki, stormed Bebeji nearby on Aliyu's behalf, Abubakar fled and was replaced by that Ahmadu whom Bello had dismissed; and following Ahmadu's death in 1897, Aliyu appointed Ahmadu's brother Muhammadu to rule at Kiru.

At Bebeji, where the loyalist chief had fled on the Yusufawa attack, Aliyu appointed his client Jibo, a Fulani from Jahun, as Sarkin Fulani Bebeji. At Rano, the Yusufawa captain, the Sarkin Yaki Yusufu, replaced his brother, the loyalist chief. At Ringim the chief, Bature, having stood by Tukur, was replaced by one of Aliyu's men. At the same time Aliyu transferred Ringim, with its subordinate settlements of Mallamawa and Biyamusu from the Galadima's administration to the Wombai, thereby reducing the Galadima's extensive fiefs. In like fashion, Aliyu replaced the chiefs of Sankara and Debi, who had supported Tukur, by Yusufawa veterans of non-royal stock. At Gwaram the chief Adamu (Adaji) fled to Kamri with Tukur and was replaced by Suleimanu, who had held and lost this office under Mamman Bello. At the same time Aliyu transferred administrative responsibility for Gwaram from the Dan Rimi to the Waziri Ahmadu. Following Suleimanu's death at the hands of the Ningi in 1896, Aliyu appointed Sule's brother Abubakar, but dismissed him in 1900 on suspicion of conspiracy with the Ningi, and chose Abdulkadir of the same family to succeed. At Gwarzo, where the village chief Garu had fled with Tukur, Aliyu appointed Garu's rival, Dambo, who had supported the Yusufawa, but dismissed him in 1898 for cowardice at the battle of Tattarawa against Zinder. Aliyu then appointed a Katsina Fulani, Dan Jika, who fled not long after to avoid Aliyu's wrath, following a fight at Gwarzo between their men. Aliyu then appointed Daba, Dan Jika's younger brother, who was killed by the British at Kotorkwashi in 1903. At Gezawa, where the "Habe" Dawaki Husaini had displaced the Fulani village chief Dabugel, Aliyu appointed Ibrahim, Husaini's son, to succeed, following Husaini's death in the battle at Tafashiya, although Ibrahim was then a minor. After the Sarkin Damagaram Ahmadu Maje Rinji attacked Gezawa and burnt the town in 1898, Aliyu restored Ibrahim and his people and helped to rebuild the town.

During the Civil War the southern frontier town of Tudun Wada, a fief of the Galadima, had been subverted by the Yusufawa adventurer Dan A'i from Garun Danga, who promised the townsfolk tax exemption if they supported Aliyu, and drove out the loyalist chief Jaye. In return for this service Aliyu confirmed Dan A'i as chief of Tudun Wada. He likewise confirmed the Sarkin Jahun Modibo who, having rebelled and seceded from Kano in Mamman Bello's reign, had visited Takai on Yusufu's revolt to declare his allegiance and support of the cause, thus restoring Jahun to Kano. Aliyu likewise confirmed the rebel Madakin Kila Ahmadu in his village chiefship, following Ahmadu's alignment with the Yusufawa when Danyaya brought the Ningi to their assistance. At Dal due south of

Garko, Aliyu also appointed the Yusufawa lieutenant, Sambo, as village chief, in place of the hereditary ruler, who had remained loyal to Tukur; but for reasons unknown, in due course Aliyu dismissed Sambo and appointed instead a *shigege* client, the Barden Sallama Abdulkadiri, thereby once more excluding the traditional rulers from their chiefship.

Such distributions of senior rural chiefships holding high rank and *tambaru* illustrate Aliyu's determination to increase his autonomy, even while fulfilling the political commitments he had inherited from the revolt. He systematically replaced Tukur's supporters by Yusufawa leaders in these rural chiefships, which he used to reward distinguished achievements, such as those of the Jarmai Dila, the Dawaki Husaini and the Dan A'i. He also restored to office at Gwaram, Kiru and elsewhere, chiefs whom Mamman Bello had dismissed, while welcoming such rebels as Modibo of Jahun and Ahmadu of Kila back to the state of Kano. However, having thus rewarded his supporters with lucrative posts, Aliyu clearly did not regard himself as obliged to retain them in office at any cost. As we have seen, on various grounds he dismissed several chiefs whom he had appointed at differing points in his reign. In each case the man dismissed discovered that he was isolated as an individual by the political context from other Yusufawa rebels, and that he risked more serious punishment by challenging the emir's decision and authority. In effect, under Aliyu appointment to office carried uncertain implications and no guarantee concerning its tenure. Each office held its holder hostage to the chief, who, having fulfilled his political obligations with the appointment, thereafter demanded loyal, efficient service in those spheres he regarded as critical.

Finally, as we have seen, Aliyu often combined the installation of a rural chief with transfer of that chief's territory from one *hakimi* to another, and sometimes to the throne. For example, both Dawaki ta Kudu and Tsakuwa had been administered by the Galadima Tukur in Bello's reign and by the Galadima Malanta in Tukur's. Throughout the civil war, and even after the Jarmai Dila had persuaded them to join the revolt, the allegiance of both these towns remained as critical for Tukur as for the Yusufawa. As we have seen, the decisive battle at Salamta was fought to determine their fate. To indicate his recognition of their significance, on promoting his brother, the Wombai Shehu, to the Galadimaship, Aliyu transferred Dawaki ta Kudu and Tsakuwa to the throne for administration by commissioned agents of his choice, including palace personnel. Besides Jahun, Dutse, Rano, Tudun Wada and Riruwe, he simultaneously removed Ringim, Malamawa and Biyamusu from the Galadima's portfolio, and restored Ringim to the Wombai who had held it in Alwali's day. By such measures Aliyu simultaneously asserted and increased his own autonomy, while redressing those territorial inflations of the Galadimaship that Mamman Bello had made to promote Tukur's power and dominance. By way of compensation, after Galadima Shehu's death in 1897, Aliyu transferred Gazara and the pleasant fief of Sarina, a *tambari*-holding chiefship, to his brother Ishi'aku, who then succeeded Shehu as Galadima on promotion from the office of Wombai. By so redistributing fiefs among the senior central offices, Aliyu simultaneously asserted his overriding powers as chief, corrected the imbalances Mammon Bello had made, and realigned the territorial administration to eliminate extraordinary concentrations of wealth and power.

The Situation of "Habe"

Aliyu's greatest difficulties in rural administration were concentrated at Getso where, as mentioned above, the "Habe" and Bedde villagers had seized the opportunity presented by the civil war to eject their Fulani chief, the Sangetso Dan Hazo and his Alkali, from the town, replacing them by a ruler of their own choice, Dahuwa, a local Habe. These developments at Getso constituted a direct revolt against Fulani overrule. Following his installation, Dahuwa had rendered allegiance to no one, neither to the Yusufawa nor to Tukur. Perhaps the Getso people hoped that Fulani rule would disintegrate in the ruthlessly destructive civil war; and they may even have hoped by their example to encourage nearby "Habe" communities to revolt and expel their Fulani rulers. However, Getso's example had no known imitators.

On assuming the throne, Aliyu could not overlook these developments at Getso since they challenged his authority as well as the Fulani dominion. To the suggestion that he confirm Dahuwa in office, it is said that Aliyu replied, "I will never make a Sangetso from among the Getso people." Certainly Dahuwa's confirmation could establish an explosive precedent. Instead Aliyu appointed Tsigi, a Fulani from Kura nearby, to replace Dahuwa. However Sangetso Tsigi failed to establish control in the face of intense local opposition; and following his ejection, Aliyu appointed Mamudu, a Fulani of Ruma in Katsina. It seems likely that Mamudu was installed as chief at Getso by a strong force from Gwarzo and Karaye. However, when the force withdrew Mamudu's troubles began. As chief, he claimed the right to dates growing on trees in the compounds and farms of his subjects, although the owners of these trees also paid an annual tax of 70 cowries, the *kudin dabino*, on each. Whether Mamudu's claims had legal or local customary foundation is not clear; but they crystallised local disaffection. One villager, Ladan, finally refused to allow the Sangetso's agents to enter his compound to pick dates from his tree. Mamudu's reaction generated public protest. The Beddes of Getso besieged his compound until Mamudu and his retainers came out and fought with them. The Sangetso reported the matter to Aliyu at Kano, who promptly ordered the arrest of all rioters, and despatched sufficient force to effect it. Mamudu accordingly sent a contingent of Getso recalcitrants to Aliyu, who placed them in the Sankurmi's gaol at Kano where many died in the filthy conditions.

Despite this success, Mamudu was soon replaced as Sangetso by Gandau, a Fulani from Daura or Kazaure, who shortly slew a villager with his sword while facing a hostile mob of Getso people. When the incident was reported to Aliyu, he chose to adjudicate it under his *siyasa* jurisdiction as chief. The case is remembered as especially difficult to decide. Some judicial assessors exculpated Sangetso Gandau on pleas of self-defence; others interpreted the evidence as demonstrating homicide. Two Getso leaders, Bala and Buna, gave witness against Gandau. In the end Aliyu removed Gandau from office, while dropping the charge of homicide. A Fulani of Getso was then appointed, following which the Bedde community withdrew en bloc from Getso to settle in a neighbouring village.[58]

These incidents illustrate Getso's continued resistance to Fulani overrule, primarily because of its oppressive, unequal character. Even as late as 1910, at Getso as elsewhere in Kano, "only the 'Habe' people are asked to do some forced labour";[59] and as we have seen from Dabo's day to Mamman Bello's and Aliyu's, "Habe" were taxed twice as heavily as Fulani. They were also virtually excluded from political and administrative office and discriminated against at law. Following the revolt of Malam Hamza and his colleagues in Usuman's reign, Fulani hostility towards their "Habe" subjects was reinforced by their fears of "Habe" sympathy and collusion with the Ningi, whose remarkable fighting power illustrated the quality of their Hausa leadership. Even without intended malice, the Fulani regime was at once corrupt, exploitive, and unequal. The Kano Chronicle casually relates that

> in the reign of Aliyu there was no famine, but people would break into the women's quarters of commoners' compounds from the rear without seeking permission. This continued until Allah sent relief when the Europeans came. Until then the commoners had a certain song, "Christians, you have waited long without coming." They (the common people) thought that when the Europeans came they would not have to do the work of subjects, they thought they would merely rest, but this was not so. Moreover, in Aliyu's reign there were many campaigns and wars until even boys of ten years old were ordered to bear quivers; if they did not, they would be arrested.[60]

Describing the judicial administration of Kano in 1894, Robinson remarks

> punishments administered ... are, mutilation, slavery and death. In some towns, if a man is convicted of stealing, his hands or feet are both cut off ... if a man is unable to pay a debt which he has incurred, his creditor may claim him as a slave. ... There is, as might naturally be supposed, a great deal of bribery practised, and it but seldom happens that a rich man is condemned, unless it be for a distinctly political offence.[61]

On March 22nd 1894, Robinson recorded the return of Aliyu to Kano in his diary. "The king came into the town this morning. It appears that he has killed Tukr. Tukr, on leaving Katsena, retreated to Kamri, one of the towns subject to Kano, the inhabitants of which were powerless to prevent his entry into their town. The result is that the king of Kano burnt this town and carried off its inhabitants as slaves."[62] Walter Miller, the missionary, who visited Kano and met Aliyu Babba in 1902, related how in Tripoli in 1899 he had met "the pick of the Hausa people, the religious, the more intelligent and educated, I heard from them before I had ever been in Nigeria, of the atrocities of these Fulani rulers, how the people everywhere were groaning under their cruel selfishness and lust for power, and how the pagan people were gradually becoming decimated by constant slave raids."[63] In his autobiography, Maimaina, a native of Lokoja, who visited Kano at the turn of the century on Lugard's behalf, disguised as a trader, to spy out Aliyu's military preparations, describing his journey north, remarks casually that "at Kafi (Keffi, a minor Fulani Emirate south of Zaria) for the first time I saw slaves in the market, women and men and children, all sitting down with their feet stretched out before them for sale, just as we sell horses or cows or donkeys nowadays."[64]

Monteil, who travelled through Hausaland in 1892, reckoned that slaves out-numbered the free population; but in Kano Robinson estimated that only one-third of the people were slaves;[65] while for the empire as a whole, Wallace esti-mated that the Fulani were "less than one-sixth of the whole population ... one-third consists of pure Hausas, and the remaining half of slaves."[66] If so, since neither slaves nor Fulani performed corvée or paid the onerous tax, the free Hausa minority alone bore those burdens together with such other inequities as the rulers reserved for their free non-Fulani subjects. Yet that Getso alone, of several hundred predominantly "Habe" communities at Kano, persistently and strenuously resisted such oppression, demonstrates how effectively the Fulani political organization isolated these subject communities from one another, and thereby ensured central control of them all.

Though little has been said directly about the conditions of Hausa commoners under Fulani rule in describing the Kano polity and narrating its development, its punitive, illiberal character should not be overlooked. There was some truth in Robinson's assertion that "the great majority of the slaves in Hausaland are obtained not from foreign or outside sources, but from villages or towns, the inhabitants of which are of the same tribe and race as their captors. ...There is no real security for life or property anywhere."[67] Despite this, popular revolts against Fulani exploitation were confined to small communities, such as Getso, Gwaram or Kila, by the insulating effects of the political and administrative organization, which could thus contain and suppress these local revolts at leisure. Perhaps the best evidence that no general revolt of Hausa or "Habe" was possible at Kano under this regime is the flight of Malams Hamza, Mai Mazari and their followers from Kano and Tsakuwa to the Ningi to preserve their lives.

Reorganization at the Center

Following the conquest, Aliyu's political difficulties lay rather with the central administration than in the rural areas. As we have seen, he could easily place his own men in those rural chiefships vacated by the flight, death or defeat of Tukur's supporters. He could also redistribute those rural units as fiefs of central offices, while reserving strategic units for his own supervision. Thus, besides Tsakuwa and Dawaki ta Kudu, Aliyu appropriated Madobi and Kura, formerly a fief of the Sarkin Dawaki Tsakar Gida, for the crown. As with Tsakuwa and Dawaki ta Kudu, by this measure Aliyu sought to demonstrate his gratitude to the people of Kura for their valuable assistance during the recent war, and to secure direct control of that strategic centre. Until Abdullahi's reign, Kura had been ruled by those descendants of the Hausa Alkali Usuman for whom the office of Magajin Malam na Hausawa was created. In 1863 Abdullahi had replaced these Hausawa by his Buzu client, Abubakar; but when the civil war broke out, Usuman's grand-son, Sa'idu, once more held the chiefship. Sa'idu sided with Tukur but was driven out by the townsfolk who supported Yusufu's claim and opened the gates of Kura to Aliyu after Yusufu's death. Aliyu then moved a large force to Kura, and from that base he reduced Bebeji and several towns southwest of Kano. As village chief of Kura he appointed a Kanuri supporter, Muhammadu dan Dalma; and after Muhammadu's promotion to the larger town of Garko, Aliyu selected another *shigege* soldier of fortune, Malam Muhutari, to rule at Kura. Meanwhile, ostensibly to assure the people of his continued interest in their welfare, he kept Kura under his own direct supervision.

At the centre, Aliyu faced more complex problems. He had first to discharge various commitments made by Yusufu or himself to their senior followers. He had also to establish Abdullahi's sons in princely positions. He was expected to distribute traditional family titles among those qualified by descent and military support to hold them. He had also to reward many ambitious and energetic adventurers and lieutenants without whose assistance the Yusufawa might not have won. Yet, while distributing these positions and powers, Aliyu had to seek out capable administrators bound to himself by ties of personal loyalty, without alienating his powerful supporters or forfeiting direct control. As we have seen, Aliyu's situation constrained him to aggrandize his office and to accumulate overriding reserves of power to the throne, in order that he could reduce his political dependence on those supporters he had satisfied by office, and on others who remained resentful, whether appointed or not.

Excluding his brother Shehu, who had retained the office of Wombai throughout Tukur's brief reign despite his revolt, none of Tukur's central officials held office under Aliyu, whatever their status as slaves, eunuchs, hereditary nobles, clients, princes, clerics or other. Many of these central executives had fled with Tukur to Kamri and fell with him at Tafashiya. Others, such as the Sarkin Bai Muhammadu Bashare, fled elsewhere, in this instance to Kazaure, thereby vacating their titles. Yet others, such as the Limam Muhammadu Dikko, had remained at Kano. In either event, all Tukur's central executives had either removed themselves or were removed by Aliyu, who then distributed their fiefs and titles among his followers.

Aliyu dismissed Tukur's Limam Muhammadu Dikko and appointed Isma'ila, probably a baGyeni and formerly Limam at Dutse, as Limam at Kano City. The Alkali Modibo, whom Tukur had appointed at Kamri on the death of Alkali Babba, was replaced by Sule, the son of Abdullahi's Alkali Zangi, whose history has been cited above. Like Limam Isma'ila, Alkali Sule was also of the Gyenawa clerical lineage.

Tukur's treasurer, the Ma'aji Son Allah, was a throne slave appointed by Mamman Bello. Aliyu replaced him by Usuman, the son of Dabo's treasurer Gado, whose techniques of prevarication and witholding payment Robinson describes vividly and at length.[68] Simultaneously Aliyu discharged the gatekeepers of the city, most of whom were Fulani, and all of whom were free and owed their appointments to the Ma'aji. Having served under Tukur, these men had closed the gates on Aliyu and his followers, and were therefore dismissed. To police each of the then thirteen city gates thereafter, Aliyu selected reliable throne slaves, whom the Ma'aji Usuman appointed and supervised, thereby reversing the status relations of the Ma'aji and gatekeepers. Under Tukur and Bello, whereas the gatekeepers were free Fulani, the Ma'aji had been a Hausa throne slave. Under Aliyu the Ma'aji was a free Fulani client with quasi-hereditary claims to the title, while the city gatekeepers were slaves bound by ties of *amana* to the throne. As before, each Sarkin Kofa (Gate Keeper) was rewarded by a *hurumi* or benefice of grain tithe (*zakka*) and by tax due on the three hundred farms nearest his gate. In addition, these gatekeepers could request small portions of any goods brought through their gates into the city, or gifts of cash in lieu thereof. Though customary and unopposed, these routine levies were illegitimate, being made without the chief's express approval.

Aliyu also reorganised the prison administration. Until the *basasa*, apart from the Gidan Shamaki, which contained the prison of last resort for high-ranking offenders, the state prisons had been administered by the Sankurmi and the Sarkin Yara. From Dabo's day onwards, these two offices had been regularly allocated to free clients; and following the dismissal of Sankurmi Musa, the son of Dabo's Hausa Galadima Ango, Abdullahi had appointed his own daughter's son, Mamudu, to that office, thereby elevating its status to the dynastic margins. It is known that the Sankurmi under Mamman Bello and Tukur, was a *shigege* freeman; and throughout the reigns of Usuman, Abdullahi, Mamman Bello and Tukur, the office of Sarkin Yara had also been filled by Fulani clients, Haburde and his lineal issue, the Sarkin Yara being then a subordinate (*lawani*) of the Galadima and, since Abdullahi's day, the *jekada* to Gaya. As mentioned above, Abdullahi had integrated both prisons under the Sankurmi's control. Aliyu seems, however, to have reorganised the prisons, leaving the Sankurmi in charge of convicted freemen, and creating a new prison for slave offenders, both public and private, under the Sarkin Yara.

Aliyu also created or revived the office of Ma'ajin Watali, whose official compound served as the public pound, lost property office and temporary jail for suspected criminals awaiting trial. In his role as custodian of such lost property (*tsintuwa*) as slaves, horses, money and commercial commodities of all kinds, the Ma'ajin Watali discharged some functions entailed by Muslim law which had formerly vested in the office of treasurer (*Ma'aji*); hence the designation of this new office, which was remunerated by allocation of hamlets near the city. But in relieving the Treasury of its responsibilities for the care of lost property and vesting these in a new office, Aliyu was primarily interested in prison reorganization. As Ma'ajin Watali he appointed Auta, a free Fulani; but at the same time he transferred the offices of Sankurmi and Sarkin Yara, in charge of the prisons for free and slave offenders, from free men to throne slaves, thereby placing both prisons directly under control by the palace. Aliyu's interest in thus reorganising the prisons is easy to understand, given the circumstances in which he came to rule Kano. Evidently, after the wave of violent reprisals that marked the Yusufawa occupation of Kano, Aliyu had reason to anticipate numerous arrests of suspected criminals and dissident subjects, both slave and free, and accordingly sought to make suitable provisions for their control.

Initially the office of executioner, Hauni, had been filled by free Fulani, but Abdullahi had transferred it to throne slaves. Aliyu maintained this tradition. He also appointed reliable slaves to the office of Sarkin Dogarai, the chief of police, who was responsible for arresting offenders, patrolling the palace precincts, commanding the emir's bodyguard, and preparing his camp on campaigns. Under Aliyu's predecessors, including Mamman Bello and Tukur, the office had generally been filled by throne slaves; but on at least one occasion during Abdullahi's reign, the Sarkin Dogarai was a free client. Under Aliyu the police, executioner, prison wardens, city gatekeepers, and the Sarkin Shanu Dan Kwari who administered the state during the ruler's absence on campaigns, were all slaves of the throne, bound to their emir by affection and respect as well as by the symbiosis institutionalised in *amana*. In addition, Aliyu had established a powerful slave force armed with rifles and harpoon-firing elephant guns (*sango*) under the new slave office of Shettima. By means of these slave formations and appointments, Aliyu brought the city firmly under his personal control; and by these means he simultaneously protected his throne against internal subversion or assault, and immobilised all opponents or rivals who remained in the city. Aliyu's search for political security directed these deployments of office among the palace slaves, who formed the unique and indispensable means of his domination; and his use of these resources illustrates his considerable political and administrative abilities. Thus Aliyu transferred the office of Kilishi from the Fulani lineage which had held it since Dabo's day, to his namesake, a slave, perhaps because as the senior court usher, the Kilishi exercised some majordomo functions which Aliyu preferred to vest in trusted slaves.

The Sultan and the Oligarchs

Of senior titles traditionally vested in founding Fulani lineages such as the Yolawa, Jobawa, Dambazawa, Danejawa and Suleibawan Jamau, Aliyu initially dispossessed only the Danejawa by appointing Abdullahi's sons, Malam Gajere and Mahamman, to the titles of Dan Iya and Dan Makwayau respectively, thus appropriating those Danejawa offices for Abdullahi's issue. As Madaki, he appointed the baYole Kwairanga, his mother's mother's son by her first husband Madaki Umaru. As Makama, following the dismissal of Mujeli whom Tukur had appointed on the death of Makama Iliyasu at Kamri, Aliyu appointed his leading baJobe follower, Hamza, the son of Dabo's Makama Isa; and when Hamza died shortly after in 1895, Aliyu gave this powerful office to his loyal supporter, the Sarkin Suma'ila Umaru, whose links with the Jobawa were traced through his father's mother, Habiba, the sister of Malam Bakatsine. Thus, as his second Makama, Aliyu set aside the traditional requisite of agnatic descent from Bakatsine's father, Malam Umaru, and appointed a Jobawa cognate on whom he could rely. As regards the Dambazawa office and fiefs, following the flight of Muhammadu Basheri to Kazaure in 1893, Aliyu rewarded Abdusallame, a grandson of Dabo Dambazau, for his active support with this hereditary title.

The Suleibawan Jamau were less fortunate, and nearly lost their lineal title in Aliyu's reign. As expected, on moving to the palace, Aliyu replaced Tukur's Sarkin Dawaki Mai Tuta by a loyal supporter, Shehu, from the same lineage; but not long after, for reasons unknown, he dismissed Shehu and appointed his younger brother, who was later dismissed for administrative blunders by the British. By these successive dismissals of his Sarkin Dawaki mai Tuta, custodian of the Shehu's flag, and his appointments of Makama, Madaki and Sarkin Bai, a senior councillor of state, Aliyu abruptly broke the historic conventions that had formerly prevented the Emir from dismissing any of those hereditary title-holders.

Title-holding lineages of lesser eminence and power fared rather rudely at Aliyu's hands. As mentioned above, besides dispossessing the Hausa Alkali Usuman's issue of their chiefship at Kura, Aliyu transferred their family title,

Magajin Malam na Hausawa, to the ex-Ciroma Musa, Abdullahi's son, who had contested his accession at Garko. At some period between the deaths of Yusufu and Tukur, Musa had withdrawn from Kano into Bauchi, perhaps in fulfilment of his threat to secede if Aliyu succeeded Yusufu. On learning this, presumably from the Emir of Bauchi, caliph Abdu had written to Musa instructing him to return at once to Kano, and tried to persuade Aliyu to communicate with him in the hope of negotiating a settlement.[69] Presumably such directives enabled the Emir of Bauchi Umaru (1883–1902) to secure Musa's return; but Aliyu sardonically gave Musa the title of Magajin Malam na Hausawa and so demoted him. Following Musa's death not long after, Aliyu returned this office to Malam Usuman's issue, and appointed Sule of that lineage.

During the civil war, Mundubawa officeholders had fought faithfully on Tukur's side, perhaps seeking thereby to preserve their two family titles, Dan Amar and Mai Anguwan Mundubawa. However, it seems that by 1897 Aliyu had transferred the title and fiefs of the Mai Anguwan Mundubawa to his *shigege* client Na ta-Allah, a son of that Sarkin Dutse Bello whom the Emir Usuman had murdered. Presumably this was done to punish the Mundubawa for their exclusive allegiance to Tukur. According to some informants, Aliyu also dispossessed the Mundubawa of the Dan Amar title; but this requires further study, since the identity of Aliyu's Dan Amar remains obscure. Likewise, it is said that Aliyu dispossessed the Balarawa of their family office, Dan Darman, the Danejawa of Dan Kade, and other Fulani lineages that had held such titles as Dan Goriba, Dokaje and Barwa, by allocating these ranks to *shigege* clients or, on occasion, to princes. However, at Minjibir he reinstated the Yerimawa lineage that held the titles of Turakin Romo and Sarkin Fulanin Minjibir by appointing his supporter Maso to replace Audu who had fled with Tukur to Katsina. Thus Aliyu proceeded pragmatically in allocating those central offices to which particular lineages had established hereditary rights. If the holding lineage had some suitable representative among his supporters whose loyalty and previous service recommended him, or someone to whom the position had already been promised, Aliyu did not hesitate to appoint them. However, if the title-holding lineage had stood solidly behind Tukur, Aliyu felt free to employ their endowments to reward his trusted and needy supporters. In either event, Aliyu's appointments were governed by his need for effective and loyal administrators, his need to reward men who had fought for him, and the need to consolidate and enhance his political authority.

The Sultan and the Dynasty

Predictably, Aliyu's greatest difficulties lay with his kinsmen, the heirs of Abdullahi, on whose behalf Yusufu had initiated the revolt. Despite Aliyu's prompt appointments of several brothers to such important offices as Galadima, Wombai, Ciroma, Turaki, Sarkin Dawaki Tsakar Gida and Dan Buram, many others remained without major office, as did their cousins descended from Dabo's other sons. Aliyu attempted to provide for these remoter collaterals by careful appointments. To Dabo's only surviving son, Sa'adu, he gave the title of Dan Isa; and to Dabo's grandsons Mai-Bene and Arabu, begotten by the Galadima Abdulkadiri and Madaki Salihi respectively, he gave the titles and fiefs of Dan

Lawan and Dan Maje. Further, having dismissed Tukur's Tafida Malanta, the son of Usuman, he gave that title to another collateral prince. On promoting Abdullahi's grandson Abdu na Gwangwazo from Dankade to Barde Babba, following the death of Jamau, Aliyu appointed another of Abdullahi's grandsons, Abubakar, as Dan Kade. Only in 1895 on the promotion of his brother, the Turaki Mamman Nakande, to the office of Wombai, following the Wombai Ishiyaku's promotion to Galadima, did Aliyu appoint any of his sons to a title, namely, Mamman, also called Dibgau, who then became Turaki. Not long after, when Turaki Mamman was killed by the Ningi in battle, Aliyu appointed another son, Mujeli, to succeed. Later, after the Wombai Mamman Nakande died as related below, Aliyu promoted his full brother Mamudu from Ciroma to Wombai, and installed his own son Abdulkadiri as Ciroma. These were the only two official positions that Aliyu conferred on his children; and it is said that he later dismissed the Turaki Mujeli for fighting with him. If so, the title fell vacant, since Aliyu appointed no further Turakis.

During his short reign, Aliyu appointed three of his brothers to the office of Galadima and four to that of Wombai. These successive appointments were associated with Aliyu's repeated promotions from Wombai to Galadima, following the death of Tukur's Galadima Malanta in 1894 and of Aliyu's appointees, Shehu, in 1897 and Ishi'aku in 1900. On Ishi'aku's death, when the former Ciroma Mamudu, who had succeeded Mamman Nakande as Wombai, became Galadima, Aliyu appointed his younger brother, the Sarkin Dawaki Tsakar Gida Abbas, as Wombai. It is not known who succeeded Abbas as Sarkin Dawaki Tsakar Gida; but clearly, by these appointments, Aliyu sought to break with the tradition of his predecessors by placing his brothers and cousins in office ahead of his sons. By such appointments, which reversed the narrow patrimonial familism of Mamman Bello, Aliyu identified his brothers firmly with his regime, and strengthened their loyalties, without thereby reducing his own autonomy.

Inevitably, since there were far fewer offices than eligible claimants, several of Aliyu's brothers were variously dissatisfied with his appointments, and on at least two occasions after the return of ex-Ciroma Musa from Bauchi, Aliyu faced the risk of revolt by dissident siblings. In 1897 Aliyu's paternal half-brother Safiyanu planned to revolt, but was rendered powerless by Aliyu's prompt action. Safiyanu had fought for the Yusufawa throughout the revolt and had apparently been promised some office (*sarauta*) without further specification when the Yusufawa won. For three years following Aliyu's capture of Kano Safiyanu waited in vain for his reward, becoming increasingly disaffected. As his impatience and hostility became known, other disappointed Yusufawa and untitled clients clustered about him as the sons of Abdullahi had clustered around Yusufu in Mamman Bello's reign. It seems likely that Aliyu learnt of this development rapidly from his spies and informants. The dissidents finally decided to repeat Yusufu's withdrawal from Kano and assemble their followers at a rural town where they could raise the flag of revolt. But on learning of Safiyanu's departure from Kano, Aliyu promptly despatched the Madakin Dan Rimi with sufficient riflemen to overawe and disperse Safiyanu's party, directing them to capture the prince and bring him to Kano, along with some of his fellow-conspirators. Aliyu then had Safiyanu bound and placed in Sankurmi's prison. It is said that later that evening he instructed his slaves to kill him. The Limamin Hausawa was summoned to read the required prayers over Safiyanu's body, and, according to this tradition, he was buried secretly that night at Gware by the slave Dan Kacalla.

In the following year, 1898, Aliyu faced another threat of revolt, on this occasion from the Wombai Mamman Nakande, who evidently felt that he should have succeeded as Galadima on Shehu's death, ahead of the Wombai Ishi'aku whom Aliyu had then appointed. It is possible that Nakande may have played some part in Safiyanu's conspiracy. He clearly knew the details of this affair. Ambitious, impatient and perhaps personally hostile to Aliyu, the Wombai on various pretexts employed his wealth to accumulate war gear, including firearms and *lifida*, chain mail and the corslets of quilted cotton worn by the slave cavalry who were sworn to die defending their chief. Despite his public denials, it seems that Nakande revealed his inclinations or intentions of revolt to his confidants not long before Aliyu's spies informed him that the Wombai had declared he would occupy the palace by force, as Aliyu himself had done. Alternatively, the allegations may have been fabricated in some intrigue. However, Aliyu at once sent his Shamaki Harisu to visit Nakande, ordering the Shamaki to bring all the Wombai's *lifida* and firearms to the palace. Nakande refused to surrender the weapons; and when Shamaki reported this reply, Aliyu declared that he would attack Wombai himself immediately. The Shamaki demurred and advised against this, undertaking to persuade Nakande to surrender his war gear without bloodshed, since a second civil war would clearly be destructive to Kano and the dynasty. While Aliyu waited, the Shamaki returned to Nakande with the same argument, guaranteeing amnesty and suggesting that, as Nakande would succeed Aliyu on the throne, there was really nothing to fight about. On these grounds the Wombai at length gave in, and handed over all his rifles and *lifida* to Shamaki for deposit at the palace. Thereafter Aliyu took no secular action against Nakande; but since the rebellious Wombai died in 1899 within a year of this incident, it is widely believed in Kano that his brother the emir employed mystical means of various kinds, in which he was thought to be skilled, to secure his early death, following which Aliyu conferred the office of Wombai on his full brother Mamudu, whose bonds of kinship and personal association guaranteed strong allegiance.

Oddly however, within a year Aliyu had to deal with yet a third arrogant kinsman, his uncle, the Dan Isa Sa'adu, Dabo's sole surviving son, who refused to turn out as required under the Wombai Mamudu for an attack on Damagaram that Aliyu had mounted. Perhaps the Dan Isa Sa'adu may by then have felt too old to go on campaign; but on appointing the Wombai Mamudu to command the expedition, Aliyu had ordered *all* Kano *hakimai* to join Mamudu with their retainers. Thus, Sa'adu's refusal to serve under his nephew, the Wombai, challenged Aliyu's authority. Aliyu at once dismissed Sa'adu from the office of Dan Isa; and, the army having already set out, he sent a message to his brother the Wombai, instructing him to appoint whoever he wished to the vacant title. This was an unprecedented honor and transfer of chiefly power to Mamudu as *tirika* in command of a force in which most Kano noblemen were then assembled. Unless equally assured of his own overriding power and of his brother's good faith and sense, Aliyu could hardly have commissioned Mamudu to take this action; that Aliyu felt sufficiently secure by 1898–99 to take this step indicates the political pre-eminence he had achieved by his appointment policies and by other means.

On receiving the Emir's instructions, the Wombai Mamudu halted the army and assembled the princes and titleholders. Having informed the assembly of Aliyu's letter, he then made two appointments in swift succession, promoting Abdullahi's son, the Dan Makwayau Muhamman, to the title of Dan Isa vacated by Sa'adu's dismissal, and appointing as Dan Makwayau another of Abdullahi's sons, Shehu (Usuman), who later became Emir of Kano under the British. Mamudu's response to his brother's commission indicated an equally high confidence in Aliyu's good faith, since, although commissioned to confer only one title, he had publicly conferred two, both appointments being welcomed by the astonished assembly, and by Aliyu, since both ennobled Abdullahi's sons, the brothers of Aliyu and Mamudu. Not long after, when the Galadima Ishi'aku died in 1900, Aliyu again demonstrated his regard for Mamudu by promoting him to that office, traditionally the most senior at Kano under the throne, and even in Aliyu's day the most powerful, despite its recent truncation and the newly created vizierate held by Abdullahi's full brother, Ahmadu. The Sarkin Dawaki Tsakar Gida, Abbas, was then appointed as Wombai.

Predictably, perhaps inevitably, in the course of these appointments, sometimes conventional and sometimes innovative, Aliyu modified the distribution of territorial fiefs among the central *hakimai* in many ways. For such new offices as the Waziri or Shettima he was obliged to furnish fiefs, generally by transfers from other titles. Thus to the vizier Ahmadu, Aliyu transferred control of Gaya, Gezawa, Gammo, Gwaram and Butubutu; to the Shettima, Harbau, Bici, Tangar and Majiya; to his slave Sarkin Shanu, Keffin Agur; to the Sarkin Dawaki Mai Tuta, in compensation for the loss of Kura, the town of Yargaya; to Shamaki Harisu, Gora, formerly a fief of the Dan Makwayau; to the Galadima, Sarina and Gazara; and to Yusufu's senior grandson, Ahmadu, the town of Daddare as a gift in celebration of Ahmadu's marriage which Aliyu had arranged. These and other fief reallocations are indicated in Table 6 that compares the territorial administrations of Aliyu and Mamman Bello. By such reallocations, Aliyu sought simultaneously to equalise the revenues of *hakimai* who held titles of comparable level, and to equalise their differential resources, status and political significance; but these territorial reallocations also demonstrated the Emir's authority and were employed to enhance his power, for example, by appropriating Rano, Dutse, Jahun Tsakuwa, Dawaki ta Kudu, Kura and other areas to the throne.

Aliyu is credited with having increased the Emir's share of rural revenues in Kano from its former level of approximately 40 per cent of the amount actually collected to nearly two-thirds, by closer supervision of the collection process through his throne slaves. As Abdullahi's *jekada* commissioned to supervise the town of Garun Malam, Aliyu had a thorough firsthand knowledge of the contemporary processes of tax collection and the various techniques of under-reporting amounts received. Those elderly informants who were familiar with the administrative methods that Aliyu employed credited his unusual success in securing the bulk of the tax receipts for the central treasury to this early experience as his father's agent at Garum Malam; but undoubtedly his extensive intelligence network and prompt dismissals of defaulting village chiefs and *hakimai* also helped to secure these increased revenues, much of which were used to purchase firearms, ammunition and other war gear for the army. Notably, unlike his predecessors, Aliyu did not increase the rates of taxation that prevailed at his accession. Instead, by exercising pressure on his administrative agents, Aliyu increased his share of the taxes, and thus had no need to raise their rates. Moreover, with the recovery of Fulani herds after the rinderpest epidemics, *jangali* collections were resumed, thereby augmenting the government's sources of revenue. Finally, having cut his ties to Sokoto, Aliyu had freed his treasury from exorbitant demands by the caliph and vizier.

Foreign Affairs: The Threat from the East

Despite the vigor and success with which he applied his domestic policies to transform the government of Kano, like his father Abdullahi, Aliyu was mainly preoccupied throughout his reign to defend a beleaguered state. While Kano was suffering the ravages of civil war, Rabeh, a Sudanese adventurer, at the head of a formidable force, well-armed and efficiently organized, had invaded and overrun the ancient Kanuri state of Bornu. In his early days, Rabeh had served as a senior lieutenant of the notorious raider Zubeir Pasha whose armies plundered the Sudanese tribes for slaves. Following Zubeir's death, Rabeh withdrew westwards from the Sudan to escape Anglo-Egyptian forces despatched to stamp out these activities and disarm or destroy the bandit armies engaged in them. For some years he lay low, while entering into politically useful relations with the Mahdi, whose armies overran the Egyptian Sudan during the eighties; and it is possible that Rabeh aided the Mahdists in their attacks on tribes in Darfur. As his arms and following increased, he moved gradually westwards from Darfur to Wadai, which he attempted to overrun without much success. He then moved on to Bagirmi southwest of Wadai where he occupied several important towns and raided widely for slaves and other loot. In vain the Sultan of Bagirmi appealed to Bornu and Wadai for help against Rabeh.[70]

Unable to overthrow the Sultan by seizing his capital, after he had plundered Bagirmi extensively, Rabeh moved west in 1893 against Bornu, devastating the settlements on both banks of the Shari river. The Shehu Kashim, grandson of Alhaji Aminu El Kanemi, first ordered Rabeh to desist, and then sent a strong force against him; but the Bornu cavalry were no match for Rabeh's disciplined troops, organised in companies or "standards" under captains, armed with rifles and supported by cannon. In three successive battles the Kanuri were defeated, following which Kashim's nephew Abba Kiari, had him killed for cowardice, and assumed leadership of Bornu. While Kiari collected his forces for a decisive battle, Rabeh attacked the capital of Bornu, Kukawa, slaughtering some three thousand inhabitants and burning all he did not remove. Rabeh then attacked Kiari's forces, defeated them, slew Kiari, and established his headquarters at Dikwa southwest of Lake Chad.[71] With Kanuri resistance thus broken and the people terrorised, until his death in 1900 Rabeh ruled Bornu and Dikwa without further opposition.

Rabeh had completed his conquest of Bornu before Aliyu entered Kano on Tukur's flight. Thereafter, like his eastern neighbours, the Fulani of Misau, Katagum, Gombe, Bauchi and Hadeija, Aliyu looked anxiously eastwards, anticipating Rabeh's attack. At Dikwa, Rabeh soon allied himself with the dissident Torodbe prince, Hayatu, a grandson of the caliph Bello, who, having failed to obtain suitable office, had migrated eastwards from Sokoto, ostensibly on pilgrimage to Mecca, only to halt northeast of Adamawa, attracted by prospects of establishing there a chiefdom of his own. It is said that Rabeh allowed his followers to represent him as an agent of the Mahdi, and that he attached Hayatu and his troops to his cause by offering to establish Hayatu as the ruler of Sokoto, following his conquest of the Fulani territories.[72] However apocryphal this widespread view of their relationship, Rabeh strengthened this alliance by giving his daughter Hauwa in marriage to Hayatu at Dikwa, where Hayatu settled, near to Rabeh's palace. Like Damagaram, the small eastern Emirates of the Fulani empire, Misau, Katagum, Jama'are and Gombe, awaited the assault by Hayatu and Rabeh they regarded as imminent. Given Rabeh's success and brutality in Bornu, these lesser emirates did not seem likely to withstand him. At Kano, Rabeh's desire to conquer the emirate was well known. Hence, while keeping himself informed about the western movements of Rabeh's and Hayatu's troops, Aliyu sought further firearms from Lokoja and Nupe against the anticipated attack.

Fortunately for Kano, following the subjugation of Bornu Rabeh's attention was temporarily diverted. In 1895 he did send expeditions westwards against the Bedde of Potiskum and against Katagum. From the Bedde, Rabeh took many slaves; but at Katagum his troops were repulsed with heavy losses.[73] The following letter from the emir of Hadeija Muhammadu to Aliyu Babba at Kano depicts the situation clearly.

> After salutations, the reason of my letter is to tell you the latest news here. Rabeh has sent twelve standards (companies) of his people to Bedde. They came there and fought with the people of Bedde and were not able to conquer them. When the Bedde people saw no way out, Sarkin Bedde Mai Duma got up, he himself with all his people, great and small, free and slaves, male and female, and came to us and remained with us. They are here now and have left Birnin Bedde. The people of Rabeh entered Bedde and the inhabitants of the villages and farms of the Bedde country were all scattered, and of them some came to us, and some went into the bush. Therefore I tell you that between us and Rabeh there is no one who has power over him save Allah. It has also been heard that Rabeh has moved and intends going to the west. Some say he is going to Kano by our road, others that he is going to you by Katagum, and others that he will go to Kano by Damagaram. May Allah preserve us both from his mischief.[74]

Another letter received by Aliyu at this time came from Muhammadu Manga, the emir of Misau.

> After salutations, to inform you of the latest news which we have received of Rabeh. He has sent out seven standards (companies) to the west, four to Bedde and three to Gujba. We have not heard where they will go next. For our part, we do not trust them in our land. He is a traitor, a mischiefmaker and a deceiver. We have driven away their people from our country. Peace.[75]

Rabeh had organised his troops in companies or standards averaging about 200 riflemen each. Fortunately for Aliyu the dreaded attack on Kano by Rabeh's forces was never launched. Instead, Rabeh's second western expedition was halted by the combined forces of Misau, Gombe and Katagum; and though Rabeh defeated these Fulani armies, "his losses were so severe that he was compelled to return to Bornu."[76] Kano thus owed its escape from Rabeh to the courage and resourcefulness of these minor emirates. Following that campaign, which took place in 1896 or 1897, Rabeh launched no more attacks on the Fulani states, but prepared to march against Zinder (Damagaram) instead.

Though his dreaded attack on Kano never materialised, Rabeh presented the greatest threat to Kano's security during the early years of Aliyu's reign. His withdrawal eastwards to Dikwa, following his costly victory over the armies of Katagum, Gombe and Misau, spread relief throughout the city; and the subsequent breach with his Torodbe ally Hayatu, which led to Hayatu's death at his hands, further weakened his chances to conquer the Fulani states, including Kano. To Aliyu's relief, after Hayatu's death Rabeh directed his attacks mainly at Bagirmi and Adamawa.

As mentioned earlier, during the civil war, Yusufu had negotiated with the emir Muhammadu of Hadeija before and during their conference with the Waziri Buhari. According to one tradition, at that meeting "Yusufu said to the Sarkin Hadeija, 'If you put me on the throne I will give you (the town of) Miga.' But although the Sarkin Hadeija came, he did not help him, returning to his own affairs. Nonetheless he seized Miga."[77] He also seized the town of Kwanda twenty miles south. On his accession, Aliyu asked Muhammadu to return Miga and Kwanda to Kano, since Hadeija had remained neutral throughout the struggle. Muhammadu declared that Yusufu had given him these towns. Aliyu rejected this reply and demanded Hadeija's withdrawal. Muhammadu then garrisoned Miga and Kwanda and repaired their walls against attack. In reply, Aliyu strengthened his alliance with the Sarkin Gumel Ahmadu, whose father Abubakar had helped the Yusufawa materially during the Civil War. As a Kanuri state, Gumel was an inveterate enemy of Hadeija; and thereafter Hadeija and Kano maintained hostilities with desultory border fighting and raids until 1901, when the Sarkin Dutse was attacked and killed by a force from Hadeija while fortifying the town of Shatari at Aliyu's orders. In response Aliyu sent Sarkin Gaya Kolo and Sarkin Kunci Dabo with sufficient forces to police the border between Kano and Hadeija. He also decreed that anyone known to come from Hadeija who entered Kano should be arrested and executed. Maimaina, the Sarkin Askira who spied on Aliyu for Lugard, witnessed such executions at Kano in 1903. Hadeija retaliated in kind; and for the rest of Aliyu's reign, relations between the two states remained tense.[78] Nonetheless, at no time did Aliyu launch a frontal attack on Kwanda or Miga, partly perhaps because he did not wish to injure their innocent inhabitants, but also because he was busy on other fronts.[79]

The Ningi were another recent ally with whom Aliyu's relations deteriorated rapidly; but in this case we do not know the specific issues that led to further fighting. Probably Dan Yaya, then the Ningi chief, claimed certain territory or prerogatives as rewards for assisting the Yusufawa. If so, Aliyu rejected these claims. Whatever the immediate "cause" of their dispute, both parties had inherited such deep historic hostilities that their continued alliance was intrinsically improbable. As Abdullahi's son, Aliyu was doubly Dan Yaya's hereditary foe; and as the heir of Haruna and Dan Maje, Dan Yaya reciprocated Aliyu's enmity. It is thus possible that in dealing with the Ningi, Aliyu determined to renege on any commitments Yusufu had made, in the belief that Yusufu would have done likewise. By 1895 Kano had resumed its war with the Ningi, and Aliyu continued to press this even though Dan Yaya made overtures of peace. In 1895 and 1897, Aliyu undertook two successful campaigns against Ningi settlements southeast of Kano. He also fortified the southern settlements of Fajewa, Dando, Kwajali, Bura, Magami and Musa against anticipated Ningi attacks.[80] However, Aliyu was never able to bring the Ningi to battle, since Dan Yaya took care to avoid his superior fire-power. The Ningi accordingly retaliated by swift destructive raids against unwalled settlements, withdrawing rapidly with their loot to avoid interception.[81]

Foreign Affairs: The Northern Enemy

To the north, Damagaram (Zinder) under its aggressive chief Ahmadu Maje-rinji (1893–1899) presented a more immediate threat to Kano's security. Ahmadu had inherited from his father, Tanimu, several hundred guns, a foundry for manufacturing cannon, and workshops for the manufacture of ammunition. In 1884, following Tanimu's death, his successor Suleimanu gave his suzerain, the Shehu Hashimi of Bornu, ten cannons and 480 muskets manufactured at Zinder.[82] It is said that Tanimu left an armoury of 6,000 muskets and 40 cannons,[83] some cannons having been mounted locally on cast iron wheels to facilitate their transport on campaigns. Tanimu had employed these exceptional armaments with signal effect against Muniyo, Hadeija, Kazaure, and other nearby states in a series of aggressive campaigns aimed at expanding the territories of Damagaram. His successor Suleimanu (1884–1893) did likewise, and attacked Madaka in Kano during Mamman Bello's reign. Ahmadu Maje-rinji pursued this program of military agression with greater vigor, stimulated by Rabeh's conquest of Bornu, by the deaths of Shehu Kashim and his successor Kiari, by the termination of Zinder's vassalage to Bornu, and by the threat of Rabeh's impending attack. While freeing Zinder of restraints from Bornu, these developments together intensified his expansive drive to forestall further moves by Rabeh to the west. Thus, in 1894–95, Ahmadu of Zinder led his troops through Zango in Daura and Kazaure to Malikawa in northwestern Kano, took the town and seized its chief and people, together with much booty, removing all to Damagaram.[84]

Since Mamman Bello's day, relations between Zinder and Kano had been strained by reports of the abuses suffered by Kano traders (*fatake*) in Damagaram. Some had been dispossessed of their goods, while others were forbidden to move freely in Damagaram. If merchants from Zinder received similar treatment at Kano, we do not know. On returning to Kano, these traders had reported their experience to Mamman Bello, and appealed to him for protection and redress. Bello had written to the Limam at Damagaram, seeking explanations and reparations; but following the deaths of Suleimanu and Bello in rapid succession, these negotiations seem to have lapsed; and throughout the civil war it seems that Kano merchants avoided Damagaram. Thus, although communications had virtually ceased between Kano and Damagaram in 1893–4, the two states remained technically at peace and without any issues that generated friction. Accordingly, Ahmadu's seizure of Malikawa in 1894 took Kano by surprise.

At Kano this assault was promptly attributed to the intrigues of Aliyu's enemy, the caliph Abdu Danyen Kasko at Sokoto. Having failed to secure Aliyu's voluntary subordination, despite his return of Kano's chiefly insignia and the refugees from Tukur's ranks, he had declared his intention of re-establishing his suzerainty by other means. It is said that initially caliph Abdu decided to lead an imperial army summoned from the loyal emirates against Kano himself, but that he was dissuaded from this by one of his kinswomen, who argued that such a course would create even more destruction than the *basasa* at Kano, and would spread general ruin throughout the Muslim (i.e., Fulani) community whose welfare remained the caliph's first charge.[85] As these incidents were well known at Kano, when Ahmadu attacked Malikawa without apparent cause or warning, it was widely believed that he had done so either at the instigation of caliph Abdu or the vizier Buhari, who thereby hoped to compel Kano's renewed allegiance.[86]

Aliyu probably accepted this interpretation of Zinder's sudden attack, but preferred to remain independent of Sokoto, even at the risk of war with Zinder. By terminating Kano's vassalage to Sokoto, he had discontinued the onerous tribute which had impoverished Kano in Mamman Bello's reign while it enriched the caliphate. He had also freed Kano of the obligation to fulfil all the caliph's numerous donations and unpredictable *ad hoc* requests for disbursements from its treasury. Thus Aliyu simultaneously enriched the Kano chiefship by abolishing its heaviest recurrent expenditures, and brought the powerful economic sanction of their lost revenues to bear on the caliph and vizier of Sokoto. Aliyu could therefore easily explain the caliph's suspected encouragement of Ahmadu's recent aggression by attributing that to his resentment at Kano's secession and the consequent fall in his revenues since Tukur's defeat. He evidently concluded that war with Zinder was preferable to vassalage to Sokoto, and undertook the risks of combat accordingly.

For some years following his raid on Malikawa, Ahmadu Maje-rinji was occupied with the conquest of Macina and Nguru, both of which were formerly subject to Bornu. He also launched an attack on Gumel, the Bornu vassal which had supported the Yusufawa in the civil war and was thus allied with Aliyu. However Ahmadu's attack on the capital of Gumel was a failure, and although his cannonades demolished one of the city gates, the townsfolk repelled the attackers.

On his expedition against Gumel, Ahmadu tried to conceal his objective by threatening the town of Sankara in northeastern Kano with assault. To this end, he wrote the Sarkin Fulani Sankara to warn that his town would shortly be attacked. Since Aliyu was then away on campaign against the Ningi, the Sarkin Fulani of Sankara, lacking the material resources to beat off Ahmadu, asked a local malam for ritual aid to defend the town. Ahmadu's failure to attack Sankara that year was promptly attributed to the spells and charms by which this malam had rendered the town invisible to the Zinder army.[87] Clearly, Ahmadu's letter had successfully misled Sankara and Gumel about his real objective.

Next year, in 1897 or 1898, Ahmadu again invaded Kano, evidently intending to attack the capital. This time his army marched due south to Gezawa, about twenty miles northeast of Kano, where Ahmadu directed his captains to rendezvous on the following day at Fage, outside the city walls. Meanwhile, on learning of Ahmadu's advance, Aliyu decided to intercept the attack, and moved his forces to Wangara five miles from Gezawa, which had already been evacuated. Early on the following day the main Zinder force set out for Fage, ahead of Ahmadu. On learning this, Aliyu ordered his drummers to beat the Zinder drum-rhythm, and so lured the main Zinder force into an ambush near Gezawa, where they were slaughtered. Ahmadu's remaining force was then attacked, routed, and driven homewards.[88]

On returning to Zinder, Ahmadu determined to square accounts with Kano in the following dry season. Meanwhile elated with his victory, Aliyu set off on a campaign against the Ningi, and marched to Burra, an important Ningi town. As usual, the Ningi withdrew before Aliyu to avoid a frontal assault; but that night they surrounded his camp and attacked it, throwing Aliyu's force into total disorder and capturing many prisoners. Aliyu himself escaped northwards with difficulty.[89]

In 1898–9, Ahmadu Maje-rinji returned to Kano via Zango, Kazaure, and the northwestern route towards Tattarawa, south of the river Tomas. Again Aliyu elected to intercept the invaders north of Kano. Learning of Ahmadu's advance, he moved in strength to Damargu, about five miles northwest of Tattarawa. Against the advice of his malams, who are said to have predicted defeat if Aliyu gave battle on the following day, the Kano cavalry under Madaki Kwairanga attacked, and at first with such success that Ahmadu directed his troops to use their muskets and cannon against the Kano horsemen. When next they charged, the Kano horses panicked at the volleys and explosions among them, and reeling backwards, spread such disorder through the ranks that Aliyu's army broke in rout as Ahmadu attacked. His army broken, Aliyu, accompanied by a few horsemen, fled direct to Kano to organise its defence. Ahmadu meanwhile moved to Panisau, Dabo's old marshalling ground (*sansani*), five miles north of Kano. Entering the town, Ahmadu seized its inhabitants and marched to Nassarawa, Abdullahi's holiday palace about a mile outside the city walls. There also, Ahmadu seized the ruler's slaves, concubines, cattle and palace stores without opposition.

Within the city, Aliyu meanwhile assembled the leading malams to invoke the aid of Allah. He also mobilised the city Arabs and placed them on the city walls, armed with rifles to defend the town. Ahmadu's failure to attack the city at this time is locally attributed to the influence of these collective prayers, for which Aliyu is said to have paid some thirty million cowries. However at Nassarawa, Ahmadu was stricken with fever and forced to abandon the prize within his grasp. From Nassarawa he withdrew northwards to Zinder without harassment, taking with him an enormous haul of booty, captives and cattle.[90]

It is possible that Ahmadu abandoned Kano and returned home, having learnt at Nassarawa of the arrival of a French expedition under Captain Pallier at the western borders of Damagaram. Having accounts of their own to settle with Ahmadu for the deaths of the explorers Cazemajou and d'Olive at Zinder in the preceding year, the French authorities at Dakar had despatched a second expedition under Pallier with sufficient force to exact retribution; and shortly after his triumphant return to Zinder, Ahmadu was defeated by Pallier's disciplined spahis at Termini, twelve miles west of the town. Ahmadu fled, but was pursued and killed at Rinji in 1899. The French then appointed his younger brother

Ahmadu dan Bassa and incorporated Damagaram in the new Territoire Militaire of Niger.[91] Pallier's victory and Ahmadu's death thus removed the most immediate threat to Kano's independence and existence as a Fulani state. In the following year, 1900, another French force eliminated the other outstanding threat to Kano's security, when Gentil defeated and killed Rabeh at Kisseri, a hundred miles within the territory allotted to Britain under the Anglo-French agreement to partition the region.[92]

The Threat from the South

The deaths of Ahmadu Maje-rinji and Rabeh in 1899–1900 thus removed the two most obvious and immediate threats to Fulani rule in Kano; but although apparently the nearest and most obvious, these were neither the only nor the ultimate threats. On January 1st 1900, the British Government had assumed those political, military and administrative powers previously vested by charter in the Royal Niger Company and which Sir George Goldie had exercised, following his clash with the Fulani emir of Nupe, Abubakar, in 1897.[93] As its High Commissioner authorised to disestablish the political and military roles of the Royal African Company, and to delimit, pacify and administer the vast territories it now claimed to protect, the British Government appointed Captain (later Sir) Frederick Lugard, an officer with wide political and military experience in India and East Africa. Anticipating resistance from the powerful Fulani emirates to the north, and particularly from Kano and Sokoto, Lugard devoted his first year in office to diplomatic exchanges with the caliph Abdurrahman at Sokoto, while assembling an army at Jebba, his headquarters on the Niger, in preparation for the coming struggle.

Shortly after takng office as High Commissioner for the Protectorate of Northern Nigeria on January 1st 1900, Lugard issued his justly celebrated Proclamation on slavery. This decreed that all children born within the new Protectorate after April 1st, 1901 were legally free, irrespective of their parents' status; that all slave-raiding and slave-trading was thenceforth illegal and punishable; and that all slaves could be redeemed or could redeem themselves or their kin on payment of £5 or its equivalent in cowries to the local Alkalai.[94] Knowing how heavily the Fulani economy and regime depended on slavery and slave-raiding, Lugard was well aware that this proclamation could not be implemented until he had broken the major centres of Fulani resistance. Indeed, during his first fifteen months as High Commissioner, he "still found it impossible to get in touch with Sokoto, Gando, Kano, and Katsena, the great centres of the northern Haussa States, but Zaria ... was ostensibly friendly,"[95] though he had already occupied Zungeru and Wushishi in the pagan areas southwest of Zaria. Realistically, Lugard did not expect that the powerful Fulani emirs would surrender their autonomies and obey his regulations without a fight; and with his limited resources of men, materials, money and political support in Britain, Lugard's two major problems were, firstly, to postpone the inevitable confrontation until he was fully prepared, and secondly, by diplomatic and other means, to avoid mobilising all the Fulani states simultaneously against him under the leadership of Sokoto.

By March 1902, Lugard was able to establish a garrison and place his representatives at Zaria when the Emir Kwassau appealed for assistance to stop his neighbour, the Torodbe Sarkin Kontagora, Ibrahim Ngwamatse, a great-grandson of the Shehu Usuman, from devastating northwestern Zaria by slave raids. Lugard sent a small force under Captain Abadie to arrest the bandit emir, and ordered Abadie to set up his base at Zaria. Thus by March 1902, the British had secured a highly strategic base at Zaria, a hundred miles south of Kano City via Makarfi and Bebeji, and two hundred miles from Sokoto.[96] Later that month Lugard reconstituted Zaria emirate as an administrative Province of the Protectorate under Captain G. F. Abadie as Resident; and in September 1902 he deposed and banished the Emir Kwassau to Wushishi for "continued slave dealing and extortion and intrigue with the Emir of Kano, who was showing marked hostility."[97]

Before the end of 1901 Lugard had sent his spy Maimaina to Kano disguised as a travelling trader to verify reports that Aliyu's troops were not only equipped with western firearms, but were also familiar with western military techniques.[98] Maimaina crossed from Zaria to Kano a month or two before Abadie arrested Sarkin Kontagora Ibrahim at Kaya in response to the Emir Kwassau's appeal.[99]

If Lugard was sufficiently concerned about Aliyu Babba's intentions and resources to despatch spies to Kano, on his side Aliyu became increasingly uneasy about Lugard's purposes, as reports came in from neighbouring emirates concerning the movements and activities of British troops. From Zaria he received the following letters with ominous news.

> (1) After greetings, the object of my letter is to inform you of the coming of the Christians. For they have increased among us, and have settled more firmly than before. As to news of the others, they have come to Kwaba and have collected stores for war. They declare that when they have finished what they are doing among us, they will go away and come to you. I have written a letter to you, that you may have the news. Peace.[100]
>
> (2) After greetings- to inform you that three Christians and their soldiers have arrived and are camped near the east of their former halting place on the Likoro road. Further, the Christians have collected men and made them work. They have given orders that every chief shall set four men to work to clear the road, and they have done so. Further, we have heard that the Christians from Bauchi are coming to join them. This is to inform you that heavy trouble has come upon us, for by Allah we can neither stand nor sit, and have no power to remain in the same place with them. May Allah protect us and you from all trouble and misfortune, by the protection of the Prophet.[101]
>
> (3) After greetings, to inform you that the Christians whom I told you were coming from Bauchi have arrived. Mai Jimina (Captain Abadie) has come, and those with him, and others. Also that you may know that they are assembling, and intend to go to Kano. May Allah think of us and protect us. He is the hearer of the prayers of those who pray to Him. We beseech Allah to scatter their company and disperse their gathering. May He instil fear and trembling in their hearts and grant you victory over them and also to all Moslems. Peace.[102]

As the "Christians" from Bauchi moved across Misau, Katagum and Azare, delimiting provincial boundaries and instructing Fulani chiefs in their new obligations, Aliyu received a stream of letters from the emirs of Jema'are, Misau and Katagum reporting their activities. From the day when the British established their garrison at Zaria, Aliyu Babba had good grounds for anxiety and concern about Lugard's intentions; but after the proclamation of Zaria Province and the deposition of the Emir Kwassau, Aliyu could hardly mistake the real alternatives that Lugard offered: submit, with or without a struggle. As he awaited further news of Lugard's plans, sundry British expeditions imposed Lugard's order on various states south and east of Kano, while other British forces assembled at Zaria City, only a hundred miles away, ready to strike at Kano.

In October 1902, Captain Maloney, Lugard's representative at Keffi, a southern vassal state of Zaria, was struck down and killed in public by the Magaji Dan Yamusa of Keffi. In the following furore Maloney's agent, Audu Tintin, was also hunted down and despatched.[103] To escape arrest, the Magaji and his accomplices fled north, avoiding the British garrison at Zaria and heading for Kano. However tense Maloney's personal relations with the Magaji and other Keffi notables may have been, his murder expressed the general Fulani resentment of British domination that crystallised after Lugard's high-handed deposition of the Emir Kwassau, the suzerain of Keffi, at Zaria in the preceding month. In killing Maloney, the Magaji Dan Yamusa had struck a blow for Fulani resistance against British demands for submission that was to have resounding consequences.

When the Magaji arrived at Kano in late October, seeking refuge and protection, Aliyu could scarcely have turned him away without thereby signifying his intent to accept British rule without resistance; had he done so, Aliyu might well have forfeited the allegiance of his officials, and therewith perhaps the throne. Instead he welcomed the refugees from Keffi with princely hospitality as Muslims who had fought for Islam against the heathen. To Lugard, news of this offered a suitable pretext for war with Kano and sealed Aliyu's fate. By welcoming the Magaji Dan Yamusa to Kano, Aliyu had aligned himself against the British administration, since Dan Yamusa had murdered a British officer and was wanted for trial by Lugard's police. British preparations for the attack on Kano acquired new urgency.

Aliyu, Sokoto and the British—1903

On October 9th, six days after Maloney's death, the caliph Abdurrahman Danyen Kasko died at Wurno; and on the 12th October, Ahmadu Attahiru, the first son of Ahmadu Zaruku, succeeded.[104] With Abdurrahman's death, the road for Aliyu's reconciliation with Sokoto was finally open; and in the prevailing circumstances, such reconciliation was equally urgent and necessary for the security of both states. Aliyu at once wrote to congratulate Attahiru on his accession and arranged to visit Sokoto shortly to render homage (*mubaya'a*), thereby terminating Kano's nine years of independence freely and in good faith. If we overlook those political and military considerations that undoubtedly influenced Aliyu's renewal of allegiance to Sokoto at this juncture, by the manner and timing of his declaration, Aliyu obliquely indicated that the deceased caliph, whose unpopularity was great, was solely responsible for the recent estrangement. Kano had already demonstrated its ability to stand alone against threats from Zinder and Rabeh; but in the presence of Christian aggressors, it behoved all good Muslims to unite under the leadership of Attahiru as amir el-Mu'minin or caliph. In these circumstances

Aliyu's resumption of allegiance on caliph Abdu's death was welcomed by the ruling Fulani at Kano, and not least by Abdullahi's issue, whose legitimacy as Kano's rulers was thus enhanced.

Before setting out for Sokoto to meet Attahiru later that year, Aliyu wrote to inform the caliph of the latest developments and to advise the vizier about the appropriate Muslim response.

> From Sarkin Kano Aliyu to Sarkin Musulmi Muhammadu Attahiru, greetings, etc. After greetings, to tell you of our latest news, with all there is to tell, whether true or false. It is that some of our neighbours tell us that the Unbelievers, the Christians, have come to them from the East and departed again. Then one of our chiefs, Sarkin Gwaram, sent to tell us that the Unbelievers, who are in Bauchi, had all gone away West to Zaria and that the Sarkin Bornu (of Misau) Ahmadu, on hearing of their movements, left his country and came to ours, to a place called Chediya, and camped at the gate of the town. After that we heard no more, but one of our chiefs, the Chief of Tudun Wada, sent to tell us of the departure of the Christians who were in Bauchi to Zaria. Any further news we may receive, we will send to you. May Allah prolong your life. My present to you is two burnous.[105]

To the vizier Muhammadu Buhari, Aliyu wrote as follows:

> After greetings, I have seen your letter and honour it. We clearly understand from it that you are following my advice, that both we and you seek for a plan which will be of assistance to our religion and to earth and heaven. I have found no more useful plan for all Muslims and for us and for you than as I wrote in my letter which my messenger brought to you, that we leave this country, all of us—this is my clear conviction—as these dogs have surrounded us and threaten to overcome us. May Allah grant that your eyes are opened speedily. May Allah assist us both and lighten our troubles. Peace.[106]

Evidently, in a preceding letter, Aliyu had proposed that the Fulani nobility should emigrate eastwards en masse under the caliph and vizier, beyond the reach of British arms, presumably on pilgrimage to Mecca. Unless Aliyu had already recognised the futility of resisting Lugard with force, this proposal could scarcely have crossed his mind. He had earlier awaited assaults on Kano by Ahmadu Maje-rinji and by Rabeh with courage and was not averse to further wars. Thus, unless the situation seemed to exclude other alternatives, neither would Aliyu have made such a radical proposal, nor could the caliph and vizier have countenanced it.

At the turn of 1902–03, and just before Lugard's force of roughly a thousand with its supporting artillery set out from Zaria to Kano, Aliyu assembled the Kano nobility and set out for Sokoto to greet Attahiru, to render homage, and to press his proposal that the Kadiriyya Fulani should emigrate as the 10,000 Tijaniyya followers of Haj Umar had already done when they fled en bloc from Masina to Sokoto in 1901 after defeat by the French.[107] Perhaps Aliyu removed the Fulani nobles from Kano in the hope of an immediate migration; but on learning that he had set out for Sokoto escorted by 2,000 horsemen, Lugard promptly moved against Kano to forestall the possibility of united Fulani resistance.

The British were marching on Kano by the end of January 1903 . Ten miles north of the Zaria border they found the walled town of Bebeji shut against them. When the townsfolk refused to surrender, Bebeji was stormed, and the column proceeded to Kano without further opposition. At Kano the main British force took up positions opposite the Kabuga gate, while two smaller detachments stood by outside the Duka Wuya and Gadan Kaya gates. On leaving Kano, Aliyu had placed the city under his slave, the Sarkin Shanu Dan Kwari, while his women-folk and young children at the palace were in charge of the Sallama Jatau. Both fought bravely but in vain; and after the Sarkin Shanu had fallen defending the palace, the Sallama Jatau fled westwards with the Emir's womenfolk to seek his master. Having pacified the city the British occupied the palace.[108]

Before he set out from Kano to Sokoto, Aliyu may have anticipated a British attack; but it is unlikely that he believed it would be launched in his absence. Nonetheless he had ordered a determined defence should the Christians attack; and his decision to leave for Sokoto at this time did not escape opposition. The Madaki Kwairanga, Aliyu's cross-cousin and staunch supporter, objected strongly. After further dispute, on crossing the Challawa River at Kanwa, Kwair-anga refused to proceed. Aliyu promptly dismissed and arrested him, and appointed Kwairanga's son, Faruku, as Madaki. Then, with Kwairanga under guard, the column continued to Sokoto.[109] There, Aliyu's proposal of collective emigration was already familiar to the inner circle of Fulani leaders grouped around the new caliph, Muhammadu Attahiru I, and the vizier Buhari; but before Aliyu's arrival, caliph Attahiru had been persuaded to defer this scheme until the British showed their hand. The following letter addressed to the caliph by his brother, the Marafa Muhammadu, to whom Attahiru owed his accession, indi-cates some of the considerations that apparently prevailed.

> After greetings, to inform you that we have no more news beyond what we have sent to you and are awaiting the arrival of the spy we sent. If we hear any news of them, we will send to you. Further, I earnestly beseech you, in God's name, let no one hear the suggestion of our departure from your mouth in this land, as this would mean ruin for our affairs. Our subjects and people, who are within the boundaries of our land, would certainly throw off their allegiance to us, on hearing such news. We should get no assistance from them of what they have promised to us. To sum up, let us sit and await the issue of the matter. Help lies with Allah alone, and if He makes easy for us this matter, He is all-powerful. If we remain in our kingdom, all will be ordered for us by the Great Ordainer.
>
> If circumstances indicating departure arise, let us depart, otherwise not. But let us only prepare—till such time as God decrees for us departure.[110]

Thus before Aliyu arrived at Wurno, Attahiru had decided to defer the order for mass emigration until the British revealed their design. In these circumstances, after further discussion, Aliyu had no alternative but to return to Kano; and so, having rendered homage and concluded his reconciliation, he set out along the homeward road with his escort of nobles.

At Daba one of the Sarkin Shanu's men met the returning column and reported the British occupation of Kano. Aliyu affected to disbelieve the report, perhaps to keep his company from flight; but a little farther on they encountered the Sarkin Fada Bagarmi who repeated the story and reported the Sallama's removal of Aliyu's womenfolk. "Some are at Wasai, some are at Gogel, and we have brought the rest with us." [111] Aliyu continued past Faru to Goga, where Sallama Jatau himself came and related what had befallen. Aliyu then took counsel with his slave commanders, the Shettima Shekarau and the Ciroman Shamaki Mahakurci, and with the Limam Ahmadu and the Limam's son, whom Aliyu had previously appointed as Magajin Malam na Cedi. The Sallama, Shettima and Ciroman Shamaki advised him to order the column to return to Sokoto, where they could settle and farm. The Chronicle, evidently recording an eyewitness account, says that Aliyu then lost his nerve. He then consulted privately with two individuals, Mai-Kano Buzu and Alhaji Baba, who offered to guide him to Istanbul. That night, having prepared his loads, Aliyu directed the Shamaki Harisu to escort his family to Sokoto, accompanied by his brother, the Galadima Mamudu, his son, the Ciroma Abdullahi, and all his other children. When the Shamaki had withdrawn, Aliyu deserted his people and slipped away into the night. On the following morning, when his absence was discovered, the Shamaki set out for Sokoto accompanied by the Limam, the Alkali, the Magaji dan Yamusa of Keffi, the Galadima Mamudu, the Ciroma and Abdullahi, and all the members of Aliyu's family. [112]

On learning of Aliyu's flight, dismay and uncertainty divided the Kano party. While the Wombai Abbas and the majority chose to proceed directly to Kano and there make peace with the British, the Waziri Ahmadu and many others determined to fight. The column accordingly divided into two parts, led respectively by the Wombai and the Waziri Ahmadu. [113] Meanwhile, at Kano Brigadier Kemball, who had taken command, received news that Aliyu was approaching, determined to fight. Leaving a small garrison at Kano, he marched out to meet them. At Kotorkwoshi near Chafe, in the district known as Katsina Laka, the small British force encountered the Waziri Ahmadu and his followers. For two hours Lugard's troops withstood twelve charges from the Waziri's party, killing 65 and dispersing the rest. Among those who fell fighting were the Waziri Ahmadu, the Sallama Jatau and several senior palace slaves. On learning that Aliyu had fled at Goga some days past, Kemball sent some officers to apprehend him. Evidently intending to find his way eastwards, Aliyu had gone north from Goga into the Hausa territory of Gobir, where he was captured, and word was sent to the British. A detachment at once rode north to apprehend Aliyu; and he was removed via Sokoto and Argungu to Lokoja, where he remained in exile until his death in 1926. [114]

The reasons for Aliyu's stealthy desertion at Goga in the middle of the night remain unknown. The Kano Chronicle puts it down to fear. [115] According to Lugard, Aliyu "fled alone in the night. He was said to be a brave man, but he mistrusted all his chiefs, who detested him, and he feared to be deserted in the battle." [116] Others say that Aliyu decided to set off on pilgrimage secretly, convinced by the fall of Kano that further efforts on his part against the British were useless. [117] It is also possible that Aliyu feared punishment if he was captured by the British for the hospitality he had extended to the Magaji Dan Yamusa of Keffi, Maloney's killer. Quite likely he genuinely believed that flight to the East was obligatory, given the conquest of Kano by heathen. However, only Aliyu could give the reasons and motives for his precipitate flight; and I know no statement of his on that matter.

Notes

1. R.M. East, *Labarun Hausawa*, Vol. 2, p. 66.

2. F. Edgar recorded two versions at Sokoto early in this century. See his *Litafin Tatsuniyoyi Na Hausa* (Belfast: Mayne & Co., 1913) Vol. 1, pp. 187–191; Vol. 3, pp. 410–416.

3. Anon., *Faid al-qadir fi ausaf al-malik al-khatir*. Unpublished Ms. written early this century by a former scribe (*Magatakarda*) of the Emirs Mamman Bello and Tukur. On file in the Palmer papers at the Museum, Jos, Benue-Plateau State, Nigeria (372,X51,52).

4. Besides oral traditions and the four versions already cited, we have accounts of the civil war by the Wazirin Sakkwato Junaidu, *Tarihin Fulani*, pp. 62–69; Dokaji Alhaji Abubakar, *Kano ta Dabo Cigari*, pp. 61–67; Malam Adamu Na Ma'aji, *Ta'rikh Kano*; contemporary observations by such travellers as C. H. Robinson and W. Wallace who visited Kano during the conflict; and many items of information scattered in the *District Notebooks*. All Nigerian accounts except the *Faid al-qadiir* exonerate the vizier Buhari and place the responsibility for the disastrous appointment and struggle squarely on the caliph Abdurrahman (1891–1903). For the author of the *Faid al-qadir*, the vizier Muhammadu Buhari is the author of the mischief and the true villain of the piece. Much that the *Faid al-qadir* reports merits further study. Unfortunately I only acquired a translation of this text several years after the field work on which this account is based.

A good brief account of the conflict is given by H. A. S. Johnston, *The Fulani Empire of Sokoto* (London: Oxford University Press, 1967) pp. 222–225. See also Murray Last, *The Sokoto Caliphate*, (London: Longmans, 1967), pp. 134–136, 173–4.

5. Dokaji Alhaji Abubakar, *Kano ta Dabo Cigari*, p. 62; see also LH, vol. 2, pp. 66. According to the *Faid al-qadir* (sheet 15), on Bello's death, Buhari, then in Kano, wrote secretly to the caliph Abdu urging that the Wombai Shehu, Abdullahi's son, should be appointed. Had this been done, there would have been no civil war. However the same account indicates that during Bello's reign Buhari had promised to secure Yusufu's appointment, and that Yusufu had given this promise wide publicity among all classes in Kano. So the public and officials probably expected Yusufu to succeed, and held Abdurrahman directly responsible for Tukur's appointment.

6. F. Edgar, *Litafi na Tatsuniyoyi*, Vol. 1., p. 187; vol. 3, p. 411.

7. LH, vol. 2, p. 66; Dokaji Abubakar, *Kano ta Dabo Cigari*, p. 62; F. Edgar, *Litafi na Tatsuniyoyi*, vol. 1, p. 188; Wazirin Sakkwato, Alhaji Junaidu, *Tarihin Fulani*, p. 62.

8. F. Edgar, *Litafi na Tatsuniyoyi*, vol. 1, p. 188; LH, vol. 2, p. 66; Dokaji Abubakar, *Kano ta Dabo Cigari*, p. 62. The anonymous *Faid Al-qadir* (sheet 16) reports that when the Galadima Tukur had arrived at his compound that night, the vizier summoned the senior throne slaves, Shamaki, Dan Rimi Sallama and the Sarkin Dogarai, handed Tukur the caliph's letter of appointment for his scribe to read, and, following this, merely instructed the slaves "there's your Emir, your *Ubangiji* (master, owner, patron).

9. LH, vol. 2, p. 66; Dokaji Abubakar, *Kano ta Dabo Cigari*, p. 62. According to the *Faid al-qadir*, having formally carried out the caliph's orders by his unusual appointment of Tukur, the vizier Buhari actively encouraged the notables at Kano to support Yusufu in the coming struggle (sheets 16 ff.).

10. Waziri Alhaji Junaidu, *Tarihin Fulani*, p. 62, says that this appointment was ordered by the caliph Abdu, following the refusal of the ex-Ciroma Musa, Abdullahi's son, to return to Kano from Takai. Probably Malanta's nomination was jointly proposed by Tukur and Buhari for the caliph's approval.

11. LH, vol. 2, p. 66. See also Dokaji Alhaji Abubakar, *Kano ta Dabo Cigari*, p. 62, who says Yusufu proceeded via Dawakin Kudu to Takai. The Waziri Junaidu, *Tarihin Fulani*, p. 62, says Yusufu moved to Takai via Gogyel and Lajawa. The author of the *Faid al-qadir* (pages 16–18) was present when Tukur learnt of the Yusufawa exodus from the city, estimated at 10,000 people. After discussing alternatives, Tukur sent to ask the vizier's permission to pursue the rebels and compel them to return. However the vizier refused to allow this, and said he would write to recall Yusufu who duly refused this summons. At Yusufu's request the vizier then forbade Tukur to send any forces from Kano against the rebels at Takai for 53 days, promising to report the affair to the caliph Abdu and secure his support. Tukur's forces were immobilized by these orders and the Yusufawa were free to overrun southeastern Kano. See also M. Adamu Muhammad, *Ta'rikh Kano*.

According to the *Faid al-qadir*, the Yusufawa halted first at Nassarawa to await further desertions from Kano, then moved to Tanagar where they seized the people's chattels, beasts and weapons without recompense, and thence via Kausani to Takai. The *Faid al-qadir* (p. 19) also says that at Takai, Yusufu swore his kin, clients, slaves and other supporters to abandon Islamic laws and rituals for the duration of the conflict, thus binding them to his cause as apostates (*kahirai*).

12. Dokaji Alhaji Abubakar, *Kano ta Dabo Cigari*, p. 62.

13. Ibid., p. 62.

14. LH, vol. 2, p. 62; Dokaji Alhaji Abubakar, *Kano ta Dabo Cigari*, p. 67.

15. F. Edgar, *Litafi na Tatsuniyoyi*, Vol. 1, p. 190; Wazirin Sakkwato Alhaji Junaidu, *Tarihin Fulani*, p. 68.

16. According to the *Faid al-qadir*, despite their formal declarations of homage to Tukur on his appointment, most of the free officials in Kano supported Yusufu and were prepared to betray Tukur in battle. The sole exception among the senior officials this manuscript notes is the baJobe Makama Iliyasu, pp. 25–27.

17. *District Note Books* Suma'ila and Wudil. Provincial Office, Kano.

18. *Anon., Faid al-qadir*, pp. 16–17.

19. *District Note Books*, Dawakin Tofa, Dambarta, Gwarzo. Provincial Office, Kano.

20. *District Note Books*, Kano, Dutse, Birain Kudu, Gwaram, Gaya, Minjibir, Gezawa. Provincial Office, Kano.

21. *District Note Books*, Jahun, Gwaram, Suma'ila. Provincial office, Kano.

22. *Faid al-qadir*, pp. 34–35, attributes responsibility for Jahun's disaffection and secession during Mammon Bello's reign directly to the vizier Buhari. "Without a doubt, the vizier Buhari was the head and source of the disobedience and deceits by which these things happened. For example, once when the Waziri passed through Jahun, he met there the Sarkin Fulani of Jahun who gave him abundant gifts. Then the Sarkin Fulani asked if the Waziri would set him up as an independent Emir paying his tribute and gifts direct to the caliph instead of Kano. This was done without the knowledge of the Sarkin Kano Bello; but the caliph Umaru rejected this request, saying "Surely, this sort of thing will start continuous rebellions." And verily, that rebellion (disobedience) continued quietly (*tana barci*)."

23. According the the *Faid al-qadir* (pp. 19–20), the Sarkin Gumel Abubakar (1872–1896) was initially dissuaded from campaigning for Yusufu by Sarkin Hadeija's threat to attack Gumel, since Gumel was not one of the Fulani Emirates, and thus had no ground for participation in their domestic conflict. However after the Sarkin Hadeija Muhammadu (1885–1906), disassociated himself from the struggle in Kano, the Sarkin Gumel apparently campaigned for Yusufu. According the the *Faid-al-qadir* (p. 30), the Sarkin Gumel Abubakar took part in the final assault on Kano City when the Yusufawa broke in, and within 3 days he enslaved between ten and twenty thousand inhabitants who were removed to Gumel as his reward. The author here says he obtained this information from some Kano residents who escaped enslavement by the Sarkin Gumel.

24. J.M. Freemantle, "A History of the Katagum Division of Kano Province," *JAS*, vol. XI, 1911, p. 62 says of these allies "Sarkin Gumel alone gave active assistance in the fighting"—but Sarkin Hadeija "did some pillaging on his own account. A great number on both sides were enslaved; as many as from ten to twenty slaves were given for a horse, and, corn being very scarce, 30,000 or 40,000 cowries were enough to buy a slave." However, v. Dokaji Abubakar, *Kano ta Dabo Cigari*, p. 62; and LH, vol. 2, p. 67.

25. Reports of this meeting by the Waziri Junaidu, (*Tarihin Fulani*, pp. 62–64), *Faid al-qadir*, pp. 19–22, and Frank Edgar, *Litafi na Tatsuniyoyi*, vol. 1, p. 188) differ. The Kano Chronicle alludes to, but does not mention, the meeting (LH, vol. 2, p. 67). The Dokaji's account omits it. Further, while Edgar's version sites the meeting at Malikawa, and the Waziri Junaidu omits its location, other accounts place it at Gunduwawa, which I have failed to locate, but which apparently lay east of the city, between Hadeija and Kano. From the Waziri Junaidu's account, which is followed here, it seems that the Emir of Hadeija brought the vizier and Yusufu together in the hope that they might arrive at some formula to suspend the conflict.

26. Murray Last, *The Sokoto Caliphate*, p. 174; F. Edgar, *Litafi na Tatsuniyoyi*, vol. III, p. 412.

27. Wazirin Sakkwato, Alhaji Junaidu, *Tarihin Fulani*, pp. 62–64.

28. Anon., *Faid al-qadir*, pp. 22.

29. Wazirin Sakkwato, Alhaji Junaidu, *Tarihin Fulani*, p. 66; LH, vol. 2, p. 67; *Faid al-qadir*, pp. 22–3, gives a useful account of the legal issues presented by the problem of these prisoners. Having agreed with those clerics who classified the rebels as apostates and heathens, on this account the vizier asked that they should all be given to him as slaves for resale rather than executed. To resolve the issue, Tukur then wrote the caliph Abdurrahman reporting recent developments at Kano and seeking instruction on how to treat them. According to this text, Abdu replied "Concerning the rules regarding your prisoners of war, if you had captured their leader, Yusufu, I would direct you to release them, since they are only our commoners (subjects) and incapable of doing us any harm on their own, like other commoners, since all are the same, and there is no difference between them in our eyes. But since need has driven them (the rebels, captives) to seize and destroy people's property wantonly by force, and they neither want high status nor to leave the country, well, if you release them all, they will simply return to Yusufu, without doubt. For this reason, the best course of action in my view is to kill them. I therefore order you to kill them all; and since they are heathen, execute them as heathen."

30. LH, vol. 2, p. 67; see also F. Edgar, *Litafi na Tatsuniyoyi*, vol. 1., p. 188; and W. Wallace, "Notes on a Journey through the Sokoto Empire and Borgu in 1894," *Geographical Journal*, vol. 8, 1896, p. 211, for an eyewitness account.

31. Anon., *Faid al-qadir*, p. 25, lists reinforcements from Katsina, Daura and Kazaure led respectively by their Kaura, Makama and Sarkin Jarmai which came to Kano at this period.

32. *District Notebook*, Minjibir, Provincial Office, Kano.

33. *District Notebook*, Gwarzo, Provincial Office, Kano.

34. W. Wallace, "Notes on a Journey through the Sokoto Empire and Borgu in 1894." *Geographical Journal*, vol. 8, 1896, p. 211; see also Wazirin Sakkwato, Alhaji Junaidu, *Tarihin Fulani*, p. 66.

35. *District Notebook*, Dawaki-ta-Kudu. Provincial Office, Kano.

36. *District Notebook, Gaya*. Provincial Office, Kano.

37. Reporting the Hadeija view, J.M. Freemantle "A History of the … Katagum Division of Kano Province," *JAS*, vol. XI, 1911, pp. 62–3, says Yusufu promised Miga and Kwanda to Hadeija in return for active help against Tukur. "When the war was over and Aliu installed, Hadeija pressed his claim to the Miga and Kwenda districts, but Aliu said he had not fulfilled the conditions of the agreement. Hadeija then seized these places."

38. LH, vol. 2, p. 67; Wazirin Sokkwato, Alhaji Junaidu, *Tarihin Fulani*, p. 66; *District Notebooks*, Dutse, Gwaram, Rano, Tudun Wada. Provincial Office, Kano.

39. Oral traditions from Kano and Sokoto. See also F. Edgar, *Litafi na Tatsuniyoyi*, vol. 1, p. 189. LH, vol. 2, p. 67; Dokaji Abubakar, *Kano ta Dabo Cigari*, p. 63; Wazirin Sakkwato Alhaji Junaidu, *Tarihin Fulani*, pp. 66–67. When Yusufu died at Garko, the Waziri Buhari was on a brief visit to Zaria. According to the *Faid al qadir*, pp. 24–25, recognising his end was near Yusufu wrote Buhari, attributing responsibility for the revolt to him and asking for his advice. In reply Buhari is said to have advised the appointment of Aliyu Babba, primarily because of his kinship with the caliph's dynasty at Sokoto. However, Malam Adamu na Ma'aji in his *Ta'rikh Kano* remarks that "After Yusufu's death at Garko, the senior throne slaves said that Aliyu should be appointed so that the caliph Abdu should be pleased, espe-cially as he had intended to send the imperial armies to Kano to overrun it. The Waziri (Buhari) worked so hard to put down the fires of the rebellion, that this led to a quarrel between himself and Saudatu. So that when they (the rebels) were victorious, he secretly persuaded Damagaram to invade Kano. And that's how the war began between Sarkin Kano Aliyu and Sarkin Damagaram," Ahmadu Maje-Rinji, 1893–99. Evidently, as the vizier played a lone hand in this situation, his visits and communications with either party invited misinterpretation by the other; and often by those with whom he dealt.

40. F. Edgar, *Litafi na Tatsuniyoyi*, vol. 1, p. 189.

41. Letter in the custody of Wazirin Sokoto, Alhaji Junaidu at Sokoto.

42. Dokaji Alhaji Abubakar, *Kano ta Dabo Cigari*, p. 63; LH, vol. 2, p. 67.

43. For Malam Adamu's remarks, v. fn. 39 *supra*. For accounts of the caliph's orders, See Anon., *Faid al-qadir*, p. 59; and Wazirin Sakkwato, Alhaji Junaidu, *Tarihin Fulani*, p. 67, which briefly reports Abdu's rejection of Aliyu's messengers and the vizier's unsuccessful attempt to mediate. At this time the vizier was in Sokoto, having obtained the caliph's permission to return. Tukur was thus at last free to send out his forces against Yusufawa strongholds in Kano; but now it was too late.

44. *District Notebooks* Kura, Gezawa. Provincial Office, Kano. Anon. *Faid al-qadir*, p. 25; LH, vol. 1, p. 67.

45. *District Notebook*, Dawaki ta Kudu; R.M. East., *L.H.*, vol. 2, p. 68; Dokaji Alhaji Abubakar, *Kano ta Dabo Cigari*, p. 64; Anon., *Faidal-qadir*, pp. 25–26.

46. For the fullest account of this battle and developments in the city during the follow-ing four days, see Anon., *Faid al-qadir*, pp. 26–29. On this account, there was a breakdown of order within the city as people feared food shortage under siege and many took advantage of the situation to seize, damage, or destroy the property of others. Tukur was unable to restore order, and was further disturbed by reports that his external allies, the Kauran Kat-sina, Makaman Daura and Sarkin Jarmai of Kazaure planned to withdraw their troops from Kano shortly. Under these circumstances he decided to lead his family and supporters from the city to seek the caliph's support.

47. R.M. East., *L.H.*, vol. 2, p. 68. See also *Faid al-qadir*, p. 30 for furrther details, including the wholesale enslavements of city folk by the Sarkin Gumel. For three days after his with-drawal, Tukur remained at Dawaki, near Tofa, while the *basasa* was at its height in Kano.

48. For a first-hand account of Tukur's stay at Kusada and Kamri, see anon., *Faid al-qadir*, pp. 30–35, the author having remained with Tukur throughout this period.

49. Since Tukur's scribe (Magatakarda), the author of the *Faid al-qadir* was present at Kamri throughout this period, presumably Tukur had other objectives and purposes in appointing Dibgau his vizier.

50. LH, vol. 2, p. 68. According to the *Faid al-qadir*, pp. 33–34, on the advice of a sup-porter, Gurshe, he also sent lavish gifts to the vizier, then at Kefin Dangi, and to the Emir of Katsina Abubakar, to secure their support before the final battle with Tukur. According to that text Aliyu secretly visited the vizier at Kefin Dangi some seeks before the final attack, travelling at night by way of Kusada.

51. Dokaji Alhaji Abubakar, *Kano ta Dabo Cigari,* p. 65. *The Faid al-qadir,* pp 31–33 credits such disobedience to contrary instructions these rulers received from the vizier Buhari at Kefin Dangi.

52. C.H. Robinson, *Hausaland* (London: Marston, Sampson & Low, 1896), p. 210.

53. Dokaji Alhaji Abubakar, *Kano ta Dabo Cigari,* pp. 65–67. Except as regards Aliyu's desire to capture Tukur alive, this account is confirmed by that of the eye-witness who later wrote the *Faid al qadir,* v. pp. 35–37.

54. Wazirin Sakkwato, Alhaji Junaidu, *Tarihin Fulani,* pp. 68–69. On this account the caliph sent the vizier Buhari to Kano to confirm Aliyu's accession as Emir. However, there was no formal installation, and Aliyu's conduct indicates his independence of Sokoto throughout Abdurrahman's reign.

55. Indeed, Aliyu occasionally upset the caliph's plans by supporting the other side, as for example Hamman Manga of Misau against Katagum in 1895–6, and the candidacy of Kwassau for the throne at Zaria in 1897. For accounts of these events, see J. M. Freemantle, "A History of the Katagum Division of Kano Province," *JAS,* vol. 9, 1910, pp. 419–420; M. G. Smith, *Government in Zazzau, 1800–1950,* pp. 193–194; and F. Edgar, *Litafi na Tatsuniyoyi,* Vol. 1, pp. 198–202.

56. Max Weber, *The Theory of Social and Economic Organisation* (London: Wm. Hodge & Co., 1947), p. 318.

57. *District Notebook,* Birnin Kudu. Provincial office, Kano.

58. Sarkin Dawaki Mai Tuta, Bello Dan Dago, "History of Getso." July 1956. In *District Notebook,* Gwarzo, Provincial Office, Kano.

59. Ibid.

60. LH, vol. 2, p. 69.

61. C.H. Robinson, *Hausaland,* p. 206.

62. Ibid., p. 216.

63. Walter Miller, *An Autobiography, 1872–1952* (Zaria: Gaskiya Corporation, n.d.), p. 23.

64. Muhammadu Maimaina, *Maimaina, Sarkin Askira* (Zaria: NORLA, 1958), p. 12.

65. C.H. Robinson, *Hausaland,* p. 127.

66. W. Wallace, "Notes on a Journey through the Sokoto Empire and Borgu in 1894," *Geographical Journal,* vol. 8, 1896, p. 217.

67. C.H. Robinson "The Hausa Territories," vol. 8, *Geographical Journal,* 1896, p. 207.

68. C.H. Robinson, *Hausaland,* pp. 108–110, 208–213.

69. A copy of caliph Abdurrahman's letter to the ex-Ciroma Musa on this matter was in the custody of the Wazirin Sokoto, Alhaji Junaidu, at Sokoto in 1959.

70. For a sketch of Rabeh's career before and after the conquest of Bornu, see A. Schultze, *The Sultanate of Bornu,* translated by P. A. Benton (London: Frank Cass & Co., 1968) pp. 284–301.

71. See H.R. Palmer, *Gazetteer of Bornu Province,* (Lagos: The Government Printer, 1929) p. 109.

72. A. Schultze, *The Sultanate of Bornu* pp. 287–8, 290–293; J. S. Trimingham, *A History of Islam in West Africa* (London: Oxford University Press, 1962) pp. 218–219; John E. Lavers, "Jibril Gaini: A preliminary account of the career of a Mahdist leader in North Eastern Nigeria." *Research Bulletin,* Centre of Arabic Documentation, Ibadan, vol. 3, no. 1, Jan. 1967, pp. 16–39.

73. See A. Schultze, *The Sultanate of Bornu,* p. 291.

74. H.F. Backwell, *The Occupation of Hausaland, 1900–1904.* (Lagos: The Government Printer, 1927). Letter No. 97, p. 61.

75. Ibid., p. 61.

76. Ibid., p. 9.

77. LH, vol. 2, pp. 69–70. On this topic, see fn. 37, *supra.*

78. *District Note Book*, Dutse. Provincial Office, Kano. J. M. Freemantle, "A History of the … Katagum Division of Kano Province," *JAS*, vol., 1911, p. 63; Muhammadu Maimaina, *Maimaina, Sarkin Askira*, pp. 12–13.

79. W.F. Gowers, *Gazetteer of Kano Province*, p. 14.

80. LH, vol. 2, p. 70.

81. Dokaji Alhaji Abubakar, *Kano ta Dabo Cigari*, p. 70; *District Notebooks*, Tudun Wada, Rano, Gwaram. Provincial Office, Kano.

82. M. Landeroin, *Documents Scientifiques de la Mission Tilho (1906–1909)*, (Paris: Imprimerie Nationale, 1911), Vol. II, p. 447.

83. Ibid., p. 446.

84. Ibid., p. 450.

85. Dokaji Alhaji Abubakar, *Kano ta Dabo Cigari*, p. 67. The anonymous *Faid al-qadir*, pp. 31–33 treats this incident at length and says the vizier Buhari blocked this, firstly by persuading the Hausa chiefs of Gobir and Maradi to raid Angamba in Sokoto and enslave its population, and secondly by persuading the *'ulama* at Sokoto to mobilise the entire population to accompany the caliph, should he attempt to set out from Sokoto for Katsina or Kano.

86. See Malam Adamu na Ma'aji, *Ta'rikh Kano*, the passage already cited in fn. 39, *supra*.

87. Dokaji Alhaji Abubakar, *Kano ta Dabo Cigari*, p. 68; *District Notebook* Ringim, Provincial Office, Kano; M. Landeroin, *Mission Tilho*, vol. 2, pp. 450–452.

88. M. Landeroin, *Mission Tilho*, vol. 2., p. 451; *District Notebook*, Gezawa, Provincial Office, Kano; LH, vol. 2, p. 69; Dokaji Alhaji Abubakar, *Kano ta Dabo Cigari*, pp. 68–69.

89. W.F. Gowers, *Gazetteer of Kano Province*, p. 14.

90. M. Landeroin, *Mission Tilho*, vol. 2, p. 452; Dokaji Alhaji Abubakar, *Kano ta Dabo Cigari*, p. 69; LH, vol. 2, p. 70.

91. M. Landeroin, *Mission Tilho*, vol. 2, p. 452.

92. H. R. Palmer, *Gazetteer of Bornu Province*. (Lagos: The Government Printer, 1929) p. 27; Commandant Chailley, *Les Grandes Missions Françaises en Afrique Occidentale* (Dakar: I.F.A.N., 1953), p. 79.

93 For further information see Sir Alan Burns, *History of Nigeria* (London: Allen and Unwin, 1948), p. 169, pp. 146–148.

94. F.D. Lugard, *Northern Nigeria, Jan. 1st., 1900–March 31st, 1901*, Colonial Reports, Annual, No. 346 (London: H.M.S.O. 1902), p. 15.

95. Ibid., p. 34.

96. F.D. Lugard, *Northern Nigeria, 1902*, Colonial Reports, Annual, No. 409 (London: H.M.S.O., 1904), p. 71, section 16.

97. E.J. Arnett, *Gazetteer of Zaria Province* (London: Waterlow and Sons, 1920) p. 23.

98. Muhammadu Maimaina, *Maimaina, Sarkin Askira*, pp. 13–14.

99. Ibid., p. 12.

100. H.F. Backwell, *The Occupation of Hausaland*, 1900–1904, p. 70, letter no. 119.

101. Ibid., p. 71, letter 120.

102. Ibid., p. 71, letter 121.

103. For further information, see H.A.S. Johnston, *The Fulani Empire of Sokoto*, pp. 243–44.

104. J.A. Burdon, "Sokoto History: TABLES of Dates and Genealogy," *JAS*, vol. 15, 1916, pp. 372–373.

105. H.F. Backwell, *The Occupation of Hausaland, 1900–1904*, p. 72, letter No. 124.

106. Ibid., p. 73, letter no. 125.

107. E.J. Arnett, *Gazetteer of Sokoto Province* (London: Waterlow and Sons, 1921), pp. 34–35.

108. LH, vol. 2, p. 70; Dokaji Alhaji Abubakar, *Kano ta Dabo Cigari*, p. 70.

109. LH, vol. 2, p. 70; *District Notebook*, Dawakin Tofa. Provincial Office, Kano.

110. H.J. Backwell, *The Occupation of Hausaland, 1900–1904*, p. 74, letter 128, and see also p. 78.

111. LH, vol. 2, pp. 70–71.

112. Ibid., p. 71.

113. Ibid., p. 71; H.A.S. Johnston, *The Fulani Empire of Sokoto*, pp. 248–249.

114. Ibid., p. 248; S.J. Hogben & A. H. M. Girke-Greene, *The Emirates of Northern Nigeria*, Vol. III, p. 446; F.D. Lugard, *Northern Nigeria*, 1902, pp. 84–88, 90–91.

115. LH, vol. 2, p. 71.

116. F.D. Lugard, *Northern Nigeria*, 1902, p. 91.

117. Dokaji Alhaji Abubakar, *Kano ta Dabo Cigari*, p. 70; H. A. S. Johnston, *The Fulani Empire of Sokoto*, p. 248.

7

Defeat and Recovery:
Abbas, 1903–1919

The British conquest closed one period of Kano's history and opened another. Neither the conquerors nor the conquered could then have foreseen the full implications of this event, nor the patterns it would unfold. To elucidate the conditions of these processes of change, I shall therefore review their contexts and sequences in detail to indicate those conflicts or convergences of personal or institutional interests that structured the changing accommodations of Fulani and British, while simultaneously preserving and transforming the Kano polity in substance and form.

Appointment

At Kotorkwoshi forty-five mounted infantry under Captain Wright had defeated one thousand horse and two thousand foot under the Waziri Ahmadu. Unable to breach the British defense because of their superior discipline and firepower, the Fulani retired to the village of Chamberawa, leaving their dead behind. At Chamberawa they were surprised and dispersed in flight by another British detachment under Captain Porter.[1] Most of the Waziri's party then rejoined that led by the Wombai Abbas and proceeded to Kano, where Lugard awaited, having arrived from his headquarters at Zungeru shortly after Brigadier Kemball had set out to intercept Aliyu.

> There, on March 4th (1903), I (Lugard) received news of the advent of the Wombai with an enormous following, and he now sent word asking for permission to enter Kano. I replied that I cordially welcomed the return of all fugitives, that the fighting was done, there were no old scores to wipe out, that I had no grudge whatever against those who had fought us fairly. I, however, insisted that they should all come in together by a specified gate, not in driblets, and that all firearms should be surrendered.[2]

"On March 6th, when the Wombai Abbas arrived with about 2,500 horsemen and 5,000 foot, he handed in 120 rifles and promised to collect more later."[3]

Aliyu's flight presented Lugard with the opportunity and problem of selecting an emir for Kano. He relates that

after the fall of Kano a representative of the elder branch of Dan Tukkur, a man named Abdul Tukkur, had arrived from Zinder where he had taken refuge on Alieu's accession. His claims were strong, but he had no following, and I found after a time that he was quite unfit for the position, being eccentric and of weak intellect. The riff-raff of the town gathered about him, and I found that they had been looting the houses of the chiefs of the rival party in their absence. I therefore turned him out. The Wombai, who was not only the heir to the emirship, but the unanimous choice of all parties, had from the first been represented to me as the best and most popular candidate, and the death of his elder brother, the Waziri, and the flight of the king's son (the Galadema) removed his only rivals. Both were very unpopular. The Wombai was a man with a most intelligent and humane face, in great contrast to the cunning, sensuality and cruelty which were delineated in the features of the ex-emir of Zaria. I summoned him, together with his six leading chiefs, and explained to them the conditions which I intended to impose.

The British Government would in future, I said, be the Suzerain of the country, but would retain the existing rulers, exercising the right to appoint not only the emirs but the chief officers of state. Rights of succession, nomination, or election, customary in the country, would not as a rule be interfered with, but the High Commissioner would retain the right of veto, and the king or chief would lose his place for misconduct. Similarly in the matter of law and justice; Mohammedan law, so long as it was not contrary to the law of the Protectorate, would not be interfered with, and the emir's and Alkali's Courts would be upheld and strengthened under the supervision of the Resident. Mutilation, and imprisonment under inhuman conditions would not be allowed, and no death sentence would be carried into execution without the prior concurrence of the Resident. Bribery and extortion would be checked, and certain classes of offence would be tried in the Provincial Court, in which alone all cases affecting non-natives and Government servants would be heard. The Government would impose such taxes as the High Commissioner might see fit, to pay for the cost of administration, but these would not be of an oppressive character. Traders and caravans would be encouraged, and were not to be taxed by the emir, whose levies would be subject to the approval of the High Commissioner. The Fulani, I observed, had lost their domination, and in future the ultimate title to land and minerals would be vested in the British Government, but owners would not be deprived of their land unless it was needed for necessary public works or Government requirements. I emphatically forbade all slave raiding and all transactions in slaves, while saying that it was not my intention to interfere with the existing domestic slaves; but these would, like anyone else in the land, at any time, have a right of appeal to the Resident, and, if they proved cruelty on the part of their masters, would be liberated. I recognised, I said, no less than they did, that labouring classes must exist, and I had no desire to convert the existing farm and other labourers into vagrants, idlers and thieves, but I hoped that they would by and by see the advantage of paid free labour, which we considered more profitable and better than slave labour. In future, I said, neither the emir or any chief would be allowed to have recourse to armed force, and the "Dogari" (gunmen) would be abolished. If the emir were unable to enforce his legitimate orders he would refer to the Resident, for in the British Government alone was to be vested the task of policing the country. Consequently firearms would not be required and must be rendered up, and unless in special cases authorised by permits from the Resident, their possession would involve punishment. All supplies would be fairly paid for, and they need have no fear in taking to the Resident all complaints against soldiers or other Government servants who might commit any violence or deal unfairly. The garrison would be located outside the town and soldiers would not be allowed to enter it with their arms. When I added that liquor was prohibited, there was a motion of appreciative assent, and to my announcement that they were absolutely free in the exercise of their religion, there was a quite remarkable expression of joy and relief. Sokoto, I said, would remain the religious head, but no tribute of slaves might be sent to him in future. I added at the close of my remarks that it was not the desire of Government to upset and to change such native laws and customs as were good, and that it would be our desire to study them so as to understand the people. I finally spoke of the advantages of a coin currency, the necessity of a fixed rate of exchange between British silver and cowries. I assured them that the British had come to stay, and nothing would ever cause us now to leave the country. I presented to the new emir of Kano the Staff of Office of the First Class, as I subsequently did to the emir of Zaria, and I later promised the same to Sokoto and Katsena, together with formal letters of appointment. It is important to note that on each occasion I had the best interpreters in the country, and the words were paraphrased into simple English ... The intelligent comments and questions of the chiefs showed that they thoroughly understood. Turning to the circumstances of Kano itself, I declined to appoint the Wombai as emir until I had returned from Sokoto, whither I proposed to go at once, judging that this period of probation would not be without good effect, while for my own part I was unwilling to act with precipitation, even though the circumstances, as I saw them at the time, seemed to leave no alternative, and though we appeared singularly fortunate in the candidate proposed. Meanwhile he was left in charge of the town, but was not to occupy the king's quarters until finally installed. I said that I had decided to occupy, as Residency and barracks, the place named Nassarawa, a suburban residence belonging to Aliyu, which was about 800 yards from the city walls, and that I would also require the emir to build a house and court house in the city near to the palace, which the Resident might occupy from time to time. This is a somewhat important matter, since I believe the people regard it as a sign of suzerainty that the British representative should have a house in the city and fly the flag there. I added that the king's buildings would be evacuated next day when I left, and I required the emir to build barracks at once for the troops before the rains set in. This order to build a Residency and barracks constituted the only approximation to a war indemnity, and since every town will be called upon to send its quota of men for the purpose, the burden was a trivial one. I had already commenced to make a broad breach in the walls opposite the Nassarawa Gate. All the chiefs who had now returned were to resume their old positions, but no vacancies in chiefships existing at this date were to be filled until my return.

With these conditions the chiefs appeared well satisfied. They had entered my room in a state of extreme nervousness, and we parted with much cordiality.[4]

On the following day, March 7th, Lugard set out for Sokoto, leaving Dr. F. Cargill as Resident of Kano. Following the fights at Kotorkwoshi and Chamberawa, Kemball's force had resumed their march to Sokoto, where they were joined by another 200 troops from Argungu under Captain Merrick. On March 15th, 1903, this British force defeated the Sokoto army under the caliph Muhammadu Attahiru I a few miles outside the city walls, thus terminating the autonomous caliphate founded by Shehu Usuman. Four days later Lugard arrived at Sokoto to receive the formal submission of the Waziri Buhari and *sarakunan karaga* (imperial council) of Sokoto. On his defeat,

> the sultan Attahiru absolved his councillors and closest followers from their allegiance and left to each of them the decision whether to accompany him into exile or return and seek the indulgence of the British ... The sultan, however, evidently felt that it was impossible for him to submit. Accompanied by his personal followers, he therefore turned towards the East and, having shaken off the pursuit, which in any case was only half-hearted, made his way to Gandi.[5]

On March 20th Lugard

> summoned the leading councillors to the sultan's house and told them that I considered it of importance either to find and reinstate the fugitive sultan, or to appoint a successor at once. I invited them to let me know whether the sultan would return, and, if not, whom they desired to appoint. After a private consultation they named Atahiru ... He now came in to pay his salutations. No mention was made of the claims of the fugitive sultan, and, in reply to my questions, all concurred, saying that no one had any notion whither he had fled.[6]

Relieved that "there was no apparent desire to restore the fugitive sultan, for he too had received the Magaji of Keffi (Maloney's murderer) with honor,"[7] Lugard appointed Attahiru II as sultan on the following day, after meticulously explaining the conditions of his appointment to the sultan and assembled councillors, following which he returned to Kano via Katsina, where he confirmed the emir Abubakar in office on similar terms.

The End of an Era, 1903–4

On April 3rd 1903, Lugard personally installed the Wombai Abbas as emir of Kano in a public ceremony at the City;[8] and within a few weeks the defeated caliph, Muhammadu Attahiru I, with a large company of followers, passed through southern Kano, heading east. Though uncertain of his plans and movements following defeat, Attahiru had belatedly adopted Aliyu's suggestion of migration eastwards; but as he moved slowly and hesitantly across the land, avoiding British stations, the ex-caliph attracted many devout Fulani who preferred to share his migration and distress rather than submit to Christian domination. The defeated caliph's journey also excited British fears of further conflict and generated a moral crisis among the Fulani, provoking deep spiritual anxieties in those communities he crossed *en route*. The ex-caliph's portentous movements prolonged the social unrest released by the shattering military and political events of preceding months, and enhanced popular uncertainty about the nature and stability of the new order among Fulani and Hausa officials and commoners alike. Many Fulani aristocrats and *'ulama* in Kano abandoned their homes to join the ex-caliph and his people as they passed through southern Kano en route to Burmi, where he was killed with 700 of his followers by Lugard's troops on July 27th.[9] According to Lugard,

The emir of Kano patrolled his eastern frontiers to prevent his people from joining the pilgrimage, and Hadeija did the same ... The posts of those who followed the ex-sultan were at once filled by new men, which acted as a deterrent. The movement was not in any way directed against the Government, but was (so far as the bulk of its adherents were concerned) a blind scare, combined with a religious enthusiasm prompting an exodus.[10]

As the ex-caliph and his people sought accommodation in villages and towns along their route, local chiefs had to make unprecedented decisions to admit or exclude them. At Tudun Wada, Attahiru and his people were welcomed, while Birnin Kudu shut its gates against them. Some leading Kano chiefs, deeply affected, abandoned their offices, families and wealth to join Attahiru. The Sarkin Dutse Abdulkadiri, who had resumed his chiefship after fighting at Kotorkwoshi against the British left Dutse to join the caliph and fought at Burmi, thereby forfeiting his office. The ex-Madaki Kwairanga, who had remained under arrest at Kanwa for forty-three days until the battle at Kotorkwoshi, had tried to reclaim the title following his release; however, as the ex-caliph passed through southern Kano, Kwairanga abandoned his quest for reinstatement, and joined Attahiru, to die with him at Burmi. Though the Sarkin Bai Abdusallami had also fought at Kotorkwoshi, he had been reinstated in office by Lugard's amnesty. Nonetheless, like the Sarkin Dutse, as the ex-caliph passed through Kano, Abdusallami set out to share his pilgrimage. While at Bima near Burmi, he received an order from Abbas to return at once to Kano and resume his office. Abdusallami obeyed, thus escaping probable death, and was reinstated as Sarkin Bai.

Not until the death of ex-caliph Muhammadu Attahiru I at Burmi in late July 1903 did the profound unrest and shock unleashed by his defeat and the fall of the Sokoto caliphate begin to subside. Lugard's Government during this period was occupied with urgent efforts to maintain calm, to restrain violence, and to prepare for further emergencies. But when the crisis terminated with the slaughter of Attahiru and his followers at Burmi, the British aroused deep resentment among those Fulani and Hausa who revered Attahiru as the caliph, successor and senior descendant of the Shehu Usuman dan Fodio. Over the next few years a considerable number of Fulani Muslims abandoned Kano and moved eastwards as pilgrims in opposition to British rule; and many of these emigrants later settled in the Anglo-Egyptian Sudan.

Following his selection as Aliyu's successor at Kano, Abbas immediately wrote to inform Attahiru I, then caliph, apparently before Attahiru's defeat at Sokoto.

From the emir of Kano Abbas to the emir El Mu'minim Attahiru: after greetings, we wish to inform you that we have met together with our people who went by way of Kotorkwoshi. From among them he died who died, and he survived who survived. When we had collected everybody, they felt it proper to make allegiance to me following their collective decision, all according to the Book and valid custom. This, in order to let you know what has befallen. Peace.[11]

Thus, following the death of Waziri Ahmadu and in the absence of Galadima

Mamudu, who had returned to Sokoto from Goga on Aliyu's orders, the reassembled Kano nobles, recognizing the urgent need for authoritative leadership, had discussed the candidates and selected Abbas as their emir. Having done so, the assembly collectively appointed him by rendering their allegiance. Accordingly when Abbas returned to Kano, unknown to Lugard he had already assumed the emirship by virtue of this collective act. He could therefore order his people to surrender their rifles as Lugard requested, without fear of protest; and by doing so he convinced Lugard of his good will, authority and capacities for leadership in the unfamiliar context of British rule. For Abbas on entering Kano, the immediate task was to secure Lugard's confirmation of his own appointment as emir. He did this partly by discrediting the claims, capacities and following of Tukur's heir, who was probably none other than the ex-Ciroma Muhammadu Lele, and by undertaking to fulfill Lugard's modest demands for accommodation in the City. Abbas thus had little difficulty in achieving his goal. By then, however, the British had defeated the Sokoto army and replaced Muhammadu Attahiru I by his namesake from the house of Mamman Bello. In reply to a letter which the new caliph probably sent shortly after his installation by Lugard, Abbas wrote as follows:

> After greetings, I have seen your letter in which you inform me that all your people have chosen you (as caliph) after you had made peace with the Europeans, and that they had rendered allegiance to you according to the Book and valid custom. Praise and thanks must be given to Allah for this event. May Allah grant relief to you throughout your life, may He assist you, may He arrange your affairs prosperously, may He reward you after all. Peace and farewell.[12]

By his method and terms of appointment, Lugard had clearly indicated to Abbas that Kano's recently resumed allegiance to Sokoto was finally ended, together with the caliphate of Sokoto. At the same time Lugard had reaffirmed the caliph's spiritual leadership, and declared that his Government would respect and uphold Islam within the Muslim communities of the new Protectorate. Following tradition, caliph Attahiru II had written to inform provincial emirs of his accession, just as Abbas had written to inform Attahiru's predecessor of his own appointment after Kotorkwoshi. In reply Abbas expressed appropriate sentiments, but mentions neither the gifts nor allegiance that were formerly obligatory on such occasions. It is possible that some tokens of loyalty and affection accompanied this and other letters from Abbas to Attahiru during the year that followed their accessions. However, direct political relations between Kano and Sokoto were now at an end, and with them the passage of tribute, the continuous exchange of reports and instructions, and all traditional restraints on Kano's autonomy that Sokoto had imposed before Aliyu's accession. What Aliyu had won from Sokoto by his victory over Tukur, Abbas received by submission following the Waziri Ahmadu's defeat at Kotorkwoshi. Kano was once again independent of Sokoto, following their brief reunion. Like Kano, Sokoto now had to deal with the British Administration independently. Like Abbas, Attahiru II, in accepting office under the British, had pledged himself to neutrality while Lugard's forces hunted down and despatched the defeated caliph Attahiru I. Both rulers had thus to some extent compromised themselves by their activities during the four months that Attahiru I wandered eastwards towards his death at Burmi; but both could justify their actions by citing their responsibilities for the welfare of the Muslim communities under their care. For Abbas this charge initially meant the defense and preservation of Islamic government, religion and law, as observed by the Fulani elite in Kano; and he thus undertook to maintain Fulani domination in the unprecedented conditions created by Fulani defeat and British overrule.

The British victory initially appeared to threaten the Fulani social order at its base by promising freedom to slaves and the end of Fulani domination to subject Hausa. Both issues found equally prompt expression and response. On leaving Sokoto after the Fulani defeat, Lugard

> had a very disagreeable task to perform. Hundreds of slaves had secretly crowded into our camp, hundreds more clambered over the walls to follow us, and no prohibition would stop them. Turned out of the line of march, they ran parallel to us through the fields or ran on ahead. I had promised not to interfere with existing domestic slaves; I had no food for these crowds, and in front of us was a desert, untraversed and unmapped, in which the infrequent wells were far apart, and could only supply a very limited amount of water. Moreover, this exodus of slaves would leave Sokoto ruined, and its social fabric a chaos. There was nothing to be done but to send these poor wretches back, and instruct the Resident to enquire into all deserving cases. We did so, and presently found that the King of Gober, who was following me with an army of 300 or 400 wild horsemen of the desert, had appropriated all he could catch. We made him disgorge them, and set them at liberty to return. Doubtless very many bolted to neighbouring towns, but I considered my obligations of honour and of necessity were satisfied, when I turned them out of my own following, and I did not enquire too curiously what became of them.[13]

As Lugard told Walter Miller in 1901, "the whole social and economic fabric of the Moslem society of Northern Nigeria was built up around slavery, and ... not all of its features were evil. He (Lugard) explained to me that his duty was to destroy and eliminate the obviously evil features first, and allow the others to die a gradual painless death."[14] Thus, having prohibited the raiding, trading and brutal treatment of slaves, Lugard freed their children born under the British protectorate, and instituted legal provisions for their redemption or self-redemption. Beyond this he did not care to move for fear of dislocating the economic and social order of the large Muslim populations under his rule. Thus, after their first naive appeals to the British for freedom, slaves learned that they could only obtain this by their own efforts, whether by absconding with all the risks of punishment that that involved, or by accumulating the equivalent of £5—100,000 to 120,000 cowries—required to claim their self-redemption through the Alkali's court. Under such conditions, until the end of 1917 only 16,612 slaves were registered as free throughout Kano Province, which then contained, besides Kano, the emirates of Katsina, Katagum, Daura and Hadeija, Kazaure, Misau, Gumel and Jema'are, and had a total population estimated at 2,750,000 in 1919, about one-third of which Robinson had classified 25 years earlier as slaves.[15] Thus in effect, while Lugard's policy forbade recruitment of further slaves to replenish existing supplies, it enabled slave owners to enjoy their customary revenues from slaves without much fear of disturbance during the lifetime of either party. As the Fulani owned most of the slaves and formed the great majority of slave-owners, such an arrangement clearly favoured them at the expense of their slaves, however much they resented restrictions on further slave raiding and trading.

As the Chronicle relates, during Aliyu's reign the commoners (*talakawa*), most of whom were Hausa, used to sing "'Christians, you delay, you do not come.' They thought that if the Europeans came, they would not have to do the work of subjects, it was said that they would be left to their own devices, but this was not correct."[16] Before the conquest and during the early years of British rule, according to the missionary Miller,

> after I had been some time in the big cities of the Hausa people, when they had learnt to know me and felt they could trust me, many a long conversation did I have with the more intelligent, free, farming and artisan class. It was always the same theme — "After the British have conquered this country, will they not restore the power and rule to those who had it for centuries before the uprising of the nomad Fulanis?"[17]

Hausa expectations of freedom from Fulani rule following the arrival of the British were freely expressed. For example when the Kano nobility fell back on Chamberawa following their defeat at Kotorkwoshi,

> the people of the villages shut their gates and thrust the Kano men from their walls when they attempted to enter, but received our party with cordiality. These gallant actions finished the opposition of Kano. A notable incident proving the attitude of the people towards us was the fact that at one time Lieutenant Wells was cut off, and would undoubtedly have been killed with the handful of men with him, had it not been for the action of a small village named Shankra, whose inhabitants, seeing his danger, came to his assistance, received him within their walls, and shut their gates in the face of the Kano army. This was a gallant act, since they could hardly expect that the handful of British would win, and our defeat would mean their own annihilation.[18]

In his Report of 1903, Lugard discusses these issues at length, with particular reference to developments at Kano.

> After the fall of Kano and Sokoto, the Fulani Chiefs of many or most of the cities owed their restoration to power entirely to the British. Dr. Cargill [the first British Resident of Kano] reports that, after I had left Kano en route to Sokoto (prior to the fight there), most of the chiefs of the big towns came and made their submission and that, when the Fulani chiefs who had accompanied Alieu of Kano to fight against us returned to their towns, the people refused them admittance and their opposition was only withdrawn by the good offices of the Resident.
>
> At first there was considerable lawlessness in the country districts; the Fulani faction were driven out, and the people refused to pay any taxes, while the slaves of the Fulani deserted them in large numbers. This caused some resentment towards the new Government on the part of the country Fulani; the peasantry showed a desire to throw off the yoke, and attacked the tax collectors, and even attacked Captain Phillips when he went to arrest the perpetrators of one of these outrages. This slight ebullition, however, subsided almost immediately and the people realised

that the Government was both able and ready to enforce just taxes and obedience to the law. It is probable that it had been caused by a few malcontents, who proposed to obey neither the Fulani nor the British, and whose cry was "No more taxes, no more slaves, no laws, and each to do as he pleases." Dr. Cargill's prompt action nipped this tendency in the bud.

The Fulani rule, in fact, had never (says Dr. Cargill) been fully accepted, even in the Kano Province, the very heart of Hausaland, and the emir stated that the peasantry had always been truculent and rebellious, that it had been necessary for the emirs to tour round their country annually, with all their forces, to ensure the payment of taxes.

The emir himself, however, and the chiefs of high standing at Kano, were not slow to appreciate the magnamity and justice with which they had been greeted. Dr. Cargill reported that when the ex-sultan of Sokoto traversed the Kano Province, the emir had sent a circular to all his towns to say that all who left to follow Attahiru would be punished on their return. He, moreover, refused any longer to pay the annual tribute to Sokoto, saying that it now belonged, of right, to the Government.[19]

The Original Accommodation

In details and outline, the conditions of this Anglo-Fulani rapprochement are clear; so too, the extraordinary rapidity of its unfolding. By May, 1903, within two months of his return to Kano, Abbas understood full well the British commitment to maintain Fulani domination over the subject Hausa, and within limits, to uphold their rights as slave owners. He also appreciated the benefits of political independence from Sokoto that the British presence assured. The latter had effectively simplified the pre-existing context of external relations in which Kano was hitherto engaged as an imperial province open to attack from Zinder, Gumel, Bornu, Hadeija and Ningi, by simultaneously controlling all these units, except Zinder, which was already under French rule. Thus, the conquest of Kano relieved Abbas of those complex, continual anxieties about the designs, resources and relations of neighboring powers that had preoccupied Aliyu. Instead, Kano's foreign relations were now reduced to its relations with the British Resident and his assistants. Moreover, the most important and frequent interactions in this relation took place between the emir himself and the District Officer in charge of Kano Division, or his superior, the Resident.

By 1906 in his *Political Memoranda*, Lugard had formulated general rules that obliged his senior Provincial staff to treat such senior emirs as Abbas, whose alliance and support were indispensable if his exiguous government was to administer the vast and varied Protectorate peacefully, effectively and economically, with the courtesy due to "natural rulers" by hereditary right.[20] Thus Abbas dealt with the Protectorate Government as a superior but foreign administration through the Resident and Divisional Officer at Kano. He was otherwise relieved of all need to handle foreign affairs, in whatever form they arose. For example, to assert Kano's claims to Miga and Kwanda which Hadeija had seized in 1893–4, Abbas could rely on British investigation and action, once the matter had been reported. The return of Kwanda and Miga to Kano when the British demarcated the Divisional boundaries between Kano and Hadeija in 1905 illustrate this clearly. Abbas was thus free to concentrate his attention entirely on the internal administration of Kano emirate and on the maintenance of suitable relations with the British.

Though the style, methods and goals of the British Administration unfolded gradually during Abbas' reign, and though his initial perceptions of these patterns were incorrect in many particulars, being based on his experience of traditional forms of suzerainty and vassalage, these Fulani models were neither entirely inappropriate nor misleading as guides to the new regime. Lugard did behave somewhat like a sultan in relation to his senior officers as well as conquered chiefs. Like Ahmadu Maje-rinji of Zinder before him, he did not hesitate to occupy the emir's quarters at Nassarawa after Kano's defeat. Like the caliphs of Sokoto, he had delegated responsibilities for Kano's administration to a Resident, Cargill, who served as his vizier. Like the vizier of Sokoto, Cargill in turn delegated Kano's immediate supervision to his senior subordinate in charge of the Kano Division, being himself simultaneously responsible for Katsina, Hadeija, Daura, Gombe, Jema'are, Misau and Katagum. To Abbas, the District Officer in charge of Kano Division thus corresponded closely to the Dangaladiman Waziri of traditional times, the Resident Kano to the vizier, and Lugard to the sultan. To heighten the parallel, Lugard also levied a tribute on the revenues of his subordinate emirs. Initially this was set at one-quarter of their total receipts per annum.[21] As suzerain, Lugard claimed

> the right to appoint not only the emirs, but the chief officers of state. The rights of succession, nomination, or election customary in the country would not as a rule be interfered with, but the High Commissioner would retain the right of veto, and the king or chief would lose his place for misconduct.[22]

With so many impressive similarities at hand, Abbas could hardly overlook the close correspondences between his current relations with the British hierarchy, and those his predecessors had enjoyed with Sokoto; but he was equally aware of the differing contents.

One corollary of this striking parallelism that Lugard designedly created and maintained was the policy of Indirect Rule through traditional chiefs. As he enunciated it in 1901,

> The Government utilises and works through the native chiefs, and avails itself of the intelligence and powers of governing of the Fulani caste in particular, but insists upon their observance of the fundamental laws of humanity and justice. Residents are appointed whose primary duty it is to promote this policy by the establishment of native courts, in which bribery and extortion and inhuman punishments shall be gradually abolished. Provincial courts are instituted to deal with the non-natives, and to enforce those laws of the Protectorate, more especially, which deal with slave raiding and slave trading, the import of liquor and firearms, and extortion from villagers by terrorism and impersonation. If an emir proves unamenable to persuasion or to threats, and will not desist from such actions (as in the case of Kontagora and Bida), he is deposed, and in each case a Fulani or other successor recognised by the people has been installed in his place. The traditional tribute (except that in slaves) paid by villages to their chief is insisted upon, and its incidence and collection are being regularised so as to prevent extortion or an undue burden on the agricultural or trading classes. I recognise the obligation of the chiefs to contribute to the revenue in return for the enhancement of their dues resulting from this system, and in

return for the protection of the roads from the robbers which used to infest them, and for the improvement of communications, etc.[23]

Under such arrangements Abbas could expect to retain his office and to exercise most of its traditional authority over the Native Administration of Kano as long as he maintained good relations with the Divisional Officer and Resident at Kano, and avoided such offences as extortion, judicial bribery, slave dealing, conspiracy or disloyalty that Lugard punished by deposition.

On his accession, Abbas had to fill a number of important offices which had fallen vacant during the past few months through the battle of Kotorkwoshi and the withdrawals of Galadima Mamudu, Shamaki Harisu and Aliyu's family to Sokoto on Aliyu's last order. By his accession, Abbas had also vacated the office of Wombai, which he gave to his elder brother, the Dan Makwayau Shehu, whom, when Wombai, Mamudu had appointed on Aliyu's authority en route to attack Zinder. Since the Galadima Mamudu had identified himself to the British as a staunch supporter of Aliyu by his return to Sokoto from Goga with Aliyu's sons, he had thereby forfeited his office, to which Abbas promptly appointed his brother Umaru. As Waziri, in place of the dead Ahmadu, Abbas initially appointed Abdullahi, son of the Tafida Muhamman and grandson of the emir Usuman Maje Ringim. The Turaki Mujeli (Maje), Aliyu's son, having forfeited his title by returning to Sokoto, Abbas appointed Salihi, a son of the emir Abdullahi, to succeed. In place of Shamaki Harisu, who had also returned to Sokoto with Aliyu's family, Abbas appointed the late Waziri Ahmadu's Shamaki Ajuji; in place of Sallama Jatau, Abu; and in place of Shettima Shekarau, a slave called Bauchi. To replace the Sarkin Shanu who had died defending Kano against the British, Abbas appointed Adam the son of Barau, whose lineage affiliations I did not learn.

Aliyu's Limam and Alkali had also forfeited their offices by accompanying Aliyu's family to Sokoto, perhaps hoping there to set out on pilgrimage. Abbas accordingly appointed two Filanin Bornu of the Zarawa clan, the elder, Ahmadu, as Limam, the younger, Muhammadu Gidado as Alkali. The Madaki Faruku, Kwairanga's son, whom Aliyu had appointed at Kanwa on Kwairanga's dismissal and arrest, had also returned to Sokoto with Aliyu's family, thereby forfeiting his office. Abbas appointed Kwairanga's brother, Husseini, to succeed. This selection appears to have been made after the ex-Madaki Kwairanga's flight to join the ex-caliph Attahiru, since Kwairanga was seeking re-installation shortly before he left Kano. Aliyu's son, the Ciroma Abdullahi, had also returned to Sokoto on his father's orders, thereby forfeiting his title. Abbas gave this to his eldest son Abdullahi Bayero, whom he promoted to the office of Waziri in 1905, but restored as Ciroma within two years. During Bayero's brief tenure of the vizierate, Abbas appointed Aliyu's son Abdulkadiri as Ciroma, but in 1907 Abdulkadiri was dismissed. On Shehu's promotion from Dan Makwayau to Wombai, Abbas appointed another of the emir Abdullahi's sons, Sa'adu, as Dan Makwayau. At Rano the chief Yusufu, who had fought at Kotorkwoshi, later joined the ex-caliph Attahiru on his eastward march. The chiefship was then transferred to Ila, another grandson of Malam Ishi'aku, the Shehu's flagbearer.

Most of Abdullahi's sons who had received titles from Aliyu claimed them during the first years of Abbas' reign. So did the Jobawa Makama Umaru, the Dambazawa Sarkin Bai Abdussallami, and the Sarkin Dawaki Mai Tuta Mamudu of Malam Jamau's lineage. In appointing Husseini to succeed Kwairanga, Abbas had also preserved Yolawa lineage rights in the Madaki title. However, on his accession the Mundubawa held none of the three offices which were traditionally theirs, neither the Dan Amar nor the Mai Anguwan Mundubawa nor the Magajin Maude. The Danejawa titles of Dan Iya and Dan Makwayau were then also filled by Suleibawa. Abbas appointed his cousin Abubakar, the grandson of Dabo's younger brother, Wombai Haruna, to the Balarawa office of Dan Darman, thereby disestablishing that lineage. He conferred the junior Yolawa title of Magajin Malam na Cedi on Salihi of Gwarzo, who may have been a baYole; and as Ja'idan-awa, he appointed Mai Bodinga, who may have been of either Mundubawa or Danejawa descent. As opportunities arose later, Abbas attempted to restore their traditional titles to the Danejawa and Mundubawa by appropriate appointments.

Shortly after Abbas' accession, the Magajin Malam na Hausawa Sule, a lineal descendant of Alkali Usuman, fled to Bima with the ex-caliph Attahiru, thereby forfeiting his office. Abbas replaced Sule by Rabi'u, a son of that Magajin Malam na Hausawa Rabi'u who had died at the Kofar Dan Agundi fighting for Tukur against the Yusufawa. When Sule returned from Burmi to Kano he found that Rabi'u held his office; but within seven months of his appointment Rabi'u died, and Sule was reinstated, almost certainly after discussions between Abbas and the British.

As mentioned earlier, on assuming power, Aliyu had appropriated control of such strategic southern towns as Kura, Tsakuwa and Dawaki ta Kudu, for the crown. On his accession Abbas transferred Kura and its dependencies to his mother Hauwa, on whom he also conferred the long-vacant title of Mai Babban Daki. His Agatawa servant, the Ma'aji Sadi, an immigrant from North Africa, besides serving as treasurer and administrative head of Kano City, was given executive control of the city environs to a radius of five or six miles, from Kumbotso in the south to Ungogo in the north where the international airport now stands. By these initial allocations of office, Abbas showed his intention to uphold traditional conventions, and, where practicable, to restore those that Aliyu had set aside. However, his appointments also followed those patterns set by Aliyu which accorded priority to the claims for office of Abdullahi's sons, the emir's brothers, over his own issue. Initially, of Abbas' sons, only Abdullahi Bayero received office as Ciroma or Crown Prince. On his accession, Abbas dismissed no one appointed by Aliyu, except those whose conduct had forfeited their offices in the eyes of the British Administration; but inevitably, not understanding his situation, the kin and supporters of those dismissed held Abbas directly responsible for their dismissal. Accordingly, within a year of his accession, there was considerable resentment and intrigue to secure his removal.

Further Upheavals

Perhaps as effects of the profound social and moral disturbances generated by the British military occupation and the eastward flight of the ex-caliph Attahiru I, the harvests of 1903–04 were very poor. Anticipating food shortages in the following year, before he set off on leave Cargill had ordered 1,200 tons of rice to be shipped from Britain to Kano; but long before the rice arrived, the peoples of Kano and adjacent chiefdoms in Nigeria and the French territory of the Niger experienced the most prolonged and intense famine since the *banga-banga* of 1857–59. The disaster impoverished all, causing widespread suffering and many deaths, and forced large numbers to quit their homes and farms in search of food. The Anglo-Fulani administrations of Kano Province set up distribution points for the limited supplies they were able to secure from Southern Nigeria. These efforts helped, but failed to relieve the general distress. By the harvest of 1905, the famine had taken a heavy toll of lives and exhausted the people.[24] Following on the upheavals of 1903, the famine of 1904 was a severe set back to the process of settling down under the new dispensation; and throughout 1905 the effects of the great famine (*Babbar Yunwa*) continued to be felt. In these circumstances the British were unable to institute administrative reforms as rapidly as they wished.

When Kemball set out from Kano to meet Aliyu's returning contingent in February 1903 he left a garrison of 254 men at the city,[25] most of whom remained there for two or three years, until the Province was pacified and they could be withdrawn. Evidently the enemies of Abbas, realising that he held office by grace of the British, thought to secure his dismissal in 1903–04 by intrigues and rumours designed to destroy British confidence in his loyalty. Writing in October 1905, Lugard records

> an event of unusual political importance in the early part of the year was the personal visit of the emir of Kano to Zungeru (Lugard's headquarters) ... A wholly causeless tension appears to have arisen at Kano, rumours circulated among the troops that the emir of Kano was projecting an attack, while the Kano people asserted that the garrison itself was meditating a similar project. The efforts of the Resident and of the emir did not avail to allay this mutual distrust, which had probably been fomented by interested parties. The emir declared his intention of visiting me in person at Zungeru to prove his loyalty. No one unacquainted with the incredible proneness to suspicion of the Fulani can realise how bold a step this was, or how striking both in its loyalty and its wisdom. Leaving the field open to his enemies in his absence, he faced a heavy march of five hundred miles, though warned by all his most trusted advisers that he would never come back alive. His reception with honour at Zungeru and his return in safety to Kano was a triumph that silenced at once the suspicions which had been entertained of his loyalty, and the projects of his enemies.[26]

During the famine of 1904, there had been some minor clashes between the mounted infantry and local people. "Two soldiers had been killed by villagers, and two villagers by soldiers at different times on the main roads."[27] The resulting tensions clearly provided a favourable field for the rumours and intrigue to which Lugard alludes.

Moreover, at the close of 1904 the political climate at Kano was again disturbed by the arrival of Abubakar, the emir of Katsina, under escort to await trial.

> The emir of Katsena has persistently given trouble since the British occupation, secretly opposing the Administration in every way, and continuing the extortion and oppression of his people for which he had always been noted. Chiefs were dispossessed and their offices sold, forced levies were made by him on the people in

the name of the Government, and revenue misappropriated, while attempts to poison our wells and to work evil to the Government Officers by means of charms were practically beyond doubt. We therefore decided, after many warnings, to depose him, and his successor was installed on my visit to Kano in December, 1904.[28]

Having banished the ex-emir Abubakar to Ilorin, Lugard summoned the senior claimant to the Katsina throne, Abubakar's senior kinsman and bitter rival, Yero. After explaining the conditions of appointment to Yero, Lugard appointed him personally in a public ceremony at Kano on January 2nd 1905, and concluded by presenting Abbas with certain installation gifts—a sword, a saddle, an illuminated Koran and a prayer carpet.[29]

Before departing, Lugard talked with Abbas, who

asked that powers of inflicting a death sentence should be granted to his native court. These powers, which, of course, have always been exercised by the emirs, I have withheld until the native judiciary should have proved itself sufficiently pure to exercise them. Sokoto and Kano have both done admirable judicial work, and I therefore concurred in the extension of his powers, provided that he obtained (in accordance with the Native Courts Proclamation) the concurrence of the Resident before a death-sentence was carried into execution ... (Lugard also) withdrew the prohibition to the restoration of the city walls, proposing that in future the customary labour of the peasantry on this work should in alternate years be devoted to this task, and to road making. He (Abbas) was, of course, much gratified by this mark of confidence."

Lugard then

told him (Abbas) of the strained relations with Hadeija, and saying that it was most distasteful to me to have to apply coercion to Fulani emirs, I suggested that he should write to Hadeija to point out the folly of his attitude. He did not appear to be very anxious to do so, but complied with my wish.[30]

In reply to Abbas' letter the Sarkin Hadeija Muhammadu wrote:

After greetings, we saw your messenger Hardo with your messages of warning and advice, regarding the guests (white men) who were coming to us. We regard the message as a token of the deep love you have for us. We have gladly followed your advice in obeying their orders and in agreeing to all they wanted. The result was good for us. Thus God saved us from the trouble which my enemies anticipated would fall on us, and I am glad to inform you that now between them and us there is peace and friendship, no trouble, and we are building them houses. For what you have done I acknowledge you from this time my best and most trustworthy friend.[31]

Thus Abbas' intercession with Hadeija at Lugard's request initially had more success than that of Mamman Bello with the emir of Misau on his own initiative in caliph Umaru's reign.

Abubakar's removal from Katsina to Kano City, followed there by his deposition and banishment, and by Lugard's public installation of Abubakar's rival Yero as the Sarkin Katsina, were dramatic events without precedents at Kano before or since the *jihad*. Neither had any Sarkin Katsina ever visited Kano since 1808, nor had Kano witnessed the deposition of any senior emir and his replacement in this manner. Such developments simultaneously expressed Lugard's overwhelming power as conqueror and suzerain, and the unpredictable modes of its exercise. Inevitably the public spectacle of Abubakar's downfall encouraged hopes among Abbas' enemies that he also might be removed.

Before suspending Abubakar, the Divisional Officer in Katsina had communicated with his superior, the Resident Cargill, at Kano, to seek his approval and advice. On Cargill's instructions, Abubakar was removed from Katsina under armed escort to Kano, where Abbas was asked to provide suitable accommodation until Lugard arrived to settle the matter. Abbas instructed the Makama Umaru to vacate his palace for Abubakar's use until Lugard came. The Makama demurred and refused to do so. Unwilling to press the issue further, Abbas then arranged for Abubakar to occupy the Nassarawa palace outside the city and took no further action against the Makama. But in the next year the British removed two Fulani dynasties established by Shehu Dan Fodio in the adjacent emirates of Daura and Katsina. At Daura the ancient Hausa ruling family was restored; and at Katsina a powerful Suleibawa lineage, with no previous claims to royal rank, replaced the Dallazawa dynasty on the deposition of Yero, Abubakar's successor, in 1906. As both emirates adjoined Kano, and fell within the Province, both came under Cargill's authority. The abrupt overthrow of their traditional dynasties inevitably disturbed many unquestioned assumptions concerning the dynastic situation at Kano. The baJobe Makama Umaru evidently interpreted these developments at Katsina and Daura to mean that the British Administration might replace the Suleibawa dynasty in Kano by the Jobawa, of whom he was the head. On learning of these seditious speculations, Abbas secured the Resident's approval and dismissed Umaru, reappointing Mujeli (also called Abdulkadir), Malam Bakatsine's grandson, who had held the title at Kamri under Tukur following the death of Makama Isa, but had forfeited it under Aliyu. When Mujeli died in 1907, his brother Dahiru was appointed, and on Dahiru's death in 1917, his son Aminu succeeded. By these successive appointments Abbas demonstrated his respect for traditional Jobawa rights; and by punishing Makama Umaru's sedition with dismissal, he warned others that he would not overlook intrigues against his authority.

Lugard's Program

Lugard's program of administrative reform and development was organised as a hierarchy of priorities. Having obliged the major Fulani chiefs to submit, Lugard disarmed their forces of modern rifles and garrisoned their capitals. Having proscribed slave raids and war, pacification followed submission as the orderly observance and enforcement of Protectorate laws and the Muslim *shari'a*. On pragmatic and symbolic grounds, Lugard demanded that his chiefs should pay the government set shares of their tax revenues; and as rapidly as his authority and resources allowed, he constituted provinces and established their administrations to supervise and guide the activities of his emirs and chiefs.

For various reasons, in Muslim areas reform and expansion of the native judiciary received Lugard's immediate attention. Mutilations and executions were forbidden, and Provincial staff were instructed to review, and, where necessary, to correct, the work of Native Courts. Emirs lost their powers of capital punishment; and, except at Kano itself, throughout the Province, all judicial courts presided over by emirs were initially abolished. The British strove to create as rapidly as they could an independent, efficient and greatly expanded native judiciary by multiplying the number of Muslim courts presided over by suitably qualified and formally appointed *alkalai* in order to furnish proper Muslim tribunals for adjudication in rural areas. Thus by 1906–07 every district in Katsina emirate had its local Alkali's court, as did many in Kano.[32] The rapid multiplication of efficient and accessible Muslim courts was essential for further administrative and social developments. In the same spirit, Lugard replaced the old state dungeons by prisons of more humane design and regime. By disarming the emirs' slave *dogarai*, he restricted them to duties of patrol, arrest, escort, bearing messages, and attendance on officials.

Even before these essential tasks were accomplished, Lugard directed his administrative staff to catalogue the forms and units of local taxation and territorial administration in order to sort, simplify and reform them. Since local taxes were still delivered to emirate treasuries by *hakimai* who held scattered towns and communities in fief, any major reforms of tax collection procedures presupposed parallel reorganizations of the territorial administration. Residents and Divisional Officers were therefore directed to investigate and record details of fief administration and allocation within the emirates under their charge in order to devise a new structure of compact territorial districts administered by local chiefs directly responsible to resident *hakimai*. Moreover, for administrative efficiency Indirect Rule required that the boundaries and internal organization of these new districts should coincide closely with traditional units of appropriate size and compactness. These requirements obliged Divisional Officers to catalogue the existing distributions of territorial fiefs in considerable detail for the emirates they supervised.

Lugard was quick to agree with Cargill that

> the more important *Hakimai* (Fiefholders) may turn out of real use to the Government after some instruction and supervision. As a class they are men of refinement and understanding, and existing abuses can hardly be laid to their charge, as their offices have hitherto been merely nominal, and their functions usurped by the big slaves.[33]

One objective of the proposed territorial reorganization was thus to exclude *jekadu* and slaves from public roles in administration and tax collection. It is true that Aliyu had increased the roles of slaves in tax collection and fief administration at Kano. However, even in his reign most *jekadu* were the free Fulani clients or kinsmen of *hakimai*, whether the latter resided at the capital, or at such district centres as Gaya, Dutse, Rano, Gwaram, Jahun, or Babura. Dealing with several emirates simultaneously, Cargill may not have drawn the appropriate distinctions between their constitutions in his reports to Lugard. At Katsina the deposed emir Abubakar had inherited a powerful slave staff whose functions he expanded by expropriating many free noble fiefholders; but at Kano, even under Aliyu, parallel developments had been restrained by various forces and circumstances mentioned above. Nonetheless, British objections to the use of slaves in public administration, amply justified by Abubakar's regime at Katsina and by similar regimes elsewhere, were applied at Kano without due attention to the different role and status of throne slaves there. Nonetheless, Lugard's objection to slave executives was quite sound. By virtue of their status, throne slaves enjoyed such immunity from public complaint and protest that they could exploit their public functions at will without much fear of punishment.

Lugard was also anxious to eliminate the traditional use of *jekadu* as political agents on economic and administrative grounds. Economically, the use of *jekadu* in tax collection would cease to be necessary once compact territorial districts were established, since village chiefs in each district would then be severally responsible for tax collection and transfer from their areas. The resident *hakimi*, having checked tax receipts from his villages against the expected returns and investigated any complaints, would then be directly responsible for transferring his district tax to the Ma'aji, after first reporting the amounts collected and due to the emir. Administratively, free *jekadu*, whatever their lineage, were at least as prone to exploit the communities they supervised as slaves holding similar roles. Under the old regime, aggrieved or oppressed commoners had such marginal prospects of securing redress for wrongs inflicted by *jekadu* that private complaints against them were probably less frequent than communal disaffection and sporadic protest. Nonetheless, in the pre-colonial regime the *jekada* institution had served important functions. Firstly, it provided administrative roles for junior kinsmen and dependents of the power elite, thereby furnishing the means of remuneration and employment necessary to support a sufficient force of military effectives to defend the state, to staff its internal communications, and to police the subject population and rural communities administered as fiefs. The *jekada* institution simultaneously provided initial training for future *hakimai*, emirs and senior officials. But above all it supported a substantial military elite between campaigns, while assuring them high political status, prospects and power. With pacification, in Lugard's view most of these traditional functions were no longer essential; and some were clearly disfunctional and incompatible with the orderly, efficient, economical and civilian pattern of administration that he sought to introduce.

In 1904 Cargill undertook the first field assessments at Gaya and its environs in an attempt to investigate the feasibility of increasing the tax revenues of the Kano Treasury, while equalizing the distribution of tax burdens. On this tour he was accompanied by Abdullahi Bayero, then Waziri of Kano, the eldest son of Abbas, and as Ciroma a former fiefholder. At Gaya, Cargill informed the chief that "we had come to assess Gaya with a view to doing away with the *jekada*." The twelve ward heads of Gaya town were summoned and instructed to assemble the householders under them. Each ward head was then asked to state the amounts that he had collected on the last occasion from his ward as *zakka*, *kudin kasa*, and so on, following which each householder was questioned about his household and recent tax payments. "The result is map, census and assessment of one district completed, and one Jakada abolished. I (Cargill) calculated it would take me up to the end of my present tour (May, 1906) to complete the map and assessment of the whole Kano District."[34] Systematic tax reforms were accordingly postponed, since territorial reorganization was prerequisite for any rationalization of the traditional tax system.

Lugard's summary of these developments illustrates their logic.

> In so densely-populated a country as Kano, an attempt to begin at once a detailed assessment before general conditions were known would have resulted in loss of time and useless work. The Resident, therefore, wisely determined not to interfere with native assessment, which ... was singularly well organised and apparently not unjust in its incidence in this emirate. Mere enquiry from local chiefs as to taxation led, however, to no useful result, since they invariably understated the amounts they had been accustomed to pay. He (Cargill) turned his attention, therefore, to the preliminary task of forming his "districts," and of appointing the headmen with the scheme described in my report for 1904. In this he has been most successful. As in most other provinces, he found that the fiefholders owned towns vicariously scattered over the whole province, but, unlike other provinces, he found no difficulty in redistribution. Picking the principal town under each fiefholder, he grouped around it, in one homologous district, a sufficient number of towns to yield a revenue equivalent to the former revenue of the fiefholder, and appointed him "District Head" of this self-contained district. He even succeeded in giving to the most important chiefs districts furthest from the capital, where their responsibility would be greater, retaining villages close to Kano itself under the direct rule of the emir. To avoid too drastic and hasty a reform, it was found necessary to allow the emir to place some of these under his head slaves as a temporary concession. In the evolution of a more complete organisation it is possible that the mode of expenditure of the official revenue assigned to the emir for public purposes may be accounted for as State funds, and that his private income may be derived from the rents of the group of estates attached to his position.[35]

However, Cargill's initial attempt to subdivide the territory of Kano into a number of compact administrative districts was not the striking success he and Lugard believed. Despite Lugard's enthusiastic account of the territorial reorganization (*gunduma*) of 1906, its subdivisions were experimental and temporary; during the next twenty years their boundaries and alignments were often redrawn. Cargill's most important achievement in the *gunduma* of 1906 was to have the *hakimai* removed from Kano City to the rural areas that Abbas assigned to their control. By that measure, and with the emir's assent, Cargill formally abolished the prevailing and traditional distributions of fiefs and constituted a provisional structure of territorial districts under resident *hakimai* simultaneously responsible for their administration and tax collection. When the *gunduma* or territorial reorganization was finally completed in 1908, shortly before Cargill's departure, the *hakimai* had already become acquainted with their new roles and duties, while the emir and supervising British officers had also gained useful experience of the new territorial administration.

Long before the Fulani emirates were incorporated into the Protectorate of Northern Nigeria, Lugard had given careful thought to the reform of their tax systems. Characterising the traditional Fulani pattern as feudal and based on tributes and rent, Lugard estimated that under the old regime an emir might receive 50 percent, the fiefholder (*hakimi*) 25 percent, the fiefholder's senior agent or "vassal" 12.5 percent, the latter's executive 6.25 percent, and the community headman 6.25 percent of village revenues on average.[36] He then declared that

> The primary object of my policy in Northern Nigeria, by dividing the country into Provinces, and deputing a Resident to the charge of each, is to effect throughout the whole Protectorate a demarcation of existing jurisdictions, and a reassessment (in accordance with the actual taxable capacity of each village) of the tribute, rent or dues which it shall pay to the overlord, to replace the present unequal incidence and the arbitrary and tyrannical levies of the past. Recourse to force for the collection of tribute, "lawful" or otherwise, by the chiefs, with its waste of life, and its continual unrest and war, is now prohibited, and the British Administration is, therefore, responsible for the enforcement of such dues as it may decide to be justly payable. In my view it is a natural corollary that the whole population should pay alike, if not to the alien Fulani, then to the Government direct ... Some progress has been made with the scheme of assessment. Simultaneously with it a census, and a geographical survey, together with the collection of a mass of statistical information regarding products, area under cultivation, etc., are being effected in a rough and ready way; but the work of fully grappling with and completing so large a task still belongs to the future.[37]

As he succeeded in bringing the Northern emirates and peoples under the Protectorate government, Lugard established provincial and divisional administrations with garrisons to police these areas and supervise their affairs. In consequence, the annual expenditures of his Protectorate Government increased rapidly from £96,457 in 1900–01 to £298,519 in 1901–02, £389,391 in 1902–03 and £498,986 in 1903–04. In 1904–05 Government expenditure passed the half million mark, but fell to the level of 1903–04 for the following two years. At this time Lugard's government derived the funds it needed mainly from imperial grants-in-aid which the British government provided annually on the basis of careful estimates of essential expenditures, and revenues from other sources. From £88,800 in 1900–01 this imperial grant had climbed to £180,000 in 1901–02 and £405,000 in the years 1903–04 and 1904–05, before declining to £320,000 in 1905–06.[38] Thereafter the imperial government, having fulfilled its undertaking to finance the occupation and pacification of Northern Nigeria, was concerned to reduce its annual contribution, and applied pressure on Lugard to ensure that the Protectorate administration secured the revenues it needed from local sources as rapidly as possible, while economising its expenditures. At prevailing levels of the regional economy, the Protectorate Government could only increase its local revenues by increasing its receipts from the taxes levied annually in the emirates and chiefdoms under its care. This, the most promising source of increased revenue immediately available, accordingly received continuous attention by the British administration. Nonetheless, though Protectorate revenues from internal taxation and excise rose rapidly from £631 in 1901–02 through £7,800 in 1902–03, £39,000 in 1903–04, £69,000 in 1904–05 to £85,000 in 1905–06,[39] those amounts were quite insufficient to relieve its Government's dependence on imperial grants in aid. In consequence Lugard and his successors continued to seek new bases of native taxation that could yield superior returns to native chiefs and the Protectorate Government.

1906: A New Accommodation

In 1906 Lugard's attempts to reorganize the territorial and fiscal bases of native administration throughout the Fulani territories were interrupted by a Hausa revolt at Satiru, six miles from Sokoto, and an expedition against Hadeija. Lugard interpreted the revolt at Satiru as Mahdist on various grounds, and suppressed it swiftly. In 1904 the village chief of Satiru had proclaimed himself the Mahdi; but he had died in the Sokoto prison awaiting trial some months before the revolt. In 1906, at the instigation of an immigrant Gobir Hausa from the French territory of Niger, the dead chief's son was persuaded to revolt, and in the ensuing fight the rebels defeated a British force despatched against them, killing three officers and 25 troops.[40] Lugard hastily prepared a larger force which overran Satiru and stamped out the revolt, but this was not, despite his assertions, merely or even primarily an expression of "religious fanaticism" since "among the slain no Fulani were found, and all bore the tribal marks of the Hausas."[41] On his own account also, before this incident,

> there was much unrest among the *telakawa* (free-born peasantry), of which he (the Resident, Sokoto) was wholly unaware, and he ascribes it to the loss of their slaves ... Racial antagonism may also have been a contributing cause to the unrest among the peasantry, for the Hausas or Habes do not love the Fulani, and may have felt that the British Administration in Sokoto was too much identified with the ruling caste, to the disregard of their interests, but the fact that the neighbouring towns held aloof and were raided and their people killed by the rebels goes to show that it was not a people's rising against their rulers.[42]

Lugard's reasoning is curious; but, whatever the "causes" and character of this revolt, its principal and immediate effect was to emphasize the dependence of the British administration on the Fulani aristocracies who ruled the Muslim states. Hitherto, according to Lugard,

> the policy of Government has been most emphatically to dissociate itself from race feeling, and, while ruling through the existing Fulani chiefs— who alone are capable of administration—to spare no efforts to hear the grievances and redress the wrongs of the Hausa, Nupe, Yoruba, or other subject tribes.[43]

Nonetheless the revolt immediately aligned the Fulani with the British.

> For the first time the troops of Government, which had been considered invincible, had been defeated and three white men killed. How would the country at large, so recently brought under administrative control, take the news? The answer was spontaneous and immediate. From every emirate it came in almost identical terms, from Yola to Ilorin, from Kano to Nupe. The latter offered armed horsemen to assist if need be, and Ilorin ... said his men would have fought on our side. Kano, Bauchi, Zaria demonstrated their loyalty ... nothing could exceed the loyalty of Sokoto and

his chiefs, who (with one exception) rallied to our assistance from every side, and the final result has been to bind them in ties of closer confidence than ever.[44]

At Satiru the British learnt the degree to which their regime depended on Fulani support; and so did the ruling Fulani. Thus the Satiru revolt served to erase some of the hierarchic features of Anglo-Fulani relations that had derived from Lugard's conquest, by transforming these into relations of symbiosis and alliance. Thereafter despite their religious differences, the two sets of rulers cooperated to maintain joint control over the large, restless and fragmented subject populations.

However, at Hadeija "the news of the Sokoto disaster was received with general rejoicing … All work on Government buildings stopped, and the emir's messenger no longer came to the Resident."[45] There, according to Lugard,

the attitude of Hadeija has been consistently marked by chronic obstruction and hostility culminating in the murder of a soldier, apparently with the sanction and in the presence of the emir. Enquiry into this matter was impossible without recourse to force. Men had been overheard in the city discussing the chances of success if the garrison were attacked by night. Co-operation between Government and the Native Administration was impossible in such circumstances, no progress could be made with the taxation reforms, nor was it safe to travel in the district without a strong escort.[46]

Thus immediately after suppressing the Satiru revolt, Lugard

sent a powerful force under the Commandant to convey my ultimatum to the emir … I demanded that the eight ringleaders should be surrendered … and that all arms should be given up. The reply was … to the effect that if we wished to arrest these men we must come and do it ourselves, and the messenger was struck in the face— a supreme insult from a Fulani. On receipt of this reply the Commandant seized one of the gates and marched his troops into the large open space which intervenes between the walls and the inhabited part of the city.[47]

On Lugard's report, his commander then directed non-combatants to leave the city, and "large numbers did so," following which

the emir and his fighting men charged the troops on horseback and were repulsed, and after five hours' street fighting the emir's walled citadel was captured, where he and three of his sons, with their retainers … died fighting. Of the eight ringleaders whose surrender had been demanded, six were killed and one captured. All possible precautions were taken to prevent looting and save the city from damage, and these proved most effectual.[48]

However, according to the missionary, Walter Miller,

Either through a mistake—the emir had sent out a white flag twice with offers to surrender—or because the Force sent up was determined to have a 'showdown,' the city was subjected to most cruel treatment: again the native troops got out of control and the city was given up to violence and murder and pillage for two days ... I wrote to His Excellency (Lugard) a strong letter of expostulation and had a most favourable reply—as usual.[49]

Of these two conflicting accounts of the sack of Hadeija, Miller's corresponds more closely with the folk tradition. Following immediately after the wholesale slaughter of rebels at Satiru, the destructive exhibition of British force at Hadeija put an end to fighting in Northern Nigeria until the Ibo riots at Kano in 1953. The dead emir of Hadeija Muhammadu (1885–1906) was duly replaced by his son Haruna (1906–9).

These incidents of 1906 at Satiru and Hadeija brought the first phase of British administration in Northern Nigeria to an end. At Satiru the protest of disaffected "Habe" (Hausa) against the Anglo-Fulani concordat had been launched in religious terms and checked in military ones. At Hadeija the emir and his court had opposed British control since 1903. On pretexts of sympathy with the Satiru rebels and the murder of a soldier, the recalcitrants at Hadeija were eliminated to discourage further resistance of that kind. Following on the heels of Satiru, the sack of Hadeija warned Fulani emirs of the penalties they risked by obstinacy. Thus, in conjunction with the abrupt replacement of the dynasties established by Dan Fodio at Katsina and Daura, the incidents at Satiru and Hadeija in 1906 clarified the nature and limits of British rule by restating its conditions and sanctions in various ways. In 1904, when Lugard wanted Abbas at Kano to mediate with Sarkin Hadeija on his behalf, he had informed him that

> it was not our policy that there should be two administrations, the British and the Native, working side by side, however harmoniously, but that both should together form an integral part of the single responsible government of the country, each dealing with its allotted part, and working in intimate co-operation with the other.[50]

Hadeija, Satiru and the dynastic changes at Katsina and Daura together—all events that occurred in 1906[51]—indicated the basic conditions, and some alternatives, of this "intimate co-operation" between the Fulani and British Administrations. Thus the events of 1906 demarcated clearly the political context in which Abbas was obliged to act as emir of Kano. As Hadeija, Daura and Katsina all adjoined Kano emirate and were all administered by the Resident at Kano, the political and administrative implications of these dramatic developments must have preoccupied Abbas, even without the Resident's commentary.

Abbas and the British Administration

To appreciate the internal evolution of the Fulani polity at Kano under British rule, we should first specify the primary objectives, conditions and terms of its British Administration, and then mention such critical events as the conflicts at Satiru and Hadeija, which substantially modified or clarified British goals and procedures. Having thus indicated the decisive features of the state's political context, and the terms of its subordination and reorganization under British rule, we may appreciate more clearly the emir's autonomy, objectives and policies within his changing historic context.

As early as 1904, when he asked Lugard to restore powers of capital punishment to his Judicial Court, Abbas had shown that as emir his immediate concern was to preserve the powers and prerogatives of his office against British expropriation. For this reason also, he sought and welcomed Lugard's permission to restore the city walls by corvée labor of the peasantry in alternate years. In 1905–06 when Cargill provisionally subdivided Kano into compact Districts under resident *hakimai*, as Lugard notes,

> the emir of course did not like the introduction of a system which would weaken his autocratic power, but has nevertheless afforded all the assistance he could, in a loyal and enlightened spirit. In recognition of this, I agreed to the concession ... by which for a time some of the villages near Kano should be placed under his ex-slaves, who formerly were all-powerful and usurped the functions of the legitimate chiefs."[52]

In short, besides seeking to recover powers initially withdrawn by Lugard from his office, Abbas negotiated strategic concessions in return for his support of particular British administrative reforms.

In these complex negotiations Abbas enjoyed certain advantages which tended to offset British military and political supremacy. Firstly, as Lugard acknowledged in 1904, the British genuinely sought the active and intimate cooperation of the emir and his officialdom in their administration of the native state. No emir was ultimately indispensable, as events at Hadeija had recently shown. Nor were dynasties indispensable, as Katsina and Daura had shown; but, provided he was prepared to negotiate flexibly with his Resident and Provincial staff, compromising and accommodating to their more urgent requirements, an emir could secure important concessions and conserve or even enhance his power, while making himself at least provisionally indispensable to the British administration of his state. For example, as Cargill tried to map the boundaries of the new territorial districts which he planned to institute in Kano, lacking knowledge of their histories and the political affiliations of their component communities, he was inevitably dependent on the emir Abbas for information and guidance concerning these pre-colonial arrangements, and had to rely on the emir's judgment of the administrative viability of the new units.

Under the canons of Indirect Rule as laid down by Lugard, the Resident also needed the emir's approval and authority to initiate this scheme within his emirate. On the other hand, only the emir as head of the Native Administration had the authority to select the new District Heads from the ranks of free *hakimai* or to decide the distribution of Districts among them. Though the Resident could veto some of these proposals, he could not formally make these appointments. It seems evident that Cargill was heavily occupied throughout 1905 to 1908 in resolving such political questions by discussions with Abbas; and in this process the boundaries of several territorial districts were changed, together with their allocations among *hakimai* of differing titles, lineage and rank.

It was open to Abbas in such discussions to accept major reforms proposed by the British after expressing various reservations, hesitations and raising questions. Such chiefly caution simultaneously served to delay an innovation, to elicit further details concerning its structure and scope from the Resident and the High

Commissioner, to purchase time in which Abbas could reconsider the scheme, to assure the protection of his own powers and interests, or alternatively to convert the proposal, where possible, to ends and goals of his own design.

As Lugard had indicated on their first meeting at Kano, emirs could be deposed for misconduct and continuous obstruction.[53] By misconduct, Lugard evidently meant slave raiding, slave trading, the illegal use of force, oppression, and "conspiracies" against the Protectorate government, activities in which Abbas neither needed nor chose to engage. Of greater relevance to him was Lugard's warning about obstruction; and by 1906, following the sack of Hadeija and eviction of their traditional dynasties from Katsina and Daura, Abbas was fully aware of its implications. Thus, however unsettling a British proposal for further reform or change at Kano might initially appear, the emir was constrained to consider it carefully within the immediate context of his political relationships with the British Provincial staff. Providing only that he demonstrated sufficient willingness to accommodate to his new political context, and to accept British administrative prescriptions, Abbas had considerable room for manoeuvre and negotiation in responding to the numerous requests and suggestions that flowed from the Residency and Provincial Office towards the palace.

At any moment there were generally several schemes for reform and development under consideration; so that by accepting the most innocuous, Abbas could defer action on troublesome proposals, while negotiating others of lesser menace to the native polity. Faced with fundamental reforms, such as Cargill's proposals to reconstitute the territorial administration and reorganize tax collection, after securing the necessary clarifications and details, Abbas could also agree in principle to the scheme, thereby demonstrating his inclination to cooperate, while criticising its particulars to secure delays in the implementation and modifications of varying scope. By such tactics, Abbas maintained the respect and confidence of the Provincial Residents and staff, who assimilated him to their stereotype of the intelligent, conservative Fulani emir who appreciated their services and proposals, but was often restrained by considerations of religion, tradition or the welfare of his people from assenting readily to them.

Abbas had yet another important advantage in this tortuous and endless series of defensive negotiations with the British Administration in Kano, namely, the constant turnover and replacement of British staff, due to leaves, illnesses, retirements, transfers to other Provinces, and the like. From February 1903 until October 1906, of five men who acted as Resident for Kano Province, only Cargill exercised all the substantive powers of that office. Of these 44 months, Cargill administered Kano for 26. For the remaining 18 months Kano experienced caretaker administrations by four Acting Residents whose uncertain tenure and powers restricted their effectiveness. By the end of 1919, when Abbas died, the Resident's office at Kano had been transferred 29 times between 4 substantive and 11 acting Residents.[54] Such turnovers of British personnel were then characteristic at all levels of Provincial administration, thereby ensuring important discontinuities in their operations. As the emir and his *hakimai* observed this ceaseless arrival and departure of Provincial staff, the differences between their own administrative positions and organization, and those of the British officials with whom they dealt, became increasingly clear.

Lugard had impressed the Fulani emirs as a great and powerful chief whose imperiousness, assurance and authority they could understand; but Lugard's deputies and successors occupied a different status, formally and substantively. As though to express this, when Lugard left Northern Nigeria in 1906, the office of High Commissioner was converted to that of Governor. More important, Lugard's successors lacked his unique personal achievements, qualities and relations with the emirs. At the Provincial level, as personnel came and went, British officials became increasingly dependent on the emir and his staff for information and guidance on local institutions, situations and history. This constant turnover of British administrative personnel accordingly strengthened the emir's position by ensuring the relative unfamiliarity of British staff with local personnel and conditions and by enhancing their dependence on the emir for guidance and support. Thus despite his formal subordination to the British officials, by 1908 Abbas had achieved an approximate parity of power in his relations with the Resident and Divisional Officer at Kano by virtue of his central role in the emirate administration, his inherited status, and his superior knowledge of Kano's history and affairs. Moreover since the British administration valued routine, despite its repeated changes of personnel, as time passed the British became increasingly aware of the difficulties that could arise if they had to replace Abbas abruptly. By 1908, when Cargill retired, having at last subdivided Kano into territorial Districts, Abbas had had five years' continuous experience of office. During that period he had established firm control over the native officialdom and had converted his initial subordination into a base from which to negotiate securely with the British. Thus in circumstances that differed radically from those of Abdullahi's or Aliyu's day, the emir of Kano still presided over its government and regulated the distributions of office, wealth and power within it, although the appointments and activities of these officials were now supervised by the British Administration.

The Gunduma of 1904–1908

Until the emirate had been effectively partitioned into compact districts under resident *hakimai*, little progress could be made in reforming traditional methods of tax assessment and collection, though special efforts were taken to ensure that the emir and the British Administration received their shares of the amounts collected without loss through peculation or embezzlement en route. By the beginning of 1908, Abbas had accepted Cargill's proposals for the apportionment of Kano into districts, and had instructed the *hakimai* to disperse to their respective rural headquarters. By then Cargill and Abbas had evidently discussed the allocation of districts among these *hakimai* at considerable length, as the resulting distribution indicates.[55] Excluding Kano and the densely populated region around it, the emirate was exhaustively partitioned into districts and sub-districts of varying population and extent. An attempt was made to equalize the populations of sub-districts approximately; but in the absence of an accurate census, such adjustments rested on estimates.

As laid down by Cargill, outside the home area around the city, each major district contained a number of sub-districts under resident *hakimai* who were each individually responsible for a district to their common superior. Thus the district administered by Wombai Shehu included the sub-districts of Majia, Buduru, Kaura, Ringim, Sankara and Dabi, all separate and under resident *hakimai* holding titles of approximately secondary rank and equal status in the traditional system. Likewise districts presided over by the Sarkin Dawaki Mai Tuta, Madawaki, Sarkin Bai, Ciroma, Galadima, Makama, Turaki Manya, Sarkin Dawaki Tsakar Gida and the Barde, each contained three or more compact sub-districts administered by resident *hakimai* under the supervision of these high-ranking officials. In effect the new district organization rested on an implicit distinction between major and minor *hakimai* which, despite its traditional foundations, now took unprecedented forms with uncertain implications. Besides the Galadima, Wombai, Turaki Manya, Sarkin Dawaki Mai Tuta, Madawaki, Ciroma, Makama, Sarkin Bai and Sarkin Dawakin Tsakar Gida, all of whom had ranked as *rukunai* or senior *hakimai* in traditional Kano, Cargill's *gunduma* placed the hereditary rural chiefs of Rano, Karaye, Dutse and Gaya in charge of extensive districts with several sub-divisions identical in status and form to those presided over by such senior central officials as the Galadima or Makama. Thus implicitly, these territorial and administrative arrangements equated the senior rural chiefs at Rano, Karaye, Gaya and Dutse with the most senior central *hakimai*. They also crystallised the stratification of titles which had guided the allocations of fiefs among *hakimai* hitherto resident at the capital.

To this pattern the major rural chiefdoms were assimilated in various ways. Thus, the Sarkin Dutse found that his chiefdom was subdivided into four parts under his Makama, Madaki, Tafida and Sarkin Yaki. Gaya district was likewise divided into four parts under its Sarkin Fada, Galadima, Waziri, and another. But while Karaye was classed as a sub-district under the Sarkin Dawaki Mai Tuta, besides administering his traditional domain, the Sarkin Karaye also supervised two adjacent sub-districts that were allotted to the village chiefs of Rogo and Gwangwam respectively, these townships having remained independent of one another and Karaye throughout Fulani times.

In the reclassification of Kano *sarautu* on which this two-tiered district organization was based, certain modifications of the pre-colonial rank alignments are evident. Under the Fulani, the titles of Madawaki, Sarkin Dawaki Mai Tuta, Makama, Sarkin Bai and Dan Iya which vested in the leading jihadic lineages were conceded seniority among non-royal ranks, and seats on the Council of State. It is said that together the Sarkin Bai, Madawaki and Makama could veto the emir's decisions, though I know no case in which they did. However, the Daneji lineage lost its exclusive right to the title of Dan Iya when Aliyu and then Abbas gave it to Suleibawa royals. Perhaps for this reason, at *gunduma* the Dan Iya was placed in charge of a compact undivided district close to the capital; yet in the pre-colonial rank order, Dan Iya followed Sarkin Dawaki Mai Tuta among the Councillors of State.

Of royal offices, the Galadima and Wombai were the senior and most powerful, followed by the Turaki Manya and Ciroma. Of these four titles, only Ciroma's was formally reserved for the ruler's son. Ideally, and to a great extent in practice also, the titles of Galadima, Wombai and Turaki Manya had been allocated to the ruler's brothers or agnatic cousins. As we have seen, each of these senior royal titles traditionally had several important fiefs; but having lost direct control of these fiefs under Cargill's *gunduma*, the four royal titles were compensated by administrative responsibilities for extensive territories. Indirectly also, in allocating such large areas to the Galadima, Wombai, Ciroma and Turaki Manya, the new territorial organization further enhanced the power of the Suleibawa dynasty throughout the kingdom by extending the territory its leading members controlled.

At the *gunduma* of 1908, the Barde Audu na Gwangwazo, the baSuleibe prince who had slain Tukur at Tafashiya, was placed in charge of a district with three sub-divisions, Miga, Jahun and Aujara, Miga having been restored to Kano from Hadeija by that date. Although a high-ranking office in Fulani days, the title of Barde was normally reserved for *shigege* clients, though periodically given to princes, and ranked well below such hereditary offices as Madawaki, Sarkin Bai, Makama, and other senior royal ranks. In Hausa days, it is true, the Barde had held a seat in the Council of Nine; and under various Fulani emirs including Aliyu Babba, the Barde had also served as a Councillor. However, by thus aggrandising the Barde's role, Abbas placed his cousin Abdu na Gwangwazo, another baSuleibe, in charge of those eastern districts that adjoined Hadeija, thereby augmenting Suleibawa control of the territorial administration.

In the densely populated core of the emirate, the city remained under the Ma'aji Ba'adamasi, an Arab, the Ma'aji Sadi having been disgraced and banished for undetermined reasons in 1908. The Tafida and Dan Isa, both Suleibawa, administered the northern and southern environs of the city respectively, from Ungogo to Kumbotso. North of Ungogo, the Dan Makwayau Sa'adu, another baSuleibe, had charge. East of Kumbotso lay the Dan Iya's district, at this time also in Suleibawa hands; and to its north were small districts under the Mai Anguwan Mundubawa Zakari, a baMundube, the Barde Kareriya Muhammadu, a son of Abdullahi, the Dan Amar, another baSuleibe, and the Dan Buram Ibrahim Cigari, another son of Abdullahi. Finally, the Ja'idanawa Mai Bodinga administered a small district centred at Kunya. Thus most of this densely settled central area was placed directly under the administration of Suleibawa princes.

Thus Abbas succeeded in converting the territorial reorganization which, under British pressure he could only delay or modify but could not prevent, to the interests of his dynasty and chiefship; yet while pursuing these goals, he was careful not to expropriate the political or territorial claims of prominent Fulani lineages either at Kano or in the rural areas. Indeed the chiefs of Rano, Dutse, Gaya and Karaye found themselves with enhanced territorial jurisdictions, administrative responsibilities, and political status. However, apart from these rural vassals, all of whom, including Gaya, claimed their offices on hereditary grounds, with few exceptions Abbas and Cargill had preserved the lineage interests of the Fulani founding families in those titles and territories they had held since the *jihad*. Thus the Jobawa Makama administered the old Jobawa territory from Birnin Bako on the Ningi border to Garko where Aliyu had died, and south from Durba and Dal to Masu on the borders of Rano. The Madaki Huseini had the old Yolawa territory from Dawanau near Ungogo west and northwest to the Katsina boundary, including the present district of Bici, which was then governed by his Shentali. The Sarkin Bai had the old Dambazawa area north of Dambarta, including Kunci, up to the Kazaure and Katsina borders. The Sarkin Dawaki Mai

Tuta initially administered the sub-districts of Karaye, Rogo, Gwangwam, Kura, Kiru, Madobi and Bebeji, all of which lay within and around the area initially claimed by Malam Jamau and his lineage after the *jihad*. Of the five founding families, only the Danejawa had lost direct administrative control over their former territory, since Dan Zabuwa now came under the Madaki. In place of this, the Suleibawa Dan Iya was given charge of Dawaki ta Kudu, southeast of Kano.

By utilising these traditional lineage claims to rural areas as the basis for allocating district headships, Cargill and Abbas avoided giving offense and generating resistance to the new territorial system among powerful lineages. Instead, by materially increasing the territories under the jurisdictions of their senior hereditary officials, they sought the support of those leading lineages for the *gunduma*. Nonetheless, while making these territorial provisions for the leading Fulani lineages, Abbas had virtually appropriated administrative control over the remaining districts of Kano for the Suleibawa dynasty, and implicitly he had restricted each of the founding families to its traditional domain or substitute. In effect, the *gunduma* presented Abbas with a unique opportunity to establish Suleibawa jurisdiction over many rural parts of Kano which had previously eluded direct dynastic control. At the same time, by scrambling the pre-colonial patterns of fief allocation and the traditional ranking and distributions of titles, official responsibilities and rewards, Cargill's *gunduma* gave Abbas unparallelled opportunities to manipulate the allocations of titles, territories and their ancillary economic rewards among his officials and seekers for office. Thus, despite its evident intention to preserve and express the colonial patterns of political organization at Kano, this new territorial allocation inevitably promoted sweeping adaptations and transpositions in the traditional alignments and distributions of office, as well as the definitions of official duties and rewards. During the next decade, Abbas continued to exploit the political opportunities that this ingenious adaptation provided as occasions arose, and further centralized the administrative control of Kano emirate under the chiefship to promote the interests of his dynasty and his sons.

Under the new territorial organization, the primary responsibilities for tax-collection and district administration fell clearly on the heads of sub-districts, who were thus simultaneously exposed to the temptations and risks of peculation, defalcation and maladministration. Being responsible solely for the supervision of these subordinate *hakimai*, the district heads themselves had limited direct responsibilities for the government or taxation of their sub-districts. They were officially required to serve primarily as channels of communication and guidance between the emir and his vizier in Kano and the heads of the sub-districts under their care. In consequence, they had little direct opportunity for tax peculation, abuse of power and other malpractices which the British were quick to investigate and punish. In effect, by this division of administrative labor, incentive and opportunity, such senior territorial officials as the Makama, Madawaki, Ciroma, Turaki Manya, Sarkin Dawaki Mai Tuta, Sarkin Bai, Galadima, Wombai, Barde, Sarkin Dutse, Sarkin Gaya, Sarkin Dawakin Tsakar Gida, and the Sarkin Rano enjoyed excellent prospects for continued tenure of office, whereas their immediate subordinates, the lesser *hakimai* who were directly in charge of district administration, faced correspondingly high risks of dismissal and punishment for administrative misconduct, particularly in the collection, report and transfer of local tax. The incidence of dismissals among *hakimai* who exercised direct responsibilities for local administration on such essentially Western grounds and criteria remained high throughout Abbas' reign, whereas only one of his senior district chiefs, the Turaki Manya Salihi, was dismissed in 1914 for tax embezzlement. In short, under Cargill's *gunduma*, senior offices invested with wide but indirect and rather vague territorial responsibilities enjoyed far greater security of tenure by virtue of their administrative situation than did territorial offices of secondary or tertiary rank, including village chiefships, which exercised direct executive responsibilities for territorial administration and tax collection.

As we have seen, in pre-colonial days most *sarautu* operated through staffs of titled *lawanai* recruited from the holder's kin, clients and slaves. Thus there might be a Shamakin Galadima, a Shentalin Galadima, a Madakin Shamaki, a Ciroman Shamaki, and the like. The senior of these titled *lawanai* normally served fiefholding officials as *jekadu*. On the establishment of the new territorial system, when the traditional fiefholders moved to their new rural headquarters, they took along their *lawanai* as official staff. In each district the supervising district Head, for example, the Madawaki or Wombai, allocated responsibilities for communications with the *hakimai* who administered specific sub-districts under his care among his *lawanai*. At the level of the sub-district, the *hakimi*'s *lawanai* were likewise allotted responsibilities for communications with and supervision of specified village chiefs in the area. It is evident that such arrangements preserved the now forbidden institution of *jekadu* by adapting it to the conditions of the new territorial organization and reducing the physical and social separation of rural communities and chiefs from the fiefholder's *lawanai*. Simultaneously, this preservation of traditional *lawanai* structures in the district and its component sub-districts emphasized the distinction between the office and title of the supervising district Head and those of his several subordinates. By thus preserving their traditional official establishments, supervisory district chiefs and executive sub-district chiefs preserved their mutually distinct identities and precluded assimilation. Thus, although the Wombai supervised the sub-districts of Taura, Ringim, Sankara, Majiya, Buduru and Dabi, the chiefs of these sub-districts were neither attached as subordinate staff to his office and assimilated to *lawanai*, nor were they brought into any structured or direct relationships with one another. Each sub-district and its chiefship remained discrete, though in many areas territorial office lacked firm hereditary ties.

1908–1910

The Chronicle relates that while Abbas

> was enjoying the pleasures of office, a certain European came called Kagil, more commony known as Mai-Gunduma, the territorial re-organiser, and he dismissed two of the emir's sons, the Waziri Abdullahi (Bayero) and the Ciroma Abdulkadir, together with his (Abbas') friend the Ma'aji Siddi (Sadi). This grieved the chief sorely. And not long after another European released several *hakimai* whom the emir had imprisoned because they had embezzled the tax. Then Abdullahi was re-appointed as Ciroman Kano while Abdulkadir went to the school at Nassarawa

which was established in 1910. Then Mr. Temple came and put a stop to intrigue between the Europeans and the *hakimai* because from the first the *hakimai* used to talk to the Europeans without the emir's knowledge. The emir then asserted his power and dismissed the vizier Alabar Sarki and made Gidado Waziri of Kano, appointing the Magatakarda Malam Ibrahim as Alkali. Following this, he apportioned salaries for the territorial chiefs, each one in proportion to their work, and likewise for the remaining officials. In addition, he initiated many different developments; for this reason the men of Kano still like Mr. Temple.[56]

The events just related took place between January 1908, when the *gunduma* was effected, and January 1910 when C. L. Temple left Kano after serving one year as substantive Resident. Following Cargill's retirement in June 1908, W.P. Hewby was appointed as Resident; but having occupied the office from July 29th to November 30th 1908, he was replaced by Temple in January 1909.[57]

In preparing the territorial reorganization, Cargill had pressed Abbas to replace his senior son, Abdullahi Bayero, who then held the title of vizier, by someone better qualified to fulfill the functions of the vizierate as Cargill conceived them. Evidently Cargill regarded the vizier as the emir's chief executive, having direct responsibility for such central administrative units as the treasury, the police, prisons, secretariat, judiciary, supervision of the capital and perhaps of its environs also. For various reasons it was preferable that such executive responsibilities should be entrusted to someone other than the ruler's son and chosen heir, and preferably to some senior cleric skilled in Muslim law and familiar with accounting and handling documents. After the expected demurrals, Abbas gave in; but to preserve Bayero's prominence and prospects, he then removed the Ciroma title from his younger son Abdulkadir, and conferred it on Bayero. As Waziri following Bayero, Abbas then appointed his slave Allah-bar-Sarki, thereby indicating his determination to direct that office, perhaps with a view to Bayero's reinstatement later on. As Waziri, the slave Allah-bar-Sarki was thus simply a cipher employed by Abbas to block Cargill's plans for the immediate development of a central vizierate less directly under his control. Abbas then bargained with Cargill to secure a suitable district as fief for the Ciroma Abdullahi Bayero.

In preparing the *gunduma* of 1908, Cargill had persuaded Abbas three years earlier to instruct his senior *hakimai* resident at Kano to proceed to specified rural towns, usually to their most important traditional fief, in order to supervise the administration of the districts around them. In 1908, when the junior *hakimai* were also directed to move from the city to the headquarters of their newly-constituted sub-districts, Abbas encountered some opposition and dissent. Some *hakimai* protested the loss of their traditional fiefs, while others protested their exclusion from the new order of sub-district heads. Despite this, Abbas implemented his part of the reorganization by placing officials of suitable rank in the unfilled district headships. However, by 1908 some *hakimai* who had moved out to the new districts during the past two years were discovered to have withheld or understated their tax receipts; and perhaps without formal trial by the Provincial staff, Abbas, whether on his own initiative or at the request of the British, placed some of these suspected or proven defaulters under arrest in the city gaol on the charge of embezzling emirate tax. After Cargill's retirement his successor, Hewby, soon requested that these delinquent *hakimai* should be released. Abbas was obliged to comply, but did not reappoint them to the titles they had forfeited.

In the prevailing circumstances such developments tended to subvert the emir's prestige and authority among the nobles and people, thereby encouraging intrigue against him. Such intrigue was directly addressed by *hakimai* and others seeking Abbas' downfall or their own advancement, to the British administrative staff, whose recent actions had demonstrated their ability to overrule and set aside the emir's decisions. For not only had Cargill compelled Abbas to replace his son Abdullahi Bayero as vizier, but his successor had also ordered the chief to release those subordinates he had sent to gaol following British directives. One consequence of these unsettling events was to encourage disloyal and subversive tendencies against Abbas' regime among his close kinsmen in office who were eligible to succeed.

In 1909, after Hewby's departure, Abbas dismissed his slave vizier, Allah-bar-Sarki, and gave the office to his Alkali, Muhammadu Gidado of the Bornawa Fulani clan. Gidado's elder brother Ahmadu, who then held the office of Limam, died shortly after, and was replaced by Abubakar, a son of Muhammadu Zarawa. As Chief Alkali, following Gidado's promotion to the vizierate, Abbas appointed his scribe, Ibrahim Maigari. Already disturbed by the *gunduma* and the new tax assessment, Cargill's departure further unsettled the political climate at Kano by apparently removing the emir's most important ally and adviser in the Provincial Administration. However Hewby was also quickly withdrawn; and C. L. Temple who replaced him halted the deterioration that had followed Cargill's illness and retirement and threatened to unseat Abbas.

Some Relevant Developments

Stimulated by such emergencies as the famine of 1904 and the rebellions at Hadeija and Satiru in 1906, the Protectorate Government had moved quickly to improve its communications with those Northern states that were geographically central, especially Kano and Zaria. In 1904 the telegraph line from Lugard's headquarters at Zungeru reached Kano, thereby enabling the High Commissioner to keep abreast of local developments. In 1907 work began on the railway from Lagos to Kano at Governor Girouard's recommendation.[58] By 1911 the railway was completed, largely by means of forced labor, and thereafter trade between Kano, southern Nigeria and Britain accelerated. In 1909 Hans Vischer opened the first Government school at Kano near to the Provincial Office and the emir's summer palace at Nassarawa. Vischer's school was designed to cater for the sons of Fulani aristocrats, including the dynasties and leading clerical lineages. It provided instruction in Hausa in Roman script and in arithmetic. Following Lugard's directive, Christian propaganda was avoided, and no Christian Missions were allowed at Kano without the emir's permission. Vischer's school introduced young ruling Fulani to those rudiments of Western education that were clearly desirable for nobles seeking administrative careers under the Anglo-Fulani regime. By thus appealing to the aristocracy to educate their sons at the school, the British tried to equip the ruling Fulani with the educational skills they would need to maintain their political and administrative dominance in the Northern emirates.

In 1908 Cargill attempted to carry out a field assessment of selected villages in the western districts under the Madawaki Huseini. The records of this survey have been destroyed, but the attempt was abandoned, ostensibly on account of the unrest and suspicion created among the peasantry. Some military patrols were needed to restore calm. In the following year, after more careful preparation and explanations of their objectives, and perhaps also some reduction in the tax rate, a more successful attempt was made at tax assessment of selected villages in the newly constituted districts. At this date, district, sub-district and village headmen were remunerated by fixed shares of the revenues that each collected; and the annual tax was generally paid in cowries exchanged at the rate of 20,000 cowries to 12 shillings in Kano.[59] Until then in the absence of any British reassessment, taxation was "based on the old native assessment. The result is not very satisfactory, there being a certain amount of discontent,"[60] perhaps because the tax was sharply increased at prevailing rates of exchange. Hitherto, no attempt had been made to reform the traditional patterns of taxation by amalgamating the various occupational, crop and poll taxes into a single land tax such as Lugard advocated; and in the absence of any systematic reassessment, neither the population figures nor the actual incidence of taxes were clearly known. For Kano in 1907–08 it is reported that "the average incidence per head of Land Revenue or Cattle Tithe is approximately per adult male 3s; per adult male and female, 1s."[61] Thus at the prevailing exchange rate for cowries, *kudin kasa* had apparently risen from its pre-colonial level of 3,000 cowries per male householder to 5,000 per adult male in the past five years. It is therefore easy to appreciate the grounds of public unrest.

Only in 1908, on the transfer of *hakimai* from Kano to the rural areas, did the Provincial Administration discover the traditional *bin kanu* arrangements for administration of transhumant pastoral Fulani.

> In past years, *Jangali* or Cattle Tithe, had been collected throughout the Protectorate on the herds, in whatever Province they were grazing, by the medium of collectors; the herds return to the Provinces of origin during the wet season and the tithe is now collected by the headmen of the district from which they emanate. This has resulted in a great improvement; a better check has been obtained, and a great increase has been shown in receipts. The effect on the Province has also been good.[62]

With the transfer of responsibilities for the collection of *jangali* from pastoralists in their home areas during the wet season to the *hakimai* in charge of these districts, the old Fulani chiefs and camp headmen were now responsible to the Heads of their wet-season home districts for the tax due from their collectivities; but although this "reform" in pastoral taxation was generalized throughout the Protectorate, the traditional *bin kanu* jurisdiction was modified in some particulars. Though remaining under the jurisdiction of their camp or lineage headmen, pastoralists now became liable to the *hakimai* of any districts in which they committed an offence, although as before, the Muslim death duty levied on their estates, like the cattle tithe or *jangali*, was paid to the *hakimi* who administered their wet season home area.

In 1907–1908 the northern frontier of Kano Province was finally delimited by an Anglo-French boundary commission, after several had traversed and re-traversed this section for some years without achieving a settlement. Following the first abortive attempt by British Divisional staff at field assessments for taxation in western Kano, some 20,000 people left that area to settle in southern Katsina a few miles away, where much fertile land had lain waste since Dan Baskore's raids from Maradi.[63] In 1907 the Administration experimented with the introduction of Native Dispensaries at Kano, but without success. "The emir of Kano sends his children and followers, but the native as a rule, the peasant, seems suspicious of modern medical science."[64] To dispel such suspicion and ignorance, but also to provide the minimum clerical staff required by the Provincial Administrations at Kano and elsewhere, when the school at Nassarawa opened, one hundred adult malams familiar with the Ajemic script were enrolled for instruction in the Roman script the British had introduced. Within a year the number of malams enrolled at the school had doubled,[65] thus helping to meet an immediate need for literate Hausa assistants in the Native and Provincial Administrations.

The Treasury and Tax Reform

In his brief period as Resident Kano, C. L. Temple presided over three interrelated developments with far-reaching implications; namely, tax reassessment and rationalization, a reorganization of the Native Administration, and the establishment of a modern State Treasury in Kano, the *Beit-el-Mal*, which the British Provincial staff could assist and supervise, as the emirate counterpart of the Protectorate Treasury.

In 1910 the work of reassessing rural communities for taxation purposes proceeded rapidly. As a result, the British were able to simplify the prevailing tax pattern by combining the various crop and poll taxes into a single *kudin kasa* which varied in incidence with the estimated incomes of householders from trade, agriculture and craft production. As before, Fulani pastoralists remained liable only for *jangali*. The statutory Muslim tithe (*zakka*), death duties (*ushiran gado*), and court fees were also collected. As malams skilled in Roman script became available from Hans Vischer's school at Nassarawa, the Administration was able to compile annual reports of the populations of all villages by households, and classified these village and district populations by their sex and physical condition. For that purpose each *hakimi* was provided with a scribe trained to prepare and check these compilations, copies of which were forwarded to the emir's office and to the Provincial Administration, thereby furnishing these central units with the systematic and verifiable information they required in order to evaluate the needs and quality of the rural administration. In essence, this attempt to base Kano taxation on careful periodic assessments, annual compilations, and routine submissions of population and tax returns, marks the introduction of bureaucratic conceptions of government and administration in the emirate, and contrasts sharply with the fiscal irresponsibility, uncontrolled tax collection procedures, and disregard for census in pre-colonial Kano.

The stage was thus set for a prolonged struggle between those bureaucratic models of government advocated by the British, and the aristocratic conceptions which the ruling Fulani had inherited and cherished as custodians of the conquest state and Islam. To Fulani aristocrats, provided they observed and upheld Islam, obeyed their superior and kept the Hausa subject, it was neither necessary to justify their official conduct, nor to balance their financial accounts; for the British, however, accurate and comprehensive assessments were indispensable for public taxation. The British also expected the revenues returned by state officials to correspond exactly with their recorded receipts, whatever principles legitimated their regime. In large part, the subsequent history of native administration at Kano illustrates the conflict between these antithetical conceptions of the aims and methods of public administration.

To secure prompt returns of population and tax assessments from the new district Administrations, to keep these and other important documents safely on file, to handle communications between the emir and his district and sub-district chiefs on matters of taxation, police, the judiciary, corvée and other routine topics, to handle enquiries addressed from district chiefs to the emir or Provincial Administration, and to supervise the central Treasury, prisons, police, the city administration, judiciary, markets and similar institutions, an adequately staffed central secretariat at Kano was essential. With Abbas' agreement, Temple developed the basis of this secretariat under the immediate control of the Waziri Muhammadu Gidado, to whom the Ma'aji, the Chief Alkali, the Sarkin Dogarai and the "Yari," as the British renamed the Sankurmi, the Prison Warder, were required to report routinely. Besides supervising these central services, the vizier was also instructed to handle and coordinate all communications between the emir and senior district chiefs, who in turn handled communications with their sub-district heads. *Hakimai* in the small districts immediately around and east of Kano City were instructed to communicate directly with the vizier on all routine administrative matters. By these means, Temple simultaneously established an executive vizierate at Kano, and effectively reorganized the Native Administration (N.A.) at the centre, so that it could handle communications between the emir, the rural and the Provincial administrations efficiently and routinely.

Clearly, by placing this central secretariat under the vizier and requiring him to record and file all important communications, reports on population, tax assessments and the like for inspection and future reference, Temple also sought to eliminate the traditional communication structures of senior throne slaves and eunuchs through whom the emirs of Kano had hitherto conducted business with their *hakimai*. However, while all official correspondence of interest to the Provincial Administration now passed through the vizier's office to the emir or district head, the old communication channels, though emptied of much contemporary business, were still available to the emir for other affairs and messages to his *hakimai*. In short, Temple's new vizierate did not immediately and totally disestablish the ancient communications structure through throne slaves and eunuchs, as he may have hoped.

In 1911 the Governor of Northern Nigeria, Sir Hesketh Bell, reviewing developments of the preceding year, remarked:

> We can only govern these people satisfactorily through their natural leaders, and it is essential that we should train up a native Civil Service which, under our guidance and supervision, could adopt the principles of honest administration in such a way

as to conflict as little as possible with the traditions, customs and religion of the country.

The most important step taken in that direction during the year was the establishment in each native State of a Treasury, to be known as *"Beit-el-Mal."* This institution regulates the expenditure of that portion of the local revenue which is annually assigned to the Native Administration of each emirate for its support and maintenance. The establishment of a *Beit-el-Mal* consolidates the rank and authority of the emirs and Chiefs in each Province. It strengthens the position of the native judiciary and diminishes extortion and corruption ...

To each emir has been assigned a fixed Civil List proportionate to the population and importance of the country. The native judges and magistrates will, in future, receive definite salaries, punctually paid, instead of being dependent on the spasmodic generosity of the emirs or more disreputable sources of profit. A fixed percentage of the taxes will be paid, as commission, to the the District administrations, and every native holding a recognised office will receive remuneration commensurate with his services. To Mr. Temple and Mr. Palmer is largely due the credit of initiating this system.[66]

H.R. Palmer had conceived and developed the first *Beit-el-Mal* in the Protectorate as the State treasury for Katsina emirate in that Division of Kano Province, for which he was administratively responsible. Following the overthrow and dispersal of the Dallazawa dynasty, his friend, the former Durbi Muhammadu Dikko, had been appointed as emir on Palmer's recommendation; and, within three years, apparently at Dikko's suggestion, Palmer had established the Katsina State treasury on modern lines with proper accounting procedures for the receipts and expenditures of state revenues.[67] As Resident Kano and Palmer's immediate superior, C. L. Temple had authorized this experiment; and following its evident success at Katsina, he set about establishing another at Kano in 1910–11. The new institution, which had excellent Muslim precedents, facilitated many other innovations which were essential if the Native Administration of the Muslim emirates was to be reformed, rationalized and assimilated to Western bureaucratic models. Hesketh Bell, then Governor of the Protectorate, was quick to appreciate its varied utility; and by 1911, at his orders, a *Beit-el-Mal* was established in every important emirate throughout Northern Nigeria.

The scope and implications of these fiscal reforms are evident in his account.

The total amount of the taxes paid by a native unit are divided into four parts. Two of these form the Government share, and are paid into the general revenue. The other two are paid into the *Beit-el-Mal* (Native Treasury). One of these is earmarked for the payment of fixed emoluments individually to the emir, his Councillors, his police, his official messengers, the officials told off by him to look after roads, buildings, sanitation, and public works generally, and to the payment of the native judges. Also to defray the cost of public works such as markets, jails, etc., road making, well making, of education, and of the subsistence of persons who, according to Muslim tenets, should receive state aid. Also towards establishing a reserve fund, in case at any time, owing to the failure of crops, it should be necessary to remit a portion of the taxes. The remaining fourth share is divided among the District and Village Heads in proportion to the amounts of rents and taxes for the collection of which each is responsible. In some Provinces, District Heads have been placed on fixed salaries, notably Bornu, but it has not been decided as to whether this system should be adopted generally.[68]

At Kano it does not seem that the district chiefs and sub-district chiefs were placed on salaries before 1915, perhaps in deference to their objections, expressed through Abbas. Till then they were remunerated by commissions through shares of the revenues they submitted to the Native Treasury from their districts. Meanwhile the emir, his vizier, the Alkalin Kano, Ma'aji and certain other officials of the central administration were placed on salaries, scaled according to their relative rank and importance in the traditional and contemporary systems. Administrative energies were then concentrated on increasing the central revenues by more extensive and detailed assessments of rural communities.

In Kano and Katsina the basic tax (*haraji* or *kudin kasa*) was then assessed on farms at standard rates of nine pence, one shilling, or eight pence per acre according to the crops and quality of the soil,[69] in addition to the Muslim *zakka* collected by the native officials. To apply this principle equitably to farmers whose cultivations varied in acreage, productivity and crop, Provincial staff were directed to survey and estimate the acreages, yields and market values of the cultivations on which tax was levied by measuring their boundaries and diagonals in paces (*taki*), so that tax burdens could be distributed in correspondence with the varying sizes and values of farmers' cultivations. Initiated in 1910, at Kumbotso, Kiru, Minjibir, Zakirai and Dawakin Tofa in the densely settled "Home districts" around Kano City, these *taki* assessments were extended annually until the entire emirate, excluding Kano City and Gwaram, had been surveyed and mapped by the *taki* technique by 1917.[70] Despite many limitations, these *taki* assessments generated substantial increases in the revenues received from rural taxation by the *Beit-el-Mal* and Protectorate Treasuries. Table 7.1 illustrates some effects of these developments by comparing Government receipts from Kano Provincial revenues for the years 1903–1912 with the estimated costs of the Provincial and Native Administrations at Kano for the year 1911–12, shortly after the institution of the *Beit-el-Mal*. These reforms increased the Protectorate's receipts from the land revenues of the Native Administrations by more than £100,000 for the year 1911–12; and the revenues of Native Administrations increased proportionately.

At Kano, Abbas clearly welcomed these developments in tax assessment, tax collection and fiscal accounting for private as well as public reasons. These British innovations promoted a rapid and continuous growth in the revenues of the Kano central administration, thereby relieving Abbas of previous difficulties in the remuneration of his administrative and judicial staff. Whereas in 1908–09, the year of Cargill's *gunduma*, the Native Treasury's receipts totalled less than £25,000, in 1911–12 they exceeded £50,000, and by 1917 they had reached £70,000. Abbas had excellent reasons for supporting the fiscal reforms initiated by Cargill and accelerated by Temple, since they probably ensured much larger revenues and higher proportions of the tax-receipts for the central Treasury than any ruler of Kano had previously received. As emir, Abbas drew a salary of £4,800 per annum, roughly equivalent to 158 million cowries at prevailing rates. His vizier, Muhammadu Gidado, received £1,000 per annum and the Chief Alkali £480. In addition, the emir retained his traditional shares in the *zakka* collected by *hakimai* from their

TABLE 7.1   Kano Finances, 1903–1912 [71]

(a) Government's share of revenues from land and cattle tax in Kano Province
    1903–1912

	£		£
1903–04	2,428	1908–09	51,842
1904–05	7,149	1909–10	56,588
1905–06	7,141	1910–11	69,659
1906–07	13,477	1911–12	70,014
1907–08	24,556		

(b) Government revenues and expenditure in Kano Province 1911–12

Government receipts	£ 70,015
Government expenditure:	£
Provincial administration	
(Personal emoluments)	9,605
Police	–
Prisons	939
North Nigerian Regiment	24,365
Internal transport	789
Total	35,698
Balance	34,317

(c) Revenues and expenditures of Kano Emirate Treasury, 1911–1912

Revenues, All	£ 51,800
Expenditure:	£
Salaries, central administration	6,436
Salaries, District administration	9,900
Salaries, Village administration	6,600
Judicial	2,760
Treasury	510
Roads recurrent	60
Police and Prisons	3,179
Public Works (minor)	3,850
Education	1,240
Land Survey	500
Medical	32
Miscellaneous	120
Total	35,247
Balance	16,583

fiefs, and distributed some of this to such central officials as the vizier, Alkali, Ma'aji and Limam, whose offices lacked adequate *hurumai* (glebes).[72]

To appreciate Abbas' response to these and other transforming innovations advocated by British officials in Kano, we should recognize the many advantages and benefits he derived from them. To conceive Abbas' role in these developments as purely passive or even resistant misrepresents the situation and his reponse. Abbas evidently welcomed these developments and participated positively in their promotion. For example, in 1909 when the Kano *Beit-el-Mal* was installed and the emir, vizier and Chief Alkali were placed on salaries, so were 283 *dogarai*, the slave police, who had previously derived their support from the emir, thereby formally relieving him of at least part of the costs of their upkeep. That year, Abbas' Judicial Council was also reconstituted to include the vizier, Ma'aji, Alkali and five learned malams selected by him. As the highest tribunal within the emirate, the Judicial Council was authorized to review and hear appeals from all Muslim courts in Kano.[73]

In 1912 when the influx of Southern Nigerians to Kano began, following completion of the Lagos-Kano railway, Abbas approved a proposal from the Provincial administration to establish a new town, the Sabon Gari, outside the city walls for southern immigrants, few of whom were Muslims. In 1913 a grand durbar was held at Kano to honor Lugard, who had returned as Governor-General to amalgamate the Protectorate with Southern Nigeria. On this occasion Abbas also had the honor of welcoming the sultan of Sokoto, Muhammadu Attahiru II, his vizier and senior chiefs at Kano, together with Fulani emirs and nobles from other states. In 1914 when the World War I began, for local and imperial reasons the Government of Nigeria decided to overrun the German Cameroons. Abbas authorised an annual contribution of £17,000 from the Kano Treasury towards the Protectorate's war expenses, thereby demonstrating his support for the Anglo-Fulani regime. He had also earlier approved an annual contribution of £1,000 per year from his Treasury to Hans Vischer's school at Nassarawa. Yet despite these outlays and its recurrent expenses, the Kano treasury was able to set aside the sum of £85,000 between 1914 and 1919 for investment as reserve against future contingencies.[74] In essence, despite substantial losses of revenue by peculations of various kinds, by 1914 the financially and administratively unstable emirate that Abbas inherited from Aliyu had been transformed into an orderly, prosperous and economically expansive state, following its conquest and the administrative reorganizations initiated by Cargill and Temple.

In 1914, for the second time in 10 years, Kano suffered severe famine due to failure of the rains. In anticipation, grain supplies had been sought in other provinces, and much food was brought in from Southern Nigeria for distribution at Kano by the new railway. To relieve public distress an attempt was made to distribute the grain tithe which the *hakimai* still collected annually from their districts. This scheme was not entirely successful, as some district heads had already sold their shares of tithe to the starving *talakawa* at considerable profit before receiving their instructions. In response to criticism, the *hakimai* protested that they had never been forbidden to sell their *zakka* receipts; but perhaps in consequence, not long after this incident, *talakawa* were allowed to distribute their *zakka* freely, to clerics or the deserving poor, thereby abolishing the *hakimai's* prescriptive rights to all of it. In 1914 also an inexplicable deficit of £742 was discovered in the Native Treasury, which led to the replacement of the Ma'aji Ba'adamasi by Babari dan Sali (Umaru), a senior Treasury clerk who had attended Hans Vischer's school. In the same year the title of Sankurmi lapsed on the death of its last holder, a throne slave. In its place, the foreign title of Yari preferred by the British was instituted with responsibility for prison inspection, records and supervision.[75]

Official Salaries, Roles and Rank

In 1915 H. R. Palmer, while reviewing the administration of Kano emirate over the year, noted that the excellent harvest of 1915 had revived the economy and people, and commented as follows:

> Decentralisation of Central Kano administration is increasingly necessary. Some steps have been taken by increasing the duties of the Ma'ajin Watali, in whom the emir had confidence, thus making it possible for the emir to keep in touch with the Native Treasury. In taxation the emir's personal influence is so important that it is almost impossible to relieve him of the direct responsibility for prompt collection ... The Ma'ajin Watali is now the public trustee and receiver in bankruptcy of Kano emirate; he also has charge of fraudulent debtors and others under detention, in addition to being the chief urban official of Kano City and the emir's representative when he and the Waziri are away. He should be recognised as ranking after the Ma'ajin Kano on the Council.[76]

As regards district administration, Palmer reports,

> salaries for District Heads and Sub-district Heads have been instituted, (but whereas) some e.g., Ciroma, Madaki, Makama, draw (good) salaries, the following of high rank, Sarkin Bai (£260), Wombai (£240), Barden Kano (£160), Sarkin Gaya (£250), Galadima (£200), must be augmenting their incomes from other sources.
>   The Kano chiefs are divided as follows and ranked in the order shown:

Hakimai (related to emir):	
(1) Galadima, salary	£200
(2) Wombai	£240
(3) Ciroma	£1,000
(4) Turaki Manya	£550

Hakimai (not related to emir):	
(1) Madawaki	£1,000
(2) Makama	£800
(3) Sarkin Dawaki mai Tuta	£420
(4) Barden Kano	£160
(5) Sarkin Bai	£260

District Heads (formerly subject to *Hakimai*):	
(1) Sarkin Rano	£300
(2) Sarkin Dutse	£380
(3) Sarkin Gaya	£250
(4) Sarkin Karaye	£600

Sarkin Dawakin Tsakar Gida has no definite precedence among the others, but comes midway on the list ...

I do not think it is a matter to be lost sight of (that) a "salary" becomes automatically a"'grade" and is a different thing to a "share" of proceeds of tax ...

In Kano the total sum paid to District officials was only reduced in 1915 by a very small amount, so that the sub-district heads have gained a very great deal in position at the expense of the District Heads. The emir now finds that the Sub-district Heads are bidding fair to usurp the position of the District Heads in some instances.

There are other things to consider besides efficient tax gathering, and inherited position is a very important asset in the administration of Kano emirate. Sub-district Heads are largely the followers and social inferiors of the District Heads ... Our future aim should be to gradually reduce the districts to somewhat smaller dimensions and also to increase the number of sub-districts within each district till they become simply towns or groups of villages ...

Taxes are still anticipated (*falle*), cattle are still concealed, as also *zakka*. Large sums are borrowed from traders to make good deficiencies which cannot be satisfactorily accounted for, and repaid again later by "*falle*."

The native mind considers that Government has no right to complain of a chief who renders to Caesar as much as Caesar can find out to be due, even though he make a good deal himself. As long as chiefs took a share of the taxes brought in, it was almost impossible to lay much stress on the distinction between Government's share and the share of the collector; but with the introduction of salaries, chiefs are bound to bring their full tribute to account, and thus find it more difficult to conceal temporary financial expedients ...

Introduction of salaries to the two larger emirates in this Province has hit the District Heads in two ways—1. By actually reducing their legitimate share (a) in Kano by handing over a good deal of it (too much I think) to Sub-district Heads: (b) in Katsina by a simple reduction of salaries by £1300. 2. By making it difficult to obtain pickings, and by forcing immediate cash payment of sums often before taken in kind, and realised at leisure.

None of the District Heads in Kano emirate should have less than £420 per annum—even if the Sub-district Heads get less (i.e. than presently). Unless the District Heads have an adequate personal salary (a) we cannot fairly come down on them for peculation or illicit exaction; (b) they will have a permanent grievance that their salaries have been greatly reduced for no fault of their own ...

In 1915 Village Heads have been paid their percentages (of revenue collected) by the emirs. In all but Kano emirate, in 1916 it is hoped to start regular monthly payments of town or group heads.[77]

This report enables us to identify in some detail Abbas' influence on the application of the financial reforms introduced by Temple and his successors. On subdividing Kano into compact territorial units, as mentioned above, Cargill and Abbas had grouped small units as sub-districts under the senior Fulani officeholders—the Galadima, Madaki (Madawaki), Makama, Sarkin Bai, Sarkin Dawaki mai Tuta, Wombai, Sarkin Dawakin Tsakar Gida, Turaki Manya, Barde—and the four senior rural chiefs, Sarkin Rano, Sarkin Dutse, Sarkin Gaya and Sarkin Karaye. At that date, 1908, district heads and sub-district heads were both remunerated by fixed shares of the taxes they returned from the units under their care. The tax ratios retained by these supervisory and executive *hakimai* adequately remunerated and distinguished them, since the supervisor retained shares of taxes received from the several executives responsible to him. Thus, Cargill and Abbas had assured for the supervisory district chiefs superior incomes in keeping with their senior status. With that objective in mind, districts had been demarcated to yield incomes proportionate to the traditional status of their rulers. For example, as the senior royal title holder the Galadima had the largest district, and should thus receive the largest annual dividend. By virtue of rank, the Wombai had the second largest, the Turaki Manya who ranked third of royal *hakimai*, the third largest, and the Ciroma, as their junior, the smallest. Of non-royal *hakimai* transferred from central Kano, the Madawaki and Makama had the two most lucrative districts, followed by the Sarkin Bai and the Sarkin Dawaki mai Tuta. By these allocations, Cargill and Abbas had tried to correlate the annual incomes, territorial jurisdictions, and relative status of these officials, ranking them primarily by reference to their titles and descent.

With the introduction of salaries for native officials, following the establishment of the *Beit-el-Mal*, the basis on which Cargill had arranged that differential remuneration of senior and junior *hakimai* was removed. New decisions had to be made concerning the amounts due as salaries to each of the senior rural officials. Such decisions could have been taken on either of several grounds, separately or together. Had the preceding formula been followed, the salaries of these rural chiefs would correspond proportionately with the amounts of revenue that each turned in to the native Treasury. Alternatively, their salaries could correspond approximately with the numbers of people and size of the areas under their administration; or officials could be paid salaries that corresponded to their relative rank in the traditional or contemporary official system. Finally, they might be remunerated differentially at the emir's whim by criteria of his own choice; and evidently that was the basis on which Abbas decided the amounts that were paid to each of his senior district heads.

Notably the Galadima and Wombai, although administering larger districts than any other royal officials, received much lower salaries than their brother the Turaki Manya Salihi, who was nonetheless dismissed in 1914 for embezzlement, while his successor, Abubakar, grandson of Sarkin Kano Abdullahi, was dismissed in 1919 for peculation.[78] The Ciroma Abdullahi Bayero, Abbas' chosen heir, despite his modest fief, received five times as much as the Galadima and four times as much as the Wombai. Indeed the Ciroma, the Madawaki (Madaki), and Waziri Muhammadu Gidado received identical amounts, being the most highly paid officials under the emir. Of non-royal district chiefs, the baYole Madawaki received the highest salary, followed by the Jobawa Makama (£800), the Sarkin Dawaki Mai Tuta (£420), and the Sarkin Bai Abdulkadiri (£260). In terms of their relative status in the traditional polity of Kano, such differentiation was clearly anomalous.

Another district Head, who received £160 per year, the Barden Kano, was mistakenly classified by Palmer as no kin of the emir. Actually Abbas' Barde Abdu Na Gwangwazo was Abdullahi's grandson, and thus his nephew. Notably, of the four rural chiefs elevated to district headships under Cargill's *gunduma*, three received salaries exceeding that of the Sarkin Bai; but the most senior, the Sarkin Rano, received only half as much as the most junior, the Sarkin Karaye, Usuman, a baSuleibe of differing lineage from the emir. Nonetheless Palmer's remark that "salary becomes automatically a grade" is not correct; rather differential salary indicated the emir's differential favour. Thus, although the Galadima received the lowest salary of all district heads except the Barde, his official pre-eminence remained unchallenged. Even so, by grossly underpaying the Galadima and over-paying the Ciroma, Abbas ensured that their unequal remuneration would facili-tate his son's succession in place of his brother; and when the Galadima Umaru died at Fogolawa, his district headquarters in 1917, Abbas appointed Umaru's son, Muhammadu Bello, to the title and district.

Evidently the British Administration respected Abbas' right as emir to decide the distribution of salaries, titles, authority, and functions among his officials without exercising their veto. Although Palmer recognised that the remuneration of district chiefs at Kano was inequitable, he also accepted his inability to change this. At most the Administration could override the emir's decision to dismiss a district chief or other official who was innocent of administrative or political offence. The British could also demand the dismissal of officials who were found guilty of illicit exactions, oppression or tax embezzlement; but they could not compel the emir to promote or enrich particular officials. The British were thus constrained to accept certain conditions as unalterable. For example, in 1916 the Divisional officials in Katsina found eleven district heads and 35 village chiefs guilty of tax embezzlement; so, being faced with risks of administrative break-down if the delinquent district heads were all dismissed, they had to content themselves with demanding repayment of the missing monies, while placing them on probation.[79]

At Kano, where the much larger population and tax revenues assured higher average returns to district chiefs, dismissals for embezzlement proceeded rou-tinely as part of the annual tax collection. In 1910 the Dan Iya Ibrahim, a nephew of Abbas, the Sarkin Dutse Halidu, a baJelube, and the Dan Isa Mamman Mai Ruwa, a brother of Abbas, were dismissed for embezzlement, while the Dan Lawan Mamman Unkulu, another of Abbas' kinsmen, was dismissed and dis-graced for providing "a gang of bandits" with political protection and cover. In 1910 Abbas had to dismiss his brother, the Dan Buram Ibrahim Cigari, who administered Wasai, Gasgainu, Sarbi and adjacent towns from headquarters at Minjibir, north of Kano. Abbas replaced Cigari as Dan Buram in charge of the same district by his younger brother Haruna. In 1911 the Dan Iya Mujeli of the Daneji lineage whom Abbas had appointed on dismissing Ibrahim the previous year, was found guilty of tax defalcations and removed; and so too Halilu, the baJelube successor of his kinsman, the Sarkin Dutse Halidu. In 1912 the Dan Tube was likewise removed from his district at Tambarawa. In 1914 the Turaki Manya Salihi and the Mai Anguwan Mundubawa Zakari were both dismissed; and Zakari's successor, his brother Mamman Taru, another baMundube, held that office for less than a year before being discovered.[80] However, of the supervisory district chiefs, only the Sarkin Dutse and the Turaki Manya, were dismissed at this period for mishandling tax or maladministration. Being primarily charged with communications between sub-district chiefs and Kano, at that date the supervi-sory district chiefs lacked executive roles and were administratively redundant.

Palmer's remark already cited that "in taxation the emir's personal influence is so important, it is almost impossible to relieve him of direct responsibility for prompt collection," suggests that sub-district heads obeyed orders emanating from the emir, rather than their district heads.

In delimiting the boundaries of his new administrative districts, Cargill had estimated their populations, since success or failure of the scheme turned on its efficiency and effectiveness in the administration of local communities rather than empty land. Even so, in 1908–10 several districts in the densely settled central area might easily have been combined, as the short distances between communities there facilitated communication and administration. Conversely, in some outlying districts, where population was thinly spread and communications poor, district subdivisions were later found necesssary to ensure effective local administration. These revisions of the territorial organization began in 1912 with the amalgamation of the sub-districts of Tambarawa and Dawaki ta Kudu following Dan Tube's dismissal.

In 1914, on Abbas' insistence, the Ciroma Abdullahi Bayero was placed in charge of the ten Home Districts surrounding Kano, namely, Kunya, Kiru, Minjibir, Gezawa, Gabasawa, Zakirai, Tsakuwa, Dawaki ta Kudu, Kumbotso and Ungogo. By this measure Abbas sought, firstly, to elevate and enhance the Ciroma's status and political prospects; secondly, to reduce his vizier's executive authority and importance by transferring to the Ciroma in the home districts those functions of communication and supervision which the vizier Gidado had previously discharged; and thirdly, to segregate the administration of the area around the city from that of other districts. However, as this experiment was no great success, it was terminated in 1916.[81] Evidently district heads in these home districts, many of whom were senior kinsmen of the Ciroma, resented being placed under him and preferred to deal, as before, with his seniors, the vizier and emir. The Ciroma himself also lacked sufficient experience to administer these consolidated districts. In 1916, when this scheme was abandoned, Ciroma Bayero was moved to Bici on the Katsina border and placed in charge of certain sub-districts formerly administered by the Madawaki (Madaki) from his headquarters at Dawakin Tofa. Thus in 1916 the large district formerly supervised by Madaki was divided into two approximately equal halves, one of which was transferred to the Ciroma Abdullahi Bayero, while the Madaki Mamudu, who had succeeded in 1914 on Huseini's death, administered the other.[82]

In 1916 also, the sub-districts of Godiya and Gwarzo were amalgamated to form a single district with its headquarters at Gwarzo under the Sarkin Dawaki mai Tuta. Getso, Karaye, Rogo, Gwangwan and Kabo, the five southern sub-districts of the district formerly supervised by the Sarkin Dawaki mai Tuta, were then placed under the Sarkin Karaye, thus splitting the large area allocated to the Sarkin Dawaki Mai Tuta in 1908 into two separate districts.[83] Again in 1916, the large area administered by the Sarkin Rano was halved when the new district of Tudun Wada was constituted by detaching the southern and western sub-districts from Rano.[84] In the same year the small home districts of Tsakuwa and Dawaki ta Kudu were amalgamated under the Dan Iya; and the sub-districts of Kura, Kiru, Madobi and Bebeji, hitherto distinct, were abolished by incorporation in a single extensive district under the Turaki Manya Abubakar dan Ayuba, a grandson of

Sarkin Kano Abdullahi, whose headquarters was Kura.[85] In 1917, on the death of the Makama Dahiru, a proposal to subdivide the large district administered by Makama from the old Jobawa centre of Wudil was mooted, but no action was taken. In the north, the various sub-districts contained in the Galadima's district were gradually amalgamated until by 1919 this consisted only of three large sub-districts administered from Babura, Garke, and from Fogolawa, the Galadima's headquarters. Thus while retaining its two-tiered form, Cargill's scheme underwent numerous changes in the decade that followed its introduction. These modifications involved the subdivision and amalgamation of some original units, and the development of new districts under the Ciroma, the Dan Kade in charge of Tudun Wada, and the Sarkin Karaye. As related below, further changes in this district organization continued to be made.

Continuity and Change in the Distribution of Office

At the executive level, the new territorial chiefships had absorbed and decentralized much of the state's routine administration. At the capital the essential central agencies, the secretariat, prisons, police, clerical and legal offices, the Treasury, and the developing Public Works Department, were all administered by the vizier under the emir's direction; and after the Ciroma's removal from Kano to Bici in 1916, Abbas also assumed personal responsibility for administration of the small districts surrounding Kano City. Beyond their perimeter, the *hakimai* exercised delegated jurisdictions over their separate districts, and were responsible for implementing the decisions of their local Alkali's courts, for nominating suitable candidates for village chiefships, for regulating the pastoral Fulani, turning in tax, corvée labor, *zakka* and other recurrent levies, arresting miscreants, settling immigrants, and the like. By 1915 the nature and implications of the dispersal of these critical regulatory functions and powers among the rural *hakimai* were clearly understood by the subject population, by experienced *hakimai* and by the emir. We may therefore review the lineage filiations of *hakimai*, sub-district chiefs and their supervisors, to examine the associations of particular titles with particular territorial districts, and to note any novel alignments as *hakimai* were transferred from one district or title to another.

Of the four senior rural chiefships converted by *gunduma* into supervisory district headships, namely Gaya, Rano, Dutse and Karaye, all except Dutse were vested in local lineages that claimed these titles traditionally by hereditary right. At Dutse, following a rapid succession of unsatisfactory local appointees, Abbas had installed the Dan Lawan Ahmadu Gurara of the Indorawa Fulani, a lineage client of the Suleibawa dynasty. After Ahmadu's dismissal for embezzlement and insubordination in 1917, Umaru, a baYole, succeeded as Dan Lawan in charge of Dutse until 1923, when that unit was split into two halves, Kiyawa being placed under the Dan Lawan Umaru, and Dutse under Suleimanu, a local baJelube.[86]

Of the large territories initially appropriated for titled heads of the founding Fulani lineages, the districts of Sarkin Bai and Makama remained under Dambazawa and Jobawa administration throughout Abbas' reign. Except for excision of a district for the Ciroma at Bici in 1916, the Yolawa domain under the Madawaki was also undisturbed. However, by 1916 the large district initially allocated to the Sarkin Dawaki mai Tuta Jamau, a lineal descendant of Shehu's flag bearer Malam

Jamau, had passed to other hands. The Sarkin Dawaki mai Tuta Malam Jamau, who was appointed in 1908, went mad in 1912 and was replaced by his younger brother Abdulkadir, who was dismissed within a year for ineptitude. On Abdulkadir's dismissal, the sub-district of Yelwa was transferred to Dawakin Tofa, and the Sarkin Karaye Usuman, of a Suleibawa lineage affiliated to Dabo's, was placed in charge of the remaining portions of Sarkin Dawaki's district on probation. In 1916, when Usuman was demoted for the administrative inadequacies noted above, the large area under his care was split into two separate districts, of which the northern unit, Gwarzo, was given to the Sarkin Dawaki mai Tuta Muhammadu Nata Allah, who belonged to one of the Dutse ruling families.[87] Thus by the end of Abbas' reign, the Suleibawan Jamau had lost their hereditary right to the title of Sarkin Dawaki mai Tuta, and with it their traditional territorial jurisdiction.

At Gabasawa, the Dan Amar Sule retained this title for the Mundubawa throughout Abbas' reign; but at Gezawa, two successive Mundubawa appointments to the senior lineage office, Mai Anguwan Mundubawa, were cancelled in quick succession, following which Ahmadu Gurara of the Indorawa lineage, attached to the Suleibawa, was appointed Mai Anguwa in charge of Gezawa. The Mundubawa thus lost one of their two hereditary offices in Abbas' reign. Following three successive dismissals of Dutse chiefs, Ahmadu Gurara was promoted from Gezawa to Dutse with the title of Dan Lawan, which had hitherto been reserved for junior royals; but on his promotion a younger brother, Yusufu, was sent to Gezawa as Mai Anguwan Mundubawa. At Babura it seems the sub-district chiefs were then either Dambazawa or Yerimawa leaders with the title of Dokaji. At Zakirai, following the death in 1918 of the Barde Kereriya Muhamman, Abdullahi's son, a baGyeni of the same name, a son of the former Chief Alkali Sule, succeeded as district head. At Kunya the district head was the Ja'idanawa Mai Bodinga, succeeded, following his dismissal in 1915 for tax embezzlement, by his ortho-cousin Zengi, both being of either Danejawa or Mundubawa descent. With these exceptions, all administrative districts and subdivisions had Suleibawa *hakimai* or supervisors. Thus in the extreme southeast, the Sarkin Dawaki Tsakar Gida Idirisu, a son of Sarkin Kano Abdu, supervised the sub-districts of Birnin Kudu, Buji, Gwaram and Fagam. After Idirisu's dismissal in 1915 for maladministration, Abdullahi, another baSuleibe, was appointed; and after his removal in 1917, Isa, a grandson of Abdullahi, succeeded.[88]

There is evidence that efforts were initially made to maintain or develop some stable associations of title, title-holding descent lines, and the new territorial divisions. Thus on Galadima Umaru's death in 1917, his son Bello succeeded as Galadima with identical responsibilities. From 1908 until 1939 all chiefs of Dawakin Kudu bore the title of Dan Iya, and most of them were Suleibawa princes. When the new district of Tudun Wada was set up in 1916, the village chief of Tudun Wada was appointed as district head with the minor royal title of Dan Kade. Following his dismissal in 1917 for embezzlement, Muhammadu Baba of the Dambazawa lineage succeeded as Dan Kade, but was removed in the following year for peculation. His successor, the baSuleibe Muhammadu, also entitled Dan Kade, went mad in less than a year, following which in succession Ibrahim, a baYole, and his son administered the district until 1955 with the title of Dan Kade. From 1908 to 1942 the district chiefs of Jahun bore the title of Barde. At Gwaram until

1945, despite the district subdivision of 1922, all district heads bore the title of Sarkin Dawaki Tsakar Gida.[89] In general, successive appointments of district chiefs throughout Kano at this period illustrate an intention to establish or preserve the associations of particular titles and territories, wherever practicable. In similar fashion, on the death or removal of a district head, some close kinsman was generally recruited to succeed. Only after two or more successive failures from the same lineage would Abbas normally transfer the title and territory to some other; but on such occasions the Suleibawa or their lineage clients were likely to profit, being numerous and disproportionately influential at court. However, as we have seen, Abbas also recruited Yolawa, Dambazawa, Gyenawa and Dutsawa to fill minor executive roles in rural areas.

Some Shigege Officials and Careers

Even so, inevitably the initial allocation of titles and territories designed by Abbas and Cargill changed significantly under the pressure of various exigencies before Abbas' death. Thus, like the Suleibawan Jamau, the Danejawa Fulani permanently lost their hereditary title Dan Iya in 1914, when Mujeli, the last Daneji Dan Iya, then in charge of Dawaki ta Kudu, was dismissed for embezzling tax and replaced by Muhammadu Nata Allah, Abbas' *shigege* client from Dutse. Nata Allah's career nicely illustrates the emergent patterns of promotional transfer which the territorial reorganization required and facilitated. Nata Allah belonged to one of the two competing Dutse lineages. Having fought for the Yusufawa, he was first rewarded by the Galadima Ishi'aku with an appointment as his *jekada* to Sarina, when Aliyu transferred that town to the Galadima in 1894. For several years Nata Allah supervised Sarina until Aliyu appointed him as Mai Anguwan Mundubawa late in his reign. However, when the Mundubawa title of Mai Anguwa was restored to them at the *gunduma* of 1908, Nata Allah was appointed Dan Isa in charge of Kumbotso. In 1914 when Tambarawa was amalgamated with Dawaki ta Kudu, following the dismissals of the Dan Tube from Tambarawa and the Dan Iya Mujeli from Dawaki ta Kudu, the Dan Isa Nata Allah was given charge of the new district with the senior title of Dan Iya and headquarters at Dawaki ta Kudu. And when in 1916 it was decided to split the large district initially created for the Sarkin Dawaki Mai Tuta Malam Jamau into two units, of which the southern remained under the Sarkin Karaye Usuman, while the northern was administered by the Sarkin Dawaki Mai Tuta, Nata Allah was promoted to that title and transferred from Dawaki ta Kudu to Gwarzo as district head, a position he held until his death in 1942.[90]

Nata Allah's career illustrates several new developments. Firstly, as a *shigege* he successively held three titles reserved for founding lineages—Mai Anguwan Mundubawa, Dan Iya, and Sarkin Dawaki Mai Tuta, the last being endowed with special prestige as custodian of the Shehu's flag, whose first bearer, Malam Jamau, slew Alwali at Burumburum. Secondly, throughout his career, Nata Allah depended entirely on the emir's favour; and his successive *shigege* appointments illustrated nicely the freedom of Kano emirs under Indirect Rule to expropriate founding lineages temporarily by transferring their official jurisdictions and titles to able *shigege* clients. In this context several traditional hereditary titles, such as the Turakin Romo, which vested in the Yerimawa Fulani, were simply allowed to lapse, following demotion and/or displacement by some central title of higher rank whose holder, often a *shigege*, now administered the area as district head. Others such as the junior Yerimawa title, Sarkin Fulanin Minjibir, escaped such displacement, being identified with *bin kanu* and village jurisdictions.

The career of Nata Allah also contrasts with that of Abbas' Indorawa Fulani client, Ahmadu Gurara, who had served as Galadiman Jarmai in the closing years of Abdullahi's reign. Like Nata Allah, Ahmadu had also fought for the Yusufawa in the civil war but received no immediate promotion. However, in 1914, following the second dismissal of a Mundubawa Mai Anguwa at Zakirai, Abbas conferred that title and district on his loyal client. Three years later, when the senior chiefship at Dutse became vacant following repeated dismissals of its hereditary claimants, Abbas promoted Ahmadu Gurara from the minor district of Zakirai to Dutse, and gave him the royal title Dan Lawan. This second honor, following so swiftly on the first, seems to have unsettled its recipient.

As Dan Lawan, Ahmadu now held a royal title, whose previous incumbents were normally linked to the emir by marriage with one of his daughters. Ahmadu accordingly sought to establish this relation by seeking a bride in Abbas' family. It is said that as Dan Lawan he made several substantial payments towards this bride-price, and was firmly convinced that the marriage could proceed. However, the Indorawa lineage, to which Ahmadu Gurara belonged, appear to have been attached to the Suleibawa dynasty as hereditary serfs and, despite the formal abolition of slavery by the British, Mamman Bello's ban on marriages between free (Fulani) women and slaves or serfs was still in force. In any event, as emir, Abbas could hardly have given his daughter to his 'serf.' During an interview with the Dan Lawan at the Nassarawa palace, Abbas refused to authorize the marriage. Ahmadu Gurara lost his temper and apparently tried to break the emir's neck. He was promptly dismissed from office for tax embezzlement and insubordination. The incident illustrates the effect of the British presence at Kano. We can hardly doubt that in pre-colonial days Ahmadu would have been despatched by the palace slaves without hesitation or trial had he ever dared to attack the emir. Instead, while losing his office, he escaped with his life.

The contrasting careers of Muhammadu Nata Allah and Ahmadu Gurara, both of whom owed their rapid rise to prominence and wealth solely to Abbas, illustrate the emir's need for *shigege* officials and for special caution in promoting them. Emirs had always found themselves in need of able supporters to whom they could entrust executive roles with confidence; but most were also aware of the risks that attached to such appointments. As an aristocrat, Muhammadu Nata Allah understood perfectly those essential differences between political and social mobility on which the Fulani regime depended; and he knew also how the requirement of *asali* (origin; entitlement by descent) determined and limited the goals and prospects of *shigege* officials. Ahmadu Gurara should have known this also. However the swift successive promotions had evidently turned his head, and hastened his downfall. Gurara's behaviour indicates that he interpreted his rapid rise in the official ranks as an ennoblement that cancelled his hereditary servile status. Abbas saw matters differently.

In like fashion, after six years in the high office of Alkalin Kano, Abbas' *shigege* scribe, Ibrahim Maigari, lost his head, intrigued against Abbas with the provincial administration, and had to be dismissed. In contrast, Muhammadu Gidado, whom Ibrahim succeeded as Alkali on Gidado's promotion to the vizierate, discharged that office with such skill and restraint until his death in 1937 that the aristocracy assimilated his family, and several of his numerous sons, including the Dokaji Alhaji Abubakar, continued to hold prominent positions in the government of Kano after Gidado's death. Indeed, some years after my visit in 1959, the Dokaji Abubakar was promoted to the viziership of Kano, an office he filled with distinction until his untimely death.

The careers of Nata Allah and Ahmadu Gurara also illustrate the emergent patterns of promotion from smaller to larger districts, from lower to higher ranking titles, and from offices with smaller salaries to those with more. Inevitably, despite the cultural preference for hereditary recruitment from particular lineages to territorial offices, such promotions and transfers became institutionalized features of the increasingly complex and labile officialdom, with its situationally shifting emphases on descent, birth status, ability, titular precedence, interpersonal relations, political alliance and prospects, administrative experience, differentiation of functions and differential remuneration. In addition, various exigencies constrained the emir to transfer *hakimai* from one district to another with or without changes of title, thereby obscuring the political character and administrative status of such movements as promotions and demotions.

When Abbas sent his client Muhammadu Nata Allah to Gwarzo as Sarkin Dawaki Mai Tuta in 1916, the office of Dan Iya through which Dawaki ta Kudu was administered became vacant. Abbas conferred it on his second son Abdulkadiri, who had lost the title of Ciroma in 1908–09 when Bayero resumed it on surrendering the vizierate. In 1916 also, when his loyal friend, the Ma'ajin Watali, who had administered the city, died, Abbas reassumed direct responsibility for supervision of the ten small districts surrounding Kano, and transferred the administration of Kano from the Waziri to the new office of Magajin Gari, which he then created to administer Kano directly under his personal supervision. As Magajin Gari, Abbas then appointed his brother Muhammadu, thereby securing direct dynastic control of Kano.

Following the dismissal of Ibrahim Maigari in 1916, Abbas appointed Muhammadu Dikko of the Zarawa lineage as Alkalin Kano. Dikko had formerly served as Limam under Mamman Bello and Tukur, but on Aliyu's triumph had been replaced. Gyenawa elders interpret Abbas' repeated appointments of their Zarawa and Bornawa rivals to the senior clerical offices as an attempt by Abbas to restore the failing fortunes of those lineages which had lost wealth and office under Aliyu.

The Status of Throne-Slaves and "Habe"

On the death of Shamaki Ajuji around 1910, Abbas reappointed Harisu, the Yusufawa Shamaki, who had presided over Aliyu's accession on Yusufu's death at Garko, and had forfeited the office by returning from Goga to Sokoto in 1903 as Aliyu had ordered. At Sokoto Harisu had learnt of Aliyu's flight, capture and removal to Lokoja by the British. After some months he accordingly returned to Kano and reported to Abbas at the palace. By then Ajuji had already been appointed, but on his death Abbas restored the office of Shamaki to Harisu, to whom the Yusufawa and Abbas himself owed so much. Not long after, when Harisu died of old age, Abbas appointed the former *jekadan* Garko, Salihi, as Shamaki.

Despite British pressure, Abbas sought to insulate the throne and conserve its power by preserving the status and roles of the senior throne slaves. Though he allowed the relatively new title of Shettima to lapse on the death of Shettima Baushe, he filled the civil slave offices of Dan Rimi and Sallama by appointing Sambo and Abu respectively. Moreover, at the *gunduma* of 1908, Abbas delegated the supervision of Dawaki ta Kudu, Tanagar and Tambarawa to the Shamaki, and gave the Dan Rimi similar functions with respect to Gogyen and two other towns. Cargill and his successors disliked but had to accept these slave executives, having transferred responsibility for the small central districts around Kano to Abbas. Both the Shamaki and the Dan Rimi had acted as minor *hakimai* at Kano before and after the *basasa*; but with the introduction of salaries, following the establishment of the *Beit el Mal*, they lost those fiefs when the towns were transferred to princes. In making these appointments, it seems that Abbas was concerned to preserve the territorial roles of these senior slaves and to find them appropriate activities and sources of income in compensation for those they had lost. When the central administration was placed on salaries, Abbas agreed to withdraw these fiefs from the Shamaki and Dan Rimi, provided they were appropriately compensated.

Restored to the palace, the Dan Rimi reassumed his traditional task of supervising the throne estates at Gurjiya, Panisau, Takai and elsewhere, besides handling communications with titled officials, city clerics, merchants and princes. The Shamaki, who had already lost some of his roles as palace treasurer and prison warder, continued to administer the palace population, the emir's slave messengers, intelligence agents, and private communications with *hakimai* and certain central officials. Thus, despite British pressure, Abbas preserved strategic positions and functions for his senior throne slaves within the central administration, recognizing that their disestablishment would severely weaken the throne and expose it to serious risks. Accordingly, at his death Abbas left his successor a powerful and well organized palace staff.

Though the British had instituted uniform tax rates for "Habe" (Hausa) and Fulani, thereby formally terminating the historic inequalities in their taxation, it seems likely that the old differences persisted substantially, at least under the *taki* farm measurements on which tax assessment was based. Unlike the Hausa, settled Fulani were not keen farmers; and in addition, the methods of *taki* assessment allowed assessors to overlook or under-report such cultivations as they wished. Since the assessors and village chiefs were predominantly Fulani, it seems probable that the preferential treatment Fulani received under this mode of taxation indirectly preserved the pre-colonial patterns of differential Habe-Fulani taxation.

Nonetheless, at least in principle the British had enunciated the novel idea that "Habe" and Fulani should be taxed equally. They also assumed that Islamic law should apply equally to both populations, and increased the number of Muslim courts to facilitate its administration. In other spheres the British did not directly attempt to challenge the pre-colonial patterns of differential incorporation by which Fulani had subjugated and ruled "Habe" from 1807 to 1903. Nonetheless, at Getso under the Fulani Sangetso whom Abbas appointed, the "Habe" protested Fulani exemptions from the onerous forced labor that was levied on them during his reign.

> The then practice was, (that) only the Habe people were asked to do some forced labor, until one Malam Habu, a Habe, gathered all the Habe people and said, "Habe people in Getso are not to do any forced labor unless Fulani do the same." Malam Habu, a limam, asked his people to resist to the last. Mass arrest was ordered by the emir (Abbas). Many people died while serving prison sentences, not through ill treatment, but through natural deaths in prison.[91]

Thus, unless Getso was unique, corvée labor continued to be levied on "Habe" only throughout Kano during Abbas' reign. Such labor was employed to build or repair roads, town walls, mosques, markets, the palaces of local chiefs, to cultivate their farms, and also the farms of the local *hakimai*. Imposed initially by right of conquest, as the emirate's expenditure for 1911–12 indicated, such labor was unpaid. Moreover, as this incident at Getso shows, those who protested such practices were likely to be arrested and imprisoned at the emir's orders, perhaps after trial for disobedience (*kin umurci*) in his court under *siyasa* jurisdiction. Many died in prison while serving their sentences. In short, while the British occupation put an end to many crude and open absuses inflicted on Hausa, it also permitted, preserved and protected other expressions of their differential incorporation in Kano society.

Village Administration

By 1916 Abbas had accepted a British proposal that village heads should be remunerated with fixed salaries rather than percentages of the tax they collected,[92] thereby converting the entire native administration from the old mode of remuneration by commission and shares, to the fixed salaries required for a modern bureaucracy. One difficulty that delayed immediate implementation of this decision was presented by the number of settlements classified as villages in Kano. There were over 4,500 such units, of varied size, age, ethnic, civic and political status. Some were large walled towns with daughter settlements, others were recently established hamlets. Some units contained only slaves, while most contained both slave and free. To place all recognized village chiefs on salaries, it was first necessary to identify them by enquiring carefully into the relative status and traditional relations of adjacent settlements throughout the emirate; and, secondly, to determine their salaries by reference to the total population and revenue of the settlements that recognized the authority they claimed.

In 1917 a pilot survey was made in Gaya District to determine the historical and contemporary alignments and pre-colonial groupings of hamlets and villages under locally resident headmen appointed by and responsible to the Sarkin Gaya for their administration.[93] This survey revealed that the many discrete groupings of adjacent settlements recognized common headmen who were normally recruited from the senior unit, which was also, as a rule, the largest and oldest. In consequence, it was possible to re-group the various rural settlements of Gaya

District into Village Areas. Headmen of the senior villages in these areas were then officially recognized as village chiefs entitled to remuneration by fixed salaries. Over the next few years similar enquiries were conducted throughout Kano, with the result that by 1920, its 4,500 rural settlements were grouped into 500 village areas under salaried village heads, who received an average of £45 per annum for their services.[94] Thus, only one in every nine heads of settlements received a salary. On the institution of officially recognized village chiefs remunerated by salary, it was also laid down that these offices should be filled by selection within the villages concerned from candidates having hereditary or other political claims to the title, approved by the village elders. Final rights to confirm or veto these nominations rested with the emir who alone, as before, could appoint or dismiss a village chief. Thus while disestablishing many traditional headmen, these rules ensured that few village chiefs would not be Fulani, thereby perpetuating Hausa subjugation. Experience soon showed that most of these new village areas were too large and unwieldy for their untrained headmen to administer efficiently. It was therefore necessary to subdivide them; and by 1934 their number had increased gradually from 500 to 1200 by splitting the original village areas and reducing their average populations from 4,500 to 1,600.[95]

Meanwhile, the immediate effect of this regrouping of rural settlements into reasonably large and administratively efficient units was to reduce the need for sub-district heads, who had hitherto dealt with all these rural settlements as separate entities. Now, as the settlements were regrouped into village areas, a *hakimi* could supervise a much larger territory and population than before, since his immediate subordinates, the salaried village chiefs, were fewer, and administered larger aggregates through hierarchies of ward and hamlet heads. These implications of the reorganization of the village administration were quickly perceived and explored experimentally at Gaya, where sub-districts were formally abolished by 1919. Over the next few years, as village regrouping proceeded, other sub-districts were abolished and their territories amalgamated, as, for example, at Kura, Kiru, Madobi and Bebeji, all of which now ceased to exist as separate divisions, being administered together by the Turaki Manya.[96] Thus, the decision to remunerate village chiefs by salaries led directly to the regrouping of rural settlements into larger administrative units, and indirectly to the obsolescence of many sub-districts demarcated by Cargill in 1908. Other implications of this far-reaching reform unfolded after Abbas' death.

Early in May 1919 Abbas died at the Nassarawa palace, having guided Kano's accommodation to defeat and colonial overrule through its most critical phases with considerable skill. At his death the two leading candidates for the succession were the Ciroma Abdullahi Bayero, who then administered Bici, and the Wombai (Shehu) Usuman, Abbas' brother, who was stationed at Ringim. Usuman, another of Abdullahi's sons, was already old when Abbas died, while Bayero, born in 1884, was relatively young. Though I have found no record to this effect, it seems likely that on learning of Abbas' death the Provincial Administration directed the Waziri Muhammadu Gidado to assemble a council of electors and seek their recommendation. Meanwhile the Wombai Shehu Usuman was instructed to administer the emirate as regent (Mukaddas) until his appointment was announced forty days later.

Notes

1. F.D. Lugard, *Northern Nigeria—Annual Report, 1902*. Colonial Reports Annual, No. 409 (London: H.M.S.O., 1903), pp. 90–91. R. M. East, LH, Vol. 2, p. 71.

2. F.D. Lugard, *Northern Nigeria—Annual Report, 1902*, p. 91.

3. Ibid., p. 92.

4. Ibid., pp. 92–94, paras. 52–53.

5. H.A.S. Johnston, *The Fulani Empire of Sokoto* (London: Oxford University Press, 1967), pp. 252–253. See also R. A. Adeleye, "The Dilemma of the Wazir: The Place of the *Risalat al-Wazir'ila ahl al-'ilm Wa'l-Tadabbur* in the History of the Conquest of the Sokoto Caliphate," *JHSN*, Vol. 4, No. 2, 1968, pp. 285–311.

6. F.D. Lugard, *Northern Nigeria*, 1902, p. 96.

7. Ibid., p. 96.

8. F.D. Lugard, *Northern Nigeria—Annual Report, 1904*, Colonial Reports, Annual, No. 476 (London: H.M.S.O., 1906), p. 240.

9. F.D. Lugard, *Northern Nigeria*, 1902, pp. 97–98 and footnote on both pages.

10. F.D. Lugard, *Northern Nigeria—Annual Report, 1903*, Colonial Reports, Annual, No. 437 (London: H.M.S.O., 1904), p. 177.

11. This letter, which is in the custody of the Wazirin Sokoto, Alhaji Junaidu, at Sokoto, was translated from Arabic into Hausa by the Waziri's student, Malam Halilu. I am grateful to them both for their assistance and courtesy.

12. Letter in the custody of the Wazirin Sokoto, Alhaji Junaidu. Translated into Hausa at Sokoto, July 1959, by M. Halilu.

13. F.D. Lugard, *Northern Nigeria*, 1902 pp. 99–100, para. 61.

14. Walter Miller, *Walter Miller, 1872–1952, An Autobiography* (Zaria: Gaskiya Corporation, n.d.), p. 29.

15. *Half-Yearly Report on Kano Province, 1917*. In the National Archives at Kaduna (unnumbered in 1959). See also W. F. Gowers, *Gazetteer of Kano Province*, pp. 41–42.

16. LH, Vol. 2, p. 69.

17. Walter Miller, *An Autobiography*, p. 23.

18. F.D. Lugard, *Northern Nigeria*, 1902, p. 91.

19. F.D. Lugard, *Northern Nigeria*, 1903, pp. 172–173.

20. F.D. Lugard, *Political Memoranda* (Lagos: The Government Printer, 1918).

21. F.D. Lugard, *Northern Nigeria*, 1902, p. 111.

22. F.D. Lugard, *Northern Nigeria*, 1902, p. 92.

23. F.D. Lugard, *Northern Nigeria, Annual Report, 1900–March 31st, 1901*, Colonial Reports, Annual, No. 346 (London: H.M.S.O., 1902), p. 27.

24. Abdulmalik Mani, *Zuwan Turawa Nigeriya ta Arewa* (Zaria: NORLA, 1957), pp. 107–111.

25. F.D. Lugard, *Northern Nigeria*, 1902, p. 90.

26. F.D. Lugard, *Northern Nigeria*, 1904, pp. 213–214, para. 6. See also Ibid., p. 241, paras. 73–74; and R. M. East, LH, Vol. 2, p. 72.

27. F.D. Lugard, *Northern Nigeria*, 1904, p. 241, para. 74.

28. Ibid., p. 241, para. 75.

29. Ibid., pp. 243–244.

30. Ibid., pp. 244–245, paras. 83–84.

31. Ibid., p. 249, para. 95.

32. William Wallace, *Northern Nigeria*, Annual Report 1906–7, Colonial Reports, Annual, No. 551 (London: H.M.S.O., 1908), p. 489.

33. F.D. Lugard, *Northern Nigeria*, 1904, p. 227, para. 33. This passage is a direct quotation by Lugard of Cargill's report.

34. Ibid., pp. 226–227, para. 33. Cargill's report cited by Lugard.

35. F.D. Lugard, *Northern Nigeria, Annual Report 1905–6*, Colonial Reports, Annual, No. 516 (London: H.M.S.O., 1907), p. 375, para. 34.

36. F.D. Lugard, *Northern Nigeria, 1902*, pp. 79–80, para. 21.

37. Ibid., pp. 110–111, paras. 80–81.

38. W. Wallace, *Northern Nigeria, 1906–7*, pp. 572–573.

39. Ibid., p. 572.

40. F.D. Lugard, *Northern Nigeria, 1905–6*, pp. 365–366.

41. Ibid., p. 370, para. 26.

42. Ibid., p. 371, para. 27.

43. Ibid., p. 371, para. 27

44. Ibid., p. 373, para. 31.

45. Ibid., p. 378, para. 39.

46. Ibid., p. 378, para. 39.

47. Ibid., pp. 378–9, para. 40.

48. Ibid., p. 379, para. 40.

49. Walter Miller, *An Autobiography,* pp. 49–50. For further details see Abdulmalik Mani, *Zuwan Turawa Nijeriya ta Arewa*, pp. 155–157.

50. F.D. Lugard, *Northern Nigeria, 1904*, p. 244, para. 83.

51. For brief references, see S. J. Hogben and A. H. M. Kirk-Greene, *The Emirates of Northern Nigeria*, pp. 153–175. For fuller accounts of these dynastic changes, see M. G. Smith, *The Affairs of Daura* (Berkeley and Los Angeles: University of California Press, 1978); and *idem, The Two Katsinas* (unpublished Ms.).

52. F.D. Lugard, *Northern Nigeria, 1905–6*, p. 375.

53. F.D. Lugard, *Northern Nigeria, 1902*, p. 92–94, para. 52.

54. W.F. Gowers, *Gazetteer of Kano Province*, p. 49.

55. Since Cargill apparently burnt the Provincial records at Kano shortly before his retirement in June, 1908, the following reconstruction is based on data from District Notebooks and oral information. On Cargill's action, see Mary Bull, "Indirect Rule in Northern Nigeria, 1906–1911," in Kenneth Robinson and Frederick Madden (Eds.), *Essays in Imperial Government* (Oxford: Basil Blackwell, 1963), p. 77

56. LH, Vol. 2, pp. 72–73.

57. W. F. Gowers, *Gazetteer of Kano Province*, p. 49.

58. E.P.C. Girouard, *Northern Nigeria—Annual Report, 1907–8*, Colonial Reports, Annual No. 594 (London: H.M.S.O., 1909), pp. 596–599, Section 20.

59. Ibid., p. 512, Section 33; W. Wallace, *Northern Nigeria, 1906–7*, p. 489.

60. W. Wallace, *Northern Nigeria, 1906–7*, p. 488.

61. E.P.C. Girouard, *Northern Nigeria, 1907–8*, p. 612.

62. Ibid., pp. 612–613.

63. Ibid., p. 613.

64. W. Wallace, *Northern Nigeria, 1906–9*, p. 489.

65. H. Hesketh Bell, *Northern Nigeria, Annual Report, 1909*, Colonial Reports, Annual, No. 674 (London: H.M.S.O., 1910), p. 693; H. Hesketh Bell, *Northern Nigeria, Annual Report, 1910* (London: H.M.S.O., 1912), p. 722. See also Mary Bull, "Indirect Rule in Northern Nigeria," pp. 71–75.

66. Hesketh Bell, *Northern Nigeria, 1910–11*, pp. 708–9.

67. H.R. Palmer, "Introduction," in Muhammadu Bello Kagara, *Sarkin Katsina Alhaji Muhammadu Dikko, C.B.E., 1865–1944* (Zaria: Gaskiya Corporation, 1957). Pages not numbered.

68. Hesketh Bell, *Northern Nigeria, 1910–11*, p. 738, Section XX.

69. Ibid, pp. 740–741; see also W.F. Gowers, *Gazetteer of Kano Province*, pp. 50–53.

70. Hesketh Bell, *Northern Nigeria, 1910–1911*, pp. 741–742

71. C.L. Temple, *Northern Nigeria, Annual Report, 1911*, Colonial Reports, Annual, No. 738 (London: H.M.S.O., 1913), pp. 788–789.

72. W.F. Gowers, *Gazetteer of Kano Province*, pp. 54–56. For salaries paid in 1909, see C.L. Temple (Ed.), *Notes on the Tribes, Provinces, Emirates and States of the Northern Provinces of Nigeria* (Lagos: C.M.S. Bookshop, 1922), p. 470.

73. C.W. Rowling, *Land Tenure in Kano Province* (Kaduna: The Government Printer, 1949), p. 28, para. 74; see also the annual chronicle of developments at Kano up till 1934, in the unpublished *Kano Provincial Gazetteer*, compiled in Dec. 1934, from which many of these details are drawn; v. File 2568, Vol. II, National Archives, Kaduna.

74. W.F. Gowers, *Gazetteer of Kano Province*, p. 54; C.L. Temple (Ed.), *Notes on ... The Northern Provinces of Nigeria*, p. 470.

75. *Half-Yearly Report, Kano, 1914*, File 2724, Vol. II, National Archives, Kaduna.

76. H.R. Palmer, *Annual Report, Kano Province, 1915*, unpublished, in File 2724, Vol. II, National Archives, Kaduna.

77. Ibid., paras. 87–93, 104.

78. *District Notebook Kura*, Provincial Office, Kano.

79. *Annual Report, Kano Province, 1916*, File 2724, Vol. II, National Archives, Kaduna.

80. *District Notebooks*, Minjibir, Kumbotso, Kura, Dawakin Kudu, Provincial Office, Kano.

81. See *District Notebooks*, Gabasawa, Ungogo, Kumbotso, Minjibir, Gezawa, Dawakin Kudu, etc., Provincial Office, Kano.

82. *Annual Report Kano Province, 1916*, File 2724, Vol. II, National Archives Kaduna; *District Notebooks* Bici and Dawakin Tofo, Provincial Office, Kano.

83. *District Notebooks*, Karaye and Gwarzo, Provincial Office, Kano.

84. *District Notebooks*, Rano and Tudin Wada, Provincial Office, Kano.

85. *District Notebook*, Dawakin Kudu, Provincial Office, Kano.

86. *District Notebook*, Dutse, Provincial Office, Kano.

87. *District Notebook*, Gwarzo, Provincial Office, Kano.

88. *District Notebooks*, Gabasawa, Gezawa, Dutse, Babura, Gwaram, Birnin Kudu, Provincial Office, Kano.

89. *District Notebooks*, Fogolawa, Babura, Dawakin Kudu, Tudun Wada, Jahun, Gwaram, Provincial Office, Kano.

90. *District Notebook*, Gwarzo, Provincial Office, Kano.

91. Sarkin Dawaki Mai Tuta Bello dan Dago, D.H. Gwarzo, "History of Getso" (July 1956), unpublished, in *District Notebook, Gwarzo*, Provincial Office, Kano.

92. *Kano Provincial Gazeteer, 1934*, unpublished, in File 2568, Vol II, National Archives, Kaduna.

93. *District Notebook*, Gaya, Provincial Office, Kano.

94. *Kano Provincial Gazeteer, 1934*, in File 2568, Vol II, National Archives, Kaduna.

95. Ibid.

96. *District Notebooks*, Kura and Kiru, Provincial Office, Kano.

8

Toward the Future

Usuman, 1919–1926

Objectives and Regime

Usuman, who was also called Shehu after Shehu Usuman, reigned seven years and two months, dying on Friday 23rd April, 1926. Throughout his reign he remained unwell, progressively enfeebled by age; and it is said that he was never able to mount a horse at any time after his accession.[1] Indeed he was by birth the senior of Abbas and Aliyu. His age and declining physical condition should be borne in mind as his reign is reviewed.

Following the death of Galadima Umaru, as Wombai, Usumanu was the senior ranking royal official. As district head of Ringim he also supervised six sub-districts. Nonetheless as we have seen, his salary was less than one-fourth of the Ciroma's; and throughout his reign Abbas seems to have kept his brother, the Wombai, isolated and uninfluential. Understandably, on his accession, Usuman sought to do likewise with Abbas' sons, the Ciroma Abdullahi Bayero and the Dan Iya Abdulkadiri. He was also eager to advance the fortunes of his own sons, the more so because, feeling his age and ill health, he could not expect to live very long. Accordingly, on his accession Usuman appointed his senior son, Abdullahi, to the vacant title of Wombai and sent him to administer Ringim district from headquarters at Dabi. Simultaneously and significantly he raised the Wombai's salary to the level of the Ciroma's. By the end of 1919, Usuman had also dismissed Abdullahi's grandson, the Turaki Manya Abubakar, who had hitherto supervised the four sub-districts of Kura, Madobi, Kiru and Bebeji. The region having been recently reorganised in village areas, the four sub-districts were then abolished, their *hakimai* removed, and Usuman's second son, Abubakar, was installed as Turaki to administer the district directly. In 1920, when the Tafida Aliyu who administered Ungogo was dismissed for tax embezzlement, Usuman appointed his own son Muhammadu as district head, Ungogo, with the title of Tafida.[2] Thus within twenty months, Usuman had appointed his three senior sons to high-ranking royal titles vested with territorial authority, adequate salaries, and political prominence. In addition he appointed a fourth son Aliyu as Sarkin Fada, and on Aliyu's death another son Muhamman (Mamudu) succeeded. The Chronicle remarks that Usuman "remained hostile to the sons of Abbas" throughout his reign.[3] That is quite possible; but of Abbas' sons, only two, Bayero and Abdulkadiri, held territorial offices on their father's death, and neither was dismissed. Whether Usuman attempted to do so but was restrained by the British, I do not know. However, without dismissing Abbas' sons, Usuman sought to establish his own in office and to promote their prospects for the succession by providing them with the requisite experience and means as territorial chiefs.

On his accession, as related above, Aliyu Babba had ruthlessly eliminated all Mamman Bello's issue and supporters from office. After the civil war, when Caliph Abdu Danyen Kasko attempted to repair the breach that he had made, he had Tukur's surviving son, the ex-Ciroman Kamri Lele, return to Kano; but he was shortly banished by Aliyu. When Aliyu set out for Sokoto in 1903, taking with him all Kano notables, Lele, then living at Zinder, kept himself informed about British movements, and when the British seized Kano in Aliyu's absence and sought a suitable person to administer it temporarily, the ex-Ciroma Lele, arriving from Zinder, was briefly placed in charge, being, as Tukur's heir, a senior claimant for the succession. The ensuing turmoil is dimly perceptible through Lugard's account. He reports that though "his (Lele's) claims were strong, ... he had no following, and ... the riff-raff of the town gathered about him, and I found that they had been looting the houses of the chiefs of the rival party in their absence. I therefore turned him out."[4] Thus, on Abbas' accession, as in Aliyu's reign, Abdullahi's issue governed Kano to the total exclusion of their dynastic rivals, few of whom then remained within the emirate. At this price Kano was freed of serious dynastic strife for twenty-five years; but following the shabby treatment Usuman had received from Abbas on his accession, as on Mamman Bello's in 1882, the stage was once more set for further dynastic segmentation and rivalry under the pressure of competing familisms. Usuman's prompt appointments of his sons as Wombai, Tafida, Turaki and Sarkin Fada crystallised these tendencies and generated factional competition between his issue and those of Abbas.

Usuman did not attempt to fill every available position with his offspring. Thus when he dismissed Ture, the son of Tsoho, whom Abbas had promoted from Sarkin Jarmai to Dan Makwayau after the Dan Makwayau Sa'adu, Abdullahi's son, had been dismissed for tax embezzlement, instead of giving this useful but minor district headship to one of his sons, Usuman appointed Muhammadu, the son of Abdullahi's Hausa Galadima Ibrahim; but in a little while Muhammadu was also found guilty of tax embezzlement and dismissed. Usuman then left the office vacant for the rest of his reign.

Usuman's unsatisfactory administration is illustrated by the history of the senior judgeship during his reign. On his accession, Muhammadu Dikko, whom Aliyu had dismissed from the office of Limam, was the Alkalin Kano. Though Dikko was only 65 years old, Usuman dismissed him on the ground that he could neither hear nor see. As Alkali, he then appointed Dikko's younger brother Aminu, another Fulanin Bornu. However, after one and a half years Aminu was dismissed at British insistence for selling a slave girl, despite the Protectorate law that forbade it. In defence, Aminu pleaded innocence of the charge, but written evidence was brought against him; after trial in the Provincial Court he was ordered to serve a sentence of three years. However, seventy days later he was released and discharged on the orders of a superior judge at Kaduna who ruled that the evidence was inconclusive. Meanwhile, Aminu having forfeited the office of Alkali, Usuman had appointed his namesake, the Alkalin Gaya; but within two years Usuman of Gaya was also dismissed under British pressure for authorising Court sales of the estate of a deceased Arab at prices so low as to constitute fraud and virtual plunder of the estate. Again the Alkali pleaded innocence, though, following correct Islamic procedure, he had approved the sales. Nonetheless, suspected of fraud, he was dismissed, and Usuman appointed a baGyeni cleric, Ja'afaru, as Alkali.[5] These successive dismissals of the senior native judges at British insistence illustrate the ambiguities of Usuman's rule. We can hardly doubt that in Abbas' reign, the senior judges may have indulged in similar conduct, despite surveillance by the Provincial staff; but whereas Abbas, an active, energetic and forceful ruler, protected his Chief Judges by political and judicial means, Usuman, secluded in the palace by age and indisposition, was either indifferent or incapable of doing so.

On his accession, Usuman's immediate objectives as emir were twofold: to place his sons in office, and to establish his personal domination of the Native Administration. The first objective was easily achieved, as related above. To pursue the second, Usuman employed those traditional communication channels from emir to *hakimai* through senior throne slaves and eunuchs that Abbas had preserved. Following the departure from Kano of W.F. Gowers, who had served as Resident from 1911 to 1920, Usuman's informal but effective revival of the old communication system appears to have escaped recognition by the Divisional staff for most of his reign; but as that proceeded, effective power was transferred from the vizier's office to the palace and centred in the Shamaki, Dan Rimi and Sallama. In consequence, the vizier, Muhammadu Gidado, progressively lost the capacity to initiate or restrain actions by the *hakimai*. Excluded from the emir's confidence, he lost control of the central and district administrations alike. Indeed, since Muhammadu Gidado had served Abbas loyally and well, Usuman apparently determined to deprive him of effective power, and soon reduced him to the status of *fonctionnaire*, head clerk of the emir's office, responsible for files and for those written communications the British wished to see, but little else. Meanwhile, Usuman developed the political realignments by which he concentrated power at the palace, between himself and his senior slaves, and beyond reach of the vizier or the British Administration.

An unpublished Provincial Gazeteer compiled in 1934 relates that since Abbas had

> governed with a firm hand and kept upstarts in their place ... control was concentrated in Kano; and after Abbas' death, when the invalid Usuman became Emir—due also to lack of supervision in the War (of 1914–18)—irresponsible favourites had slipped back into power and old abuses were again recurrent. The Emir whose Waziri, nonplussed, had faded into the background, required the stronger backing of responsible advisers ... the recognised important chiefs had ... all been established in the Districts ... and though in theory still advisory to the Emir on affairs of state and members of his *majalisa* or council, had gradually come to be ignored and had lost touch with the capital.[6]

In place of the traditional Council of State, which had been used variously by different emirs, Usuman directed Kano's affairs through the Dan Rimi Sambo, the Shamaki Salihi and the Sallama. His interests, moreover, were rather different from those of Abbas or the British. It is related that "Sarkin Kano Usumanu had a certain agent whose name was Tanko Barzo; he used to sell compounds to people and bring the money to Sarki, until the Europeans learnt about this and sent him to jail for two years."[7] Meanwhile, the Provincial Administration was occupied in designing and implementing those revisions of the district reorganization which were necessitated by experience or by Gowers' programme of regrouping villages into effective administrative units.

Pressures for Change

As occasion allowed, the British sought to eliminate sub-districts by splitting the larger districts into two or more divisions, each under a district head directly supervising the newly salaried village chiefs. For example, in 1921 when the district of Ringim administered by Usuman's son was thus subdivided, the new district of Taura was placed under the Dan Maje Zakari Ya'u, Usuman's younger brother. Simultaneously the old sub-districts of Ringim were abolished. In 1922 the Turaki's district, which had been reconstituted six years earlier on the abolition of its four constituent sub-districts, was likewise divided into two districts of Kiru and Kura, the former being placed under the Ja'idanawa, while the latter remained with the Turaki. That year the large southeastern area under the Sarkin Dawaki Tsakar Gida was also subdivided into two separate districts, Gwaram and Birnin Kudu, administered by the Sarkin Dawaki and the Sarkin Birnin Kudu respectively. As at Ringim, sub-districts were simultaneously abolished. In 1923 the districts of Dutse and Suma'ila underwent similar subdivision and simplification. The eastern half of Dutse was reconstituted as Kiyawa district under the baYole Dan Lawan Umaru who had previously administered Dutse, while the western half, including Dutse itself, was placed under Suleimanu, the baJelube Sarkin Dutse. In both units sub-districts were eliminated, and the resident *hakimai* administered them directly through officially recognised village chiefs.[8]

In 1923 when the baJobe Makama Aminu was dismissed for tax embezzlement, the opportunity was seized to subdivide his large and ineffectively administered district into two units of manageable size, with headquarters at Wudil and Suma'ila respectively. As district head of Suma'ila the baJobe Isa, a grandson of Dabo's Makama Isa, was appointed with the resuscitated title of Dan Darman; and following Isa's death in 1925, his cousin Aliyu succeeded to the title and district. At Wudil another Isa, also Makama Isa's grandson, was appointed as Makama and district head. On his death in 1926, a younger brother, Dahiru, succeeded to the title and district.[9]

In 1924 when the Magajin Gari appointed by Abbas died, Usuman replaced him with another of Abdullahi's surviving sons. In the same year Usuman's son, the Wombai Abdullahi, died, following which Usuman transferred the Wombai's title and salary to another son, the Turaki Abubakar, but left him to administer Kura district as before. Having thus released the Turaki title, Usuman gave this to his second son, the Tafida Muhammadu, who administered Ungogo, again without transfer to a larger district. Then, the Tafida title being vacant, he conferred this on his son Mamudu, aged eighteen, who was sent to Ringim as district head. Clearly, by these circuitous appointments, Usuman sought simultaneously to elevate the titular rank of his senior sons and to increase their official remunerations. As Palmer had foreseen, differential salaries now attached to particular titles, irrespective of the size and wealth of the district the title-holder administered.

Of 308 slaves freed in 1924, in Kano Province under Lugard's Proclamation, 269 were self-redeemed, while four were freed by court orders on the grounds that they had been born after 1900. In 1922 and 1923, 323 and 267 slaves had secured their freedom by these official means;[10] but since the population of Kano Province was even then estimated at nearly 3 million, of whom in 1894 one-third were said to be slaves, it is evident that very few slaves received their freedom in Kano under the terms of Lugard's Proclamation.

In the newly constituted district of Taura, administered by Dan Maje Zakari Yau, the salaries of village chiefs varied widely without relation to the relative size of their units or the amounts of tax they returned. Thus, in 1922 the village chief of Buduru who returned a total tax of £108 received £80 as salary. The village chief of Majiya received £60 as salary and turned in £131 as tax, while the village chief of Taura received £36 and returned a tax of £343. An officer's note that he had "received information that the Village Head of Bardo has been receiving tax money for some hundred farms which are not registered on the *taki* lists"[11] illustrates a common means by which village chiefs augmented their official stipends. Nonetheless, to British officials in 1924, "the organisation of the village units of Kano Emirate may now be looked on as completed."[12] This development facilitated the abolition of the remaining sub-districts, which was duly accomplished in the next two years. The Provincial staff then proceeded to reconstitute the village groups, on which the entire territorial organization now rested, by subdividing them into units that village chiefs could manage effectively, thus increasing their number and reducing their average size. However, this final stage in the development of the new territorial system did not entail direct rearrangement or modification of the district organization.

On completing their village regroupings and *taki* reassessments in 1924, the Provincial Administration, having by then identified the real basis and character of Usuman's administration, determined to act.

> Up to 1925, at the close of the reign of the previous Emir Usuman, the central administration was almost entirely in the hands of palace slaves, malams and "kofas." Abbas, Usuman's predecessor, had kept the slaves in hand, but Usuman let the situation lapse into chaos and the Government itself had allowed a loophole for the slave regime by the rigid expulsion of District Heads from the capital. Something had therefore to be done to meet a situation which had become insistent and serious. As things were, the Native Administration as such had become paralysed and the Resident found himself up against a brick wall.
>
> The first step was to abolish the slave regime, to get rid of the intermediaries. A Council was then formed which was in effect a wazirate (vizierate), composed of four waziris instead of one. It took upon itself the duties of the numerous departments of state which the Emir had been trying to perform with the existing Waziri, through slaves, malams and favourites. It was recognised that it was necessary to

"divide and rule," so to speak, and that it was impossible for one Minister to control effectively the affairs of an Emirate the size of Kano. The changes that were made in 1925 did not constitute the imposition of a new regime, but the revival of an old. It was a reversion to a system which was native in origin. It would be going too far to say that the Emir of Kano has now become ... a constitutional monarch with a cabinet of ministers, but it is true to say that he has delegated some of his powers to his Council, and is to a large extent dependent on their advice and ready to meet the wishes of his advisers.[13]

In brief, having completed the territorial reorganization, by subdividing the larger districts into units of moderate size and abolishing unnecessary sub-districts, the Resident directed Usuman to recall the Madaki and Galadima from rural areas by assigning their districts to others, and instal them as State Councillors.

No innovation was made by doing this, it being agreed that the true system (though "fallen from grace") was that of a chief assisted by responsible advisers. Kano has always been regarded, compared for instance with Katsina, as ultra-centralised, ... Drastic action had to be taken in 1925 to eliminate illegitimate holders of power.[14]

Usuman may have accepted these demands after due delay but without undue anxiety, confident that the returning "councillors" would have little part in his counsels. If so, he underestimated the determination of the British to reconstitute the "true" and "ancient" system, as required by the doctrine of "Indirect Rule" through traditional chiefs and institutions.

On the general question of the council and responsible advisers, the Resident Kano emphasised (that) it was ... a case of extricating the original functions of responsible advisers and themselves from the muck-heap into which they had fallen ... The Emir Usuman ... heartily acquiesced in the accusation of having fallen from grace, and agreed that the true system was a chief with responsible advisers, and that such was the position of old as regards the constitution of Kano, though he was suspected of saying this with his tongue in his cheek.[15]

To ensure that the new council would enjoy the chance to operate as the central agency for policy formation, the Resident demanded that Usuman expel the two senior throne slaves, the Dan Rimi Sambo and Shamaki Salihi, with whose assistance the emir had initially subverted the "true and ancient system," and to whom he had progressively lost power as his health and energies declined. Presumably Usuman perceived that he risked deposition by opposing this demand; presumably the British Resident made this point quite clear. Usuman gave in and despatched the Shamaki Salihi to Takai with a suitable pension, while the Dan Rimi Sambo was banished in January 1926. These events disarmed Usuman of his principal aides and destroyed those powerful political instruments that Babba Zaki (1768–1776) had initially devised to ensure his autocratic control and Ibrahim Dabo had revived as he reconquered Kano to entrench his power. In effect, having completed the reorganization of the rural administration, the Provincial staff were now free to reorganise and develop the central institutions of Kano.

Usuman did not survive the loss of Shamaki Salihi and Dan Rimi Sambo for very long. In 1925 there was a durbar at Kano to honour the Prince of Wales, who visited Nigeria that year. To greet the Prince, the Northern Chiefs, including the Sultan of Sokoto Muhammadu (1924–1930), assembled at Kano. As emir, Usuman played host to this distinguished assembly, greeted the Prince and honored the Sultan. This was his last public appearance. After several months of seclusion at the palace, Usuman died, politically broken, in April 1926, leaving a vast hoard of cash at the palace.[16]

Abdullahi Bayero, 1926–1953

The Appointment

The following account of the succession vividly describes the historic situation.

In April the Emir's death was expected. Intrigue and uncertainty crowded the atmosphere. The Emir died on Friday 23rd April 1926, his last public appearance having been at the Prince of Wales' durbar. In the last few months of his life the new council of big chiefs had been acepted by him—but his administration through the palace entourage had resulted in increasingly inefficient conduct of public affairs.

Rumours immediately arose of intrigues in connection with the appointment of the new Emir, there being every reason to suppose that members of the Council had hopes of succeeding. On Monday the council, consisting of the Waziri, Madaki, and Sarkin Bai, visited the Residency. The duties of the board entitled by custom to propose a new Emir were discussed, the members of the board are the Waziri, Madawaki, Sarkin Bai, Sarkin Dawaki Mai Tuta and Makama. A suggestion by the Waziri that the Council members should deal with the situation was overruled, and it was arranged to send forthwith for the Sarkin Dawaki mai Tuta and the Makama. It was pointed out that the Board was constituted by tradition of members who, having no qualifications themselves for the Emirship, were in a position to make an unbiased choice ... the Council stated that the Board, before coming to a final decision, would intimate in what direction their thoughts lay.

Meantime various measures were taken at the palace. The Council and the Alkalin Kano assumed control of the property lying therein; separate lists were made of the Emirate property and the late Emir's private property, and a considerable sum of money, undisputed possession of Usuman (£17,735), was promptly lodged at the Bank. Further, a complete list was prepared of the household slaves.

On 29th April the Electoral Board visited the Residency and stated that their unanimous choice was Abdullahi Bayero, Ciroma. (This) would accord with the views of all senior Political Officers who had recently served in the area ...

Subsequently Abdullahi was summoned to the Residency ... and it was impressed upon him that the system which had obtained in the past, of rule by the Emir through household slaves, was a matter of the past, and on no account should be revived, indirectly or directly. The responsible chiefs constituted the Council, and the Emir must rule through responsible chiefs. The activities of the Kano Emirate were now so great that it was impossible for one authority to direct them unaided. In order that public business might be conducted, there were two alternatives, administration through household followers, and administration through the chiefs. The former alternative must be ruled out directly.

Abdullahi made a clear statement that he undertook definitely, should he be appointed Emir, to accept the system which Government indicated. News of the approval of His Excellency the Governor of the appointment of Abdullahi Bayero was received at Kano on 10th May; and on the 15th May a ceremony was held at the Residency at which a public announcement was made of the approval of the appointment. A large gathering attended, and the announcement was received with prominent enthusiasm.

His Honour the Lieutenant Governor, who visited Kano on 19th May, expressed himself as satisfied with the measures taken. With a view to facilitating the pledge given prior to his accession, the Emir decided to manumit all palace slaves and to dispense with the services of a few of the slaves and eunuchs who had held outstanding positions in the household. Suitable pensions and gratuities were allowed where circumstances required. The estate of the late Emir was proved at £17,735 and distributed in accordance with Mohammedan law. Bank accounts were opened for each of the late Emir's sons; and the Alkalin Kano was appointed as Trustee for the minors.[17]

The Manumission of Throne-Slaves

In manumitting the palace slaves, Abdullahi Bayero fulfilled the undertakings he had made to the British before his accession, without however violating those traditional relations of *amana* that bound the chief and throne staff together. Bayero did not and, perhaps, could not order them to quit the palace. This vast complex, covering some 37 acres, had for centuries been so intimately identified with the chiefship of Kano that the two could not be separated suddenly without destroying them both.

For its maintenance, the palace required several thousand inhabitants, all bound to the chief by ties of unconditional obedience and mutual loyalty. Traditionally, such relations were expressed and institutionalised by hereditary slavery, although that does not accurately represent their unique and complex symbiotic character. From the palace slaves, the emir drew his servants, court attendants, messengers, *dogarai*, grooms, his heavy cavalry, confidential agents, spies, prison warders, city gatekeepers, official representatives to the Provincial Office, and such senior confidential executives as the Shamaki and the Dan Rimi. Excluding the royal harem, all other women within the palace, slave or free, enjoyed the chief's protection and economic support without demands for service. As the ruler's children increased in number and age, senior slaves would often establish special relations of "foster parentage" with young princes and princesses. In return, the children of palace slaves were welcome within the royal quarters. Relations with such depth, strength and varied dimensions could not be abruptly terminated by decree. Bayero knew this, being familiar with the palace organization and community since his youth. Accordingly, he announced the general manumission of all palace slaves without ordering their withdrawal from the palace. Legally free, these people could now choose whether to withdraw into the wider society, or to remain where they were and maintain the traditional relations and claims that guaranteed their security and fortune. Under these circumstances, it is not surprising that very few manumitted by Bayero chose to withdraw and quit the throne. Yet, by remaining at the palace despite their changed status, these ex-slaves simply reasserted the continuing validity of their traditional relations with the chief, the throne and the wider community.

In decreeing the general manumission of palace slaves, Bayero may have surprised the British by apparently over-fulfilling the conditions they had imposed on him; but substantively this decree merely served to disestablish the claims of hereditary throne staff to participate in the public administration of the Emirate by appointments to strategic positions that carried public authority and were reserved especially for them. To disestablish the ancient and central offices of Shamaki and Dan Rimi without simultaneously transforming his relation as chief to the palace community by a general manumission, would involve unilateral repudiation of the traditional *amana*, thereby inviting disaffection and intrigue within the palace itself. Bayero recognised that the slave organization of the palace community required such offices as Shamaki and Dan Rimi to order and superintend its internal affairs and to handle its external relations. In short, having had to disestablish these senior slave offices, Bayero wisely elected to convert the bases of relation between the throne and its staff from bondage to voluntary association. For this reason, he announced the general manumission of all throne slaves, undoubtedly confident that most would remain where they were, enjoying his protection and maintaining their *amana* by fulfilling their usual duties, while accepting the loss of those old political privileges that had had their fullest expression in the roles of Shamaki and Dan Rimi.

In 1959 while collecting these data, I occupied quarters in the compound of the former Turakin Soro, formerly a harem eunuch, immediately behind the palace, by courtesy of Emir Alhaji Muhammadu Sanussi and the Native Administration. During my stay the term *bawan Sarki* (emir's *or* throne slave) was used objectively and frequently in self-description and in classification of others. The term lacked pejorative qualities but asserted an individual's identification with the palace community and thus indirectly with the throne and emir. This usage indicates that Bayero's manumission enabled the palace residents to reassert their special relation with the throne in the traditional idiom of slavery and self-abnegation. For his part, by this general manumission, the emir had formally divested himself of his traditional obligations to furnish this large population with prominent political roles and subsistence. Thus by his general manumission, Bayero avoided isolating the throne by dispersing the palace community which was both its ancient matrix and, as the civil war and Aliyu's reign had shown, its prime political resource. Bayero's decree thus resolved the problem of maintaining the palace establishment while avoiding direct conflict with its members as well as the British.

The Emir as Imam

Like his father Abbas, Bayero cultivated a public reputation for piety by conducting the weekly service at the central mosque, and delivering the sermon (*wa'azi*) himself, thus fulfilling the highest Muslim ideals of chieftainship by assimilating those features of the priesthood (*limanci*) to his role as emir. By this means he identified himself as the religious leader as well as political head of his people, and simultaneously presented his government as a theocratic regime, instituted and ordered by Allah's will, in which the contemporary British overrule was merely an incident. Moreover, in thus identifying his emirship with the imamate, Bayero renewed the legitimacy of the Fulani regime in Kano by exhibiting it in the most propitious manner as the political organization of the Muslim community under God's guidance. On these pious foundations, although its development and bureaucratization proceeded apace, secularization within the native administration was restrained, diverted and obscured; but clearly these effects formed at most a minor part of Bayero's purpose in thus assuming the religious leadership.

We do not know when Bayero began these weekly addresses; but it was probably not long after his accession. Initially, by resuming his father's practice, Bayero may have wished to demonstrate his piety, learning and filial sentiment, the more clearly by contrasting his performance as emir with Usuman's. But like Abbas, Bayero also followed the Tijaniyya *turuq* (H. *tariqa*), and like his father, he was also the local head of that order. As such, he was spiritually independent of the Kadiriyya sultans of Sokoto; and as emir, he personally represented Kano's religious and political independence from Sokoto. Thus he revived and reasserted in religious form the deep secessionist currents which had first been freely expressed at Kano during the Civil War and the reign of Aliyu Babba, who was the first Kano emir openly to display his preference for the Tijaniyya order, perhaps to assert his religious independence of the Sokoto caliphate. It is possible that as a member of the Tijaniyya, Bayero was constrained to serve as his own *imam* in the Friday mosque, since he could not consistently worship under an *imam* of the Kadiriyya order. However as a Tijaniyya *imam* and head of state, Bayero's conduct and affiliations inevitably influenced many Kano Muslims, including some who had no previous affiliations with the Kadiriyya, to adopt Tijaniyya rituals and join the order, thereby augmenting his authority as emir by that of a Tijaniyya sheikh.

Predictably, as the Tijaniyya movement spread at Kano under Bayero's leadership and influence, devout Kadiriyya residents were stimulated to renew and develop their religious organization, with the result that the ensuing competition between the orders promoted a new type of religious revival at Kano, one which appeared to offer Hausa a new basis for citizenship by proclaiming a new religious universalism for members of either Muslim *turuq*. To what degree these novel expectations were fulfilled in Bayero's reign remains to be shown; but in this regard two points should be noted. First, by his identification with the Tijaniyya, Bayero divided the Muslim community of Kano into three distinct categories, two of which, the Tijaniyya and the Kadiriyya, were contraposed, while the third consisted of those Muslims who belonged to no order. Thus the religious revival Bayero helped to generate had divisive effects in the strictly religious sphere, as well as integrative ones. Secondly, although this revival persuaded many Hausa of Kano to join one or other *turuq*, they did not enrol in Fulani groupings, but preferred to establish units of their own under the immediate direction of Hausa clerics. Thus the spread of the *tariqa* failed to dissolve the historic antagonisms and mutual exclusions of the two ethnic blocs; and throughout Bayero's reign, the competing orders developed and maintained two sets of parallel but separate and mutually exclusive organizations among the Fulani and Hausa of Kano.[18]

The State Council, 1926–1930

For their part, the Provincial Administration were greatly relieved by Usuman's death, and seized the chance to reassert their direction of the emirate by redesigning its central administrative structures. In effect, the territorial reorganization had greatly increased the emir's responsibilities and his control of *hakimai* by instituting as grounds for their dismissal or demotion, ineptitude, dishonesty and maladministration, charges that could readily be levelled at various *hakimai* during these years. Initially the executive sub-district heads, seeking to avoid direction by supervisory district chiefs, had preferred to act on the emir's instructions, which were relayed initially through his vizier, and later through his slaves. Finally, at the *gunduma*, Abbas had assumed control of the central districts around Kano, while supervising others through his vizier and senior district heads. In effect, these arrangements placed district heads of either category firmly under the emir's direction. Yet not content with this situation, in 1914 Abbas attempted to tighten his control of the remoter districts and placed the central ones under his son, the Ciroma Bayero, then stationed at Panisau, thus enabling him to give more attention to the others. Although that arrangement did not last long, Abbas retained and apparently increased his central hold on the territorial administration until his death, despite the vizier's formal responsibility for communications with outlying districts.

On his accession, Usuman further subverted the vizierate by first duplicating and then displacing the official communication structure with another centred at the palace and staffed by his senior slaves. The vizier was thus stripped of political influence, authority and the emir's confidence. Until his health finally broke, Usuman apparently retained control of his senior aides, the Sarkin Fada Aliyu, the Shamaki, the Sallama and the Dan Rimi, and thus of the *hakimai* and their district affairs; but in the last two years, as his health collapsed, Usuman seems to have lost control, and in consequence, this "unofficial" structure lacked the central co-ordinating direction it initially possessed. As a result the territorial organization ceased to discharge its routine functions smoothly, the machinery of palace control was exposed, and the British were able to demand its dissolution. A new central council was then hastily assembled by recalling the Madaki, the Sarkin Bai and the Galadima to Kano to join the Waziri in discharging those administrative tasks which Usuman had recently conducted through palace slaves. However, despite the expulsion of Shamaki and Dan Rimi, the new Council organization remained inchoate during Usuman's reign, principally because he controlled communications with his *hakimai*, and the roles and responsibilities of the councillors remained poorly defined. On Usuman's death, the Provincial Administration decided to rectify this condition.

As reconstituted after Bayero's accession in 1926, the new Council consisted of the vizier Muhammadu Gidado, the Madaki Umaru and the Sarkin Bai Abdulkadiri. Later that year, when the Galadima Mamman Bello died at Fogolawa, Bayero appointed his own brother, the Dan Iya Abdulkadir, as Galadima. In 1928 he recalled the Galadima to Kano City to join the Council and restored the Sarkin Bai Abdulkadiri to Dambarta as district head.

As a former Alkalin Kano, the vizier Muhammadu Gidado was professionally competent to advise on all issues of Muslim law that came before the Council. As head of the emir's office, the vizier also received early notice of such matters. By 1927 the Council had delegated supervision of legal affairs to Muhammadu Gidado; but only in the following year, when the Galadima Abdulkadiri had replaced the Sarkin Bai on Council, were the roles of the Madaki and Galadima defined. It appears that until 1928 Bayero retained executive responsibilities for the central and outlying districts, including Kano City, even though he informally delegated certain functions and many specific tasks to the Madaki and the Sarkin Bai. When his brother joined the Council, Bayero placed the Madaki in charge of district administration, while the Galadima as district head took charge of Kano City and of all Native Administration departments within it, excluding the Treasury, Secretariat and Law Courts, which remained under the vizier.

Throughout this period, the council met twice daily at the palace. In the mornings the emir consulted the vizier, Madaki and Galadima on subjects that required administrative action. Bayero would issue the necessary instructions to the Madaki or Galadima, after which they withdrew, and left him with the vizier. Either a number of judicial assessors (*muhutai*) and malams were then admitted, or the emir and vizier would move to join them in another chamber. This group, which constituted the emir's Judicial Council, exercised exclusive jurisdiction over cases involving homicide, taxation, offences against Native Authority regulations and bye-laws, such complaints against Native Administration officials in the performance of their duties as embezzlement, oppression, or indiscipline, such political offences as disobedience, and all disputes regarding titles to land or houses, wherever these issues arose throughout the emirate. In addition the Judicial Council heard appeals from District Courts, and from the court of the Chief Alkali in Kano. It could also review cases heard by these lesser Courts and order their re-trial.

By 1932, as the emir's senior legal adviser, the vizier routinely supervised the courts of rural *alkalai* through one of his senior malams who toured the districts and read through the monthly case records of these district courts to detect any irregularities or questionable decisions. From 1926 to 1930, the Limam of Kano Usuman and the Limam of the Galadima's ward served on this Judicial Council as *muhutai*; and it seems likely that at first the Chief Alkali of Kano, Ja'afaru, was also a member. However, in 1927–28 the Alkalin Kano was removed from the Judicial Council, which the Waziri Gidado thereafter dominated by his legal expertise.

In mid-afternoon, following his daily judicial session, the emir again met with his vizier, Madaki and Galadima to receive reports on action initiated at the morning session, and any communications about developments in the city or rural areas that required attention. Thus the emir had two councils, an executive one consisting of the vizier, the Madaki and the Galadima, and a judicial one composed of the vizier and certain learned malams which adjudicated local issues by the Muslim *shari'a*. However, as before, all sentences involving capital punishment required the Resident's approval.

In 1930 the Council was expanded by addition of the Ma'aji (treasurer), Abdullahi dan Alhaji Abandi, who was of Arab descent. The Treasury was then removed from the vizier's supervision and constituted as a separate department under the Ma'aji's control. However, the Treasurer did not attend morning sessions of the Executive Council, when the vizier, Madaki and Galadima discussed political and administrative issues with Bayero. Instead he reported with the Madaki and Galadima in the afternoons when matters involving finance were discussed. Thus in 1930, although not clearly recognised by the British, on administrative matters, Bayero dealt with three councils, or alternately with two councils, one of which met as two committees. On tricky political issues, he probably consulted others. Though summoned to report and advise on issues involving state revenues, the Ma'aji was clearly excluded from sessions which dealt with confidential relations between the Native and British Administrations. As the vizier aged, although initially present at all three council meetings, he gradually withdrew from the afternoon sessions, which were of a strictly executive character, in order to keep abreast of his departmental work. The Ma'aji worked at the Treasury in the mornings; and the Galadima and Madaki directed their various departments between and after the two daily council sessions. Once weekly the councillors escorted the emir to the Resident's house for a formal discussion of Kano's affairs with him; and as necessary, the resident visited Bayero at the palace for private audience.[19]

The Emir and Council

Before describing further how routine administrative functions were divided among and discharged by the councillors, the council's status and powers should be clarified. Briefly, despite their "ministerial" roles as the emir's officially appointed executives, councillors lacked independent authority. The "Executive" Council only had an advisory status. The emir could delay decisions, or set aside the council's recommendations as he thought fit. No disciplinary powers over their subordinate staff were transferred to councillors; and all powers of appointment, promotion, dismissal, discipline, suspension, salary increases and the like, remained with the emir, subject only to the Resident's approval on the appointment of senior territorial chiefs. As the Resident himself reports in 1931,

> matters of high importance, and others, such as the appointment and dismissal of staff, changes in policy or procedure, are referred to the Emir for approval or direction as the case may be.[20]
>
> While every effort is made to encourage the Emir to delegate functions to his councillors, and to make use of their advice, they (the Councillors) remain advisers, and the Emir, under our guidance, retains his personal responsibility.[21]

Under the Native Authority Ordinance of 1925, by which the Protectorate Government assimilated the pre-colonial chiefdoms to its order, the emir of Kano had been recognised by statute as the "sole Native Authority" in the emirate. Thus, being by law endowed with all those powers and responsibilities which the Government of Nigeria saw fit to entrust to him, the emir at law could not escape his personal responsibility for their use. Accordingly, even when the Resident L.S.

Ward describes the "decentralisation of executive responsibilities" at Kano, he repeatedly notes that these delegated functions are exercised by councillors whose discretionary scope was severely restricted by prior reservation of decisions on all political, personnel or disciplinary questions to the emir.[22] In Provincial files that date from this period, the over-centralisation of Kano's government in the emir's hands forms a constant and prominent theme; yet under the Native Authority Ordinance, which legally established the emir as sole Native Authority, it could hardly be otherwise.

The emir's reservation of power to decide all issues of interest to him antedated colonial rule by several centuries. As indicated above, the meaning of Aliyu's unprecedented order to his brother, the Wombai Mamudu, to select and appoint a new Dan Iya in place of Sa'adu, and his complacency when Mamudu appointed a Dan Makwayau as well on the same day, lay in the revelation that Aliyu's confidence in his power and Mamudu's good faith made him indifferent to the particular appointments and relieved him of the invidious responsibility for these decisions. As we have seen, this event is still remembered at Kano as a unique demonstration of chiefly power, and perhaps as the most decisive evidence of Aliyu's sultanism.

The basic condition of government at Kano, as elsewhere under the Fulani, is the rule that only an emir can dismiss anyone he appoints. Implied in this formula are many subsidiary provisions which reserve to the emir all the power he needs to alter the conditions, functions, status, organization, relations and resources of the appointments he has made. At Kano from Hausa days, the chief had reserved to himself the powers to appoint village heads as well as *hakimai* and departmental heads, irrespective of their differing birth-statuses, with the sole exceptions of village heads in such imperfectly assimilated vassal states as Gaya, Rano, Dutse, Gwaram and Karaye. *Hakimai* were likewise free to appoint their own *lawanai*, and to reallocate functions, titles, fiefs and other resources among them; but while selecting prospective village heads for recommendation to the emir, or while advocating actions against those in office, they could go no further. Thus only the emir who conferred his appointment, or his successor, could initiate further action to discipline or reward a subordinate. By this principle, rulers reserved their right to investigate the conduct of lesser officials independently and at will, thereby protecting village heads against *hakimai*, and *hakimai* against one another, while retaining decisive authority over both.

In structural terms, the formally autocratic nature of this chieftaincy is thus reducible to the rule that, as the primary office, the paramount chiefship is the source of authority for all others. It accordingly regulates their distribution, tenure, scope, resources, relations and development. Moreover, it assimilates subsidiary offices to itself as organs of the same superior body, incapable of truly independent life, although autonomous in their due spheres. Substantively, as illustrated above, the chiefship delegated numerous functions and wide discretion to its official organs; and at different phases of its development under the Hausa and Fulani, relations between the chief and his officials, the chief and the nobility, varied widely. Such variation indicates that in traditional terms, in ideology and in practice alike, chieftaincy as the principle identified by ultimate power of decision and enforcement is a constitutive structural fact indifferent to functional change. Its existence was thus both sufficient and necessary to constitute and perpetuate these states. As such, it persisted with little change after Lugard's conquest and throughout the first half century of colonial rule, irrespective of British legislation or policies to modify it.

In differing ways, Abbas and Usuman had both adapted this essential discretionary power to the conditions of Indirect Rule; and after their deaths on each occasion that its critical situation changed, so did the methods by which the chief preserved his decisive power to rule. For example, despite the relatively rational and efficient decentralisation of executive functions among his councillors, Bayero retained his exclusive right to regulate official relations, procedures, responsibilities, appointments and rewards as an essential condition for the preservation and exercise of chiefship throughout his reign. It was thus by his decisions that the Galadima replaced the Sarkin Bai on the Central Council, and that the Ma'aji, a *shigege* official with purely technical duties, joined that body once the Treasury had been removed from the vizier's supervision. Thus in reviewing the changing administrative arrangements of the council during Bayero's reign, we should never at any moment forget his exclusive and final powers of decision. The British had indeed, by establishing the council, substituted free and "responsible" ministers for palace slaves. They had also substituted written for oral communications. They had not notably reduced the emir's essential power of discretion; nor could they do so without thereby subverting the basis of the state and disrupting its structure. The Council remained throughout an advisory body, which the emir could change as he felt best. Instead, by reorganising the council on functional lines, the British merely enhanced the efficiency and capacities of the Native Administration under its statutory autocrat, the emir, acting according to the Ordinance of 1925 as Sole Native Authority, despite the "true and ancient system."

It is true that the Judicial Council heard complaints against native officials and persons suspected of political offence; yet even then, the emir reserved the right to refer all such issues to his "executive" council, and as always, in the Judicial Council, having listened to the evidence and opinions of his legal advisers, he delivered the sentence. Thus, in these strategic areas also, the emir's authority could not be challenged except on those issues such as tax embezzlement in which the Provincial Administration took a very keen interest.

Orders issued by state councillors in their executive roles were all made in the emir's name. Unless such orders derived from existing rules and regulations of the Native Authority, they required Bayero's approval, privately by correspondence, or through discussions in council. Thus, devolution of functional responsibilities among state councillors proceeded without reduction or dispersal of the emir's authority.[23]

The Judiciary

Administrative reports on the jurisdiction and character of the Judicial Council at this period illustrate the great adaptive values of the emir's ultimate power. As a jurist and former Alkalin Kano, the vizier Muhammadu Gidado employed his role in the Judicial Council to extend his authority over the Alkali Courts throughout Kano. In 1927 the position was summarised as follows:

The Waziri is the chief legal councillor and is assisted by several malams. While the Emir delivers judgment in accordance with the *shari'a*, he acts on the legal opinions put forward by the malams, of whom the Waziri is the leader. The Waziri's position is entirely legal and he represents, with the malams, the legal sanction which is sometimes achieved in some Emirates by adding the Chief Alkali to the Judicial Council in important cases. (The removal by death or otherwise of the present Waziri would need reconsideration of this position, as it does not follow that every Waziri is a legal expert) ...

With (certain) exceptions, the Chief Alkali's court administers the law or *shari'a* over the whole of the Emirate, and is an appeal court from all native courts in the Emirate.

District courts are courts of first instance for the districts. Appeals against District Courts go in the first instance to the Emir's Council, which is a Court of Appeal. The Council would call for a report and if, in their opinion, there was a case for a revision on the advice of the *malamai*, the Emir would refer it to the Alkali's Court for confirmation or reversal, as the case may be. The Waziri advises the Emir in his judicial capacity, but the matter comes before the Council as such, and the Waziri has no authority to intervene personally through his agents in such cases. Complainants are always encouraged to go, but are not compelled to go to the District Courts first.[24]

Thus the vizier extended the Judicial Council's jurisdiction of first instance by admitting ordinary cases from rural areas, and then reduced the appeal jurisdiction of the Chief Alkali's court at Kano by intervening to decide firstly, whether the case appealed justified retrial, and secondly, whether this should be done by the Judicial Council or by the court of the Chief Alkali.

In 1930, discussing the Council, the Resident commented as follows:

The executive members are still hampered by an unnecessary susceptibility to *malamai* influence. The interference by the *malamai* of the Judicial Council timorously assented to by the lay members in executive matters, has again had to be checked ... It requires very careful handling ... since it is the vital spot where one finds oneself up against essentially Muhammadan tendencies and prejudices ...

The Judicial Council of Kano (still) attempts to interfere and obtain power. Farm dispute cases take up a great deal of time. These cases are dealt with by the Emir as a prerogative for the whole of the Emirate. There is interminable delay and it is doubtful if they are dealt with satisfactorily. In the past, where territorial chiefs existed as distinct from *hakimai* or headquarter fief holders, they dealt with local farm disputes. Such chiefs would be Gaya, Dutse, Rano, etc. Farm disputes are now on the increase since all heirs claim a share in land inheritance, according to law, whereas previously native custom generally left the eldest son in possession, who compensated his brothers. Now the argument is that land grows a crop worth so much (for) export, even if a man does not intend to farm it himself, he wants the use of it ...

Further investigation of District Courts has shown some undesirable features ... Several District Alkalai have been removed or changed ...

It is also considered that the central administration must devise some machinery for inspection of Native Courts apart from the inspection done by Political Officers, which cannot be very regular. With the District chiefs and their work, the central administration is in touch through the Madaki. With the Alkalai, they are not in real touch at all. The Chief Alkalin Kano is on the whole satisfactory, though there is little love lost between him and members of the Judicial Council; but I doubt if things would be any better if he was more *persona grata*.[25]

By 1932 the Waziri had established his right to supervise all Courts in the Emirate.

> In addition to exercising his functions as such in the Judicial Council, he (the Waziri) is also supervisor of the District Alkalai. In practice, the Waziri delegates to a senior malam the monthly duty of going through the cases of the District Alkalai and depends on him to detect irregularities. When such are detected, the Waziri informs the Emir and demands—in the name of the Emir—an explanation from the Court in question. Any subsequent action is taken by the Waziri's office. The Alkali is informed where it is ruled or thought that he is wrong, the matter having been first discussed in council. Any action against an Alkali for malpractice should be dealt with by the Judicial Council.
>
> The routine checking of fees and the filing and entering of cases is done in the Waziri's office by his staff of clerks (malams).
>
> The Waziri has nothing to do with the work of the Alkalin Kano. The position of the Alkali (of Kano) was not clear to me; but I gathered that he dealt direct with the Emir and Council.[26]

It seems evident that, having excluded the Chief Alkali from the Emir's Judicial Council, the vizier first dominated this group by his legal learning and experience, and then proceeded to extend its functions at the expense of the *Alkali* courts in rural areas and the city by persuading the Judicial Council to hear certain complaints of first instance from rural areas, and by assuming as vizier, on behalf of the Judicial Council, the right to review routinely decisions of all lesser courts within the emirate. By these means the vizier, himself a former Chief Alkali, personally reassumed decisive control over the judiciary. He could also deploy legalistic arguments to advocate policies or block proposals at meetings of the Executive Council. Continuing, Ward remarks,

> As regards the future, the Waziri is old and about to go to Mecca. Although senior, he is not Prime Minister (but) *primus inter pares*. His position is not very clearly defined, and there is thought to be no need that it should be (but) there will always in future be one member of the council who would be the chief legal adviser ... It appears to me that the office of chief legal adviser has created itself, owing to the present Waziri's high legal standing, but it is not the revival of a former Kano office. A scheme is under examination at the moment for the better scrutiny and control of the work of the District courts; this aims at avoiding the misunderstandings and delays of long-range examination by instituting examination and settlement on the spot of all doubtful or queried cases by staff provided for the purpose.[27]

In 1930, the 23 rural Muslim courts and 3 city courts (including the court of the *Alkalin Kasuwa* (Judge of the Market), which still functions) heard a total of 44,113 civil (*karamin shari'a*) cases and 6,898 "criminal" (*manyan shari'a*) ones. The Provincial Court under the British Resident Magistrate dealt with 20 cases that year, 19 of which were criminal suits. The Kano Judicial Council heard 48 cases involving homicide, as against 89 in the previous year.[28]

Evidently Bayero had no desire to restrict the Waziri's judicial activities, having already removed the Treasury, and with it all executive functions from the vizierate. By this means, while allowing the vizier to bring the rural courts under his control, Bayero preserved the executive from the vizier's domination. Thus instead of losing power to Gidado, Bayero employed Gidado to increase his own.

District and Central Administration

In December 1931 the Resident, L.S. Ward, described the functions of the Madaki as follows:

> There are two main branches in the Madaki's office—District administration and Revenue. The Madaki deals direct in the name of the Emir with the District heads. The annual revision of the tax is prepared in the Madaki's office. Where there is no revenue survey, the District Heads take a census to discover increases and decreases, from which adjustments are made. The Madaki regularly visits the disticts, thus keeping himself in touch with their affairs. He has no representative to act for him in his absence. It does not appear that one is necessary, as his absences are not lengthy and his office is organised well.
>
> District Heads report direct to the Madaki in the first instance. All District Heads have *mukkadasai* (deputies) in Kano City, but their function seems now to be merely that of caretakers and hosts when people visit Kano from the district ... All orders to District Heads are sent as from the Emir through the Madaki. All communications from District Heads, monthly returns, reports, etc., are sent to the Madaki, who refers the more important ones to the Emir and deals with the less important ones himself. If it is necessary to summon a District Head or Village Head to Kano, the verbal approval of the Emir is first obtained. The Madaki has no power to punish a Village Head or a District Head; this is the Emir's prescriptive right and is jealously guarded. The annual revision of the tax having been prepared in the Madaki's office (Revenue Survey with a Chief Surveyor), announcement of the tax is made through the same channel. Complainants against District or Village Heads will usually go direct to the Madaki or to the Emir. Complainants against others may first go to the *mukkadasai*. (Complainants are dealt with by the Judicial Council or may be referred to the Alkali).
>
> All roads not under the Engineer NA's care, that is, dry season motor roads, are kept up by the District Heads at the instance of the Madaki. Public buildings are similarly dealt with. District Heads are required to give a detailed estimate before being sent the money. In both cases they are made responsible for making the payments. District Heads have been given imprests for the payment of road labour, which they renew from time to time.[29]

By far the most varied and exacting role was that of the Galadima. By 1932,

> The Galadima is responsible for the following departments, each of which has a departmental head who is to a greater or lesser degree responsible to the Galadima:

	Department	Head
1	Prisons	Yari (There are 3 prisons)
2	Sanitary	Malam Sani
3	Police	Sarkin Gardi

4	Buildings	Malam Hamidu
5	Markets	Sarkin Kasuwa
6	City Wards	Masu Anguwa (Ward Heads)
7	Sabon Gari	Sabon Gari
8	Education	Middle school – M. Abubakar (son of Waziri)
		Elementary School – M. Inuwa
9	Medical	Warden
10	Works	M. Gwadabe (Wakilin Sana'a)
11	Veterinary	M. Husaini
12	Survey and Printing	(Head Malam)
13	Water and Light	–
14	Roads	(Wakilin Sana'a)

(Numbers 8 to 14 have European officers in charge)

Prisons. Yari has powers of six lashes for a prisoner and fines of two shillings for a warder. Any punishment greater than this is dealt with by the Galadima, who refers to the Emir anything beyond his jurisdiction. It is thought that the Yari in practice always refers to the Galadima before exerting his powers; but of all the departmental heads, Yari alone has disciplinary powers of punishment. He takes out his own R.I.Es (Treasury Vouchers) and is responsible for the vote not being overspent.

Sanitary. Malam Sani acts as Sanitary Inspector and reports offenders to the Galadima. The Galadima deals with petty cases by a warning. Galadima deals with the R.I.Es (Treasury vouchers).

Police. Sarkin Gadi is responsible for the discipline of the force but no disciplinary powers have been delegated. The Galadima punishes within limits but refers serious cases to the Emir. People arrested by 'Yan Gadi (police) are brought to the Sarkin Gadi, who takes them to the Galadima who passes them to the Judicial Council or to the Alkalin Kano. Appointments and dismissals are made by the Emir. R.I.Es (Treasury Vouchers) for upkeep of barracks are taken out by Sarkin Gadi; those for uniforms by Galadima.

Buildings. Malam Hamidu consults with Galadima as to what is to be done. He takes out R.I.Es and pays labour.

Markets. Sarkin Kasuwa is assisted by three malams on a system recently introduced by which all stalls are numbered and individual receipts are given. Sarkin Kasuwa is nominally responsible for repairs to stalls, but Galadima takes out the R.I.Es. Complaints against offenders and against market rules are taken to Galadima by Sarkin Kasuwa.

Ward Heads. Masu Anguwa (ward-heads in the city) are responsible for the division of tax and its collection. The tax is brought to Galadima first, as are complaints against reluctant payers. Ward Heads make daily reports to Galadima and also produce daily returns of births and deaths. Recalcitrant taxpayers are dealt with by Galadima in the first instance; he may detain them in the debtors' prison, and if necessary takes action in the Judicial Council.

The post of *Sabon Gari* (Head of Sabon Gari, the New Town outside the city walls settled by immigrants from Southern Nigeria) is a recent institution and not perhaps come to full bloom. He has no judicial powers. His position is much the same as that of the Ward Heads. There seems to be considerable liaison between the N.A. Police and the Protectorate Police, between the Galadima and the Commissioner of Police, Kano. Mutual assistance is given in the tracing of thieves and in the interchange of criminal reports. Cases not suitable for Supreme Court are sent through Galadima and District Officer for the Alkali Kano to deal with.

With regard to the departments which are under European officers (numbers 8 to 14), each has a head who is in direct touch with the Galadima. They enable the Galadima to be kept informed of routine matters, and the European (also) consults the Galadima. Minor disciplinary powers are not delegated but are reserved for the Galadima or the Emir as the case demands. In the case of the Middle School, school offences are of course dealt with therein. Truants are sought through the channel of the Galadima and if necessary the Madaki.

R.I.Es (Treasury vouchers) are in most cases taken out by the heads: No. 8, Middle School, Malam Abubakar; Elementary Schools, Malam Inuwa. No. 9, Shahuci Hospital, Galadima - but the Warden pays. 10. Works - Wakilin Sana'a. 11. Veterinary - Malam Husaini. 12. Survey - Head Malam. 13. Water, etc., - European officer. 14. Roads - Engineer, N.A. or Galadima or Madaki as the case may be.

The first six departmental heads, and to a lesser degree number 7, are directly responsible for the internal working of their departments. They have greater or lesser powers delegated to them. Only one, the Yari, has the power of punishment without reference to Galadima. Similarly Galadima, while dealing with all routine matters, less serious affairs, breaches of discipline and the like, refers the more serious to the Emir for consideration. Such matters as are referred are dealt with in Council but it does not require a full attendance of the Council; a quorum of three is sufficient. More important matters affecting the working of any department would be dealt with by the Emir in Council as a matter of course. It is perhaps the intention to develop within safe limits the discretionary powers of the Galadima, as of all members of Council. In the case of the central departments under the Galadima, it will no doubt be the aim to continue decentralisation, which has in some cases gone further ahead than in others.[30]

As District Head of Kano City, besides supervising the increasingly numerous and complex N.A enterprises at the capital, the Galadima was also responsible for its territorial administration. There were, then, some 137 historic wards in the city,

> some of them containing over 500 adult males, others only a handful; the adminis-tration is based on these small wards, which for convenience are grouped into four divisions, each of which is subdivided into a number of sanitary areas, which also form the framework of police organisation. These four divisions, with a fifth covering certain extramural areas to the east (Sabon Gari) are under the Galadima … Through the heads of the divisions he collects the general taxes and water rates, maintains the peace; he supervises the city police, the market, the prisons and sani-tation, and deals with the many problems arising.[31]

The subdivision of the city into four administrative units was effected in 1932 to relieve the Galadima. The four divisions, north, south, east and west, were placed under *wakilai* or deputies (of the Galadima) entitled Wakilin Arewa (Deputy for the North), Wakilin Kudu (Deputy for the South), Wakilin Gabbas and Wakilin Yamma (Deputies of the East and West). As might be expected, most of these new offices were conferred on Suleibawa or their leading clients. Similar considerations governed the selection of other *wakilai* as heads of the emerging central departments of Public Works, Survey, Sanitation, Police, Prisons, Education, and Survey and Printing which had grown out of the *taki* assessment of 300,000 acres surrounding the city. By 1932, when the Survey and Printing Department of the Kano NA also undertook job printing of forms, receipts, office books, ledgers and the like for other Native Authorities in Northern Nigeria, it could operate efficiently without European assistance.[32]

Complainants seeking to present their cases before the emir's Judicial Court presented themselves to the Madaki if they came from a rural district, or to the Galadima if from the city. The two councillors would then report the complaints to the Executive Council which arranged for immediate trial.

In 1930, when the Ma'aji joined the Council, the emirate's annual revenues exceeded £200,000, and its expenditures, £190,000. The Ma'aji was responsible for the receipt and banking of the revenues and for administering all disbursements. Through his staff he controlled and checked all accounts and scrutinised all requisitions for expenditures (R.I.Es) which came to him before submitting them to the emir for approval and signature. With help from the Provincial staff, the Ma'aji also prepared annual estimates of budgetary revenues and expenditures for the coming year. In 1932, district chiefs were made responsible to the Ma'aji for accounts of all expenditures on departmental or other heads within their districts. Specific projects authorised by the emir would be costed by the district head concerned, and detailed estimates submitted to the Ma'aji for the emir's approval. As work proceeded, the Ma'aji would despatch funds on requests from the district head, who supervised their disbursement.[33]

Until 1926 Kano Province incorporated nine emirates in four Divisions. While varying greatly in size, situation and wealth, these emirates required equal and continuous attention, so that the Provincial Administration, which was often understaffed and always liable to lose its experienced personnel, had little chance of promoting their economic development. However, in 1926 the Province was reduced, and Katsina was transferred to Zaria Province. Kano Province was then reconstituted as two Divisions, one of which contained Kano emirate, while the other included the emirates of Hadeija, Daura, Kazaure and Gumel. This reorganization enabled the Provincial staff at Kano to devote rather more time than before to the promotion of its technical and educational development.

Administrative Responses to Economic Developments

From 1926 to 1932 Kano hovered on the threshold that separates the medieval and the modern worlds. In 1926 the first aeroplanes landed beside the city. In 1927 the Native and Provincial Administrations approved plans for the development of electrical and water supplies for the growing town by pumping from wells dug in the bed of the Challawa river eight miles to the south. Of £330,000 this development was estimated to cost, the emirate undertook to pay £310,000 from its reserves. Work on the scheme began in 1928; and by 1931 the city and its suburbs had constant and adequate supplies of water and power. In 1929 the Native Authority (N.A) opened its first hospital at Shahuci in the City, built by the native Department of Public Works. The North Nigerian Government seconded a doctor to the hospital, which the Galadima supervised through an N.A official designated as "warden." In 1931 the hospital contained beds for 59 men, 18 women and 12 children.[34] Twenty years later it was one of the largest hospitals in Nigeria.

During 1930 and 1931, Northern Nigeria suffered heavy invasions of locusts which threatened to strip the earth of growing crops. Thanks to their district organizations, the Provincial staff and departmental personnel managed to save most of the harvest. In the same year cotton was introduced by the Agricultural Department to supplement groundnuts as a cash crop for peasants to grow for export. At Kano both the peasants and the Native Administration then relied on groundnut sales for tax payments, which averaged 7s 6d per adult male and 2s per cow in 1931 when the Kano N.A retained 70 percent of its tax receipts, and transferred 30 percent to the North Nigerian Government.

By 1925 the steady increases of strangers, motor traffic and crime in Kano and its suburbs necessitated a reorganization of the Emir's *dogarai*. Some 200 *dogarai* were selected for special training in traffic control, police duties, organization and drill. This force, known as the '*Yan Gadi* was placed under a Sarkin Gadi (Chief of the Guard), responsible for policing the city and suburbs. The remaining *dogarai* then lost their police functions within the city, though continuing to serve as police attached to district heads in rural areas, and as couriers and escorts. They were also frequently posted at railway stations, trade centres, markets, and on Native Authority premises. In emergencies, the *dogarai* and '*Yan Gadi* assisted one another, and both could also call on the Government Police, who serviced the new township outside Kano City where the Europeans lived.

By 1927 the prisons of Kano, supervised by the Yari, contained on average between 800 and 1,000 inmates. It was clearly necessary to build a hospital ward within the prison; and a reformatory was also established near the emir's fruit and vegetable gardens for the rehabilitation of delinquent boys. In 1929 the N.A. Department of Works (PWD) received new workshops and garages, new plant and further staff. In 1930 a centre for the education of girls drawn mainly from the ruling families was opened at Kano despite resistance from the vizier Gidado and Muslim intelligentsia. Within a year the centre contained 28 girls.[35]

Following the assembly of chiefs and emirs at Kano in 1925 for the durbar that greeted the Prince of Wales, in 1930, after much discussion, the Governor of Northern Nigeria initiated a series of chiefly conferences at regional centres to discuss matters of common interest and to advise on questions of Native Administration and local policy. Initially these conferences were regarded as educational by the chiefs and as politically valuable by the Administration. In 1931 a second conference of all senior Northern chiefs was held at Kaduna, the Region's capital. Accompanied by his Waziri, Madaki and Ma'aji, Bayero attended this assembly, leaving the Galadima behind to administer the chiefdom.[36] In 1934 a smaller group of emirs and chiefs again assembled at Kaduna, following which this advisory council was discontinued for some years at the direction of Sir Donald Cameron.[37] These were the first British adventures in regional consultation and policy discussions in Northern Nigeria.

By 1931 Kano emirate contained two elementary schools, a new Middle or intermediate school, a craft school, and several thousands of Koranic schools.[38] In 1928, at the vizier Muhammadu Gidado's suggestion, a legal school was established at Shahuci in Kano City to train *muhutai* for the Alkali Courts. Bayero at first appointed his old tutor, Malam Sule, as head of the school, but on the death of the Ma'aji Abdullahi dan Alhaji Abandi, he promoted Sule, a son of Limam

Isma'ilu, to the office of Ma'aji. By 1928 five experimental dispensaries had been opened in rural districts, and by 1933 there were ten.[39]

Prisoners at Kano City were finally unshackled between 1930 and 1933. At that date approximately 100 cattle were killed daily in the city markets throughout the dry season, and Kano, by Government records, also exported between fifteen and eighteen thousand cattle per annum to Ibadan, Lagos and other markets in southern Nigeria.[40]

In 1932 it was estimated that the city contained some 83,000 people, and another 25,000 during the dry season. Within 15 miles of its walls lived another 320,000 people; and within a radius of 30 miles, one million.[41] To restrain crime, the city was that year subdivided into a system of night beats manned by *'yan gadi*.[42] A trader from Sierra Leone was appointed as head of the Sabon Gari (New Town) to which immigrants from southern Nigeria and further afield came increasingly. District heads having become sub-accountants to the Native Treasury that year, trained scribes were sent to assist them and permanent district headquarters were built in ten rural towns, together with new wells, public latrines, new markets, roads, and in some cases new town layouts.[43]

With the subdivision of Kano City under four *wakilai*, each having his own staff, city sanitation received more systematic attention. A beginning was made with the still unfinished task of filling in the innumerable borrow pits in which mosquitoes and other pests flourished. On the suggestion of the vizier Muhammadu Gidado, female sanitary inspectors were trained and appointed to inspect the interiors of compounds, from which men were excluded under the institution of purdah.[44] Permanent public latrines, regular street cleaning and constant pressure gradually improved the city sanitation. During the next five years the Provincial Administration waged a vigorous campaign against some of the major diseases that affected the emirate. In 1933 the populations of Jahun and Dutse were surveyed for sleeping sickness, a new leper settlement was established, and many thousands were vaccinated for smallpox. From 1931, Veterinary Officers were busy innoculating cattle against rinderpest and improving the treatment of hides and skins for export.[45] As the rinderpest innoculation continued, the number of sanitary inspectors increased; and in 1933, for the first time, the Resident mentioned a development plan for the Emirate and specified some of its components.

The estimated surplus on March 31st 1934 is approximately £250,000. Reserves against calamities such as famines are earmarked at approximately £100,000 invested in the United Kingdom. There is therefore, at a maximum, about £150,000 available for development. This, or such proportion of it as may be considered advisable under present circumstances, and with the possibility of a shrinking revenue, is being spread over a three years' programme of development, to embrace *inter alia* the following items:

	£
Offices	25,000
Kano-Wudil-Eastern road	35,000
Town planning	9,000
Wells	15,000

Tsetse	12,000
Rural areas (Development)	9,000
City drainage	40,000

Of these items, £30,000 is expected to be spent in 1934–5. Other items for 1934–5 include Grazing Areas, Roads Improvement, Leper Colony, etc.[46]

Nonetheless, despite their desire "to galvanise the Village Headmen into activities that are not too entirely bound up with tax collection," for historical and political reasons the Resident and Provincial Administration had limited success in associating with these schemes "the elders with the Village Headman, and thereby making him a more real representative of the needs of the peasantry."[47] No attempts were made at this time to base rural development on popularly elected councils, despite Resident Lindsell's apparent desire to arouse popular support. He justified this strategy somewhat uneasily as follows: "We would appear to be building from the top, but this is not altogether so. The format of the machinery is correct, and it is a case really of supplying the sinews and life that will make that machinery more useful and active. This could not have been done with the Village Heads until the District Heads had found their feet."[48] Considerable progress had been made in redesigning and equipping the Kano administration to handle future developments.

> In controlling works in the districts, chiefs must now keep cash books and be responsible for the daily disbursement of wages to labour. With new court and school buildings, local and minor road work, tsetse clearing and new markets, there is a good deal to do, which relieves the central administration of work they never satisfactorily performed … It is now possible to send, say, £100 out to a District Chief to build a Market on an estimate duly passed, and to know that it will be properly accounted for. It will also be found, and can be verified, as I have personally done, that the labour is voluntary and duly paid according to the standard and accepted rate of 6d per day.[49]

To balance Lindsell's rosy impression of the Kano administration during these years, a memorandum written on tax collection by J.R. Patterson, who replaced Lindsell as Resident, Kano in 1934, merits notice. This memorandum discusses the indebtedness of village heads, the feasability of witholding their salaries for the December quarter when tax payments are overdue, and their reliance on *kudin falle*.

> *Kudin falle* is a payment by a peasant to a Village Head in respect of tax some time in advance of tax collection. By the peasant it is used as a bribe, so that he may be let off lightly in the apportionment of tax. The money is of course used by the village head on his personal expenditure (often to liquidate his debts); he reckons to make good in respect of tax when the collection comes.[50]

Patterson also criticises the unsatisfactory supervision of village heads by district heads; but at least in Taura District that year, the reverse obtained. There a junior District Officer reported the argument advanced by the district head of Taura, the Magajin Malam Na Cedi Ahmadu Rufa'i, a Fulani whose family had long been clients of the Yolawa, to break up five village areas of Taura District, Yangayame, Kore, Seyori, Gidan Maza and Buturanawa, thereby reducing these village heads to hamlet heads. In anticipation the Magajin Malam Ahmadu had summoned other village heads and promised them increased territories, communities and salaries, if they would make it worth his while. According to the District Officer, one village head paid £10 for this good news; and seven others were similarly exploited.[51] Probably Lindsell's optimistic assessment of the rural administration reflected his remoteness and ignorance of the reality.

Local Administration

By 1926 the *taki* method of tax assessment had been replaced with another method based on detailed assessments of selected villages. The new assessments estimated the approximate net annual values of village production in livestock and cattle, trade and "industrial" activities, on which taxes of less than ten percent would be levied. This proportion of the village's estimated income yielded the "lump sum" due as tax for the year. Under the *taki* system, since tax burdens increased with acreage, occupational taxes had been retained to balance the burdens borne by farmers; but under the lump sum assessments, *kudin sana'a*, the occupational tax, finally lapsed as the *kudin shuke* had done before, and the village chief was instructed to distribute tax burdens within his community according to his estimate of the differential wealth and taxable capacities of his people. This system accordingly enabled village and district heads to shift the tax burden from their kin and close associates to others; but as long as the "lump sum" levied against a village was paid on time and no complaints were received, the British and Native Authorities were content and pleased with the village administration.[52] Reporting on Kano in 1932–33, Margery Perham records a conversation at Bici with the Ciroma Sanusi, Bayero's son and successor, who, as district head, showed her his ledger of tax receipts with details of 96 villagers. "I collect a tax of £19,000; this year I have had some fifty complaints about the incidence, most of them were justified. The excess was shifted onto richer neighbours. Only ten complaints reached the Assistant District Officer who toured my district. Last year I had two hundred complaints."[53] Perham also remarks that "in the 1931 census 11% (of the population in Kano city) claimed to be Fulani and 77% Hausa."[54] Thus the number of taxpayers who risked the consequences of complaint was only a minute fraction of the total Hausa population.

Meanwhile village groupings had been revised and multiplied to reduce their unwieldy size. By 1934, the 500 village areas established between 1916 and 1921 had increased to 1200, while their average population had fallen from 4500 to 1600 people. However there had been little change in the total amount paid as salary to this much larger number of village heads. The total paid to the 1200 village heads on whom the rural administration was based was then £24,000.[55] By 1932 the twelve major districts established at *gunduma* had likewise increased to 27, with an average population of 75,000, though populations ranged from 20,000 in the smallest district to 150,000 at Bici, then under the Ciroma Sanusi. [56] As village areas were broken up and reconstituted into smaller, more efficient units, district boundaries were redrawn, and while some of the smaller districts were amalgamated, some larger ones were subdivided. Thus in 1928 the small central districts of Gabasawa and Zakirai were amalgamated under the Dan Amar Sule; but that year the Galadima's old district at Fogolawa was split into two, Babura and Garki, the former being placed under the Dokaji, and the latter under the Barde Kareriya who was transferred from Zakirai. Both the Barde Kareriya and the Dan Amar Sule were Suleibawa royals. In 1932 the old Dutse district, subdivided in 1923 by the removal of Kiyawa, was reunited under the Sarkin Dutse Suleimanu, a baJelube of Dutse town. Some years later, in 1944, Babura and Garki, separated in 1928, were also reunited; and so were Ringim, Debi and Taura under Usuman's son, the Tafida Muhamman, following dismissal of the exploitive Magajin Malam Na Cedi Ahmadu Ruaf'i for tax embezzlement. Thus by 1934 the emirate was sub-divided into 27 districts of varying age, population, size, wealth and levels of administrative development.[57]

District Administration: Continuity and Change

As evolutions of the traditional *hakim*-ships, district headships remained the most characteristic and prestigious forms of office within the emirate, despite the emergence of central ministers (*wazirai*) between 1926 and 1932. In like fashion, districts remained the most important type of administrative unit throughout this period. However unlike councillors, whose positions reduced their risks of removal, district heads were liable to dismissal from office and title for various offences, of which tax peculations were by far the most easily detected. Of the councillors in 1926–34, only the Galadima was eligible by descent for promotion to the throne. All other prospective candidates for the succession held district headships; but those Suleibawa princes who had failed as district heads and been dismissed, thereby forfeited their claims to the succession. Unlike district chiefships, which had their traditional prototype in the office of the *hakimi*, the emergent and still ill-defined departmental headships, including those charged with administration of the Middle School, the Public Works Department and the rapidly expanding native Hospital in Kano, were assimilated to the four *wakil*-ships of Kano City and classified as minor positions from which able men eligible by descent or political connection might be recruited to district headships. For several years these departmental offices lacked independent political status and high prestige, being subordinate to the Galadima. Thus his distribution of district headships provides the best evidence of Bayero's specifically political alignments and goals at this period.

As we have seen, the Galadima Mamman Bello's death shortly after Bayero's accession enabled Bayero to appoint his brother, the Dan Iya Abdulkadiri, formerly district head of Dawaki ta Kudu, as Galadima in charge of Kano City and the N.A. Departments centred there. As Dan Iya, Bayero then appointed his own son Aminu, who administered Dawaki ta Kudu until 1939. As Ciroma and district head of Bici, on his accession, Bayero appointed his eldest son, Muhammadu Sanusi. To the general astonishment of Kano, Bayero's accession from the office of Ciroma finally broke the age-old tradition that no Ciroma would ever become emir. This dated back at least to Alwali's day when, according to popular legend, the haughty conduct of the Ciroma called down the curse of Shehu Abdullahi at Gwale, after Dan Mama had destroyed the Shehu's farm by riding his cavalry through it.[58] Thus Bayero's accession itself signified some loosening of tradition at

Kano, and enhanced its capacity to develop and adapt to the changing circumstances and needs of the colonial era. Probably some Kano people who marvelled at the extraordinary appointment perceived these implications. Despite its basic conservatism, Kano society had already undergone quite profound transformations without destroying its fundamental unity and form; the Ciroma Bayero's smooth accession merely re-affirmed the emirate's capacity to adapt positively to these new contexts, conditions and influences.

In 1926 shortly after his accession, Bayero dismissed Usuman's son, the Turaki Muhammadu who then administered Ungogo. According to the British, Turaki Muhamman was dismissed for embezzling tax; but according to the ruling Fulani he was dismissed for *raina* (contempt, disrespect), and specifically because he refused to bow on greeting Bayero.[59] Such conduct signified his rejection of Bayero's claims to superior status, and may have stimulated the intensive study of tax administration at Ungogo which furnished grounds acceptable to the British for his dismissal. As Turaki, Bayero then appointed his younger brother, Muhammadu Inuwa, who administered Ungogo until 1931, when he was promoted to the larger district of Minjibir. In 1939, on the death of his son, the Galadima Abdulkadiri, Bayero promoted the Turaki Muhammadu Inuwa to the office of Galadima, and appointed another son of Abbas, Kasimu, as Turaki to administer Minjibir.

After dismissing the Turaki Muhammadu, Bayero took no further action against Usuman's sons, the Wombai Abubakar who was in charge of Kura and the Tafida Muhammadu, who administered Ringim from Dabi. Abubakar retained the office of Wombai throughout Bayero's reign but was dismissed in 1959 by Bayero's son Sanusi, to the horror of Kano, since he was also Sanusi's mother's brother.[60] Usuman, when emir, had pursued the policy of marriage alliances initiated by Dabo, giving daughters in marriage to the Sarkin Yaki, district head of Kiru, to the Sarkin Karaye, and to the Ciroma Bayero, Usuman's brother's son. Bayero's first son, Sanusi, was born of that marriage, and the Tafida Muhammadu and the Wombai Abubakar were his mother's brothers. Usuman had also secured a daughter of the caliph Muhammadu Mai-Turare of Sokoto as a wife for his son the Wombai. As emir, Bayero likewise employed marriage alliances to strengthen his relations with senior officials.

In 1931, on transferring the Turaki Muhammadu Inuwa to Minjibir, Bayero appointed his own son Isa as district head of Ungogo, with the title of Dan Makwayau which had remained vacant since the dismissal of Dan Makwayau Muhammadu for tax embezzlement in Usuman's reign. In 1932 the Dan Makwayau Isa was promoted without change of title to the larger district of Garki which had been created in 1928 by partitioning Fogolawa. Then, in 1939, following the death of the baJobe Dan Darman, Mamman Bello, Bayero transferred Isa from Garki to Suma'ila District with the title of Dan Darman. Thereafter, at least till 1959, the Jobawa lost their hereditary jurisdiction over Suma'ila,[61] which remained under Suleibawa princes. When the Dan Darman Isa, Bayero's son, was dismissed for tax embezzlement in 1944, he was replaced by the Dan Buram, Umaru Faruku, another of Bayero's sons, who was transferred to Gwaram without change of title in 1949. Bayero then transferred his first cousin, the Dan Amar Yusufu, a lineal grandson of the pretender Yusufu, from Jahun to Suma'ila.

At Gwaram in 1926 shortly after his accession Bayero dismissed the Sarkin Dawaki Tsakar Gida Isa, a remote cousin, for ineptitude, and appointed Isa's close kinsman Ahmadu Abassi, who died within two years. As Sarkin Dawaki Tsakar Gida, Bayero then appointed the baGyeni Muhammadu, a son of that Chief Alkali Sule whom Aliyu had appointed and dismissed. However, within two years Muhammadu was transferred to Kunya as district head, and Abubakar, another son of the pretender Yusufu, was installed as Sarkin Dawaki Tsakar Gida and D.H. Gwaram.[62] Thus unlike Aliyu Mai Sango, Abbas and Usuman, Bayero sought to provide suitable offices for the descendants of Galadima Yusufu, to whose leadership the issue of Abdullahi owed their dynastic pre-eminence.

By 1930, tax embezzlement and administrative ineptitude had been established as the two major counts on which district heads were liable to dismissal, and, in either case, at the request or insistence of the British Provincial staff. Officials dismissed for ineptitude had normally committed no punishable offence; but those dismissed for tax peculation were rarely sent to jail. Presumably, the British feared a shortage of suitable candidates for office if jail sentences attached to dismissals for tax offences. Presumably also, some of the missing monies were secured by distraints against offending district heads, to avert their dismissal. The estate of Sarkin Rano Adamu, who died in 1938 after five years in office, illustrates nicely how rewarding it was to hold a district headship even so briefly at this time. Besides 18 gowns and 7 burnouses, ten trousers, 13 turbans and much other clothing, the Sarkin Rano left two motor cars, 17 bags of rice, 19 bags of chilli peppers, 700 bundles of millet and sorghum, 40 horses, his personal property, and 18 others that belonged to the state. Adamu also left behind a hoard of 37 bottles of perfume and £1646 in his compound. The Divisional Officer commented that "the recent District Head was appointed in March 1933 and was on a salary of £480 per annum. £1600 is a lot to save on this salary in five years; and it looks as if the rumours of extortion which have been very frequent during his tenure of office have not been ill-founded," an observation with which the Madakin Kano Ibrahim agreed.[63]

Tempted by such high returns, despite the risks that attached, district headships continued to attract many eligible candidates, who canvassed their claims by the traditional means of donations (*gaisuwa*). Since such "customary presents" did not immediately involve public revenue, they were ignored by the British, though once appointed, district heads expected similar presents from village chiefs in office, and from others seeking village headships, as illustrated by the data from Taura cited above. Thus, official salaries were neither the only, and often by no means the main source, of an official's income, except perhaps for such councillors as the vizier, Madaki and Ma'aji, whose exclusion from territorial administration probably reduced their unofficial receipts. However, the risk of dismissal that attached to district headship remained rather high. In 1932 five district heads were removed,[64] including the Dan Maje Zakari Yau and the Dan Buram Haruna, both sons of Abdullahi Maje Karofi. Nonetheless Suleibawa district chiefs were far less exposed to risks of dismissal for tax embezzlement than their colleagues; and among princes this principle served equally to favour the emir's sons. For example, of Bayero's several sons who held territorial chiefships, only one, the Dan Darman Isa, was dismissed for peculation in 1943.

By 1935, the district staffs had been effectively reorganised and expanded to handle the increased tasks of district administration. Normally at district headquarters, besides the Alkali and *muhutai*, the court employed two scribes, ten to fifteen attendants who delivered summonses (*yan ijala*), and a *dan wanka* who supervised the ritual ablutions required before taking Koranic oaths. The district head had a small number of *dogarai* attached to him as police; and his headquarters also contained a temporary lock-up for short-term offenders, under a Yari whom he appointed. The average district office had a staff of three scribes responsible for preparing and forwarding to the Madaki in Kano population statistics and tax receipts of all village-areas in the district, together with monthly returns of births and deaths, the district prison register, and register of cattle statistics and *jangali* payments. At the district head's direction these scribes also conducted routine correspondence with the Madaki's office on matters of district administration. In addition the district head employed a staff of messengers for communications with village chiefs and the city. By 1935 most village chiefs were also provided with scribes to handle their population registers, tax accounts and correspondence with district headquarters. In village surveys for tax assessment and other purposes, Provincial staff aimed to examine each District thoroughly about once in six years; but on the evidence available, such reassessments were on average at best decennial.

Departmental Developments

As central departments of the Native Administration increased in numbers, scale and scope, their activities radiated from Kano into the rural districts. Besides their judicial and district establishments and staff despatched from Kano to conduct occasional surveys of limited length, most district headquarters then maintained a bush dispensary under a semi-trained malam, an elementary school with its two or three teachers, and some personnel from the Sanitary, Agricultural and Veterinary Departments of the Native Administration. In consequence at the annual conference of Northern Residents in 1935, the Secretary of the Northern Provinces (SNP) called for discussion of the appropriate administrative relationships of these departmental personnel with the district organization.

> It is maintained that there is taking place at present a process of decentralisation of departmental activities in the Districts (which has probably gone furthest in Kano). Agricultural activities, verterinary work, the formation of cotton markets, forestry activities, all necessitate a staff of people conveniently called "malams." Simultaneously, with the growth of departmental activities, special efforts are being made by the administrative staff to develop the organisation still in its infancy at each District Office. The time appears to be opportune to decide whether the various malam staffs should be purely departmental or form part of a general malam staff for each District.[65]

This problem was resolved by assigning administrative control of the departmental staff sent out to the districts to the district heads, who thus became responsible for co-ordinating and supporting the local work of these departmental officers, and for handling whatever communications and disbursements that involved, through the Madaki's office. As regards their technical activities, transfers or promotions, etc., such departmental staff remained under the direction of their departmental heads at Kano city; but any new projects of work had first to be cleared with the Emir in Council by the Galadima on briefings from the departmental head in the presence of the Madaki. This complex structure of communications and authority facilitated the dual attachments of departmental staff in rural areas to the district chief and to their departmental head. With such development of the district organization, the administrative machinery was ready to undertake routine programmes of rural survey and development in agriculture, forestry, roads, sanitation and health; and throughout the next fifteen years such departmental activities increased steadily in rural areas.

One effect of these developments in district administration was to increase greatly the number of Fulani officials empowered to inspect and direct a continuously expanding range and variety of routine activities and interests among rural people. Thus while modifying its form and severity, by reorganising and developing the district administration, the British greatly extended the range and intensity of Fulani control over the Hausa people resident in rural areas. In place of the village chief, his entourage of kinsmen and supporters, and visiting *jekadu*, the rural Hausa of Kano were now also exposed to overrule by a resident district head with an expanded staff, and by an increasing number of technical officials who carried out inspections and levied fines, many of which were illegal, on *talakawa* (subjects, commoners) who were often innocent of the departmental regulations they were said to have broken. Viewed from above or afar, the new district machinery, with its complement of semi-trained technical staff, provided a crude if effective instrument for the promotion of rural development in such spheres as sanitation, agriculture, forestry, health and the like. However, looked at from below, this multiplication of minor inspectorates armed with essentially arbitrary powers of inspection and fine, represented a significant increase in "the slings and arrows of outrageous fortune," to which the inarticulate *talakawa* were exposed. Thus, despite some token efforts at instituting village councils to increase popular compliance with their programmes, these developments of rural administration inspired by the British merely served to increase peasant subordination and burdens under Fulani rule, while ensuring that the peasants remained disorganised and inarticulate.

It is necessary to bear this situation clearly in mind as we review the development and expansion of the Native Administration. Notably, since the emir reserved to himself all but the most trivial disciplinary powers over all levels of official staff, the rules he made and the Departmental bylaws he approved permitted even the most junior native official to levy fines on the powerless *talakawa* for putative offences committed against ill-publicised departmental regulations. As Head of the Native Administration, the emir undertook personal responsibility for the punishment of his subordinates and for their protection against arbitrary discipline by their immediate superiors; but by this measure he simultaneously allowed his native officialdom to discipline his subjects at their discretion. To Hausa commoners, their relations with this new officialdom differed little from those with the throne slaves of old. Though complaints were probably no more frequent against technical staff than against inequitable distributions of tax, it should not be assumed that the official records of administrative progress and activities imply corresponding advances in public welfare or support of the Anglo-Fulani regime at Kano.[66]

Economic Developments, 1931–36

By specialising in the cultivation of groundnuts as a cash crop, which peasants grew and sold to secure the money they needed to pay tax and for an increasing range of imported goods, Kano had reoriented its economy southwards to the sea and beyond, to Britain and the world market. However, following the slump of 1929 the world market temporarily collapsed. Cushioned by its dependence on external trade with Britain, Kano did not feel the full impact of this severe depression for some years. For example, in 1931 groundnut prices increased from 90s to 190s per ton as the season waned; but by 1933–4 the price had fallen to 40s (£2) per ton, in recognition of which the Administration authorised a 5 percent reduction in direct taxes. Fortunately for Kano, during the previous three years the cultivation of cotton had become widespread, and the quality of local hides and skins, which were also exported to Britain, had improved. Thus the local economy weathered this period of severe depression with moderate hardship. By the end of 1934 the groundnut price, which served as the barometer of Kano's colonial economy, had risen to 160s (£8) a ton;[67] and on this upward turn, Bayero set out for Britain with the Madaki Mamudu and the Ciroma Sanussi to accompany the Toronkawa sultan of Sokoto Hassan and his cousin the emir of Gwandu. In Britain, where they toured extensively, Bayero and the Sarkin Gwandu had an audience with George V; and on their return, the emir and Ciroma both arranged for private tutorials in English.[68]

An elaborate and highly successful Agricultural Show, the first in Kano's history, was held in January 1934, and later that year, the Native Treasury accounts were examined for the first time by a trained auditor, who made various recommendations. The incidence of crime in the city suburbs led to further increases of *'yan gadi*, the Native Authority school for training scholars in Muslim Law received new buildings, and water consumption in the City had increased from 86 million gallons in 1932 to 134 millions in 1934, necessitating further expansions of the water supply initiated in 1931. Meanwhile an extensive programme of well-sinking had improved water supplies in rural towns, and efforts by the Agricultural Department to introduce Hausa cultivators to the advantages of animal husbandry and cattle-drawn ploughs were moderately successful in doubling the numbers of "mixed farmers" in Kano. Medical campaigns against yellow fever, leprosy, and malaria proceeded smoothly. Due to relative over-production of groundnuts, during the pre-harvest months grain shortages generated price-increases of 33 percent and stimulated the Native Authority to stockpile grain reserves against famine and uncontrolled price rises in future years.[69] By 1936 Kano's groundnut exports exceeded 265,000 tons, purchased at an average price of 169s per ton. The quality of the crop had also improved under systematic inspection over the years. With this record harvest, £290,000, or 98 percent of the tax due, was collected between November 1st and December 31st. Paper notes had to be flown out from Britain to facilitate trade by meeting the local shortage of currency generated by this economic revival.[70] Kano had shaken off the effects of the prolonged economic depression.

In 1935 the N.A. Department of Public Works completed a permanent build-ing for the Alkali's court opposite Bayero's palace. In 1936 a much larger building, which cost £20,000 and housed the Native Administration, was opened by the Governor of Nigeria with due ceremony and fanfare. This new building con-tained the legal, district, municipal and financial departments of the Native Administration, together with the offices of the N.A. Police force, the Sanitary and Agricultural departments. The new structure housed the nascent Ministries pre-sided over by the Madaki, the Galadima, the Ma'aji, and the ageing vizier under one roof, thereby facilitating further development. Village heads' scribes were now placed on the official N.A. payroll; and the City Hospital, which that year handled 3,800 in-patients and 10,000 out-patients, received new wards. Another 35,000 people were treated at the rural dispensaries. Sanitary programmes were further extended, and a plan for city drainage to cost £100,000 was approved. Some 250,000 smallpox vaccinations were administered in rural areas; an airfield was opened at Ungogo, eight miles from Kano; and a regular air mail service was initiated. The rapid expansion of motor traffic, despite a recent extension of the railway line from Kano past Hadeija to Nguru, necessitated substantial outlays on road repair and development. A Leper Settlement was opened at Suma'ila. New exports of gutta percha were developed and 350 tons of Fulani butter were pro-cessed. However Western education made little progress against the opposition of Fulani clerics, led by the vizier Muhammadu Gidado. That year only four new primary schools were opened. Tax rates varied in differing districts, but probably averaged about 10 shillings per adult male throughout the emirate.[71]

These varied data illustrate the course and conditions of socio-economic developments at Kano during the first ten years of Bayero's reign. New horizons were gradually appearing for the peasants as well as their rulers. In 1932 the vizier Gidado set out on pilgrimage to Mecca by motor, the first *hakimin Kano* in history to do so. In 1937 Abdullahi Bayero followed suit, accompanied by his younger brother, the Galadima Abdulkadiri. On their way home the two princes visited Palestine and Egypt. When Bayero repeated the pilgrimage in 1951 he was accompanied on an aeroplane by a client.[72]

Changes in the Council and Judiciary, 1937–40

In 1937 the Waziri Muhammadu Gidado died.[73] Thereafter the vizierate, first instituted at Kano by Aliyu Mai Sango, lapsed until the Dokaji Abubakar, Gidado's son, was appointed some years after my visit. Throughout his 28 years in the office, Muhammadu Gidado had only twice exercised the genuine unre-stricted vizierate and then briefly, namely, from 1909 to 1914 in Abbas' reign, and perhaps from 1925 on the transfer of power from Usuman and his senior slaves until 1928. Thereafter, of Bayero's advisory council of executive ministers, the Waziri Gidado, although the senior and most influential, had perhaps the most slender executive role. By reallocating responsibilities for departmental and urban affairs to the Galadima, and for district affairs to the Madaki Mamudu, and by removing the Treasury from Gidado's portfolio, Bayero had effectively dis-established the vizierate; and without changing its title, he had reduced its scope to legal affairs. On Gidado's death, Bayero appointed his old teacher, the Ma'aji Suleimanu, the son of Aliyu Babba's Limam Isma'ila, to the new title of Wali which he then introduced from Zaria and invested with all the legal functions and powers Gidado had held. Thus the new Wali Sule replaced Gidado as Bayero's senior legal adviser on the Judicial Council. He also routinely investigated and reviewed the case records of rural courts, advised the emir on legal appointments, promotions and transfers, and interviewed appellants, complainers and plaintiffs in cases of first instance to determine whether their suits should be brought before the Judicial Council or sent to the Chief Alkali's court. In addition, the Wali advised the emir on legal aspects of executive questions discussed in the Executive Council.

To replace Suleimanu on his promotion from the Treasury to the office of Wali, Bayero first appointed as Ma'aji a senior Treasury clerk, Salim of Hadeija, and when he was later dismissed for mismanaging the accounts, Mujir, a Kano Arab.

In 1937 the Waziri Gidado's chief rival, the baGyeni Alkalin Kano Ja'afaru, also died. In his place Bayero appointed Aminu, a grandson of Dabo's brother, the Sarkin Shanu Hasan, the first Suleibawa prince to be appointed as Alkalin Kano. Aminu retained the office till his death in 1939, following which Bayero appointed another baGyeni, Muhammadu Basheri.

In 1939, when the Wali Suleimanu died, Bayero appointed a Zarawa cleric, Abubakar, as Wali in his place without modifying the functions of the office. Following the death of the Wali Abubakar in 1948 Bayero promoted the Alkalin Kano Muhammadu Basheri as Wali; and following Basheri's death in 1952 he appointed as Wali the Alkalin Dutse Abubakar, another baGyeni. To succeed Basheri as Alkalin Kano in 1948, Bayero appointed Umaru, a son of the Zarawa Limamin Kano Usuman, whom the emir Usuman had installed. When the Limam Usuman died early in Bayero's reign after holding the *limanci* for 31 years, Bayero appointed Muhammadu Sani, the great-grandson of Abdullahi's Limam Sule; and on Sani's death, he appointed Dallatu, a son of the Na'ibi Adamu who had served Abbas.

In 1939 Bayero lost two senior councillors, the Madaki Mamudu and the Galadima Abdulkadiri. On Abdulkadiri's death, Bayero promoted his brother the Turaki Muhammadu Inuwa to the title of Galadima, but transferred him from the district at Minjibir to Dawaki ta Kudu as district head, thereby removing the Galadima from the Council. To replace Madaki Mamudu, Bayero promoted the Dan Lawan Umaru, a baYole, the lineal grandson of Dabo's Madaki Umaru, who had recently administered Kiru district after promotion from Kiyawa and Dutse. As Dan Lawan, Bayero appointed his younger brother Ibrahim Dabo; and having first put Ibrahim in charge of Garki district, he moved him successively to Ungogo, Zakirai, and finally to Jahun, without any change of title. Having thus converted the Galadima title to a district headship with Muhammadu Inuwa's appointment, on Abdulkadiri's death Bayero replaced the Galadima on the Council by his son, the Ciroma Sanusi, who was recalled to Kano from Bici, his former district headquarters. To administer Bici, Bayero transferred his son, the Dan Iya Aminu from Dawaki ta Kudu, which he placed under Galadima Muhammadu Inuwa. Thus, while promoting his brothers' interests by appointments to office, Bayero gave clear preference to those of his sons. At Kano the Ciroma Sanusi assumed all those responsibilities the Galadima Abdulkadiri had formerly exercised. Thus by 1940 the Council consisted entirely of new personnel, the Wali

Abubakar, the Ciroma Sanusi and the Madaki Umaru, all of whom lacked experience of their ministerial duties.

When Bayero promoted his old teacher, the Ma'aji Suleimanu, whom he had
initially appointed as the first headmaster of the new Legal School at Shahuci, to
be Wali on Waziri Gidado's death, he placed the Treasury under Suleimanu's
supervision and dropped the Treasurer, Salim of Hadeija, from the Council. As
former Treasurer, Wali Suleimanu was excellently suited to direct and advise on
any Treasury action required to implement Council decisions. In like fashion,
Suleimanu could present to Council the Ma'aji's queries or reports. Thus by 1940
Bayero had reduced the Council to three, all of whom, being inexperienced,
depended on his guidance. He had also vested the most complex and critical
executive functions in the hands of his eldest son and chosen heir, the Ciroma
Sanusi.[74]

The Dynasty and Lineage Offices

From 1940 to 1948, Bayero governed Kano by and through this Council. Its
only change of personnel occurred in 1947, when the Madaki Umaru died and
was replaced by Ibrahim, an affine of the Yolawa, but not baYole by descent. This
Ibrahim, an agnate of the Madaki Mamudu, had been selected by Mamudu in
1926 to administer the district of Dawakin Tofa on Mamudu's transfer from
Dawaki to Kano City as a councillor. At first Ibrahim administered Dawaki
simply as the Madaki's *wakil*; but in 1926 Bayero regularised the appointment by
reviving the recently vacant office of Sarkin Shanu, last held by slaves, and conferred it on Ibrahim. Politically, although not baYole by descent, Ibrahim was
assimilated to the Yolawa by kinship, residence, office, title, clientage and popular
classification. On promotion to the Council as Madaki in 1947, Ibrahim was succeeded at Dawakin Tofa as district head and Sarkin Shanu by Shehu Ahmadu, the
son of Madaki Mamudu, who like his father was affiliated to the Yolawa by cognatic rather than lineage ties. Thus, though ostensibly Yolawa, the new Madakis,
Mamudu, Ibrahim, and, following Ibrahim's death in 1953, the former Sarkin
Shanu Shehu Ahmadu, were not Yolawa by descent. The Yolawa thus lost the
Madaki office temporarily on Mamudu's appointment by Abbas in 1914, and
perhaps permanently on the Madaki's transfer to the Council as Minister in
charge of district affairs. Even in 1959 at Kano many believed that the Yolawa still
held the Madaki title; but after the death of Madaki Umaru, this was not strictly
correct.[75]

Meanwhile the Yolawa had been liberally compensated. The district headship
of Dawakin Tofa, bearing the former royal title of Sarkin Shanu, was now
reserved for them. In addition since 1920 when Ibrahim, a grandson of the
Madaki Umaru, was first appointed, the title of Dan Kade had been filled by
Yolawa. From 1921 till 1955 a succession of Yolawa Dan Kades administered
Tudun Wada district. Thereafter the baYole Dan Kade Muhammadu Inuwa was
promoted to Wudil, the old Jobawa headquarters, when the baJobe Makama was
demoted and sent to Ungogo as punishment for offensive conduct. In addition
the Yolawa received the office of Dan Amar in 1951, when Bayero appointed
Ahmadu Bello, a great-grandson of Dabo's Madaki Umaru, as district head of
Tofa, shortly before Dan Amar Ahmadu Bello moved to Kaduna as Minister in the

TABLE 8.1 Some Changes in the Distributions of Office Among Prominent Fulani Lineages in Nineteenth and Twentieth Century Kano

Lineages	Nineteenth Century Offices	Twentieth Century Offices
Yerimawa	Turakin Romo, Sarkin Fulanin Minjibir	S.F. Minjibir
Dambazawa	Sarkin Bai	Sarkin Bai
Jelorawa (Dugudawa)	Ma'ajin Watali	?
Zarawa ('Yan Lagi'en Gyenawa (Jelubawa)	Alkali, Limam, Sarkin Dutse	Sarkin Dutse Waziri Dokaje (1949+) Wali Barde Babba (1948+), ? Sarkin Dawaki Mai Tuta
Yolawa (Ba'awa)	Madaki, Magajin Malam na Cedi	Madaki Dan Maje Dan Kade Dan Amar Sarkin Shanu
Danejawa	Dan Iya, Dan Kade, ? Dan Makwayau	—
Zuri'an Jamau (Suleibawan Jamau)	Sarkin Dawaki Mai Tuta	—
Other non-royal Suleibawa	? Dan Maje	Sarkin Dawaki Mai Tuta
Mundubawa	Mai-Anguwan Mundubawa, Magajin Maude Dan Amar, Sarkin Dawaki Tsakar Gida	—
Jobawa	Makama	? Makama (None in ? DanDarman 1959)
Balarawa	Dan Darman	?
Fulanin Jayen	Ja'idanawa	Mai-Anguwan Mundubawa
Indorawa	—	?
Zuri'an Alkali Usuman	Magajin Malam na Hausawa	
Suleibawa (dangin Ibrahim Dabo)	Wombai, Ciroma, Galadima, Turaki Manya, Dan Buram, Dan Lawan, Tafida, Dan Isa, Dan Ruwata, Sarkin Shanu	Wombai, Ciroma, Galadima, Turaki Manya, Dan Buram, Dan Lawan, Magajin Malam, Sarkin Dawaki Tsakar Gida, Dan Maje, ? Dan Darman, Dan Ruwata, Tafida, Dan Isa, Dan Iya, Sarkin Gaya (1948 +)

Regional Government. The office of Magajin Malam na Cedi was also revived by Bayero for such Yolawa clients as Ahmadu Rufa'i, the district head of Taura mentioned above, and following him, for Mamman Sani, a baYole, who was later promoted to Kano City as district head in 1954 with the title of Sarkin Shanu. Two other senior titles recently filled by Yolawa are the former royal office of Dan Maje, long identified with the district headship of Babura, and the office of Barde Babba which remained with the Yolawa from 1920 to 1948, when its holder, Isma'ilu was dismissed for exploiting the forest reserves under his care. Thus besides the Madaki title, by 1950 the Yolawa had developed prominent interests in the offices of Barde, dan Maje, and Magajin Malam na Cedi. They also had reasonably firm claims to the titles of Sarkin Shanu and Dan Kade. The Madakiship, however, was no longer prescriptively theirs by descent. By 1958 the Jobawa Makama, Muhammadu Dahiru, was dismissed from office, having been warned on demotion from Wudil to Ungogo three years previously. Thereafter the Jobawa temporarily lost their senior hereditary office; and in 1958 the baYole Dan Amar, Alhaji Mamman Bello, was appointed to the title of Makama, thereby transferring it temporarily from the Jobawa to the Yolawa.[76]

As related above, the Danejawa and Suleibawan Jamau also had earlier lost their hereditary offices, and with them the privileged political statuses they had held since the *jihad*. No members of either aristocratic lineage held district headships at Kano throughout Bayero's reign and the years that immediately followed. Thus with the apparent expropriation of the Jobawa under Sanusi in 1959, only two of the five Fulani founding families still retained their hereditary status and titles, namely, the Dambazawa and the Yolawa. Excluding Muhammadu Baba, who was appointed Dan Kade in 1919 and dismised for peculation in 1920 by Usuman, besides their lineage office of Sarkin Bai and rights at Dambarta, the Dambazawa also held the title of Dokaji, until 1949, when that was conferred on Alhaji Abubakar, a son of Waziri Muhammadu Gidado, the former Dokaji Muhammadu Adananu being promoted to the senior Dambazawa title of Sarkin Bai.[77]

As regards the Mundubawa, their office of Mai Anguwa having passed to Indorawa serfs of the dynasty, was held successively by Yusufu and his younger brother Ahmadu until the latter died in 1940. Bayero then appointed a baMundube, Muhammadu, to the title and district headship of Gezawa; but following Muhammadu's death in 1943, Bayero appointed the Dan Ruwata Ahmadu Gwadabe, Galadima Abdulkadiri's son and senior *lawani*, as district head of Gezawa, without change of title. In 1951, on Ahmadu's dismissal over tax, Bayero installed his own younger brother Isa at Gezawa with the title of Dan Ruwata. Thus the Mundubawa also lost their lineage offices in Bayero's reign.[78]

In 1931 when the baJobe Dan Darman Aliyu who administered Suma'ila died, Bayero appointed Aliyu's younger brother Abdullahi, but had to dismiss him in 1936 for ineptitude. He then appointed another baJobe, Muhammadu Bello, a son of that Makama Mujeli whom Abbas had restored; but when Mamman Bello died in 1939, Bayero conferred the title on his own son Isa, who was dismissed five years later over tax, following which the title remained vacant for eleven years until Bayero's successor, Sanusi, gave it to his first son, Alhaji Ahmadu Tijani.[79]

Throughout Bayero's reign the offices of Sarkin Gaya, Sarkin Dutse, Sarkin Karaye, Sarkin Birnin Kudu, and Sarkin Rano, remained with their local dynasties. So too, despite repeated failures, did the district headship of Kiru. However some titles that lapsed at this time include the Ja'idanawa, Sarkin Fada, Magajin Malam na Hausawa, Magajin Maude and perhaps the Mai Anguwan Kutumbawa, at least as a territorial office, although even in 1958 a "Mai Anguwan Kutumbawa" sat with the Sarkin Sherifai on the emir's Judicial Council, neither speaking except in cases that involved their people.[80]

Excluding the rural chiefships and central offices whose lineal distributions have been reported above, in Bayero's reign the Suleibawa dynasty retained the titles of Turaki, Tafida, Barde Kareriya, Dan Amar, Dan Lawan, Sarkin Dawaki Tsakar Gida, Wombai, Galadima, Dan Iya, Dan Makwayau, Dan Isa and Dan Buram. Many new departmental titles were also appropriated by the dynasty, including the Wakilin 'Yan Doka, the Wakilin Yamma, Wakilin Arewa, Wakilin Sana'a, Wakilin Gona, Wakilin 'Yan Gardi, Wakilin Hatsi, and others within the city. Successful tenures of these junior positions were rewarded in several instances by appointments to minor district headships. Thus, while promoting the interests of his Yolawa allies, of the Gyenawa and Zarawa clerical lineages and of his Indorawa clients, and while preserving the hereditary rights of the Dambazawa at Dambarta and of the local ruling families at Rano, Dutse, Karaye, Gaya and Birnin Kudu, Bayero systematically increased the Suleibawa share of senior offices and entrenched his sons in strategic positions.

On the eve of his death in 1953, three of Bayero's sons held district headships, the Dan Iya Aminu at Bici, the Dan Buram Umoru Faruku at Gwaram, and the Magajin Malam Muhammudu Abbas at Gabasawa, while a fourth, the Ciroma Muhammadu Sanusi, supervised district administrations throughout the emirate, having assumed these functions on the appointment of Madaki Ibrahim to the council in 1947.[81]

Bayero had further advanced Sanusi's claims to the succession by assigning him the two major executive tasks, first to administer the City and central departments, and then to supervise the rural administration. By these appointments, Bayero trained Sanusi to administer the emirate and presented him to the British as the best qualified and most widely experienced candidate for the throne. Meanwhile, having thus identified the Ciroma's interests so closely with his own, Bayero had no need to fear that Sanusi would imitate Yusufu's impetuous subversion of Abdullahi. Neither did Bayero need to eliminate Usuman's sons, the Wombai Abubakar or the Tafida Muhammadu, in order to ensure the Ciroma's succession. At Ringim and Kiru those princes were so remote from the central sector, familiarity with which was now indispensable for governing the emirate, that their prospects for the succession were negligible. Finally, in training the Ciroma and promoting his candidacy, Bayero simultaneously recruited a devoted and efficient executive, increased his own power, aggrandized his son's authority, and relieved himself of many tedious exhausting tasks as his age increased.

The Central Administration—1950

In 1943 the Native Authority Ordinance (No. 17 of 1943) enacted by the Governor, B.H. Bourdillon, reasserted the Nigerian Government's conception of senior native chiefs as Sole Native Authorities. Under Section 33, the Ordinance also ruled that all chiefs should have formally constituted Advisory Councils.

"Members of such Councils may be appointed by name or office, or one or more representatives of various interests may be appointed without specifying persons by name. A chief may constitute either an Executive or an Advisory Council ... , or both. Membership for the one need not be the same as that of another."[82] Paragraph 2 of Section 33 of this Statute delegated the rights of the Governor in Lagos to approve the composition of such councils to the Chief Commissioners (Lieutenant Governors) in the various Regions of Nigeria. By 1946 the Lieutenant Governor in Northern Nigeria had transferred his powers to approve routine changes in the compositions of chiefdom councils to the Provincial Residents.[83]

Following World War II, under its new Labour Government, Britain sought to promote the development of its tropical dependencies as a prelude to decolonization. In 1946 India was partitioned and received its independence, followed shortly by Burma and Ceylon. In this penultimate phase of imperial dissolution, programmes of economic development and political participation were eagerly pressed. In these circumstances the British Administration in Northern Nigeria sought to promote the growth and differentiation of chiefly councils by increasing their memberships and specialising their functions.

By January 1950 Bayero's Judicial and Advisory Councils were clearly distinguished, the former having been re-designated as the "Emir's Court." At that date, besides Bayero, the Advisory Council had six members, the Ciroma, Alhaji Muhammadu Sanusi being Minister in charge of District Administration and Development; the Wali, Muhamman Bashari, in charge of the Native Judiciary; the Madaki Ibrahim, who retained his seat on the Council although residing in Dawakin Tofa as district head; the Galadima, Muhammadu Inuwa, who administered Dawakin Kudu as district head and remained on the Council; the Sarkin Shanu, Alhaji Shehu Ahmadu who supervised the Kano City administration, Survey and Printing Department, the City Hospital, the Veterinary, Prisons, Police, and other centrally located departments; and finally, the Honourable Mamman Bello, a baYole great-grandson of Madaki Umaru, who, besides serving as a member of the Nigerian Legislative Council, administered local education as head of the Kano Education Department. Of these six councillors, the two most senior, the Madaki Ibrahim and Galadima Muhammadu Inuwa, lived at their district headquarters within an hour's drive of Kano. Thus, while both were readily available for Council meetings when required, they did not attend unless summoned. A third councillor, the Education Officer, Mallam Bello, was also frequently absent either at Kaduna or Lagos on legislative business, or in rural areas inspecting schools.[84] Thus despite its recent increase of membership, the council with which Bayero generally worked consisted of three or four officials, the Ciroma, the Wali, the Sarkin Shanu and the Education Officer, Mallam Bello.

However, on the death of Madaki Umaru in 1947, Bayero promoted the Sarkin Shanu Ibrahim, who had administered Dawakin Tofa since 1926, to the title of Madaki, without however altering his executive duties. Thus Ibrahim continued to administer Dawakin Tofa, as he had done for the past twenty years. However, as Madaki, he was now promoted to the Emir's Council, the Madaki having always held, by right of title, a seat on the council, traditionally and since its reconstitution in 1926. Within a year it was clear that Madaki Ibrahim could not simultaneously supervise the increasingly complex district administration of the emirate and govern Dawakin Tofa. Bayero then took advantage of this situation to transfer the tasks of co-ordinating and supervising the district administration to his son, the Ciroma Sanusi, and promoted the Dan Maje Shehu Ahmadu, a Yolawa affiliate, from Minjibir Disrict as Sarkin Shanu to administer Kano City and the N.A. departments centred there. As a Western-educated aristocrat familiar with district administration, Shehu Ahmadu was well equipped for his new roles as "Mayor" of Kano and Minister in charge of central N.A. departments; but it is also likely that his lack of an independent base of political support may have recommended Ahmadu to Bayero and Sanusi for these strategic roles.

In 1949–50, when the revenues of Kano amounted to £625,612 and its expenditure was £750,126, £359,501 was ear-marked for capital development while £390,625 was recurrent. By then the Government share of local tax revenues was 14.5 percent, or £73,500 of the £504,000 that *jangali* and *haraji* yielded that year. To indicate the scale and complexity of the Native Administration, a summary of its revenue and expenditure for the year is given in Table 8.2.[85]

As mentioned above, the Judicial Council had by then been reconstituted as the Emir's Court. Besides Bayero, this Court consisted of the Ciroma, the Wali Muhammadu Bashari, the Limamin Kano Malam Usuman, who died in January 1950, the Na'ibi (Liman's deputy) Muhammadu Sani, who succeeded Usuman as Limam, and three learned malams, Alhaji Abubakar, Malam Umaru, and Malam Muhammadu dan Ahmadu. The Sarkin Sherifai and the Kutumbawa representative had seats on this court as honorary members, with restricted rights to speak. Thus the Court contained three high-ranking and three untitled clerics, the emir and his chosen successor. No *alkalai* were members; and as in the days of Waziri Gidado, the Wali Muhammadu Bashari, as senior jurist of the Emir's Court, supervised the 22 district courts and the four city courts presided over by *alkalai*. As head of the Legal Department, the Wali also recommended promotions, demotions, transfers, appointments and dismissals of *alkalai* to Bayero for decision at meetings of the Advisory Council, such matters being excluded from strictly judicial sessions of the Court. As before, the Wali also conducted routine monthly inspections of the case records of district and city courts, and selected such cases as seemed to merit re-trial. He also interviewed appellants to determine whether their complaints should be directed to the court of the Chief Alkali at Kano or brought before the Emir.[86]

Since 1937 the Treasurer (Ma'aji) had lost his seat on the emir's council. After the death in 1939 of Wali Suleimanu, who was formerly Ma'aji and finally a councillor, Treasury supervision had been transferred to the Ciroma Sanusi, on his assumption of ministerial responsibility for the city and central departments; but in 1948, when Sanusi assumed the "Ministry" of District Administration, the Sarkin Shanu Shehu Ahmadu undertook to supervise the Treasury, together with most other central departments at the capital.

Economic Developments, 1950–51

Following incorporation of the Sabon Gari or New Town for Southern immigrants in 1932 as an extramural ward of Kano City, a Mixed Court was created to adjudicate disputes within the suburb.[87] By 1950 the Sabon Gari had a population of 25,000 as against 90,000 within the walls of Kano.[88] Among its residents, immi-

TABLE 8.2   Kano Native Treasury Accounts, 1949–50

	Summary of Revenue	£
1	General tax	360,300
2	Jangali (cattle tax)	66,150
3	Native Courts	8,200
4	Interest on investments	30,661
5	Miscellaneous	38,790
1–5	Local Revenue	504,101
6	Grants etc. from Regional Funds	17,568
7	Grants etc., from other sources	6,393
1–7	Ordinary Revenue	528,062
8	Trade and Industries	74,750
	Grants: Capital Works	22,800
	Revenue Total	625,612

	Summary of Expenditure	£	Percent
1	Central Administration	24,404	6.3
2	District Administration	27,449	7.0
3	Village Administration	39,793	10.2
4	Judicial	14,910	3.9
5	Treasury	6,619	1.7
6	Police	36,606	9.3
7	Prisons	17,802	4.5
8	Miscellaneous	11,299	2.9
9	Works Recurrent	65,794	16.8
10	Veterinary	6,448	1.7
11	Education	26,910	6.9
12a	Survey	10,606	2.7
12b	Printing	8,072	2.1
13	Medical and Health	59,457	15.2
14	Agriculture	10,881	2.8
15	Forestry	5,140	1.3
16	Pensions etc.	850	0.2
17	District Councils' Funds	17,585	4.5
1–17	Ordinary Expenditure (Recurrent and Special)	390,625	100
18	Trade and Industries	234,701	
19	Works Extraordinary	124,800	
	Expenditure Total	750,126	

Source: Native Administration Estimates, 1949–50 (Gaskiya Corporation, Zaria), pp. 21–22

grant Ibo, Yoruba and Ibibio predominated in that order. Perhaps one half the suburban population were Ibo, engaged in technical, commercial and clerical occupations either on their own account or as employees of the Nigerian Government, the Kano Native Authority, or European and Lebanese firms in the nearby township. While such residential segregation of immigrants from Southern Nigeria, from other parts of the North, and from the Lebanon and Europe, restricted ethnic friction, it also fostered ethnic exclusiveness and negative stereotypes.

By 1950 Kano's economy was closely linked to the large urban markets of Southern Nigeria; and the modern communications network on which this economy depended required the technical skills of Southern Nigerians. As Kano's economic development proceeded, a new technology was introduced which included a modern airport terminal, new telephone exchanges, air-conditioned hotels, radio diffusion and transmitter stations, extensive cultivation by tractors, widespread use of chemical fertilisers and weed-killers, and the establishment of textile and groundnut factories. The local economy thus became progressively dependent on external trade and on Southern immigrants whose technical and clerical skills were indispensable to its operation.

By 1951 Kano Airport was handling about 6,600 aircraft per annum, and a new runway for commercial jets was being built at a cost of £100,000. The Kano Native Authority had established municipal bus services that linked the markets at Wudil, Bici and Dambarta as well as around the city and its suburbs. A School for Nursing was under construction to meet the needs of the city hospital, which then had 353 beds and an average daily turnover of 230 outpatients. Anti-erosion schemes, sleeping sickness surveys, reafforestations, campaigns against pleuro-pneumonia, and further developments of electricity and water supply were all in process. In 1951, 133 wells were sunk and lined in rural areas. That year Kano imported 10,000 tons of kola-nuts from Southern Nigeria and exported 3,000 tons of dried meat, 800,000 gallons of groundnut oil, and many thousand cattle in return. Late that year Bayero opened a splendid new mosque beside the Gidan Rumfa at Kano which had been mainly financed by voluntary contributions from wealthy local merchants (*attajirai*) and built by the Kano and Regional Departments of Public Works together. More than any other single undertaking, the new mosque simultaneously expressed the vigorous growth of Kano's economy and its devotion to Islam.[89] It had long been Bayero's practice, following that of his father Abbas, to conduct the Friday mosque himself, and to address the assembled congregation with a sermon (*wa'azi*) in Hausa. Thereafter to celebrate the new mosque and express his thanks, he delivered his sermons in Arabic to the delight of his audience, most of whom received his message in its Hausa translation.[90]

In 1950–51 as in 1949–50, the Kano N.A. financed capital works costing £350,000. With groundnuts then fetching £36 a ton, a boom had begun that still continued in 1959, lifting the local economy to new levels of buoyancy. 1949 and 1950 had been seasons of anxiety and near famine due to partial crop failures. In consequence as wealth had increased, the price of staple grains, millet and sorghum, had rocketed from the modest level of 25 shillings per bag at harvest to 85 shillings in the hungry months. In response the Native Administration expanded its emergency reserves of grain in 1951 to more than 3,000 tons, some of which was released as necessary the following year to reduce the market price from its peak of 60s to 45s a bag in the city.[91]

Nonetheless, with only 63 elementary schools in the Province, by 1951 Kano was suffering from its educational conservatism. From 1930 to 1950, only 630 boys had graduated from the Kano Middle School, although by 1950 the emirate contained over 2.5 million people. As the Resident observed in 1950,

> With the growth of modern institutions and the advance of social and economic development of all kinds, there is an urgent need for large numbers of educated men as teachers, clerks, dispensary attendants, etc. This has led to competition between the commercial firms, Government and Native Authorities for the services of any youth of reasonable intelligence who has passed through Middle School. It is not surprising, therefore, that the teaching profession, with its limited opportunities, has suffered.[92]

Another consequence of this shortage of educated Northerners was an increased inflow of educated Southern immigrants to Kano, where their skills were in great demand.

Government by Committee?

Meanwhile, in response to the increasing complexity and range of these economic and social developments, the embryonic ministerial system so long embedded in the Emir's Council was expanded and supplemented by numerous standing committees which were constituted to serve special needs routinely once they were recognised. Of these the first permanent committee was formed in 1943 to co-ordinate the various programs of N.A. departments. All departmental heads, one Divisional Officer, and three Executive Councillors met periodically under Bayero's chairmanship to review departmental activities and to take necessary decisions. In 1947 the three Executive Councillors were the Ciroma, the Sarkin Shanu and the Education Officer. In 1948 another permanent committee was set up to deal with finance. Besides three councillors, of whom the Ciroma and the Sarkin Shanu were two, this committee included the Ma'aji and a British Divisional Officer as ex-officio members. It was charged with preparation and review of the detailed draft estimates that were submitted to Bayero and the Resident annually.

In 1949 two more committees were constituted, one to deal with the N.A. Public Works, the other with local education. Besides the head of the N.A. Works department, the Works committee contained two councillors, the Ciroma and the Sarkin Shanu, two senior Government engineers, and one Divisional Officer. It met monthly to review the design and construction of public works, and functioned as an executive to supervise N.A. building programmes. To fulfill the requirements of a Nigerian Ordinance on education, three local education committees were constituted in 1949, one for the Sabon Gari settled by southerners, one for the European township, and one for the rest of the emirate. These committees were all composed of officials and unofficial members nominated by such educational bodies as local schools, including the Muslim Law School at Shahuci and the Christian missions in the Sabon Gari. In 1949, a special sub-committee was constituted to administer advances to Native Authority employees; however its composition exactly replicated the N.A. Finance Committee set out above.

In 1950 eight consultative committees were constituted by the Native Authority to manage labor relations within its various departments. Each committee administered these affairs for three or four N.A. Departments, giving equal representation of employer and employees, the Native Authority as employer being represented by four senior officials nominated by the Departments and approved by the Emir in Council, while employees' representatives were elected by the departments concerned, each department having one representative. In 1950 Bayero constituted yet another permanent committee to investigate complaints and recommend disciplinary action against N.A. employees. To serve on this, he nominated four senior Native Authority officials, thereby relieving the State Council of many minor complaints which had hitherto required its attention. However, even though this new committee was only authorised to take disciplinary action of the most restricted sort, it was required to report its findings and recommendations to the Emir in Council for approval. Accordingly its constitution in no way reduced the emir's original power over the native administration.[93] As no "Regulations covering the conditions of service of employees of the Native Authority" had yet been promulgated by the Regional Government for observance by the Northern Emirates, in their absence the Kano N.A. administered these affairs along traditional lines.[94] Thus the disciplinary and consultative committees introduced in 1950 were required to administer an unwritten code actuated by traditional norms of hierarchy, obedience and allegiance.

In April 1950 another important standing committee was constituted, with six sub-committees, to supervise Provincial development. Its membership, nominated by the emir and the Resident equally, consisted of native officials and British officials, and included such unofficial members as traders or others with special skills. The six sub-committees of this Development Committee, which met monthly, were charged with communications, internal and external, with education and health, industry and commerce. These several sub-committees reviewed provincial developments and needs in their respective spheres, and reported to the Provincial committee their findings and recommendations. This Provincial committee then referred any proposals for action to the Emir's Council and the Resident.

Besides the committees just described, others regulated the new Radiodiffusion programmes, the city libraries and reading rooms, electricity and water supplies. As required, various *ad hoc* committees were also constituted by Bayero in Council to deal with particular matters, such as enquiry into grave allegations against departmental or district heads.[95]

Nigerian Political Developments, 1944–50

Since 1934 there had been no further annual meetings of Northern chiefs to discuss administrative problems and policies with the Lieutenant Governor and his senior officials at Kaduna. Instead by 1946 the Northern Governor had delegated numerous functions and responsibilities to Provincial Residents, who met with him at annual conferences to review and plan the Region's political and eco-

nomic developments. There was as yet no provision for representative participation by Africans in these deliberations of the Regional Government, despite the
officially asserted principle that native populations should be governed through
their traditional rulers. In effect at Kano the emir and the Resident negotiated privately the local application of policies that either proposed. The colonial government lacked any institutional channels through which emirs could discuss
regional interests or local policies collectively with the Lieutenant Governor at
Kaduna. The regime was explicitly hierarchic and unrepresentative.

In 1946, under a new Nigerian Constitution, an attempt was made to organise
regional representation. That Constitution subdivided Nigeria into three Regions,
North, East and West, the two latter dividing the South. In the North the Fulani
emirates predominated politically and demographically; in the West the Yoruba
chiefdoms; and in the East, the Ibo-speaking peoples. Each region was administered by a Chief Commissioner directly responsible to the Governor of Nigeria. In
each, a Regional Council was constituted, empowered to advise on regional laws
and to control expenditures of regional revenues. In Northern Nigeria, the lower
house of the Regional Council contained 39 members, of whom 18 were British
officials, namely, all Provincial Residents and such senior regional officials as the
Financial Secretary, Crown Counsel, and Deputy (Regional) Directors of Education, Medical, Public Works and Agriculture. Of the 21 African members, 15 were
selected by Native Authority councillors from among themselves at Provincial
meetings. The remaining six were nominated by the Regional Government to represent interests and groups otherwise unrepresented, such as the South Nigerian
community in the North, the populations of European townships, the non-
Muslim peoples of Northern Nigeria, and traders. Thus, despite its form, this
House of Assembly also denied direct representation to the people.

The 1946 Constitution also established a Northern House of Chiefs over which
the Chief Commissioner (formerly the Lieutenant-Governor) presided. Of its 25
African members, 12 were selected by the Regional Government from chiefs of
the second class, while all first class chiefs were ex-officio members. Both Houses
of the Regional Council had identical powers. Either could debate bills laid before
them by the Regional Government, discuss Regional estimates or vote on motions
tabled by Government or by their members. They were also required to choose
four chiefs and five others from among themselves to represent the Region in the
newly constituted Nigerian Legislative Council at Lagos to discuss legislation and
budgets for the country as a whole.[96] Despite its grave shortcomings and provisional character, this constitution provided the first opportunities for regular collective consultations between the colonial government and peoples of Northern
Nigeria. However, no one could seriously argue that these councils represented
the people of the region or country. In this situation, those educated Southern
Nigerians who sought to terminate colonial rule criticised the constitution
sharply, and attempted to mobilise popular support for local autonomy through
political parties and para-political organizations. The first Nigerian political party,
the National Council of Nigeria and the Cameroons (NCNC) had been founded at
Lagos in August 1944 with Herbert Macaulay as President and Dr. Namdi
Azikiwe as General Secretary, two years before the "Richards" Constitution just
described was promulgated. In 1946 on Macaulay's death, Dr. Azikiwe was

elected President of the NCNC. This party, as its name indicates, sought to mobil- ise and represent Nigerians of all regions, religions, cultures and walks of life; but within the Northern Region, few other than immigrant Southerners knew of or supported it.

In 1948 the Yoruba leader, Obafemi Awolowo, established an association, *Egbe Omo Ododuwa*, for the development of Yoruba culture under his leadership; and in December 1949, a schoolteacher at Bauchi, Malam Abubakar Tafawa Balewa founded a parallel cultural organization for Northerners, the *Jam'iyyar Mutanen Arewa* (Northern People's Congress or NPC). Thus by 1950 Nigerian regionalisa- tion, which was formally established under the 1946 constitution, had generated new ethnic and regional associations of obscure potential among the Northern Muslims and the Yoruba.[97]

Like other educated Southerners, the Yoruba leader Awolowo and the Presi- dent of the NCNC, Azikiwe, both pressed for a new constitution which would transfer effective powers of policy formation to regional and federal legislatures elected by adult suffrage. By 1949 the Nigerian Governor, Sir John Macpherson, had accepted the need for constitutional change; and throughout the year, at his direction, Government officials sought proposals for reform from people through- out the country at widely publicised assemblies. This programme of popular con- sultation concluded with a general conference on the form of the new constitution, which met at Ibadan in January 1950. At that conference the emir of Zaria, speaking with the support of other Northern emirs, demanded that in future 50 percent of the seats in the Federal legislature should be reserved for Northerners on two grounds, namely, the larger population of the Northern Region, and the desire of its Muslim majority to forestall legislation inconsistent with Islam.[98] These Northern demands generated anxiety and resistance in South- ern Nigeria, and probably decided Awolowo to convert the *Egbe Omo Oduduwa* into a political party, the Action Group (A.G.), in March 1951, four months before the new constitution was enacted.[99] These political developments at the regional and colonial levels were followed with keen interest at Kano by the emir, his chiefs and his subjects. Their implications remained obscure; but they bore unmistakeable signs of change.

In August 1950 a new political party was founded in Northern Nigeria by rad- icals who withdrew from the Northern People's Congress, or NPC (*Jam'iyyar Mutanen Arewa*) under the leadership of Malam Aminu Kano, a baGyeni cleric whose father had been an *alkali* at Kano. The new party called itself the Northern Elements Progressive Union or NEPU (*Jam'iyyar Neman Sawaba*), criticised the Fulani emirates as feudal, autocratic, corrupt and oppressive, and demanded their immediate reform. In its declaration of principles, NEPU stated that "all parties are but the expression of class interests, and as the interest of the *talakawa* (commoners) is diametrically opposed to the interest of all sections of the master class, a party seeking the emancipation of the *talakawa* must naturally be hostile to the party of the oppressors."[100]

Not since the *jihad* of Shehu dan Fodio had Hausaland heard as radical a call for change proclaimed so clearly and boldly; but whereas the Shehu had launched his *jihad* against oppressive Hausa chiefs as apostates, Aminu Kano directed his invective at the Fulani ruling class established by the Shehu's *jihad*. As a citizen of

Kano, a devout Muslim, and member of one of the emirate's leading clerical lineages, Malam Aminu's criticism could neither be overlooked nor stamped out by traditional means. Moreover, as President of a registered political party, he enjoyed and exploited those rights of free association and speech without which popular representation could not be instituted under the revised constitution. As might be expected, Malam Aminu attracted widespread support at Kano City and further afield among certain sections of the depressed *talakawa* whose exploitation had probably increased in frequency and modes while declining in violence, as a function of their increased exposure to Fulani officials under the recent programmes of rural development. Thus in old age Bayero had to learn to tolerate and outmanoeuvre an opposition at Kano that the new colonial policies and constitution forbade him to extirpate.

The Northern Call for Reform and Its Effects

When the Northern House of Assembly met at Kaduna in August 1950, Malam Abubakar Tafawa Balewa, then president of the NPC and by descent and status a commoner, introduced a resolution:

> that this House respectfully recommends to His Excellency the Governor that he be pleased to appoint an independent commission to investigate the system of native administration in the Northern Provinces and to make recommendations for its modernisation and reform; and that the Northern Public be given the fullest opportunity to discuss and criticise the report and recommendations of the committee before their final acceptance.[101]

Abubakar moved this resolution in a carefully prepared speech which had an immediate and permanent impact on Northern affairs. Declaring, "I call for reform. We cannot afford to stagnate; we must go forward. This I maintain is quite impossible with the present machinery of government, and the sooner this is recognised and admitted, the sooner shall we take our place unhampered by the legacy of an age that is passed." He continued,

> This system which has outlived its usefulness for so long now constitutes the chief barrier to our progress ... Before Europeans came to Africa, the chief's authority was limited by his need to keep his position. He dared not become too unpopular for fear that his subjects would rise against him. Now, backed by the strong authority of central government, he may feel that he need not consider public opinion as long as he remains on friendly terms with the colonial government ...
>
> In the Native Authority Ordinance, they (the people) hardly find a place. Far from the chiefs having well-defined duties, one of the biggest defects of the system is the complete ignorance of everyone from top to bottom about his rights, his obligations and his powers ... Nobody knows where he stands, and District Officers have often assumed the role of dictator and given the executive instructions instead of the advice to which the Native Administrations are entitled ...
>
> The illiterate mass of the people recognise no change in their status since the coming of the British. They are still ruled by might, and administration is still none of their concern ... They should understand that the North enjoys freedom of speech and freedom of action within the law. It is not so today ...

> This brings me ... to the question of the Sole Native Authority. How this idea originated, we do not know, nor could we discover the circumstances which made its creation in 1934 necessary. Whatever was the reason, it is an idea which should be condemned ... I may go so far as to say that "sole Native Authority" ideas may even be said to be against the broad principles of Islam ... In the revision of the Native Authority Ordinance which is overdue, Native Authority Councils should be given real powers and their functions should be no longer advisory ... Democratisation of Native Authority Councils has now also become a necessity...
>
> Improvement is impossible as long as Native Authorities continue the practice of putting square pegs in round holes ... Unless it is dropped completely, it is bound to cause some trouble in the immediate future ...
>
> The twin curses of bribery and corruption ... pervade every rank and department. It is notorious that Native Administration servants have monetary obligations to their immediate superiors and to their Sole Native Authorities. It would be unseemly for me to particularise further, but I cannot overemphasize the importance of eradicating this ungodly evil. *No one* who has not lived among us can fully appreciate to what extent the giving and taking of bribes occupies the attention of all degrees to the exclusion of the ideals of disinterested service. Much of the attraction of a post lies in the opportunities it offers for extortion of one form or another. Unless the commission fully realise the gravity of this problem and tackle it with courage, any recommendations they make for superficial reforms are bound to fail. It is a most disturbing fact that few officials can afford to be honest.[102]

In supporting Abubakar's motion, Malam Yahaya, the Provincial Member for Ilorin, underlined its central point.

> There can never be a democratic local government until this unpopular word "sole Native Authority" is abolished. Sole Native Authority means that all powers are vested in one man or one Native Authority. May I know whether the Native Authority in whom the powers are invested has ever been allowed to use them? Certainly not ... For goodness' sake, let us abolish Sole Native Authorities and have the Native Authority system reformed so that we may have Native Authorities supported by democratic domestic councils. I am sure our Native Authorities would have no fears in adapting themselves in the changing conditions.[103]

In the ensuing debate the Secretary of the Northern Provinces who acted as President of the Council first defended the Administration's record, and then accepted the substance of Malam Abubakar's motion, while opposing his request for an "independent commission" to investigate and propose reforms in Native Administration.[104] On the following division, all 20 unofficial members voted for Abubakar's motion, and all 19 official members voted against. The motion was thus carried; but instead of an "independent commission" the Regional Government promptly appointed two Divisional Officers, K.B. Maddocks and D.A. Pott,

> to visit all Provinces and gather materials on which a survey covering the overall situation in the Northern Provinces can be prepared.
>
> (4) In addition it is necessary that as clear a picture as possible should be available re state of public opinion at all levels as to what practical means should be adopted to accelerate the processes of modernisation of Native Administrations.[105]

By circular, the Regional Secretary then instructed Provincial Residents to investigate and report factually on the current state and organization of the native administrations under their care, and to hold discussions on their shortcomings and reform, in order to generate the data required by the commissioners, Maddocks and Pott. This circular also stipulated that for such discussions any

> Provincial conferences should be bicameral in structure and should consist of the Native Authorities and their Councils on the one part, and of a larger and more representative general conference on the other. It is essential that it should be realised that the forthcoming enquiry is designed to stimulate suggestions for improvement from within. Native Authorities should therefore be the conveners and prime movers in their capacity as head of the local government system.[106]

The Provincial Conferences were instructed to evaluate the effectiveness of current measures designed to modernise local government, to suggest desirable improvements, and to recommend measures for the modernisation of district and village administration, for the devolution of responsibility, for the education of commoners in their "civic responsibilities," and for the reduction of bribery and corruption.[107] A full copy of the text of Abubakar Tafawa Balewa's speech to the Northern House of Assembly in August accompanied the circular.

In response, the Resident Kano compiled data on the N.A. Council and committees, much of which has been presented above, and estimated the emirate population at 2.6 million with an average density of 215 per square mile. Annual revenue from local tax, was then £503,600. As regards the city administration, the Resident reported that all four wards of Kano City had separate advisory councils which were then being reconstituted on an elective basis. Each ward council elected one of its members as the ward representative on the City council, which had advisory but no executive capacities. A new constitution had been approved for the Kano City Council under which there would be 21 voting members, 15 of whom would be elected unofficial members, one a nominated member, four ward heads as ex-officio members, and one other, an elected official. The new council would be given some executive powers and a small degree of financial responsibility on an experimental basis. For the southern community settled outside the city wall, an advisory board composed of nine "responsible members" nominated by the Native Authority had been established; but this was likely to be replaced by an elected body with some financial and executive reponsibility.[108]

The Resident's report on village and district administration bears quotation in full:

> 15. Village Councils. There have been many village councils with advisory functions for many years. After the war it was recognised that they were not effective, and in 1948 plans were made to reconstitute them, but only under close supervision by administrative staff. In nine districts the reconstituted councils have been established. The principle of elected unofficial membership has been introduced.
> 16. District Councils. In the same nine districts, district councils have been established. They consist of 50% Village Heads, i.e. official members, and 50% unofficial, elected by the Village Councils with the District Head as Chairman. District departmental staff are non-voting members. The Council elects its Executive Com-

mittee, usually four or five in number. The (District) Council debates matters brought up from the village councils or matters sent down from the Native Authority. Its initial function is advisory to the Native Authority, and secondly, on approval of the Native Authority of its proposals, it is given executive powers. It prepares its annual budget for the expenditure of the District Funds; and, on approval of the Native Authority, its Executive is responsible to the Council for carrying out the proposals. (District) Council funds vary from £1460 to £270 per annum. The principle is approved that the District can increase its District Council Fund (D.C.F.) allocation (now 6% per taxpayer) by as much as it is prepared to increase its normal tax incidence. Though none has yet done this, indications are that this method of raising a District rate will be adopted. D.C. Funds are spent on every form of district improvement and development, more especially on reconstruction of markets, on cement lining and topping of wells, new village layouts, construction of District and village halls. Voluntary communal labour is also encouraged.

17. To sum up, the reconstituted system of local government in village and district has introduced important principles of election, of unofficial membership, and also of a degree of financial responsibility. It has also provided a channel from the hamlet level to the district and thence to the Native Authority through which the public may voice its views and opinions. It is a matter of close supervision by administrative staff, and of time and experience for the public to become fully aware of the benefit of this system.[109]

Of equal interest is the Resident's account of the Provincial conference called at Kano to discuss the terms of reference laid down by the Regional Circular.

Membership was by invitation, and the aim was to obtain on the unofficial side as complete representation as possible of each area and section of interest in the Province.

2. After an opening speech by the chairman, the official and unofficial sides held separate meetings to consider the terms of reference in detail. At the close, each side drew up its written recommendations, and at a final joint meeting an attempt was made to reconcile these and present agreed conclusions. While successful in many instances, it was impossible to secure complete agreement over so wide a field, and a summary is therefore given of all recommendations which had the substantial support of either half of the meeting.

3. Effectiveness of existing measures. The official members, as might be expected, were more farsighted than the unofficial. Looking forward to increasing delegation of powers to Native Authorities, and ultimately to complete autonomy within the framework of the Northern Regional Government, they felt that the provision of staff qualified by education and training to take over the duties of the supervisory staff now provided by the government was of first importance. They considered that the existing measures designed to modernise local government took no account of this need, and recommended the greatest possible expansion in the Northern Provinces of Secondary and University education. As an interim measure they recommended that Northern youths should be sent abroad to study, preferably in Muslim countries, those subjects which would qualify them for the higher administrative and departmental posts which N.A. officials would in time have to fill. The unofficials had not seriously considered this aspect of the matter, but on hearing the views of the official side, accepted them in principle.

4. As regards other measures of democratisation, both sides agreed that the establishment of district and village councils was enough for the moment, and that

the pace at which these were being introduced was satisfactory, bearing in mind the need for a careful and thorough explanation of the system to the peasantry.

A council for each Emirate on similar lines deriving from the District Councils was held by all to be desirable, but there was sharp dissension between officials and unofficials on who would preside over such a council and whether any of its members should be admitted to the Advisory Council of the Native Authority. The unanimous official view was that a senior Native Authority official but not the Emir should preside, and that the Advisory Council, whose functions were mainly executive, should be composed as now of senior officials only. The unofficials felt that they should in some way be represented at the centre, with direct access to the Emir, and that a seat or two on the Advisory Council, even with no vote or executive responsibilities, would be the best means to this end.

Looking towards the future, both sides agreed that the Province was not a natural unit of administration and that Native Authorities when they claimed autonomy should be free to combine as they chose or to deal direct with the Regional Government. The further step to Provincial Council was therefore unacceptable to the conference, though it may be noted that at a later meeting to consider the election of members to the Regional and central legislature, they accepted the principle of representation by Provinces without qualm.

5. As regards modernisation of district and village administration, both sides were agreed that the appointment by the Emir of District Heads from the traditional ruling families was the best means of getting the right type of man, i.e., one whom the people would respect. The unofficials recommended that such appointments should require confirmation by the governed, and that the Emir, before appointing a District Head, should submit a "short list" to the District Council concerned, leaving the choice of the individual to them. Officials would have none of this in any shape or form, but conceded that the District Head of the future must be an educated man, though what degree of education he should possess was not stated. The unofficials agreed with this, and did not press for any definite educational standards.

6. District Councils, it was agreed by both sides, should be allowed to co-opt additional members whom they considered useful up to one-fourth of their number and to elect their own Vice-Chairman from the elected or co-opted members, the office to be held for one year with no bar on re-election. No change was proposed in the present constitution of village councils, which are in effect "free for all."

Discussion of the matter of bribery and corruption produced a greater measure of agreement than might have been expected, it being clearly conceded that those in high places were not to blame, but their underlings, paid or unpaid, and the kind of petty official—the railway, Post Office and police were instanced—whose power of inspection gave him the opportunity to demand and receive bribes. An increasing dependence on the things that money can buy and the consequent need for more cash were felt to be one of the causes of the evil. But the unofficials felt that senior officials should not be unapproachable except through intermediaries, and that the vetting of District Heads by the District Councils before their appointments would be a move in the right direction. Also that something should be done to obviate present delays and uncertainty about the date of hearing of court cases. Officials felt that more could be done by publicity and the education of the people in their rights and duties, particularly by way of district and village councils, and with the support of the unofficials, recommended that the Public Relations Officer be asked to produce suitable literature for distribution. They recommended that employees of known honesty be encouraged by promotion and honours, but some doubt was felt by the unofficials about what would be the criterion of honesty. Both sides agreed that the punishment for such crimes should be severe and public, and that a revival of morality based on religion was the best remedy of all. They therefore recommended more emphasis on the teaching of religion and morality in schools of every type.

7. Increased devolution of responsibility to district and village councils was felt by both sides to be sound policy, but both agreed that since in Kano Province the most advanced of these councils was barely two years old, it would be a mistake to increase their powers immediately. They must first learn their work and acquire a staff which could handle such things as records, accounts and estimates.

8. There was general agreement that where the district and village council system had been introduced, people were taking an interest in local government; but that elsewhere they showed little or none. Conference ... recommended that this system be extended to all districts as rapidly as possible. It was pointed out that the members of these councils, though unpaid, showed no reluctance to attend meetings, and some of them might even accept election to the regional legislature. As further means of encouragement, the conference recommended the granting of allowances to members, and if possible visits by mobile cinema units exhibiting films in illustration of local government elsewhere. On being informed that ... (a Provincial Officer) had prepared a pamphlet explaining in simple language the working of the district and village council system, the meeting recommended that the pamphlet be printed for distribution within the Province.

9. A very interesting feature of this conference was the evident desire on both sides that the powers of the Native Authorities and the Native Courts vis-a-vis Government should be increased rather than diminished. There is undoubtedly a very strong feeling among the general public in favour of greater local autonomy in conformity with the principles of Islam, in all the native authorities of this Province; and it is improbable that any revision of local government which ignores the tradition and religion of the people will find favour in their eyes.

L.R. Delves-Broughton
Acting Resident, Kano[110]

Since the official and unofficial members of this conference were selected and invited by the administration, it is possible that Bayero and other emirs used this opportunity to advocate the restoration of autonomy long withdrawn from their emirates; but it is evident from the preceding report that while official representatives conceived such developments as enhancing their authority, the unofficials desired them only if the Executive Councils of the Native Authority were simultaneously democratised. Evidently also, unofficials felt that they were more likely to secure the reforms and developments they desired by democratising the Native Administration than by political action at the regional or colonial level. Despite clear differences between the two groups concerning the desirable degrees and modes of N.A. democratisation, their evaluations and recommendations illustrate a surprising consensus, even with due regard to the careful selection of the conference personnel. Presumably N.E.P.U. radicals, if at all present, were a very small minority. The conference report accordingly illustrates the state of conservative and moderate "public opinion" concerning local democracy and government in Kano Emirate on the eve of constitutional reform, party politics, and decolonisation. It should not be assumed to represent "public opinion" freely or fully. Nonetheless the conference was a truly revolutionary event and marked the end of an era. For the first time in its history, and after nearly 50 years of British rule, some representatives of the people of Kano had been convened to discuss political reforms and developments as a group with their officials. So utterly unprecedented an event was pregnant with future implications.

The End of an Era, 1951–53

In December 1951 under the new "Macpherson" Constitution elections were held throughout Nigeria for the new Regional Houses of Assembly. "The election was by a pyramid of electoral meetings called 'colleges.'"[111] In the North, only adult males were allowed to vote, but in other regions, adults of either sex could vote. Under the system of electoral colleges used in Northern Nigeria, each village-area elected one or two residents to represent it at the district level, where delegates from all villages in the district constituted a college which chose two or three representatives from their ranks to the emirate college, according to population. At that level, district delegates were supplemented by others nominated by the emir; and this college elected members from its ranks to represent the emirate at the provincial level, where some delegates were selected from the assembly by vote to represent the province at the regional level. In like fashion the Regional House of Assembly elected from its members a certain number to sit in the Lower House of the Nigerian Legislative Council. The Regional House also selected some members to sit on the Regional Executive Council. In Northern Nigeria beside this "elected" House of Assembly there was also a House of Chiefs, which met under the presidency of the Lieutenant-Governor of the Region and consisted of 13 first class chiefs, 37 other chiefs, one adviser on Muslim law, and three expatriate officials. Under the new constitution the House of Chiefs and the House of Assembly had identical powers, and could therefore veto one another's decisions in case of conflict;[112] but to my knowledge no such occasion arose in Northern Nigeria.

The constitutional developments of 1951 introduced and institutionalised popular elections throughout Nigeria, thus initiating bold, unprecedented and perhaps irreversible changes in the bases, range, scope and distribution of political power within the country. In preparation for this series of collegial elections, the Sardauna of Sokoto, Sir Ahmadu Bello, joined with Abubakar Tafawa Balewa to revive the relatively dormant N.P.C. and used it as a political organization to assure a Muslim majority at the Regional and Federal levels.[113] Thus by the end of 1951 the North possessed two Muslim parties, the radical NEPU and the moderate or centrist NPC. A third party, the Middle Zone League, had already been founded in 1950 by David Lot and others in Southern Zaria to organise and represent the large non-Muslim populations from which the Muslim Kanuri, Fulani and Hausa had for centuries recruited slaves.[114] Thus the electoral process had rapidly generated political parties divided by ethnic criteria as well as ideology and programmes.

Since the Northern chiefs had rested their demands for one-half the membership of the Federal Legislature on demographic grounds, the Nigerian Government duly carried out a census of the country's population in the summer of 1952, the first for twenty years. Carefully prepared and conducted, that census provides a useful account of Kano's population at the close of Bayero's reign and the end of fifty years of Indirect Rule. In 1952 the emirate contained 2.9 million people, an increase of 970,000 since 1931, when the last census was held. Its sex ratio was relatively even, with 948 males per 1,000 women. Approximately 40 percent of the emirate's population was less than 15 years of age. In the emirate, 34.4 percent of the males were children, while 51.7 percent were engaged in agriculture, 6.9 percent in crafts, 2.7 percent in trade and clerical work, 1.3 percent in administrative, technical or professional activities, and 2.9 percent in other occupations.

Of the emirate population, 62.5 percent were Hausa and 29.4 percent Fulani. Kanuri accounted for 4.3 percent and Ibo 1.4 percent, Yoruba 0.3 percent, and other Southerners 0.3 percent. Only 0.1 percent of the emirate's population were non-Nigerian. Of the total population above 7 years of age, 20,900 or 0.9 percent were literate in Roman script; and only 0.5 percent had completed standard 4 in the Elementary school. In contrast, 178,000 or 8.2 percent of the population were literate in the Ajemic script which had been employed in pre-colonial days. Within the emirate 97.9 percent were Muslim, 1.7 percent animist (pagan), and 0.4 percent Christian, the latter being mainly Southern Nigerians. At this date Kano City contained 93,000 people and the Waje, its environs or suburban communities, including the Sabon Gari, 34,000. The township dominated by Europeans and Lebanese had less than 3,000.[115]

In May 1953 Kano experienced the first popular riots in Northern Nigeria against Ibo immigrants from the South. According to the official report, 36 were killed and 241 injured between the 16th and 18th of May. Property damage was estimated at over £10,000.[116] The Resident blamed "hooligan elements" in Kano for this violence.

> It began with the crowds that jeered the Northern members at the House of Representatives in Lagos in April. The anti-Northern press campaign and the much-publicised Action Group tour in the North followed in May, and all the seeds of hatred and fear of Southern domination had been sown. The hooligan elements had found conditions in which to flourish and fell upon the Southern people in Sabon Gari. Reprisals and mutilations inevitably increased the violence of the emotions aroused, yet it was possible by skilful use of the police and military to contain and in the end to disperse the forces of disorder without a shot being fired or any loss of life due to their arms.[117]

More recent outrages in Kano and other Northern centres against Ibo immigrants suggest that these initial race riots were not entirely attributable to the "hooligan element" in Kano.

Later that year the City trembled on the edge of further violence between NEPU and NPC activists. According to the Resident,

> For nearly three years the Northern Elements Progressive Union had been carrying on a campaign of villification against the Native Authority. In July the Northern delegates to the London conference, among them the Emir of Katsina, were subjected at the Airport to a shower of abuse from its (NEPU) members. Arrests were later made, and the accused were brought before the court of the Junior Alkali of Kano. Fifteen were found guilty and sentenced to three months' imprisonment for insulting words and behaviour. They obtained a writ of *certiorari* and the case was quashed in the Supreme Court on a technical point on the jurisdiction of the

court. The accused were re-arrested and the case was tried *de novo* by a different Alkali. They were again found guilty and sentenced.

There is no question that the quashing of the case was not understood in Kano City and was interpreted there as an endorsement by the European administration of the conduct of Northern Elements Progressive Union. Overnight a party calling themselves the *"Mahaukata"* or "Madmen" bent on the destruction of Northern Elements Progressive Union appeared and began to hold unlawful assemblies. Hooligans, in entirely different circumstances, had again found a political temperature to suit their activities. Against Northern Elements Progressive Union, they could count at least on the passive support of all members of the extreme Right in politics. On October 16th the Native Authority imposed a "Preservation of the Peace Order" prohibiting public meetings for a month, and the same day two detachments of Nigerian Police arrived from Kaduna.[118]

In December 1952 the death of Wali Muhammadu Basheri provided the Resident with an opportunity to press for further changes in the Council's composition. "There was something unreal about the old Council which made it dramatically reminiscent of Sheridan's Critic—'When they do agree on the stage, their unanimity is wonderful!' It was essential to find more independence of opinion."[119] This remark is excellent unintentional evidence of Bayero's success in maintaining autocratic control of the emirate despite his obligation to govern through a ministerial council, the growth of popular politics, administrative efforts at decentralisation, and the many, varied developments of his final years. It also suggests that many NEPU strictures on the Kano N.A. were by no means inappropriate.

To replace Muhammadu Basheri, Bayero appointed the Alkalin Dutse Abubakar as Wali. Simultaneously the Madaki Ibrahim, district head of Tofa, was retired on grounds of blindness. Next "The Honourable Bello, Minister for Community Development, resigned his portfolio to take his place with the title of Dan Amar."[120] Either Mallam Bello, who had formerly sat on the Council as head of the Kano Education Department, was thus following the emir's instructions, or he attached greater value to the traditional role of district head than to his modern role as Minister of Community Development. To broaden the Council the district heads of Dambarta, Jahun and Ungogo were also appointed, with some interesting consequences. The Sarkin Bai Muhammadu Adananu having been appointed to the Council, retired as district head within a year in favour of his eldest son, Muhammadu Mukhtari, while retaining his personal seat on the council. On the retirement of the Madaki Ibrahim for blindness, the Sarkin Shanu Shehu Ahmadu succeeded as Madaki, while the title and office of Sarkin Shanu was conferred on the district head of Jahun, the Magajin Mallam Muhammadu Sani, a baYole.

At Ungogo the Dokaji Alhaji Abubakar, the Waziri Gidado's son and historian of Kano, was promoted to the Council with responsibility for Medical and Health services, which were then separated from other departments under the Madaki Shehu Ahmadu's supervision. The most notable innovation in the composition of the Council was the appointment of the wealthiest Hausa trader at Kano, Alhaji Alhassan dan Tata, as a non-executive member to represent commercial interests. According to the Resident, "the Council, thus enlarged to ten members, is a far more representative and vocal body than many of its predecessors. If seven of its members come from traditionally great families of Kano, it is because these were the first to welcome modern education and the best qualified to benefit by it."[121] Indeed, with the sole exception of Alhassan dan Tata, all councillors were drawn from ruling Fulani lineages, including three from the Yolawa.

To supplement this exclusive N.A. Council, and implement the recommendations of the Maddocks-Pott Report in 1952, an Outer Council of delegates elected from districts had been instituted to afford some popular participation in the emirate government. At biennial meetings, the Outer Council received reports from departmental heads of the Native Administration, and raised questions, criticisms and suggestions regarding current and future programmes. In addition,

> District Councils have been established in all districts ... Three Districts in Kano now hold a delegated financial responsibility. They have done well with this. The Kano City Council operates as a District Council, meeting quarterly, and is elected partly on an occupational basis, partly territorial; guilds elect members and so do wards.[122]

However when the council of the Sabon Gari, which had a mainly South Nigerian population, voted not to co-operate with the Kano Native Authority following a rise in the water rates, it was suspended for six months, and the rates were levied.[123]

Bayero was now in his 70th year. Late in 1953 his health broke down. On December 24th he died and was buried beside his father, Abbas, at the Nassarawa Palace.[124]

> On Christmas Day the traditional electors assembled at 1 pm and at 2 pm announced that they had unanimously elected the Ciroma Alhaji Muhammadu Sanusi, eldest son of the late Emir, to succeed.
> Before he had been 24 hours in office, the new Emir had already begun to institute some valuable changes and reforms. In a broadcast speech to his people he promised to put their interests before all else, and to consult his council in all things. He planned to hold all sessions of the Emir's Court in public in future, and was making immediate changes in its personnel. To prevent repetition of former criticisms that the administration of Kano was too centralised, too autocratic, too much in the hands of one family, he said he would never at any time appoint a close relative of his to any one of the three highest offices on the council, the Wali, in charge of the city, or in charge of the districts. He also asked his Council to reorganise for him his personal household, limiting it to those who were pensionable from the Treasury or rightly a charge against his privy purse, and removing all others.
> There is no question that these immediate reforms have been welcomed throughout Kano. As a result a great wave of loyalty and confidence has greeted him on his accession.[125]

Thus Bayero was equally successful in his end and his beginning. By establishing the Ciroma as the only feasible successor, he had relieved the Electoral Council of any problem about this decision; and by manumitting all his slaves on his own accession, he had ensured their continued residence at the palace, thus obliging his successor to seek the Council's aid in reducing his responsibilities for their support.

Having lamented the passing of Alhaji Abdullahi Bayero, the Resident, A.T. Weatherhead, concluded his review of developments at Kano in 1953 with the following comparative observations:

> We have just completed half a century of British rule in Kano. In that time we have telescoped five hundred years of political development. One does not expect Pitt or Fox fifty years after Simon de Montfort. Nevertheless, Kano is already on the eve of an industrial revolution on a small scale. It is leaving a strictly aristocratic society and entering on an era when the middle class and those engaged in trade are beginning to be a power in politics. We could hardly be living at a more interesting and enlivening time.
>
> There may be some who seem at this moment to despair—they are expecting too much. They look only at the short-comings; at the lack of integrity in public life; at the still limited demand for education; at the lack of vocation in our African Nursing Service; at the violence of communal riots; at the perversity of those who cant of liberty; the irresponsibility of the press; and at the lack of respect for established authority. All these have their parallel in England in the last 200 years.
>
> *Integrity* - At the end of the Eighteenth Century in England statesmen regarded the Civil Service "chiefly as a means of rewarding supporters and providing for younger sons."
>
> *Education* - In 1815 "compulsory State Education would have seemed to Englishmen an intolerable invasion of private liberty."
>
> *Nursing Services* - In 1851 the physician of a large London hospital wrote, "Nurses are all drunkards, sisters and all, and there are but two nurses whom the surgeons can trust to give the patients their medicine."
>
> *Communal Riots* - In 1780 the Gordon Riots directed against Catholics raged for six days and disgraced England in the eyes of Europe.
>
> *Liberty* - Wilkes' "unabashed purpose was to see how full he could fill his pockets by trailing his coat."
>
> *The Press* - In Eighteenth Century England "scurrilous abuse was characteristic of everything that came from the press of either side."
>
> *Hooliganism* - Lady Mary Wortley-Montagu wrote of the idleness and ignorance which were the breeding ground of vice and hooliganism; "catcalls of a well-paid canaille" were a feature of Eighteenth Century politics.
>
> *Respect for Authority* - Authority is respected where it is deserved. Our own monarchy has survived because since Victoria it has given an outstanding example of devotion to public duty and service.
>
> I have paid my tribute to the Emir of Kano Alhaji Abdullahi Bayero. If his successors show the same steady virtues of integrity amid the changing political scenes of the future, there is no need to doubt the stability of the Emirate tradition.[126]

This studiously inappropriate comparison nicely illustrates the paternalistic orientations of successive Regional Governors and Residents at Kano. With such assumptions and orientations, the British Administration had stabilized and developed Fulani control of Kano by adapting and preserving its autocratic government. But with Bayero's death, Kano entered a new and turbulent historical era; and in rapid succession it experienced decolonization, independence, regional politics, pogroms, civil war and military governments. The critical factors in Kano's history under Bayero's successors are still half-hidden by their past and present shadows. Its rulers, exposed by British withdrawal to more aggressive pressures at home and beyond, must undoubtedly sometimes recall with nostalgia those halcyon days when, deliberately or otherwise, British Residents guarded the emirate's integrity and the essentially absolute nature of its kingship. As an illustration of their prevailing attitude, Weatherhead's peculiar parallel provides an apt conclusion to this narrative of the political evolution of Kano until 1953.

Notes

1. LH, Vol. 2, p. 73.

2. *District Notebooks*, Ringim, Kura and Ungogo, Provincial Office, Kano.

3. LH, Vol. 2, p. 73.

4. F.D. Lugard, *Northern Nigeria*, 1902, p. 92.

5. M. Adamu na Ma'aji, *Ta'rikh Kano*, supplemented by oral accounts of these turnovers.

6. *Kano Provincial Gazetteer*, December, 1934, File 2568, Vol. 2, National Archives, Kaduna, p. 29.

7. LH, Vol. 2, p. 73.

8. *District Notebooks*, Ringim, Kura, Kiru, Gwaram, Birnin Kudu, Suma'ila, Provincial Office, Kano.

9. *District Notebooks*, Wudil and Suma'ila, Provincial Office, Kano.

10. E.J. Arnett, *Annual Report on Kano Province, 1924*, File 2724, Vol. II, National Archives, Kaduna.

11. *Report on Taura District*, 1922, File 203A / 1927. National Archives, Kaduna.

12. E.J. Arnett, *Annual Report on Kano Province*, 1924, File 2724, Vol. II, National Archives, Kaduna.

13. L.S. Ward, *Decentralization in Kano N.A.*, January–December 1931, File 693, National Archives, Kaduna, paras. 2 and 3.

14. *Kano Provincial Gazetteer*, December 1934, File 2568, Vol. II, National Archives, Kaduna, p 29.

15. L.S. Ward, *Decentralization in Kano N.A.*, File 693, National Archives, Kaduna, p. 29.

16. *Annual Report on Kano Province*, 1926, National Archives, Kaduna; see also LH, Vol. 2, p. 73.

17. *Annual Report on Kano Province*, 1926, National Archives, Kaduna; Anon., *Sarkin Kano, Abdullahi Bayero, C.M.G., C.B.E.* (Zaria: N.R.L.A., 1954), p. 8.

18. For a much fuller account of the development and organization of the Tijaniyya *turuq* at Kano, and the role of these Islamic orders in the political integration and social life of Kano, see John Paden, "Aspects of the Emirship in Kano" In Michael Crowder and Obaro Ikime (Eds.), *West African Chiefs: Their Changing Status under Colonial Rule and Independence* (Ile-Ife: University of Ife Press, 1970), pp. 162–186; also John Paden, *The Influence of Religious Elites on Political Culture and Community Integration in Kano, Nigeria*, (Ph.D. dissertation, Department of Government, Harvard University, 1968). See also, John Paden, "Aspects of Political Legitimation and Integration in Nineteenth Century Kano Emirate," paper presented to the Boston University African History Colloquia, April 1967 (unpublished).

19. These data are drawn from the Annual Report on Kano Province, 1930, File 438, National Archives, Kaduna; correspondence between Residents H.O. Lindsell and L.S. Ward on decentralization in Kano Emirate, National Archives, Kaduna; and H.O. Lindsell's memo on 19th July, 1927, on "Relations of the Emir's Council to the Alkali's Court and District Courts, Kano Emirate," File 693, National Archives, Kaduna. See also Margery Perham, *Native Administration in Nigeria* (London: Oxford University Press, 1937), pp. 81–112.

20. L.S. Ward, "Decentralization of Executive Responsibilities in Kano Emirate," December 1931, File 693, National Archives, Kaduna, para. 1.

21. Margery Perham, *Native Administration in Nigeria*, p. 87.

22. See L.S. Ward, "Decentralization of Executive Responsibilities in Kano Emirate," December, 1931; and his correspondence on this with H.O. Lindsell, his successor as Resident, Kano, in File 693, National Archives, Kaduna.

23. For official documents that provide the basis of these observations, see *Annual Reports on Kano Province*, 1926, 1930 and 1934, on File in National Archives, Kaduna; also *Kano Provincial Gazetteer*, December, 1934, in File 2568, Vol. II, National Archives, Kaduna; L.S. Ward, "Memo on ... the Decentralization of Executive Responsibilities in Kano Emirate," December, 1931; and his correspondence with H.O. Lindsell on this memo, in File 693, National Archives, Kaduna; also *Annual Report on Kano Province* 1934–5, File 1073, National Archives, Kaduna; and *Memo on Village Administration*, 1933–4, File 2087, National Archives, Kaduna. For other views of Kano at this period that have differing emphases, see Margery Perham, *Native Administration in Nigeria*, pp. 81–112; C.R. Niven, "Kano in 1933," *Geographical Journal*, Vol. 82, 1933, pp. 336–343; and Anon., *Sarkin Kano, Abdullahi Bayero, C.M.G., C.B.E.* (Zaria: NRLA, 1954), pp. 8–14.

24. H.O. Lindsell to Secretary Northern Provinces. "Memo on Relations of the Emir's Council with the Alkali's Courts," on File (?693) in National Archives, Kaduna.

25. *Annual Report on Kano Province, 1930*, File 438, National Archives, Kaduna.

26. L.S. Ward, "Decentralization of Executive Responsibilities in Kano Emirate," December, 1931, File 693, National Archives, Kaduna, para. 13.

27. Ibid., para. 14.

28. *Annual Report on Kano Province*, 1930. National Archives, Kaduna.

29. L.S. Ward, "Decentralization of Executive Responsibilities in Kano Emirate," File 693, National Archives, Kaduna, paras. 17–25.

30. Ibid., paras. 26–38.

31. C.R. Niven, "Kano in 1933," *Geographic Journal*, Vol. 82, 1933, pp. 340–341.

32. L.S. Ward, "Decentralization of Executive Responsibilities in Kano Emirate," File 693, National Archives, Kaduna, para. 39; *Annual Report on Kano Province*, 1932, on file, National Archives, Kaduna.

33. *Annual Reports on Kano Province*, 1930, 1932; L.S. Ward, "Decentralization of Executive Responsibilities in Kano Emirate," para. 40; M. Perham, *Native Administration in Nigeria*, p. 96; C.R. Niven, "Kano in 1933," *Geographical Journal*, Vol. 82, 1933, pp. 336–343; *Kano Provincial Gazetteer*, December, 1934, File 2568, Vol. II, National Archives, Kaduna.

34. *Kano Provincial Gazetteer*, December, 1934, File 2568, Vol. II, National Archives, Kaduna; *Annual Report on Kano Province*, 1926, on file, National Archives, Kaduna.

35. Nigerian Government, *Annual Report on the Northern Provinces of Nigeria* (Kaduna: Government Printer, 1932), pp. 24–25, paras. 153–55, 158–9, 168.

36. Ibid., p. 24, para. 152.

37. See M. Perham, *Native Administration in Nigeria*, pp. 126–131.

38. Nigerian Government, *Annual Report on the Northern Provinces of Nigeria*, 1931, p. 26, paras. 166–167.

39. *Kano Provincial Gazetteer*, December, 1934, File 2568, Vol. II, National Archives, Kaduna; and Nigerian Government, *Annual Report on the Northern Provinces*, 1933 (Kaduna: Government Printer, 1934), p. 38, para. 206.

40. Nigerian Government, *Annual Report on the Northern Provinces, 1933*, p. 40, para. 218; p. 44, para. 245.

41. C.R. Niven, "Kano in 1933," pp. 336–337, 339.

42. Nigerian Government, *Annual Report on the Northern Provinces, 1933*, pp. 41–42, paras. 225–227.

43. Ibid., p. 37, paras. 198–199; L.S. Ward, "Decentralization of Executive Responsibilities in Kano Emirate," File 693, National Archives, Kaduna, paras. 17, 25, 35; and Correspon-

dence with H.O. Lindsell in File 693; *Kano Provincial Gazetteer, 1934*, File 2658, Vol. II, National Archives, Kaduna.

44. For a summary account of the contribution of his father, the Waziri Muhammadu Gidado, see Dokaji Alhaji Abubakar, *Kano ta Dabo Cigari*, p. 86; see also Nigerian Government, *Annual Report on the Northern Provinces, 1933*, p. 40, para. 217.

45. Nigerian Government, Annual Report on the Northern Provinces, 1933, pp. 38–40, paras. 205–28; pp. 42–3, paras. 233–236.

46. Ibid., pp. 44–45, para. 248.

47. Ibid., pp. 37–38, paras. 200–201.

48. Ibid., p. 38, para. 200.

49. Ibid., p. 37, para. 198.

50. J.R. Patterson, *Village Administration, General, 1934*, File 2087, National Archives, Kaduna.

51. Taura District file 203A/1927, National Archives, Kaduna.

52. For official discussions of the "*taki*" system of tax assessment in Kano, see "*Taki* Assessments," File 1708A, National Archives, Kaduna. On the 'lump sum' method, see Margery Perham, *Native Administration in Nigeria*, pp. 104–105.

53. Margery Perham, *Native Administration in Nigeria*, p. 108.

54. Ibid., p. 86.

55. *Kano Provincial Gazetteer*, 1934, File 2568, Vol. II, National Archives, Kaduna.

56. C.R. Niven, "Kano in 1933," p. 338; M. Perham, *Native Administration in Nigeria*, pp. 106–112.

57. *Kano Provincial Gazetteer*, 1934, File 2568, Vol. II, National Archives, Kaduna.

58. Dokaji Alhaji Abubakar, *Kano ta Dabo Cigari*, p. 41; LH, Vol. 2, p. 74; Anon., *Sarkin Kano, Abdullahi Bayero, C.M.G., C.B.E.*, p. 8

59. *District Notebook*, Ungogo, Provincial Office, Kano; and oral information from Kano.

60. For notice of this replacement, see *Nigerian Citizen*, March 11, 1959, p. 6.

61. *District Notebooks*, Ungogo, Garki and Suma'ila, Provincial Office, Kano.

62. *District Notebook*, Gwaram, Provincial Office, Kano.

63. For this inventory and correspondence, see Kano File 2724, Vol. 2, National Archives, Kaduna. Evidently, bearing in mind the estate of a late 19th century Madaki catalogued by M. Hiskett (see, *idem*, "Materials Relating to the Cowrie Currency of the Western Sudan," Part I, *BSOAS*, Vol. 29, 1966, pp. 122–142), it seems likely that many items were omitted from this list of the Sarkin Rano's possessions.

64. M. Perham, *Native Administration in Nigeria*, p. 106.

65. Secretary of Northern Provinces (SNP) - Circular of 19th August, 1935, to Residents on "Decentralization of Departmental Activities in Native Administration," para. 2; on File (?693) in National Archives, Kaduna.

66. For discussion of these developments at Zaria, see M.G. Smith, "Historical and Cultural Conditions of Political Corruption among the Hausa," *Comparative Studies in Society and History*, Vol. VI, No. 2, 1964, pp. 187–193; also *idem, Government in Zazzau, 1800–1950*, pp. 230–233, 271–276, 288–292.

67. Nigerian Government, *Annual Report on the Northern Provinces of Nigeria, 1931*, p. 27, para. 175; *idem, Annual Report on the Northern Provinces, 1934*, pp. 29–30.

68. Anon, *Sarkin Kano, Abdullahi Bayero, C.M.G., C.B.E.,*, pp. 16–20. S.J. Hogben and A.H.M. Kirk-Greene, *The Emirates of Northern Nigeria*, p. 208; Nigerian Government, *Annual Report on the Northern Provinces, 1934*, pp. 30–31.

69. Nigerian Government, *Annual Report on the Northern Provinces*, 1934, pp. 30–34.

70. Nigerian Government, *Annual Report on the Northern Provinces, 1936* (Kaduna: The Government Printer, 1937), p. 30.

71. Ibid., pp. 30–33.

72. Dokaji Alhaji Abubakar, *Kano ta Dabo Cigari*, p. 86; Anon., *Sarkin Kano, Abdullahi Bayero, C.M.G.,C.B.E.*, pp. 20–22.

73. Dokaji Alhaji Abubakar, *Kano ta Dabo Cigari*, p. 86

74. Oral information, gathered at Kano in 1959, corroborates and amplifies the lists compiled by Malam Adamu na Ma'aji, *Ta'rikh Kano*. See also Dokaji Alhaji Abubakar, *Kano ta Dabo Cigari*, p. 88.

75. *District Notebooks*, Dawakin Tofa, Minjibir, Dawakin Kudu, Dutse, Ungogo, Jahun, Bici, Provincial Office, Kano.

76. *District Notebooks*, Dawakin Tofa, Wudil, Suma'ila; Provincial Office, Kano, and Dokaji Alhaji Abubakar, *Kano ta Dabo Cigari*, pp. 88–92.

77. Dokaji Alhaji Abubakar, *Kano ta Dabo Cigari*, pp. 92–93; *District Notebook*, Dambarta, Provincial Office, Kano.

78. *District Notebook*, Gezawa, Provincial Office, Kano.

79. *District Notebook*, Sum'aila, Provincial Office, Kano.

80. Dokaji Alhaji Abubakar, *Kano ta Dabo Cigari*, p. 83.

81. B. Sharwood Smith, *Kano Survey, 1950*, on file in National Archives, Kaduna; see also Dokaji Alhaji Abubakar, *Kano ta Dabo Cigari*, p. 77.

82. Government of Nigeria, *Native Authority Ordinance (No. 17 of 1943)*, Section 33 (Lagos: The Government Printer, 1943).

83. Circular No. 343 of 12/12/1946 from the Secretary of the Northern Provinces to Residents. In File NAC/43 on Local Government, Provincial Office, Kano.

84. B. Sharwood Smith, *Kano Survey, 1950*, on File in National Archives, Kaduna. See also reply of 13/10/1950 from Resident, Kano to Circular 207/1950 from Secretary of Northern Provinces in File NAC/53, Provincial Office, Kano.

85. *Native Administrations Estimates 1949–50, Kano Province* (Kaduna: The Government Printer, 1950), pp. 21–22.

86. Resident Kano's reply of 13/10/1950 to Circular 207/1950 from SNP; File NAC/53 Provincial Office, Kano; B. Sharwood Smith, *Kano Survey 1950*, Section (vi), Courts.

87. B. Sharwood-Smith, *Kano Survey 1950*, Section (v); Annual Report on Kano Province, 1932. Both on file in National Archives, Kaduna.

88. These figures are extrapolated from the *1952 Population Census of the Northern Region of Nigeria* (Lagos: Department of Statistics, n.d.), Table 8.2, pp. 34–35.

89. Northern Region of Nigeria, *Provincial Annual Report, 1957* (Kaduna: The Government Printer, 1953), pp. 40–46.

90. Anon., *Sarkin Kano, Abdullahi Bayero, C.M.G., C.B.E.*, pp. 21–22.

91. Northern Region of Nigeria, *Provincial Annual Reports, 1951*, p. 44, para. 30, p. 46, paras. 39–40, p. 40, para. 2.

92. Ibid., p. 42, para. 16; Reply of Resident, Kano, 13/10/1950 to Circular 207/1950 of SNP, File NAC/53, Kano Provincial Office, para. 20.

93. Reply of Resident, Kano, 13/10/1950 to SNP's Circular 207/1950, File NAC/53, Provincial Office, Kano, para. 11.

94. To my knowledge, these regulations were first formulated and published for employees of the new Kaduna Native Administration in 1956 by the Government of the Northern Region.

95. Reply of Resident, Kano, 13/10/1950 to SNP's circular 207/1950, File NAC/53, Provincial Office, Kano, para. 11.

96. C.R. Niven, *How Nigeria is Governed* (London: Longmans, Green & Co., 3rd Edition, 1958), pp. 58–60.

97. K.W.J. Post, *The Nigerian Federal Election of 1959: Politics and Administration in a Developing Political System* (London: Oxford University Press for the Nigerian Institute of Social and Economic Research, 1963), pp. 27–28, 31–33, 40–43.

98. M.G. Smith, *Government in Zazzau, 1800–1950*, pp. 248–9, 277–278. For some immediate results of these demands, see C.R. Niven, *How Nigeria is Governed*, pp. 77–78.

99. K.W.J. Post, *The Nigerian Federal Election of 1959*, pp. 32–33.

100. Ibid., pp. 71–76. For quotation see para. 6, footnote 1, p. 76.

101. This speech was published fully in the Hausa newspaper, *Gaskiya to fi Kwabo*, no. 415, of August 23, 1950. It is also recorded in full in the reports of that meeting of the Northern Region House of Representatives, in Hausa and English versions. The text quoted here is taken from the official English translation circulated by the Regional Government to Provincial Administrations in file NAC/53 at the Provincial Office, Kano. See also Sir Ahmadu Bello, Sardauna of Sokoto, *My Life* (London: Cambridge University Press), pp. 73 ff.

102. File NAC/53, Provincial Office, Kano. His emphasis.

103. Ibid.

104. Ibid.

105. Circular 199/1950 of 29/9/1950 from Secretary, Northern Provinces to Provincial Residents, in File NAC/53 at Provincial Office, Kano, para. 3.

106. Ibid., paras. 7–13.

107. Ibid., para. 10.

108. Reply of Resident, Kano, to circular 207/1950 of 9/10/1950 from Secretary of Northern Provinces, File NAC/53, Provincial Office, Kano, Sections A-C, paras. 1–14.

109. Ibid., paras. 15–17.

110. Letter no. 2325/30A of 10/11/1950 from Resident, Kano to SNP in reply to circular 199/1950 of 29/9/1950. File NAC/53, Provincial Office, Kano, paras. 1–9.

111. C.R. Niven, *How Nigeria is Governed*, p. 60 ff. See also Sir Ahmadu Bello, the Sardauna of Sokoto, *My Life* (London: Cambridge University Press, 1962), pp. 62–72.

112. C.R. Niven, *How Nigeria is Governed*, pp. 60–63.

113. Sir Ahmadu Bello, Sardauna of Sokoto, *My Life* (London: Cambridge University Press, 1962), p. 85.

114. M.G. Smith, "Kagoro Political Development," *Human Organization*, Vol. 19, No. 3, 1960, p. 137–149. See also K.W.J. Post, *The Nigerian Federal Election of 1959*, pp. 77–80.

115. Department of Statistics, Nigeria, *Population Census of the Northern Region of Nigeria 1952* (Kaduna: The Government Printer, n.d.). Data cited here are drawn from Tables 1–9, pp. 12–37.

116. A.T. Wetherhead, "Kano Province 1953," in Northern Region of Nigeria, *Provincial Annual Reports 1953* (Kaduna: The Government Printer, 1955), p. 79, para. 1.

117. Ibid., p. 79, para. 2.

118. Ibid., p. 79, paras. 3–5.

119. Ibid., p. 80, para. 11.

120. Ibid., pp. 80–81, paras. 11–14. Quotation from para. 13, p. 81.

121. See D.A. Pott, *Progress Report on Local Government in the Northern Region of Nigeria* (Kaduna: The Government Printer, 1953). A.T. Wetherhead, "Kano Province, 1953," p. 81, para. 16.

122. A.T. Wetherhead, "Kano Province, 1953," p. 81, para. 17.

123. Ibid., p. 81, para. 18.

124. Ibid., p. 80, para. 7; Anon., *Sarkin Kano, Abdullahi Bayero, C.M.G., C.B.E.*, pp. 29–30.

125. A.T. Wetherhead, "Kano Province, 1953," p. 80, paras. 8–10.

126. Ibid., pp. 88–89, paras. 84–86.

9

Analysis

Introduction

Some Historical Reservations

In preceding chapters, I have described the political institutions and development of Kano as far as my data allow. Like all ethnographies and histories, this account is clearly provisional and subject to reservations that increase with the temporal remoteness and complexity of events. For example, as regards the advent of Islam, which the Kano Chronicle sets in Yaji's reign, 1349–1385 A.D., on the basis of a recently discovered Arabic text written at Kano in 1061 A.H. (1650–1651 A.D.), certain scholars hold that "the balance of evidence according to our present knowledge about the spread of the Wangarawa (Mandinka Muslim missionaries to Kano) seems to favour the 15th century A.D. rather than the 14th,"[1] and that in fact Islam reached Kano simultaneously from the West and the East in the reign of Muhammad Rumfa (1463–1499 A.D.). Unfortunately while this document claims that the Shaikh Abdal-Rahman (Zagaiti) b. Muhammad reached Kano with his companions in Rumfa's reign and not that of Yaji, it confirms that Islam was already established at Kano,[2] and thus suggests the opposite conclusion to that quoted above. In short, the document leaves open the possibility that Yaji was converted by Wangarawa Muslims who came under an unidentified leader.[3] It therefore seems wise to suspend judgment on this issue in the hope of decisive evidence.

The puzzling sequence of events which the Chronicle reports for the reigns of Abdullahi (1499–1509) and Muhammadu Kisoke (1509–1565) include Abdullahi's campaigns against Katsina and Zaria, the preparations of Dagaci, who may have been Bornu's delegate resident at Kano, to revolt, Abdullahi's dismissal of Dagaci after placating the Mai of Bornu at Gunduwawa, and the summary statement that Abdullahi's successor, Kisoke, "ruled over all Hausaland, east and west, south and north."[4] This last fits so neatly with the recollections of Leo Africanus[5] that it seems likely that at this time Kano passed briefly from the suzerainty of Bornu to the Songhay empire, probably in 1513–1514 A.D. when the Askia Muhammad al-Hajj led his army against Katsina,[6] before that fell under the dominion of Kotal Kanta, the ruler of Kebbi, who revolted against the Askia in 1516[7] and subsequently brought Kano and other Hausa vassals of Songhay under his control. As noted above,[8] it seems likely that Kanta's death soon after the sack of Nguru, in which Kisoke participated, gave Kano complete independence from Bornu and Kebbi alike; but this conclusion is inferential.

So too is the thesis that Bornu re-established its suzerainty over Kano in the reign of Kumbari (1731–1743 A.D.) when Mai Muhammad ibn Hajj Hamdun (1731–1747 A.D.) besieged Kano for seven months, according to a Bornu manuscript, or for three nights according to the Kano Chronicle.[9] Certainly, if the information Hornemann obtained at Mourzouk is correct, Kano, Katsina, Daura, Gobir and Zamfara were tributary to Bornu in 1800;[10] and so too was Zazzau or Zaria, whose Hausa historians date their subjugation to 1734 "when the Beriberi of Bornu made war on all the Hausa states."[11] These are surely not the only problematic features of our historical record of Kano under its Hausa chiefs. Indeed, even the dynastic genealogy remains obscure, and the Fulani period also presents various uncertainties, chronological and substantive. For example, it remains uncertain when the first Fulani emir of Kano, Suleimanu, was appointed, and when and for how long the Fulani governed Kano collegially. The precise nature and organisation of the revolt against the second emir Dabo are also obscure; and we need more information on the Ciroma Dan Mama's relations with the Fulani, on Dan Tunku's position from 1804 to 1826 when Kazaure achieved independence, on Kano's relations with the small northerly emirate of Daura, and with the eastern Fulani emirates of Misau, Hadeija, Katagum, Jamaare, Gombe and Bauchi, before, during and after the civil war of 1893–94. There are good reasons to believe that after defeating Tukur and rejecting Sokoto's offer of reconciliation, Aliyu Babba actively promoted the Tijaniyya *turuq* at Kano as a religious alternative to the Kadiriyya caliphate, and even that Aliyu was himself converted to Tijaniyya teachings, though he may not have joined the order. However, for neither of these possibilities do I have specific data. These and other ambiguities, omissions and errors certainly characterise the preceding account as an imperfect historical and ethnogrpahic record of Kano. However, similar qualifications inevitably attach to any historical or ethnographic record. Such inevitable imperfections cannot in themselves deprive analysis of those documents of value and interest, though naturally they affect any features of the analysis that depend on erroneous or misinterpreted data.

In the following discussion I shall therefore assume that the preceding account of Kano under its successive regimes is substantially correct and adequate for our analytic purposes, despite its obvious incompleteness. Where the analysis assumes particular events, data, or interpretations of data that are open to question, I hope to show that in its essentials the analysis would be little affected, should those questionable data be replaced, corrected, or supplemented by others. Meanwhile, as remarked above, this account may perhaps stimulate others to supplement or correct its data, and so promote a superior knowledge of Kano's history.

The Analytic Aim

The ultimate object of this study is to try to advance our understanding of the processes and conditions of political change. This objective may be pursued by two routes, or by some combination of them. Either we may attempt to improve our understanding by reasoning abstractly from some general statements about the nature of political change; or we may proceed by analysing the historical experience of change in empirical polities, provided that the historical information provides adequate detail on the conditions, contexts and processes in which the unit and its components underwent change.

There are many persuasive reasons for pursuing the enquiry along the latter route, provided only that we can secure historical accounts that are adequate and relevant; but only two considerations in favour of this approach need be cited here. First, the study of empirical sequences of change requires both deductive and inductive methods of study, while the alternative approach relies primarily on deduction in constructing the framework of discourse as a general theory or set of models for the subject matter, and in adducing particular propositions or theorems about the conditions of change. Such logico-deductive theoretical structures are clearly of great value in the study of change, and other topics. However, their utility can only be assessed by applying them to the analysis of adequately documented sequences of empirical change; and any analysis of such empirical sequences requires some logico-deductive constructs or models as a guide. There is thus an obvious advantage in pursuing the development and refinement of our logico-deductive constructs by detailed analyses of empirical sequences of change.

This is especially necessary for a second reason, namely, that by no conceivable processes of pure reasoning can we deduce and catalogue all the innumerably varied and challenging combinations of factors and circumstances that history presents as ordinary contexts and conditions of change. But clearly any deductive scheme, however elegant and appealing, which could not accommodate these varied and often perplexing empirical conjunctures would be of limited use in the study of political change as that actually proceeds in human societies. It is not difficult to devise a theoretical structure that appears to illuminate a selected series of situations and sequences in which change proceeds. The problems that historical reality presents in this field are vastly more complex and significant; and we have no other way of apprehending their character except through history.

However, the conclusion that there are advantages to be gained by studying change as it has proceeded in historical contexts imposes its own criteria of adequacy on historical accounts selected for such analysis. Above all those accounts must provide systematic, clear and reliable information on all units, conditions and factors which are central to the sequence and to the analytic scheme that will be brought to bear on them. They should also document adequately the contexts, events and processes by which the changes they relate developed, and identify their institutional features and correlates. Unfortunately, few accounts prepared by historians with other interests are likely to fulfil these specific requirements sufficiently to sustain a close analysis. Accordingly, scholars who intend to study the forms and conditions of change as this occurs in historical contexts may often find that they have themselves to assemble the historical information they require to allow their analyses to proceed. Primarily for these reasons, but partly because of the intrinsic interest of the Hausa-Fulani emirates and their histories, and partly also because such studies provide excellent opportunities for testing and refining these techniques for studying history by combining oral and other kinds of information, I have tried to assemble the various data presented above, these being clearly required for analytic study of political change at Kano.

Concepts and Theory

The Orientation to Enquiry

What can we say about the structure and conditions of political change over the past 600 years at Kano, using traditional approaches and concepts that are not purely or mainly descriptive? Our account relates, for Hausa days, repeated struggles between chiefs, their officials and their kinsmen for executive supremacy at Kano. Such struggles proceeded apace whether Kano was independent or under the suzerainty of Bornu. Under Sharifa (1703–1731) and Babba Zaki (1768–1776) these conflicts seem to have issued in a dominant chiefship that administered the state through a highly centralised official hierarchy that communicated with the chief through two or more distinct sets of channels which checked and neutralized one another. This was the model of the regime that Dabo revived with Sokoto's assent after Sulemanu's ineffectual reign and in the teeth of opposition from the oligarchy established by the *jihad*. Yet by his death in 1846, Dabo had established the basis for that rapprochement between the chiefship and the oligarchy which persisted in outline without change until caliph Abdurrahman and his vizier Buhari overrode the warnings of senior officials at Kano and appointed Tukur in 1893, thus precipitating the civil war, the *basasa*, and the brief but vigorous period of autocratic chiefship under Aliyu Babba (1893–1903).

Abbas, appointed first by the Kano nobles after their defeat at Kotorkoshi, and later more stringently by Lugard, inherited the structure that Aliyu had built. British actions revealed their intentions, firstly to weaken the immunity of officials against complaint by commoners; secondly, to rationalise and simplify the Fulani administration, thus increasing its efficiency and capacity; thirdly, and belatedly, as it might seem to some, to reduce the emir's domination over the Fulani government by eliminating his throne slaves and re-establishing committees and councils of free men as critical organs of government. The introduction of elected councils in 1951 was the most radical expression under British rule of these intentions; but it was not entirely unprecedented. Nonetheless the centralized chiefship that Abbas had inherited from Aliyu, and Aliyu from his ancestors, Abdullahi and Dabo, persisted under Abdullahi Bayero despite British efforts to reduce it, and passed to Sanusi on his father's death.

This briefly summarises the evolution of one aspect of the Kano polity since Yaji, initially under three dynasties of Hausa rulers, and then, after successive conquests, under the Muslim Fulani and Christian British. There are of course many details and changes of fortune even in the chiefship that have been ignored in this summary statement. Such details are surely relevant; but, within the traditional terminology and approach of social science to the analysis of political change, can they add much to the summary, or can we say anything more useful or illuminating about these developments than the summary says? Can we in fact pass beyond the ideal type concepts of Max Weber[12] and penetrate the specific contexts, stages and conditions of Kano's political evolution in order to enhance our understanding of the processes of political change it illustrates? At present I rather doubt that; and even though Weber clearly urged his successors to develop and supersede his analysis, that is in any case inappropriate in detail for Kano, since the officialdom, which so frequently opposed, restrained and even removed the chief, cannot correctly be regarded as the chief's staff since many, and especially the leading officials, had independent rights to the offices they held on grounds of descent and status. Surely if it is true that, with our present terminology and approach, we can say little more about the sequence of political changes at Kano than Max Weber could without the knowledge of that history, it is time to make a new start and try again.

It is always useful, before embarking on the study of any subject, to pause and ask three questions: What do we really want to know about the subject? What should we want to know in the interests of science, humanity, or some other abstraction? And finally, what, given all the circumstances of the subject, of our methods of enquiry and limitations, can we reasonably seek to know, and how may we best try to learn this?

Clearly, all three questions involve conceptions of knowledge that may either amuse or provoke epistemologists. However, as laymen we may, I suggest, treat as knowledge any statements about events or their properties that are confirmed but not disconfirmed by the experience of others. By experience I mean not merely those selective combinations of observation, experiment, reasoning and inference that enable us to support Darwin's theory of evolution through natural selection, or historical traditions of Napoleon's existence and activities; but also the theories of number, of probability and communication, whose foundations are variably removed from our everyday observations.[13] In brief, on this argument the critical tests of objective "knowledge" are twofold—independent, objective verifiability, and lack of dis-confirmation. On this basis, we may consider the three general questions raised above.

First, what do we really want to know about the subject of political change, and what should we seek to learn? Answers will clearly vary with individual interests and orientations. From Kautilya, Confucius and Plato through Machiavelli and Marx to the present, thinkers have tended to seek three types of answers to this question. They have sought to unlock the logic that underlies the courses of political change, either in order that they could show their fellows how to anticipate it, or how to manipulate and direct it for their own ends, or because, like Rousseau, with this knowledge they hoped to devise constitutions for human societies that would increase their collective capacities to pursue some ideal goals and regulate change. Contemporary orientations in the "policy sciences" illustrate all three points of view; yet despite sustained efforts and interest, to date our achievements in this field have been limited and trivial, primarily perhaps because we have persisted in asking the wrong questions, or some right questions in inadequate ways because, as put, our questions yield answers that are empirically untestable.

Though generally implicit in the writings of influential authors, it seems clear that by political change they mean some significant shift or shifts in the nature and/or the distribution of political relations and power. Many writers seek to identify the factors or conditions that underlie these changing distributions in order either to predict or promote future developments, or to devise appropriate safeguards and policies to forestall them. In either case, those factors or conditions that are assumed to underlie observable changes tend to be reified as generative forces or causes, while the changes they are said to underlie become their effects. The consequence, as I have pointed out elsewhere,[14] is to confuse the enquiry, which by the mere variety and nature of the phenomena with which it deals must initially be abstract and general, by conceptualizing it as a field where a number of discrete and relatively constant forces articulate to produce, in differing combinations, a wide range of diverse and specific effects.

For various reasons such causal assumptions and objectives condemn these enquiries in advance either to futility or to illusion. First, in social studies, while we can readily adduce correlations, we can very rarely demonstrate specific causal relations between successive events of any collective significance and complexity. In historical studies, the difficulties are far greater than in comparative studies of contemporary peoples and situations, not simply because historical sequences can neither be replicated nor manipulated to permit their controlled comparison; but primarily because each is a relatively unique series of events that unfolds in a specific socio-cultural context, distinguished from its proximate antecedents and successors, as well as from similar developments elsewhere, by situationally changing and specific combinations of ecological and other constraints, resources, opportunities and priorities. Inevitably, such complex and labile collocations of precise particulars articulated through specific and shifting relations oblige exponents of causal analysis to formulate conceptions of causes and causal relations which are sufficiently abstract and general to facilitate comparative study of similar situations or sequences. However, in order that these general notions may apply to concrete case data, it is necessary to discount all situationally specific particularities by one means or another, including the principles of *ceteris paribus* and "imaginary experiment." It is equally necessary, having thus reduced the sequence to an abstract series that fits the causal hypothesis, to regard that correspondence as simultaneously an "explanation" of the sequence and a "demonstration" of the causal relations and factors invoked. Unfortunately, by such procedures we can remodel the most recalcitrant and intricate data to fit neatly any causal moulds, flow-charts or sets of boxes that we prefer; but we can do so only by conceding that others are free to do likewise, or to employ other principles of exclusion and inclusion, so that the same series of data may equally well illustrate contrary causal models. Yet even when scholars agree on the criteria and procedures of exclusion and inclusion, and on causal concepts and relations, these latter must normally remain sufficiently imprecise and vague to account plausibly for the phenomena they are held to explain. This is so because in social science—and even more so in history—we are rarely able to isolate, measure and demonstrate the precise way in which any single condition or factor has contributed to the occurrence of a given event in all its recalcitrant and multidimensional actuality. That being the case, despite so many generations of intellectual effort to specify the causation of social and cultural events, we shall have to pursue our enquiry by some other route.[15]

Given the present unsatisfactory state of the subject, despite prolonged and persistent enquiries, the appropriate answer to our second question, namely, what should we seek to learn about political change, must surely be the same as that to the final question, namely, what can we reasonably seek to know, and how may we best try to learn this? For indeed to students of any subject, including political change, there is no acceptable alternative to learning all that their circumstances permit, however disappointing the results of such study may appear, when compared with the high expectations that novices and laymen may hold.

Political Structure and Change

It is necessary then, as our very first step, to formulate precise and operational conceptions of change, and specifically of political change. As this has already been the subject of extended discussion I shall here only summarise my definitions of these phenomena.[16] By change we mean two closely linked conditions: (1) any alterations in the structure of a given unit that involve some modifications of its characteristic properties and relations; and (2) the processes or events by which these alterations occur. By "political change" we accordingly mean first, any alterations in the structural components or relations that constitute a political unit which modify their characteristic properties; and secondly, any processes or events by which such developments occur. If, as is usual, a polity is the unit, we must first identify its boundaries in space and time, then distinguish its structural components with their characteristic properties and relations, and finally look for evidence of alterations in these particular phenomena and in the inclusive unit.[17]

It will be obvious that by change I mean both changes of structural components and relations within discrete social units, such as polities, and changes in the relations of these units and external features of their environment, together with the processes by which these developments occur. Such conceptions accordingly exclude simple circulation of individuals through roles, together with any reductions or expansions of an aggregate that are not accompanied by structural modifications in its components or in its internal or external articulations. Thus change, in this sense, is always structural and develops processually.

By structure, I mean the set of units and their articulations that constitute a larger aggregate having distinct form, properties and boundaries. Such an aggregate not only possesses a structure, the arrangement of its parts, but is a structure, that is, a relatively discrete and organised unit. This is equally true of all those components that enter into the structure as durable elements with determinate forms, boundaries and properties. Thus, large structures include smaller ones that compose them; and these in turn may be composed of still smaller structures, down to the minimal level of the institutionalised status and role. All social structures then, whatever their scale and complexity, consist simply of institutionalised and non-institutional units and their interrelations. As the units differ in their bases, forms and place in the structure that includes them, they will differ also in their properties, operational processes, requirements and implications, and in their appropriate relationships with other units in their immediate environments.

Political change accordingly consists in changes of political structure, that is changes in the bases, properties, forms and relations of those units that together constitute the political structure. Most political units are readily segregated from other kinds of social unit by their simultaneous possession of the following four formal attributes, namely, the presumption of perpetuity, unique identities, closure by fixed rules of recruitment, and determinate memberships at any point in time. Units that have these characteristics are corporations, and while all are either the means and agencies or the objects of public regulation, they always provide its structures. Besides such units, public affairs may also be regulated by other agencies which we may call quasi-corporations, since they have some but not all the formal attributes that distinguish a corporation. They are thus in various ways imperfect, most notably in their lack of permanence.

A political structure is a structure that regulates public affairs, a structure of collective regulation. What may be included in this category of public affairs will vary with the nature and circumstances of the public; but all publics are corporate groups, and all corporate groups constitute publics for their memberships, since at the very least, these units can and do regulate their own collective affairs.

Collective Regulation

Such collective regulation is both the substance, the purpose, and the object of political processes, since politics or government consists simply in the regulation of public affairs. This collective regulation proceeds within and through corporations because, as the most durable, clearly bounded and often the largest social units, they are both the most appropriate for such regulation, and always include those units with the best endowments of resources, organisation and manpower to ensure its effectiveness.

Collective regulation proceeds variously, according to its context, means and immediate objectives, but it always employs authority or power, and normally combines them. Authority is the institutional right to take certain decisions and actions in specific situations subject to conditions laid down by relevant rules and precedents, while power is the capacity to take effective action, despite material and social obstacles. Collective regulation always requires and employs these two principles, since without sufficient power to enforce it, authority remains ineffective and loses credit, while without authority, power constrains but lacks the moral legitimacy to justify its distribution and use. Accordingly collective regulation, which is continuous, however intermittent in certain societies, requires and combines both authority and power, although in mixtures that vary with circumstances, means and objectives.

Although by general usage such collective regulation is described as political, there is much to be gained by distinguishing it as government, and by restricting the term political, for analytical purposes, to those actions, relations, processes and structures that either involve the exercise of power or mediate and influence its distribution. In like fashion, those actions or decisions that involve the exercise of public authority may be distinguished for purposes of analysis as administrative. Government or collective regulation accordingly combines two analytically distinct structures and sets of processes, the administrative and the political, which can be identified and separated by reference to the complementary but contrasting principles that constitute them, namely, authority and power. Regulation, since it involves both of these principles in variable mixtures, is inevitably more complex than either in its character and conditions.[18] Government is thus most simply the process and structure of political administration.

In human societies authority and power are always distributed unequally, almost as if by definition. However, these two unequal distributions differ sharply in their bases, nature and stability. Authority, as we have seen, is endowed by culture and social tradition to those who occupy certain institutional statuses. It is also conditional and limited by requirements of conformity to the rules and traditions that govern its form and exercise. Power differs in all these respects. It is acquired, used, held and lost by individuals or groups acting within their circumstances, and is neither conferred nor defined and restricted by institutional rules, since it is often sought and used specifically to violate or override these norms and can never, by definition, be transferred as an institutional endowment, since that would simply convert it into authority.

Associated with these and other contrasts in the natures of authority and power, there is a fundamental difference in their distributions. While the distribution of power, being uninstitutionalised, is always inherently uncertain and unstable, labile and changing in its efficacious bases as well as its modes, authority distributions appear to its holders and to the collectivities they regulate as firm, persistent, and only subject to revocation or other changes under certain unlikely conditions. These differences, which reflect the institutional basis and nature of authority, and the contingent character of power in the absence of such foundations, persuade societies to identify their structures, boundaries and continuity with an established and prevailing distribution of authority. Max Weber first grasped the salience of this relation between continuity of authority distributions and the structures of total societies in his penetrating typology of authority structures in human societies and the conditions and course of their change.[19]

However, authority distributions as structures cannot constitute governments solely of themselves, and Weber's discussion suffers from his attempt to fuse the disparate principles of authority and power in the undifferentiated concept of *Herrschaft*, which has been translated as "domination," "imperative control" and "authority," but which corresponds closely to "regulation" as defined above. Societies do indeed identify their boundaries and futures with the maintenance of their structures of authority; and those structures are essentially patterned distributions of differential authority across the range of institutional statuses. But such authority structures are neither of themselves sufficient to regulate societies, nor are they ordinarily likely to generate those changes of a normative or operational kind which are a normal feature of social experience. Necessarily, alongside and complementary to these authority structures there are power distributions which, however uncertain, labile and contingent, being non-institutional, can only be understood by reference to the institutional order which defines the bases and modes of authority, together with the opportunities for assembling power and the modes and objectives of its exercise. For power, though always non-institutional, always develops within the institutional framework that distributes authority. And without this complementary alternative distribution, which proceeds within and across particular authority structures as well as beyond them, those presumptively perpetual distributions of responsibility, immunity and the right to command would be insulated against all effective pressures for change that could conceivably arise *within* their societies. Yet, however secure and immutable authority structures may seem to their incumbents and subjects, they do change, and their changes modify the social organisation that surrounds them; but without pressures from the complementary distributions of power, such changes could occur only through the agency of external forces.

Nonetheless, given their resilience, institutional entrenchment, and the quicksilver lability of power, authority structures are unquestionably as a rule the most stable features of human societies. In consequence, we distinguish as revolutions their abrupt transformations from other equally abrupt reallocations of authority which do not overtly transform the structure, such as coups, successful rebellions, or mere changes of administration. Beneath such distinctions lies a very general assumption that is also substantially true, namely, that as long as the prevailing authority pattern persists without change, the social order will continue much as before.

Constitutions and Concrete Structures

For this reason among others, the constitutional arrangements of human societies are commonly and correctly equated with their structures of collective authority. Specifically political relations and processes, which assert and employ quanta of power of differing modalities within, between, across and around these discrete hierarchies, either uphold a given authority structure and seek to preserve it against change, or move within, beyond or against it with differing explicitness, intensities, means and purposes. Invariably also, over sufficiently long spans of time, these pressures, intended and unintended, conservative and otherwise, promote successive modifications in the actual procedures, composition and articulation of the authority structure that furnished the society with its constitutional model; but normally such changes are neither fully perceived nor admitted by those concerned. This is so since societies identify their structures and continuity with their constitutions, and accordingly hesitate to admit the uncertainties inherent in such fundamental changes. However, such failures of collective recognition can rarely insulate a constitution against pressures for further change. There is always some tension and discrepancy between an antecedent authority structure as idealised and petrified in a constitutional model and the empirical structure of government, of which the authority structure is merely one feature, however important. It is therefore necessary for us to distinguish sharply between the concrete reality to which these constitutional models refer, and the more complex and dynamic distributions of authority and power by which governments regulate their publics and simultaneously develop and evolve, adapting to the changing exigencies of their internal and external situations. I shall therefore first distinguish the constitutional model from the concrete structure to which it refers; and then distinguish this concrete structure from the more complex and labile reality of which it is the foundation, framework and primary focus; and as this latter is manifested through events and processes that express relations of authority and power, I shall refer to it as the analytic structure, since these principles and relations can only be distinguished analytically.

By a concrete structure, I mean a set of institutional units and positions, each with its specific membership, distinguished *inter alia* by the authority with which it is endowed, and articulated together as a unit by appropriate patterned relations. The units of such a structure are either non-corporate or corporations or quasi-corporations, having responsibilities and capacities for collective regulation. Though quite diverse, the forms that such units may take are finite, and include, besides corporate groups, offices and colleges, or permanent councils, which are always located within corporate groups as their official regulative agencies, and those quasi-corporations or commissions which are either created independently by outstanding individuals, or exercise powers delegated to them by units authorised to do so. Such units always possess the four requisites of positive corporate action, namely, a comprehensive or representative organisation that articulates their memberships, an exclusive body of common affairs, and the necessary autonomy and appropriate procedures to regulate those affairs. Corporations of another variety lack these four essential requisites of united positive action, and are thereby constituted as closed perpetual categories or unorganised aggregates, even when their memberships are divided between a number of organised groupings, corporate or non-corporate. Lacking the organisational preconditions of common positive action, such corporate categories can neither adequately represent nor regulate themselves or any other units, and are therefore subject to regulation either by external bodies or by rules regarded as binding and more or less sacred on traditional grounds.[20]

Authority structures abstract the regulatory capacities and relations of the corporate units that distinguish societies as differing forms of corporate organisation. Constitutional norms and models, although based on such concrete structures, distort and misrepresent their nature by further abstracting and elaborating their authority structures, while either assimilating thereto all the power exercised by such units as organs of authority, or disregarding or treating as illegitimate the power dispersed or exercised by others in the collectivity. However, as governmental structures, such concrete units must always integrate and exercise power as well as authority. Those principles, being clearly distinct and complementary essentials of collective regulation, can neither be disregarded nor assimilated to one another in reality, despite the constitutional models which are formulated to represent and idealise the concrete structure as it existed—or was believed to exist—at a certain moment of its evolution.

However accurately such constitutional models may describe concrete structures at particular moments or phases of their development, divergences inevitably develop with time as the concrete structure continues to evolve in response to external pressures and to those generated within it. For not only must a given concrete structure or any of its components maintain a highly specific set of satisfactory arrangements with all other units in its environment to persist unchanged; such perfect stasis also assumes equivalent changelessness of the units and articulations that gave the structure its precise form; and such internal stasis is only possible if all its components have maintained between and within themselves mutually satisfactory relations that routinely fulfil their respective operational requisites and entailments. This possibility diminishes the greater the number and variety of corporate units in the structure, since each of these will have its own specific set of requisites and entailments.[21]

Moreover, as units of collective regulation, corporations deploy authority against their members and against outsiders, who are normally members of another corporation of similar or differing kind. Such exercises of corporate authority inevitably provoke reactions among those they directly or indirectly affect. So too does the allocation of positions and resources of authority within and between corporations. In consequence the establishment and exercise of corporate authority can rarely proceed without assuming or generating political responses within and between corporations which frequently anticipate the administrative action that mobilizes them. Such essentially political reactions within corporate groups may assert, evaluate or deny the validity, rationality and efficacy of administrative action taken by or on behalf of these units; and, whenever such actions appear to affect the interests and status of other corporations, directly as units, or indirectly through their members, these external bodies also respond in ways that they regard as appropriate for the maintenance or promotion of their interests and status.

Two critical features of all corporations and quasi-corporations that are capable of positive regulatory action ensure that any corporate actions that appear to affect their interests will elicit political responses, that is, reactions that express relations of power. These are the need of each corporation for collective assurance of its individual autonomy, or right to administer its exclusive affairs according to its own procedures and interests, free of outside interference; and its need for collective reassurance regarding its scope, that is, those sets of common affairs which are exclusive and specific to the corporation, however similar in compass and content each unit's set may be to those of other corporations of identical form and base. Since corporate units are committed to pursue their own perpetuity, and since that requires the unimpaired preservation of their scope and the autonomy required for their effective management, each of these units is understandably wary of any developments within or moves by others that appear to reduce or trespass on either of those essential conditions. In like fashion, each corporation is keenly concerned to maintain the delicate balance in the distribution of material, moral, ideological, fiscal and human resources to which its capacity to maintain its appropriate autonomy and scope is tied. In consequence, corporations are structurally jealous of their own and one another's autonomy, resources, activities and interests, so that any novel action by one of them typically evokes political responses mediated by power from the rest. Corporate authority always operates, therefore, within two variably related fields of pressures and power, that is, of political relations, one of which is internal and the other external to the corporation. As a product of these overlapping sets of political responses, the common authority structure which articulates these units is subject to continuous instability and change from the many diverse corporate pressures and demands that it generates and must accommodate and contain to preserve its unity, form, scope and regulative capacity. It is this changing distribution of power and political relations, with which the changing forms and scope of administration is linked, that I denote as the analytic structure of the polity.

Corporations and Analytic Structure

This analytic structure consists of two distinct but complementary and interdependent structures whose composition and relations are continuously subject to change. These components can only be identified and segregated by means of analytic concepts, since empirically they overlap and are often interwoven, like elements in a chemical compound, which fuse together in differing proportions to produce substances with quite new properties, while themselves remaining distinct, although submerged. Although analytic, they are no less real and significant than the complex of corporate units in which they are rooted and which together they serve to transform. One component of the analytic structure consists in specifically political relations and actions, distinguished from other kinds of relations and actions by the power they manifest and by their use of or relation to the distribution of power to regulate collective affairs. The second set of relations and activities are specifically administrative and are identified by the authority they exercise to regulate public affairs. Both sets of relations and activities are found in the set of corporations and quasi-corporations that constitute, with their articulations, the concrete structure of the polity. But each set is abstracted from this matrix by means of the analytic criteria set out above, so that neither corresponds fully with the complex articulations that hold within and between the various corporations that constitute the concrete structure as an empirical and ordered ensemble of discrete membership units, each having its own distinct autonomy, scope, resources, articulations and other properties.

As pointed out above, each of the corporations that enter into this concrete structure, by virtue of its *form* (that is, as a corporation of particular type, such as a college, a category or a corporate group) and by virtue of its *base* (that is, the principles on which it recruits its members and excludes others), has a minimally necessary scope, or set of affairs, and autonomy to regulate these affairs, without which the unit can neither operate nor persist in its normal way. As all such units (including the society itself, which is simply the most inclusive corporation), whether constituted as organised groups or as categories that lack organisation, are located in milieux that contain other bodies of similar and/or differing type, each is impelled to realise the conditions which are necessary for its adequate operation and continuity, and has certain requisites that must be met and maintained by appropriate relations among its members and with these external units. In like fashion, by the simple facts of its existence and operation as a unit of specific form and base, each of those corporations has certain inescapable implications for others in its milieu. These logical requisites and implications of the various types of corporations within a society must be appropriately integrated with one another, in order that the whole may operate smoothly as an inclusive unit with that particular form, range and composition. Thus the articulations of those corporations and quasi-corporations which form the concrete structure relate to the forms and bases of these units as their logical requisites and implications. Given appropriate adjustments, these articulations should accordingly preserve the inclusive structure and each of its components against change, by fulfilling adequately the requisites and implications of each corporation. However, the empirical situation diverges from this pattern variably, due not only to unavoidable differences in the resources and rates of growth of corporations, but, for reasons given above, far more directly, to the mutual anxieties they have about one another, which arise from their individual concerns to maintain the autonomy, scope and resources that each requires to operate and persist effectively and without significant change. Thence derives the widespread emphasis on relations of power, such as opposition, alliance, direct and indirect reciprocities, dependence, coalitions and the like, as well as authority relations, by which these units pursue the interests inherent in their corporate constitutions, and simultaneously generate an analytic structure of political and administrative relations that commonly differs in some particulars from the network of appropriate articulations that aligns them in the concrete structure.

Moreover, those shifts that remove the analytic structure of unstable but actual distribution of power and authority between and within corporations, from the pattern prescribed by and embedded in the concrete structure, modify the latter progressively by materially aggrandizing certain corporations, often at the expense of others, which accordingly suffer some diminution of the autonomy they need to manage essential affairs, and, being thus weakened, are liable to lose more, until they can no longer sustain themselves. In such situations corporations generally redouble their political efforts to secure their futures against further erosion, and do so by various means; by strengthening old alliances and creating new ones, by various innovations that seem appropriate, by replacing leaders or procedures that have apparently failed to assure success, by challenging the legitimacy of authority that impairs their interests, by manufacturing accounts of events that discredit their opponents and favour themselves, by modifying the principles on which their members are recruited and allocated to different positions, and by other means. Often such stimuli provoke counter-actions by those who think, however mistakenly, that they are the targets of these developments, with the result that a self-propelling set of processes is established, which operates to modify still further the concrete structure of the polity, first by maximising those features in which the actual distributions of authority and power deviate from the antecedent pattern, and then, providing that this distribution achieves relative stability and appears irreversible, by institutionalising those modifications in the character and properties of the corporate units and their reciprocal articulations that are necessary to correspond with the prevailing distribution of power and authority.

The Categories of Latent Structure

We can now give some partial answers to the questions with which we began, namely, what can we reasonably seek to learn about political change, and how should we go about it? For if political change consists in successive modifications of the concrete structures of collective regulation which follow those changes in the distributions and nature of power and authority that arise from internal processes of the operation of the concrete structure and from its changing relations with the environment, we should first seek to specify as precisely as we may how the properties and relations of the corporate units that make up its concrete structure are affected by specific developments within or beyond the polity. We should also try to specify exactly how these same events and processes have modified the immediately antecedent distributions of authority and power, that is, the analytic structure which mediates between the concrete structure and the events or developments that affect it. We may then ask precisely how such shifts in the distributions of authority and power relate to simultaneous changes in the relations and properties of the concrete units which are produced by these events; and in these detailed summary statements of changes in the analytic and concrete structures associated with specific events and processes, we should look for any regularities of sequence and sets of relations or variables linked with internal or external developments of the same or differing kinds. Particularly we should seek any invariant relations within the sequences of change in those variables and relations at both the concrete and analytical levels of the structure. For though we cannot expect to find causal relations within the sequences of change, those are not the only possible relations of invariance; and we should seek within these series for all examples of invariance ordered by relations of logical necessity, the *principium rationis* of Aristotle.[22]

But for relations of logical necessity to be possible, we must first define carefully the variables or conditions under study, and then arrange these propositions in an order of logical priority. This inverts those relations between antecedent and consequent that establish the *principium rationis*, and asserts that one concept or proposition, Q, presupposes a specific antecedent, P, to be conceived. One implication of ordering our conceptions of conditions and variables in their relations of logical priority is that thereafter the contents of any category in the series can only be changed by successive modifications of the contents of all those antecedent categories its conception presupposes. This implication has two aspects: first, it lays down an order of invariant relations among the concepts or categories that together constitute the structure as a fixed form, and implies that those categories may only change their content or substance in that order. Secondly, it excludes the possibility that such changes in the specific contents of form can proceed simultaneously, thereby implicitly distinguishing structural changes which proceed *seriatim* in an intransitive order, from changes of substance or properties which may proceed simultaneously and transitively.

In earlier studies of change in the governments of two Hausa states, Daura and Zaria, I have found it useful to formulate a set of concepts, ordered by such relations of logical priority, that together describe all essential features of those governments throughout the phases of their development recorded for analysis. The conceptions or categories are analytic devices of my construction, and were fashioned expressly in relations of logical priority so that I could apply them as a set to the historical data to see whether the recorded changes of content in these formal elements proceeded in the expected order.[23] In that respect both enquiries yielded positive results, and the general thesis, that specifically structural changes, i.e., changes in the forms or relations of units, proceed always in a fixed and irreversible order, while specifically substantive changes in the properties of these units normally proceed in simultaneous and transitive relations, will be tested again below against our data from Kano.[24]

There are several reasons why that should be done. Firstly, it enables us once again to test the two major conclusions of the study of political developments at Zaria, namely, that empirical changes in the contents of these logically ordered formal categories always proceed in the sequence of their relations of logical priority and succession, and secondly, that such changes are always mediated by redistributions of power, that is, by changes in the analytic structure. Secondly, and of greater significance, we need to examine the evidence of changes in the contents of these logically ordered categories in detail, since together as a series they embrace all requisite elements of the Hausa constitutions, including those that held sway at Kano from 1350 until 1953. Accordingly these categories together define the latent structure that underlies the changing constitutions and concrete structures on which they are modelled. Successive concrete structures as articulated sets of regulatory units with discrete memberships and corporate qualities thus differ in the ways in which they express the abstract general categories of the latent structure; but as long as the forms and features of those concrete structures are all covered by the abstract categories of the latent structure, then changes of those concrete forms figure as changes in the contents of those categories, and can only develop in the order of logical priority that aligns them.

There is however one category which must be added to the list employed in analyzing political changes at Zazzau to distinguish corporations from other kinds of social unit.[25] With that addition the latent structure that underlies the changing governmental regimes at Kano consists of the following categories, which are listed below in their order of logical priority and given the alphabetical symbols by which they are denoted in the analysis that follows.

(a) Status differentiation.
(b) Corporations differentiated as unique, perpetual status-units.
(c) Offices distinguished from other corporations.
(d) Offices differentiated by status criteria of eligibility.
(e) One office differentiated as supreme and most senior.
(f) Rank organisation of offices.
(g) Role differentiation of offices.
(h) Alignments of offices having similar status qualifications in
     exclusive promotional series.

Comparison of this list with those set out in the studies of Zazzau and Daura[26] shows that besides inserting the category of corporations in the list above, I have replaced the original concept of kingship, (d) in the earlier lists, by one that is looser and more general, and which includes presidential and dictatorial positions as well as monarchies. This extension illustrates the hope, based on these analyses, that with little further elaboration the concepts aligned as related above are sufficient to describe and analyse the constitutional changes in centralised polities that have supreme presidial offices of any kind, including regimes that distinguish executive and ceremonial supremacy and allocate them to differing offices, such as the Japanese shogunates, modern Britain, and the Federal Republic of West Germany. Clearly, if this set of concepts can help us to analyse changes in such diverse and complex regimes as well as Kano, its utility and significance will be greatly increased; but once these objectives and possibilities are noted, we need not discuss them further here.

One last feature of the list of latent categories merits attention, namely, its preoccupation with the conditions and organisation of office. This reflects the fact that these categories were formulated especially for the analysis of Hausa governments, which are organised as structures of office and which operate through them. For these reasons, while the present list of categories fits the forms of Hausa government nicely, it is clearly quite inappropriate to describe polities that lack offices as regulative organs, or for the analysis of official structures that lack a supreme central office. For acephalous regimes, it is therefore necessary to formulate another set of categories, designed for those regimes, first by translating each of their formal features into general abstract categories, and then by reformulating those to establish an order of logical priority among them.

Clearly then, this set of categories has been formulated analytically to include all elements required to establish governments of the Hausa type. However, being constructed to assist the analysis of changes in these governments, no category in the list specifies the precise properties and articulations of any concrete unit or feature of the regime. The list merely asserts the necessity and sufficiency of these abstract and formal categories to constitute the regime and to encompass all the changes to which it is subject as modifications in the properties and articulations of those components that give concrete expressions to the abstract forms of these latent categories. Accordingly any event or process that assumes the serial revision of the specific contents of two or more of these latent categories should entail modifications in the articulations and properties of some or all units of the concrete structure. The converse may not always apply. It is quite conceivable that certain developments may modify the properties and relations of concrete units so slightly that they presuppose no changes in the contents of these latent categories. In the following analysis we shall try to test this possibility.

The analytic relations of these latent and concrete structures to events that express or precipitate change differ sharply in two respects: first, being deliberately abstract, the categories of latent structure only undergo change in their contents, that is, in the particular concrete structures that express them. Thus changes in the contents of these latent categories always proceed formally in the order fixed by the relations of logical priority among the categories themselves. By contrast, when concrete structures undergo change, this normally involves those external and/or internal articulations which together establish their forms, and some of their properties or substance. Thus changes in concrete structures are generally more complex that changes in the latent structure, and involve variables of two different kinds, namely, substance and form.

Events and Processes

The analytic relations of latent and concrete structures to events that express change differ also in status and temporal reference. Briefly, while our analytic statements of changes in concrete structures always attempt to describe the implications of these events as modifications of the properties of units of concrete structure, similar statements about the latent structure seek to specify prior changes in the contents of those categories which are essential formal preconditions of the events and processes under study. In other words, summary statements of changes in the contents of the formal categories of latent structure specify the necessary formal preconditions of those events whose substantive effects are represented by statements that refer to the concrete structure, from which we may derive other statements that describe the implications of these events for the analytic structure. Thus while summary statements of change in the contents of latent categories specify the formal prerequisites of a given event or process involving change, parallel statements that relate the event to the concrete and analytic structures specify its implications for each of them, in differing detail and precision. We can thus attempt to specify for any political process or event, its formal preconditions as defined by categories of the latent structure, its concrete implications as manifested at the level of concrete structure, and its analytic implications for the distributions of authority and power that together form the analytic structure.

For this among other reasons, it is particularly important in isolating a process or incident for study as a moment of change to identify its temporal conjuncture as precisely as possible in order that the three complementary analyses should refer to identical phases of the process and states of the inclusive structure. There are clearly far fewer difficulties in conceptualising incidents such as the conversion of Yaji to Islam, or his conquest of Santolo, the defeat and flight of Muhammad Alwali II, or the appointments of Suleimanu, Dabo and other emirs as events that occurred at single instants of time, than in doing the same for processes which unfolded as a sequence over longer periods. However, it is possible to treat as single events those sequences which are homogeneous in their character, development and content, that is, in their elements, their requisites and implications, provided that the governmental order can also be treated as homogeneous and constant throughout all phases of the sequence. With these conventions, we can assimilate such processes to the model of an event that occurs at an instant in a particular milieu, and so isolate sharply those aspects or features of the sequence that we wish to examine. We may then formulate statements to summarise the formal preconditions of the process as necessary states of the latent categories, and others that describe its implications for the concrete and analytic structures to which it relates.[27]

Clearly, such procedures can only apply to homogeneous processes of limited duration that unfold in milieux at relatively steady states. Complex sequences of heterogeneous elements and character, or simple sequences of greater duration that proceed within unstable milieux, are not amenable to study by these means. Instead, it is necessary to divide such sequences into a succession of relatively homogeneous segments, each of which may then be conceptualised as a single event for further analysis. This indeed is the procedure we shall employ in analysing the development of government at Kano. But clearly that leaves open the question whether political processes of any kind, duration, complexity or heterogeneity in their requisites, elements and implications, are equally amenable to this analytic procedure. Moreover, our approach says nothing directly about the concepts and procedures appropriate for study of relations between government and other institutional areas of social life such as religion, economy or kinship.

As regards the first point, our analytic procedures can only be safely applied to homogeneous processes which may without violence be summarised as single events that occur in stable milieux. If these processes are heterogeneous in their composition, or if they develop in unstable milieux, that is, in contexts that are changing independently of those developments, we cannot analyse them hypothetically as single events. However, we can in part overcome this limitation by isolating a series of specific significant events that occurred in the context of these developments, and by analysing their conditions and implications separately in series. We may also do this for each of the homogeneous strands in a complex process; and, if the data allow, we should also be able to establish the differing states of the milieu before and after the process ran its course. By such successive segmentations of the process and its field, we should be able to indicate the preconditions and implications of its differing phases and components. To some degree it is hoped that the following analysis of developments at Kano may illustrate the utility of these procedures.

Environmental Relations

Another question mentioned above concerns the capacity of our analytic tools and procedures to study the important, complex and changing relationships of government and other institutional structures such as economy, religion, kinship, stratification and the like. Clearly, insofar as such relations affect or alter the conditions and activities of government, any analysis of political change has to take them squarely into account. However, as our enquiry is expressly restricted to political change, we shall not be concerned with the reciprocal effects of government on these other institutional structures, unless such effects are materially relevant to the governmental order.

In our conceptual scheme, relationships between the political order and other institutional sectors are features or conditions of the concrete structure. Strictly conceptual conditions or assumptions of that concrete structure are listed as categories of the latent structure, while specifically political and administrative aspects of this concrete structure together compose its analytic level. These three structural levels accordingly differ in scope and specificity. For while the latent categories simply state those axiomatic conceptions that underlie the concrete structure, since that structure includes all social units that undertake collective regulation, these latent categories must also specify their conceptual foundations.

As we have seen, the concrete structures of a polity consist of its regulatory membership units and their relations. The essential features and properties of all such units can be listed as follows.[28]

(a) The unit's *internal articulations*, that is, its components and their relations.
(b) The unit's *external articulations* with other units.
(c) The unit's *autonomy* to regulate its affairs and members.
(d) The unit's material, ideological, human and technical *resources*.
(e) Its *range*, that is, the territorial and demographic extent of its regulative validity.
(f) Its *scope*, or the set of affairs that it regulates.
(g) Its *capacity*, that is, its ability to regulate its affairs more efficiently, or, without further resources, to regulate other affairs as well.

It is evident that two of these categories, resources and range, will register any relations of a unit with other institutions and any changes in those relations, be they religious, economic, technological, ecological or demographic. Relations of kinship are also included in these categories as ideological and human resources. Accordingly all changes of input to a unit from extra-political institutions will appear in categories (d) and (e) of this list; and if such changes modify the values of other variables in the list, these shifts should also be apparent. Accordingly our analysis does include changes in the relations or implications of demographic and ecological conditions as well as other institutional sectors for government, but it treats these changes as given data, and makes no attempt to elucidate them, unless they arise from the governmental process itself.

This, stated abstractly, completes our outline of what we presently hope to learn about political change, and how we shall try to do so. To recapitulate briefly, political order or government is conceived as a structure with three levels, namely, a set of latent categories that underlie the concrete structure of regulatory units and their relations, that is, of corporations; and an analytic level which consists of the specifically political and administrative aspects of the concrete structure, identified by the changing distributions of collective authority and power that its operation generates. These changing distributions of power and authority express and promote realignments and modifications within the concrete structure which themselves presuppose appropriate revisions of the relevant conceptual categories of the latent structure before they can occur. Subsequent modifications in the concrete structure may or may not stabilise new distributions of power and authority by providing them with firm bases in the new alignments and properties of the concrete units; but these modifications may equally well generate pressures or counter-pressures for further change in various directions; and in any event the concrete structure like its components presupposes a specific set of relations with its environment in order that it may operate routinely without disturbance. Any important change in these external articulations is likely therefore to precipitate internal changes of the concrete structure as necessary adjustments.

Method

Notations and Referents

We shall therefore proceed to examine significant historical events at Kano in chronological order to determine the changes associated with each at each of these three levels of structure. We may then examine these three sets of structural changes to determine their relations; we can also re-examine each of these series to detect any regularities of sequence in the changes recorded, and to identify for further study any patterns in these sequences of structural change associated with events of similar or different kinds.

To indicate latent categories whose substantive revisions are implicit preconditions of specific events, we shall employ the set of alphabetical notations presented above,[29] and to describe the changes of concrete structures that flow from these events, we shall employ the notation given above.[30] For each event selected for study, we shall formulate descriptive statements of latent preconditions and concrete implications as formulae with the aid of these symbols; and in this exercise we shall follow the methods of deriving and presenting these formulae set out in the first volume of this series with one or two modest improvements described below.[31]

As we have seen, by virtue of the relations of logical priority and succession that order the categories of latent structure in our series, their contents can only undergo change successively in that sequence. Thus we may summarise a set of changes in all eight categories of the series by the formula a b c d e f g h, denoting succession by intervals, and the order of change by the sequence of symbols. Accordingly any formula that inverted this alphabetical order would disconfirm the basic generalisation derived by analysis, that "changes of form develop successively and in a constant order."[32]

By contrast with these purely formal developments that express revisions in the contents of the latent categories, changes in those properties that together define the substance of the units of concrete structure have been found often to change simultaneously and in a wide variety of combinations. To distinguish between successive and simultaneous changes of these variables, following conventions adopted in the study of Daura, I shall represent the former, as above, by intervals between symbols set out in the order in which the changes occurred, while indicating simultaneous changes of specified variables by writing such symbols as d/e or e/d or c/d/f/e. Moreover, as it now seems possible and useful to indicate the general directions of these changes as increases or decreases of value in the variables concerned, wherever the data allow I have added qualifiers to the symbols for the variables modified. To represent unqualified increases in the value of any variable, such as autonomy, resources or range, the plus sign is thus attached to the relevant symbol, as c+ d+ e+ etc. If there has been an unqualified decrease in value of a variable, this is represented by a minus sign, as c− d− e−, which indicates first that these three variables altered, secondly, they did so successively and in that order, and thirdly, that the value of each was reduced. Finally, if the value of a variable modified by an event is simultaneously increased in some particulars and reduced in others, both positive and negative signs are required, the first indicating my judgment of the direction of greater change, on the data available. For example, if in my judgment a given event *simultaneously* modifies the autonomy and scope of a concrete unit by increasing these properties in one or more directions and reducing them in some others, and consequently reduces the unit's capacity, these modifications are represented as follows: [c+−/ f+− g−]. Moreover to simplify statements that two or more variables have altered simultaneously or successively in a single unqualified direction, formulae indicating increases are written as [p+ (x/y z)] where x and y have altered simultaneously but before z and after p, and where the values of x, y and z have all increased without corresponding losses, however unequally. Finally, where the data are inadequate, or where uncertainty arises concerning changes in the value of a particular variable or variables, I have inserted ? before the relevant symbol, to indicate probability but lack of knowledge, as in the following examples: [a b ?c/d ?e ?f], which might also be written as [a b ?(c/d e f)], no qualifiers being attached to these symbols to indicate increases or decreases of the variables concerned.[33]

As in the preceding analysis of political changes at Daura, I have selected three concrete structures as constant reference points for formulaic statements of changes associated with particular processes or events. These are the supreme office, namely, the chieftaincy under the Hausa, and the emirship after 1808–09; the government, identified as the set of all titled offices involved in regulating the polity; and the state, which is the total social unit identified with the government and chiefship, and subject directly to their regulation. As a series, these units are progressively more extensive, and together include all governmental structures and processes. Thus government includes the chiefship and all other offices, while the state includes the populace and territory as well as government. In consequence, relations between the state and government are internal for the state but external for the government. Likewise relations between the chiefship and the government are internal for the government, since the chiefship is one of its organs, but external for the chiefship. The internal articulations of chiefship strictly consist solely in the organisation of its components and staff in the same way that the internal articulations of government consist of all governmental units, including the chiefship, their staffs and relations with one another.

The internal articulations of Kano state consist of relations between the government, the people of Kano, and others resident in the country. The state has external articulations with populations outside its range, and so do the government and chiefship, but these latter structures also have external relations with the people and territory they govern; finally, as we have seen in reporting changes of concrete structure, relations between the chiefship and government are represented as internal to either structure. However, to allow us to discriminate between changes in the relations of the chiefship with the rest of the government on the one hand, and those with the state and foreign bodies on the other, I employ the symbol a to denote relations of the chiefship to the government as well as to its staff, and reserve the symbol b for relations of the chiefship to the state, including its territory and population, and also to foreign units. This anomaly is necessary if we are to distinguish changes in the relations of the chiefship to the government from changes in its relations to the state and to foreign bodies; and these distinctions are necessary since, as we shall see, the chiefship is peculiarly sensitive to changes in those articulations.

Together these sets of internal and external articulations define the form of the structures to which they refer, while their scope, range, resources, autonomy and capacity together define their substance by specifying all their properties. Accordingly statements of changes that affect these concrete structures refer equally to their formal and substantive features, while formulae that summarise changes in the categories of latent structure are formal statements of changes in the contents of the structures that express these categories. To derive statements that summarise changes in the structures of authority and power associated with changes at the concrete levels of chieftaincy, government and the state, we must first state these changes of concrete structure as precisely as we can, and then examine them to determine whether changes associated with a given event are all homogeneous and either positive or negative, or whether they are heterogeneous mixtures of these modes for one or other of the reference units. We then have to consider carefully how such changes in the concrete structures have altered the immediately antecedent distributions of power and authority among the chiefship, the government excluding the chiefship, and the state distinguished as the polity from both the government and the chiefship. Having done so, we may then rank those units in the order in which, in our judgment, they appear to have gained authority and power relative to one another from the development under study.

If all three seem to have suffered material reductions in these respects, and if these losses were unequally distributed, we may still rank them in the order of least loss, assigning numerals and plus and minus signs to denote the relative order of these increases or reductions. Instances for which no firm judgments are possible should be left blank and unranked. Clearly, these rankings of relative gains or losses of authority and power between the chiefship, the government and the state, are subjective and open to error, even more so than those subjective judgments of changes in the articulations and properties of the concrete structures on which they are based. Accordingly, to reduce the scope and significance of such errors as far as possible, though we can never hope to exclude them entirely, several independent assessments of changes of all types associated with each event were made at irregular intervals, in order to identify specific differences in these several statements, to isolate the factors that underlay these differences, and, by repeated analysis, to reduce the scope for error inherent in these subjective judgments as far as possible.[34]

To prepare the following formulae that describe modifications in these latent and concrete structures, six independent assessments were made over a period of more than two years, before they were collated for comparison and analysis. Likewise, to prepare formulae summarising changes of analytic structure associated with these events, having arrived at the final formulae recording changes of concrete structure, I made three independent assessments over a period of two months which were then collated and analysed with the results shown in the Table that follows.

The Analysis of Events

Before we confront the results of our analysis, it should be helpful to elucidate the meanings of two sets of formulae that describe any two events or processes in the series, in order that readers may be able to interpret the others exactly. Certain other features of Table 9.1 also require explanation.

The Table lists four sets of formulae for each event. A single formula summarises those changes in the contents of the categories of latent structure made explicit by the event. The three following formulae describe changes associated with the event in the concrete structures of chiefship, government and the state. To facilitate analysis, separate columns list the different formulae required to describe these changes in chiefship, the government and the state for each of these events. Next, changes in the analytic structure promoted by these events are indicated by numbers with qualifying plus and minus signs to indicate relative gains and losses by the chiefship (C), government excluding the chiefship (G) and the state, excluding both the government and the chiefship (S).

Formally, the numerical range of these rankings runs from +3 to −3. In practice, on our rankings few events exceed a total range of 4, and zero values are only assigned to units that were imperceptibly affected by events. The sign +3 against a given concrete structure indicates that, in my judgment, that unit had the greatest gains of authority and power from a given incidents +2 indicates that that structure has had a substantial increase of power and authority from the event, while

TABLE 9.1 43 Moments of Change at Kano, 1349–1953

1	2	3	4
		Changes of Latent Categories	Changes of Concrete Structure
No.	Event		Chiefship
(a) The Hausa Period, 1349–1806			
1	Yaji converts to Islam (1349–85)	abcdefg	ba+(c/d/e/fg)
2	Yaji conquers Santolo (1349–85)	abcde	ba+(c/d/e/fg)
3	Kanajeji apostasizes (1390–1410)	abcde	abc+/d+−/f+− ?e+−g+
4	Dagaci arrives from Bornu (1421–38)	abcde	bac−/f+?e?d?g
5	Abdullahi Burja submits to Bornu (1438–52)	abcde	bc−/d−/f+−?g
6	Galadima Dawuda's slave campaign (1438–52)	abcdefg	ab+(c/d/e/fg)
7	Galadima Dawuda and Atuma (1452)	abcdefg	a−(cdg)
8	Rumfa's innovations (1463–1499)	abcdefg	a+(c/d/fg)
9	Kisoke's independence from Bornu (1509–65)	abcdefg	ba+(c/d/fg)
10	Instability at the throne: Yusufu and Dawuda (1565)	abcdefg	a−(c/d/fg)
11	Shashere elevates the eunuchs (1573–82)	abcdefgh	a+(c/d/fg)
12	Kutumbi's innovations (1623–48)	abcdefgh	ab+(c/d/e/fg)
13	Instability at the throne, 1648–53; Alhaji (1648); Shekarau (1649–51); Kukuna (1651–52); Soyaki (1652); Kukuna (1653)	abcdefg	a−(c/d/fg)
14	Muhammadu Sharifa's oppressive innovations (1703–31)	ab	b+(c/d/fg)
15	Babba Zaki's administrative reorganisation (1768–76)	abcdefg	a+(c/d/fg)
16	Alwali destroys Dirki (1781–1804)	−	ac+/d−?g
17	The *jihadis* revolt, 1804–05	abcde	ab−(c/d/e/fg)
18	Alwali's defeat and flight (1806?)	abcdefgh	ba−(c/d/e/fg)
(b) The Fulani Period, 1806–1903			
19	The interregnum and Fulani collegial government, (1806–?1808)	ab	None
20	The appointment of Suleimanu, 1808–09	abcde	ba+(c/d/e/fg)

TABLE 9.1   *(continued)*

5	6	7	8	9	10	11	12
Changes of Concrete Structure		*No. of Formulae*	*Ranked Changes of Power and Authority*				*Nature and Source of Event*
Government	*State*		*C*	*G*	*S*	*All*	*Event*
ba+(c/d/e/fg)	ba+(c/d/e/fg)	1	+3	+1	+2	+	I–E
ba+(c/d/e/fg)	ba+(c/d/e/fg)	1	+3	+1	+2	+	I vs E
abc+/d+−/f+− ?e+−?g+−	abc+/d+−/f+− ?e+?g	3	+3	+1	+2	+	I vs E
bac−/f+?e?d+?g−	baf+?c−?e−?d−?g	3	−3	−2	−1	−	E
bc−/d−/f+−?g	bc−/d−/f+−?g	1	−3	−2	−1	−	E
ab+(c/d/e/fg)	ab+(d/e/fg)	2	+2	+3	+1	+	I vs E
a+(cfg)	ad+−f+g+	3	−1	+3	+−2	+−	I
a+(c/d/fg)	a+(c/d/fg)	1	+2	+3	+1	+	I?E
ba+(c/d/fg)	ba+(c/d/fg)	1	+3	+1	+2	+	∅
a+(c/d/f)?g	af+d+−?g	3	−1	+3	+−2	+−	I
ad+?g+	ad+?g+	2	+3	−1	?	+−	I
ab+(c/d/e/fg)	ab+(c/d/e/fg)	1	+3	+1	+2	+	I>E
a+(c/d/f)?g−	af+d−g	3	−1	+3	+−2	+−	I
							E = external
							I = internal
b+(c/d/fg)	a+(f/d?g)	2	+3	+1	−2	+−	I
a+(fdg)	a+(fdg)	2	+3	−1	+2	+−	I
ad−?g−	ad−?g	3	−	−	−	−	I
ab−(c/d/e/fg)	ab−(c/d/e/fg)	1	−3	−2	−1	−	I/E
ba−(c/d/e/fg)	ba−(c/d/e/fg)	1	−3	−2	−1	−	E
a+(c/d/e/fg)	a+(c/d/e/fg)	1	None	+3	+1	+	E/I
ba−(c/d/f)?g	ba+(c/d/f)?g	3	+3	+1	+2	+	E

(continued on the next page)

TABLE 9.1   *(continued from the previous page)*

1	2	3	4
		Changes of Latent Categories	*Changes of Concrete Structure*
No.	*Event*		*Chiefship*
21	The appointment of Dabo, 1819	abcde	ba+(c/f)?g
22	Dabo revives Hausa political forms (1819–?1824)	abcdefgh	ba+(c/d/e/fg)
23	The revolt against Dabo (?1820–26)	abcde	ab–(c/d/e/fg)
24	Kazaure's independence recognized, 1825–26	abcdefgh	ba–(c/d/e/fg)
25	The accession of Usuman, 1846	abcde	ba+(dg)
26	Abdullahi seizes the throne, 1855	abcde	ba+(c/f)?g
27	The appointment of Tukur, 1893	abcde	ba–(d/eg)
28	Yusufawa withdrawal and revolt, 1893	abcde	ab–(c/d/e/fg)
29	Aliyu drives out Tukur, 1894*	abcde	ba+(c/d/e/fg)
30	The *basasa*, 1894–95	ab	abc+/f+/d+–/e–g+
31	Aliyu rejects the rule of Sokoto, 1895	abcdefg	bac+/f+d+–g+
32	Aliyu renders homage at Sokoto, 1903	abcdefg	bc–f+/d+g+
33	Aliyu deserts the Kanawa, 1903	abcde	ab–(c/d/e/fg)
34	Defeat at Kotorkoshi, 1903	ab	None
35	The Kanawa appoint Abbas, 1903	abcdefg	ab+(c/d/e/fg)
	* Treated from Yusufawa perspective – Aliyu, not Tukur, as reference point		

(c) Kano under the British, 1903–53

36	Lugard appoints Abbas, 1903	abcdefg	ba–(c/f)d+–/e+–g+
37	Cargill and Abbas make *gunduma*, 1909	abcdefgh	bac–+/f+d+g+
38	Usuman dismisses Shamaki and Dan Rimi, c. 1924	abcdefgh	ba–(c/d/fg)
39	The selection of Bayero to succeed, 1926	abcdefg	ba–(c/d/f?g)
40	Bayero manumits the palace slaves, 1926	abcdefgh	ba–(c/d/fg)
41	The first Nigerian elections, 1951	abcdefg	bac–+/d–+f+?g
42	Riots against Ibos at Kano, 1953	ab	b–(c/d)f+?g
43	The selection and appointment of Sanussi, 1953	–	bag+

TABLE 9.1   *(continued)*

5	6	7	8	9	10	11	12
Changes of Concrete Structure		No. of Formulae	Ranked Changes of Power and Authority				Nature and Source of Event
Government	State		C	G	S	All	
ba–(c/f)?g	ba–(c/f)d+?g	3	+3	+1	+2	+	E
ba+(c/d/e/fg)	ba+(c/d/e/fg)	1	+3	+1	+2	+	I+E
ab–(c/d/e/fg)	ab–(c/d/e/fg)	2	–3	–1	–2	–	I
ba–(c/d/e/fg)	ba–(c/d/e/fg)	1	–3	–1	–2	–	E
bac–/f–d+?g+	ba+(dg)	2	+3	–1	+2	+–	E
ba+(c/f)?g	ba+(c/f)?g	1	+3	+1	+2	+	I vs E
ba–(c/fe/dg)	ba–(fe/dg)	3	–2	–3	–1	–	E
ab–(c/d/e/fg)	ab–(c/d/e/fg)	1	–3	–2	–1	–	I/E
ba+(c/d/e/fg)	ba+(c/d–/e–/fg)	2	+3	+2	+1	+	E/I
abc+/f+e–d+g+	ac+/f+d–/e–?g	3	+3	+2	–1	+–	I
bac+/f+d+–g+	bac+/f+d+–?g	2	+3	+1	+2	+	Ɇ
bc–f+/d+g+	bc–d+/f+g+	1	+3	+2	+1	+	I–E
ab–dc+/f+g	abd–g–	3	–3	–2	–1	–	I
b–(c/d/eg)	b–(c/dg)	2	None	–3	–2	–	E
ab+(c/d/fg)	a+(c/d/fg)	3	+3	+2	+1	+	I
							E = external, I = internal
ba–(c/f)d+–/e+–g+	ba–(c/fdg)	2	+–1	+–2	+–3	+–	E
bac–+/f–+d–+?g	ba+(fdg)	3	+3	–1	+2	+–	E
ba–(c/d)f+?g	ba–(c/df)?g	3	–1	+1	?	+–	E
ba+(c/fdg)	ba+(c/fg)	3	+2	+3	+1	+	E
ba–(c/d/f)?g	ba–(c/d/f)?g	2	+2	+3	+1	+	E
bac–+/d–+f+?g	ba+(c/d/fg)	2	–1	+1	+3	+–	E
b–(c/d)f+?g–	ab–(c/d)f+?g–	3	–1	–2	–3	–	I
ba+(c/f/dg)	ba+(c/fg)	3	+2	+3	+1	+	E

+1 denotes a lesser gain of authority and power by the relevant unit than those received by the other two units. In the rare cases where one of these three structures does not exist at the time of a given event, it is omitted from the rankings assigned for that event. If an incident clearly reduced the authority and power of one or more of these three structures, that which lost most is given the largest number preceded by a minus sign, while that which lost least will have the smallest number preceded by a minus sign. If it seems uncertain whether the authority and power of a given structure was altered by a particular event, this uncertainty is indicated by a question sign before the numerals. If a given event simultaneously increased the authority and power of any or all of these three concrete structures in some respects and spheres, while reducing them in others, these dual effects are indicated by combining the plus and minus signs and placing that one first which corresponds with the direction of greater change. Thus +–3 indicates that the unit given this value gained most from the event to which it relates, but that while gaining in certain respects from that event, the unit concerned also lost certain authority and power it originally had, though less than it gained. In several cases an event reduced the relative power and authority of one unit while enhancing those of another, as indicated by the signs that qualify these numbers.

For most events that changed the analytic attributes of these concrete structures in the same direction, the order and estimated values of gain or loss are represented by numbers running from 3 to 1; but sometimes it has seemed appropriate to indicate particularly uneven shifts in these distributions by an irregular order of numerical rankings, such as +3, +1, –1. These and all other numerical assignments are not presented as absolute measures of changes in these aspects of the concrete units for the simple reason that I have found no criteria and techniques to assess and measure such shifts in any objective quantitative scale. Instead, these numerical values and rankings merely state *my* assessments of the directions of change in the power and authority of the three concrete structures associated with each of these events, of the relative gains or losses sustained by these units, and of their magnitudes relative to one another. In short, the values +3, +3, +1 should not be regarded as equal for any two events, despite my efforts to standardise them. At most these numbers may represent correctly the relative order and magnitude of the shifts to which they refer.

A fourth column indicates whether the value shifts associated with a given event are positive or negative for all three structures, or whether they are a mixture of these modes.

The final column distinguishes these events by their source and orientation as follows:

I   = events whose source and orientation are both internal.
E   = events whose sources are wholly or primarily external.
I – E   = events whose source is internal, but which are oriented peacefully and positively to external bodies or influences.
I vs E   = events whose source is internal but which are oriented aggressively and negatively to external bodies.
I + E   = events of internal source that require external assent and support.

I ? E = events that may reflect external models or influences, though this is uncertain.

/   = events that free the state of Kano from external domination or suzerainty.

I/E   = events in which an internal component becomes an independent external body.

E/I   = Events in which an external body becomes the supreme internal one.

I>E   = events by which external bodies are incorporated as subordinate internal components.

The Reign of Yaji—An Illustration

For illustration, let us first examine the changes associated at Kano with Yaji's adoption of Islam, sometime between 1349 and 1385. We take the following data as given:

(1) that Yaji, then chief of Kano, as reported by the Chronicle, received Islam from Mandinka Muslim missionaries who came from Malle;

(2) that prior to this Mandinka mission, two distinct cults flourished at Kano, one practised by the Gaudawa ruling stratum, the other by the natives they had conquered;

(3) that like his predecessors, Yaji ruled through a set of titled offices that were held mainly if not exclusively by men of Gaudawa stock, the natives of Kano forming the subject population;

(4) that relations between the Kano natives and their Gaudawa rulers were hostile, the natives refusing to marry the Gaudawa, resenting the invaders' attacks on the shrine of their god Cibiri, and perhaps allying themselves with the community at Santolo which had successfully resisted all Gaudawa assaults.

On these assumptions, we can list in their order of priority the changes in the contents of latent categories that were expressed by Yaji's conversion as follows:

(1) The preceding structure of status differentiation was revised to include the new statuses of Muslims and immigrant Mandinka.

(2) The preceding corporate structure was revised to include the Muslim Mandinka as a new corporate group, and the House of Islam, to which these Mandinka belonged, as a wider corporation which local people could enter on accepting Islam.

(3) The preceding structure of offices was revised to include the Muslim offices of Imam, Na'ibi and Kadan (ritual butcher), together with that held by Abdurrahman Zaite or his predecessor as head of the group.

(4) The eligibility criteria for offices at Kano were thus modified to reserve Islamic offices for Muslims.

(5) The supremacy of Yaji's chieftainship was altered by the arrival of the Muslims, to whom the chiefship was a heathen office, incompatible with Islam. To the immigrants, Yaji's conversion to Islam re-established the

chiefship as the supreme office at Kano by identifying it with Islam and thus incorporating the Mandinka as subjects.

(6) Yaji's conversion also altered the preceding rank organisation of Kano offices by establishing a new order of offices reserved for Muslims.

(7) This new order of Muslim offices likewise modified the preceding role differentiation of offices, since the roles of these Muslim offices were defined by Islam.

(8) These developments did not alter the preceding promotional alignments of offices with similar status qualifications, since at this time the future distribution of the new Muslim offices remained obscure.

Accordingly, those revisions in the latent categories associated with Yaji's conversion can be summarised in the formula $a\ b\ c\ d\ e\ f\ g$. It should be noted, firstly, that these changes are all purely formal, though all express revisions in the preceding contents of these categories; and secondly, that they develop serially in the order of logical priority that aligns the latent categories.

Proceeding next to examine the implications of this event for the three concrete structures of chiefship, government and the state, it will be recalled that while the state includes the government which includes the chiefship, in order to distinguish the chiefship's relations to the rest of the government from its relations with the state, including the subject population, or with foreign bodies, we shall treat the former as internal to the chiefship as well as the government, while classifying the relations of both these units with the state and with foreign bodies as external.

Yaji's conversion to Islam first altered his relation with the Mandinka immigrants who were a foreign group, with the House of Islam, and with the hitherto heathen state of which he was head. These changes in turn altered Yaji's relations with the Gaudawa and the rest of his government. Conversion enhanced the autonomy of his office by suspending many traditional restraints as invalid. It increased the resources of the chiefship by attaching to it the Mandinka immigrants. It extended the demographic range of the chiefship by incorporating these and any other resident Muslims; it increased the scope of the office by adding Islamic rules and interests to those affairs it had formerly regulated; and, as a consequence of these changes, it enhanced the capacity of the chiefship to regulate its traditional concerns more efficiently as well as additional affairs, without the addition of any new resources. Moreover, while initial changes in the external and internal articulations of the chiefship proceeded serially, increases in its autonomy, resources, range and scope proceeded together, simultaneously, and increased its capacity.

We may therefore summarise the implications of this event for the chiefship by the following formula: b a +(c/d/e/f g), where the + sign denotes that all the bracketed variables increased their values, while symbols separated by sloping lines (/) represent variables that changed simultaneously, and those spaced apart indicate successive changes, in the order as set out.

Parallel examination of the implication of Yaji's conversion for the government and the state, both of which include the chiefship, will show that they both experienced successive changes in their external and internal articulations, and simultaneous increases in autonomy, resources, range and scope. The capacities of both government and state to regulate new interests were enhanced. Accordingly, one formula, b a +(c/d/e/f g), describes the implications of this event for the government and the state as well as the chiefship, even though its significance was not identical for each of these units.

Analytically, Yaji's conversion to Islam substantially modified the prevailing distributions of authority and power between the chiefship, the rest of the government, and the state by changing their bases abruptly. As a Muslim chief, Yaji attached to himself the group of Mandinka immigrants from the more advanced state of Malle, some of whom were literate and learned, while most were probably better informed and more sophisticated and mobile than the Gaudawa. On becoming a Muslim, Yaji had to a large but uncertain degree freed himself from many traditional restraints that were formerly binding. Most of these suspended restraints probably restricted the autonomy of the chiefship in relation to the government, since the Gaudawa, organised as a corporate group under their chief, then ruled Kano, while the subjugated natives were administered as a category.

By adopting Islam, Yaji had therefore very sharply increased both his authority and his power over the government, which now contained two counterposed groups of officials, the immigrant Muslims who apparently had Yaji's support, and the heathen Gaudawa, of whom he was head. By that act, Yaji greatly enhanced his control over the government; but simultaneously he enhanced the power and authority of the state, which was thenceforward identified as a Muslim chiefdom on the basis of its ruler's adoption of Islam. The enhanced authority, security and power which the chief's conversion brought the Gaudawa state are evident in Yaji's establishment of the new Muslim offices of *alkali* (judge) and *limam*, in his suppression of pagan opposition to the new mosque, and in his conquest and incorporation of Santolo, with the help of the Mandinka. Altogether, in my judgment, while the chiefship gained most from this event in authority and power, the state gained rather more than the government. These changes may thus be represented in the following way: C (chiefship) = +3; S (state) = +2; G (government) = +1. However, these numerals merely indicate my judgment of the relative gains made by these three structures. Nonetheless, as all three structures gained from the event, though unequally, we may assign a simple positive sign, +, to indicate that Yaji's conversion simultaneously strengthened the chiefship, the state and the government.

Finally, while the motives and considerations that persuaded Yaji to convert may be classified as internal to himself and his polity, the conversion expressed his peaceful and positive orientation to the external units and influences the Mandinka represented. Thus as regards its internal or external derivation, this event may be represented as I – E, to correspond with the glossary of these notations (previously given).

Cargill's Gunduma

For a second example, let us consider the *gunduma* carried out by Abbas at Cargill's direction in 1905–08, since this illustrates a different pattern and presents some intriguing problems. First, although the first reorganisation of the emirate's territorial administration unfolded over at least two years, I shall treat it as a single event on the grounds that its components, its requisites and implications were homogeneous, and the process unfolded at a time when the political and administrative situation of Kano, following on Satiru and the sack of Hadeija, was otherwise stable. The circumstances and conditions of Lugard's confirmation of Abbas as emir have been reported above, together with the context in which the *gunduma* proceeded and its place in Lugard's program for reorganisation of the Native Administrations.[35] We are clearly much better informed about Kano in 1905–08 than in Yaji's day, but unfortunately most details of this *gunduma* disappeared in the fire of 1915 that destroyed the Provincial Office, if indeed they escaped Cargill's destruction of the provincial correspondence on his retirement in 1908.[36] The *gunduma* itself consisted in replacement of the preceding pattern of territorial administration through *hakimai* resident at the capital who supervised their scattered fiefs through staffs of titled and untitled *jekadu*, by an exhaustive subdivision of the emirate into coadunate districts and sub-districts, each administered by a resident *hakimi*. At the same time, traditional forms of taxation were replaced by taxation fixed in volume on the basis of lump sum estimates of the values produced by sample communities in a given year, and the new heads of districts and sub-districts were made responsible for the collection and transfer of these taxes under conditions the British regarded as fair and efficient, with penalties for malperformance. Sufficient details of the introduction and consequences of these measures have been given above[37] for us to proceed with their analysis without further description.

In the chronological series of events analysed in the table that follows, the *gunduma* of 1905–08 follows Lugard's appointment of Abbas as emir. Since nothing had happened at Kano during the interval to modify the relations and conditions laid down in 1903, we shall treat the structures that prevailed from Abbas' accession as the base-line against which to assess developments linked with the *gunduma*.

(a) At the level of the latent categories, *gunduma* modified the antecedent structure of status differentiation sharply by redefining *hakimai* as resident district heads and sub-district heads, and by arranging them in local hierarchies that often violated antecedent orders of precedence.

(b) *Gunduma* likewise replaced fiefs as the traditional corporate units of territorial administration by a new structure of compact sub-districts and districts, each of which was constituted as a corporate group.

(c) *Gunduma* likewise assumed offices as unique presumptively perpetual status-units with regulatory capacities, but presupposed certain redefinitions of the offices of *hakimai* as set out in (a) above.

(d) *Gunduma* likewise assumed that the criteria of eligibility for offices of *hakimai* were revised to stipulate residence in the districts and accountability to the emir and the British administration for tax-collection and local administration.

(e) *Gunduma* assumed a supreme senior office, the emirship, but revised its relationships with the *hakimai* and implicitly redefined criteria of eligibility for the emirship for eligible senior princes to include successful local administration as a *hakimi* and as a central administrator.

(f) *Gunduma* presupposed revision of the antecedent organisation of offices by rank, reduced sharply the numbers of fiefholders (*hakimai*), and replaced that order by two ranks of district heads and sub-district heads.

(g) *Gunduma* involved agreed redefinitions of the roles of the *hakimai*, the emir, the central administrative officials, and many lesser officials with regard to territorial administration, tax assessment, tax collection and transfer, and proper accounting and use of emirate revenues, to meet criteria laid down by the British. At the same time, *gunduma* disestablished many former fiefholding offices of their territorial administrative roles.

(h) *Gunduma* involved new promotional alignments among offices with similar status qualifications in at least three ways. First, by segregating offices of resident *hakimai* from other fiefholding ranks, it modified antecedent promotional series that included both, and substituted two sets of promotional series for the inclusive set that had existed before. Secondly, by aligning some *hakimi* offices as sub-district heads under others as district heads in combinations that sometimes violated traditional precedence orders and promotional ladders, *gunduma* expressed the suspension of those preceding promotional alignments and features of the traditional precedence order. Finally, in substituting a smaller number of district heads and sub-district heads for many fiefholders, it assumed a selection that was in fact a new kind of promotion for some and demotion for others.[38]

Revisions in the concrete expression of the latent categories that *gunduma* presupposed and expressed should therefore be written as

a b c d e f g h

since all categories were affected serially and in the order shown, thus illustrating the relations of priority and succession among them.

As regards changes associated with *gunduma* in the concrete structures of chiefship, the government excluding chiefship, and the state, changes in the chiefship will be considered first. *Gunduma* assumed and expressed the dominant relation of the British administration vis-à-vis the emir Abbas, but it involved a significant change in these relations by authorising Cargill and his officers to redesign and supervise the territorial and tax administrations. It accordingly transformed relations between Abbas and many of his officials. Some lost their former rights of territorial administration and/or tax collection, while those who continued to enjoy both as resident *hakimai* were obliged to do so on quite novel conditions of supervision and accountability to the emir and the British.

Gunduma thus reduced the emir's autonomy in several ways. Especially he was obliged to establish and administer new patterns of taxation and territorial administration designed by the British and in association with them. But *gunduma* also enhanced the emir's autonomy by suspending the antecedent allocation of fiefs, territorial and tax-collecting authority, thereby enabling Abbas first to delimit the new districts and sub-districts at his discretion, and then to redistribute these redefined functions among officials as he thought best, to strengthen his control over the government and country.

Gunduma thus greatly increased the scope of the emir's authority by placing the selection and allocation of *hakimai* to the new districts in his hands, and by increasing his responsibilities for supervision of tax assessment, collection and territorial administration. Moreover, though clearly different, these changes of autonomy and scope proceeded together and simultaneously, as the account of their contents shows.

Consequent on these changes, the emirship also gained increased resources, especially through the new arrangments for tax assessment and supervision; but *gunduma* in no way modified the demographic or territorial range of the emir's office. However it did increase the emir's capacity to supervise and control the government and the country by disestablishing the antecedent patterns of territorial and tax administration and by establishing in their place new conditions for the tenure of territorial office and the supervision and care of state revenues.

Thus the following formula correctly describes those formal and substantive changes in the emirship associated with *gunduma*:

$$b\ a\ c-+/f+d+g+$$

Excluding the emirship, the rest of the government did not fare so well from *gunduma*. Most important offices in the traditional polity previously enjoyed territorial jurisdictions and tax-collecting powers. As we have seen the *hakimi* was the model or prototype of the official in Fulani Kano. The sudden and severe reduction in the number of these territorial offices that accompanied their transformations at *gunduma*, coupled with the loss of privileges, immunities and powers that this transformation involved, together represented substantial losses of autonomy, scope and resources to the officialdom at large.

These changes began with British insistence on the need for a new territorial organisation which they undertook to supervise with, through and for the emir. This radically redefined the antecedent relations of the British administration to the Kano officialdom. It also involved sharp changes in the relations of the officialdom to its head, the emir; but, as shown above, those internal changes presupposed and followed other changes in their external relations with the British.

These changed external and internal articulations subtantially reduced the autonomy of the Fulani officialdom in tax and territorial administration and tenure of office, notably by demanding accountability from *hakimai* under heavy sanctions. At the same time the autonomy of this officialdom was increased by *gunduma* in other ways, notably by placing resident *hakimai* in direct control of rural populations, tax collection, and cognate administration.

In like fashion, *gunduma* reduced the scope of the Kano government—other than the chief—by exposing its officialdom to active and direct British surveillance on the one hand, and by redefining more narrowly the powers of *hakimai* as tax collectors and territorial administrators on the other. Yet, by involving the *hakimai* in these functions, and by establishing new criteria and arrangements for the administration of state revenues, *gunduma* simultaneously increased the scope of the offcialdom.

Gunduma reduced the resources of the central officialdom in some ways, notably by proscribing a variety of customary imposts and modes of domination and extortion, while increasing it in others, notably by ensuring, through central assessment and administration of revenues, their rapid annual increase from 1908 to the present.

Whether these developments in any way modified the capacity of the government to manage its traditional affairs remains uncertain; but *gunduma* in no way altered the range of this government. Its implications for the officialdom, i.e., for the Kano government excluding the emir, are thus as follows:

b a c +f/+d +?g

For the state, *gunduma* first meant abrupt changes in its external relations with the British administration, which thereafter exercised direct supervision of local *hakimai*. This was followed by substantial changes of internal relations between the emir and his officials on one hand and the *hakimai* and subject population on the other. Substantively as a product of these changed articulations, the state increased its scope to include territorial and tax administration according to British standards and procedures. In consequence of this it also increased its resources, notably its revenues from local taxation. It accordingly increased its capacity to discharge these functions more efficiently, and consistently improved their performance; but it also increased its capacity to undertake new administrative tasks without extra resources, and demonstrated that later. These three sets of changes proceeded serially, the later presupposing the former, but neither the autonomy nor the range of the state was affected by *gunduma*. We may thus describe the implication of this event for the state as follows:

b a +(f d g)

Thus, as the formulae indicate, that event affected each of these three concrete structures differently.

It will be noticed that in none of the six formulae which describe changes of concrete structures in these two examples are the symbols that denote internal or external articulations qualified by plus or minus signs as positive or negative. All that these symbols indicate is that the internal or external articulations of these structures were altered in certain particulars by the specified event. To determine whether these changes are plus or minus, we need first to specify their substantive correlates or products on each of these concrete structures, and then to evaluate their implications with reference to the preceding distributions of authority and power. These assessments proceed at the analytic level of structure, and with reference to the *gunduma* they indicate that the emirship increased its authority and power substantially; and that the state also enhanced its strength, while the officialdom suffered material losses of autonomy and power from this development. The authority of the state was enhanced by *gunduma* because it eliminated many abuses the people had formerly borne, thus increasing their support for the regime, and so the power of the state. To indicate these shifts I have assigned the following values: C= +3; S= +2; G= –1. This yields a summary statement of the total shift as = +– which signifies a mixture of gains and losses of authority and power among the three structures. In the case of *gunduma*, the state and the chiefship gained authority and power, while the officialdom lost in both spheres.

It is also abundantly clear that *gunduma* was initiated and imposed on Kano and Abbas by the British Provincial Administration. Accordingly it is external (E) in its origin.

These two examples illustrate the analytic procedures and criteria that underlie the various formulae and evaluations in Table 9.1. Their exposition should also enable interested readers to check the various formulae by working out their own summaries and evaluations of changes associated with the events listed below. It should be clear then that Table 9.1 presents my subjective assessments of changes in the polity associated with 43 events or processes selected from the much larger number that are known to have occurred at Kano between 1349 and 1953. For each event the table presents formulae indicating the change in the content of latent categories presupposed by the event, together with those changes in the articulations and properties of three concrete structures—the chiefship, the government and the state—that are direct implications of the event. Changes promoted by each event in the distributions of authority and power among these three structures are also indicated as described above; and the events are classified by their source and orientation as internal and endogenous or external and exogenous.

The Selection of Events for Study

Of 43 events analysed in Table 9.1, 16 occurred before the start of the Fulani *jihad* at Kano, and another two before the Fulani established their rule. 17 occurred between 1806 and 1903 when the Fulani governed Kano, and 8 between 1903 and 1953 when the British supervised the state. These 43 events are clearly only a very small fraction of the total we could have analysed. They are certainly by no means the only incidents that expressed or generated change in the polity between 1349 and 1953. Indeed two of these events involved no changes in the prevailing contents of the latent categories, and one, the destruction of Dirki by Muhammad Alwali II (1781–1807) also had no effect on the prevailing analytic structure. I have nonetheless included these two events despite their limited significance, partly to illustrate the sensitivity and discriminating power of our analytic tools, but also because together they represent a large category of events whose dynamic import was either illusory or limited.

The remaining 41 events or processes analysed in Table 9.1 together provide a broad chronological outline of the main trajectory of political developments at Kano under the Hausa, Fulani and British. There are of course many other important incidents, especially during the Hausa period, of which we know too little to assess their developmental significance and allow analysis. For example, we do not know clearly the contexts, processes or effects of the successive dynastic changes at Kano before 1804. We cannot even say surely whether or not the Gaudawa, Rumfawa and Kutumbawa dynasties were linked genealogically. Likewise with the data available we cannot assess adequately the implications of the successive Kororofa assaults on the concrete and analytic structures of Kano government. To undertake such assessments, however hesitantly, we need sufficiently detailed information about these structures immediately before and after the event under study, in order that we may determine their requisites and implications. Unfortunately for many intriguing incidents and processes that took place before the *jihad* at Kano, we lack such necessary details. For many others that were wholly or primarily endogenous, our information indicates that firstly, these merely replicate certain events included in Table 9.1, and secondly, that while they certainly entailed and expressed significant changes, these neither persisted nor modified the polity in any permanent way.

There are also several such cyclic developments in the history of Kano before the *jihad*. They tend either to illustrate the central struggle between the chiefs and the senior officials, or the practice of certain chiefs to aggrandize their mothers and favourites as instruments of personal or family rule at the expense of their senior officials. Such developments are equally characteristic and important features of the Hausa polity, but they are adequately illustrated by events analysed below. In selecting these 18 events and processes from the period of Hausa rule at Kano, I have tried to include all the decisive steps by which the government developed the form and substance it possessed in Alwali's day, together with its experience of foreign domination so far as our data allow, and those internal crises that best illustrate the problems and forces that underlay its development. Though grossly incomplete, I believe that these 18 events and processes fairly represent the historical growth and experience of the Kano polity under its Hausa chiefs and include most of the adequately documented events that marked its major changes of fortune and organisation.

For the Fulani and Anglo-Fulani periods, although uneven and often incomplete, our data are much richer and firmer. Again, I believe that the events selected from each of these periods outline economically the main course of political developments at Kano from 1806 to 1903 and from 1903 to 1953, and include most or all of the major events through which these developments proceeded. In sum then, the 43 events selected from these three eras together describe the course of political evolution at Kano under its Hausa, Fulani and British rulers, and include the major incidents that promoted, arrested or threatened that growth, namely, foreign domination, the loss and recovery of independence, coups, revolts and struggles for the throne, the Fulani *jihad*, the civil war of 1893–4, the British conquest and administrative reorganisation, the disestablishment of the throne slaves, introduction of elections, and first wave of ethnic riots that expressed Hausa resentment of their Southern partners and rivals in the emerging federation of Nigeria.

To determine the changes associated with each of these events, it is necessary to formulate precise ideas of the state of the relevant structures, latent, concrete and analytic, immediately before and after the event occurred. This can be done approximately by reference to the formulae that describe the event immediately prior in the list. Such formulae together define the base situation against which changes associated with the next event listed can be identified and analysed. However, to determine the extent to which and the ways in which these structures may have changed during the intervals between successive events, we need only review the relevant section of the historical record and summarise its implications in formulae that detail changes in the forms that express the latent categories more fully. There is no need to construct parallel formulae for the concrete and analytic structures immediately preceding a selected event, since such formulae always denote the specific implications of an event, and these can be derived by relating the event to the formulae that summarise its immediate antecedent. Such formulae describe changes of antecedent states of these structures entailed by the events to which they refer, while the formulae that summarise developments of latent structure specify the formal prerequisites of such events. For our present purposes it is therefore sufficient to set each event against the state of the polity described by the formulae that detail the changes associated with the preceding event. Thus, as the events and processes form a series which includes all the major developments, upheavals and changes of fortune in the history of Kano for which our data are sufficient to sustain the analysis, the series represents the principal moments of change, and the events it lists can therefore be adequately contextualised by comparison with their immediate antecedents.

Analysis

The Variety of the Series

These 43 events trace the major development of government at Kano from Yaji's conversion to the accession of Muhammad Sanusi, a span of 550 to 600 years. Of these 43 events, eleven (nos. 1, 8, 11, 12, 14, 15, 22, 34, 38, 40, 41) consist of innovations that modified and developed the governmental organisation; and perhaps we should add to these nos. 19 and 20, the collegiate interregnum that formally ended with the appointment of Suleimanu as the first Fulani emir. Another 15 events consist in transfers of chieftainship, if Aliyu's seizure of the throne in 1894 after expelling Tukur, and his desertion in 1903 are included. These are nos. 7, 10, 13 and 18 from the Hausa period, nos. 20, 21, 25, 26, 27, 29, 33 and 35 from the Fulani era, and nos. 36, 39 and 43 from the period of British rule. Notably, all four transfers dating from the Hausa period involve the forcible removal of reigning chiefs; and if we exclude Alwali's overthrow by the Fulani *jihadis*, the three preceding incidents together involved the depositions of eight Hausa chiefs, one of whom, Dakauta (1452) was a deaf mute, appointed, according to the Chronicle, in the hope that he would thereby be cured. This instability of the Hausa chiefship from 1452 to 1653 contrasts sharply with its security of tenure under the Fulani and British. From 1808 until 1953, only two Fulani emirs lost the throne before their death, namely Tukur after defeat in the civil war which began soon after his accession, and Aliyu by desertion on the eve of the battle at Kotorkoshi.

Three of the events listed in Table 9.1 refer to important revolts, namely no. 17, to the outbreak of the Kano *jihad*; no. 23 to the severe revolt against Dabo in which Dan Tunku of Kazaure played a major part; and no. 28 to the Yusufawa revolt against Tukur that initiated the civil war. Another incident listed, no. 42 in 1953, refers to the first of a series of spontaneous popular assaults by Hausa on Ibo immigrants from southern Nigeria settled in the Sabon Gari (New Town) outside the city walls.

Two events in this list occurred when Kano was formally chiefless, namely, no. 19, when the Fulani *jihadis* ruled collegially after expelling Alwali and before Suleimanu was appointed; and no. 34, when the Kanawa faced the British at Kotorko-shi after their emir Aliyu had fled.

Two incidents, no 18, Alwali's destruction of the fetish Dirki, and no. 43, the appointment of Sanussi, apparently had limited effects on the governmental structure.

Five events, nos. 5 and 9, 31, 32 and 36, refer to changes of status to and from vassalage and independence. Of these, nos. 5 and 9 refer to the early period of subordination to Bornu, while nos. 31 and 32 report Aliyu's changing relations with Sokoto, and 36 represents the point at which Lugard imposed British rule in confirming Abbas as emir.

Two events, nos. 14 and 30, consist of unprecedented aggression by chiefs, Muhammad Sharifa (1703–31) and Aliyu Babba, against the populace. Two others, nos. 2 and 24, consisted in conquest and defeat, territorial gain and loss.

Of these 43 events, only 12 are entirely internal in their origins and orienta-tion, namely nos. 7, 10, 11, 13, 14, 15, 16, 23, 30, 33, 35 and 42. Fifteen events, including the three revolts mentioned above, express local responses to external forces and influences. Sixteen events were generated externally, namely nos. 4, 5, 18, 20, 21 24, 25, 27, 34, 36, 37, 38, 39, 40, 41 and 43. Of eight incidents selected from the British period, seven were exogenous in source. Of seventeen incidents chosen from the Fulani period, six were exogenous in source; but of 18 incidents from the Hausa period, only 3 are wholly exogenous, while 7 are wholly internal in source and focus alike. These numbers neatly illustrate the progressively restricted autonomy of Kano under its Fulani and British overlords. Together they show how heavily developments at Kano were provoked or influenced by exter-nal factors even under the Hausa chiefs. To discriminate Kano's differing relations with external bodies, we need nine categories. These differing patterns show clearly that we cannot treat Kano as an isolated unit which developed purely or primarily under the direction of its own logic and forces; but neither can we regard these developments as simple products of external factors. Many of Kano's responses to foreign bodies and influences were aggressive and successful; for example, nos. 2, 3, 6, 9, 12, 26, 29, 31 and 35. Others were apparently spontaneous, peaceful and positive, for example, nos. 1, 4, 8, 22 and 32. Yet others were unsuc-cessful, e.g., nos. 5, 18, 24, 34; but, as we have seen, even under close supervision by the British, the rulers of Kano were able normally to exercise sufficient auton-omy to maintain and enhance their position. It is perhaps nearer the truth to regard most of the events that took place between 1903 and 1953 as illustrating mutual Anglo-Fulani accommodations rather than simple Fulani obedience to British directions. Beginning with Yaji's conversion, we may also regard several earlier responses of Kano to external pressures and influence as accommodative; but this designation is not analytically useful since it obscures differing types and degrees of constraint to which the rulers of Kano were subject in those situations.

Dialectically Linked Clusters

Considered chronologically, many of the events listed cluster to form short sequences of development through which the structure accommodated the impact of some event that initiated the series. For example, Yaji followed his con-version by leading his army of Muslims and pagans against Santolo, thus eliminating an important threat to Kano's local domination. Yaji's successor, Kanajeji, was even more aggressive, but after suffering defeat in Zaria, he apostasised and adopted the cult of the Kano pagans, thus basing his power on their support, rather than the Muslims and Gaudawa. These two latter events illustrate the main responses of Kano chiefs to the advent of Islam, and notably Kanajeji is the last known pagan chief.

A second short sequence unfolds in events 4–6. This indicates Kano's initial responses to expansion by Bornu. The sequence starts with the arrival of the deposed Mai Othman Kalnama and his party at Kano to the consternation of the reigning chief, Dawuda (1421–38), whose successor, Abdullahi Burja, was obliged to submit to Bornu as a tributary vassal. These developments obliged Burja to collect slaves for the Bornu tribute. Perhaps to ensure that Dagaci and his large Kanuri community had little chance for mischief at Kano while the army was away on campaign, Burja decided to remain at the city and despatched his forces south against the pagans under the command of his Galadima Dawuda. Burja thus initiated the status of *tirika* (pl. *tirikai*), which thereafter was gradually extended to the Wombai and certain other senior officials, whose high status qualified them for field commands.

This innovation had several important consequences. The Galadima's campaign succeeded beyond all expectations, thereby validating Burja's innovation and establishing *tirikai* as the category of most powerful senior officials, or *rukunai* (s. *rukuni*). Besides furnishing the Bornu tribute, Dawuda built and supplied for the throne 21 slave-estates (*indabu*), each equipped with one thousand adults, thus endowing the chiefship with a sufficiently large and organised staff of slaves to reduce greatly its dependence on Muslims and free noble lineages for the power to rule. Dawuda's campaigns thus converted the basis of chiefly power from support by free noble lineages to command of slaves. In response, Burja unwisely rewarded Dawuda by placing him in charge of the new slave estates, thereby making Dawuda by far the most powerful man in the state. In consequence, on Burja's death in 1452, the Galadima was able to dictate the succession, and after two rapid enthronements and depositions, with Dawuda's backing, Yakubu, a son of Burja, became chief. In effect, Burja's innovations and the Galadima's successes had together destabilised the throne by disproportionately aggrandising its senior non-royal official.

Rumfa's constitutional and administrative innovations, which were clearly modelled on Bornu, can best be understood as an imperfectly successful attempt to insulate the chiefship against domination by any single powerful official, such as Burja's Galadima. Kano traditions describe Rumfa (1463–1499) as founder of the dynasty that bears his name; and while most likely a native of Kano, he may have owed his chiefship to the support of Bornu. In magnifying the office, increasing its grandeur and elaborating its establishment, Rumfa simultaneously exploited the vast numbers of slaves with which Burja's Galadima had endowed it, and copied the style and organisation of chiefship as practised by his suzerains in Bornu. Thus, for successful resolution of the unstable relations between the chiefs and senior officials which Burja's novel commission to the Galadima promoted, Rumfa's constitutional and administrative innovations presupposed continuity of stable relations between Kano and its suzerains in Bornu. Songhai's attacks on Kano, Katsina and Zaria shortly after Rumfa's death dislocated this relation; but we lack sufficient information to discern in detail the pattern of local developments linked with Kano's brief subjugation first to Songhai and then to Kebbi. Evidently Kisoke (1509–1565), under whom Kano resumed independence from Kebbi, Songhai and Bornu alike, ruled securely if unconstitutionally with the help of his mother, the Iya Lamis, his grandmother, the Madaki Hauwa, and her brother, his grand-uncle Gulle. But this regime was no less unstable than that of Burja's later years. After Kisoke's successor Yakufu had reigned 4 months and 20 days, Gulle deposed him and appointed Dawuda. The Galadima, presumably supported by other senior officials, opposed such unconstitutional actions, and in the brief civil war that followed, Gulle was killed and his nominee replaced by Abubakar Kado (1565–73), who was himself deposed.

These events provided the contexts and driving forces for the remarkable political development of Kano during the following two centuries, which began under Shashere (1573–82), who succeeded Kado and sought to strengthen the chiefship by appointing eunuchs to such senior offices holding seats on the State Council as Wombai and Sarkin Dawaki, which may previously have been filled by princes or by free nobles. While this move formally strengthened Shashere, it clearly infuriated his opponents, royal and other. His free soldiers deserted him in battle against Katsina, and the princes plotted his assassination. On both occasions Shashere was saved by his eunuchs and slaves.

Shashere's successor, Muhammad Zaki (1582–1618) sought security from internal and external enemies by means of ritual, and reinforced the throne with two fetishes, Chokana and Dirki, but nonetheless had to flee Kano when the Kororofa (Jukun) attacked. Under Nazaki, who succeeded, the Wombai Giwa established a preponderant position at Kano, and was sent to rule Karaye and wage war on Katsina.

Kutumbi (1623–48) sought solutions to the conflict between the chief and his council of senior officials partly in expansion, and partly in personal rule through a series of favourites whom he set up as ministers. However his expeditions against Bauchi, Gombe and Katsina were not unqualified successes, and some say he died in Katsina on campaign. His greatest achievement was to incorporate the pastoral Fulani at Kano, to oblige them to pay tax (*jangali*), and to establish an official structure to administer them. Kutumbi allocated some of these new *sarautu* to his slaves. That, together with his preference for favourites as instruments of personal administration, perhaps provoked the intense political reactions of officials and royals which, within four years of his death, found expression in the removal of three chiefs, the last after a brief civil war between the Madawaki and his supporters on one side, the Galadima, Dan Iya, Makama, Sarkin Dawaki and Sarkin Gaya and theirs on the other. The Madawaki lost and was humiliated. Kukuna (1652–60), previously deposed, was recalled from Zaria and reinstated, and the unstable situation persisted for three reigns and fifty years until Muhammadu Sharifa (1703–31) succeeded.

Sharifa aggrandized the government—that is, the throne and officialdom—by increasing its demands on the population of Kano in various ways, thus augmenting the status and incomes of his officials, while increasing his own. His successor Kumbari (1731–43) had to face another assault from Bornu and may have been forced to pay tribute. Babba Zaki (1768–76) finally resolved the struggles of chiefs and senior officials for domination by distributing the latter in two distinct communication structures which served to cross-check one another. Thereafter until Alwali was overthrown by the Fulani, there was no governmental power to threaten or balance the chiefship. Babba Zaki thus laid the basis for chiefly despotism at Kano.

These developments can be traced back to the initial imposition of suzerainty by Bornu and to Burja's unsettling appointment of Galadima Dawuda to command his army on its great southern raid for slaves. Faced with the extreme concentration of authority and power in the chieftainship that Alwali had exercised, and facing divisions and rivalries among themselves, it is easy to understand why the jihadic leaders hesitated to have an emir and tried instead to rule the country they had conquered collegially. With Suleimanu's appointment in 1808–09, the stage was set for a second struggle between the leaders of an entrenched nobility, in this case the leading *jihadi* clans, and the new chiefship created and backed by the suzerain at Sokoto. Dabo's long reign (1819–46) was critical for the outcome of this struggle. Dabo revived the basic forms of Hausa government but accepted the "founding" oligarchy's demand for security of office, and agreed that Sokoto should assure their rights. By the time of Dabo's death, the chief and the nobles had found a *modus vivendi* which continued under his sons, Usuman, Abdullahi and Mamman Bello (1885–1893) and allowed both to consolidate their positions free of internal threats.

Sokoto's ill-advised appointment of Tukur to succeed Bello in 1893 precipitated the sequence of events listed as nos. 28–32 which concluded formally with Aliyu's belated visit of 1903, on the eve of Lugard's attacks on both these states. Aliyu's desertion on his homeward journey initiated the short sequence (nos. 33–36) that ended with Lugard's confirmation of Abbas as emir. Thereafter under the aegis of Indirect Rule, the British strove to reform and redesign the Fulani administration of Kano by rationalizing taxation and the territorial organisation, by instituting a State Treasury with audited accounts, pressing for the abolition of slave officials, and finally, in 1951, by introducing elections to public councils. The Fulani rulers, meanwhile, strove with considerable success to secure their autonomy and interests against erosion by change. Each of these measures and adjustments strengthened the native government, but they also greatly increased its organisational complexity and scale, while strengthening the chiefship.

By 1953, when Sanusi succeeded, the emir's position seemed as secure and powerful as in the days of Abdullahi.

Sources and Implications of Events

It is instructive to examine those columns of Table 9.1 that summarise the changing distributions of power and authority at Kano in light of this brief review of the successive short sequences that together form the chronological series of events. The first three events were all unqualified gains for Kano, while the two that followed reduced the power and integrity of the state. Dawuda's successful slave raids enhanced Kano's strength, but the succession crises of 1452 were not an unqualified gain. Rumfa's innovations and Kisoke's achievement of independence from Bornu both further strengthened the state; but the succession crises of

1565 and Shashere's elevation of eunuchs to the state council had rather mixed implications. Kutumbi's incorporation of the pastoral Fulani strengthened the polity, but Sharifa's oppressive innovations and Babba Zaki's aggressive centralization both had mixed effects. Alwali's destruction of Dirki affected nothing, but the *jihad* and Alwali's defeat, while destroying the Hausa regime, left the polity intact for the Fulani conquerors.

The interregnum under collegial government, and the appointments of Suleimanu and Dabo, all served to strengthen and establish Fulani rule, and to assure the continuity of Kano as a unit. Dabo's resurrection of Hausa political institutions further strengthened the state, but general revolt and the secession of Kazaure weakened it. The circumstances of Usuman's appointment in 1846 consolidated Suleibawa rule but denied Kano the freedom to choose its emirs. This provoked Abdullahi's assumption of power in 1855, an act of defiance which greatly enhanced the solidarity of the state, and set a pattern that Abdullahi's sons, Yusufu and Aliyu, followed later.

The circumstances and consequences of Tukur's appointment in 1893 again weakened the state, while Aliyu's victory reasserted its power. The *basasa* of 1894–95 had very mixed implications, but laid the basis for Aliyu's despotism. His initial rejection and final acceptance of Sokoto's suzerainty, both in their immediate contexts, benefitted and strengthened Kano, while his desertion and the defeat at Kotorkoshi reduced its power. In selecting Abbas to succeed, the defeated Kanawa reaffirmed the solidarity of the state, and Lugard's appointment later confirmed this, though with severe limitations. The series of British-inspired changes that followed cumulatively strengthened the polity, often by reducing the interests of the chief or the officialdom while protecting or promoting those of their subjects.

This brief sketch of the changing fortunes of Kano summarises the fourth column in Table 9.1 which lists the implications of these events for the polity as a whole. It will be noticed that all events which contributed positively or negatively without qualification to the polity had identical implications for each of the three concrete structures to which the preceding columns refer. If we classified these events by their positive (+), negative (–) or mixed (+–) contributions to these concrete structures, and by their source and genesis as primarily external (E), primarily internal (I), or mixed (E/I), the following distribution results, the subtotals of the categories being set in brackets.

Thus of these 43 events or processes, one had no effect on either of the three concrete structures, 19 enhanced the polity and its three principal structures, 11 had negative implications for all three structures, and 12 were positive for some and negative for others. These distributions show clearly how mistaken it is to conceive all changes of analytic structure on the model of a zero-sum game. On 19 of these 43 occasions, the polity and all three of its major structures—the chiefship, the government and the state—gained in power and authority, however unequally, while on 11, all suffered, though differentially so. Only 12 of these 43 occasions corresponded in their form to the model of a zero-sum game, in the sense that one or more units gained while others lost power and authority, and in several cases their equations did not balance. It is thus inappropriate to think of the analytic structure of the polity as a closed system with a fixed volume and distribution of authority and power that may only be reallocated by simultaneously augmenting some units and reducing others. Our analysis shows unqualified gains and losses for the polity and its three major concrete structures in a total of 30 of these 43 events, but no discernible change in one other.

Of those events that were wholly endogenous in genesis and focus, three were negative in all respects, while seven had mixed implications, one had no effects, and one simultaneously enhanced all three structures and the polity.

The 16 events that were external in their genesis and implementation are almost equally divided with reference to their effects on the polity and these concrete structures. Five strengthened and six weakened all, while five had mixed implications.

Of 15 locally generated events which were oriented to external factors, 13 were wholly positive and 2 were wholly negative in their implications for the polity and all three concrete structures.

Table 9.3 groups these 43 events by their sources and orientations as external, internal or mixed, and by their implications as neutral, positive, negative or mixed for the power and authority exercised by the chiefship, government and state when each event occurred. The neutral category in this table is indicated by 0 and includes two events that occurred when the chiefship was vacant, two that probably did not affect the state, and one which altered nothing. The analytic implications of each event are assessed with specific reference to each of the concrete structures.

While the state and the chiefship were each unaffected by three events, two of those incidents occurred when the chiefship was vacant. Of the 43 incidents, 26 increased the power and authority of the government, 24 strengthened the chiefship, and 23 strengthened the state. The chiefship and government suffered losses in 15 events and the state in 13, but neither were these occasions identical for all three structures, nor did they lose equally from events that affected them all. Of the latter, four strengthened the state in some respects while reducing its power in others, and one of these four events had similar implications for the chiefship and government. From 16 events of exogenous origin, the state had unqualified gains on 9 occasions, the chiefship on 8 and the government on 7. From 12 endoge-

TABLE 9.2   Moments of Change Classified by Source and General Implication

	External (E)	E/I	Internal (I)	All	
0			1	(1)	1
+	20, 21, 39, 40, 43 (5)	1, 2, 3, 6, 8, 9, 12, 19, 22, 26, 29, 31, 32 (13)	35	(1)	19
−	4, 5, 18, 24, 27, 34 (6)	28, 17 (2)	23, 33, 42	(3)	11
+−	25, 36, 37, 38, 41 (5)		7, 19, 11, 13, 14, 15, 30 (7)		12
All	16	15	12	43	

nously generated events, the government gained on 6 occasions and the chiefship on 5. Three internal events had mixed implications for the state, while two yielded unqualified gains. All but two of these 15 events initiated at Kano and oriented to external bodies were wholly beneficial to the officialdom and the state, while 12 of these augmented the chiefship. This category of events accounts for exactly half of the total occasions on which the chiefship and government both gained, and for more than half of the total that strengthened the state. Table 9.1 shows how in my judgment the implications of each of these 43 events differentially affected the state, the chiefship and the officialdom.

A Serial Survey of These Changes

To grasp the contributions of these events to the changing bases, volumes, nature and distributions of authority and power in Kano, we need to examine them serially and typologically. In its chronological order, the series in Table 9.1 may be usefully divided into 10 or 12 short sequences as sketched above. The first sequence which spans the first three events was entirely positive in its effects on the polity and its three major structures. Nos. 4 and 5, which were entirely negative for all three units, gave rise to no. 6, which considerably strengthened the polity and all three structures. However, the distribution of this additional power destabilised the government and weakened the chiefship, as Atuma's deposition in 1452 at the Galadima's insistence—event no. 7—revealed. This incident further strengthened the officialdom vis-à-vis the chiefship, thus strengthening the state and polity in some respects and weakening it in others, especially by the precedent it established.

As remarked above, Atuma's deposition probably stimulated Rumfa's efforts at constitutional development and reform (event no. 8); but while strengthening the state and the chiefship, these innovations also consolidated and enhanced the power and authority of the officialdom.

Kano's resumption of independence from Bornu during the reign of Kisoke (1509–65), closed this sequence, and was clearly an unqualified advantage for all, but left the constitutional issues and political tensions between the chiefship and officialdom unresolved. Indeed, Kisoke seems to have aggrandised his maternal kin as a means of strengthening his patrimonial rule. In the action that followed swiftly on Kisoke's death—event no. 10—the officialdom reasserted its power over the chiefship, thereby enhancing the internal autonomy of the state while dislocating its most senior and sensitive organ.

Events 11 and 12 denote successive attempts by Shashere (1573–82) and Kutumbi (1623–48) to re-establish the executive dominion the chiefship evidently enjoyed in the days of Yaji and Kanajeji; but while Shashere appropriated power and authority from the officialdom, he neither strengthened nor weakened the state. By contrast, Kutumbi's incorporation of local Fulani pastoralists as a subordinate category of the state did significantly strengthen the polity and its three major structures.

Even so, Kutumbi's death was promptly followed by successive reassertions of its superior power by the officialdom—event no. 13; and almost certainly at this time Shashere's patrimonial allocation of senior offices with seats on the state council to eunuchs was revoked. Those developments established a framework

Analysis

which persisted without structural change until Muhammadu Sharifa (1703–31) increased the government's authority and resources by laying new burdens on the people. While the chief and officialdom both benefitted from Sharifa's innovations, the population suffered. These innovations were accordingly rather mixed in their implications for the state as a unit.

So was the overall effect of Babba Zaki's masterly reorganisation of communications and responsibility within the government. This effectively centralised administrative authority in the throne and greatly increased the chief's power at the expense of his officials, while correspondingly strengthening the state. It was left to Babba Zaki to resolve the prolonged struggle between the throne and the officialdom for supremacy and executive control; and his solution brought the Hausa state as close to sultanism as it came before the reign of Aliyu Babba (1894–1903).

Alwali's anxieties, illustrated by his destruction of the Dirki fetish, the beginning of the Fulani *jihad* at Kano, its final victory, and the collegial administration that followed Alwali's flight, form a separate sequence which ended with the appointment of Suleimanu as emir. The implications of each of these events for the Hausa state and its structures are set out in Table 9.1.

Dabo's appointment and revival of Hausa governmental forms and procedures both brought advantages to all the structures of government; but local resentments at these reforms, at Dabo's appointment, at the mode of his selection, and at the claims of the emirship to supremacy, which he pressed, found expression in a general revolt which resisted Dabo stubbornly for several years and only concluded with the loss of Kazaure to the dissident Yerimawa chief, Dan Tunku.

Sokoto's autocratic appointment of Usuman as Dabo's successor strengthened the Suleibawa emirship and the state, but denied its officialdom a voice in the choice of their ruler. That pattern perhaps provoked Abdullahi's forcible assumption of power after the death of Usuman. Abdullahi's action may in turn have hardened the ears of caliph Abdurrahman against the many warnings he received of the dire consequences of appointing Tukur to succeed his father, Mammon Bello, in 1893. The implications of each of these appointments for the throne, the officialdom and the state are fully set out in Table 9.1.

Tukur's appointment initiates the sequence of the civil war and Aliyu's reign (nos. 27–32). For the nine years that followed Aliyu's victory, Kano was an independent sovereign state; but in 1903, anticipating the British attack, Aliyu belatedly sought a rapprochement with Abdurrahman's successor at Sokoto and made formal allegiance. His desertion, the defeat at Kotorkoshi, the brave and wise selection of Abbas as emir by the defeated nobles, and Lugard's confirmation of Abbas on his own terms, complete, in another brief sequence, Kano's history under the Fulani, and are analytically described in Table 9.1.

The British thereafter remodelled the Fulani government at Kano to their own design through the *gunduma*, the institution of the Treasury, and cognate measures, and finally by insisting on the disestablishment of throne slaves (events 37–40). Each of these measures strengthened the polity, but some, notably the *gunduma* and the dismissal of throne slaves, disadvantaged certain units in the process. Table 9.1 summarises their implications.

Two of the last three events in this series are without precedent in the history of Kano, namely the introduction of elections in 1951 and the ethnic riots of Hausa against Ibo at Kano in 1953. While elections weakened the chiefship, they supported the government and supplied the state with the popular affirmation of consensus it had never previously received or dared to seek. However the Ibo riots of 1953 were uniformly negative in their implications. Sanusi's appointment as emir following Bayero's death in 1953 reaffirmed the state and particularly the structure of its electoral council, but otherwise altered little formally. With Sanusi's appointment, Kano finally moved across the threshold into the contemporary period.

The Typological Alternative—Empirical Version

This serial treatment of the changing distributions of authority and power associated with these 43 events reaffirms our preceding discussion of the chronological relations of these developmental sequences, but otherwise adds little to our understanding of change at Kano. The typological approach must therefore be tried; and that approach comes in at least two versions, one empirical, the other analytic.

Empirically, we may classify events, as above, according to their salient features in such categories as chiefly innovations, administrative or political; chiefly appointments and depositions; revolts or internal strife; and incidents that marked turning points in Kano's foreign relations with suzerain states.

Of 11 incidents in our list that mark administrative and/or political innovations, 5 benefitted the polity and its main components, however unequally— namely, nos. 1, 8, 12, 22 and 40. None of these five events were wholly internal in genesis and orientation. All involved external factors in one way or another. The remaining six innovations, nos. 11, 14, 15, 37, 38, 41, all had mixed implications for the polity, since the advantages they conferred on some units were balanced by disadvantages conferred on others.

Of ten chiefly appointments included in these 43 events, seven occurred during Fulani rule and three under the British. Of the seven Fulani appointments, five events, nos. 20, 21, 26, 29 and 35, strengthened the polity and all three concrete structures; one, no. 25, had mixed effects; and another, no. 27, was wholly negative in its implications. Of the three chiefly appointments made by the British, two events, nos. 36 and 39, had mixed implications, while the third, which was wholly beneficial, left the categories of latent structure unchanged.

All three sets of chiefly depositions—events nos. 6, 10 and 13,—took place before the *jihad* as incidents in the prolonged struggle of Hausa chiefs and their officials for control of Kano. All had mixed implications for the polity and state, since they strengthened the government at the expense of the throne.

All three revolts, events nos. 17, 23, 28, had negative implications for the polity, the chiefship, the government and the state.

Of ten exogenous and externally oriented events, four refer to military campaigns, nos. 2, 6, 24 and 34. Of these, the first pair were victories that augmented the authority and power of all three structures at Kano, while the second pair were defeats and had the opposite effect.

On four occasions in this list of events, Kano was obliged to accept foreign suzerains—nos. 5, 18, 32 and 36. On the first two of these occasions the state, the government and the chiefship all lost authority and power; on the third, namely Aliyu's belated acceptance of Sokoto's leadership in 1903, all three structures gained formally; and on the last occasion, when Lugard imposed British rule, gains and losses were mixed.

Twice in this record Kano recovered its independence of foreign rule; and on both occasions—events nos. 9 and 31,—the state and all its structures enhanced their power and authority.

The results of this typological review are not in general surprising; but they reveal certain distributions that we could not anticipate, for example the mixed implications of innovations listed as events nos. 11, 14, 15, 37, 38 and 41; of the appointments of the emirs Usuman, no. 25 and Bayero, no. 39; of the three sets of chiefly depositions in Hausa days, events 6, 10 and 13; and of Kano's submission to the British, event 36. These unexpected insights illustrate some advantages of studying political developments systematically; but they add little to our general understanding of the conditions and structure of the processes of political change. To advance our knowledge in this area, we must deal with these events in more abstract and analytic terms.

The Relations of Structural Levels in Events: An Example

We have found it necessary and useful to distinguish three structural levels in order to examine changes of political organisation, namely, the conceptual level of latent categories that underlies the level of concrete units and their articulations, and finally, a third analytic level which consists in the distributions of authority and power that structure governmental relations among and within these concrete units. As the eight categories of latent structure which together define in general terms the type of regime that prevailed at Kano throughout its development from 1350 until 1953 are aligned by relations of logical priority and succession, we argued first that any structural modification of concrete structure which expressed those latent categories could only proceed in the order of logical priority that governed their relations; and secondly, that such changes of latent structure, that is, changes in the content of these logically ordered formal categories, were presupposed by the events that expressed them—in other words, that such changes in the content of formal categories were prerequisites of those events that superficially seemed to generate them.

To illustrate and clarify this point, let us consider an extreme case which should provide an exacting test, namely, the arrival of Dagaci, who was probably Othman Kalnama, a former sultan of Kanem-Bornu, in the reign of Kanajeji's son Dawuda (1421–38),[39] with a large entourage that included malams, musicians, "musketeers," horsemen and flagbearers. The Chronicle gives a vivid account of this incident.

> In his (Dawuda's) time, Dagaci, a great prince, came from south Bornu with many men and mallams. He brought with him horses, drums and trumpets and flags and guns. When he came, he sat down (settled) at Bompai (beside Kano city). The Sarkin Kano went to see him. When he saw that he was indeed a great prince, he returned

home and took counsel with his men and said, "Where is this man to stay?" The Galadima Babba said, "If you let him settle elsewhere than in Kano town, he will soon be master of that part of the country." The Sarki said, "Where can he stay here with his army—Kano is full of men—unless we increase the size of the town?" The Galadima was sent to the Dagaci and returned with him, and built a house for him and his men at Dorayi (inside the city). The Sarki said to his men, "What shall I give him to please him, and to make his heart glad?" The Galadima Babba said, "Give him whatever you wish, you are Sarki, you own everything." The Sarki said nothing. At that time he was about to start for war with Zaria, so he said to Dagaci, "When I go to war I will put all the affairs of Kano into your hands, city and country alike." So the Sarkin Kano went to war, and left Dagaci in the town. Dagaci ruled the town (and country) for five months and became very wealthy. Then the Sarki returned.[40]

Evidently Dawuda, his Galadima Babba and senior officials were so impressed with Dagaci's status and the size and splendour of his company, that they all regarded his presence as a serious threat to the chief and the traditional regime. Kano had never witnessed anything comparable since Bagauda came south from Daura.

Dagaci's arrival accordingly questioned the supremacy of the local chiefship and thus involved significant changes in the concrete structures that expressed those formal conceptions that underlay the government of Kano. These changes began with revisions in the preceding structure of status differentiation which distinguished the immigrants as a quite unique corporate group under a leader who was given the new titled office of Dagaci, thus modifying the preceding complements of corporations aggregate and sole at Kano. Those developments in turn raised questions about the criteria and qualifications which would govern recruitment to the office of Dagaci while excluding its holder from the chiefship at Kano; and these questions in turn involved the supremacy of the chiefship at Kano over Dagaci and his entourage.

Altogether the redefinitions in the contents of these five latent categories, **a b c d e**, are presupposed by Dawuda's actions to define his relations with Dagaci and his Kanuri companions. Clearly, neither did those categories entail Dagaci's arrival, nor did his movement west to Kano presuppose the categories; yet, given the circumstances of Dagaci's arrival and entourage, the local perceptions of this event and reactions by Dawuda and his senior officials not only presupposed those five categories, but indicated recognition of the substantial changes of their contents experienced at Kano by virtue of Dagaci's arrival with his people. Without these presuppositions, Dawuda's behaviour remains unintelligible. He clearly, on the account cited above, recognised the Kanuri immigrants as a powerful corporate group having a different status from his subjects at Kano, and regarded their leader as "a great prince" who, by virtue of his royal descent, political connections and military strength, might either claim autonomous jurisdiction over his community, thereby suspending the chief's territorial authority, or attempt to seize control of Kano at Dawuda's expense. To indicate his recognition of Dagaci's eminence and unique status, Dawuda commissioned him to act as regent of Kano during his absence at Zaria on campaign. Such behaviour is only intelligible as a response that recognises substantial changes in the first five categories of the latent structure, namely **a b c d e**, serially and in the order of their logical relations, as just shown.

It follows then that while the formulae in Table 9.1 that refer to changes in the analytic distributions and concrete structures denote implications entailed by events, those that refer to latent structure denote their prerequisites. These prerequisites will either consist in the persistence of some or all of these formal categories, with no changes in their empirical expressions or content or in the necessary prior revision or changes of some or occasionally all of the concrete structures and arrangements that presuppose and manifest these categories.

Accordingly, to increase our understanding of the structure of the processes of political change, we should try to determine how changes of concrete and analytic structures that are the substantive implications of discrete events relate to those changes in the manifest contents of the latent categories that are prerequisites of those events.

Typological Analysis of Latent Structure

To pursue this question, we should first group events that express changes of identical sets of categories, and then examine their concrete analytic implications. On these lines the 43 events fall into the following five classes. Two events, nos. 16 and 43, involved no changes in any categories of latent structure. Five, nos. 14, 19, 30, 34 and 42, assumed changes in the first two categories, namely (a), the structures of status differentiation, and of (b), corporations. These changes are summarised in the formula, **ab**. Fourteen events presupposed and expressed changes in the first five of these latent categories, namely, the structures of status differentiation, corporations, offices, the criteria that governed their allocation, and chiefship as the supreme and senior office. These events, nos. 2–5, 17, 20, 21, 23, 25–29 and 33, are represented in Table 9.1 by the formula **abcde**. Another 14 events involved changes in the rank organisation and role differentiation of offices, as well as the five preceding categories. These events, nos. 1, 6–10, 13, 15, 31, 32, 35, 36, 39 and 41, are all represented in Table 9.1 by the formula, **abcdefg**. Finally, there is a class of 8 events, nos. 11 and 12, 18, 22, 24, 37, 38 and 40, which involve changes in all eight categories of latent structure. These events are indicated in Table 9.1 by the formula, **abcdefgh**.

If changes in latent categories are linked with changes in concrete or analytic structures by specific kinds of invariant relations, we should expect to find significant differences in the formulae and rankings that register the concrete and analytic changes for events that involve changes in different sets or numbers of latent categories. Conversely, we should expect to find changes of the same kind and content in the concrete and analytic structures entailed by events that involve revisions of content in the same set of latent categories. The latter expectation is more easily checked; and clearly it does not hold.

Two events that involved no changes in the contents of these latent categories, nos. 16 and 43, between them entailed 5 different changes in the 3 concrete structures of chiefship, government (including chiefship) and the state, out of a possible maximum of six. Of these two events, one left the preceding analytic structure unchanged, despite some positive modifications of the properties and relations of all concrete structures, while the other formally modified the antecedent distribution of power and authority. In brief, neither do all changes in the properties or relations of concrete structures presuppose revisions of the contents of latent categories, nor is it always inevitable that changes of concrete structures should generate changes in the distribution of authority and power. These three structural levels are evidently less directly and rigidly associated with one another than the hypothesis of invariant relations between them could allow.

This conclusion is supported by the patterns of change in concrete and analytic structures associated with five events, nos. 14, 19, 30, 34 and 42, that involve redefinitions of the first two categories of the latent structure. Of a maximum possible total of 15, these five events have 10 differing sets of implications for the three concrete structures. Moreover, in my assessment, no two of these events have identical implications for the analytic structure. Those 14 events, 2–5, 17, 20, 21, 23, 25–29 and 33, that express changes in the first five latent categories, could between them at most generate 42 distinct sets of changes in the chiefship, government and state. In fact, their implications require 25 distinct formulae for description. As regards the changes of analytic structure entailed by these 14 events, those form six distinct patterns. Five events—2, 3, 20, 21 and 26—yield increases distributed as follows: C +3; G +1; S +2. Another five events—4, 5, 17, 28 and 33—yielded decreases distributed as follows: C–3; G –2; S –1. Each of the remaining four events yields a distinct pattern of gains and losses. For 23 this is C –3; G –1; S –2; for 25, C +3; G –1; S +2; for 27, C –2; G –3; S –1; and for 29, C +3; G +2; S +1. In short, 7 of these 14 events affected all three structures negatively, and six of these weakened the chiefship most of all. Six events positively strengthened all three structures, and especially the chiefship. One event strengthened the state and the chiefship but weakened the officialdom. Clearly, the analytic implications of events that involve substantive revisions of the first five categories of latent structure are very various indeed.

So too are the analytic implications of 14 events that expressed changes in the content of the first seven latent categories. Three of these events, 1, 9 and 31, yield the pattern, C+3, G +1, S+2; for three, 6, 8 and 39, this is C +2, G +3, S +1; and for another two events, 32 and 35, C+3, G–1, S +2. One event, 15, has the following: C +3, G –1, S +2. For three events, 7, 10 and 13, the implications are C –1, G +3, S +– 2. The two remaining events, 36 and 41, have the following effects: C +–1, G +–2 and S +–3 for 36; and C –1, G +1, S +3 for 41. Thus of these 14 events, eight enhanced the authority and power of all three concrete structures without qualification, while the remaining six had mixed implications in these respects.

Of eight events—11, 12, 18, 22, 24, 37, 38 and 40—that involved revisions in the contents of all eight categories of latent structure, six had individually distinct analytic implications, while two, 12 and 22, had the following pattern: C +3, G +1, S +2. Two of these 8 events, namely 11 and 38, probably did not change these properties of the state as a unit; three others, 12, 22 and 40, were wholly beneficial in their implications for all three concrete structures, while two, 18 and 24, were wholly negative. Of three events, 11, 24 and 38, which had mixed implications, two, 11 and 38, probably had no effect on the power and authority of the state as such.

Thus neither do all developments that involve identical sets of latent categories have the same implications for the power and authority of the polity and its three concrete structures, nor are these implications uniformly advantageous or disadvantageous for any of these units. Indeed, while two events that modified the distributions of authority and power between the chiefship, officialdom and the state involved and expressed no changes in the contents of any latent categories, on two other occasions, 11 and 38, events that assumed and expressed revisions in the contents of all eight categories of latent structure seem neither to have increased nor decreased the power and authority of the state. Clearly the implications of change in the contents of these latent categories for the distributions of authority and power in the polity and its three principal concrete structures are at most very indirect, uncertain and variable. Indeed, it seems unlikely that even the most ingenious and sophisticated set of partial differential equations could represent these relations as moments of a single coherent system.[41]

Negative Conclusions: Grounds and Measure of Variance

There are at least two reasons for the high degree of variance in relations between these two levels of the political structure. Firstly, each formula that lists changes of latent categories presupposed and expressed by a particular event refers explicitly to those changes of content in these categories which had developed since the change that immediately preceded them. This is equally true of the ranked advantages and disadvantages that directly follow each event and distribute authority and power relatively among the three concrete structures. In consequence, either series of formulaic statements compounds the cumulative modifications of latent and analytic structures that proceeded historically, with the result that very rarely can any pair of such formulae, except those chronologically juxtaposed, refer to identical states of the structures whose modifications they summarise. In brief, the significance of these latent formulae and analytic rankings is purely formal; and so formally identical statements will often vary in their substantive significance. In part the widely variable connotations of identical formulae reflect the differing states of the structures to which they refer, as produced by the cumulative modifications of history in these categories and distributions. Thus rarely indeed could any two or more formulae or rankings refer to identical prior states of these concrete and analytic structures.

Secondly, besides their strictly formal reference, these formulae and rankings are qualitative and relative, not absolute statements. Both summarise all discernible changes in their referents, without distinguishing the greater from the less, or attempting to state their absolute coefficients. In consequence, identical statements of either kind will often have starkly diverse connotations. Indeed, as we have seen, changes in the distributions of authority and power among concrete structures may proceed without prior or consantaneous changes of latent structure. The converse holds equally. Some modifications in the contents of these latent categories may have no discernible implications for the power and authority of the state. In either case, formulae or rankings of identical character may denote events of radically different significance and kind, partly because these statements are both purely formal and thus indifferent to differing values of the changes to which they refer; partly because they are qualitative and merely register the elements that have changed without assessing the absolute values of these changes; and partly because identical formulae can always only refer to different

TABLE 9.3 43 Numbered Events Classified by Their Sources and Analytic Implications for the Chiefship, Government and State

		External (E)		E/I		Internal (I)		Total
Chiefship	0	34	(1)	19	(1)	16	(1)	3
	+	20, 21, 25, 37, 39, 40, 43	(7)	1, 2, 3, 6, 8, 9, 12, 22, 26, 29, 31, 32	(12)	11, 14, 15, 30, 35	(5)	24
	–	4, 5, 18, 24, 27, 38, 41	(7)	17, 28	(2)	7, 10, 13, 23, 33, 42	(6)	15
	+–	36	(1)	–		–		1
Total			16		15		12	43
Government	0	–		–		16	(1)	1
	+	20, 21, 38, 39, 40, 41, 43	(7)	1, 2, 3, 6, 8, 9, 12, 19, 22, 26, 29, 31, 32	(13)	7, 10, 13, 14, 30, 35	(6)	26
	–	4, 5, 18, 24, 25, 27, 34, 37	(8)	17, 28	(2)	11, 15, 23, 33, 42	(5)	15
	+–	36	(1)	–		–		1
Total			16		15		12	43
State	0	38	(1)	–		11, 16	(2)	3
	+	20, 21, 25, 37, 39, 40, 41, 43	(8)	1, 2, 3, 6, 8, 9, 12, 19, 22, 26, 29, 31, 32	(13)	15, 35	(2)	23
	–	4, 5, 18, 24, 27, 34	(6)	17, 28	(2)	14, 23, 30, 33, 42	(5)	13
	+–	36	(1)	–		7, 10, 13	(3)	4
Total			16		15		12	43

states of a given structure which has changed in various ways, by incorporating the cumulative implications of many preceding events. In consequence, rarely can two events, however similar in form and character, have identical implications of a substantive or analytic kind for the polity and its concrete structures, simply because the relations and properties of these units will differ on these occasions as the cumulative products of changes brought about by intervening events.

These general remarks are strongly supported by variations in the substantive implications of events that involved changes in the same sets of latent categories for the three concrete structures, namely, the chiefship, government and the state. As noted above, two events that developed without any changes in the antecedent states of the latent categories entailed five distinct changes of a possible six in the relations and properties of these three concrete structures. Likewise, five events that expressed changes in the first two latent categories produced ten distinct changes of a possible 15 in these three units. Of 42 distinct possibilities, those 14 events that involved changes in the first five latent categories generated 25 differing effects in these three concrete structures. Likewise, 14 events, 1, 6–10, 13, 15, 31, 32, 35, 36, 39 and 41, that expressed changes in the first seven latent categories, between them entailed 23 different patterns of change in the relations and substantive properties of these three units. The final group of eight events, 11, 12, 18, 22, 24, 37, 38, 40, presupposed changes in the contents of all categories of the latent structure, and generated 11 distinct sets of implications for the three concrete structures. Altogether, these 43 events had a total of 60 distinct sets of implications for these three concrete structures out of a possible 129. Eighteen events chosen from the period of Hausa rule required 23 formulae to describe their substantive implications for these structures, while 17 events from the Fulani period required 22, and 8 events from the period of British rule required another 15 to describe their specific substantive implications for these concrete structures. These 60 alternative formulae are, it seems, distributed independently and almost at random in relation both to the changes of latent structure that were their prerequisites, and to those changes of analytic structure that they directly implied. Neither is any invariant relation discernible between changes at this substantive level of structure and the two other levels; nor have I been able to detect, however faintly, the presence of any submerged mediators that might readily bring all the formulae and rankings that describe these different sets of changes into any single set of coherent relations.

There are, as we have seen, several very cogent reasons why this should be so. Firstly, the first two sets of formulae both indicate the order in which specific categories, relations or properties have changed, but say nothing about the magnitude of these changes. Formulae that describe changes in the relations and properties of concrete units do, it is true, indicate the nature and direction of changes in these properties, but not their magnitude. In consequence we cannot assume that identical formulae denote quantitatively equivalent changes in the values of the variables to which they refer. The referents of these formulae are all qualitative; and this is equally true even of numerical rankings that indicate the relative order of gains or losses of authority and power to the chiefship, the government and the state, that flow from these events.

The second reason for the marginal correlations of formulae that describe the patterns of change associated with discrete events at these three levels lies in the continuing evolution of their structure, and the fact that each formula refers precisely to its state at the instant of a given event. Application of such disjunctive formulae to a continuously changing structure necessarily isolates the state of that structure at the moment of each event as the reference-point for identification of any changes presupposed or implied by the event. In consequence, identical patterns of change reported for concrete structures at two or more distinct phases of this evolutionary process can never denote alterations of identical magnitude and significance. At best, they only specify the order and direction in which the properties and relations of these units were modified at precise moments by different events, and say nothing about the extent of these changes.

Positive Conclusions: Two Modes of Invariance

It might seem then that this elaborate analysis has proven sterile and adds nothing to our knowledge of the processes and conditions of political change. Fortunately, our results do not fully support such negative assessment. Table 9.1 shows clearly that all changes in the contents of the latent categories prerequisite for the substantive changes of concrete structures presupposed by those events proceeded serially and in the order of logical priority that aligns these categories themselves. This partly confirms the generalisation that

> all change in the form of a governmental system will develop in a single order, since this order is governed by principles of logical priority which define the relations of constitutive forms. Formal change is therefore always sequential, and the order of such change is fixed and irreversible, being logically necessary.[42]

To test or confirm this proposition fully, we must re-examine all 129 formulae in Table 9.1 that summarise the changes entailed by these events in the forms and substance of the three concrete structures that together constitute the polity of Kano. Table 9.1 shows, firstly, that in every instance changes in the properties or substance of these structures are preceded by changes of their internal or external articulations or both; and, secondly, that whenever both sets of articulations change together, they always do so serially and in succession, never simultaneously. These features sharply distinguish the patterns of change exhibited by their articulations on the one hand, and by the substantive properties of these units on the other. In most, though not all, instances, changes in these substantive variables involve some simultaneous shifts, and in many instances all the variables affected changed simultaneously. Since the actual form of a social unit at any moment is defined by its external relations with other units and the sum of internal relations between its parts, the uniform precedence of relational shifts over changes in the substance of these concrete units demonstrates that "the form of a system limits the range and development of its content."[43] Moreover, these changes of internal and external articulation are always stochastic, and whenever concurrent proceed sequentially, like those changes in the content of the latent categories to which they give structural expression. However, since these two sets of articulations are not ordered by relations of logical priority, changes in either set of articulations (often) occur independently ... Their relative freedom to change in various sequences or contexts independently of one another probably reflects their role as mediators between the formal and substantive levels of the concrete structures.[44]

As mediators, these articulations respond sensitively and in variable order to external or internal conditions that modify the forms and properties of these units. Notably, neither does our analysis of the changes entailed by these events in the three concrete structures selected as diagnostic reveal any instance of such substantive changes that is not preceded by some change in the articulations of the unit affected, nor does it provide any instance in which such changes in a unit's articulations was not followed by changes in some or all of the unit's properties. With the qualification noted below, these patterns thus confirm the generalisations that "resistance to changes in the content of a system varies according to their significance for the maintenance of the current structure;" and that "attempts to change the form of a system by changing its content are self-defeating."[45] The amendment that this statement requires is replacement of the term "system" by some other such as structure, or unit; for our analysis of political change at Kano shows clearly that its government was not a system in the sense of systems theory or in any meaningful sense of that term. As societies exist in time as well as space, and in pursuing the conditions of their persistence, develop, change and evolve, any adequate conception of these aggregates as systems must accommodate this diachronic dimension and its experience. Anyone who supports this thesis and is willing to test it against empirical developments is invited to analyse the preceding record of Kano's political history within that framework.

Instead of conceiving the polity as a system, we have repeatedly described it as a "unit" or a "structure"—that is, as a bounded unit with, at any moment, a determinate structure, consisting of units or of parts and the relations within and between them.

As we have seen, this structure has three levels, each of which has a structure of its own. Of these, the empirical level of concrete units that have distinctive features and properties is directly open to observation, together with their mutual relations. At the analytic level, we can isolate structures of authority and power and determine distributions within and among these concrete units at successive moments. Underlying the ensemble of concrete structures and their relations, and the ideal of constitutional order that they express, is the set of latent conceptions aligned by relations of logical priority and succession as a structure of categories which these constitutional models, concrete units and analytic relations express in temporally successive and particular forms. We have found that changes at this conceptual level invariably underlie changes in the relations and properties of concrete units, and that changes at that level in turn always underlie or generate those changes in the distributions of power and authority within and among them that modify or sustain the antecedent analytic structure.

Finally, the relevant columns of Table 9.1 indicate that, in my judgment, redistributions of authority and power among these concrete structures are always unequal, whether all units gain or lose from an event, or it has mixed implications. This conclusion, which summarises the rankings of Table 9.1, is perhaps the most interesting feature of our analysis. It may also be the most questionable. In either case, it acknowledges the elasticity of the analytic structure, while demonstrating how inadequate is the view that politics and political change are intelligible as zero-sum games.

Notes

1. Muhammad A. Al-Hajj, "A Seventeenth Century Chronicle of the Origins and Missionary Activities of the Wangarawa," *Kano Studies*, 1:4 (1968) pp. 8–16; for quotation, v. p. 9. Thomas Hodgkin, *Nigerian Perspectives: An Historical Anthology*, (London: Oxford University Press, 1975) 2nd edition, p. 100, fn. 2.

2. v. Muhammad A. Al-Hajj, *op. cit.*, "When he (the Shaikh Muhammad b. Abd al-Karim, Sidi Fari) arrived (at Kano), he found the jurist Ahmad and the jurist Abdullahi well-established as the indisputable scholars of this land. They met him outside the city" (p. 11). Also, "In fact Muhammad Rumfa, the jurists Ahmad and Abdullahi, the commander of the cavalry and a few other men were perfect Muslims" (Ibid p. 12).

3. Genealogical data included in this text list seven or eight generations of Shaikh Abd Al-Rahman Zagaiti's agnatic descendants at Kano in 1650–1651 when the text was compiled. This could suggest that the Shaikh arrived during Rumfa's reign, which would then require modification of the Kano Chronicle's earlier references to Zagaiti's appearance in Yaji's day. However, as furnished this genealogical information is equally consistent with the earlier date for Zagaiti's arrival; and in any event Yaji may have received other missionaries from Mali whose identity was confused with Zagaiti by the early chroniclers. v. Muhammad A. Al-Hajj, *op. cit.*

4. KC, p. 79; and LH , p. 39.

5. See Chapter 3, above. Leo Africanus, *The History and Description of Africa*, trans. by John Pory. The Hakluyt Society, London (Cambridge University Press 1896), vol. 3, p. 830.

6. Mahmoud Kati, *Tarikh El-Fettach*, translated by O. Houdas and M. Delafosse (Paris: Adrien-Maisonneuve, 1964) pp. 129–130.

7. Ibid.

8. See Chapter 3, above. Also H.R. Palmer, *The Bornu Sahara and Sudan* (London: John Murray, 1936) pp. 226–228.

9. H.R. Palmer, 1908, *op cit.*, p. 90; *idem*, 1936, *op. cit.*, p. 253; Y. Urvoy, *Histoire de l'Empire du Bornou*, Memoires de l'Institut Français d'Afrique Noire, no. 7 (Paris: Libraire La Rose, 1949) p. 86.

10. E.W. Bovill, *Missions to the Niger*, vol. 1. The Hakluyt Society, Second Series: no. 123 (London: Cambridge University Press, 1964) pp. 115–117. However Urvoy does not list Kano and other Hausa states within the Bornu empire at 1800. v. Urvoy, 1949 *op. cit.*, Figure 6, p. 65, and pp. 87–92.

11. Hassan (Sarkin Ruwa, Abuja) and Shu'aibu (Mukaddamin Makaranta, Bida), *Makau, Sarkin Zazzau na Habe*, and *Tarihi da Al'adun Habe na Abuja*, 2 vols. (Zaria: Gaskiya Corporation, 1952). Trans. by Frank Heath as *A Chronicle of Abuja* (Ibadan: The University Press, 1952) p. 5.

12. Max Weber, *The Theory of Social and Economic Organization*, trans. by A.R. Henderson and Talcott Parsons (London: William Hodge & Co., 1947) pp. 297–389.

13. Bertrand Russell; *Human Knowledge: its scope and limits* (London: Allen & Unwin, 1948).

14. M.G. Smith, *Corporations and Society* (London: Duckworth & Co., 1974, and Chicago: Aldine Publishing Company, 1975) pp. 167–170. *The Study of Social Structure*, 1997.

15. For further discussions, see M.G. Smith, *Corporations and Society,* pp. 167–170; *The Study of Social Structure* (1997 in press); R.M. MacIver, *Social Causation* (New York: Harper Torch books, 1964) pp. vii–xiii, 382–393; Bertrand Russell, *Human Knowledge: Its scope and limits,* pp. 332–333, 471–493.

16. See "A Structural Approach to the Study of Political Change" in M.G. Smith, *Corporations and Society,* pp. 165–204.

17. Ibid., pp. 170–175.

18. For further discussions, see M.G. Smith, *Government in Zazzau, 1800–1950,* (London: Oxford University Press, 1960). pp. 15–33; and *idem, Corporations and Society,* pp. 26–37, 104–105, 175–176.

19. Max Weber, *Theory of Social and Economic Organization,* pp. 43–119, 297–360.

20. On the typology and properties of corporations, v. M.G. Smith, *Corporations and Society,* pp. 43–45, 91–105, 176–180, 208–211, 254–257, 333–337, etc. For the distinction between concrete and analytic structures, v. M.G. Smith, *The Affairs of Daura,* (Berkeley and Los Angeles, University of California Press, 1978) pp. 385–387, 440–442.

21. For a fuller discussion, v. M.G. Smith, *Corporations and Society,* pp. 180–204; *idem, The Affairs of Daura,* pp. 386, 432–437, 441–444; and *The Study of Social Structure,* Ch. 4.

22. For a critical discussion of this approach, v. R.M. MacIver, *Social Causation,* pp. 48–56.

23. M.G. Smith, *Government in Zazzau,* pp. 294–329; *idem, The Affairs of Daura,* 440–441, 481–483.

24. M.G. Smith, *Government in Zazzau,* pp. 297–308, 319–321; *idem, The Affairs of Daura,* pp. 444–462, 481–490.

25. M.G. Smith, *The Affairs of Daura,* pp. 18–19, 385–387, 440–441, 487–488.

26. Smith, *Government in Zazzau* pp. 298–302; *idem, The Affairs of Daura,* pp. 440–441, 470.

27. M.G. Smith, *The Affairs of Daura,* pp. 471–473.

28. M.G. Smith, *The Affairs of Daura,* pp. 432–433, 437–438, 442–443, 476, 479.

29. p. 621 above.

30. p. 623 above.

31. M.G. Smith, *The Affairs of Daura,* pp. 470–481.

32. M.G. Smith, *Government in Zazzau,* p. 307.

33. For fuller discussion of these notations, v. M.G. Smith, *The Affairs of Daura,* pp. 470–481.

34. For further discussion of the problems, criteria and method involved, see M.G. Smith, *The Affairs of Daura,* pp. 470–481.

35. For details see chapter 7, above.

36. See chapter 1 (e) and footnote 1. Also chapter 7, footnote 55, above.

37. See chapter 7, above.

38. See chapter 3 above.

39. See chapter 3 above

40. KC, pp. 74–75; and LH, p. 34. Palmer's spelling in this passage has been adjusted to conform with East's.

41. On this point, see Bertram A. Gross, "Social Systems Accounting" in Raymond A. Bauer (ed.), *Social Indicators,* (Cambridge, Mass., M.I.T. Press 1966) pp. 178–179, 185, and the contrary view of Ludwig von Bartalanffy, *General Systems Theory* (Harmondsworth, Eng., Penguin Books, 1971) pp. 55–56.

42. M.G. Smith, *Government in Zazzau,* p. 302

43. M.G. Smith, *The Affairs of Daura,* p. 485.

44. M.G. Smith, *Government in Zazzau,* pp. 319–320.

45. Ibid., pp 319–320

Index

About the Book and Author

This history of the African kingdom that included the famous trans-Saharan trading city of Kano is the third in the late M. G. Smith's series of histories of the Hausa-Fulani kingdoms in West Africa. Combining the approaches of social anthropology and history, Smith provides a fascinating account of this kingdom's complex political and administrative organization from medieval times to the threshold of Nigerian independence.

The book relies on written sources in Arabic, Hausa, and English, but it is supplemented by in-depth interviews with Fulani rulers and councilors who were intimately familiar with the organization of the Muslim emirate of Kano before the British arrived in 1903. In the final chapter, Smith continues his analytical inquiry, begun in his earlier books, into the processes of change in political units.

M. G. Smith, who died in 1993, was professor of human environment and anthropology at Yale University and the author of *Government in Zazzau* and *The Affairs of Daura*.

Riley

St. Louis Community College
at Meramec
Library